The Big Book
of Home Learning

Volume 2: Preschool &
Elementary

Also by Mary Pride

The Way Home
All the Way Home
Schoolproof

With Bill Pride

Pride' Guide to Educational Software

The Big Book of Home Learning

FOURTH EDITION
Volume 2: Preschool & Elementary

Edited by Mary Pride

A PRACTICAL HOMESCHOOLING® BOOK

The Big Book of Home Learning Fourth Edition
Volume 2: Preschool & Elementary
©1999 by Home Life, Inc.

Clip art images on pages 1, 3, 5, 36, 441, 447, and 478 provided by ©1990 Dynamic
Graphics, Inc. Stock photo images on cover provided by ©1998 Corbus Corp Digital
Stock, ©1999 Eyewire, and ©1997–1998 PhotoDisc.

Quotes from *Phyllis Schlafly Report* are reprinted by permission from the Phyllis
Schlafly Report, PO Box 618, Alton, IL 62002. This is an indispensable source of cut-
to-the-chase, thoroughly documented information on the major threats arising to our
freedoms of education, family life, and citizenship. Well worth the $20 annual subscrip-
tion fee.

Library of Congress Cataloging-in-Publication Data:
Pride, Mary
    The big book of home learning / Mary Pride—4th ed.
        p. cm.
    Include bibliographical references and index
    Contents: v. 1. Getting Started — v. 2. Preschool &
Elementary — v. 3. Teen & adult.
        1. Home schooling—United States. 2. Home schooling—
United States—Curricula. 3. Education—Parent participation—
United States. 4. Child rearing—United States. I. Title.
LC40.P75 1999
ISBN 0-7403-0007-5

Liability Disclaimer

Trademarks

Table of Contents

How to Use This Book

If you want to find the *best* academic resources for individual school subjects for preschool through grade 6 . . .

. . . or you want to supplement your existing packaged curriculum with some carefully-chosen quality resources . . .

. . . or you are "afterschooling" your elementary-schooled child and want to get the most out of the time you are squeezing in. . .

. . . or you realize that quality elementary resources often beat "remedial" resources for junior high and high school students . . .

. . . you've come to the right place!

What You'll Find in the Other Big Book Volumes

If you're new to homeschooling, or just thinking about it, you should also pick up Volume 1 of the Big Book series. In that volume you'll find answers to commonly asked questions about homeschooling, basic contact information to get you in touch with the movement, an introduction to homeschooling methods and styles, and the Curriculum Buyer's Guide with reviews of complete packaged curriculum for all the school subjects, including correspondence programs and online academies. "Packaged" curriculum means "I buy one year's worth of curriculum all from the same supplier," and it's often a good way to dip your toe into the homeschool waters.

If your child is at the borderline of the elementary years, or you simply want to "get a feel" for what lies ahead in the teen years and start mentally preparing for getting your child into college someday, Volume 3 of the Big Book series is a good investment. This has hundreds of reviews of the best educational material for the junior high through college years, plus *detailed* information on all the testing and planning needed for college. If you plan to have your elementary-aged child try to qualify for one of the "Talented Youth" programs, which often require taking the SAT I at an early age, the resources in Volume 3 will be invaluable.

Using This Book's Special Features

The new format of the Big Book series was designed to make it easy for you to do your "shopping." All the information you need to contact the

New Features of This Edition

- Hundreds of all-new reviews. These are marked with the notation "NEW!" next to the review in the margin.
- Complete updates of all reviews from previous editions. In almost every case, the price and ordering information has had to be updated. Only those products that have significantly changed since the last edition have the notation "UPDATED!" in the margin.
- Supplier addresses, phone numbers, and fax numbers are right alongside each review now, instead of in a separate index. (You asked for it, you got it!)
- Plus many reviews include email addresses and World Wide Web addresses for the supplier. Technology marches on!
- For the first time ever in a homeschooling book, we have taken photos of most of the products reviewed. See them for yourself!
- Brand-new chapter introductions bring you up-to-date on the latest homeschooling methods for each subject.
- Sidebars and other highlights provide commentary and additional points of view on chapter subjects.
- Finally, we felt it would be appropriate to celebrate the achieve-

ments of our wonderful home-schooled children by featuring some of the children themselves! So every section begins with a picture and brief description of a homeschooled student and his or her special achievement. These students were all originally featured in the "Show & Tell" section in *Practical Homeschooling,* and we are very proud of them!

supplier of a product is in the margin right next to each review. Product photos are included too, where available. Feel free to use the rest of the margin space to jot down your own thoughts, or to "star" the products you are most interested in.

Thanks to the way products are separated into chapters, and then presented in alphabetical order in each section inside a chapter, it shouldn't be hard to find any product you're looking for. If you have any trouble, the handy index in the back of the book will help you out.

Prices are for Comparison Only

You will note that the reviews include product price information. As always, the information in *The Big Book of Home Learning* is as current and up-to-date as we could possibly make it. After the reviews were written, they were sent back to the suppliers for verification of prices, addresses, and other such information. Even so, *it is always wise to write or call the supplier to check on prices before ordering.*

The prices in this book are included to help you compare different products for value and are not permanently guaranteed. Prices go up and down. Too, you will sometimes have to add state tax (depending on whether you and the supplier are in the same state or not, or whether the supplier has additional offices in your state). Both you and the supplier will feel better if the supplier does not have to return your order because the check you enclosed was not for the right amount.

Introduction

"**M**ommy, please read to me!" "Daddy, show me how to do that!" From the beginning of time, children have wheedled their parents into teaching them things the children wanted to know. Then someone invented school . . . and suddenly kids discovered that they didn't really want to learn anything any more!

You Can Make a Difference

Well, that's not *exactly* how it happened. Still, it's smart for us parents nowadays not to rely solely on the public (or even private) school system to teach our children everything they need to know. For one thing, God never gave schools that job. For another thing (and I know you already know all about this), public schools today are failing rather spectacularly to fulfill these enormous expectations. I'm not going to dwell on the reasons for that, other than to merely hint that giving more money to the same people who caused the mess is *not* terribly bright. We don't need more of the same; we need quite a bit less of it. On the other hand, you and I didn't cause the mess. (This is also true of the kind of teacher who is willing to read this book!) So we're the logical people to clean things up.

Does that mean becoming a full-time educational revolutionary? Heavens, no. It just means cleaning up the mess in front of our own front doors and in our own classrooms.

The good news is that you don't need to move to the country's best school district, get elected to your local school board, or buy stock in a textbook company in order to positively influence American education. You can positively influence *your own children's* education, starting right now, and without waiting for permission from the state textbook approval committee. It's fun, it's easy, and your kids will love you for it. All you need is access to some good resources, and you're holding that in your hands. Now that you have this book, with the teensiest little bit of effort you can buy or put together a preschool and elementary program that will beat anything your local school can offer.

In the two other volumes of this series you will find resources for getting started with home education, and resources for junior high and up. This volume is dedicated to the little kids, from the wide-eyed newborn to the rough 'n ready preteen turning cartwheels on the lawn!

Is Your Child Ready for More?

Since this is the Preschool and Elementary volume, I have limited it to resources at the typical skill level of that age group in modern American public schools. However, be prepared for the fact that home-taught children tend to be ready for teen and adult resources years before they are actually teenagers. My six-year-old has read *Robinson Crusoe*, and my 10-year-old has read *David Copperfield*—totally without pressure from me, I might add. The books were on our shelves, and they decided on their own that they wanted to read them. Similarly, our oldest son,ß Ted, started his first algebra lessons when he was nine years old, and all of the children have learned to type at age seven or thereabouts.

I'm not saying that young children interact with great literature on the same level as an adult would, or that they mature by the age of seven if they are taught at home, but that we must be careful not to dumb down our expectations to what is currently expected of children. Children are capable of learning a lot more than we give them credit for. This is not a pitch for superbabies— just a gentle hint that you might find some items of interest in the *Junior High Through College* volume of this series, even before your children are technically teens!

What You'll Find in This Book

This volume of the Big Book of Home Learning series has everything you'll need to take control of your young child's education:

- **Readiness** activities for babies through toddlers
- **Learn-to-read programs,** including what works and what doesn't, and a *free* six-step outline you can use to create your own program
- **Bible and character education**
- **Creative writing** resources, plus reasons why you should *not* start every paragraph with a "topic sentence"
- **Grammar,** including a Grammar Self-Test that will reveal how good (or bad) your child's grammar really is
- **Handwriting** resources, including a visual demonstration of major handwriting styles
- **Keyboarding** resources, because after all this is the Computer Age
- **Ways to improve spelling and vocabulary**
- **Literature** resources
- **Math manipulatives**—what are they? Are they worth it? Can you make some yourself?
- **Math curriculum,** up to and including calculus lessons for kids age 7 and up!
- **Origins: creation v. evolution.** You won't get this in public school!
- **Science** materials for this age are especially appealing when designed for home use
- **Health, safety, and anatomy.** A head start for future doctors!
- **Engineering** lessons can start in first grade at home!
- **Geography**—we've got some *really* fun ways to learn what used to be a dull subject!
- **History**—world history in first grade? American history kids will actually remember? Toss the textbooks and check out the resources here!
- **Economics and politics**—it's never too early to start understanding how the world *really* works
- **Art and music**—how to make it, how to appreciate it
- **Physical education** curriculum and equipment
- **Even a bonus section** on what the U.S. Constitution actually says and what it *means*. You won't find *this* in any school textbook!

Do It Now!

Our nation may be educationally at risk, as the experts inform us, but our kids still can be winners. All they need are the right resources and a little loving teaching.

Go for it!

PART 1

Preschool

Katharine Danae Lelina, a homeschooler from Sylmar, CA, received an honorable mention at the '99 CURAD Design Your Bandage Contest. She's had some of her artworks framed on display at a children's shoestore in Glendale, CA. 7 years old, Danae has been drawing since she was a mere one year of age. She loves to write stories and enter contests. Some day, Danae wants to produce her own animated movie. Maybe she will; her artwork has already impressed a Disney animator.

CHAPTER 1

A Great Start at Home

Want to get in on the ground floor of a a dynamic preschool with a one-to-one teacher/student ratio? The teachers in this incredible preschool truly love the students, and even spend their own money on classroom supplies. What's more, the students truly love the teachers and were born wanting to please them! Better yet, this school accepts *any* child, even the most severely handicapped, and charges nothing whatsoever for its 24-hour services!

Got your pen out, ready to sign up?

Go take a look in the mirror.

This marvelous preschool is *your own home!*

Kids, Grownups, and the Real World

Am I saying that your home can be as good a learning environment as a good preschool?

No.

Your home is a *better* teaching environment than any preschool!

Look at what you've already accomplished, or (if your child is still a baby) plan to accomplish. Learning to speak is harder than learning to read, and you know you don't need a school to teach your child to speak. Potty training is harder than learning to write, and I've never heard of a child whose parents didn't manage somehow to potty train him.

"But doesn't my child need to spend hours every day around other people's children, and their dangerous childhood diseases, in order to develop intellectually?"

Not really.

It turns out, you see, that the greatest predictor of genius, the factor that shows up most often in case studies of geniuses, is the *large* amount of time they spent with adults and the *small* amount they spent with agemates.

Of course, this refers to adults who actively spend time with their children. Plopping in front of the TV with your baby in your lap may be cozy, but it's not very instructive. But when children spend a lot of time helping adults, watching adults, talking to adults, going where they go and seeing what they see, those children grow intellectually by leaps and bounds.

You would expect this to be so, once you stop to think about it. Getting in touch at a young age with the adult world, including the world of adult thoughts and language, these fortunate children who do so are getting the raw data that will prepare them for *real* thinking about the things grown-up people really think and talk about. Children isolated in a special little peer group of their own, on the other hand, are deprived of this exposure to adult thinking and ideas. They are being encouraged to remain childish and to function only in the artificial setting of the age-segregated group, a setting they will never again encounter outside of school.

Preschool or Homeschool?

Preschool kids always used to be raised at home. But something happened. Governments discovered that they could appropriate huge amount of funds, and build enormous bureaucracies, by doing for the family what the family used to do for itself. Simultaneously, Big Business discovered it didn't have to pay a family wage to its workers if enough women could be lured into the workforce. So now miles of forest are felled to produce propaganda asserting that children can only fulfill their potential if they are snatched from the very breast and plunked into an institutional setting.

This plan is very appealing to the hordes of eager young would-be teachers who have been enticed into selecting Early Childhood Education as their major, and even more appealing to the schools, bureaucracies, and industries which have made Early Childhood Education into a lucrative business. But in our view, it is disastrous to children.

Why?

Because, for very young children, playing *is* learning, or at least the essential precursor of learning. Without raw data to chew over and digest—without a chance to become familiar with *ideas* and *objects* before being taught *rules*—learning difficulties multiply. The relatively sterile "learning environment" of a preschool center can't begin to compare with the messy richness of your own home and your own backyard.

The "school is best" types also tend to forget that children are people with emotions and a need to belong and be loved. To a social theorist, any "care giver" is as good as any other. Love and a permanent commitment to the child aren't important. In fact, a 22-year-old caregiver who has taken some college courses in the latest theories is usually assumed to be a *better* choice than a child's own parents. But to children, social theories don't matter. To children, adults are not interchangeable parts. Your child wants security, stability, immense amounts of love and attention—in short, he wants *you*.

This doesn't mean that formal instruction has absolutely no place in our children's lives; rather, that for formal instruction to succeed, it must be preceded by a period of getting familiar with the new materials and ideas in a completely non-threatening, take-all-the-time-you-want, non-graded way.

The earlier the champions of early childhood education get their hands on our children, the better the chances that your son or daughter will be labeled "dyslexic" or "learning disabled" or, for heaven's sake, "hyperactive." *All* young children are dyslexic when first learning to read, and *no* normal three-year-old wants to sit for hours gazing at an adult's face. Ram schooling

Your child wants you.

down younger and younger children's throats, and soon they *all* will be labeled "learning disabled"!

Mom and Dad are well aware of the pitfalls awaiting Junior in the halls of academe. That is why, if they can afford it, they do their best to sign Junior up for a "quality" preschool, and maybe even a private school. But why should we knock ourselves out paying for the best preschool, at stiff rates, to be followed perhaps by years of expensive private school and years of outrageously expensive college, when we could be providing a far better education, without guilt, if only one or both parents would consider working at home?

When you teach your own, the more you have, the more you save! It takes $3 earned to equal $1 not spent, counting in taxes, donations, extra cars, office clothes, and other business expenses. So if you give one child a $5,000 per year education, it's like earning $15,000 a year. If you have two, you're making $30,000. Think about it!

There's No Place Like Home

When you look into it, you discover that the home, in contrast to institutional settings, is an ideal environment for preschool learning. It's quite humorous to leaf through the catalogs of preschool materials and see how many of them are copies of items found in any home. Play stoves, play pots and pans, little squares of different textures, trays for sorting little objects (remember Mama's button box?), dress-up clothes (what happened to raiding Mom and Dad's closet?) are just some of the products schools buy in an attempt to copy the home environment. Many more of the products you can easily make yourself, like beanbags and sandpaper letters. Any you *can't* easily make or copy are now available to you from suppliers listed in this book, or over on the shelves at your friendly local teacher's store.

So what's Ye Snobbe Academy got that you haven't got—besides high prices, the risk of handing your baby over to strangers, and a fertile breeding ground for serious childhood diseases?

You are your child's best teacher. Kids are born wanting to please their parents, and nobody knows a kid better than his own mother and father. Your job is far easier than the challenge faced by a 22-year-old with an education degree facing a room of 20 preschoolers who would all rather be home. The "experts" can't do a single thing for your child that you can't do—and most of the time, they aren't all that "expert" anyway. If all you ever do with your preschooler is read to him, admire his crayoning, play with him, and answer his questions, you will *already* be providing a richer educational environment than the harried preschool teacher of 20 kids. Remember, it's one-on-one time that counts the most!

Good resources do help, of course. There's plenty out there—more than any one family could ever realistically use. (We know. We've tried!) In this section alone, we've assembled *dozens* of excellent programs to give Baby a head start, your toddler a complete "readiness" education, and your kindergartner everything he or she needs to be ready for formal education. Even if you purchased *all* of these programs, it would cost less than you'd have to pay for daycare and preschool if you sent your child away from home to these establishments.

As you'll find, most of the skills that go to make up "readiness" come naturally in the home environment. With just an inexpensive book or two, and common items lying around your house, you can provide far more stimulating activities than any institution. And if you have the vision to include your preschool child in some of your *adult* activities:

Parent to baby sitter:

"Oh, by the way, while we're gone 19 other kids will drop in. We expect you to take excellent care of all 20 *and* teach them something." Sound ridiculous? Then why do we expect daycare workers and teachers to perform such miracles?

—Based on a question raised by Dr. Robert Doman in his *Miracles of Child Development* seminar

- letting him "help" in your workshop
- letting her stir and measure ingredients when you cook
- teaching him to listen quietly when your friends come over for Bible study or other adult meetings
- inviting her to watch the kind of wholesome, nonviolent films that appeal to you, and not just "kiddie" entertainment (*Anne of Green Gables* as opposed to Barney)
- taking him along sometimes to work or to your volunteer activities
- reading ever-longer classic stories to her, not just "picture books"
- and especially answering all his questions and discussing the books and films you experience together

you'll be giving him or her a head start that puts him miles ahead of daycare and preschool kids. This extra freedom and extra adult attention is probably why homeschooled children test, on average, *seven years* ahead of institutionally-schooled kids in reasoning skills!

What a relief to know you don't have to spend a fortune to give your child a rich education.

Just give her yourself!

CHAPTER 2

Baby Steps

Before we start, allow me to congratulate you on the birth or adoption of your baby. Babies are *wonderful,* and so are people who are willing to welcome these little gifts of God into their homes (that means you!). But you're going to do even more than provide clothes and hugs. You're going to *spend time* with your baby (which Baby will love), doing all kinds of fun things together. I know this is true 'cause you're reading this chapter!

Lots of us are willing to spend time with our little ones, but haven't the faintest idea of how to play with, entertain, or teach a baby. Let's face it: high school and college are usually baby-free environments. So are the Office, the Truck, the Warehouse, the Married-Without-Children Apartment, and all those other adults-only places where we spend our lives before Baby arrives.

Me and My Baby

So here it is. You're alone with the baby. First you try "This Little Piggy Went to Market." That's always good for a few laughs, if Baby is old enough to appreciate it. Kisses and hugs are also fun. You change a diaper and wipe up some spitup. Another hug and kiss. Now you're stuck! You rack your brains for the games your own folks played with you when you were that age. If you didn't have little brothers and sisters, or nephews and nieces, you are likely to come up blank. Time to reach for the Johnson & Johnson toys you bought at Expensive Trinkets 'R Us. These hold Baby's attention, all right—for five minutes or so. You are starting to discover an important truth; store-bought toys *do* provide "hours of fun," but not all at once. It's more like "minutes of fun," with constant breaks to switch toys.

Here's where most parents wimp out. They switch on the TV, or the electric lullaby-gizmo, or wind up the baby swing, and leave, figuring they have spent "quality time" with Baby. If this is their first baby, they are thinking, "I've never felt so exhausted in all my life!" Already they are on their way to the Yellow Pages to check out prices at the local day-care center, because, as all the articles in "parenting" magazines tell us, "you gotta have a break away from the baby."

Take courage! If you don't give up and hand your baby over to other people (like those terribly well-trained high-school dropouts at the local Kiddie Heaven Day Care Zoo), you will learn to keep Baby happy *and* learning without even thinking about it. But first, you have to put in your apprenticeship. This means taking time to maybe make a few baby toys yourself, reading some books about baby games, and not forgetting the hugging and kissing! In an incredibly short time, you will learn how to amuse a baby for an entire half-hour armed with nothing more than a diaper that happened to be hanging over the arm of your sofa. What's more, you will be able to do all this while simultaneously catching up on your reading (in snatches, since Baby gets jealous if you don't give him enough attention). You will learn all this in record time, since mothering hormones make every woman a genius when it comes to keeping her baby happy, if she can keep away from those Madison Avenue types who keep urging us to "have it all" (meaning large paychecks, emaciated bodies, fancy hairdos, STDs, guilt, and heart attacks). Fathers don't have special father hormones, but babies are naturally inclined to love Daddy to pieces, and this translates to a willingness to be happy when cradled on Daddy's arm or shoulder.

Now comes the amazing secret that you never learned in Home Ec class; babies are *fun!* You've just got to learn their language and culture. Once you do, you will find yourself enjoying activities that the gang at the office would never have believed, such as rolling tomato paste cans back and forth on the floor with your toddler. You will learn to lighten up, stop being so dignified, and take pleasure in little things, like an unexpected wildflower growing by your mailbox.

Children have a gift of joy and gratefulness that can nurture our morose adult spirits. They are not perfect little angels from Over the Rainbow, of course, any more than *you* are a perfect little angel from Over the Rainbow. But children are born trusting and willing to appreciate the good life brings. This great gift of childlike faith is why Jesus said we must change and become like little children before we can enter the Kingdom of Heaven—and there's no better way to soak up all the good qualities of a little child than showing him how to use his God-given abilities constructively and introducing him to the best parts of this beautiful world of ours.

Learning in Baby Steps

"Go play nicely with the baby, dear." Good idea, Mom! But *how* can a little kid play with the baby or toddler without causing pain, sorrow, distress, or even boredom?

Now, here in one book, **Baby and I Can Play & Fun with Toddlers**, are activities that older kids can pursue with the babies or toddlers in their families; plus developmental information presented on a preschooler's level so older brother or sister can understand what to expect from a baby or toddler and what they are *not* ready to tackle. The author, a social worker, unfortunately believes the popular myth that older kids naturally have times of longing for the baby to disappear. This is strictly a matter of how your kids are trained in the virtues of affection and sharing. I was the oldest of seven and I *never* wanted to "send back" any of my little brothers and sisters! *Mary Pride*

The delightful ten-video **Baby's First Impressions** series is "readiness while you watch." Everything normally taught in a "readiness" curriculum is covered:

- *Volume 1—Shapes* teaches the standard circle, triangle, rectangle, and square, but goes far beyond showing familiar shapes. Much of the fun is in picking out the shapes from the footage of real objects. Could you see a spinning pinwheel as a "circle," for example?
- *Volume 2—Colors* presents black, white, red, blue, green, yellow, brown, and pink. See moppets modeling cute little colored suits! See animals and real-world objects and pick out their colors!

Baby and I Can Play and Fun with Toddlers (one combined volume)
Preschool. $7.95 (paperback) or $17.95 (library binding). Plus shipping.
Parenting Press, PO Box 75267, Seattle, WA 98125. (800) 992-6657. Fax: (206) 364-0702. Email: office@parentingpress.com. Web: www.parentingpress.com.

NEW!
Baby's First Impressions video series
Ages 8 months–5 years. $14.95 each. Add $4.75 shipping per order.
Small Fry Productions, 4016 Flowers Rd., Suite 440, Atlanta, GA 30360. Orders: (800) 521-5311. Inquiries: (770) 458-2330. Fax: (770) 451-0330.

- *Volume 3—Letters* teaches the names of the capital letters. Oversized letters, such as you can find at a good teacher's store, are major props for the kiddie cast to handle in this video.
- *Volume 4—Numbers* teaches the numbers 1 through 20, plus some simple addition and subtraction. Again, real-world objects and oversized hands-on numerals are used.
- *Volume 5—Opposites* shows just about every "opposite" pair taught in a typical readiness curriculum. The video format is perfect for these concepts, since you can *show* left and right, up and down, over and under, etc., much more easily on video than in a workbook.
- *Volume 6—Animals* introduces pets, farm animals, zoo animals, and insects of all kinds. Kids are shown watching the zoo animals and playing with the farm animals and pets.
- *Volume 7—Sounds* plays sounds while showing pictures of what is making the sound, .e.g. house sounds—various telephones, sound of water running from a faucet, then down the drain, popcorn popping, etc.; farm sounds—donkeys, kittens, roosters, goats, etc.; miscellaneous big and little sounds—big saw, little saw, big river, little river.
- *Volume 8—Seasons* shows scenery and objects associated with the different seasons. It also explains many holidays so your child can tie them to the seasons they occur in.
- *Volume 9—Head to Toe* teaches a little one how to find his nose, fingers, and toes and shows him what can be done with them.
- *Volume 10—Food Fun* teaches the basic food groups and the difference between fruits and vegetables. It emphasizes table manners, good nutrition and basic food groups.

All six videos star an assortment of cute, happy babies and toddlers. This was an inspired idea, as babies love to watch other babies! The children mainly play with toys you can find at a teacher's store, playground equipment, and small animals. The only adult presence is a soft female voice saying the name of the letter, number, opposite, or whatever you are currently seeing. There's no frenetic drill *á là* Sesame Street—just a few simple "What is this?" reviews, where appropriate. No cartoon characters, purple dinosaurs, or middle-aged adults in funny costumes appear. The result is a bright, educational series that children of this age will gladly watch over and over again. *Mary Pride*

Bright Baby Books, a company founded by occupational therapist Barbara Sher, a lady with a lot of experience in movement and exercise training for children, publishes a whole series of physical development books with easy activities and games for different age groups. **Homegrown Infants**, for babies 0–8 months, has a slightly risqué cover (crude pen sketch of undressed mom holding baby in such a way that he covers her torso). Its interior graphics are also on the amateurish side. The text contents, however, have good suggestions for stimulating and developing each muscle area, as well as general balance and mental stimulation. **Homegrown Babies**, for ages 8–12 months, has better graphics. Like the first book, this is nicely arranged in logical topics, such as Movement, Self Care, Exploring and Experimenting, and Social Awareness. *Caution:* Suggested toys for baby in both these books include some that are *not* safe for him to be left alone with, since he might choke on them. The author intends for you to be there with your child as he plays with these items. Finally, you might be interested in the Bright Babies **Toy Gym instructions**, which gives you the plans for making a versatile device for hanging toys over baby's head when he's at the age to play, but not to roll and crawl. **Extraordinary Play With Ordinary Things**, for kids 5–12, shows you

Bright Baby Training for Children

Ages 1–12. Toy Gym instructions, $2.50. Homegrown Babies, $4. Homegrown Infants, $4. Extraordinary Play With Ordinary Things, $10.95. Other toys and books available. Shipping extra.
Bright Baby Books and Videos, 101 Star Lane, Whitethorn, CA 95589. (707) 986-7693.
Email: momsennse@asis.com. Web: www.unm.edu/~asher/barbara.html.

how to turn mateless socks, hula hoops, and carpet squares into instant games. These are really good, doable activities that don't involve a lot of fuss. Just reading these books awakens you to new possibilities for physical development. *Mary Pride*

NEW!
Janice VanCleave Play and Find Out About Math

Ages 2–7. $12.95 plus shipping.
John Wiley & Sons, 1 Wiley Drive, Somerset, NJ 08875. (800) 225-5945. (732) 469-4400. Fax: (800) 597-3299. Web: www.wiley.com.

Have you ever heard "I wonder . . . how can I draw a star?" Our preschoolers are full of wonder. Janice Van Cleave uses that wonder to ignite the desire to learn. **Play and Find Out About Math** is filled with 50 simple activities to help your child discover the answers to the many questions that jump out of his little head each day. Each activity includes illustrations, a list of materials, and simple instructions.

The topics covered in this book include counting, numbers, time, shapes, patterns, measurements, and quantities.

On page 84 of this 122-page paperback book is the question, "I wonder . . . How tall am I?" The items needed to answer this question are a roll of adding machine paper, masking tape, pencil, scissors, and a yardstick. Your child proceeds to roll the adding machine paper out with one end touching the wall, taping it to the floor as he goes. Then he lies on the floor next to the paper, with his feet against the wall. You mark across the paper even with the top of your child's head. Cut the strip equal to the length of your child, and tape it to the floor. Using a measuring stick, help your child measure his height. There are other suggested activities to go with this assignment.

Play and Find Out About Math is written in a clear, straightforward manner, making it easy to use. The activities are sure to keep your child's attention and he gets to answer his own questions along the way. What more can you ask for? *Maryann Turner*

NEW!
My See, Point, and Learn Bible Book

Ages 2–7 (pre-readers). $9.99 plus shipping.
Baker Book House, PO Box 6287, Grand Rapids, MI 49516-6287. Orders: (800) 877-2665. Inquiries: (616) 676-9185. Fax: (616) 676-9573. Web: www.bakerbooks.com.

Even non-readers can learn biblical principles with **My See, Point, and Learn Bible Book**. Traits like kindness, fairness, thankfulness, obeying, and many others (42 in all) are covered in this 93-page book. In addition to learning the 42 traits, your child will learn to count, name animals, identify colors, make animal sounds, and learn listening and pre-reading skills.

Each character trait is presented on two pages. The first page introduces the trait and shows a Biblical picture that represents that trait, along with questions to aid the child in "reading the picture." The second page has a Bible verse at the top of the page, a picture that your child will be able to relate to. The pictures are well-done, very colorful, and understandable even to very young children.

The first trait covered is friendship. The first page has a picture of Peter denying Jesus. Jesus is being lead away by two soldiers, a women is pointing at Jesus, and Peter is looking away from Jesus with his arms crossed. The "Let's Read the Picture" questions are:

> *There are some soldiers in this picture. Can you count the soldiers? The soldiers are taking Jesus away. Point to Jesus. Can you find Jesus' friend Peter in the picture? What is the woman with Peter doing? Is Peter being a friend to Jesus? Should you always be a friend to Jesus? Will Jesus always be a friend to you? Say, "Hooray for Jesus!"*

The second page shows the Bible verse "A friend loves at all times." (Proverbs 17:17) on the top of the page. The picture on that page shows two boys mowing the yard. One is pushing the mower and the other is raking. A cat and mouse are sleeping in the yard. The questions are:

> *These two boys are Michael and Joey. What are the boys in the picture doing? Do you think these two boys are friends? Why? Say, "Hooray for friends!" How many boys are in the picture? What color are the leaves? Can you point to some other friends in the picture? Should real friends be friends all the time or just some of the time? The Remember Rhyme is "Don't pretend be a friend."*

All 42 traits covered in the book are listed on the Contents page. Page 92 lists all the Bible stories that are used for the Biblical pictures. Use this to expand the lesson for older children by having them read the story to find the trait, then discuss it with you.

If you have or work with young children, this is one of the books you must have. I know it will become a well-worn book in my library. *Lynn Smith*

Slow and Steady, Get Me Ready, a complete readiness curriculum in one 324-page book for children from birth to age 5, is now in its third printing. Most readiness programs start only at age three or four: *Slow and Steady, Get Me Ready* starts in the crib, providing one new activity for every week of your child's first five years of life—260 activities in all. These are really good activities, using materials found around your house and taking only 10 minutes or so a day.

Let's look at a sample activity for age 3, chosen totally at random. Judge for yourself if your child will find this interesting:

> *Suspend a nerf ball, sock ball, yarn ball or a stuffed paper bag from an open doorway by attaching a piece of yarn or string at the top of the door frame and tying it to one of the balls or the bag. The yarn or string should be long enough so that the ball hangs at the child's eye level.*

The author continues with instructions on how to teach your child to successfully hit the hanging object using a bat or yardstick, and suggests extending the activity by having the child count how often she can hit the ball.

Major changes in this edition: a section entitled "Tips for Solving Behavioral Dilemmas," 100 new illustrations, and a revised back cover. The tips mostly involve games and distractions. They may or may not solve your child's behavioral dilemmas, but they're worth a try before you resort to more drastic measures.

The other new part of this program is a video which enables you to "see, hear, and discover the joy of using homemade play activities from the book." The author of *Slow and Steady, Get Me Ready*, June Oberlander, narrates and describes some of the activities in the book while parents and children demonstrate. The video is low-key, unintimidating, and comfortable to watch. There are no slick graphics or fancy camera work, but the viewer gets the idea that a normal, everyday parent could do this stuff with his child as well as anyone.

My suggestion would be to order the book first, since you only get a small discount when you buy the book and video together. Then, if you're having trouble visualizing or carrying out the activities, or if you just want some encouragement and reassurance, buy the video. *Sherry Early and Mary Pride*

UPDATED!
Slow and Steady, Get Me Ready
Birth to 5. Book, $19.95. Video, $19.95. Both, $35.90. Volume discounts available. Postpaid. *Bio-Alpha, Inc. PO Box 7190, Fairfax Station, VA 22039-7190. Orders: (800)753-6667. Inquiries: (703)323-6142. Fax: (703) 323-0743. Email: bioalpha@erols.com. Web: www.home-school.com/mall/bioalpha/bioalpha.html*

SLOW AND STEADY GET ME READY

The How-To Book That Grows With Your Child

June R. Oberlander

260 Weekly Developmental Activities From Birth to Age 5

NEW!
Usborne's Board Books

PreK. $3.95 each. Kid Kits, $10.95 each. Shipping extra. Catalog, $2, comes with a $2 coupon good on first order.
EDC Publishing, Division of Educational Development Corporation, 10302 East 55th Place, Tulsa, OK 74146. (800) 475-4522.
Fax: (800) 747-4509.
Web: www.edcpub.com.

NEW!
Usborne Farmyard Tales

PreK. $4.95 each. Shipping extra. Catalog, $2, comes with a $2 coupon good on first order.
EDC Publishing, Division of Educational Development Corporation, 10302 East 55th Place, Tulsa, OK 74146. (800) 475-4522.
Fax: (800) 747-4509.
Web: www.edcpub.com.

Usborne You & Your Child series

Ages 3–6. Each book, $6.95 (paperback) or $14.95 (library-bound). Shipping extra. Catalog, $2, comes with a $2 coupon good on first order.
EDC Publishing, Division of Educational Development Corporation, 10302 East 55th Place, Tulsa, OK 74146. (800) 475-4522.
Fax: (800) 747-4509.
Web: www.edcpub.com.

NEW!
Williamson MathPlay

Age 2–6. $12.95 plus $3 shipping.
Williamson Publishing Company, Church Hill Road, Charlotte, VT 05445. (800) 234-8791.
Fax: (802) 425-2199.
Web: www.williamsonbooks.com.

These are the Kid Kits.

Usborne's Board Books are wordless books with a little animal hiding on each page. Your preschooler develops perception skills and talks about the scenes on each page while finding the animal. Titles include *Find the Duck, Find the Teddy, Find the Piglet, Find the Puppy, Find the Kitten,* and *Find the Bird.* Corresponding Kid Kits, including finger puppets, are available for all titles but *Find the Bird. Mary Pride*

The **Farmyard Tales series** covers life at Apple Tree Farm, where Mrs. Boot, the farmer, her children Poppy and Sam, and their dog Rusty encounter gentle misadventures. Each book includes simpler text at the top of the pages, for beginning readers, with more detailed text at the bottom, for Mom or an older sibling to read. Stephen Cartwright's charming illustrations make these books favorites with our children. The set currently includes 16 books, with titles as *The Grumpy Goat* and *Pig Gets Lost.*

You'll be encountering Usborne Books frequently throughout this volume, and I won't have the space to repeat this every time, so take note—the catalog is *not* free. It costs $2, but to soften the blow it does come with a $2 coupon good on your first order. *Mary Pride*

Usborne You & Your Child series is terrific! Each book has 32 pages loaded with instructions and step-by-step full-color illustrations of fresh and original projects for 3–6 year olds. The *Playdough* book for instance, shows you have to make pigs (and a pen to house them), sheep (and a field with shrubs and flowers for them to lie in), hedgehogs, the ever-popular "snakes in a basket," a Christmas nativity scene, play food of all sorts, playdough jewelry, and more.

These are really doable projects, with great suggestions for project variations. Text accompanies each illustrated step, making it super-simple to follow. The book itself, with its cheerful, colorful illustrations, is bound to inspire young children (and their older siblings), and the text is easy enough for older children to read by themselves. The activities gently promote basic readiness skills, while helping children see the creative possibilities all around them. *Mary Pride*

Introducing your little ones to math should be simple and fun. **MathPlay** is full of ideas—and black-and-white, child-appealing art—to help familiarize your babies with counting, sequencing, numerical recognition, pattern identification, manipulating shapes, and measuring. There are over 80 noncompetitive games and activities revolving around nature, art, crafts, and food, with lots of counting and sorting thrown into this 141-page paperback book.

The variety of activities are sure to spark your creative energies, and you will soon surround your preschooler with math opportunities. *Maryann Turner*

CHAPTER 3

Readiness Programs

What is "readiness"? It's meeting the numbers and letters. It's lots of arts and crafts activities. It's learning "concept" words, like *up* and *down* and *more* and *less*. It's everything short of reading 'n writing 'n seatwork—short, zingy activities geared to a preschooler's interest span. Readiness workbooks are big and splashy and each page takes little time to complete. No writing required: just tracing, cutting, and pasting! All this helps children get ready for their academic studies while having a whole bunch of fun.

Readiness programs are typically called *nursery, preschool,* or *kindergarten.* For the purposes of this book, academic (non-readiness) kindergarten programs are listed separately, in the Kindergarten chapter.

What's the difference? Well, academic kindergarten programs are like a mini first grade. These normally include phonics, simple math, and often art, music, simple history lessons, and other activities as well. Readiness, on the other hand, is more like what we've traditionally thought of as preschool and kindergarten. It involves a lot of creative play, exploring various art media, doing simple dramatics, becoming familiar with colors and shapes, listening to stories and nursery rhymes, and becoming acquainted with seasonal activities. Towards the end of the school year, counting and letters are usually introduced in a very low-key way.

So, which should you start with, readiness or kindergarten? Assuming that Johnny is young enough for this to be a serious decision, I recommend always starting with a readiness program, for three reasons.

> **(1) Readiness programs give kids a really positive attitude** towards school, because they are so much fun.
> **(2) Readiness is also a gentle way** for you to ease into your new teaching responsibilities—a whole lot less pressure than starting right out trying to teach Johnny to read.
> **(3) Readiness helps kids get *ready!***

You don't want Suzy to be struggling with her kindergarten studies because she has never learned how to handle crayons and scissors, or doesn't know the concepts "before" and "after." Readiness programs make sure any such gaps in school readiness are eliminated before they can cause any serious trouble.

Academic kindergarten programs are like a mini first grade.

Readiness is more like what we've traditionally thought of as *preschool* or *kindergarten*.

**Best Books for Getting Started with Little Ones
Teaching Preschoolers: It's Not Exactly Easy But Here Is How to Do It
Teaching Kindergartners: How to Understand and Instruct Fours and Fives**

Preschool–K. $9 each.
Education Services, 8825 Blue Mountain Dr., Golden, CO 80403. (800)421-6645. Fax: (303)642-1288.

Ruth Beechick is a lady who knows a tremendous amount about teaching. Her books on teaching preschoolers and kindergartners, though written for Sunday school teachers, are loaded with insights and practical tips useful in general home schooling as well. Dr. Beechick brings up *and deals with* topics you may never have thought of, such as "How do children think? Do they learn differently at different ages? What is the best way to teach memorization? Are behavioral objectives in Christian curriculums good or bad?"

Dr. Beechick takes a middle of the road position on when preschool teaching should start. She believes in a developmental approach, based on when children are ready, but does not strongly urge putting off formal academics to age 8, as some do. Beyond her Christian view of child development, you also get explicit instruction in how to teach each age group about Christ, sin, salvation, and essential doctrines. She also deals with the mundane how-tos such as how to present flannel-board and puppet lessons, the uses of singing games, and so on. *Mary Pride*

Getting Ready for Readiness

So now you want to enrich your home with exciting stuff? The place to start is the School Supply people. Teacher's stores (sometimes now called "parent and teacher's stores") and school supply catalogs carry a huge variety of fun and clever learning tools. You can craft homemade versions of many of these products, and this is well to keep in mind when flipping through such a catalog. We have, for example, made our own jumbo-size flannelboard and our own beanbags. I collected the tops of gallon milk jugs to use for arithmetic counters and game markers, and used the styrofoam trays meat comes packed in as collage trays. Large disposable diaper boxes make excellent puppet theaters. Ingenious woodworkers can make jigsaw puzzles, beanbag targets, and building blocks (well sanded, of course!). Ingenious seamstresses can save fabric scraps to make their own doll clothes, stuffed puppets, and felt figures. Virtually any arithmetic manipulative can be made at home with the right tools. You can make a bug house out of an empty peanut butter jar with holes drilled in the lid. You can make your own play dough and other crafts mixtures. If fingerpaint you must, you can even make your own fingerpaint.

Packaged Readiness Curriculum

Trying to separate "readiness" from "academic" programs can be quite confusing when reading companies' brochures. That's why I've separated them out for you! Full reviews of these programs, plus addresses and ordering information, are contained in the Curriculum Buyer's Guide in Volume 1 (there simply wasn't room to repeat it all in this volume).

You can purchase a prepackaged readiness or academic curriculum from these suppliers, or make up your own from the great resources in this chapter. If you lack teaching confidence, and especially if this is your first encounter with home schooling, a prepackaged readiness curriculum is your best bet.

Of the list of packaged readiness curriculum, I am partial to Calvert's Kindergarten I. It is fun, complete, easy to use, and does a fine job of helping a mother (or father) learn to teach. You can't go wrong with Calvert! However, other programs are less expensive and have features Calvert lacks, such as Bible content (A Beka, Bob Jones, etc.), a particular doctrinal emphasis (e.g., Catholic or Mennonite), or a greater emphasis on history and geography (Ann Ward's Learning at Home program), and so forth. As you can see, you have plenty of options.

Not every packaged preschool program comes from companies, like those above, that supply educational curriculum for many grade levels. Here are some more curriculum choices.

Prepackaged Readiness Curriculum

- A Beka Books (nursery for two- and three-year olds)
- Advanced Training Institute (preschoolers have activities in Parent's Guide, but no separate program available for preschoolers)
- Bob Jones University Press (K4 readiness)
- Calvert School (kindergarten is a readiness program)
- Clonlara School (any age, whatever kind of program you want)
- Hewitt Child Development Center (readiness program for children aged five to seven)
- Home Study International (preschool readiness)
- Landmark's Freedom Baptist (preschool readiness)
- Learning at Home (preschool is combined with kindergarten in one-volume curriculum).
- Oak Meadow School (kindergarten—readiness with Waldorf storytelling and artistic approach).
- Seton Home Study School (kindergarten—readiness and phonics).
- Sonlight (preschool is a readiness program).
- Sycamore Tree (readiness and phonics both available).

More Curriculum Choices

The **Attributes** series from Bookstuff is utterly unique. What you get are spiral-bound books full of perception-training riddles. You open the book. Staring at you are a bunch of matrices. I mean, 2 x 2" or 3 x 3" squares. On the top and left side of each box of squares are items arranged to show differences. For example, in *Alphabet Attributes* you might find a tiger standing up and a tiger lying down on the left side, while on the top you see blades of grass leaning left, standing up straight, and learning right. The idea is to cut out the page of accompanying pictures and paste each picture into the correct spot. Thus, the picture of a lion standing up near an uppercase L goes in the row with the lion standing up and in the column with the uppercase L. This exercise promotes visual discrimination, fine motor skills (cutting and pasting), pre-math readiness (graphing, counting, coordinates, etc.), and logic (the Midwest Publications thinking-skills series uses a similar user interface, for example).

Alphabet Attributes has animals corresponding to alphabet sounds—a total of twenty-six 2 x 2" matrices. For ages 4–6.

Doing Dinosaurs has (naturally) dinosaurs. Twelve 2 x 2" and 3 x 3" matrices altogether. Ages 4–8.

Toy Chest Attributes is more challenging. Designed for ages 5–8, it features toy chest objects such as roller skates, teddy bears, and toy ships, in 12 matrices up to 4 x 5" in size.

Attributes Activity Book, for ages 4–7, is 15 matrices ranging in size from 2 x 2" to 4 x 4". Most have a whimsical animal motif—e.g., a mama kangaroo with a pig or a turtle in her pouch.

Bookstuff's **Patterns** is 26 worksheets containing a total of 130 patterns. Each page represents a letter of the alphabet. For example, the letter "p" page has a pig, panda, and penguin. Cut out the answer and paste it in. It can be used for enrichment with a phonics program.

The artwork is adequate. However, the discussion questions have absolutely nothing to do with working the puzzles. For example, in Alphabet Attributes for the letter *A* they ask, "How many apple dishes does your family enjoy?" What?

Paste the puzzle pieces in the matrix or laminate each puzzle matrix and pieces to use them over and over again. *Mary Pride*

Before Five in a Row is a "Treasury of Creative Ideas for Learning Readiness." It includes 24 literature-based "units" for toddlers and preschoolers built around 24 very simple children's picture books. The second half of the book is a compendium of ideas for activities to do with your children while shopping, cooking, at bathtime, etc. There is information on selecting toys, playing games, exploring all of the fine arts, and more.

Before Five in a Row strongly encourages parents to treasure these few precious preschool years and to maximize this time to build closeness and intimacy as they play with their children in creative ways—preparing them for the lifetime joy of learning. Like *Five in a Row* (see review in "Unit Studies" chapter in Volume 1), you read each story book aloud several times, and there are no pre-scheduled daily activities. Instead, for each book you read you are given a storehouse of ideas and activities to prepare children for learning, organized by subject headings.

For example, when studying the library book *Yellow Ball*, the subject headings are Bible, Art, Playing Ball, Pastels, Follow the Ball, Science, and Sequencing. Each of these subject headings includes one or more activities. Activities under "Follow the Ball" include finding the ball on every page,

UPDATED!
Attribute series
Ages 4–6. Alphabet Attributes, Toy Chest Attributes, Attributes Activities, $8 each plus shipping. Doing Dinosaurs Attribute Book, Math Attributes, $7 each plus shipping. Patterns, $14 postpaid. Send SASE for information. *Bookstuff, 21534 Saint James Place, West Linn, OR 97068. (503) 638-4806.*

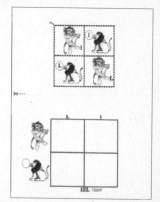

NEW!
Before Five In A Row
Ages 2–4. $24.95 plus $5 shipping. *Five in a Row Publishing, 14901 Pineview Dr., Grandview, MO 64030-4509. (816) 331-5769 for inquiries or to send for catalog. Fax: (816) 322-8150. Email: fiveinarow@aol.com. Web: www.fiveinarow.com.*

learning perspective by noting how the ball looks bigger or smaller (and a real ball looks bigger and smaller) when seen from varying distances, naming as many actions as possible on one page, and viewing fish from different angles. As you keep re-reading *Yellow Ball* to your child, each day you will pick one or more activities to follow your reading.

Just about every readiness activity is covered, with the exception of tracing and other pre-handwriting exercises. It would be a good idea to pick up some TREND or Frank Schaeffer preschool workbooks for extra cut-and-paste, pre-handwriting, number recognition, and letter recognition practice.

Books you'll read for *Before Five in a Row* are: *Jesse Bear What Will You Wear? Yellow Ball, My Blue Boat, The Little Rabbit, Ask Mr. Bear, Blueberries for Sal, Goodnight Moon, The Big Green Pocketbook, The Runaway Bunny, The ABC Bunny, If Jesus Came to My House, Caps for Sale, The Carrot Seed, The Snowy Day, The Quiet Way Home, Play with Me, Prayer for a Child, I Am an Artist, Angus Lost, Katy No-Pocket, We're Going on a Bear Hunt, The Red Carpet, Corduroy,* and *Jenny's Surprise Summer.*

It will take some pre-planning to use this readiness curriculum. You'll have to read through all the activities for a book to ferret out the additional books, supplies, and field trips you'll need to do the activities you select. Getting the books out from the library also may be difficult without pre-planning; the more people use this curriculum, the more likely it is that the book you want will already be checked out! Program author Jane Claire Lambert suggests filling out library request cards for all the books at once, then submitting a few each library trip for books you want that aren't in or can only be obtained through interlibrary loan. Even if you break down and buy all the reading books, though, your total cost for a year's readiness program won't be outrageous.

If you like to read aloud and share worthwhile experiences with your child (and what homeschool parent doesn't?), you ought to love *Before Five in a Row. Renee Mathis and Mary Pride*

NEW!
BJUP Foundations K4

Age 4. Foundations Home School Kit, $89.
Bob Jones University Press, Greenville, SC 29614. (800) 845-5731. Fax: (800) 525-8398. From other countries: Call 1-864-242-5100, x3349.

BJUP's Foundations Home School Kit, designed for four-year-olds, is a "readiness" program that includes:

- home teacher's manual with daily lesson plans for "Heritage Studies" (BJU-speak for social studies), science, English skills, math, story time, art and crafts, motor development, and music
- student activity packet with over 100 preschool activities
- teacher's cassette with sound effects and stories used in the program
- home teacher packet with all the visuals, patterns, and other help you need to complete the program

Foundations leads children through all the preschool skills, and introduces them to letter sounds. The Foundations Home Teacher's Manual is as detailed and helpful as Calvert's. Like Calvert's, it's based on years of actual classroom teaching experience, transferred to what is needed in a home setting. Also like Calvert, Foundations includes lots of songs, stories, and art experiences. Unlike Calvert's Kindergarten 1, letter-training is woven throughout the curriculum, instead of being introduced briefly at the end. Overall, the tone of the Calvert program is warmer and gentler, while Foundations is more crisp and to-the-point.

Bible is available as a separate subject, not included in the kit. However, Foundations still has a Christian flavor. *Mary Pride*

The **Brown Paper Preschool Books** are really nice, containing information on how to begin teaching your toddler different skills, such as science and math. The style of each 48-page book is easy to follow and the full-color cartoon-style drawings are cute. Each book contains many useful activities, cleverly disguised as games, that will keep you and your toddler busy for a while. For example, the Pint-Size Science book helps sharpen perception by having you make "smellers" (cans filled with different scented objects), "shakers" (what sound do the objects inside make? can you tell what they are?) and "feelies" (stick your hand inside and see if you can tell what you're touching). That's just one of the 23 activity sets in this book, all of which involve simple around-the-house items such as ice cubes, soap bubbles, mirrors, and so forth. Each book also includes "learning notes" to teach the teacher, and a skills list and index.

Books in this series are: *WordsAroni* (word play), *Eenie Meenie Miney Math!* (math play), *Razzle Dazzle Doodle Art* (creative play), and *Pint-Size Science* (finding-out play). These will be loved by one and all. *Sarah Pride*

Calvert's Kindergarten I program is great. Grab it if you want a truly fun "readiness" (as opposed to "early reading") style kindergarten. Lots of songs, poems, games, stories to read aloud, cut-'n-paste, arts-'n-crafts, holiday activities, kindergarten math from Macmillan, pre-reading, and pre-writing. The Home Teacher's Manual includes detailed daily lesson plans. Using it is like having a master teacher warmly giving you personal lessons in teaching.

Kindergarten I comes with *all* materials needed, even the paper (large amounts of five kinds), scissors, wool, tapestry needle, crayons, clay, paper, watercolor, pipe cleaners, paper clips, and Elmer's glue. With all that's available, this is still the program we use. Highly recommended. *Mary Pride*

This "Curriculum Guide for Parents of Preschoolers and Kindergartners" was written and published by Jean Soyke, a homeschooling mother of four. She says **Early Education at Home** is a "low-pressure, flexible, inexpensive curriculum for preschoolers," and guess what? It is!

The 137-page book starts off with a short article introducing the concept of homeschooling, a skills checklist for kindergarten, and some suggested home schedules. The curriculum section of the book begins with some lists: 46 suggested activities to teach letters and sounds, 37 activities to teach numbers and numeration, 26 activities to teach shapes, and 14 activities to teach colors. These activities are to be integrated into the weekly units which make up the core of the curriculum. Each weekly planning

---

NEW!
Brown Paper Preschool Books

Preschool. Each book, $8.95 or $9.95.
Little, Brown, and Company, 3 Center Plaza, Boston, MA 02108. (800) 759-0190. Fax: (800) 286-9471.

UPDATED!
Calvert School Kindergarten I

Preschool. Kindergarten I, $285. Normal UPS domestic shipping included.
Calvert School, 105 Tuscany Rd., Baltimore, MD 21210. (410) 243-6030. Fax: (410) 366-0674. Email: inquiry@calvertschool.org. Web: www.calvertschool.org.

NEW!
Early Education at Home

Ages 4–6. $19.95 plus $3 shipping.
Jean Soyke, 2826 Roselawn Avenue, Baltimore, MD 21214. Inquiries: (410)444-5465. Cannot take credit-card orders. Email: jsoyke@juno.com. Web: www.athomepubs.com.

sheet is two facing pages, and there's space for the teacher to write in plans for teaching the letter of the week or the color or whatever.

Most weeks the child learns one letter or number and one color or shape. Some weeks are set aside for review. There are also language and social studies activities, science activities, suggested read-aloud books, suggested Bible stories, a character quality to emphasize, field trips, and even a suggested snack (red foods or applesauce for the week you study the letter *a* and the color red).

There's not nearly as much "stuff" here as in some kindergarten programs; however, if you're just beginning to feel the need for a plan in teaching your preschooler, simplicity is an advantage. **Early Education at Home** supplies plenty of good material to keep a four- or five-year-old busy and learning for a year or more. *Sherry Early*

NEW!
McClanahan Toddler Time series

Ages 2–3. $2.95 each plus shipping. *McClanahan Book Company, Inc., 23 West 26th St., New York, NY 10010. (212) 725-1515. Fax: (212) 779-7347.*

Toddlers will love these full-color activity books. Each **McClanahan Toddler Time workbook** is sixteen pages long, with four more pages of stickers and punch-outs. On the paper next to each sticker, there is a number telling which page it is to be used on.

These books definitely need adult supervision, like the publisher says. Not only will your toddler not normally be able to read these, it is doubtful as to whether they will understand the instructions. Besides, children that young are likely to purloin the stickers for placing on miscellaneous spots on the wall, or stick them all over one of the pages where they don't go.

The lessons these books teach are helpful and memorable. Each page has a large colorful picture with an explanation beneath of how to use the stickers or punchouts with that page, plus some brief additional questions or activities. Sample exercises are: (*Sorting*) Understanding relationships between adult and baby animals, (*Thinking*) Sorting objects by where they belong and (*Little Explorers*) showing "in" and "out."

Books in this series:

- *Observing* (same and different, what's missing)
- *I Can Do It!* (readiness activities related to children's activities—e.g., sorting by size on the "Build a Sand Castle" page)
- *My Busy Day* (workbook activities related to parts of a child's day teach big/little, in/out, same and different, etc.)
- *Numbers*
- *Sizes*
- *Shapes*
- *Going Places* (workbook exercises with a "places to go" theme, e.g., zoo, train station, airport, park, museum, etc.)
- *Little Explorers* (readiness activities with an outdoor environment theme, such as a backyard, pond, beach, garden, and farm)
- *Thinking* (the readiness concepts of on/off, in/out, over/under, location, summer/winter, same and different, adding details, first/next)
- *Sorting* (by color, by category, by families, where something belongs)

It's a pity that the books in this series with special theme—e.g., *I Can Do It!, Going Places, My Busy Day,* and *Little Explorers*—don't include any suggested activities for the real-world environments they mention, or even any noticeable information about those environments. They really are just additional "readiness" books. *Sarah Pride*

The **McClanahan High Q Preschool-Kindergarten Workbooks** begin where their Toddler Time books finished, and require proportionately greater reading ability. Using McClanahan's same colorful style, these books will likely be a hit with your pre-readers. Each 32-page book has a small, full-color, four-page, pull-out storybook. There are also two pages of full-color stickers, for children to place on the appropriate book pages. The regular exercises are printed in black and orange ink, and require adult oversight.

Sample exercises are: (All About Me) drawing a picture of yourself, (Follow Me) matching animals to what they eat and (Rhyming Words) finding a picture that rhymes with a word.

The books in this series are:

- *My First Math Book*
- *My First Numbers*
- *My First Words* (words grouped by category, e.g., "beach words")
- *My abc's* (lowercase)
- *My ABC's* (uppercase)
- *Get Ready to Read* (same and different, adding details to a drawing, perception training by finding objects in a picture, directionality, sequencing alphabet letters, beginning sounds, rhyming, sequencing parts of a story)
- *Rhyming Words*
- *What Belongs?* (classifying and sorting)
- *Colors, Shapes, and Sizes*
- *My Book of Opposites*
- *Following Directions* (sequencing)
- *All About Me* (not self-esteem, but "facts about me"—what I look like, where I live, my family, etc.)

As usual, these McClanahan books are delightful for both parent and child, and educationally valuable as well. Recommended. *Mary and Sarah Pride*

The **Perception Publications IQ Booster Kit** is a perception-training program I really like. Drawing on her ten years as a classroom teacher, author Simone Bibeau, M.Ed., produced a four-workbook series that exercises your child in these four areas: Motor (left-right tracking, mazes, eye movements, hand-eye coordination), Visual (similarities, memory, figure ground, space orientation), Auditory (similarities, memory, rhyming), and Comprehension (categories, sequence, language, awareness).

This all sounds very complicated, but really it's not. The exercises are laid out in a carefully graduated sequence of fun activities. None of these require strain on your or your child's part. He practices drawing lines from here to there without running his lines into the "obstacles," he solves mazes, he colors the happy face if the birdies look alike and the sad face if they don't. For the auditory exercises, you might need to ding a spoon on a cup or thunk a book on the table while Junior listens with his eyes shut. Even this small effort can be removed by buying the accompanying cassette with the auditory exercises on it.

We bought this series for our oldest son when he was four, and he absolutely loved it. "When do I get to play 'Same and Different?'" Ted would ask. We could almost visibly see his mind sharpening up as he did the exercises. Let me mention that when the IQ Booster Kit has been tested, 95 percent of all children tested significantly increased their learning abilities by using the program.

NEW!
McClanahan High Q Preschool-Kindergarten Workbooks
Ages 3–5. $2.25 each plus shipping. *McClanahan Book Company, Inc., 23 West 26th St., New York, NY 10010. (212) 725-1515. Fax: (212) 684-2785.*

Perception Publications IQ Booster Kit
Ages 2½–8. Complete Kit (containing IQ Booster Kit cassettes, Developing the Early Learner workbook series, and 151 Fun Activities), $89. 151 Fun Activities, $25. Shipping extra. *Perception Publications, Inc., 8711 E. Pinnacle Peak Rd., #345, Scottsdale, AZ 85255. Orders: (800)338-5831. Inquiries: (602)585-6989. Fax: (602)451-9372.*

The art is engaging, and since the books are all black and white your child can have the added fun of coloring them in. If your son or daughter is old enough to hold a crayon, he or she is ready to start on the first book of the series. By the time a child gets to book four, he is solving complicated mazes and figuring out the answers to questions like "House is to tent like glass is to—?"

Each book contains a diagnostic Progress Chart and suggested exercises for testing and remedying perceptual handicaps, as well as identifying certain special and gifted skills.

You get four cassettes with the complete IQ Booster Kit. The first two share the program's educational philosophy and train you to use the kit effectively. On the last two are the auditory exercises.

151 Fun Activities for Children is a two-tape set with accompanying manual and binder. Down-to-earth explanations of how and why to train your child's thinking and motor skills, plus 151 easy-to-do activities that develop those skills. Since the last time I revised this book, Simone has thrown it in along with the IQ Booster Kit—and lowered the price as well! She reduced the price of the kit to include the *151 Fun Activities* book "because we believe so strongly in educating our parents. Too many parents just give the books to their children—they are used as busy work and so much of the valuable skill development is missed. All learning does not take place in a workbook—thus the need for games and activities to enhance the child's perceptual growth." In other words, she believes you will get much more out of her program if you get the entire package including the workbooks, IQ Booster cassettes, and *151 Fun Activities* book, rather than just purchasing the workbooks. If you do not have much of a background in child development and perception training, I believe she is right; however, if you can't afford the entire program, even just the workbooks, used according to directions, can make a significant difference in your child's mental sharpness. *Mary Pride*

Potter's Press Preschool Curriculum

Preschool. Curriculum, $37.95 with binder; $32.95, without. Correlated Learning Aids, $5.95. Add $5.95 shipping.
Shekinah Curriculum Cellar, 101 Meador Rd., Kilgore, TX 75662. (903) 643-2760. Fax: (903) 643-2796. Email: customerservice@shekinahcc.com. Web: www.shekinahcc.com.

Potter's Press Preschool Curriculum contains cute-as-a-button intros to letters, numbers, colors, shapes, and Bible stories (Adam-Zaccheus). You get 32 ten-page workbooks plus a *very* brief teacher's brochure. The latter gives teaching hints, suggests a follow-up phonics method, and outlines a simple approach to science and history that you can easily add to your preschool program. Starting with *How Hermie the Glow Wormie Got His Name*, every booklet has a little story (Bible stories start in book 3) and simple exercises built into the booklet's basic theme. Example: count the food items on the Ark and color in the rainbow. Time required: only a few minutes a day.

Correlated Learning Aids include black-and-white Alphabet Flash Cards (short A is for Adam, long A is for Abel), 17 Practice Printing sheets, and Reading with Vowels, a mini-course in combining letter sounds to form words.

If you're not really excited about baking pretzels with your kids or planting rose bushes together (and all the other creative activities in regular readiness programs), or if you'd like some Bible-based prereading and premath to supplement one of those activity-laden programs, you won't find anything simpler or cuter than Potter's Press. *Mary Pride*

Readiness Set Go!

Ages 2–6. $49.95 plus 15% shipping. Preschool Readiness book only, $19.50. Exercise video, $7.95.
Alpha Omega Publications, 300 N. McKemy Ave., Chandler, AZ 85226. Orders and inquiries: (800) 622-3070. Fax: (602) 940-8924. Web: www.home-schooling.com

When Mary reviewed this complete preschool program a couple of years ago, it included a lot more and cost about twice as much ($79.95). As far as I can tell, all the other material is still available separately and for $49.95 you still get all the basics.

Three main components make up the program: a parent's book, a preschool exercise video, and a materials starter package.

The **Preschool Readiness Book**, by Mary Ellen Quint Ph.D., consists of instructions for activities to teach colors, shapes, size, position and direction, matching and grouping, language development, and math readiness.

The exercise video, **Teeny Time Tune-Ups**, features two perky-looking teenage girls leading the exercises and a class of preschoolers following. The exercises are done to music, mostly contemporary Christian kids' music or traditional preschool songs, and the whole thing is lively, engaging, and lots of fun.

The materials starter package includes all the "harder-to-find" materials you need for the program: colored counting bears, tangram puzzle set, safety scissors, right angle prism, magnifying lens, and a play coin set. *Sherry Early*

Rod and Staff's preschool/kindergarten series consists of six workbooks and a Bible story book.

Adventures with Books teaches basic preschool skills, such as tracking from right to left and top to bottom, following simple directions, learning the colors, cutting and pasting, drawing with lines and circles, recognizing simple shapes, and learning important preschool concepts such as *up-down* and *big-small*.

Counting with Numbers is a pre-math book designed to teach children about the numbers from 1–10, including how to write them, what quantity each represents, what number comes before or after, and simple numerical concepts like *more/less* and *empty/full*.

Bible Pictures to Color encourages children to color neatly with realistic colors, and even includes color-by-number pictures. The companion book, *Bible Stories to Read*, has 60 Biblically-accurate stories written on the preschool level: 36 from the Old Testament and 24 from the New Testament. Each comes with a few discussion questions and a memory verse.

Do It Carefully teaches how to write the letters and recognize their sounds.

Everywhere We Go reviews the concepts introduced in the first four workbooks: colors, shapes, numbers, letters, and sounds. The book's 64 pages include lots of matching, coloring, listening activities, writing letters, cutting, and pasting.

Finding the Answers develops thinking skills through matching activities, comparison and contrast, sequencing, and listening activities. The flavor here is simple, unpretentious, cozy, and God-honoring. The goal, according to the people at Rod and Staff, is "an excellent, obedient, cooperative spirit." Who can argue with that? *Mary Pride and Sherry Early*

From the people who brought you the delightful *Sing, Spell, Read and Write* reading program comes a preschool kit. It includes a Teacher's Manual, short vowel cards, a music tape, a learning game, and a pair of preschool readiness workbooks with a Raceway theme: **On Your Mark** and **Get Set**.

On Your Mark has a pair of shoes pictured on its back cover, with punched-out holes and real shoelaces for practicing lacing. This workbook covers colors, shapes, visual discrimination, matching, opposites, classification, sequencing, and seasons. *Get Set* has a giant clock with turnable handles on the back cover, and includes letter shapes and sounds and recognizing beginning letters. The accompanying Teacher's Guide is friendly and helpful, and includes readiness activities to go along with the workbook exercises. *Mary Pride*

Readiness Activities for Toddlers

I had originally intended to call this section "Preschool Widgets" or "Preschool Accessories," but the first one sounded like a kiddie hardware store and the second sounded like we would be talking about designer handbags for moppets. Below you will find all kinds of readiness goodies: floor puzzles, shape and color sorters, clean-up gear for kiddies, wipe-off books, preschool learning games, and other neat extras!

Kids can learn many of the basic preschool and kindergarten concepts just as well with these goodies as with a packaged curriculum, even if the process is somewhat less formal and methodical.

Some of these resources teach skills not found in any regular packaged program, such as geometric logic (otherwise known as *puzzling*) and practical life skills (otherwise known as *mopping the floor*). If you're like me, your birthday shopping buck might stop right here!

NEW!
BipQuiz Play & Discover Series
Ages 4 & up. Books, $2.95 each. BipPen, $4.95. Shipping extra.
Sterling Publishing Co., Inc., 40 Saw Mill Pond Rd., Edison, NJ 08837. (800)367-9692. Fax: (212) 213-2495. Web: www.sterlingpublishing.com.

A BipPen is an electronic pointing device that tells you whether you've chosen the correct answer. You press the tip of the BipPen (which doesn't really write) on a black shape next to the answer you think is correct. A correct answer gets you a pleasant beeping sound and a flashing green light; incorrect gets you an annoying "eerp" noise and a red light. You can use the same pen for all of the books in the **BipQuiz Play & Discover Series**.

These colorful 8 x 10 inch books each contain 30 games of increasing difficulty. Some activities involve choosing the object that is correct, and often there is more than one that is correct. Other activities involve finding the correct path to follow, by pressing the BipPen on black shapes along possible paths.

The first three books—*Numbers, Shapes,* and *Colors*—contain activities where the choice is just a picture and no reading is required. However, each page has a short paragraph at the top; sometimes you can't tell what's ex-

pected of you unless you can read that paragraph or have it read to you. Other pages can be figured out without having to read this paragraph. Though these titles suggest concepts that are learned in the preschool years, the activities go beyond simply recognizing colors, shapes and numbers.

The other five books—*Letters, First Words, Rhyming Words, Time,* and *Feelings*—contain many activities that require reading of at least a few single words in order to be able to answer correctly. These books still contain plenty of big, colorful pictures, and the reading is not overwhelming. They would work best with children who are reading somewhat independently.

The BipPen technology is a built-in self-check that should allow a child to use these books on his own. However, the format of many of the pages is confusing to younger children who are not yet reading independently. Therefore these books work better when used with a parent or older sibling who can read the instructions and explain to the child what is expected.

While the BipPen is not meant to write, dragging it across the page does produce a black smudge. Continued use by a child who likes to "write" with the BipPen causes marks to be made on the pages that can "give away" the correct answer to any child who uses the book later on. Parents should also note that the pen's plastic contains several openings; if any liquid (including saliva, if you have children who still put things in their mouths) is poured into these openings, the pen keeps beeping until either the liquid has evaporated or you dismantle the pen and cut the wires, rendering it permanently useless. Overall, the technology worked well, but it wasn't perfect. *Melissa Worcester*

You've seen a lot of bead mazes, I'm sure, but here are some reasons I'd like to recommend **Educo Bead Mazes** to you.

- They surpass strict North American and European child safety standards.
- Each maze comes with a carefully written activity guide, to help you get extra educational mileage out of what otherwise would only be a toy.
- Their family of 78 bead mazes includes some of the most innovative models available anywhere.
- They have been making these mazes for 15 years, during which time they have won over 40 international awards.
- Educo mazes are the world's #1 best-selling bead and wire mazes.

Bead mazes, by their nature, consist of small objects children could swallow and long wires that can cut children or poke them in the eye. This is not a problem as long as the wires are fastened securely into the base. Educo's special fastening process is *extremely* durable. I know, because we have several of these mazes, and our not-very-gentle youngsters have played with them almost daily for over three years—including non-approved uses such as standing on them and dropping them. Yet each maze looks as fresh as the day it arrived. This might not prove to be the case with the "bargain" knockoff you think is such a deal at the discount store. I would also urge you to *never* buy a bead maze at a yard sale or flea market, since you have no way of knowing how much damage the former owner inflicted on its internal fastenings, and the few bucks saved are *not* worth the potential risk.

My personal favorite, and one I own, is the "Rings Around a Row-sy." This large bead maze has five play wires that form a ring around a figure eight and a central circle. It has both tiny beads, and larger beads that slide over them. A square "pusher" bead can move the whole group at once. The parent guide explains how you can use this maze to teach *inside/outside* and *round/square*, as well as colors, shapes, counting, and of course, fine and gross motor skills.

Other specially innovative mazes: "Springtime" has regular beads, as well as two removable "Springalongs," bead people whose heads and bottoms are connected by a spring. "Funny Face" is a maze with wire twisted into a goofy face shape. "Purple Parade" has both regular and "puzzle beads," beads that snap together to make bead flowers. There's much, much more, and I'm sure a new batch of maze models will be out by the time you read this! *Mary Pride*

Janice VanCleave's Play and Find Out series currently includes these titles: *Science, Bugs, Human Body, Math,* and *Nature.* Each book is paperbound, 128 pages, and around 10 x 8" in size. Each of these amazingly cute (but not trivial) books includes 50 simple and fun demonstrations designed to answer questions kids often ask about the book's topic.

Each demonstration is its own little chapter. I call these "demonstrations" rather than "experiments" because they are mostly designed to model the answers to questions such as, "Do plants have bones?" (no, they don't; you simulate a plant's outer wall with gelatin, grapes, and a shoebox) or, "How does my back bend?" (you model a spine using thread spools, construction paper, and a piece of string). Each chapter starts with a question posed by a cartoon child, a "Round Up These Things" materials list, a "Later You'll Need" materials list, step-by-step demonstration instructions, a "So Now We Know" section that explains what the demonstration's all about, plus "More Fun Things to See and Do" follow-up activities. For example, after constructing your model spine, you are given the follow-up activity of measuring your height in the morning and evening of the same day. Amazingly, you shrank.

These books are printed in two colors, with large, airy print and illustrations for extra eye appeal. With all this kid appeal, the books still use genuine science terminology in the text. All this, plus a glossary and an index. No wonder so many copies of these books have been sold! *Mary Pride*

Lauri makes an enormous array of wonderful hands-on learning stuff. Here are some of their best products for preschoolers:

- **Shape and Color Sorter**. Every kid age 2 and up could use one of these! You get a rubber base, five colored pegs, and 25 pieces of double-thick colored crepe rubber cut into squares, circles, triangles, stars, and hearts. Your little one can sort them either by shape or by color: red, yellow, blue, green, and orange. This is the closest I have seen to a toy that really *does* provide "hours of fun," and it teaches colors, shapes, and hand-eye coordination as well!

- **Lacing goodies**. Lacing is a pre-needlework skill that also develops fine motor skills, and is a wonderfully soothing activity to pull out when the kids are frazzling your nerves. I got a review sample of the Lace-a-Puppet, and had to beat off our girls long enough to look it over myself! The Lace-a-Puppet has six "people" to lace up, while the Lace-a-Saurus and Lace-a-Pet-Puppet each have three lacing critters. Each kit includes precut

NEW!
Janice VanCleave's Play and Find Out series

Ages 4–7. Each book, $12.95. *John Wiley & Sons, 1 Wiley Drive, Somerset, NJ 08875. (800) 225-5945. (732) 469-4400. Fax: (800) 597-3299. Web: www.wiley.com.*

Lauri Hands-On Learning Products

Preschool–grade 6. Free catalog. Most items under $10. Shape and Color Sorter, $13.95. Lace-a-Puppet, $11.95. Lace-a-Saurus and Lace-a-Pet Puppet, $8.95 each. Needles for Lacing, 36/$4.95. Laces for Lacing, 24 36" laces, assorted colors, $4.95. Beads 'n Baubles, $6.95. Shipping extra. *LAURI, PO Box F, Phillips-Avon, ME 04966. Orders: (800) 451-0520. Inquiries: (207)639-2000. Fax: (800) 682-3555.*

felt body shapes, plastic needles, yarn, and lots of remnant felt pieces so your kids can decorate their finished hand puppets. And for those of you who are always losing your lacing needles, Lauri has those, and lacing laces for regular lacing projects, too.

- **Beads 'n Baubles**. Stringing is a slightly different skill than lacing, but is just as quiet and satisfying. Your little ones will enjoy stringing the 100+ variously-sized and colored crepe rubber pieces on the three tipped laces. If they are like mine, they will also quickly catch on to the idea of stringing the rubber pieces on in pretty patterns—by color, shape, or both—another readiness skill! *Mary Pride*

As I mentioned, **Lauri** produces their own crepe rubber preschool learning goodies, which cover just about every important preschool skill, all at extremely good prices. Let's run through just a few of their hundreds of wonderful, colorful, fun-to-use puzzles.

- **Fit-a-Space**. This was Lauri's first product, and it's still a winner. You get 16 round crepe foam rubber disks, each with small colored shape cutouts that fit inside—52 fit-in shapes in all. This one set provides enough mini-puzzles for a flock of preschoolers, or a real challenge for one lucky kid.
- **Crepe Rubber Puzzles**. I should have put these first, since after all these puzzles are what Lauri is most famous for. Brightly colored, washable, impervious to curling or tearing, quiet, and, most of all, beautiful puzzles that can be put together and taken apart again and again for years and years. Lauri has puzzles in all difficulty categories, from very easy puzzles like their Fit-a-Space to the Big Puzzles with up to 92 pieces. You might also want to try one or more of Lauri's "See the Difference" Puzzles. These are readiness aids, designed to help kids learn to discriminate between similar shapes. One puzzle has butterflies, each with a slightly different shape; another has fish, another cars 'n trucks, and yet another cookie-cutter-style kids engaged in a variety of activities.
- **The A-Z panels** and **1–10 Panel**. I consider these essential learning aids. These are inexpensive crepe rubber panels into which you fit alphabet letters (uppercase or lowercase) or numbers. You can take the letters and numbers out and use them separately to practice alphabetic or numeric sequencing. You can use the nubbly letters or numbers for kids to rub their fingers over, thereby learning how to form the letters. Or you can simply use them as puzzles, while your kids become unconsciously familiar with the basic letter and number shapes. Very highly recommended. *Mary Pride*

Have you ever wished your preschool child would listen more carefully? Then you might want to try a tape and worksheet program called **Listen and Do**. With two levels available, the child listens to simple instructions from the tape and follows the instructions on the worksheet. Each session is approximately 10 minutes long and the tape provides self-correction for the child. Worksheets may be copied for use by multiple students.

In Level 1, some of the activities include identifying the source of

Lauri Puzzles

Preschool–grade 6. Free catalog. Most items under $10. Early Learning Picture Puzzles, $7.50 each. Chubby Puzzles, $6.50 each. Beginner Puzzles and Picture Puzzles, $7.50 each. Big Puzzles, $14.95 each. "See the Difference" Puzzles, $7.50 each. Fit-a-Space, $11.95. A-Z Panels, $8.95 each for uppercase or lowercase. 1-10 Panel, $5.95. Shipping extra. *LAURI, PO Box F, Phillips-Avon, ME 04966. Orders: (800) 451-0520. Inquiries: (207)639-2000. Fax: (800) 682-3555.*

NEW!
Listen and Do

Ages 2–5. $64.95 plus shipping. *Living and Learning Company, 2400 Turner St., Grand Rapids, MI 49544. Phone: (800) 253-5469. Fax: 800-543-2690. Email: instructionalfare@tribune.com. Web: www.instructionalfare.com.*

sounds, following instructions to make shapes, ordering activities and predicting what happens next. The tape narrators' delightful English accents encourage and praise the child for his efforts.

Level 2 extends the skills of Level 1. Children identify sounds, make inferences, draw conclusions, follow directions and recall sequences.

This tape and workbook series is a pleasant way to expand children's listening skills with self-correcting activities which require little parental supervision. *Christine Field*

Montessori Kid-Sized Tools

Young children. Tools: 40¢ to about $15 each.
Montessori Services, 836 Cleveland Avenue, Santa Rosa, CA 95401. (707) 579-3003. Fax: (800) 483-9822. Email: monserv@sonic.net.

I read somewhere that boys who grew up doing chores had more success in business, happier marriages, and a sunnier outlook on life as adults than boys whose parents did all the picking up. (Don't you just love studies like this?) Extrapolating from the data, I surmise that the same would be true of girls. The problem is, *how* to get the kids to help?

If you start while the children are young enough, and if you don't make the fatal mistakes of grouching about your own chores and trying to shove off all the worst jobs on the kids, you are halfway there. But only halfway. No matter how willing a little child may be to help, he just won't be strong enough to shove around an adult-sized broom or use the other standard-sized cleaning implements we all take for granted.

Decades ago Maria Montessori, an Italian physician, discovered the amazing fact that kids do a *much* better job of helping out if they are given tools their own size. There is, of course, a lot more to the Montessori philosophy than this. However, since we're being practical at the moment, let's focus on the large array of kid-sized tools available from **Montessori Services**, a company founded to produce and distribute products necessary to Montessori education. For the two- to seven-year-old set, Montessori Services carries **kid-sized household tools**. Would you believe a kid-sized scrubbing board (you can't even find adult-sized scrubbing boards nowadays!). Child-sized clothespins? Vinyl and cloth aprons for all ages of children? Kid-sized apple corers and brooms and washbasins? Mops, brooms, dustpans, baking equipment, and so on, all sized for little hands? Good quality, not like that discount store stuff. Montessori schools shop from this catalog, so if it will hold up for their classes of kids, it should hold up for yours.

Not a lot of high-tech stuff here, you'll notice—no kiddie vacuum cleaners—but everything your child needs to take care of the house the way Grandma used to. *Mary Pride*

NEW!
Rock 'N Learn Preschool Tapes

Ages 2–5. Each tape/workbook combo, $9.95. Shipping extra.
Rock 'N Learn, Inc., P.O. Box 3595, Conroe, TX 77305. Orders: (800) 348-8445. Inquiries: (409)539-2731. Fax: (800) 801-5481.

Rock 'N Learn offers an energetic, colorful way to introduce early learning concepts to your child with a cassette tape/workbook combination. Lessons (in the form of rock music) are light, peppy and fun. The accompanying workbooks are colorful and engaging for preschool children.

Pre-readers can learn from *Rock N Learn Alphabet* and *Rock N Learn Colors, Shapes and Counting*. The cassette tapes guide your child from page to page by picture references as opposed to page number. For example, page 19 is the page with the frog at the top. Though this may seem a bit patronizing, it helps very young children listen and follow along independently.

In **Rock 'N Learn Colors, Shapes and Counting**, the child learns all shapes, colors and the numbers from 1 to 20 in 28 engaging pages of text and music. At the beginning of the little workbook are additional, simple activities that parents can use to reinforce the concepts.

In **Rock 'N Learn Alphabet,** the cheery songs guide the child through all beginning letters of the alphabet, both capital and lower-case. There is a special song for each letter and fun musical games. Additional activities are presented for parents to extend the learning.

These tapes are great for learning in the van or during a regular day at home. The catchy music and colorful illustrations ensure that your child will look, listen, remember and learn. *Christine Field*

Now we come to some *real* preschool essentials—**TREND's Wipe-Off Card** sets. These are double-sided, oversized, plastic-coated cards that you can write on again and again, preferably with TREND's plastic wipe-off crayons. These are the exact same exercises you get in the better preschool readiness workbooks, except they are full-color and can be repeated again and again! Series includes *Let's Count* (writing numerals, circling the correct number of objects, etc.), *Follow the Path* (great pre-handwriting practice), *Finish the Picture* (great pre-art practice), *I Can Print* (now we're getting into real manuscript writing), *See It, Make It* (simple designs to copy using basic geometric figures), *Match the Letters* (capital to capital, lowercase to lowercase, capital to lowercase), *Colors and Shapes* (tracing and matching), and the wonderful perception-training set, *Same or Different.*

I wouldn't want to be without TREND's colorful write 'n wipe handwriting books. The pre-handwriting book lets children trace the different shapes and strokes they will use in writing. The numbers book gives practice in writing numerals and in counting. You can use the manuscript book as a pre-cursive intro by just having your student start some letters differently and using one continuous stroke. TREND even has a cursive book, with a silly race car theme. The **Wipe-Off Books** are great for practice, lively and colorful, and can be used again and again by every kid in a family of twelve.

TREND'S **Wipe-Off Crayons** for use with the books are super cheap and come in assorted zippy colors. *Mary Pride*

You've been tossing and turning at nights wondering what to do with your leftover deodorant bottles, crumpled paper, and wallpaper scraps, right? Your problem is solved. **1•2•3 Art: Open-Ended Art Activities for Young Children** is possibly the biggest and best collection ever of wacky art activities using common household objects.

I've seen lots of art-with-simple-things books, but this one has special features. For one thing, the layout. All the "Painting With . . ." activities, like painting with shaving cream or food coloring or ice or Q-Tips and so on, are all in the same section. Ditto for the Painting On, Gluing, Glue Substitutes (can you see peanut butter as a glue substitute?), Printing With, Prints of, Modeling With, Marking With, Tearing or Cutting, Lacing, and Miscellaneous Art. A Seasonal Index directs you to activities appropriate to that season and its holidays (e.g., forget painting on snow in June). Every page lists materials needed, preparation required, hints, and variations on the activity, plus there is a cute cartoon of a bear doing the activity. These activities are suggestions submitted by teachers from all around the country, and represent true creative thinking. Gonna get us some squeeze bot-

TREND Wipe-Off Products
Ages 4 and up. Wipe-Off Cards, $6.99 per set. Wipe-Off Books, $3.79 each. Wipe-Off crayons (#T-593), $1.49/box (eight assorted colors). Wipe-Off markers (#T-598), $5.99/box (four assorted colors). Add shipping and applicable sales tax.
Trend Enterprises, Inc., PO Box 64073, St. Paul, MN 55164. (800) 328-5540. Fax: (800) 845-4832.

Warren 1•2•3 series
Ages 2–7. 1•2•3 Art, 1•2•3 Colors, $14.95. Special Day Celebrations, Small World Celebrations, $15.95. 1•2•3 Puppets, $7.45. 1•2•3 Murals, 1•2•3 Books, $1.75. 1•2•3 Games, $8.95 each. Shipping extra.
Frank Schaffer Publications, PO Box 2853, Torrance, CA 90509-2853. (800) 421-5533. Fax: (800) 837-7260. Email: fspinfo@aol.com. Web: www.frankschaffer.com.

tles, spray bottles, and tongue depressors and paint us up a storm.

Warren Publishing House remains *the* place for activity books for preschoolers. Their lineup also includes *1•2•3 Puppets, 1•2•3 Murals* (these are designed to be made and used in large classroom formats), *1•2•3 Games, 1•2•3 Books* (easy books kids can make), *1•2•3 Colors, Small World Celebrations,* and *Special Day Celebrations.* Each of these books has a strong hands-on flavor, with easy-to-follow directions for every activity. *Mary Pride*

NEW!
Williamson "Little Hands" Books

Ages 2 and up. Each book, $12.95. Shipping extra.
Williamson Publishing Company, Box 185, Charlotte, VT 05445, Phone: (800) 234-8791. Fax: (802) 425-2199.

"Mommy, what can I do. I'm bored." How many times have you heard this from your pre-schooler? Or your elementary students? While school is in session and the little ones have nothing to do, get out one of these **Williamson "Little Hands" books**:

- *Rainy Day Play—Explore, Create, Discover, Pretend*
- *Stop, Look & Listen—Using Your Senses from Head to Toe*
- *Shapes, Sizes & More Surprises!—A Little Hands Early Learning Book*

These amply illustrated books give a myriad of ideas for your young ones to do. Step-by-step instructions and black-and-white line drawings provide both inspirations and explanations. You can make letters, scratch and sniff paints, or rainbows and mobiles. You can float eggs, play in puddles, dance, and make your own music. Explore the world outside and inside. Grow your own herb garden. Collect leaves.

Many of these ideas you've seen elsewhere or picked up from friends and other homeschoolers but now they're all in these volumes. With well over 50 activities per book, it will be a long time until you run out of ideas. Many of the activities your children will want to do again and again.

With hints for you and special notes for your children, these books from Williamson Publishing could add the finishing touches to your preschooler's school day. *Barb Meade*

CHAPTER 4

Academic Kindergarten Programs

Kindergarten is a German word. It means literally "child garden." The German educator who invented it back in 1837, Friedrich Wilhelm August Froebel, believed that certain basic readiness activities such as paper cutting, clay modeling, and weaving were the building blocks of later vocational skills, and that children should be exposed to them in a happy, child-centered environment guided by an ever-understanding and loving teacher—a veritable garden of children.

If you're over 30, the kindergartens you and I attended when we were kids more or less fit this mold. We cut and pasted. We fingerpainted. We pretended we were little flowers raising our tiny faces to the sun. We listened to stories about Mr. Busy Bee and Mrs. Robin Redbreast. We ate cookies and milk. We napped. We learned which hand was the right hand, which color was orange, and that God was great and good and we should thank Him for our food.

But somewhere during the years we were in college or going out into the world, the bright boys who are responsible for the current illiteracy fiasco in the public schools came up with a theory that has, in effect, eliminated old-fashioned kindergarten. They reasoned that, **since they weren't able to teach kids to read in grades 1–12, they should start one grade earlier,** and that would make all the difference.

So today, "kindergarten" is often really a mini first grade. Kids are expected to learn reading, addition and subtraction, handwriting, and other skills traditionally reserved for the six-year-olds. This leads to all kinds of parental and child distress, as the pressure mounts to keep Junior from "falling behind."

Kinder Boot Camp or Kinder Garden?

Now, I happen to think that kids of that age *are* capable of learning these things—but not necessarily in a formal, lockstep, institutional setting. Kids learn in fits and starts, especially little kids. You can show a little

---

When Are Children Ready For "Real" Kindergarten

When children reach Step 9 [of the Kellogg Hierarchy of scribbling levels], what Kellogg called the *humanoid,* they usually name the person drawn. At that point we know that the child is cognitively ready to learn about abstract symbols such as alphabet letters or numerals because the child has already drawn an abstraction (something that represents something else).

To try to teach young children to write alphabet letters before the humanoid spontaneously appears is probably counterproductive and possibly harmful to some children.

—*Donna Reid Connell,
Lesson Guide to* itl *Integrated Total Language: A Draw to Write to Read Program*

Packaged Curriculum

- A Beka Books (K4, K5—accelerated phonics/academic approach, Christian)
- ACE School of Tomorrow (choice of two academic learning-to-read programs, Christian)
- Advanced Training Institute (academic kindergarten *without* math and phonics, which must be purchased elsewhere, Christian)
- A Beka Video School (academic kindergarten, Christian)
- Alpha Omega Publications (Horizons kindergarten includes math and phonics, Christian)
- Alta Vista Homeschool Curriculum (K–1 two-year integrated program: need separate phonics and math curriculum, Christian)
- Bob Jones University Press (K5 phonics, Christian)
- Christ Centered Publications (preschool program is actually more like kindergarten, Christian)
- Christian Liberty Academy (junior and senior kindergarten—academic programs, Christian)
- Christian Light Education (academic kindergarten, a Learning to Read worktext program, Mennonite)
- Clonlara School (any age, whatever kind of program you want, secular)
- ESP Publications (kindergarten— *My Yearbook* huge supplemental workbook, secular)
- Home Study International (academic kindergarten, Seventh-Day Adventist)
- Landmark's Freedom Baptist (Champion Kindergarten program, Christian)
- Learning At Home (preschool is combined with kindergarten in one-volume curriculum, Christian)
- KONOS (K–6 integrated manual: choose your activities: need separate phonics and math curriculum, Christian)
- Rod and Staff (kindergarten—phonics, Mennonite)
- Seton Home Study School (kindergarten—readiness and phonics, Catholic)
- Sonlight (preschool and kindergarten, Christian)
- Sycamore Tree (readiness and phonics both available, Seventh-Day Adventist)
- The Weaver (K–6 integrated curriculum, Christian)

kid how to make the numeral "2" dozens of times, to absolutely no effect, and then all of a sudden one day he will "get it." The same goes for blending letters to make words, or understanding the concept of "same" and "different." You can't pick a day and say, "*Achtung!* On this day all five-year-olds across America will be ready to learn to write the lowercase alphabet!"

This would not matter terribly much, except that in school you are labeled *stupid* if you fail to learn what the schedule book says you should learn on a given date. Oh, pardon me, not *stupid*—"learning disabled," or "minimal brain dysfunction," or "attention deficit disorder," etc. This last one is particularly interesting. It means, "Johnny is bored with his lessons and would rather run around the room or sit staring blankly at the clock." Just think—after all these years, I finally discovered that I suffered grievously from attention deficit disorder—just like a million other perfectly normal kids with boring teachers!

As the schools become more inflexible about what kids should learn at what age, homeschool parents have a golden opportunity to both recapture a little of the fun of our crayon-lovin' childhoods and ease our little ones more gradually into the academic mainstream. The secret is to give our kids readiness training before launching into academics, and to take the academics at whatever pace is comfortable for the kids.

What this all boils down to, is that I see no reason for teaching kindergarten at home, unless you are determined to place your child into a formal school setting for first grade. As preparation for today's first grade classroom, an academic kindergarten is fine. Otherwise, here's what I'd suggest:

- **Pick a good readiness program.**
- **Add a bunch of readiness goodies**, such as puzzles, Lauri lacing activities, art supplies, and Frank Schaeffer preschool workbooks. (See previous chapter for reviews).
- **Go straight from readiness** into a real phonics program and a real first-grade math book.
- **Add a bunch of library books**, including many in the areas of history and science, that you will read to your child.
- **Skip kindergarten.** It's just more readiness plus not enough phonics.
- **Skip first grade.** The history at this grade level is a joke in every packaged curriculum I've seen, just as it is in school. You're lucky if you learn the Pledge of Allegiance and the meaning of a few holidays. Social studies is mostly I am a Wonderful Me (Yes, I Really, Really Am!) and Francine the Firefighter is Your Friend. Science for first-graders is likewise rinky-dink—buy the Usborne science book of your choice and your child will be getting about 500 percent more instruction than in any school science text. The phonics is better in a phonics program, plus a good phonics program will include instruction in spelling and handwriting. You already have a math book.
- **Go directly to second grade.** You are now one year ahead and have spent about one-third the time, money, and effort of those who felt the need to struggle through kindergarten and first grade.

Packaged Kindergarten Curriculum

All that being said, it's now time to take a look at some kindergarten programs designed especially for you to use at home. These are *not* readiness programs; those are covered in the last chapter. In fact, these aren't kindergarten at all, in the classic, Froebelian sense of the word. Think of these as the transition from babyhood to student, for kids who are ready for more formal instruction than a readiness program.

The suppliers in the sidebar on the left-hand page offer many complete grade levels of curriculum, including complete *academic* kindergarten programs. I have listed their religious emphasis, if any. "Christian" indicates "nondenominational Bible-believing Christian." If the curriculum has a specific denominational emphasis, that is mentioned in lieu of the less specific "Christian." For more information, see the complete reviews, addresses, and ordering information in Volume 1.

Other Kindergarten Materials

Not every kindergarten supplier has curriculum for lots of grade levels. You can find math materials just for kindergarten in chapter 25 of this book. Many of the phonics materials in the phonics section of this book can be used with kindergarten-aged children. Finally, here are reviews of individual kindergarten programs and kindergarten-level resources *not* found in Volume 1.

Delightful, very gentle introduction to typical kindergarten skills—letter names and sounds, writing, drawing—and some quite untypical kindergarten skills like research and basic science experiments.

Alphabetiks is subtitled "Alphabet Activities for Young Children, ages 5–7," and that's what it is, plus some. You get three spiral-bound books: the curriculum manual, a manuscript writing tablet, and a dictionary tablet. The curriculum manual includes the following alphabet activities for each alphabet letter: a small rectangle containing information and the shape of the ancient letterform from which our modern letter is derived; a dictionary word beginning with that letter; a list of tools whose names begin with that letter; a suggested drawing subject whose name begins with that letter; an "ideas" list from which you can build your own mini-unit study (again, each idea name begins with that letter); a thought question for discussion around the dinner table; a short list of recommended picture books whose names begin with the letter; one or two extremely clever art or science projects; and a list of snacks whose names begin with the letter.

The Manuscript Handwriting Tablet has one page for each letter. In the illustrated border of the page you will find one or more objects whose names begin with that letter. At the top of the page are illustrated letterforms showing you how to construct the letter using a pre-cursive approach. Underneath that are uppercase and lowercase copies of the letter to trace. Below that are a few lines for the child to write copies of the words beginning with that letter that are listed on the left side of the page.

Remember the dictionary words I mentioned in the curriculum manual? These are "big" words like *aqueduct* and *fabricate*. Parents look up the word for the child, thereby teaching an important research skill while increasing the child's vocabulary. The child then traces the word in the Dictionary Word Tablet and writes the word on the line provided. He also makes up a sentence using the word, which the parent copies down in the space provided for this. Finally, the child makes a drawing about the word, using the suggested sentence in the curriculum manual. For example, he might draw an ant pulling a piece of apple across an aqueduct. The parent is supposed to explain what the objects he is trying to draw look like before he starts drawing. If the child is not ready to produce a drawing that complicated, Alphabetiks' authors urge you to simplify the task.

Alphabetiks

Grade K–2. $19.95 (includes manual and both tablets) plus shipping. *Bookstuff, 21534 Saint James Place, West Linn, OR 97068. (503) 638-4806. Email: cjreinold@msn.com*

Manuscript Handwriting Tablet

Sample Page

Let me share just one letter's worth with you, to give you the flavor of this excellent program. The letter is *B* and the dictionary word is *burrow*. Tools are "simple balancing scale, binoculars, balloons." If you have these around the house, introduce your child to them and show him how to use them. Then have your child draw a bear balancing on a barge, crossing under a bridge. The "Ideas" are balloons (hot air or helium), balance, bones, building, bridges. Using a blackboard or a large sheet of paper, list what your child "knows or wants to know about each of these topics, branching down and out." For example, the progression might be, "BONES —> Rover has bones —> I have bones —> Are my bones different from Rover's?" Pick one of these topics to explore in depth, using the library or any resources you might have around the house. (You keep the results in a journal.) The recommended picture books are *Blueberries for Sal* and *Benjamin and Tulip*. Letter B has two projects: BUILD strong bridges and make a BOOK about one of the B ideas. The bridge project includes experimenting with different shapes for the bridge (which is made out of plasticine clay) and seeing how long a bridge your child can make (measure it!) and how many objects such as paper clips it will hold (count or weight them!). The book project instructions tell you how to construct and reinforce a simple book. Finally, you get a list of simple snacks: banana bread, bagels and butter, etc.

This curriculum is easier to use than any other kindergarten program. You just do one letter a week. The authors recommend that you teach a few consonants first, then a vowel or two, so you can start teaching your child to read simple three-letter words. Along the way the child will learn to use a variety of useful household tools, be prodded to think more creatively and scientifically, have a variety of excellent children's classics read to him, do some fantastic art projects and science experiments, pick up any readiness concepts he might be missing, and have a whole lot of fun.

For families with little time to spare for teaching, but who still want to give the kindergartner an unpressured, yet rich learning experience, *Alphabetiks* is a great choice. Just add a kindergarten math program and you've got it made! *Mary Pride*

NEW!
BJUP Beginnings K5

Age 5. Beginnings Home School Kit, $155. Math K5 Home School Kit, $53. Music K5 Home School Kit, $79.
Bob Jones University Press, Greenville, SC 29614. (800) 845-5731. Fax: (800) 525-8398. From other countries: Call (864) 242-5100, x 3349. Email: bjup@bju.edu. Web: www.bju.edu/press/home.html.

What comes after four-year-old kindergarten? Kindergarten for five-year-olds—the **Bob Jones University Press Beginnings K5** program.

Basically, this is a language-arts program. Here you get into actual phonics lessons, using the "word family" method and using songs and charts. Each lesson begins with science and Heritage Studies activities, and listening comprehension—the foundation of eventual reading comprehension—is built with a story in every lesson.

Handwriting is taught with BJU's "Practi-Slate," a magic slate by another name. You place a "handwriting insert"—a piece of paper with a handwriting example printed on it—under the transparent top sheet, and press down hard to write. When you take the insert away, you can see the letters formed on the underlying black waxy surface. Personally, I have always found these hard to use. They have a tendency to self-destruct, and even at best it's hard to keep the top sheet flat enough to keep air bubbles from messing up the letters. A whiteboard and erasable Magic Marker work much better. That said, BJUP's precursive script is easy to learn and teach, and quite attractive.

Also included are teacher's manual, worktexts, reader, song cassettes, student response cards, and three flip charts.

Again, Bible is a separate subject, not included in the kit. At this level, math and music are also available as separate subjects. All are engaging, pleasing to the eye, and reasonably easy to use. *Mary Pride*

Calvert Kindergarten II
Grade K. First child, $325. "Group" enrollment for additional child, $275. Optional Advisory Teaching Service, $200 per child.
Calvert School, 105 Tuscany Road, Baltimore, MD 21210. (410) 243-6030. Fax: (410) 366-0674. Email: inquiry@calvertschool.org. Web: www.calvertschool.org.

Calvert's Kindergarten II is an academic kindergarten designed to bridge the gap between the very fun, arts and crafts, stories, and songs of Calvert's traditional "readiness" Kindergarten and the highly academic Calvert First Grade. Think of this one as the "real" kindergarten and the original Kindergarten course as a preschool course for four-year-olds.

This incredibly fun and solid course includes Calvert's own phonics readers, plus math manipulatives, poems, music, science, and tons of crafts materials and activities.

When we opened a Calvert box for our children's courses we were always amazed at the amount of materials we got. Calvert Kindergarten II is no exception. You get

- the Calvert School Kindergarten II Teacher's Manual
- a "teacher aids" book (flashcards associating letters with pictures, sight word cards, key picture cards, and "sliders" that enable you to make lots of little words by sliding a consonant strip up and down or back and forth)
- reading worksheets
- *Sounds and Letters* (a workbook with one page apiece for most alphabet letters, starting with *Mm*, *Bb*, and *Cc*)
- science and math activities worksheets
- a read-aloud book entitled *Poems and Prose*
- Calvert's own set of 20 beginning phonics storybooks
- Macmillan/Mcgraw-Hill's *Mathematics in Action*, (a book with dozens of neat colored cardboard punch-out manipulatives built right in)
- Macmillan/Mcgraw-Hill's *Science in Your World* (a Weekly Reader-style softcover text)
- Harcourt Brace Jovanovich's *Rainbows Level R* (simple phonics activities plus classic read-aloud poems, with punch-out alphabet flashcards built in)
- *Arts & Crafts From Things Around the House*
- two kindergarten music tapes including an assortment of Christian songs, Hannukah songs, nursery rhyme songs, classic children's songs, patriotic songs, and a very few new songs (lyrics for every song on the tapes are printed in the teacher's manual)

You also get math manipulatives: a magnetic tray with multicolored shapes, and 30 unifix cubes. For your school supplies (a Calvert specialty),

If you choose to enroll in the optional Advisory Teaching Service, you'll send Calvert samples of your child's daily work and the current set of progress sheets. Calvert will evaluate these materials and return them to you with helpful comments.

you get newsprint paper, watercolor paper, index cards, sidewalk chalk, watercolors, paste, yarn, metal brads, glue sticks, Elmer's school glue, scotch tape, Calvert pencils, a pencil sharpener, pipe cleaners, masking tape, rubber bands, crayons, modeling clay, flexible magnets, a ruler, a pink eraser, paper clips, a pair of scissors, lots of colored construction paper and manila construction paper (bring back memories?), two folders with pockets inside, and a "Calvert pad" of lightweight plain paper.

Bound into the Teacher's Manual every 20 lessons are something new for a Calvert kindergarten course: "progress sheets." These ask you to identify how well your child is doing in various academic areas (e.g., "Can he order numbers 1 through 12 correctly?") and various readiness areas ("Is the pupil able to catch and throw a large ball?"). There are also some rather invasive questions that ask you to reveal your child's personal behavior and seem to judge your parenting skills (e.g., "Does he have a regular bedtime routine?" . . . "Can he work well only on things he really enjoys doing or thinking about?" . . . "How does your child choose to spend his leisure time?" . . . "Does he adjust to changes in a new situation without becoming fearful?"). Considering homeschoolers' concerns about public school "attitudinal" and "personal preferences" tests, I think Calvert would be well advised to remove these questions altogether. If the authors of this grade level think it is important to offer advice in such areas, it would be much better to simply include a list of such questions, with suggested responses, in the back of the manual.

Aside from the unnecessary psychological "progress" questions, this is a *wonderful* curriculum. It has warmth, charm, and depth. It has loads of hands-on goodies. Little kids will love it . . . and learn from it. *Mary Pride*

Christ Centered Curriculum for Early Childhood

Grades K–2. Basic Program, $177.95 (usable ages 3–7). Student/teacher workbooks and readers: K4, $39.95; K5, $63.95; first grade, $46.95. Math Manipulatives Kit, $61.95. Components available separately. Shipping extra.
Christ Centered Publications, Inc., PO Box 968, Tullahome, TN 37388. (800) 778-4318. Fax: (800) 884-7858.. Email: ccpcurriculum@ficom.net. Web: www.christcentercurriculum.com.

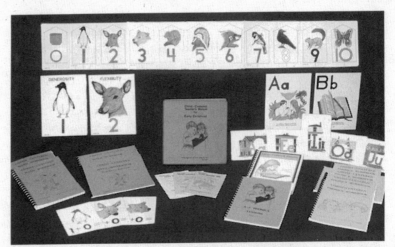

Christ Centered Curriculum for Early Childhood may be the most serious attempt yet at a truly Christ-centered kindergarten and early grades program. Author Doreen Claggett, a schoolteacher of many years and a firm believer in early childhood as the time to begin scholarly studies, has assembled a workbook curriculum focusing mainly on phonics and math, with some art and other activities built in. The basic homeschool version Teacher's Manual ($15) outlines the full early childhood education program and explains how to do seatwork with young children. Included is an article entitled "Detecting Learning Disabilities." The Basic Program also contains Bible, phonics, and math lesson plans in separate binders plus related visual aids. The program's philosophy appears in Mrs. Claggett's book *Never Too Early.*

OK, OK. Now where does the "Christ-centered" part come in? Well, would you believe math starting with the days of creation? Each day's work begins with a Bible verse and ties in as many Biblical examples as possible. Drawing upon the traditional Biblical numerology (seven as the number of perfection, three as the number of Trinity), numbers are presented as they relate to their occurrences in the Bible. Colors also have their own (slightly more strained) typology: purple for royalty, blue for heaven, orange for "the completeness of Christ's crosswork" and so on. Along with this you get flash cards reminiscent of Thoburn Press's *Animal Families* curriculum, with Mr. One Penguin and his chick 1+0, and so on. The math flash cards come with stories derived from Bill Gothard's Institute of Basic Youth Conflicts animal character sketches.

Similarly, CCP's phonics program uses Bible names and words as key words for the phonics sounds. The full program includes phonics work-books, a *Phonics Drill Reader*, three little readers, phonics flash cards, alphabet wall cards, and other teaching devices. See the separate writeup of the phonics program in chapter 7.

CCP's math program teaches the addition and subtraction facts in a somewhat roundabout way based on amounts less than or greater than 10. According to the author, this has caused no problems for the more than 2,000 students who have used CCP math in her school's classrooms over the last 22 years. The children have achieved very well on standardized achievement tests. Still, for the higher levels of math I personally would substitute Bob Jones University Press texts.

Spiritually, most people get excited by the program's intense concentration on spiritual application—some so much so that the author has to warn against the temptation to use too much time preaching the lesson's spiritual theme at the expense of academics! CCP certainly is a far cry from the stray-Bible-verse-here-and-there or add-one-missionary-plus-one-missionary approach of much Christian curriculum. Send for the free information and you will see what I mean. *Mary Pride*

UPDATED!
Commonsense Kindergarten Program
Grade K. $63 plus shipping.
Common Sense Press, P.O. Box 1365, Melrose FL 32666. Call (352) 475-5757 for a retail store near you; they do not sell retail themselves. Email: LearnCSP@aol.com.

Designed for four- and five-year-olds, the **Commonsense Kindergarten Program** includes readiness exercises, Bible, pre-reading, pre-writing, math, thinking skills (unusual for a kindergarten program), manners (ditto), safety, art, and ideas for role play and physical education. Program contents include:

- **Early Education at Home** by Jean Soyke. This oversized, spiral-bound teacher's manual provides 36 weekly lesson plans. These are called "planning guides" because they are somewhat adaptable—you are given choices such as reading a Bible story about "Bartimaeus, or other character starting with B." This rather complete book has a handy index in the back for all the suggested activities (thanks, Jean!), a bibliography, and one appendix each with ideas for learning centers, tangram shapes to duplicate, software for young children, and reading programs for home instruction, as well as reproducible planning sheets. There's also a skills checklist, a list of suggested activities you can insert into the program as you wish, and more.

- **A Study in Wisdom** by Dr. Dale Simpson is a slim 28 pages. First he explains the importance of wisdom. Then several verses from Proverbs are used to teach "wisdom" lessons. Finally, you are instructed to create a chart that you fill in as you read Bible stories as a family, in which you answer the questions, "What do you learn about God?" Who is wise?" and "Who is foolish?" This is meant to teach you the attributes of God—and of wisdom.

- **Language and Thinking** by Dr. Ruth Beechick and Jeannie Nelson (Mott Media). A wonderful book! Includes units of how to get the most out of telling and reading stories (plus six complete classic children's stories to read), activities to improve vocabulary and language skills (nutrition vocabulary, traffic vocabulary, numbers, measurement, classifying and organizing), language games (these are excellent!), items to memorize (personal info, letters, numbers, prayers, Bible verses, poems, hymns, patriotic songs, the calendar), telephone use and manners (including emergency phoning skills), poems (from baby poems to one-liners, funny poems, and rope jumping rhymes), manners (a very important unit that teaches polite words, how to accept and give compliments, how to meet and greet people, special manners for boys and girls, and public manners for church, library, store, and restaurant), and how to get the most educational value out of field trips (including suggested field trips).

- **Common Sense Math** by Yuriko Nichols. This manipulative-based program teaches counting, sequencing, patterning, symbols, shapes, addition, subtraction, odd and even, and skip counting. You get nine colored cubes, onto which you are supposed to apply pregummed stickers with shapes, dots, and numbers. You also get 20 see-through colored bingo chips, cards for a bingo game, symbol cards, a Clothespin Math Game (with no clothespins), and a Hundred Chart.

- **The First Learning Activity Books series** from EDC Publications: four colorful activity books covering counting to ten and simple addition, pre-reading readiness, opposites, and pre-writing skills. These are not reusable workbooks, unfortunately—once your child writes in the EDC workbooks the first time, that's it for them. *Mary Pride*

Fast Progress

Ages 4–7. $36 plus $6.95 shipping. *Shekinah Curriculum Cellar, 101 Meador Rd., Kilgore, TX 75662. (903) 643-2760. Fax: (903) 643-2796. Email: customerservice@shekinahcc.com. Web: www.shekinahcc.com.*

Designed for four- to seven-year-olds, this nifty game is the only one I've ever seen that teaches communication skills needed for success in school.

Fast Progress is a colorful game board of the move-along-the-straight-path variety. It comes with 180 game cards, die, timer, six player pieces, 10 blank cards, and complete instructions. Someone who knows how to read needs to read the cards to the young players. Average playing time ranges from 20 minutes to an hour.

Each small blue card has two questions on it, directed to different readiness levels. This simple device means children of different ages can play competitively. Simply have the younger children answer Level I questions while the older ones answer Level II. Cards with one right answer are answered on the Answer List. Some questions, such as, "What is your name?" are not answered on the answer list. You only use the one-minute timer if necessary to keep the game moving along.

To play, pick as many cards as you think your child is up to answering. Each player rolls a die, and the highest number goes first. When it's his turn, each player takes a card and tries to answer that question. If he can answer it correctly, he rolls the die and moves that number of spaces. If the card he draws gives a direction (e.g., "If you are on red, move to the next nearest blue") he follows the directions first and then rolls the die to move again. The object is to arrive exactly at the "Finish" space.

Questions are an intriguing mix. Some require kids to think out the answers, while others test what kids know. All use the typical communication skills required in school. Topics cover those kids need to be familiar with before entering first grade: body parts, personal data, time concepts, directionality (right/left, up/down), classifying, making analogies, antonyms (words that are opposites), rhyming, describing, vocabulary, math concepts, and general practical knowledge. The game author encourages you to have the children answer each question in a complete sentence, if they are old enough to make this feasible.

Here are a few sample questions:

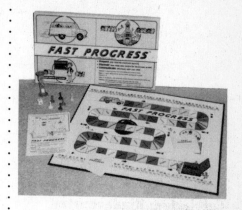

- (Level I) *How many sides does a triangle have?* (Level II) *Which is more money, a quarter or a nickel?*
- *After you touch a green box on the board, touch a white one.*
- (Level I) *What do you wear that comes in a pair?* (Level II) *What number is at the bottom of a clock?*
- (Level I) *Name three things that could be below you.* (Level II) *Name the months of the year.*
- (Level I) *How does a mother cat clean her babies?* (Level II) *What is hail?*

I really admire the questions in this game. They really cover an amazingly broad range of stuff kids need to know and be thinking about.

Now, is *Fast Progress* fun to play? You betcha! It really moves fast. And is it really educational? For sure. This is not another boring educational game—it's more like Preschool Student's Educational and Thinking Trivia. Any kid whose parents play this game with him before he starts his school studies (whether at school or in home school) will have a definite edge on most kids who don't. *Mary Pride*

Training Wheels is a hefty, spiral-bound, 345-page readiness curriculum. The book contains 40 week-long units. Each unit begins with goals for the week in the areas of Bible, social studies, language, math, science, health, music, and art. If you buy the complete program, you'll also get a felt human body package (for learning anatomy), a food groups pyramid, and a set of upper-/lower/case letters and numerals, so children who aren't ready for handwriting can still practice recognizing letters and forming words.

The Bible portion of the curriculum hits the high spots of the entire Bible in one year—from Creation to the Apostle Paul's missionary journeys. Each week's lessons also include a suggested memory verse.

The language activities are designed to teach the alphabet, upper- and lower-case letters, letter sounds, and some phonograms and their sounds. You'll also do a lot of conversation, vocabulary development, storytelling, and story reading.

Math activities teach recognition of shapes, counting up to 100, and identification of numerals. In addition, the child will practice lots of other math skills: sequencing, measurement, calendar reading, coin skills, etc.

Social studies covers Bible-time customs, modern-day customs, manners, and relationships. Science consists mostly of hands-on nature activities. Health covers safety rules, hygiene, and some simple anatomy. Music activities involve singing, rhythms, and music appreciation. In art, the emphasis is self-expression using a variety of media.

In keeping with the Hewitt philosophy of hands-on early childhood education, there's little or no workbook-type stuff in this curriculum. What you will find is lots and lots of learning activities for parent and child to do together. There's enough material here for each day to last me for two or three hours. *Sherry Early*

Champion Baptist Kindergarten is a first-class, total kindergarten package! It comes in two parts. The teacher's kit includes everything you will ever need to thoroughly teach kindergarten concepts. Included are: Daily Lesson Plans, *The Beginner's Champion Phonics Reader*, *McGuffey's Eclectic Primer*, "Teaching Phonics Sounds" Cassette Tape, 31 Alphabet Flashcards, 20 Number Flashcards, 0–100 Chart, 36 Bible Memory Verse Cards, five Phonics Charts, and 19 Phonogram Towers.

The Student Kit includes: Report Card, Diploma, ABC Bible Memory Verse Chart, three Letters and Numbers Pads, Letters Writing Pad, Numbers Writing Pad, Small Number Cards (0–9), *The Beginner's Champion Phonics Reader*, and *McGuffey's Eclectic Primer*.

The program is carefully designed to leave no room for failure. The *Lesson Plan Manual* is practical and simple to use, right down to the spiral binding. All the material is spiral bound, making it easy to handle . . . just one of the many neat features of this program. I even liked the fact that a copy of each of the readers is included for both parent and student. No more trying to lean over to figure out what word they are struggling with!

This phonics-based program is totally eclectic. *The Beginner's Champion Phonics Reader* emphasizes building fluency and speed for your young readers. It has a *Victory Drill Book* flavor . . . and did I mention that I love the spiral binding? McGuffey Readers are used throughout the elementary literature part of the program to help your child with reading comprehension. The math is "no-nonsense" as well, with a strong emphasis on the basics.

This is structured program does require some work from your kindergartner, but the quality of the program helps guarantee success if your child is ready! Landmark's Freedom Baptist Curriculum took the best of a variety of programs and rolled them into one. This program compares favorably with any of the "long-time, big-names" in the home education movement. In fact, the eclectic nature, well-thought-out design, and low cost make it a first-rate choice. *Maryann Turner*

My Father's World From A to Z: A Complete Kindergarten Curriculum uses quality children's literature and a unit-study approach for a complete kindergarten curriculum. The author draws on the ideas presented by Susan Schaeffer Macaulay in her book *For the Children's Sake* in developing this curriculum, which is designed to be used in either a homeschool or a classroom. There are separate instructions for the homeschool in many cases, and this program does not have the flavor of a classroom program adapted for homeschool use.

What you get is a spiral-bound teacher's manual, a set of 5 x 8" full-color flash cards, and a student "workbook" which is actually a stack of separate pages at least an inch thick. The flash cards are one-sided so they can be hung on the wall, and feature the 26 letters of the alphabet along with one picture for each letter. You will also need a set of 2" textured alphabet letters, 27 file folders, twice that number of envelopes and various common school and art supplies, and your Bible. You also need access to the literature selections, which will be available in most public libraries (alternates are suggested if you have trouble finding a specific selection).

NEW!
Landmark's Freedom Baptist Curriculum Kindergarten

Age 3–6. Champion Baptist Kindergarten: Teacher's Kit, $125; Student's Kit, $75.

Landmark's Freedom Baptist Curriculum, 2222 E. Hinson Ave., Haines City, FL 33844. (800) 700-5322. Fax: (941) 422-0188. Email: lfbc@juno.com. Web: www.landmark-baptistchurch.org/lfbc.

NEW!
My Father's World From A to Z

Grade K. Complete program, $89.95. Alphabet flashcards alone, $7.95. Sample, $3, comes with $3-off coupon. Shipping extra.

My Father's World, PO Box 1674, Corvallis, OR 97339-1674. (541) 745-5421. Email: mfw@dnc.net. Web: www.dnc.net/users/triad/mfw.

My Father's World can be started with a child who does not know all the letters of the alphabet, and by the end the child will be reading simple sentences with short vowel sounds. The reading plan uses a multisensory phonics approach using blend ladders. In addition, science, math, Bible, art, children's literature and creative thinking are covered in this 166-day program.

The first 10 days have a different format from the rest, during which the days of creation are taught and the letters of the alphabet are introduced. Each of the following 26 lessons covers six days. On the five weekdays you have reading and math activities (and student pages that go along with these) as well as a science or art activity. The sixth day is Book Day!

The student pages have a simple, uncluttered look. Each 60–90 minute lesson concentrates on one letter of the alphabet, presented not in alphabetical order but in an order that goes along with the phonics part of the program. The picture on the flash card is an object (usually an animal) that starts with that letter, and each unit's activities center around that object.

The teacher's manual has the reading plan on separate, yellow pages, followed by the lessons. This means you will have to flip around a bit as you are teaching the lessons, but you should quickly get used to the format. Some of the activities involve singing; the words are provided and they are either common songs or sung to the tune of common songs. Those of us who are musically challenged would appreciate the addition of a tape containing the songs; for now you have to manage the songs on your own. *Melissa Worcester*

The partnership of teaching and television will never get better than the **Rusty and Rosy series of educational videos**! Over thirty minutes of engaging, educational music and language come alive when you pop one of these four tapes into the VCR.

Nursery Songs and Rhymes brings us 26 animated rhymes of various cultures. The skills stressed combine to offer your child a language lesson that can be repeated time and again for reinforcement, or even just for fun! Colorful animation and catchy harmony elevate this video past mere education, into the realm of pure "edutainment."

ABCs and Such uses a variety of musical arrangements to teach the alphabet. Children with prereading skills can read along with Rusty and Rosy and will be enthralled by the diversity of graphics used to represent each letter. The videos use quality classical music, which may appeal to parents who desire classical accompaniment to the learning process.

Letter Sound Songs is just as innovative. Four songs teach letter sounds, while two songs teach vowel sounds. Beautiful illustrations teach the child how to carefully recreate each letter of the alphabet. The one concern a parent might have: their child may become so engrossed with this video that they stand or sit too near the television screen as they learn to make lowercase letters. The glimpse of wigs to represent the letter "W" might be too brief for some children to comprehend, but does not detract from the overall superiority of this video.

Last, but in no way least, **Sing Around the World** will certainly become a favorite! While developed for children ages 2–6, the possibility of using this video in world history education should not be overlooked. *Sing Around the World* is not merely a selection of favorite children's songs, Rusty and Rosy treat the subject as a geography lesson and use a map to indicate the origin of each piece in the collection. Twenty-seven songs appear on this video, representing cultures from India, Japan, Wales, Africa, Jamaica, New Zealand, and more. Each song is played twice in the English language, then read in English, and finally performed in its original foreign language.

The addition of a Native American selection and the complement of a hauntingly beautiful melody make this video a tremendous success in understanding the culture of the earliest Americans.

The new **Sing, Spell, Read & Write Kindergarten Combo Kit** includes the entire Sing, Spell, Read & Write program reviewed in the Phonics Programs chapter, as well as all the following

- *All Aboard* and *On Track*, the kindergarten worktexts. These include age-appropriate lessons for the kindergarten child.
- Instructor's Directions, a supplement to the Teacher's Manual, with directions for teaching the kindergarten materials. This basically amounts to one page of instructions per book. You don't need any more than this, since every page of the student worktexts has teacher directions printed in small type at the bottom of the page.
- Six additional full-color Storybook Readers just for the kindergarten child, five featuring adorable little bug characters, and one featuring a variety of talking animals. Exercises in the worktexts are correlated with the readers.

All Aboard introduces name and different, tracing, classification, pattern completion, following directions, and other reading readiness skills. *On Track* introduces letter recognition, letter sounds, manuscript writing, word blending, vocabulary, beginning reading, comprehension, spelling preparation, listening, and speaking skills. *On Track* also includes 10 tear-out, color-and-read storybooks.

This is a really cute and adorable program. Everything is four-color, very eye-appealing, and easy to use. If you plan to use SSR&W for your phonics instruction, it makes sense to get this Combo Kit, and use it for your kindergarten as well. *Mary Pride*

NEW!
Sing, Spell, Read & Write Kindergarten Combo Kit

Grades preK and K. $235 plus shipping.
International Learning Systems, 1000 - 112th Circle N., Suite 100, St. Petersburg, FL 33716. (800) 321-8322. Fax: (813) 576-8832. Web: www.singspell.com.

The Kindergarten Combo kit introduces these items, plus everything in the SSR&W Home Kit

PART 2

Learning to Read

During 1998's summer reading program at Carbondale (IL) Public Library, homeschooler Olivia Davis, age 6, read 400 books written for well beyond the reading level of the average six-year-old, like the Boxcar Children, Bobbsey Twins, easy readers of all kinds, and so on. Olivia has also completed two AWANA Sparks handbooks, review patches, and workbooks. She looks forward to starting Latin in 2000.

How old do you have to be to learn to read? Some of our nine children were ready at age 4, others at age 6 or 7. Here our daughter Lillian gets ready for reading by playing with a book. Books are favorite toys in the Pride household.

CHAPTER 5

The Reading Mystery Revealed

Reading is like toilet training; until your little one does it, you're afraid he never will. And if you send your child to public school, there is a good choice that your fears are justified. This is odd, because of the 24 million functional illiterates the Department of Education estimates live in the USA, virtually all have had between eight and 12 years of compulsory public schooling. This is more than enough time to teach kids to read, one would think!

Once the public schools actually did teach kids to read. As educational historian Sam Blumenfeld documents in his book *NEA: Trojan Horse in American Education*, statistics compiled by the Bureau of Education showed, "Of children from 10 to 14 years of age there were in 1910 only 22 out of every 1,000 who could neither read nor write." In 1910, nine states and the District of Columbia actually reported only *one* child in 1,000 between the ages of 10 and 14 as illiterate. And let me point out that when they said in those days that Johnny could read and write, they meant he could handle literature that's now beyond most Harvard freshmen.

As Mr. Blumenfeld notes, "Apparently they knew how to teach children to read in 1910. Also, there was no such thing as 'functional illiteracy,' that is, a kind of low, inadequate reading ability. . . . The illiteracy of 1910 was the result of some children having *no* schooling" (Emphasis mine).

How did those old-time schoolteachers work this miracle? With longer school years? No way! In rural districts school often was only in session from six weeks to a few months at a time several times a year. With more years of reading instruction? Nope. Kids frequently dropped out at early ages to help out on the farm. How about Head Start and other get-'em-early programs? Didn't exist. Johnny and Janie often didn't start school until age 7 or 8. Higher pay for teachers? Dream on! Schoolteachers were paid in room and board and very little more. Teachers were also often required to be single, for the very good reason that a married man couldn't possibly support a family on a teacher's pay.

People keep saying that we can't turn back the clock. Maybe not. But we can get it fixed and wind it up again! So first let's find out what went wrong, and then we can see what we should do about it.

> Many schools give high grades and happy report cards to children who are good at guessing and memorizing words, so parents don't realize that their children are being taught to guess instead of to read. Self-esteem is a higher priority [in those schools] than literacy.
>
> —*The Phyllis Schlafly Report*

PHONICS

"cat"

c – a – t

| The sound of c=/k/ | The sound of a=/a/ | The sound of t=/t/ |

LOOK-SAY

"cat"

The word is now a hieroglyph with its unique shape (outline) that must be memorized.

Why Johnny Can't Read

So why can't so many kids read today? Johnny can't read, quite simply, because *Johnny was never taught properly how to read.* Forget all the self-serving piffle about learning disabilities, underfunded schools (when they get an average $5,325 per pupil per year!), nutritional deficiencies, etc. We can also see through and reject the subtle racism of those who try to blame illiteracy on increased immigration and the larger numbers of "inner-city" (they mean minority) kids in the public schools. Black and Hispanic kids can learn to read English just as well as the Hungarian and Polish immigrant kids of the 1910s.

What I really want to do is to get the resources into your hands to make your kids literate. But first, you need to know what's going on. For the past 40 years, the teacher-training colleges have been indoctrinating eager young teachers in the doctrine of whole-word memorization. This approach, sometimes called "look-say," but more recently rechristened "Whole Language," consists of having children *memorize* words by their *shapes.* Typically, kids are "taught" to read this way by seeing large labels on objects around the classroom, having the same sentences in the same books read to them again and again until the child can "read" the sentence (I put "read" in quotes, because he's actually *memorized* the sentence), having flash cards flashed at them hundreds of times, guessing at the word from "context clues" and "picture clues" in books (unbelievably, this kind of guessing is actually taught separately as an essential "reading skill"!), and literally hundreds of stupid, trivial, and irrelevant activities only dimly related to reading, such as making a collage of objects that begin with the letter R. (The latter is a perfect example of the "phony phonics" activities that always accompany look-say programs. More on phony phonics in a minute.)

If you wonder whether your child is being taught to "read" by look-say, do what one mother did. Take the book your child is "reading" from in school, write some of the words on flash cards, and see if he can read the words *without* picture and context clues. If he can do that, then make up some similar *nonsense* words and see if he can read *them*! For example, if he can "read" the sentence, "John looked at the fish," he should be able to read the nonsense words *mooked* and *bish.* If he can't do this, you'd better keep reading this chapter.

Where Did We Get "Look-Say" Reading?

Interestingly, look-say was not invented to teach normal American kids to read. It was invented for the benefit of *deaf* kids! Here's how it happened. Once there was a good man, a reformer, named Thomas Gallaudet. Mr. Gallaudet was concerned about deaf children. He wanted to help them learn to read. Deaf children could not sound out words like hearing children, so to get around that difficulty Mr. Gallaudet devised a method of picture-word association. The child would be shown a picture of a cat and the word *cat.* By memorizing the configuration of the word the child could build up a very limited reading vocabulary. The reason his vocabulary would of necessity be limited is that so many words look like each other: *bag* and *bay, ball* and *bell, play* and *ploy.* As the child tried to memorize more and more words *by their appearance alone,* sooner or later his memory would give out. This method was, however, useful in its limited way and for its original audience.

As Kathryn Diehl, the author (with G. K. Hodenfield) of *Johnny STILL Can't Read—But You Can Teach Him at Home,* says, "Why it was ever decided that this would be an effective way to teach children who *can* hear and speak remains a mystery to this day." But that is exactly what happened! Since good readers read whole words, someone decided it was time to skip those silly phonics lessons and get right into "real" reading—sort of like skipping the swimming lessons and trying to swim the English Channel.

At this point, entire publishing empires have been built on supplying the hundreds of little vocabulary-controlled readers and millions of consumable workbooks that look-say requires. More than a few inflated reputations in those teacher-training colleges are at stake, not to mention big bucks in remedial education programs and years and years of employment for reading teachers, as reading instruction now continues beyond the elementary level, yea even unto college itself. These entrenched interests aren't about to let the look-say goose that is laying them such big fat golden eggs get killed without a struggle. These are big bucks. Over $3 billion dollars a year goes to the illiteracy mafia just in ECIA Chapter I funds alone. That is the real reason for our reading crisis.

Under the present setup, the more kids fail to read, the better life is for their school districts, as the federal money showers money on school districts for "remedial" programs and "special education." This may explain why New Hampshire, with the highest SAT scores in the nation (35 points above the national average), has the lowest per-pupil spending—$3,400 per pupil as opposed to New York's $11,000 per pupil. New York kids manage to score a whopping 105 points lower on the SAT than Granite Staters, so naturally those "teaching" them get almost three times as much per kid! If New Hampshire teachers would quit teaching the kids to read, they too could get more federal money.

Whole Language: Activities Instead of Training

Now, we Americans aren't totally stupid. We know something is wrong with what we fondly call "our" public schools, and we demand reforms. So every few years a "new" reading method is unveiled in the government school system. This time around it's the "Whole Language" method. When you boil them down, though, the supposed "reforms" *always* turn out to be sight-word reading, "phony phonics" (e.g., a few phonics principles introduced here and there in no systematic sequence), and tons and tons of expensive non-reading-related classroom materials. What's missing in this picture is always some *systematic* method of instructing the child in the sounds of the letters and combinations of letters that make the words of his country's language. Instead, we get "creative teaching methods" that jump around from one thing to another like a dog that just stepped on a porcupine. We get literally *millions* of kids labeled "learning disabled," when it's really the reading methods that are "teaching disabled"!

The currently fashionable Whole Language method, for example, believes in "immersing the child in print." The child is supposed to "do lots of reading and writing," but somehow he is never really *taught* to read and write. It is believed that kids will learn to become superb readers if they just have enough comic books, newspapers, play scripts, and can wrappers thrust before their noses. Coming to school dressed as Little Red Riding Hood is supposed to help, as is putting on a play circus and taking the parts of various animals. (I'm not making this up—these are actual Whole Language activities I've seen written up in teacher's magazines and supplier's catalogs!)

The reading problem is theorized, by Whole Learning advocates, to be merely a lack of motivation—those stupid kids don't *want* to learn to read—and a lack of access—their equally stupid parents are depriving

☺ **Whole Language is great once a child has already learned to read.**

☹ **Whole language fails when it is used to teach reading**

California came in last in national fourth-grade reading tests, set up a state task force to find out why, held legislative hearings, discovered that the state's Whole Language method is a disaster, and earmarked $100 million for new textbooks and teacher training to switch the schools back to phonics.

Governor Pete Wilson is even requiring that schools districts spend their federal Goals 2000 money on reading instruction. Wilson's spokesman, Sean Walsh, was blunt. "Whole Language was an utter failure. Our curriculum taught to kindergarten to third-graders, quite frankly, stinks."

—*The Phyllis Schlafly Report*

> Whole Language teaches children to guess at words by looking at the pictures on the page, to memorize a few dozen frequently used words, to skip over words they don't know, to substitute words that seem to fit, and to predict the words they think will come next. The child who is taught those bad habits, instead of how to sound out the syllables, will never be able to read big words or become a good reader.
> —*The Phyllis Schlafly Report*

them of a rich print environment. Kids are told to write their own books and plays when they haven't learned to decode words yet. Any activity involving letters is sacred, yet they are never systematically taught the letters' *sounds*. Maybe that's why one school using this method had *double* the usual number of "learning disabled" kids in the very first class taught by Whole Language methods.

Now, some of the Whole Language objectives are noble, such as the objective of getting kids reading real literature instead of crummy Dick-and-Jane vocabulary-controlled basal readers. But noble *goals* and noble *results* are two different stories, unfortunately. Without a systematic method for teaching kids to decode new words *without* having to memorize them, reading success is limited to those who are able to guess the rules on their own.

Phonics to the Rescue!

So what does work? Phonics. Since 1910, 124 studies have compared the look-say approach with phonics programs. *Not one study showed the look-say approach to be superior.* The reason is simple. Phonics is a logical approach that helps kids organize their way of attacking new words. Once children have learned a few rules, the exceptions won't knock them for a loop. In fact, even the "exceptions" have some phonetic elements. The three common "sight" words *do*, *the*, and *said*, for example, are at least 50 percent phonetic, and the irregular sounds can be easily figured out from the sense of the sentence. In fact, even *do* is 100 percent phonetic in some phonics methods I have seen, where more than one sound of the letter O is taught! The look-say approach, in contrast, is *all* exceptions. Each and every word has to be memorized on its own, and there is no end to this task. No wonder children give up in despair!

One of the most exciting things about teaching phonics is the way it brings back hope to children who have been taught by the schools to consider themselves stupid. You need no gimmicks or frills to accomplish this miracle—just time-tested phonics.

I am delighted to announce that there are literally dozens of home phonics programs that really work just as well as the public schools used to work in 1910. If you have "teaching blood," some excellent books can give you the whys and hows of teaching reading. If you haven't a teaching bone in your body, several methods have the teacher on the record, or provide programmed instructions that tell you everything you have to say. Prices range from a few measly shekels to over $200 for a complete language arts program that includes all your child could ever hope to learn in this area from the best private school in the country. Or you can start with my *free* step-by-step program—found in the next chapter!

Six Steps to Reading Success

So here you are. You want to teach your child, or the neighborhood children, or the kids in your class, to read. What now?

Step 1: Knowing What to Expect

The first thing you need to do is to *honestly* assess your teaching ability. If you have never taught children, or have had little success with your teaching efforts in the past, you might run into the **Rule of Three**. This rule states that whatever program you use first won't work. The second one might not either. But the *third* phonics program will work wonderfully well!

I discovered this rule when I started getting letters from some people complaining that Phonics Program A didn't work, but that the problem disappeared when they bought Phonics Program B, while others wrote that Phonics Program B was no good and *their* child had learned to read in no time with Phonics Program A. Yet others complained that neither A nor B was any good, but that C had solved all their problems. And so on.

After a while I began to catch on to what was really happening. Little kids always learn in spurts. So, when Johnny started on Program A, he did fine for a while, until he hit his next learning plateau. At that point his parents despaired and bought Program B. Faced with a fresh new approach to phonics, Johnny again picked up speed for a while, but then hit another plateau. Enter Program C. By now Johnny had seen phonics presented in lots of different ways, one of which was bound to make sense to him eventually. So when his next learning spurt came along, he spurted all the way to real reading.

Sometimes it also happens that Program A stresses auditory skills more than Program B, which stresses hands-on learning, while Program C is more visual in its approach. Under these circumstances, parents who are unaware of their child's learning style will stumble along until they happen on a program that fits that style, and then conclude the other programs are "no good."

> You don't have to continue until every last phonics rule and obscure sound is mastered. You can start off systematically teaching a list of sounds. But at some point your child will take off and fly with her reading skills. She forms her own rules and doesn't need the rest that you planned to teach. Let her fly.
>
> —*Ruth Beechick*
> *Author of* A Home Start in Reading

I might point out that parents also have different *teaching* styles. A very organized, time-consuming method might not work for a mother who refuses to be organized and systematic about how she teaches, whereas with a program that only requires using a few flash cards once a day she might have great success. Typically, it's not so much that the first one or two phonics programs failed, but that the parents didn't understand the directions or follow them consistently.

Teaching phonics is not terribly difficult. It's just that the average parent has a learning curve to follow before becoming a phonics expert. One way to accelerate up the learning curve is to use several phonics programs in succession. This makes you familiar with a number of teaching approaches, and also helps tamp down in *your* mind just how phonics works. Once you start comparing phonics methods in your mind, and figuring out which one you consider superior, you are a teacher!

Now let me ask you again—how good a teacher are you? If you have any doubts on this score at all, the number-one thing you should be looking for in a phonics program is *good, clear instructions,* especially instructions in how to recognize and overcome the typical trouble spots. It doesn't matter how thorough or clever a program is if you can't figure out how to use it, or if you're lost every time Johnny doesn't "get it" right away. Parents with teaching experience or talent can be successful with just about any program, but the rest of us need to stick with something safe, no matter how tempting the glitzy games in another program might be. Keep this in mind as you look through the programs reviewed in this book.

Since the biggest hurdle in phonics instruction is just getting clear in your mind what you're trying to teach, here, free to the readers of this book, is a sequential list of what your child needs to know, along with some bare-bones teaching suggestions. This alone might be enough to teach your Johnny to read! And if not, since many of us have to foul up with at least one phonics program before we get good at teaching phonics, at least I've making it easy for you to foul up for free!

Step 2: "Read To Me, Daddy!"

The second step in successful phonics instruction is to forget all about phonics instruction. Read, read, read to your kids! Kids need to be read to and to see lots of different sorts of print to build up a picture of reading in their minds, which the phonics method can then tie together. You may think you have no skill whatsoever as a teacher. If you read to your children, though, you are giving them the foundation without which even skilled teachers have difficulty succeeding.

To paraphrase the old rock 'n roll song, "You gotta scribble, babble, and hear" before you can write, talk, and read. Children need to be read to in order to build up an understanding of what reading is. When Suzy snuggles up to you and begs for *The Cat in the Hat* for the hundredth time, she is not being a nuisance; she is requesting pre-reading instruction.

Children who are read to learn that the little black squiggles on the page always say the same words. They discover the different book forms—adventure, mystery, fairy tale, poetry, Bible—and become aware of rhythm and rhyme.

You can start reading to a baby. Pick books with interesting pictures and just a few words per page. When Baby gets just a little bit bigger, you can start pointing out interesting happenings and characters in the pictures. A little bit bigger than that, and you can ask him to point them out to you! Flap books, pop-up books, poke-the-finger-through-the-hole books, furry books, and gloriously illustrated board books are excellent first books. Use your sense of drama. Let the lions ROAR and the field mice squeak! Make lazy characters yawn and type-A characters talk fast and choppy. Hush your voice for dramatic buildups. Make sound effects: a zooming noise for a race car, bubble-blowing noises for a fish. This helps your child (1) learn how to get involved in a story plot—to see it in his mind's eye, and (2) develop his dramatic abilities. More on the latter in the Speech and Drama chapter!

So read, read, read to Johnny. Leave all kinds of reading material around for Johnny to pick up and pretend that he's reading to himself. And let him see you reading for pleasure and enjoying it. That's all we Prides do, and every single one of our kids has preferred books to any other toys from the age of one on up.

The more print of all sorts a child gets to see, the better his chances of understanding what's happening when the grown-ups decide it's time to teach him to read. (This is *not* the same thing as substituting "print immersion" for phonics, as the Whole Languagers do!) Or, in the case of those laid-back folks who insist that children should initiate their own education, the more likely it is that Johnny will someday ask you to teach him to read. He will have imbibed the necessary data. When you give him the framework, it will not strain his little brain, but will fill in the answers to his own unspoken questions.

One more point that reading methods rarely mention, but that has a major effect on your child's reading potential—if you are *really* committed to your children's educational success, try junking your TV, or at least substituting a TV-free video player for it. Print just can't compete with the moving image, and, even worse, TV *teaches* kids to have low attention spans. There is also some evidence that it can prevent the ability to imagine stories in your own head from fully developing in some children. This ability, of course, is absolutely essential to successful reading. So control the TV, and if you can't (be honest now!—nine out of 10 people are TV addicts), get rid of it.

Step 3: Write On!

It is important for children, if at all possible, to learn to write at the same time they learn to read. Because of a muscle weakness our oldest son was not able to write when he learned to read. Teddy, being a very visually-oriented little chap, learned nonetheless. Joseph, on the other hand, kept switching his *b*'s and *d*'s around until he learned to write them himself. By feeling and manipulating letters, and ultimately writing them, children with the dreaded "dyslexic" tendency can learn to read as well as anyone else.

Kids don't have to write *before* they can learn to read, though. The two skills reinforce each other, but are not interdependent. Reading is for pleasure; writing is for communication. Few kids love to write for its own sake. If you force your child to write every blessed thing he is learning to read (as a few methods would have it), he may never learn to love to read.

Step 4: "Now I Know my ABC's . . ."

The next chapter lists resources for alphabet-learning practice. Let's move on now, to actually teaching phonics itself. Look in the sidebar for the alphabet sounds a child must know:

This more or less covers it. Some people manage to come up with one or two more sounds for the vowels, but they are so close to the sounds above that you don't really need to bother to try to teach them. All kids

SOUNDS TO LEARN

a as in *at*

b as in *bag*

c as in *cat*

d as in *dog* (make sure he's not confusing lowercase *b* and *d*)

e as in *egg*

f as in *fan*

g as in *gas* (handwritten g and q are identical except for the direction of the tail)

h as in *ham*

i as in *in* (watch out for *i* getting confused with *j*, and *I* getting mixed up with *l*)

j as in *jam*

k as in *kid*

l as in *lap*

m as in *man* (kids also confuse capital w and m)

n as in *nap*

o as in *ox*

p as in *pass* (lowercase p sometimes gets confused with lowercase *q*)

qu (pronounced together as "kw") as in *queen*

r as in *rat*

s as in *sat*

t as in *tap*

u as in *up*

v as in *van*

w as in *wax*

x as in the ending sound of *ax*, *fox*, and *wax*

y as in *yell* (we'll save the ending sounds of y for later)

z as in *zoom!*

If you prefer to teach all the sounds of each letter at once, add the following:

a as in *late* and *pa* (teach at the same time as the first A sound, if you are using this method)

e as in *Eve*

i as in *I*

o as in *oh* and *do*

u as in *cute*

y as in *baby* and *by*

c as in *cent*

g as in *gym*

s as in *bags* (a *z* sound)

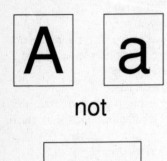

need is enough information to sound out a word, after all—they're not applying for a Ph.D. in linguistics!

It's important to isolate the pure sound of the letter: say the sound *b* with just a little puff of sound, instead of saying "buh." If this is difficult for you, try isolating the consonant sounds at the *ends* of words—e.g., *b* as in *cab*. Vowel sounds can be dragged out until Johnny can hear and repeat them clearly.

I always teach this stage with flash cards with no pictures, so our little ones won't end up "reading" the pictures instead of the letters! I made my own set years ago with a few chopped-out sheets of heavy white cardboard and a Magic Marker. They have the capital letters on one side and the lowercase letters on the other. Now, you can teach the alphabet sounds lots of ways, but this is how we do it. We simply flash the cards several times in alphabetical sequence, showing the letter and making its sound at the same time. I ask my child to repeat the sound after me. I also go through the deck once and have him trace each letter with his finger (make sure he does it right!). There's no testing at all until we've done this for several days. Then I let him try to "get" the cards without me saying the sound first. Those he "gets," he holds, while we run through the remaining cards several times with me making the alphabet sounds and him repeating. Throughout the day, I also ask him to find, say, all the ys on the Cheerios box, or all the bs on one page of a book I am reading to him. Do this enough days in a row and your children will know the alphabet sounds.

Of course, this is not the only way to begin. Some programs teach *all* the sounds of each letter at once. Some teach only uppercase or lowercase letters, or teach the letters in a particular order. All are good approaches, based on good reasons, and all of them work. Don't worry about this! I'm just trying to give you an overview of what you're going to accomplish, not telling you exactly how to do it. I haven't even discussed other ways you can help children learn the letters, such as tracing them, writing them on the blackboard, air writing, sand writing, sandpaper letters, writing them in pudding, walking around a letter outlined on the floor, and so on. All this detailed information is in the books at the end of this chapter or in the programs in the next chapters. Remember, we're just looking at the *steps* of phonics instruction here!

Step 5: Blending

After your learner has mastered the basic alphabet sounds, it's time for the next big step: **blending them into words.** A typical first word is *at.* The child makes the "aaa" sound, then makes the "t" sound. You show him how to blend the two together: "aaaaat—at." You show him some other words (on a chalkboard, paper, or flash cards, if you're doing this all by yourself without a phonics program) and let him try them: *Sam, sat, rat, pat, fat, man.* You will notice I only included words using short vowel *a* in that first reading list. There's a reason for that: the short *a* sound is the easiest for kids to distinguish. Most phonics programs initiate blending practice, therefore, with short *a* words of three letters. This step can take anywhere from 10 minutes to 10 weeks, depending on how ready your child is to learn to read. If he doesn't get it, no matter how often you explain it, give it a rest and come back to it in a couple of days or weeks.

Try to stay cheerful and relaxed, but don't beat yourself over the head if you catch yourself pushing too much. Almost everybody pushes too hard the first time he or she teaches phonics. Just apologize and go do something fun together!

Once your child has blending under control, you move on to words with short *o* (the next easiest short vowel), then words with short *e, i,* and *u.* Ideally, Johnny is reading sentences and even whole stories in a simple phonics primer by now.

Step 6: Finishing the Job

At the point when a child is able to read his first books a lot of parents figure their child is reading and they don't need to teach him any more. Not so! He still has to learn about long vowels—the silent *e* that turns *man* into *mane*—and blends, diphthongs, and digraphs. These latter three imposing terms have fancy technical definitions which only make life more confusing for people who don't already know what they mean. For our purposes, blends are two-or-more consonant combinations like *br, bl, st,* and *spr,* where the individual sounds of the letters are heard. Diphthongs are two-vowel combinations like *ai* and *ou* that actually combine two sounds (*ai* sounds like *ah-ee* if you say it slowly enough). Digraphs are two letters that make a single sound, like *th, ch, sh,* and *wh* and *oa, ee,* and *ui.* And then there are the *tions, ighs, oulds,* and other weirdo combinations. Finally, a few words really ought to be taught as sight words: *the* and *come,* for example.

What happens in real life is that you don't actually end up teaching all this. At some point, the child starts to figure out new combinations on his own. You'd better oversee the process, though, or you'll end up with a child who thinks, like I used to, that pigs eat out of something pronounced a "trow"!

To practice blends, just run your kid systematically through words using them, and some nonsense words too: *brat, drat, frat, blat, flat, slat,* etc. The phonics drill books listed at the end of Chapter 9 make this task much easier, if by this time you still don't have a complete program that includes this kind of drill. Diphthongs, some of which have more than one sound, are considerably trickier. Kids have to puzzle over questions like, "Is the *ai* in 'bait' pronounced as BAYT or BITE?" Digraphs can be tricky too. Consider the two sounds of *th* in *think* and *that,* and the word *read,* which can be pronounced either "reed" or "red." Just to make life more complicated, that same *ea* diphthong can also be pronounced "ay," as in *bear.* If you're very smart, you can figure all this out and how to teach it. If you're too busy for this, then at this point you're definitely ready for an official phonics program.

Now, should we teach phonics and spelling *rules,* or just expose kids to the *patterns?* I personally think we should do both. Knowing the rules gives kids a sense of confidence, and running through the word-family patterns turns those words into words the kids can read on sight. Knowing the rules *alone* is not enough. Picture a kid sitting there with the world *child.* According to one method, he would have memorized a little four-line jingle that shows all the ways long *i* is used in words. Can we realistically expect him to hum through this entire jingle, sorting it out from all the other jingles, every time he sees a new word? The "phonogram" method, where *ild* is memorized as a sound unit, and then the child is drilled in words using the two sounds of *ild* (e.g., *child* and *gild*), works a lot better for instantaneous recall.

Learning the phonics rules does fit very neatly into learning the *spelling* rules, since they are often one and the same. You might also have noticed that once a child knows the basic alphabet sounds and can sound out *at,* he immediately is able to read *bat, cat, fat, hat, mat, Nat, pat, rat, sat, tat,* and *vat.* Twelve words for the price of one! In the look-say method, he would have had to learn each of these words by its "configuration"—in

other words, its outline. This gives you a clue as to why intensive phonics is such a powerful learning method.

The most important thing for your child to learn is what Frank Rogers, the author of the TATRAS phonics program, calls the "phonics habit." This means the habit of *decoding,* or *sounding out,* words rather than guessing at them. I would urge you to beware of "phonics" programs that present an excessive number of words for kids to memorize as sight words. Once a child gets into the habit of guessing at a word, rather than trying to decode *all* words, it's awfully hard to break. The worst part is that often parents don't suspect this has happened until the child hits third or fourth grade, when he moves out of the strictly vocabulary-controlled readers of the early grades. This delayed reaction makes it possible for people to claim great results for their sight-word-larded programs, since *at first* it looks like the kids are really learning to read.

The true test of a phonics program is not how quickly a child can learn to parrot vocabulary-controlled readers, but whether he has learned the phonics habit and has enough tools when he finishes the program to decode *any* word. Properly taught, a six-year-old child should be able to decode the words in a college text with reasonable accuracy. He won't *understand* the college text, but that's because comprehension is not the same thing as reading. I can *read* Einstein's writings on relativity, but I won't promise you I'll *comprehend* them!

A sure sign that a reading method is tainted with look-say is that the author will try to pit comprehension against reading. It's like pitting digestion against eating. Although it's possible to eat something too inedible to digest, there's no way to digest without eating. A child who reads, "See the nice pony," when the words on the page actually say, "Look! A nice horse!" is neither comprehending nor reading, and the minute he hits third grade, the whole world will know it.

Now that you have a general idea of what you want to accomplish, I hope you see that you *can* teach phonics. There are a finite number of steps, and only a few really big "new" things to teach. The main learning plateaus seem to occur at the alphabet-learning stage (learning to tell *b* from *d* and *l* from capital *I*, for example), at the word-blending stage, and at the point of adding that elusive silent *e* to the end of words. Aside from that, with a good intensive phonics program, it's all smooth sailing. And the better phonics programs will even tell you how to get past those learning plateaus. It's just a matter of time and practice. Results guaranteed!

Instruction for Future Phonics Teachers

There isn't space in this book to list all the diphthongs, digraphs, etc. (often known by the simpler names of "phoneme" or "phonogram," meaning "bunch of letters frequently used together in words"), or to provide teaching help for the plateaus. This would bother me a lot if I were the only person in the world who knew how to teach kids to read; but happily, I am not. Others have written helpful books on this subject, and here they are!

A basic reference work designed to help the teacher help his students understand all the rules and exceptions of phonics and spelling. The main body of **The ABC's and All Their Tricks: The Complete Reference Book of Phonics and Spelling** is laid out in alphabetical order (e.g., Z as in zebra followed by Z as in waltz, ZE as in sneeze, Z as in azure, and ZZ as in buzz). This makes the book very simple to use. Plus it contains all you need to know about root words, syllables, vowels, consonants, suffixes, and much more. A truly useful encyclopedia of phonics information that will make you an expert. Mary Pride

The ABC's and All Their Tricks

Parents. $22.99, or $14.50 if you belong to the book club. Plus shipping. *Mott Media/Homeschooling Book Club, 1000 E. Huron St., Milford, MI 48381-2422.* (800) 421-6645. *Fax:* (248)685-8776.

Mary Pecci's At Last! **A Reading Method for EVERY Child**! trims the teaching of reading down to seven steps (compare this with the so-called "Mastery Learning" method of over one hundred steps!). A book purchase also entitles you to *free* telephone consultations from the author, a reading expert.

Mary Pecci begins by teaching the alphabet in order, so children by looking at an alphabet strip can help themselves find the letter they need. She then teaches the consonants, divided into "good guys" who make a sound like their name and "tough guys" who change their sounds or don't sound like their name. Next the blends (*bl, br, scr, . . .*) and digraphs (*ch, sh, th, wh*). Now, vowels, both short and long, followed by the other standard phonemes (*ay, oo, er, tion, . . .*). That's it! The rest of the book shows how to teach this information by getting children to ask, "What's the family?" (*at, cat, sat*) and "What's the clue?" (teaching them to approach weird words like *do* and *friend* by connecting with the regular sounds in the word). Very well-organized, easy-to-use approach. Can be used with a variety of readers (not just the typical "Cat sat on a mat" phonics readers). Supplementary workbooks are also available. *Mary Pride*

Mary Pecci's simplified reading program is designed for easy step-by-step use. But if you haven't taught using this method, you may have trouble putting the steps together for your individual situation. The **At Last! A Reading Method for Every Child video workshop** will explain and demonstrate the method in ways a mere book can't.

The video is meant to be viewed while following along in the book *At Last! A Reading Method for Every Child!* You will also need charts which can be made by enlarging certain pages in the book using a photocopier, and home-made flash cards which are shown and demonstrated in the video. Also highly recommended are her Super Seatwork workbooks, various pages of which are shown and demonstrated in the video. Also you need a set of basal readers—you can choose any basal readers that you desire.

Mary Pecci herself presents the material in this three-and-a-half hour workshop. She shows step-by-step procedure for all phases of the program and demonstrates many of the techniques, using her assistant as a pretend student. At times she suggests that viewers pretend to be the student as well, to see what the student will experience. At other times she gives opportunity for the audience to stop the tape and practice their technique before viewing her demonstration of the same technique.

The setting is the front of a classroom with Mary Pecci standing behind a teacher's desk. Behind her is a white board on which she frequently tapes enlarged charts or writes letters and words to demonstrate the techniques she is discussing. Her assistant sits at a table in the foreground on which is propped an open copy of the book. She turns the pages as Pecci clearly states which page the viewers should be looking at, though not enough of the book is legible to make this video a substitute for the book itself. The assistant also acts as a pretend student to demonstrate the students' responses in the various phonics exercises. The video is not of professional quality; however, the audio and video are clear and the content does not suffer for the lack of professional expertise in video production.

The Pecci reading method consists of a no-nonsense approach to teaching phonics. You teach only the reliable phonics facts (meaning, you don't teach more than one sound per symbol), which cover 90 percent of the information needed to read. Mary Pecci says students can figure out the other 10 percent on their own. The class time is divided into the phonics period, when all students are taught phonics skills together, and the reading period, when students are divided into reading groups to proceed at their own pace. The

phonics skills are taught in the following order: letter recognition, consonants that you can sound out (the "good guys"), consonants that you can't sound out (the "tough guys"), digraphs, short vowels, long vowels, and sight families. Once students have mastered the phonics skills, words are introduced using two methods, "what's the clue?" and "what's the family?" Though most of the time is spent discussing the techniques which will be used in first grade, mention is made of what will be covered from kindergarten to grade 5.

All this is presented in a clear and easy-to-follow way so that you as a teacher understand what you're supposed to do for every stage. According to Mary Pecci, every student will succeed because of the following qualities of the teaching technique: self-checking, clear-cut categories, daily review, reinforcement, testing, and the use of all learning modalities. *Melissa Worcester*

Eagle's Wings Comprehensive Handbook of Phonics (revised edition)

K–adult. $19.95 plus $3.50 shipping.
Eagle's Wings Educational Materials,
PO Box 502, Duncan, OK 73534.
Information: (580) 252-1555.
Fax: same, call first.
Email: info@eagleswingsed.com.
Web: www.eagleswingsed.com.

Although the Handbook's primary emphasis is on phonics for spelling, the authors also address phonics for reading. A set of phonogram flashcards ("Tell-a-phone" cards) is included with the handbook. Teaching directions are given in the first unit. The Handbook includes many more extras: lists of prefixes, suffixes, and roots; lists of synonyms, antonyms, and homonyms; specific instructions in poem form on how to form the lower-case manuscript letters; pages of phonics games; and an assortment of stories and "fun forms" from the Eagle's Wings *Alphabet Island Phonics* program.

Eagle's Wings Alphabet Island Phonics (reviewed on page 75) is a rule-based phonics program with a lot of unique features. Rules are in poem form and tell you when each sound has each spelling. The number of rules is far less than in other programs, and each rule is more complete.

I wished, when I first saw it, that the clever features of Alphabet Island were available separately, without all the workbooks, games, etc. The authors have such a unique, useful way of breaking down English spelling and decoding into just a few rules that it would be really worthwhile for anyone seriously involved in teaching reading to learn this approach. Now **Eagle's Wings** has made it possible for you to inexpensively master their approach with their new **Handbook of Phonics & Spelling**. It contains "the essence of the program without workbooks or reference manuals," and can be used as a phonics and spelling program from grades K–8, or as a supplement to any other phonics program. As they say,

> *When a rule is taught, it is important to know if it holds true for five words or 500. No longer do you have to take the word of the "experts," because complete word charts allow you to see the patterns for yourself and to judge the validity of any rule.*

Rules are often made memorable by giving them "personality." For example, the "boy" vowels are *a, o,* and *u,* while *e* and *i* are "girl" vowels. Thus it's possible to clue kids into the two pronunciations of *c* by pointing out that Clever C sounds like *k* when he's playing with the other boys, but makes a silly *s* sound whenever he's around the "girls." Other rules that don't easily fit around the letter personalities are cram-jammed into as little space as possible. Here's an example, just one of many, the different ways to spell the long sound i.:

What makes a long 'i'?	Example
To make a long 'i', use 'i' with silent 'e',	mine
But at ends of words, a 'y' will usually be.	sky
And then 'i' is long with 'igh' or 'ind',	high/find
And again with 'ign' or 'ild'.	sign/child

This covers all the options in just four rhyming lines. Then the program expands on the poem. For example, the *igh* phonogram is found in only 16 common words. So you get a story poem using all 16 words, along with a picture illustrating the poem and labeled with the words.

To find a particular word or topic, you can either locate it in the Table of Contents or in the comprehensive charts of consonants and vowels. Each chart deals with a particular pattern or concept, and an explanation is usually given on the page across from the chart.

The Handbook will provide you with many insights into the generally unrecognized regularities of the English language, or if you have a little teaching ability you can use it as an inexpensive phonics program all by itself. *Mary Pride*

Is $4 too much to spend for understanding the five steps of teaching reading? **A Home Start in Reading**, written by Dr. Ruth Beechick, gives the outline of how to teach reading and allows you to use *any* readers you choose, from cereal boxes to easy books from the library. Step 1, "Pre-reading," answers the questions of how to prepare your child for reading and when is the right time to start. The next three steps, "Beginning," "Blending," and "Decoding," provide the simplest possible way for a child to move from learning his first letter to sounding out any word on sight. Dr. Beechick provides a chart of all the basic sounds you need to teach. Finally, Step 5, "Fluency," shows how to stretch your child toward total fluency without frustrating him with too-hard reading. This chapter also deals with comprehension.

The essence of the Beechick approach is (1) streamlining—decluttering the educational process and (2) freeing the child from the stranglehold of a strict inch-by-inch approach. Dr. Beechick recognizes that children can leap ahead and learn on their own, and that what she calls "the messiness of phonics" make some words or syllables easier to learn on their own rather than according to an abstract rule.

For a phonics program based on Beechick's ideas, see the Learning Language Arts Through Literature Common Sense Reading Program on page 86. *Mary Pride*

A Better Path to Literacy
Frank B. May, Ph.D.

Much can be said about the advantages of one-on-one learning. Unfortunately, many of the materials homeschoolers use are actually geared for classroom use and therefore have to be adapted for use at home. That's what makes **One on One Learning: a Better Path to Literacy** different. All of the material in the book is presented with the assumption that you are going to be spending one-on-one time teaching reading and writing skills.

This 187-page paperback book contains 12 chapters such as "Reading and Writing Work Hand in Hand," "The Art of Producing a Good Reader," "Phonics Through the Right Side of the Brain," and "Advanced Vocabulary for Age 8 and Above." Although it is not a curriculum *per se*, it can be the foundation of your reading program, especially if you like a relaxed approach to learning. The book is easy to read and contains lots of ideas for games and activities which help to promote literacy. If you're looking for something with a lot of structured lesson plans, you'll need to look elsewhere, but if you simply want something that will point you in the right direction, this book might be just the thing you need. *Rebecca Livermore*

The 351-page **Reading Reflex** book is a comprehensive guide to take your child all the way from learning beginning letter sounds to advanced phonics and spelling. Everything you need is in the book, no kidding!

The best part about *Reading Reflex*, besides the sensible advice and good reading research references, is the fact that you begin by pinpointing your child's exact reading developmental level and needs. If you've become dissatisfied with your present phonics program and would like to try something else, but don't want to begin at the beginning again, this book will be a great aid. In fact, you'll feel like a professional reading teacher by the time you finish it!

A Home Start in Reading
Preschool–grade 3. $12 for the set (part of a "3 R's" set also including A Strong Start in Language and An Easy Start in Arithmetic).
Mott Media/Homeschooling Book Club, 1000 E. Huron St., Milford, MI 48381-2422. (800) 421-6645. Fax: (248)685-8776.

NEW!
One on One Learning: A Better Path to Literacy
Parents. $14.95 plus shipping.
Spice of Life Educational Publishing, 820 16th St., Suite 410, Denver, CO 80202. Orders: (888) 441-5119. Inquiries: (303) 893-1635. Fax: (303) 893-1637. Email: Spice@spicebooks.com. Web: www.spicebooks.com.

NEW!
Reading Reflex
Grades K–3. Hardcover, $30 plus shipping.
The Free Press, An Imprint of Simon & Schuster, Attn: Order dept., 200 Old Tappan Rd., Old Tappan, NJ 07675. (800) 323-7445. ISBN #: 0684-83-96-60. Web: www.simonsays.com.

THE FOOLPROOF
Phono-Graphix™ METHOD
FOR TEACHING YOUR
CHILD TO READ

Carmen McGuinness
Geoffrey McGuinness
Founders of Read America, Inc.

NEW!
The Three Ingredient
Reading Program
Parents. $14.95 plus $3 shipping.
Blue Bird Publishing, 1916 W Baseline #16, Mesa, AZ 85202. Orders: (888) 672-2275. Inquiries: (602) 831-6063. Fax: (602) 831-6728.
Email: bluebird@bluebird1.com.
Web: www.bluebird1.com.

You will learn that the three success factors for good readers have been pinpointed: an early start, knowledge of the letter sounds, and an ability to blend and segment sounds. Your child will be taught and tested for the last skill, not left to figure out how to do this work on his own.

You start with the lesson your child needs and repeat the elements of that lesson until your child has mastered that "chunk" of phonetic knowledge. The book builds phonics into your child; it doesn't try to bend your child to some method. I tested a child whose mom decided to homeschool him because he wasn't doing well in school. He had been given lots of extra reading instruction, but it wasn't helping. After testing him, we pinpointed his areas of weakness, Mom went to work, and he began to master reading, one skill chunk at a time. We were both so excited! I was so pleased to have something so easy to use to help this new mom and her son find success in homeschooling.

You will have to spend a little time copying and cutting materials, and part of each day presenting a lesson to your child(ren). Reading really can't be taught by a better method than the tutorial process. Sorry, a computer program or tape set won't do it for you. The good news is, if your child catches on quickly, he'll whiz through the lessons. If he needs help, you'll know exactly how to help him.

My only quibble: I wish the book had given some logical strategies for older children which would aid them in spelling beyond what is in the book. All in all, probably the best phonics instruction I've seen so far.
Kathy Von Duyke

All you need to teach your child to read is a copy of this book and a set of linguistically- structured reading books. **The Three Ingredient Reading Program** gives step-by-step instructions and hints on how to help a child through possible sticking points. Examples of actual dialogs between parent/teachers and their children are provided, showing how the specific steps actually work. Also included is a discussion of why it is beneficial to teach a child to read at an early age, and the theories and methodology are supported with research throughout the book.

What are the "three ingredients"? First, your child will "read" letters—not say the letter names, which aren't needed in order to sound out a word, but say the letter sounds. The book includes pages you can cut out to make letter cards for teaching purposes, as well as step-by-step instructions on how to use them. When your child can read the letters, you move on to reading simple words; the book contains instructions for making first books which contain single words with short vowel sounds (no sentences, just words). The complete list of words to use in these books is included. When your child can read all of these, you move on to the third ingredient, using linguistically-structured books to learn and practice more complex words and sentences. The author claims to know of only one such set of books, and includes ordering and pricing information for these. Also included are sample pages from several of the books from the set she refers to; these are not enough for you to use to teach with, but they will be enough for you to be able to decide whether a set of books you may already have would work for this program.

Though this book does not give a lesson-by-lesson plan, each step is clearly explained. You are also told when to go on to the next step and what to do if your child encounters problems. *Melissa Worcester*

CHAPTER 7

Phonics Programs

Phonics programs differ in many ways. Otherwise, there'd only be one program you could buy and this chapter would be a lot shorter!

In one way they are all alike: **phonics instruction starts with recognizing the alphabet letters**. Some methods teach both the names and sounds of the letters; others teach only the sounds. The reason for teaching the letter names is that this makes it easier for the teacher to give directions to the students—e.g., "Johnny, write an *A* on the blackboard." Those who prefer to teach only the sounds also have a valid point, namely that one less thing to learn means one less chance of confusing young kids, who need the letter *sounds* to read but only need the letter *names* for later classroom exercises. Resolving this issue, it seems clear that bright kids can be taught sounds and letters simultaneously, while slower (though not necessarily less intelligent) learners should be taught alphabet sounds first, and the letter names later, once they are reading successfully.

Some phonics programs present the letters or letter sounds in alphabetical order, while others present them out of sequence. Again, each method has its advantages. Learning the alphabet sequentially as A-B-C prepares the way for later alphabetizing skills, plus you can use the alphabet song (or some variation). Learning the alphabet "out of sequence" may mean learning it in order of how easy the letters are to write, or how easy it is to make words with just a few letters, or some other reason that makes sense to the program author.

Learning to write the letters also has a practical advantage, especially for kinesthetic learners, who memorize letter shapes much better when writing than when just looking at them. The downside is that some kids are ready to read before they are ready to write. It is possible to be mentally more advanced than you are physically. This was true in the case of our first son. However, whether reading is taught first or together with writing, learning to write can't help but improve reading skills, just from the extra opportunity to practice spelling and letter shapes.

Teach the

- **Letter Names** (as in the ABC song)

- **Letter Sounds** ("A says /a/ as in apple.")

Alphabetical . . . or not

Write makes might

Here are some more ways phonics programs differ:

- **Many programs use "key words" and "key pictures"** for each letter sound. This is fine, as long as the key words and pictures don't appear on the flashcards, and the uppercase and lowercase letters don't appear together on the same side of a flashcard. You need to be *sure* the child is remembering the letter shape—not the picture, not the word, not the associated upper- or lower-case letter.

- **Some programs use a "ladder letter" approach** to blending: *ba, be, bi, bo, bu.* Others use a "word family" approach: *bat, cat, fat, hat.* I lean towards the "word family" approach, as this fits the way we think. However, if good blending skills are taught, the child will quickly learn to sound out entire words, regardless of which method is used.

- **Some programs start with lots of writing and almost no reading.** Others leap into reading as early as possible. Proponents of "writing to read" feel that it teaches children discipline—life is not a bowl of cherries. Others respond that kids taught this way miss the joy of learning to read, and may in fact fixate more on the phonograms than on reading itself. My bias here is with the "jump right into reading" crowd. A kid who enjoys reading will pick up any missing phonograms, but a child who thinks of reading as unending flashcard drill is not likely to sneak off in a corner with a book.

- **Some programs are loaded with games and fun activities.** Others eschew these and concentrate solely on reading drill and practice. In general, young children appreciate the games, and these add more of an element of parent-child bonding than hours of pure drill are wont to provide. On the other hand, the games-free programs are very inexpensive and streamlined, and have the added benefit of appearing "grown up" to kids who need remedial lessons.

- **Some programs feature whimsical animal puppets or animations.** Little kids appreciate these. Older children who need remedial phonics often dislike these, considering them "cutesy."

- **Some programs have songs that teach phonics facts.** Proponents point out that song have "sticking power"—like ad jingles, a good phonics song is not easily forgotten. There is also a certain charm and sense of community associated with singing along with other children. Opponents stress that songs are "right brain" tools, remembered in order (like a tape) and not accessible easily out of order (like a computer disk). A child may have to mentally replay part or all of a song to remember a certain fact on it.

- **Many programs come with instructional videos or audiocassettes.** These are close to a necessity for parents who do not know how to form the pure phonics sounds. The more recent crop of videos are kid-appealing, adding motivation.

- **A few programs have excellent packaging** that allows you to quickly put away all program items, quickly take them out again, and easily transport the whole kit and caboodle from place to place. This makes your job much easier.

Here are a few other things to consider:

- **Are you buying this program for one child, or do you plan to reuse it?** If so, is it made up mostly of nonconsumable items, or are replacement workbooks, etc., readily available?

- **How much phonics do *you* know?** The less you know, the more likely it is that a "fancier" program with videos, audiocassettes, and other helps will be worth your while.

- **How much time do you have to teach phonics?** If you only have a few minutes a day for this, a program that requires lots of preparation time (making puppets or flashcards, playing lots of games) may not be your best choice.

- One last thought: **Is it really worth skimping on a phonics program?** $200 may seem expensive, but it's less than the cost of *one* college credit in most universities. Even if you bought three or four of the most expensive phonics programs, it would cost less than *one* college course. Keep that in mind if you are one of the many who don't experience wild success with the first program you try. Parents routinely plan on spending tens of thousands on a child's college education. A fraction of that will get the best phonics tools available, *and* if your child learns to read and study well, he can earn his own way through college!

Phonics Programs

NEW!
10 Minutes a Day to
Reading Success
Grades K–2. Each book, $9.95.
Houghton Mifflin, 1900 S Batavia,
Geneva, IL 60134. (800) 733-2828.
Web: www.hmco.com.

Looking for a way to spice up your phonics program? Look no further than **10 Minutes a Day to Reading Success**! This three-book series is an excellent source of activities to motivate your young reader. Though this is by no means a complete phonics program, it is chock full of ideas, activities, games, worksheets, and art projects that provide opportunities for your child to actually use his growing reading skills.

If you like to plan unit studies, this series is for you. Each book is divided into units. At the beginning of each unit are the teacher's notes that provide a brief overview of what will be taught and exactly what to expect from your child at each level. Reading strategies such as drawing conclusions and prediction are also explained in the teacher's notes.

Icons are scattered throughout activity pages and are a real highlight of the book. For example, the time icon let you know exactly how long an activity should take. Teacher's note icons are helpful because they instruct the parent on what to do if your child seems to be struggling with a concept. For example, in the Grade 1 book, an alphabet dot-to-dot activity is introduced. If your child falters or seems confused, you are instructed to sing the alphabet with the child.

Reading Success K contains hundreds of different ways to reinforce letter learning. One activity I particularly liked was making a Beginning Sound Dictionary. Even though this activity has a rainy day icon on it, I feel this is something my child could work on continually throughout the year. All you do is write the letter *S* at the top of a piece of construction paper. Your child then draws or cuts out pictures of things that begin with the letter *S*. When your child's dictionary is finished, he will have a nice book to show his family. The activity is easy and requires a variety of skills.

Reading Success for Grade 1 contains even more ideas for singing games, recipes, book creations and books to share with your child. In the unit entitled "Family Fun," instructions are included for making your own fishing game. Each fish has a digraph printed on it. Your child will have to read it before he can catch it. Just a change of pace like this can be a real help for struggling reader. Afterwards, make your own menus and fix yourself a healthy lunch with recipes included in the book.

Reading Success 2 is filled with interesting ways to teach prefixes, suffixes, literary genres, and compound words. In fact, each book in the 10 Minutes to Reading Success series is overflowing with ideas. Buy all three in the series to motivate your young reader at any grade level. *Irene Buntyn*

A Beka Phonics

Preschool–grade 3. Basic Phonics Charts, $9.20. Basic Phonics Flashcards, $20.20. Clue Word Cards, $9.20. Basic Phonics Sounds Cassette, $8.45. Blend Practice Cards A, $8.20. Blends Practice Cards B, $9.20. Phonics Charts and Games, $17.20. Blend Ladders, $16.20. Letter Picture Flashcards, $12.20. Large Alphabet Flashcards, $11.20. Felt Upper-Case & Lower-Case Alphabet, $15.20. Nursery school phonics materials: Letters and Sounds, $7.50. K4 phonics materials: Little Books 1–10, $5.75. Little Owl Books, $5.75. ABC-123, $9.85. Miniature Alphabet Flashcards, $2.60. K5 phonics materials: Basic phonics reading program (12 books), $11.40. Reading for Fun Enrichment Library, $23.20. Four Big Owl Books, 95¢ each. Letters and Sounds K, $9.65. K5 Phonics/Reading/Writing Curriculum, $59.95.
A Beka Book, Box 19100, Pensacola, FL 32523-9100. (800) 874-2352. Fax: (800) 874-3590. Web: www.abeka.com.

NEW!
ABC Discovery Book

Grades preK–1. $12.95. Audio tape, $8.95. ABC Discovery Kindergarten Reading Program, including other two items listed here, worksheets, phonetic reader, teacher's manual, visuals, $59.95. Shipping extra.
ReinCo Educational Services, PO Box 862, Spring Lake, NC 28390. (800) 952-9427. (910) 497-2871.

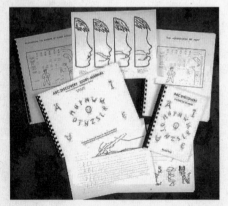

A Beka Book Publications is a major Christian publisher of school materials for all subjects and ages, including **phonics materials** for all ages from age 2 on up. They publish oodles of supplementary phonics aids: flash cards, charts, games, readers, workbooks, writing pads, etc. Or you can sign up for their complete correspondence courses or video correspondence school (as reviewed in Volume 1). Each correspondence option includes all the phonics goodies for that grade.

A Beka uses the "ladder letters" approach rather than the "word families" approach. This means teaching the blends *ba, be, bi, bo, bu* rather than teaching, say, *at* and then *bat, cat, fat,* and *mat*. They also use "key words" for not only the basic letter sounds, but for other phonograms. This very aggressive phonics program, which starts in nursery school, works well for some kids but not for others.

BEST FEATURES: Very complete line of supplemental aids. Many can be used with other programs. Lots of adorable little readers. Integrated supplies for handwriting, Bible, etc. Quality production.

WORST FEATURES: Pace of learning and early acceleration may be too much for some children. Not as easy to use as some other programs. Classroom-oriented. The "ladder letters" approach doesn't work for all children. *Mary Pride*

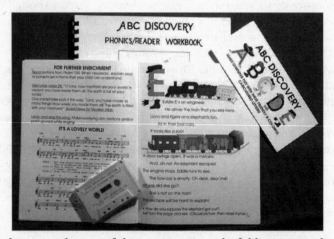

This has got to be one of the cutest, most colorful beginning phonics programs that I've ever seen! The **ABC Discovery Book** introduces each letter as a cartoon figure. For instance, *a* is "Abigail A," an acrobat with apples on her hat. You will introduce her to your children with a cute little story featuring the short *a* sound. Your child will learn to make the sound and will trace big colorful letters in the book with his or her finger. "A Lesson for Living" will be about apples and their seeds, and that will be an introduction for a brief story about creation. Then you can read Genesis 1 or a Bible storybook creation story to your child. The words and music to a song about creation are right there in the book; the song is also on the audio tape available from ReinCo. After that, you can go on and meet "Billy B." The first part of the program is designed to be so easy to use that even an older child could teach beginning phonics to his younger sibling.

The audio tape includes accompanying rhymes, songs, letter-sounds, and Bible verses. Also available is an entire kit for kindergarten. One of the unique aspects of this approach arises from the author's background in linguistics. She stresses correct pronunciation and gives all sorts of little-known tips on how to help your children pronounce the sounds correctly. In fact, there is even a game to teach your children to conquer that pesky *r* sound, and a complete workshop on pronunciation of other necessary sounds! There are also terrific follow up reading materials available. *Rebecca Prewett*

Sam Blumenfeld's **Alpha-Phonics: A Primer for Beginning Readers** (168 pages) is a home-school classic. You get a step-by-step phonics program that has both instructions and reading exercises in the same oversized book.

Alpha-Phonics presents one vowel or phonetic sound at a time. Then the learner gets to practice reading all the possible word families of that sound. By the time you have finished the last lesson, you have covered all the phonics and phonetic spelling a child needs. Very systematic and thorough.

The words are hand-printed by a calligrapher in a very large size. Some lessons include word lists only (set up to show the natural phonetic patterns), and others have practice sentences, some delightfully goofy. The amount of reading required at any lesson is not overlarge, and the book is paced so children can move right along.

Mr. Blumenfeld starts blending right at the beginning, and adds letters as he goes. Everything you need is right in the (reusable) book, including some very brief pre-reading exercises and suggestions for introducing cursive handwriting. Minimalist lesson plans are found in the back of the book.

You really ought to spend some time with flashcards teaching the basic letter sounds before starting with Alpha-Phonics. If you have not ever taught phonics before, this task will be easier if you also purchase the Alpha-Phonics Audio Tapes (two cassettes for $20). These include instructions on how to teach anyone to read, verbal explanations of all 128 lessons, and the 44 speech sounds clearly pronounced. An excellent Oral Reading Assessment Test is also available for $19.95 plus $3 shipping.

Preparation time required is almost nil. Just listen to the cassettes; after that everything is in the book. You will have to add handwriting and spelling exercises based on the words just studied, if desired, as these are not included in the program. *Mary Pride*

Whoa! This is *not* the humble one-book *Alpha-Phonics* I have been recommending for years as the simplest phonics program around. We're almost into the 21st century, and here comes the 21st-century version of this classic homeschool phonics program.

NEW!
Alpha-Phonics: A Primer for Beginning Readers

Ages 6–9 or remedial. $29.95 plus $3 shipping.
Paradigm Company, 3500 Mountain View Drive, Boise, ID 83704. (208) 322-4440.

ADDITIONAL MATERIALS REQUIRED: Pencil and paper or other writing materials such as chalkboard and chalk (if you choose to teach handwriting). A set of readers is optional; book includes sufficient reading exercises for practice purposes. CONSUMABLE PROGRAM ITEMS: None.

SUBJECTS COVERED: Phonics and spelling. Minimal handwriting instruction.

BEST FOR: Ages 6 and up; remedial; adults. Lack of fun and games means learners need self-discipline and decent attention span; also means the program will appeal to older children and adults who get turned off by other programs' child-oriented features.

NEW!
Blumenfeld's Alpha-Phonics Reading Program Kit

Ages 2–8 and remedial. $239.95 plus shipping (ask about homeschool discount).
Literacy Unlimited, Inc., 31566 Railroad Canyon Rd., Suite 657, Canyon Lake, CA 92587-9446. Orders: (888) 922-3000. *Inquiries:* (909) 244-0485. *Fax:* (909) 244-1965. *Web:* *www.alpha-phonics.com.*

BEST FEATURES: Twaddle-free. Well organized. Never silly or baby-ish; can be used by all ages, from preschool through adult, without embarrassment. Based on a proven program that has worked for years.

WORST FEATURES: The introductory cassette, and the introductions to the lesson cassettes, are scripted like a radio interview. "Hello, I'm Helen Fabian and with me is Samuel Blumenfeld, creator of Alpha-Phonics. Sam, I'm so excited that we're working together . . . " Puh-leeze! Straightforward instruction would have worked better than this contrived banter.

BEST FOR USE BY: Serious parents and students of all ages. The methodical-minded will especially appreciate it. This is not a "games" program. That doesn't mean children won't enjoy it, just that their enjoyment will come from the joy of learning, not from games, colorful pictures, prizes, and the like.

Yes, **Blumenfeld's Alpha-Phonics Kit** still includes *Alpha-Phonics: A Primer for Beginning Readers* by famed homeschool speaker and writer Sam Blumenfeld. The new edition is spiral-bound, but otherwise it's pretty much the same old book. Only now it comes with a slew of other wonderful helps, all packed in a lovely cardboard suitcase:

- **Play Me First!** Side of this audiocassette is an overview of how this program works. Side two, on which you get to hear Sam Blumenfeld sing his version of the Alphabet Song, explains how to teach the alphabet.
- **A Video Introduction** See how the program works and what all the program components are for. Meet Sam Blumenfeld, and learn from him why an alphabetic language should be taught phonetically, not as a bunch of word shapes. Watch as former high-school teacher Carlo DiNota explains how to teach the first group of lessons.
- **Alpha-Phonics Instruction Manual** A small spiral-bound book that introduces phonics in general and this program in particular. Lesson-by-lesson teaching instructions are found here. These are more or less the same instructions you used to find in the back of the old *Alpha-Phonics* book.
- **Alpha-Phonics Audio Lesson Tapes** Six color-coordinated audiocassettes lead the learner through each lesson word by word. Good for developing proper pronunciation, and a great help for anyone trying to use this program on his own—e.g., the crowd *Hooked on Phonics* has been famous for aiming their commercials at. The difference being that, in my opinion, *Alpha-Phonics* is far more likely to do the job.
- **Alpha-Phonics Flashcards** Seven packs of color-coordinated flashcards. Each pack is bound together with a large white ring. Again, *Hooked on Phonics* had the idea of ring-bound flashcards first, but *Alpha-Phonics* has way better cards. You start with the alphabet letters, then move to simple two-letter words using the letter *a*, and so forth. Cards are coordinated with the lessons, and have no distracting pictures on them.
- **Alpha-Phonics First Readers** Lack of primers for additional reading practice was probably the biggest single gripe of users of the old *Alpha-Phonics*. Again, someone was listening, and this set of 11 readers is the result. Color-coordinated and matched to the lessons, these small books take you from simple sentences all the way through reading *America the Beautiful*. No pictures are included, to prevent word guessing.
- **Alpha-Phonics Flip Book** What fun! Flip the left, middle, and right pages to form a variety of three-, four-, and five-letter words.
- **Writing Tablet** For handwriting practice.

This is a step-by-step, lesson-by-lesson program. You don't need to prepare a thing; it's all done for you. Just go straight through the workbook's 128 lessons, using the tapes, flashcards, and readers with the lessons indicated, and doing the handwriting practice. You'll begin with learning the letters of the alphabet by name, and then start learning the sounds of individual letters. Once you have learned the sounds of *a* and *m*, you read your first word: *am*. From there, progression is straightforward, from short *a* words, to short *e* words, and through all the short vowels. Here things get a little unusual. Instead of immediately progressing to long vowels, instead

Sam introduces plurals, possessives, *sh/ch/wh,* words of more than one syllable, final blends, and initial blends *before* finally introducing the long sound of *a* in lesson 72. All the remaining phonics needed to read any English word—from diphthongs such as *oy* and *oo* to "exceptions" such as the silent *t* in *hustle/bustle/rustle*—are covered in the remaining lessons.

On top of all the help from audiotapes, video, and the instruction manual, as an Alpha-Phonics purchaser you can also call their **telephone tutors** between the hours of 9 A.M. to 5 P.M. Pacific Standard Time, to request help with any phonics-related question. If in spite of your best efforts, your student doesn't "get it," a little expert counseling might just do the trick. *Mary Pride*

"We're off to see the letters . . . the wonderful letters of Oz!" No, **Alphabet Island Phonics** (a production of Eagle's Wings Educational Materials) does not include this song, but it does have a little of the flavor of Oz. Here we have a fantasy land populated by people with letters on their bodies. From Active "A" to Zany "Z," each letter person's personality corresponds to phonetic rules. Active "A," for example, says, "W-a-a-a-ah" (the short *a* sound is the drawn-out "a-a-ah"), and can only be baby-sat by Innocent "I" and Yours Truly "Y" (*ai* and *ay* are the only two diphthongs beginning with *a*). Each letter also has his or her own poem to introduce its formation as a lowercase letter. Example:

> *For active 'A' draw a circle nice and round.*
> *Close it up and come back down.*

You have to admit this is cute and clever. But of course, the program consists of more than little people and little poems. The authors, two home-schooling sisters, have a definite educational philosophy. They introduce letter formation through writing letters in the air following the poem's directions. Lowercase letters are taught first. Vowels are introduced before consonants, which are then taught alphabetically. The "word family" approach is used rather than the "ladder letter" approach. In other words, *at-cat-fat-hat* are introduced together, rather than teaching children to say "ba-be-bi-bo-bu" and then add a consonant at the end. Complete word lists are given for every rule, including the exceptions. Where a limited number of words share a common element, such as the tricky *ough,* they are made into a poem or little story.

The kindergarten course includes three parts: *Getting to Know Alphabet Island,* in which children learn to recognize the alphabet characters by sight and sound and write them in lowercase; *Learning to Read in Alphabet Island,* where uppercase letters, alphabetizing, and rhyming are introduced, as well as three-letter words; and an attractive three-ring organizer with cassette tape, flash cards, and games. A kindergarten math course is also included.

You get the workbooks and teacher's manuals for all three parts, a cassette tape of songs and stories (now fully orchestrated), four color laminated Alphabet Island Alphabet Cards for yourself and your student, a game board and cards, five readers, and sheets of cut-'em-out flash cards. All of this material is tucked into a printed vinyl organizer.

As the brochure warns, the workbooks make no sense without the teacher's manuals. These have a definite desktop-publishing look: crisp, clear, and easy to follow. The lesson sequences have also been improved since I first reviewed this program. The letters A–Z are introduced in order, with no funny business about teaching *ph* at the same time as *f*. Another improvement: a previous edition of this program featured Quivering "Q."

UPDATED!
Alphabet Island Phonics
Grade K–3. Alphabet Island Phonics I (includes Alphabet Island I and Kinder-Math), $69.95. Alphabet Island II, $84.95. Complete Alphabet Island Phonics (includes level 1 and 2), $119.95.
Eagle's Wings Educational Materials, PO Box 502, Duncan, OK 73534. Information: (580) 252-1555. Fax: same, call first. Email: info@eagleswingsed.com. Web: www.eagleswingsed.com.

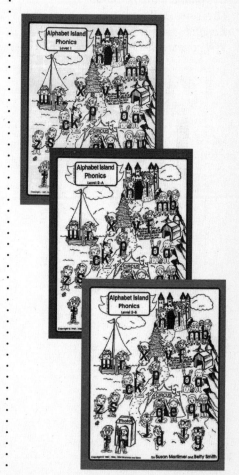

BEST FEATURES: Poems for letter and numeral formation. Characterization of phonics rules (very well done and unique). Cuddly approach works well with little children, especially girls. Alphabetizing emphasis. Less rules than other rules-based program; rules are more complete. Rules are rhymed and sung for added memorability. Uses all learning styles. Spelling emphasis. Kid-appealing.

WORST FEATURES: Vowel dot-to-dot exercises are too complicated for many preschoolers.

Ball-Stick-Bird

All ages and remedial. Set #1 (Books 1–5 plus instructor's manual), Set #2 (Books 6–10 plus instructor's manual), $92.45. Both sets $175.95 postpaid.
Ball-Stick-Bird Publications, Inc., PO Box 13, Colebrook, CT 06021. Information: (860) 738-8871. Fax: same, call first. Email: bsbpub@snet.net. Web: www.ballstickbird.com.

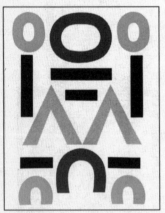

All capital letters can be formed from these "ball," "stick," and "bird" shapes!

improvement: a previous edition of this program featured Quivering "Q." Although Q is still missing a leg, and needs his friend Understanding "U" to help him get around, he is now Qualified "Q," a much superior characterization. Some of the phonics activities still are too complicated, though. For example, a child might be required to cross out the consonants and connect the dots in numerical order when he is not really competent in distinguishing consonants and vowels and has not even learned the numerals yet! Letter names and sounds are introduced together, another potential stumbling-block for the slower student. And I still can't figure out why such emphasis was placed on introducing the lowercase letters via Alphabet Island people, while the uppercase letters are just introduced as letters. The characters are cute, but the letters in the middle of their bodies don't stand out as much as they should. Quibbles like these make the program unsuitable for children with perceptual problems or difficulty in learning.

The average child can learn to read with Alphabet Island. He (or especially, she) will enjoy it very much. *Mary Pride*

Ball-Stick-Bird, a phonics program invented by research psychologist Dr. Renée Fuller, was found to teach even certified, institutionalized retardates to read (people with an IQ of 60 or less)!

Dr. Fuller's first breakthrough is her system for breaking down the capital letters into three strokes: the Ball (a circle), the Stick (a line), and the Bird (two lines joined at an angle, like the cartoon of a bird in flight). These basic forms are color-coded to make the difference between the strokes even more dramatic. Capital letters are taught first, in a sequence designed to make it as easy as possible to "build" each letter out of its forms. Lowercase letters, which are harder to form and present potential reversal problems, come later. Eventually the student learns all his letters and basic phonics.

Ball-Stick-Bird's second unusual feature are its science-fiction fables. Dr. Fuller contends that "story readiness," not some mystical amount of motor Skill Readiness, is the real preparation for reading, and that successful reading itself grows out of the basic human desire to understand one's own life as a story. Therefore her stories, although funny, present some heavy-duty moral lessons. Using an invented colony of aliens, the Vooroos from Venus who want to conquer everyone, she is able to teach many lessons about human nature: the lust for power, the foolishness of sloganeering, how experts use their authority to stifle criticism of their actions, and so on. (Fear not: good guys like Vad the robot man, his space cat Dick and comet friend Mimi, and the fun-loving Jet Set of Jupiter overcome the Vooroos in various clever ways.)

It is easy to see why labeled people—like the "mentally retarded," "gifted" and "special education" children—lap up these stories. Dr. Fuller tells it like it is. She literally gives them the words that explain their experience as the powerless victims of experts.

Another unusual Ball-Stick-Bird feature is the amount of review built in. Unlike all other phonics manuals, the B-S-B manual encourages the teacher to let the student keep reading the next book, even if he hasn't mastered his current lessons. So much review is built in that he is bound to catch on sooner or later.

The Instructor's Manual has page-by-page lesson scripts. It also includes games, vocabulary lists, and comprehension questions for the stories. No handwriting, spelling, or composition is included; this is a *reading* program only. *Mary Pride*

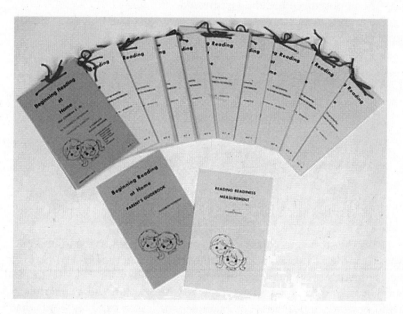

The really cute **Beginning Reading at Home** is just enough to get you started without overburdening you with bunches of teacher's directions. You get 10 take-apart kits, a short Reading Readiness Measurement test, and a parent's guidebook. The take-apart kits are hole-punched 5½ x 8½" colored cards tied together with orange yarn. Kits have four parts. Blue cards have letter names and sound cards. Green cards are letter-touch cards, with tactile letters for your learner to trace. Orange cards are for practicing sounding out words, and yellow cards have stories on them. You take apart a kit and work through the concepts on each card. Each kit is about 15 cards or less, making it easy to master one kit in a short time. This is highly motivational stuff—your kids will beg for lessons! The entire program covers most introductory phonics, stopping short of diphthongs and some digraphs, and is an excellent choice for the three- to six-year-old set, for whom it was designed. *Mary Pride*

ADDITIONAL MATERIALS REQUIRED: Pencil and paper or other writing materials such as chalkboards and chalk (if you choose to teach handwriting) or a computer. No handwriting is necessary; challenged students can construct at least the capital letters from the "balls," "sticks," and "birds" provided.

CONSUMABLE PROGRAM ITEMS: None.

SUBJECTS COVERED: Phonics. Ethics (good v. evil).

BEST FOR: Young children, especially those who are "too young" to use other systems. Older remedial students, especially those with genuine mental handicaps and the gifted.

Beginning Reading at Home

Ages 3–6. $35 postpaid. *Individualized Education Systems/Poppy Lane Publishing, PO Box 5136, Fresno, CA 93755. (559) 299-4639. Email: Bette1234@aol.com.*

BEST FEATURES: Simple. Fun. Clever. Takes little time to do and no preparation time at all. Inexpensive.

WORST FEATURES: None.

Calvert Come Read with Me

Grades preK–1. $175.
Calvert School, 105 Tuscany Road,
Baltimore, MD 21210. (410) 243-6030.
Fax: (410) 366-0674.
E-mail: inquiry@calvertschool.org.
Web: www.calvertschool.org.

A section on the interconnectedness of things introduces a story, not published by Calvert, titled *The Earth and I*. The story goes like this:

The Earth and I are friends . . . I tell
*   her what's on my mind.*
She listens to every word.
Then I listen to her.
She helps me to grow.
I sing for her. I dance for her.
She sings for me. She dances for me.
When she's sad, I'm sad.
When she's happy, I'm happy.

After the reading, the gelfins reinforce the message of the book, by praising it as a good book and affirming its message. Personally, I think talking to the Earth has to fall either into the category of prayer (for those who literally believe "she listens to every word") or just plain squirreliness ("I used to talk to the wall, but I find talking to the Earth is more fulfilling. When I listen, I hear her little voice inside my head. She loves the way I do the lambada."). And what the heck does it mean when the earth "dances for me"? Earthquakes, maybe?

Calvert tells me that nobody has complained about this book, so either it's just me or everyone else is working around it or everyone else isn't watching the videos with their kids. Or we've all become so used to overblown praise of the earth and the environment that we don't even notice when it ascends into the realms of worship/loopiness.

Come Read With Me is Calvert's unusual pre-reading course. It doesn't teach phonics per se. Instead it introduces story readiness, alphabet sounds, context clues, and picture clues in the setting of a video saga about little creatures in a fantasy land. The muppet-like creatures, including the "wise creature," an iguana with red eyes, are trying to find out about the past history of their country, Zigzat, with the help of a friendly archaeologist. The importance of reading is stressed.

Like most Calvert courses, this one comes with a lot of kiddie-friendly supplies:

- Eight videos
- Come Read With Me guidebook that leads you through the 40 lessons
- Come Read With Me Activity Workbook
- *Me? A Mess?* storybook
- Two "gelfin" finger puppets (a gelfin is one of the little creatures that lives in Zigzat)
- Lots of construction paper and newsprint drawing paper
- Two Calvert pencils
- Yarn
- Two boxes of large crayons
- Pencil sharpener
- Glue stick
- Kid-sized, round-tip Fiskars scissors

Here's the story line. Russ Green is an archaeologist trying to find out what happened to all the people who used to live in the big city there. He meets a bunch of little critters, like the gelfins Dilsey and Nik, the tropical bird Jando, and the iguana Tam. Together they explore the wonderful world of words and stories. For example, one lesson explores words that start with *b*. Russ uses a stone he found in the ruins that has on it a series of pictures of objects whose names start with *b* to illustrate to Dilsey and Nik that a story has a beginning, middle and end. The next episode explores words starting with *t* with Jando and Tam, including Russ's tools and toolbox and of course Tam's name. Russ reads a book called *Tools* by Ann Morris. They share a riddle and a song. And so it goes. A lot of story reading and story telling. A little phonics. A lot of language activities emphasizing non-phonetic ways of guessing words.

This program has the students trying to read words before they learn all their letters. Also, the words are grouped, not by their phonetic similarity, but by categories like "color words." Sometimes the groups of words are not related at all, e.g., *brown, red, cat, green, map, yarn, yes*. In one spot in video 8, someone asks: "What is that word again?" and is told, "Look at the picture!"

Come Read With Me is cute and charming without being saccharin. The videos are all TV-quality and entertaining. This course does introduce the letters and their sounds, Sesame Street style, one letter a day over a period of weeks. If a child is having difficulty hearing the sounds in words, it is bound to help. It certainly does emphasize—again and again and again—the importance and worth of learning to read. The ancillary activities are fun. It has even won a Parent's Choice Award. Even so, I can't agree with its approach in the areas I outlined above. The buying decision, however, as always is up to you. *Mary Pride*

Carden Reading Method materials are very different from other phonics programs. Developed in the famous Carden Schools (see Carden review in Volume 1), this reading method only goes up through second grade. Why? Because by the end of second grade, your child should be able to read *anything*.

The method consists of a series of old-fashioned clothbound readers, paired with workbooks. The workbooks teach handwriting, reading comprehension, spelling, and vocabulary.

Unlike other methods, after the child learns the alphabet and consonants, the next step is long vowels. Plus, the readers have *no* pictures! There is absolutely no way for the young reader to "word guess," or be distracted from figuring out the sentence. Stories are interspersed with pages of word families for straight word reading practice.

The books are color-coded. In first grade, the sequence is Red Book, Blue Book, and Green Book. The stories are sweet and old-timey, with no fantasy settings. Many occur outdoors and on the farm. In grade 2, the yellow Junior Book is followed by the Bluebird Book. The latter is all "talking animal" stories about bluebirds and elephants.

The workbooks are pretty straightforward. Layout looks like it was produced on a typewriter. You may not be able to figure out exactly what all the exercises are teaching without the help of the teacher's edition of each workbook.

This is a comforting, soothing reading method. No political agendas, and what a relief to have love of nature taught without eco-guilt! The Carden Reading Method is homey without being home-made, and it's always nice to know your children are learning the same way that students in a visionary group of private schools have successfully learned for decades. *Mary Pride*

We wrote this Christ-centered kindergarten and early grades program up in some detail in Chapter 4. Let's look at its **Christ-Centered Phonics** component now.

The Lessons Guide is a teacher text, replacing the former *A–Z Phonics Lessons*. This book can not be used on its own. It requires the phonics flashcards and other materials available from the publisher.

CCP's phonics program uses Bible names and words as key words for the phonics sounds. Lessons contain phonics drills, introduction of the letter sound using a picture card, listening exercises, visual discrimination exercises, vo-

NEW!
Carden Reading Method
Grades 1–2. Grade 1: Red Book, $11.55. Red Book Workbook: student, $6.70; teacher, $15.55. Blue Book, $12.90. Blue Book Workbook: student, $6.80; teacher, $15.60. Green Book, $14.30. Green Book Workbook: student, $6.80; teacher, $15.45. Grade 2: Junior Book, $13.60. Junior Book Workbook: student, $6.15; teacher, $14. Vocabulary from the Junior Book with Exercises: student, $6.70; teacher, $15.55. Bluebird Book, 13.10. Bluebird Book Workbook: student, $6.30; teacher, $13.85. Grade 2 Spelling Book, $9.15. Spelling Workbook Two, $7.30. Comprehension Techniques Workbook 2, $7.55. Graduation Book Two, $9.20. Workbook for Mother West Wind's Children, $8.75. Science in Rhyme, $10.20. Language Workbook Two, $8. Old Mother West Wind: hardback, $16.95; paperback, $9.95. Mother West Wind's Children: hardback, $16.95; paperback, $9.95. The Story About Ping: hardback, $14.99; paperback, $4.99. Language of Numbers Unit Two, $12. Teacher Techniques book, $5.60. Shipping extra.
Carden Educational Foundation, PO Box 659, Brookfield, CT 06804-0659. (860) 350-9885. Fax: (860) 354-9812. Email: carden@cardenschool.org. Web: cardenschool.org

Christ-Centered Phonics
Ages 3–7. Level A (K4): Phonics Lessons, $24.95; Workbooks/Readers, $24.95. Level B (K5–1): Phonics Lessons, $35.95; Workbooks/Readers, $39.95. Level C (1–2): Phonics Lessons, $33.95; Workbooks/Drill Reader, $47.95. Phonics visual aids for Levels A and

B, $46.95. Shipping extra.
Christ Centered Publications, Inc., PO Box 968, Tullahoma, TN 37388-0968. Orders: (800) 778-4318. Inquiries: (931) 393-4150. Web: www.christcentercurriculum.com.

Of the phonics programs we have seen, this is definitely the one that is most successfully Christ-centered, with a heavy emphasis on Scripture and biblical values. The King James Version is used throughout and children will end up learning much more than reading skills.

NEW!
Christian Light Learning to Read

Grades 1–2. Grade 1: Learning to Read Lightunits (10), $22.90; I Wonder Reader, $6.95; I Wonder Learning Sheets, $6.95; I Wonder Teacher's Guidebook, 5.95; Learning to Read Teacher's Handbook, $5.95; Word Flash Cards, $9.95; Phrase Flash Cards, $13.95; I Can Read reader, $3.95; Wall Picture Cards, $6; Sound Slider, $10.95. Grade 2: Reading 200 Lightunits (10), $22.90; Helping Hands Reader, $7.95; Helping Hands Teacher's Guidebook, $5.95. Happy Hearts reader, $7.95. Happy Hearts Teacher's Guidebook, $5.95. Shipping extra.
Christian Light Publications, PO Box 1212, Harrisonburg, VA 22801-1212. (540) 434-1003. Fax: (540) 433-8896. Email: Orders@CLP.org.

cabulary development (introducing words like *idol, omnipotent, endurance,* and names of Bible characters), enrichment activities, and a spiritual application. For example, for short *A* the rhyme goes, "To remain in *Adam* all shall die/But in Christ, eternal life is nigh." The flash cards illustrate this rhyme with beautiful color pictures.

The lessons are well organized and even spell out what the teacher is to say. However, somehow I (Rebecca) can't imagine saying to a tiny child, "God's nature is reflected in His creation which has both unity and diversity . . . in God's nature, unity speaks of the fact that the three Persons of the Godhead are 'alike'; they are the same . . . the doctrine of the Trinity is difficult even for adults . . ." My four-year-old would no doubt interrupt with, "I don't understand!"

The Phonics Workbook is for independent readers. Visually attractive and well-organized, it involves a lot of writing, using ball-and-stick manuscript style, and it reinforces phonics skills with an emphasis on spelling. For every new phonogram, you get a page of "phonics art"—pictures for you to draw piece by piece while your children copy, until one of them is able to guess what the picture is. (Hint: each of the four pictures per lesson begins with the letter or sound you are studying.) Our kids love this! You also get a page of tracing/writing practice for every new sound, as well as lots of vowel practice. The latter is particularly helpful, since preschoolers often confuse their vowels.

The Teacher's Guide provides answers and teaching helps.

CCP also offers a *Phonics Drill Reader* very similar to Victory Drill Book, timed drills and all. Nice laminated color cover, pages very light card stock. More: little readers (Creation: *God Made Me*, Fall: *God Loves Me,* Flood: *God Saves Me*) contain the same principles, but fewer words for younger children. Along with this you can purchase phonics flash cards, alphabet wall cards, and other teaching devices. No matter how many add-ons you get, the program is easy to use, thanks to the basically logical workbook format. *Rebecca Prewett and Mary Pride*

The 90 lessons in the **Learning to Read** reading course from **Christian Light Education** take your first grader from letters to simple stories. Squeaky-clean morality and Christian piety are features of this reading program originally designed for Mennonite schools. Directions are for classroom teachers, but easily translated to the home environment.

Learning to Read's pace is slow and gradual. The first Lightunit teaches only the letters *a, d, s, m,* and *f,* for example. However, it does teach children diacritical marks and terms such as *macron* and *breve* that other curricula call "long vowel sign" and "short vowel sign," or even "line" and "smile." This technical terminology, necessary for those German-speaking Mennonites for whom English is a second language, has been a stumbling-block in the past to those who did not grow up with it. To their credit, CLE has simplified it quite a bit over previous editions.

Visual discrimination is mostly taught through the "same and different" picture exercises woven throughout the first Lightunits. Handwriting, spelling, and listening skills are also taught.

In this approach, every sound is associated with a picture. Each picture has an associated story and rhyme, which use words with the new sound.

The updated **Learning to Read** program contains:

- Ten Learning to Read Lightunits—workbooks with sturdy covers and a nice airy format
- Learning to Read Teacher's Handbook—you need this!
- Set of 79 Word Flash Cards—the program does teach sight words
- Set of 79 Phrase Flash Cards—phrases such as "for Dad" and "should treat others"
- Set of Wall Picture cards: 21 consonant cards, 5 long vowel cards, 5 short vowel cards, and 4 digraph cards—*sh, ch, wh,* and *th*
- Sound Slider—a clever gizmo that enables you to quickly practice syllables beginning or ending with a vowel

The **Reading to Learn** curriculum takes up where Learning to Read leaves off. Intended for the second half of first grade, it includes: *I Can Read* Grade 1 Primer, *I Wonder* First Grade reader, Learning Sheets for *I Wonder,* and Teacher's Guide for *I Wonder*

This second-grade program continues with:

- Ten Reading to Learn Lightunits (201-210)
- *Helping Hands* reader (goes with Lightunits 201-205)
- Reading Teacher's Guide to *Helping Hands*
- *Helping Hearts* reader (goes with Lightunits 206-210)
- Reading Teacher's Guidebook for *Helping Hearts*

If you want a "school" style phonics curriculum, here it is. *Mary Pride*

Challenge your auditory learner. Get extra reading practice in the car. Improve your child's reading skills . . . all for the cost of a large pizza.

The two levels of the **Fab Phonics** book and tape sets will lead you from the review of the alphabet to *r*-controlled words. Between the glossy covers of these bound books are eight lessons and short workbook exercises that will reinforce learning.

For more details about **Christian Light Education's overall curriculum design,** see the review in Volume 1.

NEW!
Fab Phonics
Grades K–3. Each level, $13.95. Shipping extra.
Learning Quest, P.O. Box 1698, Carmichael, CA 95609. (916) 332-9544. Web: www.ns.net/~lquest

Fab Phonics would be ideal for the auditory child who could use extra help with his reading skills or for the older child who has never had any previous phonics instruction. Because of the small amount of reading practice in each section, it can not stand alone. I would definitely supplement this program with a good set of readers that would help your child practice each reading skill as it is learned.

NEW!
First Reader System

Ages 4–adult. $79.95 plus $7 shipping.
First Reader Systems, Inc., PO Box 495, Alton IL 62002. (800) 700-5228. Fax: (618) 462-8909. Email: info@firstreader.com. Web: www.firstreader.com.

UPDATED!
Gift of Reading Phonogram Materials

Prereading to adult. Phonogram cards, $17.95. Phonogram tape, $7.95. Kit, $55. Book, $14.95. Shipping extra.
Gift of Reading Program, 423 Maplewood Lane, San Antonio, TX 78216. (210) 828-5179. Email: sanantonio@hotmail.com.

The heart of this program is the audiotapes. The minute your cassette player starts to whir, an engaging song called, *"Readers are Leaders"* begins encouraging your child to succeed. The next thing the tape does is explain what phonics is. The novice homeschooler will be pleased to hear how simple it can be to teach her child to read. Upbeat music and song tunes—most derived from popular children's songs—provide pizzazz. The dialogs between a mom and dad and their two children—conversations that you could be having with your own children—provide instruction and humor. The entire program generates an "I can't wait until I learn to read" type of attitude.

Level 1 begins with a short alphabet review and continues with an introduction to consonants. Long vowels are introduced briefly and aren't really discussed again until level 2. The introduction to short vowel sounds is short but can be reviewed by playing the tape again.

One highlight of *Fab Phonics* is that it explains in detail different reading strategies to help the struggling reader, such as context clues, prediction, and pictures. Though some parents may object to this not-entirely-phonetic approach, it is a genuine help for the child who is struggling with his reading skills. Alternate sounds of *g, c, x,* and *s* finishes out the level one book. Level 2 continues with blends, digraphs, diphthongs, long vowels and *r*-controlled words. *Irene Buntyn*

Famed conservative activist Phyllis Schlafly has always been good at eliminating the confusion surrounding political issues and leading her audience right to the main point. Her phonics program, the **First Reader System**, is just as streamlined as her speeches.

Those of us who went to elementary school before 1965 will feel right at home with the look and feel of this phonics system. The winsome illustrations, the quality 183-page oversized hardbound text, the ball-and-stick handwriting lessons. Yes, this is one slick, up-to-date package. Phyllis has taken the traditional intensive phonics approach as taught in popular programs such as Sam Blumenfeld's *AlphaPhonics* and improved on it (forgive me, Sam!). How? With *color* text for the word parts the child is currently practicing, an accompanying workbook that teaches manuscript printing while it provides phonics practice, and two cassette tapes narrated by Phyllis that explain the whole program. All is neatly packaged in a handy binder, into which two oversized pencils are also fitted.

Needless to say, the First Reader System is totally wholesome: the innocence of yester-year without any contrived nostalgia. The reading selections are classic: Thomas Miller's *Evening Prayer*, Mother Goose rhymes, Aesop's fables, Robert Louis Stevenson's poems. Although lacking in games and hands-on activities (e.g. cut and paste), for visual learners this system should be near perfection. *Mary Pride*

Trudy Palmer, a lady with years of experience as a classroom teacher and tutor, was having such success with her phonogram-based phonics method that other people started asking her to teach them how to use the method with their children. Out of these requests was born her home business, which publishes her excellent phonogram cards and tape, as well as the *Gift of Reading* book.

Trudy's **Gift of Reading Phonogram Cards** look like they could have been produced by a million-dollar company. The set of 73 8½ x 4¾" cards can almost be used to teach reading by itself! Each card has a phonogram in lowercase letters on the front. Remember, a phonogram is a set of letters that makes a single sound. Sometimes one phonogram can have two or more separate sounds, like the phonogram *oo* which can either say *ew* as in *moo* or *euh* as in *book*. Teaching these is no joke. So on the back of each card you'll find a list of example words that use the phonogram . . . instructions for the teacher to say to the student . . . teaching tips, spelling rules, and explanations of the phonogram's peculiar features for the teacher . . . and a list of "exception" words that include the phonogram but are *not* pronounced according to the usual rules. The accompanying tape includes both teaching tips and the sounds of each phonogram, so you'll know exactly how to teach your student the sounds. Unique feature: the tape is recorded in such as way as to mimic one of Trudy's tutoring sessions—in other words, it sounds as though she is speaking directly to your child. This provides you with a model for your own home teaching.

The Gift of Reading Kit is a conveniently-packaged phonogram program. Opening up the cardboard box you find *The Gift of Reading: What Every Parent and Teacher Should Know*, a set of 73 large Phonogram Flash Cards in a handy zip-loc bag, an audiocassette that presents sample lessons as well as the sounds of each phonogram, a spelling notebook with rules and instructions, and a spelling list with rules and instructions.

This program teaches spelling using sequential, categorized lists organized by syllabication and spelling rules. An optional marking system can be utilized if the parent desires. However, because of the organization of the lists, this marking system is not mandatory. The method is more complicated than Total Reading's, since it involves placing "rule" numbers above or below some letters.

Trudy's new **The Gift of Reading book** (137 medium-sized pages) is perhaps the best part of this program. It is the best-organized presentation of the phonogram method we have yet encountered. It includes not only an excellent discussion of how and why to use this method, but also daily lesson plans, teaching tips to overcome problem spots, how to diagnose your child's reading level from listening to him read aloud, and even an appendix on penmanship! Unlike other books on this subject, it does not skip back and forth between endless charts, lists, and special instructions.

Also available from this source: composition books and paper, various "school" series used for reading comprehension, spelling lists for K–5, a writing workshop on tape, a book on auditory processing and listening skills, and language arts materials for K–12. *Mary Pride*

You've heard the commercials. Memorized the phone number. Read about the controversy. Now you're wondering: is the new **Hooked on Phonics** any good?

I was impressed when I opened the box. If the packaging, look, and feel of the materials could teach your child to read, this would have to be the best phonics program around. The program is divided into two main sections. First, the phonics part of the program. You get nine cassette tapes, color-coded to match the books, and nine sets of flash cards. The flash cards wowed our little ones right away. They are the size of playing cards, each set kept in order by a little metal ring (the first major improvement). Alas, the children quickly ceased saying "wow" once the tapes started. No

ADDITIONAL MATERIALS REQUIRED: Composition book. Pencils and paper. Set of phonics readers.

CONSUMABLE PROGRAM ITEMS: None.

SUBJECTS COVERED: Phonics, handwriting, spelling, and prereading skills.

BEST FOR: Ages 6 and up. The Phonics Treasure Chest is separately available to provide games for phonogram practice. Well-organized material is less demanding than other phonogram-based programs; reading starts sooner than with the Small Ventures program, for example. Spelling component is overly complicated; I'd skip the optional notation system and just use the spelling rules and lists. Good for "Teacher" types who want to really understand all about phonics, spelling, and handwriting.

NEW!
Hooked on Phonics
All ages. $249.95 plus $25 shipping (California residents add tax).
Gateway Learning Corporation, PO Box 26167, Santa Ana, CA 92799-6167. (800) ABC-DEFG.
Fax: (714) 429-2293.
Web: www.hookedonphonics.com.

ADDITIONAL MATERIALS REQUIRED: Another phonics program, to teach you what Hooked On Phonics didn't. Packaging materials and postage to return Hooked On Phonics to the publisher.

CONSUMABLE PROGRAM ITEMS: None.

SUBJECTS COVERED: Phonograms and some look-say words presented but not really taught. No feedback mechanism to determine if student is reading words correctly. No handwriting.

BEST FOR: Nobody. Designed for adults.

PHONICS KNOWLEDGE REQUIRED: A lot. Hooked on Phonics does not teach you how to teach phonics, nor does it outline or follow through on any of the major steps.

TEACHING ABILITY REQUIRED: The program is intended to be self-instructional. Actually, the user has little hope of teaching himself; he needs someone to tell him if he is reading the words right and to explain the spelling and phonics rules. Therefore he requires an excellent teacher, since no such materials are supplied.

NEW!
In The Beginning . . . Teach a Child to Read

Grades K–2. $169 plus shipping.
In the Beginning, HC 63 Box 19,
O'Neill, NE 68763. (402) 482-5906.
Fax (402) 482-9191.
Email: begin@inetnebr.com.
Web: www.beginningreader.com.

one liked the chant/soft rock style in which they were supposed to learn the alphabet. If they weren't paying close attention and turning the cards as quick as they were supposed to—and didn't know how to read the numbers from 1 to 26 that were whispered on the tape—they ended up lost.

Once your child learns the alphabet and the letter sounds, he will be mysteriously required to memorize by sight a list of words such as: *read, out, loud, now, sounding, words,* etc. so that he can "read" the instructions in the books. Periodically, the child is tested by being told to read through a card deck while the voice on the tape pauses before saying each letter or word (second improvement). Short vowels are taught in the same chanting way. So is blending (third improvement) and everything else. Little or no instruction is given, only practice.

The tapes were so endlessly tedious in their approach and the rhythm became so grating, that I find it remarkable that any child could finish this entire program without bribery or coercion. We certainly couldn't.

However, should your child finish, he is now presumably ready for "Your Reading Power": 100 SRA Power Builders. If the child can't read the stories yet—not to worry. He can listen to them on tape. The stories start out extremely simple and not very well written and rapidly progress to an adult level. Some parents would probably rather not have their children reading about myths presented in a factual way, politically correct environmentalism, naked men, and science fiction stories with aliens planning to eat all of us. Even if you removed the questionable stories, what's left isn't that great either.

BOTTOM LINE: Rebecca's mother has tutored at least one "graduate" of this program who could not read at all. If this was the only phonics program in existence, you could probably adapt it and improve it. However, don't think that you can sit your child down, hand this over, and he will soon be reading like the children in the commercials. At least they have a 30-day money back guarantee.

TUNE UP: There's no way to make this program acceptable. If you already know phonics well enough to sit with the student and follow up on his reading practice, you don't need the course. If you want just the minimal help the Hooked On Phonics flashcards and reading extracts provide, don't waste your money on this; get *Alpha-Phonics* instead. *Rebecca Prewett and Mary Pride*

The author of **In The Beginning . . . Teach a Child to Read** taught public school for 27 years. This program contains a 2-hour video that is the next best thing to sitting down with Lois Caroll at her kitchen table to learn her techniques for teaching beginning reading. The somewhat homemade-looking video also shows the author using the program with her granddaughters over the course of a school year. It is helpful to see the techniques used with actual children in a home setting: the younger girl is initially distracted by the camera, the doorbell and the phone occasionally ring, a dog barks, the girls make typical mistakes—and you see how the author handles these situations.

What you get with this program is the video (meant to be viewed by the parent in preparation for teaching), 100 phonetic cards and a blending box, a file box containing 300 cards with sentences for the child to read and write, 40 reading books, a short instruction booklet for the teacher, and a writing tablet. The phonetic cards and the blending box go together and are a strong point of this program. The box has 3 sections and you get 3 sets of cards containing lower-case letters with which the child can build one-or-two-syllable words. These cards are also used earlier in the process when you are instructed to teach the letters to the child using a technique called skywriting, where the child forms the letters in the air with her finger. The file box contains label card dividers with instructions on how to introduce new concepts to the child. The 40 reading books are 5½ x 4¼" booklets, plain black and white with no distracting pictures.

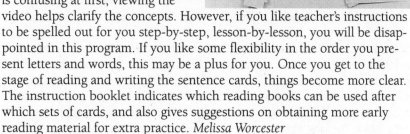

The teacher's instruction booklet is confusing at first; viewing the video helps clarify the concepts. However, if you like teacher's instructions to be spelled out for you step-by-step, lesson-by-lesson, you will be disappointed in this program. If you like some flexibility in the order you present letters and words, this may be a plus for you. Once you get to the stage of reading and writing the sentence cards, things become more clear. The instruction booklet indicates which reading books can be used after which sets of cards, and also gives suggestions on obtaining more early reading material for extra practice. *Melissa Worcester*

The **itl learn-to-read program** has always been remarkable for its unusual approach to phonics instruction. I reviewed it way back in the first edition of *The Big Book of Home Learning,* but it's gone through two more publishers since then and a lot of revising. For all practical purposes, this edition can be counted as a new phonics program.

Not because the method used has changed. Just as before, the program introduces lowercase letters first, and in a special sequence designed to match children's motor-skills abilities. *I, t,* an *l* are the first three letters introduced—hence the name *itl.* This is a "Draw to Write to Read" program, so the author, Donna Reid Connell, is concerned first with the ease of forming each letter. *I, t,* and *l* are the three easiest letters to form, so they come first. Second, she understands the value of stories to learning to read, so each letter has an animal character and story associated with it. *I* is an inchworm, for example. Third, and this is quite different from other programs, the letter sounds introduced in *itl* correspond to animal *noises,* not to the first word of animal *names,* as in virtually every other phonics program.

This last feature was invented by Donna's four-year-old son, Michael, who added yet another feature: the letter shapes in this program are "animal skeletons." This doesn't mean you see gruesome bones, but rather that each letter shape forms the "backbone" of an animal whose sound is associated with the letter. Each letter also has a motion associated with it, for total body involvement.

Just because the author listens to her preschooler when he has something insightful to say, don't get the idea that this program is just another off-the-top-of-the-head job. The lesson manual makes it abundantly clear that each *itl* feature is there for a reason. The letters were each assigned a "difficulty index" and then presented in increasing order of difficulty. Uppercase letters are presented last because they are much harder to write than lowercase letters, and also more subject to reversals. Writing is stressed because research shows that children who begin writing early (and this includes scribbling) also begin reading earlier. Even the letter shapes themselves were based on painstaking research into the effectiveness of various alphabets. Readiness lessons are also included right along with the phonics lessons. You're even given an index of difficulty for children's drawings, which tells you exactly when your child is ready to start using the program based on the level of drawing ability they have achieved.

NEW!
ITL: Integrated Total Language
Ages 4–7. $42.95 plus shipping. *Addison-Wesley Publishing Company, PO Box 5026, White Plains, NY 10602-5026. (800) 872-1100. Fax: (800) 551-7637. Email: info@awl.com. Web: www.awl.com/dsp.*

Every homeschool support group should have a copy of this program. The information about "drawing readiness" alone is worth it. Especially recommended for kinesthetic-tactile learners and for boys, who often are ill-served by other programs to the point of being falsely labeled "developmentally delayed" or even "learning disabled."

The *itl* program comes with:

- Two audiocassettes with all the lesson stories on them
- The lesson manual
- A huge set of blackline masters, with everything from letters to parents (not terribly needed in the homeschool setting), to directions for making an *itl* sock puppet, to patterns for games, to 134 student handouts, plus teacher materials such as lower- and uppercase alphabets with directional cues, hand signs, and lots more
- A poster showing every animal character in the *itl* alphabet

Intended for classroom use, the lesson manual includes some unnecessary features, e.g., expecting you to buy or make hand puppets for each letter of the alphabet and perform stories using these puppets and additional props. Suggestion to Addison-Wesley: a videotape of these puppet stories would meet the bill here and save teachers (and moms and dads) a lot of extra work. Besides, these days just about every new phonics program has a lessons video included. *Mary Pride*

NEW!
Jolly Phonics

Ages 3–6. Phonics Workbook (Volume 1–7), $1.99 each. Finger Phonics (Volume 1–7), $48.30 set. The Phonics Handbook, $27.50. The Phonics Videos (2-video set), $29.95. Phonics Wall Frieze, $8.95. Jiglets (pack of 4), $13.95 each. Stencilets (pack of 8), $15.95. Phonics Box—one of everything, $187.50. Shipping extra.
Jolly Learning, Ltd., c/o AIDC, 12 Wintersport Lane, Williston, VT 05495. USA orders: (800) 488-2665. USA fax: (802) 864-7626. UK orders/inquiries: (011-44) 181-501-0405. UK fax: (011 44) 181-500-1696.

This charming phonics program from England is packed with unique features. Here are a few:

- **Little animal characters** appear throughout the course in the videos, books, worksheets, and other phonics accessories.
- **"Finger Phonics" board books** introduce each letter with a key word, additional words, and pictures loaded with items beginning with that letter.
- That's not too unusual so far, but **each letter also has a physical movement** associated with that letter. For the letter *m*, for example, the child says "mmmm" while rubbing his tummy.
- Even more unusual, **each new letter is engraved right into the page** with a dot for its starting point and little lines pointing which direction you should draw it in. Children can slide their finger along the engraved groove and "feel" the letter. Hence the name "Finger Phonics."
- **Letters are introduced in an unusual sequence**, starting with the letters *s, a, t, i, p,* and *n* in the first Finger Phonics book.
- **Additional unusual accessories,** such as Jiglets and Stencilets, are available. We'll describe these in a moment.

The animal characters are un-Muppet-like puppets. For one thing, Inky Mouse's mouth never moves. Bee is moved about by a stick, which can clearly be seen in many of the lessons. Phonic is a computer with an animated face. Snake is the most Muppet-like of the group, having a mouth that opens and shuts and a big puffy body. However, these characters are surrounded by an above-average environment. Some scenes take place indoors, while others occur in various naturalistic outdoor environments, with everything to scale so the trees and leaves are H-U-G-E compared to the small animal characters. It even rains and thunders outside the open mousehole door on occasion, providing a real feeling you are looking into a small, self-consistent world.

The stories on the videos begin with Inky Mouse looking for good scenes to snap with her camera. She is looking for items beginning with the "S" letter for the first page of the Finger Phonics book. What she finds, much to her fear, is Snake. Happily, Snake is just teasing when he says she looks like supper! So Inky takes the picture. Inky has met Bee, who is lost and can't find her beehive. Inky shows Bee a sign, causing Bee to see how useful reading is and express a wish to learn to read. Already both major themes of the videos are in place:

(1) **The animal characters are learning to read.** They often make mistakes, thus showing kids how to overcome these mistakes and at the same time getting out the message that it's OK if you don't "get it right" the first time.

(2) **The Finger Phonics books and workbooks are tied together with the videos,** because on the videos you see the animal characters working at finding photos for the books! After a certain number of snapshots have been taken, Phonic the computer pushes a new completed book out his slot. Thus, the whole series comes across not as another committee-written product for kids, but as something made for them by little creatures whose worries, failures, and triumphs are very similar to their own.

What matters is if the method is easy, if it's complete, if it works, and if it's fun. Jolly Phonics comes up roses in all three categories. Not only is it story-based—and remember, "story readiness" is an important part of getting ready to read—but it teaches kids all 42 sounds of the English language using nothing but fun activities. Kids act out the letter sounds, act out the stories, color in pictures that reinforce the letter sounds, and trace letters. One good sign is that the **Phonics Handbook** that accompanies the course devotes almost three times as much space to reproducible materials for your flashcard work, activities, and games as it does to instructions on how to use the program. Another good sign is that there is exactly one **Phonics Workbook** for each **Finger Phonics book.** Each workbook includes prewriting activities that teach stylus skills, practice in writing the letters (in this program, they are a form of precursive), and an Activity Page with just a few simple additional activities, usually based on one of the animal characters. For instance, you might cut paper in a spiral and pull on it to create a snake you can hang up on a string. By the time you get to Phonics Workbook 7, children are ready to read the included story about a bad-tempered billy goat.

The **Jiglets** and **Stencilets** I mentioned earlier are, respectively, sets of two word puzzles each and stencil sets that allow you to trace a word and an accompanying picture. These are both quite skippable. You can only make the one word "car" out of the car Jiglet, for example. Cute, but not necessary.

It would not be an exaggeration to say that this series has taken England by storm. As of March 1996, publisher Christopher Jolly told the *Guardian* that he estimates his program has gone into 20 percent of British primary schools. Not bad for a program that only came out in 1992. In Canada, the response has been even more enthusiastic, with Canadians now buying as many copies of Jolly Phonics as Brits. Even New Zealand, a country where pushing Whole Language has been a tourist attraction for many years, is now showing some interest in this program. Such interest is based on the results Jolly Phonics has produced, even in classrooms with kids from disadvantaged socioeconomic strata.

My only serious complaint about the Jolly Phonics program is the way it teaches blending. In the videos each individual letter is pronounced very distinctly, rather than truly blending them. Thus *cat* is "blended" as "cuh," "aaa," and "tuh." The only concession to actual blending techniques is that you are told to pronounce the first letter louder and whisper the others. This merely yields "CUH-aaa-tuh." Instead, each consonant should be pronounced as its distinct sound, without any following "uh," and vowel sounds should be *held*. You may therefore want to invest in a copy of *Teach Your Child to Read in 100 Easy Lessons*, which has the best teaching on blending available but isn't too great on phonics after it teaches blending, and substitute its lessons on blending in place of the Jolly Phonics lessons on this topic.

While I'm nitpicking, it's not easy to do "left to right practice" at the end of Finger Phonics 2 when the letters need to be matched to pictures that surround them on all four sides. Also, inexplicably, the pictures shown of proper hand position in each workbook do not show how "lefties" should hold a pencil. But these are minor quibbles. If you have young children who enjoy cute (but not gooey) stories and an enthusiastic, use-your-whole-body method of learning to read and write, Jolly Phonics may well be for you. *Mary Pride*

Fans of Ruth Beechick, take heart! This gentle, easy-to-teach program has been designed to implement her philosophy of language arts education. Here is what you get in the nice sturdy box:

- **The Blue Book**—A step-by-step guide to teaching each lesson, a booklet of supplemental materials, sight word cards, sound picture cards, consonant and vowel cards, blend cards, game cards.
- **Bob Books**—12 cute little short vowel readers.
- **Bridge Story Readers**—Three readers containing six stories in all,
- **Educational Insights**—10 long vowel readers, and a cube game designed by Ruth Beechick.

This is a complete language arts program. It begins with reading readiness activities and progresses through a phonics-oriented approach to reading. In addition, you will be reading library books out loud to your child, using reference books with your child, having him narrate or retell stories, teaching your child how to write a story, memorizing Scripture, and teaching him penmanship, using either italic handwriting or another method of your own choosing (the Italic Handwriting Book can be included for an additional $4.95). Along the way, you and your child will discussing and analyzing what you read together, and your child will be embarking on a lifelong relationship with good literature.

Those who have enjoyed using other books in the **Learning Language Arts Through Literature** series will enjoy and welcome this high quality program. I would highly recommend it for anyone looking for a complete, enjoyable program that could, with little work, become the springboard for an entire unit-study-based first grade curriculum. *Rebecca Prewett*

NEW!
Learning Language Arts Through Literature Common Sense Reading Program

1st grade. $95 plus shipping.
Common Sense Press, P.O. Box 1365, Melrose FL 32666. Call (352) 475-5757 for a retail store near you; they do not sell retail themselves.
Email: service@cspress.com.
Web: www.cspress.com.

Literacy Primer Packet

Ages 6–9. $38.50 plus $2.75 shipping. Extra spelling board for second child, $3.50.
Literacy Press, Inc., 24 Lake Drive, DeBary, FL 32713. (407) 668-1232.

ADDITIONAL MATERIALS REQUIRED: Pencils and paper. Letter flashcards. Chalkboard.

CONSUMABLE PROGRAM ITEMS: Literacy Primer, if children are allowed to write in the book or color the pictures.

SUBJECTS COVERED: Phonics, handwriting, creative writing, and spelling.

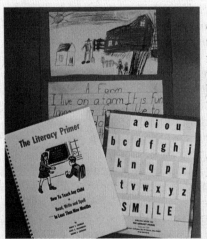

This small mail-order firm has an offer that's hard to beat: if, after trying their **Literacy Primer Packet** reading program with your most difficult pupil, you aren't satisfied that it's the best method you've seen, "return the USED BOOK with the shipping label for a full refund." The kit is designed, in the publisher's words, to "Teach Any Child to Read, Write, and Spell in Less Than Nine Months." Used as directed, children will read independently in eight to ten weeks, and be writing well-spelled compositions at the end of nine months.

How does it work? You get a **Literacy Primer**, which contains the lessons (in large type) and teacher's notes (in small type). The *Primer* is reusable, since children finger trace and say the letters in the book, writing them on separate paper (provided in the Spelling Kit) or a chalkboard. The trace-and-say method is supplemented with a **Spelling Board Kit**, consisting of a sturdy cardboard frame with accordion pockets into which single letters are placed to spell out words. The many kinesthetic drills using tracing and the Spelling Board reinforce reading concepts, and are a great help for those children who the schools like to label "learning disabled." Moreover, using the Spelling Board Kit, children can spell all the words they can read even *before* they learn to write. This is a feature not found elsewhere. (You can buy the Spelling Board separately.)

The **Teacher's Supplement**, also provided, is a mini-course in how to teach reading, spelling, and composition skills. Classroom teachers will find the teaching tips absolutely invaluable. These include time-tested motivational ideas and helps for getting problem pupils over the "humps."

And then there are the accompanying **Homestead Readers**. These delightful little books (*Jon and Jim on the Homestead*, *Homestead School*, and *Jon and Jim Discover Alternate Energy*) include drawing activities and questions for the children to show their comprehension of the story. Very thoughtfully, the writers have provided an appendix of simplified line drawings for this purpose. These drawings, like the rest of the art, are rather amateurish: not gorgeous, but acceptable.

In *Homestead School*, each story describes how to do some pioneer activity, like making soap. In *Alternate Energy*, you guessed it, the stories tell about alternate energy sources. Stories contain some Christian emphasis.

The people at Literacy Press have a lovely attitude, as this quote shows: "We do not feel that others who are promoting LITERACY are our competitors. The need is wide." Amen! *Mary Pride*

Lockhart Reading Systems

Phonics is a completely non-consumable, reasonably-priced, and absolutely clutter-free program. The only supplies you need are a blackboard or markerboard and something to write on it with. (We made our own lined blackboard, from instructions in the manual.)

Charlotte F. Lockhart ("Char-L, the Biphonic Woman"), the program's author, sounds like an interesting person. Her program has been tested and proven effective all over the country—as well it might, being written by a lady with years of experience as a teacher and principal.

You don't have to know a thing about phonics to use Char-L's system, and your child doesn't have to know a single thing about it either. Discover Intensive Phonics for Yourself starts right at the beginning, with letter recognition. Children learn to write letters at the blackboard. (Char-L even tells you how to make a blackboard, if you don't have one!) Lesson one starts with consonant *b*. Next comes *f*, then *d*, *g*, and *a*. Your children then learn the "slide," blending a consonant and vowel together. After that they learn the rest of the letters . . . and then the real fun begins!

Char-L has broken down the entire decoding process into 42 sounds. Your child will also learn spelling rules, contractions, and stuff like suffixes

---

BEST FOR: Ages 5 and up; remedial or English as a second language. Home teacher should know how to pronounce phonics sounds accurately, understand how to teach blending, be prepared to review the first few lessons many times before proceeding on. It might be helpful to pick up some additional materials for teaching the basic letter sounds and beginning blending (e.g., Mary Pecci's book and Sam Blumenfeld's Alpha-Phonics Audio Tapes) rather than relying on this program alone. Not recommended for adults or very young children. Some motivational activities: drawing stick-figure pictures, comprehension discussion questions. Spelling Board is excellent for use with children physically unable to write.

BEST FEATURES: Great guarantee. Systematic approach, easy to use. Spelling Board allows kids who aren't ready to write to spell out words. Cute readers include clever comprehension exercises.

WORST FEATURES: Amateurish production quality.

Lockhart Reading Systems Phonics (formerly CHAR-L, Inc.)

Ages 5–12. Shipping extra. Level III Basic Phonics program, $174. Teacher's Phonics Manual, $108. Reverse Listening Card Set, $33 (primary/remedial set); $19 (intermediate set). Posters (2-8½ x 11"), $6. Parent's Homeschool Program, $148 level 1 and $134 level 2. *Lockhart Reading Systems, 1420 Lockhart Dr., Kennesaw, GA 30144. (800) 501-6767 or (770) 428-6796. Fax: (770) 419-1900. Email: info@lockhartreading.com. Web: www.lockhart-reading.com.*

BEST FEATURES: Step-by-step lessons start at the beginning and assume nothing. No clutter. Active learning at the blackboard. "Nonsense" words make sure your student really understands. No need for separate reading groups when used in a classroom. Whole program is completely reusable. All components available separately.

WORST FEATURES: Instructions could be more systematic and easy to follow.

and synonyms. The big orange manual tells you what to do every step of the way. An enclosed cassette teaches you the sounds and explains the program. Two big orange posters (you assemble them out of six included pieces of cardboard) show the 42 sounds, blends, and special vowel combinations your student will be learning.

Unique to this program are the included Reverse Listening Cards. These are 324 cards printed on cheerful colored card stock. Every card is different. You are supposed to laminate the cards or cover them with contact paper, then cut them out.

What is "reverse listening"? Char-L explains it like this:

Even before I had written my material, a teacher once complained that her students could write and spell anything that she dictated, but when they saw the same words in print, they could not read them. This gave me the idea of reversing the process—to use cards with words on them so the students would see the letters and words (instead of hearing them all of the time).

With the Reverse Listening cards, they see the words in print, they copy the words on the chalkboard, following the instructions, then read the words aloud to the teacher, who checks to see if they have mastered the skills involved.

"Nonsense words" are included to see if the student is really reading and understanding or just memorizing word shapes.

Char-L's new set of Mini Reverse Listening Cards was designed just for homeschoolers. Its 18 8½ x 11" sheets for a total of 176 Reverse Listening cards are also (I *think*) included in the basic kit price.

Char-L's program can be used with a whole school class at once, without any need for segregating the kids into ability groups, by the way. Teachers who hate making little slow Johnny feel bad definitely should look into this program which includes him right along with everyone else, with no extra effort for them!

Every component of this program looks really professional and sharp. Char-L doesn't miss a trick. And she'll even answer your questions once you are using her program. If you can't live without games and activities, this isn't the program for you. But if you just want your children to *read* . . . and you want to enjoy teaching them . . . this is a great little program. *Mary Pride*

NEW!
Modern Curriculum Press "Plaid" Phonics

Grades K–6. Student editions: Level K, $6.40; Level A, $7.95; Levels B and C, $7.85 each: Levels D–F, $7.55 each. Teacher resource guides: each level, $38. Phonics Power Pack: K, $120; A, $160; B, $185. Power Pack items also available individually. Picture cards: level K, $46; level A & B set, $57. Flashcards: set 1 (levels A & B), $33; set 2 (level B only), $33. Starting Off with Phonics Program Sampler (includes all six student books and teacher's book), $47.95.

The **Modern Curriculum Press "Plaid" Phonics** curriculum has been an unadvertised staple for many homeschool families for years and years. The reason? While other publishers switched wholesale first to "sight words" then to "whole language," MCP ignored the fads and stuck with genuine, step-by-step phonics. Beginning with alphabet sounds and moving logically to one-syllable words with short vowels, blends, digraphs, long-vowel words, and so on, the famous "Plaid Phonics" series concentrated on actually teaching children to read.

Newly revised in 1998, the series now sports an entirely different look. How so? Most classroom phonics programs rely on pictures, rather than dictation, for children's practice assignments. A workbook page will show an illustration of a hand, and the child is supposed to write "hand" underneath it, for example, or pick it out as one of the words that begins with *h*, or one of the words that rhymes with *and*.

A big problem with this type of program is that children often see an illustration and have trouble figuring out *what* the word is that the illustration is intended to convey. Sometimes it is simple confusion: is the word supposed to be *chicken* or *rooster* or *hen*? Sometimes the art is so bad the child doesn't know if he's looking at a *hat* or a *bat*.

Modern Curriculum Press has partly solved this problem in their 1998 Plaid Phonics edition by including *full-color photographs* of every object the child is asked to identify. These are clean photos of just the object, with no extraneous elements—an "Eyewitness Book" style look, if you are familiar with that series. (Black-and-white editions are available for a few pennies less, although I can't imagine why anyone would want one.)

Of course, you get a lot more than photos. Each lesson comes with a step-by-step lesson plan, strategies for teaching kids with different learning styles and needs (including ESL, gifted, and special students), suggested "favorite books" to reinforce the lesson (don't feel obligated to rush out to the library for these—the selection are more "trendy" than "classic," none are needed to teach reading, and some are pretty obscure), cross-references to their AstroWord phonics software line for extra practice, and "Curriculum Connections" for suggested writing and spelling activities. That is, assuming you buy the Teacher Resource Guide for the level you are currently teaching. I personally wouldn't bother; these huge, spiral-bound manuals are not necessary for teaching the lessons in the student workbook to one child at home.

MCP Plaid Phonics comes in seven levels. Level K is for pre-reading. This is not followed, as you might guess, by Level 1. Like most publishers these days, MCP declines to print grade levels on their books. This is supposed to help the self-esteem of kids assigned lower levels than the rest of their class, although in reality kids are not fooled by the difference between being in the "green" book and the "red" book. In MCP's case, the levels are named A–F. By the time you get to level D, you're doing language arts (grammar, alphabetizing, test prep, reading comprehension, etc.), and phonics is being reviewed, not introduced. That's why the books for levels D through F are called "Word Study" instead of "Phonics."

A "Phonics Power Pack" is helpful, if not absolutely necessary, to teach each phonics level. This includes between 30 and 47 phonics posters (depending on the level), up to 176 phonics picture cards, up to 512 phonics flashcards, and a different set of cassettes for each level. The level B set includes the flashcards and picture cards found in the level A pack, allowing for some savings by just purchasing the additional items necessary when you move up to level B. To save some money, home-schoolers will probably only need the flashcards and picture cards for each level.

I haven't had the time to check the entire new edition for political correctness—the bane of most publishers' reading programs, whether phonics-based or not. Since this program was revised so recently, MCP will deserve extra credit if they have managed to keep their workbooks on target. This seems likely, judging by the titles of their readers, which deal with "kid's world" subjects like chickenpox, animals, and friends, rather than the political fads of adults. The K and D levels, which I have seen, were quite conservative in their outlook. In the selections about dinosaurs, for example, evolution and "millions of years" are never mentioned, just known facts about dinosaur types. Love for family members, including grandparents . . . old-fashioned types of community service (e.g., a Scout troop cleaning up a park) . . . how to make a snow globe . . . these are typical of the reading selections in level D. Patriotic handling of the United States flag was even one of the reading selections! *Mary Pride*

Schoolhouse Phonics (levels A–C): each student book, $11; each teacher's book, $16.75. Phonics is Fun (levels 1–3): each student book, $8.90; each teacher's manual with answer key, $12.90. Shipping extra. *Modern Curriculum Press, 4350 Equity Dr., PO Box 2649, Columbus, OH 43126-2649. (800) 321-3106. Fax: (800) 393-3156. Web: www.mcschool.com.*

SUPPLEMENTARY NOTE: MCP has a number of alternative phonics series. **Starting Off with Phonics** is a six-book, mostly black-and-white, kindergarten program. **Schoolhouse Phonics** is a three-level series of supplementary workbooks, this time with pages in two colors. **Phonics is Fun** is a three-level series that allows students to learn all of phonics at a faster pace than Plaid Phonics. While all three employ line-art illustrations, and consequently are nowhere near as beautiful as the new Plaid Phonics, *Starting Off with Phonics* and *Phonics is Fun* are a more streamlined (and less expensive) way for cash-strapped families to cover the phonics basics.

The MCP catalog claims that Plaid Phonics is the program that "has helped 50 million children learn to read" in the past 40 years. In other words, a very significant fraction of all the people in the USA who now *can* read learned to read with an ancestor of Plaid Phonics. While some of the material in the new edition is overkill for home educators, it has been improved overall. Definitely worth a look, especially if you are only familiar with the old version.

Penny Primer and the S & H Reading Package

Grades K–4. Penny Primer Starter Set, $12.95. The Great Saltmine and Hifwip Reading Package, $38.50 (includes manual in 3-ring binder and following items: wall chart, two dictation notebooks, and two audiocassettes). Shipping extra. *Teach America to Read and Spell, PO Box 44093, Tacoma, WA 98444. (253) 531-0312. Email: tatras@juno.com.*

BEST FEATURES: Elegant phonetic approach uses a minimum of phonograms and rules. Multisensory. Inexpensive. Teacher-training emphasis directed at parents, with a complete explanation of why phonics works and look-say doesn't, as well as how to use the program. Free phone consultations. No burdensome overemphasis on writing, although writing is taught. Timings make it easy to record progress, motivate student. Only phonics program to concentrate on the MOO (Most Often Occurring) words that comprise more than 50 percent of both children's and adult's literature. Lessons are short.

WORST FEATURE: The manual alone *looks* disorganized (though it's not) and makes you have to work harder than you should. The new TATRAS #2 cassette, "Introduction to the S&H Manual," and the free telephone counseling make the manual easier to understand.

Here's an inexpensive, phonogram-based program quite different from the famous phonogram-based Spalding Method. Author Frank Rogers believes that "reading is the road to writing," rather than that writing is the road to reading, as Spalding says. His set of phonograms also differs markedly from Spalding's. It is based on computer analysis of the English language, and makes it possible to decode most of the MOO (Most Often Occurring) words, unlike other programs in which many of these words are taught as "sight" words. Also unlike Spalding and other methods, the phonics rules in this program are not mixed with spelling rules.

Frankly, I was really impressed with all the program components, from the **Penny Primer** starter set to the **Great Saltmine and Hifwip Reading Package**. (S A L T M I N and E are the first eight phonograms taught in this system, in case you're curious. Hifwip stands for High Frequency Words in Print.) The Penny Primer starter set serves as an inexpensive introduction to this phonics system, *and* the first eight phonograms of the program! (These are also repeated in the program manual.)

WHAT YOU GET: Comb-bound instruction manual complete with word lists, step-by-step program outline, daily lesson format, and a separate "Fast Track" sequence with special "Confidence Builder" word lists for remedial students of all ages, and two audiocassettes that explain various features of the Penny Primer and the manual and how to use them. Phonogram flash cards. A blue and red-lined dictation notebook. A "finger clock" card for teaching students proper letter formation (e.g., *a* starts at two o'clock . . .). Pencils and pencil gripper, to teach proper finger position while writing.

Saltmine and Hifwip is a "vertical phonics" program. That means you teach all the sounds of each phonogram at once. The three sounds of *a,* for example, are presented as "/A/t /AY//AW/." This means that the first sound is the *a* in *at,* the second sound (called the "long a" by other systems) sounds like *ay,* and the third sound is pronounced like *aw.* The Penny Primer and teaching cassette explain exactly how to present the material, right down to suggested wording for the teacher to use with the student. Possible obstacles are acknowledged and you are told how to overcome them.

The bottom line of The Great Saltmine and Hifwip Reading Package is to get kids reading *for pleasure* as soon as possible. That's why so much attention is focused on those MOO words. Typical phonics programs ignore those words, or teach many of them by whole-word memorization. But TATRAS deliberately attacks these words—*and* lets you know which still remain irregular in this phonetic system! (Less than 3 percent.)

The flash cards are rather unusual. Phonograms in black are on one side, phonograms in red are on the other. The black phonograms are those that occur most often, while the red ones occur less often but must be taught for spelling purposes. Sounds and teacher instructions are on the opposite side of the card from the corresponding phonogram. This means the teacher can see the answer but the student can't. Phonograms are printed in the upper left corner, so the flash cards can easily be staggered to spell out words (a good feature for kids whose motor skills are not yet up to writing).

This is about the best-thought-out phonics program I have seen. I just wish the author had provided more structure in the manual. You *can* figure out how to use the manual, but I know I'm not the only one who initially found the format confusing. Word lists, rules, phonogram charts, irregular words, abbreviations, etc. are all clustered together, while the lesson format and program outline is in the front of the books. The word lists themselves are littered with (admittedly useful) subscripts and icons. These indicate such things as "spoken word has two spellings" or "first word to use newly introduced phonogram." All this technical stuff is perfectly clear to veteran phonics teachers, but a bit unnerving for the novice. The new "Introduction to the S&H Manual" cassette walks you through it all, which helps; be sure to take notes in your manual as you listen!

If you're interested in this program, and your child is five years old, be sure to start with the Penny Primer starter kit. Play that cassette a couple of times and *take notes*! If your child is older than five, you will want to start with the full S & H package. *Mary Pride*

Phonics for Reading and Spelling is a kit, not just a book. Seven-ring binder with phonogram audiocassette mounted inside. Eighteen cardstock pages of phonogram cards for you to cut out, tucked into a binder pocket. Huge tabbed manual includes not only program background and instructions, but spelling word lists, spelling evaluation tests for levels from kindergarten through college, handwriting instructions, and reference charts covering phonic sounds, spelling rules, and basic grammar.

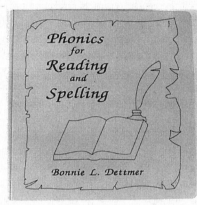

Features of this program: (1) Spelling is taught before reading (as in the Spalding Method). (2) Precursive is taught using pictures as reference points around a circle—e.g., "Start at the star." (3) Seventy-two phonograms are taught, beginning with the small letters. Letter sounds are taught before letter names. (4) Child copies his own reference charts from dictation. These show the spelling and phonics rules. (5) The appendix includes Greek and Latin word roots, for vocabulary-building as well as for help in spelling.

Daily lessons follow a pattern. First, oral review of the phonograms using the flashcards. Next, written review from dictation. New material is then introduced in a very structured way, with scripts for the parent to follow, and both the new and old material are practiced via dictation.

Other materials available from Small Ventures include the Phonics Fun game ($15.95 plus shipping, includes two sets of phonogram cards and instructions for several games) and a nice selection of language arts resources. *Mary Pride*

Phonics Pathways was originally a one-book intensive phonics program that used an incremental approach to teaching reading. Since then, a whole range of ancillary products has been added. It can be used with children of all ages and can be used remedially as well. Older students would not find this perfect-bound manual insulting or baby-ish.

First, the short vowel sounds are introduced, along with their diacritical marks. Then two-letter blends are introduced. I have noticed that intensive phonics programs tend to follow one of two different philosophies on how to

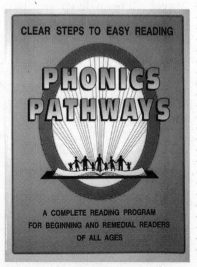

CLEAR STEPS TO EASY READING

PHONICS PATHWAYS

A COMPLETE READING PROGRAM FOR BEGINNING AND REMEDIAL READERS OF ALL AGES

NEW!
Phonics for Reading and Spelling

Ages 6–9 or remedial. $69.95 plus shipping.
Small Ventures, 11023 Watterson Dr., Dallas, TX 75228. (972) 681-1728. Fax: (972) 681-0139.

ADDITIONAL MATERIALS REQUIRED: Pencil, notebook, loose paper, red pencil (for proofreading), flip charts, whiteboard or chalkboard, readers (once spelling is well under way).

CONSUMABLE PROGRAM ITEMS: None.

SUBJECTS COVERED: Phonics, handwriting, and spelling—in that order.

BEST FOR: Ages 6 and up. Main emphasis is on spelling and organized thinking, not on reading per se. Lack of fun and games means learners need self-discipline and decent attention span. Home teacher must be organized person who can handle significant lesson preparation. Expect to put in about 10 hours learning how to use the program. "Teacher" types who want to really understand all about phonics, spelling, and handwriting will be ecstatic.

NEW!
Phonics Pathways

All ages. Phonics Pathways, $29.95. Short Vowel Dictionary, $5.95. Wordwatch, $35. Blendit!, $35. The Train Game, $9.95. The Dorbooks, $9.95. Pyramid, $17.95. All of the above, $125. Shipping extra.
Dorbooks, PO Box 2588, Livermore, CA 94551. Orders: (800) 852-4890. Inquiries: (925) 449-6983. Fax: (925) 447-6983. Email: dor@dorbooks.com. Web: bookzone.com/feature/phonics.html.

Phonics Pathways set

"Ugly" from the Short Vowel Dictionary

teach two-letter blends. Some phonics programs teach in word families, such as the *at* family, consisting of *cat, hat,* etc. The reasoning behind this is that beginning readers need to be trained to look ahead to the end of the word, as it is the letters following the vowel that determine its sound. Phonics Pathways adopts a different approach. After learning the short vowel sounds, children practice reading and saying *sa, se, si,* making the short vowel sounds. After introducing two-letter blends, the child learns to read three-letter words by sounding them out from left to right, *sa, sa-d, sad.* Ending digraphs and consonant blends are taught, followed by long vowels, suffixes, multi-syllable words, etc. By the end of the book, students will be reading words such as *impression* and *indispensable.*

I like the format of this book. It is written in a large, easy-to-read type-face. Each page is visually interesting and uncluttered. Instructions and suggestions appear in the text, written in a smaller typeface. Every once in a while there are little cartoon sayings, such as "Sometimes people are lone-ly because they build walls instead of bridges" or a word of encouragement to the student.

If you want a no-frills approach to phonics that almost teaches itself, this book is certainly worth considering. One concern: the picture that goes with "U for UGLY" might scare young children—it looks demented, with its one staring, bloodshot eye and wild hair, not just ugly!

Now, onto the supporting materials! Developed by program author Dolores G. Hiskes, who has tutored reading for over 30 years, and is a member of a half-dozen reading organizations, the materials in this pro-gram are approved for legal compliance by the California State Department of Education.

Short Vowel Dictionary helps kids learn to distinguish the vowel sounds. It is a kid-sized comb-bound book with instructions in the front, review in the back, and one spread for each of the five vowels in the mid-dle. On the right page of each spread is an upper-case and lower-case vow-el. The letter "A" is shown twice, once showing how "a" is printed, the oth-er showing how it is written. On the left page of each spread are pictures of words starting with the short sound of the vowel on the opposite page. Under these are the words for the pictures and two sentences loaded with words with the short vowel sound in them. For example, "Jan's crafty black cat smacked and grabbed the fat crab as it sat in Jack's black hat." The "UGLY" character appears in large size in this book.

The Dorbooks are a series of three books and a cutout model of Dewey the Bookworm, the series mascot. Dorbook Number One is a little 24-page book for teaching the short vowels. Dorbook Number Two is twice as big and 21 pages. It teaches two-letter blends. Dorbook Number Three is twice as big again, 15 oversized pages, and teaches how to build three-letter words. The "U is for UGLY" character also unfortunately appears in these books.

Pyramid is an 80-page spiral bound oversized reader with an unusual approach, designed to strengthen eye tracking and develop reading skills. Each page, or two-page spread, has a vocabulary list of phonetically related at the top or on the left-hand page. At the bottom, or on the right-hand page, is a pyramid. The first line is one word long. The second line is two or three words long, and so on until the last line, which may have 10 or more words. So the child might read,

Kit.
Kit hid.
Kit hid six.
Kit hid six figs.
Kit hid six figs in Jim's.
Kit hid six figs in Jim's dish.

See the pyramid shape?

The Train Game is a set of 64 "train car" cards, one for each phoneme taught in this program. These two-sided cards have a phoneme on one side, and the same phoneme on the other side along with a picture beginning with or using that sound.

The Long and The Short of It is a way to practice adding suffixes beginning with short vowels. A set of 36 "train car" card has words printed on one side and the spelling rule for how to add suffixes to that word on the other side. Another set of cards includes 8 common suffixes. You practice adding suffixes, then turn the card over to see if you did it right. The instruction sheet has a summary of all spelling rules.

Blendit! and **Wordwatch** are both sets of 12 card games. For both these games, you have to cut out the playing cards. Be careful not to cut up the gameboards by mistake!

Blendit!, the more elementary game, reinforces simple spelling patterns. You play the game bingo-style by placing cards over the matching gameboard squares. Each game can be played competitively or until everyone wins, by two to four players. Skills drilled are short vowels and consonants, two-letter blends, three-letter words, double-consonant endings, "Y" endings, twin-consonant endings, C/K/CK words, SH/TH endings, CH/TCH endings, NG/NK endings, long-vowel review, and EA/EE.

Wordwatch is more advanced, but still played the same way. Skills drilled are double-consonant endings and ING/ANG/UNG/INK/ANK/UNK, short-vowel ED endings, long-vowel ED endings, phonemes that make long vowel sounds, vowel diphthongs, R-modified vowels, phonemes that make the AW sound, and phonemes that make the AIR sound.

The book and teaching materials have lots of personality, and are certainly not a clone of anyone else's products. Kids should enjoy the games. I advise you find stickers for *umbrella* or some other innocuous "U" word and cover up the "U is for UGLY" character, unless you're teaching an older boy, who will probably think it's cool. *Rebecca Prewett and Mary Pride*

Play 'N Talk, a homeschool classic that has been around for over 35 years, now has leapfrogged into the 21st century! This complete and comprehensive phonics-based program teaches reading *and* spelling right up to the college level, plus suffixes and prefixes (as opposed to most phonics programs, which only teach children how to read). For years the program

UPDATED!
Play 'N Talk

Ages 5–9 or remedial. $250 for cassette version, $350 for CD version, $395 for CDs with 3.5" diskettes (last option requires IBM-compatible computer with CD-ROM drive). Literacy First Aid Kit (90-minute cassette, samples of 3 Play 'n Talk lessons, and 88-page Resource Manual), free upon request. All prices postpaid (U.S. orders only). There is a budget plan available, with up to eight monthly payments. *Play 'N Talk, 7105 Manzanita St., Carlsbad, CA 92009. Orders: (760) 438-4330. Inquiries: (800) 472-7525 Fax: (760) 438-9288. Web: www.playntalk.com.*

If you would like to sample this program, just request the free **Literacy First Aid Kit**. This comes with a 90-minute cassette tape with three sample lessons, a phonics reading test for grades 1–3, a sample bingo game, a sample slide rule, and the 88-page Play 'N Talk "Phonics in Action" Resource Manual, Volume II. The manual shows how to use Play 'n Talk as a spelling program, including rules for spelling. It is crammed with testimonials, reports, letters, nutritional information, biographical backgrounders on Mrs. LeDoux, case histories, and even an order form for vitamins! At the price, you can't miss . . . right?

TUNE UP: To organize your new Play 'N Talk materials, purchase a lap desk if possible. The kind with a write-on surface is ideal. Rubber-band each game inside its box, so the game pieces won't spill out. Place the games, flashcards, and manual inside the lap desk, along with a pencil and small pad of paper. Put the video wherever you normally keep your videos and the recordings near the record, tape, or CD player.

If you don't want to keep swapping recordings in and out of your stereo, feel free to skip the daily "Riddles 'N Rhymes," or save them up and play many at a time. I'd also regard the enrichment activities as strictly optional; only do them if your child needs extra help.

Use precursive (single stroke) letters instead of the ball-and-stick method the program shows.

Do not plan on leaving a child alone to listen to a recorded lesson for the first time. You need to follow along, to make sure he's doing it right. This is not as necessary when reviewing lessons.

Play the same lesson repeatedly. Review the last few lessons before going on to a new lesson.

Two short study times a day work better than one long lesson.

was only available on records—now you also have your choice of cassettes, CDs, and even a computer-enhanced option.

Those of you who have not seen Play 'N Talk for a few years might remember it as a huge set of colorful materials that you had trouble organizing into a coherent program. This has all changed with the introduction of the Amplified Instructor's Manual, recently revised and expanded to 144 pages. New information includes historical documentation of the origin of Play 'n Talk, testimonials by professionals and users, and comparisons between Play 'n Talk and other programs. You'll also find information on the role of proper nutrition in educational success. This material used to be included as loose pages in your information packet; it's definitely more handy to have it all bound with the manual.

The heart of the manual, of course, is the day-by-day lesson plans you need to tie the course together. After the introductory program outline and teaching tips for different types of learners, the manual is broken into 12 units and further divided into enough lessons to fill up a school year, with plenty of review and break time built in. Unit 1 starts with basic readiness and alphabet learning, including lots of suggested activities you may not have thought of unless you have taught phonics before. Units 2–12 go through the entire course and tell you exactly when to use each program component. The accompanying 3-hour teacher-training video is packed with additional information, such as how to overcome common reading problems, how to use each program component properly, how to say the phonics sounds, and so forth.

You don't get flash cards. Instead, you get a 96-page Flash Card Pattern Book. Every time you need a new set of flash cards (old cards do get worn if you use the program with several children), you photocopy up a new set of cards. The pattern book itself remains untouched. The flash cards contain vocabulary words all the way up to college level.

The heart of Play 'N Talk remains the same, except that instead of LPs you now have the choice of cassettes or CDs. You get a whopping amount of teaching aids, more than any other phonics program, including:

- **A Reading Readiness kit,** consisting of Sing 'n Sound with the alphabet song, big double-sided alphabet flash cards, 10 singing lessons on phonics sounds, a musical score for the songs for both piano and guitar, a giant phonics chart, and a colorful manuscript handwriting chart with directional arrows.
- **The Play 'N Talk Basic Course.** Series I has 32 recorded lessons, plus an 80-page large print text. Series II has 60 lessons and a 66-page text. Between them, these cover all the basic phonics skills taught in most courses.
- **The Play 'N Talk Advanced Course.** Series III comes with a 56-page book and Series IV comes with a 76-page book. Between them, these 125 recorded phonics and spelling lessons include all the rules your child needs to become an advanced speller, right up to college level.
- **Slide 'N Sound** is a clever word-making kit for practicing phonics skills. You get a plastic-coated picture of a bay, including dock and lighthouse. Using two plastic-coated slide rules that fit into slots in the picture, young learners are able to construct a large variety of words. Example: using the beginning consonants and the family "at," how many words can you construct? At, bat, cat, fat . . . The maximum totals for each combination are given in the accompanying book. You can build over 1,800 one-syllable words twiddling those little

slides! This kind of hands-on word construction is great for preventing or curing letter reversals and other learning problems.

- **Spell Lingo** is a set of 24 Bingo spelling games that covers all the phonograms taught in the program. By using the game cards, you can pinpoint your learner's spelling problems as well as provide practice in overcoming them. This is the best set of phonics Bingo games we've seen.
- **Ring 'N Key,** a simple touch-typing course, is one of Play 'n Talk's most unique features. I am not aware of any other non-software-based phonics program that starts children with typing, yet in our computer-literate age this makes perfect sense. Typing or keyboarding is also easier for young children than handwriting. You get three sets of color-coded rings (small, medium, and large) and two sets of color-coded dots with the keyboard letters printed on them. The finger with red belongs on the red row, and so on. The accompanying lesson book begins immediately with simple short-vowel-family words. A very motivational method, especially good for older learners and those with dyslexic tendencies.
- **Riddles 'N Rhyme,** a set of recorded phonics riddles with three accompanying 28-page booklets, is cute but not essential, in my opinion. Listening to the clues and answering the riddles is meant to improve both listening and deductive skills. However, the program itself contains plenty of that. Consider the riddles an optional motivational goodie.

The twelve 12-inch LPs originally offered with Play 'n Talk are being discontinued. Frankly, I can see no reason for purchasing the LPs, which are so hard to store and relatively easy to destroy, considering that the course costs the same with cassettes as with LPs. CDs are even better; given an extra $100, we would pick the CDs every time. How convenient to sit back with your remote and zip to the exact spot where your lesson starts! Both the cassettes and CDs come in nice binders, making it easy to keep them clean and organized.

How does Play 'N Talk work? You put the recording on and turn to the correct place in the accompanying book, illustrated by a Disney artist. The teacher on the record takes it from there. All instructions are on the record (except for instructions on when to use the accessory items, which you'll now find in the Amplified Instructor's Manual). A group of children do all the exercises right on the record, and your child is supposed to chorus along with them, reading his part out of the appropriate book.

With the computer-enhanced option, you get the same seven CDs, along with six floppy disks. Just pop the CD into your computer's CD-ROM drive. The computer software allows you to select the appropriate lesson.

In Play 'N Talk, your children meet the alphabet family and different word families. All the phonics groups are portrayed as people. For example: "Here are Mr. and Mrs. Digraph, and their children. WH is a fat one. He puffs out his name!" "Long Vowels wear straight hats. Short Vowels wear laughing hats. They turn up like the corners of our mouths do when we laugh." Very sweet and innocent .

A perfectly delightful young lady with just a slight upper-class English accent did the narration of the first records, and Marie LeDoux, the producer of Play 'N Talk, did the rest. The only songs are the alphabetic songs in the Readiness portion. This is because Mrs. LeDoux believes background music may distract the student. Genteel mood music written

ADDITIONAL MATERIALS REQUIRED: Pencil and paper. You will also need to photocopy and cut out flashcards. Enrichment activities require a variety of household items. Correlated readers are optional; program includes sufficient reading exercises for practice purposes.

SUBJECTS COVERED: Phonics, diction, spelling, typing. Extremely detailed and thorough spelling instruction covers all phonics and spelling rules. Some beginning handwriting instruction.

BEST FOR: Young children (ages 5 to 8). Lots of fun and games, child-oriented recordings.

PHONICS KNOWLEDGE REQUIRED: None. The parents will learn how to teach phonics by using PNT.

TEACHING ABILITY REQUIRED: Some; you should understand principles of drill and review, be able to follow daily lesson plans, be able to eliminate unneeded activities, be able to "reteach" and take it slower at difficult spots. The only major complaints we have heard about PNT have come from parents who (a) were using the old program (which lacked the videos, instruction manual, and flashcard patterns), (b) new to home teaching, and (c) expected the program to be mostly self-instructional. We have never heard of a classroom teacher failing with this program.

BEST FEATURES: Play 'n Talk covers everything and is very motivational. The games are lots of fun and involve all learning styles. It's a nonconsumable program you can use again and again with additional children without needing to purchase anything more. (If you should lose or break any of the items, replacements are available.) Play 'N Talk has been used in tens of thousands of homes and thousands of schools over the past 35 years. All items in this program are approved under all Federal Fund Titles NESEA. Mrs. LeDoux offers free telephone consultations and will answer your questions about the program before you buy it.

by the son of Harpo Marx sets the stage at the beginning of each lesson, and each lesson comes to a definite musical close. No frenetic "rap" or "rock" here!

Play 'N Talk takes the "word family" approach. Children are taught to blend the sounds at, and then practice reading words from that "family," such as *bat, cat,* and *fat..* Short vowel words are taught first. Play 'N Talk presents long vowel words ending in "E" as "Magic E" words, and drills children in seeing the difference between rows of words with and without the final "E." Since this is one of the common "sticking" points for learning to read, we appreciate the detailed presentation and drill. (By the way, the "magic" reference has nothing to do with the occult—it was written back in the Fifties. The program author is an evangelical Christian.) Other long-vowel blends, consonant blends, and other phonograms are then introduced in a logical sequence. Finally, the program takes children through a complete phonetic spelling course.

Play 'n Talk's most special ingredient is love. It was not created to fill a "market niche." The program author truly loves and cherishes children, and wants them to succeed. This gives Play 'n Talk a timeless, gentle charm, and makes it a treasured experience for many users. *Mary Pride*

Professor Phonics

Ages 6 and up. 4-part Primary Kit, $33. Five-part Master Kit, $48. Components available separately. 2½ hour training videotape, $40. Shipping extra.
Professor Phonics, 4700 Hubble Rd., Cincinnati, OH 45247-3618. (513) 385-1717. Fax: (513)385-7920. Email: sue@professorphonics.com. Web: www.professorphonics.com.

BEST FEATURES: Least-expensive total phonics program around. Time-tested. Explains *what* you are doing; you'll learn how to teach phonics, instead of just using a program without understanding it. Anticipates and solves learning problems. Best suited for parents with "teaching instinct."

WORST FEATURES: Teacher's instructions are not the easiest to follow. Repro quality of both books and tape is not the best.

Professor Phonics is an inexpensive program that works well for children six years of age or older, for whom it was designed.

The Primary Kit includes a combined practice book/reader that contains a total intensive phonics program. The accompanying manual gives page-by-page instructions. Alphabet picture flash cards and a spelling and reading word list round out the package. For a few extra dollars, the Master Kit also includes *A Sound Track to Reading* and its built-in manual. This is a more advanced book that can be used with teens and adults, as well as with kids who have finished the Professor Phonics book.

Marva Collins, a woman who has had phenomenal success in teaching inner-city, minority children, recommends Professor Phonics highly as being "one of the simplest methods of teaching children to read." That it certainly is. What it lacks in tinsel and pizzazz Professor Phonics provides in simplicity.

Reading begins on the very first lesson page, as children learn the sounds of *m, s, t,* and *a* and immediately blend them into words. This immediate reading, and the association of pictures with the sounds, differentiates Professor Phonics from the other systems.

Professor Phonics has a really simple method of presenting vowel sounds. They are either short, long, the "third sound," or diphthongs. For example, the first (short) sound of *a* is found in *apple.* Its second (long) sound is found in *ate.* Its third sound is heard in the word *all.* The three diphthongs are the *ow* sound as in *owl,* the *oi* sound, and the *ur* sound. Vowel digraphs, i.e., two vowels that together make a single sound, like *oa* in *boat,* are taught separately, along with the other advanced phonograms.

Sister Monica Foltzer, the program author, really knows her stuff, and I was anxious to view her new videotape. Unhappily the soundtrack on the new Professor Phonics videotape is very murky. We had real trouble hearing what Sister Monica had to say. (It was possible to make most of it out, with intense concentration and a bit of lip-reading!) The video explains how to teach intensive phonics with the Professor Phonics Master Kit system. Sister Monica, a Roman Catholic nun, has been teaching others how to teach intensive phonics for years and years. Her experience is that many first-graders can learn to read (and she means *really* read) in one semester, using her method. *Mary Pride*

Saxon Phonics is a heavy-duty phonics program—including reading, spelling, writing, and (in *Phonics 2*) vocabulary—done up in true Saxon fashion. Although it has some games, it lacks the "fun" level and charm of a program such as *Sing, Spell, Read & Write.*

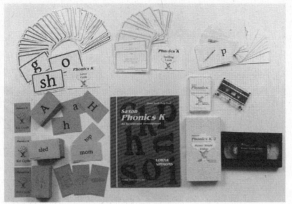
Saxon Phonics K

But if you like Saxon Math, you will be very impressed with Saxon Phonics. Everything is included, and every lesson is "scripted" to tell you exactly what to say and do.

Each grade level includes the spiral-bound teacher's manual, a set of teaching tools, and the student material. In the teaching tools box, you will receive a video that explains how the program works, a cassette that demonstrated how sounds are to be pronounced, a rule book, and several decks of cards. The cards include a spelling deck, a picture deck, a letter deck, and color-coded cards to be used for specific activities. The student materials are an alphabet strip with D'Nealian precursive letters on one side and block manuscript on the other, letter tiles (*Phonics K* and *1* only), a reader collection box, readers for the particular grade level, and student workbooks. You really get everything you need in each kit!

Saxon Phonics 1

Saxon Phonics lessons are designed to take 30 minutes each day, four days a week, not counting the actual reading time with the readers or any extra enrichment activities.

As an example, Lesson 18 in the *Phonics K* concentrates on learning the letter *T.* A gray box at the top of the page lists lesson preparation materials and things to do the night before. For this particular lesson, you need a ball for rolling or throwing, and your review deck of cards and spelling sound sheet 1/worksheet 19. The lesson is divided into an alphabet activity, phonemic awareness activity, review of cards, spelling sound sheet activity, and worksheet.

The alphabet activity has you and your child seated on the floor with the ball. In bold print, the teacher's manual tells you what to say to your child, "Let's say the alphabet while we roll this ball. I'll begin with *A* and roll the ball to you. After you catch the ball, say *B* and roll the ball back to me. I'll say *C* and roll the ball back to you. We'll continue until we complete the alphabet."

The phonemic awareness activity also includes the ball. You say to you child, "I am going to say a word and then roll this ball to you. After you catch the ball, tell me with what sound the word begins. Let's begin. *Lid.*" The activity progresses as you roll the ball and say words.

NEW!
Saxon Phonics

Grades K–2. Kindergarten Homestudy Kit, $110. First grade kit, $130. Second grade kit, $125. Shipping extra.
Saxon Publishers, 2450 John Saxon Blvd., Norman, OK 73071. (800) 284-7019. Email: info@saxonpub.com. Web: www.saxonpub.com

Phonics K teaches a new letter or "letter cluster" (their term for phonogram) every week, with constant daily review. Letters are not taught in alphabetical order: the first five taught are *L, O, G, H,* and *T.* Blending words (for reading) and "unblending" (for spelling) are also taught, as are the "long vowel" (silent *e*) rule, the digraphs *sh, ch,* and *th,* and *ar, er,* and *or.* A few suffixes and prefixes are also covered.

Phonics 1 picks up the pace. In this program, the student is taught a letter a day, with an occasional time-out for assessment of progress to date. By the end of week 10, most of the material in *Phonics K* has already been covered, and by the end of the course you have taught every phonogram in the English language.

Phonics 2 again begins with a total "review" of the letters and phonograms. Of course, this will all be new material to a student starting with this book. It carries on with more advanced reading assignments, tougher spelling words, and a thorough study of prefixes and suffixes. The child's vocabulary studies not only include vocabulary words, but an introduction to the history of the English language.

Saxon Phonics 2

For the review of the decks activity you show your child letter cards 1–5 in random order. Your child should name the letter on each card. Then you show your child the picture cards 1–5 in random order. Your child should name the keyword and sound for each picture card.

Next you move on to the spelling sounds activity sheet. For this activity your child has to practice spelling sounds that they have learned. You shuffle the spelling card deck and call out the sounds on spelling cards 1–5. Your child should echo each sound and name the letter that makes the sound as he writes the letter. Then he turns over his spelling sound sheet to reveal his worksheet. The worksheet includes several activities to reinforce learning the sound of the letter *T,* as well as review of 2 letters your child has already studied.

Just like this lesson, the entire program is in keeping with the Saxon philosophy as each lesson builds on prior learning. There is a lot of repetition to make sure your child succeeds. The lessons are short and move at a smooth, uncluttered pace. Each volume assumes the student knows no phonics at all before beginning. Handwriting is taught at all levels.

Saxon Phonics assumes the parent has no prior knowledge of how to teach phonics. Extremely thorough in its presentation, this course is designed for success for both teacher and student. *Maryann Turner and Mary Pride*

NEW!
Scaredy Cat Pre-Reading Kit
Scaredy Cat Reading System

Ages 5–15. Level 1—Pre Reading Kit, $39.95. Level 2—Beginner's Book (with audio tape), $34.95. Level 3—Advanced Beginner's Book (with audio tape), $49.95. Level 4—Rules . . . and Fun! (with audio tape and story book), $49.95. Shipping extra.
Greenleaf Press, 3761 Hwy 109 N., Unit D, Lebanon, TN 37087. Inquiries: (615) 449-1617. Orders: (800) 311-1508. Fax: (615) 449-4018. E-mail: Greenleafp@aol.com. Web: www.greenleafpress.com

Joyce Herzog initially designed the **Scaredy Cat Reading System** to be taught with learning disabled students, but it is now being used with students of all types and learning styles. The idea behind this program is to present phonics in a way that is fun, humorous, and makes sense.

The **Level 1 Pre-Reading Kit**—a notebook, an audio tape of songs, and the *Lettermaster Storybook*—is designed to teach the letter sounds and consonant blends. Students will learn a different alphabet song than most of us did: "A,B,C,D,E,F,G, Jesus loves you and me. H,I,J,K,L,M,N, He died to save us from our sin. Amen! O,P,Q,R,S,T,U, What the Bible says is true. V,W,X,Y,Z, Pray to Him to be set free." After completing the activities outlined in the notebook, students will be ready for the next level of the Scaredy Cat Reading System.

Level 2 includes the *Beginner's Book* and an audio tape (complete written script is provided) reviewing the alphabet and teaching the short vowel sounds.

Level 3 includes an *Advanced Beginner's Book* and an audio teaching tape.

Level 4 includes the *Scaredy Cat Rules Book*, a song tape, and the *Lettermaster Storybook*. The *Rules Book* contains the "meat" of the program and teaches the 15 phonics rules. Students will be reading multisyllable words by the completion of this course.

I could see where this program would be great for a student who had burned out on phonics which had not been taught well. The rules are presented in such a different way, that they are completely non-intimidating. However, some children might find this a bit confusing and would perhaps prefer a more straightforward approach as opposed to: "When a vowel goes last or a close friend pokes, a Scaredy Cat says its name!"

Parents looking for a different approach might also wish to investigate the new and improved editions of this program. *Rebecca Prewett*

UPDATED!
Sing, Spell, Read & Write
Version 2
Ages 5–8. Version 2 Home Kit, $175. Preschool Readiness Collection for Little Scholars, TBA. Kindergarten Combo Kit, $235. Level II kit, $57.90. Level III kit, $33.50. Shipping extra.
International Learning Systems, 1000 - 112th Circle N., Suite 100, St. Petersburg, FL 33716. (800) 321-8322. Fax: (813) 576-8832. Web: www.singspell.com.

Sing, Spell, Read & Write is an award-winning total language arts program for grades K–3 including—what else?—singing, spelling, reading, and writing! It has recently been upgraded to include many new features, so let's talk about them!

The kit used to come packed inside a lap desk. Now it comes in a sturdy cardboard box. Contents include

- Completely updated and expanded full-color Teacher's Manual—it's *so* pretty!
- Separate assessment/reading comprehension book with 17 book-end assessments for the Phonetic Storybook Readers and three achievement tests
- Two student worktexts, *Off We Go* and *Raceway Books*, each with a dry-erase writing "slate" on the back cover
- Six color-coded song cassettes, and a CD also containing the same songs
- 17 colorful phonics readers
- Five reading and spelling games, including Bingo chips and colored cards, now with circular plastic containers for each game to make them last longer
- A large, colorful raceway chart that you can stick on your refrigerator, plus vinyl sticker "cars" to place on the raceway
- A–Z Phonics Song Placemat whose back side can be used as a dry-erase "slate" for handwriting practice
- A cardboard Treasure Chest stuffed with dozens of nifty little prizes
- A 69-minute video in which program author Sue Dickson leads a homeschool mom through the entire program, demonstrating each part
- Even a wipe-off pen and cute little felt eraser!

The Teacher's Manual does not have daily lesson plans. Instead, it tells you what you need to do to progress through each of the 36 program steps. Sheer common sense is enough to fill in the rest. If you follow our Tune-Up hints below, read the manual carefully, and watch the video, even a total

More About Sing, Spell, Read & Write

ALSO AVAILABLE: For preschoolers, a brand-new kit, the **Preschool Readiness Collection for Little Scholars,** will be out in September 1999. It includes a laminated placemat with the A–Z Phonics Song pictures, and on the flip song a new song, "Alphabet Lane" pictured. A laminated Number Line to accompany the Counting to Ten and Counting Backwards songs. On the flip side of the number line is an alphabet to accompany an updated Alphabet Song. Hundreds of activity sheets will cover all traditional readiness areas, with 314 activities in all. For colors alone, there are 36 activities. Many activities are more than seatwork. For example, there's a special song for children to follow while marching around in the shapes of triangles, rectangles, circles, and such.

For kindergartners, there's a **Combo Edition** that includes the entire Sing, Spell, Read & Write program *plus* additional kindergarten material designed to ease a youngster into the world of phonics. See review in the Kindergarten chapter.

For **grade 2,** Level II includes *Down the Track* and *To the Finish* books plus a teacher's manual. It teaches creative writing, transition to cursive, synonyms, antonyms, sentences, 1500 spelling words, and a Mastery Level review of the 36 reading/writing/phonics steps.

For **grade 3,** Level III "Trophy" Kit covers middle-elementary language arts: grammar, alphabetization, cursive writing, and so on. It comes with *Trophy 1* and *Trophy 2* worktexts, Parts of Speech song cassette, and teacher's manual.

TUNE-UP: To organize your materials, first take the videos and recordings out of the suitcase. Place them near where you will be playing them. Put the Treasure Chest in a secret location after showing your children its contents. Place the Storybook Readers up high somewhere, so nothing can happen to them before you get around to using them. Keep the worktexts, manual, and games inside the suitcase. Then add several colored erasable markers, a pencil, blunt-tipped scissors, and a glue stick. You'll have everything you need for each lesson right at your fingertips! All you'll have to do is pick up the suitcase to start a lesson.

If your child has difficulty hearing the phonics sounds in the songs (this happens with some children), you learn the songs and sing them to him slowly as you work around the house. Once he can "hear" you making the sounds, he will be able to "hear" the tapes. He'll also be able to hear the sounds better when he sees the teacher and class singing the songs on the videotape.

Watch the tapes and listen to the songs with your children.

When your child is learning to blend with the Ferris Wheel song, check him by holding different consonant cards up to the vowels in random order and seeing how quickly he can say the sounds—e.g., *be, da, fi, gu, jo* . . . At all stages of the program, check his understanding, whether of basic letter sounds or individual blends or words, by occasional random testing like this. Drill to fill any "holes" in his speed and understanding.

To make sure your child is learning properly and getting enough review, first make your own set of letter-only flash cards. These should have the uppercase letter on one side and the lowercase on the other. Flash each card as you say its sound. Do all the uppercase letters first (in alphabetical order), then the lowercase letters (also in alphabetical order.) When you have gone through the deck several days, let the child try to say the sounds as you flash the cards. He gets to keep each card he calls correctly. Keep doing this until he "gets" all the cards. Keep this up each day until the child can whiz through the letters even when you shuffle them out of order; review periodically afterwards.

Second, as your child learns to write each letter, have him start each day by writing the letters he has learned on the placemat writing surface. Once he has learned the whole upper- and lowercase alphabets, have him start each day by writing them on the placemat.

Third, once your child has learned to blend, each day dictate a few spelling words he has already learned to read. Have him write them on the placemat. (This can substitute for writing the words in the worktext, if your child has trouble writing "small" or holding a pencil.)

Fourth, once he has learned to read a little, have him read a little each day from readers he has previously completed.

If you do these steps each day, they will provide the review and reinforcement the program currently lacks.

ADDITIONAL MATERIALS REQUIRED: Pencil, erasable marker, scissors, glue stick. I also recommend that you make yourself a set of letter-only flashcards. Optional wall charts are very nice to have.

CONSUMABLE PROGRAM ITEMS: Inexpensive worktexts.

SUBJECTS COVERED: Phonics, spelling, handwriting, reading comprehension. Inexpensive follow-up worktexts cover grammar, punctuation, other typical elementary language arts topics. Readiness worktexts also available; these cover preschool language arts.

BEST FOR: Young children (ages 5 to 8). Lots of fun and games, child-oriented recordings. Separate "Winning" program is designed for older children, adults, remedial.

PHONICS KNOWLEDGE REQUIRED: None. The parents will learn how to teach phonics by using SSR&W.

TEACHING ABILITY REQUIRED: Some. You should understand principles of drill and review, be able to create daily lesson. Program provides "steps" with objectives and material to cover; you figure out which game, reader, or worktext pages to do first and how much repetition is required. Follow our Tune-Up Hints and watch the video for assistance with this. No special "lesson preparation" is required; merely a decision about what to do first and for how long. The only complaints we have heard about SSR&W have come from parents who (a) were new to home teaching and (b) expected it to be completely self-instructional. Those who have any teaching experience at all, or merely a good dose of common sense, love it. We have never heard of a classroom teacher failing with this program.

homeschooling novice should have all the tools needed to teach phonics successfully.

SSR&W teaches pre-cursive script (one point in its favor) and acquaints children with both the printed and type alphabet symbols (another good point). We are not aware of any other program that does both these things. The worktexts are delightful—just enough exercises, not overdone, and a lot of fun reinforcement. (Caveat: don't ask very young children to do all the writing in the worktext. See Tune-Up below.) The games are likewise delightful. And what kid could resist a chance to win lots of prizes?

SSR&W takes a "ladder letters" approach rather than Play 'N Talk's "word families" approach. Using the teaching device of a large Ferris wheel, children hold consonant cards before each vowel in turn as they sing "Ba - be - bi - bo - bu . . . Ca - ke - ki - co - cu . . ." You note that the child alternates between *c* and *k* when going around the Ferris wheel. That is because, from the very beginning, spelling rules are integrated with the program. *C* followed by *e* or *i* makes an *s* sound, so the children sing the hard *k* sound and present the proper consonant.

The songs are the heart of the program. They teach such things as the alphabet, short and long vowel sounds, and digraphs and diphthongs. They have catchy lyrics and nice tunes and are sung by children with professional orchestration. Learning the songs is no strain—just let kids play them! When our youngest daughter was two years and could barely talk, she could sing the entire Alphabet Sounds song!

The little phonics readers are cute stories about various children, pets, talking bears and bugs, and so on with a strong family emphasis. There's one book for each short vowel, then they progress through the long vowels and other phonograms. Vocabulary for each book is strictly controlled to make sure the child has first learned all the sounds needed to pronounce each word. Each book is illustrated in color and sturdily bound.

Our verdict: this is the most motivational program around, and with the new teaching video and materials, one of the easiest to use. We are using it ourselves. *Mary Pride*

Teach Your Child to Read in 100 Easy Lessons (ISBN 0671-631-985) is a one-book, 100-day program for home use, adapted from the Distar Fast Cycle Reading Program used in public schools. It uses a "programmed" approach, in which everything the teacher says and does is spelled out for him word by word. The method introduces letter sounds before letter names. It also uses special orthography—e.g., "funny print"—in which the letters are printed different ways depending on how they are pronounced. Silent letters are shown much smaller than voiced letters. Simple reading comprehension exercises are introduced right along with the decoding skills.

All the reading and drill material is provided right in the book. This includes huge lowercase letters with balls and arrows underneath them, so your child can follow your finger moving from right to left with exactly the right tempo (as explained in the book), and (in the later lessons) multitudes of silly stories featuring bugs, ants, ducks, girls, and eagles.

Teach Your Child to Read in 100 Easy Lessons is probably the best resource around for teaching a child to "blend" letter sounds. Some time is spent in every early lesson on having your child practice slowly saying the letter sounds he has learned. You say words using long, drawn-out sounds—e.g., mmmmaaaannnn. He first repeats the word slowly, then says it fast. Since when a child is first learning to blend he will be saying the sounds very slowly, these exercises help him learn to "hear" a slowly-spoken word. He also traces and writes two letters per

---

NEW!
Sing, Spell, Read & Write ESL Spanish Manual
Ages 5–12. Student books, $9.75 each. Teachers manual, $39.95. *International Learning Systems, 1000 - 102nd Circle N., Suite 100, St. Petersburg, FL 33716. (800) 321-8322. Fax: (813) 576-8832. Web: www.singspell.com.*

A new SSR&W ESL Spanish Manual is now available for teaching students whose native language is Spanish to speak, read, and spell English. It provides side-by-side pages with Spanish translations for all the pictures and words in the Off We Go and Raceway books (those cover the alphabet letter sounds and the 36 phonics steps). *Mary Pride*

UPDATED!
Teach Your Child to Read in 100 Easy Lessons
Ages 6–9. $17.95 plus shipping. *Simon & Schuster, Att: Order Dept., 200 Old Tappan Rd., Old Tappan, NJ 07675. (800) 223-2348 ext. 6. (800) 445-6991. Web: www.simonsays.com.*

ADDITIONAL MATERIALS REQUIRED: Whiteboard or chalkboard, erasable markers or chalk.

CONSUMABLE PROGRAM ITEMS: None.

SUBJECTS COVERED: Mix of phonics and look-say.

BEST FOR: Parents who need some quick help in teaching basic blending skills. NOT recommended as a child's sole course; NOT recommended that you use the whole book, as it does tend to develop the habit of "phonogram guessing."

UPDATED!
Total Reading

Ages 6–13. Basic Package, $150. Advanced Primary Package, $250. Prices are postpaid.
Total Reading, PO Box 54465, Los Angeles, CA 90054. (800) 358-READ. Fax: (310) 327-1434. Email: tot_read@ix.netcom.com. Web: www.totalreading.com.

Remedial packages are available for young children ($190; includes everything in the Basic Package plus a set of comprehension questions for easy-to-read library books and a teacher's supplement, *Decoding with Phonograms*) and older students or adults ($85; different materials are used for this package). Bilingual materials are also available, as is an Intermediate Student package that takes a child from fifth grade to eighth grade in language arts.

day on the chalkboard (you can substitute paper and pencil). In the early lesson, he does simple rhyming exercises. Once he starts reading simple sentences, he is asked to identify individual words in the sentences. This prevents "guessing" at words. You then ask him several questions about the story and the picture that goes with the story (questions are provided in the text).

The book is designed to teach reading skills up to the second grade level. Since the book does not teach phonics rules, this means that after teaching blending its usefulness rapidly degenerates. Children need the help of genuine phonics to bridge the gap between sounding out words and knowing which sounds to use in every word. For example, the "magic E" rule tells kids that mad is pronounced with the short sound of A, while made has the long sound of A ("the A says its own name"). This rule is not taught in the book. *Mary Pride*

Total Reading is a complete language arts program for the elementary grades. The Basic Package program combines phonics, spelling rules, dictation, penmanship (pre-cursive and cursive), speech development through narration, literature, vocabulary, and stresses reading comprehension as well. The Advanced Primary Package assumes the child can already read on a good second-grade level. This package includes grammar, creative writing, proofreading, and higher-order comprehension skills, plus content area reading for social studies and science.

The **Basic Package**, which is what most homeschoolers choose to get, includes a *Primary Homeschool Manual*, a dictation cassette that teaches you how to dictate words the Total Reading way, one set each of Sound Cards (flashcards with the phonograms only; no pictures) and Word Cards (spelling words marked to indicate the phonics sounds), levels I through III of the course (workbooks and word cards), an *I Can Read by Myself* reader, comprehension questions for 1000 read-aloud library books, and two posters that introduce the Total Reading phonograms and vowel code.

Designed for homeschoolers, the new *Primary Homeschool Manual* is a welcome addition to the current *Primary Manual*, a huge spiral-bound book designed for classroom teachers.

The **Advanced Primary Package** includes three higher-level workbooks, reproducible masters for writing new words and practicing cursive, placement tests, to decide where to start, *I Can Read More Stories* reader, comprehension questions for 3000 library books, including books covering science and social studies material appropriate for this age level.

No matter what package you choose, your children are encouraged to read a wide variety of library books. Total Reading has comprehension question sets for over 2,000 of these books, plus the basal readers from many publishers, including A Beka. The Advanced Primary Package also includes content area reading for science and social studies—which is about all kids need for those subjects at that age. Add a math course and a timeline, and you have practically an entire curriculum.

Total Reading uses a "vowel code" of diacritical marks to speed up beginning reading (diacritical marks are the line, curve, and dots used to tell vowel sounds apart). Words are printed on the Sound Cards just the way they are spelled, with these additional marks added to the words. Children learn to mark new words themselves according to the "vowel code," thus concentrating on penmanship, correct spelling, and correct pronunciation at the same time. This beats the "funny-looking letters" that some other publishers foist on unsuspecting home educators. Since these marks are only added to the correct spellings, instead of substituted for them, it's relatively simple to make the switch to mark-free reading.

The "comprehension questions" are really more than that. The Read Aloud Comprehension set included with the Basic Package first introduces the new vocabulary words for each book, then follows this up with page by page "what happened" questions and questions about whether the story could have happened, the sequence of story events, and the story's main idea. The Easy to Read set included with the Advanced Primary Package shows new words marked according to the vowel code, then includes multiple-choice vocabulary and content questions (answer key is included).

Phonics is used not only for decoding but for spelling (e.g., the hard k sound at the beginning of a word is spelled K before i and e). Comprehension is taught through literal (who, what, when, where, why?), evaluative (what is the main idea?), and interpretive (relating it to other experiences) questions. Give Total Reading credit for going beyond fill-in-the-blanks to more important "thinking" questions.

Be aware that the free 62-page "Total Reading Success Story" booklet was designed for teachers. As a marketing tool for home educators, it makes the program sound much more complicated than it really is. However, it comes with a $10 coupon good on your first order. A word to the thrifty! *Mary Pride*

Touchphonics is phonics by the trays! Using a "phoneme" approach, it teaches your child to recognize the individual letters and letter combinations, or "phonemes," that make up the sounds of the English language. The "touch" in Touchphonics comes from the nubbly crepe rubber letters and letter groups that make up the heart of the program, and that are stored in corresponding outlines on a set of four large plastic trays.

You get four Touch-Unit trays, 200 color-coded Touch-Units (the crepe rubber letters and letter combinations), a slim teacher's guidebook, a thicker teacher's word list, a video with program demonstrations and instructions, a

---

BEST FOR: Ages 6–13 and remedial. Choose the package that suits your child's age and attainment level. Home teacher should count on spending a fair amount of time getting acquainted with the program (hint: inservice Total Reading workshops for school teachers last up to four days!). Homeschool consultant is available to help you over rough spots: you're not just buying the books! New homeschool manual (due out in August) should help trim down preparation time.

ADDITIONAL MATERIALS REQUIRED: Pencil, paper, library books.

CONSUMABLE PROGRAM ITEMS: Workbooks, comprehension questions in the Advanced Primary Package.

SUBJECTS COVERED: Phonics, listening, spelling, dictation, penmanship (pre-cursive and cursive), oral narration, literature, vocabulary, and reading comprehension. Content area reading in Advanced Primary Package covers science and social studies. Complete correlated creative writing course also available.

NEW!
Touchphonics

Ages 5–8. Touchphonics, $299. Touchphonics with magnetic tiles, $299. Complete kit, $548. Shipping extra.
Touchphonics Reading Systems, 4900 Birch St., Newport Beach, CA 92660. Orders: (800) 928-6824. Inquiries: (714) 975-1141. Fax: (714) 975-1056.

If you already have tried another phonics program with less than total success, the Touchphonics materials may be just what you need to get "over the hump." However, if you plan to use this program for your basic phonics course, I strongly suggest you also purchase one of the inexpensive and excellent phonics teaching books favored by homeschoolers, such as *AlphaPhonics* or Mary Pecci's *At Last! A Reading Method for Every Child,* as well as a good set of phonics primers.

As for the teaching instructions themselves—for overwhelming success in the home, these should have been more step-by-step. For example the teacher's guidebook asks you to have a class full of kids bring in examples of "environmental print," e.g., words printed on common household items such as cereal boxes or newspaper headlines. The kids are then supposed to sort the words by their initial sounds, and spread them around the classroom. This is the very first exercise in the teacher's word list book, and it requires kids to be great at alphabetizing who are supposed to just now be learning the letters.

Victory Drill Book

Ages 4–7 or remedial. Book, $14.95. Teacher's Guide, $17.95. Cassette tape, $6.95. Worksheets and learning activities, $22.95. Predrill Book, $8.75. Shipping extra. California residents add sales tax.
Victory Drill Book, PO Box 2935, Castro Valley, CA 94546-0935. Phone/fax: (510) 537-9404.

BEST FEATURES: Everything in one book. The learner knows exactly what he is supposed to do and how he's doing at all times. Not cutesy.

WORST FEATURES: Short on teacher instructions. Not a good choice for kinesthetic (or just not well-disciplined) kids. Best for visual learners.

whiteboard on which write with a wipe-off marker or to form words with your Touch-Units, and a handy little spiral-bound set of cards used to diagnose which phonemes your child already knows—or doesn't know.

About those trays. The first is the consonant and diagraph tray. This includes two of every consonant, plus three of those that have more than one sound, like *c* and *g*. Digraphs, namely *ch, sh, th,* and *wh*, are in the middle of the tray. Consonant combinations with silent letters, such as *gn* are nearby. Regular consonants are yellow. Silent consonants, such as the *c* in *ck,* are white.

The second tray is for vowels, broken down into single vowels, vowel combinations that always make the same sound, vowel combinations such as *oo* which can make two sounds (e.g., *oo* as in *moon* or in *book*), vowel combinations such as *ou* which make more than two possible sounds, vowel combinations that make the same sound but look different (*au* and *aw,* for example), and *r*-controlled vowels. The color-coding on this tray is red for vowels, yellow for the *r*'s, and white for the ostensibly silent *e, i,* and *u* part of *er, ir,* and *ur.*

Tray 3 is your blends and "borrowed sounds.". Blue for initial consonant combinations, such as *st* and *fl*; green for final consonant combinations, such as *nd* and *sk*; brown is for what they call the " borrowed sounds" of *gh, ph, ci, si, ti,* a "schwa," an apostrophe, and an accent mark.

The last tray takes you all the way through spelling and vocabulary development, with prefixes (in orange) and suffixes (in purple).

The Touch-Units are large and easy to handle. The tray layouts make it easy for both children and adults to understand the underlying logic of English phonetics. This setup would make an excellent hands-on and visual addition to any intensive phonics program. *Mary Pride*

Phonics program based on step-by-step learning and timed drills. You get the **Victory Drill Book**, a Teacher's Guide, a cassette tape of the phonetic sounds, along with teaching tips, worksheets, and a predrill book that teaches short vowels and consonants and how to write a ball-and-stick alphabet.

The heart of the program is the *Victory Drill Book* itself. This very attractive hardbound book consists of word lists and sentences. There are no stories or pictures, except for the initial alphabet pictures at the beginning of the VDB. Students learn the phonetic sounds and then practice their skills with *timed drills* on the word pages. After achieving the speed considered necessary for his age level, the student goes on to the next phonetic combinations and the next page. After finishing the VDB the first time, he can freely read anything he wants. The publishers recommend that students go through the VDB a total of three times to ensure that total mastery has taken place.

The VDB was developed for Christian schools and includes prayers to God and references to preachers and church.

If you are looking for phonics worksheets, the VDB worksheets beat any others, in my opinion. The type is large enough for very young learners, there are just enough exercises to practice the concepts, and you do *not* get endless pages of pictures to "color if the object pictured begins with the letter *p*." The focus is on words, not illustrations, as it should be.

The VDB emphasis on *timed* drill keeps you alert to where your learner actually is. At home, you can time drills just for the fun of it and avoid the invidious comparisons of the classroom.

VDB also makes sure the *teacher* is able to teach phonics. Get the cassette tape if you are at all unsure of yourself in this area.

VDB students have achieved outstanding scores on standardized tests. VDB is used all over the USA and in other countries. *Mary Pride*

CHAPTER 8

Phonics Primers

Could you hit a golf ball hundreds of yards down the fairway the first time you picked up a club? Did your first soufflé rise to majestic heights . . . and stay there? Did you swoop gracefully around the rink the first time you put on ice skates or roller skates? Did you bowl a perfect game the first time you stuck your fingers in a bowling ball? (OK, so you've *never* bowled a perfect game. Join the club!)

Perfection in any pursuit is achieved step by step, through learning all the little skills that make up a perfect golf swing or a towering soufflé. It take practice, too. That's why, at first, beginning readers need primers.

Yes, I know, some kids just seem to learn to read by magic. (The "magic" usually consists of hours and hours spent looking at the pages while Mom or Dad reads to them.) But *expecting* Johnny to learn to read from street signs, or dumping any old library book in Janie's lap and expecting *that* to be all the practice she needs to accompany her phonics lessons, is a mistake.

Whole Language advocates rightly point out that phonics primers are confined to pretty slim story material. "The cat sat on the hat" is a typical example. What they miss, though, is that the cat-sat-hat stage is *very brief*. (At least *at home* it's brief. Schools have a way of prolonging the agony through endless "reading groups" and "reading comprehension" exercises for grade after grade.) Furthermore, using phonics primers doesn't mean kids can't *try* their fledgling reading skills on any "environmental print" they may happen to encounter.

What phonics primers provide is step-by-step *practice* and thorough *review*. If a kid can read his whole set of primers, he knows how to sound out *all* the basic English sounds. From that point on, each new book will represent less and less of a reading challenge.

You *can* avoid the primer stage by letting your child "read along" in library books, sounding out the words he knows while you read the rest. Unfortunately, you sometimes can't be sure he is sounding out words as much as guessing context clues, and you definitely can't be sure he knows *all* the sounds he'll need. The very klunkiness of phonics primers makes it harder to guess words, and a good set of primers provides plenty of practice for all the sounds it covers.

The good news is that many phonics programs now include primers, and that many of the newer phonics primers are much more fun to read.

> To learn to read,
> Get up to speed.
> With primers your plans
> Will succeed!

Make the effort to work through at least one of these sets, while reading a lot to your child and letting him try the easier words in the books with large print, and you'll have the best of both worlds!

Phonics Primers & Readers

Because of Love is a simplified version of the gospel of John written with new readers in mind. Printed with large type and simple wording, the book targets children, immigrants, and adults who are learning to read.

Each lesson contains three parts: "Things to Know," a background to the reading; "Now For the Story", the Bible reading; and "To Think About", questions designed to encourage discussion. Every page has an "Easy Read Diction Guide" which offers a pronunciation guide to unfamiliar or difficult words. The pronunciation guide is not standard and can cause some problems. For example, the pronunciation for law is *LO*. My first thought was low, not law.

Included are 70 readings that cover Psalm 23, the book of John, parts of other gospels and some epistles which complete John's record, and John's description of heaven from the Revelation.

The text is simplified but not babyish. This could be useful as a reader for older children or adults who need practice reading. *Terri Cannon*

Your child can approach the "Starting Line" and become a winner in the reading race with the new **Starting Line Readers**. This 12-book set comes attractively packaged in a gift bag. Suggested for children in kindergarten or first grade, I feel they are a perfect link between Bob Books and more difficult readers. Start this series as soon as your child can read short vowel words.

As soon as your child picks up the book, his eyes will be drawn to the beautiful full color illustrations. The 8 x 5" size is perfect for little hands. The first short vowel reader, *The Tent*, is eight pages long and has one to two sentences per page. Your child will be thrilled to finish a whole book! If you flip to the last page of the book, you will see a reading guide that contains wonderful teaching tips, a book overview, and comprehension questions. No need to lug a heavy teacher's manual to the table; everything is included in the book. At the end of the story, vocabulary is listed that was used in the story along with any sight words. Each book also lists enrichment words, such as *Mr.* or *Moses,* which do not follow regular phonics rules. A valuable addition to your library. *Irene Buntyn*

The **Bob Books** get their name from their author, schoolteacher Bobby Lynn Maslen. These books (3 sets available) are sized for little hands, printed on heavyweight paper, and illustrated with charmingly naive drawings using shapes even little children can draw. Book covers are different colors, just to be pretty.

The first series of 12 books, **Bob Books**, starts off easily. Book 1 teaches only four sounds—*m, a, t, s*—and the word "on." Each of the books in this first series has only eight pages of actual reading material, for instant reading success, and is written using only three-letter words with short-vowel sounds. By the end of the series, kids have learned all the letters of the alphabet except Q. The enclosed instruction sheet explains the series philosophy, summarizes the plots of the books, and gives some wonderful pre-reading and reading teaching techniques.

Series 2 (8 books), **More Bob Books**, continues the short vowels taught in series 1, and adds more letter combinations and longer words. Silent e words are introduced, as well as easy consonant blends such as *nd* in *land*

NEW!
Because of Love

All ages. $15 (Canadian funds) plus shipping.
Esme James, 100 Fir Street, Sherwood Park, Alberta T8A 1Z7, CANADA. (780) 467-7359. Email: wejames@telusplanet.net.

NEW!
BJUP Starting Line Readers

Grades K–2. Set of all 12 books, $19.95 plus shipping.
Bob Jones University Press, Greenville, SC 29614. (800) 845-5731. Fax: (800) 525-8398. Web: www.bju.edu/press

UPDATED!
Bob Books for Beginning Readers

Ages 4½ and up. Each set of books, $15.95 plus shipping.
Scholastic Professional Books, 2931 East McCarty St., Jefferson City, MO 65102. (800) 724-6527. Fax: (800) 223-4011. Web: www.scholastic.com.

and *mp* in *bump*. Color words are introduced as sight words in book 7 of this series. This series has eight books, but more total reading pages than series 1.

Series 3 (8 books), **Even More Bob Books**, is another set of eight books. Here long vowel words are introduced, and so are compound words.

A new series, **Bob Books Plus**, is geared to fall between series 1 and 2. I haven't seen it yet, but it includes eight beginning readers and two activity books, packaged in a red lunch box with pencil and eraser.

The Bob stories are all warm and friendly. The characters sometimes get into trouble, or even quarrel, but everything always turn out all right in the end. There's quite a strong emphasis on kindness, sharing, and forgiveness. Recommended. *Mary Pride*

This is the most unusual set of primers you will see in a long, long time. You go through and fill in the blanks in each 8½ x 11" booklet with your child's name and the names of family, friends, and pets where appropriate. While doing so, you notice the large number of rebuses (pictures of things instead of words). This allows the authors to include words like "camel" and "monster" in the very first book. The primer/workbook also includes space for the neophyte reader to copy some of the simple words in Bookstuff. A yellow instruction sheet is tucked in to help anxious parents understand what we are doing. Book 2 has room in the back for the child to write his own story, or for a mom or dad to write a dictated story.

Each page has a separate little sequence of sentences. Rather than stories, in **My First Bookstuff** these sentence sequences ask the reader questions, like, "Can a [picture of lion] make a [picture of kite] go? Can a [picture of mouse] stop a [picture of boat]? Can you make a [picture of kite] go? Can you stop a [picture of boat]?" **My Second Bookstuff** has some little real-life stories.

The art, and artistic hand-printing of words, are very nice. Content is modern and secular.

Also available from the curriculum specialist and art-and-science teacher who invented Bookstuff are **Attributes Activity Book** (cut and paste format of increasing difficulty to help children learn colors, shapes, etc.) and **Thinking Things** (a set of pages featuring one question of the "How is a caterpillar like a butterfly?" variety per page. Other Bookstuff products, including their great kindergarten program *Alphabetiks,* are reviewed in the Preschool chapter. *Mary Pride*

Written many years ago for use in the private schools founded by Miss Mae **Carden**, these hardbound **primers** hold true to Miss Carden's philosophies. She believes pictures distracted young readers, as well as encouraging "word guessing," so these books have lots of large print instead. Correlated with the phonics sequence taught in Carden schools, they go from the Red book (easiest) to the Bluebird book (hardest). Accompanying workbooks provide an opportunity for introducing and practicing phonics skills. The flavor throughout is gentle and wholesome. See review in previous chapter for more details. *Mary Pride*

Bookstuff Primers

Ages 4–6. My First Bookstuff, My Second Bookstuff, $5.95 each or $10.95 for both. Thinking Things, $5.95. Attributes Activity Package, $6.95. Send SASE for information. Shipping extra.
Bookstuff, 21534 Saint James Place, West Linn, OR 97068. (503) 638-4806. Email: cjreinold@msn.com

NEW!
Carden School Primers

Ages 4–8. Red book, $11.55. Blue book, $12.90. Green book, $14.30. Junior book, $13.60. Bluebird book, $13.10. Workbooks for: Red book, $6.70. Blue book, $6.80. Green book, $6.80. Junior book, $6.15. Bluebird book, $6.30. Shipping extra.
Carden Educational Foundation, PO Box 659, Brookfield, CT 06804-0659. (860) 350-9885 Fax: (860) 354-9812. E-mail: homeschool@cardenschool.org. Web: www.cardenschool.org.

NEW!
I Can Read a Rainbow

Grades K–2. Set of all 6, $12.
Wild Pony, 2418 Sixth Street, Berkeley, CA 94710. (925) 228-5117.

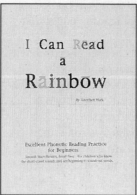

This comb-bound black-and-white book includes six different readers, each about 10 pages long, instructions, and simple black-and-white clip-art for teaching phonics. If you are looking for early phonics readers with no distracting pictures, here's a set to last a year. The large lettering and spacious margins in **I Can Read a Rainbow** are easy on the eyes, though Mom will have to provide the motivation. This series of readers is unique in that all reading selections have markings like those in a dictionary to alert the young reader to unusual letter sounds. In theory, it will help a beginning reader decipher larger words, and will help with recognizing pronunciation patterns. *Kathy von Duyke*

NEW!
Literature Links to Phonics

Grades K–3. $22. Shipping is free if prepaid.
Teacher Ideas Press/Libraries Unlimited, P.O. Box 6633, Englewood, CO 80155-6633. (800) 237-6124.
Fax: (303) 220-8843.
Email: lu-books@lu.com.
Web: www.tip.com.

I wish I had the **Literature Links to Phonics** book when I was teaching my daughter to read. I spent many hours at the library looking for books that were interesting and which contained only the letter sounds that she had already mastered.

Literature Links to Phonics is a 150-page oversized softcover reference to 472 children's books that contain high-frequency words and common phonetic elements. It is divided into sections on the alphabet, general phonetic rules and high-frequency rules. Although the format of each section is consistent, each section uses a different format.

- **The alphabet section** discusses how children are introduced to the sounds that letters make. A list of books, publishers and descriptions are given.
- **The 14 chapters on phonetics** explain each rule, the connection to writing and spelling, and a sample lesson.
- **Each chapter has a table** which lists the associated books, author, publisher, a one-line description of the book, reading level on an A-B-C scale. (Using this scale, D. Crews' *Freight Train* is an A-level, and A. Lobel's *Frog and Toad Are Friends* is a C-level book.)
- **Core word lists** contain the most frequently used words and are often taught as sight-reading words. The books are categorized by the core word that they emphasize and include publisher, A-B-C reading level and the number of words in the book.

The book's appendices provide the phonics rules, core word list and the addresses of all the publishers. *Teresa Schultz-Jones*

NEW!
The Little Companion Readers

Ages 6–10 and remedial students. Ten book set, $19.95 plus $3 shipping.
The Paradigm Co., P.O. Box 45161, Boise, ID 83711. (208) 322-4440.
Fax: (208) 322-7781.
Web: www.howtotutor.com.

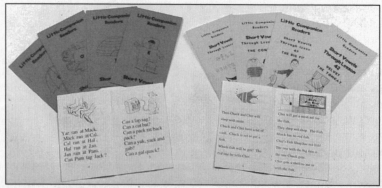

Samuel Blumenfeld fans, wake up! Now you can get readers and workbooks to accompany Sam's books. Mr. Blumenfeld, whose book *Is Public Education Necessary?* has been a homeschool classic for years, is also the very popular author of the *Alpha-Phonics* learn-to-read program.

The **Little Companion Readers** are a set of 10 small 12-page books. Very large type, jagged black-and-white computer art. But you're not buying these books to look at the primitive pictures, you're getting them to practice the phonics principles taught in *Alpha-Phonics* and other phonics programs. You get one book for each of the short vowel sounds, plus five more that gradually add digraphs and blends to the short vowel sounds. The series ends at lesson 71 of *Alpha-Phonics,* just before long vowels are introduced. *Mary Pride*

If your child is just beginning with phonics and likes animals, the **My First Pets Phonetic Readers** series might interest you. Each of the five 5x7 inch books has a home-made look because they were produced by a homeschooling family that has its own home-based business. Most of them were charmingly illustrated by the children, Casey and Kiley Queen, and all were written by their mom, Sandi.

Each book introduces a new short vowel sound, in alphabetical order, and also reinforces the previously-learned sounds. Each has a different, bright-colored cover and is about the adventures of a different animal. Only one-syllable words are used. Exception: book 5 uses two two-syllable words (*tummy* and *bunny*). Each book features a list of all of the words used in that book, most of which are phonics words. A few sight words are used in each book, and these are listed separately.

Though the second book introduces the short *E* sound, most of the words in that book contain the short *A* sound. But the rest of the books contain more short-*E* words, so this compensates for that lack. Also, the sight word *the* is introduced in the fourth book; it is my feeling that the lack of the use of this word in the earlier books makes some of the sentences awkward.

The stories are humorous and the characters all interact in a nice way. The dog even helps the rabbit get through the fence after it eats too many vegetables to fit through the fence posts! *Melissa Worcester*

Pathway Publishers created their **delightful series of clothbound readers** for the Amish community. This series stresses "character building" with a capital C. Starting with easy readers for very little children, the series goes up through the eighth grade level. True stories, animal stories, fictionalized history, poems, and straight fiction are mixed artistically to create books my  children couldn't put down. Every reading selection in these books has a character-building emphasis, too, from stories in which children learn not to make fun of classmates to accounts of Anabaptist martyrs. And, since the writers are Amish, the story settings manage to be both old-fashioned and modern at the same time. Your children will get to experience a different culture in which children milk cows by hand, boys go fishing (infrequently) *after* doing hours of chores (or "choring," as the Amish say it), girls feed the chickens and watch the baby, and Mom and Dad are strict disciplinarians. Life is not all dreary drudgery, though. Story characters have plenty of personality and face realistic dilemmas as their fallen sinful nature conflicts with what they know Mom and Dad want them to do!

Nothing smarmy or phony in this series. Animals are seen from a farmer's point of view, not as the almost-human (and biblically incorrect) characters in *Bambi* and other Hollywood fantasies. Children in these stories love their dogs but sometimes get irritated with the family cows. This is real life, as Bill informs me. He spent a summer working with cows when he was a teen, and he tells me that such an experience does not breed romantic feelings!

NEW!
My First Pets Phonetic Readers Series

Grades K–3. Set of all 5 books, $7.95 plus $2 shipping.
Queen Homeschool Supplies, P.O. Box 245, McClellandtown, PA 15458. Information: (412) 737-1340. Orders: (888) 695-2777 pin# 5780 for orders. Web: www.hhs.net/queenshss/. Email: queenhss@hhs.net.

Pathway Readers

Grade 1 readers, $6.80 each. Grades 2 and 3 readers, $7.90 each. Grades 4–8 readers, $9.05 each. Complete set of 13 books, $93. Workbooks, $2.55 each. Teacher books, $5.75 each. Shipping extra.
Pathway Publishers, 2580 N. 250W, La Grange, IN 46761. No phone/fax numbers available. Available through many homeschool catalogs.

Pathway Publishers also has a complete line of workbooks to accompany this series. Each has an accompanying teacher's manual. In grades 5–8, additional vocabulary workbooks are available for each grade level, entitled *Working With Words.* The workbooks are optional—I wouldn't personally consider getting them unless you are planning to make this series the heart of your language-arts curriculum. Kids will enjoy the readers much more if they are just storybooks, not curriculum. (It's only fair to mention here that Pathway tells me at least 75 percent of home schoolers who buy their readers get the workbooks as well, so maybe I'm not on target this time!)

NEW!
Programmed Reading

Grades K–6. Programmed Reading books 1–23, $13.32 each. Introductory offer: books 1–7, $69.93. Teachers Guides: for books 2–7, for books 8–15, and for books16–23, $24.96 each.
Phoenix Learning Resources, 2349 Chaffee Dr, St. Louis, MO 63146. (800) 221-1274. Fax: (314) 569-2834.

Rod & Staff Bible Nurture and Reader series

Grade 1: Reader Unit 1, $5.10. Reader Units 2 & 3 (one book), $9.05. Reader Units 4 & 5, $11.25. Reading

Grade 1 books are *First Steps, Days Go By*, and *More Days Go By*. Grade 2 books are *Busy Times, More Busy Times*, and *Climbing Higher*. Grade 3 books are *New Friends* and *More New Friends*. Grade 4–8 have one reader per grade; *Building Our Lives, Living Together, Step By Step, Seeking True Values*, and *Our Heritage*. Books are about 400 pages each, except for the "beginner" readers.

My experience is that older children enjoy the little kids' books, so you might just want to go ahead and get the series as a wonderful character-building treat for your children. As you can see, prices are very inexpensive for all Pathway Publishers materials. *Mary Pride*

Programmed Reading was designed as a stand-alone reading course, but is probably most useful for homeschoolers used as primers alongside an intensive phonics program.

The Programmed Reading series has an unusual format. These 144-page, saddle-stitched books are "flip books." You work your way from front to back always staying on the right-hand page (left hand pages are upside-down), then you flip the book and work on the right-hand pages going the *other* way through the book. They are heavily illustrated, in color for the most part, although books 17–20 are black and white.

The exercises are self-checking. Readings, questions and exercises are on the right side of the page and answers are in a narrow margin to the left. You cover the answers with a strip of paper and as you answer the questions, you slide the paper down to reveal the answer without showing the answer for the next question.

You first have to teach your child to recognize and write the alphabet and know letter sounds, but as soon as you start to get into short-vowel three-letter words and beginning blending, you could start to use book 1 of Programmed Reading.

Words are introduced in these books in a systemized way. The first words introduced are "short *a*" words—for example, "Am I an ant?" (You have to teach one "sight" word, the word "I," which is unique phonetically anyway.) Questions are a mixture of yes/no, multiple choice, and fill-in-the-blank.

After the "short *a*" words, Programmed Reading Book 1 mixes in some "short i" words, then a couple of *th* words. Around page 54 you get the first two syllable word and the *ing* sound, etc. By book 3 you are getting into "short o" words, blends like *dr, bl*, etc., and sentences like, "Did Rip sit on the hill?" Book 6 starts the student reading little stories and answering questions about them—beginning reading comprehension. The flip side of book 6 has the first story that continues from page to page. As you go on, the type gets smaller, and the stories get longer and more involved. Book 9 has a complete fairy tale with many chapters. Book 13 features a fable with a talking rose and talking birds. The questions after the stories include vocabulary questions along with the comprehension questions. The stories have blank spaces left where either letters or whole words need to be filled in. Books 22 and 23 use Greek myths for stories.

The first books of this series would be great practice primers along with your phonics program. The later books are good reading comprehension practice. I don't think the teacher's manuals are necessary for homeschoolers. *Bill Pride*

Rod and Staff, a publisher of Mennonite textbooks, has come out with a revised edition of their popular **Bible Nurture and Reader** series. This is the *only* complete phonics program whose readers consist of solid Bible stories without added flights of fancy. Systematic approach uses the same lesson plan every day.

Unlike other phonics programs, this utilizes the diacritical marks extensively. Diacritical marks are those fancy symbols used in dictionaries to indicate the exact pronunciation of letters.

Previous editions of this program were, to put it mildly, difficult for young children. We used them with our own first two children, and I can remember Joseph crying in frustration because he couldn't handle the extensive writing and difficult questions. The revised edition has kept the biblical content while simplifying the texts and exercises. Another difference: the major phonics review now is in grade 2 rather than in grade 3, as previously. The revised program still requires quite a bit of writing at an early age.

Grade 1 of the Bible Nurture and Reader series is broken into five units with 30 lessons in each unit. Each lesson has five divisions: reading from the Reader, working in the Reading Workbook, working in the Phonics Workbook, doing a worksheet, and optional printing practice. Grade 2 also has 5 units of 30 lessons each, but just three divisions in each lesson: reading from the Reader, working in the Reading Workbook, and working in the Phonics Workbook. Together, these books cover reading, phonics, language skills, spelling, and penmanship. Grades 3 and 4 do not include separate phonics workbooks.

In grade 1, the first unit, "We Learn About God," covers the Creation and the Fall. The second unit, "We Learn More About God," reviews Creation and goes on to Cain, Abel, and Noah, with some practical applications. The third unit, "Poems About God," is poems about history from the Creation until after the Flood. The fourth unit is stories about Abraham, Isaac, and Jacob. The fifth unit contains stories about Joseph, the son of Jacob, and stories about Jesus from the Gospel of Matthew.

Unit 1 of **grade 2** reviews Genesis. Unit 2 is "Moses Leads God's People," while unit 3 covers "More About Moses," "Balaam," and "Israel in Canaan." Unit 4 is "Stories from Ruth and 1 Samuel." Unit 5 goes through the Gospel of Mark.

Grade 3 leads off with "Stories About David and Solomon," followed by "Stories of the Kings—Rehoboam to Jeroboam" and "Stories of the Last Kings and Prophets." Unit 4, "God's People During and After the Captivity," includes parts of Ezekiel, Daniel, Ezra, Nehemiah, Esther, and Jonah. The fifth unit works through the Gospel of Luke.

Grade 4 has only one reader, with noticeably smaller print than that of the earlier grades. It includes three units: "The Gospel of John," "The Book of Acts," and "Job, Psalms, Proverbs."

Plans are in the works to provide a new chronological Bible curriculum for grades 5–7, which will then fill in any Bible books not covered by the Bible Nurture and Reader series.

As you can see, the books are God-oriented rather than man-oriented. This makes a welcome change from the too-typical "God Love Me . . . I Learn About Me . . . Wonderful Me" emphasis of other publishers. The stories also are very carefully kept close to Scripture, without any flights of fancy. *Mary Pride*

Workbook (5 units in 3 books), $4.05 each. Phonics workbook (5 units in 3 books), $4.20 each. Worksheets Unit 1, $2.85. Worksheets Units 2–4 (one set), $6.60. Worksheets Unit 5, $3.05. Teacher's manuals (3 for the grade), Unit 2–3, $6.95; Units 4–5, $7. Vocabulary flash cards (250 cards), $12.55. Phrase flash cards (222 cards), $15.30. Phonics flash cards (186 cards), $13.55. Total set, $136.65. Grade 2: Reader Units 1–3, $10.55. Reader Units 4–5, $9.85. Reading workbooks (5 books), $3–$5 each. Phonics workbooks (5 units in 3 workbooks), around $2–$4 each. Teacher's manual for reading, $9.50. Teacher's manual for phonics, $7.80. Grade 3: Readers (2 books), around $11.80 each. Reading workbooks (5 books), around $4 each. Teacher's manual, $7.90. Total set, $49.50. Grade 4: Reader, $10.80. Reading workbooks (3 books), around $3 each. Teacher's manual, $5.90. Journeys of Paul map, $3.85. Postpaid.

Rod and Staff Publishers, Box 3, Hwy 172, Crockett, KY 41413-0003. (606) 522-4348. Fax: (800) 643-1244 or (606) 522-4896.

The (classroom-oriented) teacher's manuals for grade 1 include instructions in both phonics and reading, unit by unit. In grade 2, there are separate manuals for phonics and reading, and each covers the entire year. Teacher's manuals for all grades include answers for the workbook exercises, plus teaching tips, oral drill exercises, and lesson plans.

Flash cards are used with the program. The Vocabulary Word Cards cover each reading word introduced in the first two units of grade 1. Phrase Cards include phrases from those same two units. The Phonics Cards are divided into 10 sets as follows: 26 alphabet cards, 21 consonant sounds, 17 vowel sounds, six combination sounds, 23 digraphs, 39 consonant blends, four diphthongs, eight letters with more than one sound, 27 letter sounds with certain letters, and 15 silent letters (e.g., *kn* and *gn*, in which *k* and *g* are respectively silent).

NEW!
Shared Reader—Psalms

Beginning readers. $9 plus $3 shipping.
Caring Communications, PO Box 486, Camas, WA 98607. (360) 834-0554 (evening & weekends only). Email: caricom@pacifier.com. Web: www.pacifier.com/~cari.com.

NEW!
Sing, Spell, Read & Write Storybook Readers

Ages 6–9. $75 plus shipping.
International Learning Systems, 1000 - 102nd Circle N., Suite 100, St. Petersburg, FL 33716. (800) 321-8322. Fax: (813) 576-8832. Web: www.singspell.com.

NEW!
To Grow By Storybook Readers

Ages 6–9. $45 (set of 18 readers) plus $3 shipping.
Play 'N Talk, 7105 Manzanita St., Carlsbad, CA 92009. Orders: (760) 438-4330. Inquiries: (800) 472-7525 Fax: (760) 438-9288. Web: www.playntalk.com.

Years ago, tiny tots learned to read at their parents' knees, often straight out of the Bible. "Here, this verse says 'Oh Lord my—' you can read that next word, can't you?" And the child would pipe up, "God!" "That's right!" his mother would say. "Let's go on!"

Ellen Dana has written a thin book, **Shared Reader—Psalms**, that explains this method of teaching. She includes ten Psalms, in the KJV, with the words for the child to read printed in a large, bold type. A typical phonics approach is used, presenting short vowels first, and progressing from there until more and more of the words are printed in bold type.

Your child will not only hear these Psalms and learn to read them with you, but he or she will learn the content and background of these ten Psalms as well.

In addition, there are stories illustrating certain truths that you will read out loud to your child.

This method is extremely simple to use. You don't need to know a thing about phonics or about the Psalms. I look forward to using it in our home, with our little frustrated beginning reader. This is just the sort of gentle approach I think she would enjoy. *Rebecca Prewett*

Correlated to the Sing, Spell, Read & Write program, the set of 17 durable **Sing, Spell, Read & Write Storybook Readers** cover every phonics rule in the program. Each book concentrates on a particular phonogram: the short vowel a or the digraph ch, for example. Many, many words containing the phonogram are used in the story, plus phonograms taught in previous lessons.

Each book is 32 or more pages long, completely illustrated in color, and opens with a list of vocabulary words used in the story. The vast majority of words are regular phonetically, according to the rules systematically taught to that point in the program; a few "rule-breakers" such as the and has are included.

The stories are all good-humored and family-oriented but not distinctively Christian. Art is friendly but not slick. The only drawback is that the text sometimes wiggles around on the page, following the picture. This could perhaps cause problems for some children, especially those who have difficulty tracking from left to right. *Mary Pride*

If you're looking for readers packed with Christian morals and lessons, look no farther than this set of 18 readers plus two activity books all slipcased in a colorful cardboard box.

The **To Grow By Storybook Readers** are meant to be read aloud by parent and child as a team. The child reads the underlined words, which are phonetically sequenced to correspond to the words he learns as he goes through Play 'N Talk or other intensive phonics programs, and the parent reads the rest. So, for example, in the first book, which concentrates on the "at" word family, you'll find sentences such as "Mat and his rat sat. . . . 'My hat! My hat!' said Mat." Note that not all words using the short "a" sound are underlined—just those ending in "at." This is because Play 'N Talk takes the "word family" approach.

As some of you immediately realized, nothing is stopping you from getting easy-reader library books and reading them this way with your children. You simply point to the words you want the child to sound out. Just make sure the books have nice large print!

The "To Grow By" books are small (20–28 pages each), paperbound, and lightly illustrated with realistic black-and-white drawings. Price seems somewhat steep. *Mary Pride*

…eries is a set of classic chil-
…gether. The parent reads the
…d page, which has simple be-

…ve unfortunately see his

…Bunny (Grades 1–2)

…ts letting the little one sound
…r book.
…ks when we tried them with
…w threw her for a loop. Sure,
…hen she'd start word guess-

…ll have only simple one-syl-
…we need, and there will be

…Flavors

…on of the original
…o educate America. Charles
…the reviews they write for
…e readers and added a
…ur paperback readers and
…hild in reading skills and
…de. Project assignments
…ublic speaking skills, and
…your child gets older.
…the first year to staging a
…d to help you judge/grade

…rs and the quality of this
…ernative to the modern
…e: This is not a phonics
…The Burgers include sug-
…r study guide. *Maryann*

…dial McGuffey as with re-
…has published a very suc-
cessful **Christian School Edition** of the revised edition of 1880. These readers, which McGuffey actually had nothing to do with, are much more useful for actually teaching reading than McGuffey's first edition, since they follow a more phonetic plan. Compared to the Mott Media version, they moralize more and evangelize less. *Mary Pride*

Mott McGuffey Readers

Grades 1–12. McGuffey Boxed Set with teacher's guide, $109.99; without teacher's guide, $99.99. Individual books available separately. Parent/Teacher Guide by Ruth Beechick, $12.99. Shipping extra. *Mott Media/Homeschooling Book Club, 1000 E. Huron St., Milford, MI 48381-2422. (800) 421-6645. Fax: (248) 685-8776.*

Mott Media prides itself on offering **the *original* McGuffey Readers**, *a la* the 1836–37 version compiled by Rev. McGuffey himself. Their hardbound version is not an exact reproduction; words have been changed, the grammar has been amended, and the layout has been revised. The early volumes of "original" McGuffey do not follow the normal pattern of introducing short vowels first, long vowels second, and exceptions last. Furthermore, presenting your child with an archaic vocabulary at the same time as asking him to tackle reading is a bit much. These McGuffeys work much better as supplemental literature than as phonics readers. *Mary Pride*

CHAPTER 9

Phonics Games & Tools

Many phonics programs include their own games. That's because "drill and practice" is always more fun if it comes disguised as a game.

But if your phonics program doesn't include games . . .

. . . or you'd like to supplement with *more* games . . .

. . . or you'd like a phonics program that is *all* games . . .

check out this chapter!

Drill & Practice

What do *bab, cab,* and *dab* all have in common? They are all words that can be made with **Flipping Phonics**. Flipping Phonics is a tool which can be used to help young children progress in their reading ability. It is a spiral-bound deck of 4 x 6" cards which have been cut into thirds. Most cards contain either one or two letters. Other cards have been left blank to allow you to add in letters of your choosing. New words are created when either the teacher or student flips one or more of the cards, exposing a new letter or combination of letters. This can be done in random order, or you can focus on a specific family of words. For instance, you can focus on words which end in *ack* by changing only the first letter in the stack, one letter at a time, coming up with words such as *back, cack, dack, fack,* and so on—some of which actually exist! The "nonsense" words are valuable, too, as a way to make sure your child is really sounding out words phonetically and not "word guessing."

Flipping Phonics also contains easy-to-follow instructions, information about common word patterns, and a free-standing base which allows you to stand it up on a table or desk. It can also be hand-held by either the parent or the child. A good supplement to any phonics-based reading program—and fun to use, too! *Rebecca Livermore*

For the beginning reader, the **McClanahan High Q** series makes great workbooks. Each 32-page book includes a full-color pull-out storybook, plus two full-color sticker pages, plus lots of regular workbook pages in black and one other color. The workbook pages are where your child will be placing the stickers.

The workbook pages are well designed, with friendly (not grotesque) child-pleasing line art and lots of simple, well-planned exercises that cover all the basic activities normally found in early-learning materials, such as simple crosswords, coloring a happy face if you hear the sound and a sad

face if you don't, tracing letters, filling in missing letters, coloring pictures, and drawing lines between letters and words that start with that letter. Each page is self-explanatory and takes only a few minutes to complete.

The books in this series are:

- *Letters and Sounds*
- *Beginning to Read*
- *Key Words to Reading*
- *We Can Read*
- *Phonics Vowels*
- *Phonics Consonants*

Enjoyable, educational, easy to use, fun for little children, and recommended. *Mary and Sarah Pride*

NEW!
Noah Webster's Reading Handbook

Grades K–2. $7 plus $4 shipping. *Christian Liberty Press, 502 West Euclid Ave., Arlington Heights, IL 60004. (847) 259-4444.*
Fax: (847) 259-2941.
E-mail: enquire@homeschools.org.
Web: www.homeschools.org.
They take credit card orders, but not over the phone. Any other contact method will work.

This small, 138-page book is an "updated and modernized" version of Noah Webster's famous **Blue-Backed Speller**. Webster, who among other things produced the first authoritative dictionary of American English, was very concerned about the education of American young people. Generations of children in one-room schoolhouses were taught from his *Blue-Backed Speller*.

This new edition makes use of some technologies that were unavailable or too expensive in Webster's day. For example, two-color printing is used to emphasize the letter or letter combination being drilled on any given page.

Starting with the alphabet, with each lower-case letter accompanied by a "key word" and picture, you proceed to a page each for short vowels, long vowels, and consonants. The short-vowel sounds then get a page apiece, with words to sound out. Some words are in two colors and associated with pictures; others just have the short vowel in boldface and no picture. After a page of short-vowel review, consonants are introduced in the order *s, t, b, h, f, m, c/k, d, j, r, g, l, n, w, p, v, qu, y, x, z.* Long vowels then make an appearance, as part of two-vowel combinations. Next come consonant blends, diphthongs, and the remaining less-common phonograms, such as *ue* in *guess*.

Blending is taught in "ladder letter" fashion, e.g., first you say "t," then "ta," then "tap." Reading practice is provided on every page, first with words alone, then with sentences, and finally with short excerpts straight out of Webster.

You need to know the phonics sounds and have some teaching experience in order to use this book successfully. No writing practice or activities are provided, and instructional tips are almost nonexistent. However, it is a nice, inexpensive phonics drill book, and very useful for anyone who wants to provide a quick phonics refresher for an older student. *Mary Pride*

Phonics Made Plain

Grades 1–3. $19.99 plus $3.50 shipping.
Mott Media/Homeschooling Book Club, 1000 E. Huron St., Milford, MI 48381-2422. (800) 421-6645. Fax: (248) 685-8776.

Phonics Made Plain is essentially a large set of phonogram flash cards, a wall chart listing all the phonics rules in this program and the phonograms to be learned, and two sides of one card giving *very* streamlined instructions on how to use the program. The writer assumes you know how to teach, and thus throws out teaching hints rather than giving programmed teaching directions. You can teach the phonograms in whatever order you think best, although the wall chart does present a particular order for those who want some guidance. Designed to be used with any set of readers, this is a very flexible approach to phonics. *Mary Pride*

Phonics Games

The **Phonogram Fun Packet** includes a two-sided game board, eight "Go the Row" game cards (bingo cards with progressively harder phonograms on each color card), 72 phonogram calling cards for the bingo games, two sets of 70 phonogram playing cards, two sets of 34 spelling rule playing cards for the board games, 24 wild cards for the board games, 100 plastic bingo chips, 6 teddy bear playing pieces, one die, a master sheet for spelling rules, and directions for 10 games.

The two games, on alternate sides of the game board, are called *Teddy Bears on a Picnic* and *Tubin' Down the River.* The game board itself is nicely laminated, colored, and cute, printed on heavy stock. The Bealls suggest that you "bend the board to a flat position and hang it on the wall"—a storage solution that might help to preserve it a little longer if you have the wall space. The various game cards are printed on brightly colored card stock and not laminated. So, if you want them to last, you'll have to laminate or cover them with clear contact paper. The games are designed specifically to reinforce *Writing Road to Reading*, *Teach Your Child to Read in 100 Easy Lessons*, and *Total Reading*, hence the 72 phonogram cards. However, the games could be used with any phonics program. These games are designed for reinforcement and review and should be adequate for those purposes.

Also available from the homeschooling Beall family: two Math Facts Fun Packets, U.S. Geography Packet, and a Bonanza Packet including all the above plus some American documents and Bible Memory "Review" cards. *Sherry Early*

This charming set of games and videos is designed to precede The Phonics Game or another full-fledged phonics program. **The Jr. Phonics Game** teaches the individual letter sounds, plus how to blend them into short-vowel words such as *Ed* and *odd*. If you are up on your phonics, you can accomplish the same thing with a set of homemade flash cards and a few phonics primers, but it won't be nearly as much fun.

The Jr. Phonics Game comes in a designer cardboard box and thoughtfully includes little ziplock bags for storing the game cards in between uses. Each of the three included videos in this attractively-packaged set goes with a wall chart and a game.

Here's what you get:

Video 1 teaches the alphabet song, letter shapes, and their names. With this video, you use the included:

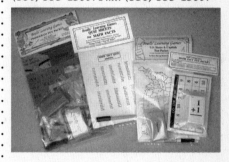

- Alphabet Chart with lower- and upper-case letters only. Sized for attaching to a wall.
- Cover-Up Game Boards (Bingo with lowercase alphabet letters)
- Cover-Up Markers (colorful little circles featuring "Ed," a character who looks like a Muppet, with a Kermit-sized grin and oval nose)
- Cover-Up Card Deck (letters for use with the bingo-like game)

Video 2 teaches letter sounds. With this video, you will use

- "Sound Chart" to put on your wall, with all the alphabet letters in upper- and lower-case, each with an accompanying word and picture
- The Fat Cat Game Board and Spinner—full-color and durable, with a trail of letter squares you have to follow to get to "Ed"
- Fat Cat Game Markers—these are heavier cardboard than the "Ed" markers and feature cats with different color circles around them
- Fat Cat Card Deck is small cards with short-vowel words on them
- Fat Cat Stickers for rewards

Video 3 introduces basic blending of short-vowel words. Now it's time to break out the following:

- "Ed Chart" featuring the phrase "At Ed's it's odd up (there)" used to teach short-vowel sounds, plus a picture of the odd treehouse with Ed in it
- Middle Match Card Deck A gives you words to read, and your little reader can double-check his reading with the picture on the back
- Middle Match Card Deck B has words on the front and nothing on the back
- *Red Ed Book* is a little 12-page reader with two words on each page.

The **Junior Phonics Playbook** is your instruction guide for all the above. It provides game instructions, follow-up activities, smaller version of the wall charts, self-test sheets, and certificates. *Mary Pride*

NEW!
Paper Chains

Ages 4–8. Paper Chains set 1 & 2, $12 each. Paper Chains phonics, $29. Shipping extra.
Living and Learning Company, 2400 Turner St., Grand Rapids, MI 49544. (800) 253-5469. Fax: (800) 543-2690. Email: JAmes@tribune.com.

The name of this game really threw me off: I kept envisioning a chain made out of paper, like paper dolls, but there are no paper dolls involved in this very unique and fun card game. The "chains" are more of a figurative nature, being the "link" between different cards in a set. Let me explain. **Paper Chains** comes with a self-sorting tray containing 25 card sets with 8 cards in each set. You spread out the cards of one set so the picture side of each faces up. One card has a big arrow on it: read the word on the reverse side of that card (for set 1, the word is *cat*) and then find the card with the corresponding picture. Flip that card over (set 1's *cat* card has the word *dog* on the back) and find the picture that matches that one, and so on. If you do it correctly, the back of the very last card in the "chain" has a big check-mark on it to show you that you've correctly completed that set. My son was fascinated to see this work, like it was magic or something.

The colorful picture cards are laminated and about the size of business cards. Each set has different words, but works the same way. Each card has its set number printed on it in case the toddler of the family dumps the whole box on the floor and you need to be able to sort them again. Sets 1–15 contain simple consonant/vowel/consonant words. The words in sets 16–25 also contain consonant blends and the digraphs *sh*, *ch*, and *th*. Once the concept is explained (which takes seconds) the child is able to play independently, because of the self-checking concept. Very neat . . . and recommended. *Melissa Worcester*

Phonics Adventure, "The Game That Helps You Learn to Read," is a really nifty game with many levels for helping you practice and recognize decoding principles. You will have to teach your child the ABC's and their basic sounds before you can really use this game. However, once they have mastered this first step, you can practice beginning through advanced phonics painlessly with this easy-to-use game.

You get a colorful game board with the usual tokens, dice, and trek from Start to Finish interspersed with squares that let you jump ahead and others that make you gain or lose a turn. You also get three color-coded sets of cards. Level A (yellow) lets your child practice matching sounds to letters, telling sounds, reading simple sight words, and describing vowels and consonants. Level B (green) goes on to consonant blends, more vowel sounds and sight words, contractions, and a very good section of phonics rule questions that make the child *think*. Level C (orange) continues with advanced vowel/consonant combinations (such as *tion* and *sion*), more sight words and advanced phonics rules, prefixes and suffixes. These two latter levels can be used to teach the phonics as well as to review it.

The cards explain themselves—you need no professional phonics knowledge to use Phonics Adventure, although at least one experienced reader needs to play to help the others. The game is very complete, and can be used as a card game (if you answer correctly you keep the card) or as flash cards, if you prefer a change from the board-game format. Some fancy dictionary marks are used—circumflex, dot, dieresis, and so on—but you can easily ignore these if your phonics program doesn't use them. It takes about two minutes to figure the whole game out, and there is no clutter of hundreds of strange little pieces to sort out. A nice, professionally-presented, quality game that will make phonics drill and advanced phonics much more simple and fun. *Mary Pride*

"Forty-two million Americans can't read!" the advertisement proclaims, and with that startling figure **The Phonics Game** proceeds to offer their reading solution. This multisensory system is attractively packaged in a customized plastic case.

A warning to first-time users: put aside the game play book, or you may become overwhelmed! Forty-seven pages explain the steps of phonics reading in a methodical, if not complicated, manner. You're better off to first pop the accompanying video in the nearest VCR. This energetic video tape demonstrates correct phonics pronunciation, as well as how to play the game. The narrator outlines each game on the video, relegating the playbook to the role of reference manual. Don't have a VCR? Then use the five audio cassettes also included.

Players learn the sound codes—provided on two 8 x 11" cards—and then play these five phonics games:

- **In the Beginning** drills one-syllable, short-vowel words such as *cat*
- **Silent Partners** practices "final e" and two-letter combinations that make a long vowel sound
- **Copy Cats** mostly practices the rule for when a *c* or *g* is pronounced soft, i.e., like *s* or *j*
- **Double Trouble** is for letter combinations that are spelled differently, but pronounced the same, like *oi* and *oy*
- **Oddballs** tackles the leftovers, such as the *ue* in *guess* and the *tion*
- **Divide and Conquer** teaches syllabication

The Phonics Game substitutes these games for boring exercises and repetitive drills. However, you still need to find a way to teach the basic letter sounds. Just using a single card with all the letters on it isn't as effective. That's why the makers of this program hope you'll first purchase their **Jr. Phonics Game** (see its review earlier in this section), which uses additional videos, wall charts, card decks, and games to teach the alphabet letters and their sounds.

Adaptable to a single student learning alone or to a family learning together, 1–6 players may play each game in the course. The whole-family approach may prove effective, as the involvement of parents and older children makes a big difference.

The kit includes a money-back guarantee with the purchase of this product, but requires a few stipulations. A disclaimer hastens to point out that younger children will receive the most benefit of this teaching tool, while adults with poor reading skills may require more playing time to reach proficiency. Considering the high cost of the product, the guarantee makes purchase a less stressful choice. You may return the course within 30 days for a full refund. *Lisa Mitchell*

NEW!
Phonics Treasure Chest

Ages 4–8. $19.95 plus shipping.
*Gift of Reading Program, 423 Maplewood Lane, San Antonio, TX 78216. (210) 828-5179.
Email: sanantoniored@hotmail.com.*

Phonics Treasure Chest includes two sets each of the following: 73 phonogram cards, four laminated bingo-type game cards, a couple of laminated 9 x 12" game board cards, two dice, two game pieces, a fishing pole with a magnet attached, and instructions. The games are designed to accompany Trudy Palmer's *Gift of Reading* program but can be used to reinforce other phonics-based reading programs, too.

This set of games is similar in scope and quality to *Beall's Phonogram Fun Packet*. The other set includes more games and activities, but these game boards are already laminated. In **Phonics Treasure Chest**, you'll get instructions for eight games along with variations. 72 phonograms or 73? Take your pick. Either set of games will provide simple, enjoyable review and reinforcement. *Sherry Early*

NEW!
Small Ventures Phonics Fun and Tape

Grades preK–3. Phonics Fun game, $16.95. Basic Phonograms cassette tape, $5.95. Shipping extra.
Small Ventures, 11023 Watterson Dr., Dallas, TX 75228. Phone/Fax: (972) 681-1728.

Phonics Fun is two decks of phonogram cards without any special directions on the back. These cards can be used with any phonics programs. One deck has a pink square pattern on the back, while the other is blue. Each deck is divided into sections by a symbol which appears in the top right corner of each card. The circle represents single letter phonograms. The square and triangle are for multi-letter phonograms. The star is for the most advanced phonograms, e.g., *gn*. Cards are laminated, jelly-proof, business-card size. Complete directions for four games are included. Three are similar to the well-known card games of Concentration, Old Maid, and Fish. In the last game, players combine cards to form words within a time limit.

For parents and teachers who have difficulty figuring out the sounds of the phonograms from written instructions only, Small Ventures also provides a **Basic Phonograms Tape**. This is an audiocassette with the sounds of the phonograms and their rules narrated for you. *Mary Pride*

Wordo

Grades K–3. $12.50 plus $2.50 shipping.
*Success House, 556 Ludlow Avenue, Cincinnati, OH 45220-1579. (513) 861-2688. Fax: (513) 861-9688.
Email: mathgames@hotmail.com*

Five simple card games that provide reading practice and vocabulary development. You get one set each of 27 orange and 27 blue cards, plus a yellow instruction booklet. Blue cards have word beginnings like *w* and *pl* on their top left and bottom right corners, while orange cards have word endings like *ay* and *ill*. If this sounds like you are going to play word-building dominoes, you're right. You also can play variations on Tic-Tac-Toe, Concentration, Rummy, and Solitaire. The **Wordo** Word Checking Chart in the middle of the instruction booklet tells you which word combinations are licit, of the possible 1,054. *Mary Pride*

Phonics Toys

When lawyer Michael Wood tried to teach his toddler son phonics, he discovered that many toys could say the letters of the alphabet, but none taught the phonetic sounds necessary to learn to read. Inspired by a client who manufactured a sophisticated voice chip, and funded by a grant from a weapons lab that needed to convert to consumer products, he invented . . . Small Soldiers! Nope. Though I really didn't make up that bit about the weapons lab. Actually, Mr. Wood launched a company dedicated to designing durable phonics toys that talk. These toys have won all sorts of awards, and keep getting better every year.

Take, for example, **Hug & Learn Little Leap**, or as we call him around here, The Big Green Frog. Press his palm to turn his voice chip on or off. He says, in a young boy's voice, "(Giggle giggle) I'm Little Leap. Let's play. Please press a red square to play a game." Then press a red square on the bottom of his tummy to learn the letters (displayed on his tummy) or numbers (on his fingers), play a couple of games that involve finding the correct letter or number, or to make The Big Green One say, "Please." If you press a letter, Little Leap will tell you its name and sound(s), as in, "A says *ay* or *aaa*." If you choose a game, Little Leap will either ask you for a specific letter or number (depending on whether you click the contact under the letters or numbers in the square when you choose the game), or will give you color and direction clues to find a mystery letter or number. If Little Leap forgets to say, "Please," you are supposed to press the "Please" box, thus learning etiquette along with your phonics.

The voice is clear and easy to understand. Both long and short vowel sounds are given. However, consonants are pronounced "buh" or "muh," not with the consonant sound isolated. Also, you have to press pretty hard to select a letter or number. My five-year-old couldn't press hard enough to turn Little Leap on in her first three tries. The contacts do loosen up over time, making it easier.

Little Leap is the most engaging and cuddly of LeapFrog's offerings. The other phonics toys they offer look more like traditional alphabet toys: a phonics bus, a phonics desk, etc. Those were older models, so we asked to see two newer ones: the Phonics ProReader and Think & Go Phonics.

The **Phonics ProReader** is the upscale model. Not only can it say the name and sounds of each of the lowercase pressable letters prominently displayed on its front, it comes with an interactive LCD display that is used in many of the teaching and game options with which this toy is packed, and an area for interactive talking word cards (20 are supplied; you can purchase additional sets of Blends, Long Vowels, Complex Consonants, Complex Vowels, and Vowels with R, for a total of 100 additional cards). Learning options are selected by sliding a pointer along a bar. "Learn" asks you to press a letter: its upper- and lower-case forms then appear in the LCD area. "Quiz" gives you a letter name, and asks you to press it. "Spell" asks you to spell a word. If you can't, it will show you letter by letter in the LCD window. "Create" asks you to push three letters to make your own word. If you hesitate, you'll be told, "C'mon, you can do it!" "Read" tells you to push the letters on the word card. When you do so, it sounds out the word. "Rhyme" asks you to find two words that rhyme with the word on the word card. You do so by picking a new initial consonant that makes a valid rhyming word. Hit the "phrase" button to hear a phrase, and see it spelled on the LCD area, such as "fox in a box." Hit the "help" button if you lose your way, or check out the included Parent's Guide & Instruction Manual. In all, you can create and hear 450 three-letter words with this toy.

NEW!
LeapFrog Phonics Toys
Ages 2–7. Hug & Learn Little Leap, $39.99. Phonics ProReader, $54.99. Additional card sets for ProReader, $6.99 each. Think & Go Phonics, $29.99. Shipping extra.
LeapFrog, 1250 45th St., Emeryville, CA 94608. (800) 701-LEAP (5327) or (510) 595-2470. Fax: (510) 595-2478. Email: custserv@leapfrogtoys.com. Web: www.leapfrogtoys.com.

The word cards can be stored in a handy click-shut compartment on the back of the ProReader. Each card has a picture of the object, and shows rhyming words as well. Finally, the whole thing comes with a handy carry handle, *and* batteries installed!

Think & Go Phonics, the budget model, also comes with a handy carry handle. Here, you turn a pointer to select the options: push a letter to hear its name, find a letter, push a letter to hear its sound, find the letter that makes a sound, make a word by pushing the letters, or push three letters to make your own word. If the word does not exist, Think & Go will sound it out anyway—with the exception of derogatory words such as *wop* or *fag*. There are no word cards or LCD, but on the other hand, it only takes 10 seconds to learn how to use this toy, and all its parts are attached.

For any of these, your best approach is to sit down, take the time to show your little one how it works, and then run to the other end of the house before the cheery electronic voice drives you nuts. Any of these are a great add-on to your home phonics lessons, and a great way to keep little ones happy and busy while you have other things to do. *Mary Pride*

NEW!
Read Spin

Grades preK–2. $10 plus $4 shipping.
Geospace International, 1546 NW Woodbine Way, Seattle, WA 98177. Orders: (800) 800-5090. Inquiries/fax: (206) 365-5241. Email: debink@gte.net. Web: www.spingames.com.

Read Spin comes with eight ten-sided, colorful magnetic wheels that you can turn around, break apart, and lock together with very little effort. The wheels are designed to facilitate learning the alphabet, vowels, and consonants. It comes in your choice of uppercase and lowercase versions.

Three wheels are devoted to the alphabet letters in order. One is for vowels, and another is for extra consonants. The remainder include a combination of letters, plus characters such as ampersand and apostrophe. You teach the alphabet—forwards and backwards!—with the first three wheels, then the vowels with the vowel wheel, then progress to making simple short-vowel words, and so forth. Another use: have your child use Read Spin to spell words you call out. Great practice, especially for youngsters whose fine motor skills lag behind their reading abilities. A neat and tidy alternative to having him handwrite endless lists of words.

As with other magnetic products, don't store Read Spin on top of your disk drive or with your videotape collection. *Mary Pride*

PART 3

Building Good Kids

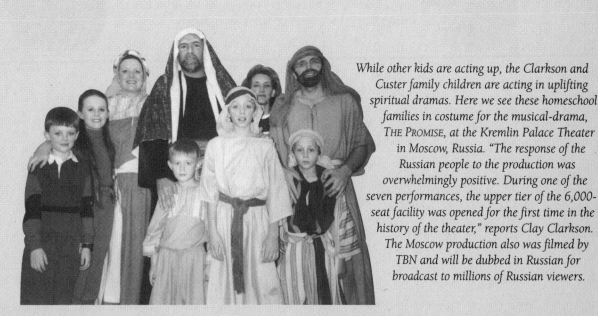

While other kids are acting up, the Clarkson and Custer family children are acting in uplifting spiritual dramas. Here we see these homeschool families in costume for the musical-drama, THE PROMISE, at the Kremlin Palace Theater in Moscow, Russia. "The response of the Russian people to the production was overwhelmingly positive. During one of the seven performances, the upper tier of the 6,000-seat facility was opened for the first time in the history of the theater," reports Clay Clarkson. The Moscow production also was filmed by TBN and will be dubbed in Russian for broadcast to millions of Russian viewers.

Aubyn Burnside (13) and Jason Crowe (11), both homeschooled kids, were named by U.S. Senators Robert Kerrey (Nebraska) and Tim Hutchinson (Arkansas) as two of ten National Honorees of the Prudential Spirit of Community Awards at a ceremony at the National Press Club in Washington, D.C. Aubyn and Jason each received $5000 and a gold medal commemorating their awards.

Aubyn Burnside founded a program that collects and distributes used suitcases for children in foster care. After learning that the belongings of kids being moved from one foster home to another are usually transported in garbage bags, Aubyn dedicated herself to ensuring that every foster child would have a suitcase of his or her own. Suitcases for Kids has collected almost 4,500 suitcases to date and is now expanding to other states.

Jason Crowe actually provides two services, for all practical purposes. He produces a newspaper, By Kids and For Kids, which showcases young talent in writing and art. Jason then donates the profits to the American Cancer Society.

CHAPTER 10

Bible Curriculum

Here's what you'll find in the Bible-related chapters in this section. First, we're going to look at Bible curriculum—products meant to teach actual Bible content, e.g., "What Judge was found by an angel threshing wheat in a winepress?" (Helpful hint: It wasn't Sandra Day O'Connor!)

Second, we're going to review Bible memory products and products to teach devotional skills, e.g., prayer and worship. (A note to suppliers: most of the material available for devotional training for kids ranges from weak to nonexistent. A market niche if I ever saw one!)

Third, we're going to check out ways to "get into" Bible Stories through the eye-gate and ear-gate.

Last, we're going to look at Bible references, tools for learning the books of the Bible, and other teaching aids.

Funsy-Wunsy Cutesy-Poo

Sometimes someone else says what you wanted to say so well that you don't have to say it. Here's Clifford E. Miller, editor of the Rapids Christian Press catalog, with some words on the best way to teach kids the Bible:

Children's voices were heard, seriously singing, "Jesus, help me to remember some sweet lessons from Thy word. . ." It was a fitting ending for a three-hour session of Vacation Bible School. The time had been spent on two Bible lessons (the main emphasis for the day), memory work, singing, a 15-minute recess, some notebook work for older children and handwork for the little ones, and perhaps a brief object lesson. Children loved it! There were no puppets, no cassettes, no skits, no imaginative adventures. Just Bible. And kids found it delightful! The program was not designed to make them laugh, but they said it was fun!

"But that was 50 years ago," you say. "They're smarter, so they wouldn't be able to stand two Bible lessons in a forenoon. They're used to being entertained, so we have to amuse them."

NIV = New International Version, a popular translation among evangelicals

KJV = King James Version, the traditional Elizabethan English translation produced in the 17th century at the order of King James of England, and used in most Protestant churches until recently.

NKJV = New King James Version, slightly updated modern edition with current words substituted for archaic words.

What we really need in a Bible curriculum is:

- **Chronological knowledge of Bible events.** This includes some understanding of the cultural framework of these events, which the Bible itself readily supplies.
- **Book-by-book knowledge of what is in the Bible,** so you can find your way around in it.

These first two types of biblical knowledge provide the framework for what is to follow:

- **Knowledge of how to understand the Bible** (exegesis), **how to apply its teachings, and which teaching applies to which situation.** The Bible calls this "wisdom" and says only those who belong to God and practice what they already know of His commandments ever achieve it.
- **Knowledge of the basic Bible teachings** about God, man, sin, redemption, creation, eternity, the meaning of life, etc. We all know what the world teaches about such things. Trust me, the Bible says something different.

Granted, today's children are different. They are much more knowledgeable about sin, sad to say. But their hearts are the same. They are all sinners who need, not more hilarity and excitement, but the living Word of God. Is there someone among our readers who would dare to conduct a new kind of Vacation Bible School this year, the kind that used to be common but has been all but forgotten? Hebrew 4:12 is still true. Let's make it a BIBLE school this year!

With that in mind, and at the risk of sounding old-fashioned, I would like to mention that great old standby for teaching Bible. It's called, "The Bible."

What with all the puppet lessons, flannelgraphs, Bible stories, Bible videos, Bible dolls, and so on, sometimes our Bible programs end up missing the mark. For some reason, Bible curriculum designers have been really heaping on the fun 'n games lately. They load us up with "easy activities," like finding the puppet figures, dragging out flannel pieces 22A-24F, or correcting a Friends of Jesus Crossword Puzzle. That's OK for fun on Sunday afternoon, but it does get rather old after a few school weeks.

So how about just *reading the Bible to your children* instead? They are going to pay attention because, after reading, you will have each one *tell you the passage in his own words.* Alternatively, the children can act out the passage (with or without costumes), draw pictures that explain the passage, model it in clay (quick, and you don't have to save the results forever unless you want to), or write it out.

With a little creative imagination, your children can be actively listening and retelling all of Scripture to you in their own words. And that even includes the "tough" passages like the genealogies in Chronicles. Try making name tags for the important characters and have the children sort them in order as to who begat whom.

How to Teach Bible

The above approach works for all ages and levels of Bible literacy—and it's free. But some of us feel like we need more of a helping hand. That's OK, provided the Bible curriculum we choose actually helps!

Here are some questions to ask when shopping for Bible resources.

- **Is it complete?** In too many programs, well-worn stories appear again year after year, while major events like the downfall of Jerusalem in 586 B.C. are either passed over quickly or completely ignored. (As one curriculum author complains, "A lot of these programs never get out of the wilderness"—referring to the tendency to start again and again at Genesis and poop out at Exodus, with only a few brief excursions into the rest of the Bible.) If your only contact with the Bible was through some of these programs, you would never guess that Leviticus, Deuteronomy, large sections of Judges, the two books of Chronicles, most of the message of the major prophets, or any of the minor prophets even existed. Since these are just the areas in which most parents are weak, it makes sense to keep looking until you find a program that shores up your own weak areas instead of tiptoeing around them.
- **Is it easy to understand?** I'm not asking, "Does it use easy words?" but "Is the teaching systematic?" Does one thing follow another in logical sequence, or does the curriculum hop-skip-and-jump all over the place? Is the program designed to help the child remember his lessons . . . or do the authors simply throw a lot of unorganized data at the children?
- **Does it have depth and thoroughness?** Don't assume that because it's a Bible curriculum the authors necessarily know what they are talk-

ing about. Surrounding material may be frivolous, irrelevant, or downright wrong. One Bible program I know cites Goliath as an "example of courage." Sure. A nine-foot bully would have to be pretty brave to face a young unarmored Israelite! Another turns the story of Moses in the bulrushes into a sermonette on Miriam's courage, in which Miriam is made to constantly state that she trusts in the Lord and will not be afraid. Good sentiments, except they appear nowhere in this passage. Still another shows young David zapping tin cans off a fence with his slingshot. Only problem is, tin cans weren't invented until this century. Why these silly treatments of important passages? Because the authors are trying too hard to jam every lesson into one shoebox—a moral of the week. A really good curriculum, rather than grasping for a "moral of the week," will teach students to get deeper and deeper into every passage, finding dozens of applications.

- **Does the program challenge children to grow spiritually?** Or does it assume they are only interested in fun and games? Even when the lesson claims to teach the story's basic message, often so much time is given to side activities, like making puppets of David and Goliath, that the actual message vanishes in the creative swirl.

- **Is preaching substituted for teaching?** Do the curriculum designers prefer to sermonize about, say, the need to avoid drugs rather than tell us what the difficult words in the Bible passage mean? Are children taught how to handle Scripture study tools like concordances and given a systematic outline of Bible history? Are they given an understanding of Bible cultures (Hebrew, Egyptian, Assyrian, Canaanite, Philistine, Babylonian, Greek, Roman, New Testament Jewish . . .), and a workable Bible memory program? Or does an unbalanced appeal solely to the emotions replace solid teaching for the intellect?

- **Does it trivialize the sacred?** A crossword puzzle is a crossword puzzle. And Jesus Christ did not die on the cross to get His name into a crossword puzzle. Often Bible curriculum, in an attempt to be clever or relevant, focuses more interest on an activity than on the person or doctrine supposedly being taught. I think, for example, of the cutesy idea of having children write modern-day news reports about Jesus' birth or other Biblical events. Game-show formats, "interviews" with Biblical characters, and other such activities all tend to trivialize the Bible's message. Should prophets of God, before whom kings trembled, be reduced to interview subjects for snide eight-year-olds? (I seem to recall that a gang of irreverent youth once got into serious trouble for taking the prophet Elisha lightly.) Right in line with this is the practice of "dumbing down" Scripture into a small, easily-memorized list of clichés and slogans. Should children be taught to be satisfied with pigeonholing Jeremiah as "the weeping prophet" without ever really hearing his message?

The main purpose of Bible teaching is to provide us with enough *understanding* of the Word of God so that the Holy Spirit, through His appointed means of preaching and meditation, can apply it to our hearts.

At home, we parents don't need a load of sermons-in-workbook-form as much as we need resources for sharing the vast amount of *information* in the Bible with our children. Before we go flying off into the air with all kinds of great applications of Scripture, we have to know what the Bible *says*.

Seminaries today are forced to provide remedial Bible classes for students who have graduated from Bible college and attended Sunday school all their lives—all because of this overeagerness to get to the preaching and the application before children even know Hosea from Joshua. You don't want this to happen to your family!

A Beka Bible Study

Grades K–6. Flash-a-Card series: Salvation Series, $18.20. Mini Salvation Series 1 and 2, $2.60 each (personal-size for student). Other series cost $9.70–$18.50 each. Bible Curriculum Materials Kits: nursery, $175.55. K4, $176.50. K5, $241.05. Grade 1, $252.90. Grade 2, $248.15. Grade 3, $249.60 Grade 4, $258.10. Grade 5, $258.70. Grade 6, $258.20. Daily Bible curriculum plans (included in Bible Curriculum Materials Kits), $12.95 for nursery, K4 and K5. $14.95 for other grades. Shipping extra.

A Beka Book, Box 19100, Pensacola, FL 32523-9100. (800) 874-2352. Fax: (800) 874-3590. Web: www.abeka.com.

Bible Curriculum

A Beka's unique approach to Bible study for grades K–6 is based on large full-color cards and does not require the use of notebooks. Starting in Genesis with the story of Creation, the series includes

- *Salvation Series*: five stories illustrated on 35 cards.
- *Genesis* 21-lesson series: Creation/Adam/Cain, Enoch/Noah/Babel, Abraham and Isaac, Jacob, and Joseph
- *Life of Moses* 20-lesson series: Moses in Egypt, Journey to Sinai, and Journey through the Wilderness.
- *Joshua*: 7 lessons on 35 cards.
- *Judges*: 6 lessons on 34 cards.
- *The Tabernacle*: three lessons on nine cards.
- *Elisha*: eight lessons on 42 cards.
- *Elijah*: six lessons on 38 cards.
- *Daniel*: six lessons on 32 cards.
- *Samuel*: four lessons on 18 cards.
- *Ruth*: three lessons on seven cards.
- *Life of Christ* includes five series, with 35 lessons in all: The First Christmas, Boyhood and Early Ministry, Jesus Heals and Helps, Later Ministry of Jesus, and Crucifixion and Resurrection.
- *Paul 1* series has five lessons on 26 cards.
- *Paul 2* series has nine lessons on 34 cards.
- Also available: *David I, II,* and *III; Ezra/Nehemiah; Esther; Daniel;* and *Jonah.*

Helpful lesson guides are provided with each set. The illustrations are outstanding.

If you prefer, you can also obtain a Bible Curriculum Materials Kit for each grade level. Each includes several Flash-a-Card series, a songbook for hymns and choruses, a daily curriculum guide, and Bible Doctrinal Drills. *Mary Pride*

Alpha Omega Bible LIFEPACs

Grades 1–12. 10 LIFEPACs per grade. Levels 100–1000 (grades 1–10), $3.50 each or set of 10 for $34. Levels 1100–1200 (grades 11–12), $2.95 each or set of 10 for $28.50. Boxed set (includes all teacher and student materials for the year): Grade 1, $61.95; Grades 2–10, $41.95–$51.95; Grades 11–12, $38.95–$51.95. Shipping extra.

Alpha Omega Publications, 300 N. McKemy, Chandler, AZ 85226. Orders and inquiries: (800) 622-3070. Fax: (480) 785-8034. Web: www.home-schooling.com.

Alpha Omega's Bible LIFEPACs courses contain seven major themes: Christian growth, theology themes, attributes of God, Christian evidences, Bible literature, Bible geography and archaeology, and a special theme for each level. Each one-year course includes nine workbooks, with full instructions built in, plus one workbook that reviews the entire course. The teacher handbooks include all answer keys, LIFEPAC test keys, additional tests, enrichment activities, and discussion questions.

Let's go through this curriculum grade by grade. In **grade 1,** the LIFEPAC titles are: *God Created All Things, God Loves His Children, We Can Pray, God Wants You to Be Good, Old Testament Stories* (men, women, and children of the Old Testament), *God's Promise to Men, Jesus Our Savior, God Calls a Missionary, New Testament Stories* (men, women, and children of the New Testament), and *God Gave You Many Gifts.* **Grade 2:** *Who Am I?* (subtopics: God Made Use, God Loves Me, God Helps Me, and God Helped Daniel), *The Story of Moses, God and You* (subtopics: God is Great, God Keeps His Promises, You Should Obey God, and God Rewards His People), *How the Bible Came, David's Sling, God is Everywhere, The Story of Joseph, God and the Family, God Made the Nations* and *God, the Word, and You.* **Grade 3:** *Why Am I Here?* (answers: to love, obey, praise, and worship God), *The Life of Jesus Christ, O Joseph! What Was God's Plan for You?* (Joseph, the son of Jacob, not Joseph the husband of Mary), *You Can Use* *the Bible* (how to study and memorize Scripture), *God Takes Care of His People*, *How Do I Know the Bible is the World of God?*, *Archaeology and the Bible*, *God Gave Us the Need for Friends* (teaching about Christian love and personal needs), *God Wants Man to Help Man*, and *God's Word, Jesus, and You*. **Grade 4:** *How Can I Live for God?*, *God's Knowledge* (how to become wise), *Saul Begins to Live for God* (Saul the Apostle Paul, not Saul the king of Israel), *The Bible and Me* (studying, memorizing, and living out the Bible), *God Cares for Us* (Jesus, David, and Daniel), *How Can I Know God Exists?*, *Geography of the Old Testament*, *God-Given Worth* (self-esteem), *Witnessing for Jesus*, and *God's Word Is Perfect*. **Grade 5:** *How Others Lived for God*, *Angels*, *The Presence of God*, *Bible Methods and Structure* (parts of the Bible), *The Christian in the World* (behavior at home, school, and work), *Proving What We Believe*, *Missionary Journeys of Paul*, *God Created Man for Eternity* (the final judgment and rewards), *Authority and Law*, and *Angels, the Bible, and Living for God*. **Grade 6,** the basic Bible survey, is broken up into: *From Creation to Moses*, *From Joshua to Samuel*, *The Kingdoms of Israel*, *The Divided Kingdom*, *Captivity and Restoration*, *The Life of Jesus*, *The Followers of Jesus*, *The Apostle Paul*, *Hebrews and General Epistles*, and *Revelation and Review*.

As a whole, I do not think the "seven-themes" approach is the best, since it doesn't stick with a subject long enough to build a really good framework. Grade 6 is the exception, covering the entire Bible without any special units on apologetics and self-esteem.

On the positive side, you can hardly find a more inexpensive or easy to use set of Bible worktexts. All Alpha Omega's products encourage thought—there is little rote fill-in-the-blanks, and students write an increasing number of sentence and essay answers as they go up the grade levels. On the negative side, the first few grades are rather rinky-dink, in my estimation, and the constant emphasis on "I am a very special person" and "I must love myself" wears thin. Things pick up in grades 3–5, with the exception of the unfortunate unit on self-esteem in grade 4. The grade 6 chronological Bible Survey course is quite good, including maps, timelines, and detailed explanations of Bible times practices. It covers *all* the Old Testament prophets (rare in an elementary Bible curriculum) and includes a mid-course review of the Old Testament, before getting into the New Testament. *Mary Pride*

The Bible is the Best Book—Why? covers ten different topics in 33 pages. Each lesson is three pages long. Each lesson contains a section to read, an activity page, and a page to color. It also has suggested Bible Memory Work to match the lessons. The questions for each lesson are"

- Lesson 1: Where did the Bible come from?
- Lesson 2: How does God give his word to us?
- Lesson 3: Is the Bible true?
- Lesson 4: How much of the Bible is true?
- Lesson 5: Are there any mistakes in God's word?
- Lesson 6: How long will the Bible last?
- Lesson 7: What did the Lord Jesus say about his words?
- Lesson 8: Will everything God has foretold really happen?
- Lesson 9: How is the Bible different from every other book?
- Lesson 10: What is the Christian's only weapon?

This is easy enough to incorporate for either individual Bible study or devotionals. It would be nice to see a larger devotional put together by this author to be used as a daily devotional throughout the year. I like the short, direct lessons and everything I have seen by this author is based soundly on the Word of God. *Lynn Smith*

In the early grades, the Bible course is integrated with language arts instruction, which means you get word exercises, phonics drills, and so forth. You will still need a separate grammar, spelling, and phonics program to use along with the Bible course.

NEW!
The Bible is the Best Book—Why?
Grade 2–6. $2 plus $1.50 shipping. *Gunderson Publications, PO Box 717, Ferndale, WA 98248. Phone/fax: (360) 384-1747. Email: GundersonWV@juno.com.*

Bible Study Guide for All Ages

All ages. Volumes 1–4, $29.95 each. Teaching Plans, $11.95 each. Worksheet sets, $4.95 each (3 units apiece available for non-reading, low-reading, and regular reading). Wall Map/Time Line packets, $19.95 each. Numbered picture & label packets, $9.95 for #1-52 and $5.95 for all others. Children's a capella song tape, $12.95. Shipping extra.
Bible Study Guide Publishers, PO Box 2608, Russellville, AR 72811. (800) 530-7995. Fax: (501)890-6262. Email: mlwbaker@cei.net.

Bible Study Guide for All Ages *really* is for all ages. Each volume contains 104 lessons and could cover a full year with two lessons a week or two years at one lesson a week. The entire Bible is covered in the four volumes.

There's no written work required at all for this program—another plus in the eyes of many of us. Designed originally for use in family study times, it is infinitely adaptable to any number of individual or group situations for Bible students of all ages. On a scale of 1 to 100, I give this one a 100.

The program moves back and forth between sections of the Old and New Testaments, with review lessons providing natural transitions. This means you don't have to wait forever to teach your children about Jesus, and since the segments are organized logically—e.g., "Divided and Conquered Kingdoms"—your children won't get confused.

Bible Study Guide for All Ages is one of the few Bible courses available for children that actually concentrates on teaching them Bible *knowledge*. Although life applications are not neglected, the main emphasis of this curriculum is on *facts:* knowing *all* the Bible stories cold (not just a few often-repeated favorites), knowing what happened when, knowing what happened where, and knowing Bible verses and Christian songs. However, this is not a dour "medicine" style program! For sheer numbers of engaging visuals and hands-on activities, it outranks just about every other Bible curriculum I've seen.

Each lesson includes drill work (e.g., practicing saying the 10 Commandments), review of important questions from previous lessons, seven questions on the Bible chapter for this lesson (you read the chapter aloud), a song, an applicable Bible verse for meditation or memorization, prayer time, and a visual. Some lessons also have an "additional Scriptures" section, with a few verses to read from other sections of the Bible that help explain the passage of the day, and/or an "According to the Dictionary" section that explains unusual words or customs occurring in the passage. Map work is also included where appropriate. All this is on *just one page for each lesson*, making it super easy to use.

Already this program towers head and shoulders above all others for sheer usefulness. Find me another program that the whole family, from preschooler to Grandpa, can study together at once, let alone one where the entire lesson is so well organized it fits on one page!

Bible Study Guide for All Ages also includes all sorts of visual-aid cutouts, flap pages, and drawings, plus literally dozens of suggested Bible games to help pep up your lessons. These are contained in the optional wall map/time line packets. Besides the maps and timeline, the packets contain all the cutouts needed for the lessons, the printed names of Bible people and small pictures of Bible events to put on the time line, and the place names to put on the map. Two wall map/time line packets are available: one for non-readers, and one for readers.

If you'd like even more help, you can get worksheets that cover the first three quarters of the first year of Volume 1. Separate sets of worksheets, each containing 13 separate four-page lessons, are available for the following reading levels: non-readers (preschool through grade 1), low readers (grades 2 and 3), and regular readers (grades 4 and up). These worksheets are really super to look at, fun for the kids without losing a smidgin of reverence for the Bible, and easy to use.

Each **non-reading worksheet** includes memory work (e.g., "Say these books of the New Testament: Matthew, Mark, Luke, John"), time line review, a memory verse with a picture to draw or color, a "rebus" Bible story (with pictures in place of many of the words, so the little one can "read" along), questions and activities about the story, and application questions related to a large coloring picture on the back (e.g., "What is big sister Gracie doing? Is God pleased with Gracie?"). Words fail me to describe how cute and appealing these full-color worksheets are, yet without the least bit of off-putting cutesiness.

Low-reading worksheets include memory work, review questions to keep previous lessons fresh in the child's mind, a "Tell a Story" or "Sing a Song" activity that requires narration or singing of a previously-learned Bible story or song, a "Things to Know" section that teaches one or two Bible vocabulary words, a visual Bible story outlined in cartoon style (with just enough pictures and words to help the reader remind the whole story), time line activities using the time line across the top of the double-page spread, map activities using the large half-page map printed right in the worksheet, an application lesson, and more. All this is in the liveliest, most engaging visual format you can imagine.

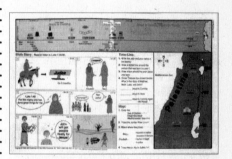

Regular-reading worksheets have the same general format, with more text that the low-reading worksheets. An additional "Think!" section provides thought questions for discussion. For example, in reference to Joseph's brother's coming to hate him because of their father's favoritism for Joseph, the question is, "How does 'hate' cause a person to act?"

Each set of worksheets comes nested in an outer cover, with a game or activity printed on the inside of the cover. Just one more extra!

Teaching notes are available for each worksheet set. Non-reader teaching notes mainly aid in telling the Bible story. On your side of the two-page spread, you have the story text. On the kids' side are the cast of characters in large pictures, so you can point to each as he or she comes into the story. Additional instructions for teaching the lesson are found on the inside cover of the teaching notes wrapper. Low-reading and regular-reading teaching notes are more traditional lesson plans, including filled-in versions of the student worksheets.

If you have the time to do more than just hand your kids a Bible curriculum workbook, this is the most outstanding Bible program I've seen. Highly recommended. *Mary Pride*

The **Bible Truths for Little Children series** is a revision of a classic five-book set written a hundred years ago. The revision retains the McGuffeyesque character of the original, now translated into "proper English and children's language." Highly moralistic, it includes comments on the stories along with an interactive style in which children are asked questions during the telling of the story. Example:

> *You have heard how the Israelites came into the land of Canaan. I shall tell you what happened to them in Canaan after Joshua died. Do you know who was their king? God was their king. Joshua was not their king, though he used to tell them what God wanted them to do . . .*

An example of the moralizing style:

> *Among the worshippers at the tabernacle, was a man who had two wives. Men long ago could have more than one wife, though they must not now.*

Bible Truths for Little Children series

Grades K and up (if a grownup reads); Grade 3–6 (child reads to himself). $6.75 each. If you order all 5, mention the Big Book of Home Learning to get a 50% discount on the set.
Triangle Press, 23 Fifth Ave. SE., Conrad, MT 59425.
Phone/fax: (406) 278-5664.
Email: published@tripress.com.
Web: www.tripress.com.

One of these wives was a very Godly woman named Hannah. She had no child. The other wife was unkind, and she acted very wicked. The unkind wife laughed at Hannah. She told Hannah that God gave her no child because He did not love her. This was not true, for God loved Hannah very much. Poor Hannah used to cry when the other wife spoke so unkindly to her . . .

As you can see this type of storytelling is very lively and involving, since the author isn't afraid to ask the readers to identify with the good guys and hiss the bad guys.

Volume 1 covers Creation through the story of Joseph, son of Jacob. Volume 2 is the story of Moses and the Israelites. Volume 3 is the stories of Samuel and David. Volume 4 carries on with Solomon and the other prophets and kings of Israel and Judah. Volume 5 is the life of Christ. All are written on a third grade reading level, so children can read them to themselves. *Mary Pride*

BJUP Bible Curriculum

Grades 1–6. Student Worktext K4 children's packet, $12. Student Worktext K5 and grades 1-4, $9 each. Student Worktext Grades 5 and 6, $10 each, Teacher's Edition, $37 each grade. Cassettes, storybooks, etc. extra. Shipping extra. *Bob Jones University Press Customer Services, Greenville, SC 29614. Orders: (800) 845-5731. Fax: (800) 525-8398. Web: www.bjup.com.*

The first two grades of the **Bob Jones University Press Bible Truths** series provide a chronological overview of the entire Bible. These books impart some solid knowledge along with the salvation emphasis, covering the Children's Catechism along with the Bible and emphasizing simple "Bible Action Truths." Both K and 1 include enjoyable memory and handwork activities. Grades 2 through 4 systematically study the fundamental doctrines of the Christian faith. Grade 5 is a New Testament survey, while grade 6 surveys the Old Testament.

Like all other Bob Jones products, the art, layout, and general quality of these books is impeccable. The content is clean, clear, educationally excellent, and contains nothing "iffy." Eschatology is handled separately from other subjects, making it possible for families with diverse eschatological views to use these books.

In the lower grades, the teacher's manuals make a big difference. You get teaching tips, explanations of the activities, and supplemental activities.

The series was designed for use in daily Christian schools, making it deeper than Sunday school-style materials. *Mary Pride*

NEW!
The Blessing of the Lord

Grades 1–7. $20 (hardbound) plus shipping.
Wm. B. Eerdmans Books for Young Readers, 255 Jefferson Ave. S.E., Grand Rapids, MI 49503.(800) 253-7521. Fax: (616) 459-6540. Email: sales@eerdmans.com.

Explore 25 different Bible stories, 15 from the Old Testament and 10 from the New, in **The Blessing of the Lord**. Each is written from different points of view. These are not the everyday Bible stories like what you study in Sunday school. They are written to answer questions that you may ask yourself as you read stories straight from the Bible.

The author states how these stories are written much better than I can, so here it is in Gary D. Schmidt's own words:

"What must the sons of Leah felt have felt when Jacob so clearly favored the sons of Rachel? What must Elisha have felt when he lost Elijah, even though Elijah went up to heaven in a storm of fire? What must Purah have thought when he was walking behind Gideon in the midst of thousands of Midianites all ready to kill him? What must Abraham and Mary have thought when confronted by an angel of the Lord? Did Noah become discouraged? Was Ananias confused? Was the centurion at Calvary surprised?"

The Bible does not answer these questions directly, but the author does, as he shares his ideas of how others must have felt in the various stories he presents.

> *"Each of the stories is set in a moment of crisis, when human frailty comes face to face with God Almighty, and when through grace God teaches and cajoles and leads Us to Himself. Some of the stories are told by characters on the periphery, who see God's hand but can not understand it. Others are told by characters who see that same hand and respond to love and faith."*

The pictures in the book are beautiful watercolor paintings. Each painting adds to the beauty of the stories. Each story has the scripture references that the author used to re-tell the story listed at the end. After you read the rewritten story, go to the Bible and compare the two. My children love this book and I imagine yours will too. Recommended. *Lynn Smith*

These excellent workbooks, designed for self-study with some teacher involvement, emphasize learning Bible history, developing strong Christian character, and establishing a biblical worldview.

The **Christian Liberty Studying God's Word** series starts with book A (for kindergarten). This 160-page workbook covers many of the major events in the New and Old Testaments and is enhanced with many two-color illustrations and black-and-white photographs. Unlike the other books in this series, Book A has 45 units. Each unit is a well-told Bible story for you to read aloud, with a few brief comprehension questions at the end.

Book B (for grade 1) is doctrinal in tone, going through the questions of the Children's Catechism. It has 36 weekly units. For each week, Lesson 1 is a catechism drill, Lesson 2 is a Bible reading and vocabulary lesson, Lesson 3 is a Bible reading with application, Lesson 4 is a written exercise, and Lesson 5 is an activity.

Book C (for grade 2) covers the Old Testament and D (for grade 3) covers the New. Book E (grade 4) starts over again with Genesis through Ruth, F (grade 5) covers I Samuel through Malachi, G (grade 6) covers the Message and Ministry of the Lord Jesus Christ, and H (grade 7) covers the Book of Acts. The series uses the KJV but could be adapted for other translations.

Each of the 29 weekly lessons in book C and the 30 weekly lessons in book D includes a few paragraphs in large text introducing the Bible topic, a Bible reference to read, a memory verse, and simple but fun seatwork activities. Parents will need to help children who are not yet reading, or who might find the reading or writing a bit difficult. Both books have pages in the book of items to cut out for the cut-and-paste activities in the books.

Lessons for grades four and up includes a timeline or map, Bible reference to read, memory verse, principles from the text and applications for the stu-

Reverent in tone, the illustrations and personal applications do not distract from God's Word but rather illuminate the lesson. You won't waste your time collecting craft materials, designing object lessons, or pretending to fly around in spaceships and time machines. This curriculum is completely twaddle-free.

If you want your children to be well-grounded in the Word, equipped for every good work, able to discern truth from error, and to articulate and defend their faith, these books are definitely worth checking out.

dent or society today, questions, and activities. In addition, the books also contain map studies, unit tests, backgrounds of the Bible books, suggestions for reference materials for your home library (of great value in itself), a glossary, and a complete timeline. Answer keys are available for books C and up. *Rebecca Prewett*

Come, Ye Children is a solid Dutch Calvinistic Bible storybook. Author is the well-known Bible curriculum author Gertrude Hoeksema. 200 Bible stories, each ending with a thought to remember, accompanied by realistic drawings. Durable, hardcover binding in a convenient 7 x 10" size. *Mary Pride*

Come, Ye Children

Ages 4 and up. $39.95 postpaid.
Reformed Free Publishing Association, 4949 Ivanrest, Grandville, MI 49418. (616) 531-1490. Fax: (616) 531-3033. Web: www.iserv.net/~rfpa.

NEW!
Covenant Home Champions

Grades 5–adult. $15.95 plus 8% shipping. Includes study guides.
Covenant Home Curriculum, 17800 W. Capitol Dr., Brookfield, WI 53045. (414) 781-2171. Fax: (414) 781-0589. Email: educate@covenanthome.com. Web: covenanthome.com.

In the spirit of the McGuffey Readers, Dale Dykema has written a solid, meaty book that seeks to challenge young minds. No Dick and Jane fluff in **Champions**!

The stories are taken from the books of Judges and Samuel and center around Deborah, Samson, Gideon, David, and Solomon. Using short stories and personal journals, the themes of conquest, deliverance, and the sin of man are illustrated. Proper names are italicized and syllabicized to make them easier to pronounce. Comprehension questions for all thirteen stories are included in the back of this 102-page book.

The first story tells of Deborah, a faithful woman called to leadership, during a time when men did not assume this rightful role. The battle between the Israelites and the army led by Sisera is recounted and concludes with Jael, the woman who killed Sisera with a tent peg. After reading the story, the author suggests reading the corresponding scripture and answering or discussing the questions.

The questions do not rely on simple answers, but encourage the student to think and dig for nuggets of truth. The reading level is appropriate for 5th or 6th graders and up and stimulates thought about the people God used to foreshadow the coming of His Son. Very good. *Marla Perry*

Covenant Home Doré Bible Pictorial Briefings

Grades 5–10. Set A, or Set B, $12.95 each. Both sets, $24.95. Shipping extra.
Covenant Home Curriculum, 17800 W. Capitol Dr., Brookfield, WI 53045. (414) 781-2171. Fax: (414) 781-0589. Email: educate@covenanthome.com. Web: covenanthome.com.

Covenant Home Curriculum is a full-service K–12 home-school curriculum provider with a Reformed bent. Their materials tend to be innovative, beautiful, and thought-provoking, and the new **Doré Bible Pictorial Briefings** are no exception.

You might recognize the name of Gustave Doré. His famous etchings of Bible scenes made the 1860 Doré Bible, which featured these etchings, a financial success. The Pictorial Briefings are four-page (8½ x 11") booklets, each with a Doré Bible illustration on the cover. Inside are comments on the illustration, Scripture references, questions based on the illustration, and further questions based on the passage. Example, from the "Creation of Light" booklet:

> *The eye > What is the focal point of the picture?*
>
> *The eye focuses first on the light source coming from behind the angry clouds. It then follows the rays and draws down to the surface of the earth. Finally, it circles up into the dark, turbulent clouds, completing a counter-clockwise rotation.*
>
> *The emotions > Does the bright light convey the idea of great power? Is there something in the clouds that causes you to feel the energy and brooding of the Spirit of God? Do you sense the anticipation in the scene?*
> 1. *Why did the artist make the clouds dark and foreboding?*
>
> 2. *Make a list showing the order in which everything was created.*
>
> 3. *Do a word study tracking the word "light" through a book, such as the Psalms. Note all the usages of this key word.*

Set A of Doré Pictorial Bible Briefings includes *The Creation of Light, The Formation of Eve, Isaac Blessing Jacob, The Egyptians Drowned in the Red Sea, Moses Coming Down from Mt. Sinai*, and 16 more.

Set B includes *Joshua Commanding the Sun to Stand Still, Samson and Delilah, Solomon Receiving the Queen of Sheba, Elijah Taken Up to Heaven in a Chariot of Fire, Jehu's Companions Finding the Remains of Jezebel, The Vision of the Valley of the Dry Bones, The Vision of the Four Chariots, Job and His Friends* and 21 more.

These sets are very easy to use and an excellent choice for an intellectual, artistically-minded student. *Mary Pride*

The **Explorer's Bible Study Curriculum for the Young Scholar** is currently three curriculum series, with more to be added. When complete, they will combine to form a comprehensive Bible-study solution for the school years.

Doré's illustrations are powerful, make no mistake about that. As Dale Dykema, the Pictorial Briefings author, says,

> *Many of the themes which he capably executes are those which are avoided or ignored by modern day Christian teachers and illustrators. The glorious judgments of God upon the disobedient and upon His enemies is one. His awesome vindication of His people is another . . . These are prominent themes in the Doré drawings . . . The disarming insights made obvious in many of the pictures by Doré are not the typical fare of religious art today.*

NEW!
Explorer's Bible Study Curriculum for the Young Scholar

Grades preK–12. Bible Beginnings (ages 2–4): And It Was Good: Old Testament Lessons For Little Listeners, $19.95. Bible Foundations Read-Along Edition (grades K–1), TBA. Bible Foundations (Grades 2–3): Old Testament Overview, New Testament Overview: Student Workbooks, $14.95 each; Home School Teacher's Manuals, $16.95 each; Answer Keys, $6.95 each. Bible Discovery (Grades 3–6): Genesis; Exodus through Joshua (God's People, God's Land); Words of Wisdom: Job, Psalms, & Proverbs; and Luke & Acts (Promises Fulfilled): Student Workbooks, $18.95 each; Home School Teacher's Manuals, $19.95 each;

Answer keys, $6.95 each. Bible Quest (Grades 7–12): Genesis; Exodus through Joshua (God's People, God's Land); Words of Wisdom: Job, Psalms, & Proverbs; and Luke & Acts (Promises Fulfilled): Student Workbooks, $18.95 each; Home School Teacher's Manuals, $19.95 each; Answer Keys, $6.95 each. Explorer's Bible NKJV, $15.99.

Explorer's Bible Study, PO Box 425, Dickson, TN 37056-0425. Orders: (800) 657-2874. Inquiries: (615) 446-7316. Fax: (615) 446-7951. Email: tom.ebs@mcione.com. Web: www.explorerbiblestudy.org.

What is Spiral Learning?

An example of how spiral learning works: In Bible Foundations, a first- through third-grader will be asked to describe the world before the Creation. In Bible Discovery, a third- through sixth-grader will be asked, "In what words did God command light to appear?" Finally, in Bible Quest, a teenager will be asked, "How do the first verses of Genesis deny atheism?" As you can see, while older children will be studying the same Bible passages as the younger ones, they will be analyzing them in the light of developing a Christian worldview rather than merely parroting back the Bible facts, as is more appropriate for younger children.

A Home School Teacher's Manual is now available to accompany each workbook. This includes everything found in the Answer Key, plus additional home teaching helps, without adding all the extraneous (to home-school) info in the classroom teacher's

Explorer's Bible Study Curriculum has some similarities and differences to other Bible curricula. Like most other programs available today, it is "spiral." That is, children study the same material repeatedly at different levels. In Explorer's case, they will go through many Bible portions four times during their school years: once in preschool, once in the early elementary grades, once in the later elementary grades, and once in the middle-school/high-school years. But Explorer's takes the spiral concept a bit farther. Every child in a family from grade 3 and up can be studying the same passages in the same week. That's because the Bible Discovery and Bible Quest workbooks run in "parallel." Similarly, once the Bible Beginnings workbooks are out, all preschool through grade 2 or 3 children in a family will be able to study the same Bible portions together, because Bible Beginnings and Bible Foundations will be designed with parallel Bible lessons.

The curriculum as a whole concentrates on teaching Bible facts in chronological order and in context. The workbooks are designed to be self-directed, and the lessons require practically no teacher preparation. In keeping with the factual emphasis, the courses are non-denominational, not seeking to present any particular emphasis or agenda.

Bible Beginnings, the preschool course, is in the process of development. When completed, it will have the same format as Bible Foundations, presented at a simpler level for the younger child. There will be one workbook each for Old Testament Overview and New Testament Overview, and Home School Teacher's Manual.

Bible Foundations is currently being revised. Both the old and new edition include two courses, each with 30 lessons intended to cover a school year: Old Testament Overview and New Testament Overview. Although the classroom teacher's edition lays out a "three-day schedule" and "five-day schedule" for each lesson, actually you can do each in just one day at home. (In fact, the Home School Teacher's Edition doesn't even include schedules at all!) That's because the five- and three-day schedules both include loads of repetition: reading the story day after day, saying the guided prayer day after day, practicing the "Bible words to remember" memory verse day after day, and so on. The school-week schedules also include time for "guided activity" and "Bible drama," neither one of which appear in the student workbook and both of which are totally skippable.

Happily, all this busywork has been removed from the new Home School Teacher's Edition. What you end up with is a provided Bible story to read, a little prayer to say, a Bible verse to memorize, about a dozen vocabulary words the child is supposed to learn (with definitions supplied), and some questions to ask and answer.

Although you couldn't call the "Foundations" courses complete (Old Testament Overview skips Cain and Abel, the Tower of Babel, most of the Judges and Kings, and all the minor prophets except Jonah, for example), you'll be following them up with courses that cover all of this. The Foundations courses hit the high spots and give you a fairly painless way to ease your children into systematic Bible study. In fact, an hour once a week on Sunday afternoon should be enough time to do it all.

Bible Foundations is followed by **Bible Discovery**. These workbook courses are designed to help the student learn to systematically study out Bible portions verse by verse. The "inductive" method is taught starting at this level. Expect a lot of questions about what happened, who did it, when it happened, and so forth. Lessons also include vocabulary words with definitions, and map studies as appropriate. At this level, count on 30-minute lessons, five days a week.

Bible Quest is the capstone of this curriculum. It continues to teach the inductive method, while introducing "worldview" topics as appropriate.

Expect a lot of questions designed to make the student think about *why* the Bible uses a particular word and *why* a Bible personage acted as he did. Study notes at the end of each lesson provide additional background information, answer questions that the lesson may have raised, and provide additional worldview applications. It would be good to have an hour per weekday to allow enough time for discussing all the important questions Bible Quest raises.

Words of Wisdom: Job, Psalms, and Proverbs are now available in both the Bible Discovery and Bible Quest levels. Eventually, these will be joined by *Judges, Prophets and Kings: Judges–Malachi* and *New Testament Epistles and Revelation.* This will result in five years at each level, plus one elective (*Words of Wisdom*).

This is not the curriculum for hands-on, funsy-wunsy activities. It's designed to efficiently make your kids into Bible experts and Bible thinkers, with as little fuss and wasted time as possible. If that's what you're looking for, then Explorer's Bible Study delivers. *Mary Pride*

"Relationship—a state of affairs existing between those having relations or dealings." (*Merriam Webster's Collegiate Dictionary*) How many people know who Jesus is, but don't really have relations or deal with Him? The goal of this one-year **Family Discipleship Manual** curriculum is to lead your children into a *relationship* with Jesus Christ.

The 120 lessons (planned for 20–30 minutes a day) and their reproducible activity pages come in a three-ring binder. The curriculum is age-integrated and non-consumable. Most materials will already be in your home.

Teacher preparation is negligible. Read through the lesson, gather necessary materials, and jump right in. You begin with an introduction designed to capture their interest and spark discussion of the day's topic. Hand out the activity page and move right on into the lesson (everything you need to say is scripted). Children mark in their Bibles, using specific colors to designate scriptures dealing with salvation, personal responsibilities, God's promises, and warnings. After this, the children narrate the lesson back to you, explaining what they've learned in their own words. Finally, you work on scripture memorization and end with prayer.

The author, Susan Gaddis, has a positive attitude toward children. She encourages you to interact with your children, to listen to them and ensure that they understand. Her lessons are interesting, tempting you to read for your own pleasure. The activity sheets include "Whiz Kids" activities for more advanced students, and there are answer keys for everything—no fumbling around and hoping you get it right.

The layout of the book is basic, but not boring, and the activity pages are varied and interesting. This being a loose-leaf notebook, I would add tab dividers to make it easier to find the activity pages and the different units. Other than that, I've no complaints. *Tammy Cardwell*

Begin with Genesis? What an unusual idea!

Okay, so there is chronological Bible curriculum out there. This **Firm Foundations** one, however, really impresses me. Originally designed for use on the mission field, this approach to teaching the Bible has been so beneficial that New Tribes Mission now offers a Sunday School curriculum that is easily adapted for use in the home.

You get five paperback books containing detailed instructions for each step of every lesson, a generous supply of appealing charts, maps, timelines, and other visuals. (Plus, also available at an additional cost are a stack of reproducible line drawings to use as coloring pages. These drawings are punched, ready to insert into a three-ring binder.)

manuals. If you also want the song cassette and song book for each curriculum level, you can buy them separately. The sections of the Home School Teacher's Edition include an introduction, a curriculum overview (in which we learn that this curriculum is geared to "develop mental thinking and comprehension" and follows the "spiral" theory of presenting the same material repeatedly at different grade levels), guidelines and rules for effective teaching, a weekly schedule for Bible memory work, and finally a complete copy of the student workbook with answers to all the questions in boldface.

NEW!
Family Discipleship Manual #1: Relationship With Jesus
Grades 2–6. $35 plus $7.50 shipping. (California residents add tax.) *Eternal Foundations Curriculum, Tom & Susan Gaddis, PO Box 1213, Atascadero, CA 93423. Inquiries: (805) 466-1910.*

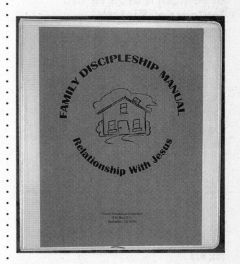

NEW!
Firm Foundations: Creation to Christ: Children's Edition
Grades 3–4. Curriculum, $39.95. Optional reproducible line drawings, $15.60. Shipping extra. *New Tribes Mission Bookroom, 1000 E. First St., Sanford, FL 32771-1487. (800) 321-5375. Fax: (407) 330-0376. Email: books@ntm.org. Web: www.ntm.org.*

Book 1 introduces the curriculum. Much of it is testimonies, accounts of natives who have come to a clearer understanding of salvation after studying from "In the beginning . . ." to the ascension. This is the primary purpose of this curriculum, to lead the child through the Bible, showing God's plan at each step. After seeing it foreshadowed over and over in the Old Testament, the child is much more prepared to comprehend the fullness of what Jesus did for him on the cross. At the end of book 1, you find detailed instructions on using the lessons.

The fifty lessons, with their skits and reproducible visuals, are divided among the remaining books. In Sunday Schools the fifty lessons would take one year to complete; the homeschooler could work through the curriculum much more quickly.

Each lesson begins with review. Classroom teachers would have the students fill out the optional review sheets. Not being worried by large classes, the homeschooler is free to simply spend time discussing the previous lesson(s). Next, take parts and read a short skit aloud—skits only have three or four characters. You may either make copies of the skits and hand them out to your children or simply gather around the book and read your parts directly from it.

Presenting the lesson is easy. Everything you say and do is scripted and notes in the margins cover almost any question you might have. This is one of the best Sunday School curriculums I've ever seen and is easily adapted to the home school. If you're looking for a Bible curriculum, one designed to lead your children to a clear understanding of the price Jesus paid, this one's a keeper. *Tammy Cardwell*

NEW!
Greenleaf Guide to Old Testament History

Grades 1–6. $10.95 plus $4 shipping.
Greenleaf Press, 3761 Hwy 109 N., Unit D, Lebanon, TN 37087. Inquiries: (615) 449-1617. Orders: (800) 311-1508. Fax: (615) 449-4018. E-mail: Greenleafp@aol.com. Web: www.greenleafpress.com

Do you want accurate, realistic, educational Bible study? If so, you'll love the **Greenleaf Guide to Old Testament History.**

This book goes through some of the most interesting stories in the Old Testament, realistically. It has a total of 196 lessons, each with a bit of reading straight from the Bible and interesting questions to discuss or use as topics for papers in each lesson. If you do a lesson a day, this is a one-year course. You will have read all the historical books of the Old Testament and discussed most of it by the time you finish this book.

The Greenleaf Guide to Old Testament History was recently chosen by *Practical Homeschooling* readers as their favorite educational product in the "Bible" category. That's an endorsement of some consequence, and it's deserved, because this book perfectly fits the "Homeschool Way" of teaching this subject. No twaddle, no time-wasting activities, simple to use and thorough in coverage. If you like realism in your Bible study, and you have a few minutes every day to go over the questions and answers with your kids, then this is the book for you! *Joseph Pride*

NEW!
Gunderson Doctrine Books

Grades 2 and up (must be good readers). The Dangerous Bandit, Saved on Monday, $3.25 each. The Secret Room, $5. Shipping extra. *Gunderson Publications, PO Box 717, Ferndale, WA 98248. Phone/fax: (360) 384-1747. Email: GundersonWV@juno.com.*

Good safe interesting reading is hard to come by these days. *The Dangerous Bandit, Saved on Monday, and the Secret Room* are just about as good as it gets. Each book covers 10 principles of the Christian walk. At the front of each book 10 verses are listed to interest and encourage children to memorize scripture. These same verses are included on the text cards to color and used in the stories. At the back of each book are several songs that may be used to enrich the time spent in the books.

The Dangerous Bandit is a 72-page collection of interesting stories. Each story shows the Power of God's Word and how the Lord cares and protects His own. Learn about why we need to be saved, in whom we believe to be saved, whether there is any other way to be saved, and whom the Lord Jesus said is the only way to heaven.

Saved on Monday is a delightful 65-page book that outlines the steps of getting saved and addresses the question "Is it dangerous to neglect salvation?" This is a must read for young children who have difficulty understanding the message of salvation.

The Secret Room is a 127-page book that focuses on Creation. It answers the questions, who made the earth, who made us, and why did God make us?

Also in this series: *Wrong Road, Over the Cliff,* and *Enemy Guest.*

The text cards to color cover each of the Bible stories. Each packet has 10 pictures. The verses and pictures change, but the purpose does not. Use these for review after reading the story to students. For slightly better readers, let them read the stories to you. If you buy copies of the books for each student, you can let them color the black-and-white pictures in the books themselves. The text cards are nicely done; it would be neat to see this author publish a coloring book. *Lynn Smith*

The **New Testament on Cassette Curriculum**, an innovative approach to Bible instruction, comes in a sturdy case containing four binders. One of those binders contains 100 reproducible lessons (with teaching suggestions) for either primary, middler, or junior age students. (Each level comes in a separate binder.) The other three binders contain high-quality recordings of the NIV Testament on cassette, dramatically read and complete with sound effects. The readings are divided into individual lessons. The tapes for the primary grades are followed by a song that the children can sing. (These tapes can also be used with older children.)

This is an extremely easy curriculum to teach and would be especially ideal in Sunday school classes. (An instruction cassette is provided for Sunday-school teachers. It tells you everything you need to know and do, even if you've never taught before. It also contains wonderful teaching suggestions for each age level.) Basically, each child follows the taped lesson by reading in their own Bibles (or for nonreaders, by listening only). Then they answer the questions and do the activities on the lesson sheets, memorize Scriptures, and do any additional activities selected by the teacher.

Some of the multiple choice questions are on the silly side. I was impressed with the quality of the tapes and with the concept of this curriculum but found the lesson materials not as serious and as in-depth as I had hoped. *Rebecca Prewett*

Vivian Gunderson, noted Sunday school material author, has prepared what she calls a **Scripture Catechism**. Consisting of two cards for preschoolers, four for kindergartners, and 38 more for primary-aged and older children, covering a total of 30 topics, her *Bible Answer Cards* series is a graduated, topical Scripture-memory program that runs from preschool through high school, using Bible verses for the answers to its questions.

This idea is not new: such types of catechisms were used long ago. What is new is the correlated storybooks, color-it-in texts, and memory work certificates for successful learners.

Each card has either five or 10 questions on it. Each question is answered by a complete Bible verse.

The two Nursery Class cards, "Verses About God" and "Verses I Can Learn," each have five questions. The four Beginner Cards, "The Greatness of God," "God Saves Sinners," "Clean Hearts," and "Bible Verses for Me," each also have five questions. All the rest of the cards in the series each have 10 questions. This includes the Primary Cards and the Topical Cards. Primary cards are "Learning About God," "About the Lord Jesus," "Good Behavior," "Learning About Sin," "Learning About Heaven," "Learning to Serve God," "Learning to Pray," and "Learning Right Words." Topics cards cover the Bible, creation, man's responsibility to God, conduct toward God,

> I like the way these little books are used with the text cards to color. Even reluctant readers will enjoy the time spent on these books full of stories. Since each story takes a mere 1–3 pages, the lessons will not take long to teach.

NEW!
New Testament on Cassette Curriculum

Ages 5–12. Price for entire curriculum (50 tapes & lesson plans) $125. Set of 12 tapes, dramatized, $29. Undramatized, $22. lesson plans only (no tapes) $25.
Hosanna, 2421 Aztec Road N.E., Albuquerque, NM 87107-4224. (800) 545-6552. Fax: (505) 881-1681. Web: www.faithcomesbyhearing.org.

Rapids Christian Press Scripture Catechism

Bible Answer Cards, $4 (set of 44). Certificate for learning one card, $1/dozen, 10¢ each. Set of 10 assorted text cards, $1.50 (includes permission to make copies for local use). Correlated short stories for text cards, $3.25 each book. Shipping extra.
Rapids Christian Press, PO Box 717, Ferndale, WA 98248. Phone/fax: (360) 384-1747. Email: GundersonWV@juno.com.

An example from card 41,"Our Words":

1. **What should we always speak?**
   "Speak every man truth with his neighbor." Ephesians 4:25
2. **What kind of lips does the Lord hate?**
   "Lying lips are abomination to the Lord: but they that deal truly are His delight." Proverbs 12:22
3. **Should we say unkind things about others?**
   "Speak not evil one of another." James 4:11

NEW!
Scripture Activities for Family Enrichment (SAFE)

I John: Love, Light and Life; Life of Christ; People in Proverbs
All ages. Getting Started, $2. Unit books (one per family), $7. Activity books (one per child age 2–7), $3. Video, $9. Postpaid.
SAFE, 1300 9th St., Greeley, CO 80631. (970)356-1166. Fax: (970)352-7880. Email: chessmates@aol.com.

God's gifts, giving to God, God the Son, the work of Christ, the Resurrection, Satan, sin, salvation, conduct toward others, God the Holy Spirit, the Christian life, the Christian and the Law, Bible study, faith, prayer, eating and drinking, love, joy, peace, angels, our works, our words, our thoughts, Heaven and Hell, and soul-winning.

Also available from this company, and useful for simple Bible memory work: **Text Cards to Color.** Each 8½ x 11" card has a picture and a Bible verse to color. You color both the picture *and* the verse, since the letters of the verse are large and outlined. Cards come in sets of 10. For classroom use, you can buy quantities of each card at a very good price. The Bird Text Cards each have a verse about speaking like a Christian. The Farm Animal Text Cards each have a salvation topic. The Flower Text Cards have commandments. The Wild Animal Text Cards are all about sin. The Wildflower Text Cards are about obedience to the Lord. The new Australian Animal Text Cards has verses about the Bible, plus info on the card's envelope about the animals! A book of correlated short stories is available for each topic mentioned in this paragraph. Each book has 10 stories, with each story emphasizing the truth of one Bible verse. *Mary Pride*

Are you looking for a family-based, age-integrated Bible curriculum? **SAFE** may be just the thing for you. SAFE materials were designed to be used by families meeting together as a unit in place of the traditional Sunday School class. The program can also be used in the homeschool to learn biblical principles as

a family. Currently, 13 units are available. A unit contains lessons for 13 weeks.

Getting Started is a 15-page introduction to using SAFE. It includes preparation instructions, philosophy, and evaluation helps. The information will assist you in setting the atmosphere for using the other materials.

Each SAFE lesson includes a project sheet, a supplement sheet, and an activity sheet. The project sheet is divided into two columns, Milk and Meat. The milk projects are for younger Christians. The meat projects are for older Christians. Projects are divided into Bible Study, Character Development, and Life Application. Supplement sheets have more explanations and answers to activities on the project sheet. Activity sheets are handwork items for the children to do. There is one activity sheet per lesson.

For any lesson, the family meets together and Dad leads the family through the key verses for the lesson, and prays through a scripture. Each lesson is keyed with a character trait. Then, together, the family chooses projects from the project sheet to be worked on through the week. The projects are fun and easy to accomplish. When studying I John 1:1-4, the character trait is joyfulness. One character development project is to begin dinner each evening with a rousing chorus of "I Have the Joy, Joy, Joy, Joy Down in My Heart." This is a group program; parents learn and work with the children. Parental involvement is required. *Terri Cannon*

Yes, Virginia, there really is a Bible study series named **Suffer Little Children**. Those of us with little Bible study in their backgrounds might naturally wonder at such a title. "Struggle, little children? Hurt, little children? Make your Bible study an ordeal, little children? What in the world does that title mean?" In reality, it is based on Christ's words in the King James Version, "Suffer the little children to come unto me and hinder them not, for of such is the kingdom of Heaven."

As so often happens with denominational literature, we have to get by the title and get by the author's assumption that every reader has been raised from the cradle as a member of the denomination (in this case, Dutch Reformed). Once we do so, we find that Gertrude Hoeksema, the author of this series, has put together a really decent three-year curriculum that goes through the entire Bible, with the exception of some of the minor prophets.

Let me digress here for a minute. I am unusual in that the first thing I do when I get a new Bible curriculum is run to check if it covers the minor prophets: Joel, Amos, Obadiah, Jonah, Micah, Nahum, Habakkuk, Zephaniah, Haggai, Zechariah, and Malachi. Jonah, although he is a minor prophet, is always covered. The others never are. One publisher explained it was because "People aren't interested in these prophets. I'd lose a barrel of money if I put them in my curriculum." Is he right? Are we really unwilling to share anything but "Bible stories" with our children?

Back to *Suffer Little Children*. Ignore the unfortunate title. Your children will not suffer with this curriculum. This is not your average cut-and-paste-and-color bunch of Bible stories and crafts. Thanks to solid Dutch Calvinism, your children are expected to *learn* something.

You get a large teacher's manual for first grade (Book 1), with the program's philosophy and teaching instructions built right in. Since the children are supposedly not readers at this stage, there is no workbook. For second and third grade, workbooks are supplied.

Once you get by the overwhelmingly intellectual introduction to Book 1, you find a well-thought-out series of lessons that carries you from Creation to Saul's last battle. Each lesson lists a Scripture passage (covered in chronological order), gives a background/introduction for you to read, outlines the lesson, provides low-key lesson applications, gives one or at most two simple suggested activities, and a Bible verse to memorize. To keep memory work simple, the verses are all listed in chart form in the back with a box for you to check off when the verse is mastered. You may photocopy that page for use with all your students.

Books 2 and 3 proceed in the same fashion. Book 2 covers the rest of the Old Testament; Book 3, all of the New.

The new **Show Me Thy Ways** series follows the same historical divisions as *Suffer Little Children*, but with more historical, cultural, and geographical detail. You'll need the workbooks in order to follow all the geographical references in the text. The texts have approximately 100 lessons, and the workbooks have one lesson for each three text lessons. *Mary Pride*

Have you ever wanted to take your children on a treasure hunt in the Bible? **The Treasure Study Bible**, a Thompson Topical Study System New International Version children's Bible, attempts to do just that. This small-print, thin-paged thick book makes every effort to assist your children with finding hidden treasure in God's Word.

The book is laid out with an index of the books of the Bible, a daily reading guide called "Daily Treasures from God," the Treasure Map, the Bible, and the Treasure Chest. There are also pages on how to use the Treasure Map and the Treasure Chest.

Suffer Little Children Bible series

Grades 1–5. Shipping extra. Suffer Little Children: Book 1, $18.95. Books 2 and 3, $11.95 each. workbooks for book 2 and 3, $4.95 each. Complete set of all five books, $45.95. Show Me Thy Ways textbook, books 4–6, $20.95 each. Workbooks, $5.95 each. Postpaid. *Reformed Free Publishing Association, 4949 Ivanrest, Grandville, MI 49418. (616) 531-1490. Fax: (616) 531-3033. Web: www.iserv.net/~rfpa.*

One remarkable feature of this curriculum is the extensive amount of map work. Outline maps are provided throughout, with instructions on how to fill in the place names, peoples, and other important items, so the student can "make" the map himself. The section of review questions and true/false questions is also very helpful. The whole program is delightfully easy to use: no shades of *Suffer, Old Teacher* here!

The author's father-in-law was a theologian of renown, and his daughter-in-law appears to be a theologian herself. Each lesson could be viewed as a child-sized commentary on the Bible passage. It all is very solid—no hype or tinsel, and definitely none of this wretched pandering to self-esteem with which so many newer Bible programs are loaded.

NEW!
The Treasure Study Bible

Grades 3–6. Softcover, $19.95. Hardcover, $24.95. Prices postpaid. *B.B. Kirkbride Bible Co, Inc., PO Box 606, Indianapolis, IN 46202. Orders: (800) 428-4385. Inquires: (317) 633-1900. Fax: (317) 633-1444. Email: sales@kirkbride.com. Web: www.kirkbride.com.*

The way the system is designed, you look up one of five hundred topics in the Treasure Map; for example, Angels. Under the title "Angels" is a little additional information: "God's messengers. Does every person have a guardian angel? What do angels do?" Then a verse is listed for where our search begins: Exodus 14:19. They also suggest related topics to look under. When you look up the verse, there is part of a treasure map showing the reference and a new reference to look up or else a picture of a treasure chest if it is the final reference used. If you see the chest, you go to the Treasure Chest section at the end of the book and look up your topic again. It lists all references used and reiterates what you should have learned from these references in regards to the questions from the Treasure Map.

In most of the topics we looked up, everything seemed to work fine; but, there were a couple where the verses and information in the Treasure Chest were inappropriate.

For those who love a good hunt, this would be a great addition to your library. If you prefer your Bible without games, stick with something else.
Barbara Buchanan

NEW!
What's the Bible Like? series

Grades 2–6. $2 each, plus shipping.
Gunderson Publications, PO Box 717, Ferndale, WA 98248.
Phone/fax: (360) 384-1747.
Email: GundersonWV@juno.com.

If you are looking for a short, simple and direct study that teaches about the Old and New Testament books, you can stop looking. These two books provide just enough but not too much to accomplish the task. Each lesson has a section to read an activity to do Bible memory work, and a page to color for each verse. Everything is black and white typed text.

What's the Bible Like?—New Testament takes up a mere 36 pages, the first four containing the title page, table of contents, a listing of the 30 different topics covered in about a page each. The topics are in question form. Learn all the names of the New Testament books. Learn about the four of the men who wrote the New Testament, the books of the New Testament, what an epistle is, or how the Bible is like honey. These are just five of the topics covered in this course's 30 lessons. Bible verses are also here to aid you in memorizing scripture. The lessons contain many important or interesting questions. See if you can answer the questions without looking up the answers. Some are quite tricky.

What's the Bible Like?—Old Testament is laid out much the same as the one for the New Testament, except that several of the lessons are two pages instead of three. This allows some lessons to be covered more thoroughly. Learn how the Bible is different from every other book; why we should be interested in the history of Israel; how the Bible is like a mirror; who wrote Proverbs, Ecclesiastes, and the Song of Solomon; how the Bible is like a hammer; and 25 more topics.

This should work well for either younger children or older children who have had little or no Bible training. These books work great because you can adapt them to fit your own needs and still cover the basics. Highly recommended for anyone in need of some devotional time with the children.
Lynn Smith

CHAPTER 11

Bible Memory and Devotion

The elementary-school years are the best time for children to start memorizing. Memory work just comes naturally to little kids, and why not? *Their* minds aren't cluttered with trying to remember monthly bills, the phone numbers of 100 friends and relatives, house maintenance task schedules, and the names and supposed qualifications of the fifty or so candidates running for political offices in your area at any given time!

Today's little tykes certainly are able to remember hundreds of Bible verses. In the 1800s, it was not uncommon for children to memorize entire Bible chapters, and even whole Bible books, before they turned ten. The point, of course, is not that we prod our children to become show-offs, but that they understand and remember enough of the Bible to make a difference.

During the Vietnam War, the prisoners in one Vietcong POW camp were able to reconstruct the Christmas story by pooling the verses each had memorized as a boy. That's a heartwarming story, but it's also a reminder that some parts of the Bible can bring real comfort when you are deprived of ready access to the Book itself, whether through sickness, blindness, or extreme circumstances such as imprisonment or disaster.

Now, here is my personal Bible memory study tip:

Ignore the verse number!

It takes four times as much effort to remember both chapter and verse as it does to just remember the chapter—but if you know the chapter, you can quickly find the verse.

To do so, of course, you need to have memorized the books of the Bible in order: Genesis, Exodus, Leviticus, Numbers, Deuteronomy, and so on. For a fun family game, try calling out a Bible reference, and see who can look it up the quickest!

What to memorize?

You could just go through the Bible, picking key verses from each book. Or you could follow the topical approach and select key Scriptures that illuminate important truths of the Christian life, like most of the programs below. Some combination of the two is probably most helpful. You don't want your children to grow up quoting verses out of context, but you also want them to quickly remember verses related to essential topics.

I'd suggest the following, for starters:
- The Ten Commandments
- The Lord's Prayer
- Psalm 23
- The Christmas Story
- The Sermon on the Mount

If you manage that much, you've done better than 99 percent of churchgoers today! Feel free also to pick key verses related to important issues in your family life. That's probably the best way to handle the Epistles, for example, which are hard to memorize in their entirety but easy to pluck notable verses from.

NEW!
Audio Memory Bible Songs

Ages 2–12. $12.95 plus shipping.
Audio Memory, 501 Cliff Dr., Newport Beach, CA 92663. (800) 365-SING. Fax: (949) 631-1150. Web: www.audiomemory.com.

NEW!
Bible Memory Challenge

All ages. Laminated Large Flashcards, $10. Audio Cassettes with small flashcards, $7. Small flashcards, $3. 26 multi-colored flashcards with Personal Contest Packet, $5. Many sets available. *Bible Memory Challenge, 5309 Walzem Rd., Suite #177, San Antonio, TX 78218-2124. Inquiries: (210) 657-9136.*

NEW!
Catechism for Young Children with Cartoons

PreK–grade 6. Vol. 1 and II, $1.75 each plus shipping.
Vic Lockman, 233 Rogue River Highway #360, Grants Pass, OR 97527. Fax: (541) 479-3814.

Memory

Audio Memory Bible Songs comes with a sing-along book and cassette tape, all in a handy reclosable plastic case. In the back of the sing-along book, you'll also find cartoon illustrations of the Ten Commandments and poster-style Bible verses. These can be colored in, removed, and placed on your child's wall, if desired.

Eleven songs on one side of the tape teach important Bible facts; accompaniment tracks on the flip side of the tape let you sing alone. Tunes are easy listening or light pop. Vocals are mostly sweet, with a little extra "punch" when needed to convey the personality of a Bible personage.

Some of the lyrics are original paraphrases of Bible texts. Others are taken from *The International Children's Bible.*

Songs include The Rich Man and Lazarus, Ask and You Shall Receive, The Lord's Prayer, No Other Name, The Ten Commandments, The Mote in Your Brother's Eye, Books of the Old Testament, Books of the New Testament, Forgive Others, The Apostles' Creed, and Treasures in Heaven. *Mary Pride*

Memorizing Bible verses is a major goal at our house. Many of the methods or materials I've tried to use for this purpose are too flashy or burdensome to keep my children interested. We have come to find out over the years that the Bible is without doubt the most effective teacher. **Bible Memory Challenge** Ministries has developed a durable, eye-appealing set of memory verse flashcards using the King James Version of the Bible. They are available in several sizes, on laminated, cardstock paper that can withstand the normal stresses of homeschool life (toddler's jelly fingers, etc.). The larger size (10 x 6") is easy to use to quiz our children's memory, and the smaller pocket size cards are excellent to tuck in our purse for use at those unexpected, opportune moments while waiting. The smaller size is also great for children to use to study on their own.

Bible Memory Challenge Ministries also have "The Perfect Ten Audio Cassette" which contains the "Perfect Ten" song and a narration of Exodus 20:1–17 and a collection of Bible passages form the Old and New Testaments. Both their audio cassettes are set to a background of peaceful piano music. Another flashcard/audio set we liked is "God's Word on Women." All passages on these cassettes are straight from the King James Version of the Bible. "God's Word on Women" was designed to help parents "train up" godly young ladies.

If hiding the Word in your child's heart is a major goal for you, then Bible Memory Challenge Ministries have top quality, "no frills" products that can be used over and over to successfully help you train your children in God's Word. *Maryann Turner*

While involved in junior high ministry, my husband and I grew quite concerned over how little these young people, raised in the church, knew of the fundamental doctrines of our faith. We decided that our children would be taught more systematically, just as previous generations were taught. Instruction by catechism is a proven, godly, and valuable method to use in our families.

A catechism consists of questions and answers. This two-volume **Catechism for Young Children with Cartoons** begins by asking "Who made you?" The provided answer is "God." The first few questions teach children that God made all things for His own glory, and that we glorify God by loving and obeying Him. Next, the child learns about the nature and attributes of the Godhead, about the nature and fall of man, about

sin, about grace and salvation, etc. The questions and answers, in a systematic fashion, help children to memorize and retain the important concepts of our Christian faith. Scripture references are given for each question.

Since we use the catechism by asking the questions to our children and teaching them the answers, we didn't find Vic Lockman's cartoon illustrations extremely important. We found ourselves sort of ignoring them, but still other families would likely find them useful, especially as a springboard for discussion.

Mild caution: those who do not believe in infant baptism will probably want to skip questions 129 and 130. While this catechism is written from a Reformed perspective, that was the only potential stumbling block I saw for those who are outside of the Reformed camp. Everything else is pretty basic. *Rebecca Prewett*

Hiding God's Word is a simple and attractive approach to Bible memorization. It consists of a folder with 36 verses (one per week, with one week per quarter for review) attractively printed and illustrated in black and white. The verses are all in KJV. (My pet peeve: curricula that use several versions for memorization! It's bad enough that I have memorized in the KJV, RSV, NASB, and NIV—do I have to wish such a fate on my children? Thankfully this curriculum sticks to one version.)

Children using this will memorize, in order, key verses from Genesis, Exodus, Psalms, John, Romans, and I Corinthians. In addition, they will memorize the names of the books of the Old and New Testaments.

I appreciate this low-key approach. Even though we use something else for our memory work, we are looking forward to displaying these verses in our home. *Rebecca Prewett*

Are you a visual learner? Are you someone who no matter how hard he tries, can't memorize Bible verses merely by hearing them spoken or saying them in his head? This nifty little program might be just the thing. **Heart Hider**s is designed for children to help make Bible memory easy and fun for them and to help even non-readers to be able to decipher the meaning of a verse, but the cards work as great mnemonic devices for adults.

Each verse is coded in rebuses, like an eye for the word "I," or a leather book with a cross on the front, an obvious Bible, for "word." Some of the pictures are more like charades, acting out the word or idea. Why is that guy pushing against the wall? That little picture represents the word "against." Now that I have seen the translation, I will know to say "against" when I see that picture.

Now, how about a show of hands: How many of you have heard your preacher say, "The word for sin in this verse comes from an archery term meaning to miss the mark . . . ?" If so, you can recognize the picture of a target with arrows scattered all over representing a really poor showing with the bow to be a representation of the word "sin."

Put this all together and you have a composite picture of Psalm 119:11, "I have hidden your word in my heart that I might not sin against you." All you have to do is to remember the picture, and you have the verse.

If you finish Heart Hiders Volume 1, you will have mastered 42 passages totalling 68 verses. All you really need is the inexpensive volume itself. But for extra reinforcement for little learners, there's a coloring book with most of the verses. Older learners can use the flash cards for "on the road" drill and practice. This program is an easy and entertaining way to put God's Word into your heart. *Bill Pride*

Covenant Home Hiding God's Word

Grades K–3. Only available with their kindergarten Bible module, which also includes Come, Ye Children; quarterly exam; a course blueprint; and a schedule and exams. Total cost is $62, plus shipping. *Covenant Home Curriculum, 17800 W. Capitol Dr., Brookfield, WI 53045. (414)781-2171. Fax: (414)781-0589. Email: educate@covenanthome.com. Web: covenanthome.com.*

NEW!
Heart Hiders

Grades 1–adult. Heart Hiders Volume I, $9.95. Heart Hiders Coloring Book, $6.95. Heart Hiders Flash Cards, $7.95. Value pack of all three, $21.95.
Off the Curb Publishing, 306-N West El Norte Pkwy Suite 352, Escondido, CA 92026. Orders: (800) 294-2397. Fax: (760) 738-6038. Web: www.hearthiders.com.

NEW!
Illustrated Bible Chapters

Ages 3–10. Psalms 23, $10.95. All others, $12.95. Free brochure.
Thy Word Creations, Route 76, Box 28, Glenville, WV 26351. (800)347-WORD. Fax: (304) 462-5589.

Each **Illustrated Bible Chapter** comes with an oversized soft cover book and cassette tape. The child listens to the tape while following along in the book, turning the page each time he hears a bell ring. Verses are written in large, bold print and illustrations are black and white line drawings, suitable for coloring.

I especially enjoyed Psalms 23. First, there was a song that children can learn to sing. Then the Psalm was read out of the KJV in the cutest, clearest little child's voice! After that, there was the word-for-word song to learn. The songs are timeless and peaceful; nothing trendy and disturbing here. Children will love hearing other children learn and sing.

Psalm 23, the Lord's Prayer, The Ten Commandments, The Beatitudes, the temptations of Jesus, and Isaiah 53 are available in the KJV. I Corinthians 13, Psalm 91, and Psalm 139 are available in the NKJV.

The books also contain the words and music to the songs, teaching guidelines, and suggestions for further activities. What a beautiful way for children to hide God's Word in their hearts! *Rebecca Prewett*

Memlok Bible Memory System

All ages. $49. Shipping extra.
Memlok Bible Memory System. 420 E. Montwood Ave., La Habra, CA 90631-7411. (800) 373-1947. Fax: (714) 738-0949. Email: memlok@pacbell.net. Web: www.memlok.com.

Memlok is an exciting new approach to topical Bible memorization, based on flash cards with pictures symbolizing the first key words of each verse. For example, the front of the card might say, "SOVEREIGNTY. John 1:22." Under this is a picture of an outline "F" with an eye in it. When you turn over the card, you find the verse is, "If I want him to remain until I come, what is that to you? You follow Me!"

As opposed to other "visual" systems, Memlok does not try to present an entire verse in pictures. This means less strain on your brain (in my opinion), and avoids the problem of associating Bible teaching with silly mental images. You are asked to spend only five minutes a day, five days a week, learning one new verse a week. The author calls this a "long range — low pressure" system. By the end, you will have memorized verses from every New Testament chapter, Old Testament book, and every chapter of the book of Proverbs. Memlok is the only topical system I know about that has such complete Bible coverage.

You select your own verses from 48 topics totaling 700 verses. Each topic has an illustrated summary card, with a kooky sentence made up of the beginning illustrations from each of the memory verses. All the cards and summary cards are included in the binder, in pre-perfed pages of 12 cards per page. Also included are instructions in how to use Memlok, a sample Covenant of Accountability to use with a memory partner, a completion record, memory tips, a complete alphabetical and topical index of all the verses, plastic Monthly Cardholders for all the cards you are reviewing, and of course the cards themselves! The cards are printed on sturdy colored cardstock, professionally illustrated, and look really sharp.

I am really impressed with Memlok. The packaging is really great, and the cards are kid-appealing. Available in KJV, NKJ, NIV, and NASB versions. Recommended. *Mary Pride*

NEW!
Memlok Say the Books!

All ages. $8. Add $2 shipping (15% Canada, 10% overseas surface).
Memlok Bible Memory System. 420 E. Montwood Ave., La Habra, CA 90631-7411. (800) 373-1947. Fax: (714) 738-0949. Email: memlok@pacbell.net. Web: www.memlok.com.

Memlok's newest product addition is **Say the Books!** In the Memlok way you can learn to say all 66 books of the Bible in order. This book offers two methods for learning the books. One is the picture method, one picture for each book with a story to go with it. The other method is to travel through the Old Testament Library, one room for each book and the New Testament House.

I'm a left-brain thinker and the house was much easier for me to follow than the pictures. The pictures are cute, though the story can stretch a little farther than I can. When the "dew toe" was going to "run on me" for Deuteronomy, I gave up.

If you like the Memlok system this is a good way to learn an important subject. *Terri Cannon*

For those who want the world's most inexpensive, bare-bones Bible memory approach, Visual Education's **Selected Bible Verses** flash card set is 1,000 cards with verses from the KJV in the order they appear in the Bible (NIV available soon). Each card has book, chapter, and verse number on the front, as well as the topical category, and the verse itself on the back. You also get a pamphlet with study hints and verses by category. The verses are well-chosen; this is a fine resource for parents who believe in teaching key verses from each Bible book. It works equally well as a mini Biblical theology on cards. Work through the cards to get an overview of all the major Bible doctrines. *Mary Pride*

Can your child give a brief summary of the book of Ezra? Can you? Here is a simple program designed to help you remember the theme of each book of the Bible. Volume I is currently available and covers Genesis through the Psalms.

The 44-page **Sing Through the Bible** song book has an overview, a selected passage and a short song for each book of the Bible. The program also includes two tapes. The first one is "The Songs." Using side one, the student learns the songs with someone singing along. Side two is just the music without the singing. Your children can perform for family devotions or for your homeschool group. The second cassette, "The Bible," contains a narration of the overview, the passage and the song.

Most of the songs are catchy and easy to remember. A few of the songs seemed unusual. I felt funny about singing about the children of Israel's disobedience to a swing tune. *Terri Cannon*

Devotion

Now those of you who have never sung the Psalms at home can give it a real shot! The brand-new **Psalm Tune Tape Set** (four tapes) includes all 425 selections from **The Book of Psalms for Singing** (clothbound edition.) Each selection is played through once with all four parts together, emphasizing the melody. Every selection is announced in order. No singing. This sure beats trying to sight-read your way through those old tunes! (Remember, many Psalter tunes are the exact same hymn tunes you sing every Sunday.) Get a set today and warm up your family devotions! Other Psalm tapes available, with *a cappella* singing.

Also, Crown & Covenant now has the Psalm tunes on CD. This makes it even easier to sing along, because instead of fast-forwarding to the (hopefully) correct spot you can now jump directly there. *Mary Pride*

John Bunyan's all-time bestseller *Pilgrim's Progress* has got to be the greatest character-building book of all time. Based on Bunyan's book, **Dangerous Journey** features the truly excellent, detailed illustrations of Alan Parry and excellent narration besides. The art fits the old-fashioned flavor of Bunyan's book, and the length of the series give the narrator plenty of time to cover much of Bunyan's best ground.

Selected Bible Verses
Grades 5–adult. $10.95 plus $2.50 shipping.
Visual Education, 581 W. Leffel Lane, Springfield, OH 45501. Orders: (800) 243-7070. Inquiries: (937) 325-5503. Fax: (937) 324-5697.
Web: www.vis-ed.com.

NEW!
Sing Through the Bible Volume I: Genesis through Psalms
All ages. Tapes, $4 each.
The Homeschool Advantage, 311 S. 12th St., Griffin, GA 30224-4116. (770) 228-9053.

UPDATED!
Book of Psalms for Singing
All ages. Book, $13. Psalm Tune Tape Set, $27. Psalm Tune 5-CD set, $37. Shipping extra.
Crown & Covenant Publications, 7408 Penn Ave., Pittsburgh, PA 15208-2531. (412) 241-0436. Fax: (412) 731-8861. Email: Psalms4U@aol.com. Web: www.psalms4u.com.

Dangerous Journey
Ages 6–12. $19.99 for one video, teacher's guide, and Scripture guide. Hardbound color storybook, $19.99. Shipping, $3.95 for one or $4.95 for both.
Vision Video, PO Box 540, Worcester, PA 19490. Orders: (800) 523-0226. Fax: (610) 584-4610. Email: visionvide@aol.com. Web: www.gatewayfilms.com.

Instead of animation, the producers used camera angles and special effects to move the story along. I had worried that our children would be bored because of the lack of animation, but what we lost in animation was more than made up for by the vividness of the illustrations. Warning: the monsters in this series do look monstrous. (Not that it bothers our crowd!)

NEW!
Glory and Grace

All ages. $5.95 plus $3 shipping. *Homeschooling Basics Series, Tabletop Academy Press, R.R. 1 Box 114, Blue Mound, IL 62513. (217)692-2849. Email: dcgaskins@juno.com.*

NEW!
Lord, Teach Us To Pray

All ages. $10 plus shipping. *Mark and Kathi Wilson, PO Box 583, Bowmansville, PA 17507-0583. (717) 445-6151. Email: Wils@epix.net.*

NEW!
Memlok Devotional Tools

All ages. $4. Shipping extra. *Memlok Bible Memory System. 420 E. Montwood Ave., La Habra, CA 90631-7411. (800) 373-1947. Fax: (714) 738-0949. Email: memlok@pacbell.net. Web: www.memlok.com.*

The new version of *Dangerous Journey* includes nine programs on two full-color VHS videotapes, plus a *Dangerous Journey* 128-page color story book, a teacher's guide, and a Scripture guide, all in a gift pack. Tape 1 includes the Slough of Despond, the Interpreter's House, the Hill Difficulty, the fight with Apollyon, and the Valley of the Shadow of Death. Tape 2 takes you to Vanity Fair, Doubting Castle, the Dark River, and the story of Christiana. A good deal, especially since they've dropped the price $40 (it used to be $59.95). *Mary Pride*

The first chapter alone is worth the price of this booklet! In **Glory and Grace**, authors Randall and Marilyn Kok write that we need to get the focus off of lists of rules ("do this") and lists of character traits ("be this") and onto the task of knowing God. As Christ Himself teaches, obedience flows out of love.

Specific ideas for helping your kids know God better are the focus of the rest of the book. Using the inductive Bible study method presented here, all you need are a Bible, a notebook, and a dictionary. Instructions and examples are provided for pre-writers, writers, and older teens.

The authors give plenty of examples of their own children's work in case you need further illustration. I appreciate their flexible attitude as they recognize that every family's study will be different—not a duplicate of what the Kok children have done.

One chapter deals with how to memorize (and review!) passages of Scripture. The appendix offers suggestions for verses to begin with as well as ways to extend your study into other subject areas (art, crafts, and written compositions). An inspiring little book! *Renee Mathis*

When we think about teaching our children to pray, we remember the disciples asked Jesus to teach them to pray. With this in mind, we start with the Lord's Prayer, just as Kathi Wilson does in her reprint of a book by Elisabeth Scovil, *Prayers for Girls*. Mrs. Wilson retitled the book **Lord, Teach Us To Pray** to make the intent more clear. This small book, only 88 prayers in all, would be a wonderful addition to anyone's collection. It is useful for adults as well as for instructing children on how to pray. These prayers are short enough to be memorized, just as we have memorized the Lord's Prayer. Some of the topics: Against Gossip, Against Worry, For Friendliness, For Knowledge of Self and Others. Don't expect to read this book straight through, but use it in your daily prayer life! *Barbara Buchanan*

Now that we've whetted your appetite for devotional activities, take a look at a year-round devotional aid: **Devotional Tools from Memlok**. This set of reproducible cardstock sheets (make as many copies as you need for your family!) includes seven "tools" to transform your family devotional time. The "Forgiveness" sheet takes you through a list of questions, with accompanying Scriptures, to help you free yourself from a bitter spirit. The "Adoration" sheet lists 100 descriptions of God, along with Bible citations and pictures from those topics in the Memlok Bible Memory system. The "Intercession" sheet provides a way to organize your prayer list. "My Own Requests" helps you keep track of personal and family prayer requests. "The Daily Journal" helps you focus your Christian growth. "Meditation" helps you pull more out of the memory verse of the week. "Ambassador Prayer" organizes your prayers for the salvation of others, with specific suggestions for shared activities as well! A sheet of ministry ideas helps you use the tools effectively, as much or as little as you can manage. Nifty! *Mary Pride*

CHAPTER 12

Bible Audio & Video

Hear it. See it. Dramatize it. Live it! This is the chapter for resources that make the Bible come to life . . . with sound effects and living color!

Audio

Dramatizing the Bible is always a difficult task, similar to preaching a sermon. The dramatist has to decide what points he wants to make, how he thinks the characters sound, and what their motivations are. Plus he has to accurately recreate the entire cultural milieu of a different millennium, right down to the sound effects.

The Bible in Living Sound makes a respectable, but not perfect, effort to meet all these goals. The authors take some liberties with the biblical text in order to present their view of what *might* have happened. For example, the serpent in the Garden of Eden says he ate of the fruit of the tree of knowledge of good and evil . . . and that's why he could talk. Noah's ark is depicted as a favorite vacation spot for the skeptics of his day, where they gathered to laugh at Noah's preaching and to view his huge boat. Paul and his disciples chat about why Paul is writing various letters to the churches. I am not saying the interpretations presented on the tapes are necessarily wrong—in fact, many of them are quite plausible—just that they aren't spelled out anywhere in the Bible.

The tapes skip over some of the more violent Bible events, such as Samson's wife and father being burned alive by vengeful Philistines. There are also the usual slip-ups, almost inevitable with a project of this size, such as Samson's parents calling the "man of God" who visited them an "angel" before he revealed that he was one.

Dramatically, this series is fascinating. While I did not always agree with the authors' interpretation of the stories behind the Bible events, the way they were presented does lead you to ponder them more deeply. You find yourself asking questions such as, "Did huge crowds come to hear Noah? Why didn't they believe him?" The awesomeness of the Flood, and the folly

The Bible in Living Sound

Collector's Club: First CD, $4.99; or first two cassettes, $3.99. Each month after that: next CD, $7.95; or tape, $6.95. Any 10 CDs, $59.50. Any 10 cassettes, $49.50. Entire series (75 CDs or cassettes in 8 CD wallets or cassette albums): CDs, $446.25; Cassettes, $371.25. Entire Old Testament (40 CDs or cassettes in 4 CD wallets or cassette albums): CDs, 238; Cassettes, $198. Life of Jesus (20 CDs or cassettes in 2 CD wallets or cassette albums): CDs, $119; Cassettes, $99. Paul & Apostles (15 CDs or cassettes in 2 CD wallets or cassette albums): CDs, $89.25; Cassettes, $74.25. Workbooks, $6.95 each. All prices are postpaid.
Bible in Living Sound, PO Box 234, Nordland, WA 98358-0234. (800) 634-0234, ext. 8699. Fax: (360) 385-1124. Email: bls@olympus.net. Web: www.BibleInLivingSound.org.

Workbooks are available to accompany the Old Testament, Life of Jesus, and Paul series. These are pretty standard fare, with the usual crossword puzzles and other busywork.

NEW!
A Visit With Mrs. G: Adam and Eve

Ages 4–104. Each tape, $8 plus shipping.

A Visit with Mrs. G. Ministries Inc., PO Box 150, Station O, Toronto, Ontario, Canada M4A 2M8. (416) 755-5918. Fax: (416) 423-3895.

The World's Greatest Stories from the World's Greatest Book series

Ages 5–adult. $6.95 each add $1.50 shipping.

World's Greatest Stories, PO Box 711, Monroe, CT 06468. (888) STORIES. (203) 459-4554. Fax: (203) 459-0807. Email: georgesarris@juno.com. Web: www.greateststories.com.

Storyteller George Sarris has a Bachelor of Science degree in Speech from Northwestern University and the Master of Divinity from Gordon-Conwell

of those who "almost" believed, come vividly alive—to name just one example.

If you sign up for the cassette- or CD-of-the-month offer, your first two tapes or first CD will be episodes from the Life of Christ.

You can also purchase these tapes or CDs as series. That way, they come with nice albums and shipping is free.

Our advice: listen to these tapes or CDs the first time along with your children, to ensure they understand which parts are straight from the Bible and which are speculation or interpretation. Handled in this way, The Bible in Living Sound is sure to spark much lively discussion and inspire deeper Bible study! *Mary Pride*

Who is **Mrs. G**? She is Dr. Kitty Anna Griffiths, who tells Bible stories on the "Through the Bible Story by Story" series of tapes and also has a weekly radio program broadcast throughout the world. She is an excellent, vivid storyteller. I found myself wishing I could adopt her as an extra grandmother for my children.

While Mrs. G provides details in her stories that make them "come alive," she does not embellish the Scripture. My nine-year-old, a stickler for detail, listens to her radio program early Saturday mornings and ensures me that her stories are quite accurate. (I'm too sleepy at that time to be sure.)

The **Adam and Eve** tape tells the story of God's creation, what was created on each day, how His beautiful creation was spoiled by sin, the story of Cain and Abel, and God's plan of redemption. An accompanying book is available for each tape in the series, but I have not seen a copy. The tapes can be ordered singly, as part of a Cassette-a-Month Club, or in series at reduced prices. *Rebecca Prewett*

These are the best Bible-narration tapes I have ever heard. **The World's Greatest Stories from the World's Greatest Book** series includes five tapes: *Beginnings, Joshua & Esther, The Prophets, Joseph & his Brothers* and *The Life of Christ* narrated word by word from the New International Version and King James Version translations of the Bible. What makes these tapes different is the terrific interpretation of the characters and setting by actor George W. Sarris. Nebuchadnezzar *sounds* like a tough Middle-Eastern emperor. His descendant Belshazzar, frightened by the writing on the wall, mumbles his fears in an alcohol-slurred voice (totally accurate, since he had been drinking heavily all day). The Bible characters cry, or threaten, or do whatever they do with amazing realism. But more than this, even the strictly descriptive portions are read in a way that makes them come to life. Mr. Sarris can make even the words, "Nebuchadnezzar, king of Babylon," describe the man's personality. Plus the well-chosen special effects and music do a great job of helping us "see" how it was. And the production quality and packaging are first-class.

You probably realize by now that I'm really tough on Bible resources when it comes to accuracy. So tough, in fact, that I haven't even bothered to include several series of Bible tapes that I went to the trouble of listening to, since they consistently made obvious mistakes. These tapes are different. They're really great. And I'm not the only one who thinks so. Bill Gothard's Institute in Basic Youth Conflicts ordered 14,000 of these tapes in the first two years after they were published!

The *Prophets* tape has these stories: The Burning Fiery Furnace, The Handwriting on the Wall, Daniel in the Lions' Den, Elijah and the Prophets of Baal, and The Prophecy of Jonah. The *Life of Christ* tape includes The Real Story of Christmas, The Baptism and Temptation of Jesus, The Healing of the Blind Man, Things Jesus Said and Did, and The Real Story of Easter.

If you're not a Christian, or have always thought of the Bible as a boring book, these tapes will revolutionize your thinking. If you just want to turn your children on to Bible study, or want to learn how to read the Bible in a way that makes the text jump up and turn cartwheels, these tapes will do it for you. Get them today! *Mary Pride*

A winner many times of our *Practical Homeschooling* Reader Award in the Educational Audiocassette category, **Your Story Hour** is a name you can trust for excellent Bible stories, history and biography dramatizations, and character-building tales. Over the years these folks have built up an impressive library of cassette albums. Here's what's available now:

- **First, the freebie.** Send for Your Story Hour's Bible lessons, complete the initial set of four they send you, return them, and you'll get one free New Testament cassette plus four more lessons. Keep this up at the rate of one Bible lesson per week for a year, and you'll end up with the entire series of New Testament story tapes in a year. When you've finished all the lessons, they'll send you a handy album to keep the tapes in, too. The only requirement is that the person doing the lessons be age 9 or older.
- **Bible Story Albums.** Four 12-cassette albums of dramatized Old Testament history, and one of New Testament history. The New Testament album is identical with the tapes you can get free for completing the Bible lessons.
- **U.S and European History Albums.** Two 12-cassette albums with dramatized biographies of famous people: explorers, inventors, statesmen, scientists, writers, preachers, and more.
- **True Life Adventures.** Four 12-cassette volumes of character-building fictional stories.
- **Great New Stories.** Two six-cassette albums with a mix of fictional stories and dramatized biographies. No overlap with the history albums.
- **Acts of the Apostles.** A brand-new 8-cassette album with dramatized stories from the book of Acts.

Each cassette is a full hour long, so you can see the price per tape is pretty low. *Mary Pride*

Video

"Wow!" That was my reaction after watching every single one of the **Animated Stories from the Bible** and **Animated Stories from the New Testament** videos. They are beautiful! Inspiring! Awesome! Movie quality!

Produced by the man who brought us the animated movie *The Swan Princess*, these videos make a serious effort to present Bible stories accurately. Some characters are "fleshed out" more than you'll find in the Bible, but

NEW!
Your Story Hour

Ages 4 and up. New Testament, 13 tapes, 1 free for each 4 Bible quizzes completed. Other 12-tape albums, $43.50 each. Great New Stories, volume 1 & 11 (6 tapes each), $21.50 each. Acts of the Apostles (8 tapes), $28.50. Ask for 10% homeschool discount. Shipping extra.
Your Story Hour, PO Box 15, Berrien Springs, MI 49103. (800) 987-7879. Inquiries: (616) 471-3701. Fax: (616) 471-4661. Email: ysh@aol.com. Web: www.yourstoryhour.com.

NEW!
Animated Stories from the Bible
Animated Stories from the New Testament

Ages 4–13. $29.95 each. Library of tapes, $239.40 (any 12 videos from one series including 12 workbooks.) Additional workbooks $4.50 each. Shipping extra.
Nest Entertainment, 6100 Colwell Blvd., Irving, TX 75039-9833. (800) 447-5958. Fax: (972) 402-7182. Web: www.nest-ent.com. Sold direct through independent home distributors and independent TV networks, or by calling (800) 447-5958.

The Old Testament series currently includes the following titles: *Abraham and Isaac, Joseph in Egypt, Joseph's Reunion, Moses, Ruth, Samuel, David and Goliath, Solomon, Elijah, Elisha, Daniel,* and *Esther.*

The New Testament series currently includes: *The King is Born, John the Baptist, Forgive Us Our Debts, Bread from Heaven (feeding the 5,000), The Kingdom of Heaven, Treasures in Heaven, The Prodigal Son, The Miracles of Jesus, The Greatest is the Least, The Good Samaritan, The Righteous Judge, Jesus–the Son of God, He is Risen, Saul of Tarsus,* and *The Ministry of Paul.*

NEW!
In the Beginning

Ages 2–adult. Each video, $11.99. Set of all 25, $249.99. Study guide, $12.99. Shipping extra. Available in English and Spanish.
CCC of America, 8080 Tristar Drive, Suite 106, Irving, TX 75063. Orders: (800) 935-2222. Inquiries: (972) 929-3360. Fax: (972) 929-3366.

the character interpretations are realistic for people of the times. The boy who shared his loaves and fishes, for example, is presented as a "street rat" type—which may well have been true, as otherwise why weren't his parents mentioned? The apostles' and prophets' appearance and personalities are in tune with the way they are portrayed in the Bible and in church tradition. Peter is bluff and impetuous; Elijah is strong and hairy; Gehazi is crafty and greedy. (If you don't know who Gehazi is, maybe you need the *Elisha* video!)

Meticulously researched, the backgrounds and costumes are historically accurate. Some nitty-gritty realism has been sacrificed to make these acceptable modern kiddie cartoons: the scenery has that lush "movie" look, and bloody scenes take place off camera, are only hinted at, or are skipped over altogether. You won't see the confrontation between Elisha and the mocking youths, for example. (You really *need* to get that video!) However, the fact that people had to be strong, and sometimes suffer and die for their faith, certainly comes through. Miracles, angels, and the devil are shown to be real. It is clearly taught that Jesus is the Son of God.

Each video comes with a reproducible workbook designed to reinforce material presented in the video. Nest Entertainment allows you to photocopy the pages for your own family's use. The workbooks for the New Testament series are divided into two parts. "Level 1," for preschool through first grade, is coloring pages, dot-to-dot, and other simple exercises based on the video. "Level 2" exercises come in three levels of difficulty—easy, intermediate, and difficult—and are intended for 8- to 10-year-olds, though really they can be used by any child or adult who reads well. Workbooks for the Old Testament series contain "Level 2"-type exercises only. All workbooks come with answer keys and Certificates of Achievement in the back.

These inspiring videos will surely motivate deeper love for God . . . and deeper Bible study as well! Highly recommended. *Mary Pride*

In the Beginning is a series of 25 animated videos covering much of Old Testament history (with the notable exception of the book of Judges), animated under the direction of the great Japanese artist Osamu Tezuka, who some of us may remember as the creator of Astroboy and other TV cartoon series. Mr Tezuka is considered the foremost animator of all time by those who are fans of Japanese-style "manga" illustration. His work is known for its charm, detail, and stunning effects.

It's impossible in a series of this type to tell the story in traditional video style without adding some scenes and words that aren't in the Bible itself.

For that reason, a parent or knowledgeable older child ought to watch the series along with the younger children and point out where the video story "adds to" or diverges from the biblical account.

The accompanying study guide begs the question of whether the Bible stories are historical or not. The author's sympathies appear to be with those who hold that only parts of some of the stories really happened. However, in order not to offend the conservative Christian parents who are the most likely market for this series, he does acknowledge that their point of view exists. When it comes to pointing out the moral and spiritual *lessons* of the stories, however, the guide is surprisingly good. The author doesn't flinch from pointing out the parallels between Pharaoh's "throw the boy Hebrew babies into the Nile" and modern government attempts at population control, for example. All the "tough" themes of the Bible stories are brought out and dealt with, including how to present them to children, even when these themes don't appear on the videos themselves.

Because Osamu Tezuka designed the stories as well as the art, these videos don't have any particular denominational "bent." He was trying to tell the Bible stories in as effective a visual manner as possible, not to make any specific doctrinal points. The result is an artistic masterpiece that children and adults will *enjoy* watching again and again, without the smarmy puppets, time-transporting kiddies, and other banalities of most American-produced series.

BOTTOM LINE: although it may not be perfect, if you know the Bible well enough to distinguish between the facts on these videos and the fiction added to fill out the story, this is a wonderful animated Bible video series. *Mary Pride*

"Tell us a story . . . a true story!"

George W. Sarris answers this cry in a 24-minute video entitled **The Real Story of Easter.** Standing in a church sanctuary, armed only with a scarf, Sarris tells the story of Easter verbatim from the Gospel of John. His facial expressions and actions, combined with creative use of the one prop, make the pertinent characters come to life before your very eyes. The scarf, wrapped around his neck, brings out Pilate; with one end draped over his shoulder, it produces the angry Jewish leaders; covering his head, it makes Mary Magdalene plainly visible. This video is an example of the art of storytelling at its finest being used to share one of the greatest of all stories.

In a case such as this, the storyteller portrays the characters as he sees them. As a result, there may be instances where Sarris depicts a character differently from the way you have always envisioned him or her. Those who only accept the King James version of the Bible will also want to note that Sarris speaks from the New International Version. Other than these two things, I see no room for complaint. This is excellent. *Tammy Cardwell*

Videos in this series are: *Adam and Eve, Noah's Ark, The Tower of Babel, Abraham the Forefather, Sodom and Gomorrah, Isaac and Ishmael, Abraham's Sacrifice, Joseph in Bondage, Joseph's Triumph, Moses the Egyptian, The Burning Bush, Moses and Pharoah, The Exodus, The Ten Commandments, The Golden Calf, Journey to the Promised Land, The Fall of Jericho, One King for Israel, David and Goliath, King David, The Wisdom of Solomon, The Exile of Israel, Release from Babylon, Prophets in the Desert,* and *The Birth of Jesus.*

NEW!
The Real Story of Easter

All Ages. $9.95 plus $2.25 shipping. *World's Greatest Stories, PO Box 711, Monroe, CT 06468. (888) STORIES. (203) 459-4554. Fax: (203) 459-0807. Email: georgesarris@juno.com. Web: www.greateststories.com.*

CHAPTER 13

Bible Teaching Aids

Timelines. Atlases. Dictionaries. Charts. Think of the resources in this chapter as useful background information for your actual Bible studies.

Charts & Timelines

The Adam and Eve Family Tree is a colorful wall poster that shows who was related to whom and what they were up to for all of Bible history until Christ, plus giving selected Scripture references for further study. Talk about genealogical research! The Chart is accurate and easy to use, and will provide hours of educational browsing for any Bible lover. And it's so handy to have a *laminated* chart which the little folks can't shred before they're old enough to appreciate it!

The Chart comes in both laminated and plain paper styles, both colorful and very beautiful. You can also get a tape that explains how to use it. *Mary Pride*

Reader Mrs. Paul Steigerwald from La Pryor, Texas wrote, "I thought you might like to know about a laminated Bible time line that I purchased for $5.95." Yes, indeed, I was interested!

The **Bible Overview Chart** is full-color, 25½ x 11", printed on card stock and laminated on both sides. It folds to 8½ x 11" so you can carry it with your Bible for ready reference. It provides a bird's-eye view of the entire Bible, with a ton of information in an easy-to-follow format. For each book, the chart has a mini-map above the time line, color-keyed to the time line itself. The name of the Bible book is on the time line, with its general content, chapter numbers, chapter content, special map references, significant events highlighted, book's author, place of writing, and more! This is not all jumbled together, but presented visually in a way that a seven-year-old can understand. At this price, almost everyone can afford this wonderful resource. *Mary Pride*

Adam and Eve Family Tree Wall Chart

Laminated chart(38 x 25") & one tape, $30. Cassette tapes (60 minutes each), $10. Study Booklet, $10. Shipping included.
Good Things Company, Drawer 'N', Norman, OK 73070-7013.
(888) 482-6552.

The Bible Overview Chart

Grades 1–12. $5.95. Larger version available for $12.95. Shipping extra.
Heritage Products, Inc., PO Box 38, Wheeling, IL 60090. (800) 346-2395. Fax: (847) 419-8831.

Books of the Holy Bible charts

Grades 1–12. Small chart (8 x 10" full-color and laminated) $6, Small chart in black-and-white outline without book titles $2, Large chart (20 x 24" full-color laminated) $12, Large in black-and-white outline without book titles $4. Shipping $3, free on orders over $14.
*Good Things Company, Drawer 'N', Norman, OK 73070-7013.
(888) 482-6552.*

NEW!
Illustrated Bible Timeline

Grades 3–12. $22.95 plus shipping.
*CLH Publications, 9235 Kingsridge Dr., Temple Terrace, FL 33637.
(813) 985-5046.
Email: crystalhunter@juno.com.*

NEW!
The Simplified Bible Time Line

Grades 2–6. $9.99. Shipping extra.
*Standard Publishing, 8121 Hamilton Ave., Cincinnati, OH 45231. (800) 543-1353. Fax: (513) 931-0904.
Email: standardpub@attmail.com.
Web: www.standardpub.com.*

NEW!
Standard Bible Time Line

Grades 4–8. $10.99. Shipping extra.
*Standard Publishing, 8121 Hamilton Ave., Cincinnati, OH 45231. (800) 543-1353. Fax: (513) 931-0904.
Email: standardpub@attmail.com.
Web: www.standardpub.com.*

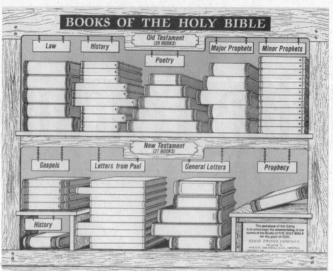

Good Things Company's **Books of the Holy Bible** poster is a very useful visual tool that shows the books of the Bible stacked on two shelves, one for the Old Testament and one for the New. Above each stack of books is a label, like Law or History or Minor Prophets. The books are in the order of the Bible. We started off our little ones with this chart by reading it, and letting the ones who can talk repeat each name after us. "Genesis." "Gen'sith." "Exodus." "Ex'dith." "Leviticus." "Cus." Great stuff! In no time at all, they are getting the idea. You can also get plain paper outlines of this same chart with the book titles left out, for your youngsters to fill in. Very simple, well-organized way to understand how the whole Bible fits together and get used to the names of Bible books. *Mary Pride*

The **Illustrated Bible Timeline** stretches to 10 inches high by 28 feet long when the 15 separate full-color panels are all displayed. This timeline covers from Creation to the Second Coming of Christ, with an emphasis on Bible characters (85 shown on the timeline) and Bible books (all O.T. prophets shown in chronological order). The very simple format emphasizes the plan of redemption, while Bible characters are shown smiling or frowning depending on whether they were good or evil. Ultra-simple format makes this the easiest timeline to actually learn from. Too bad it only comes in a "classroom" size and price! *Mary Pride*

The **Simplified Bible Time Line** is a set of four colorful picture charts designed for teaching children from grades 2–6. These depict Bible events (with associated symbols), Bible books, and events in surrounding cultures, in chronological order. Accompanying teaching instructions explain how to make the most of the time line. Our only quibble: why in the world are Buddha and Confucius mentioned on this time line? They may be important historical figures, but have nothing to do with Bible events. *Mary Pride*

Standard's regular **Bible Time Line** is one large, colorful wall chart covering the time period from creation to A.D. 100. Suitable for use with preteens through adults, it contains more information than the simplified time line reviewed above and uses a different format. Bible Time Line lists main events and eras across the top, and Bible books, major people, and events vertically underneath. Once again Buddha and Confucius make an appearance, but since the section in which they appear has a black background you can easily remove them if desired with a smidgen of black Magic Marker. *Mary Pride*

Reference Books

This gorgeous hardbound book gives you more than double for your money. First, **The Amazing Expedition Bible** is a chronological retelling of 60 major Bible stories. Second, its historical timelines (featured at the top of each new "Bible Event" chapter) and its historical sidebars tell you what was going on when in the Bible . . . *and* in other parts of the world at the same time. These background "fun facts" and features cover the areas of science, technology, and growth; daily life; history and politics; literature and theater; religion, philosophy, and learning; visual arts; and music. Plus interest-sparking "Bible Mysteries" and "History Mysteries" (example: "Which Bible queen had a heavenly name? Answer: Esther. Her name means 'star'"), full-color illustrations on *every* page, and more!

Coming from Baker Book House, you expect *The Amazing Expedition Bible* to reflect traditional Protestant views of religion and biblical chronology, which it does. Gods and goddesses, where mentioned, are always referred to as *"false* gods," just to make sure there's no confusion. Creation and the Flood are treated as historical events in a "young earth" chronology, Jesus is definitely the Son of God, and the Bible is inerrant and inspired. Just what most Christian parents expect, and not enough Christian publishers deliver.

The high visual appeal and large print makes this a book you can read to your littlest ones, and that preteens will want to browse on their own. A real standout. *Mary Pride*

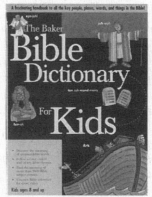

This most excellent, colorful, hardbound handbook is just the sort of present every Christian kid should get this Christmas. With easy-reading definitions for each person/place/concept, easy-reading pronunciations for each word that don't include any strange symbols or diacritical marks, color illustrations on every page, Bible references for each entry appearing in the margin next to it, highlighted key themes, full-color mini-maps right next to important place-name entries that pinpoint that place, color-coded tab locators to help you quickly zero in on the beginning letter of an entry, cross-references to other related entries, and straightforward definitions you can trust, it's hard to see how they could have made **The Baker Bible Dictionary for Kids** any better! Over 2,000 entries in all; 503 pages, from *Aaron* to *Zuzites*. Also recommended for adults who have trouble remembering who those Zuzites were. *Mary Pride*

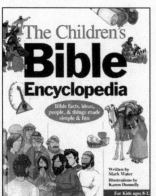

Baker's **Children's Bible Encyclopedia: The Bible Made Simple and Fun** is a 320-page hardcover book. This encyclopedia covers a multitude of topics such as:

- Angels: God's messengers
- Bible Translations
- End of the World
- Hobbies and Games
- Suffering
- Work

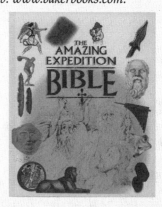

Each topic covers one page, with some topics being broken down into subtopics. For example, information pertaining to Jesus is covered in 23 subtopics.

Mark Water had good intentions in writing *The Children's Bible Encyclopedia*. In trying to simplify various topics from the Bible, Mr. Water left out some important ideas. He also added details that were not found in the Bible, but were based on other information gained about that time period. For example, in the section on Hobbies and Games, it is mentioned that "archaeologists have found squares scratched on the pavements, as if for hopscotch." The Bible does not mention hopscotch; this is Mr. Water's way of making the Bible more fun for children.

If you intend to use this encyclopedia in the classroom, it may not answer most of your questions. I have a smaller children's dictionary that gives much better information in two to four sentences than what Mr. Water gives in an entire page. Conclusion: this colorful book is best used to motivate your children's interest in Bible topics, rather than for in-depth curriculum instruction. *Barbara Buchanan*

NEW!
Victor Journey Through the Bible

Grades 3–adult. $34.99 plus shipping.
Veritas Press, 1250 Belle Meade Dr., Lancaster, PA 17601. (800) 922-5082. Inquiries: (717) 397-5082. Fax: (717) 397-6544. Email: Veritasprs@aol.com. Web: members.aol.com/Veritasprs.

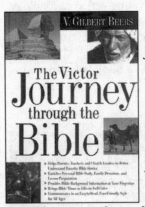

Here is a little (well, not so little) gem I discovered in the Veritas Press catalog. **The Victor Journey Through the Bible** takes you from Genesis to Revelation in chronological order, helping you understand the historical and cultural background of many Bible events. In its amply illustrated 416 hardbound pages, you'll find background summaries, photos of Holy Land sites mentioned in the text, illustrations of objects and people of the times, maps, time lines, family trees, and much more. For example, the entry for "Naboth's Vineyard" has a summary of the Bible story, a photo of the site of Jezreel where the story took place, a backgrounder on King Ahab (who stole the vineyard by having Naboth falsely accused and executed), a photo of a vineyard along with five paragraphs of text about vineyards in Israel, and information about seals (the kind used to verify who sent a message) along with a large full-color illustration showing five different types of seals used at the time.

Mostly straightforward in its facts, *The Victor Journey Through the Bible* does dance around a bit when it comes to questions like whether Moses crossed the Red Sea (requiring a miracle) or the Reed Sea (which dries up at certain times of the year). In such cases, both points of view are presented, although the book is careful to never say a miracle *couldn't* have happened.

With over 200 entries, and a wealth of easy-to-use information organized in a can't-miss fashion, it's no wonder the folks at Veritas named this one of their two "Favorites of the Year"! *Mary Pride*

CHAPTER 14

Character Education

True character means never having to say you're sorry—and if you *do* have to say you're sorry, saying it. It means doing what's right when it hurts, even when Mom and Dad aren't watching and nobody's going to pat you on the back for it. It means keeping your promises, telling the truth, and looking out for other people, not just for Number One.

Are human beings born with this kind of character? That's an interesting question. Some of us naturally find it easier to be truthful. Others, who struggle against a constant temptation to embellish the truth, may have a natural extra dose of courage, or kindness, or something. The bottom line is that all of us need help, and some of us need a *lot* of help!

So how can we help our children develop good character? First, we have to stop expecting today's schools to do this for us. Character education in the schools is a hodgepodge of:

- "What do *you* want to do, Johnny? Have you clarified your own personal values for yourself?"

- "Obey the teacher. Why? Because she says so!"

- "If it feels right, it must be right."

- "Just say no."

- "Smart kids don't do drugs."

See what's missing in this list? It's three little letters that have been banned from all public school classrooms since the fifties. Those letters are G-O-D.

Every "character-building" program in the schools can only appeal to two authorities: *force* (your teacher can *make* you do things, the judge can *make* you go to reform school) and *self* (do it to be successful, because you want to, to impress others or make them like you, because you're so special, etc.). True character, though, is based on doing what is *right,* even in *the face of* external force and your own less-than-worthy desires.

We already have a nice short list of righteous character traits supplied to us in the Ten Commandments. "Thou shalt not steal. . . . Thou shalt not

> The goal of the schools now is to inculcate self-esteem in schoolchildren instead of to give them the skills necessary to individual achievement. The schools have been pumping up kids with inflated notions of their self-worth and importance, eliminating the discipline of competition, insulating them from failure, and shielding them from the knowledge that poor performance can be remedied by hard work and perseverance.
>
> —*The Phyllis Schlafly Report*

> At best, teaching self-esteem is a waste of precious classroom time and, at worst, it's teaching the wrong lesson that it's okay to feel good about doing poorly in school.
>
> Self-esteem should be the reward that comes from achievement and hard work. It should be earned.
>
> —*The Phyllis Schlafly Report*

murder. . . . Thou shalt not commit adultery. . . . Thou shalt not bear false testimony against thy neighbor. . . . Thou shalt not covet anything that is thy neighbor's. . . . Honor thy father and mother." Almost everyone can see the sense in these. The first three commandments, to have no gods before God, to honor His name, and to keep the Sabbath, might only make sense to Bible believers, but that doesn't make the other seven irrelevant. Try running a society without them, as we have been doing for about forty years now, and you'll see the results. Try keeping the last seven, though, and the first three might suddenly start making a lot more sense!

Character Education Resources

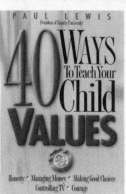

Ways to Teach Your Child 40 Values would have been a much better title for this insightful book by Paul Lewis. Lewis does a wonderful job listing the various skills, attitudes and values that most parents would like their children to understand. In all, **40 Ways to Teach Your Child Values** introduces thirteen skills, thirteen attitudes, and fourteen values. Yes, only fourteen actual values, but the other twenty-six items can also be construed as values or at least closely related!

Lewis takes a skill, such as "learning the art of friendship," and breaks it down into manageable segments. He starts by discussing the purpose of learning the skill. He then lists from three to ten or more ways to achieve your goals. The goals are broken out by ages if appropriate. After the lists, he summarizes the entire chapter once again.

Each chapter is only three or four pages and can easily be read in five minutes. Lewis suggests, and it's easy to see why, that you only read a couple of chapters at a time; otherwise, you will be overwhelmed by the amount of information. The information given is not necessarily new, but it inspires you to say, "Why didn't I think of that!" It is an excellent book for assisting parents in our efforts to raise godly children. *Barbara Buchanan*

Christian character training and a touch of evangelism in radio soap operas with a science-fiction-and-fantasy twist. Somewhere in all this mix of ingredients must be something the public wants, because **Adventures in Odyssey** is tremendously popular.

If the phrases "Imagination Station" and "Room of Consequences" are already familiar to you, then you don't need to read the rest of this review. If, on the other hand, you have no idea what I'm talking about, then here's the scoop.

Odyssey is a small, friendly, nonexistent town where one John Avery Whittaker, known as Whit, presides over his "ice cream and discovery emporium" called Whit's End. Whit's End is home to the state's largest handmade electric train set, an kid's inventor's corner, the "Kid's Radio" station, a library, a theater, a bookstore, a soda shop, a couple of secret rooms, the Room of Consequences, and the Bible Room, where kids can take a trip into actual Bible events via the amazing Imagination Station. With all this architectural splendor, it's hard to figure out why nobody has turned it into a CD-ROM game yet. But I digress.

The basic plot of each Odyssey episode is as follows: Someone has a problem or exhibits a character flaw. Through their interactions with Whit and the other Odyssey characters, or through their experiences in the rooms at Whit's End, a lesson is learned. This worked for *Leave it to Beaver*

NEW!
40 Ways to Teach Your Child Values

Parents. $9.99 plus shipping. *Zondervan Publishing House, Attn: Order Processing, 5300 Patterson Ave., Grand Rapids, MI 49530. (800) 727-3480. Web: www.zondervan.com*

NEW!
Adventures in Odyssey

Ages 8–12, albums 1–5. Ages 12 and up, albums 16–31. Cassette albums, $22.99 each. CD albums (Chronicles, Kings, & Crosses; Welcome to Odyssey; and albums 16–29), $24.99 each. *Tommy Nelson Publishers, PO Box 141000, Nashville, TN 37214. (800) 251-4000. Also available at a significant discount from Library and Educational Services, PO Box 146, Berrien Springs, MI 49103. (616) 695-1800.*

and *The Andy Griffith Show,* but the kids in Odyssey aren't exactly like Beaver, and Odyssey isn't exactly like Mayberry. Instead of heart-warmingly perfect role models, the writers decided to make Odyssey more '80s (and now, '90s), by having the characters exhibit some sharp edges and some not-instantly-resolved conflicts. Even grandfatherly old Whit loses his temper at times. And the kids on the show, while employing only G-rated vocabulary, often display snotty and disrespectful attitudes which go largely uncorrected.

Thirty-one six-cassette albums are currently available. Each cassette contains two 30-minute episodes from Focus on the Family's radio drama, Adventures in Odyssey. They are best listened to in order, as the characters in the stories grow and change in their relationships with each other, just as in real life. Or, if you prefer to select episodes on specific character topics, you could purchase a copy of *The Complete Guide to Adventures in Odyssey* ($20 postpaid from Focus on the Family Publishing, (800) 232-6459). This most excellent oversized paperback has handy summaries of each and every episode, with study/discussion questions at the end of each. It also has a guide to episodes by Scripture verses covered, as well as by character topic, plus an introduction to the series (its authors, the actors, its history, and more), and a lot more of interest to any Odyssey fan. Simply as a buying guide to help you pick the episodes you want, it's well worth the price. *Mary Pride*

The format of the video series **Adventures from the Book of Virtues** is always the same. Cartoon kiddies Annie Redfeather (a Native American) and Zach (a white boy whose last name I'm not sure is ever given) visit Socrates, Aristotle, and Plato. Of course, this being TV-land, you aren't going to see any trio of wise old Greek philosophers. "Plato" is a buffalo, "Aristotle" is a gopher, and "Socrates," shortened to "Socks," is comic relief in the form of a bumbling bobcat. In the course of straightening out Annie and Zach's problems, Plato tells the kids three stories and (usually) one poem.

The individual story segments are well done, as far as animation and storytelling is concerned. What I don't understand is the way the stories are censored. Following the example of the print version of *The Book of Virtues,* parts are left out, and not always for obvious reasons. The entire 23rd Psalm is presented, for example, *except* for the line, "He prepareth a table before me in the presence of mine enemies." Huh?

Some of the story choices also seem strange, given the "virtue" being taught. Some examples: Aesop's mice who did not dare to bell the cat *didn't* have "courage," the theme of that video. The spoiled brat who finally let his

NEW!
Adventures from the Book of Virtues
Age 2–8. $12.95 each. Volumes 1–6, $59.98. Volumes 7–13, $69.98. *PBS Home Video, 1320 Braddock Pl., Alexandria, VA 22314. (800) 344-3337 or (800) 645-4PBS. Fax: (703) 739-8487 or 739-8131. Web: www.pbs.org/adventures/.*

At present, the following videos are available:

- **Faith** Daniel in the Lion's Den, Harriet Tubman, Psalm 23 (Faith in a sort of generic God, or faith in faith itself, appears to be the message of this video)
- **Courage** William Tell, Theseus and the Minotaur, Aesop's Belling the Cat, "If" by Rudyard Kipling
- **Honesty** The Frog Prince, George Washington and the Cherry Tree (a myth from American history that never actually happened), The Indian Cinderella, "Truth"
- **Compassion** The Good Samaritan, The Legend of the Big Dipper, Androcles and the Lion, "The New Colossus"
- **Self-Discipline** The Golden Touch (a story that's *really* about not being greedy), Genghis Khan in The King and His Hawk, The Magic Thread, "For Everything There is a Season"
- **Work** How the Camel Got His Hump, The Bundle of Sticks, Tom Sawyer Gives Up the Brush

- **Responsibility** Icarus and Daedalus (a Greek myth that's *really* about obedience and humility, not responsibility), King Alfred and the Cakes, The Chest of Broken Glass
- **Generosity** Old Mr. Rabbit's Thanksgiving Dinner (in which he gives away all his winter stores to provide a feast for the other animals who didn't save anything for the winter), Rocking-Horse Land, Gift of the Magi (an O. Henry story of futile generosity in which a wife cuts her hair to buy her husband a watch chain and he sells his watch to buy her combs for her hair), "Count That Day Lost"
- **Humility** The Emperor's New Clothes, King Canute at the Seashore, Phaeton of the Sun, "Serenity Prayer"
- **Friendship** Why Frog and Snake Don't Play Together, Waukewa's Eagle, Damon and Pythias, "New Friends and Old Friends"

Coming soon to video: episodes on Loyalty, Respect, and Perseverance.

NEW!
Animated Hero Classics Series

Ages 4–13. $29.95 each. Library of tapes, $239.40 (any 12 videos from one series including 12 workbooks.) Additional workbooks $4.50 each. Shipping extra.
Nest Entertainment, 6100 Colwell Blvd., Irving, TX 75039-9833. (800) 447-5958. Fax: (972) 402-7182. Web: www.nest-ent.com. Sold direct through independent home distributors and independent TV networks, or by calling (800) 447-5958

magic rocking-horse go free only when he did not need it any more is not exactly a great example of "generosity."

Some of the Annie-and-Zach segments also left me scratching my head. In one, Annie falls while running a hurdles race, and decides to never run again. After being told some stories about courage, she runs and wins! But what exactly does this teach us? If she wasn't any good at hurdling, would it have been wrong of her to quit? Is winning a race the proof of your courage? Is it OK to whine and throw tantrums when something goes wrong? What's the message here?

These videos stop far short of declaring the God of the Bible to be the true God. Myths from various cultures are presented in the exact same way as Bible stories. God's name is even left out of stories that it should appear in—e.g., King Canute and the Sea. Where King Canute gave glory to God, this video refers to "one far more powerful than I, who alone controls earth and sea and heaven." Exactly who is that "one"? It's not stated. The "God" referred to elsewhere in these videos is generic. However, there is no ambiguity as to the righteousness of recycling.

The real problem with this series, in my opinion, is found in the opening song: "The thrill of knowing that it's up to you." This is humanism, my friends. Maybe that's why Zach and Annie are learning these lessons from a buffalo, instead of from their parents. *Mary Pride*

The **Animated Hero Classics** are terrific! These high-quality animated stories of real-life heroes and heroines have the production qualities of a movie, well-crafted (and well-researched) stories and dialog, great mood music and songs (no rock or rap!),and a "fun factor" that make them watchable again and again. Unlike other "character-building" materials that reduce their "heroes" to silly caricatures, Hero Classics treat the heroes with respect; unlike other materials that practically worship the heroes, Hero Classics show their human personalities as well. Each hero's particular character strengths come out naturally in the course of his or her life story, without unnecessary preachiness.

The Animated Hero Classics currently include the following titles. They are listed below, in more or less historical order, along with any points I thought you might find the tiniest bit questionable. I didn't personally have a problem with watching all of these with our own children—these videos are squeaky clean morally, and after all, I can always build discernment by commenting on anything I disagree with! If I didn't say anything about a video take that as a 100 percent vote of confidence for it.

- Maccabees: The Story of Hanukkah
- Marco Polo (the only video in this series that disappointed me, for the following reasons: (1) we only saw disjointed fragments of his travels, (2) we never were told *how* he got "in" with the Khan, (3) the scene where he jumps into the hand of a giant idol to save himself from a crocodile and says "The Siamese gods gave me protection" is meant to be funny, but monotheists won't like it, and (4) the video's basic point, "An honest man dies in peace," can be taken as meaning that salvation is not necessary)
- Joan of Arc (from the Catholic point of view, with Joan as a genuine saint)
- Leonardo da Vinci
- Galileo (be sure to point out that Galileo was *wrong* when he says, "The Bible teaches us how to get to heaven, not how heaven was made!")

- Christopher Columbus
- William Bradford: The First Thanksgiving
- Pocahontas (a shaman tries but fails to heal Pocahontas of the flu)
- George Washington
- Benjamin Franklin (this one features a clergyman who believes lightning strikes only sinners—which Ben scientifically disproves; be sure to point out that, although some people have always believed disaster only visits the wicked, the Bible specifically says this isn't so!)
- Harriet Tubman
- Abraham Lincoln
- Florence Nightingale
- Louis Pasteur
- Alexander Graham Bell
- Thomas Edison
- The Wright Brothers
- Helen Keller
- Marie Curie

I only noticed two factual errors in the bunch; Marie Curie received the Nobel Prize *after* becoming a professor at the Sorbonne, not *before,* and the Maccabean revolt actually started when officials of Antiochus Epiphanes tried to make local Jews sacrifice a pig.

Each video comes with a reproducible 48-page workbook designed to reinforce the video. The workbook exercises come in three levels of difficulty—easy, intermediate, and difficult. "Easy" activities are for K–2, "intermediate" activities require third or fourth grade skills, and "difficult" activities require fifth or sixth grade skills. In addition, each activity is labeled with one or more "subject codes" : *a* for art, *cd* for character development, *c* for culture, *g* for geography, *h* for history, *la* for language arts, *m* for math, *mu* for music, *ps* for problem solving, *sc* for science, *sp* for spelling, *va* for "video awareness" (e.g., comprehension of the facts and story presented on the video), and *w* for writing. Exception: the *Christopher Columbus* and *William Bradford* workbooks follow an older format, of coloring pages for little kids followed by puzzles, games, and activities for older kids. All workbooks come with answer keys and Certificates of Achievement in the back.

I really enjoyed watching these videos. The kids loved them, too. They have genuine educational content and are genuinely inspiring. Highly recommended. *Mary Pride*

This bestselling, 831-page book, a compilation of literary selections, has even inspired an animated series (reviewed earlier in this chapter). However, after reading **The Book of Virtues**, I believe most people who bought it were responding more to the *premise*—that kids should be taught what virtue is—than to this particular book's follow-through on that premise.

Author Bill Bennett has selected a number of stories, poems, etc., to illustrate the virtues of self-discipline, compassion, responsibility (including social activism), friendship, work, courage, perseverance, loyalty, and faith. All stories are chosen, or rewritten, to appeal to a mainstream, only marginally conservative audience.

Many selections in *The Book of Virtues* practically shout, "Don't take me seriously!" These include poems about the gruesome fates that await little kids who break the rules, which here take on a nudge-nudge wink-wink

NEW!
Book of Virtues
Moral Compass
Parents. Hardcover, $30 each.
Softcover, $16 each.
Simon & Schuster, Att: Order Dept., 200 Old Tappan Rd., Old Tappan, NJ 07675. (800) 223-2348 ext. 6.
Fax: (800) 445-6991.
Web: www.simonsays.com.

flavor inviting us to jeer at those old-time folks who sought to imprint character so heavy-handedly. Seeing a single book mix such poems, genuine classic literature, popular snippets, and civil-rights hagiography is a unique experience.

Bottom line: If you're looking for the book of *classic* virtues, this isn't it. For a book of modern, mainstream virtues, it's about what you would expect.

About the same size and edited by the same men, the 824-page **Moral Compass: Stories for Life's Journeys** is divided into eight sections designed to complement *The Book of Virtues*: Hearth & Home, Into the World, Standing Fast, Easing the Path, Mothers & Fathers, Husbands & Wives, Citizenship & Leadership, and What We Live By. The latter, a collection of Christian and Catholic stories, including retold Bible stories and legends of saints, is unlikely to offend anyone of any (or no) religion, since the way the stories are presented makes it easy to treat them *all* as myths.

Like *The Book of Virtues*, *Moral Compass's* stories are drawn from myths, folklore from around the world, classic literature, and the Bible. The Bible stories are always rewritten versions created for this book.

Aside from the bonus of political correctness reaped from including works from every continent, why *this* particular collection of literature is so popular—and why people believe reading it will actually build character—remains a mystery. *Mary Pride*

NEW!
Character Building For Families

Grades preK–8. Volumes 1 and 2, $13 each postpaid. $25 for both. *Full Gospel Family Publications, 419 East Taft Avenue, Appleton, WI 54915. (920) 734-6693. Email: pilgrims@juno.com. Web: www.angelfire.com/wi/ characterbuilding.*

Sure you want obedient children, but have you taken them systematically through a series of Bible lessons that teach and reinforce obedience? **Character Building For Families** (108-page, comb-bound volume) covers 12 biblical qualities for the whole family to learn. Written by a mother, these lessons are designed to be led by the parent either as devotions or as part of your homeschool lessons.

This volume covers obedience, orderliness, diligence, loyalty, deference, cheerfulness, gentleness, contentment, gratitude, truthfulness, service, and hospitality.

Ranging in length from 7 days to 23 days, each character trait is outlined for study. Day one typically defines the trait and introduces scripture. Subsequent days offer review, memorization, application, and practice. Some comments in the outline are scripted, giving exact words for the parent to say to the child. Usually these comments are in the form of questions, opening discussion and encouraging children to participate in what the Bible says about that quality. Each day can be expanded or condensed according to your needs.

Newly available is Volume II, which covers five more character traits (indepth lessons on Stewardship, Teachableness, Mercy, Patience, and Desire for Jesus) in its 105 pages.

Our family has eagerly begun using this book in our evening devotions as a framework for studying what God wants us to be and do. *Terri Cannon*

Christian Character

Grades 5–9. Christian Character $14, answer key $2. Christian Manhood, $17 for student text, $8 for teacher's guide. Shipping extra. *Plain Path Publishers, PO Box 830, Columbus, NC 28722. (828) 863-2736. Email: plain@juno.com*

Christian Character *is a book that provides an intensive examination of the character that should be found in the lives of our young people. Christian Character is Scriptural, practical, and convicting; clearly examining the lives of young people who use the book, and then guiding them in setting short-term, specific goals.*

That's what the flyer says. Can any book live up to it? This one sure comes close! **Christian Character: A Guide for Training Young People to Have the Habits That Will Lead to Godly Character** is a series of lessons, in alphabetical order, on 28 major character traits. Each lesson includes a brief introduction defining the character trait in everyday language, with supporting Scripture citations, one or more student exercises, a personal evaluation, and a goal-setting section. One type of student exercise requires the student to answer questions about Bible verses pertaining to the character trait. Another type asks the student to apply what he knows about that character trait to a number of hypothetical situations. The personal evaluation usually is a pretty comprehensive checklist whereby the student can evaluate how well he is doing as far as that character trait is concerned. The questions are quite discerning and interesting to work through. In the goal-setting section, the student is exhorted to set a specific short-term goal for improvement in that area.

Although originally designed by a teacher for classroom use, *Christian Character* works beautifully in the home. The answer key gives the answers to all the exercises that aren't open-ended, and the whole program couldn't be easier to use.

Author Gary Maldaner's point of view is staunchly fundamentalist. He is opposed to rock and contemporary Christian music and is for treating girls and women with special honor (if this be male chauvinism, make the most of it!). He believes in modest dress and the rightness of fighting in a just war. None of these points is beaten to death in *Christian Character;* you could presumably disagree with him on every one of them and still use it by skipping over the questions when they crop up.

Also by the same author, *Christian Manhood: A Guide for Training Boys to be Spiritually Strong Young Men* is for boys ages 10–14. This 45-lesson text doesn't flinch from any of the "tough" areas, from sexual identity to a kid's choice of entertainment. Good biblical common sense, along with a fair amount of insight into spiritual warfare. The author's fundamentalist beliefs are much more basic to this course. The student text has a similar format to the *Christian Character* text, except that lessons are arranged topically rather than alphabetically. You'll also need the teacher's guide, which includes lesson objectives, suggested memory verses, vocabulary from those verses, explanation of the lesson goal, introduction, pointers on leading the classroom discussion, additional activities, discussion questions, and answers to the student exercises. *Mary Pride*

Are you looking for new ideas to plan your unit studies? Or perhaps ideas to enhance your child's character development? **Developing Godly Character in Children** is a resource you don't want to miss! Like KONOS and other similar unit studies, it can be adapted for all ages. It's also very flexible. It focuses on 10 basic character traits, and you design your units from ideas and resources listed in the book. It is Bible-based with no doctrinal position. There is approximately three years' worth of material in one book, so it saves money! You can use the book in any order, depending on the particular needs of your child and family.

The major character qualities studied in the book are: *Wisdom, Loyalty, Brotherly Love, Faith, Fear of the Lord, Integrity, Joy, Obedience, Responsibility, Virtue,* and *Love—God's Grace.*

Each unit includes a key verse for each character quality, a working definition, memorization for meditation of longer scripture passages, Bible facts of important related concepts, hymns and choruses, scripture passages for devotional or study purposes, project suggestions for practical, hands-on growth, and resources for supplemental materials.

Also included: lots of practical advice and sheets for planning your units.

The amount of organization, ideas, and flexibility in *Developing Godly Character in Children* is impressive. There are ideas that can be used in every home, Sunday School, or Christian homeschool support Group. It gives you insight into planning unit studies that the whole family can participate in! *Maryann Turner*

The author's point of view is best expressed in his own words: *After Salvation, the constant indoctrination by example of the "live as you please" philosophy (through TV, music, adults in the world, etc.) produces young people who lack standards, and therefore are also weak in character . . . So that provision is not made to fulfill the lusts of the flesh, a young person must be busily engaged in putting into practice principles from God's Word by forming habits of behavior—these behaviors in total forming the various areas of character development . . . We must teach the Word of God faithfully (Deut. 6:6, 7) and then train young people (Prov. 22:6) by expecting habitual conformity to God's Word as it has been taught. It is a mistake to only teach and then leave the "doing" entirely to the discretion of the child. We . . . cannot produce children with strong character through the philosophy of the world—teach, and then leave them alone to allow them a free choice . . . Setting goals should become a life-long habit whenever they learn about something that God requires of them and make a decision to do it. A decision without further action is worthless.*

NEW!
Developing Godly Character in Children, 5th edition

Grades 1–12. $20 plus shipping. *Hands to Help, PO Box 2364, Orange, CA 92865. (714) 637-1733. Fax: (714) 282-0496. Email: caruso@xc.org. Web: www.ioc.net/~abba/Home.htm.*

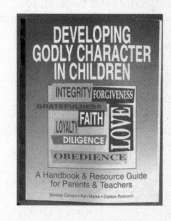

DEVELOPING GODLY CHARACTER IN CHILDREN
INTEGRITY FORGIVENESS
GRATEFULNESS
LOYALTY FAITH
DILIGENCE LOVE
OBEDIENCE
A Handbook & Resource Guide for Parents & Teachers
Beverly Caruso • Kim Marks • Debbie Peterson

Doorposts has many character-training materials. Let's look at four of these.

Checklist for Parents. Featuring Pam Forster's beautiful calligraphy, these questions and Bible verses are designed to evaluate our actions and attitudes in light of God's Word. The six categories of questions pertain to areas of responsibility towards our children: love, prayer, instruction, protection, provision, example. This is thought-provoking, convicting stuff. This simple checklist, with its accompanying suggestions, is probably far more edifying and practical than the vast majority of parenting books on the market.

For Instruction in Righteousness. Where do you go for advice in child training? What is the basis for the rules we make for our children? Is not the Scripture sufficient? Pam Forster believes that "God's Word has the answers to our questions." She has compiled a wonderful big book full of Scripture references on all sorts of topics, from disobedience to complaining/ingratitude to covetousness to fear to laziness to haste to immodesty to bullying to unkind speech to poor manners . . . the list goes on and on. But this is more than a lengthy listing of Bible verses. Pam Forster has creative suggestions for illustrating and living out these verses for our children. For example, for I Timothy 6:10, you can draw a picture of a plant with a dollar sign for its root and theft, envy, covetousness, lying, etc. for leaves. There is enough material here for several years, even a lifetime, of character education.

Stewardship Street. This is not just a program to teach your children (ages five and up) how to earn and budget their money, it's a clever craft project as well. You decide how your children will earn their money, help them divide their earnings into budget categories (suggested categories are charity, living expenses, tithe, short-term savings, spending, long-term savings, and dowry or preparation for marriage), use the enclosed pattern and instructions to turn milk cartons into a "street of savings houses," memorize related Scripture verses, and help your children along "a road to financial faithfulness." The modest price for all this is certainly money well invested. Who knows? You might find yourself on the road to greater financial faithfulness as well!

Watchwords. Here is where Pam Forster's calligraphy really shines. Inspired by the Scripture, "You shall write them on the doorposts of your house and on your gates," Pam has beautifully written out twelve verses, mostly from the King James Version, suitable for framing or other artistic projects that Pam suggests. They can be ordered on either white or cream paper. Since my attempts at calligraphy have been less than pleasing, I plan to use these to decorate our home and touch our hearts at the same time. *Rebecca Prewett*

As you know, child training takes a carrot and a stick. This course provides guidance for both.

The **If-Then Char**t is the stick. This large (16 x 22") wall chart lists common kid misbehaviors on the left, along with a cute cartoon of each problem area. Next to each misbehavior is a Scripture verse commenting on that misbehavior. For example, next to "Arguing, Complaining, Whining" is the verse, "Do all things without murmurings and disputings" (Phil. 2:14). A blank column on the right is where you will fill in the agreed-on consequences of each misbehavior. The If-Then Chart comes with a list of suggested consequences for each sin. These include additional work, loss of a privilege, fines, double restitution, asking forgiveness, and a specified number of swats with a spanking spoon. The authors make it clear that these are only their suggestions; each family is free to choose its own disciplinary measures. You can cut out the pre-lettered and illustrated "consequences" and glue them onto your chart or write in your own.

The **Blessing Chart** is the carrot. It's the same size and format as the "If-Then" chart, except that *good* character qualities are listed and illustrated down the left-hand side. The Blessing Chart comes with a little booklet, *How to Use the Blessing Chart,* that has some really clever ideas for Scriptural methods of rewarding your children. For example, one of the two verses for the character trait of "Truthfulness" is, "Righteous lips are the delight of kings, and they love him who speaks what is right" (Prov. 16:13). So here are some of the ideas they associate with that verse: Prince-for-a-Day (with crown, robe, and servants); go to work with Daddy; a family parade in honor of the truthful child; special clothing; special privilege; and a blank space for you to write in your own ideas. Patterns for some of the recurring reward ideas are also available. These include a flag to fly from your front porch with the child's name on it, felt banner and patches, certificates, medals of honor, and a cloth crown.

More products from Doorposts: a **Service Opportunities Chart** for organizing chore assignments and a set of **Armor of God** patterns, with instructions, so you can make a set of armor for your children like that mentioned in Ephesians 6:10–17.

These materials all look really friendly and professional. Excellent lettering, illustrations in the style of Joshua Harris. Combine these with Gregg and Josh Harris "courtesy" materials in the Social Skills chapter for a really great jump start on your character training program. *Mary Pride*

"Dear God, You promised that when I hurt inside I can talk to You. I know You love me. Well, I did something wrong today." Each of the little 14-page books in the **God, I Need to Talk to You About . . . series** tackles a great big sin in a simple, conversational way. Written in the form of a prayer from a child's perspective, the process of confession (both to God and to any offended parties) and reconciliation/restitution are modeled realistically. A simple reading level and the small size (5½ x 4") add to the appeal of these books. Light-hearted black and white cartoons illustrate each page.

The series includes titles on cheating, vandalism, hurting others, sharing, paying attention, bad temper, stealing and lying. Each one is balanced, honest and offers hope through Christ of both forgiveness and heart change. Our own family has a well-worn copy of *God, I Need To Talk To You About My Bad Temper,* read and re-read by our child who struggled mightily with a temper bigger than he was. He saw that he wasn't alone with this problem each time he thumbed through this little book.

The only title in the series I had difficulty with was the one about paying attention. There are children for whom a lack of focused listening skills fall into the category of laziness, and that sin needs to be addressed. However, there are other children for whom a lack of the ability to attend to words or tasks is a day-to-day struggle. This struggle isn't rooted in laziness. *God, I Need To Talk To You About Paying Attention* is *not* for those kids!

On the whole, however, this series of books is encouraging and balanced. As your children learn to deal with their sin, they may find a hand up and a child-friendly pattern of prayer in each little book. *Michelle Van Loon*

Godly Character Under Construction is a simple-to-use tool that helps build your child's character and appeal to his conscience. It helps you get away from the "because I said so" mentality that we busy parents sometimes fall into. It uses a really easy technique to help your child deal with what he has done wrong and discover what he should have done instead.

The program is in a 3-ring binder workbook format and includes index cards and a dry-erase marker and pencil. Included in the binder is an explanation to parents of how the program works, as well as instructions and a list of Scriptures for parents to use as prayers. The workbook is designed for parents and children to use together to build godly character.

NEW!
God, I Need To Talk To You About . . .
Ages 5–10. Each booklet, 99¢. Shipping extra.
Concordia Publishing House, 3558 S. Jefferson Ave., St. Louis, MO 63118. (800) 325-3040. Fax: (800) 490-9889.

NEW!
Godly Character Under Construction
Ages 2–16. $14.95 plus shipping.
Sower's Press, P. O. Box 666306, Marietta, GA 30066. (770) 565-8202. Fax: (770) 977-3784. Email: jcwood@charactercorner.com Web: www.charactercorner.com.

In the back of the workbook is an "offense" section . You are supposed to refer to this section when your child has a specific character trait that needs to be worked on. Let's say his problem is "arguing." On the page for "arguing" are listed four different Bible verses for your child to study and ponder. After this step, your child turns to the Learning and Building page. This page is laminated, so that your child can fill it in with a dry-erase marker. On this page your child is asked "What did I do wrong? What does God say about what I did? What could I have done instead?" There is a prayer to be filled in asking God's forgiveness for the particular sin. Then your child has to answer the questions of "Is there anyone else I need to ask to forgive me? Is there anything else I need to do to make things right?" After your child works through this process and reviews the answers with you, the slate is wiped clean, as an object lesson of God's forgiveness.

Godly Character Under Construction is simple to use and very effective. It gives immediate results and is also a powerful reminder to us parents that our children need to be trained up in a godly fashion constantly and consistently. *Maryann Turner*

This 50-page book of read-aloud selections has a wonderful, old-fashioned flavor. The **Lessons from the Farmyard** stories, about a family of rabbits, were adapted from the French of Madam Colomb. You will read about little Trottino and how his unthinking disobedience and greediness get him into all sorts of scrapes, and how he eventually becomes a much better rabbit. The book includes teaching suggestions that you can use to review and emphasize the principles found in these stories. Appropriate Scripture references are given for you to read to your children. This is a delightful character resource— one that will have your little ones begging, "Don't stop now! Please read some more!" *Rebecca Prewett*

NEW!
Lessons From the Farmyard

Ages 4–6. $3.50 plus $4 shipping. *Christian Liberty Press, 502 West Euclid Ave., Arlington Heights, IL 60004. (847) 259-4444. Fax: (847) 259-2941. E-mail: enquire@homeschools.org. Web: www.homeschools.org. They take credit card orders, but not over the phone. Any other contact method will work.*

UPDATED!
Patch the Pirate Adventures

Ages 4–12. Cassettes, $10.98 each. Treasure Chests 1 and 2, $59.95 each. CDs, $14.98 each. Choral Books, $5.95 each. Shipping extra. *Majesty Music, PO Box 6524, Greenville, SC 29606. Orders: (800) 334-1071. Inquiries: (864) 242-6722. Fax: (800) 249-2117. Email: info@majestymusic.com. Web: www.majestymusic.com.*

Patch the Pirate is the invention of Ron Hamilton. After losing an eye to cancer, Ron was forced to wear an eyepatch. Hence the moniker "Patch the Pirate." Making the most of this unhappy situation, Ron decided to dress up as a pirate and tell Christian stories. One thing led to another, and that's how we got the Patch the Pirate series.

Patch is a very straight-arrow pirate. In fact, he does nothing piratical at all except sail the sea and use sailor talk.

Instead of a crowd of squirmingly cute stuffed animals or unbelievably adorable children whose adventures resemble nothing on this earth or the next, the Patch adventures are parables of the Christian life. They feature really bad villains who do not roll over and play dead if you just smile sweetly at them. Hence their interest for our family.

All the Patch the Pirate adventures have cute characters (Sissy the Seagull is almost *too* cute!), dashes of daft humor, memorable songs your children will love to sing, and plots designed to get children thinking about basic Christian virtues.

Unlike other "character-building" audio series, these do *not* look at the world through rose-colored glasses. Patch knows there are good guys and bad guys, just as there are character virtues and character flaws. Sometimes bad guys can be converted into friends; but sometimes they can't.

Here is a list of titles in the series, and their themes:

- *Giant Killer* (courage)
- *Mount Zion Marathon* (finish the course)
- *Harold the King* (putting Christ first, especially at Christmas)
- *Down Under* (you reap what you sow). When Sissy Seagull is romantically duped into getting engaged to a nasty octopus, Patch and his gang have to make some enemies into friends quickly! Great Aussie characters
- *Once Upon a Starry Knight* (servanthood, somewhat overdone as our hero Starry Knight gives away everything he has when at times the people he encountered only needed a loan or smaller gift)
- *The Friendship Mutiny* (choosing friends wisely and ignoring peer pressure)
- *The Custard's Last Stand* (recognizing ways the Christian home is being attacked). Generalissimo Homewrecker is out to get the Custard family. Beware the Magnetbox TV (the soap opera send-up scene is hysterical!) and other major family-busters!
- *Camp Kookawacka Woods* (the Second Coming—includes a great song about Hoo Flung Chow's camp stew made out of "greasy grimy gopher guts" that your kids are guaranteed to sing at the dinner table)
- *The Calliope Caper* (bearing spiritual fruit)
- *The Evolution Revolution* (creationism)
- *The Misterslippi River Race* (trusting Christ)
- *The Great American Time Machine* (patriotism). Patch and his crew escort a delegation of two from Bonkinland back through American history to discover the secret of America's greatness. The Bonkers only understand coercive power (in Bonkinland every higher Bonker gets to bonk everyone lower than him to keep them in line), and the sight of George Washington kneeling in the snow at Valley Forge and Dwight L. Moody preaching in Chicago, among other peeks into American roots, amaze them. Lots of good songs and nice effects, like the Statue of Liberty speaking with a Bronx accent.
- *Kidnapped on I-land* (putting Christ first). An action-packed excursion into the kingdom of the nasty King Me-First. Silas Sailor, found floating on a raft by Patch and his crew, succumbs to the blandishments of King Me-First, who promises him a marvelous life on his own if Silas will just determine to always put himself first. With Silas firmly chained to him, King Me-First flies off to I-Land and flings Silas into Pity-Party Pit, a particularly dark corner of the Prison of No Sing-Sing. Patch and friends set out to rescue Silas, who is slated to become a barbecued sailor steak, courtesy of King Me-First's pet, Torch the Dragon. Silas finally decides to put Jesus first, at which point the castle disappears, Me-First shrinks into nothingness, and all is well. The whole adventure resembles John Bunyan's *Pilgrim's Progress* (on a somewhat lower literary level) and is characterized by frequent clever jokes and lots of bright, happy music.
- *Patch the Pirate Goes to the Jungle* (growing in Christ)
- *Patch the Pirate Goes West* (family unit)
- *Patch the Pirate Goes to Space* (growing in Christ)

You can also get sets of eight cassettes at a discount as "Treasure Chests." These come in an attractive cassette binder, for easy storage. **Treasure Chest 1** includes *Sing Along with Patch the Pirate*, plus the following adventures: *Goes to Space, Goes West, Goes to the Jungle, I-Land, Time Machine, Misterslippi River Race,* and *Calliope Caper*. **Treasure Chest 2** includes *Camp Kookawacka Woods, Custards' Last Stand, Friendship Mutiny, Starry Knight, Harold the King, Down Under, Mt. Zion Marathon,* and *Evolution Revolution*.

We have just about every Patch tape, and have played them numberless times. If you get them, so will you. *Mary and Ted Pride*

NEW!
Pictures from Proverbs

All ages. $12 per set. Coloring book with all sets, $4. Postpaid.
Ornament Publications, 2301 South Country Club Rd., Garland, TX 75041. Fax/Phone: (972) 278-5965.

NEW!
The Pilgrim's Progress/ Christiana

All ages. Pilgrim's Progress, $25. Christiana, $25. Shipping extra.
Orion's Gate, PO Box 430, Dobbins, CA 95935. Fax/Phone: (530) 692-1124. Email: orion@oro.net.
Web: www.orionsgate.org.

NEW!
Plants Grown Up: Projects For Sons on the Road to Manhood

All ages. $40 plus shipping.
Doorposts, 5905 SW Looking Glass Dr., Gaston, OR 97119. Phone/fax: (503) 357-4749.
Email: Doorposts@juno.com.
Web: www.lyonscom.com.

Here is a different approach to character studies based on the book of Proverbs. Each set of **Pictures from Proverbs** includes 18 full-color drawings on 8½ x 11" cards. The drawings illustrate various proverbs that are based on analogies. For example, one of my favorites asks, "Who is like a jewel of gold in a pig's nose?" and shows a prize pig in a ruffled skirt with a jeweled ring in her nose. The back of the card, written for the parent, includes the proverb, its explanation, an example or illustration from the Bible, and questions to ask your children. This is a wonderful way to provoke interest and curiosity in your children and to encourage lively discussion. *Rebecca Prewett*

My older brother read an increasingly more tattered version of *Pilgrim's Progress* countless times as a child. I can still remember him weeping over parts of it and cheering over other parts. However, the first time I tried to read it, I had an almost impossible struggle with the Old English. I've wanted to introduce this wonderful classic to our family, but have not liked any of the abridged or simplified versions and have not wanted to discourage my little ones with the archaic language either. Maybe you feel the same way. If so, this audio rendition of **Pilgrim's Progress**—a set of six cassette tapes in a handy album case—might be just the answer.

Seventy-seven actors were involved in recording over six hours of John Bunyan's classic book. It is "virtually unabridged." (I'm not sure what that means; I didn't notice anything missing) and features sound effects and music. The Old English of the original has been only slightly simplified—it retains the flavor, yet is more understandable than I remember.

These tapes are beautiful. They make the incredible story come alive and will be a blessing to your family. This is probably one of the best timeless lessons in "character education" that your family can enjoy.

An eight-hour dramatized version of the story of **Christiana**—Bunyan's sequel to *Pilgrim's Progress*—is also available and just as nice! *Rebecca Prewett*

This book is an answer to my prayers! A good reviewer avoids "gosh-wow" statements and looks for ways to improve a product. Well, I tried. If Pam Forster has left anything out of this book, I'm not catching it.

Plants Grown Up has an enthusiastic attitude that relaxes and encourages, giving you hope that you really can raise up strong men of God. It gives you thorough instructions for using these projects as part of your homeschool life—even a section specifically for single moms. Forster interjects Scripture throughout the introduction, presenting it in a fitting and helpful manner, leaving you to deal with it yourself—she doesn't "preach." Even the layout is professional and appealing, right down to the choice of a font that appears handwritten.

This character builder's oversized spiral bound book has over 500 pages of ideas for developing godly character and practical skills in boys of all ages. It contains 48 chapters, each dealing with a specific area of godliness and listing anywhere from 17 to 54 projects designed to cover that area. The lists progress from basic Scripture memorization to projects that require research and effort from the older student. Some of the more advanced projects: studying what the Bible says about things like abortion and capital punishment, repairing something around the house, and designing and implementing a unit study.

The vast array of projects makes this a book you can use year after year. It is good for both the child who can't read and the young man preparing for marriage. It is non-consumable and, whenever a project calls for filling out a chart or other such thing, you find a reproducible copy within that very chapter.

Forster indicates appropriate school subjects for each project, assisting those who keep academic records. Each chapter ends with notes to the parents and a checklist to help you evaluate your son's progress. All memory verses are in the back of the book (in King James Version), listed by topic with a check box so you can track which ones have been assigned/learned. Again, you may copy these lists.

This is a quality product, well worth the money you're investing. *Tammy Cardwell*

The Richest Christian is my children's favorite board game. The aim is to learn biblical principles of money; but *The Richest Christian* emphasizes how money is earned as well as how it is spent. The game is for two to six players, who need to know how to read. One player, the cashier, needs to know how to add and subtract large whole numbers.

The large, illustrated gameboard is easy to read and use. Most spaces have a topic and Bible verse at the top, a picture applying the verse in the middle, and a game action at the bottom. Other spaces tell you to draw a Disaster card or give you a chance to earn game rewards if you have performed a prescribed pious action recently, e.g., if you can quote a Bible verse you learned this month. Opportunity cards may be chosen once you have passed the first round, assuming you aren't in debt at this point. These give you the opportunity to do a good deed with some or all of your game money, thereby earning Eternal Treasures. The game is over when all Eternal Treasures (pretty gold-foil cards with their value printed on them in blue) have been passed out. The player with the most Eternal Treasures wins.

Watch out for the ominous green paths on both sides of the board. If you land on a shady transaction space, you make some money on the deal, but then have to suffer through a series of disasters, some brought on by your own evil character (you make unwise investments and lose most of your money, for example) and some visited on you directly by the Lord.

The Richest Christian admirably teaches principles of diligence, inventiveness, thrift, and generosity, while exposing the pitfalls of get-rich-quick thinking, laziness, dishonesty, show-off giving, and selfishness. It's also easy to learn and fun to play. Can't ask one board game to do much more than that! *Mary Pride*

You can taste the wisdom as the author of **School Days**, a grandmother of 19, teaches God's Word in unique lessons designed to build character.

The 534-page paperback includes 180 lessons, divided into 36 weeks of 5 days. Each week centers on a specific theme such as obedience, habits, and peer pressure. A special page for each week highlights the theme, a memory passage, a song (cassette included), and a poem. History and nature content are included, as are review questions. Posters and clip art offer fun reinforcement. Each lesson includes servant attitudes and gratitude attitudes that relate to the theme. Ready-made visual aids, object lessons, quizzes, and true-life experiences round out this program.

One rather unusual, though memorable, example: "A Fruitful Funeral" (day 5 of week 6) wraps up the theme of habits. The first page introduces

The Richest Christian

Ages 6 to adult. $23 postpaid. *Ornament Publications, 2301 South Country Club Rd., Garland, TX 75041. Fax/Phone: (972) 278-5965.*

HERE'S WHAT THE SPACE FOR TOO MUCH TALK SAYS:
"... *The talk of the lips tendeth only to poverty.*" *Proverbs 14:23*
[Picture of a man in business clothes, feet up on desk, chatting with a friend holding a cup of coffee]
You are a salesman who wastes too much time talking with other salesmen. Lose $400.

NEW!
School Days: Devotional Praise

Grades 3–8. $21 plus shipping. *Bechtel Books, 36107 SE Squaw Mt. Rd., Estacada, OR 97203. (888) 621-3293. Fax: (503) 630-4606.*

the topic, provides clear instructions, and presents a large rose, appropriate for a funeral. Another page features a tombstone—PRETTY PROUD, cause of death SELF-CONGESTION, Proverbs 16:18. A paragraph above explains, "Pretty was so full of herself that she couldn't breathe a thought for anyone else." A flower lies beneath the tombstone next to the word HUMILITY. Under the flower it states, "Humility is a lovely flower which does not draw attention to itself." This pattern repeats for 18 more habits.

Teenagers might find some of the lessons just a little too cute. A separate package for artwork would make displaying and photocopying easier. And poetry memorization depends on a book not included. Overall though, *School Days* is simply scrumptious. *Gail Rivera*

This curriculum, written by a homeschooling mother, consists of 20 weeks of daily Bible lessons to be used with the entire family. The goal of **Searching for Treasure** is to involve your family in Bible reading and memorization. (The Bible version used is the NIV.) The topics studied come out of the book of Proverbs and are divided into the following sections: Understanding Wisdom, Developing Right Relationships, Controlling Yourself, Controlling What You Say, Avoiding the Way of the Wicked, and Following the Way of the Righteous.

Younger children will learn a verse or a section of a verse per week, while older children will memorize more. Activities are simple and don't require a lot of preparation time or a lot of materials. You will need to cut out the Bible Memory cards and the game cards, which are printed on heavy stock. Also, you may want to copy the illustration for each lesson for younger children to color. Any additional materials depend on whether or not you choose to do the crafts, but most are items easily found in homes with children.

The lessons are easy to teach, as they are organized well and include everything you need to know. They include an explanation of the reading passage, discussion questions, prayer emphasis, and craft and game ideas. This is one of the best family-oriented studies I have seen and is completely non-intimidating, yet solid.

This curriculum can also be used in a family class. There is even a section on how to organize a "Family Night" program. *Rebecca Prewett*

How often have we read our children a cute little storybook and thought to ourselves, "Huh?" Some books out on the market have no moral value whatsoever. They do nothing to teach us good or bad morals.

Vigen Guroian has taken favorite childhood stories and found a new way to ensure understanding of morals in his book **Tending the Heart of Virtue: How Classic Stories Awaken a Child's Moral Imagination**.

Guroian has taken some of the classics—*Pinocchio; Charlotte's Web; The Lion, the Witch and the Wardrobe,* to name a few—and opened our eyes to see their real value. These are not just interesting, fun stories; these are stories that teach our children and us. He discusses both good morals and bad. For how can we know something as good, if we never see something that is bad? Thus, he discusses evil and then explains the need for redemption.

Parents will be well served by reading this book and taking it to heart. Not just for seeing the lessons the classics teach; but as a reminder that a good story will instruct. We should be on the lookout for these good stories and avoid the junk that is all too available. *Barbara Buchanan*

NEW!
Searching for Treasure: A Guide to Wisdom and Character Development

All ages. $19.95 plus $3 shipping.. *Noble Publishing Associates, PO Box 2250, Gresham, OR 97030. Orders: (800) 225-5259. Inquiries: (503) 667-3942. Fax: (503) 665-6637.*

NEW!
Tending the Heart of Virtue

Parents. $22 plus shipping. *Oxford University Press, Inc., 2001 Evans Road, Cary, NC 27513. (800) 451-7556. Fax: (919) 677-1303. Web: www.oup-usa.org.*

PART 4

Language Arts

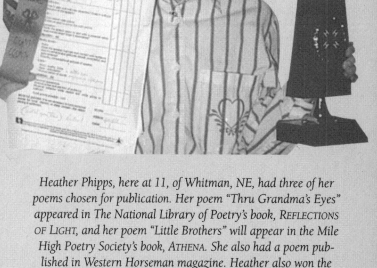

Heather Phipps, here at 11, of Whitman, NE, had three of her poems chosen for publication. Her poem "Thru Grandma's Eyes" appeared in The National Library of Poetry's book, REFLECTIONS OF LIGHT, and her poem "Little Brothers" will appear in the Mile High Poetry Society's book, ATHENA. She also had a poem published in Western Horseman magazine. Heather also won the Pre-Junior division and the Public Service Announcement division at the 4-H District Speech contest.

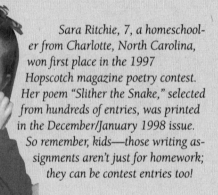

Sara Ritchie, 7, a homeschooler from Charlotte, North Carolina, won first place in the 1997 Hopscotch magazine poetry contest. Her poem "Slither the Snake," selected from hundreds of entries, was printed in the December/January 1998 issue. So remember, kids—those writing assignments aren't just for homework; they can be contest entries too!

CHAPTER 15

All-Purpose Language Arts

Though many homeschoolers use separate products for phonics, reading, creative writing, grammar, spelling, handwriting, literature, and vocabulary, many prefer a curriculum that integrates all these subjects.

Most major homeschool curriculum publishers package this together in an "English" course. Expect these to follow a sequence comparable to public schools, although the content of the reading exercises is usually more family-friendly. For something more suited to the homeschool schedule (who needs to study grammar for 8 years?), check out the products below.

Language Art for the Homeschool

Change English drudgery to English delight! The writers of *Journey Through Grammar Land* and *Jensen's Grammar* have come up with **English Fun Stuff**, 80 pages of fun puzzles and games that will stretch your use of the English language, bound in heavy paper stock. Yes, I admit that I tried some of these games with a group of homeschool moms and we not only had a great time but we were challenged!

"Pretentious Proverbs," the first part of this book, is a list of proverbs given in unfamiliar language. Have your child try this little saying with those naughty neighborhood kids. "Splintered wood and mineral chunks can rupture my skeletal system, but nomenclatures do not impair me." Stumped? "Sticks and stones may break my bones but words will never hurt me."After your kids have done one, they will be begging to do more. They will really be searching their mental rolodexes for forgotten vocabulary words.

The next exercise is "Idioms and Metaphors." You will really have to think about what all those interesting sayings really mean. "Wordhai" and "Shakespearean Cryptograms," games of logic, will challenge your play on words. In addition you will find parlor games, word games, and research treasure hunts. All of these activities can be done orally or on a few sheets of paper within a few minutes.

Have your children try these games and puzzles on their anti-homeschooling relatives. This will really prove to them what a superior education your children are getting. *Irene Buntyn*

NEW!
English Fun Stuff
Grades 5 and up. $11 plus shipping. *Wordsmiths, 1355 Ferry Road, Grants Pass, OR 97526. (541) 476-3080. Cannot take credit card orders at this number. Email: frodej@chatlink.com. Web: www.jsgrammar.com.*

AlphaBetter

Grades 3–12. $17.95 plus shipping.
Providence Project, 14566 NW 110th St., Whitewater, KS 67154.
(888) 776-8776. Fax: (316) 799-2192. Email: info@providenceproject.com.
Web: www.providenceproject.com.

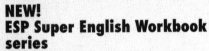

"To improve your vocabulary, look up all new words in the dictionary." But how's a kid going to look anything up if he's not comfortable with the alphabet both forwards and backwards?

Good question. And **AlphaBetter** is the good answer.

Like the other modules of the Character and Competence Series from Providence Project, AlphaBetter is designed to "bridge the gap between learning what-and-how-to-do and doing it well." It takes students over the hump of alphabetizing with simple four-minute timed exercises, each on a single sheet. The first exercises begin by dividing the alphabet into eight overlapping groups of five letters each and drilling these combinations. The next exercises drill rapid recall of every letter's position in the alphabet relative to every other letter. Carefully planned alphabetizing drills come next, followed by exercises that translate these skills into actual use with reference book formats. Students try to "beat the clock" each day, doing the same sheet over and over until they are able to beat the time limit. The excitement of trying to beat the clock provides motivation sadly lacking in typical textbook alphabetizing drills, and the extra time spent on making this skill as effortless for the child as walking or talking pays rich dividends in confidence with all reference and alphabetized materials. Twelve sheets each of 16 drill exercises, printed on colorful bond paper. *Mary Pride*

NEW!
ESP Super English Workbook series

Grades 3–6. Student book, $15.95 each grade. Teacher edition with answers, $15.95 each grade. Shipping extra.
ESP Publishers, Inc., 7100 123rd Circle North, #100, Largo, FL 33773. Orders: (800) 643-0280. Inquiries: (727) 532-9100. Fax: (727) 539-6071.

The ESP Super English Workbooks are recommended by the publishers of several unit-study programs as accompaniments to their programs. So I had to see what all the fuss was about.

ESP is not afraid to make *big* workbooks, and these are no exception! 400 pages apiece, each book includes a variety of composition and grammar exercises, with 33 two-page quizzes built in. At the rate of two pages per school day, your child can finish one of these books in a school year.

Each book covers all the grammar and composition skills for its grade level, presented in a logical sequence. In addition:

- Grade 3 also includes a series of pages on reference skills
- Grade 4 has a series of exercises on common misspellings
- Grade 5 teaches you how to research and write a report
- All grades teach sentence diagramming, building from the simplest (grade 3) to most complex (grade 6)

Teacher books are identical to student books, except they have the answers printed in them. You probably won't need them for grades 3 and 4, but as the diagramming becomes more complicated with each grade level, you may want to invest in the grade 5 or 6 teacher edition as well as the student book.

The black and white layouts are attractive and straightforward. No cute bunny-wunnies, licensed characters, or political correctness. Just good old-fashioned step-by-step education. It doesn't get much easier to use—or more thorough—than this. *Mary Pride*

Romalda Spalding, lace up those track shoes; Kay Milow may give you a run for your money! While Spalding's formidable *The Writing Road to Reading* provides the classic intensive phonics approach, Milow's **Language Arts From A to Z** streamlines the process—even while adding rules—and incorporates vocabulary, grammar, reading, and composition for a pretty comprehensive language arts program.

NEW!
Language Arts From A to Z
Grades 1–6. $50 for entire curriculum. Shipping extra.
Milow Enterprises, 5508 S. 169th Street, Omaha, NE 68135. (402) 895-3280. Fax: (402) 895-7049. KayMilow@aol.com.
Web: www.members.aol.com/ kaymilow/index.htm.

While Spalding teaches 54 of 70 total phonograms before a child begins reading and writing, Milow provides a vowel and a few consonants in the "no-picture, no-letter-name" style to get beginners reading and writing right away. Most of the 124 phonograms are packed into first grade, but all the phonograms are reviewed at the beginning of each level, so older students needn't start with Level A (first grade).

Week 7 of Level A is typical: the week's dozen new words (*has, hen, lot, tip,* etc.) are introduced on Monday and Tuesday, tested Tuesday and Wednesday, and fully tested Friday with three review words (*gum, zip, mud*). On Monday students review the 20-odd phonograms learned thus far, practicing hearing, saying, reading, and writing them. Tuesday introduces Grammar Rule 7 (articles) and Wednesday reviews Grammar Rules 2 and 3 (subject/predicate and declarative sentences) with oral sentences. On Thursday students discern *thee* and *thuh* and *a/an* in context and identify subjects and predicates in dictated sentences. Note: Regional pronunciation oddities crop up: *gulf=golf, broad=brode.*

By Level D (fourth grade), Milow believes students should be able to work independently. By Level F (sixth grade), the student exercises new words and grammar rules by taking dictation, diagramming sentences, writing book reports, and fashioning stories, letters, and a brief autobiography.

The Reading Manual is Milow's compilation of classic and popular titles appropriate for each grade level. Each day of the first twelve weeks in Level A, the parent reads a story and "recalls facts" with the child. After this point the child is expected to read independently from the titles and even has a book report assigned near the end of the year, but without much guidance. At Level A the student might read *Are You My Mother?*, then tell where the baby bird looks for his mother or draw a picture of her own mother. At Level E, the student reads *Caddie Woodlawn* and makes a commemorative stamp for Caddie or a report on Wisconsin. Because the titles are not specifically keyed to the program, you might prefer reading lists geared to your other curricula.

Parents wanting true composition instruction for elementary-grade students will be disappointed with the bare instructions in this curriculum: "Report on . . . Write a story . . . Create a bibliography . . . ." But Milow has done a good job of drawing together the threads of phonics, spelling, grammar, and sentence-level composition, with an eye to incorporating reading and larger compositions as well.

With the sturdy spiral-bound (and partially consumable) student text, the teacher text, the Spelling/Grammar Rules Manual, the Phonograms Kit (includes manual, cards, audio tape), the Teacher's Training Kit (includes booklet, video tape, handwriting aid), and your own plans for library trips, review games, and more composition help, you can feel confident that you're set to cover language arts from A to Z! *Cindy Marsch*

NEW!
Learning Language Arts Through Literature

Grades 1–12. $18–$20 per level; each level corresponds to one or two years of school. New edition expected out soon. 1st grade will be $95, 2nd grade $85, others $25 each. *Common Sense Press, P.O. Box 1365, Melrose FL 32666. Call (352) 475-5757 for a retail store near you; they do not sell retail themselves. Fax: (352) 475-6105. Email: service@cspress.com. Web: www.cspress.com.*

All the books excerpted in the program are available from Family Learning Services, PO Box 9596, Birmingham, AL 35220, (205) 854-6870.

Learning Language Arts Through Literature is a highly-thought-of total language arts curriculum.

Since I first wrote it up many years ago, the program has been improved in several ways.

- New books have been added, taking LLAL from first grade right through high school.
- The books were retypeset, making them far more attractive and easy to read and use.
- Student Activity books ($16 each) were added for the Red, Yellow, Orange, Purple, and Tan levels (these correspond to grades 2–6), making the program super easy to use. Now all your student's work can be neatly done in the workbooks, which include the Student Models for copying exercises, room to write all the assignments, and additional helps such as cut-out cards for some activities.

Most of the books in the LLAL series provide weekly lesson plans and exercises based on a weekly excerpt from some classic book. Exercises cover the gamut of language arts, from labeling parts of speech in your copied excerpt to composition assignments based on the type of excerpt you are studying. Exceptions: the Orange, Purple, Green, and Gold books take a "unit" approach, with more traditional units on, for example, poetry and how to write a research paper. You will probably also need the inexpensive supplementary books *Learning Grammar Through Writing* ($10; grades 2–6) and *Write Source 2000* ($10; junior high and up) to organize your teaching of grammar and writing skills.

LLAL has quickly become one of the most popular homeschooling language arts programs. It could still be improved, though. Although it claims to be based on the Ruth Beechick method, and in fact carries endorsements from Dr. Beechick, the composition exercises rarely encourage students to copy the style of the writer being studied. Yet the study of writers' styles is at the heart of the old-time creative writing approach, which Dr. Beechick is popularizing in her books. We would like to see the curriculum provide more help with the serious philosophical issues raised in some of the books studied. The authors presuppose you are Christian, but leave you on your own to discern just what is wrong with the outlook of the some of the authors studied. This laid-back approach to life-and-death philosophical questions assumes you can figure out the answers to these questions on your own without much help, and could possibly impart the feeling that the right answers to these questions aren't all that important or even that there are no "right" answers. In addition, five out of 30 excerpts in the Tan book feature suffering and death, subjects most parents feel no need to strongly emphasize with sixth-graders. *Mary Pride*

The **Learning Beat language-arts series** apply the concept that "Catchy songs make learning to read fun and easy!" Each workbook and audiocassette in this series addresses one of the vital areas of learning necessary to make your child a great reader. As a resource, these cassettes and workbooks can be used to enhance any reading program, but parents should be aware that preparation may be needed to make these tools really come alive in the education of their child.

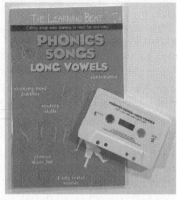

Both the *Short Vowels* and *Long Vowels* cassettes use two-verse songs to teach each vowel sounds. The second verse of the song has words omitted, so that the child participates by reading the words which fit into the gaps. Other activity suggestions are offered in the workbook, but may not be sufficient for strong reinforcement.

Spelling Songs uses catchy tunes and fun lyrics to teach the common rules of spelling. Lyrics are provided, as well as a worksheet for each song. While exercises are not sufficient for full comprehension, they are an added bonus to this thoroughly delightful language arts program. A handy answer key is provided in the back of the workbook, but parents may prefer to do each brief exercise right along with their child.

By far *Grammar and Punctuation Songs* is the most complicated of the series, and deserves more parental attention. Twelve fun and entertaining songs address the comma, vowels, quotation marks, syllables, nouns, and other common basics. Worksheets and answer key are also provided. However, children will enjoy the variety of pop, country, rock, and rap tunes so much that this cassette is bound to become their favorite of all The Learning Beat cassettes. *Lisa Mitchell*

Smart Start in Language Arts is a 463-page worktext with 140 days of lessons. It teaches letter sounds and sight words systematically, with daily review of concepts. Lessons progress so that the child identifies the differences between short and long vowel words, words with silent *e*, and vowel combination sounds. As soon as possible, sounds are practiced in the context of sentences which later become stories. In this way comprehension is emphasized simultaneously with decoding skills. This is rather a shame because children focused on early decoding aren't really enjoying the story anyway. The teaching parent can help by rereading the story before asking questions.

My least favorite spelling rule is included and stated worse than normal, "When two vowels come together, the first one says its name and the second one is silent." This rule is *not* true for many words, but is usually stated to jump-start the child through the initial introduction. I think it would be wiser to simply introduce vowel combinations within a set of words with the same pattern.

Other than this quibble, the phonics lessons are well laid out. Spelling is taught at the same time as reading. The program reinforces letter sounds with brief tests and reviews, plus activities that involve fixing misspelled words and identifying differences between short and long vowel words. Later lessons introduce the parts of speech, punctuation, and sequence story writing. I doubt you could find a more comprehensive course for the price. *Kathy von Duyke*

NEW!
Learning Beat series
Grades K–4. Each audiocassette/ workbook combo, $9.95.
The Learning Beat, 10 Pineview Dr., Media, PA 19063-4337. Orders: (800) 232-8244. Inquiries/fax: (610) 892-7055. Email: lebeat123@aol.com.

Editor's Note: Two new titles have been added to the series: *Multiplication Songs, Addition Songs.* Coming soon: *ABCs.*

NEW!
Smart Start in Language Arts
Grades 1–2. $38.95 plus shipping.
Books for Results, 94 Deerview Terrace SE, Calgary, Alberta T2J 7C1 Canada. (403) 271-9085. Fax: (403) 278-1160.

UPDATED!
Super Seatwork Series

Grades K–3. $12.95 each, except Word Skills, $18.95. All books for $8. Shipping extra.
Pecci Educational Publishers, 440 Davis Court #405, San Francisco, CA 94111. Information: (415) 391-8579. Email: pecci@sirius.com.

Use this sunny workbook series to "fill in the holes" (even for slow learners) in any K–3 language arts program. **Mary Pecci's friendly Super Seatwork series** is a real lifesaver. Since each book progresses step by step through a single subject area, confusion is eliminated. Mary Pecci knows kids are put off by pages stuffed with problems, so each page has only a few exercises. Her lively hand-drawn illustrations and hand-printed instructions convey an air of joyfulness, and simple yet clever activities make these workbooks fun. Each activity takes only a few minutes, yet has solid learning value. I know what I'm talking about—we've used them for years!

Each book is made of sturdy paper with a durable softcover. They are printed in black and white, to encourage coloring. The books are thick, ranging from 106 to 238 pages.

With the exception of the phonics books, all the workbooks include seasonal and holiday activities. These are designed for use in public schools, so include a few typical Halloween and Santa Claus pages. We just remove these—they aren't needed for anything—and enjoy the rest of the workbooks.

Correlated with her book, *At Last! A Reading Method for EVERY Child!* (reviewed in chapter 6), the **Phonics Grab Bag** (138 pages) has 12 different fun types of exercises, organized in the order in which phonics sounds are normally taught.. The book includes matching, cut-'n-paste, phonic picture puzzles (cut out the strips and paste so the phonics sound matches the small picture on the side), spell-the-picture spelling practice, add-a-vowel, drawing pictures to match words, and a variety of "word wheels" to cut out and pin together with brads. These latter are a device much beloved of phonics teachers. A "wheel" with a phonics family on it (e.g., digraphs or short vowels) is bradded to a picture with holes cut in it. Turn the wheel and different words appear. As with all Mary Pecci's seatwork, the book is big and the pictures are simple and entertaining.

Linguistic Exercises (106 pages) is a terrific workbook even for the struggling reader. It includes simple phonics rules, sets of word families and syllables (not too many to a page), and easy-to-complete reading and writing exercises. A page, for example, may feature repetitions of *ore, ote, ove,* and *oze.* Some the student just reads. Towards the end of the book he does some writing and drawing. This pattern-building is the way our brains construct frameworks for storing the data we feed them, unlike short-term "rote" memory which quickly fades away unless refreshed.

Content Areas (154 pages) is packed full of cut-'n-paste activities. For example, kids cut out pictures of furniture and place them near the proper labels in the bedroom picture. It's a fun way to increase vocabulary, and to take some of the "wiggle" out of your wiggle-worm!

Number Words (120 pages) helps kids learn and practice both cardinal (1,2,3 . . .) and ordinal (first, second, third . . .) numbers. A typical activity: match the sets of eggs to the right bunnies (each bunny has a number on his cap). Kids write numbers, draw sets of objects corresponding to numbers, color the right number of objects, do simple number word puzzles, cut and paste objects in the correct order, and so on. Each activity is simple and fun.

Color Words (130 pages) is really a variety of art and craft exercises. Kids color, cut out, and put together a variety of seasonal, historic, and holiday models, including (among many examples) a pioneer covered wagon complete with horses, jack-in-the-box, snowflake, Valentine folder, and my favorite, the log cabin. Super fun!

Letter Recognition (104 pages) includes lots of games and flashcards; dot-to-dot activities; matching activities, and more. Easy to use pre-reading fun.

Word Skills (238 pages) is a treasure trove for kids just learning to read. It effortlessly teaches all the tricky spelling stuff: roots and endings, how to add endings to a word (no more agonizing over words such as *swimming* or *babies!*), compound words, possessives, contractions, prefixes, suffixes, syllables, and even dictionary skills. Our nine-year-old daughter who *could not* learn to spell picked it up in a flash with the help of this book. Very highly recommended—as is the whole series. *Mary Pride*

Wouldn't it be nice if teaching language arts were simple? Wouldn't it be nice if someone would figure out a way to keep all the subject areas in one place, centered around one book? Someone has. **Total Language Plus** (which has nothing to do with the "Whole Language" phonics substitute found in public schools today) is a a comprehensive language arts curriculum with a Christian perspective and a unit studies flavor. The child reads a book considered to be first-rate literature (most are Newbery Medal or Honor award winners), then completes the corresponding Total Language Plus workbook. Spelling, vocabulary, critical thinking, writing, grammar, dictation, reading comprehension, and even some fun projects are all a part of this novel-centered program.

Designed to take 90 minutes of your time for five days a week, each consumable workbook will take approximately seven weeks to complete. It is recommended that you use one workbook per quarter with one to two weeks of breathing space between unit studies.

Author Barbara Blakey has written study guides for age levels from fifth grade all the way up to honors high school English. You can plan on finishing one book per quarter, and the guides are conveniently priced in sets of four (you choose the titles, novels not included). Definitely plan on purchasing the teacher's manual. For under $5 you get a thorough overview of the program as well as teaching hints for each of the subject areas. It's well worth it!

First things first: TLP gets an A+ for their well organized and super-informative catalog. Each study guide description includes the overall themes of the novel as well as a heads-up for any possible controversial subject matter. While all the books may not be written from a Christian perspective, all the study guides most certainly are. Each novel has been chosen for its ability to withstand several weeks of study, its literary merit, and its interest to both boys and girls.

While it's possible that younger students have read some of the novels, it's recommended that TLP be used no sooner than fifth grade. By this age,

NEW!
Total Language Plus
Grades 5–12. Elementary student study guides, $16.95 each or 4 for $65. High school study guides, $18.95, 4 for $65. (one year's worth, if you do a book each quarter). Teacher's manual, $3.75. Shipping extra.
Blakey Publications, P.O. Box 12622, Olympia, WA 98508. (360) 754-3660. Fax: (360) 754-3505. Email: tlp@integrityol.com. Web: www.integrityol.com/tlp.

About the only thing lacking are instructions for the teacher on how to grade the writing assignments. If you are not comfortable in this area, you won't find a lot of help here. If possible, try to enlist the aid of another homeschool teacher who is proficient in this area, or even find an off-duty English teacher. (Homeschoolers may want to check out Cindy Marsch's Writing Assessment Services for help: *members.aol.com/cmarsch786/index.htm*)

All of the study guides follow the same format, with the exception of the upper-level high school guides. Your week's worth of activities, each designed to coordinate with specific chapters in the book you are reading, consists of:

- Reading: assignments of typically 40–45 pages, followed by reading comprehension questions in the study guide. You can do part of these in writing and part orally if you wish.
- Grammar: three days' worth of dictation passages, some from Scripture, some from the novel. The fourth day is always a grammar activity based on one of the passages.
- Spelling: words come from the novel and are studied thoroughly using a variety of methods (flash cards, etymologies, games, word analysis).
- Vocabulary: same as the spelling words, four days' worth of activities (context clues, matching dictionary definitions to words, creating your own glossary, puzzles, and word analysis).
- Enrichment: Choose from various options for each week. The four categories are Projects, Pictures, Pen and Paper, and Personal Thinking. This is the critical thinking "meat" of the program. The activities allow for a variety of creative styles and interpretations and lend themselves well to both discussion and written assignments.

NEW!
Word Arcade

Grades 1–6. $49.95. Lesson Sets, $14.95 each. Optional AC adaptor, $9.95. Shipping extra.
Educational Insights, Inc., 16941 Keegan Ave., Carson, CA 90746. (800) 995-4436. (310) 884-2000. Fax: (800) 995-0506. Web: www.edin.com.

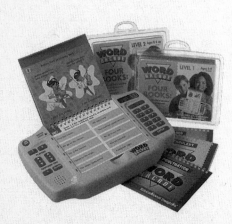

students are well grounded in the basics of reading, writing, and grammar. They can construct a decent sentence and paragraph, they are up to the task of tackling a novel in depth, and their abstract and critical thinking skills are developed more fully.

Teacher prep time is kept to a minimum. A planning grid in the front of each consumable guide tells you exactly what to cover each day in all the subject areas. An answer key is provided in the back of the book (just tear it out if you'd rather not tempt your student). Although it isn't mandatory that you read the novel being studied, I can't imagine not being able to interact over the subject matter. Moms, read the books!

The author, Barbara Blakey, stresses that you may do as many, or as few of the activities as you like. In fact, she put all of the activities at the front of the book so that we homeschool moms won't put ourselves on a guilt trip if we don't do *every* single activity relating to each chapter of the book our child is studying! Very considerate!

Let's take a look at some examples. The activities for *My Side of the Mountain* included researching wild plants, making a pole calendar and using it, hand sewing a garment, illustrating Sam's mountain in each of the four seasons, writing a report on barometers, composing a psalm, and listing the items you would bring along if you were to live in a wilderness area near your home. You can see how these types of activities would help the child internalize the book.

The study guides are workbook in format and are well laid out and easy on the eyes. No pictures or color, but an enthusiastic teacher can compensate for that.

How do these compare to other products on the market for homeschoolers? Probably most similar to the Progeny Press study guides (which I also like, and you can find in the Literature chapter). However, TLP offers a more cohesively packaged product. If you are strictly looking for literature study, then Progeny Press is always a great choice. But for an all-in-one language package, Total Language is tops. *Renee Mathis and Cynthia Madsen*

Word Arcade is a small electronic machine that drills basic language arts. It comes with special little books to teach and drill with. Every page has a code on it. You enter the code into the Word Arcade machine and it's ready to go. You can play with one player for solitaire or with two players for competition. The Word Arcade will flash a light next to the multiple-choice question on the book that you need to answer. Then you type the number corresponding to your answer. If you get it right, the machine will make a bunch of beeps and bloops, and if you get it wrong the machine will give you a rather inharmonious blat sound.

Word Arcade's drill books open upwards instead of sideways like most books. This way they can fit into the Word Arcade's book holder. Lessons are arranged in double-page format. One page will have the lesson, the next page will have the test. Every page of every drill book is full-color.

Word Arcade drill books come in sets of four books, each set containing a total of 100 lessons. Primary is for grades 1–3. Intermediate is for grades 3 and up. The Primary and Intermediate lesson sets each include one book apiece for vocabulary lessons, spelling lessons, grammar, and punctuation. These may involve, for example, matching words to their synonyms, or deciding whether a group of words is alphabetized correctly or not.

The Word Arcade is made of hard plastic, has nice rounded corners, a little door to close in your drill book, and a compartment for another book. It measures about ten inches wide by six inches tall by two inches thick. Due to being a lot smaller than the other Educational Insights drill machines, the Word Arcade makes a great car game. *Joseph Pride*

CHAPTER 16

Creative Writing

Writing receives less attention in the public school curriculum than any other core subject. It takes time to teach children to write well, and teachers are overburdened. It takes attention to detail, and many teachers have been taught to believe that details are petty. It takes, most of all, an appreciation and understanding of good writing, and the present generation of teachers has itself been denied this instruction.

To give you an example of how ridiculous the teaching of creative writing has become: Have you ever heard of "topic sentences"? Here's how children are actually being taught to write a paragraph:

(1) Write a topic sentence. This states the theme of the paragraph.

(2) Add several "supporting" sentences. These give extra details and support the theme.

(3) Write a concluding sentence to summarize the paragraph.

This approach leads to lively writing of the following sort:

Scott is a good dog. He comes when I call him. He never wets the rug. He doesn't bite the letter carrier. Yes, Scott is a good dog.

Workbooks are actually available, with titles like *How to Write a Paragraph*, that teach kids this is the right way to write.

Too bad nobody was around to teach these rules to Robert Louis Stevenson (I pick him almost by random). Take a look at the second paragraph of *Treasure Island:*

I remember him as if it were yesterday, as he came plodding to the inn door, his sea chest following behind him in a hand-barrow; a tall, strong, heavy, nut-brown man; his tarry pigtail falling over the shoulders of his soiled blue coat; his hands ragged and scarred, with black, broken nails; and the sabre cut across one cheek, a dirty, livid white. I remember him looking round the cove and whistling to himself as he did so, and then breaking out in that old sea-song that he sang so often afterward:—

Six Quick Ways to Revive a Dead Sentence

1. Substitute "action pictures" for dead adjectives and adverbs.

BEFORE: Dick was very happy.

AFTER: Dick leaped for joy . . . screamed for joy . . . beamed . . . glowed with delight . . . tingled with joy . . .

BEFORE: Dick was unhappy.

AFTER: Dick felt his heart breaking into sharp flinty pieces, each leaving a jagged wound.

2. Substitute more colorful adjectives whenever you see "very," "kind of," and other dead words.

BEFORE: Dick was very happy.

AFTER: Dick was elated . . . euphoric . . . exalted . . . delighted . . .

3. Tell us who is doing what. Be concrete.

BEFORE: It has often been felt that excessive spending reflects poorly on Congress. [Questions: *Who* feels this? *What* are they feeling? *About what* are they feeling it?}

AFTER: Average citizens [that's *who*] get grumpy [that's *what*] when Congress keeps spending more money than it should [that's *about what*].

4. Don't overdo the adjectives. Show instead of tell, when possible.

BEFORE: The big, fat, old, bald man walked past me as a strong breeze blew.

AFTER: I'm not saying he was big as an elephant, but I definitely felt the ground shake as the old gent wallowed by, the wind whistling in what would have been his hair if he'd had any.

5. If you're tempted to rant and rave, try understatement instead.

BEFORE: *Eyeball Stew* was absolutely the most disgusting, putrid, awful movie I've ever seen!

AFTER: *Eyeball Stew* was sadly lacking in socially redeeming quality. In fact, it was sadly lacking in quality of any sort. If you feel a real need to regurgitate, this is the movie for you.

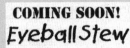

COMING SOON! *Eyeball Stew*

Quality . . . This is the movie for you!

6. To make the mundane sound exciting, use warlike and/or sports imagery. This is how writers of business books keep their readers awake.

BEFORE: I tried to convince my boss to use the new slogan.

AFTER: I led the charge for the new slogan.

BEFORE: We're going to try to increase our market share.

AFTER: We're going to pound the competition! Take no prisoners! Squash them like bugs!

BEFORE: The sales team had a meeting and decided to hand off the responsibility to the engineering department.

AFTER: The sales team went into a huddle and decided to pass the puck to Engineering. [Note: it's OK to mix sports metaphors when talking to business types, since few play any sports.]

> Fifteen men on the dead man's chest—
> Yo-ho-ho, and a bottle of rum!
>
> in the high, old tottering voice that seemed to have been tuned and broken at the capstan bars. Then he rapped on the door with a bit of stick like a handspike that he carried, and when my father appeared, called roughly for a glass of rum. This, when it was brought to him, he drank slowly, like a connoisseur, lingering on the taste, and still looking about him at the cliffs and up at our sign-board.

We translate this now, according to the rules of topic sentences, supporting sentences, and summary sentences:

> *I remember what a character the old seaman was. He was tall and strong. He was heavy and tanned. He had a tarry pigtail. His coat was blue and dirty. His hands were ragged and scarred. His fingernails were black and broken. He had a sabre cut across one cheek. Yes, he was a real character!*
>
> *The old seaman did strange things. He looked around the cove and whistled to himself. Then he sang a sea-song: "Fifteen men on the dead man's chest, Yo-ho-ho and a bottle of rum!" He sang it in a high, old voice. Then he rapped on the inn door with a stick. He called for a bottle of rum. He drank the rum slowly, enjoying the taste. All the time he was drinking he was looking about him at the cliffs and up at our sign-board. Yes, he was a strange person!*

These are the kinds of sentences and paragraphs kids are learning to write in school. They are bad sentences. They are bad paragraphs. Yes, kids are learning to write badly in school!

You may be wondering why I chose the second paragraph of *Treasure Island* for an example of the great gulf fixed between real literature and topic-sentence writing. That's because the *first* paragraph of *Treasure Island* is a single sentence!

The first antidote to topic-sentence hack writing, then, is to read *real* literature. The second? See the resources below.

How to Teach Writing

Writing is easy to teach at home. All you have to do is (1) get a copy of **Any Child Can Write** by Harvey Weiner, and (2) put it into practice. *Any Child Can Write* is absolutely the best book ever written, and quite possibly the best that ever *will* be written, on teaching children to write. It's simple. It's inspiring. It's thorough. It's based on the author's own extensive experience teaching in schools, and on his experience teaching his own daughter at home. Melissa Weiner was writing and illustrating before she was four, and by the time she was five she was coming up with imagery like this:

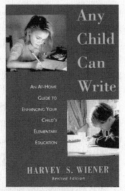

> *This is me. I like to dance and sing a song like a robin. I love to ice skate in red skates. I slip and slide and go errrrr on the freezing ice.*

Thanks to Bantam Books, this fantastic book is finally back in print.

I can't tell you anything about writing that Dr. Weiner hasn't already put in his book. Here are some of the high points for beginning writers.

Writing begins with speaking. Encourage complete sentences, and draw your children on to describe what they see and feel as crisply as possible. Once a child learns to write, *let* him write! Letters to Grandma and shopping lists make things really happen. Mom or Dad can act as secretary and write out Johnny's stories if handwriting is still a struggle. Then Dr. Weiner shows you how to help your kids make their ideas come alive by inserting adjectives and adverbs, choosing sparkling nouns and verbs, adding word pictures, and all the other gambits that separate the real writer from the topic-sentence hack.

Dr. Weiner's great contribution is in showing parents how to nourish the creative process. The vitality and joy that children pour into their poetry and prose when they have discovered how to see the world with an artist's eye make this book a delight to read. Very highly recommended. *Mary Pride*

Want to be a success in homeschooling? Then realize that your job is to learn the subject you want to teach! Once you know a subject, and know how to teach it, you can use virtually any resource and teach it successfully.

So, if you want to teach kids creative writing, learn how to teach it first. To learn how to teach it, get Ruth Beechick's *You CAN Teach Your Child Successfully* (from Education Services) and get **If You're Trying to Teach Kids to Write, You've Gotta Have this Book!** by Marjorie Frank. The title says it all. Packed into these 220 pages are more thoughts, tips, philosophy, examples, resources, and helps for teaching creative writing than you'll find in any other one spot except Mrs. Beechick's book. Sections like "100 Alternatives to *What I Did on My Summer Vacation*" take you beyond the typical loser writing lesson. Find out how to motivate the reluctant writer, the gifted writer, the very young writer. How to recover from floppo lessons. What to do with the finished writing. How to criticize writing constructively (wish all *my* critics would read that section!). How to start "word collections" of words like *smithereens* and *bamboozle* that are fun just to say. People-watching: an essential skill for writers of fiction and non-fiction alike. Tons more, all shared from the heart of a writer who evidently loves writing and cares about helping your children do likewise. *Mary Pride*

Helping your young child learn to write can shake your confidence and send you scrambling for reinforcement: "Do other kindergartners make up letters? Can I fix her errors without discouraging her? How can we use our computer?" If you don't have access to veteran homeschoolers in a support group, **Let's Write: A Practical Guide to Teaching Writing in the Early Grades** can help.

Nancy Areglado, Mary Dill, and the three other contributors all teach at a Virginia elementary school. Their yearbook-type manual full of photos gives an inside look at how writing works at Rolling Hills School. The samples alone should spark new ideas and quell anxieties about your child's performance. And although many suggested activities are best suited to a classroom, most of the photos show children working alone, with one other child, or with a teacher—a clear advantage for homeschoolers!

This large-format quality paperback presents standard educational concepts, such as the teacher's role, planning, and assessment, but within each chapter nestle the everyday how-to's these teachers use. You'll learn to motivate with paper colors and formats, use kinesthetic punctuation for read-alouds, get past common problems in invention and mechanics, create nifty "publishing" formats like flip books and shaped or "double door" books, and keep track of student progress.

Of special interest for the neat and organized are the 20-odd reproducible pages in the back, including assessment records, grade-level goals

If You're Trying to Teach Kids to Write, You've Gotta Have this Book!

Parents. $16.95 plus shipping. *Shekinah Curriculum Cellar, 101 Meador Rd., Kilgore, TX 75662. (903) 643-2760. Fax: (903) 643-2796. Email: customerservice@shekinahcc.com. Web: www.shekinahcc.com.*

NEW!
Let's Write

Grades K–2. $13.95 plus shipping. *Scholastic Professional Books, 2931 East McCarty St., Jefferson City, MO 65102. (800) 724-6527. Fax: (800) 223-4011. Web: www.scholastic.com.*

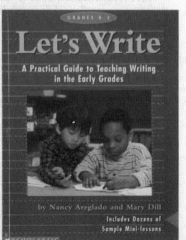

for the children to "own," student revision checklists, a couple of composition templates, and award certificates. This book should be of special help to any writing co-op teacher.

Note: The easy-going approach to grammar and spelling may clash with a very formal language arts curriculum. *Cindy Marsch*

Don't cross this pricey item off your homeschooling budget quite yet! Offering over six hours of seminar, a workbook with reproducible charts, toll-free consultation and evaluation, and a grade-specific workshop tape for your child, this package delivers. Not quite convinced? Try a money-back guarantee. In the IEW newsletter, Andrew Pudewa's happy students rave that it's the best money they've spent on curriculum.

The **Teaching Writing Video and Correspondence Seminar** is a worthy investment in professional development for homeschool teachers. Carefully outlining the written communication pathway, which includes taking notes, summarizing from notes, and creating non-fiction and fiction for almost every writing task, Pudewa previews both the course of the seminar and the suggested development of an individual student writer. He shows us simply, step by step. Students read a sample paragraph. They write three-word notes. They summarize from the notes. Into the midst of the structure sneaks the style. Even second-graders use dress-ups (specific grammatical features) and openers (variations to start a sentence.) Following the pathway, because it is clear, students and parents travel smoothly from non-fiction paragraphs and story retellings to research reports and literature critiques.

Like ingredients in a complex recipe, the Structure and Style elements can be prepared separately and used later in a variety of combinations. Mastering the notes, polishing the reconstituted paragraphs, and planning the use of dress-ups and openers, students perfect individual short pieces. But then comes the surprise. Cleverly the teacher assigns a groaner "report"—then reveals that it's already half-written! The individual pieces plug into an outline and, with the addition of a framing introduction and conclusion, create a stick-to-your-ribs concoction.

It's not just hype. My seven- and nine-year-olds worked with me on a paragraph from an American Girls story about a horse. Originally one sentence read, "One morning, after Felicity had been visiting her for a few weeks, Penny took the apple right from her hand." Because we had just three words to summarize, we wrote "weeks from hand." Of course Mom helped *and* held back, but here's our result: "It took a few short weeks for Penny to get used to lipping the apple from Felicity's hand willingly." Though we debated the placement of "willingly," and though it needs more work, we agreed it is better than the original.

Invest in the foundation of your homeschool writing program with Teaching Writing: Structure and Style. The videos and practicum inspire and build confidence, and the reproducible checklists and reminder signs provide practical help. Slavishly adhering to the techniques may stifle, and Pudewa is a bit loose about how to grade the final results, but he stresses teacher choice in all these things. As an added value, the seminar techniques should enhance your own skills—I used them to write this review! *Cindy Marsch*

Writing is not a secret art, but a natural part of life, to be nurtured and encouraged, according to Cherie Fuller, an experienced teacher and workshop leader. Because it is not a set curriculum, her book **Teaching Your Child to Write** may help you "shake out" from a stifling programmed curriculum, especially if you are relaxing your homeschool.

Fuller cites plenty of educational research, mostly common sense: read stories to children and they'll be interested in reading and writing stories. She guides parents with clues on what to foster or avoid, and she sets forth mostly informal projects—email, diaries, book reports, homemade books, and stories, with an especially strong set of ideas on poems. Budding authors will find hints on publishing, and a helpful appendix includes a condensed approach to grammar and writing assessment keyed to grade levels. *Cindy Marsch*

Writing from Home is great! This book is much more than "a portfolio of homeschooled student writing," as its subtitle modestly implies. True, editor Susan Richman first got the idea for the book from the student portfolios she was evaluating (Pennsylvania law requires such portfolios). But, being the unique lady she is, she had the additional idea of including the children's and parents' thoughts about the children's writing right along with the writing itself.

This book has not only hundreds of inspirational examples of student writing (inspirational in the sense that your child will be inspired, not overawed, by what other children his age have accomplished), but dozens of ideas for helping our children improve their writing. I am hardly ever tempted to say a book has everything, but this one comes mighty close. From a whole chapter on how to create a productive writing environment, to the final index of books on writing and major writing contests your children can enter, I don't see how anyone can read *Writing from Home* and not be surprised and excited about the possibilities captured between the covers of this book. Kids will feel the same way. Thanks to the book's non-patronizing tone, they can read it right along with you! *Mary Pride*

This extremely useful book, written by Dave Marks, begins by explaining why parents should encourage their children's writing. It then pinpoints nine conditions which make the teaching of writing difficult and gives tips to alleviate those problems. Following this is a very worthwhile section about common problems which affect the quality of a composition. Writing problems such as the unconscious repeating of words or phrases, ambiguity, and pronoun reference and agreement are defined and solutions given to correct them.

In one of the most helpful sections of the book, Dave Marks actually models the evaluating process for you. There are seven examples of student compositions spanning **Writing Strands** Levels 2–5 for you to peruse. He includes both the rough draft and final draft of each composition, and then proceeds to evaluate the student's work. He gives an example of a conversation he might have with the child both praising the positive aspects of the

---

NEW!
Teaching Your Child to Write

Parents. $12 plus shipping.
Cherie Fuller, PO Box 770493, Oklahoma City, OK 73177. Phone/Fax: (405) 749-1381. Web: www.cander.net/~cheri.

NEW!
Writing from Home

All ages. $8.95 paperback, $15.95 hardback. Shipping extra.
Pennsylvania Homeschoolers, R. D. 2, Box 117, Kitanning, PA 16201. Phone/fax: (724) 783-6512. Email: richmans@pahomeschoolers.com. Web: www.pahomeschoolers.com.

NEW!
Writing Strands: Evaluating Writing

Parents. $19.95 plus shipping.
National Writing Institute, 810 Damon Court, Houston, TX 77006-1329. (800) 688-5375. Fax: (713) 522-1934. Email: info@writingstrands.com. Web: www.writingstrands.com.

composition and picking out one mechanical error or element of the composition which could be improved.

Evaluating Writing also includes guidelines for drafting papers, suggestions for teaching spelling, and definitions of commonly confused words.

Also included is **Fixit**, a DOS computer program which helps solve mechanical problems in writing. Once DOS is booted, the program is activated by typing FIXIT. The menu displays the writing problem directing the user to the definitions, rules, and examples of the rules in operation. This program, which you get on a 5¼" diskette, functions well as a quick grammar reference. *Cynthia Madsen*

Writing with Results is a 315-page manual on how to develop writing assignments for children based on a skills checklist. Different types of writing are covered at appropriate grade levels. These include story writing, poetry, newspaper articles, journals, book reports, letters, reports, essays, autobiographies, biographies, sentences, paragraphs, and how to begin with young children.

Author JoAnne Moore, holder of a bachelor's degree in education, notes, "The moral imagination seeks to encourage the reader to develop virtue and to face life's hardships with right choices and faithfulness. The idyllic imagination seeks only to escape from life's hardships and provides no model for how to face them." Hence the writing lessons in her book are based on stories that inspire the moral imagination more than the idyllic imagination.

A very useful writing growth chart helps the teaching parent quickly determine the difficulty of an assignment before giving it to the student. There are seven levels based on the amount of planning responsibility the child has for the setting, character, plot, and resolution. The more planning a child has to do, the more difficult the assignment. Next, keys to dynamic writing are presented. Children learn to "show" rather than "tell" in their writing by developing a vocabulary based on verbs, describing pictures, and using word banks to add in the telling. Rather than telling the reader his character is upset, the child will learn to describe facial expressions, body language, speech, and inner thoughts.

This would be a very useful guide for those using unit studies, or who have a curriculum with very little guidance in teaching writing. It isn't a get-in-and-drive program, though; you'll have to be motivated yourself to digest the information within the book and translate it into assignments for your child. *Kathy von Duyke*

Writing Curriculum

Parents who thought Scholastic Books only made pocket paperbacks should take a look at this magnificent instruction book for creative writing! This 45-page book begins with full directions on how to make a creative writing course productive and successful, whether in the classroom or home. **325 Creative Prompts for Personal Journals** suggests that five or ten minutes of journal writing each day has the potential to evolve into complete writing assignments. Steps and procedures are outlined, as well as instructions on how to create more and more journal prompts. Seven chapters of sparkling prompts range from Memories, Current Affairs, and Quotations to the intriguing subject of Multicultural Connections and Personal Experiences. One suggested prompt to "Invent the Best Dessert in the Whole World" led to some amazing experiments in the kitchen! The prompt "List Everything That is Valuable or Precious to You and Tell Why You Value It" led to some particularly in depth soul searching.

NEW!
Writing with Results
Grades 1-6. $28 plus shipping.
Books for Results, 94 Deerview Terrace SE, Calgary, Alberta T2J 7C1 Canada. (403) 271-9085. Fax: (403) 278-1160.

NEW!
325 Creative Prompts For Personal Journals
Grades 4–8. $10.95 plus shipping.
Scholastic Professional Books, 2931 East McCarty St., Jefferson City, MO 65102. (800) 724-6527. Fax: (800) 223-4011. Web: www.scholastic.com.

This instructor's manual will help students become better writers, better thinkers, and better feelers, while enriching any language arts curriculum. The sparks are here . . . parents need only supply a notebook, a pencil, and a child! *Lisa Mitchell*

NEW!
The Better Letter Book

Grades 3–6. $6.95 plus shipping. *The Learning Works, Inc., PO Box 6187, Santa Barbara, CA 93160. Orders: (800) 235-5767. Fax: (805) 964-1466.*

Though **The Better Letter Book** is for kids in grades 3–6, don't be surprised if your older children want to use it, too. This letter-writing guide has it all! Through excellent detail and directions, students learn the different types and parts of a letter and ways to make their writing exciting, appealing, and effective. Divided into four parts, this workbook is full of fantastic graphics and provides activities in an assortment of writing skills, including complaints, apologies, and condolences. Perhaps the most fun activity is the assignment to write a to public official. Addresses for all U.S. and Canadian public officials are included, as well as the titles by which they are to be addressed. Activities in creating stationery and postcards move this 64-page workbook into the area of arts and crafts, and easy-to-follow directions will surely make for an afternoon of fun. An explanation of zip codes completes the book, and there is also a handy list of state and province abbreviations for quick reference. *The Better Letter Book* can become a resource to any home, used by children and parents alike for years to come. *Lisa Mitchell*

Easy Writing

Grades 2–9. $24.09 postpaid. *ISHA Enterprises, PO Box 12520, Scottsdale, AZ 85267. Orders: (800) 641-6015. Inquiries: (480) 502-9454. Fax: (480)502-9456. Web: www.easygrammar.com.*

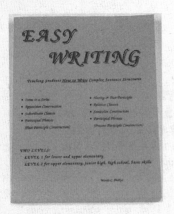

Easy Writing, by Wanda Phillips, author of *Easy Grammar,* is a big, thick workbook full of carefully sequenced and graded exercises to help students spiff up their sentences by the use of more complex sentence structures. In other words, instead of "Bill ran. Ann ran, too. They were screaming. They ran to the house," the student will learn to write, "Screaming, Bill and Ann ran to the house." An improvement, no?

The book has several innovative features. For one thing, each unit comes in two levels. Level 1 is for lower and upper elementary students, while Level 2 is for upper elementary on up. Her book is also very logically laid out, with one unit each on writing items in a series, semicolons, appositives, participial phrases (both past and present participles), the use of "having" plus the past participle, and subordinate and relative clauses. If this all sounds rather gruesome, it really isn't so when you get into it. You get clear instructions, lots of examples, and doable exercises. Each exercise set fits on two pages and should take only about 15 minutes to complete. There's lots of repetition in both the instructions and the exercises. None of this here-today gone-tomorrow outlook about *Easy Writing!*

This book definitely has its merits. It's extremely simple to use. Everything is explained right in the lesson. No preparation time is needed. The exercises are easy to grade with the answer keys at the end of each section. You can use this one book with children of all ages—a whole *Cheaper by the Dozen* family, if they write the answers on separate paper! There's enough repetition to learn the concepts, without so much as to cause unutterable boredom. If you balance the one-size-fits-all suggested answers with a dash of William Zinsser's *On Writing Well*, your child will be scribbling better sentences than 97 percent of today's American high school graduates. *Mary Pride*

This series of three books lets students put their language-arts training to use. This is great for really "cementing" what was previously only theoretical knowledge of spelling, grammar, and usage.

Each **Editor In Chief** workbook includes 33 editing exercises. These are in the form of essays or letters, each accompanied by a visual with additional information. For example, along with an article about "finding fingerprints" there is an illustration of fingerprint powder being dusted on a jewelry box, captioned, "A grey or black powder is used to dust hard surface for fingerprints. Chemicals are used on soft surfaces."

Your student, as the "editor in chief," has the job of finding and correcting all the errors in the written material. Each exercise includes at least one *content* error (described as "a discrepancy between the illustration/caption and the writing sample") and five to eight errors in spelling, mechanics, and grammar. Following the editing checklist at the beginning of the book, your child tracks down and corrects the errors. Answers are in the back of the book, along with explanations of what type each error was. A Guide to Grammar, Usage and Punctuation is also built into each of these workbooks, so students have detailed information about these rules, along with examples to demonstrate the rules.

Levels A-1 and B-1 include lines below each exercise for the student to rewrite it properly, or to catalog the errors. By the time you get to level C-1, it helps for the student to know common editing symbols, as there is no space to completely rewrite the lengthier essays in this book (as if anyone would want to!).

The written material your student will be editing is itself educational, and the program is easy to use. I just wish there were more exercises! *Mary Pride*

The Essay Handbook is designed to lead the student through the process of essay writing. The basic essay as it is taught in this program consists of four sections—setting, problem, reflection/solution, and conclusion—and is built in four steps:

- Essay Outline Note Forms. The writer uses a key word or short phrases to respond to questions that create the building blocks for each section.
- Essay Planning Sheets. The student transforms the words and phrases from Step 1 into key sentences and simple paragraphs.
- Rough Draft Writing Forms. Sentences and paragraphs are filled out, giving attention to capitalization, punctuation, and grammar.
- Final Draft Writing Forms. The budding essayist completes the final draft.

The book includes a basic essay model which can be used for elementary students and for remedial junior high and high school students and an advanced essay model which can be used by regular junior high and high school students. You also get a list of suggested essay themes. Very little preparation or background is required, besides a good grammar handbook. *Cynthia Madsen*

A simple cure for "idea amnesia," Michelle Van Loon's slim booklet **From Heart to Page: Journaling Through the Year for Young Writers** inspires children with seasonal topics for the common writing journal. She vividly describes cultivating young writers as orchardists' espalier fruit trees: "The disciplines of spelling, grammar and vocabulary study are the fence upon which we train our young writers. But the growth will be hard

NEW!
Editor In Chief
Book A-1 (grades 4–6), $14.95. Book B-1 (grades 6–8), $15.95. Book C-1 (grades 8–adult), $16.95. All 3 books, $42.95. Shipping extra. *Critical Thinking Books & Software, PO Box 448, Pacific Grove, CA 93950-0448. (800) 458-4849. Fax: (831) 323-3277. Email: ct@criticalthinking.com. Web: www.criticalthinking.com.*

NEW!
The Essay Handbook
Grades 5–12. $13 plus $3.20 shipping. *Christian Family Resources, PO Box 405, Kit Carson, CO 80825. (719) 962-3228. Fax: (719)962-3232. Call only between 1:00 PM-5:00 PM MST.*

NEW!
From Heart to Page
Grades K–12. $5 postpaid. *Michelle Van Loon, 2833 Lincolnshire Court, Waukesha, WI 53188. (414) 542-2998. wvanloon@worldnet.att.net.*

and woody if we're not willing to feed the soil, and help their young roots sink deep into rich earth." The booklet then opens to "Autumn" and includes topics like these:

- Write a letter to your mom today. Ask her 3 questions. Have her write back to you in your journal.
- Describe your perfect autumn day.
- Have you ever been lost? Can you describe a time when that happened? How did you feel?

If you have difficulty coming up with creative writing exercises, these gentle ideas may help train your writers to more productively bring forth the fruit of their hearts. *Cindy Marsch*

NEW!
Hayes Learning to Write Poetry

Grades 3–6. $4.95 plus shipping. *Hayes School Publishing Co., Inc., 321 Pennwood Ave., Pittsburgh, PA 15221-3398. (800) 245-6234. Fax: (412) 371-6408. Web: www.hayespub.com.*

Hayes is the undiscovered treasure trove of homeschooling, with a wonderful—and large—line of basic and supplemental workbooks for all elementary grades and subjects. **Learning to Write Poetry** is another winner. Activities encourage children to play with words, create word pictures, laugh with words, and experiment with sound and rhyme. The book uses light, witty poetry to draw children in. The student works through activities involving similes, metaphors, and synonyms. He also learns poetry forms, including couplets, haiku, and limericks. Only a few activities have correct or incorrect answers, which allows great freedom of expression. Activities build on each other. There is an excellent poetry glossary, an answer key, and perky illustrations. Playing with words and writing in a funny way are important skills for poets, and this book provides a great sense of fun and play. *Cynthia Madsen*

NEW!
Listen to This: Developing an Ear for Expository

Grades 4–12. $14.95 plus shipping. *Maupin House Publishing, PO Box 90148, Gainesville, FL 32607-0148. (800) 524-0634. Fax: (352) 373-5546. Email: jgraddy@maupinhouse.com.*

Too often our children clamor for creative writing and balk at essays. They think nonfiction is daunting and dull. Prove them wrong! Go in the ear gate, the eye gate, and the tastebud gate with **Listen to This: Developing an Ear for Expository**.

This 120-page paperback opens with a "primer." Go through its many features slowly, especially with younger writers. Then come a variety of essays, simple to complex, emphasizing argument appeals, organization, and features of lively writing.

There are no specific writing assignments, only notes to "try this technique in your next piece," so you'll need to look elsewhere if you want a full writing curriculum.

For an example of the kind if exercises in this book, read the piece entitled "Chocolate" to your students. Let them roll a Hershey's Kiss around in their mouths as you read. Then see if they remember Aztec, Montezuma, and the gooey white pulp the secret beans hide in. See if they can identify the hook at the beginning, the secret of the introduction repeated in the conclusion, and the chronological development throughout. Having found these, they should be able to incorporate them more fully in their own work.

Other pieces (mostly persuasive) of the eighteen found in this book include "Don't Run With Those Scissors!," "Kids Who Are Different," and "Myths of the Milky Way." In the back a handy grade-specific bibliography suggests further good reading.

Perhaps the most valuable function of this text is to help develop an ear for expository writing so that you find excellent examples from your own family readings to study for expository technique. Carry out the techniques in frequent writing and your children will learn that essays can be creative, too! *Cindy Marsch*

"Come and play!" What child doesn't love to hear an invitation like that? **Pencil Playground** invites your children to come and play creatively . . . with words. For your elementary-level children, creative writing can be like recess: a time to stretch their imaginations and have fun. And Pencil Playground looks like fun!

Inside the three-ring binder, you'll find nine colorfully tabbed, four-week units. They are written in inviting, child-friendly language. Lots of clean black-and-white graphics and easy-to-follow directions make it easy for your child to jump in and begin writing fearlessly.

For example, one unit encourages you to act as a reporter, putting together a story about an older relative or friend (the older, the better). Your child begins by listing all of the older relatives in their lives, delivering an invitation to one of them to spend time being interviewed, brainstorming a list of everything he or she knows about the interview subject, and writing them in note boxes in the text. Your child is encouraged to use a tape recorder to ask the interviewee questions in the text: "How did you meet your husband or wife?" "What event would you say was the most difficult in your life?" "What were your parents' occupations?" Afterwards he or she can use the tape to help them record the answers in more note boxes. Next, your child will cut out all the completed note boxes and arrange them in groups on construction paper. Finally, your child is encouraged to send a thank-you card to the interview subject.

You can receive a certificate of completion by sending in the story or project from each of the nine units, if you'd like. However, the emphasis is on process, not product. A friendly tone, the ability to teach several skill levels at once, an approachable look, and an imaginative presentation make this product a terrific "playmate" for your beginning writer. *Michelle Van Loon*

The Write Source, published by the company of the same name, is an excellent English grammar, writing, and general information handbook. I am delighted that Shekinah is carrying it, because the publisher was not set up to handle individual orders and I thought I'd have to leave it out of my book!

The *Write Source* handbook includes a great deal of information useful to students in grades 4–9. Writing skills covered: the writing process, the classroom report, the book review, the short story, the poem, the letter, thinking and study skills, vocabulary and spelling skills, library skills, and speech skills . . . for a start! Other useful information includes the United States Constitution, U.S. and world maps, computer terms, and more! It's a bit hard to describe such a compendium of everything-you-need-to-know-about-everything. Suffice it to say that this is a great source of information about writing, loaded with facts writers find useful. The Write Source has the write stuff, all right!

Shekinah is also making the rest of the *Write Source* line of workbooks available. These are designed to be used with the handbook. **Basic Writing** concentrates on creative writing skills activities. **Mechanics of Writing** includes lessons on punctuation, usage, capitalization, plurals, abbreviations, etc. **Revising Process** shows you how to spot subject-verb mismatches, fragments, run-on sentences, wordiness, and other bloopers; how to replace bland adjectives with zippy ones; how to add supporting details; how to kill off passive sentences; and so on. *Mary Pride*

NEW!
Pencil Playground

Grades 2–8. $34.95 postpaid (also available in German and British). Add $10 shipping outside USA. *Estella Graphics, RR #3, Box 369, Montrose, PA 18801. (570) 278-4504. Fax: (570) 278-4230. Web: www.pencilplayground.com.*

Shekinah Writing Books

Grades 4–9. The Write Source, $15.95. Basic Writing, $11.95 for student book or teacher's edition. Mechanics of Writing and Revising Process: Student book, $7.95. Teacher's edition, $11.95. Shipping extra. *Shekinah Curriculum Cellar, 101 Meador Rd., Kilgore, TX 75662. (903) 643-2760. Fax: (903) 643-2796. Email: customerservice@shekinahcc.com. Web: www.shekinahcc.com.*

A Strong Start in Language

Grades K–12. $12 (includes A Strong Start in Language and two booklets about teaching reading and math), plus $3.50 shipping. *Education Services, Mott Media, 8825 Blue Mountain Dr., Golden, CO 80403. (800)421-6645. Fax: (303)642-1288.*

NEW!
The WIN Program

Grades preK–12. Story Writing by Dictation, $6. Level I, $6. Level II and III, $20 each. Essay Handbook, $13. Term Paper Handbook, $10. Expository fee (with purchase of book), $7. Shipping extra. *Christian Family Resources, PO Box 405, Kit Carson, CO 80825. (719) 962-3228. Fax: (719) 962-3232. Call only between 1:00 PM-5:00 PM MST.*

Ruth Beechick does it again! **A Strong Start in Language** presents a powerful *natural* method that will help anyone become a good (maybe even great!) writer. Starting from the very beginning with a student who can physically write but has no understanding of sentence structure, Dr. Beechick's 13-step method can take you as far as you want to go. Ben Franklin used this method; so did Jack London. Included are grade-level guidelines, 14 sample lessons, instructions for spelling improvement, and some sample Bible sentences for writing practice. No supplies necessary except good library books, paper, and pencils. *Mary Pride*

People are talking about **the WIN program**, a step-by-step method for teaching story writing. Can good stories really be written "by the numbers"? Naturally we had to take a look!

Story Writing by Dictation: The Three Step Introduction to WIN, is designed for K–1 students whose written language skills are as yet undeveloped. Students begin learning the meaning of each of the four story parts (setting, problem, solving the problem, and conclusion) by answering the questions posed on "Dictation Forms." The Dictation Form is a logical framework for building simple stories. Everything the teacher has to do is spelled out—great for harried moms.

Level I, " A Simplified Introduction to Story Writing: The Seven Sentence Story," introduces paragraphs. Seven basic sentences form a story. The first paragraph answers the questions "when, who, and where?" The second sentence is the "starting event sentence" which indicates something interesting that is going to happen. In the next paragraph, the "problem paragraph," one sentence describes the conflict of the story. The third paragraph, "solving the problem," consists of two sentences—one which elaborates on the conflict, and one which tells how the conflict is solved. Finally, in the last paragraph, "the conclusion," two sentences tell what the people in the story feel and what they learned. "Detail sentences" can be added to the basic seven sentence story to add information which helps the reader better understand the story. Again, worksheets found in the back of the book walk the student through the seven-sentence story.

Level II, "Story Writing: The Four Parts of a Story," consists of model stories and accompanying specially designed learning sheets that direct and enable students to easily identify the major sections of a story and their components. In order to help the student understand how to put stories together, we meet a unique feature of WIN—the "connecting sentence." Students learn that these sentences, which are much like a summary, create a framework around which the rest of the story expands. Thirty user-friendly lessons give lots of examples and very detailed explanations.

Level III, "The Story Writing Program," adds dialogue and examines descriptive writing.

Cindy thought WIN is an excellent program, and plans to use it with her children. Mary thinks it is OK as a start, especially considering that the average high-school graduate nowadays can't even write any coherent simple story. *Cynthia Madsen and Mary Pride*

You are an apprentice at a newspaper. During your term on the job, you will get to try all the writing jobs on the newspaper. Such is the premise of **Wordsmith Apprentice**. Sound cutesy? Be surprised—this book manages to carry it off!

There's a method behind author Janie B. Cheaney's madness. You notice it the minute you open the spiral-bound book's table of contents. At the "editor's desk" you study nouns by making many different kinds of lists. You study verbs while writing "Help Wanted" ads. Caption writing, invitations, letters, and headlines also turn out to be handy for teaching sentence-related writing skills.

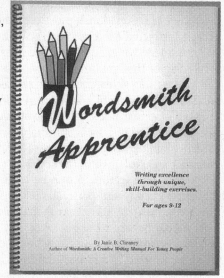

In the next section, which covers modifiers and more-complex sentences, the author craftily employs everything from "Tom Swifties" to real-estate ads to make her writing points—and provide you with fun exercises. Finally, things get advanced when you start writing *very* short news stories as a reporter, in the last section.

Comics-style sequences involving the editor and his crew of crazy characters both introduce writing skills and enliven the book. Writing examples of the before-and-after sort also make things clearer, which the author cajoles and exhorts you to do the job right. An excellent program, perfect for homeschool. Highly recommended. *Mary Pride*

What John Saxon does for mathematics, Dave Marks does for creative writing. Written with gentle wit and good humor, Dave Marks incorporates the "incremental approach" to writing. Each level in the series of seven books is a complete program in itself, and can be bought separately.

Level one, which includes a cassette, is loaded with engaging activities for parents to do with children ages two through eight, teaching them that language is rich and diverse. The games are designed to be adapted to different learning levels.

Levels two through seven are organized using the same basic format. Each level allows the student to progressively work more independently. The in-depth writing exercises in each level of the **Writing Strands** series generally explore these four common forms of composition: argumentative, explanatory, research and report, and creative. Each book is designed for 90 days of training and the student should produce a finished composition at the completion of each assignment. The assignments can be modified to accommodate your child's individual learning needs.

Skills and objectives to be mastered in each assignment are presented at the beginning of each book. All assignments are arranged to be completed within a week, and include specific, daily directives about what the student should accomplish. At the end of each assignment is a "problem list" in which the student and teacher identify any errors made in the assignment and correct them. As the student completes a writing assignment, the teacher and he will pick out just one mechanical error that can be worked on to make the paper better. Working on structure and grammatical problems incrementally in this way, over a period of time the child will thoroughly master the rules of writing.

The grammar philosophy advocated by the National Writing Institute is that "there is no relationship between the study of grammar as a separate skill in abstracted exercises and the ability to write." The rules of writing are introduced when children need to know them to do their assignments. While I agree that grammatical concepts must be taught in tandem with concrete writing skills, that doesn't mean that you don't need to have a good understanding of grammatical rules. Although the author feels that "any old grammar book will do," you will need to find a grammar program that you understand, feel comfortable with, and which will enable you to explain grammatical concepts to your children, because not all the rules of grammar are explained in the series.

Questionable feature: A number of the examples include unnecessarily unpleasant family and personal relationships, presented with little or no moral comment. While it is true that bad families exist, children of this age level should be writing about what they know—and bad families don't spend time and money on fancy homeschool curricula! We would like to see this corrected in a future edition.

This writing series has a very upbeat, positive attitude toward the writing process itself. The concept that student papers do not have to be perfect puts the student at ease. The injunction to the teacher to "praise, praise, praise" the student's efforts creates confidence. *Cynthia Madsen*

CHAPTER 17

Speech

Calling all curriculum providers! How can you expect homeschooled kids to win debates, make thrilling presentations, star in stage productions, and amaze adults everywhere with their verbal dexterity if you make them wait 'til they're 13 before you develop any speech and drama curriculum for them? Hmmm?

Not that *schooled* kids, as a group, are that terrific in these areas, either. Is that a new market niche I smell?

Here's all I could dig up to help shy kids speak up and innocent kids become verbally streetwise. Next edition, this chapter will be bigger, I bet!

Speaking up with Style

Want to "enjoy a warm and loving time together" with your family, "sharing thoughts and feelings and discovering new things about each other"? Feel like you need an extra little help to get your strong, silent family members to unclamp their strong, silent lips?

Designed by a family therapist, the **Chatter Matters** game is designed to enhance family communication. Before starting to play, everyone picks their secret wish on the pre-printed pad that comes with the game. These sound like lots of fun: family video night, breakfast in bed, later bedtimes, or an outing to the park, to name a few. As you advance your token around *Chatter Matters'* simple game board, you take turns answering questions such as:

- "In your family zoo, which animal would each person choose to be?"
- "What kind of ice cream cone would you be?"
- "Sing a little song that describes something unique about someone in your family."

This is an easy game to learn and play. As Bill says, "A minute to learn, a minute to master." *Chatter Matters* cards are color-coded to correspond to the spaces around the edge of the gameboard. Yellow, Green, and Pink cards are questions about you. Blue cards are questions about the person in the family to whom the spinner points. Red cards are questions the whole

family gets to answer. Multicolored spaces allow the player to pick a card from a deck of his choice.

The game ends when a player reaches the FINISH space by an exact roll of the dice. The winner shares his wish, and the rest of the family is supposed to do their best to make the wish come true.

I think this is a sweet game. It's doubtful you'd think of these questions on your own, and as you can see, they are fun for kids and adults to answer. The only rule has to be "Say something nice or say nothing at all," as some of these cards could lend themselves to mean remarks, if this rule is not followed. *Mary Pride*

NEW!
Fun with Speech & Language Arts

Grades 1–6. $19.95 plus shipping.
Quality Speech Materials, PO Box 579, Laurens, SC 29360. (864) 862-7640. Email: qualityspeech@usa.net. Web: www.qualityspeech.com.

If you want to get your young 'uns comfortable with all sort of speaking situations—public speaking, answering a phone, presenting memorized pieces, telling jokes, and lots more—**Fun with Speech & Language Arts** is the book for you! In 68 pages, author Wendy C. Collins gives you basic speaking tips to pass on to the young fry (such as "What to do with your hands and feet?"), plus 24 games and activities involving public speaking. Some of the assignments are basically verbal essays, while others deal with practical speaking situations. A word of advice: make sure your child does not try the "911 call" for real. One of our sons did that repeatedly on a phone he thought was disconnected, and we did *not* enjoy the policeman's visit! *Mary Pride*

NEW!
Speaking Up, Speaking Out

Grades 4–8. $8.95 plus shipping.
The Millbrook Press, PO Box 335, 2 Old New Milford Rd., Brookfield, CT 06804. Orders: (800) 462-4703, extension 3034. Inquiries: (203) 740-2220. Fax: (203) 740-2223.

Written especially for preteens and early teens, **Speaking Up and Speaking Out : A Kid's Guide to Making Speeches, Oral Reports, and Conversation** covers all types of public speaking, from social occasions to formal speeches on a stage. More specifically, this 79-page paperbound book has chapters on: speaking in social occasions; reading aloud; stage fright and how to overcome it; oral reports and presentations; and speeches for every occasion, such as impromptu speeches or chairing a meeting. The nice, open format speaks directly to the kid reader, occasional cartoons liven it up, and quotes from other kids make it more real.

For each section and subsection, *Speaking Up* has a detailed description of how best to conduct yourself and what the people or person you are addressing will be looking for. For example, in the chapter on social occasions, you learn how to introduce people to each other, how to make "party talk" as a host or guest, and how to handle yourself on the telephone. This last section is especially helpful. It gives both right and wrong responses to a number of situations, as well as the reasons *why* each response is right or wrong. How to respond when someone other than the person you called answers the phone, what to do if you dial a wrong number or answer a wrong number, how to talk to an answering machine, and how to take messages are all covered. Phone safety is not forgotten, either, as it sometimes is in "etiquette" or "speaking" books. There's even a glossary and an index!

This book would be a definite help to all those who blush at the very thought of going to a party or making a speech. *Sarah Pride*

CHAPTER 18

Grammar

Admit it—you used to hate grammar when you were a kid. You used to grouch about the grammar homework old Mrs. Pickle sent home with you. You failed to leap for joy when the class discussion topic was gerunds. Way down deep, you figured you would *never, ever* learn or use all those rules, anyway, so what was the point?

Now, in that remorseless way life has of rolling on and over us, you have a child. A child who needs to learn grammar. Rules. Such as, that these last few sentences are all ungrammatical and *wrong, wrong, wrong*! I can just see old Mrs. Pickle getting out her red pen right now. "Mary is a bright girl, but her grammar needs improvement . . ."

So do we all. After reading thousands of magazines and newsletters, I can say with confidence that most people need to refresh their grammatical training. Our whole society is losing the ability to distinguish the proper uses of *its* and *it's*, for example. *Its* is the possessive pronoun, as in *The boat slipped from its moorings*. *It's* is short for *it is*, as in *It's raining outside*. Yet over just the past few years I have seen the two mixed up everywhere. I really wince when I see fancy curriculum products with *its* where *it's* should be, and vice versa. This common mistake, like many others, is easy to fix once the teacher (namely, *you*) learns the rule.

A Quick Grammar Self-Test

1. Identify every part of speech in the following sentence by writing its abbreviation over each word. For example, if the word is an adjective, write ADJ; if an adverb, write ADV. Also identify subjects, verbs, direct and indirect objects, and objects of prepositions, if any. Check your work with the answer at the end of the chapter.

> These are the harrowing times in history that
>
> vigorously try men's souls.

(Yes, we know this is not the original quote. We added some words and phrases to make it more of a test.)

ABBREVIATIONS FOR USE IN SELF-TEST

ADJ = Adjective
ADV = Adverb
ART = Article
CONJ = Conjunction
D.O. = Direct Object
I.O. = Indirect Object
INF = Infinitive
H.V. = Helping Verb
N = Noun
O.P. = Object of a Preposition
PRO = Pronoun
PREP = Preposition
V = Verb
Subject is underlined once.
Main verb of predicate is underlined twice.

Here's a chance to see how up-to-date you and your family members are on commonly tested grammar skills!

To use the following self-test with more than one person, photocopy the test sentences or have each person copy them by hand.

2. Now, *diagram* the above sentence. The answer is at the end of the chapter.

3. Circle each mistake in the following vignette, and write the correct word(s) above it.

> "Its a beautiful morning", Sally said. "Lets go out and play!"
>
> "Id like to invite the Smith's", Julie replied. "Whose gonna call them?"
>
> "I guess I will," Sally said. She picked up the phone. "Hey its not working!" she cried. "Well Julie what are we going to do?"
>
> The girls were startled; to hear the doorbell ringing.
>
> It rang four times; once loudly, twice softly, then again loudly.
>
> "Thats Jacks signal"! Both girl's rushed to the door.

Again, the answers are at the end of the chapter.

We have just gone through the three ways grammar is taught:

1. **Identifying parts of speech**—what does what in a sentence. This comes in handy when studying other languages.
2. **As rules to learn,** that you can apply when editing writing selections (yours or those of other people).
3. **Diagramming**—a visual way of seeing how the parts of even complicated sentences relate to each other.

Below you'll find resources that teach grammar all three ways.

Grammar Curriculum

Caught'Ya!
Grades 3–12. $14.95 plus shipping. *Maupin House Publishing, PO Box 90148, Gainesville, FL 32607-0148. (800) 524-0634. Fax: (352) 373-5546. Email: jgraddy@maupinhouse.com. Web: www.maupinhouse.com.*

Bored middle-school kids. Hate grammar. Frustrated teacher. Wants kids to connect grammar skills taught in class to real life. Serendipitous synergy results in . . . **Caught'Ya!: Grammar with a Giggle**. Appalling (but memorable) title, this. (Endless possibilities: *Math with a Mumble. Science with a Sneer. History with a Hiss.*)

Back to real sentences. Believing that "frustration has to be the real mother of invention," teacher Jane Bell Kiester developed a simple, 10-minute-a-day technique that reconnects writing with grammar. *Caught'Ya!* outlines the technique, which has been classroom-tested in Florida public and private schools for 10 years.

Her approach: soap opera. Every day the teacher writes a sentence in the ongoing saga on the blackboard. Each day's sentence contains five to 10 mistakes that must be discovered and corrected. A mistake is only counted wrong if the student doesn't catch it during the self-grading time, when the teacher explains all the mistakes. This means everyone, even the dullest stu-

A Free Grammar Program for You

Here's a simple solution to your panic over teaching Junior his grammar. A really simple solution.

First, **you learn correct grammar.** You're bigger and tougher than Junior—you make the sacrifice. Then, once you have learned the grammatical rules, you can easily teach them to Junior, using any program you like. In fact, you won't even need a program. Once you understand grammar, you can teach it from classic literature and/or the Bible, working in handwriting, spelling, vocabulary improvement, and every other language art skill at the same time.

Here's one way of doing this. Every day, have Junior **read a chapter from the Bible** and **narrate the chapter back to you** (Bible study, speech practice, thinking skills, oral creativity). Then have him **write out a paragraph** from that chapter in his best handwriting (handwriting practice). Next, have Junior **identify every word** in that paragraph. He can write N over a noun, V over a verb, ADJ over an adjective, PREP over a preposition . . . you get the idea. If Junior is a little older, and you understand diagramming, he can **diagram the sentences.** The Bible is a fairly complicated book, so sooner or later Junior will run into every grammatical construction. This takes care of grammar. Now, **dictate another paragraph** (or sentence, or phrase, depending on Junior's age) to Junior from that chapter. Check for spelling mistakes. Have Junior **rewrite every misspelled word** five times and put the word in his personal spelling notebook. There's your spelling instruction. If you like, Junior can **act out the visual scenes,** if any, in the chapter (drama). **Vocabulary improvement** will take care of itself as long as you're available to tell Junior what the words mean that he doesn't yet understand, assuming you aren't using one of those dumbed-down pseudo-translations.

This same method can be used with **classic literature.** In both cases, Junior can also **pick his favorite extracts** and **copy them** in a creative writing notebook. He can then use the form of each extract to **produce a creative sentence or paragraph** of his own (creative writing). For example, take Shakespeare's "Parting is such sweet sorrow/Let us say goodnight, till it be morrow" as an example. A typical 10-year-old takeoff on that might be "Eating is such great delight/Let's eat all day, till it be night!" This may seem like a trivial exercise, but becoming familiar with the style and phraseology of the great authors is what learning to write creatively is all about.

This method can only succeed, of course, if you are absolutely certain of your own grammar, since you won't find an answer key anywhere that has the whole Bible diagrammed into sentences and the individual parts of speech all identified. (Hint to suppliers: The King James Version is copyright-free, so if you want to create a "Bible as literature *and* spelling *and* grammar *and* vocabulary *and* dramatic reading skills *and* handwriting" program using the method I just outlined, feel free.)

However, the freedom to pick your own source material for language arts study is what makes this kind of teaching really fun. So, why not pick your favorite grammar resource from this chapter and whip through it yourself? You're a lot older and wiser than when you first struggled with the subject, and your earlier school experience will make it much easier for you to learn all this the second time around. Then you can either use that same resource (with which you will be very familiar and comfortable) with your children, or add the best tips and ideas you gleaned from it to a literature-based method such as I outlined above.

dent, has the chance for a perfect score. Result: kids start concentrating on grammar, improving their writing, and enjoying English class!

The book both explains the technique and provides three 100-sentence sample soap opera sagas, complete with a new vocabulary word each day and the corrections needed for each sentence. These soap operas are pretty bad. Romeo and Juliet go to the mall. Students trip about the world with magic purple umbrellas. Hairy Beast suffers from a hopeless crush on a fickle female. Kids learn from these sagas that rudeness pays, revenge is fun, and that kids should keep secrets from their parents. Be glad you don't have to use the pre-written soaps to use the easy, fun, and effective techniques taught in *Caught'Ya! Mary Pride*

Need grammar review more than grammar instruction? Want to fill in the punctuation, capitalization, and usage skills that programs such as Winston Grammar and Understanding Grammar (both reviewed in this chapter) leave out? You can always get **Daily GRAMS: Guided Review Aiding Mastery Skills**. All the big Daily Grams workbooks have the same format. Exercise #1 on each page is always capitalization review. Exercise #2 is always punctuation review, and #5 is always a sentence combining exercise. Exercises 3 and 4 are general reviews of grammar us-

Daily GRAMS

Grades 3–8. Daily GRAMS, $18.95 each. Daily Guided Teaching & Review, $16.95. Shipping extra. ISHA Enterprises, PO Box 12520, Scottsdale, AZ 85267. Orders: (800) 641-6015. Inquiries: (480) 502-9454. Fax: (480)502-9456. Web: www.easygrammar.com

age, sentence types, and (in the third and fourth grade levels) dictionary skills. Concepts are repeated every 20–25 days.

Big improvement in the new editions: answers have been moved to the back of the book. They used to be found at the bottom of each page, so you either had to have your student cover the answers or transcribe the questions.

There are four overlapping Daily Grams workbooks. The books are reusable for student after student as long as you don't write in them. The first is for use in grades 3 and 4. The second is for grades 4 and 5, the third for grades 5 and 6, and the fourth for grade 6 and up. What used to be Daily Grams for grades 2 and 3 has been changed to **Daily Guided Teaching and Review for Second and Third Grades,** and is intended as an introductory language text.

All levels of Daily Grams contain 180 daily reviews, one per teaching day. A GRAM a day only takes ten minutes or so, including correction time. Add five minutes to that if you prefer to write the questions on the blackboard. No fuss, no sweat. *Mary Pride*

NEW!
Diagramming

Grades 5–6. $15.95 plus shipping.
Builder Books, Inc., P.O. Box 5789, Lynnwood, WA 98046. Orders: (800) 260-5461. Inquiries: (425) 778-4526. Fax: (425) 771-4028.

Diagramming: the Key to Understanding Grammar is an easy-to-use spiral-bound book written especially for homeschoolers. Answers are in the back, so you won't have to suffer for long wondering if you got it right. Some "just for fun" composition exercises are included as well.

The diagramming instruction in this book is great. Methodical, step-by-step, you can do your diagramming right in the book, and as a bonus you learn (or review) all the parts of speech in order to diagram them properly.

Covered are: nouns, verbs, adjectives, adverbs, pronouns, prepositions, direct objects, indirect objects, predicate nouns and pronouns, subjective and objective forms, using who and whom, predicate adjectives, compound modifiers/subjects/predicates/sentences, complex sentences of all kinds, participles, gerunds, infinitives, appositives, nouns of direct address, and parenthetical material. All in a nice, open, nonthreatening format that practically guarantees success without fear or strain. Recommended. *Mary Pride*

Easy Grammar

Grades 4–10. Text, $28.95; workbook, $13.95 (each level). Shipping extra.
ISHA Enterprises, PO Box 12520, Scottsdale, AZ 85267. Orders: (800) 641-6015. Inquiries: (480) 502-9454. Fax: (480)502-9456.
Web: *www.easygrammar.com.*

Isha Enterprises' popular **Easy Grammar** course is the easiest grammar instruction around. That's probably why it's the perennial winner of our *Practical Homeschooling Reader Survey Award.* The *Easy Grammar* text (505 pages) includes all workbook exercises plus teaching instructions. The *Easy Grammar Workbook* takes zero lesson preparation time. It is easy to teach, easy to understand, and easy to correct.

Author Wanda Phillips, a schoolteacher for many years, begins by teaching your children prepositions first. They learn to cross out the prepositional phrases in normal sentences. In theory, this enables them to easily find nouns, verbs, and so on.

Rather than diagramming, Mrs. Phillips employs a system of underlining and notation. The course is complete, covering everything from antecedent pronouns and appositives through how to write a business letter. Grammar is introduced step by step. Each unit also contains material from the previous units, for a continuous review.

If you choose this course, count on taking a few weeks for your younger children to thoroughly master what prepositions are all about. Don't skimp on reviewing this part of the course, as until it is mastered the rest just won't work. *Mary Pride*

For younger children, Cyndy Shearer's revision of Mary F. Hyde's **English for the Thoughtful Child** (119 pages) is a one-book grammar and composition text that follows the Charlotte Mason approach: dictation, memorization, oral composition (narration), and lots of excerpts from good literature such as *Aesop's Fables* and poems by Robert Louis Stevenson. Like *Simply Grammar* (reviewed below) it includes full-page nineteenth-century pictures; not quite so many of them, but nicer ones. Also like *Simply Grammar,* lessons ask the child to write or talk about the pictures. The 62 lessons cover introductory grammar terminology, punctuation, and capitalization, and include some rinky-dink lessons (e.g., when to use *is* and *are*). Nice large print with teacher notes in small type. Best features: simplicity, ease of use, good literature. What it lacks: more meaningful usage exercises based on the mistakes children normally make in their speech and writing. Questionable features: two classic Greek myths, one starring Apollo and the other Jupiter, presented in the style of the nineteenth century, when people treated them like fables. Good for second-grade students. *Mary Pride*

The **Grammar Key** by Robert L. Conklin is a well-organized group of grammar rules, mnemonics for these rules, lists of words to memorize, and simple practice exercises that covers all the grammar your student will ever need.

The key to the program is a set of questions that help you quickly identify exactly which part of speech you're looking at. You also learn a simple method of labeling sentences to identify their parts of speech. The sequence goes like this: first simple and complete subjects and predicates, then determiners, subject and object pronouns, verb helpers, verb links, adjectives, conjunctions, and interjections. We've just glanced at what's covered in the Beginning step—one side of an oversized folded sheet of cardstock. Next comes Intermediate, then Professional. By the time you're done, you've covered everything, from simple diagramming right up to gerunds and participles. (Admit it—you don't even remember what a gerund is!)

Along with the Grammar Key sheet comes a Punctuation Rules sheet, a 28-lesson workbook loaded with memory aids, and a set of worksheets and tests.

Just like the man said, this system does simplify English grammar. It does "accomplish in minutes what you believed would take hours."

Hot off the presses: the updated workbook now includes over 100 pages of new practice sentences, plus some writing practice assignments. The exercises are easy to do and grade, and insure your student will "overlearn," that is, totally master the concepts. Graduates of this program should have no trouble with the grammar self-test at the beginning of this chapter..

Best features: well-organized, clever memory tricks, streamlined. Questionable features: none.

The **Grammar Key Software** contains the workbooks for all grades, now as computer software for PC and Macintosh. This lets you print your own worksheets or make your own workbook.

Too new to review: a new software program, **Grammar Key Volume 2,** that runs on PC or Macintosh, and The Grammar Key for grades 1–3. This product line just keeps growing! *Mary Pride*

NEW!
A Guide to Teaching Grammar Using the Principle Approach

Parents. $12 postpaid.
Dorothy Robbins, 11037 Erickson Way #79, Redding, CA 96003. (530) 241-1149. Email: der76@juno.com.

Hayes Learning English

Grades 3–8. $7.95 each grade. Teacher's key included. Shipping extra.
Hayes School Publishing Co., Inc., 321 Pennwood Ave., Pittsburgh, PA 15221-3398. (800) 245-6234. Fax: (412) 371-6408. Web: www.hayespub.com.

Humpties

Grades 2–9. Humpties, $8.95. Building Sentences with the Humpties, $9.95. Both books, $17.95. Shipping extra.
Builder Books, Inc., P.O. Box 5789, Lynnwood, WA 98046. Orders: (800) 260-5461. Inquiries: (425) 778-4526. Fax: (425) 771-4028. Email: Books@televar.com.

A Guide to Teaching Grammar Using the Principle Approach by Dorothy Robbins (37 pages; spiral-bound) is not a grammar course but an inspirational teacher-training aid. You may judge its tone from the sentences "In the beginning God created—grammar!" and "Lacking the ability to communicate our thoughts accurately, the Gospel, the only basis for freedom and liberty, is lost." Emphasis is on why we should study and teach grammar and the methods we should use. Mrs. Robbins outlines what must be studied, but doesn't provide lesson plans. These are for you to develop as you apply the "Four Rs" of the Principle Approach: *researching, reasoning, relating,* and *recording.* A fine introduction to the subject, it also includes specific information on how and why to keep a grammar notebook. *Mary Pride*

Learning English is a series of cleverly-designed, inexpensive 86–156 page workbooks. Books are divided into sections, each with its own diagnostic test, practice lessons to reinforce any skills found wanting on the diagnostic test, and a mastery test to check the student's work after finishing the unit. Diagnostic tests are at the end of the book. Mastery tests are in the middle of the book, pre-perfed for easy removal. All workbooks except that for grade 8 have a pull-to-remove answer key with answers for all tests and practice exercises.

The diagnostic tests are designed to help your child avoid any unnecessary drill work. Each question is linked with a lesson practice page. If the child misses the question, you can assign the exact page to drill that particular skill. This means only necessary practice gets assigned. Lesson practice pages do more than drill; they teach the skill with both rules and examples, as well as drill exercises, thus quickly bringing your child up to speed.

For further ease of use, each workbook is divided into 6–13 units, each dealing with one topic. For example, the grade 3 units are Sentence Sense, Capital Letters, Correct Usage, Composition, Letter Writing, and Word Study. For grade 7, the units are Mastering the Sentence, Building Paragraphs, Nouns, Pronouns, Verbs and Their Uses, Classification of Modifiers, Adjective Modifiers, Adverbial Modifiers, Prepositional Phrase Modifiers, Classification of Sentences, Punctuation and Capitalization, General Review, and Letter Writing. Individual units can be studied in any order. An excellent, clutter-free series for learning or drilling grammar and usage.

Hayes also has an *Exercises in English* series, with a similar format to their *Reading Comprehension* series. *Exercises in English* is much less thought-provoking, more fill-in-the-blankish. I would definitely choose *Learning English* over Hayes' *Exercises in English* series. *Mary Pride*

Humpties: Parts of Speech with "Eggceptional" Personalities by Ellen Hajek lives up to its promise that "At last grammar can be fun!" This cute and innovative program introduces parts of speech through little Humpty-Dumpty "egg" people. The conjunction, for example, poses with both arms outstretched to show how he joins words, phrases, or complete thoughts together. The pages of the book introduce the "Humpties" and provide sheets of small pictures of them for you to cut out. These pictures are then placed under the appropriate parts of speech in the sample sentences included. Large type, good cumulative reviews, answer key. Parts of speech covered: noun, verb, conjunction, pronoun, adjective, adverb, preposition, interjection.

A follow-up volume, **Building Sentences with the Humpties** (45 pages), whizzes through simple and compound subjects and predicates, diagramming, objects, and sentence types, plus a few just-for-fun activities that actually are fun (no tedious crossword puzzles!). Best features: fun characters make grammar terms memorable, short lessons. What it lacks: more volumes to cover the rest of grammar, more exercises to make sure students thoroughly master each concept. Questionable features: none. *Mary Pride*

A Journey Through Grammar Land uses an allegory format. Designed for fifth through seventh grades, it follows the adventures of Tank, a young man with grammar and writing problems, as he wends his way through Grammar Land.

If you've ever seen the movie *The Phantom Tollbooth* or read the book, you might have an idea of how this works. Tank meets characters such as Capitalization and Coach Substituter and visits locations such as Naming Part Auditorium. The characters he meets tell him about their jobs. Vivid allegorical descriptions and line-art illustrations help the student remember grammar principles. For example, when learning about proper nouns, Tank walks down People Corridor. It is lined with names, titles, races, and nationalities. You can see a picture of this corridor in the worktext, as well as the place where it joins up with Places Passageway and Things Hallway.

At certain spots in his journey, Tank is asked to stop and fill out a "scroll." This is code for a grammar exercise, to be found in the back of the workbook. Where necessary, additional explanations are included before the exercises. Answers to the exercises are in the far back of the workbook.

Volume 1 of **Grammar Land** covers nouns and pronouns (Namers and Substituters, in Grammar Land lingo). **Volume 2** introduces verbs and auxiliary verbs. Punctuation is taught throughout all books. **Volume 3** teaches adjectives and adverbs. **Volume 4** is about prepositions and conjunctions.

Don't get too excited about the "professional" artwork said to illustrate the Grammar Land series. It's really pretty murky and bad (body parts out of proportion, etc.). The main virtue of this series is the story line itself, which is quite interesting and memorable. Good for younger children and slow learners. *Mary Pride*

For those who themselves have a reasonable command of grammar and wish to help others, whether children or adults, who are not so fortunately endowed, this is a wonderful tool. "The central idea of **Learning Grammar through Writing** is to teach grammar to students by having them write compositions regularly and then correct their own work, by applying numbered grammar and punctuation rules." The book is divided into 13 sections—e.g., Verbs, The Sentence, Punctuation. Within each section you will find all the necessary rules

and examples in nice large print. This helps, since your student has to either look up or memorize the rules and examples in order to use them to correct his work. The book is inexpensive and reusable. *Mary Pride*

A Journey Through Grammar Land

Grades 5–7. $15 per volume. Shipping extra. *Wordsmiths, 1355 Ferry Road, Grants Pass, OR 97526. (541) 476-3080. Email: frodej@jsgrammar.com. Web: www.jsgrammar.com.*

Learning Grammar through Writing

Grades 3–8. $8.95 plus $4 shipping. *Educators Publishing Service, Inc., 31 Smith Pl., Cambridge, MA 02138. (800) 225-5750. Fax: (617) 547-0412. Email: epsbooks@epsbooks.com. Web: www.epsbooks.com.*

UPDATED!
Rod and Staff Building Christian English

Grades 2–8. Inexpensive. Prices vary by grade.
Rod and Staff Publishers, Box 3, Hwy 172, Crockett, KY 41413-0003. (606) 522-4348. Fax: (800) 643-1244.

BEST FEATURES: consistent, simple explanations and review. Solidly Christian. Extremely wholesome. WHAT IT LACKS: not enough emphasis on getting *le mot juste*. Little training in how to present strong emotions or persuade others. QUESTIONABLE FEATURES: none.

Rules of the Game

Grades 5–9. Books 1, 2, and 3, $8 each. Answer key for books, $3.70 each. Shipping extra.
Educators Publishing Service, Inc., 31 Smith Pl., Cambridge, MA 02138. (800) 225-5750. Fax: (617) 547-0412. Email: epsbooks@epsbooks.com. Web: www.epsbooks.com.

Rod and Staff Publishers, a Mennonite textbook publisher well-known to homeschoolers, has been updating their **Building Christian English** series. The series, which goes from grades 2–8, covers traditional language-arts skills. Sentence examples and literature selections go beyond wholesome to include Bible stories (told with no imaginative additions), family life ("Uncle Bill waved and smiled"), nature vignettes, and many sentence sermonettes on courtesy, kindness, generosity, obedience, and so forth. Illustrations are violence-free and feature Mennonite dress and hairstyles.

In keeping with Rod and Staff tradition, the series is moderately priced and many of the books are reusable. The revised Grade 3 edition, for example, includes a hardbound Pupil book ($10.85 for 321 pages), larger hardbound Teacher book ($13.55 for 406 pages), worksheets ($2.75), and tests ($1.10). You can save even more by only purchasing the Teacher book, which includes the entire text of the Pupil book in reduced form, and creating cardboard "masks" to cover the teacher instructions and answers on the outside of the pages. We would recommend this for our budget-minded readers rather than the more common expedient of getting a Pupil book without a Teacher book.

Also in keeping with Rod and Staff tradition, Building Christian English requires lots of writing—although not as much as older editions of this series. This is fine for schools, where children need to be kept busy all day, but not necessary in the homeschool situation. Feel free to do most activities orally (after all, you have time to listen to your child!).

Overall, *Building Christian English* spends much time on traditional skills of identifying parts of speech and learning grammar terminology, and relatively little on improving composition skills. Many types of compositions are presented (e.g., poetry), but few ways to make your compositions better (e.g., substituting active voice for passive voice). The writing models presented are self-effacing, not flamboyant, thrilling, or hard-hitting.

We give this series the full five hearts for piety, and three hearts for a good, solid, if unexciting presentation of traditional English skills. *Mary Pride*

Rules of the Game: Grammar through Discovery is inexpensive and easy to use. Using the inductive approach, the three workbooks (one each for grades 5–7, 6–8, and 7–9) lead students to discover grammar rules and definitions. Example: "In the following sentences, underline any words that name people, animals, places, things, ideas, or feelings." When the student does this, he discovers those words are called nouns.

Workbook 1 has just enough exercises to carry you from parts of speech through punctuation, capitalization, and sentence structure, to subject and verb agreement. Book 2 teaches direct and indirect objects, linking verbs, predicate nouns and adjectives, and more. Book 3 includes work on dependent clauses, complex and compound-complex sentences, gerunds, participles, and infinitives.

The exercises use both traditional and innovative approaches. Many exercise sets consist of sentences that form a narrative about a particular subject—for example, Strange but True Baseball Facts or the Underground Railroad. Other exercises ask students to follow sentence patterns, write their own sentences, choose effective modifiers, or combine sentences.

As with all public school workbooks, these workbooks repeat material learned in previous volumes: 18 pages of review on Book 2 and 21 pages in Book 3. Occasional bits of public-school propaganda. Watch out for these and you'll be OK.

Answer keys are available separately for each book. *Mary Pride*

NEW!
Shurley Grammar
Grades 1–8. Homeschool kit, $65 plus shipping.
Shurley Instructional Materials, Inc., 366 SIM Drive, Cabot, AR 72023. (800) 566-2966. Fax: (501) 843-0583.

Shurley Grammar has seven levels in all. Highlights of the rest include:

- Level 2—complete/simple subjects and paragraphs, simple 2 point paragraph, capitalization
- Level 3—transitive verbs, direct/indirect objects, verb tenses,
- Level 4—singular/plural possessives, punctuating quotations, expanded paragraph writing, outlines, changing verb tenses
- Level 5—helping verbs, compound subjects/predicates, double negatives, irregular verbs, types of paragraph writing, beginning research skills.
- Level 6—compound verbs, conjunctions, interjections, pronoun antecedent agreement, continued work with different types of paragraphs (informative, compare/contrast, descriptive), writing a report.
- Level 7—more sentence patterns, verbals, conjugation, clauses, and in-depth pronoun study.

As "Classical Education" becomes the homeschooling buzzword of the 90's, many parents are looking for materials that correspond to Dorothy Sayer's trivium model of learning. It's not always easy to find "classical in a box," so many of us do the next best thing: Find out what successful and well-respected classical Christian schools are using. Logos School (Moscow, ID, founded by Douglas Wilson) has been using **The Shurley Method: Grammar Made Easy** for several years now and homeschoolers are starting to follow suit.

The Shurley Grammar method corresponds perfectly to the "grammar" stage of learning. Although very young children may not have the maturity to fully comprehend all that there is to learn of grammar, they begin acquiring the vocabulary from the very beginning. There is much memorization and repetition in younger grades, a constant review and reinforcement of previously learned material, and application of grammar skills to original writing. Speaking and writing in complete sentences is emphasized, as is learning grammar concepts in the context of sentences.

A distinguishing feature is the use of something called the Question and Answer Flow. This is a highly structured oral recitation where students and teacher practice classifying and labeling sentences. Definitions are learned by the use of chants and rhymes that are practiced daily. Instead of a textbook, teachers follow up instruction with student worksheets. These, by the way, are administered *after* the initial teaching and review with the teacher at the chalkboard. In other words, the worksheets are used as a practice and a check, not as the primary teaching tool.

Between all the hearing, seeing, saying, and doing, there is something here for every learning modality. This is definitely a teacher-directed program and you'll need to allow time to familiarize yourself with the teaching methodology. Although it's directed to classroom teachers, don't let that scare you away. The teacher helps are all very detailed, even giving you scripts to follow. The basic structure and layout actually change very little from year to year. Take the time to hone your teaching skills the first year, and following years will be a breeze. (And don't be surprised if you find your own grammar skills taking some leaps in the process!)

Here's a welcome addition: Each year the lessons begin with a review of basic study skills and good habits, including following directions, listening, and staying organized.

What about diagramming? While you won't be drawing all the lines and figures, the classification of the parts of speech, as well as the sentence pattern types, is every bit as detailed. (If you really want to, you can go ahead and draw the lines.)

Your kit consists of a cassette tape so you can listen to all the jingles, definitions, and question/answer flows for every sentence you'll work on that year; a student workbook; a teacher's manual with teaching instructions for each lesson; a teacher's resource book; and a video workshop featuring Brenda Shurley, the author, guiding you through the teaching process. Don't be put off by the classroom emphasis of the video—just concentrate on getting the big picture.

Right from the start, first graders will learn to identify subjects, nouns, verbs, prepositions, objects of prepositions, adverbs, adjectives and articles. They'll learn what comprises a complete sentence, practice simple paragraph writing, and compose friendly and thank-you letters.

Choose the level that corresponds closest to your child's grade level. Although the grammar study is a grade or two ahead of most programs, the reading difficulty is right on grade level. Each year begins with the basics (nouns and verbs) and progresses from there. So don't worry if your child is new to this program. Give them a few weeks and they'll be whizzing right along.

If you're looking for a quick-and-dirty, "let's get grammar over in one year" kind of program, then this will not appeal. Likewise, if you're planning to delay formal grammar until later years, the idea of first graders chanting parts of speech may seem absurd. However, if you want a solid program that will build grammar skills into your students from day one; if you like to sing, chant, and recite; if you want to capitalize on your young child's ability to memorize, then this program will be both effective and fun. Shurley Grammar respects students without patronizing, believes enthusiasm for learning is contagious, and knows that kids will enjoy learning when they are successful.

How do you make a great program even better? Brenda Shurley is writing a special version of her grammar just for homeschoolers (grades 1–8). If you didn't care for the classroom emphasis in the earlier version, you won't find any of that in the latest one. Look for it by the time this book is out, featuring an expanded and more detailed creative writing section. *Renee Mathis*

NEW!
Simply Grammar

Grades 4–8. $24.95 plus $3 shipping.
Charlotte Mason Research and Supply,
PO Box 1142, Rockland, ME 04841.
(207)593-9063.
Web: www.charlotte-mason.com.

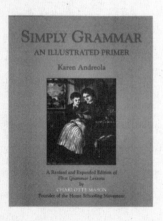

Simply Grammar: An Illustrated Primer (178 pages; oversized paperback) is a revised edition of the original work *First Grammar Lessons* by Charlotte Mason. *Practical Homeschooling* columnist Karen Andreola did the revision. Intended for students anywhere from fourth grade to eighth grade level, this one-book program takes a highly "oral" approach. Students spend relatively little time writing. Instead, they practice narrating ("telling") stories back and learning terminology. Large nineteenth-century illustrations serve as story-starters, with students making up stories about the pictures, using the grammar rules. Students also learn professional grammar terminology—nominative case, intransitive verbs—introduced as simply as possible by explaining the meaning of these words' Latin roots. The main instruction method is "guided conversation" between teacher and student, with the text providing the outlines of what the teacher is to say. This program takes less time than any of the others, being designed for 10–15 minute lessons, and only one lesson per week. Best features: Fairly thorough coverage of grammar terms, short lessons, imaginative composition exercises, minimal writing required, only one grammar rule per lesson. What it lacks: systematic review, exercises to train children out of making common usage errors, instruction in correct punctuation. Questionable features: a few mentions of fairies and goblins in the appendix of 19th century poetry.

Since *Simply Grammar* and *English for the Thoughtful Child* are each designed for a different age range, there is no reason why, if you favor their classical Charlotte Mason approach, you can't use both. *Mary Pride*

This two-workbook series for third-graders or bright second-graders is not quite as inspired as the rest of the *Sing, Spell, Read and Write* program, but the **Trophy books** still beat the standard public school texts. Book I covers alphabetical order, kinds of sentences, capital letters, and punctuation. Book II has Writing Letters, Writing Stories, Word Usage, Language Manners, a "Parts of Speech" song, Articles, Nouns, Adjectives, Pronouns, Verbs, Adverbs, Conjunctions, Prepositions, Interjections, and Practical Everyday Reading Skills. Both books have a spelling section in the back, with 10 words for each of 95 days, and accompanying puzzles, crosswords, word searches, and other games. Together they cover in one year what regular schoolbooks drag out over ten. *Mary Pride*

Understanding Grammar is a slim easy-to-follow spiral-bound book. It chronicles the method author Mary Schwalm invented to teach her own four sons grammar at home. Starting with simple word games (about 20 creative games are included), your whole family learns the three basic sentence types, the parts of speech, verb tenses, sentence diagramming, and how to create personal grammar notebooks.

Step follows step in a very simple, clutter-free fashion. You are taught how to teach the concepts. Many examples and exercises are provided. Most exercises can be done orally. The sentence diagramming instruction is very well done: both simple and concise.

Since *Understanding Grammar* only covers parts of speech and sentence analysis, you will have to add instruction in capitalization and punctuation, grammar rules such as subject-verb agreement, and usage rules such as the difference between *lie* and *lay*. The book is non-consumable: you are expected to do the written exercises on separate paper.

When combined with a complete English grammar handbook, *Understanding Grammar* can noticeably accelerate your student's grammar progress. In fact, after using this program to get acquainted with grammar, it could take as little as a year of daily, supervised instruction to pick up all the remaining grammar you'll ever need. Bonus: your student should be able to diagram sentences such as this: "The King of Cebu and his people listened eagerly while Malacca Henry described the wonders of Spain, and then the king asked to come aboard the 'Trinidad.'" One-half point off because you have to make up your own exercise sentences. Questionable features: none. When the student workbook comes out, which should be soon, this will be a five-heart resource. *Mary Pride*

I love detective stories, and I love the Usborne books from EDC Publishing. Put them together, and what have you got? Inspector Noun and Sergeant Verb and the other goofy characters in **The Word Detective**. Laid out like a Richard Scarry book, each page of this oversized, fully illustrated, colorful book features a part of speech. Inspector Noun, for example, tracks down thieves in a supermarket by passing by displays of all the different fruits and vegetables—all nouns, of course. Or we see Sergeant Verb performing all the duties of a busy crook-chasing day—all verbs, of course. *Mary Pride*

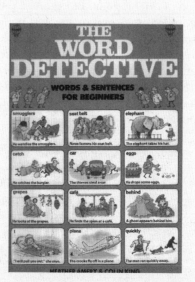

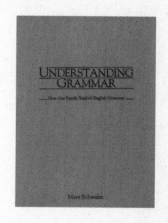

UPDATED!
Winston Grammar

Grades 3–8. Volume 1, $36 plus shipping.
Hewitt Homeschooling Resources, PO Box 9, Washougal, WA 98671. Orders: (800) 348-1750. Inquiries: (360) 835-8708. Fax: (360) 835-8697. Email: hewitths@aol.com.

Here's a product that actually makes grammar fun, even for little kids who aren't neat and orderly types. It's called the **Winston Grammar** series and it teaches grammatical constructions to students of all ages by pattern-building with colored flash cards, rather than by diagramming.

Volume 1, *Winston Grammar*, is designed for grades 3–8. Volume 2, *Advanced Winston Grammar*, is for grades 9–12 and is reviewed in Volume 3 of *The Big Book*. Volume 1 costs more because it comes with a really fancy custom vinyl packet, with space for adding the advanced kit later.

Volume 1 teaches parts of speech, noun functions, prepositional phrases, and the principles of modification. All in all, it's supposed to take you 50–75 sessions to complete this course, including the frequent review lessons.

Children identify the parts of speech in worksheet sentences by laying out their part-of-speech cards in the proper order. For example, in the first lesson, when children have just learned articles and nouns, they would lay out the sentence, "The boy and the girl saw a man eat an apple" as article-noun-blank-article-noun-blank-article-noun-blank-article-noun. Later on, they learn more parts of speech and eventually are able to lay out even complex sentences without using blank cards. (The cards, by the way, have "clues" on one side and the part-of-speech name on the other, for added learning value.) They also learn to identify parts of speech and constructions by underlining and writing abbreviations above the words in a sentence.

Each Winston Grammar program includes a set of worksheets bound with a pre- and post-test; a teacher's manual; quiz keys; and the color-coded noun function cards and parts-of-speech cards.

The courses only cover parts of speech and sentence analysis. You will have to add instruction in capitalization and punctuation, grammar rules such as subject-verb agreement, and usage rules such as the difference between *lie* and *lay*.

Since this program uses a nonstandard notation to mark sentences, and does not teach diagramming, those pursuing a classic liberal-arts program should not make it their first pick. However, it's a great choice for "wiggle worms." *Mary Pride*

Grammar Through Song

Audio Memory's Grammar Songs Kit

Ages 6–12. $19.95 plus $3 shipping.
Audio Memory, 501 Cliff Dr., Newport Beach, CA 92663. (800) 365-7464. Fax: (949) 631-1150. Email: emily@audiomemory.com. Web: www.audiomemory.com.

The **Grammar Songs** kit from Audio Memory Publishing provides a ton of teaching for your money. You get 16 professionally-performed pop/light rock grammar songs performed on cassette, plus an illustrated songbook and workbook, answer key, progress chart, and teacher's guide.

Auditory learners—kids who like to snuggle up to the stereo or who run around wearing headphones— will enjoy this way of painlessly learning about nouns, verbs, adjectives, and so on—even Greek and Latin prefixes and suffixes! The lyrics really educate. For example, part of the first Verb Song goes:

I'm running, jumping, singing—that's because I am a verb.
I'm hopping, dancing, ringing—that's because I am a verb.
I'm coming, going, hitting, throwing,
Humming, rowing, sitting, blowing,
Riding, hiding, gliding, sliding—
Because I'm a verb.
I'm a verb, verb, verb—I'm an action word.
So put me where the action is 'cause I'm an action word.

Other verses list examples of helping verbs and linking verbs, and explain that verbs can describe what you're doing in your head—"The action isn't physical, it's in my mind instead."

Well, that covers one of the Grammar Songs. The kit also includes songs for nouns, sentences, pronouns, adjectives, adverbs, apostrophes, prepositions, direct objects, capitalization, plurals, commas, quotation marks, and even Greek and Latin prefixes and suffixes! The workbook includes explanations, exercises, and just enough drills. The slim teacher's guide has the instructions and answers, plus a couple of verbal grammar games. Really a fun package.

The tape and book are sufficient to learn the eight parts of speech and other basic rules, but don't expect this kit to do the whole job of teaching all the complexities of grammar. Do expect it to make your child comfortable with grammar terminology, so that later grammar lessons will go down easily. *Mary Pride*

Rock N Learn Grammar Volume 1 features a cassette and a 21-page booklet, which, when combined with a tape player, gives you everything you need to listen and learn about nouns (both proper and common), pronouns, verbs (regular and linking), and verb tense.

Lyrics and music, instead of paper and pencil, present each part of speech. The lyrics and questions are included in the booklet and there are no obnoxious words here, just little jingles to help remember the parts of speech being learned. Immediately after each song, the entertainer walks you through the questions one at a time. The questions are always related to the topic just sung about. After the entertainer reads the question, a short tune is played and you are supposed to answer. If you need more time to figure out the answer, just pause the tape. This method provides immediate practice on the new skill.

The booklet contains suggestions to extend the learning beyond the tape and booklet. Find out what a "whopper letter" is, for example!

At first the title rather scared me because "rap" music is not my favorite type. But this particular presentation is good because the songs are rather short and do not go on and on. If you have a child that just does not seen to grasp the basic parts of speech, give it a try. *Lynn Smith*

Grammar Games

Punctuation Bingo comes with 36 playing cards, 25 calling cards, a calling mat, who knows how many little red chips, and a reference sheet. The rules of the game are simple—this is just bingo with a grammatical twist.

Each playing card has eight squares, each square containing a sentence that is missing some type of punctuation (question mark, comma, etc.). Calling cards each contain one type of punctuation and, when you 'call' them, the players search their cards for a sentence needing this particular item (i.e. "APOSTROPHE—To indicate that a letter or letters have been left out in contractions"). Once you've called a card, place it on the calling mat and call another. When a player cries "Bingo!," pull out the reference sheet. This sheet gives the solutions for each of the playing cards, and it is an easy matter to compare the solutions on the reference sheet to the list of cards you've called.

This game is fun, simple, and a great way to reinforce basic punctuation rules. We're sure to use it in our home. *Tammy Cardwell*

Did you identify all 12 words correctly?

# Correct	Rating
11 or 12	You're a parts-of-speech whiz!
9 or 10	Pretty good, but some review is needed.
5–8	Needs work.
0–4	Time to buy a couple of the books in this chapter!

Does your diagram look like this one?

This is a fairly simple diagram, following standard rules of diagramming. If you missed a fine point or two, one of the books in this chapter that teaches diagramming can help you. If you didn't even know where to start, these books can *really* help you!

Answers to Self-Test

```
        PRO   V   ART     ADJ        N   PREP  N-O.P.   PRO
        These are the harrowing times in history that

            ADV      V    N*    N-D.O.
        vigorously try men's souls.
```

*Men's is a possessive noun acting as an adjective modifying *souls*.

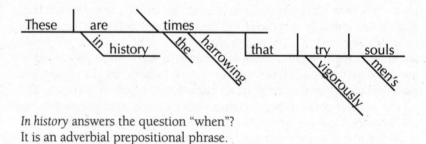

In history answers the question "when"? It is an adverbial prepositional phrase.

Did you find all 17 errors?

If you found . . .

16 or 17	You're a punctuation whiz!
13–15	You're better than most high-school grads!
10–12	Needs work.
7–9	Needs *lots* of work.
0–6	Do your parents know you're writing in their book?

It's
"Its a beautiful morning," Sally said. "Lets go out and play!"
I'd   Smiths   Who's going to
"Id like to invite the Smith's," Julie replied. "Whose gonna call

them?"

"I guess I will," Sally said. She picked up the phone. "Hey its not
                                                              it's

working!" she cried. "Well Julie what are we going to do?"
        no semicolon
The girls were startled; to hear the doorbell ringing.

It rang four times; once loudly, twice softly, then again loudly.
That's Jacks   girls
"Thats Jacks signal"! Both girls rushed to the door.

CHAPTER 19

Handwriting & Keyboarding

It has been said, in educational circles anyway, "Kids don't really need to learn to write any more. They can just learn to type on a computer keyboard. After all, everything's computerized nowadays." Sorry, but that's not true. Human beings sometimes need to write down ideas when they are more than six feet away from a wall outlet, and we don't all have laptop computers permanently welded to our belt buckles. Plus, some forms of literature aren't well suited to electronic input. Henry David Thoreau would have had a pretty poor time trying to write *Walden* at a computer console.

So let's just give up and admit it; children should learn to write legibly. Now comes the crunch: *how* shall we teach them?

Today four major methods are contending in the handwriting field. They are:

- **Ball and stick.** One group favors manuscript writing ("ball and stick") for young children because it is so easy to teach (all strokes begin on a line) and it resembles print, thus making the teaching of reading less confusing. Unhappily, ball and stick degenerates into a hash of bouncing balls and chopped-up sticks when students are trying to write fast, and once a child has started with ball and stick he has to make the dreaded transition to cursive from scratch.

- **Precursive.** Recognizing the flaws of ball-and-stick manuscript, a number of companies are now vending a type of manuscript handwriting closely allied to cursive. Letters are formed with a single stroke rather than with several as in ball and stick, and generally they follow the cursive form. What's left out are the connectors. Precursive moves smoothly to cursive, with only a few letters changing (such as *b* and *f*). The goal here is to end up with legible cursive writing.

- **Starting with cursive.** It is possible to begin with a simplified cursive script and stick with it, thus making no transitions at all. Drawback: for beginning readers, the large difference between cursive and book print may confuse matters.

- **Italic.** Here the ultimate goal is to develop a beautiful and functional calligraphic hand based on calligraphic italic, rather than the standard

Why "Ball-and-Stick Handwriting Was Invented

In the early decades of this century it was common practice to use metal-tipped pens, liquid ink, and rough-surfaced newsprint for writing exercises. The pen often snagged on the paper fibers on the upstrokes of letters and splattered the paper with ink. In 1922, Marjorie Wise, a concerned British educator, invented a new start-and-stop form of lowercase letters made entirely with down strokes. To help students avoid ink blots, she separated lowercase letters into separate strokes, like capitals (Gray, 1979). This form of letter is usually referred to as *ball-stick* or *manuscript*. Wise did not realize she was creating the same problems young children have with start-and-stop capitals: requiring students to determine which direction to go with each new stroke. As with capitals, reversals were common with Wise's alphabet. Within two years she admitted her error and urged teachers to return to continuous-line lowercase letters.

—*Donna Reid Connell*, Lesson Guide to *itl* Integrated Total Language: A Draw to Write to Read Program

Handwriting Styles

This A Beka handwriting sample should look very familiar to anyone who attended grade school in the 1950s or early 1960s. Note the slant, and the loops at the bottoms of letters.

The Lord is my shepherd;
I shall not want.
Psalm 23:1

A Beka cursive

Bob Jones University Press teaches a slightly more streamlined, but still very traditional, cursive. The pre-cursive is extremely streamlined, as you can see. It differs from traditional ball-and-stick manuscript in that (1) it slants and (2) the letters are formed in the cursive way, rather than as a melange of balls and sticks.

The Lord is my shepherd
I shall not want. Psalm 23:1

Bob Jones University Press pre-cursive

The Lord is my Shepherd
I shall not want. Psalm 23:1

Bob Jones University Press cursive

Calvert School's cursive is even more streamlined than BJU's. Note the manuscript-style capital letters and the absence of "lead-in" lines. The transition to their cursive is not effortless, though, as they retain the fancy lowercase "s" and "r" which cause many children trouble.

The Lord is my Shepherd
I shall not want.
Psalm 23:1

Calvert School cursive

As you can see, Christian Liberty Academy's cursive is our old friend, traditional cursive, again. Note the ornate capital letters and the introductory lines leading into the small "n" and "w."

The Lord is my Shepard
I Shall not want.
Psalm 23:1

Christian Liberty Academy cursive

from Plain to *Fancy*

The Lord is my Shepard I shall not want. Psalm 23:1

Spencerian cursive

The Lord is my shepherd, I shall not want. Psalm 23:1

Handwriting Without Tears "European" style cursive

The Lord is my Shepherd; I shall not want. Psalm 23:1

Portland State University/Getty-Dubay Italic—slower "practice" style

The Lord is my Shepherd; I shall not want. Psalm 23:1

Portland State University/Getty-Dubay Italic—faster everyday writing style

The Lord is my shepherd. I shall not want. Psalm 23:1

Zaner-Bloser cursive

Joan Donaldson, who wrote a lovely article about Tasha Tudor in Practical Homeschooling #6, crafted this sample of Spencerian handwriting for us. Believe it or not, she writes her correspondence by hand, and it all looks this good!

The Spencerian method requires precise practice. It is actually easier to write many letters in Spencerian than in traditional cursive, and it certainly is elegant.

The capital letters in this example have extra flourishes. A nib pen adds flair as well.

See Volume 3 for sources for Spencerian handwriting instruction

The easiest type of handwriting to learn, Handwriting Without Tears employs the European "two-line" paper rather than the American "three-line" paper. Children find it easier to place letters correctly with just a baseline and midline to guide them. The script is almost as simplified as Calvert's, but includes looped capitals.

Portland State University's cursive italic employs a precise slant and simplified capitals and is built for speed, as opposed to traditional italic which is more of an art form than a usable handwriting.

A second sample of Portland State University cursive italic.

Zaner-Bloser is the king of handwriting suppliers to the public schools. Zaner-Bloser cursive is traditional and elegant. Note the similarities and differences between Zaner-Bloser, A Beka, and Christian Liberty Academy. These are all based on the traditional "Palmer method" taught in schools for decades.

cursive. The new italic hands do not require special pens, but can be written with anything from a ballpoint pen to a fine tip marker or even a pencil. Students begin with precursive and move towards italic mastery. A big difference in this system is that the capitals are the manuscript forms, rather than the fancy and hard to read cursive capitals. Furthermore, since calligraphy is an art form, children are encouraged to develop their own style rather than to adhere to a uniform model.

In the homeschool market, several additional methods are now becoming popular:

- **Old-Timey Handwriting.** The curls and flourishes of Spencerian handwriting are beautiful, plus this is the way Grandma used to write. Not to mention John Hancock!

- **European Style.** Europeans teach basic letterforms using *two* lines on their graph paper instead of *three*. This makes it much easier to see which letters "stick up" or "hang below."

In the final analysis, handwriting style is a matter of personal choice. If your daughter is learning at home and she just loves old-fashioned copperplate writing, indulge her. Similarly, if she likes to print everything, let her (although she *will* have to learn to *read* cursive sooner or later). The only reason schools struggle with standardized handwriting systems is that they don't have the resources to deal with students as individuals. As a parent, you do have these resources. As long as the results are legible, you and your children are free to choose any system at all—so pick the one you find most fun!

Handwriting

Anyone looking for a real workout in handwriting should try the **Callirobics Series**. *Callirobics-For-Kids* is designed for ages four through seven, while *Callirobic Handwriting Exercises to Music Exercises* is for the student seven years to adult. Each booklet comes with its own cassette tape, and each lesson is accompanied by a song. By doing 10 simple lessons to music, students can quickly develop a smooth flowing hand, balance and coordination, and a much improved enjoyment of writing!

Callirobics-For-Kids complements each lesson with an attractive picture for your child to color, a gentle reminder of their handwriting workout. However, parents, take warning! The songs are so enjoyable your youngster may be begging to go to sleep by "The Sleeping Moon" and wake up to "The Bunny's Ears"!

While he is having so much fun, the young student improves small muscle skills and prepares to print or write in cursive. The soft, soothing music of *Callirobics* relaxes the older student and enables them to place more concentration on the balance and flow of making letters. They learn to take their time and pay special attention to details.

While these workouts do not teach handwriting, they are very innovative in their approach. Your handwriting can improve as daily, self-guided exercises are applied with the rhythm of music. Many of these exercises are similar to those in Dr. Richard Stoller's *Psychology of Penmanship*; however,

NEW!
Callirobics Series
Grades preK–adult. Callirobics-For-Kids, $19.95 ($2 discount available for homeschoolers). Callirobics Handwriting Exercises to Music, $26.95 (both with workbook and audio-cassette; 7 and up includes teacher's guide).
Callirobics, PO Box 6634, Charlottesville, VA 22906. (800) 769-2891. Fax: (804) 293-9008. Email: cal-avir@cfw.com. Web: www.callirobics.com.

children using the Callirobics series will enjoy the exercises so much, they won't even realize they are building confidence in their ability to write! The positive influence of motivational quotes with each lesson could encourage even the worst handwriting student.

Practice pads are available for the series, but aren't absolutely necessary. Stickers, and even a Diploma in Callirobics for older students, provide extra incentive for an already outstanding product. Both *Callirobics* and *Callirobics-For-Kids* come in a nice, protective case which makes the books easier to store, and also creates an attractive gift. *Lisa Mitchell*

Christian Liberty Academy's handwriting program, based on the traditional Palmer method (manuscript and cursive), takes 15 to 20 minutes a day, introduces cursive after a year's practice with manuscript, and combines patriotism with Scriptural themes and everyday life. Each slim book (60 to 76 pages) also includes teaching instructions, eliminating the need for separate teacher's manuals. The publishers include a free writing practice pad with each book.

For four- and five-year-olds, Book 1, **In the Beginning,** has 20 pages of fun readiness instructions before children are introduced to the manuscript alphabet (in alphabetical order) and the numerals. Book 2, **Writing with Diligence,** starts with just a few pages of readiness activities, then settles down to drilling the manuscript stroke groups (i.e., letters that use similar strokes). This book, intended for first- and second-graders, follows each group of stroke drills with a page of independent writing and an self-evaluation page—four in all. Book 3, **Writing with Prayer,** starts with manuscript review and finishes up with cursive, introduced in stroke groups. Also directed at first- and second-graders, Book 3 handwriting exercises include punctuation practice.

Writing with Grace is designed for third- and fourth-graders. It has four sections: Difficult Lowercase Cursive Letters, Manuscript Maintenance, Uppercase A-N Cursive, and Uppercase O-Z Cursive. Each section contains a varied mix of activities, such as unscrambling a poem, a crossword puzzle, making outlines, writing sentences to describe the action in a series of pictures, and so on. The mild emphasis on grammar continues, with some alphabetization work and the introduction of homonyms and quotations. Each section also draws attention to a "Home Education Model." You get a brief biography of a famous person who was educated at home, such as Abraham Lincoln, Thomas Alva Edison, or Helen Keller. Toward the end of this book, creative writing begins to take the place of the previous copy-this-sentence and rewrite-that-sentence-according-to-this-grammatical-principle exercises.

Writing with Power, a new book, provides a review of the principles of advanced cursive for children in grades 4–8.

These books mix a few language arts activities in with the handwriting practice. Otherwise, the format is simple, logical, and concise. *Mary Pride*

The hardest part about learning cursive writing is learning to form the connections between the letters. Those connections are the emphasis of **Cursive Connections**, thus the name. It is designed to build fluency and confidence in writing using the traditional style of cursive.

Included are instructions for teachers, a description of the vari-

A Traditional Style
Cursive Connections
Letter Drill
Letter Connections
Fluency Development
Workbook and Guide for Student, Parent and/or Teacher

Christian Liberty Press Handwriting Program
Grades K–4. $5.50 each workbook. Shipping extra.
Christian Liberty Press, 502 West Euclid Ave., Arlington Heights, IL 60004. (847) 259-4444. Fax: (847) 259-2941. Email: enquire@homeschools.org. Web: www.homeschools.org. They take credit card orders, but not over the phone. Any other contact method will work.

**NEW!
Cursive Connections**
Grade 3 and up. $9.99 plus $3 shipping.
KEL Publications, P.O. Box 260, Gilbert, AZ 85299-0260. Phone/Fax: (480) 539-0125. Email: cursive@goodnet.com. Web: www.goodnet.com/~cursive

ous strokes, and examples of how to correctly slant the letters (examples of how *not* to slant show which way is correct). There is also a sample alphabet, which the author suggests you photocopy and laminate for reference.

The 80 pages of this book introduce the lower case letters first, then capitals. There are additional teacher hints at the beginning of the capital section. A typical page contains an example of the featured letter at the top, formed in both manuscript and cursive; the cursive example includes arrows showing the correct order and direction to use in writing it. This is followed by four lines of letters, letter combinations, and words, each followed by a blank on which to copy the example above it. The guide lines are two solid lines ½ inch apart with a dotted line in the middle. After the first few pages, which are more introductory, many pages have a phrase written in manuscript which you are supposed to copy into cursive. *Melissa Worcester*

The same people who brought us *A Reason For Writing* now present parents with a manuscript writing workbook for beginners. **God Made My World** is an ideal starting point for early learners. Each lesson is methodical, thorough, and fun! Without overloading on exercise, the workbook offers parents the option of either a one- or two-page lesson per day. The use of a tree house to orient the student to line spacing may cause a moment of confusion to some youngsters, and parents may have to explain exactly what a tree house is, but the teaching concept flows throughout the workbook and can actually be an asset as the child learns to work between lines.

While lessons are sequential, they are not necessarily alphabetical. Shapes and sounds replace the old A, B, C order of handwriting. The workbook begins with instructions on how to hold a pencil, how to make lines, and how lines and shapes make letters. As they move through the basic techniques of printing letters, the student then discovers the way grouped letters create words. Easy words are accompanied by a bold full-page picture to color. Each illustration depicts an object in the living world around them so that parents can easily use the activity to enhance other lesson areas. Capital letters are addressed in the last third of the workbook. Supplement exercises combine both lowercase and capital letters and round out this 136-page workbook. This workbook requires little preparation to use, and can be the highlight of your day. *Lisa Mitchell*

The **Handwriting Without Tears Method** by occupational therapist Jan Z. Olsen is the gentle way to teach your child to write. Especially good for slow learners and children with weak motor skills, these books, which follow the European method of using only two lines to anchor each letter, are all you'll ever need to introduce and instruct your child in basic manuscript and cursive handwriting. Children find the two-line method easier to follow than our American three-line method. They can much more easily see which letters have parts that "stick up" or "stick down." There are also special techniques which help prevent or correct reversals.

You begin with **Handwriting Without Tears,** a book for parents/teachers which explains the whole system. It also presents the kindergarten readiness activities, such as using wood pieces to construct capital letters and using an old-fashioned slate for teaching capitals and numbers. Then comes **My Printing Book,** a beginning book for first-graders. Here your child learns the basics: the alphabet, all numbers, and simple words. Each lesson is accompanied with a picture and plenty of practice space. Though capitalization is included in the book, most time is spent learning to form lower-case letters.

Printing Power continues the same easy-to-follow lessons for grades two and above. After reviewing the alphabet, lessons move on quickly to teach words, sentences, and simple paragraphs.

NEW!
God Made My World
Grades K–1. $10.98 plus shipping. *Concerned Communications, PO Box 1000, Siloam Springs, AR 72761-9797. Orders: (800) 447-4332. Inquiries: (501) 736-2244. Fax: (501) 549-4002. Email: areasonfor@aol.com. Web: www.areasonfor.com.*

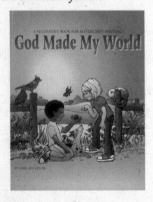

NEW!
Handwriting Without Tears
Grades 1–4. Handwriting Without Tears course book, $6.50. 26-piece capital wood pieces, $22.50. Slate, $2.50. My Printing Book, Printing Power, Cursive Handwriting, Cursive Success, $4.75 each. Teachers Guides, $4.75 each. Print or Cursive display cards, $3.75 each set. Shipping extra. *Handwriting Without Tears, 8802 Quiet Stream Ct., Potomac, MD 20854. (301) 983-8409. Fax: (301) 983-6821. Email: jan@hwtears.com. Web: www.hwtears.com.*

Cursive Handwriting introduces each letter in the vertical style of cursive handwriting. The connecting of letters to create cursive words is taught in a thorough manner before sentences are finally constructed, with plenty of practice space allowed. The series wraps up with the fourth book, **Cursive Success.**

Unlike other exercise books, each model is copied just once, and there is no attempt to integrate handwriting with history, geography, math, careers, or skateboarding. The *Cursive Handwriting* book uses a simplified vertical (straight up-and-down) cursive. Accompanying teacher's guides for the first three books are available.

These books form a cohesive, complete instruction in handwriting. Children will love the pictures and workbook style. Display cards can be ordered for those needing visual aids. I particularly love the 22-piece set of wooden letter pieces used to construct capital letters. Designed for preschool and kindergarten children, these wooden pieces are an excellent teaching tool. Children can actually see and feel the letter they are learning to write.

Last of all, the teacher's guides provide a rich supply of extra instruction. Information is included for left-handed writers. The lesson-by-lesson approach adds up to a guarantee of success. This series cannot be praised enough! *Lisa Mitchell*

HANDWRITING WITHOUT TEARS

The **Let's Write series** from Hayes competently covers penmanship skills taught in grades 1–6. Originally written in 1967, it has a serene, Leave-it-to-Beaver flavor.

Book 1, **Let's Write Manuscript,** does just that. Step-by-step presentation of manuscript basics plus space allotted on each page for the student to copy the example letters, words, and sentences. Excellent teacher's notes in the front of the book explain just how to present each new skill. For grades 1–2.

The transition from manuscript to cursive is difficult for many children. Book 2, **Let's Write Cursive,** makes it as painless as possible. Again, exercise space and a teacher's guide are built in. For children making this transition, anywhere from grades 2–6.

Books 3 and 4, **Let's Drill Cursive** and **Advanced Cursive Writing,** follow a similar format. Book 4 is especially endearing. Written examples in this book include patriotic source material (portions of the Declaration of Independence, Bill of Rights, Gettysburg Address, etc.) and sage sayings and maxims from our own good ol' Western culture.

The presentation in these books is remarkably clutter-free. You cover a lot in just 44 pages!

Each book looks just like a regular workbook (which it is). Since these are considered "blackline masters," though, you have permission from the publisher to copy each page for use with all the children you are teaching. I personally would just get each of my children his own workbook, but if you want to penny-pinch, you can! *Mary Pride*

Hayes Let's Write series

Grades 1–6. Books 1–4, $4.95 each (specify blackline masters). Shipping extra. *Hayes School Publishing Co., Inc., 321 Pennwood Ave., Pittsburgh, PA 15221-3398. (800) 245-6234. Fax: (412) 371-6408. Web: www.hayespub.com.*

At a price anyone can afford, **Integrated Writing** provides an easy, pleasant method of teaching writing skills.

Enhancing this five-workbook series is the Integrated Writing Fonts program for PC or Macintosh. This allows simple writing to cross curriculum lines, as parents use the IW Fonts to produce study materials and have children practice their handwriting in all areas of learning. While not an absolute necessity, the 64-

NEW!
Integrated Writing

Grades K–12. Exercise Books, $3.95. Teacher's Manual, $9.95. IW Fonts (PC or Mac), $9.95. *Golden Educational Center, 857 Lake Blvd., Redding, CA 96003. (800) 800-1791. Fax: (530) 244-5939. Email: rlw@iname.com. Web: www.goldened.com.*

page Teacher's Manual provides excellent foundation and sequence directions. Each workbook contains a single page of teaching instructions; however the Readiness workbook contains two, covering the necessary basics needed to begin teaching handwriting. But it is only in the Teacher's Manual that you find all the more crucial helps, like how to teach a left-hander and visual-motor skills.

Each 64-page workbook is finished in a bright cardstock cover, with pages printed in bold black, white and gray ink. Handwriting is taught in sequence from Readiness, to Print, to Script, then Transition and finally Cursive with a smooth progress from workbook to workbook.

Parents who select this approach to handwriting should strongly consider applying the IW Fonts computer program to the total educational process. *Lisa Mitchell*

Dr. Stephen Morgenstern has published a handwriting manual/workbook specifically for parents of the **left-handed** child. While we might have wished for more detailed instructions, this no-frills manual/workbook has the benefit of photographs to assist parents in teaching their left hander correct writing techniques to avoid cramping wrists and awkward positions. The explanations of push and pull muscles may help the right-handed parent better understand their child's writing inclinations, but the paragraphs on poor wrist alignment may be of greater benefit. Each letter of the alphabet is provided in the workbook section, first in bold letters, then in dots for the child to trace. Finally there is a practice line offered, but parents will need to have another tablet on hand for additional exercise. This brief guide can be an asset to parents of the left-handed and can be used to avoid common mistakes the right-handed do not experience. *Lisa Mitchell*

Believe it or not, some public school systems are getting into teaching italic handwriting. The series they are using is published by **Portland State University**. It begins with prewriting exercises in Book A and goes all the way to a very professional italic hand. The series is spread out over seven grades, starting with kindergarten, like most public school courses; but you don't need to buy all the workbooks if you are using them at home.

Portland State University's third edition of the **Getty-Dubay Italic Handwriting Series** maintains the same smooth continuity of learning, with emphasis on an easy mastery of italic handwriting. The instruction manual has been completely revised and expanded to include creative student activities and many hints for parents. It covers techniques for teaching and evaluating the course, as well as many special considerations for both left and right-handed writers.

NEW!
Left Handed Handwriting Skills

For parents of children grades 1–3. $18.95 plus shipping.
Dr. Stephen Morgenstern, 6 Norman Court, Bix Hills, NY 11746. (516) 549-8232. Fax: (516) 271-8074.

Portland State University Getty-Dubay Italic Handwriting

Grades K–6. Books A through G and Instructor's Manual, $5.75 each. Basic Blackline Master Practice Sheets for Homeschoolers (covers books A, B, C) and Cursive Blackline Master Practice Sheets for Homeschoolers (covers books D, E, F and G), $6.75 each. Classroom Wall Charts, two sets: Basic Italic Alphabet and Numerals, Cursive Italic Alphabet and Numerals, $6.75/set. Alphabet Desk Strips (specify Basic Italic or Cursive Italic,) $6.75 (set of 30). New "Write Now!" instruction video, $29.95. Shipping extra.
Portland State University, School of Extended Studies, Continuing Education Press, PO Box 1394, Portland, OR 97207-1394. Orders: (800) 547-8887 x4891. Inquiries: (503) 725-4846. Fax: (503) 725-4840. Email: press@ses.pdx.edu. Web: extended.pdx.edu/press/.

The series contains seven books, A–G, plus an instructor's manual. Each can be used on its own; you do not need all the previous books in the series. Book A begins with the kindergarten age student, while Book G is designed for any student from the sixth grade up to adults. With all the creative ideas and suggestions in the instruction manual, parents should have no trouble encouraging more practice.

Barbara Getty and Inga Dubay are the two ladies who invented this simple italic teaching method. Differences between the Getty-Dubay approach and other public-school handwriting programs:

- **How many letters change shape** when making the transition from manuscript to cursive? Only two capital letters and one manuscript letter change shape in the Getty-Dubay approach. Compare this to the 18 capital letter changes in the D'Nealian system and the 26 capital letter changes in Palmer, Bowmar-Noble, and Zaner-Bloser, and to the 13 lowercase letter changes in D'Nealian and 26 in Palmer, Bowmar-Noble, and Zaner-Bloser.
- Getty-Dubay is the only public-school method in which **capital cursive forms are based on the manuscript forms**.
- Getty-Dubay uses **no loops**, aiding both legibility and ease of teaching.
- **Capital letters, ascenders, and descenders are in the same proportions as those found in book typefaces**, allowing closer writing without tangling letters together. Other methods use ascenders and descenders which frequently become tangled. Example: try writing the word *fly* in cursive handwriting and then writing *fall* directly underneath. If you learned from one of the other methods, the loops of the *f*'s will be getting tangled, and so will the bottom loop of the *y* in *fly* and the top loops of the *l*'s. The same words, written in Getty-Dubay script, don't tangle at all.
- **Letter slope** can be a problem. In Palmer, Bowmar-Noble, and Zaner-Bloser, the slopes changes from 0° in the manuscript books to 27 degrees in the cursive books. The D'Nealian slope remains at 17 degrees for both manuscript and cursive. Getty-Dubay script slopes at only 5 degrees, which they feel is a more natural slope better suited to both manuscript and cursive.

You can also get an instructor's manual, which includes teaching techniques, a scope and sequence, and the theory behind the course. Blackline masters contain follow-up practice exercises. Portland State University has recently put together two sets of blackline masters (which include permission to photocopy) just for home schoolers.

New: a **43-minute training video** for the parent or teacher explains how to teach handwriting the Getty-Dubay way. Letters are introduced in the video by family groups: one-stroke letters, two-stroke letters, letters with arches, etc. While the audio is not always completely clear, the instructor was animated and entertaining. One possible distraction is the shadows created on the paper by background lighting. Overall the ease of usage and instruction override these simple drawbacks. Parents interested in teaching italic handwriting will greatly appreciate this long-awaited product.

My inclination would be to skip Book A, which is merely the italic alphabet with one letter per page. There are no review pages in the book—for these you need the blackline masters—so the student could easily forget all the early letters by the time he gets to the end of the book, unless he practices using the lined paper masters supplied in the instructor's manual. Joins are first introduced in Book C, and thereafter the letter size gets smaller and smaller. Books B through E seem the most valuable of the series, if you don't want to buy the entire set. Or, if you want only one book for yourself or an older student, Book G has a self-teaching approach to the whole system.

This is the most complete italic handwriting series you will ever want, covering all of the alphabet and numerals in an easy transition from basic printing to italic cursive, no matter which book you begin using. The homeschooled child should have no difficulty at all in following this innovative and delightful course. Directions are easy to follow with minimal preparation. All instructions and side notes have been typeset using a new font designed to be a replica of the italic style. This provides a unique opportunity for the child to see in print what he is learning to write! There are plenty of exercises, as well as a fun activity at the end of the book. *Mary Pride and Lisa Mitchell*

ReadyWriter

Ages 4–7. $17.95 plus shipping.
Providence Project, 14566 NW 110th St., Whitewater, KS 67154. (888) 776-8776 or (316) 799-2112.
Fax: (316) 799-2192.
Email: info@providenceproject.com.
Web: www.providenceproject.com.

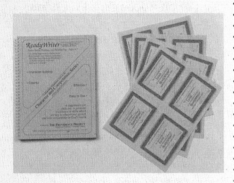

A Reason for Writing

Grades K–6. Student books $10.98 each. Instruction Guidebook, $12.98, covers all grades. Quantity discounts available on student books. Shipping extra.
Concerned Communications, PO Box 1000, Siloam Springs, AR 72761-9797.
Orders: (800) 447-4332. Inquiries: (501) 736-2244. Fax: (501) 549-4002.
Email: areasonfor@aol.com.
Web: www.areasonfor.com.

Could Junior's horrible handwriting stem from a simple lack of stylus skills? Has he ever really learned how to make neat lines, zigzags, spirals, and circles? If not, why not take a couple of minutes a day to practice these skills with the fun, motivational **ReadyWriter** program from Providence Project?

Each ReadyWriter practice sheet features a scene on Farmer Brown's farm. You read the paragraph-long "story" of the day, and your student gets to work filling in the missing parts of the picture. Example:

> *Mrs. Brown has just fixed a big batch of the Brown family's favorite dessert—brownies (naturally)! They've cooled off just a bit, so now let's help her cut them. Start at the top of the page, and with your pencil "cut" one panful at a time, first from top to bottom and then from left to right. Try to make nice square brownies of the same size, and try not to cut into the middle (shaded area) of the brownies. It might be a good idea to have some real brownies sometime, too!*

What red-blooded kid could resist helping Mrs. Brown cut out her brownies? Your child repeats this sheet every day until he's making nice unjiggly lines. Then he moves on to helping Farmer Brown sharpen his saw blades (zigzags), helping the sheep wake up by coloring in their eyes, drawing spirals on the ends of Farmer Brown's logs, helping Farmer Brown fix his roof by tracing the lines that slant in different directions . . . . you get the idea. Even when we had finished this program, our children were begging to do it again!

ReadyWriter comes with 12 sheets for each of the 16 exercises (enough for several children, if they learn quickly) and an instructor's guide with the stories and directions for use. Very highly recommended. *Mary Pride*

A Reason for Writing is the only K–6 handwriting curriculum using Scripture verses (from *The Living Bible*) as the total subject material. Children in grades K–2 learn manuscript, and in grades 4–6 practice cursive. Either second or third grade is set aside for making the transition between these two handwriting styles.

All of the workbooks are printed in black and white on sturdy newsprint paper, with each page pre-perfed for easy removal. The glossy covers are printed in full color. The format is simple and the procedure for using the books is clearly spelled out in the Instruction Guidebook. This contains three pages of general guidelines introducing the program's philosophy and format, followed by:

- 33 pages of guidelines for introducing beginning students to manuscript writing, including comments about formation of each letter and other hints
- 30 pages of information on basic manuscript, including letter formation, a vocabulary list and a skills list index for each book
- 14 pages of information about the transition between manuscript and cursive
- 18 more pages about teaching cursive

You'll also find blackline masters of a lined practice page and another of the manuscript alphabet . For each stage, there is an explanation of how to evaluate the student, and also some extra projects for the older students who need extra practice.

God Made My World, the kindergarten book, focuses on God's creation. There are some pre-writing exercises, followed by practice pages. Each perforated page introduces one letter on one side of the piece of paper, with three sets of lines on which to practice the featured letter. Some letters are dotted and some you must write on your own. The reverse side of this page contains a large picture of an animal or item starting with that letter and the word identifying that object in dotted letters for you to trace. Lower-case letters come first, followed by capitals.

Words of Promise, the first-grade book, provides plenty of practice in manuscript writing. There are 34 pages of letter formation practice, each containing six sets of lines on which to write (each set is two solid lines with a dotted line in between). These pages show the proper formation of the letter on a sample with arrows, followed by space to write your own. Following the practice pages, 29 weekly lessons pull you into the main concept of *A Reason for Writing*, writing a verse of scripture. On days 1, 2, and 3 you are to read the verse of the week aloud and work on pages containing four lines of practice containing words or letters used in the verse. On day 4, you write the verse on practice paper once or twice and choose a border sheet from pages at the back of the book, then write the verse in your best writing. On day 5 you get to decorate the border, which is a coloring-book-style illustration with lines for writing the verse. The verses in *Words of Promise* are from Psalms and Proverbs.

Words of Jesus is the second-grade book. This teaches manuscript and transition to cursive, with verses from the gospels of Matthew, Mark, Luke and John. You start with 30 lessons in manuscript with the same five-day format as in the book above. There are then 28 practice pages covering transition, and then 10 actual lessons in the five-day format which use cursive writing. The size of the writing on all of these pages is the same as in the book above. The only difference is that the practice pages each contain 11 lines of practice writing.

Words to Live By, the third-grade book, works with verses from the New Testament epistles and concentrates on transition and cursive writing. It has 30 practice pages followed by 25 weekly lessons in the same five-day format used in the above books. The difference here is that the size of the writing expected in this book is smaller than in the two previous books, and that the practice pages each contain 17 lines of writing.

Words of Love, the fourth-grade book, provides cursive handwriting practice from the gospels of Matthew, Mark, Luke and John.

Words of Praise, the fifth-grade book, offers cursive practice from the book of Psalms.

Words of Wisdom, meant for sixth grade, contains cursive practice from the book of Proverbs.

All of these books for grades 4–6 include 33 weekly lessons in the same rive-day format, with the same size writing as in the third grade book.

This is an excellent program for anyone who wants to combine handwriting training with biblical devotion. *Melissa Worcester*

NEW!
Rol'n'Write

Ages 2–7. Alphabet, $65.95. Numbers, $39.95. Activity book, $19.95.
Ideal Instructional Fare Publishing Group, 2400 Turner Ave. NW, Grand Rapids, MI 49544. (800) 253-5469. Fax: (800) 543-2690. Email: instructionalfare@tribune.com. Web: www.ifair.com.

These blue plastic letters are really unique! The **Rol 'n' Write** alphabet set holds all 26 from the lowercase alphabet and 6 ball bearings. What are the ball bearings for? Well, the blue plastic letters are raised, with a groove down the middle. You place a ball bearing in the groove where the letter starts, and the ball bearing rolls all the way through the letter in the exact way you would write it! This is because the grooves on the letters are ingeniously tilted in just the right directions. The ball bearing never sticks or stops in the middle, either, because the plastic is completely smooth.

Your children will just sit and play with these for hours, especially the *M*. Of course, they can also trace each letter by placing a finger in the groove, and they'll know the right direction from watching the ball bearing. (You'll have to supervise, of course, since a little kid might decide to try putting the ball bearing in his mouth if left alone.)

This is the most ingenious learn-to-write aid we have ever seen. It actually engages a child in hands-on practice *and* reinforces what he's learning visually at the same time. Recommended, if you can afford it. Perhaps your support group would like to add it to their library? *Sarah Pride*

NEW!
Writestart

Ages 3–6. $15.95 plus shipping.
Ideal Instructional Fair Publishing Group, 2400 Turner Ave., NW, Grand Rapids, MI 49544. (800) 443-3976. Fax: (800) 543-2690. Web: www.ifair.com.

Writestart is like a deluxe cousin of the popular *ReadyWriter* from Providence Project. My four-year-old filled up all fifteen double-sided cards in two obsessed hours. We'll work on precision another day.

The first few cards instruct the child to "lead the donkey to the carrot" or dog to the bone in a large circle, square, or triangle maze. Then the cards graduate to connecting dots and completing "m," "u," and "w" patterns, both isolated and in context of themed pictures in cheerful colors. By card 9 the child is copying letters in an almost-cursive italic style with cute pictures for extra practice—like "g's" to fill in a goat's haunches and legs and to complete a comic face.

The capital letters deviate a bit from classic italic style, especially the "G." The final card features a "framed" blank space for a self-portrait and, on the reverse, four lines of manuscript rule for further practice.

The creators of *Writestart* have included a brief brochure with additional tips on developing young students' stylus skills, and the high-quality slick cards are just the right size (8 x 8") for little ones. But isn't there an easier way to handle the write-on, wipe-off mess? The grease/wax pencil (with rubber grip) didn't rub off much on the child, but it also won't rub off easily from the cards for the next go-round! *Cindy Marsch*

Keyboarding & Typing

Today's kids do need to learn to "keyboard," that is, type on a computer keyboard. Personally, I favor using software for this task. My favorite typing/keyboarding program is *Mavis Beacon Teaches Typing* (not to be confused with *Mavis Beacon for Kids*). However, for the benefit of those readers who do not have computers, but do have typewriters, here are some non-software programs that will do the trick.

Color-code your fingers and keyboard with little colored dots. Learn to type the alphabet letters first, in familiar alphabet order. Then review upper- and lowercase. Practice the 70 most-often-occurring words. Practice capitalization and single caps. Learn the top row keys. Practice typing some typical facts and figures (names, addresses, dates, telephone numbers). Learn centering and tabbing. Practice typing state names and abbreviations. Finish with a number of timed-typing exercises.

You get 16 lessons in all, in one spiral-bound book. You can prop the book open, making it easier to use while practicing your typing. The inside back cover is a practice keyboard.

The **AlphabeTyping** method has worked with regular and intellectually-behind children and adults of all ages. It's *very* simple, starting as it does with something you already know—the alphabet—as opposed to virtually all other typing programs, that start with "home row" keys (ASDF). It's also color-coded. A worthy contender to Educators Publishing Service's *Keyboarding Skills* program (see next page). *Mary Pride*

AlphabeTyping

All ages. $13.95 plus shipping. Beaumont Books, PO Box 551, Westminster, CO 80030. (303) 477-4349. Fax: (303) 433-9192. Email: beaubooks@aol.com.

The **Herzog System of Keyboarding** is perfect for the homeschooled child. This course does away with the old *home row* method of learning to type. Instead, it introduces special sensory locators called *Hub Key Sensors*. Adaptable to either computer keyboard or typewriter, these little key "caps" position your fingertips on four keys: D, K, 3 and 8. Letter locations are then taught alphabetically, a method that is much easier and allows elementary age students to learn the skill of typing well before when they would have learned with the old home-row method. Students grasp the Herzog method quickly and build confidence as they learn to locate letters around the *Hub Key Sensors*.

Presented in a straightforward style, this course is simple for the parent to teach, and easy for the child to understand. In no time at all your child will be typing!

The system is available in either the Elementary Fast Track or the Secondary Fast Track, with each level covering the alphabet and number keys. Common punctuation, shift keys and basic computer terms are also introduced in both books.

Though it would seem that the Secondary Fast Track would have more computer terms, this is not the case. Nor does it address any specialty computer keys or the numeric keypad. The only variation in computer use is that Secondary Fast Track adds a page on protective care of floppy discs.

Nevertheless, this is an outstanding typing series with additional help and suggestions offered in the teacher's guide. The books are spiral-bound with firm cardboard covers that open into an easel, making the book self-supporting. For those with children who are challenged, this system has proved successful in public special education classes. *Lisa Mitchell*

NEW!
Herzog System Keyboarding

Grades 2–adult. $30. Optional wall chart $7.50. Plus $4.50 shipping. Herzog Keyboarding, 1433 E. Broadway, Tucson, AZ 85719. (520) 792-2550. Fax: (520) 792-2551. Email: office@HerzogKeyboarding.com. Web: www.HerzogKeyboarding.com.

Keyboarding Skills

Grades 1–12. $12.50 plus shipping. *Educators Publishing Service, Inc., 31 Smith Pl., Cambridge, MA 02138. (800) 225-5750. Fax: (617) 547-0412. Email: epsbooks@epsbooks.com. Web: www.epsbooks.com.*

Here's an innovative touch-typing system developed for dyslexics but usable by anyone. Like *AlphabeTyping*, **Keyboarding Skills** starts with the alphabet in its normal sequence, rather than the usual "home row" approach of ASDF and JKL. By saying the name of a letter and pressing its key—a motor process with kinesthetic reinforcement—most students master the alphabet on a typewriter in less than an hour. Next come words of increasing length, phrases, capital letters, and sentences. Numbers, symbols, and punctuation marks complete the course.

Keyboarding Skills is designed for rapid success and ease of use. The spiral-bound top and heavy covers let you stand *Keyboarding Skills* up like an easel, with the copy then in an easy-to-read position. On top of each page is an illustration of the keyboard parts corresponding to the letters freshly introduced. Younger students can use it as soon as their hands are big enough, and the method, though simple, is not too babyish for older students or adults. *Mary Pride*

Type It

Grades 1–12. $12.50 plus shipping. *Educators Publishing Service, Inc., 31 Smith Pl., Cambridge, MA 02138. (800) 225-5750. Fax: (617) 547-0412. Email: epsbooks@epsbooks.com. Web: www.epsbooks.com.*

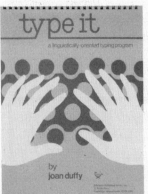

Type It is the best non-software beginning course in touch typing for the money. This is real touch typing, starting with home row keys and covering the entire keyboard except for the special characters above the numbers. It's also *linguistically-oriented* touch typing. The words chosen for the exercises are phonetically regular, so you can use *Type It* for children as young as six.

Type It now has a bound-in standing easel, so you can simply prop the *Type It* manual open at the ideal height for typing. The manual is spiral-bound, with exercises set in large type. Eight lessons in all, with 16 exercise sets per lesson. Kids can check off completed exercises on the Progress Chart on the inside of the back cover.

There's no magic here—just do the exercises in order, according to the one page of directions at the beginning of the book. You'll need to hover around to make sure your child is using the right fingers, as bad typing habits are easier to prevent than to break. Aside from that, you have nothing to do except *ooh* and *aah* over Junior's newfound typing skills. *Mary Pride*

CHAPTER 20

Literature for Kids

Your daughter knows how to read. Wonderful! Now . . . *what* is she going to read?

In all the concern about teaching our children to read, it is well to remember that the purpose of learning to read is to read *something*. If the only printed matter in the world were the backs of cereal boxes, the need to read would be far less urgent. If our children are only going to read popular magazines and the instructions on government forms, it's hard to see why we don't just switch over to phonetic spelling, which is much easier to learn. (Example: "Lets Invayd Sum Small Kuntree Sum Ware, Prezident Sez.")

The only legitimate reason our kids struggle through the odd English orthography is so they can read books written before today—preferably, the better of these books, otherwise known as The Classics.

Please note, gentle reader: **school "basal reading series" are *not* The Classics**. Often they *include* snippets from a classic or two. When they do, the snippets are often edited or abridged, sometimes totally contrary to the tone of the original writing. But the bulk of virtually every modern series of "readers" is made up of modern works, often written expressly for the series.

To put it as bluntly as possible, **"readers" are *not* literature**. They may *include* some literature, just as a soft drink may include fruit juice. But they also include a lot of *other* stuff. When parents object to the offensive items included in a public school reader, such as stories promoting witchcraft or suicide, the publishers can then point to the "classics" and paint the parents as people who "want to censor *The Wizard of Oz*." Never mind that the publishers have already censored most of the Western classics out of their books in the first place!

Now, when we talk about "the classics of Western civilization," I don't mean *Amelia Bedelia* or *Frog and Toad are Friends*. Such books may be several decades old—kids may love them—they may be bestsellers or good literature—but they are not *classics*. *David Copperfield* by Charles Dickens, on the other hand, *is* a classic. It has been regarded as such for generations. It has affected our culture. It deals with significant issues with stylistic excellence.

Sadly, your child is likely to emerge from his school experience having read *Amelia Bedelia,* but not having read *David Copperfield.* "So what?" someone asks. Well, among other things, it is a grave loss to our cultural

Truth and Fiction

Every book human beings produce has an element of fiction in it, except the better sort of instruction manuals! "True" stories, to be readable, must contain fictional elements. Rare is the person who can remember the weather and everything he said on a given day; thus, historical biographies contain "reconstructed" dialogs and "best guesses" at weather conditions, the appearance of characters and their surroundings, and the like.

Good true stories are as faithful as possible to the historical details. Good fiction is "true to life." And, as Gregg Harris notes, all good literature (including fantasy, which is neither true to history nor true to life) is "true to principle." Are good and evil portrayed realistically? Do the characters make realistic choices? Are their behavior and surroundings consistent with what we know about the time period and culture? If the author does a good job in all these areas, he has, *whether he wanted to or not,* created a powerful vehicle for teaching character lessons.

Such a Character!

A parent's response to the stories his child reads and hears also has a powerful teaching effect. If Mom thinks Scarlett O'Hara was a bimbo who got what she deserved, Suzy Q will look at Scarlett in an entirely different way than Janie, whose mom secretly wishes she could have *been* Scarlett!

vocabulary. Time was when everyone knew what you meant when you say, "Mr. X is a Uriah Heep," or "Mrs. Y is a regular Betsy Trotwood." It's also a grave loss to our combined wisdom and discernment, as it is very handy to know about the Uriah Heep character type and to be able to recognize him when he tries to ooze his way into power. The Dickens novels are almost a complete course in character traits, presented as memorable stories.

And that's just *Dickens*.

In Praise of Old Books

Ah, those good old books! This is what a child gets when he spends hours, weeks, and months immersed in classic literature:

1. **Grammar.** This subject can be "caught" as well as "taught." Correct usage was considered essential in previous generations, and the sentence structure of their books reflects this.
2. **Vocabulary.** This almost goes without saying. Children can vastly increase their passive vocabulary by reading old books (though they may need to consult a dictionary in order to pronounce the words correctly). Today the trend is towards dumbing-down literature, in hopes an

Faith-Destroying Fiction

Character training through stories is as old as stories themselves. Æsop's *Fables*, Homer's *Iliad* and *Odyssey*, and the Bible are all examples of how a story can be used to involve and motivate the listener.

In our desire to turn Johnny and Janie into great readers, though, we need to remember that bookstores and libraries today contain a mix of bad books and good books. Not that everything kids read has to be great literature, but there's a definite difference between "junk food for the mind" and "poison for the mind" that we parents need to be aware of.

Sanctified Unreality Good and evil never struggle in most modern stories. In Christian kiddie fiction, evil scarcely exists; the "bad" characters are only poor lonely souls with unmet needs who immediately blossom into sanctified goodness the first time someone smiles at them. This trivial view of temptation and sin also extends to a trivial view of faith and perseverance. The "character-building" hero immediately succeeds once he learns his "lesson," rather than having to struggle on in faith, believing that in time his faith will be rewarded. All it takes is a few of life's hard knocks to make kids cynical who have been brought up on this type of unrealistic nonsense.

Unsanctified Unreality In secular kiddie fiction, on the other hand, evil often is the star. I bring to your attention the best-selling *Goosebumps* horror series, to name just one. In these stories, evil is as likely to triumph as good. The net effect is to teach *nihilism,* the doctrine that there is no point to life and nothing really matters. And *Goosebumps* isn't the worst thing out there. Many bestselling books for preteens now include themes of witchcraft, murder for trivial reasons, hate-filled family relationships, and sexual predation, all with a nihilistic dash of hopelessness mixed in.

Avoid both these kinds of faith-destroying fiction at all costs. Young readers desperately need a universe they can count on. They need certainty; they need to know that reality is real and that right and wrong do matter and that, though it's a struggle, good will eventually win. Without this certainty, the options of suicide, psychopathy, and apathy all begin to look reasonable.

increasingly illiterate population will be able to read it. Not so then. Even barefoot boys of Huck Finn's generation read the King Arthur and Robin Hood legends, archaic language and all. Give kids a good plot, and they'll make the effort to pick up the extra vocabulary needed to understand it.

3. **Spelling.** This varies from child to child, but in my experience visual learners can pick up correct spelling simply by reading a lot of books containing correct spelling.

4. **Creative writing.** In the past, youngsters learned the techniques of good writing by copying extracts from great writers. Without going to the effort of actually writing paragraphs out, those who read a lot of great writing still unconsciously absorb its forms.

5. **History.** Even if the old book in question isn't a historical book *per se*, it is historical by virtue of being old. A book written in 1920 can't help presenting us with 1920s ideas, architecture, fashions, and so on.

6. **Worldview.** Another benefit of reading old books is that they enable you to become aware of different ways of thinking. In today's world, where our national motto seems to be, "It's the economy, stupid," old books remind us of when passion, honor, and nobility of character were treasured. There *was* life before Dilbert!

Keep in mind that I'm only listing benefits kids pick up *without* extra study. Children who read lots of old books will come by improved grammar, vocabulary, spelling, creative writing, historical understanding, and a more thoughtful worldview whether or not they ever write book reports or take tests. I would, in fact, argue against book reports and tests, except possibly for an occasional one thrown in just for practice. Literature has power because is it so enjoyable. Turn it into an assignment and most of its appeal disappears.

In any case, effortful assignments based on kids' reading aren't necessary. Good books spark interest in further study all by themselves. Kids who read Jules Verne novels are almost guaranteed to develop an interest in science, geography, and engineering, just like kids who read Sir Walter Scott's books can often be found engaged in swordplay using cardboard swords and trashcan lids for shields. Any "book" place that can be located on the map teaches geography in a way not easily forgotten. Any "book" event can spark further historical study. Your job will be just to find the resources to satisfy your child's new interests.

Why You Don't Need "Reading Comprehension" Quizzes

The literature programs available for homeschoolers have increased since we put together the last edition of this book. Some publishers have put together "reader series" of classic stories, or collections of classic stories on audiocassettes. Others have come out with study aids for classic children's books, so you can squeeze more juice out of your reading assignments.

What you won't find here are lots of "reading comprehension" tests, workbooks, or courses. "Reading comprehension" is really a substitute for the book reports, oral reports, and essay questions teachers used to assign. As "look-say" phonics began to cripple kids' ability to read and write, "reading comprehension" was discovered. So what if kids couldn't sound out words properly? *Understanding* was what counted—and understanding would be measured by multiple-choice questions that required *no* writing and practically no ability to read. Smart kids learn to look for "key words" in the questions, or phrases that duplicate those in the reading passages,

Heroes & Villains

Here are some rules to remember while evaluating the character lessons a work of literature teaches:

1. If there is a "good" character or "hero," the reader will naturally identify with him or her.

2. Exception: To be a hero, you must valiantly and nobly overcome obstacles. If the main character never has any problems or disappointments, or if the main character is a smarmy idiot who seems oblivious to how serious the problems are he faces, the reader will *not* identify with him. Especially bad in this regard are the multitude of personality-free Christian stories in which kids are taught that evangelism is a trivial process that requires no more from you than letting the neighborhood bully play in your games or giving him some cookies. Teaching kids that life is easy, and that every good work is instantly rewarded, is *wrong*.

3. If there are no good characters, or the main character is an anti-hero, or the hero's efforts are made to seem pointless, the reader will find that consuming sizeable amounts of that kind of literature for pleasure will exert a draining effect on his own character.

and fill in the blanks accordingly. In other words, "reading comprehension" is a scam designed to *hide* from kids, teachers, and parents that the kids *can't* really read and comprehend.

At home, you can just ask your kids to narrate back what they read. If they can tell you what the book or story was about, obviously they read it. Once they start talking about the book characters as if they were real people, including wondering what would have happened if the characters had done things differently, or how the characters would act in settings outside the book, you *know* they understand the book! When you hear them arguing about whether Robinson Crusoe or Friday is the better man, or what would have happened if Robinson Crusoe had taken Friday up on his offer to become an evangelist to his tribe, or see them acting out story scenes ("I'm pretending I'm Robinson Crusoe and my room is his cave"), the literature has passed from "a book" to part of their lives. And that's what it's all about!

How & What to Read

More than just a list of must-read books for children, **Babies Need Books: Sharing the Joy of Books with Children from Birth to 6** by Dorothy Butler is an important inspiration and guide. It's an excellent baby-shower gift, especially for a young and inexperienced expectant mother, more important than nursing gowns. Scientific evidence shows the importance of reading to children, even from birth. Reading broadens horizons, establishes speech patterns, develops imagination, nurtures creativity, forges relationships, promotes communication, and fosters positive attitudes toward reading and learning.

Now you know *why*, and with this 261-page book you will have suggestions on *what* and *how* to read as well. More than just a list of books, Butler offers guidelines to help adults evaluate books for small children—books that will endure and become favorites of parents and children. *Anne Brodbeck*

NEW!
Babies Need Books

Parents. $15.95 plus shipping. *Greenwood Publishing Group, PO Box 5007, Westport, CT 06881. (800) 225-5800. Fax: (203) 222-1502, mark it "Attention: Customer Service." Web: www.greenwood.com.*

Books Children Love
For the Children's Sake

Parents. Books Children Love, $14.99. For the Children's Sake, $12.99. Shipping extra. *Crossway Books, 1300 Crescent St., Wheaton, IL 60187. (800) 635-7993. Fax: (630) 682-4785.*

You want more than reading lists? **For the Children's Sake** is a wonderful book about how children learn which, among other things, shares the idea of learning through "living books"—real masterpieces—rather than committee-written textbooks. Based on the writings of British educator Charlotte Mason, *For the Children's Sake* presents a natural, rich style of learning founded on Christian principles and suited to all times and cultures.

From the same publisher, **Books Children Love: A Guide to the Best Children's Literature** goes far beyond a reading-list approach. Most reading lists deal exclusively with fiction, but *Books Children Love* lists hundreds of books from more than two dozen subject areas, with comments on each one. Author Elizabeth Wilson has selected "excellently written, interest-holding books on as wide a range of topics as possible—books that also embody ideas and ideals in harmony with traditional values and a Christian worldview." Susan Schaeffer Macaulay wrote the foreword to this lovely thick book. *Mary Pride*

A family reading program that reflects American patriotism, the Foundation for American Christian Education's **Family Program for Reading Aloud** contains discussions of more than 200 literary classics. In Part I, three chapters introduce reading aloud and the listening-learning skills. Three more suggest books to read to the youngest (FACE is pro-Mother Goose). Six chapters introduce American themes, including immigrants and ethnic groups, pioneers and Indians, and even American horses, and give a sample of how to teach the Principle Approach using historical biographies. The last two chapters help you evaluate your family reading program.

The new second edition now includes a Part II on reading in depth for high-school students. Some topics: the ocean, pioneers, teaching and learning, and the French Revolution. Some authors covered in depth: Charles Dickens, Sir Walter Scott, Washington Irving, and Nathaniel Hawthorne. A section on restoring heroes and heroines in literature includes Richard E. Byrd, Charles A. Lindbergh, Eddy Rickenbacker, Anne Bradstreet, Lydia Darrah, and Mercy Otis Warren. The last section highlights people who preserve our history and the Mount Vernon Ladies Association who pioneered historical preservation in America. *Mary Pride*

Have I got a book for you! Zondervan's **Honey for a Child's Heart**, subtitled *The Imaginative Use of Books in Family Life*, is the most fantastic, inspiring book about books that I have ever read. Gladys Hunt, the author, expertly deals with the questions of what makes a good book a good book and explains how to make family reading a rich part of your life, as well as providing 224 pages of suggested reading for different age levels. The book is illustrated with pictures from recommended books and is an absolute delight to read. Gladys Hunt says everything I wanted to say about literature, and says it better. Highly recommended. *Mary Pride*

Literature Curriculum

Beatrix Potter: Her Life and Her Little Books is **Calvert School's** second foray into literature units. This program comes with the following:

- The Reading Guide
- *The Story of Beatrix Potter*, a hardback biography
- Ten little hardcover books: *The Tale of Peter Rabbit, The Tale of Squirrel Nutkin, The Tailor of Gloucester, The Tale of Benjamin Bunny, The Tale of Two Bad Mice, the Tale of Mrs. Tiggy-Winkle, The Tale of Mr. Jeremy Fisher, The Tale of Tom Kitten, The Tale of Jemima Puddle-Duck, and The Tale of the Flopsy Bunnies*
- Supplies: Notebook, crayons, Beatrix Potter writing set, Beatrix Potter stickers, Jemima Puddle-Duck eraser, Mrs. Rabbit pencil sharpener, Fiskers kid-size round-tip scissors, glue stick, watercolor paint set, watercolor pad, modeling clay, a few pieces of tracing paper, and an adorable set of Beatrix Potter stickers, featuring characters from her books.

A Family Program for Reading Aloud (second edition)
Parents. $18 plus $4.50 shipping. *Foundation for American Christian Education (FACE), PO Box 9588, Chesapeake, VA 23321. Orders: (800) 352-FACE. Inquiries: (757) 488-6601. Fax: (757) 488-5593. Email: info@face.net. Web: www.face.net.*

Honey for a Child's Heart
Parents. $10.99. *Zondervan Publishing House, 5300 Patterson Ave. SE, Grand Rapids, MI 49530. (616) 698-6900. Fax: (616) 698-3439. Available in Christian bookstores.*

Calvert Beatrix Potter Literature Unit
Grades K–3. Entire course, $125. Reading Guides only (includes guide, biography, and activity supplies), $65. Regular UPS shipping included. *Calvert School, 105 Tuscany Road, Baltimore, MD 21210. 410-243-6030. Fax: 410-366-0674. Email: inquiry@calvertschool.org. Web: www.calvertschool.org.*

The Reading Guide covers the biography chapter by chapter, then has a lesson apiece on each little book. This amounts to 20 lessons in all—perfect for a summer unit study of one to two lessons per week. At the back of the Guide is a glossary of words from each little book. This comes in handy, since unless you are British, you probably are a bit confused by words such as *bolster* and *pipkin*.

Each lesson has tons of activities and discussion questions. You get to do many cute little literature-related crafts, such as making your own little book, making papier maché foods (as in *The Story of Two Bad Mice*), hosting a tea party (like Mrs. Tiggy-Winkle) or a dinner party (like Mr. Jeremy Fisher), making a vest for a stuffed animal (like the Tailor of Gloucester), and making a lavender sack (as in *The Tale of the Flopsy Bunnies*). Paper-and-pen activities include crosswords, decoding messages, word searches, drawing pictures, writing an adventure story, and putting sheep-shearing pictures in order.

These are just a few of the craft and non-craft activities. You'll also learn about Beatrix Potter's life, the period of history in which she lived, the English Lake District, watercolors, nature study, and a lot more. Plus, of course, you get to read and re-read some of the most beloved children's books in the English language.

If you've ever wondered what unit studies are really like, this is a cute way to start! *Mary Pride*

NEW!
Calvert Reading Guides: The Little House Books by Laura Ingalls Wilder

Grade 3–adult. Complete course, $125. Reading Guides + Laura Ingalls Wilder Country, $90. Reading Guides only, $70. UPS surface shipping included.
Calvert School, 105 Tuscany Rd., Baltimore, MD 21210-3098. (410) 243-6030. Fax: (410) 366-0674. Email: inquiry@calvertschool.org. Web: www.calvertschool.org.

How does Calvert's course compare to *The Prairie Primer*? Like apples to oranges! Prairie Primer's focus is more discovery-oriented. Where Calvert offers a paragraph explaining panthers, Prairie Primer would have you look them up and write a short report. If you're using The Prairie Primer, then adding Calvert would round things out beautifully.

These books are a treasure trove that will surely delight all Little House fans everywhere! Rich in background information and bursting at the seams with trivia and tidbits, **Calvert's Reading Guides** will turn the **"Little House" books** by Laura Ingalls Wilder into an educational gold mine for your family.

Volume 1 covers books 1–4 (*Big Woods* through *Farmer Boy*) and is recommended for ages 6–8. Volume 2 picks up with *Shores of Silver Lake* and goes to *The First Four Years*; suggested ages are 9–11. These could easily stretch to cover two year's of study. While the guides are written directly to the student —a nice touch—Calvert urges parents to be a vital part of the study. Indeed, these would make wonderful additions to your family read-aloud time.

It's important to note here that there are no specific assignments included in these guides. Although the author might make a suggestion or two ("You might have fun making up your own story . . . ") there are no organized vocabulary lists or tests.

Each new book is introduced in the reading guides with chapter summaries as well as a discussion of the themes to be aware of in that particular book.

The guides are organized into lessons which cover about 50 pages of reading from the books themselves. Gray boxes in the margins of the Calvert guides direct the reader to the page numbers in the Little House book being discussed. Comprehension questions, vocabulary enrichment, elements of literature, and historical background all serve to deepen the reading experience. In addition, there are several musical selections and recipes from the *Little House Songbook and Cookbook*.

The author of the guides, Calvert teacher Ann W. Dahl, has really done her homework in ferreting out Wilder lore from many different sources. The guides are illustrated not only by the Garth Williams drawings that we are all familiar with, but also with drawings from the original illustrator, Helen Sewell. What a difference in styles!

Calvert's guides offer you and your family a wonderful opportunity to meet the Wilders. *Renee Mathis*

Ann Ward fans, read on! If you love classic literature, and if you like Ann Ward's material (see the review of her Learning at Home curriculum in Volume 1), you'll love **The Classics at Home**.

This 121-page study guide covers the following four story books: *The Complete Tales of Beatrix Potter, Charlotte's Web, Winnie the Pooh,* and *The House at Pooh Corner.* If you count each "Summary" as one lesson, you get 122 lessons in all. It is clear this is meant as a one-year course; at the rate of three lessons per week, you could cover the book in a slightly extended school year of 40 weeks.

The guide is non-consumable. It is suggested that you purchase a notebook for each child, to be used for answers to questions, drawings, and information on various topics,.

Each lesson tells you which pages to read from the book and contains vocabulary words, questions which can be answered either orally or in writing, and a section on learning more. The questions in the first half of the course are mostly about facts, while in the latter half more discussion questions are included. Unfortunately, definitions of the vocabulary words are *not* included. Since a single lesson may have as many as 60 vocabulary words (20–40 is average), and many are strange to modern Americans (e.g., *groat* and *paduasoy*), looking them up so the child can copy definitions into a workbook is a major waste of time.

The Learning More section briefly draws in other topics. Here's an example of one day's Learning More assignment:

> *(1) Find Gloucester on a map of England. (2) Feel (with clean hands!) different kinds of fabrics. Which kinds do you like best? (3) Which illustration from this part is your favorite and why? (4) Draw a picture of your favorite part of this section of the story. (5) Make up sentences using at least twelve of the vocabulary words.*

If you're looking for a good introduction to writing and classical literature for your young child, look no further. *Rebecca Livermore and Mary Pride*

If you're attracted to the Principle Approach, you may find the literature curriculum you're looking for within the 368 oversized pages of the **Noah Plan Literature Curriculum Guide**. Authored by Principle Approach cofounder Rosalie June Slater, its five massive "chapters" (other books would call them "sections") outline the philosophy and how-tos you need.

Principle Approach education involves following and filling out a lot of forms and charts. Chapter 1 includes multiple-page charts for each grade level that explain the purpose of the course and define "literature," as well as providing key definitions (e.g., of *prose, poetry, rhythm*), teacher objectives, methods, student performance, books you need to teach the course, enrichment activities, and a list of literature selections to study. Sample forms and instructions for writing lesson plans are included, as well as many pages of sample student notebook work.

Chapter 2 examines how to teach the literature of the Bible (as opposed to teaching the Bible "as literature"). A sample study of the Bible book of Amos is included.

Chapter 4 goes extensively into how to teach Shakespeare. The premise here is that Shakespeare is the "bard of the Bible," and studying his works will ennoble your vocabulary and thought life. You are introduced to Shakespeare's England, including the educational methods and drama of the time. A history of drama, including its relationship to what FACE calls the "chain of Christianity," leads into a discussion of Shakespeare's style and how to teach Shakespeare. A sample study of *The Merchant of Venice* is included.

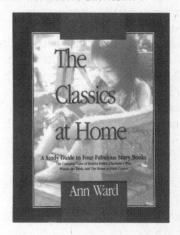

Chapters 3, 5, and 6 include the elementary, junior-high, and high-school literature programs respectively. You get teaching instructions for each type of literature—from fairy tales to modern classics—along with lists of literature for study and in-depth sample studies of some works.

You get your money's worth with this *Guide*, but realize you must plan to spend a lot of time studying the *Guide* and creating your own lessons based on its forms, principles, teaching suggestions, and reading lists. *Mary Pride*

NEW!
Penguin Whole Story Series

Grades 4–adult. Tom Sawyer, Around the World in 80 Days, Treasure Island, $17.99 each. Heidi, The Jungle Book, The Call of the Wild, $14.99 each. Shipping extra. *Veritas Press, 1250 Belle Meade Dr., Lancaster, PA 17601. (800) 922-5082. Inquiries: (717) 397-5082. Fax: (717) 397-6544. Email: Veritasprs@aol.com. Web: members.aol.com/Veritasprs.*

You can get unabridged editions of these children's classics for around $5 in any bookstore, and I've seen abridged versions on sale for as little as 99¢ each. So why are the **Penguin Whole Story series** editions of *The Adventures of Tom Sawyer, Around the World in 80 Days, Treasure Island, Heidi, The Jungle Book,* and *The Call of the Wild* worth from $14 to $18 each?

Three words: *beauty* and *educational value*. These are more than gorgeously illustrated, larger-print versions. Just about *every page* is illustrated—often in full color—with pictures that *show* what the text is talking about. Rather than just pictures of the book's action, you'll find what trains of the period looked like, or a photo of the old city of Frankfurt, or styles in gentleman's clothes of the period. Sidebars give further details and explanations. You end up with a painless, thorough understanding of the history, geography, social customs, architecture, literature, science, and animal life of the time and place the book covers. It's like mini unit studies on every page!

Having just struggled through a non-Penguin edition of Jules Verne's *20,000 Leagues Under the Sea* with my second-oldest daughter, I sincerely hope the publisher expands this series to include *all* Jules Verne's books, not just *Around the World in 80 Days*. With this kind of help, Mr. Verne's incredible scientific vocabulary and descriptions would practically be a natural-science education in themselves! *Mary Pride*

NEW!
The Prairie Primer

Grades 3–6. $45 plus 10% shipping. *Cadron Creek Christian Curriculum, 4329 Pinos Altos Rd., Silver City, NM 88061. (505) 534-1496. Fax: (505)534-1499. Email: marigold@gilanet.com. Web: www.cadroncreek.com.*

If you've often thought that there is enough material in the Little House books to fill an entire school year, you're right! Margie Gray has designed a year's worth of unit studies around this classic series. You take one book each month—nine in all. Each month is broken down into four weekly sets of activities, as well as a few general activities for you to work on the entire month.

As unit studies go, **Prairie Primer** has something special to offer: a beginning and an end! These units are very well organized, right down to the planning lists for the beginning of each month. You'll probably find that you can't do all the activities in this 335-page book, so there is a degree of flexibility built in.

While it's easy to imagine using this book with your daughters, there's no reason to leave your sons out of the excitement. There are plenty of activities to hold their interest as well: Pa Ingalls, fatherhood, hunting, guns, railroads, and more.

Even if your children have already read the Little House books they will find themselves appreciating the books on a deeper level.

Each section is divided into four weeks of four days each. At the beginning is background information for the teacher, suggested books for further reading, materials to gather, and a list of possible field trips. Each day's plan consists of reading assignments and comprehension questions followed by a list of activities in the various subject areas: Bible, Character, Health, Science, History, Crafts, Language Arts, and Living Skills. All lessons are thoroughly Christian and include Biblical references where appropriate. There is a super section on courtship that accompanies *These Happy Golden Years.*

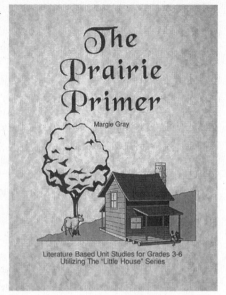

Mrs. Gray draws from a wide variety of outside resources in addition to providing you with plenty of information in the Primer itself. You'll still have to come up with your own phonics and math programs, but armed with the Primer, a Bible, and your local library you can provide an excellent year (or more)'s worth of study. *Renee Mathis*

No one wants to kill a great book by studying it to death. Thanks to the **series of literature guides offered by Progeny Press**, you won't have to. These are well-crafted tools designed to encourage you to dig a little deeper, enhance your reading experience, and end up with literature that lives and breathes.

The guides are a snap to use! Each includes a synopsis of the story, author biography, and background information. The books themselves are broken into manageable chunks to read and study. The basic comprehension questions are kept to a minimum. There are just enough to let you see if the book was read and understood. Vocabulary exercises vary from looking up definitions, matching definitions, and defining the word in context for yourself. There are suggestions for written assignments as well. Every chapter includes opportunities to evaluate the literature in light of the Bible. This is the kind of material that develops deep thinkers. In case you haven't read the book yourself, or if you'd like another view, the answers are included in the back of each study guide. *Renee Mathis*

NEW!
Progeny Press Bible Based Study Guides for Literature

Grades 1–12. Prices for home editions, which may not be photocopied: Elementary School titles, $5.49 each; Middle School, $6.99 each; and High School, $8.99 each. Prices for larger classroom editions, which may be copied for students: Elementary School titles, $13.95 each; Middle School, $15.95 each; and High School, $19.95 each. Shipping extra.
Progeny Press, 200 Spring St., Suite A, Eau Claire, WI 54703-3225. (877) 776-4369. (715) 833-5261. Fax: (715) 836-0105.
Email: progeny@mgprogeny.com.
Web: www.mgprogeny.com.

Elementary School titles available: *The Bears on Hemlock Mountain, The Best Christmas Pageant Ever, The Bridge, Clipper Ship, The Courage of Sarah Noble, Crown and Jewel, The Door in the Wall, The Drinking Gourd, Frog and Toad Together, The Josefina Story Quilt, Jumanji, Keep the Lights Burning, Little House in the Big Woods, The Long Way to a New Land, The Long Way Westward, The Minstrel in the Tower, A New Coat for Anna, Ox-Cart Man, Sarah Plain and Tall, Sam the Minuteman, The Two Collars,* and *Wagon Wheels.*

Middle School titles: *Carry On, Mr. Bowditch, The Hiding Place, The Indian in the Cupboard, Johnny Tremain, The Lion, The Witch, and the Wardrobe, The Secret Garden, Shiloh,* and *The Sign of the Beaver.*

High School titles: *A Day No Pigs Would Die, Hamlet, Heart of Darkness, The Merchant of Venice, Out of the Silent Planet, Perelandra, The Red Badge of Courage, Romeo and Juliet, To Kill a Mockingbird,* and *The Yearling.*

New titles are always forthcoming.

Quizzes for 220 Great Children's Books: The Quest Motivational Reading Program

Grades 4–8. $24.50 postpaid.
Teacher Ideas Press/Libraries Unlimited, P.O. Box 6633, Englewood, CO 80155-6633. (800) 237-6124. Fax: (303) 220-8843. Email: lu-books@lu.com. Web: www.tip.com.

The "220 great children's books" covered in this program include Newberry and Caldecott winners and runners-up, such as *The High King* and *Sounder*; some classics; and popular books, such as *Ramona and Her Father, The Black Cauldron,* and Judy Blume's *Superfudge.* "Pop" selections definitely outweigh the classics—I wouldn't agree that *all* of the books are "*great* children's books"—but it is quite a representative selection.

To author Polly Jeanne Wickstrom's credit, she includes multiple books by the same author, instead of unnecessarily hopscotching around. Laura Ingalls Wilder, Marguerite Henry, Mary "The Borrowers" Norton, and Beverly Cleary are all well represented, for instance.

NEW!
Greathall Storytime CDs

All ages. $14.95 each CD, minus 10% if you order more than one. Also on tape for $9.95 each. $2.50 shipping any quantity..
Greathall Productions, PO Box 5061, Charlottesville, VA 22905-5061. (800) 477-6234. Fax: (804)296-4490. Email: greathall@greathall.com.

Hate book reports? I'm with you. Here's an alternative that can help you determine what, how much, and how well your children read.

Quizzes for 220 Great Children's Books is just what its name implies. The idea is that your child will read some or all of these books. Books are ranked by difficulty level, with more points granted for more difficult books. After reading a book, the student takes the quiz. (Hint: Do *not* let your child write on the quiz sheet, thus making it unusable for other students. The teacher's manual describes how to prepare and photocopy standard answer sheets.) Various record-keeping forms let you track your child's progress and motivate him (hopefully) to read more. All together, these form the "Quest Motivational Reading Program."

The quizzes themselves are your basic true-false and multiple-choice variety, designed for simplicity of grading in the classroom. You might want to let your child take the tests both before *and* after reading the book—the questions are great interest-sparkers!

Quizzes includes a teacher's manual, a Children's Catalog with books sorted by book topic, the quizzes themselves, and answer keys for all the quizzes. The teacher's manual has student record sheets and instructions for using this simple program.

Although I can't recommend every single book selection in this program, by and large it gives you the best of several worlds. You get a recommended reading list with just enough info to help you decide whether a book might be worth reading. You get a simple method to both spark interest in reading the book and find out how much of it your child actually understood. (There are no trick questions on the quizzes—any child who actually reads the book with interest should be able to answer the questions correctly.) You also get a way of keeping track of your child's reading—useful for your record-keeping. Your child can either pick books by topics (thus following up an interest and maybe launching a unit study) or simply by difficulty level. Looks good! *Mary Pride*

Audio Literature

I am coming to believe more and more that we all learn best through stories. **Greathall Productions** feels the same way. They produce recordings of a storyteller *telling stories*, as opposed to other companies which record people *reading books*. This takes more time and effort, but has earned them numerous awards.

If, like the Shearers, you believe Greek mythology is worth studying as a set of enjoyable fairy tales embedded in our cultural heritage, you will enjoy Greathall's "Greek Myths" tape. The storyteller explains several times that these are made-up stories, and points out the morals they contain. The moral of "King Midas," for example, is, "Many things are more important than gold." Other tapes we have heard from this company include "King Arthur and His Knights," and "Sherlock Holmes for Children." They all are excellent; great for car trips or just for easy listenin'. *Mary Pride*

Audio tapes have been a big part of our schooling for years, helping us to take advantage of moments spent on those inevitable tasks. This classics collection on tape has been very popular around our house since it first arrived.

Each volume contains 40 high-quality, long-playing stereo audiocassettes. **The Children's Classics Library** contains such favorites as *Pinocchio, The Wind in the Willows, Aesop's Fables, The Adventures of Huckleberry Finn* (unabridged), and others including a tape of nursery rhymes. **The Family Classics Library** contains *A Tale of Two Cities, Call of the Wild, Lés Miserablés, A Christmas Carol,* and more.

The publisher has been faithful to record most books in their complete form on tape. When my husband, Tim, taped himself reading *A Christmas Carol* to our children it took up three full tapes, which is how many tapes you'll find on this same book in the Classics collection. Unlike our home-made readings, the Classics Libraries are enhanced by music and sound effects, with parts read by several actors.

The literature in the classics series is not necessarily Christian. You will find some tapes contain difficult ideas. *The Adventures of Huckleberry Finn* by Mark Twain contains some racial slurs we wouldn't use, but the tape reminds parents that these are used in the story to show the negative character of those who use them. The Children's Library tales has one story called "Little Red Shoes" of the folk variety having scary overtones which may seem unacceptable. The Family Library has more material that contains concepts inappropriate for younger children, including some tales by Poe and the story "The Outcasts of Poker Flat" which talks about a town casting out its low life consisting of gamblers, charlatans, and prostitutes.

While we chose to skip some tapes, the older children benefited from discussing the issues presented in others. Fiction allows children to peek into the characters of people from different walks and times of life. This helps them to gain an understanding of the internal thinking that motivates outward behavior. As they examine thinking in light of Scriptures, they discern violated principles, yet with compassion. We so enjoyed *Lés Miserables* (not the complete book, which is voluminous!) that we found the play on video, read about the production of the play, Victor Hugo's life, and I read the book itself, with my oldest breathing down my neck to get the copy for himself. *Katherine von Duyke*

Special Books

These wonderful **reprints of classic children's literature by Bethlehem Books** are the type of material that makes you want to shout "I *love* these books!" They are exactly the kind of material that you can embrace joyfully, and feel the richer for reading together with your children. Whether it is a book with strong family values like *The Mitchells: Five For Victory* or *The Cottage at Bantry Bay* (both by Hilda Van Stockum), nicely done renderings of ancient heroic tales like *Beowulf the Warrior* (retold by Ian Serraillier), or a piece of literature that also teaches math and science concepts (*Archimedes and the Door of Science* by Jeanne Bendick), each of Bethlehem Books' contributions is of high value and quality.

The Winged Watchman by Hilda Van Stockum is an excellent example. Set in Holland during World War II, this book is historical fiction at its finest. Originally published in 1962, *The Winged Watchman* follows the adventures of the Verhagen family through the later days of the war. The Verhagens' involvement with the Dutch Resistance, as well as their unselfish ways of dealing with those in need around them, demonstrate courage and strength. The characters are not moral paper dolls; they come through as flesh and blood real people. And your children won't quickly forget them.

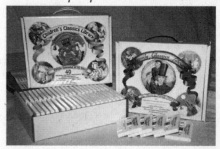

Nice introductions by Lydia Reynolds of Bethlehem Books found in many of the books help to put the material in an educational context. You will find the truth, power and excellent writing in these offerings full of delightful, educational virtue. Highly recommended! *Michelle Van Loon*

NEW!
Classics of Adventure

Grades 4–college. Each volume, $48.25. You receive a new book each month.
The Easton Press, 47 Richards Ave., Norwalk, CT 06857. (800) 211-1308. Fax: (203) 831-9365.

If you love beautiful books, and if you remember the childhood joy of reading the great adventure books—such as *Robinson Crusoe, Robin Hood, Treasure Island, The Black Arrow, King Arthur and the Knights of the Round Table*—then this 14-volume set of leatherbound books is an extravagant gift you might just want to give your children.

Classics of Adventure feature the dazzling full-color illustrations of N.C. Wyeth, including one on the cover of each book. With their large print, lush feel, and even a ribbon marker to keep your place, these are the books to set young hearts thrilling and young minds dreaming of heroic deeds yet to be done. *Mary Pride*

NEW!
G.A. Henty Series

Grades 7–adult. Each book, $19.99 (hardcover) or $13.99 paperback. Shipping extra.
Preston Speed Publications, RR #4, Box 705, Mill Hall, PA 17751. (570) 726-7844. Fax: (570) 726-3547. Web: www.prestonspeed.com

G.A. Henty, known in the last century as "The Boy's Own Historian," wrote approximately 144 books, plus numerous magazine articles, all with the desire to make accurate history live in the hearts of his readers. Preston Speed Press, the brainchild of a homeschooling family, is lovingly reprinting these classic books in hardcover format, on acid-free paper. These books are meant to be read, and re-read, and handed down to your grandchildren.

Each story uses the device of a fictional boy interacting with real-life historical figures. For instance, *By Pike and Dyke* introduces you to Edward Martin, a young English sailor who becomes a part of the Dutch struggle for religious independence against Spain in the late 1500s. The text's 351 pages detail Edward's service to William of Orange, and to the cause. You'll watch Edward transformed from a boy into a selfless, courageous man, and you will learn about a period of history that you may not know much about in the process.

Coming soon: *Winning His Spurs: A Tale of the Crusades, St. George for England,* and *With Wolfe In Canada.* More titles are coming. Preston Speed plans to release all of Henty's work at the speed of one volume every four to six weeks. Audio editions of some of the books will also soon be available.

Books so far in the series include:
- *The Dragon and The Raven (or The Days of King Alfred)*—a look at the battle between the Saxons and the Danes, set in 870 A.D.
- *For The Temple: A Tale of the Fall of Jerusalem*—based on Josephus' narrative
- *In Freedom's Cause: A Story of Wallace and Bruce*—The war for Scottish independence at the end of the 13th century is nothing like the recent movie *Braveheart*
- *By Pike and Dyke*—a late-Reformation era struggle, as discussed above
- *Beric The Briton: A Story of the Roman Invasion*—A time of great transformation for England during the later years of the Roman empire

Additional titles available: *A Knight of the White Cross: A Tale of the Siege of Rhodes, Wulf the Saxon: A Story of the Norman Conquest, The Cat of Bubastes: A Story of Ancient Egypt, Under Drake's Flag: A Tale of the Spanish Main, Saint Bartholomew's Eve: A Tale of the Huguenot Wars, By Right of Conquest: or with Cortez in Mexico, With Lee in Virginia: A Story of the American Civil War,* and *The Young Carthaginian: A Story of the Times of Hannibal.*

Henty is a stickler for detail, and an almost bottomless well of historical knowledge. (One exception can be found on page 6 of *For The Temple*: as part of a meal served to a visiting rabbi, "kid's flesh seethed in milk" was served. No self-respecting rabbi would have eaten this meal, which is specifically prohibited in Exodus 23:19.) That aside, these books are well worth your time. History texts can only outline events; Henty's action-packed narratives fill in the details. And in the process, they invite noble, courageous young heroes into your life. *Michelle Van Loon*

CHAPTER 21

Spelling & Vocabulary

How do good spellers *get to* be good spellers? And what are the stages of learning to spell? Research tells us that good spellers "see" the word they intend to spell in their mind's eye. Bad spellers, on the other hand, try to "sound out" each word using whatever spelling rules they know.

So a good speller "sees" the word *success* and spells it *s-u-c-c-e-s-s.*

A bad speller tries to spell it like it sounds: *s-u-k-s-e-s-s.* Or maybe he "sort of" remembers the letters that are supposed to make up the word, and tries *s-u-c-e-s-s* or *s-u-c-c-e-s*

Whoa! Does this mean that phonics is *no help* when it comes to spelling? Do sight words and "look-say" rule after all?

No. That is like comparing apples and orangutangs. Phonics teaches you how to "sound out" or *de-*code a word, for the purpose of reading or speaking it. Even phonetically irregular words can be sounded out, because *most* of the letters in such words *do* make their regular sounds. For example, in *success,* the initial *su* and the final *ess* are perfectly regular. Actually, even the initial *suc* (pronounced *suk*) and the final *cess* (pronounced *sess*) are perfectly regular if you know the phonics rules about syllables and the "soft" sound *c* makes when it's followed by *e, i,* or *y.*

There is only one correct way to pronounce most words. (Exception: A few, like *tear* and *row,* have two or more separate meanings and pronunciations.) The reason spelling is so difficult is that there are often *several* phonetically correct ways to *en-*code, that is, to spell a word. *Suxess, suksess,* and *success* are *all* phonetically correct. *Pneumonia, newmoaneeyah,* and *neumoniah* all sound alike, and are all phonetically correct.

The life cycle of a good speller, then, goes like this:

Invented Spelling. All young children go through this stage. The child wants to write, but doesn't know the correct spellings for most words. So he spells them like they sound. That's cute, and fine for a while. Unfortunately, in the ongoing and ill-considered crusade to give American school children the highest (and most unearned) self-esteem in the world, many schools are now treating invented spelling as a *teaching method.* The idea is that teachers *won't* correct kids' spelling. Kids are just supposed to magically pick up correct spelling on their own, just like they magically pick up reading, writing, and manners.

Y Kids Kant Spel

The anti-competition movement is galloping across America. Schools are getting rid of their honor rolls, honors courses, class rankings, academic prizes, and even valedictorians. Spelling bees are out. In fact, even correct spelling is out; it's replaced by inventive spelling (so students can spell words any way they want.)
The Phyllis Schlafly Report

The cynical among us might note that many teachers are not good spellers, and this is a great excuse to save such teachers the embarrassment of not knowing how to spell *potato* any better than a former vice-president of the USA. Those even more cynical might theorize that this is another symptom of the underlying flight from rules in America today. Teaching spelling rules is so . . . restrictive. Telling kids they can soak up correct spelling without any effort, and praising their own incorrect spelling, is so New Age. Lead me to the hot tub. Don't wurry, bee happee.

Learning Spelling Rules and Patterns. Assuming we made it out of the tub, the next phase in the life cycle of a good speller is learning the spelling rules. There *are* quite a few of them, you know. For example, if you hear the sound *il* at the end of a word, it's spelled *ill*. (Exception: the name *Phil*.) "*I* before *E* except after *C*, or when sounding like *ay* as in *neighbor* and *weigh*," is another handy rule you might remember. Some rules, like "*I* before *E*," are best taught as rules, but most spelling rules really work better as *patterns*, or "word families," that children encounter during their regular phonics training. Exceptions can easily be remembered in the context of their word family. So if kids are studying the family of words that end in *ave*, such as *cave*, *gave*, *pave*, in all of which the letter *A* makes the "long" sound, thanks to the silent *E* at the end of the word, the word *have*, in which the letter *A* makes the "short" sound, can be taught at this point as an exception to the rule.

Play 'N Talk and *Alpha-Phonics* are just two of the quality phonics programs that teach spelling rules *and* spelling patterns in this fashion, thus giving kids a real head start on future spelling success.

Lots of Reading. The next step in the normal life cycle of a good speller is lots of reading. *If* a child is a visual learner, and *if* she reads a tremendous amount of high-vocabulary books, *then* she may well pick up a large mental vocabulary of correctly spelled words. This is what the "invented spelling" people are counting on.

This worked fine for me. I was one of those kids. But most kids aren't visually-oriented bookworms. And even visually-oriented bookworms have to study to win spelling bees.

Lists of Spelling Words. So how *do* good spellers study? Probably the least successful method is the "spelling words list" made up of random words of a similar difficulty level. Since there's no pattern to the words, each has to be memorized by brute force. What's more, you may not even want to use any of the words in your own writing until months or years after you studied the list.

Homeschoolers around the world have discovered that the easiest way to come up with lists of spelling words is to compile words your child has misspelled in his own writing. These are words he *does* use. You certainly don't want him to get into the habit of misspelling them!

Your child needs to expand his vocabulary, too, and not just use the same words over and over for the next 70 years. So how can new spelling words be introduced?

Those who study for spelling bees get lists of words organized by topics: "medical words" or "flower words." This is a useful way to study words that builds vocabulary at the same time as it builds spelling skills.

Adding new vocabulary words from your school studies also works. Again, have the child attempt to spell each word. Only words he misses belong on a list of spelling words to study.

Several publishers also offer lists of most commonly misspelled words. It's a good idea to go through a list like this, since these words are likely to trip your student up if he encounters them without assistance.

Greek & Latin Roots

One really neat way to quickly improve your spelling and vocabulary is to learn the Greek and Latin word roots found in so many English words. Just one example: the Greek root "phon" means "sound" and "caco" means "harsh." Now isn't it easier to remember the meaning of the English word *cacaphony*? Not to mention *dictaphone*, *homophone*, *microphone*, *phoneme*, *phonics*, *quadrophonic*, and *telephone*? (Hints: *dicta* means "to speak," *homo* means "same," *micro* means "small," *eme* means "structured unit," *quadra* means "four," and *tele* means "distant."

Study Methods. Some spelling programs use flash cards. Others ask students to use a blank card or piece of paper to cover each word, so you sneak a peek and then see if you can remember it. Quite a few ask you to write down the word, sometimes multiple times.

Whatever method you use, remember that you are trying to learn to "see" the word in your mind. If your handwriting is poor, it will be hard to visualize the scrawled word. In that case, you may benefit from printed flash cards or a computer drill program. For words you simply can't remember, special memory gimmicks may help, such as chanting the word ("M-i-S-S-i-S-S-i-P-P-i" is a favorite) or visualizing it with the troublesome letters enlarged or making up little mental phrases. "You *RANT* because you're *IGNORANT*" will help you remember that the word *ignorant* ends with the letters *ANT*, for example.

All of this means nothing, of course, unless you know what the word means and can use it correctly. That's why we recommend you learn to spell your vocabulary words, and learn the meaning of your spelling words. It's also why you'll find vocabulary improvement resources at the end of this chapter, right after the spelling programs!

How to Win a Spelling Bee

Valerie, Natalie and Huntley Tarrant, also known as the Spelling Sisters, have sold their original spelling materials since 1983. All three have made it to the first round of the Scripps Howard National Spelling Bee, and all their products show their knowledge of what you actually need to be a competitive speller. And I'm not the only person who shares that opinion. In the 1998 National Spelling Bee 54 out of 250 participants (22 percent) used their products, and four out of the top five placers. These gals are *good*!

Valerie's Spelling Bee Supplement was the first book they produced, and it's my personal favorite. When I was studying the *Paideia* (the booklet of words to study for the regional spelling bees), the thing that most annoyed me was the organization of the words, and that I had no idea how to pronounce the majority of them until I looked them up. **Valerie's Supplement** solves both these problems. The words from the *Paideia* for the current year are organized into three categories: Novice, Junior Varsity and Varsity. Each word is listed with a short definition and a phonetic pronunciation, which although unique is very understandable. Listing them this way greatly cuts down on the time needed for dictionary research and leaves you better able to drill the words. I only wish I had known about this book before I reached my last year of competition! For use with this book are the **Talking Webster Audio Tapes**, which are available in two versions. The full version gives a pronunciation and short definition for each word, in the order it appears in **Valerie's Supplement**. The short version pronounces each word twice with a pause in between to give time for a student possibly to write it.

The **Spelling Rules Book**, or **"Why Isn't 'Phonetic' Spelled the Way It Sounds?,"** discusses (it seems like) just about every English spelling rule, gives examples of how the rule is right, and then lists several categories of exceptions to each one. This spiral-bound book truly amazes me with the amount of information contained in its 171 pages. Some categories it covers are suffix rules, prefix rules, more suffix rules, plural rules, possessive rules and tricky word endings. Plus it holds a totally impressive list of Latin and Greek prefixes, suffixes and roots—in addition to many pages of words containing and combining them. Also it includes, just for fun, lists of words with funny first letters and funny double-letter combinations. Examples of these are: *bhikku*, which I could proudly say I knew how to spell; *dghaisa*, which I could not; *saturniid* and *schokker*. This book alone could be used as spelling curriculum for a few years.

Calvert Spelling and Vocabulary CD-ROM

NEW!

Grades 5–7. Each grade, $20.
Calvert School, 105 Tuscany Road, Baltimore, MD 21210. (410) 243-6030. Fax: (410) 366-0674. Email: inquiry@calvertschool.org. Web: www.calvertschool.org.

Although I resolved not to include software in this edition of *The Big Book of Home Learning,* for every rule there must be a few exceptions. **Calvert's Spelling and Vocabulary CD-ROMs** are an exception because (1) this is a major product from a major homeschool supplier that many families will use, and (2) it teaches both spelling *and* vocabulary at once.

Each of Calvert's Spelling and Vocabulary CD-ROMs is a complete one-year course. The program is not designed to be a game, but to be a teacher. Graphics and sounds are used to liven things up, but mostly the program quietly and patiently drills you in the words of each lesson.

If you choose spelling, the program displays a list of lessons by week, i.e., Lessons 1–4, Lessons 6–9, Lessons 11–14, etc. The four numbered lessons are for Monday through Thursday. Friday of each week is for the weekly review.

In the spelling section, you select a week on the lesson menu. On this menu you have a choice of each of the four numbered lessons, the weekly review, or your study lists. The study lists menu gives you the opportunity to study either your current weekly word lists, your review list (compiled out of the words you missed on your weekly review quizzes), or your personal list of words to practice that your teacher put into the program. If you want to, you can select one of these lists and practice it in the "lab."

A spelling lesson consists of up to ten words. First you do a pretest on the words. The program pronounces each word, says a sentence that defines the word in context, then repeats the word. You then type the word and press "return." The program goes on to pronounce the next word, etc. When you reach the end of the list, the "check" button appears. You can click the button to check the words, or you can change any word that doesn't look right to you first, and then click "check." The program puts a check mark on the numbers of words that are correctly spelled and an X on the numbers of the ones that are wrong.

You must correct the words that are wrong before you can go on. You do this by clicking on the "ear" symbol that will be placed next to one of the Xs. The program displays the word spelled correctly, and the word as you spelled it. It speaks the word, and spells it out loud for you. You have to click on the letters in your version that are wrong, then press the "type again" button and type the word from memory. If you spell it right, you can go on to the next word. Otherwise, the program spells it for you again, and you type it again. Once you have corrected all the words, you go on to the lab.

In the lab, you interact with each of the words you got wrong on the pretest. In order to get through the lab, you have to do at least one activity with each of the words. The activities are: 1. Write—fill in the blanks by clicking on a letter, then clicking on the blank in which to put it. When you are done, you get to type in the word from memory; 2. Look—find your word in a large array of letters and click on each of the letters; 3 Touch—move scrambled letters to blanks for the word in the right order.

The vocabulary portion consists of 16 units of 8 lessons and two activities apiece. Lessons are either teaching lessons or review lessons. Each teaching lesson consists of up to four words. You pick a word to review. The program puts up three possible definitions for the word. You choose one. If you are right, the program congratulates you with a little graphic animation. If you are wrong, the program blats at you. Ether way, the program displays a screen defining the word, illustrating the word (sometimes animated), and giving an interesting derivation of the word. Click next to go on to the next word. Review lessons give a definition. You choose the correct one of three possible words. Activities consist of giving a definition and you either fill in the blanks or descramble the letters.

The grammar game is designed to correlate with the spelling lessons. The program displays a sentence with one of the vocabulary words in green and a dart board with the balloons labeled with names of the parts of speech. Throw a dart at the balloon with the part of speech corresponding to the green word in the sentence.

Let's face it, this program is not the most exciting educational program in the world. On the other hand, it does have enough bells and whistles that a child will enjoy playing it and will learn to spell a whole lot of words in the process. If you're already using the Calvert course, you definitely should get this program. *Bill Pride*

The **Etyma Notes** books are intended to introduce and teach Latin and Greek roots, prefixes and suffixes. They succeed admirably. On each page until number 35, there are eight elements and their meaning(s), related Latin or Greek words and four English words, with pronunciation and definition, showing each Latin or Greek element in use. Starting at page 35, you'll find an alphabetical list of every example word in the book. This would help if you knew a certain word was featured and wished to find which roots it contained, or if you wanted to find out how many different elements could create a word beginning with the same letters. Finally, each book has several pages of words from SAT study lists to practice your word analysis. Books in this set so far are *Basic Latin*, *Basic Greek*, and *Intermediate Latin*.

The National Spelling Bee always has some "surprise rounds," or rounds for which Scripps-Howard provides no words for study. **Nat's Notes** is designed specifically for these rounds. Holding over 10,000 of the toughest words from *Webster's Third Dictionary*, UIL high-school words, *Death By Spelling* words, old National Spelling Bee surprise rounds, regional bee surprise rounds and *Words of the Champions*, this book is truly intimidating. On each page there are about 50–55 words, the sources of which are indicated to the left by a letter or number key explained at the beginning of the book. Each word is listed with a pronunciation guide and a short definition. For future or current NSB contestants, this book would really be handy. However, as it is little more than a list of "arcane aberrations" in the world of spelling, it would not be too useful otherwise.

Also helpful in studying for the National Spelling Bee are **UIL Notes** and the **UIL Spelling Complements** for use with the software **UIL Mentor**. In the 1995 National Spelling Bee, the percentage of words per round in Nat's Notes was 59 percent on average. In the **UIL Notes**, the percentage was 60 percent. Together, the words contained in each round was 79 percent on average. You can see that this gives contestants a considerable advantage. **UIL Notes** basically contains the last six years of words for UIL high-school competitors before UIL changed their dictionary source. The **UIL Spelling Complements** basically provide every bit of the dictionary work for the UIL spelling lists. There is a pronunciation guide, definition, description of what part of speech the word is, and a sentence for each word. *Sarah Pride*

Spelling Instruction

This crop of oversized softbound books may include one or two for you!

1000 Instant Words is a 64-pager subtitled "The Most Common Words for Teaching Reading, Writing, and Spelling." Words are presented in very large type in groups of five and in the order of their frequency of use. The first 300 words—words like *the*, *of*, and *look*—make up 65 percent of all written material. All 1000 words together make up 90 percent! The book also includes instructions for teaching the words, an Instant Word Test to determine the lesson at which your learner should start, and a set of 100 illustrated Picture Nouns, common words in large type next to pictures of these words.

Phonics Patterns is 44 pages of *cab-dab-gab-lab*. Each phonics family—for example, *ab*—appears as a column of words that use that word pattern. The phonics patterns are in semi-traditional order, with short *a* patterns first, followed by long *a*, long *a* and *r* (-*air*, -*are*, -*eigh*), broad *a* and *r* (-*ard*, -*art*, -*arge*, etc.), and broad *o* (-*alk*, -*aught*, -*aunt*, etc.). The other vowels are next, followed by the diphthongs. In all, you get about 320 families of rhyming words, each ending in a different phonics pattern. Good for spelling and reading practice.

NEW!
1000 Instant Words
Phonics Patterns
The Beginning Writers
Manual
Grade 1–4 and remedial. 1000 Instant Words, $6.95. Phonics Patterns, $6.95. The Beginning Writers Manual, $14.95. Shipping extra.
Teacher Created Materials, 6421 Industry Way, Westminster, CA 92683. (800) 662-4321.
Fax: (800) 525-1254.
Email: custserv@teachercreated.com.
Web: www.teachercreated.com.

The Beginning Writers Manual is a desk reference book for young writers in grades 3–8. It contains a 7,000-word spell checker to look up the correct spelling, grammar rules, letter forms, punctuation, story starter ideas, etc. *Mary Pride*

After a child has learned to read using phonics, **Beyond Phonics—Reproducible Text/Workbook for Christian Schools** can be used to build his spelling skills by reinforcing those phonics concepts. Each lesson contains a word list for a specific word pattern, followed by a story using those words. The stories incorporate Christian character and biblical principles, and can be read aloud and/or dictated to the child. The accompanying reproducible workbook contains activity pages using these same word lists. Most of these are the same story again, with the word list words replaced by blanks for the child to write them in. There are also some word search activities and crossword puzzles.

Here's the beginning of the phonics story for the second sound of "OU:"

As rain *poured, four* weary *souls* finished the *course* . . .

You can use the over 100 lessons in any order, though the author does suggest an order if that flexibility overwhelms you. You can also use this program alone or in conjunction with other spelling programs. It could be easily adapted to many ages by simply using the easier words with the younger words and more difficult words with older students. *Melissa Worcester*

NEW!
Beyond Phonics

Grades 2–6. Text/Teacher's Manual, $29.95. Workbook, $19.95. Complete program, $49.95. Shipping extra.
Training for Life Publications, PO Box 66303, Scotts Valley, CA 95067-6303. Orders: (800)51-TEACH. Inquiries: (831) 439- 8123. Fax: (831)439-8123. Email: trn4lifepub@aol.com. Web: www.beyondphonics.com.

NEW!
BJUP Spelling for Christian Schools

Grades 1–6. Grade 1: Student Worktext, $10; Home Teacher's Edition, $20; Grades 2–6: Student Worktext, $11; Teacher's Edition, $20. Skill Charts, $15. Shipping extra.
Bob Jones University Press Customer Services, Greenville, SC 29614. Orders: (800) 845-5731. Fax: (800) 525-8398. Web: www.bjup.com.

Designed to be used with or without *First Grade English Skills*, **Spelling for Christian Schools 1** (Home Edition) lays out daily lesson plans for the entire school year. This spelling program focuses on phonics principles, taking advantage of the many regularities of English spelling. It emphasizes understanding patterns and generalizations rather than memorizing lists of words. In addition to the Teacher's Guide, which I reviewed, other instruction materials needed are the Spelling Worktext, the Write-It Flip Chart, and the Practi-Slate.

On the first day the student is given a pre-test. After checking the test, the student erases misspelled words and rewrites the word correctly. Then the teacher explains the particular phonetic or structural spelling pattern that will be focused on that week. Each lesson also has "memory words"—word which are harder to remember because they do not follow a specific pattern.

On the second day, there is a Bible-verse activity and a "reinforcement" page which has activities designed to bolster the child's understanding of the spelling skills. Each lesson also has an optional hands-on activity designed to instruct the kinesthetic learner. For instance, one activity suggests that you let your student help you to prepare instant pudding. Place a large spoonful of pudding on a piece of wax paper, and ask him to "fingerwrite" his spelling words. On the third day another trial test is given after additional practice and dictionary skills are taught. The fourth day focuses on journal activities. And finally on the fifth day the student reviews his spelling words and takes a final test.

This is a very thorough spelling program. You can feel confident that your first grader will be getting an excellent spelling foundation.

Spelling 2 introduces pliable spelling patterns and introduces the most common structural generalizations. It teaches fundamental dictionary skills, and provides systematic composition experience.

Spelling 3 applies generalizations to word families and provides extensive practice in adding suffixes. It expands dictionary skills with weekly practice and continues to give opportunity for original writing.

Spelling 4 add structural generalizations and other extended spelling skills. It includes activities that deal with word histories and more advanced dictionary skills.

Spelling 5 features pairs of related words as an aid to spelling and the fifty state names as spelling words. It continues to provide writing experience and a word etymology in each lesson. Also featured is a special dictionary section with a game, "The Dictionary Game," which has a sports theme.

Spelling 6 focuses on common Greek and Latin word origins and more pairs of related words. A special dictionary section follows detective Dick Shanary through six exciting cases, climaxing in his capturing the criminal Werds and his accomplice, Miss Spelling. *Mary Pride and Cynthia Madsen*

Building Spelling Skills is a Christian spelling series based on phonics. Starting in grade 5, a good deal of vocabulary is also systematically taught.

This very clean and well-designed spelling curriculum is definitely *not* dumbed down. The perfect-bound workbooks are clearly laid out with simple but excellent illustrations, a nice airy format with lots of room for student writing, and instructions in large type. Each workbook has 36 weekly units with daily lesson plans, plus forms for the weekly unit tests in the back of the workbook.

Book one contains good teaching suggestions based on the author's and editor's belief that "the best approach to the teaching of spelling is through the process of incorporating phonics rules. Yet a number of words in the English language do not follow a logical phonetic pattern and therefore must be mastered through the process of memorization." Therefore, the series seeks to incorporate both a phonetic approach and exercises employing rote repetition of word writing. Sections include short vowels, blends, long vowels, and digraphs. These are taught with thematic stories, with the a rule first and then a sentence which illustrates its use.

Book two teaches all the vowel sounds, consonants, consonant blends, digraphs, double consonants, compound words, syllables, diphthongs, roots, prefixes, and suffixes. Six lessons at the end are devoted to "Stories for Spelling." In these lessons, you are given a list of words, then a character-building story. You are supposed to circle the list words in the story, then on subsequent days do more exercises with the list words.

NEW!
Christian Liberty Building Spelling Skills

Grades 1–8. $8 each. Answer Keys, $3 each. Shipping extra. *Christian Liberty Press, 502 West Euclid Ave., Arlington Heights, IL 60004. Inquiries only: (847) 259-4444. Fax: (847) 259-2941. Email: webmaster@homeschools.org. Web: www.homeschools.org. Orders only by mail, fax or web.*

Each weekly unit includes five lessons and a test. A box contains a description of exactly what you'll be working on and the specific spelling rule. There are also different games to reinforce the spelling words learned. An optional answer key is available for books two through eight in the series.

Book three goes through beginning consonant sounds, short and long vowel sounds, consonant blends, *th/wh/sh/ch*, *y* and *w* as vowels, hard and soft sounds of *c* and *g*, *r*-controlled vowels, vowel digraphs, diphthongs, *ch/ck/kn,gn/wr/ph*, words ending in *le*, and suffixes such as *s* and *ing*.

Book four contains thematic vocabulary and spelling guides. It includes a section on thinking about spelling: how to form the past tense, adding suffixes and prefixes, etc. It also contains a section about fitting a vocabulary or spelling word to a definition.

Book five has a a theme: "The World of Words." The first six units are devoted to studying country names. Two units follow on the names of the states. The rest of the book units study words in groups: e.g., "The World of Astronomy" teaches spelling words associated with this science. Unit topics also include flowers, music, business, geography, birds, sports, buildings, anatomy, forms and offices of government, titles for civil officers, scientific and technical instruments, law, trees, health, economics, food, the elements, animals, pets, church terms, the elderly, arts and entertainment, travel and transportation, and books. Continent maps showing the locations of each country are included in the back.

Book six units are based on the sounds within the word. For example, Unit 1 has as its topic the long sound of *a*. Units on the other vowel sounds, consonant sound, and digraphs follow. This book includes a number of units on "Tricky Trailers." These are word endings such as *cy* and *sy*, or *ance* and *ence*, which are easily confused by beginning spellers. Prefixes and suffixes are dealt with in more detail than the earlier book, including those from other languages. There's a unit on learning to find the proper use of each synonym, and one on how to tell where the stress is placed in a word such as *escort* that can be used as either a noun or a verb.

Book seven is entirely devoted to suffixes and prefixes. Considerable dictionary work is required with this workbook, and considerable vocabulary is built. I've seen SAT vocabulary reviews that didn't teach this much vocabulary, let alone how to spell it!

Book eight has the theme of "words and word parts from other languages." You'll learn words derived from Greek, Latin, Latin through French, Arabic, Celtic languages, Dutch, Hebrew and Persian, American Indian languages, Asiatic and African languages, Anglo-Saxon, Scandinavian languages, French, Italian, and Spanish. You'll also learn words used in early English poetry, English literature, and world literature.

If there is such a thing as a spelling and vocabulary course to get a student ready for classical education, this is it. Recommended. *Cynthia Madsen and Mary Pride*

NEW!
How to Teach Any Child to Spell
Tricks of the Trade

Grades 3 and up. How to Teach Any Child to Spell, $8. Tricks of the Trade, $12. Shipping extra. *Lasting Lessons, 1209 Avenue 'N', Suite 11, Plano, TX 75074. (800)820-LAST. Inquiries: (972)398-1834. Email: lastinglessons@msn.com. Web: www.lastinglessons.com.*

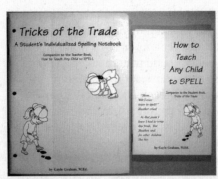

Your child reads like a librarian, but spells like a can of alphabet soup. You know memorizing spelling lists doesn't work. Reviewing all those phonics rules (again) doesn't seem to make a dent, either. What to do? Veteran homeschooler Gayle Graham offers her solution to the spelling dilemma in **How to Teach Any Child to Spell**. Inspired by Ruth Beechick, this slim volume has 25 pages of spelling instruction, plus a brief appendix of some basic spelling rules. Her theme? She suggests lots of reading, lots of writing, and systematic categorization of all your child's misspelled words into an individualized spelling notebook. Some wonderful tips (have your child concentrate on spelling words by syllable), ladled out with a dollop of reassurance, make this an easy-to-use resource, especially if you are of the "reading *is* homeschooling" bent.

The **Tricks of the Trade** student book is comprised of two sections: a listing of basic spelling rules presented in an easy-to-read kid-friendly format, and fill-in-the blank pages, each captioned with the phonetic bugaboo. For example, in the consonants section, each possible combination of the pairs with one letter silent is listed, along with some handy memory tips (*kn* in *knife*: In Old England they pronounced the *k*. Try it!). There are ample blank lines that you and your child will be able to use to record every misspelling that comes along in your child's writing. Error patterns will likely present themselves as you capture mistakes. The notebook then serves as a springboard for spelling study. Though this might be too informal for some, you may find this method fits your child to a "T." *Michelle Van Loon*

Finally, teaching the *Writing Road to Reading* has been made simple! This book, written by Katherine von Duyke and originally appearing in the *KONOS Helps!* newsletter, is described as "a dialogue for teaching the *Writing Road to Reading*," which many homeschoolers simply refer to as the "Spalding method."

One of the complaints I have frequently heard about using the otherwise excellent Spalding method is that it is not at all teacher-friendly and that parents are often bewildered at how exactly to implement this method with their children. Now there is hope!

The Month by Month Spelling Guide was not "officially" approved by the Spalding Foundation and certain aspects of the *WRR* program have been modified or revised. Katherine von Duyke brings her own expertise as a homeschooling mother of mixed-aged children and offers practical suggestions as to how to implement *WRR* step-by-step and month-by-month.

You will learn how to teach the phonograms, how to involve both older children and toddlers. You can use any method of handwriting, even teaching manuscript to younger children and cursive or calligraphy to older children—and all of this is just on the first six pages! This book will provide daily lesson plans along with detailed teaching instructions, real life homeschooling examples, and answers to questions like, "What do you do when you have several children in several different sections of the spelling list?" *Rebecca Prewett*

If you have a really bad speller, **My Kid Can't Spell** is for you! Or you might actually have a good speller, but the curriculum you trust is making unreasonable requests of your child. This book will give you several tools:

- A means to analyze your spelling program
- An argument for teaching spelling in kindergarten (i.e., use phonics early)
- How to recognize and encourage the five stages of spelling ability
- A spelling placement test for grades 1–8 that really works!
- A list of good strategies for the poor speller

Arm yourself with knowledge; spelling is a tough area! If you have a child that isn't getting it, don't blame the child, learn how to mentor him to success. *Kathy von Duyke*

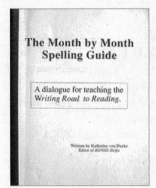

NEW!
Pickle Lee by Barry Ross

Grade 5–7. Entire curriculum
$19.95 postpaid.
*Pickle Lee Productions, 4174 St. Clair
Parkway, Port Lambton, Ontario N0P
2B0, CANADA. (519) 677-5598.
Email: picklee@kent.net.
Web: www.globalvillagemall.com/
~spelling/index.shtml.*

This no-frills program consists of 27 pickle-colored sheets per lesson set, stapled at the corner. 140 lessons are included in the entire four-set program.

The target of the **Pickle Lee** program is to teach all the rules for adding suffixes to root words. Some spelling programs string these lessons out over so many lessons the child can't develop a comprehensive picture of how to handle all endings. Other excellent phonics programs teach the whys of rules on comprehensive charts, but leave it to the parent to present lessons.

All the work of presentation has been done for the home teacher on these sheets! A spelling rule is introduced to the student, then the student rewrites the root word with the ending in three columns. The first column consists of one-syllable words (for younger children), the second of two-syllable root words, and the third column of three-, four-, five-, or even six-syllable words. Each student starts in the first column and works up to his frustration level. Every few lessons, a new rule is introduced and previous rules are continually reinforced. Eventually, the rules become innate.

The Pickle Lee rule comes in Set Two. It says that when a word ends in -*ic*, to add an -*ly* you must insert an -*al* hence *ic-al-ly*; pickle lee, cute!

I think this is a great program targeted to the tricky parts of spelling, and probably a sufficient spelling text for most children who do better knowing the "why" of spelling then memorizing lists of words. To use the program with greatest efficiency, I would wait until a child has had a few years of phonics, has built up a visual word bank from reading and is ready for analytical thinking. *Kathy von Duyke*

NEW!
S.T.A.G.E.S.

Grades K–8. All five books, $25
plus shipping.
*Can Do Books, 2119 Lone Oak
Avenue, Napa, CA 94558. (707) 224-
0197. Email: napaitl@aol.com.*

S.T.A.G.E.S. is an acronym for **Sequential Tasks to Assist the Growth of English Spelling**. If the name sounds complicated and hard to follow, well . . . Essentially, this is a complete spelling program designed by Dr. Donna Reid Connell for use in public school classrooms, for grades K through eight. It comes as five oversized, spiral-bound books, plus two loose sheets (left out when the books were published) containing an index and a teaching plan.

The teacher's manual contains much of Connell's book *Writing Is Child's Play* as well as specific helps for teaching spelling, including eighteen spelling games. The blackline masters book contains reproducible masters for all handouts, as well as sheets of spelling clues (picture clues to help children remember difficult spelling rules). Books one through three contain the actual lessons.

Lessons are ungraded, which is good in homeschool situations, but are divided into stages, which is simply a way of labeling the different skill levels. Pre- and post-tests for each level let you know where to start with your student, what things to emphasize, and what to pass over. Stage one assumes the child has some familiarity with sound-symbol correspondence and is able to correctly form most of the lower case letters. The final stages contain lessons for eighth grade.

The lessons are highly formatted, telling you exactly what to do at every step. Each lesson clearly explains your objective, the understandings you want to reach, and the materials needed. The lessons guide you through activities (games, etc.) and provide a script to use in explaining the day's lesson. Extended activities reinforce learning.

The program is not especially user-friendly but, once you've seen how it all goes together, it's not that hard to work with. Remember that this a public school curriculum. Adjust it to your family's needs just as you would any other programmed curriculum. *Tammy Cardwell*

I have a friend who insists that there's a spelling gene that scientists have yet to discover: "How else can you explain the fact I'm a lousy speller and my kids have really strong spelling skills?" Besides the good phonics base she's given to them, it could just be that her analytical children intuitively picked up on spelling patterns and the exceptions as they read and wrote. Genetic excuses aside, most folks find that spelling is a skill that needs daily doses of training "vitamins." Instructional Resources Company offers three spiral-bound, softcover books that offer you a traditional word-list approach to spelling bugaboos.

Spelling Plus: 1000 Words Towards Spelling Success is based on mastery learning of a 1,000-word core list. Though structured for classroom use, *Spelling Plus* can easily be adapted for home use. Weekly word lists are broken down by grade level and are grouped according to patterns (words ending in *-le* and beginning with *pro-*, for example). Each word list comes with notes that offer teaching hints. The other component of this program is guided daily dictation of four new sentences each day that puts the spelling words as well as other writing skills into some sort of context. Audiocassettes of the spelling lessons and dictation sentences will soon be available as well.

The **Dictation Resource Book** offers not only ready-made sentences, but a handy writing and grammar reference section and a fun section on word histories (did you know that the word "weird" was spelled "wird" in Middle English and became popular after being used by Shakespeare in *Macbeth*?)

A separate **Homophone Resource Book** isolates and drills troublesome sound-alikes. Each set of homophones is keyed to the core word lists found in Spelling Plus. After a quick look at meaning, you can hand your child a simple 20 question worksheet that offers him a bit of fill-in-the-blank practice.

Note that these are teacher manuals. There are reproducible masters of all student handouts, which may mean a few visits to a copier in preparation. However, Instructional Resources Company has developed a consumable student work packet for homeschool use. *Spelling Plus* is a relatively painless way to get a good basic spelling vitamin into your elementary learner's diet each day. *Michelle Van Loon*

Spelling—Your Key to Better Communication is a wonderful new spelling series that is sure to please both students and teachers. Each of the six books is 64 handy-sized pages long and contain 26 nice short two-page lessons. The first page has the phonics lesson and identifies the pattern of the words for that lesson. The second page is a "Spelling Workshop" with activities to help the student remember the correct spellings of the words. For review, each book has a section called "Before you go on" about halfway through the book and a section at the end entitled "How did I do?"

The words in books A and B are presented as printed words. In books C, D, E, and F, the presentation is cursive.

- **Book A/Grade 1** has eight words per lesson. Topics are alphabetical order, word groupings, rhyming words, match the word to the number and creative sentences.
- **Book B/Grade 2** has eight words per lesson. Topics include word grouping, rhyming words, alphabetical order, and compound words.
- **Book C/Grade 3** has 12 words per lesson. Topics include using guide words, does it look right?, word grouping strategy, words are for writing, making contractions, make compound words, and build your lesson words.
- **Book D/Grade 4** has 15 words per lesson. Topics include using guide words, word grouping strategy, creative sentences, contractions, possessive words, suffixes, homographs, and compound words.

NEW!
Spelling Plus second edition
Dictation Resource Book
Homophones Resource Book
Grades K–6. Spelling Plus, $19.95. Spelling Plus Work Packet (with consumable worksheets), $15.95. Dictation Resource Book, $12.95. Homophones Resource Book, $15.95. Shipping extra.
Instructional Resources Company, P.O. Box 111704, Anchorage, AK 99511. Orders: (800) 356-9315. Inquiries: (907) 345-6689. Fax: (907) 345-6689. Email: santhony@alaska.net. Web: www.alaska.net/~santhony.

NEW!
Spelling—Your Key To Better Communication
Grades 1–6. $4.95 per level. Set of six for $29. Shipping extra.
ELP (Essential Learning Products), P.O. Box 2590, Columbus, OH 43216-2590. (614) 487-2718. Fax: (614) 487-2272.

- **Book E/Grade 5** has 15 words per lesson. Topics are homophones, using guide words, proofreading strategies, creative sentences, synonyms, antonym, word grouping strategy, prefixes and suffixes, using a dictionary, creative sentences, and spelling demons.
- **Book F/Grade 6** has 20words per lesson. Topics are using a dictionary, proofreading, self test strategy, spelling demons, dissecting words, word grouping strategy, creative sentences, and synonyms.

The words are common everyday words—no strange ones here. The difficulty level increases slowly, so even poor spellers will do well. The activities are back to the basics; there is no fluff, just the filling. The books have a space theme on the covers and are very colorful and eye-catching. The inside text is black only. Most exercises are fill-in-the-blanks, with some creative-writing exercises using the book covers as story starters. This should provide some very interesting stories.

This series is well written and easy to understand. It would work well for remedial spelling work or as a stand-alone spelling program for each grade. *Lynn Smith*

NEW!
Super Spelling, Book 1

Grades 1–2. $19.95 plus shipping.
Pecci Educational Publishers, 440 Davis Court #405, San Francisco, CA 94111. Information: (415) 391-8579. Email: pecci@sirius.com.

Paperback yet sturdy, this 243-page book is the latest offering by Mary Pecci, author of the Super Seatwork books reviewed in Chapter 15. Although intended specifically for classroom use, it is easy to see how **Super Spelling, Book 1** could be used in a homeschool. It outlines day by day exactly what the teacher should do, and what precisely should be said while introducing new material. While this may seem extremely structured, her method does appear useful. Most specifically, she deplores the way many teachers force first-graders to try to write original stories when they have not yet taught them how to write or spell the necessary words. In this book she instead suggests teaching students rudimentary spelling words and grammar, then slowly having them write preset sentences to teach them how the rules are used firsthand. After they have learned this, they can begin to actually write. *Sarah Pride*

English from the Roots Up

Grades 3–12. $27.95 plus $4 shipping. Flashcard sets $17 plus $3 shipping per 100 cards.
*Literacy Unlimited, PO Box 278, Medina, WA 98039. (425) 454-5830. Fax: (425) 450-0141.
Web: www.literacyunlimited.com.*

Since the program was originally designed for classrooms, you will have to slightly adapt it for home use. ADAPTATION #1: a chalkboard is not really necessary. A few children can copy the information straight from the book to their cards. ADAPTATION #2: since

Vocabulary

I like it! If you can get your hands on a set of red, green, and blue Magic Markers and 100 index cards, you can use this excellent step-by-step system to teach kids as young as second-grade level 100 Greek and Latin word roots. By the time you're done with the book, your children will have also learned about 800 new English words and be able to figure out literally thousands more.

English from the Roots Up (spiral-bound, 125 pages) is based on author Joégil Lundquist's years of teaching this system in her classroom. She starts with Greek roots such as *photo, tele,* and *graph* that quickly fit together to make many English words. The child gets a card with that word on one side. He uses Magic Markers to draw a border on the outside of the index card—green for Greek, red for Latin. Then on the back he copies the word meaning, and a list of English words based on that word, with their etymologies and definitions. Examples of two words from the graph card: *telephoto* and *telephone*. As you can see, your child will learn additional Greek (or Latin) roots almost automatically.

Each lesson fits on one page. At the top is the information you need to fill out both sides of the card. Below that are teaching notes that give more information and suggested follow-up activities for each of the new English words, plus an "extra words" section that introduces words not covered on the card. Bonus appendices teach the Roman numerals and explain an "auction bidding" game that can be used to review cards already studied.

Aside from the time spent preparing the cards, which amounts to about 15 minutes per card, this program takes just minutes a day. It's simple, neat, usable, and even fun! Five stars. *Mary Pride*

you are home, just ignore the section saying that the index cards should never be brought home.

Add to your word power with the board game **Ludi at the Circus Maximus.** In this fast-paced game you race your chariot pieces around a racetrack by attempting to come up with words using Latin prefixes. Prefixes are listed and defined on the racetrack. An included word booklet tells you which words are legal for each prefix. Too bad it doesn't include word definitions, too! Extremely easy to use and play, especially educational if you take the time to look up some of the words in the booklet. 4,000 words in the booklet, 57 prefixes. *Mary Pride*

Ludi at the Circus Maximus

Grade 3–adult. $30 plus shipping. *Discere, Ltd., 6336 Mountain Rd., Macungie, PA 18062. (610) 966-3782. Fax: (610) 966-2230.*

Rummy Roots is a card game with two sets of cards—one set of Greek and Latin root words and one set of English equivalents. You can play four different games with the cards. The purpose of the simplest game is to learn the Greek and Latin root words and their English meanings. The next three games aim to increase your English vocabulary by teaching you to put these root words together to make various English words. **More Roots** follows the same format, but includes different word roots.

We use the book *English from the Roots Up* at our house to teach these same root words, and these card games are a good companion to that curriculum. The games are easy to figure out, fun to play, and useful for teaching or reviewing 42 Greek and Latin roots. *Sherry Early*

NEW!
Rummy Roots

Grades 3–12. Rummy Roots and More Roots, $11.95 each plus shipping. *Eternal Hearts, PO Box 107, Colville, WA 99114. Fax/Phone: (509) 732-4147. Email: eternalheart@aol.com.*

The **Usborne Children's Wordfinder** is a colorful picture dictionary with 3,000 words of high interest to preteens. When I say "picture dictionary," I mean in this case that you get many labeled pictures, instead of text with occasional pictures thrown in. Every page is the equivalent of dozens of visual vocabulary flashcards. You can easily use this to build vocabulary with a child who can read English sounds. *Mary Pride*

Usborne Children's Wordfinder

Grades 2–8. $9.95 plus shipping *EDC Publishing, Division of Educational Development Corporation, PO Box 470663, Tulsa, OK 74147. (800) 475-4522. Fax: (800) 747-4509. Web: www.edcpub.com.*

Word Spin, like the other spin games from Geospace, comes with ten-sided, colorful magnetic wheels that you can turn around, break apart, and lock together with very little effort. The regular game and junior game each come with eight wheels; the deluxe and challenge game each include ten wheels. The regular, challenge, and deluxe versions all assign points to the rarer letters; the junior game doesn't.

Each player is given a certain number of these wheels, and turns them to make as many words as possible *all at the same time*. Very challenging

NEW!
Word Spin

Grades 3–12. Regular travel version or junior game, $6 each. Challenge Game, $7. Deluxe Game, $12.50. Shipping extra. *Geospace International, 1546 NW Woodbine Way, Seattle, WA 98177.*

Orders: (800) 800-5090.
Inquiries/fax: (206) 365-5241.
Email: debink@gte.net.
Web:www.spingames.com.

Wordly Wise series

Grades 2–12. All books $7.10 each.
Teacher's keys, $5.50 each.
Shipping extra. Quantity discounts
are available.
Educators Publishing Service, Inc., 31
Smith Pl., Cambridge, MA 02138.
(800) 225-5750. Fax: (617) 547-0412.
Email: epsbooks@epsbooks.com.
Web: www.epsbooks.com.

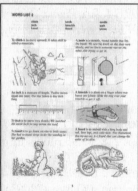

A page from Wordly Wise Level B

and fun; a good vocabulary-builder and a great, non-messy travel game.
No wonder it was voted 1995 Game of the Year by the Australian Toy
Association, and the Best Mind Game of 1995 by the American chapter of
Mensa (the exclusive group for those with well-above-average IQs).

As with other magnetic products, don't store Word Spin on top of your
disk drive or with your videotape collection. *Mary Pride*

Unlike other alleged vocabulary-building series that I've seen from secular publishers, Educators Publishing Service's **Wordly Wise** is interesting,
entertaining, and useful. Several major home school correspondence programs include it in their materials.

Wordly Wise A, B, and *C,* for grades 1–3, are the first books in the series.
Each introduces about 100 vocabulary words. Books A and B have 10
lessons each; Book C has 12.

Books 1–5, for grades 4–8, introduce about 375 words each. Each lesson includes about 12 new words, studied in a variety of ways. For each
lesson, exercises A–C present words in context, show their multiple meanings (if any), and allow students to practice using the words in sentences.
Exercise D reviews the lesson and earlier lessons. Exercise E is self-checking—when completed correctly, the student discovers part of a quotation,
poem, or riddle. The Wordly Wise section in each lesson discusses words
with interesting histories and distinguishes between commonly confused
words. Each third lesson has a crossword puzzle to fill in, using words
studied in those three lessons.

Books 1–3 each have word glossaries. Beginning in Book 4, the student
needs a separate dictionary, and each lesson has an extra exercise focused
on roots, prefixes, and suffixes.

So much for dry, cribbed-from-the-catalog copy. Here's a sample of part
of one lesson:

> *Wordly Wise 4*
> *ABYSS is pronounced a-BISS.*
> *NAIVE is pronounced ny-EVE.*
> *TUMBREL may also be spelled* tumbril. *The rolling of the tumbrel*
> *brought fear into the hearts of noblemen during the French Revolution,*
> *for this was the cart that carried prisoners to their execution. Its desti-*
> *nation was the guillotine (pronounced GEE-yo-teen in French, GIL-a-*
> *teen in English), a machine for chopping off the heads of those sen-*
> *tenced to death.*

As you can see, words are not introduced according to common roots or
other methods of organization, but they *are* introduced memorably.

If you aren't wedded to the Greek-and-Latin approach to vocabulary
study, you could do worse than *Wordly Wise. Mary Pride*

CHAPTER 22

Classical Languages for Kids

It's never too early to start with Greek, Latin, or biblical Hebrew. Most of the work in learning a new language is memorizing vocabulary, and that's especially easy for young children. Picking up simple phrases is just as easy. Grammar and lengthy reading assignments in the classical language of your choice can wait until the student has fully mastered reading and writing in English.

Why classical languages? So you can . . .

- Study the Bible in its original languages
- Read the classic authors of Greece and Rome
- Read just about any important work written by Europeans before the year 1700
- Understand those cryptic phrases with which the loftier class of author loves to dot his works
- Impress your friends
- Improve your vocabulary
- Join the Junior Classical League!

Greek

I strongly suggest you teach your young children the Greek alphabet. This will give them a great head-start on high-school math and science, where Greek symbols frequently appear, as well as making it far easier for them to jump into Greek itself later on. *English from the Roots Up* and *Rummy Roots* (both reviewed in the vocabulary section of the last chapter) also teach a number of Greek roots.

Finally, for advanced preteens, you could try the Greek programs reviewed in volume 3.

The **Trivium Pursuit** catalog was developed *by* homeschoolers *for* homeschoolers. Harvey and Laurie Bluedorn and their homeschooled children are devoted to reviving classical education, which is based on a grammar–trivium–quadrivium sequence. (To find out what that means, see the chapter on Classical Education in Volume 1!)

Unlike other classical education promoters, the Bluedorns feel it is important to study Greek and Hebrew as well, not just Latin. Here are their Greek materials for younger students:

**NEW!
Trivium Pursuit Greek Materials**
Grades 3–12. Alphabet for Biblical Greek, $4. Alphabetarion workbook, $12. Audio tape, $5. Greek alphabet flashcards, $4. Greek alphabet banner, $4. Greek Primer for Windows95, $10. Shipping extra.
Trivium Pursuit, 139 Colorado Street, Suite 168, Muscatine, IA 52761. (309) 537-3641. Email: trivium@muscanet.com. Web: www.muscanet.com/~trivium.

- **The Alphabet for Biblical Greek** is a small comb-bound book printed on heavy card stock. Each Greek letter is on a left-hand page, with a right-hand facing page explaining its sound and an ink illustration to associate with the letter sound. A folded Greek Alphabet Chart is also included.
- **A Greek Alphabetarion** is an oversized, wide-format, comb-bound workbook that teaches everything you need to know about the Classical and Biblical Greek Alphabets. It is divided into two sections. Younger students are only expected to complete the first section.
- **Alphabetarion Audio Tape** includes a "cadenced" (rhythmical chanted) recitation of the Greek alphabet, plus how to pronounce each Greek letter.
- **Greek Alphabet Flashcards** are just that. Capital and lowercase Greek letter on one side, pronunciation on the other.
- **Greek Alphabet Banner** is really eight oversized cards that you stick in sequence on the wall. It shows both the uppercase and lowercase alphabet.
- **Greek Primers for Windows95** is inexpensive computerized alphabet drill, for use with the *Alphabetarion*.

For older students, Trivium Pursuit offers their **Homeschool Greek** course. See review in Volume 3. *Mary Pride*

Hebrew

Again, with Hebrew, It's important to teach the alphabet (in this case, the *aleph-beth*) as early as possible, since the strange new letters are the rocks on which many a would-be Hebrew scholar first runs aground.

NEW!
Behrman House Hebrew Resources

All ages. Free catalog. Sam the Detective, $5.95. Ivrit Alfon, $6.95. Shipping extra.
Behrman House, Inc., 235 Watchung Avenue, West Orange, NJ 07052-5520. (800) 221-2755. Fax: (973) 669-9769. Web: www.behrmanhouse.com.

The large **Behrman House** catalog is chock-full of Hebrew language resources for learners from preschool through adult; Jewish heritage courses by grade level; books on rabbinical wisdom; and more. Some choice items: *Sam the Detective's Reading Readiness Book* teaches kindergartners the Hebrew letters. *Ivrit Alfon: A Hebrew Primer for Adults* teaches the Hebrew letters, phonetic reading, and a basic 100-word vocabulary. Much, much more, all from a Reform Jewish perspective. *Mary Pride*

NEW!
Tall Tales Told in Biblical Hebrew

Grades 4–adult. Book and set of tapes, $59.95. Book only, $16.95. Tapes only, $44.95. Shipping extra.
EKS Publishing, 1029-A Solano Ave., Albany, CA 94706. (510) 558-9200. Fax: (510) 558-9255. Email: eks@wenet.net. Web: www.ekspublishing.com.

Tall Tales Told in Biblical Hebrew is a cheerful add-on to any Biblical Hebrew course. The familiar tales of Aesop, Grimm, Perrault and others, translated into Hebrew, make for an interesting change of pace for those learning Biblical Hebrew. The tales are taken, with minor changes, from *The First Hebrew Primer* by Ethelyn Simon (also from EKS Publishing), and parallel the grammar and vocabulary lessons of that primer.

The vocabulary is largely high-frequency Bible words. With the repetitiveness of children's stories, these tales reinforce the lessons of the language course. A word bank is located at the beginning of the book, and there is a list of new words and grammar points at the beginning of each tale. Translations and a glossary are provided in the back of the book.

The only thing I could think of to improve this product would be to enclose cassette tapes or CDs with the sounds of the language. *Anne Brodbeck*

The Alphabet for Biblical Hebrew is a small comb-bound book printed on heavy card stock. Each Hebrew letter is on a left-hand page, with a right-hand facing page explaining its sound and an ink illustration to associate with the letter sound. A folded Hebrew Alphabet Chart is also included. *Mary Pride*

Latin

Thanks to the burgeoning popularity of Classical Education in the homeschooling community, the number of Latin products and courses for preteens is growing apace. I think you'll find this a pretty complete listing.

Although it was designed for junior-high and high-school students, Waldo Sweet's **Artes Latinæ** programmed language Latin course is so easy to follow, a dedicated seven-year-old who is a good reader can use it by himself.

This secular course (no Christian content) begins with a series of cassette lessons correlated with the attractive programmed text. These teach the student how to use the course. Artes Latinæ then proceeds to teach Latin pronunciation and a number of "Basic Sentences." These Basic Sentences are famous quotations from famous classical writers and the Bible. Each Basic Sentence gives the student a grammatical form—like the basic subject-verb-object sentence *Vestus virum reddit*. By adding vocabulary words, the student can create an infinite range of new sentences using the basic models. At the same time he is exposed to Latin thought and introduced to classical literature.

Graded readers correlated with the student text contain proverbs, poems, and other readings, plus Latin question-and-answer exercises. The Reference Notebooks give your learner a place to record what he is learning. These are not bare sheets of paper. The page for Principal Parts of Verbs, for example, has places for students to write out the first conjugation of a number of listed verbs. Unit tests and teacher's guides for those tests let you know right away how your learner is doing. The drill cassettes provide painless practice in Latin pronunciation, and make it unnecessary for the parent or teacher to know Latin before embarking on the course. Teacher's manuals explain the whole program and provide extra activities. Plus you can get two sets of filmstrips, one on the Basic Sentences and the other on Roman culture, and even Latin buttons featuring the basic sentences A new CD-ROM featuring the early lessons is also available—see review on the next page. *Mary Pride*

NEW!
Trivium Pursuit Alphabet for Biblical Hebrew
Grades 3–12. $4 plus shipping. *Trivium Pursuit, 139 Colorado Street, Suite 168, Muscatene, IA 52761. (309) 537-3641. Email: trivium@muscanet.com. Web: www.muscanet.com/~trivium.*

Artes Latinæ
Grades 5–12. Level I (traditional format), Books 1 & 2, $27 each. Unit Test Booklet, $10. Graded Reader, $15. Reference Notebook, $7. Set of coordinated drill cassettes, $14 each. Two sets of 5 Artes Latinæ filmstrips, $60 each set. Level II materials available at similar prices. CD-ROM, $212. CD-ROM package, $270, also includes all level 1 materials except filmstrips. Shipping extra. *Bolchazy-Carducci Publishers, Inc., 1000 Brown St., Unit 101, Wauconda, IL 60084. (847) 526-4344. Fax: (847) 526-2867. Email: orders@bolchazy.com. Web: www.bolchazy.com.*

Software for Artes Latinæ

Artes Latinæ CD-ROM

Ages 10 and up. CD only, $212.
Level 1 Package, $270. Win 3.1x,
CD-ROM drive.
*Bolchazy-Carducci Publishers, Inc.
1000 Brown St., Unit 101, Wauconda,
IL 60084. (847)526-4344. Fax: (847)
526-2867. Email: latin@bolchazy.com.
Web: www.bolchazy.com.*

Everybody's favorite Latin curriculum is now even easier to use,
thanks to modern technology. No
more tapes and tape recorders to
keep track of. No more rewinding
the tape to repeat pronunciations.
No more forgetting where you are in
the book. **Artes Latinae on CD-ROM** even lets you keep track of
multiple students.

Using a "programmed learning"
approach, Artes Latinae teaches the
course in little snips called "frames."
In almost every frame you're required to pronounce, repeat, echo,
finish a sentence, or type in an answer. Feedback is immediate as
you're told if you got it right or if
not, where you made your mistake.

The program's interface is clean
and crisp. The same black and white
line drawings that are in the book
are here as well. Unlike the book,
you only see one frame at a time,
which makes for a less cluttered approach overall.

Pronunciations have been expanded from just one (American

Scholastic) to three: Restored
Classical and Italian/Ecclesiastical.
Just pick which option you prefer.

The icon bars at the top of each
frame allow you to navigate back and
forth through all the frames, hear a
pronunciation (as many times as you
like!), see the words in print that the
teacher is saying, or give the illustration its own separate window. The
"review" function allows you to see
unit summaries, takes you to vocabulary review sections, shows you what
you'll need to know for the test, and
plays particular sound clips.

One minor quibble: In order to
have your place in the program
saved, you have to remember to use
the "file exit" command. If you forget
and double-click on the top corner
of your screen, too bad!

For those of you familiar with
Artes Latinae, this CD replaces the
books and cassette tapes. You'll still
need to buy the test booklet, reference notebook, and graded readers.
Moms and dads, this CD-ROM isn't a
stand-alone program. Your kids need
to do the written work to get the
most from Artes Latinae. These are
integral parts of the program, so buy
everything you need! In fact, some
homeschoolers like to have the textbook available for a backup when
the family computer is in use. *Renee
Mathis*

Jake's Latin Flash Cards

5¼" disks $12, 3½" disks $13, post-paid. IBM/compatible, 640K,
EGA/VGA, hard drive and mouse
recommended. Not copy protected.
Only available direct from Jake.
*Jake La Foret, PO Box 166,
Fountainville, PA 18923.*

Now those of you using the Artes
Latinae curriculum from Bolchazy-

Carducci Publishers have an inexpensive electronic helper to drill the
material covered in that curriculum.

Because of its programmed instruction design, Artes Latinae doesn't
have lists of vocabulary words to
study or numbered exercises. This
makes it hard to drill the material
covered in the books.

Jake LaForet and his dad have
provided the solution to this problem with Jake's computer program,
Jake's Latin Flash Cards. This program drills all the vocabulary and
basic sentence structures in Artes
Latinae Level 1, Book 1, Units 4–15
(all of Book 1). In the works and
soon to be released is a second program to cover the vocabulary and
sentences in Level 1, Book 2, Units
16–30 (all of Book 2).

Up to 14 students at a time can
keep track of their scores. The program records your performance for
each and every word and sentence,
so by looking at your scorecard, you
can immediately see which ones you
need to work on.

Jake's Latin Flash Cards provides
options to test you in just about
every way you are likely to want—
vocabulary words only or sentences
only; type in the answer or multiple
choice; words presented in totally
random order or so that the ones
you mess up on the most are the
ones you see the most; Latin to
English or English to Latin. You can
test only the unit you are currently
working on, or review everything
up to and including the current
unit.

This computer program greatly
increases the usability of Artes
Latinae. It is perfect for review, especially if you are taking Latin self-study. *Bill Pride*

Want to learn Latin while studying the Bible? Then **Biblia Sacra** is the program you want. Throughout both levels of this Latin curriculum, students work with Bible passages from the classic fourth-century Latin version of the Bible translated by the scholar Jerome. Also called the "Vulgate," because the common ("vulgar") person could read it, the Vulgate is noted for its beauty of style. Biblia Sacra creator Scott Bayer attempts to build on this reverent atmosphere by filling the spiral-bound workbooks with lovely illustrations and using the music of Bach as background on the accompanying audiocassettes.

Level 1, based on Bible readings from the life of Christ, mostly concentrates on building vocabulary. Level 2, based on Bible readings from the book of Genesis, includes a thorough study of Latin grammar, with lots of drill and practice. Both levels include vocabulary drills, matching exercises, translation exercises, and point out English words based on the Latin words you are studying. In addition, reinforcement of new words is provided via crossword puzzles and other more gamelike activities. Answer keys and glossaries are included in each workbook as well.

The four tapes that accompany each workbook help you learn ecclesiastical (also called medieval) Latin pronunciation. This, rather than classical Latin, is the type of Latin recommended by Dorothy Sayers. It enables you to go on to study the great treasury of literature and theology from the era of Christendom, whereas classical Latin is directed to study of the writings of the great pagan Romans.

The Biblia Sacra courses are designed for self-study, which of course works better at higher age levels. If you're planning to try Level 1 with an eight-year-old, don't just leave him or her alone with the workbook. A high-school student will probably be able to do the course alone, if properly motivated. Also, don't expect glitz—the workbook reproduction looks rather cheap. These courses are a labor of love, not written for mass-market packaging and marketing. Little attention has been paid to them until now, not for any reason of educational quality, but due to the lack of advertising and reviews. Let's see if that changes! *Mary Pride*

The people at **Canon Press** have designed two courses for children who want to learn Latin. Or (let's be honest) for children whose parents want them to learn Latin! Both are based on the courses taught at Logos School in Moscow, Idaho, where Latin is taught starting in third grade.

The new edition of **Latin Primer, Book I** (117 pages, spiral-bound) can be used as early as grade 3. It starts with a brief pronunciation lesson. Following this are 27 weekly word lists in large print. Many of the lists are followed by a chant for the students to memorize, beginning with that all-time favorite, "*Amo, amas, amat . . .*" The children learn Latin noun declensions and verb conjugations by chanting them. A brief section of Latin selections to translate follows the weekly word lists, and is in turn followed by a set of weekly worksheets. Finally, all the chants are listed on the last few pages of the book.

Latin Primer, Book II (137 pages, spiral-bound) follows the same format. Intended for use in fourth grade, its 70 lessons employ only 15 word lists. For fun, kids get to see some college seal inscriptions, in both Latin and English. Chants for nouns, verbs, and pronouns are taught with "chant charts."

Latin Primer, Book III, which I have not seen, is designed for the fifth grade level. By the same author as the other two, it continues to add vocabulary, translation exercises, and basic grammar.

After Book III, you can continue on with Canon Press's Latin Grammar, as I'll explain in a minute.

The spiral-bound teacher's edition for each Latin Primer includes general information on Latin grammar, a list of Latin quotations to use in the weekly lessons, lesson plans, songs, games, reproducible exams with answers provided, and solutions to the weekly worksheets. No separate answer key is now necessary or available.

Latin Grammar for Christian Private and Home Schools (199 pages, spiral-bound) has different authors and starts somewhat differently. Intended for students in grade 6 and up, it begins with pronunciation and parts of speech and quickly moves on through the typical material of a traditional Latin course, all the way up to the fourth conjugation and fifth declension. Christian content is found in the translation exercises, e.g., translating the phrase "Christ is God" from English to Latin. This book includes explanations of what you are studying, so no separate teacher's manual is required. The accompanying solution key has answers to all the exercises.

Latin Grammar is much simpler to use than other traditional school Latin courses I have seen (e.g., Cambridge Press and Longman's). The streamlined format, with everything in one spiral-bound book and accompanying solution key, is a lot easier to use than juggling the teacher's editions, textbooks, workbooks, and readers from other publishers. The course teaches sentence translation only, with no long selections to work through, so you still will need a set of Latin readers eventually. Maybe this can be Canon Press's next publishing project! *Mary Pride*

Now this brings new meaning to the word "classic"! When I first heard about this **Elvis Songs in Latin** CD via an online chat, I just had to get it. So I tracked down the gentleman who had mentioned it, and asked him to buy me one the next time he was in Finland.

Why Finland? Because the incredibly talented Dr. Jukka Ammondt (a professor of Literature at the University of Jyvaskyla, believe it or not) whose rich voice sings these Elvis songs in Latin, is Finnish, and that's where the CD was recorded.

The kids and I were wondering just how "Hound Dog" would come across in Latin. We're still wondering, because all the songs on this CD are Elvis ballads. Remember "Love Me Tender?" Now it's "Tenere Me Ama." "Can't Help Falling in Love" is "Non Adamare Non Possum." Plus many more!

Something this unique can't be kept a secret. Not only is this CD now a hot seller in Europe, but the American Classical League hosted an enthusiastically-received "Elvis in Latin" concert with Dr. Ammondt in 1997. (Picture a group of classical scholars screaming for multiple encores—the mental image is alone worth the price!) Our "Artes Latinae" friends at Bolchazy-Carducci Publishers were there and couldn't resist, and so now this painless way to pick up Latin vocabulary (and fit into the *frigidus* Junior Classical League in-crowd!) is available right here in America, complete with a little booklet of the Latin lyrics and their English translation. What a gift for that Latin student in your life! *Mary Pride* (P.S. *Frigidus* is Latin for "cool." *Frigidissimus* is Latin for "way cool." You now have the power to be cool in Latin—use it wisely!)

NEW!
Elvis in Latin

All ages. $20 plus shipping.
Bolchazy-Carducci Publishers, Inc., 1000 Brown St., Unit 101, Wauconda, IL 60084. (847) 526-4344.
Fax: (847) 526-2867.
Email: orders@bolchazy.com.
Web: www.bolchazy.com.

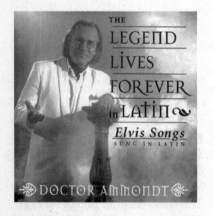

First Latin

Grades 4–7. Student activity books, $10.52 each. Teacher's guides, $41..96 each. Cassette, $22.40 Cue cards, $64.60.
Addison Wesley Longman, One Jacob Way, Reading, MA 01867.
(800) 822-6339. Fax: (800) 367-7198.
Web: www.awl.com.

First Latin can be used as a FLEX program (foreign language exploratory course) or spread out however you choose as a first basic Latin course. First Latin's special charm is that it is designed to be taught by people who may not necessarily know any Latin at all. Since this is 99 percent of average American parents, read on.

First Latin's teacher's guide and pronunciation cassette explain everything you need to know to use this program, assuming you are familiar with the terminology of basic English grammar. All Latin expressions are translated, and you are led step by step through every lesson. If you can manage to read one lesson ahead of your learners, you can teach this course.

Students first listen and speak, then they read the Latin and write it in their activity book. The program starts with oral question/answer dialogues and songs, and follows up with readings in the activity books. Grammar emerges in the Language Discovery sections.

The complete program includes two student activity books, two teacher's guides, one audiocassette, and Picture Cue Cards. The latter are large cards with outline drawings on the front and Latin questions, with English translations, on the back. You point to the card and ask the questions. Say you ask in Latin, "Who is he?" while pointing at the card with a picture of a Roman boy. The student, having done the lesson, is supposed to answer in Latin, "He is Lucius." You use the cassette and cards with both books.

First Latin is designed as a self-contained introduction to all second-language study, and therefore is not as comprehensive in its coverage of Latin forms and grammar as a regular Latin I course. Its other goal, of improving students' English vocabulary, is reached through studying Latin roots and their English derivatives. A third goal is acquainting children with the pagan Roman culture, which could at times be pretty raw. Lesson 1, for example, jumps right in with the story of Romulus, the mythical founder of Rome, murdering his brother Remus and the story of Mucius Scaevola burning his hand off to impress the barbarians. Part 1 of Book 1 ends with a visit to a temple and learning about the gods and goddesses of Rome and Greece. You'll also find a bit of liberal preachifying about lifestyles, brave girls rescuing helpless boys, and so on, mixed in with a lot of helpful cultural notes about everyday Roman life.

Tons of supplementary material is included: songs, activities, games, competitions, greeting cards, toga-making, ideas for writing a Roman soap opera, and so on. Never a dull moment with this program. *Mary Pride*

Linda McCrae has packed more than 149 pages with methods, materials and ideas to make Latin lively, fun, and useful. Some of the methods in **Latina Vivit! A Guide to Lively Latin Classes** are ancient (we remember them from our own high-school classes) and some are as modern as the Internet addresses included in the resources. There are reproducible pages, motivational activities, projects for fun and skill building, answer key, bibliography, reading, and resources. Although designed with the classroom teacher in mind, with a little ingenuity they can be modified for home use. *Anne Brodbeck*

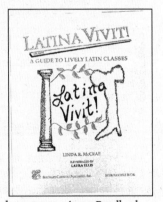

If you've had the impression that **The Latin Road to English Grammar** by Barbara Beers is an English grammar course that just happens to use Latin as a teaching aid, then wipe that impression away. This is, first and last, a Latin course. Just like any other Latin course that teaches Latin grammar, it will enhance your understanding and knowledge of English grammar. However, although this course will teach you all the *advanced* English grammar you need, it is *not* a substitute for teaching the *basics* of English grammar. In fact, the teacher needs to know those basics pretty well in order to teach this course.

Having disposed of possible misconceptions, let's look at this as a Latin course. First, the packaging. Each "volume," which includes many items

Unlike other courses, Latin Road to English Grammar teaches students study skills (through preparing their own study notebooks) as a part of the course's basic design. Each student sets up his own notebook with the following sections: vocabulary, pronunciation, definitions, grammar, cases/declensions, conjugations, text work, worksheets, word study, and tests. He fills these in by copying the relevant sections out of his student book as each new topic is studied. The teacher's manual explains exactly what needs to be copied and when.

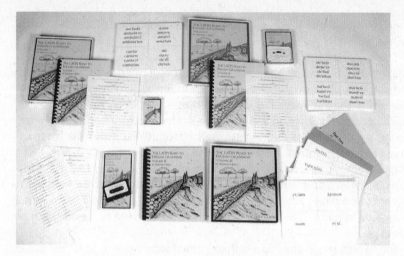

we'll discuss in a moment, comes neatly packaged in a plastic drawstring bag with the "Latin Road to English Grammar" insignia emblazoned on it. What a great organizing idea!

Second, the contents. Each volume includes

- Comb-bound student book with sturdy laminated cover—daily lesson text and readings in the front, Latin-English and English-Latin vocabulary pages in the middle, and perforated tear-out worksheet pages in the back
- Teacher's manual in looseleaf binder includes daily lesson plans, maps and conjugation charts, and answer keys for daily exercises/worksheets/tests, plus section tabs for Pronunciation, Definitions, Grammar, Cases/Declensions, and Conjugations, to be filled in as the teacher does the work along with the students
- Cassette or cassettes to teach pronunciation—Volume 1 has one tape, Volume 2 has two in a neat little cassette binder, Volume 3 has three in a neat little cassette binder
- Color-coded sheets of flashcards, four to a sheet, printed in very large type, for you to cut apart—masculine nouns on blue cards, feminine nouns on pink cards, neuter nouns on yellow cards, verbs in blue ink, adjectives in brown ink, and prepositions in red or green ink, depending on what case governs them
- Set of tests in a three-hole-punched sheet protector

The first two volumes are divided into 14 lessons and the third into 18 lessons. The student is expected to take about two weeks to master each lesson. The first volume covers all the cases of first and second declension nouns and adjectives, all the tenses of first conjugation verbs, imperative mood, prepositions, and adverbs. The second volume adds second and third conjugation verbs, third declension nouns and adjectives, passive voice, specialized uses of some of the Latin cases, pronouns, and numbers. The third volume rounds out what is normally covered in a second-year Latin course.

Typically, each volume starts with a review, then introduces new material. So **volume 1** starts with a review of English grammar, then an introduction to Latin grammar, pronunciation, parts of speech, syntax, and derivatives, all in lesson 1. You then study nouns, verbs, adjectives, and so forth in detail in future chapters. This approach—in which everything about a topic is initially laid out for you, to be studied later in detail—allows you to "predigest" the subject matter and learn it thoroughly.

Latin taught is ecclesiastic, or "church," Latin—the Latin of the Middle Ages. This is the Latin that Dorothy Sayers, author of the famous essay, "The Lost Tools of Learning," recommends.

Readings for each volume include a mix of Bible verses, Christian prayers and songs, famous American texts, and texts related to Roman and Greek history—all in Latin, of course!

Volume 1 readings are the Lord's Prayer, Pledge of Allegiance, "America," O Come All Ye Faithful, The Christmas Story, "To Us Is Born Emanuel," the Ten Commandments (in three parts), "The Star-Spangled Banner," "God Bless America," and Psalm 1.

Volume 2 readings are John 1:1–5, state mottos and sayings about the duties of the President and legislators, famous verses about the "heart" from the Vulgate Bible, the Lord's Prayer (this time the student is able to totally translate it, not just part of it), some paragraphs about Britain by Julius Caesar, more famous verses from the Vulgate, the Pledge of Allegiance, an adaptation from Caesar's *Gallic Wars,* a reading about gladiators, a comparison of the meanings of "love" in Latin, Genesis 1:1–13, and a description of the Colosseum.

Volume 3 readings are titled Spartacus, The First Seven Kings of Rome, The Romans Kill the Christians (don't worry, there are no graphic descriptions of *how* this was done), Before a Roman Judge, American Geography, Psalm 119:97–104, The Senate and The Forum, The Trojan Horse, Map of Italy, Who Is Truly Free? Cicero, The Apostles' Creed, Quiz on American History, Columbus, The Second Punic War (three parts), and Ecclesiastes 3:1–8.

This very attractive program is suitable for use with any child who reads well, understands quickly, and has a solid knowledge of the parts of speech. *Mary Pride*

Latina Christiana: An Introduction to Christian Latin shares with Artes Latinae and Latin Road to English Grammar the distinction of being a course usable by young learners. However, where Artes Latinae is a self-checking, self-teaching course, Latina Christiana needs to be taught by a parent or other instructor. And where Latin Road to English Grammar has everything you would find in a high-school course but paced for use by pre-teens, Latina Christiana was designed for younger students from the beginning and is thus less demanding on both student and teacher as well as less comprehensive and rigorous.

The premise on which this course was designed is "the teaching practices of past centuries, when grammar schools taught Latin grammar—and little else." As author Cheryl Lowe, who has been teaching Latin grammar to students in grades 3–8 for over a decade, says,

> *In those schools Latin instruction began around age 8 and was completed about age 14. Latin was the center and the focus of the grammar school years, not an add-on to an already overloaded curriculum. . . .*

Fans of Romalda Spalding's *Writing Road to Reading* program, which author Barbara Beers has taught for years, will love the very organized, systematic way that Latin Road to English Grammar methodically teaches Latin. They will also be familiar with, and appreciate, the requirement that the child create his own Latin notebook. Principle Approach families will also find much to like about this program, as will anyone who appreciates thoroughness.

NEW!
Latina Christiana
Grades 3–12. Latina Christiana I, $35. Latina Christiana II, $35. Henle Latin I, $16. Henle Grammar, $9.50. Henle Latin II, $16. Shipping extra.
Memoria Press, PO Box 5066, Louisville, KY 40255. (606) 238-2148. Fax: (606) 236-6643. Email: magister@memoriapress.com. Web: www.memoriapress.com.

Overall, I'd say both courses of Latina Christiana combined amount to about "Latin ¾," as opposed to "Latin 1." Not bad if you're in third grade—not as impressive at the junior-high or high-school level.

For those who wish to continue beyond Set 2, Memoria Press recommends the classic Henle Latin 1 and 2 courses, which they carry. Written by a Jesuit priest, these books may be used by fifth- and sixth-graders who have complete Latina Christiana, or seventh-graders and up who have not yet had a Latin course.

Henle's *Latin: First Year & Grammar* has a controlled vocabulary of 500 Latin words, and enough exercises so you won't need a separate workbook. *Latin: Second Year* covers grammar not dealt with the the *First Year* book, and introduces the student to reading Julius Caesar's *Gallic Wars.*

Both of these classic texts have been popular for years with Latin teachers. They include both Christian and classical content, teach parts of Roman and American history, and have a character-building emphasis. The virtues of the Roman "natural man," which were not insignificant, are contrasted with the virtues of the Christian man. The second-year book emphasizes leadership, with studies of Julius Caesar, Vercingetorix (the leader of the Gauls, who almost succeeded in defeating the Romans, as fans of *Asterix* know), and Jesus Christ. Some Catholic content, but non-Catholics can easily skip over it if desired.

Because Latin teaches so much about English grammar, vocabulary, spelling, history, and culture, it is a nearly complete course in and of itself. it makes the modern bevy of textbooks, workbooks, and subjects redundant.

No previous Latin knowledge is necessary in order to teach this course. The lesson plans and student exercise pages are a model of clarity. Each course progresses slowly and systematically. Ecclesiastical (Italianate) Latin pronunciation is taught rather than classical Latin pronunciation. The "Christiana" part comes into play through the many readings from Christian doctrine, history, and songs. One Catholic song, "Ave Maria," is included in the appendix of book two, but can easily be skipped by non-Catholics.

Latina Christian Set I includes a comb-bound teacher book, saddle-stitched student book, and pronunciation audiocassette. Set II contains the same except the student book is comb-bound.

Set I covers:

- 200 Latin words
- 25 Latin sayings, two prayers, and three songs
- Grammar—including definitions of noun, verb, and adjective; concepts of tense, number, gender, and person; first and second conjugation verbs in the present, imperfect nd future tenses; declining first and second declension nouns and adjectives; singulars and plurals of nouns; agreement of subject and verb; agreement of adjectives and nouns; and the names of the five Latin cases and how to spell them correctly
- Derivatives—learn that many English words derive from Latin and learn the meanings of a lot of them and how to use them in sentences
- Lots of Roman history, culture, and geography, with questions to research using the first 13 chapters of Greenleaf Press's *Famous Men of Rome.* Oddly, the lesson plans themselves don't say when to study which chapter or answer which questions.

Set II covers:

- Review of the 200 Set 1 Latin words, plus 200 more new words
- 20 more sayings and additional prayers, passages and songs
- More grammar—prepositions, third and fourth declension verbs in the present and imperfect tenses, principle parts of regular and irregular verbs, the remaining three declensions of nouns, translate simple sentences with direct objects in either direction.
- More derivatives
- More Roman history (using *Famous Men of Rome*) and early Christian history, again without specific daily directions in the lesson plans

As you can see, this leaves out study of the perfect and pluperfect tenses, the passive voice, all moods besides the indicative, dative/ablative/vocative/locative cases, participles, infinitives, gerunds, gerundives, and other topics normally covered in high-school level courses. Such topics *are* covered in Latin Road to English Grammar, so keep this in mind when comparing these two courses. *Mary Pride*

CHAPTER 23

Foreign Languages for Kids

When I was very young, I was given a scholarship that enabled me to attend a private school for several years. There, we had lessons in the normal school subjects—math, English, history, and science—*and* classes in elocution, French, art, and ballet.

I was poor at elocution, ponderous at art, and pitiful at ballet. But I really enjoyed French class! Learning all those new words was like learning a new code. Picking up the patterns of French was like entering a new and beautiful world. Such elegance. Such vitality!

I continued French in junior high and high school, and picked up German as soon as I got the chance. In college, I dabbled in Russian. In seminary, Greek. For me, this was fun.

Now, the scorecard:

- I have never been to France, or Germany, or Russia.
- I don't know anyone who speaks these languages well enough for me to practice my rusty language skills.
- The only French books I've seen in the library are the same miserable existentialist books I was forced to read in high school.
- My German isn't good enough for reading anything but kiddie books.
- The library has no German kiddie books. Dittos for Russian.
- I rarely have the time to play with New Testament Greek.

So all those years of language study were a total loss, right? Wrong! On the plus side of the scorecard:

- I frequently run across phrases in one or more of these languages while reading.
- When snatches of these languages are spoken in a movie, I can usually understand them.
- Someday I hope to brush up all these languages—when I finally get to visit Europe!

- "Target language" means the language you are trying to learn to speak.

- "Native language" means the first language you learned to speak. For most of us, this is English.

- "Native speaker" means someone whose native language is the target language.

Delightfully confusing, *n'est-ce pas?*

Learning French and German helped me a lot with my English vocabulary, since English is descended from these two languages. Learning Greek helped me with my Bible studies. I'll grant you, Russian has never been all that useful for me, but I'm still not sorry I took that Russian class.

In your case, Spanish or Japanese or Korean may be a better choice. But I can say from experience that whatever language you choose, studying it will enrich your life and broaden your horizons.

Is learning a second or third language that hard? Look at it this way—just about every immigrant child ends up knowing two languages: his native tongue and English. If they can do it, often without a lot of wonderful resources and in spite of "bilingual" education mandates that prevent them from getting good English instruction, so can you!

How to Teach Languages

"I hear and I forget. I see and I remember. I do and I understand." This is the philosophy behind **Hooked on Languages.**

This 276-page, spiral-bound book by Penilyn Kruge is designed to engage your student in foreign language learning using non-traditional methods. For example, you teach pronouns by using drawings of raindrops and puddles. Single object pronouns are written inside the raindrops and double object pronouns are inside the puddles. Pictures of little ghosts help to teach direct and indirect pronouns.

The book is full of activities for the auditory, visual, verbal, and kinesthetic learner. The only problem is that you, the teacher, have to know the target language in order to use this approach. Spanish is the predominant language used, but there are also French and Latin examples. Learn vocabulary by singing the words to the tune of "Frere Jacques" or "The Farmer in the Dell." The goal is to provide "hooks" for easier learning and better retention.

Hooked on Languages! is written for teachers in the classroom setting. It is not a student workbook, but if you're looking for techniques to make language learning fun, this may be the ticket. *Marla Perry*

Courses Available In More Than One Language

When I was a child, I read a novel whose main character learned new languages by studying a Bible in the target language. This method could work well if you (1) know the Bible very well and (2) only want to read the new language, or (3) also have cassettes to help you with pronunciation. If you're a Christian and want to talk about Jesus in a foreign country, it wouldn't hurt to have some Scripture memorized in that language.

American Bible Society has the Bible in many languages. Avoid the "classical" translations that correspond to our King James Version; nobody overseas understands these any better than we understand Elizabethan English today.

ABS's free *Scripture Resources in Many Languages* catalog lists Scripture publications in the forty most popular languages, about half of the languages they normally have available. Many Scriptures can be specially ordered even if they are in a language ABS does not normally offer for sale.

All ABS materials are inexpensive. *Mary Pride*

You know the quality will be high with products from an established and well-known company like **Berlitz**. I am not disappointed with **Adventures with Nicholas—The Missing Cat**. This 60-minute cassette tape and accompanying 64-page story book has eight stories in French, with an English translation on each page (also available in Italian, German, Spanish and English). The stories are all read in the target language on the tape, but tape time is not wasted on translation of the stories. Each story presents carefully-selected units of vocabulary, which are reviewed at the end of both tape and book. Cheerful and familiar songs to go with each story make the learning more fun and increase retention of language skills. The only complaint I have is that there aren't *more* of these sets! *Anne Brodbeck*

Calvert's Beginning French and Spanish courses are designed for children in grades 4–8, though in reality I see no reason why older students couldn't or shouldn't use these courses. You do not have to be enrolled in the Calvert K–8 curriculum to sign up for Beginning French or Spanish. Unlike other programs, which either concentrate solely on reading and writing or on speaking, the Calvert courses have it all. Detailed pronunciation instruction, examples, and practice. Dialogues. Spelling. Vocabulary. Plus the famous Calvert step-by-step instructions, perfected in their day school classrooms since 1897, which make it possible even for a parent who never learned French to teach this course!

Children taking Calvert's Beginning French or Spanish courses learn the French or Spanish alphabet and pronunciation. They listen to taped dialogues and pronunciation examples. They learn to follow directions in French or Spanish, acting out such commands as, "Go to the table. Touch the eraser." They make their own Pronunciation Notebooks, listing the rules of French or Spanish pronunciation. They do workbook exercises that drill vocabulary and grammar in a fun, visual way. They pick up tidbits of French etiquette or Spanish culture. What more can you expect from a beginning language course you can use with your fourth grader?

Beginning French Level I and **Beginning Spanish Level I** come with five audiocassettes, a set of crayons, an eraser, a 166-page spiral-bound workbook with exercises in front and tests in the back, a Lesson Manual with detailed teaching instructions, a Tape Script with every word on the cassette tapes, and an answer key to everything except the tests. The theory is that if you want to get your tests graded, you should sign up for the Advisory Teaching Service. However, grading the tests is a snap for anyone who has followed the lessons, especially if you already have a grasp of the language. Save even more by using the course with several of your children at once; materials for an extra student cost a lot less than the initial course price

Beginning French Level II includes all the same ingredients, at a higher level of course, plus an illustrated children's book in French, *Caroline Visite À Paris.*

Beginning Spanish Level II, just introduced, is not as closely patterned after the French Level II course. It comes with two books: *Getting to Know Spain and Spanish* and the Spanish book, *El Señor conejo y el Hermosa Regalo,* written by a famous children's author and illustrated by a popular children's illustrator.

Each course has 96 lessons, plus review lessons and tests. Calvert suggests a Monday-Wednesday-Friday teaching schedule, which would make

each course fit precisely into one school year. Together, the two courses are equivalent to one year of high-school French or Spanish. Although they teach you a lot of vocabulary, more than you would learn in a year in high school, and give you a great chance to pick up a genuine accent, you only learn the present tense of French verbs. Calvert now needs to develop third-level language courses, to take us through the other verb tenses. And, while we're at it . . . Latin, anyone? *Mary Pride*

French for Kids, Spanish for Kids, and English for Kids

Ages 2–12. French for Kids and Spanish for Kids, $19.95 each. English for Kids, $14.95. Shipping extra.
OptimaLearning Co., 885 Olive Ave., Suite A, Novato, CA 94945-2455. Orders: (800) 672-1717. Inquiries: (415) 898-0013. Fax: (415) 898-1654. Email: barczak@optimalearning.com. Web: www.optimalearning.com.

I am impressed! Here is a foreign-language mini-course for children ages 2 and up that really works with almost no effort on your part. You get two cassettes (one with just the songs plus some supplementary vocabulary at the end, to play throughout the day for reinforcement, and one with both lesson vocabulary and songs), and an activity book with parental guide. Dialogues are spoken, and songs are sung by fluent French speakers. The woman has a beautiful voice, and the original music is very sweet and pleasant.

The **. . . for Kids** program is based on the OptimaLearning educational method. They ask you to use a special symbol associated with the study of the language, a special place where you have the lessons, and a little "alerting technique" ritual to announce that the lesson is coming. This sounds a bit new-ageish, but actually is just a way of shedding the day-to-day environment and entering into a proper frame of mind for study. Memorization is *not* stressed. Rather, it is considered important to expose the young child to the rhythms and intonations of the foreign language, before he begins to lose his ability to reproduce these sounds. Exactly what those sounds *are* is explained quite well in a special Pronunciation Guide in the activity book. Each lesson also includes phonetic pronunciation as well as English translation for each phrase, right under the phrase where it does the most good.

You are supposed to go through the lesson with the child, perhaps explaining what it all means, and then he can play the song tape as often as he likes during the day until he memorizes it without any effort. This, of course, would accomplish little if the songs did not aid building vocabulary and expression. For this purpose, the course is set up very well. Each lesson introduces one set of vocabulary. Here are the lesson topics from the French for Kids edition:

Greetings, what's your name, my name is . . . , face parts, animal names, what is this?, more animals, how do they sound?, water and rain, body parts, directions, where do you live?, friends, counting, fruits, vegetables, shopping, I'm hungry, meal time, bedtime, and good night greetings.

Supplementary vocabulary is found on the second side of each tape. Vocabulary words are read "with special intonations to affect receptivity" against a background of Baroque music.

You don't need to know the target language to use this very cuddly, motivational program. For its purpose—presenting the target language to kids —it's about as simple as you can get. *Mary Pride*

UPDATED! International Linguistics "Learnables" Courses

Grades 1–college. Courses in English, Spanish, French, German, Chinese, Hebrew, and Russian. Intermediate series available in English and German only. Full set for any foreign language, $175. Full

A homeschool classic, **the "Learnables" series** teaches foreign languages in a way that's family-friendly and fun! This is the first complete language program designed especially for children ages 7 and up. They now offer English, Hebrew, Spanish, French, German, Chinese *and* Russian.

You get a book of numbered cartoon-style drawings (10 lessons, 100 drawings each, plus comprehension checks) and a series of cassettes in a binder. You learn to count to ten on the tape, then look at pictures (numbered 1–10), hear the sentences illustrated in the picture, and learn the

set for Intermediate English or German, $170. Book 1 plus 5 cassettes in binder, $45. Book 2 plus 6 cassettes in binder, $51. Book 3 plus 5 cassettes in binder, $45. Book 4 plus 5 cassettes in binder, $45. Books 5–8 plus their accompanying cassettes, $45 per book/cassette combo. Extra books, $8 each. Basic Structures Book 1: French, German or Spanish with 4 cassettes, $45; Hebrew with 6 cassettes, $65; Russian with 5 cassettes, $60. Book 2: French, German, or Spanish with 6 cassettes, $59. Book 3: French, German or Spanish with 5 cassettes, $55. Additional Basic Structures books, $18–$28 each. Shipping extra. *International Linguistics Corp., 3505 East Red Bridge Road, Kansas City, MO 64137. Orders: (800) 237-1830. Inquiries: (816) 765-8855. Fax: (816) 765-2855. Email: learn@qni.com. Web: www.learnables.com.*

language. All instruction is in the target language. It works, too! I know, because our children (studying the French) are making up whole new sentences inspired by the lessons—crazy stuff, like *"La grosse pomme mange la maison,"* accompanied by the sounds an apple might make while eating a house.

Unlike other programs, which stress repeated sentences, grammar, and drill, International Linguistics teaches language through word-picture association. Cassettes accompany picture books; each sentence or phrase goes with a picture. This results in "natural" learning, the way a baby learns. No written words are in the text, either English or in the other language. International Linguistics is insistent that you must learn through sounds only.

Pictures are in amusing but understandable cartoon style. The stories are clever. Our sons love the sequence with the baby throwing eggs at the window and the harried mother rushing about looking for a paper towel to wipe up the mess. All languages use the same picture books, so learning more than one language with this approach is a breeze. You start with common nouns (bread, table, ear) and quickly move to simple verbs (to eat, to drink) and prepositions (under the tree, by the tree . . .).

Book 1 has 1,000 sentences, as does Book 2. Stories begin in Book 2, and you are introduced to prepositions and pronouns. Book 3 has more complex stories and gets into verb tenses. Book 4 has complex sentences. The Beginner Series of all four books contains a total of 3,000 basic words and grammatical constructions. The Intermediate series, available only in English and German, teaches 1,500 words and advanced grammatical structures.

When you buy a whole series (Beginner or Intermediate), International Linguistics throws in a vinyl cassette case. You can buy a little at a time and easily branch out into new languages.

I recommend that you buy a separate picture book for each learner (they are not expensive), as otherwise squabbles develop over who gets to hold the book. We found that mealtimes are a good time to turn on the cassette player and learn a little French, and you might try it too, if you don't mind getting the pages greasy!

For those who want to learn to read and write, as well as to speak, in the target language, **Basic Structures** are now available to accompany Learnable Books 1, 2, and 3. These workbooks use many of the same drawings, teaching students to associate the printed word with the spoken word, and providing many "pick the correct picture" exercises.

You first complete Learnables Book 1, *then* Basic Structures Book 1. I also strongly suggest you get each child his own books. *Mary Pride*

NEW!
Muzzy Language Courses from the BBC

Ages 3–12. Muzzy Level 1 or Level 2, $178.50 each postpaid. Languages available: Spanish, French, Italian, and German. Each set includes complete English-language materials. Muzzy Junior has foreign-language material only, $113 postpaid each level. Payment plans also available.
Early Advantage, 25 Ford Road, Westport, CT 06880. (888) 327-5923. Fax: (203) 259-0869. Web: www.early-advantage.com.

The new BBC Vocabulary Builder video, sadly, does not include written text along with the illustrations and spoken vocabulary, thus robbing us of an opportunity to pick up written language along with the spoken. It stars the Muzzy characters and is organized logically by groups of words. First you learn the numbers 1–10, then objects in a classroom, garden objects, clothing (we get to see Norman's wife in her paper-doll-like underwear), numbers 11–20, transportation, house and home, people and family, parts of the body, shapes and colors, positions, numbers 21–30, directions, shop names, outdoor objects, tools, musical instruments, toys and games, sports, occupations, animals, pets, more numbers, food and drink, fruit and vegetables, times, and big numbers. In all, 514 words are learned from this video alone.

Note to owners of previous Muzzy editions: You can purchase an "Upgrade Set" including the *Muzzy at the Seaside* CD-ROM and BBC Vocabulary Builder video, not included in the original product edition, for $79 plus $5.50 shipping.

He's a big blue guy who eats clocks. His friend, John, the palace gardener, is in love with the Princess Sylvia. Who is he? **Muzzy**, an engaging cartoon character who stars in the best foreign-language video series for children we have ever seen.

Developed by the BBC, who are famous for high-quality programming, the Muzzy program consists of two levels in each target language. Each level comes in a huge, colorful binder. Level 1 includes two videos and corresponding audiocassettes in the target language, plus an activity book in that language; two videos in English; a "vocabulary builder" video; a Windows CD-ROM of language activities, usable for any combination of target and support languages from the available five languages (including English); and a booklet with the script for the videos in all five languages. Level 2 includes the same number of videos and audiocassettes, minus the vocabulary-builder video; two activity books; a video script book; and a Windows CD-ROM. Each level includes as much vocabulary as a grade of high-school instruction in that language, but considerably less formal grammar, as you might expect from a video series you can use with your four-year-old!

Here's how it works: you watch all or some of the French (or German, or Spanish, or Italian) video. It cuts back and forth between the ongoing trials and triumphs of Muzzy and his friends, and segments featuring a nerdish little fellow named Norman. Norman, who lives with his wife in an old clock tower and who gets about by bicycle, acts out the new vocabulary words in each segment. This is often quite humorous, as when he tries to order some food in a restaurant and gets a waiter who tosses it to him. You can pick up a lot of vocabulary this way. You then watch the English version, which helps you figure out whatever words you missed.

The Muzzy story line is very wholesome and pro-family, much more so than typical American cartoons. In Level 1, cartoon characters John and Sylvia want to get married . . . and actually do! The entire extended family is involved in both levels, including John and Sylvia's baby in Level 2. Muzzy himself is no superhero, just a big cuddly teddy-bear type who happens to own a space ship (this makes for some interesting plot wrinkles).

Kids will watch these videos over and over again. I know, because ours do! They also actually learn to use the language . . . at least, if you encourage them to. Typical dinner-table question at our house: *"Pouvez-vous me donner un hamburger, s'il vous plaît?"* Remember, just watching TV or videos doesn't teach correct speech to anyone. This is why inner-city kids, who watch hours of TV each day, don't talk in the Midwestern accents of the TV announcers.

The Muzzy series price seems high, but includes a lot. You get a break when you want to order a second set in another language—they give you 22 percent off the price of a set. The current edition does include more than the old did. Is the extra fun and motivation worth the money? I'd say, "Yes, if you have children of the appropriate grade levels to benefit from Muzzy, and if you can afford it." *Mary Pride*

The Adventure Begins?!? Most of us would hardly think of learning a foreign language as an adventure, at least until we got our hands on it. I have only finished the first tape of the six-tape series in the **Powerglide** Russian language course, but with the mnemonic devices, songs and dialogues, I am beginning to feel comfortable in Russian!

Even the alphabet is not as formidable as expected. The series is introduced with an intriguing adventure, in which you star; and you must learn Russian to survive. I almost believed it. The engagement of imagination, music, jingles, and dialogues weave narratives which, along with mnemonic devices, make this the most effective, intensive, and thorough language course that I have used.

Unlike other higher-priced courses, the approach does not contain repetitive drills, is not strictly listen-and-repeat, and does not promise subliminal learning. It is fast-paced and takes full concentration. The use of the full-sized textbook (223 pages) included with the tapes makes it a more comprehensive course than others with twice the number of tapes. It is probably equivalent to a good first year college course. With our super-motivated homeschoolers, we can do it in less than a year. Because of the combination approach, it is suitable for a whole family to use together.

So far I have found nothing more objectionable than a brief mention of Santa Claus in a child-oriented story. All this, as well as the great price, practical vocabulary, and grammar make Russian "The Adventure Begins" a best buy.

Power-glide Spanish, as expected, moves more quickly than Russian, as Spanish is much more familiar to most of us. It is not a retranslated rehash of Power-glide Russian, although they do share many features. There are more games and more explanations in the Spanish. The narratives appear again, adding more and more Spanish, and using less English. Pictographs are used liberally to help reduce reliance on translation and help the student to go directly from concept to Spanish. By the end of the six tape set and textbook, the student should be well on the road toward fluency. The French and German courses are similar to the Spanish. Japanese has a different format. The new Latin course has its own unique adventure! *Anne Brodbeck*

The Level 1 CD-ROM is very versatile. You can pick both your target language and your native language. This means you can use it for vocabulary-building in English, as an ESL program, or for practice in French, Spanish, German, or Italian. The CD-ROM deserves a longer review of its own (this we'll have to save for our separate book, *Prides' Guide to Educational Software*), but suffice it for now to say that you can watch a story, with highlighted text, play with a picture dictionary, practice recording your voice, play a game with up to four players, and much more.

NEW!
Power-glide "The Adventure Begins"

Grades 2–adult. Complete Course (includes the 6 tapes, a workbook, a test book, test tape and a Learners' Guide), $119.90. 6-tape series with textbook, $89.95. Additional workbooks, $29.95. Russian, Latin, Spanish, French, German, and Japanese available. Shipping extra.
Power-glide Language Courses, 1682 W. 820 North., Provo, UT 84601. (800) 596-0910. Fax: (801) 343-3912. Email: deloyh@power-glide.com. Web: www.power-glide.com.

NEW!
Teach Me . . .
Teach Me More . . .
Teach Me Even More . . .

Ages 2–12. Teach Me, $12.95 each language; teaching guides, $6.50 each. Teach Me More, $13.95 each language; teaching guides, $6.95. Teach Me Even More (Spanish or French), $14.95. Inquire about CD editions. Shipping extra.
Teach Me Tapes Inc., 9900 Bren Rd. E, Suite B1-100, Minnetonka, MN 55343. Orders: (800) 456-4656. Inquiries: (612) 933-8086. Fax: (612) 933-0512. Email: teachme@wevetech.com. Web: www.teachme.com.

NEW!
Usborne First Language at Home Series

Grades 3–8. $6.95 each. Shipping extra.
EDC Publishing, Division of Educational Development Corporation, 10302 East 55th Place, Tulsa, OK 74146. (800) 475-4522. Fax: (800) 747-4509. Web: www.edcpub.com.

All over the world, we parents sing, laugh, dance, and play with our children as we teach them to talk and tell them about their culture. If there is anything to teach, we do it with music: nursery songs, lullabies, wake up calls, alphabet songs, and counting songs.

So do the **Teach Me . . .** tapes. Cartoon characters Marie and Peter are your hosts for this series of foreign language programs. Favorite songs and basic vocabulary are introduced via a 20-page coloring book with written text and a cassette with songs performed by native children accompanied by professional musicians. English translations are included (thanks, guys!). The songs are a mix of classic children's songs and more "pop"-style modern songs. No rock.

The coloring book that accompanies each tape is charmingly and clearly illustrated, with the words of the 21 songs in the second language and the English translations in the back. Other captioned illustrations accompany several short narrations and a dialogue about things all children think about.

The Teach Me series is available in French, German, Hebrew, Italian, Japanese, Russian, Spanish, and ESL. An additional set, **Teach Me More** extends the experience for French, German, Italian, Japanese, English, and Spanish. The author has wisely used the same format for all languages, so children can go from one to the other with a feeling of comfort and familiarity.

The *Teach Me . . . Italian* tape lasts 45 minutes, but children will ask for many replays. It is easy to work with, and inviting enough to children that they will gladly carry the tape and coloring book everywhere with them. We found nothing objectionable to anyone.

You really are better off thinking of these as "culture introductions" than as foreign-language-learning courses. The spoken vocabulary is not introduced step-by-step or simplified, but rather serves to introduce the songs. The songs are not "learning" songs per se, but regular songs that children might sing just for fun. "Old McDonald Had a Farm" and "Day-O" were not written to introduce vocabulary, after all! These programs are best suited to parents who don't want to spend any time systematically teaching and just want to expose the kids to a foreign language through coloring-book exercises and songs. *Anne Brodbeck and Mary Pride*

First French at Home and **First German at Home** are the first in a new series that now also includes **On Holiday** and **At School** volumes for each language. Each book follows the adventures of a slightly goofy family (the French Noisettes or the German Strudels), with different scenes and activities on each double-page spread. The books include games, puzzles, and songs to encourage speaking.

Each double-page spread introduces one new language element, plus a learnable amount of new vocabulary. Once introduced, new material is then reviewed farther on in the book. The clever illustrations—which are the same in both the French and German editions—make word meanings abundantly clear.

We hope Usborne will quickly come up with cassettes to accompany these charming "First" books as well—they look like winners! *Mary Pride*

Usborne's **First Hundred Words** and The **First Thousand Words** are now available in a slew more languages. *The First Hundred Words* now comes in French, German, English, and Spanish. *The First Thousand Words* is available in (are you ready?) French, German, English, Spanish, Italian, Japanese, Russian, and Hebrew.

These are foreign-language vocabulary books for young children with a consistent user interface. Each book has the same pictures on each page as the others in the series, making it at least theoretically possible to add on new languages with little effort. Each page illustrates an environment (the kitchen, a street corner . . .) full of labeled objects. Even the margins contain more labeled pictures. Those familiar with Richard Scarry's word books will recognize this format. In the back of each book is a foreign language/English dictionary.

On every page of *The First Thousand Words* a little yellow duck is hiding. Finding this duck fascinates my children—more than learning the target words, to be frank.

Since the format for each hardbound book is identical from language to language, if your child can follow the book for one language he can easily pick up the written rudiments of another. In either case, these adorably-illustrated picture-word books are a great first exposure to a foreign language.

These books, while wonderful for teaching vocabulary, have not been so great for teaching children how to *say* the words. Among other things, the pronunciation guides in the back of each book were designed with British youngsters in mind. Thus, you are told to pronounce the French *non* as "naw," which in American sounds nothing like the French word!

To remedy this, Usborne has launched an edition of *The First Thousand Words in Spanish,* with an accompanying cassette tape including words from the book and some music as well. This long-overdue tape at least triples the usefulness of *The First Thousand Words*. We hope tapes for the other languages will also soon be forthcoming.

For follow-up vocabulary development for the preteen crowd, the new Usborne **Beginner's Dictionary** in French, German, Italian, or Spanish is just wonderful. These fully-illustrated, full-color, witty picture dictionaries group vocabulary words together in context or by word type. Thus the numbers are all on one page, with a picture of a man holding many balloons. Body parts (no genitals) and things you do with your body are all shown on another two-page spread. Each noun, action, or phrase is clearly labeled in both English and the target language. The English-target language word list in the back of the perfect-bound book also gives a rough pronunciation for each word. (Too bad the pronunciations weren't alongside the words in the book itself; this would have made it a lot more useful for use by parents and students who are not fluent speakers of the target language.) You could easily use these dictionaries as the heart of a vocabulary-development course, after running the kids through some simple introduction to the language. This is also a really quick way for adults who once took, but never used, the language to brush up on our vocabulary—and learn some new words, too! *Mary Pride*

Audio-Forum has done it again. They continue to supply our children with high quality, introductory foreign language teaching aids.

The **Winko Teddy Bear** package includes an audiocassette tape and 78 oversized flashcards.

Winko Teddy Bear introduces your young child to Spanish (or French, or German, depending on which set you get) in a playful atmosphere. Your child is greeted with a story about Winko, the Spanish-speaking teddy bear. Winko is found in an attic by children that teach Winko to do many things he doesn't already know how to do. In return, Winko teaches the

Usborne Vocabulary books

Grades preK–8. The First Hundred Words, $8.95. The First Hundred Words Sticker Book, $7.95. The First Thousand Words, $12.95. Beginner's Dictionary (French, German, Italian, or Spanish), $10.95 each. Usborne Essential Guides series: Essential Dictionaries (German and French), $6.95 each. Shipping extra. *EDC Publishing, Division of Educational Development Corporation, 10302 East 55th Place, Tulsa, OK 74146. (800) 475-4522. Fax: (800) 747-4509. Web: www.edcpub.com.*

Accompanying sticker books are now available

NEW!
Winko Teddy Bear series

Grades K–6. Each set, $21.95. Available in Spanish, French, and German. Shipping extra. *Audio-Forum, Dept. W, 96 Broad St., Guilford, CT 06437. (800) 243-1234. Fax: (203) 453-9774. Email: info@audioforum.com. Web: www.audioforum.com.*

children Spanish (or French, or German). The flashcards are used in unison with the latter part of the tape. The most commonly used phrases, nouns, and verbs are on the illustrated flashcards. The target language words as well as the English words are pronounced on the tape for your child. The tape is easy to follow.

Trying to keep all of the flashcards in the proper order might prove to be difficult for a younger child, but with parental supervision, this should not be a problem. *Maryann Turner*

NEW!
Words for the World

Grades 1–8. $23.50 postpaid (includes book and cassettes).
Comprehensive Language Communications, 811 Old Valley Way, Houston, TX 77094. Phone/fax: (281) 398-8815. Email: full5quiver@juno.com. Web: www.home-school.com/HSMall/ COLC/COLC.html. Server is case sensitive.

NEW!
World of Language audiocassette series

Grades preK–3. Each audiocassette/book combo, $7.95. Going to Grandma's video, $14.95. Shipping extra.
Worldkids Press, 5900 Sussex, Troy, MI 48098. Orders: (800) 824-2184. Inquiries: (248) 641-8115. Fax: (248) 641-8115. Email: wkds@ix.netcom.com. Web: www.webpub.com/worldkids.

Words for the World is a beautiful full-color hardbound book with charming illustrations introduces children to the language and cultures of France, Spain, Italy, the Soviet Union, Germany, Norway, Holland, and Sweden. Accompanying eight-cassette set in sturdy binder teaches basic phrases and Bible verses in each language. Super introduction to foreign languages for young kids. Nothing like it anywhere else. A great bargain; highly recommended. *Mary Pride*

Although not quite a real introduction to foreign languages, the **World of Language audiocassette series** are entertaining and amusing. However, if you are interested in a particular foreign language, you will not necessarily find that language in all of the sets. German, French, Italian, Hebrew, Japanese, Swedish, Polish, Hungarian, Russian, Spanish, Portuguese, Hawaiian, Arabic, Swahili, Korean, and Greek are among the languages that appear in at least one of the sets.

The **Around the World series** focuses on traditional celebrations, such as Christmas, birthdays, and visits to Grandma's. While the main goal is not to stress the spiritual value or origins of these feasts, the focus is more on customs around the world. In some places, Christmas is a predominantly Christian holiday. In America, it is not. *Going to Grandma's* includes a few interesting facts about each featured country. A video of *Going to Grandma's,* which won the *1998 Parents' Choice Approval* Honors Award, is now available.

The **Bible Story series** tells favorite Bible stories and gives historical information which make them more interesting. However, there are a few small inaccuracies, like calling Judah a city rather than a region or tribe. There is also an unnecessary comment that Saul probably suffered from some form of mental disorder.

The **Sing, Color, 'n Say series** consists of an audiocassette tape plus a 32-page coloring book. Tapes are about 25 minutes per side, with side two being exactly the same as side one. The songs are mostly folksy. First your child listens to the sing-along song, follows along with the words in the coloring book, and learns to sing the easy-to-remember song. As your child colors, he learns fun facts about people and places around the world. Then he will learn to pronounce the theme phrase in several different languages. A pronunciation guide is included. *Anne Brodbeck and Maryann Turner*

French Only

The Carden Educational Foundation provides training and textbooks to scores of private Carden schools around the country. These are based on the philosophy of its founder, Miss Mae Carden, a Christian woman of great energy and spirit. Like good private schools of the days gone by, Carden schools offer French courses. For preschool, it's **French for the Young Child**. Grades kindergarten and 1 study **French for the Elementary School**, while grades 2–5 have **Le Français pour les Éleves Americains**. Starting in grade 6, French literature and serious grammar study is introduced.

Although I have not yet had the chance to see these materials, if they are at all like the other Carden materials you will find serious study for children presented in a way that challenges and respects them.

Carden materials were all designed for classroom use, meaning that the teacher's manuals are not the simplest books to zip through. If you can't attend Carden Basic Training, you will be well-advised to obtain the teacher instruction cassettes for subjects and grades you want to teach, as these will greatly enhance your ability to get the most out of Carden materials.

For more information, see the writeup for Carden Educational Foundation in the Curriculum Buyers' Guide of Volume 1. *Mary Pride*

Carden Educational French Courses
Grades 1–6. French for the Young Child, $9.95. Manual, $17.80. Cassette, $9. French Songs for the Younger Children (lyrics only), $4.85. French for the Elementary School, $9.95. Manual, $15.15. Cassette, $13. Le Français pour les Éleves Americains, $9.95. Manual, $18.45. 2 Cassettes, $22. Shipping extra.
Carden Educational Foundation, PO Box 659, Brookfield, CT 06804. (860) 350-9885 Fax: (860) 354-9812. Email: carden@cardenschool.org. Web: www.cardenschool.org.

Spanish Only

It is easy and fun to learn everyday children's vocabulary while singing and playing 12 traditional songs and nursery games. An Argentine teacher and her class sing quite nicely on the 15-minute cassette tape. **Arroz con Leche** comes with a comb-bound 32-page song book with the words, music and directions for playing the games. The songs are sung and printed in Spanish and loosely translated into English. You can hear the local color, for *se comen los eses:* some of the s's are only lightly hinted at, not clearly pronounced, but the Spanish is still easily understood. *Anne Brodbeck*

NEW!
Arroz con Leche
Grades K–4. $17.95 plus shipping.
Audio-Forum, division of Jeffrey Norton Publishers, Inc. 96 Broadstreet, Guilford, CT 06437. (800) 243-1234. Fax: (203) 453-9774. Email: info@audioforum.com. Web: www.audioforum.com.

Canta Conmigo is authentic Mexican folk music, with Mariachi-style band and singing with clearly pronounced Spanish. It's also one of the best reasonably priced extra resources for Spanish language learning available.

I love CDs and cassettes of authentic music to take in the car on long rides. The time not only passes quickly but we learn so much of the authentic language usages, idioms and patterns, intonations, and inflections.

The Canta Conmigo series now includes two volumes. Included in Volume 1 of this series is a teacher's guide, song book, and

NEW!
Canta Conmigo
Ages 2–adult. Each CD, $17. Each audiocassette, $17. Shipping extra. *Niños, PO Box 1603, Secaucus, NJ 07096-1603. (800) 634-3304. Fax: (201) 583-3644.*

cassette or CD. The songs are divided into 13 learning songs, two listening songs, five traditional Mexican favorites, and two advanced Spanish learning songs. Also included is a charmingly related folk tale—in English—that Mexicans tell to explain the appearance of two mountains near Mexico City. I wish that the folk tale had been told in Spanish. Some may object to reflections of the ancient Aztec culture in the tale, while others will rejoice in them. *Anne Brodbeck*

NEW!
Spanish for Gringos

Grades 3 and up (younger children with parents). $14.95 plus shipping.
Production Associates, 1206 W. Collins Ave., Orange, CA 92867. (800) 535-8368. Fax: (714) 771-2456. Email: mikecash@worldnet.att.net.

Even with the included 51-minute video and 24-page pamphlet, **Spanish for Gringos** is not a year's worth of Spanish classes. But if you need to go to Latin America and only have five hours or so to prepare, this might be just what you need.

The *profesor* (Spanish for teacher) says "This is Real Spanish," not classroom grammar or dialogue drills. You learn only the basics, but not street Spanish, slang, or haphazardly chosen vocabulary. Profesor Bill Harvey gives techniques for building vocabulary, and demonstrates usage, but not in a dry boring academic formula. He uses humor—OK, silliness—to get the idea across as briefly and painlessly as possible. Watching the video about three times should not be difficult, and with a few additional hours of practice, you should have the basics. *Anne Brodbeck*

NEW!
Spanish Made Fun

Grades K–6. Course 1 with test packet (includes reproducibles & 6 cassettes), $55. Methods and Techniques, $2. Tricky Words and Travel Tips, $2. Reproducible Activity Calendar, $5.
Spanish Made Fun, PO Box 35832, Tulsa, OK 74153. (918) 665-8245. Web: www.trisms.com.

Ready for a one-year Spanish course with a lot of unusual features? Such as the "talking fruits" that occasionally show up in the dialogues. And tips for travelers, suggestions from missionaries and teachers, and tons of activities.

Written and illustrated by homeschooling moms, **Spanish Made Fun** has a Christian perspective. It also has a lot of "stuff"—the hefty loose-leaf notebook (150 pages) comes with six cassettes in a special binder, many duplicating sheets for flash cards, activity sheets, and vocabulary lists, plus a very complete teacher's guide and a good resource list. There are songs, many ideas for games, and other projects like telling time and restaurant service. Especially designed for parents teaching young children, this course is a useful resource for adults learning the language, too. Course 2 is now available. *Anne Brodbeck*

NEW!
Spanish Songs for Children

Grades K–6. $14.95 plus shipping.
Audio-Forum, division of Jeffrey Norton Publishers, Inc. 96 Broadstreet, Guilford, CT 06437. (800) 243-1234. Fax: (203) 453-9774. Email: info@audioforum.com. Web: www.audioforum.com.

If you're looking for folksy little songs that will encourage your children to learn more Spanish, this **Spanish Songs for Children** tape is for you. There are 16 songs on one cassette as well as the lyrics in Spanish, of course.

So what do Spanish children sing about? Shepherds who move their sheep from pasture to pasture, a mother who washes her baby's clothes in the river, a little girl who prays over her doll who has caught a cold and then tries to put the doll to sleep by adding numbers, and a Spanish version of "London Bridge is Falling Down" are just a few.

There is no English translation, so keep your dictionary handy. Also, remember that these songs are meant for younger children, so your teens may find them less than exciting. *Marla Perry*

If you're looking for glitz, tinsel, professional mood music backgrounds, and a va-va-voom brochure, you came to the wrong place. But if all you want is to give your children (and maybe yourself) an inexpensive, simple, excellent elementary Spanish course with biblical content, **Speedy Spanish** may interest you!

The Bechtel family, who have homeschooled and who attend many West Coast conventions as Christian Light representatives, have put together a really fine course here. I'm not talking about the graphics; all you get is basic typewriter-and-photocopy quality in the manual. I'm not talking about the accompanying cassettes, either; these are strictly bare-bones here's-the-words-in-English-and-Spanish. But the 36 lessons of **Speedy Spanish** have what it takes to teach you over 500 vocabulary words, many basic phrases, basic grammar, Spanish Bible songs, and Spanish Bible verses.

With the cassettes, Speedy Spanish is self-teaching and self-correcting. You get a total of 30 lessons plus six review lessons. Each lesson introduces about a dozen new words and is planned to take one school week. On Monday, you look at the words and practice with the tape. On Tuesday, you read sentences in English and practice them in Spanish with the tape, learning Spanish sentence structure. On Wednesday, you do a matching exercise. First you color and cut out the vocabulary cards for the week. These are printed on the same paper as the rest of the manual, so you will want to laminate them, or at least cover them with clear contact paper, to make them last longer. You then put the vocabulary cards in the Word Bank until Friday. Thursday is Memory Day. Now it's time to memorize your Spanish Bible verse and song for this week. On Friday you review and play "Quiznish," matching your vocabulary cards to the game chart included for that lesson. After five lessons, the review lesson gives you a chance to master the extra vocabulary words you have been picking up in your Bible verses and songs.

Speedy Spanish II adds more than new vocabulary words. students learn conjugation of verbs and translation. They also begin writing Spanish sentences. Both *Speedy Spanish I* and *II* are perfect-bound books so they lay flat nicely.

The Bechtels' Spanish background includes three years of Spanish study, one year teaching three third-grade Spanish classes, three adopted children from Guatemala, and a son who is a missionary in Guatemala. As far as this non-Spanish speaker can tell, the accent on the tapes certainly sounded authentic. And the price is quite inexpensive for a program that will really get you started on this language. *Mary Pride*

Modern Greek

Here is a treasure chest of age-graded materials for learning modern Greek. For the adult, *Modern Greek*, Parts I and II is used by high schools, colleges, and universities as a two-year course. Learn the language yourself and you can then teach it to the kids! Preschool Greek resources include **I Learn by Coloring** (133 drawings which introduce the Greek alphabet), and **Preschool Reader** (one letter per lesson, leading up to a 130-word preschool vocabulary). Primers, readers, tests, tapes, and workbooks are also available for grades 1–7. *Mary Pride*

Speedy Spanish: Elementary Spanish Book

Grades 1–12. $12.95. Set of 4 90-minute tapes, $32.95. Book II, $12.95. Set of 5 90-minute tapes, $40.95. Tests and keys, $4. Shipping extra.
Speedy Spanish, 36107 SE Squaw Mt. Rd., Estacada, OR 97023. Orders: (888)621-3293. Inquiries/Fax: (503) 630-4606.

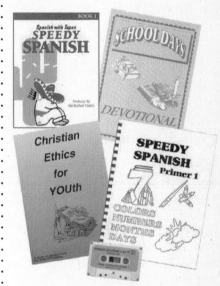

Speedy Spanish and two other books by the same publisher

Papaloizos Publications Greek Resources

Grades preK–college. Modern Greek Part 1: text, $15; workbooks, $5; set of 8 cassette tapes, $32. Modern Greek Part 2: text, $13; workbook, $5; set of 6 cassettes, $26. I Learn by Coloring, $6. Preschool Reader: text, $7; workbook, $5; cassette, $5. Grade level sets of readers and workbooks, $11/grade. Shipping extra.
Papaloizos Publications, Inc., 11720 Auth Lane, Silver Spring, MD 20902. (301) 593-0652. Fax: (301) 681-3390.

NEW!
Say, Sing, and Sign video series

Ages 3–adult. Each video, $14.95. ABC CD set, $14.95. Shipping extra.

Production Associates, 1206 W. Collins Ave., Orange, CA 92867. (800) 638-4397. (714) 771-6519. Fax: (714) 771-2456. Email: mikecash@worldnet.att.net.

Timberdoodle Sign Language Materials

All ages. Signs For His Glory: Complete course, $55; Standard workbook, $12; Children's workbook, $11; Little one's workbook, $8. Sign With Me: Volumes 1 & 2, $48 each. The Joy of Signing: Book, $22; Video series, $295. Shipping extra.

Timberdoodle, E. 1610 Spencer Lake Road, Shelton, WA 98584. (360) 426-0672. Fax: (360) 427-5625. Web: www.timberdoodle.com.

Sign Language

The **Say, Sing, and Sign** video tape series is so much fun, you may never want to sing again without signing along! You will learn six to nine American Sign Language (ASL) songs centered around a specific theme, each ranging from 20 to 30 minutes. The range of songs start from ABC basics to colors, numbers, Mother Goose and other children's rhymes, animals, patriotic, and Christmas carols and hymns.

The series includes 10 videos, each teaching 100 to 200 words and word phrases. The ABC video is the exception, since it focuses on learning the alphabet and words associated with them. This video is 45 minutes long and has an accompanying booklet. A music CD includes all of the songs from the series, for those of you who want to sign without the video teacher's help.

Four different instructors appear, each with his or her own style of signing instruction. The pace is comfortable as they define, sing and sign, and review. The setting is creatively put together with colorful backgrounds, with sound effects and singers to accompany you.

Beware! You'll never know what style of music will be used with the songs. These tapes are geared toward children, so for the most part, you will get children pleasantly singing background with acoustic guitar. Once in a while, you will get zinged with some funky blues or rock and roll. The song selections are excellent, except for a Halloween counting song on the *Songs Volume 1* video, which counts jack-o-lanterns, witches, skeletons, and ghosts. "The Snowman's Hat" on the *Colors* video is another odd one. The song was too long and it seemed to focus on the teacher's dance moves, instead of her signing. One other problem was the amateur use of lighting and camera angles in the *Colors and Nursery Rhymes* videos. I felt as if I were on rough waters at sea. Apart from these discrepancies, the videos were professionally and tastefully done for the children's market.

As a series or individually used, *Say, Sing, and Sign* videos would be a creative way to spice up your ASL class and get your students motivated to put their newly learned language to use. *Toni Clark*

Deb Deffinbaugh of **Timberdoodle** says that research indicates "babies who learn to sign can communicate at an earlier age than those who learn verbal communication alone." Interesting. And to help you learn this wonderfully expressive form of communication, the Deffinbaughs offer a wide array of sign language materials for use in your homeschool.

Signs For His Glory is a complete course that teaches over 500 signs using the included workbook and two videos. **Sign With Me** takes a secular approach to teaching sign language, while **The Joy of Signing** provides a thorough instruction in American Sign Language. *Mary Pride*

PART 5

Math

Playing chess is a great way to build mathematical thinking skills. Homeschoolers Matthew Peterson, here at age 5, and David Peterson, at 10, of Manukau Heights, New Zealand, won awards at the Papatoetoe Junior Chess Tournament. Matthew, who was by far the youngest contestant in the tournament, played against and beat many teenagers to win fifth place. David also faced older opponents on his way to winning third place.

Barnum Software hosts an annual national speed math tournament. Here are two more homeschooled winners. Daniel Fry participated in the Second Grade tournament and placed second out of 125 students nationwide. Alex Fry competed at the Fourth Grade Level in two |topics—he placed third out of 35 students in mixed problems and first out of 126 students in multiplication facts.

CHAPTER 24

Math Manipulatives

You can study math three ways:
(1)   Manipulating the *numbers*.
(2)   Manipulating *theoretical abstractions* such as *sets* and *subsets*.
(3)   Manipulating *manipulatives*.

The Old Math: Math by the Numbers

The old-fashioned way of teaching math worked this way. First, you taught a child to count. Then you taught him the "math facts"—that one plus one equals two, two plus two equals four, and so on. Typically at this stage the child worked lots of pages of problems illustrated with pictures of one duck plus one duck equalling two ducks, etc. When he had learned all the addition and subtraction math facts up to nine plus nine equals eighteen, you introduced him to skip counting by 2's, 3's, 4's, and so on. This laid the foundation for multiplication and division, which were also taught as sets of "math facts" up to the point of two-digit-and-up multiplication problems and long division, which were taught as a series of steps to be memorized. Next came fractions, demonstrated on paper by pies and rectangles divided into appropriate portions, and decimals and percents.

Children were expected to learn all this with the aid of workbooks and flashcards alone. Math was presented as a series of computational exercises, each building logically on what came before. Most work was done with the numbers themselves: the pure abstractions of value. "Word problems" were seen as applications of the principles already taught in math class.

The New Math: Math by the Sets

In the mid-Sixties, a number of math eminences proclaimed that the old-fashioned "rote" method of teaching math wasn't working well enough. "Children taught this way lack true understanding of math," they moaned. "We need to teach children to think like mathematicians!"

In practice, this meant that instead of studying concepts like *one* and *two,* little children were exposed to "the set of one object" and "the set of two objects." Instead of proceeding logically from computational skill to computational skill, kids wandered in a wilderness of subsets and Venn diagrams.

How to Make Your Own Manipulative-Based Curriculum

Creative Math Concepts K–4
Grades K–4. $4 postpaid. *Creative Teaching Associates, PO Box 7766, Fresno, CA 93747. Orders: (800) 767-4282. Fax: (559) 291-2953. Email: cta@psnw.com. Web: www.mastercta.com.*

If you'd like to develop your own math program for the elementary years based largely on games and manipulatives, Creative Teaching Associates, a publisher of math games and manipulatives, can accommodate you. **Creative Math Concepts K–4** contains (1) a step-by-step review of each math concept your child must learn, (2) suggested activities you can do around the house, and (3) brief lists, where appropriate, of Creative Teaching Associates games that help with a particular concept. The slim booklet makes it really easy to figure out where your child is mathematically and what should come next. Pre-math teaching steps are generally spelled out; for higher levels, you need to either know how to teach the concept, or buy the suggested games. *Mary Pride*

New New Math = Know No Math

Mathematics, so chivalrously called the queen of the sciences, is being neutered into "math appreciation."

A major explicit goal of the National Council of Teachers of Mathematics (NCTM) is elimination of the "gender and non-Asian minority gaps" that widen as the math curriculum advances. Recent assessments, such as a 1996 study of fourth-, eighth-, and twelfth-graders in California, show that while overall performance is at a standstill or sliding backward, boys and girls have begun to do equally badly in math. The NCTM's 258-page "Curriculum and Evaluation Standards for School Mathematics," which has been undergoing implementation since its publication in 1989, makes the tactics of this crippling strategy clear:

Verbalization and visualization of problem solving. Real mathematical thinking may be preverbal or postverbal or subverbal or supraverbal, but in any case it is definitely not "word processing." Teachers now require pupils to write out in words how they get their answers. The parents' group Honest Open Logical Debate (HOLD) reports that "teachers in middle and high school are actively discouraging the use of mathematical symbolism and penalizing students who write correct but short mathematical arguments using such notation." This is equivalent to penalizing those with any genuine mathematical gift, while rewarding those without, especially girls, who studies have shown process math better verbally than abstractly, i.e., directly. Similarly, using pictures instead of numbers also sidesteps the basic abstraction of mathematics.

A parent named Charles L. Beavers (on the Internet at *www.intres.com/math/*) recently confronted an educrat named Ruth Parker who came before her school district with a "New New Math" trick called the "Turkey Problem." Briefly, the problem could be, and in the past would have been, solved by establishing that a ratio between the known amount and fraction equals the ratio between the unknown amount (x) and fraction and then solving for x. This method, Beavers pointed out, always works, no matter what the amounts and fractions involved. Parker's solution, which diagrammed the problem as nine little circles which the student then divides up physically into a jumble of half-circles and quarter-circles ultimately adding up to x, "works, graphically, for one carefully chosen problem" only. Parker refused to discuss Beavers' observation, suggesting he get input from schoolchildren if he were "curious."

"The problem with the ratio method, and standard methods in general, is not that they don't work," comments Beavers. "Indeed, they have immense mathemati-

cal power. The problem is that too few people, including many elementary teachers who explain them to our children, understand the simple mathematical manipulations behind the methods." He is too kind. If fools have been sent to teach math to our children, they have been sent knowingly and with malice.

Traditionalist Marianne M. Jennings laments in her critique of the new algebra curriculum (*Wall Street Journal*, December 17, 1996) that current textbooks "have all but eliminated numbers. . . . By taking the math out of math, educators have stripped the discipline of its beauty." While it may be true that most of us "innumerate" masses will never revel in the sheer joy of number theory or bask in the reflected glory of Fermat's elusive Final Theorem, that beauty is the heart of the mathematical enterprise. Never to glimpse it is to live in a kind of twilight; to be taught to not look for it is a crime against human nature.

Use of manipulatives. These are basically toys of various kinds—counters, cubes, sticks, marbles, grids, and so on. Even the NCTM admits in its Standards that manipulation of manipulatives is incapable of proving any mathematical proposition, yet it advocates such a hands-on approach well into the fifth grade.

This approach is closely related to verbalization/visualization in that it is innumerate, antitheoretical, anticonceptual, and anti-abstract. Remember the multiplication principle, or basic set theory? To determine the total possible number of sets of certain variables, one multiplied the quantity of the first group of variables and the quantity of each other group. But not any more. Now students are instructed to make an "organized list." This means writing down, line after line, all the possible combinations of variables, after which you add them all up. This chore may then be followed by the manipulative exercise of coloring and cutting and pasting little paper representations of your sets, which are not of course called "sets." Math is now a lot of dull busywork.

William G. Quirk, a Connecticut software consultant and former university math teacher, has battled the math establishment for years on these issues. He has posted what he calls "The Truth About the NCTM Standards" on the Internet (*www.webcom.com/~wgquirk/welcome.html*) and has this to say about manipulatives: "Prolonged reliance on concrete 'pacifiers' interferes with the most important social reason for studying math, the development of the average citizen's ability to think abstractly." It does indeed. Are we beginning to get the idea that the average citizen's ability to think abstractly is not something ardently desired by those in positions of authority?

by Marian Kester Coombs

Repetition. The same ground is covered in grade after grade, especially in elementary school. The "organized list" business, for instance, has been handed my children in both second and fourth grade, without any conceptual difference between the presentations. My fourth grader, by no means a math whiz (possibly thanks to the new mathless math), was instantly able, however, to grasp real set theory, remember it, and apply it; so the rationale that "kids aren't ready for it" is not supportable.

Guess and check. Otherwise known as trial and error, this "strategy" says brightly (actual example): "Sometimes you can solve a problem by identifying two conditions. You can guess at an answer that satisfies Condition 1. Then you can check to see whether your guess also satisfies Condition 2." Sometimes students can stumble upon the solution, too, if they recognize it as such. How many diagonals can be drawn inside a four-sided figure? Guess. Four? Okay, draw them. No, only two. What about a pentagon? Five? Three? Yes, five. A hexagon? Six! No, nine. And so on. Guess, then draw the tiny lines. The teacher told my fourth grader, "There's a formula for this, but I don't remember what it is, and you don't need to know it."

"Everyday problems" or "real-world" math. The New New Math argues that math instruction must be related to everyday life and practical solutions. They call this a switch from "skills orientation" to "meaning orientation." Arithmetic does of course help children tell time, make change, count their Halloween candy, and so forth. But as William Quirk points out, "Most math has no 'everyday' application." Mathematics is an abstraction that exists solely as a result of human mentation. "Who will build those bridges in the 21st century?" asks Quirk. "Right now, it looks like the Asians."

Teamwork vs. individual effort. Used sparingly, the team approach can be an exhilarating change of pace within the school day as well as a valid means of arriving at new knowledge. In the context of the New New Math, though, it is just another means of devaluing the concept of a teacher teaching objective facts and skills to students who need to pay attention and learn, memorize and practice them in order to get—yes!—the correct answer. The theory behind having teams of ignorant students wrack their empty little brains to arrive at estimated approximate solutions is called "constructivism" or "discovery" learning. Needless to say, since the teacher is no longer conveying a body of knowledge but presiding over a vague "discovery process," the testing of these "discoveries" is necessarily problematic and to be avoided.

Perhaps the most disturbing statement in the NCTM's entire document is this: "Students might like mathematics but not display the kinds of attitudes and thoughts identified by this standard. For example, students might like mathematics yet believe that problem solving is always finding one correct answer using the right way. . . . Although such students have a positive attitude toward mathematics, they are not exhibiting the essential aspects of what we have termed mathematical disposition."

Most students who "like mathematics" do so precisely because it offers a "right way" to arrive elegantly at the "correct answer." The NCTM seems to be implying that such students are in need of "disposition" modification. And it seems to be imposing just that upon our hapless young.

Forget memorization. The NCTM Standards call for a curriculum focused "on the development of understanding, not on the rote memorization of formulas." Here is proof positive these folk do not know what thinking is. The content of human memory is what "thought" operates upon: no content, no operation. It's like trying to open a computer file without an application program. Without stored knowledge of facts, sense cannot be made of past or current experience: there is literally nothing for "understanding" to build with. To downplay memory is to disable the brain itself. According to Jack Youngblood, a teacher who advocates the Kumon method to undo the damage of public school math, "You can't teach 'concepts' without teaching *math*."

Use of calculators. Astonishingly, the NCTM Standards declare, "There is no evidence to suggest that the availability of calculators makes students dependent on them for simple calculations." Do math educators never witness the agonies of young cashiers when the register goes down? The Council promotes calculators in the classroom and proclaims they have transformed the way math is understood; they have freed humanity from the need to compute; we can now forget about number facts and concentrate on "meaning." Meanwhile, even with calculators, American students trail the industrialized world in math, and they not only can't do sums but don't know what they "mean," either.

Excerpted from an article originally published under the title "Dumb and Number" (Chronicles: A Magazine of American Culture, *October 1997). Used by permission.*

Chronicles: A Magazine of American Culture *is a publication of The Rockford Institute, 928 N. Main St., Rockford, IL 61103, (815) 964-5054, rkfdinst@bossnt.com. I've subscribed for years.*

Why the eminences decided that *set theory,* rather than, say, topology, or a dozen other mathematical disciplines, was what kids needed in order to "think mathematically," we may never know. Or why in order to "think mathematically" it was felt necessary to expose kids to an added layer of abstraction at an age when all research shows they do best with simple memorization of facts.

The upshot was predictable: the New Math was a disaster. Parents, who had never studied math this way, could no longer help kids with their math homework. This was a major complaint, because the kids needed major help with that homework. Instead of morphing into mathematical geniuses, kids exposed to a strict diet of New Math couldn't even do the simple computations that used to be the backbone of math class.

New Age Math: Strategize and Grow Confused

Hating to admit they were totally wrong, the math eminences decided to hang on to the theory that children should learn to think like mathematicians. Flash cards and memory work were allowed back into the curriculum, thanks to heavy public pressure. But there was no return to the simple step-by-step math classes of the olden days. Instead, all sorts of extras were injected into the math curriculum:

- **Smaller doses of set theory** (the New Math, trimmed down)
- **An emphasis on "problem-solving,"** meaning "thinking about strategies for solving math problems" or even "holding group meetings to discuss strategies for solving math problems" as opposed to "knowing the math needed to solve the problems"
- **More kiddie geometry** with geoboards and tangrams
- **Using calculators** to solve problems Grandma solved in her head
- **Math videos**
- **Math puppets**
- **Math manipulatives** by the bagful

Somehow, again, the eminences have missed the boat. Math isn't about "strategizing to solve problems." It's about *solving* problems. In the real world, the only people who are paid to "strategize" about math problems are the Ph.D.'s who invent new algorithms for code encryption and decryption, or who create search strategies for databases. Everyone else *uses* the techniques that *already exist* to solve their math problems. And learning corporate groupthink methods prepares you for nothing, except life as a minor character in the *Dilbert* cartoon strip.

But this cloud has a silver lining. Now that the National Council of Teachers of Mathematics hath decreed, in its new set of standards for how math shalt be taught, that Math Manipulatives Shall Be Used With Children of All Ages, we have a plethora of inexpensive hands-on math devices to choose from.

Math Manipu-What?

Math manipulatives are those colorful little sticks, blocks, and cubes sold to schools. Manipulatives are supposed to spark "discovery" learning. By handling the objects, children theoretically figure out arithmetic patterns for themselves.

My father taught me math through the eighth grade level by the time I was seven years old. He didn't use any manipulatives, just an experimental set of workbooks written by a colleague of his at Boston College. (I'm sorry; I don't know what the name of these workbooks is or how to find a set anywhere. If I did, I'd certainly recommend them!) *After* I had already learned all this math from my father, the well-meaning teachers at my school made me spend hours playing with Cuisenaire rods. What I learned from this experience is:

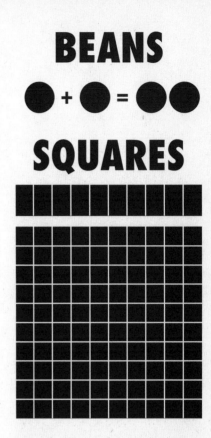

(1) **If you're an abstract thinker, you don't need fancy manipulatives** to learn math. They can even be an irritant, if the teacher insists you work out problems with them, instead of using paper or doing the problem in your head, both of which are much faster.

(2) **However, they are fun play toys** for building and making pattern pictures with.

(3) As far as "mathematical thinking" goes, **I enjoyed my books of math riddles more**, and got more out of them.

Since then, I have also learned that

(4) In the hands of a capable teacher, **math manipulatives are good for *demonstrating* how a math concept works**. But don't count on kids discovering all math by themselves using manipulatives. They'd rather build block towers. See (2) above.

The toughest thing to learn when first checking out math manipulatives is *which manipulative type is best suited to which topic*. Although you can, in theory, demonstrate just about any math concept with just about any math manipulative, it's a lot easier to teach place value with cubes and rods or an abacus than with snap cubes. It's easier to teach perimeter with a geoboard than with links. It's easier to teach fractions with fraction manipulatives than with pattern blocks. Keep this in mind. Crazed math teachers have spent months concocting curriculum encouraging the hapless novice to use the wrong manipulative to teach basic school topics. Enamored with their set of links or tangrams, they want to ensnare you in hours of pointless struggling, forcing the manipulative to fit the topic. The results are like substituting a radial arm saw for a screwdriver and vice versa. Much better to get the right tool for the job in the first place.

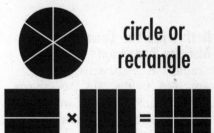

What Are My Choices?

The dazzling array of manipulatives settles out into just a few categories.

First, the "beans" programs. Lots and lots of similar items that kids count, arrange, or string together. Snap cubes. Links. Kitty-cat counters. Chips. Abacuses fit into this category, since they are basically beans on wires. These are used for demonstrating math facts the old-fashioned one: "See, one chip plus one chip equals two chips. If I divide six chips into groups of three, I'll have two groups, so six divided by three equals two."

Next, the "cubes" programs— rods and cubes used to teach base-10 concepts. Sometimes these snap together, sometimes they don't.

Third, fractions programs. You remember the classic fractions manipulatives—a pie shape cut into wedges. Newer fractions manipulatives come as transparent square overlays, so you can criss-cross the square marked in halves with the square marked in thirds to produce sixths, and so forth.

Fourth, the Hundred Board and its cousins. These are great for showing the patterns of numbers in our base-ten system, since a Hundred Board, is basically one hundred numbers arranged in rows of 10, like so: ----▶

1	2	3	4	5	6	7	8	9	10
11	12	13	14	15	16	17	18	19	20
21	22	23	24	25	26	27	28	29	30
31	32	33	34	35	36	37	38	39	40
41	42	43	44	45	46	47	48	49	50
51	52	53	54	55	56	57	58	59	60
61	62	63	64	65	66	67	68	69	70
71	72	73	74	75	76	77	78	79	80
81	82	83	84	85	86	87	88	89	90
91	92	93	94	95	96	97	98	99	100

Fifth, temperature-telling manipulatives (oversized cardboard or plastic thermometers with a red ribbon you adjust to indicate a particular temperature).

Sixth, time-telling manipulatives (clocks and calendars).

Seventh, geometric and pre-geometric manipulatives (pattern blocks, geoboards, etc.).

Eighth, weighing and measuring devices.

Ninth, funny money.

Tenth, everything that doesn't fit into the first nine categories!

Math Manipulatives of All Kinds

Beans. Links. Snap cubes. Counters. Poker chips. You can demonstrate numbers, counting, adding, subtracting, and other introductory math concepts with all or any of these.

You don't need instructions for how to make your own set of "beans." Use real beans! Or M&M's, or milk bottle tops, or pennies. Whatever you have on hand that is small, comes in a uniform size, and doesn't roll off the table will work.

Or you may prefer to buy your "beans," in order to get the teaching instruction or just because plastic is less edible than M&M's.

"Rod" programs are a bit harder to duplicate. In fact, unless you have exceptional woodworking skills and lots of time to waste, it's not worth even trying. Besides, math rods have additional play value as building toys, so you're really getting two products for the price of one.

These are a sampling of the different manipulative types available—including some of the most popular. Remember, all of them work best when used to *demonstrate* a concept. Solving hundreds of problems the slow way, with manipulatives, may actually *delay* abstract math skills.

Activities for Learning Abacus Programs

Grades 1–8. AL Abacus, $25. Abacus Activities, $18. Worksheets for Abacus, $25. Math Card Games, $18. Six decks of math cards for games, $20. Place Value Cards, $5. Base 10 Picture Cards, $2.50. Fraction charts, $6. Drawing Kit for Geometry, $12. Suffix Flow Charts, $4. Complete kit (all 10 items), $120. Shipping extra.
Activities for Learning, 129 SE 2nd Street, Linton, ND 58552-7118. (701) 254-0128. (800) 593-7030. Fax: (320) 587-0123.

Complete abacus-based elementary math calculations curriculum developed for her son by Dr. Joan A. Cotter, a lady with an impressive list of credentials. In 1980 she formed a company, Activities for Learning, and started publishing some of them. We're talking about doing math with an abacus and at the same time learning how all the math operations work.

The **Activities for Learning Abacus** is a very nice-looking piece of work, with its wooden frame, ten strong wires, and 100 beads. The beads come in your choice of three color combinations: purple and pink, purple and yellow, or blue and yellow. The price is definitely right, and you can also purchase both an activities book with pre-K through grade 6 activities and a volume of worksheets designed for use with the abacus and book.

More about **Activities for the Abacus**. This is the second edition (a good sign, since loser books never have second editions!). Like the worksheet books, it has an oversized spiral-bound format. This book is *very* complete. For example, in Unit Five, Introducing Subtraction, you get Simple Subtraction (oral subtraction, written subtraction, subtracting from 10, subtracting 1), Subtractions < 10 (subtracting tens, subtracting single-digit numbers, subtracting double-digit numbers), Subtraction Results (greater than, equal to, or less than; remainders and differences; subtraction twins; equations; checking), and Special Effects (minuend decreased by 1, subtrahend decreased by 1, counting up, and the complement method). This is just one of the 11 units, which cover everything from how to read the abacus and basic math concepts to fancy stuff like squares and percentages, millions on the abacus, and how to use both the Japanese and Chinese abacus. The associated worksheet volumes contain correlated exercises on both paper and the abacus.

Math Card Games is an oversized spiral-bound book with games for every math concept from numeration (we know this as "counting"!) through all four basic arithmetic operations, clocks, money, and fractions. You will need to get the six decks of special cards from Activities for Learning to play the games outlined in the book. These include **Basic Cards** (12 of each number from 0 to 10), **Product Cards** (numbers for products from 1 x 1 to 10 x 10), **Money Cards** (50 cards using 5 coins), **Corner Cards**, **Clock Cards** (24 cards with numbers from 1 to 12 and :00 to :55), and **Fraction Cards** (72 fraction cards and 20 percent cards).

Joan also has **Place Value Cards** (36 plastic cards for composing numbers from 1 to 9999 by overlapping) and **Base 10 Picture Cards** (87 pictures of the base 10 blocks, including 26 each of ones, tens, hundreds, and nine of the thousands).

All the Activities for Learning materials I've seen (and I've seen most of them) were *very* professionally done, nice to look at, durable, easy to follow, and even fun! Another great resource for kinesthetic learners. *Mary Pride*

Base Ten Fries is the next generation of base-ten manipulatives. What genius had the idea of taking bright yellow "ten rods" and packaging them by tens in bright red boxes that look like French-fry containers? Suddenly, the fear factor is gone and kids are highly motivated to play with the manipulatives!

The Starter Kit comes with 100 "ones," two sets of "tens" in the aforementioned bright red containers, and one flat "hundred," all packaged in a plastic fast-food-style container. The extension kit is a box with ten sets of "tens" in their red fry-style boxes.

Base Ten Fries Activities is designed for use with the two sets above. It covers all the basic math skills, plus place value, in its over 60 activities and games. Game pieces and answers are found in the back of this 138-page oversized reproducible book. *Mary Pride*

Given a choice from a box of new math products, my kids, aged 5 to 14, all wanted to play with the **Connecting People** first. The set includes a teacher's guide and 96 little plastic people (four sets of all possible combinations of four colors, three sizes, and two sexes). You've probably used this type of product before for sorting, counting, patterning, and multiplying activities, but these connect, so you can use them for measuring, and because they're people, they're perfect for story problems. The guide describes games to teach simple and advanced concepts (like probability).

The only drawback I can see to this product is that the little plastic people start taking on personalities, and then the younger ones will want to put them to bed, and make dollhouses, and . . . well, they might get lost. *Kim O'Hara*

SECOND OPINION: I'll second that! Kim never got all 96 little people, because *my* little people kept playing with them and refusing to put them back in the package. *Mary Pride*

Cuisenaire Rod Sets

Grades PreK–2. Jumbo Rods Set (154 with self-sorting tray), $64.50. Jumbo Rods Teacher Set (56 rods), $22.95. Cuisenaire Rods Intro Set (74 rods with wall poster and 36-page booklet in plastic tray), $10.25/plastic or $11.50/wood. Starter Set (155 rods with self-sorting tray and 36-page booklet), $35/plastic or $37.50/wood. Supplementary Trays of 155 rods, $17.50/plastic or $19.95/wood. 100-cm Rod Track, $5.50. 50-cm Rod Track, $3.25. Shipping extra. *Cuisenaire Company of America, 10 Bank Street, PO Box 5026, White Plains, NY 10602. (800) 237-0338. Fax: (800) 551-7637. Web: www.cuisenaire.com.*

> Reader Edith Best of Detroit, Michigan pointed out to me that Cuisenaire rods and Cuisenaire's Base Ten blocks "work just fine with Mortensen books and methods." I had come to the same conclusion independently, and feel it's worth repeating here, since the Cuisenaire materials cost far less than Mortensen.

Cuisenaire Snap Cubes

Grades K–6. Set of 100 (10 each of 10 colors), $13.95. Set of 500, $53. Set of 1000, $87.50. 1–100 Operational Board, $17.95. 100 Track, $32.95. 1–10 Stair, $7.95. Add 10% shipping. *Cuisenaire Company of America, 10 Bank Street, PO Box 5026, White Plains, NY 10602. (800) 237-0338. Fax: (800) 551-7637. Web: www.cuisenaire.com.*

Cuisenaire Rods are my favorite all-purpose math manipulatives for basic arithmetic operations. Their metric size (1 centimeter per side for the unit cube) and weight make them ideal for measuring and weighing activities. Their patented color-coding lets you tell a 4 from a 5 at a glance (not true of snap-together cubes, which you must count every time). Their shape and balance are wonderful for free play. Many of the best manipulative-oriented programs require the use of these rods.

Let me pause for just a moment to tell you what on earth we're talking about. Picture a unit cube. Color: natural (if wood) or white (if plastic). The 2 rod is red and twice as long. The 3 rod is light green and three times as long as the unit cube. And so on up to the orange 10 rod. None of the rods are marked in any way, save for their color, so you can call them ones, tens, *Xs*, or whatever.

Now perceive the beauty of this system. To show 5 + 5 = 10, I need merely take two yellow rods and show that their combined length is the same as an orange rod. If I were doing this with counters, unit cubes, color tiles, or snap-together cubes, I would first have to count out five items and then either group or snap them together. After repeating this process, I would then have to count the total number of items. That's about 19 steps more than the Cuisenaire rod approach requires—just for that one problem!

To make life even easier, use the 50 or 100 cm Rod Tracks. Here, to work the problem *6 x 7 = ?*, simply take either six black rods or seven dark green rods. Lay them end-to-end on the Rod Track and read off the answer: 42. Without a rod track, you would have to build a parallel rod of four orange 10 rods plus one red 2 rod to find that the answer was 42.

Since Cuisenaire rods come in one-centimeter multiples, and since that means the shorter rods are rather small, Cuisenaire Company has developed **Jumbo Rods**—and hidden them in a completely different section of the catalog than the section featuring regular Cuisenaire rods, which is why I'm going out of my way to tell you about them. Jumbo Rods are exactly double the length of Cuisenaire rods in each dimension, making the volume of a Jumbo Rod eight times the volume of its corresponding regular Cuisenaire rod. While the smaller Jumbo Rods are still too small to be safe around babies, they are just perfect for preschool and the early grades. Not too many accessories are available for Jumbo Rods, but it doesn't matter, since you'll mainly be using them to introduce the rods and do some simple math (and a *lot* of building!).

You can get by with just the **Teacher Set of Jumbo Rods** (a mere 56 rods packed loose in a box). For the regular-sized rods, you should get at least a dozen of each size. This means at least two Supplementary Trays. If you want the booklet *Idea Book for Cuisenaire Rods at the Primary Level* you need one Starter Set and one Supplementary Tray. If you can live without a self-sorting tray but you still want the *Idea Book*, three of the Introductory Sets will do you (this is the least expensive option). Rods are actually more accessible, though not as neat, in the unsorted trays.

All sorts of books and accessories are available for Cuisenaire rods, from sets of logic games and puzzles to pads of one-centimeter graph paper. My very favorite is still *Miquon Math* (see review next chapter). *Mary Pride*

Cuisenaire Company's new **Snap Cubes** are ¾" on all six sides. One side of each cube has a jutting circular peg; the other five sides have circular indentations into which a peg can fit. Thus, when the catalog tells you the cubes "connect on all six sides," know that it takes a certain amount of ingenuity to design solid constructions using these cubes.

Snap Cubes are the same size as Unifix cubes, and can be used in all the same ways. Snap them together end-to-end for counting and arithmetic manipulations. Additionally, you can snap them together into solids, which is useful for demonstrating squaring and cubing and for 3-D work. All sets, no matter how large or small, come with equal numbers of cubes in each of 10 colors. This is handy for demonstrating that 2 + 5 = 7, since your set of two snapped-together cubes and your set of five snapped-together cubes can be different colors.

Snap Cubes have brighter colors than Unifix cubes. They fit together (and stay together) beautifully. Since any two rows only connect at one point, these irresistible little building blocks are great for showing rotations, flips, and transformations of solid objects.

Cuisenaire Company has a group of accessories just for use with Snap Cubes. Of these, the products that look like they'd be of most interest in the home are:

- **The 1–100 Operational Board.** This is our old friend the Hundred Board, gridded so that a single Snap Cube (or Unifix cube, etc.) can fit over each numeral.
- **The 1–10 Stair** is a series of connected shallow trays, each topped with a numeral. The 1 stair only can hold one Snap Cube; the 2 tray can hold two; etc. Your child practices counting and numeral recognition by building the stair.
- **The 100 Track** is ingeniously designed so each ten-number section is a separate piece. Slide them together to form the track. Use the track to demonstrate that 17 + 8 = 25, or 4 x 9 = 36, or whatever your little heart desires. (I still feel that Cuisenaire rods and the Cuisenaire Rod Track are better suited to this work, since you don't have to count up and snap together cubes every time you want a 5 or a 9.) *Mary Pride*

Years ago Eunice Coleman, author of the Literacy Press's fine literary program, designed a math manipulative that is also a lovely room decoration and furthermore can be used to teach *every* arithmetic operation, even clocks, money, and fractions. No kidding.

The **Hundred Board**, Mrs. Coleman's invention, is a ten-by-ten grid with little color-coded sequentially numbered tags hanging off brass cup hooks. Starting with skip counting (e.g., counting by 2s, 5s, 6s, 10s), the **Early Math Literacy Packet** leads the student through addition, subtraction, multiplication, division, and even fractions, all using the Hundred Board. All no sweat, all high-interest. In Mrs. Coleman's classroom the children never lost a Hundred Board tag in eleven years and showed remarkable math gains in less time than you'd imagine.

Along with the manual and Hundred Board plans and ingredients you get three Continental Press workbooks (grades 1–3) and 30 blackline masters for Hundred Board seatwork. You have to provide the training to keep your littler ones from flinging the tags madly about the room. They are endlessly fascinating to children; our little ones' first math lessons include putting the tags back on the board in the right place! *Mary Pride*

Fun At the Beach is fuzzy and wonderful. You get a felt beach scene; five felt children of various races; ten each of beach buckets, toy boats, fish, starfish, shells, beach balls, and seals; symbols and numbers; three different sizes of the five basic shapes; nine nests with baby birds; twenty-five coconuts and two bunches of ten coconuts each for teaching place value. Oh, I forgot the five fraction circles. Along with this gloriously colorful stuff comes a short-and-sweet manual that explains how to teach counting, adding, subtracting, fractions, place value, multiplying, and dividing using the felt manipulatives. All very warm and cuddly and easy for little chil-

Early Math Literacy Packet
Grades K–3. Complete Kit (manual, 30 blackline masters, 100 printed but uncut tags, 100 brass cup hooks, 3 math workbooks, and Hundred Board kit instructions), $72.50. Custom handcrafted 20 x 25" Plywood Hundred Board, $33.50. Shipping extra.
Literacy Press, Inc., 24 Lake Drive, DeBary, FL 32713. (407) 668-1232.

Fun at the Beach
Ages 4–8. Complete set (including file box and flannelboard), $40.95. Felts only, $17.95. Felt Counting Set, $12.95. Shipping extra.
Sycamore Tree, 2179 Meyer Place, Costa Mesa, CA 92627. Orders: (800) 779-6750. Inquiries: (949) 650-4466. Fax: (800) 779-6750. Email: 75767.1417@compuserve.com. Web: www.sycamoretree.com.

dren to understand, not to mention marvelous *fun* for them to try! You will have to cut out the pieces; but to make up for your extra effort, a file box is included in the basic set, and along with the box you get flocked sheets with outlines of each shape, for easy storage. The felts are airbrushed and gorgeous. You will need a flannelboard to use with this set. *Mary Prid*

This fascinating new math tool shows kids how equations literally "balance out." It's a scale with pegs numbered 1–10 sticking out on the arms, and a base with more pegs for storing the included weights. Place a weight on 3 and a weight on 1 on one side; see that one weight on 4 on the other side balances it, proving 3 + 1 = 4. Feel more sophisticated? Try 32 divided by 5. After placing six weights on the pegs numbered five, you discover that the sixth weight is too much. Experimenting, you find that one extra 2 balances the scale—so 32 = 5 x 6 + 2.

You can hang a maximum of eight weights both fore and aft on the pegs for a number, thus proving combinations up to 80, or even more if you are creative. 99, for example, could be eight tens plus one nine plus two fives. You can also label the included stickers any way you like and place them on the provided spots on the backside of the scale, thus adding even more educational value. The little eight-page booklet suggests labeling the back side as fractions (¼, ½, ¾, etc.).

The **Invicta Math Balance** is durable, easy to set up and balance (just slide the little thingamajigs back and forth until the arms are horizontal), and made of excellent European plastic. It's self-checking, open-ended, and can be used to demonstrate every arithmetic operation in a very satisfying way.

The Balance Book (not included with the balance) is 94 pages of balance activities, presented as 5 x 8" tear-out task cards. These range from simple discoveries of what plus what equals what to more sophisticated problems like discovering which numbers can be balanced with exactly four weights. The book covers addition, multiplication, division, place value, problem solving, logic, and factoring. You need this book if you get the Invicta Math Balance. With both the book and the balance, you have an elementary math manipulative program that only lacks geometry. *Mary Pride*

Kitty Kat Counters are great for teaching numbers, colors, or just for replacement playing pieces in some game. Each set has five bags of little plastic kitty cats, each bag with a different color. About twenty counters per bag. Absolutely will not break. Believe me, my brothers and sisters have tested them. Use them to teach colors. "Find the blue one and I'll give you a cookie." (Cookies not included.) Or to teach math. "If I have 5 of these little whatever-they-ares and you take away 2, how many do I have left?"

Invicta Math Balance

Grades K–8. Invicta Math Balance, $24.95. Additional weights, $10.95. The Balance Book, Grades 2–8, $7.95. Shipping extra.
Cuisenaire Company of America, PO Box 5026, White Plains, NY 10602-5026. (800) 237-3142. or (914) 328-5487. Fax: (800) 551-7637. Email: info@awl.com. Web: www.cuisenaire.com.

NEW!
Kitty Kat Counters
Dinosaur Counters

Ages 3–7. Each set, $14.95 plus shipping.
Educational Insights, Inc., 16941 Keegan Ave., Carson, CA 90746. (800) 995-4436. (310) 884-2000. Fax: (800) 995-0506. Web: www.edin.com.

The kids will like these. Just don't lose them down the side of the couch or you may never see them again; they're only about ¾ of an inch tall. Also, they constitute a choking hazard. And they look like candy. So look out.

Dinosaur Counters are exactly the same; they just look like dinosaurs. For that little boy who just doesn't like "Kitty Kats" but would prefer a T-rex. *Joseph Pride*

The real problem with Mortensen is that it doesn't come organized into one easy-to-use-and-put-away set. **The Homeschool Kit** does come in one shipping box, but includes dozens of kits and books. There's so much to choose from! I imagine I'm not the first would-be buyer who has been paralyzed by all the choices. The thing to do is, first, forget for a minute about which basic rods set you are going to buy, and second, concentrate first on the specialty kits. We're going to look at them one by one.

Let's start with the inexpensive **Numeral ID Kit**. Your child can learn the numbers and numerals 1–10 with this kit. You get a molded plastic tray, into which the colorful rods fit in ascending order. The idea is to place the card with the right number under the rod to which it corresponds. The backs of the cards are color-coded to the rods, so the child can check his own work. When not in use, the rods and cards store neatly in their own pockets on the tray.

Next comes the **Number/Picture Fun Kit**. This really fun set has five molded plastic puzzles. Children fit the colorful plastic rods into the indentations on the puzzle trays in order to "fill in" the pictures (a palm tree, a camel, etc.). This familiarizes them with the rods and develops thinking skills and hand-eye coordination (puzzling is the ultimate pre-math activity). As a bonus, it turns out that the tray for each puzzle into which the loose pieces are stacked has a width corresponding to a different number. Puzzle 1 has units: puzzle 2 uses both units and twos; puzzle 3 uses units, twos, and threes; and so on. As children put away their puzzle pieces after a session, they discover that a "one" and a "one" fit into the same space as a "two."

Both the Number Discovery Kit and the Number/Picture Fun Kit come with outer plastic trays, in which you can store both the puzzles and all the number rods.

These two items are so colorful and exciting for little kids that you could give them as birthday gifts, no questions asked. They are designed for children between the ages of 3 and 8—toddlers under the age of 3 might be inclined to munch the smaller counting rods.

The **"-n-Stuff"** and **Smiley Face** series introduce the manipulatives. The "-n-Stuff" booklet asks children to fill in the bars and boxes in the pictures of boxes, animals, or vehicles with the correct manipulative. The Smiley Face series asks your child to either match a Mortensen Math symbol with the appropriate number (the *Counting* book) or do some simple multiplication (*Multiplication* book). Your child peels back the sticker of what he thinks is the right answer to see if the smiley face is underneath. The Smiley Face series requires very little writing.

The **Addition/Subtraction Kit** comes with a set of problem cards. You get the usual molded plastic tray, with indentations where you store the problem cards and bars, and two sets of unit bars (two each for the numbers 1–9). As in all the Mortensen materials, the 1 bars are all green, the 2 bars are orange, the 3 bars are pink, and so on, for easy recognition. At the bottom of the tray are two long grooves, in which you solve the problems using the unit bars. Say the problem is "8 + 4." You join the 8 bar to the 4 bar in one of the grooves. In the next groove is a 10 bar. You see that you need to add a 2 bar to the 10 bar to make a rod of equal length to 8 + 4.

Mortensen Math Manipulatives

Grades 1–8. Numeral ID Kit, $15.95. Number/Picture Fun Kit, $25.95. Addition/Subtraction Kit, $16. Very Basic Basic Operations Kit, $34.95. Combo Kit, 91.90. Curriculum Starter Kit: includes Combo Kit (with skip-count underlays), Home Fractions Kit, Multiple Tens Kit, pieces from Very Basic Basic Operations kit, Level 1 workbooks and teachers manual, IBM-compatible multiplication software, Multiplication Facts Mastery workbooks, and audio tape with coloring book, $303.25. (Discounts available for Math Discovery Club members.) Animals-n-Stuff booklet, $5.28. Smiley face series (set of 50 books), $37.50. Many other manipulatives sets available. Shipping extra. *V.J. Mortensen Co., PO Box 98, Hayden Lake, ID 83835-0098. Orders: (800) 4PLUS4-8. Fax: (208) 667-9438. Email: request@mortensenmathdirect.com (catalog requests only). Web: www.mortensenmathdirect.com.*

The prices shown here are club pricing; in order to enter the club, you must make an initial order of $39.95 minimum, then the renewal fee is $24 per year. Also, if you're a brand-new customer, you can request a catalog packet and receive a certificate for 15% off your first order.

For reviews of Mortensen books, see page 320.

The answer, then, is 10 + 2, which is 12. For subtraction problems, you reverse the process. As straightforward as it can be. Another good point is that, unlike straight "beans" manipulatives, this manipulative method emphasizes 10s, which are so important when it comes to carrying and borrowing later on. If you like this, then get the Addition Tray and a set of subtraction cards to round it out.

The **Multiplication Facts Tray** is another really neat resource. It's a molded plastic tray in which reside nine each of the colorful multiple unit bars, skip count cards to place underneath the unit bars, and multiplication fact cards with the answers on the reverse side. On the bottom of this tray are four long grooves. In two of them are stored, end to end, ten 10 bars. You can solve a given problem, say 4 x 9, either by removing that number of bars from its storage area (thus revealing the answer underneath), or check it out physically by placing the bars end to end and checking the answer against the number of 10 bars. For example, 4 x 9 is as long as 3 of the 10 bars plus a 6 bar, so the answer is 36. This kit is great for teaching what multiplication is (adding multiples of a number) and cementing its base-10 nature (all answers are seen in terms of how many 10s fit into them). You can always use the cards for regular flash card drills, while the student can check every answer for himself.

These kits are pretty—really pretty. The Addition and Multiplication Trays are easy to keep neat, since everything has its own storage spot. Although the pieces are all compatible, you do not want to start mixing and matching between these sets. It's not necessary, since each contains all the pieces needed for its own operations. You also don't want to have more than one of these kits out at a time, since each takes up quite a bit of space.

Personally, I find the Series A manuals (which explain how to use the manipulatives) much more useful than the workbooks. With the addition of a **Combo Kit**, **Very Basic Basic Operations Kit**, and **Home Fractions Kit** (all written up in the Fractions chapter), you have a complete, impressive math manipulatives program. *Mary Pride*

NEW!
The New Math Builder

Grades preK–6. $59 (special discount price).
Novo Lore, PO Box 251111, West Bloomfield, MI 48325. Orders: (800) 405-MATH. Inquiries: (248) 661-8910. Fax: (248) 661-3800. Email: rayhilde@ix.netcom.com.

When you see the **New Math Builder**, you'll wonder why it wasn't invented before! The New Math Builder combines an abacus with place values to create a very practical hands-on math board.

The New Math Builder is a 10 x 12" wooden frame with four rows of counters. There are nine counters in each column with columns for units, tens, hundreds and thousands. The counters are wider towards the left of the board and have numbers painted on them corresponding to their place value. The units value in each number is painted red, the tens are painted green, etc. reinforcing the place value concepts. When you flip the board over, you'll find the multiplication table (one times one through nine times ten) painted on the counters.

In addition to the math board, the New Math Builder comes with a videotape explaining how to use it and six brightly-colored spiral workbooks covering:

- Counting
- Basic addition and subtraction (numbers less than twenty)
- Major addition and subtraction
- Multiplication
- Decimals and fractions
- Using decimals

The books are not a complete math program—combined there are only 133 pages, but they do contain simple exercises and tests to check whether your child understands the concepts at each level. The instructions are clear and the only preparation you'll need is to read through the lesson beforehand. A typical lesson introduces a concept, shows how to use the math builder to solve the problem and lets your child explore the concept with related problems (e.g. adding different combinations of numbers to make six, subtracting ones, multiplying by eights, etc.). The approach is well suited to kinesthetic learning styles.

The New Math Builder may seem an unnecessary luxury supplement to your math program, but it's hard to find a one-piece math manipulative that is as well designed and durable as this one. *Teresa Schultz-Jones*

Success House's Whole Number Path to Math and Magic Multiplier kits give you the "square" view of math at a fraction of the price of other manipulative kits. The downside is that the materials aren't as thick or easy to handle, and they won't come back with a smile if you spill your coffee all over them.

The **Magic Multiplier** is one colorful, preprinted square piece of heavy cardstock and one L-shaped "framer" to use in framing any multiplication problem from 1 x 1 to 10 x 10. To use the Magic Multiplier, your child must know how to count money using quarters, nickels, and pennies, since it works the same way. Clear as mud? Really, it's quite simple. By using a 5 x 5 gridded rectangle, 1 x 5 rectangles, and a red square (value 25) on the printed card, your child can figure out the answers to multiplication problems by adding. It's really a cute, unusual little visual device.

Whole Number Path to Math comes in a couple of ziplock bags. You will appreciate this, because the little pieces could easily get lost otherwise. You get:

- 29 yellow "ones." These are half-inch yellow matboard squares.
- 11 orange fives—matboard rods as long as five ones
- 15 red tens—rods of length ten
- one green twenty-five (a 5 x 5 square)
- two purple fifties (a 5 x 10 rectangle)
- one blue hundred (10 x 10 square)
- two Place Value Boards (heavy cardstock, with tens and ones marked)
- a multiplication mat with a square grid
- a division board
- three colored, numbered dice (two 10-sided, one regular)
- a 16-page instruction book describing 19 activities and 14 games of addition, subtraction, multiplication, and division. These are not solitaire games; you will need to play them with your child, or teach the children to play them together. All games have an element of chance. Alternatively, you can use the manipulatives simply as teaching devices.

Success House also sells a **Fraction Path to Math** kit (addition, subtraction, multiplication, and division of fractions) and **Tic Tac Frac**, a two-player game which "gives meaning and practice in reducing fractions and in changing improper fractions to mixed numerals." *Mary Pride*

Sometimes the simplest ideas can be powerful. Whoever thought of making these counters with one side red and one side yellow stumbled onto something.

Counters, as you know, are sets of uniform objects used in schools for counting practice. They can be cute little plastic kitty cats, clear poker chips, beans, raisins, forks, spoons, or even children. The **Two-Color**

Success House Math Kits

Grades 1–6. The Magic Multiplier, $5. Whole Number Path to Math Kit, $20. Fraction Path to Math Kit (addition, subtraction, multiplication, and division of fractions), $25. Tic Tac Frac, $5. Shipping extra. *Success House, 556 Ludlow Avenue, Cincinnati, OH 45220-1579. (513) 861-2688. Fax: (513) 861-9688. Email: mathgames@hotmail.com*

Two-Color Counters

Grades K–12. $9.50/set of 200. *Cuisenaire Company of America, 10 Bank Street, PO Box 5026, White Plains, NY 10602. (800) 237-0338. Fax: (800) 551-7637. Web: www.cuisenaire.com.*

Counters happen to be thickish plastic circles, a sandwich of yellow and red plastic.

"So what?" you ask. So did I. I wasn't even going to review them until Maggie Holler of Cuisenaire Company pressed them on me.

They arrived. I opened the ziplock bag, noting the included instruction booklet. I grabbed a handful. They smell a little funny—like the Monsanto plastic factory I once worked in—but feel *good*. Satisfying. Chunky. They don't slip around like poker chips. Next, I started doing problems with them. 3 + 3 = 6 becomes three red counters plus three yellow counters equals six counters in all. Hmm. That's a lot easier to see when the counters are different colors, and it's a lot easier to do when you can simply flip over a counter to get a different color. How about showing the fraction $\frac{4}{5}$? Easy—four counters yellow-side-up and one red-side up. Five counters in all, of which four are yellow. Obviously $\frac{4}{5} + \frac{1}{5} = 1$. When presented this way any child can see it. Hmm again. Now how about some simple probability experiments? How often in 20 tosses will six counters come up with three yellow and three red? Try it! Keep records! Along the way your kids will pick up graphing and notetaking, plus experimental techniques.

As you can see, Two-Color Counters do a lot more than poker chips and kitty cats. They are especially useful for finding combinations (e.g., "What are all the pairs of numbers that add up to 10?"), single-operator math problems, working with fractions, and simple probability experiments. Simple is beautiful. *Mary Pride*

CHAPTER 25

Arithmetic

Kids are natural mathematicians. "Not true," you say? I can prove it! Here's a simple experiment:

Take four young children and eight cookies. Divide the cookies among them as follows: three to child A, three to child B, one each to children C and D. Immediately children C and D will begin to demonstrate their math abilities, as follows:

"THAT ISN'T FAIR! A AND B GOT *MORE* THAN WE DID!"

Is this practical math or what? C and D can count and compare, and they're barely out of diapers! (A and B can count, too, but they're too smart to rock the boat while *they* have the extra cookies!)

For a more stringent test, take your classic blueberry pie. Divide it in unequal pieces and pass them out to a crowd of children. Every single child in that crowd will infallibly comment, in uncomplimentary terms, on the intelligence of the person who cut the pie. When challenged as to how *they* would have divided the pie more fairly, they will prove they already have the rudiments of division "built in."

No, **kids aren't confused about math. *Grownups* are confused.** Our national confusion about arithmetic arose, you'll remember, with the introduction of the New Math. Hailed as a breakthrough in math instruction, the New Math taught kids mathematical principles in place of rote instruction. In this way, the math profs reasoned, children would be prepared for real math when they had mastered arithmetic. Unhappily, the New Math generation didn't ever learn their arithmetic!

NCTM = National Council of Teachers of Mathematics.

The NCTM standards are a list of the particular skills and concepts the NCTM currently says should be taught at each grade level. Many of the curricula in this chapter were designed to meet the NCTM standards.

Be aware there is no *legal* requirement that a math curriculum meet NCTM standards. There is also no edict from Mt. Sinai affirming that these "standards" are valid, or even that they define a good way to teach math. Finally, it's worthwhile remembering that the math scores of American schoolkids have been *falling* during the same period that the NCTM has been exerting influence on curriculum design.

For a critique of the NCTM's standards and philosophy, see the article on pages 280 and 281.

Now that "math anxiety" and "math failure" are so widespread, what should we do about it? Well, how about trying some of the programs in this chapter?

Preschool & Kindergarten Math

We learn best by first assembling raw data and then fitting it into a framework. So expose your kids to some real-world arithmetic first. Count things with the children. Add pennies. Subtract forks. Children don't have to be able to count or add in order to benefit from simply seeing it done. This initial number play is essential to producing the raw arithmetic data that children's minds need to work on.

When a child learns to *count* (which he does by rote repetition) he is well on his way to learning *arithmetic*. Counting is adding by one. Subtraction is counting backwards. Multiplication is adding by groups (2 x 3 is the same as adding two three times, 2+2+2). Division is subtracting by groups. All of these concepts grow directly out of counting. If counting is an abstract series of noises, so is arithmetic. If counting is what you do to find out how many buttons are on your jacket, then arithmetic is much more likely to seem real to a child.

I personally believe in showing children the patterns ("principles") of arithmetic and, after they are comfortable with them, then drilling on the actual "facts." The "9s" pattern is that adding nine to a number is the same as adding ten and then counting backwards once. Whether a child discovers these patterns or you reveal them to him does not seem to me as important as making sure that he does become aware that arithmetic is full of patterns.

Elementary Math Programs

Schools make basic arithmetic drag on far longer then needed. In the 1800s, a child could go to school for three six-week sessions for four years and know more math than one of our high school graduates today. Great-Great-Grandpa put in less than one-fifth the time, yet he could solve tough compound-interest problems and figure the height of a pole by knowing the length of its shadow and the angle of the sun. To bring this more up to date, kids in Sweden, Germany, and Ireland all whomp American kids on those international math tests. Coincidentally, in those countries they all complete basic arithmetic courses years earlier than we stop teaching it in the USA.

Arithmetic, after all, is logical. One step follows another. The key to success, in my opinion, is not interrupting this logical progression with all kinds of absurd classroom "activities" and unrelated topics. Measurement, for example, while it uses math, is really a *science* topic. The same goes for clocks, calendars, and even geometry. I know from experience it's possible to buzz along in arithmetic right up through algebra without having the foggiest idea of how to figure the circumference of a circle, given its diameter. All these other studies are worthwhile, but they do *not* belong in the basic arithmetic course, any more than the spelling class ought to be studying the geography of Mesopotamia. When arithmetic is mixed with any other subject, arithmetic (being abstract) is what loses out.

Your child won't necessarily fail to learn arithmetic by following the typical private- or public-school sequence, which mixes arithmetic with set theory, measurement, clocks, calendars, riddles, crossword puzzles, famous people of history, important dates, geometry, money, and so on.

He just won't learn it as fast.

With a little creativity, these "basic" courses can be (and have been) dragged on to last into high school and even college. The reason is that so much time is spent on everything *but* arithmetic.

Happily, homeschoolers are no longer confined to programs written for the current school scope and sequence. Some publishers have reprinted the math books our forefathers used. Others have developed their own streamlined programs, as you'll see below. Please note that curriculum listed in this section may or may not include kindergarten levels.

Whichever approach you choose, below you'll find an abundance of colorful, exciting programs for your littlest learner.

How to Teach Math

The cover of **Understanding Mathematics: From Counting to Calculus** states that it is "the only math help book you'll ever need." While you might think that sounds a bit overdone, by the time you've finished examining this thick book you'll probably agree that it's the best *overview* of mathematics that exists.

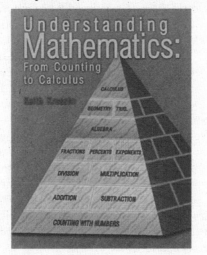

There are lots of books about how to teach math, what to teach, and even why to teach it. *Understanding Mathematics* is none of these. Instead, it provides an overview of mathematics from counting through calculus, and in so doing, gives you the big picture—making it obvious how everything fits together.

Each chapter introduces the key points for its subject and provides examples, written in an easily understood style (with the exception of that first chapter). Definitions are boldfaced to make them stand out, and shaded step-by-step boxes provide methods for solving standard problems. The examples provided are easy to understand and illustrate the practical applications of each area of math. At the end of each chapter there are summaries of the math laws, definitions and topics that were covered. Practical examples combined with some illustrations help make the book very readable and more eye-appealing than most.

It's impossible for even a 340-page oversized math book to cover everything, so while you'll find out how to solve problems about two cars travelling toward each other, parabolas aren't specifically mentioned. And while the softcover makes it look like a workbook, you won't find any problem sets like other math books. *Understanding Mathematics* also avoids chapters on things like estimation and calculator math by emphasizing *understanding the concepts* rather than problem solving—making it a refreshing change from most other math books.

Advanced topics are not covered in as much depth as the earlier ones, but basic concepts of calculus are presented in a way that's easy to understand.

I would not classify *Understanding Mathematics* as a *help* book, but as an overview that makes it easy for you to understand what you'll be teaching. You could even think of it as a math appreciation book. In either case, *Understanding Mathematics* will help you get a solid grip on your family's homeschool math program. *Teresa Schultz-Jones*

NEW!
Understanding Mathematics: From Counting to Calculus
Grades 1–12. $19.95 each. Shipping extra.
K Squared Publishing, Inc. P.O. Box 5354, El Dorado Hills, CA 95762-5354. (916) 933-9350.
Email: k2publish@aol.com. Web: users.aol.com/k2publish/mainpage.html

Don't be intimidated by the chapter on numbers and counting—which is the most abstract and hardest to understand section in the book. The rest of the book is much better, with chapters on:

- Elementary Mathematics
- Addition and Subtraction
- Multiplication and Division
- Fractions
- Percentages
- Negative Numbers
- Exponents
- Pre-Algebra
- Intermediate Mathematics
- Solving One Algebraic Equation
- Solving a System of Equations
- Word Problems
- Functions
- Graphing
- Geometry
- Measurement of Geometric Figures
- Trigonometry
- Advanced Mathematics
- Logarithms
- Complex Numbers
- Finding Geometry Using Algebra
- Introducing Calculus
- The Derivative
- The Integral.

NEW!
Calculus By and For Young People

Ages 7 and up. Spiralbound handbook, $13.95. Book of worksheets, $22.95. Changing Shapes With Matrices book, $9.95. Infinite Series with 6-Year-Olds and Up video, $42.95. Iteration to Infinite Sequences with 6- to 11-Year-Olds video, $42.95. "A Map to Calculus" wall chart, $7.95. Complete set, includes all above, $124.90. Add $4 shipping.
Don Cohen—The Mathman, 809 Stratford Dr., Champaign, IL 61821-4140. (800) 356-4559. Fax: (217) 356-4593. Email: mathman@shout.net. Web: www.shout.net/~mathman.

Advanced Math for Little Kids

It's small. It's cute. It's the spiral-bound "textbook" (if you don't mind calling it that) of **Calculus By and For Young People (ages 7 and up)**. The "ages 7" part is indeed part of the title; Don Cohen the Mathman, the author, doesn't want anyone to miss the point that Y-O-U-N-G P-E-O-P-L-E are the target students for this series.

You can fit this book in the palm of your hand, if you have a big hand. Its 177 pages explore some of the neater things about calculus, including ways young kids have found to describe it. Think of how to divide six cookies among seven people, for example. Using index cards to represent the cookies, cut the six cards in half, yielding 12 pieces. Give one to each of the seven people, so each person has a half cookie. Now take the remaining five pieces. Divide *them* in half and hand out seven. Now everyone has ½ plus ¼ cookie, and you have three pieces left. Divide them in half; it's not enough. Divide again, and you're back to 12 pieces. From here on out, clearly the whole series will keep repeating again and again. The bright boy who figured this out just after he graduated second grade provided you a way to visually demonstrate infinite converging series.

The "textbook" may be small, but the workbook is B-I-G! This oversized perfect-bound book has 324 pages with exercises *and* explanations.

A wall chart that shows where all the topics on Don's videos and in his books fall in relation to classic calculus is also available. This will make no sense at all to you at first. "What is a 'snowflake curve' and why is it next to 'square numbers' as one of the offshoots of 'area'?" you will ask. Don't worry. It will all make sense once you've watched the tapes and read the books. Some of it will make sense even earlier than that. It's easy to see that counting squares on a geoboard is related to the topic "area under curves," for example. The chart just serves as a handy way of organizing all these topics—handy, that is, if you like to think in terms of lots of arrows pointing in different directions and even crossing each other at times to show what is related to what.

On each of the two videos, Don Cohen first introduces a concept, then he talks a child through demonstrating the concept, then he explains what it means. For example, he introduces the function $2 \cdot x \longrightarrow x$, substituting in 3 as the first x. This yields the sequence 6, 12, 24, etc. Jane, a six-year-old, then appears. She chooses the number 5 for the first value of x, and before our eyes without any help (except Don encouraging her to write out the next step) she figures out the sequence 10, 20, 40, 80, and 160. Don then takes over again, and shows us that by substituting $2x$ for x each time we can wind up with something that looks like $2 \cdot 2 \cdot 2 \cdot 5$, where 5 is the initial value of x. This can then be rewritten as $2^n \cdot x$, where n is the number of iterations in the sequence.

Moving in a slightly different direction, *Changing Shapes with Matrices* is a whole book dedicated to multiplying a very crude "doggie" shape by matrices that consist of nothing but plus or minus values of 1, and 0. Because of the very simple shape and the very simple transformation matrix, you don't even need graph paper to do this, just an X and Y axis. Why fiddle with matrices? It's good preliminary practice for techniques that will be used in advanced math courses. It's not the advanced math itself, though, because all of the set theory and theorems that govern matrix math are missing—it's just a *taste* of the math.

And that's what this series is all about. Playing with interesting aspects of math—the Fibonacci sequence, for example—and learning to think mathematically. None of these materials offer a step-by-step instructional sequence, like a regular math course. Instead, these are *explorations* in math, a veritable hands-on museum of activities for young children in areas where high-school students fear to tread. A Japanese version will be out soon. *Mary Pride*

This is such a find! For *years* I've been saying that young children can and should be exposed to the terminology and concepts (just not the calculations!) of upper-level math and science. But where were the resources for this?

G is for Googol is the answer, in the area of math. This "alphabet" book is *not* for teaching little kiddies to read. Instead, this 57-page, oversized, fully illustrated hardcover is devoted to explaining advanced math to the young. Starting with "A is for abacus," in which we see an abacus, learn its history, and see how it works, each letter stands for one or more important topics beloved of mathematicians.

I'm not talking about wimpy stuff like addition or fractions, either. Cast your ovoid oculars on this list:

> Abacus, Binary, Cubit, Diamond, Equilateral, Exponent, Fibonacci, Googol, Googolplex, Hundred, "If," Jupiter, Königsberg, Light-year, Möbius Strip, Nature, Obtuse, Probability, Quantity and Quality, Rhombicosidodecahedron, Symmetry, Tesselate, Unit, Venn Diagram, "When are we ever going to use this stuff, anyway?," X, Y-axis, Zillion.

Each concept is explained in easy-reading detail, with full-color drawings and diagrams. As a bonus, for each letter you'll also find a list of other math concepts starting with the letter in question. So *A* is for *Abacus* (the main entry), and also for *acute, algebra, angle, art, architecture, area, asymmetry, average,* and *axis*. No definitions are provided for the bonus list, but any parent with a smidgen of mathematical training can use this list for inspiration for further explanations and explorations. So why isn't this book in the MIT Museum Shop catalog, already? *Mary Pride*

TrigO is the second in a series of educational games from Lewis Educational Games. The first game is ElementO, a game about Chemistry (reviewed in Chapter 31). TrigO is quite obviously about Trigonometry.

With TrigO you get a game board, rules, six each of six different colors of playing pieces, and a die. Each playing piece has the name of a trigonometric function.

In the TrigO Beginner's game, you start at a red circle on the vertex of a right triangle. You move from there according to the throw of a die in whatever direction you choose. You have to move in such a way that you trace the outline of a right triangle. You can add a wrinkle to this by paying attention to which direction you are moving. The arrows that run around the edges of each playing piece tell you which direction that piece is moving.

The third game adds knowledge of the definitions of the trig functions into the mix. You can only start your playing piece at vertices next to sides used in defining the function whose name is on the piece. For example, the Tangent piece would have to start so that its next move would proceed down the side labeled "opposite" and then to the adjacent side, because the tangent of an angle is the length of the opposite side divided by the length of the adjacent side. Additional rules can be added as you become comfortable with the play at each level.

This game will teach the names of the Trig functions, which sides of a triangle are used to compute each function, and whether a function is posi-

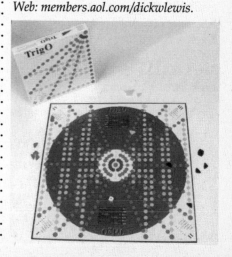

tive or negative in each quadrant of the coordinate plane. I am not aware of any other product designed to teach all this to such young children. *Bill Pride*

Beginning Math at Home

Ages 3–6. $13.50 postpaid.
Individualized Education Systems/Poppy Lane Publishing, PO Box 5136, Fresno, CA 93755. (559) 299-4639. Email: Bette1234@aol.com.

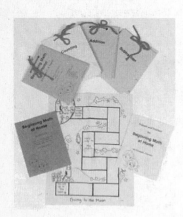

BJUP Math for Christian Schools K5

Kindergarten. Student Worktext, $12. Student Materials Packet, $5.50. Teacher's Edition, $22. Optional supplementary math Kindergarten Activity Sheets are available. Shipping extra.
Bob Jones University Press Customer Service, Greenville, South Carolina 29614-0062. (800) 845-5731. Fax: (800) 525-8398. Web: www.bjup.com.

Regular Math for Little Kids

This delightful little program for children ages 3–6 has the same format as *Beginning Reading at Home,* by the same author. You get four "kits," each designed to teach a different math concept. Each kit is a set of 3½ x 5" colored cards tied together with orange yarn. You also get a pre- and post-test, for checking how much your child has learned or needs to learn from **Beginning Math at Home** and a very short program guidebook explaining what it's all about and how to use it.

Oh, I almost forgot—a game, *Going to the Moon,* and a chart showing the correct way to write the numerals are also included.

The kits are Shapes, Counting (0–12, plus more than, less than, and time telling to the hour), Addition 0–10, and Subtraction 0–10. No writing is needed, except tracing the numerals. All manipulatives and practice cards necessary are built in. You just cut out the little clock and its hands, the little number cards, less than, equal to, and the question cards for the Going to the Moon game.

This little program is the perfect example of a well-designed program for home use. It costs almost nothing, is ultra simple to use, has no unnecessary clutter, is charming to look at, involves the children right away, and includes everything except a brad for attaching the clock hands and a pair of scissors for cutting!

If author Elizabeth Peterson could only be persuaded to invent a *Beginning Math II* kit, with counting up past 100, skip counting, reverse counting from 20, money, and time to the quarter hour, with those two itty-bitty programs you'd be able to do everything it took the University of Chicago experts pages and pages of instructions and $200 of manipulatives to accomplish (see the *Mathematics Their Way* review on page 315). Do it, Elizabeth! *Mary Pride*

Here's my personal favorite kindergarten math program. **Bob Jones kindergarten math** not only is cute—featuring Farmer Brown and his pet mouse Cheddar as ongoing characters—but covers all beginning math so efficiently and in such an interesting way that I don't mind using it again and again with child after child (and I have *nine* children!).

The 165 lessons in this course only take about 15 minutes each. The first 85 lessons "are rather informal and require a minimum of written work—none of which is in the worktext." In other words, you need the teacher's manual, because without it you only get work for half the course. The teacher's manual also includes work center activities, calendar activities, time telling and all that manipulative pre-math to get kids ready for their first math workbook—*without* requiring that you purchase any manipulatives!

You will need the inexpensive Materials Packet, which includes numeral, money, and dot flash cards for you to cut out. Other manipulatives, such as a demonstration clock, are built right into the workbook (see p. 31 for a really fun clockface with a real face in it!).

What makes this program really inspiring and great is that kids absolutely love it. They love the gentle pace. They love the colorful workbook pages, each new, fascinating, and doable. They love Farmer Brown. They love Cheddar. They love the comfortable, family-like activities. So I love it, too. *Mary Pride*

When I first was looking into homeschooling, I had trouble understanding how people could successfully teach math without using a structured math curriculum. After reading **Family Math For Young Children: Comparing**, I not only understand *how*, but I can see *why* it works for so many people.

Family Math For Young Children: Comparing is the first volume in a planned series of math books for children four to eight years old. Already out for older children are two other books, *Family Math* (K–8), and *Family Math—The Middle School Years* (grades 5–8).

In this oversized softcover book, you'll find 200 pages of ways to explore math with your young child. Some of the activities seem very math-oriented (if I have a box with one button and another box with two buttons, how many buttons are there altogether?). Some are more like craft projects (such as the share-a-square mobile), and there are some creative movement activities (hop twice inside a circle, jump three times outside the circle, and slide four times around the circle). All are fun and provide the basis for important math skills that children will build upon as they grow.

The set of directions for each activity follow the same format, telling you what skills are practiced, required materials, setup, directions, and comments. Not every activity requires materials, but when they do, it is most often common items found around the home. Many of the activities are open-ended and varied to suit every learning style.

Other sections in the book provide:

- ways to encourage your child's mathematical skills through everyday estimation and questions that promote mathematical thinking
- ideas on how you can practice sorting and classifying skills as you build a collection of treasures
- questions and common sense advice to assess how your child is doing
- suggestions, checklists and forms for using *Family Math* in a group
- references to other math resources

Family Math For Young Children sets the right tone for making math an enjoyable experience for you and your children. If their future books are as good, the entire series may provide a complete math program. *Teresa Schultz-Jones*

Frank Schaffer has about the cutest, most fun, easy to use workbooks for young children around. The simple activities in his books are a great way to introduce kids to math, handwriting, and a host of other subjects.

Right now we're looking at math, so I pulled a few of the most applicable workbooks off my shelf. All the workbooks are 24 pages of simple activities, such as counting and coloring a certain number of objects, writing numbers, counting objects and circling the correct number, and so on. *Kindergarten Math Activities*, a more ambitious 80-page workbook, covers number recognition 1–20, counting and sets 1–20, quantitative representation of numbers 1–20, basic shapes, patterns, one to one correspondence, ordinal and cardinal numbers. In this book kids color, match, trace, do dot-to-dots, and all the stuff in all the other books combined. These are great for keeping little ones happy and busy while you teach the older ones!

You can generally find these workbooks at your local teachers' store. Why not take a look at them the next time you pop in? *Mary Pride*

NEW!
Family Math For Young Children

Grades preK–3. $18.95 plus shipping.

EQUALS Publication, University of California, Berkeley, CA 94720-5200. (800) 897-5036 or (510) 642-1910. Fax: (510) 643-5757. Email: *equals@uclink.berkeley.edu.* Web: *www.equals.lhs.berkeley.edu*

While this is a new book, the group responsible for it has been around since 1977 running workshops around the world to teach people how to learn and think about math. (You can read more about them at *equals.lhs. berkeley.edu/fm.lhs.html.*)

Frank Schaffer Math

Kindergarten. Kindergarten Math, Numbers, Beginning Activities with Numbers, and Getting Ready for Math, $3.98 each. Kindergarten Math Activities, $9.95. Shipping extra. *Frank Schaffer Publications, 23740 Hawthorne Blvd., Torrance, CA 90505-5927. (800) 421-5565. Fax: (800) 837-7260. Email: fspinfo@aol.com. Web: www.frankschaffer.com.*

NEW!
Janice VanCleave's Play and Find Out About Math

Ages 4–7. $12.95.
John Wiley & Sons, 1 Wiley Drive, Somerset, NJ 08875. (800) 225-5945. (732) 469-4400. Fax: (800) 597-3299. Web: www.wiley.com.

Saxon Math Grades K–3

Grades K–3. Math K, $55. Math 1, $85. Math 2, $87.50. Math 3, $90. Shipping extra.
Saxon Publishers, 2450 John Saxon Blvd., Norman, OK 73071. (800) 284-7019. Email: info@saxonpub.com. Web: www.saxonpub.com.

Janice VanCleave's Play and Find Out About Math is a really cool addition to any preschool or kindergarten curriculum. This 128-page wide-format paperback has 50 simple and fun demonstrations on the topics of counting, addition and subtraction with fingers and toys, fractions, time (seconds and days), shapes, symmetry, patterns, measurements (length, circumference, and weight), area, and volume.

Each demonstration has its own little chapter that starts with a question posed by a cartoon child—for example, "How can I draw a circle?" Next comes a "Round Up These Things" materials list (in this case, a one-hole punch, a cardboard strip, poster board, and two pencils—your child won't be drawing freehand!), a "Later You'll Need" materials list (in this case, lids and caps from different-sized bottles and jars, a sheet of typing paper, and a pencil), step-by-step demonstration instructions, a "So Now We Know" section that explains what the demonstration's all about, plus "More Fun Things to See and Do" follow-up activities. For example, after learning how to make circles two different ways, you are shown how you can make a bear design out of nothing but circles!

Fun, easy to do, and not time-consuming at all. You'll enjoy the airy, large text and illustrations; your child will love the simple math play. *Mary Pride*

We have received more questions about these math kits than any other math product in recent years. Not surprising, as the original Saxon Math for grades 4 and up is a homeschool best seller! (See its review in the next section of this chapter.)

Saxon Math has become famous for its "incremental" approach. Every new topic is followed up again and again with exercises in following lessons. This method has tripled the success rate in schools using John Saxon's algebra books.

Saxon Math for grades K–3 is not written by John Saxon, and includes none of his trademark wacky sentence problems. Instead, it employs lots of math manipulatives, has a script for the parent to follow ("say this . . . do that"), and features daily calendar and pattern-recognition exercises. Unlike the upper-grades Saxon courses, which reflect Mr. Saxon's authoritative personality and wry sense of humor, these courses have a typical gentle early-grades look and feel. With one difference: the lessons use correct mathematical terminology instead of the cutesy terms so often inflicted on children by early math books.

WHAT YOU GET: The Home Kits for Math 1, Math 2, and Math 3 each include a large spiral-bound Home Study teacher's manual, a "meeting book," two thick student workbooks, and flash cards. The Home Kit for Math K has the teacher's manual and meeting book, but no separate student workbooks or flash cards.

Each day's lesson includes two parts: The Meeting and The Lesson. The "incremental," or continuous review, portion of the program occurs during The Meeting. For each grade, the "meeting book" includes calendars you fill out day by day. In kindergarten, The Meeting also includes counting, patterning, and telling time. As you progress through the grades, the meeting books add weather tracking, temperature graphing, measurements, and other non-computational skills. New skills, such as subtracting and multiplying, are introduced in The Lesson.

The teacher's manuals are very well organized. Each day's lesson is easy to find, lesson preparation materials and activities are fully described at the top of the page, and the lesson itself is fully scripted; it tells you exactly what to say and do. Reproducible masters needed for some lessons are at the back of the manual. A copy of each worksheet used in the lesson, sized smaller and with answers filled in, is included in the information for that lesson in the teacher's manual.

Math K. Besides the manipulatives available from ETA (see spread below), you will need some "common household items" for doing the various lessons. These are colored construction paper, envelopes, index cards, round and rectangular crackers, paper napkins, glue, scissors, tape, crayons, coins, measuring cups, clear containers, plastic drinking straws, a deck of playing cards, baskets (for storing teddy bear counters, pattern tiles, etc.), a small plastic bag (ziploc will do), and a large bag (for carrying items from your pretend "store").

The pace is gentle, as befits a child's first academic experience. Beginning with mostly play, the course ends up covering counting by 1's, 5's, and 10's, using manipulatives to solve addition and subtraction problems, comparing and ordering numbers, identifying common shapes, recognizing and creating patterns, and creating and reading graphs, among other things.

Twelve lessons are taught each month, so you only need to teach three lessons per week. Starting with lesson 27, there is a brief oral assessment of the child's skills every seven lessons or so.

Math 1. In this course, and those following, you shift to a schedule of four lessons per week. Good of Saxon to notice that for many homeschool families, Friday is field trip day!

"Common household objects" required for this course include crayons, paper, scissors, coins (you'll need five bags of 100 pennies each, so plan a

NEW!
"Saxon Math K–3" Manipulatives kit

Complete manipulative kit, $57.95 plus 10% shipping. Individual items available separately. Minimum order $25. *ETA, 620 Lakeview Parkway, Vernon Hills, IL 60061. (800) 445-5985. Fax (800) ETA-9326. Web: www.etauniverse.com.*

You need **a set of manipulatives to use with Saxon Math K–3**. The easy way to get them: in a complete kit from a company named ETA. (It stands for "Educational Teaching Aids.") These folks make *solid* math manipulatives! In hundreds of hours of kid-testing, the only piece that didn't hold up was the Hundred Number Chart. A plastic chart would make this kit perfect.

Here's what you get:

- A plastic balance, consisting of a base and a piece you lay across it with two large platforms for resting items on
- Two student Judy clocks—the standard time-telling trainers used by millions of kids
- A set of 100 plastic pattern blocks (like the kind you find in parquetry kits)
- Two geoboards, complete with colored rubber bands in different sizes
- A Hundred Number Chart (this is great for all kinds of number facts training and pattern-recognition exercises)
- Two rulers to measure both inches and centimeters
- A set of four tangram puzzles (you know, those geometric pieces you put together to form different shapes)

- A set of 100 square colored tiles
- A set of 100 MathLink cubes (they snap together)
- A set of 10 two-color counters (for probability experiments)
- A set of 48 Baby Bear counters
- A set of dominoes

Items required for the Saxon courses that are not included in the kit (but that are available from ETA) are the folding meter/yard stick ($4.50) and outdoor thermometer ($9.95). I guess the folks at ETA thought most families already have one of these. Optional items are a Learning Clock ($13.50) and a neat set of foam geometric solids ($10.95).

If you have toddlers, I strongly recommend that you purchase an additional set of the Baby Bear counters ($5.95) and an extra set of MathLink cubes ($10.75). These two items absolutely fascinate young children, who will run off with them and use them for toys in their bath, in odd corners of the living room, in the sandbox . . . Keep the extra sets in a high cupboard and use them to replace the pieces that will inevitably be lost.

I liked the sampler set of "Manipulite" math manipulatives they included with the Home Kit. This foam material has a great "feel" and is totally quiet to work with, unlike the clackety-clack of wood or plastic manipulatives. Just about any math manipulative you might want is available in colorful Manipulite.

ETA has complete math and science catalogs loaded with killer projects, experiments, manipulatives, and equipment. Collect them all! *Mary Pride*

OUR CONCLUSION:

I see pros and cons here. This is an easy program to *follow*—just get the materials and repeat the script—but not necessarily the easiest program to *use*. You keep switching from one activity or manipulative to another. In other words, this program is *organized*, but not *streamlined*. If you have lots of time to lavish on math, you should do fine. It's hard to see how any child could fail with the step-by-step instruction, fun activities, and constant review. Saxon Math K–3 does follow the "incremental" approach very carefully for time- and date-telling, math facts, and pattern recognition. However, some skills, such as measuring volume, are introduced without immediate follow-up. We would have liked to see *all* skills handled incrementally.

trip to the bank or start saving pennies!), grid paper, glue stick, tab board, brads, toys (used in many lessons—stuffed animals, dolls, action figures, or small trucks will do), paper towels, a cutting board and knife, envelopes, index cards, pencil, eraser, basin, funnel, newspaper, masking tape, marker, a small bell, a cup of shelled peanuts, a blender or food processor, vegetable oil, measuring cups and spoons, crackers, celery stalk, napkins, empty food cans or boxes, tape, construction paper, paper plates, assorted veggies, food coloring, and cups. The list of ingredients sounds like "John Saxon meets Jessica Hulcy," doesn't it?

You start by building short towers with the linking cubes, and end by writing numbers in the hundreds and memorizing all the subtraction facts. Along the way you do a lot of work with coins, time, simple geometry, and basic math. Comes with a set of number cards and flash cards for all the addition and subtraction facts.

Math 2. Cooking supplies make more of an appearance at this grade level, while the stuffed animals bow out after lesson 10. Aside from that, the list of extra materials you have to supply is pretty similar to that in grade 1. Activities at this grade level include creating and reading Venn diagrams, making and labeling an array, and locating points on a coordinate graph. Lots of work with money, number patterns, geometry, and math facts, too.

Some simple multiplying and dividing. Comes with flash cards for all the math facts, plus pre-perfed colorful geometric shapes.

Math 3. You get to grow beans, measure liquids and solids using a variety of containers which you supply, chart temperature, multiply and divide multi-digit numbers, do lots of geometry, and more. The ingredient list is somewhat smaller than for second grade. You'll have to add a set of paper money, unless you happen to have lots of $50 and $100 bills lying around your house (I wish!). The flash cards have more multiplication and division than those for grade 2—a complete set of math fact cards.

Upon completion of Saxon K–3, you should be ready to use *Saxon 54* (the "5" stands for "fifth grade," and the "4" means that advanced fourth-graders can handle it). Accelerated learners who can handle two math lessons per day can finish all four grades in one year. From that point on, an average child with no special coaching can manage two Saxon courses a year, so conceivably your nine-year-old could be doing algebra if you work at it! *Mary Pride*

NEW!
Wiley Math for Your 1st and 2nd Grader

Grades 1–2. $12.95 plus shipping. *John Wiley & Sons, 1 Wiley Drive, Somerset, NJ 08875. (800) 225-5945. (732) 469-4400. Fax: (800) 597-3299. Web: www.wiley.com.*

Math without the twaddle! If you like books like *Teach Your Child To Read In 100 Easy Lessons*, then you'll like **Math for Your 1st and 2nd Grader**. This book contains seventy-eight mini lessons that cover most of the basic math skills that your child will need to learn by the end of second grade.

This 274-page book provides a no-nonsense approach to early math. Steve Slavin, author of *All the Math You'll Ever Need*, introduces each lesson by telling you what you will be teaching, why it should be taught and how to tell if your child is ready for the material. Then he tells you how to teach it, providing appropriate exercises and answers. "Extra Help" boxes give further explanation to concepts that may not be easily grasped the first time.

Concepts are introduced in the following order for first grade: counting, adding single-digit numbers, subtracting single-digit numbers, translating words into numbers, understanding zero, filling in the missing number, double-digit addition, counting money, word problems, telling time, ordinal numbers, calendars, fractions, and counting by 2s, 5s, and 10s to 100.

Second-graders build upon their skills by doing more complicated problems, such as three-digit addition with carrying, and are introduced to inequalities; three-digit addition and subtraction; regrouping; expanded notation; multiplication; division; fractional parts and measures; yards, feet, and inches.

Math curriculums all vary, so it is hard to say that this doesn't cover everything that a first- or second- grader should know. I would have liked to have seen sequencing, sets, basic geometry, and bar graphs included in this book.

If you spend 20 or 30 minutes each weekday, *Math for Your 1st and 2nd Grader* can be completed in four or five months. Because it covers a lot, the exercises are minimal, and you may want to give your child more practice using the student workbooks from another curriculum. And just because of the title, don't wait to buy *Math for Your 1st and 2nd Grader* before your child is ready for first grade, because many of the beginning lessons are suitable for preschoolers.

Steve Slavin reassures us that it is more important that your child really understand each concept before moving ahead. He writes in a very conversational style. (When was the last time you could say that about a math book?) *Teresa Schultz-Jones*

All you need to know to be your child's best teacher

Math for Your 1st and 2nd Grader

Steve Slavin

Traditional Curriculum

Drill, drill, drill. Pages and pages of problems. If you think this approach is character-building, **A Beka** has the **math workbooks** for you. Each day's work takes a single page and is easy to grade with the answer key. (I personally feel it's not necessary to do *that* much drill—how about assigning *part* of the problems on each page, like real schoolteachers often do?) Work progresses more or less sequentially, so if you understand basic math there's not all that much to helping your students use these books. *Mary Pride*

If you like colorful illustrations and good, thorough math instruction, you'll like **Horizons Math**! In this new series, **Alpha Omega Publications** has left behind the familiar LIFEPAC approach for a workbook style of teaching, which they feel is more effective for the lower elementary grades.

The coverage is *very* thorough, especially if you use the teacher's handbook (more on that later). The approach is a spiral, continuous review, like Saxon (which reviews everything every lesson) or A Beka (which reviews at regular intervals). Children will see concepts reviewed at specific, planned intervals. (Alpha Omega will send you a copy of the Scope and Sequence if you ask.)

This series gives children an early introduction to plane and solid geometry (shapes, symmetry, perimeter, area, volume, congruency, lines,

Supposing you decide to purchase the teacher's handbook, what does it include? Easy-to-follow lesson plans, extra worksheets, instructions on daily oral practice (counting by two, five, etc.; math facts; calendar drill), timed drill sheets, math manipulative suggestions, and answer keys. If you do get it, and find you don't need it, you can return it for a full refund within 30 days.

rays, and angles), graphs (bar, line, picto-), symbols (less than, greater than, not equal to), metrics (linear, liquid, and weights), ratios, money, time, and fractions (equivalents, mixed numbers, reducing, and addition). Carrying for addition is introduced late in first grade, borrowing early in second grade, and carrying for multiplication in the middle of third grade. The curriculum continues up through the normal coverage of fractions, decimals, and percent in grade 5. Grade 6 introduces long division and a bit of pre-algebra. Each year includes 160 lessons, presented in two student books. The Teacher handbook has detailed daily lesson plans.

For those who like to compare publishers, Horizons moves faster than A Beka (but it is *not* harder), and I like several of their explanations better, especially for division and telling time. A Beka is earlier in only two areas: thermometer reading, and terminology such as "sum" and "subtrahend." Also, although the Alpha Omega people strongly recommend that you purchase a teacher's handbook (even if you have to share it with other families), I found Horizons easier than A Beka to use with the workbooks alone.

Horizons is an excellent choice for a math curriculum for almost any child. It is especially appealing to children who like to move fast and hate busy work. *Kim O'Hara*

Alpha Omega Math LIFEPACS

Grades 1–12. Complete boxed set: grade 1, $61.95; grades 2–6, $41.95 each; grades 7–10, $47.95 each; grades 11 and 12, $45.95 each. Shipping extra.
Alpha Omega Publications, 300 N. McKemy, Chandler, AZ 85226. Orders and inquiries: (800) 622-3070. Fax: (480) 785-8034. Web: www.home-schooling.com.

As you recall, the **Alpha Omega** system is set up with 10 **LIFEPACs** per grade. These are consumable workbooks, fairly slim, with full instructions and how-to examples built in. The new LIFEPAC Gold format means full-color workbook pages and attractive page design.

Alpha Omega is currently revising their entire math program to conform to the typical course of study followed in public schools. Among other changes, there are now separate teacher's booklets (grades 1–9) including answer keys, tests, and test answers. The upper-grades revision won't be out until next year.

Additional games, workbooks, and manipulatives for each LIFEPAC grade level are offered in the Alpha Omega catalog. These are well chosen, inexpensive, and recommended as a way to make this more than "just a worktext" curriculum. *Mary Pride*

Math for Christian Schools is a well-regarded and well-rounded set of math courses. Each grade level offers systematic step-by-step instruction, activities, practice, and review, with 165 lessons divided into 20 chapters. Manipulatives are used when appropriate to demonstrate concepts. Math topics covered are the same at each grade level as in typical public-school texts.

If you remember your elementary math well, you *can* teach these courses with just the student book for your grade level. This is a kivar-covered worktext in grades 1–4, and a hardbound textbook in grades 5 and 6. You'll have to solve the problems along with your student to check his or her answers. Or you can purchase some or all of the other materials available for each course.

Your best deal is the Home School Kit for each grade level. This includes:

- Home Teacher's Edition
- Home Teacher Packet
- Student worktext or textbook
- Student Materials Packet
- Teaching Chart Flip Chart
- For grades 4–6: tests and answer key

The Home Teacher's Edition for each grade level includes scaled-down versions of student pages, with answers noted. The manual tells you *how to* teach each lesson, provides additional activities not included in the student book, and explains how and when to use the manipulatives.

The Home Teacher Packet comes with ready-to-use visual aids and flash cards, fact review drills, and essential teaching examples.

The Student Materials Packet has the manipulatives you need for the lessons, such as counters, play money, Base Ten kit, fraction kit, measuring tapes, or number line—whichever of these is appropriate for your grade level. These are *not* "real" manipulatives, but items you cut or punch out from heavy, colored cardstock. Additional "real" manipulatives are available separately in the Bob Jones University Press homeschool catalog.

Teaching Charts Flip Chart are different for each grade level. These provide an oversized visual introduction of the important concepts and skills for that grade, and are the most skippable item of the bunch. *Mary Pride*

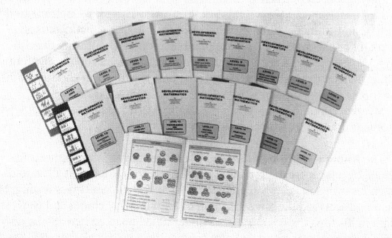

Developmental Math is a series of 16 workbooks that can teach a kid basic arithmetic faster than any other curriculum on the market. The series was written by a math teacher with a Ph.D. from the University of Birmingham in England, where they still know how to teach math. It is based on his series of elementary math textbooks that for over 25 years has been the official math series in Egypt, with over 200 million copies in

NEW!
BJUP Math for Christian Schools 1–6

Grades K–12 available. Home School Kits: grades 1–3, $57 each; grade 4, $64; grades 5 and 6, $72 each. Home Teacher's Edition, $22 each. Home Teacher Packet, $8 each. Student Worktext (grades 1–4), $12 each. Student Text (grades 5 and 6), $23 each. Student Materials Packet, $5.50 each. Teaching Charts Flip Chart, $15 each. Test set with answer key, $10 each. Shipping extra.
Bob Jones University Press Customer services, Greenville, SC 29614. Orders: (800) 845-5731. Fax: (800) 525-8398. Web: www.bjup.com.

Other materials available, but not included in the Home School Kit, are test sets with or without answer keys, activity workbooks (*Spread Your Wings* series provides extra help for struggling students; *Spring Into Action* series provides extra practice for regular students), a video on how to teach using math manipulatives, and additional math manipulatives.

Developmental Math

Grades K–10. $200 for a complete set of 16 student books (level 1–16), 9 parent's guides (level 1–9), 7 teacher's editions (level 10–16). Partial set available (student workbooks and parent's guides/teacher's editions). Inquire about single workbook prices. Shipping extra.
Mathematics Programs Associates, PO Box 2118, Halesite, NY 11743. (516) 643-9300. Fax: (516) 643-9301. Email: mpa@greatpyramid.com.

Developmental Math Contents

UPDATED!
Kumon Mathematex Worksheets

Grades preK–12. $30 one-time registration fee. Monthly fee, $75 at Center/$80 Correspondence. *Kumon Educational Institute, 300 Frank Burr Blvd, Teaneck, NJ 07666. (800) ABC-MATH (222-6284). (201) 928-0444. Fax: (847) 640-6340. Web: www.kumon.com.*

print. The English-language series is the culmination of a 10-year project involving several schools, hundreds of students, and many teachers.

What you get is a really clean, efficient program covering all your child's basic math. Kids are first taught concepts with real objects. In step 2, the concepts are represented with symbols (e.g., circles). Step 3, once the concept is learned, drills for speed using numerals-only problems. Step 4 is application with word problems. Each workbook comes with a diagnostic test, so you can quickly slot your child into the right workbook or figure out which pages of the workbook he needs to work to catch up on concepts he might be shaky on. The series is both "sequential" and "incremental." This means concepts are introduced step-by-step in logical order, and old concepts are reviewed periodically to make sure they aren't forgotten.

The series explains itself. Teacher's manuals are just student books with the answers in brown—no complicated explanations or projects necessary.

The series is called "Developmental Mathematics" because it *develops* math concepts, rather than presenting them as isolated skills. For example: Children are drilled on combinations of numbers that add up to 10, in preparation for teaching them "regrouping," which we used to know as "adding with carrying." They then learn that $7 + 8 = 7 + (3 + 5) = (7 + 3) + 5 = 10 + 5 = 15$. This sounds more complicated than it is, as the workbook presents base 10 addition first with pictures. When I say it's not complicated, I mean that my six-year-old daughter is already at Level 7 (a fourth-grade level), zooming along and really enjoying her math! My non-mathematical 9-year-old is also picking up new math skills more quickly than with any other program I have seen.

At the rate of two pages per day, your child would be through K–6 arithmetic in 3½ years. At the still-quite-reasonable rate of four pages a day, it will take less than two years! I *know* this is possible, because my father taught me math up through the eighth-grade level the summer I was six, using a series very much like this one. I grant that I had an aptitude for math, but even spotting me a couple of years, the average home-schooled child should be able to whiz through his arithmetic studies, using these workbooks, about two to four times as fast as the average public-schooled child—and know his math a *whole lot better* in the end!

All you'll need to teach your child on your own is (1) how to tell time and temperature and (2) weights and measures. These have nothing to do with basic arithmetic, but are usually thrown into basic math courses, breaking up the systematic course of instruction and confusing the children. A systematic proceed-at-your-own-pace arithmetic course, with time-telling and so on taught separately, is the best way to teach children computational math, in my opinion.

My own children have been, or are, all going through this program, with excellent results. Recommended. *Mary Pride*

The **Kumon Method** of learning is a systematic set of worksheets invented by a Japanese math teacher named Mr. Toru Kumon. It all started when his own son got a bad grade on a second-grade test. Investigating, Mr. Kumon discovered the same infection of "enrichment" clutter and New Math in his son's math text that has undermined math ed here. So he devised a series of worksheets, concentrating solely on calculation ability, with the ultimate goal of allowing his son to proceed step by step until he could solve all high school math problems (Japanese high-school math is like college math here in the dumbed-down USA). The idea is to work through one sheet a day under trained adult supervision. The next day the student would self-correct any problems the adult had marked incorrect. This process is repeated until the student can do that worksheet perfectly in an allotted time period. He then goes on to the next worksheet. This takes about 20 minutes a day for young children, and 30–40 for older ones.

Kumon starts with exercises in line drawing and use of puzzles, and progresses all the way through calculus and statistics (see what they learn in high school in Japan?). You don't get geometry and word problems, but that's no big deal, as they should be taught in a different way anyway

In Japan, Kumon is used by about 1.92 million schoolchildren at present, all studying in classroom settings run by approved Kumon instructors (generally outside school hours).

As of four years ago, Kumon was trying to sell the same approach here in America, charging a monthly fee to "tutors" who are expected to hunt up students and sit with them every day. This meant that homeschoolers couldn't just buy the worksheets. Instead, they wanted you to attend a Kumon seminar and pay a rather steep monthly fee for each child enrolled. This entitled you to get the needed worksheets doled out in one-month-at-a-time batches. I couldn't get it through their heads that they would probably have had 100 times as many people using it if they would make the series available directly to parents.

Who says nobody ever listens? They now have a correspondence program, for $5 extra per month per child above and beyond the cost of enrolling in a center. *Mary Pride*

If you're into classics, you'll be glad to hear that Mott Media has resurrected a whole series of the texts America used in the days of Reverend McGuffey and Laura Ingalls. One of these

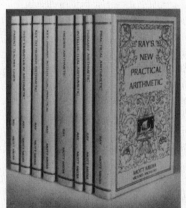

selections is the **Ray's Arithmetic** series. The series goes from kindergarten to high school, with a strong consumer-math emphasis in each grade.

Mental arithmetic in this series precedes written, and some of it is tough (your students will have to think!). Example: "If 3 lead pencils cost 18 cents, how many cents will 5 pencils cost?"

Primary Arithmetic starts with counting concrete objects and proceeds to counting, writing, and reading numerals. Word problems appear from the start.

Intellectual Arithmetic, Practical Arithmetic, and *Higher Arithmetic* carry on with old-fashioned word problems and solid business math, right up to compound interest.

Be sure to get the great parent/teacher guide! *Mary Pride*

The revised Rod and Staff **Mathematics for Christian Living** series

- emphasizes Mennonite biblical values
- emphasizes thorough mastery of number facts in the lower grades
- presents concepts, computation, and applications in a balanced mix
- exercises a thorough review pattern in the daily lessons
- includes reading or reasoning problems that involve a spiritual lesson, a Biblical principle, or other character-building emphasis

Grade 1 covers the facts up to sums and minuends of 10 with a strong memory emphasis, and two-digit addition and subtraction. Other concepts

Ray's Arithmetic series

Grades 1–12. Complete set with teacher's guide, $99.99. Primary Arithmetic (grades 1–3), $7.99. Intellectual Arithmetic (grades 3 and 4), $9.99. Practical Arithmetic (grades 5 and 6), $16.99. Key for those three books, $12.99. Test Examples in Arithmetic, $12.99. Higher Arithmetic (grades 7–12), $20.99. Key for Higher Arithmetic, $12.99. Parent/teacher guide for all books, $10.99. Shipping extra. *Mott Media/Homeschooling Book Club, 1000 E. Huron St., Milford, MI 48381-2422. (800) 421-6645. Fax: (248) 685-8776.*

UPDATED
Rod & Staff Mathematics for Christian Living Series

Grade 1, all materials, $54.80 (2 workbooks, teacher book, tablet of speed drills, blackline masters for extra practice, flash cards). Grade 2 materials, $56.90 (5 workbooks, 2 teacher books, blackline masters). Grade 3 student book $11.35, teacher book $13.00, speed drills tablet $4.20, blacklines $3.85. Grade 4 student book $12.95, 2 teacher books $15.25

and $16.40, speed drills $4.20, tests $1.10. Grade 5 student book $12.90, 2 teacher books $15.25 and $16.40, speed drills $4.35, tests $ 1. 10. The revised series is available through grade 7 with following levels in preparation. Shipping extra.

Rod and Staff Publishers, PO Box 3, Highway 172, Crockett, KY 41413-0003. (606) 522-4348. Fax: (606) 522-4896.

Saxon Math Grades 4–8

Grades 4–8. Home Study Kits: Math 54 (2nd edition), $48.95; Math 65 (2nd edition), $49.95; Math 76 (3rd edition), $50.95; Math 87, $50.95. Each Home Study Kit includes student text, answer key, and tests. Shipping extra.

Saxon Publishers, 2450 John Saxon Blvd., Norman, OK 73071. (800) 284-7019. Email: info@saxonpub.com. Web: www.saxonpub.com.

include counting, time, place value, fractions, money, and skip counting. The teacher's book shows a reduced copy of the student's page and has answers filled in. Detailed directions are given for teaching the concepts in class, and directions are not printed in the workbooks. **Grade 2** introduces the facts from 11 to 18, three-digit addition and subtraction, and carrying and borrowing. Multiplication and division of ls, 2s, 5s, and 10s is optional. **Grade 3** has a hardcover textbook instead of workbooks. Multiplication and division tables through 9 are taught, each table going up to 12. Roman numerals are introduced and measure equivalents are drilled. **Grade 4** teaches the 10s to 12s tables, long division, and two-digit multipliers. Adding and subtracting fractions, decimals to hundredths, and graphs are introduced. This level shows written explanations and examples in the student's textbook. The teacher's book shows student's pages full size with answers filled in, and teacher's instructions expand the material to a two-volume manual. **Grade 5** extends basic computation skills and introduces multiplying and dividing fractions, percents, metric system, and early geometry. *Mary Pride*

What modern crusader has upset the math establishment and raised children's math scores by incredible amounts? **John Saxon,** that's who!

When this ex-Air Force officer took to teaching, he wondered why only 20 percent of his algebra students passed the final exam. Unlike so many modern teachers, who have been trained to blame the students, Saxon blamed the textbook. Moreover, he decided to try an experiment. He invented lesson plans that not only simplified math concepts, but reviewed the same types of problems again and again, once introduced, rather than moving on immediately to new ideas.

This "incremental development and continuous review" approach to math teaching produced unbelievable results. Students, for the first time, had a chance to let math settle into their bones. Instead of desperately treading water, trying to cope with new idea after new idea, Saxon's students had time to become familiar with all the ideas through long-term practice. They also had a chance to experience success, because once they had learned and were required to use a skill, that same skill continued to be included in their problem sets. Math became, as Saxon says, a time for "showing off" instead of for failure. Another Saxon saying: "Time is the elixir that turns things difficult into things familiar."

Saxon Myths

The first editions of Saxon's books drew the ire of some Christian homeschoolers because of occasional word problems that referred to fairy-tale creatures such as gremlins (in red suits, no less) and fairies (counting toadstools to make sure there are enough seats for all those attending the fairy convention), or characters from Greek and Roman mythology (e.g., two Greek gods guessing at the weight of Athena's armor as she springs full-grown from the forehead of Zeus).

Saxon had trouble understanding these concerns at first. After all, he didn't believe in these creatures; he was just trying to get students interested in math. Eventually he took out the more noxious characters, but a few fairy-tale and mythological folk remain.

Having read *all* the story problems in these books, and being familiar with the cultural references, I can testify that Saxon is *not* trying to sneak in New Age or occult thinking here. If you look carefully at these word problems, they all treat the fairy-tale and mythological folks *irreverently*. Lacking altogether is that serious, worshipful tone in which goddess-worshippers and others trying to revive ancient religions like to refer to such imaginary beings. In any case, the few word problems that refer to myths are only a tiny subset of all the historical, cultural, and scientific references Saxon builds into his problem sets. Two minutes with a Magic Marker can banish the six or ten sentences of this nature from your math book, if they bother you.

Saxon's books look quite somber: black and white text, only simple illustrations. Full color and 3-D airbrushing, common to elementary-school math books these days, are conspicuous by their absence. The excitement comes from the learning itself. Saxon's texts support and encourage the student, not by babyish Behavior Modification ("You're doing great! Keep it up!") or glitzy eye candy, but by allowing him to go step by step and *rewarding him for learning*.

The problems themselves sparkle with personality and expose children to fun facts from other school subjects. Example:

> *Genghis Khan was born in 1167. In 1211 he invaded China. How old was he then?*

> *The Arctic Ocean is almost completely covered with the polar ice cap, which averages about 10 feet thick. About how many inches thick is the polar ice cap?*

Let me explain the numbering system used in these books. Math 54 is for "fifth graders and bright fourth graders." Math 65 is for "sixth graders and bright fifth graders." Etc. If you're not sure where your child should start in this sequence, the simple diagnostic test built into the middle of the Saxon Math catalog will help you figure it out.

Saxon's **Math 54**, **Math 65**, **Math 76,** and **Math 87** are wonderful for home use, with the separate teacher's booklet with problem answers, tests, and test keys all in one place. The incremental approach means children practically teach themselves, only requiring infrequent explanations of some new concepts.

This is the most popular math series for homeschoolers today. *Mary Pride*

Manipulatives and Activity-based Curriculum

Multiplication Teaching and Learning Made Easy, a program originally designed for the classroom, now has been updated for the home. The complete program teaches kids all the multiplication facts in six weeks and includes:

- A simple, effective philosophy of how to teach multiplication
- Teacher's Manual with detailed instructions, daily lesson plans, six complete games, and two bulletin board ideas
- Coloring/Activity Book (bound together with the Teacher's Manual in the set I received). This includes 18 color-by-number pictures, 12 "just fun" coloring sheets, and activity sheets
- File folder games, bulletin board ideas, incidental learning suggestions, and other classroom-oriented extras
- Precoded flash cards for the weekly drills
- Three computer games for the computer: *Heart Chase* (basic), *Flash Fill* (intermediate), and *Math Invaders* (advanced).

The formatting and layout of *Multiplication Teaching and Learning Made Easy* are excellent. The philosophy is easy to follow, also. You start by explaining that multiplication means adding the same number again and again, and showing students on a multiplication table that they do *not* need to memorize many of the facts (like 0 times, 1 times, and 10 times), since simple rules govern these multiplications. You also cross off the duplicate facts on the table (e.g., 3 x 4 = 4 x 3, so there is no need to memorize them

Addition Teaching and Learning Made Easy
Multiplication Teaching and Learning Made Easy
Addition, grades 1–3. Multiplication, grades 2–7. Book and flashcards, $16 each postpaid. Computer Game, $30 postpaid. *Addition • Multiplication Teaching & Learning Made Easy*, PO Box 1482, Conway, AR 72033. (501) 327-1968. Web: *www.conwaynet.com/mult-add*.

This program was originally too pricey for the home market, so the publisher listened to us and came out with a very affordable home edition. Now you can get the teacher's instructions, lesson plans, games, coloring and activity pages, and so on all in one handy workbook, plus a set of flash cards as well. The computer games are also available separately now.

separately). You then concentrate on a few facts each week in *random* order (to prevent guessing and counting), using color by number, flash cards, activities, tests, and games to reinforce the facts. If you have a computer, you can go one step farther and get the computer disk. Then use the three computer games on your disk for math fact drill.

Addition Teaching and Learning Made Easy is also available, teaching the addition facts with a similar approach. *Mary Pride*

Hands-On Equations Learning System.

Grades 3–8. Single student kit (comes with instruction manuals, game pieces, and worksheets), $34.95. Class Set (Teacher and ten students), $195. Two hour instructional VideoManual, $79.95. Shipping extra.
Borenson and Associates, PO Box 3328, Allentown, PA 18106. Orders and Inquiries: (800) 993-6284. Fax: (610) 398-7863. Web: www.borenson.com.

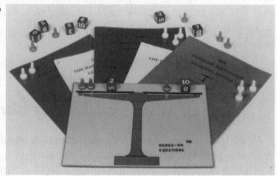

Here's something *really* new—a hands-on approach to algebraic linear equations! You know what those are: fun stuff like $2x + (-x) + 3 = 2(-x) + 15$. Most parents enjoy teaching this as much as visiting the dentist, and the kids feel likewise. But now, with **Hands-On Equations** from Borenson & Associates, learning pre-algebra and solving simple linear equations can be as fun and easy as playing a game. Kids age eight and up simply set up any such equation using pawns and cubes. They then perform various "legal moves" (according to the simple instructions) and thus solve the equation.

Level I, seven lessons, is designed for third- or fourth-grade level. It takes students from setting up simple equations on a laminated representation of a balance scale through teaching them to solve equations as complicated as $2x + x + x + x + 2 = x + 10$ on paper. **Level II** gets into equations with negative variables (-x). **Level III** introduces equations with negative whole numbers, including subtracting negative numbers. Again, the students learn to replicate the process on paper. Each level is supposed to take about two weeks of succeeding years in the average classroom.

The Hands-On Equations Learning System comes with manuals for Levels I, II, and II, a set of 26 worksheets plus answer keys, and one student kit of game pieces with a laminated picture of a balance. Game pieces included are eight blue pawns and four red number cubes (introduced in Level I), eight white pawns (to represent negative variables—Level II), and four green number cubes (to represent negative numbers—Level III). There is no dice-rolling or chance involved—the pieces are simply used to represent numbers and variables.

The Class Set includes worksheet masters with permission to make up to ten copies and a teacher's demonstration balance scale. This kit and the VideoManual are all you need to teach this course. The cost for the Class Set and Video together ($275) is pretty steep for one family, but the publisher envisions it being used in a cooperative homeschool group where the cost could be spread around.

Henry Borenson, Ed.D., the gentleman who invented this system, suggests that you simply replace some class time spent on mental math or basic facts worksheets with his Hands-On Equations.

Why start so young? Four reasons:

1. It's *easy* for the kids.
2. It gives them "a tremendous sense of mathematical power and self-confidence."
3. It increases interest in math.
4. It lays a "concrete, intuitive foundation" for facing equations and thus improving future math performance.

Bottom line: Hands-On Equations is not a substitute for ninth-grade algebra (nor is it meant to be), but it is a wonderful, systematic, fun, empowering preparation for it! *Mary Pride*

Making Math Meaningful is a curriculum for homeschoolers that

- tells you, the teacher, exactly what to do and say (this is called "programmed" learning)
- uses manipulatives and real-world objects wherever possible to introduce and demonstrate math skills
- spends as much, if not more, time on math *concepts* as on math *skills*
- has both a teacher and student workbook for grades 1–4 (level K has one book for parent and child to use together, while levels 5 and 6 are written directly to the student and thus only have a student workbook)

Each lesson includes a list of materials needed, a description of the concept or skill being taught, a "What I Am to Do" section (on the left side of the page) and a "What I am to Say" section (on the right side of the page). Lessons each are one of three types: *exploring* a concept (you demonstrate it for the child), *naming* the concept (learning terminology and/or skills), and *applying* the concept (the child practices the skill). Answer keys are at the end of each lesson.

Each "chapter" deals with a single topic—e.g., "Addition and Subtraction with Real Objects"—and has a number of "Activities" grouped under it. Some "Activities" can take a week, while others can be just a day's lesson. A suggested teaching schedule in the front of the parent book shows how to arrange activities throughout a 36-week school year.

This is not a drill-and-practice curriculum or an incremental-review curriculum. Like Miquon, it stresses understanding, discovery, and moving from the concrete to the abstract. However, it's actually easier to use than Miquon, thanks to its more logical organization.

Level K introduces the numbers 0–20. **Level 1** presents the addition and subtraction math facts form 0–20, plus writing and solving equations with those facts, equal/not equal, and less than/greater than. **Level 2** works with numbers up to 99, introduces the multiplication facts through 10 x 10, and addition/subtraction with borrowing and carrying. **Level 3** pro-

UPDATED!
Making Math Meaningful
Grades K–6. Each level (one year), $40, except level K, $30. Manipulatives kit for K–3, $15. Add 10% shipping ($3 minimum). *Cornerstone Curriculum Project, 2006 Flat Creek Pl., Richardson, TX 75080.* (972) 235-5149. *Fax: (972) 235-0236. E-mail: dquine@CornerstoneCurriculum.com. Web: www.CornerstoneCurriculum.com.*

Making Math Meaningful student workbooks look like a cross between Math Program Associates workbooks, Miquon workbooks, and mass-market workbooks. Like classroom workbooks, they have computation problems, time and money problems, word problems, graphs, and so on. Like Miquon workbooks, they give children challenges to solve with manipulatives (Unifix cubes, links, etc.). Like Math Program Associates workbooks, you'll find a lot of work with grouping, and place value is introduced *very* slowly.

UPDATED!
Mastering Mathematics

Grades 1–6 and remedial. Entire program, $129.95. Set of six extra workbooks (sold with complete series only), $187.95. Add/Sub, $54.95. Mult/Div, $54.95. Point/Fractions, $58.95. Extra workbooks, $10.95–$13.95 each. Finishing Fractions, $33.95. Drill Practice Disk (PC only), $9.95. Shipping extra. *Mastery Publications, 90 Hillside Lane, Arden, NC 28704. Phone/fax: (828) 684-0429. In Canada: The Learning House, 8 Dunlop Dr., RR #4, Goderich, ON, CANADA N7A 3Y1. Phone/fax: (519) 524-5607. Email: masterypub@aol.com. Web: www.masterypublications.com.*

gresses to numbers up to 999, larger addition and subtraction problems, and more work with fractions. **Level 4** finally gets into numbers up to millions, larger multiplication problems, and writing equations with fractions. **Level 5** works with place value up to the trillions, introductory long division, adding/subtracting/multiplying/dividing fractions, and decimal equivalents. **Level 6** introduces place value to the right of the decimal point—tenths, hundredths, and thousandths—ratios and proportions, and more work with decimals. All levels review previous skills and build on them. So, for example, after multiplication and division is introduced in level 3, all subsequent levels teach and practice bigger and tougher multiplication and division problems. Time, measurement, money, and even cooking recipes are built in to each level.

Thanks to the wide variety of activities and problem types, your student is not likely to get bored with this curriculum. It's easy to use and thorough. Maybe that's why it's so popular. *Mary Pride*

Mastering Mathematics is not at all what I expected it to be. From the titles of its component programs—*Attacking Addition, Subduing Subtraction, Mastering Multiplication, Defeating Division, Perfecting the Point,* and *Finishing Fractions*—I had expected a series of single-skill workbooks similar to those sold in teacher's stores. Instead, it's a complete elementary curriculum.

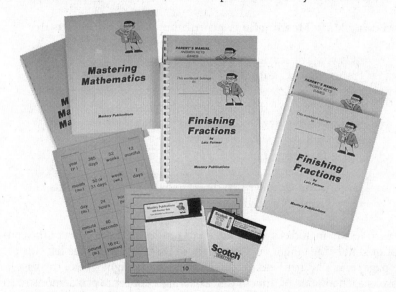

Mastering Mathematics has many unique features. First, this is a Christian program. The Christian content is not overly evident in the *Attacking Addition* workbook, apart from an occasional problem that mentions Sunday School. Many pages of *Subduing Subtraction*, though, are devoted to problems involving biblical time lines, and the curriculum repeatedly refers to Jesus, Creation, the Flood, and other Christian teachings.

Also noticeable is the rapid progression to problems using large numbers. Curriculum author Letz Farmer rightly notes that young children can do problems with many numbers as easily as problems with few. It is no harder, for example, to add 2543 + 5344 than to add 3 + 4, 4 + 4, 5 + 3, and 2 + 5 as individual problems.

Another special feature is the pretests. Unlike other programs, Mastering Mathematics allows your child to "test out" of any subject areas he has already mastered.

Still another special feature is that kids don't study subtraction and division facts in this program. Mrs. Farmer figures that if you know your addition facts, and a few other basic math principles, you automatically know your subtraction facts. That's because 3 + 4 = 7 really describes the same concept as 7 - 4 = 3.

The teacher's manual includes separate instructions for how to teach time, money, weights and measures, etc., using oral and real-life examples and homemade manipulatives. Pretests are included in the front of each student workbook, with an additional copy in the teacher's manual.

Kids can do most of the work on their own. Assignments are short, in large print, and have lots of white space for problem solving.

Mastering Mathematics comes with special flash cards, board games, manipulatives, and self-checking fact wheels. You have to cut these out and assemble them. Beyond these, you will need some coins or play money, a clock with movable hands, a demonstration thermometer, and a few other manipulatives you can make yourself. Directions for making these manipulatives are provided. These are used while teaching time, measurement, money, temperature, and other non-computational concepts.

Purchasers are now allowed to make sufficient copies for immediate family use. However, you'll probably find it cheaper to buy extra bound workbooks.

A drill practice disk for PC compatibles is also available. You fill in the grid practicing addition and multiplication facts. Choose random or consecutive facts presented in a timed or untimed manner. Record keeping of each child's three fastest times allows him to compete against himself.

New manipulatives are also available for the Mastering Mathematics curriculum. These resemble cardboard Cuisenaire rods. A "Go to the Bank" game is also included, as are weight/measure/money/time flash cards.

It would be nice if the reproducible appendix worksheets came in drill packs, like CalcuLadder, of sets of 10 or more. As it is, you'd be smart to use the plastic page protector (included) along with erasable pens (included in the complete set) over each workbook page, to avoid having to photocopy pages or buy extra workbooks when your child merely needs to do the same page over several times.

This is a good program—I used it with my own daughter Sarah, until she was ready to switch over to Saxon Math. Excellent explanations, easy to use for kids of all ability levels. *Mary Pride*

Because of Mrs. Farmer's background in special education, she developed this program to work with special needs children as well as average and gifted children. Thus her program minimizes the need for memorization, and memory facts are reinforced with flash cards, board games, and self-checking fact wheels. For the severely disabled learner, she recommends that only multiplication facts be memorized, since they can always do addition and subtraction on their fingers, but not multiplication! With an attitude like this, it's not surprising that children with IQs as low as 45 have been able to learn with her program. Conversely, kids with IQs as high as 138 who used this program have placed five years above grade level in mathematics within months.

Professor Elmer Brooks' Math It series leads kids through the basic math principles *and* drills them on arithmetic facts. Instead of memorizing tables, kids learn how to derive the answers (e.g., adding nine is the same as adding ten and subtracting one). Kids then practice adding nine (for example), until they can give all the plus-nine math facts instantly.

Pre-Math It involves exercises with dominoes (included). **Math It** tells you "How Stevie Learned His Math" and includes the *Addit*, *Dubblit*, and *Timzit* games, along with the *Math Concepts Book*. **Advanced Math It** has *Percentit* and *Dividit*. Each kit is nonconsumable and covers several years of arithmetic (no time telling or measurement, etc.).

With Math It and Advanced Math It, you get pre-perfed math facts cards for each game, color-

Math It series

Grades K–8. Pre-Math It, $41.95. Math It, $47.95. Advanced Math It, $24.95. Math Concepts Book (covers math learning for all three sets), $13.95. Shipping extra.
Hewitt Homeschooling Resources, PO Box 9, Washougal, WA 98671. Orders: (800) 348-1750. Inquiries: (360) 835-8708. Fax: (360) 835-8697. Email: hewitths@aol.com.

Packaging has improved a lot since the first edition of this product. It now comes in a fancy binder, with professionally-printed books and materials. If you follow the directions, your child is bound to learn his math facts, and enjoy it, too!

coded as "facts families"—the +9 family, the +8 family, the doubles, the "neighbors," and the "leftovers" for Addit, for example. You also get game boards, facts sheets, envelopes for storing your cards and games, and an instruction book that covers not only the basic games, but extra math tricks, such as how to quickly "reduce" a complicated multiplication problem to check your answer, or how to add long columns of figures like a flash. The approach gets kids thinking mathematically, and is a lot more motivational than traditional memorization-only methods. (In plain English, it's *fun!*) *Mary Pride*

NEW!
Math Sense

Grades 1–6. Math Pack, $38. Math Bag, $26. Math Sense Manual, $16. Shipping extra.

Common Sense Press, P.O. Box 1365, Melrose FL 32666. Call (352) 475-5757 for a retail store near you; they do not sell retail themselves. Fax: (352) 475-6105. Email: service@cspress.com. Web: www.cspress.com.

When it comes to manipulatives-based homeschool math programs, **Math Sense** wins the award for packaging. "Manipulatives" mean items such as blocks, rods, fraction circles, and the like, with which the teacher can physically demonstrate the math principles the class is studying. Instead of lots of pieces and no place to put them, or at best a cardboard box, you get either a mini back pack with an external pouch for storing the manipulatives and space in the pack itself for the *Math Sense Manual*, which comes with it, or a small roll bag with room for the manipulatives and a tiny instruction guide. The sturdy pack and bag both sport an attractive two-color look, with their names and the Common Sense Press logo in white. To see them is to want them.

Each of thee comes with the same 104-piece set of **Math Sense Blocks**. These Lego-like blocks have a snap on the top for each unit of size and a different color for each size block. Units, for example, are white, while 2's are purple and 3's are green. You can tell each block's number by either counting the squares on the side or the snaps on top. Teaching arithmetic is literally a "snap" with these blocks. Snap two together for addition, or snap two together and see how many snaps are "left over" for subtraction. Build rectangles for multiplication, or see how many of one size "go into" a number for division. There's even a 100 square for doing work with place value, and a pair of dice for simple work with probability.

The **Math Sense Manual** contains complete instructions for using the manipulatives to teach all these concepts, of course. This spiral-bound, two-color manual is divided into sections for use with K–3 children and children in grades 4–6. A handy glossary of mathematical terms, and equally handy reproducible sheets for use as graph paper, hundred chart, and "Number Express" activities, are also included.

By and large, the instructions and illustrations make everything clear. However, the manual urges you to introduce 11, 12, and the other "teens" as "one ten and one," "one ten and two," etc. This is supposed to keep children from getting confused about how to write these numbers. But you are never told when to switch back to standard numbers, and I am not convinced that using odd terminology really makes things easier in the long run. Another thing: you are asked to do exercises using a "Number Express" train. However, not until many lessons later is it ever made clear which part of the train is the Cargo Car, Engine, or Tanker Car. This should have been illustrated when the Number Express was first introduced.

Finally, multiplication is taught in an unusual way. Let's say you're multiplying 5 by 4. Other manipulative programs would either simply ask you to snap four set of 5's together, or they would have you lay out the two factors—5 and 4—and then form the product between them. Math Sense, for some reason, asks you to place a 5 on its side, and then snap that number of 4's together. This neither demonstrates that multiplication is a product of two numbers, nor does it have the benefit of only having the answer on the table with no stray pieces lying around to confuse the issue.

With these exceptions, this is a very nice, slick program that is easy to use, motivational, and (best of all) easy to put away. *Mary Pride*

Moving with Math is the most thorough math course based on math manipulatives I have ever seen. The program spans the range from kindergarten through basic high school skills, and is completely manipulative-based. They don't teach you *anything* without "showing" you how it works with real-world objects. Even better: through careful design, they have trimmed down the numbers and types of manipulatives needed with the program, to the point where it won't break your budget to use it.

The program is organized into four levels. Level A covers grades 1 and 2; Level B, grades 3 and 4; Level C, grades 5 and 6; Level D, grades 7 and 8, or remedial high school. The sequence covers between 90 and 100 percent of the curriculum objectives your state board of education requires for math in those grades, depending on which state you live in. A Pre-Kindergarten/Kindergarten level is also available. Level C, Part II: Fractions, Decimals, and Percents has been restructured and includes lots of new games. New Home School Instruction packets for levels A through D are available to help adapt the package to home use. Separate programs for grades K–2 are also now available, for parents who want to have one pupil book per year.

Each level includes diagnostic tests, workbooks, teacher instructions that tell you how to use manipulatives to illustrate lesson concepts, post-tests, answer keys, grading sheets for record-keeping, and regular "maintenance" tests that constantly review you on material you have already studied. It is all organized carefully, but rather confusingly. For example, they don't explain anywhere that their "diagnostic tests" are the same as their "pre-tests" for each level. (Most publishers use "diagnostic" tests for once-a-year placement, and "pre-tests" for weekly or monthly progress checking.) They do tell you that you have permission to reproduce the tests for use in your classroom, but instead of emblazoning this permission on the jacket holding the tests, it's in small print here and there, and only visible by inference on the instructions for giving the tests. Likely a lot of unwarned home schoolers end up giving Junior the master test to write on before discovering this error.

As an alternative, a consumable test and review booklet is available at half the cost of the reproducible format. Workbook pages are keyed directly to the objectives on the pre-tests, but you have to reference the teacher book to find out which pages of the student book go with which objectives. Each objective may correspond to several workbook pages, as well. Wish they had used one consistent keying method instead of two different ones!

Once you figure their system out, you're golden, but Bill and I had to struggle with it for over an hour just to figure it out.

Math Teachers Press has published a new Home School Instructions manual to fix the above problem. This guide lists the objectives with the page numbers of the activity sheets that go with them, so parents don't have to study the teacher's manual before starting to teach the course.

NEW!
Math Teachers Press "Moving with Math" Curriculum

Grades preK–8. Student Activity Book: Grade K, $11.95; Grade 1, $15.95; Grade 2, $15.95. Student Workbooks (Levels A–D), $4.95–$6.95 each. HomeSchool Student Sets: Level A, $54.90; Level B, $54.90; Level C, $49.95; Level D, $61.95. Reproducible sets $20 extra each. Teacher Guides with answer keys: Level A, $29.95; Level B, $29.95; Level C, $34.95; Level D, $49.95. Teacher's Guides with tests (grades K–2), $49.95 or $69.95 each. Shipping extra.
Math Teachers Press, 5100 Gamble Drive, Suite 375, Minneapolis, MN 55416. (800) 852-2435. (612) 545-6535. Fax: (612) 546-7502. Email: mtpckp@aol.com. Web: www.movingwithmath.com.

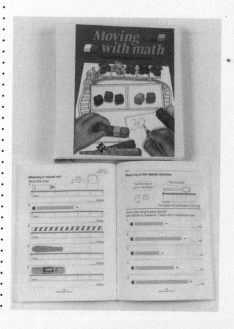

Here's what we found:

- *Math Capsules,* the jacket with papers inside it, holds the objectives, pre- and post-tests, daily review quizzes, record-keeping sheets, and answer keys to the tests and daily reviews. You can reproduce the tests and quizzes for use in your own "classroom," that is, with your own children.
- A number of Moving With Math workbooks are included. You need a set of these books for each student, as they are not reproducible.
- Each Moving With Math workbook has an accompanying teacher's edition with lesson plans and answers to the exercises.
- *Skill Builders Using Action Math* books are reproducible, since they are "black line masters." Black line masters look exactly like any other workbook—you just have permission to copy a set of them for your classroom. Each level has one of these books. Teacher's notes are in the front of the book. Answers are in the back, as are some very useful masters for drilling math facts, making game boards, grids and ruled paper, and the like.
- Some levels also include a book from a series entitled "Using Models." Each of these books explains how to use manipulatives to teach an entire area of math, e.g., multiplication and division.
- Manipulatives can be purchased separately (and fairly inexpensively) from Math Teachers Press, or in some cases you can make your own. I doubt the value of trying to save the $2.95 cost of a geoboard by banging your own nails into your own piece of wood, though!

Math Teacher Press materials are inviting. Lesson plans are "scripted," so you know exactly what to say to the student. Workbook pages are illustrated with simple line art drawings and are easy to comprehend. Grading is quick and easy, as is record-keeping. Even the manipulatives don't get out of hand, since you only need a few sets, and they are reused from level to level. Recommended materials for a kindergarten child are less than $40, including manipulatives. Home School Student sets for each level cover two grades each, and aren't that expensive to begin with. Manipulatives average $20 per level for grades 1–8. Supplies for a second child using the same program amount to only about $10 per school year in the original format or $22 per year in the consumable format.

Math Teachers Press thoughtfully provides free Sampler Packs for each level, showing sample sheets from all the different materials in the level. Their Sampler Pack also outlines their program philosophy and shows how it meets NCTM standards. Of course they throw in a current price sheet! A homeschool video is offered free with qualifying orders, too. They also offer a 100 percent money-back guarantee, so I guess you'd have to say they're pretty confident you'll like what you get. *Mary Pride and Kim O'Hara*

Lots of you have asked us about the **Math-U-See** program, and finally we had time to check it out. What I can tell you is this:

- **Steve Demme**, the program author and video teacher, is **the most incredible math teacher** I have ever seen. If there's a clever way to explain a math concept that will help children remember it, this guy knows it.
- **The manipulatives are sensible, usable, and well-organized.** The fraction manipulatives actually come in a storage pouch, so you won't lose those slippery little items. The rods are kind of like Cuisenaire rods, except they're stackable. Bill calls them "a cross between Cuisenaire rods and Lego bricks!" The algebra and decimal inserts are smooth green pieces that snap into the back of the hundred blocks, plus blue snappable rods for tens or tenths, and red snappable "units." Trust me—the video makes it all clear.

Kids who pick up abstract concepts easily probably don't need all the extra help of these videos, manipulatives, and workbooks, although even they will most likely find the Math-U-See manipulative approach more fun than others. But for kids who are the slightest bit math-phobic, or who don't like math, or who are being taught by parents who had trouble with math, this is one great program. *Mary Pride*

This activity-centered program for early childhood math education is "the most popular activity-centered mathematics curriculum in use today." Over the years it keeps popping up in homeschool magazines, especially those of the unschooling persuasion. So I finally begged a copy from Cuisenaire Company, expecting great things.

After working through **Mathematics Their Way**, I have to honestly say I don't like it for home use. For one thing, it's just too much work for too little content. This is the familiar curse left to us by John Dewey, the father of the "if you don't experience it you don't learn it" educational philosophy. In a classroom, where children's backgrounds differ so widely, there may be value in approaching each new concept from twenty different angles, thus ensuring that even the dullest child can't help but catch on, but at home this is just a lot of unnecessary work. Kids can learn patterning, for example, without having to make dot charts *and* Unifix cube patterns *and* pattern blocks *and* stand in lines *and* do rhythmic clapping *and* decipher letter patterns.

Secondly, the program requires gazillions of different math manipulatives. Cuisenaire offers a "bargain kit" of manipulatives for use with this program—only $209.50, and it includes its own seven-drawer storage unit. This doesn't even include all of the materials you will need for the program. You'll still have to make your own counting audiocassettes, dot pattern cards, dot chart, dot-to-dot templates, egg carton graphing boards, geoboard sequence charts, graphing plastic, magic box and magic box numbers, milk carton graphing boxes, milk carton scale, junk box, number flips, numeral sequence cards, etc. 'Nuff said.

NEW!
Math-U-See

Grades K–10. Videos: Foundation, $30; Intermediate (set of 2), $35; Advanced (set of 2), $40; Basic Algebra & Geometry (set of 3), $60. Student workbooks: Foundations, Intermediate, Advanced, Basic Algebra & Geometry, $15 each. Manipulatives: blocks, $30; fractions overlays, $30; algebra & decimal inserts, $20. Teacher's manual: Foundations, Intermediate, Advanced, $20 each; Basic Algebra & Geometry, $25. Additional worksheets, $17.50 per level. Shipping extra.
Math-U-See, 905 County Road 214, Eureka Springs, AR 72631. Contact local representative to order. (888) 854-MATH. Fax: (501) 253-2177. Email: mcdonald@ipa.net. Web: www.mathusee.com.

Mathematics Their Way

Grades K–2. $39.95 (includes pad of blackline masters). Add 10% shipping.
Cuisenaire Company of America, 10 Bank Street, PO Box 5026, White Plains, NY 10602. (800) 237-0338. Fax: (800) 551-7637. Web: www.cuisenaire.com.

Thirdly, the author for some reason has seen fit to use the ugly and ungrammatical constructions *hisorher* and *sheorhe* throughout the book. Like mosquitoes, these minor annoyances become more aggravating each time you see one. They also betray the fundamental insecurity and sterility informing this program. John is a *he*. Mary is a *she*. But we never meet John and Mary: only *hesandshes*. One comes away with a feeling that the curriculum considers children as objects to be manipulated, just as all the manipulatives called for in the program are not enjoyed for their beauty of color and shape but only pressed into service for detached scientific explorations. Kids are allowed to use the manipulatives for "free play" before getting down to real work with them, but it's only because this free play time is "the foundation for later development," not because we enjoy watching happy children at play. The atmosphere is tense: kids have to *deduce* things and *explore* things under the guidance of a watchful adult, who makes sure things stay on track. This I don't object to in a straightforward 1 + 1 = 2 program, where we're all here to work, and no funny business, but it does seem a bit unfair to lead kids to chocolate pudding and fingerpainting and not let them play.

Part of the problem is that, as is the nature of early childhood education, the teachers are wearing themselves to a frazzle trying to explain concepts that come almost automatically to children a few years older. Problems raised in the book, such as, "What do I do for the child who thinks there are more windows in the room than pencils because the windows are bigger?" disappear once kids reach age 7 or 8. Home teachers have a great advantage over school teachers here, since we don't have to justify an early childhood education program by pushing concepts on kids who aren't ready for them.

Another advantage of home education is that many of the lessons in *Mathematics Their Way* come quite naturally as part of everyday living: measuring recipe ingredients with Mom in the kitchen, sorting the laundry, counting plates to set around the table. In fact, it is possible to think of *Mathematics Their Way* as a partly effective attempt at recreating in the classroom the rich mathematics possibilities inherent in the home. This probably explains why unschoolers are always talking about it. The program justifies their own approach to education.

If you want a really good course on basic mathematical thinking, the Miquon Math program is much better suited to home use. It covers lots more ground in lots less time, uses a more coherent set of manipulatives (love those Cuisenaire rods!), treats kids like kids, and is structured beautifully for home use. See review below. *Mary Pride*

Miquon Math

Grades 1–3. (Primary) Orange Book, Red Book, Blue Book, Green Book, Yellow Book, and Purple Book, $5.95 each. Miquon Lab Sheet Annotations, $13.95. Miquon Notes to Teachers, $5.95. Miquon First Grade Diary, $5.95. Complete set, $53.95. Add 10% shipping.
Key Curriculum Press, 1150 65th St., Emeryville, CA 94608. (800) 995-MATH. Fax: (800) 541-2442. Email: orders@keypress.com. Web: www.keypress.com.

Miquon Math is a laboratory approach to math, so called because children are encouraged to demonstrate and discover how and why math principles work. It's called "Miquon" Math because it's based on clever lab sheet activities, some teacher-invented, some student-invented, pioneered 27 years ago at the Miquon School in Miquon, Pennsylvania.

Miquon Math is *math*, not a gussied-up arithmetic course. Lots of abstract thinking here. Children using this program do work with the real world mathematically, but the worksheets themselves are heavy on numerals and symbols. In other words, Miquon sets are more likely to include circles and squares than frogs and mittens.

More unusual features: In a world of "Dress for Success" and hyped packaging, Miquon Math makes no attempt to dazzle the children with gorgeous color graphics—although the sheets do have a certain gracefulness of design.

Most unusual of all, often the same sheet can be used for a number of quite different activities. For example, on the very first sheet of the very first book you find a number of sets of circles. In anyone else's program, you'd find instructions asking the student to perhaps count the circles or find all sets of 3 circles. The Miquon approach, instead, is to take the teacher through a discussion of all the topics to be taught under the broad heading of counting. For that particular sheet, here are a few of the suggestions:

1. *Pupils match each element in each set (picture group) with an object such as a rod or a bead.*
2. *Pupils check off each element in a set with a tally mark. [An illustration shows how this might be done.]*
3. *Pupils match each element in a set with a white [Cuisenaire] rod to get a model set. Then they arrange the rods in a row and exchange the row of white rods for a single rod of that length. [An illustration demonstrates this process.]*
4. *Pupils count the elements in each set and match each set with a numeral card.*
5. *Sample questions appropriate for all three [first lab sheets]:*
6. *Which collection (group, set)*
   . . . is the smallest (the least?)
   . . . is the largest (most?)
   . . . has one more than three things?
   . . . has twice as many as two things?

The list goes on and on with even cleverer suggestions. This is real math teaching, not cookbook arithmetic.

The core of the Miquon Math program is the lab workbooks and *Lab Sheet Annotations*. There is no answer key: although the *Lab Sheet Annotations* book contains miniature copies of every page in the entire curriculum (several pages reduced to fit on one *Lab Sheet Annotations* page), answers are not filled in, as they usually are in math teachers' books. So how are you supposed to check your children's work? You are supposed to be right there with them, observing and guiding. (This is not the program for parents who like to set kids working and leave the room!) Mrs. Rasmussen expects you to go through an entire set of workbooks, solving each problem yourself. Your set of completed workbooks will then be your answer key.

This is indeed wonderful preparation for teaching this course, but you'll need to take extra preparation time *and* purchase an extra set of workbooks. A less costly and time-consuming idea would be to stay just a few lessons ahead and simply write in the answers, in cases where each problem has just one answer, on the scaled-down copies of the lab pages in the *Annotations* manual. Thus you can have your own personalized answer key without buying (or toting around) an extra set of workbooks.

Teaching suggestions are scattered where necessary among the copies of student workbook pages in the *Lab Sheet Annotations* book. There is nothing in the nature of formal lesson plans of the "Do this on day one" variety.

Another unusual twist is that the *Lab Sheet Annotations* books lists lab sheets, and comments on them, in the order of the concepts on the sheets, not the order in which they appear in the workbooks. The *Orange Book*, for example, has 24 pages on the subject of counting, followed by 12 on addition, four on subtraction alone, 25 on addition and subtraction combined, 12 on multiplication, and so on. In *Lab Sheet Annotations*, however, all the addition sheets for all six books are listed sequentially, with corresponding teaching philosophy and tips, followed by all the subtraction sheets for all six books, etc.

Miquon Math Lab materials include a set of six workbooks (the *Orange Book, Red Book, Blue Book, Green Book, Yellow Book,* and *Purple Book*, designed to be used in that order), a hefty volume entitled *Lab Sheet Annotations and Mathematics for the Primary Teacher*, another slimmer book entitled *Notes to Teachers*, and the most intriguing book of all, the *First-Grade Diary*. The latter is a literal diary, following the experiences for one year of one first-grade class taught by Lore Rasmussen, author of the Miquon Math materials. You find out not only what the children were told to do, but how they responded to the activities, including activities they invented on their own. The diary is not intended as a teaching guide, but as an example of math teaching in action. If you're fascinated by learning and teaching math, you'll love the *Diary*. If not, skip it and stick with the straight curriculum.

In contrast to the practical emphasis of the *Diary,* the *Notes to Teachers* book is Lore Rasmussen's educational manifesto. Here you discover the philosophy behind the Miquon program (rather similar to that of John Holt—by the way, John Holt used a Miquon-style approach in his own teaching!), plus various appendices. The most essential of these, from the point of view of the home teacher, who already knows her pupils quite well, are Appendices B and E. Appendix B, "Beginning Play with Cuisenaire Rods," shows free play activities with the rods and how these prepare the children for Miquon Math. Appendix E lists all materials and supplies you need for your entire math lab program, and gives instructions for making your own number lines, Hundred Board, square geoboard, meter sticks, and yard sticks.

In the Miquon curriculum, concepts are broken down into 26 areas, each labeled with a letter. Concepts include counting, odd-even, addition, subtraction, multiplication, fractions, division, equalities and inequalities, place value, number lines and functions, factoring, squaring, simultaneous equations, graphing equations, geometric recognition, length/area/volume, series and progressions, grid and arrow games, mapping, clock arithmetic, sets, and word problems.

Mortensen Math Curriculum

Grades 1–8. Animals-n-Stuff kit, $8.82 for book and manipulatives. Smiley face series (set of 50 books), $110, $2.20 each. Algebra, Arithmetic, Problem Solving, Measurement, and Calculus (each 3 levels), $110 per level, 50 books per level. Teacher's manuals: level 1, $13.20; level 2, $14.41; level 3, $16.83. Many other manipulatives sets available. Shipping extra. *V.J. Mortensen Co., PO Box 98, Hayden, ID 83835. Orders: (800) 4PLUS4-8. Fax: (208) 667-9438. Email: request@mortensenmathdirect.com (catalog requests only). Web: www.mortensenmathdirect.com.*

For reviews of Mortenson Math manipulatives, see chapters 24 and 26.

Editor's note: The Mortensen books are being changed into a new format; three-hole-punched, normal white paper, as opposed to greyish newsprint paper. The prices shown here are club pricing; in order to enter the club, you must make an initial order of $39.95 minimum, then the renewal fee is $24 per year. Also, if you're a brand-new customer, you can request a catalog packet and receive a certificate for 15 percent off your first order.

Kids are supposed to finish two books a year, completing the entire program by the end of third grade. Here kids who attend most public or private schools will have a real problem—they will already know everything the schools plan to teach them for the next three years. Home-taught children using this program should probably go straight to John Saxon's *Math 65*, or possibly even *Math 76*. Alternatively, they could pick up the Key Curriculum Press *Key to . . .* series, which covers decimals, fractions, geometry, pre-algebra, and all that other upper-elementary stuff.

If all you want is for your kids to be fast with the math facts, then you need another program. If, however, you are excited by the sight of your children thinking, pondering, discovering, and inventing . . . if you want the best program around for developing mathematical thinking skills and accelerating your children's native intellectual ability . . . this just might be the one. *Mary Pride*

Putting math in a box. That's literally what **Mortensen Math** does. Creator Jerry Mortensen has developed a unique visual math analogy of boxes and squares to present not only the basic arithmetic operations, but such esoteric subjects as algebra and calculus.

For multiplication and division, the process is obvious. 3 x 4 is three rows of length four, or a square with surface area 12. Simple. In algebra, simply substitute *x* and *y* for any specific numbers. To present $(x + 1)(y + 2)$, you end up with a square of surface area *xy* flanked on one side by a bar length *y* and on the other by two bars length *x*, and two little squares (each valued at 1) in the corner to make up the total square. Clear as mud, right? Maybe you'd better catch the demonstration.

For manipulatives, you get large squares, bars, and tiny unit-value squares. For counting practice, stack the lined bars in order of length . . . 1, 2, 3, and so on. For adding, add the bars. For subtraction, subtract. In multiplication and division life gets a bit more complicated. However, the workbooks creep along at a snail's pace repeating the same sort of problem over and over so your child is not likely to get lost.

The **"-n-Stuff"** and **Smiley Face** series introduce the manipulatives. The "-n-Stuff" booklet asks children to fill in the bars and boxes in the pictures of boxes, animals, or vehicles with the correct manipulative. The Smiley Face series asks your child to either match a Mortensen Math symbol with the appropriate number (the *Counting* book) or do some simple multiplication (*Multiplication* book). Your child draws a smiley face on what he thinks is the right answer.

The **Arithmetic** series goes through the basic four operations: adding, subtracting, multiplying, dividing. **Algebra** goes a bit further with *x*s and *y*s. Due to the physical limitations of representing all algebraic equations using manipulative units, tens, and hundreds, you are limited to equations with two factors. The people at Mortensen say it is possible to represent higher order polynomials, but I haven't seen it done. Consider this more as pre-algebra than as a substitute for a real algebra course. Ditto the calculus workbooks, which only in Book 5 get around to introducing the idea of taking delta *x* to zero. There is much more to calculus than can be represented using manipulatives.

At each level, there are arithmetic, algebra, problem-solving, measurement, and calculus workbooks. The teacher's manual for each level follows the workbooks. If your goal is just to understand how to introduce math concepts using Mortensen manipulatives, though, the Series A manuals (a set of 10 books) are probably enough. They show how to introduce addition, subtraction, multiplication, division, fractions, equations, functions and relationships, algebraic operations, and algebraic story problems. The set also includes a games and activities book.

The entire Mortensen series sticks firmly to the math-as-a-square vision. But math is not about making squares out of everything; it is about solving real-life problems. This entire reliance on an (admittedly helpful) abstract analogy makes it more helpful as a second chance for children with math troubles or an explanatory tool to accompany regular math lessons than as a complete or primary teaching tool. Personally, I find the Series A manuals (which explain how to use the manipulatives) much more useful than the workbooks. *Mary Pride*

Think & Do

What do you get when you take a classic and rewrite it to introduce math concepts? You might end up with **Alice in Pastaland** and **Sir Cumference and the First Round Table**. These thirty-two page softcover illustrated tales attempt to illustrate mathematical ideas by twisting them into a classic tale.

In *Alice in Pastaland*, Alice falls into a wonderland where pasta is the only common denominator. This book must have been challenging to write, because it was designed to not only parody Lewis Carroll's story, but to also incorporate the NCTM standards for teaching math plus Howard Gardner's multiple-intelligence theories on learning and to be used with *Pasta Math*, a book by Mary Chandler that uses pasta as math manipulatives.

In spite of these challenges, *Alice* comes across as an amusing story that will be enjoyed by children of many ages (though I suspect it's more suited to children older than the age recommended on the book). I particularly like the borders around the illustrations which include all the ways to add numbers that total six, adding twelves, and more.

Sir Cumference and the First Round Table is reviewed in the Geometry chapter.

Both books can be enjoyed as stories, or as introductions to various math concepts. It makes you wonder what other books could be next in the series? Perhaps *Gulliver's Adventures in the Lands of Large and Small*? *Teresa Schultz-Jones*

Some of the over 200 "fun and challenging math puzzles, game, designs, and projects" in this attractive spiral-bound book you might not immediately recognize as "math." If you define "anything having to do with shapes" as geometry, for example, than making paper models of geometric shapes is "math." Or if you define matching numbers to letters as math, then constructing a secret code wheel is "math." Not that there's anything wrong with this. I just didn't want you to think that **Barron's Math Wizardry for Kids** was mainly about addition and subtraction.

The book is printed in two colors (the colors are red and blue) and comes loaded with lots of line-art illustrations, and a surprising amount of built-in teaching, some obviously useful and some pretty ersatz (e.g., the origin of the word *googolplex*). The book's 336 pages also include a list of math signs and symbols, an appendix on how to construct basic angles and shapes using a protractor and compass, a glossary of math terms, and an index. If you purchase the full kit, you also get a lot of hands-on activities to complement the book.

One use for this book that I bet nobody else has suggested is to get a gander at the sort of "math" skills the National Council of Teachers of Mathematics wants your child to have. Most are of almost no use in learning the basic arithmetic on which all actual math is based.

Kids who already know their arithmetic and who enjoy problem-solving can certainly sharpen their minds and learn fun facts in a fun way with this

book or kit. Kids who don't already have the math facts at their fingertips had better start with them first. *Mary Pride*

NEW!
Dealing With Addition

Ages 2–8. Jacketed reinforced binding, $15.95, or paperbound, $6.95. Shipping extra.
Charlesbridge Publishing, Inc., 85 Main St., Watertown, MA 02472. (800) 225-3214. Fax: (800) 926-5775. E-mail: books@charlesbridge.com. Web: www.charlesbridge.com.

Dealing With Addition is not a book about card games, although it does include instructions for a "Dealing with Addition" card game in the back. Its 32 oversized colorful pages teach kids about the card suits, the values of the face cards, how to make pairs, and how cards can be combined to form each number from one to ten. Most kids who are allowed to play with cards learn this on their own—but if you'd like to make it more of a math lesson, and less of a games lesson, here is the book. *Mary Pride*

Family Math

Grades K–8. $18.95 plus shipping.
EQUALS Publication, University of California, Berkeley, CA 94720-5200. (800) 897-5036 or (510) 642-1910. Fax: (510) 643-5757. Email: equals@uclink.berkeley.edu. Web: www.equals.lhs.berkeley.edu/

Family Math is a collection of activities originally invented for community family-math classes. The book, however, is definitely meant for use at home. Activities require only common household objects (beans, toothpicks, paper, pencils, etc.), although you may want to photocopy some of the gameboards. Sample pages of graph paper are included for the activities requiring it.

The activities in *Family Math* were chosen because they allow parents and children to play with, discover, and experience math together. An icon at the top of each page indicates which age groups can do the activity.

The activities in *Family Math* are really satisfying. My only complaint about this book is that the illustrations are so grotesque. Many feature children in threatening situations—e.g. measuring an enormous, ugly snake with a huge bulge in his middle (he has evidently just eaten something or somebody). Tongues, claws, and overwhelming size are recurring features in the illustrations. There's a sense of alienation and of the universe being out of joint. For a book meant to empower kids to stress the themes of children's tininess and powerlessness seems odd, to say the least.

The motive behind *Family Math* was to make math accessible to those who otherwise might fear and fail it, notably girls and minorities. This explains why *housewife* and *mother* are not in the list of careers that use math at the back, but not why businessmen and executives (some of the world's biggest math users) are left off the list.

On balance, this is an excellent math (as opposed to arithmetic) course full of ugly pictures. The first math exercise I'd do with this book is calculate how many stickers it will take to cover up the unappealing portions of the pictures! *Mary Pride*

NEW!
Figure It Out

Grades 1–6. Student Books, $4 each. Teacher's Books, $8 each. Shipping extra.
Pennsylvania Homeschoolers, RD 2 Box 117, Kittanning, PA 16201. (412) 783-6512. Fax: (412) 783-6512. Email: richmans@pahomeschoolers.com. Web: www.pahomeschoolers.com.

If you could get your own personal math whiz to sit down with your kids and tell them his secrets of solving tricky math problems, you'd have the human version of these delightfully appealing **Figure It Out** books. Simple illustrations and clear text help kids to realize that there are lots of different ways to tackle a problem, and lots you can learn from it afterwards. (The *Mathematical Olympiad for Elementary Schools* poses the same kinds of problems.)

The publisher only sells these in sets of 10, but Pennsylvania Homeschoolers (otherwise known as Susan and Howard Richman, occasional contributors to *Practical Homeschooling*) offer them individually. For people who buy just the student book and run into an occasional sticky problem, the Richman kids will write a detailed solution for you and send it free. (How's *that* for service!) *Kim O'Hara*

Janice VanCleave's Math for Every Kid covers all the subjects that elementary math texts usually fail to teach well. The book is divided into four sections. "Basics" includes chapters on fractions, fractional parts, equivalents, averages, and multiples. "Measurements" covers centimeters, millimeters, perimeter, diameter of a circle, circumference of a circle, area of rectangles and squares, area of triangles, area of circles, surface area, volume of cubes and rectangular prisms, volume by displacement, liquid capacity, mass, weight, and temperature. "Graphing" teaches bar graphs, line graphs, pictographs, and circle graphs. Geometry introduces angles, what a protractor is, using a protractor, polygons, symmetry, and reflections.

Each chapter starts with a definition of the chapter's purpose (e.g., "To determine the surface area of objects with different shapes"), basic facts and explanations of terms, a question or situation that requires kids to apply these facts, a step-by-step solution accompanied by detailed diagrams, exercises with practice problems (and solutions), and a hands-on activity that enables the student to apply his or her new knowledge to the real world.

Real mathematical terminology is used throughout. Each new word is defined when first introduced, and also included in the glossary at the end. An index is also included.

This book makes it possible for you to use a "computation skills only" math curriculum, such as Developmental Mathematics from Mathematics Programs Associates, and still teach all the "other" math skills tested on standardized tests. You might also want to purchase some "drill" workbooks, once the skills have been introduced, for further practice on measurements and graphing. The "Key to Measurements" and "Key to Metric Measurements" series reviewed in Chapter 27 would be great for further measurement practice. *Mary Pride*

This book presents such a simple idea that it's surprising how few math curriculums cover it: children should be *creating* (and not just solving) math problems. **Math by Kids** is a 74-page softcover book packed with ideas, problems and solutions. Susan Richman, who edited the book, explains in the introduction that the problems were written by Pennsylvania homeschoolers (ages 4–17) and are provided to solve and inspire you.

The 11 categories of problems are organized from easiest to hardest within each category and include:

- Trading and Comparing,
- Cooking,
- Working and Earning,
- Mystery Numbers – Can You Guess Mine???
- Shopping for Math Problems,
- Time, Traveling, and More . . .

The original problems provide a glimpse at how children at different ages look at math. One 4-year-old wrote: "There were six dogs at our house. Four dogs got lost. Maybe they went in the forest. We went to look and found seven dogs and brought them home. How many dogs are now at home?," while a 12-year-old came up with this intriguing question: "If a triangle has zero diagonals, a quadrilateral has two, a pentagon has five, how many diagonals does a hexagon have? Hint: Check for number patterns."

The back of the book contains the answers, explanations, and sometimes what inspired the problem's creation. Richman points out that writing solutions teaches you as much as solving math problems.

Mini-certificates at the end of the book provide an informal lesson plan by prescribing a set number of problems to write in each category. *Teresa Schultz-Jones*

NEW!
Janice VanCleave's Math for Every Kid
Grades 3–6. $12.95.
John Wiley & Sons, 1 Wiley Drive, Somerset, NJ 08875. (800) 225-5945. (732) 469-4400. Fax: (800) 597-3299. Web: www.wiley.com.

NEW!
Math by Kids
Grades preK–8. $6.95 plus shipping.
Pennsylvania Homeschoolers, R. D. 2, Box 117, Kitanning, PA 16201. Phone/fax: (724) 783-6512. Email: richmans@pahomeschoolers.com. Web: www.pahomeschoolers.com.

Cook It!

The Gobble Up series of books have a novel approach to avoid kids' school projects accumulating throughout your house. Eat them! (Well, most of them anyway.)

These 9 x 8½" consumable—but inedible—136-page softcover books are full of math activities and science experiments that you can whip up in your own kitchen. The other book in this series, *Gobble Up Science,* is reviewed in the Science Experiments & Activities chapter.

Gobble Up Math provides a fun start—or gentle assist—to basic math. In it you will find 88 delicious math activities that teach you about patterns, sets, geometry, measurement, number operations, fractions and estimating. You'll make things like fruit-loop necklaces and peanut butter raisin crackers to learn about pattern sequences. For addition, you'll create a code with alphabet cereal and and use it to write simple number problems. Graham crackers are perfectly perforated to teach about fourths and when halved and "glued" with peanut butter, they can be used to learn about cubes!

There is very little actual cooking needed—mostly you use crackers, snack foods, raw fruits, and vegetables. The most complicated preparation is a recipe for edible play dough that's used for several activities. As the book advances from sets and patterns to fractions and estimating, the activities become slightly more complicated. Each chapter introduces the topic and has a related food guide pyramid activity. The activities within each chapter are open-ended, use foods that you either already have or can easily get, and can be set up within minutes. At the end of each chapter is a certificate of completion, suitable for coloring.

After some activities, you may find yourself cooking up frozen vegetables and pasta and making juice—all in all, a much healthier alternative to M&M math manipulatives. *Teresa Schultz-Jones*

When you combine math and cooking into a book, how do you organize it? This 180-page paperback book arranges its recipes by type of math problem. **The Math Chef** includes sections on measuring, arithmetic, fractions and percents, and geometry. Other sections and appendices include kitchen tools, cooking skills, safety in the kitchen, nutrient content of the recipes, nutrition and the food pyramid, food poisoning, molds, etc.

The Math Chef is primarily a cookbook with added math problems. Cooking typically requires some basic math skills—and each of the recipes in this cookbook has a related math problem such as converting between measurement types, multiplying or dividing to change the number of servings, estimating amounts of ingredients or calculating an area. The beginning of each section gives some background for the math required and a related math activity. All answers are provided in the back of the book.

The format of the book makes it easy and appealing. There are attractive line drawings throughout illustrating foods, ingredients, math concepts and people. Each recipe indicates preparation and cooking time, difficulty, ingredients, required tools and number of servings. The recipes are broken down into simple steps and numbered, making it easy to keep track of where you are.

Written for beginning and advanced chefs, all but your youngest will be able to follow each simple step of the 55 recipes, and your whole family will enjoy the resulting soups, cookies, pasta dishes, snacks and more. *Teresa Schultz-Jones*

CHAPTER 26

Fractions & Decimals

Yes, this deserves a separate chapter. Fractions and decimals are the shallows in which many students first founder. Unlike basic arithmetic, which mainly requires sheer memory power, handling fractions and decimals with confidence requires some glimmering of mathematical logic. Why is dividing by a fraction the same as multiplying by its inverse? Why is 25% the same as ¼ and the same as .25 of a unit? Where does the decimal point go? If your student needs more help with such topics than your math curriculum provides, this chapter may help you find some relief.

Developmental Math and Mastering Mathematics, both reviewed in the last chapter, both have separate books to teach fractions and decimals.

Curriculum

You won't beat this guarantee. Steven Rasmussen, the publisher of the **Key To . . . series**, says, "I unconditionally guarantee that *Key to . . .* worktexts will substantially improve your students' math skills and enjoyment. If, for any reason, you are not satisfied, return your books—even if they're used—and I'll give you a 100 percent refund. No questions asked."

Why is Mr. Rasmussen so confident? Because these workbooks assume *nothing.* Each workbook leads the student step by step, with abundant explanation and review. Only one concept is handled per page. Wherever possible, black-and-white visuals are used to illustrate the concept. Examples are worked out step by step. New terms are explained and underlined. Vocabulary is kept simple. Instructions are directed at the student, so he can do the work on his own. Students get plenty of workspace and lots of exercises which gradually increase in difficulty. Based on years of classroom experience, the workbooks anticipate and solve your student's difficulties *before* they occur.

Updated since the last edition of *Big Book,* these series are now typeset (no more handwritten exercises) with updated visuals, and many more of them!

Key to Fractions includes the following workbooks. Each has 37 pages of exercises:

- Book 1: Fraction Concepts
- Book 2: Multiplying and Dividing Fractions
- Book 3: Adding and Subtracting Fractions
- Book 4: Mixed Numbers

Key to Series: Fractions, Decimals and Percents

Grades 5–8. Key to Fractions (set of 4 workbooks), $9. Decimals (set of 4), $9. Percents (set of 3), $6.75. Answers & Notes, $3.25 each subject. Reproducible tests, $9.95 each subject. Shipping extra.
Key Curriculum Press, 1150 65th St., Emeryville, CA 94608. (800) 995-MATH. Fax: (800) 541-2442. Email: orders@keypress.com. Web: www.keypress.com.

Key to Decimals features real-world uses of decimals—such as pricing, sports, metrics, calculators, and science. Each workbook has 45 pages of exercises. The series includes:

- Book 1: Decimal Concepts
- Book 2: Adding, Subtracting, and Multiplying Decimals
- Book 3: Dividing Decimals
- Book 4: Using Decimals

Key to Percents also has 45 pages of exercises per book. The series includes:

- Book 1: Percent Concepts
- Book 2: Percents and Fractions
- Book 3: Percents and Decimals

There is one *Answers & Notes* book for each series, which I strongly suggest you buy. The "notes" in this case take up just one page of basic suggestions for teachers. The "answers" are the pages from each book with correct answers filled in. For space reasons, these are printed with four workbook pages on one *Answers & Notes* page.

My feeling is that you can do without the *Reproducible Tests* books for these series. These just include one final test and diagnostic test for each book in the series, plus answer keys (the test pages with handwritten correct answers). Parents who grade their kids' work know whether the kid is learning or not without the extra bother of separate tests.

Anyone who knows arithmetic can succeed with these series. I highly recommend them. *Mary Pride*

Mastering Fractions' subtitle is "The Most Complete Book on Fractions." At three-and-a-half pounds, 548 pages, and no pictures, that's easy to believe.

The author, Said Hamilton, was inspired by a textbook he had in high school. It explained math in simple terms and provided examples with answers. Hamilton wanted to provide a book that would build a solid foundation for an increasingly technological world.

The oversized softcover book is very comprehensive—it progresses in an orderly fashion from the basics of parentheses and brackets, to explaining what fractions are, and then onto operations with integer, decimal and mixed fractions.

Each chapter begins by stating the objective and the contents. Rules are stated and methods for solving are followed by several examples. Explanations are terse and none of the examples are annotated. At the end of each section, ten problems are given. The answers—and all the intermediate steps—are in the back of the book. There are over 1600 solved problems in the book!

This is a cookbook approach to fractions: you can match your fraction problem to a similar problem in the book and follow the steps to solve it. You may have to break the problem into smaller parts and flip to different parts of the book to solve each part. This approach does not work for everybody, but if this is your learning style, *Mastering Fractions* is wonderfully complete. *Teresa Schultz-Jones*

NEW!
Mastering Fractions

Grade 6–adult. $49.95 plus shipping.
Hamilton Education Guides, PO Box 681, Vienna, VA 22183. (800) 209-8186. Phone/fax: (703) 620-3960. Web: www.hamiltonguides.com

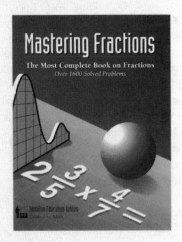

NEW!
Mastering the Math Monsters

Grade 3–6. $5.95 plus shipping.

Have your kids experienced the satisfaction that comes from the "Aha!" of finally "getting" a math concept? If not, maybe what's needed is a different way of explaining the material. In **Mastering the Math Monsters**, Denise Gaskins slays these monsters by giving you practical ways to approach the common bugaboos: decimals, long division, multiplication, and fractions. Emphasizing the use of games and puzzles to stimulate our kids' thinking muscles, the author's enthusiasm is contagious. Armed with this book and a few of the suggested resources, your kids can go from just number crunching to problem solving in no time.

This 64 page booklet is full of affordable, practical, twaddle-free help. Keep your highlighter handy; the hints and tips are packed onto every page! *Renee Mathis*

Fractions & Decimals Manipulatives

How to make your own fractions manipulatives:

Pie shapes. Take felt or colored cardboard. Cut in uniform circles. Cut individual circles into halves, thirds, fourths, fifths, etc.

Square shapes. Take several sheets of transparent acetate—the kind businessmen use for overhead transparencies. Mark out and cut a uniform set of large squares. Mark individual squares with lines dividing them into halves, thirds, fourths, etc.

A set of rods can be made into a place value/decimals/powers of ten set by adding a couple of large squares equivalent to a ten-rod by a ten-rod. Making the big Hundred Square is less of a challenge than making the rods, so possibly you might aspire to this. Or you could just get one of the sets below.

Fractions are easy to teach with Cuisenaire rods. I haven't seen the book *Everything's Coming Up Fractions with Cuisenaire Rods*, but can assume its 64 pages manage to explain how to do it.

Connecting Fraction Circles are notched on the back to fit onto a ring, making them easy to organize and use. Each pie-shaped section is marked—e.g., ½, ¼—and color-coded. The set includes halves, thirds, fourths, sixths, and eighths. No instruction booklet, but the wily parent can readily remove two ⅛ sections and substitute one ¼, thus proving that 2 x ⅛ = ¼. Other manipulation possibilities will occur, besides the obvious use of this set for demonstrating what ¾ and ⅚ look like (and which is larger).

Avoid the **Fraction Circles** and **Square Fraction** sets. Although you get more unmarked pieces for your money, they don't snap together in any way, making them an absolute bear to put back into the case and not as easy to use. *Mary Pride*

Homeschooling Basics Series, Tabletop Academy Press, R.R. 1 Box 114, Blue Mound, IL 62513. (217)692-2849. Email: dcgaskins@juno.com.

Cuisenaire Fraction Manipulatives

Grades 3–6. Everything's Coming Up Fractions with Cuisenaire Rods (#030950), $9.95 (does not include rods). Connecting Fraction Circles (#035033), $6. Fraction Circles Set (#035034), $7.95. Square Fraction Set (#035037), $7.95. Add 10% shipping. *Cuisenaire Company of America, PO Box 5026, White Plains, NY 10602-5026. (800) 237-3142. or (914) 328-5487. Fax: (800) 551-7637. Email: info@awl.com. Web: www.cuisenaire.com.*

NEW!
Decimal Dog

Grades 3–8. Decimal Dog, $15.98. Decimal Dog Activities Guide, $15.98. Shipping extra. *Delta Education, 80 Northwest Blvd, Nashua, NH 03063. (800) 442-5444. Fax: (800) 282-9560. Email: Mathew@delta-ed.mv.com. Web: www.delta-ed.com.*

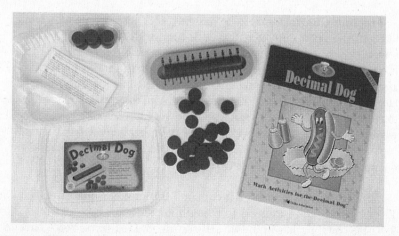

Decimal Dog is the sort of educational tool kids mistake for a toy and love on sight. This unique manipulative comes with:

- one plastic "bun" with markings for decimals (1–10, with tic marks for halves and quarters) and fractions (¹⁄₁₀–¹⁰⁄₁₀)
- one realistically-colored plastic hot dog, sized to exactly fit into the curve of the "bun"
- 10 "bites," each one-tenth of a dog
- 30 "slices," each one-tenth of a bite
- a sheet of instructions in how to use the above to teach decimal concepts
- all attractively packaged in a three-chambered plastic fast-food holder

Just adorable, and so easy to use! My kindergartner was "getting it" almost immediately when I used Decimal Dog to introduce decimals and fractions.

The *Decimal Dog Activities Guide* is designed for use with Decimal Dog, and includes 3 games and 42 activities, plus answers, in its 114 reproducible pages. *Mary Pride*

Let's talk **Fraction Burger**. This funky foam manipulative comes with ten layers, each a unit divided into a different set of fractions, except the two buns, which both stand for a unit of 1. The burger is in two halfs; onion is thirds; cheese is fourths; relish is fifths; tomato is sixths; lettuce is eighths; mustard is tenths; and special sauce is twelfths. When wet, the pieces will stick to white boards or chalkboards. When not, they are velvety soft to the touch (but not very compressible or easy to hurt). Activity suggestions are included.

Two separate reproducible activity books are available, both designed for use with the Fraction Burger. *Fraction Burger Activities* is a regular reproducible workbook, with over 50 activities and games. Game pieces and answers are found in the back. *A Feast of Fraction Activities* has more personality. Featuring the ongoing character of Googol Gourmet, it covers similar fraction concepts in about half the pages and two-thirds the price. *Mary Pride*

Fraction Charts seems to be designed for those people who would like a fraction chart but don't have the time or desire to make it themselves. (If you would rather make your own, *Math Card Games*, a book from the same company, tells you how to construct and use the charts.) The two identical white vinyl charts show ten 1 inch by 10 inch bars labeled with halves, thirds, fourths, and so on, to tenths. You're supposed to cut one apart and leave one whole. To get full use out of these, you'll want to get the book; however, most of the other activities in the book require decks of math cards ($20 for six different decks). Discounts for quantities of 10 or more. *Kim O'Hara*

The **Mortensen Combo Kit** contains 10 hundred squares, 40 ten bars, 12 unit bars each of values 1 to 6, and nine unit bars each of values 7 to 9. These come packaged in two self-sorting molded trays. You'll have to study the setup for awhile, but after you do, it's easy to find the right place for every item.

NEW!
Fraction Burger

Grades 4–8. Fraction Burger, $9.98. Fraction Burger Activities, $12.98. Feast of Fractions Activities, $8.98. Shipping extra.
Delta Education, 80 Northwest Blvd, Nashua, NH 03063. (800) 442-5444. Fax: (800) 282-9560. Email: Mathew@delta-ed.mv.com. Web: www.delta-ed.com.

NEW!
Fraction Charts

Elementary. Fraction Charts, $6. Math Card Games, $18. Shipping extra.
Activities for Learning, 21161 York Rd., Hutchinson, MN 55350. (800) 593-7030. Fax: (320) 587-0123. Email: joancott@hutchtel.net.

Mortensen Decimal Manipulatives

Grades 2–8. Very Basic Basic Operations Kit, $34.95. Combo Kit, $91.90. Shipping extra.

Like other powers-of-ten material, the Combo Kit doesn't include enough material to demonstrate problems like 52 x 46. For that you would need 20 hundred squares. To solve a problem like 96 x 99 you'd need 81 hundred squares, or more than eight Combo Kits' worth of hundred squares! That's why the Mortensen workbooks tend to use 10, 11, 12, and 21 as the second multiplier. You also have to use a large number of 10 rods for each problem, since the Combo Kit does not include multiple ten bars.

If you merely want to *demonstrate* decimals, multiplication, algebra, and basic operations, the Combo Kit works very well. The multiple unit bars make life easier than the single unit cubes in most other companies' powers-of-ten material. They do not work as well, however, for simple place value operations like 79 + 86 + 95, where it is beneficial to actually see 79 as seven tens and nine units. For these basic powers-of-ten operations, Mortensen has the **Decimal Half Tray**. I haven't seen this particular kit, but from the catalog picture it appears to include two whole units (also usable as hundreds), 20 tenths rods (also usable as tens), and 50 hundredths cubes (also usable as units), which is less than you get in the similar set from Cuisenaire Company.

Mortensen's **Very Basic Basic Operations Kit** helps you take powers of ten concepts up to the ten thousands. The Very Basic Basic Operations Kit contains 10 thousand bars, 10 hundred strips, 10 hundred squares, 20 ten bars, and 20 units. These items are all much smaller in scale than regular Mortensen manipulatives and made out of thin plastic rather than rodlike in shape. The units are almost impossible to handle, meaning you won't want to use this set for much basic multiplying. Its main virtue is the ability to show 100 as both a square and a strip, and 1000 as 10 hundred squares end-to-end. The set can be used for numbers up to the ten thousands and decimals to the ten thousandth. It can also be used to introduce algebra formulas including $x3$ and $x4$. The kit comes with a molded plastic tray for storing the units, squares, strips, and bars.

Both the Combo Kit and the Very Basic Basic Operations Kit are included in the Homeschool kit—see review on page 299. *Mary Pride*

Mortensen's fraction kits introduce new types of manipulatives. Until now we have been looking at Mortensen kits with multiple-units bars. These bars are all the same width—one unit wide—but different lengths, depending on the numeral with which each is associated. Now we are going to meet "multiple-ten bars." These are all 10 units wide, but different lengths, again depending on the numeral with which each is associated.

Fraction units are thin, square pieces of colored plastic, each divided by white lines into a number of equal pieces. The green fraction unit represents one unit (no white lines dividing it). The orange fraction unit has a white line down the middle, indicating it comprises two halves. (Note that orange is the color for 2 in the Mortensen system). The pink fraction unit is divided into thirds (pink being the color for 3), and so on.

Fraction bars are slices of colored plastic that fit into the divisions on the fraction units. Two orange fraction bars, each with an individual value of ½, fit side by side to make one whole square. Three pink fraction bars, each with a value of ⅓, make one square.

The **Home Fractions Kit** includes two colored and two clear Fraction units for halves, thirds, quarters, etc., up to ninths, plus one set of strips for each quantity, i.e., two half-sized bars, three third-sized bars, up to nine ninth-sized bars.

V.J. Mortensen Co., PO Box 98, Hayden Lake, ID 83835-0098. Orders: (800) 4PLUS4-8. Fax: (208) 667-9438. Email: request@mortensenmathdirect.com. Web: www.mortensenmathdirect.com.

Mortensen Fractions Manipulatives

Home Fractions Kit, $49.45. Multiple Tens Set $20.63. (Prices for Math Discovery Club members.) Shipping extra.
V.J. Mortensen Co., PO Box 98, Hayden Lake, ID 83835-0098. Orders: (800) 4PLUS4-8. Fax: (208) 667-9438. Email: request@mortensenmathdirect.com. Web: www.mortensenmathdirect.com.

The **Multiple Tens Set**, very useful in multiplication and division work, includes one of each tens multiple from 10 to 100, plus a tray, but no fractions units or strips. These have a grid side for arithmetic and a smooth side for representing multiples of "x" in algebraic expressions. *Mary Pride*

NEW!
Picture Grids for Fractions and Decimals

Elementary. Order #020272. $14.95 plus shipping.
Cuisenaire Company of America, PO Box 5026, White Plains, NY 10602-5026. (800) 237-3142. or (914) 328-5487. Fax: (800) 551-7637.
Email: info@awl.com.
Web: www.cuisenaire.com.

Picture Grids for Fractions and Decimals clearly illustrates fraction multiplication and equivalencies. Vertical lines divide these transparent acetate squares into halves, thirds, fourths, fifths, sixths, eighths, tenths, or twelfths, with different numbers of the parts shaded. (You also get two hundredths grids, thus the "decimals.") On the white cardboard backing (provided) you can see through the shaded grids to identify equivalent fractions, or you can cross two grids to show multiplication. Crossing a grid with no shading (for example, thirds) with a shaded grid (for example, $\frac{3}{5}$) illustrates equivalent fractions in another way ($\frac{9}{15}$). Depending on your child, these could inspire either sudden comprehension or "why-do-I-need-*this*?" shrugs. *Kim O'Hara*

Games

NEW!
Fraction Mania

Grades 1–12. $24.95.
Math Concepts, Inc., 445 State Route 13 N, Suite 26-372, Jacksonville, FL 32259. (800) 574-9936.
Fax: (904) 287-0363.
E-mail: mathconcepts@leading.net.
Web: www.mathconcepts.com.

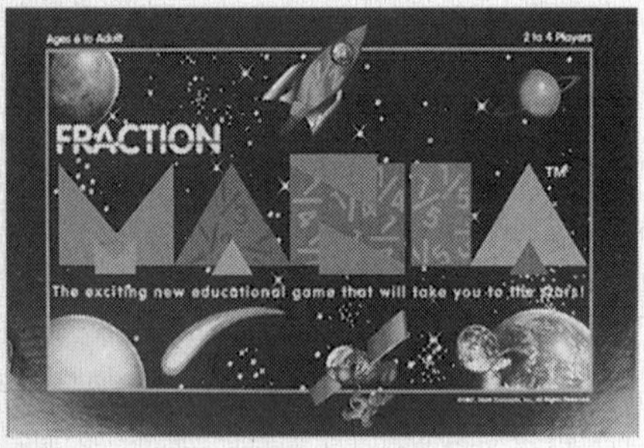

You don't play games to learn fractions ("Oh, boy! I'm gonna learn fractions!") You play games to have fun. This fast-paced game looks like fun and I can't wait to play it with my kids.

Fraction Mania has a solar system theme. Your goal: gather fractions to fill up the planet circles on your playing board. Each planet is divided into a different number of pieces. For example, Earth is divided in half and Venus is divided into eighths. The size of the piece you get to pick is determined by the roll of a die.

In the first game, you merely have to roll the die and select a piece that matches the fraction on the die. the first person to fill all the circles wins. You have to verbalize all moves: "I am putting a $\frac{1}{4}$ piece into the circle for Jupiter," or lose the piece.

The second game adds the wrinkle that you have to trade fractions up to the largest possible piece, even if you have to trade down to do it. For example, if you had two $\frac{1}{6}$ pieces, you would have to trade them in on a $\frac{1}{3}$ piece, or if you had a $\frac{1}{6}$ piece and a $\frac{1}{3}$ piece, you would have to trade the $\frac{1}{3}$ down to two $\frac{1}{6}$ pieces and trade up to a $\frac{1}{2}$ piece. If you miss a chance to trade up, you can be challenged by the other players and lose the piece for that turn. Another wrinkle is that each turn you take a card which can affect your move.

The other two included games, *Double Mania* and *Action Mania,* add even more challenges. By the time your student gets proficient at all four games, he will know his fractions down to eighths. He will understand how fractions can get reduced to lower terms, i.e., that $\frac{2}{8}$ is really $\frac{1}{4}$ by another name. By trading up, then adding he will have the foundation at least to understand adding fractions by getting both fractions to have the same denominator before adding.

Fraction Mania really teaches you how fractions work, and it does it better than any manipulative or game I have ever seen. Recommended. *Bill Pride*

CHAPTER 27

Time, Money, & Measure

Telling time, identifying money, making change, measuring, graphing, and charting—typically these skills are brushed by in the middle of each week's math curriculum, taught little by little and rarely, if ever, reviewed. If you think this is the right way to teach such things, tell me quickly—how many pecks in a bushel?

My personal belief is that "calculation" skills (addition, subtraction, multiplication, division, and so on) and "practical" skills (those in this chapter) should be taught *separately*. The practical math skills could as readily be considered part of the *science* curriculum. Why interrupt a child's math instruction to teach him about gallons and o'clocks, when they can be handled as complementary, but separate, subjects?

Time

No, these are not functioning timepieces. However, if you want to teach your kids how to read time, **Student Clocks** are nice "clocks" to do it with. There are five clocks to a set. Each clock is hard plastic, with hour and minute hands fairly firmly attached. It also has a blank area under the clock face to write on with wipeoff crayons or markers. Each clock has the hours marked in red, and a red hour hand. Likewise, each has the minutes marked in black, and a black minute hand. Much better than the little cardboard clocks you see in the back of many math books, and certainly more durable. You probably won't need five, though.

Clock-O-Dial is a self-checking way to learn time-telling skills. The green plastic base has a clockface with movable hands, and a window. Close the window and you only see a written time (e.g., "10:30"). Set the clock's hands to what you think are the correct positions. Then open the window to see a clockface with the correct positions on it. Comes with four double-sided lesson wheels (the part you see behind the window). An affordable solution for the homeschool.

Discovery Clock is the deluxe model. It's a clockface with movable hands: the hours in red and the minutes in blue. You pick a time and set the hands in what you hope is the correct position. Then slide the "ringer" to one side, and a set of "portholes" open, revealing the minutes in five-minute increments. Not as interactive or self-teaching as Clock-O-Dial, but great for nailing down how to read minutes. *Mary and Joseph Pride*

NEW!
Educational Insights Teaching Clocks
Grades K–2. Student Clocks, set of 5 for $15.95. Discovery Clock, $29.95. Clock-O-Dial, $17.95. Shipping extra.
Educational Insights, Inc., 16941 Keegan Ave., Carson, CA 90746. (800) 995-4436. (310) 884-2000. Fax: (800) 995-0506. Web: www.edin.com.

NEW!
The Time Book

Grades 1–6. $13 plus shipping.
Klutz Press, 455 Portage Ave., Palo Alto, CA 94306. Orders: (800) 558-8944. Inquiries: (650) 424-0739. Fax: (650) 857-9110. Web: www.klutz.com.

The Time Book also includes, as a bonus, "A Complete Collection of Time Facts, including: The Truth about Bedtime, Why Commercials Always Take So Long, and What to Get Ready For When Your Parents Say, 'I'll only be a minute.'"

Klutz has another winner in **The Time Book**, the only book on the subject that comes with a working electronic watch with an old-fashioned "real" watchface (you know, numbers around the edges, long and short hands, sweep second hand).

Educationally sound, too. *The Time Book* has the best and simplest instructions on the subject I've ever seen. And I quote:

> *Every time the short hand points exactly at a number, it is exactly that hour.*
>
> *If it points exactly at 3, it is exactly 3 o'clock.*
>
> *But MOST of the time, it is NOT pointing exactly at a number. It's pointing BETWEEN the numbers.*
>
> *That's OK. Here's how to deal with that.*
>
> *If it's a little past the 3, say, "It's a little past 3."*
>
> *If it's a lot past the 3, say, "It's a lot past 3." Or, you could say, "It's almost 4." Means the same thing.*
>
> *But what if it's right in the MIDDLE? Right between the 3 and the 4. Then what?*

Gotcha! I just know you're dying to turn the page and find out what to say when it's right in the middle.

All this is illustrated with the goofy full-color drawings of watch faces, little kids, gorillas, dinosaurs, and others curious to tell the time that you can expect from the gang at Klutz.

Did I mention that *The Time Book* is printed on sturdy cardboard with spiral binding, and the accompanying watch and band are in screaming two-tone neon? I loved my first Timex, but I would have loved it better in two-tone neon! *Mary Pride*

NEW!
The Usborne Time Kid Kit

Grades preK–2. $10.95 plus shipping.
EDC Publishing, Division of Educational Development Corporation, PO Box 470663, Tulsa, OK 74147. (800) 475-4522. Fax: (800) 747-4509. Web: www.edcpub.com.

A chunky plastic practice clock with movable *synchronized* hands. *The Usborne First Learning—Time* book. Both together for the first time in a reclosable plastic pouch. What could be a neater (in all senses of the word) introduction to time-telling?

The **Time Kid Kit**'s synchronized clock hands mean that, as you move the minute hand, the hour hand moves realistically to its proper position. At 10:30, the hour hand points halfway between 10 and 11, as it should. Made by the pros at Learning Resources, this clock can take a licking and keep on . . . whoops, better not mess with any trademarked phrases here! No ticking is involved, just a lot of talking, as you lead your young child through the book spreads on sequencing, day and night, seasons, times of day, day of the week, and number practice, before finally getting down to serious business with the final seven clock-reading pages. Reusable from child to child (especially if you don't let them write in the book). Recommended. *Mary Pride*

Money

Creative Teaching Associates manufactures a wide variety of educational consumer math games. I asked which would be most suitable for home use, and of the two they sent, **Allowance** is the clear winner.

The skills practiced in *Allowance* are counting and money math. Kids get an allowance each time they circle the board, which they either augment by extra chores or spend on movies, clothes, and other kid stuff. Take-A-Chance cards add some unpredictability to the mix. In the process, kids find out that savers and workers always beat spenders—a worthwhile lesson, for sure!

At every turn in this game someone has to make change. One person is supposed to act as the Cashier, but if this is Mom or Dad the kids will miss out on a lot of math practice. Game includes play money and small cards labeled with coin amounts. *Mary Pride*

TREND's **Money Match Me Flash Cards** provide a unique way to drill money recognition and counting. Each card has a different combination of coins pictured on the front, with its value on the back in either decimal notation (e.g., *35¢*) or spelled out (*thirty-five cents*). They come in 26 sets of two, so you can play the matching games described on the inside box cover. A little work with these cards will make your child a money expert!

Four mix-and-match game instructions included, plus instructions for a game that gives practice counting large amounts of change.

The Match Me series also includes *Telling Time, Numbers 0–25,* and *Alphabet. Mary Pride*

Measurement

Centimeter Gram Cubes have one claim to fame: each has a mass of one gram, and each measures one centimeter on each edge. Easy to snap together, they also make comparing mass to volume a snap. Cube-O-Gram cubes are also usable for any other basic math manipulations for which you'd use snap-together cubes or unit rods. A good idea taken one step further. *Mary Pride*

Measurement is one area (pardon the unintentional pun) where kids mess up frequently. Why? Because it's introduced erratically, at best, in most math programs. Like, "We interrupt our regularly scheduled math lesson to bring you a few minutes on the topic of measurement. Don't change that dial, because we'll be back in just a few months with your next measurement lesson."

Here is the answer: the **Key to . . . series** books on measurement. Like the other Key to . . . books, each 44-page workbook leads the student step by step, with abundant explanation and review. Only one concept is handled per page. Wherever possible, black-and-white visuals are used to illustrate the concept. Examples are worked out step by step. New terms are explained and underlined. Vocabulary is kept simple. Instructions are directed at the student, so he can do the work on his own. Students get plenty of workspace and lots of exercises which gradually increase in difficulty. Based on years of classroom experience, the workbooks anticipate and solve student's difficulties *before* they occur!

Key to Measurement includes:

- Book 1: English Units of Length
- Book 2: Measuring Length and Perimeter Using English Units
- Book 3: Finding Area and Volume Using English Units
- Book 4: English Units for Weight, Capacity, Temperature, and Time

Key to Metric Measurement introduces kids to the measurement scheme used in the scientific world and just about every country except the USA and England. For extra zest, you'll find problems using these measurements from other countries. The series includes:

- Book 1: Metric Units of Length
- Book 2: Measuring Length and Perimeter Using Metric Units
- Book 3: Finding Area and Volume Using Metric Units
- Book 4: Metric Units for Mass, Capacity, Temperature, and Time

Don't have a ruler or tape measure with the right units to do the activities? No problem: there's a set to cut out inside the back cover of the first three book in both series!

There is one *Answers & Notes* book for each series, which I strongly suggest you buy. The "notes" are brief teacher notes for each page in each book, with additional teaching suggestions and solutions for mistakes students commonly make. The "answers" are the pages from each book with correct answers filled in. For space reasons, these are printed with four workbook pages on one *Answers & Notes* page.

These are really good books. Even reluctant learners enjoy them, and though they are *not* reproducible, for the price you can afford a set for each child in your family. Recommended. *Mary Pride*

Graphing & Charting

Imagine you have your own copy of **Math-O-Graphs**. Your kids are busy, calling up everyone they know to fill in an interesting graph. When they are done, you'll pose a related problem that really makes them think. How will they solve it? Will they graph it? Math it? Or come up with their own unique approaches?

This book is all about getting to a solution by many different paths, involving your whole family in the process, and learning. A few minor difficulties: Because it is aimed at classroom use, you may have to adjust some graphs for smaller groups. And in one question that concerns charting popular holidays you may want to substitute more worthy ones than Halloween and April Fool's Day. Reproducible. *Kim O'Hara*

First published in 1981, the **Tables & Graphs** graded workbook series is still an effective introduction to tables and graphs. Twenty-four lessons per book will teach you to understand, use, and make your own example of each of five or more different types of graphs. Simple and straightforward, with exercises based on graphic subjects that appeal to kids (cars, food, bugs, etc.), this series does a nice job of showing how practical graphs can be. One exercise in Book A that advertises prices for Halloween costumes (witch hats, Dracula fangs) can be omitted without losing much. Black-and-white; not reproducible. *Kim O'Hara*

CHAPTER 28

Geometry for Kids

In the elementary grades, geometry is mostly about recognizing simple shapes, with a dash of area and perimeter calculations mixed in. Typically, this is taught using a host of manipulatives.

For some reason, elementary math teachers like to have kids construct shapes using a **geoboard**. This is usually a square with rows of small pegs solidly affixed. Kids stretch rubber bands around the pegs to make the shapes.

Geometric shapes (circle, triangle, rectangle) can easily be cut from felt, light cardboard, or even construction paper. Use different colors of felt and different sizes to teach colors and size at the same time. You might also consider adding fancier geometric shapes, such as the parallelogram, square, rhombus, trapezoid, hexagon, and so forth. Although schools only teach little kids the names of a few shapes, we at home can push for a little more vocabulary development!

Geometric solids are harder to make, but can be found all around the house. A soup can is a cylinder. A cereal box is a rectangular solid. A piece of paper can be twirled into a cone, or use a sugar cone (the kind that crunches and holds ice cream). Ice cubes are cubes. Bath drops are itsy-bitsy spheres.

For area and perimeter, a good old **ruler** can be used to measure the sides of a book, or the size of your living-room carpet.

Tangrams are a set of seven geometric pieces—six triangles of various sizes and shapes and one square—used in an ancient form of puzzling. The puzzler is given an outline, which he must fill in exactly using the seven pieces. The number of potential puzzles is enormous, and the similarity of the pieces can make any given puzzle quite tricky. Tangrams, like other sophisticated puzzles, aren't just for kids. As one book on the subject explains, Napoleon Bonaparte, Lewis Carroll, Edgar Allan Poe, and John Quincy Adams all enjoyed tangrams. Educational value of tangrams: like other puzzles, they develop your problem-solving and spatial skills. A "store" set costs very little; most of your cost will be the books of tangram puzzles.

Pattern blocks are similar to what we called "parquetry" when we were children. The sets of colorful hexagons, trapezoids, parallelograms, and triangles are used to fill in outline shapes, just like tangrams. Since more shapes are included, often the same outline can be filled in a variety of

This is a tangram

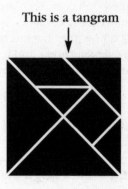

These are the standard pattern-block shapes

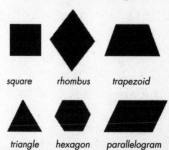

square   rhombus   trapezoid

triangle   hexagon   parallelogram

How to Make a Geoboard

Obtain a thick piece of non-warping wood, 20 cm x 20 cm. Paint one side black (the better to see the rubber bands, my dear). Pound in 25 roundheaded nails in a 5 x 5 array, each 4 cm from the next, and the outside rows 2 cm from the edges. Take care that the nails don't go all the way through! Now, while you're at it, make four more just like that one. Stick velcro on the sides, so when you connect the geoboards in a 2 x 2 square, they all stay together nicely. Now you can do percentage and decimal problems, since you have 100 pins to work with. Alternatively, make a 10-pin x 10-pin geoboard (a fairly hefty size). Draw lines with Magic Marker separating it into four 5-pin x 5-pin sections. Either way, you have 100 pins.

Got your rubber bands? Good! Now that you have your geoboard, you can slip rubber bands over those nails to make triangles, rectangles, squares, and all sorts of odd-shaped polygons. You can move your rubber bands around and watch how the shapes change. You can calculate areas and perimeters. It's instant geometry.

Creating Line Design series

Grades K–9. $5 each. Shipping extra.
Timberdoodle Company, 1510 E. Spencer Lake Rd., Shelton, WA 98584. (360) 426-0672. Fax: (800)478-0672. Email: mailbag@timberdoodle.com. Web: www.timberdoodle.com.

ways. Because the blocks fit together geometrically, children can pick up geometric relationships by working with them. Educational value of pattern blocks: problem solving, spatial skills, pre-geometry. Too hard to make at home; don't bother.

Attribute blocks also often come in geometric shapes. The shapes may or may not relate geometrically, depending on brand. The same shape will come in a variety of colors, sizes, and thicknesses. Attribute blocks are mainly used for logic puzzles, not geometry. Example: "Find all the blocks that are red *and* thick. Now find all the blocks that are small, not blue, not thick." Educational value of attribute blocks: logic, problem solving, occasionally pre-geometry and fractions (depending on brand). You *could* make your own set, out of colored cardboard or felt, but the plastic and wood commercial sets are *much* nicer.

Regular puzzles, the kind you buy at the store, teach much the same skills as tangrams and pattern blocks. At least one highly successful Japanese program uses puzzles as its pre-geometry curriculum.

An enterprising teacher can beat pattern blocks to death as educational tools, forcing children (for instance) to graph how many blocks they think will be needed to solve a problem and how many they actually used. I've seen a number of these workbooks. Avoid them. Tangrams can be similarly forced to tell children about symmetry, area, perimeter, and other concepts best introduced with mirrors, geoboards, and rulers. Attribute blocks, which lend themselves well to dominoes-like games, are fun to sort and classify—their basic use.

It's not fair to give a child what looks like a set of colorful toys and demand that he fill out endless workbook pages with exercises that incidentally use these toys. By puzzling with tangrams and pattern blocks, kids will squeeze out the legitimate educational value of these materials. By playing logic games, kids will get the best use of their attribute blocks. Let fun be fun and work be work!

In a previous edition of this book, I spent many pages reviewing geometry manipulatives such as I described above.

This time I'm going to just suggest that you check out the selection at your local teacher's store, or in the Cuisenaire catalog. Instead, let's look at products that teach spatial skills, pre-drafting, and geometry terminology. Ready? Let's go!

Good Geometry Stuff

Learn pre-drafting skills through this series that trains a child's visual perception and memory. OK, that sounds pretty fancy. What are we talking about here? We're talking about the **Creating Line Design** series. You use a straightedge to connect numbers ranged along the sides of a box. Simple, right?

Well, at first it is. In book 1, designed for kindergartners, you just connect numbers. This produces a variety of designs. Check yourself with the inset completed design to see if you did it right. In book 2, you have to connect pairs of letters as well as numbers in order to produce more complicated designs. Book 3 designs require you to lift your pencil occasionally while connecting dots, since the square now contains different shapes around which you must maneuver. In book 4 (intended for grades 7 through 9) the designs are very challenging, but even young children can complete them after finishing the first three books.

Making the designs is fun. You can color the finished product and display it. Some of the designs could be pasted on cardboard and made into puzzles. Whatever—the Creating Line Design series takes no teaching effort; kids like it; why not get it? *Mary Pride*

I can tell you one thing: any geometric program based on colorful foam blocks of interlocking shapes is guaranteed to appeal to kids. All you have to do is open the **DIME Geometry** box.

OK, you've opened the box. The children, from the preteens on down, will immediately flock to the box and start building with the blocks. (The teenagers are watching out of the corner of their eyes and scheming to secretly play with the blocks in the privacy of their rooms after the little kids are in bed.)

Now you enter. "It's OK, kids—go ahead and have some fun with those blocks. When you're done, I've got some books here with diagrams of stuff you can build with the blocks." Nobody will be left out, since the DIME books start with two-dimensional puzzles even the preschoolers can work and progress to 3-D solids that will give you a challenge. In the process, children (and adults) discover mathematical patterns and relationships and develop amazing spatial skills.

The *3-D Build Up Book* 1 briefly explains the program and is mostly full of problems your kids can solve themselves. First they must learn the nomenclature. The large square is an F block. The L-shaped one is an L. The S-shaped one is an S. The small square is a 1, the rectangle twice that length is a 2, and the rectangle three times that length is a 3. The first page of the book is a set of labeled outlines, asking the children to fill the outline with the block of the right name. The next seven pages have more outline shapes for children to fill in with the prescribed combinations of blocks, e.g., "Fill the shape with LL," meaning "Use two L-shapes to fill in this outline." After this, kids make the jump to concocting increasingly complex shapes shown in isometric 3-D outlines.

The DIME program is a self-correcting activity, of the sort beloved by Montessori teachers. Children can see for themselves if they have found an answer, and can usually figure out new ways of attacking the problem if an answer is not immediately forthcoming. The teacher's role is simply to provide a supportive environment, observe the process, and *ooh* and *aah* over the results. No reading is required to solve the problems, an additional plus for parents of special-needs children, some of whom are brilliant at spatial tasks, though they may be slow with reading and writing. *Mary Pride*

Drawing Kit for Geometry combines several useful geometry tools into one package. You get an 11 x13" drawing board, T-square, 30°/60° and 45° triangles, a compass (without sharp points), a protractor, and a booklet that shows you several activities you can do with them.

In my mind, the booklet is the most valuable part of the package, but it probably wouldn't be used much without the rest of the kit. Easy-to-follow exercises include drawing an equilateral triangle with T-square and 30°/60° triangle, then dividing it into halves, thirds, and fourths; drawing tangrams; and drawing to show depth. Good for geometry exercises but not enough for an art or drafting student. *Kim O'Hara*

Janice VanCleave's Geometry for Every Kid explores both plane geometry and solid geometry. Each concept is introduced in easy-to-follow language, using correct mathematical terminology. Then the student's understanding is immediately tested, and he is given a hands-on activity to "cement" what he has learned.

Here's how it works. Each chapter starts with a "What You Need to Know" introduction to the chapter subject, "Let's Think It Through" questions and puzzles to solve using the information from the introduction, answers to the above, application exercises, a step-by-step activity, line-art charts and illustrations, and solutions to the exercises. The hands-on activi-

DIME Geometry

Grades K–9. DIME Geometry Blocks (required to use books), $17. 3-D Build Up Book 1, Sketching Book 2, and Sketching Book 3, $7 each. Shipping extra.
Timberdoodle Company, 1510 E. Spencer Lake Rd., Shelton, WA 98584. (360) 426-0672. Fax: (800)478-0672. Email: mailbag@timberdoodle.com. Web: www.timberdoodle.com.

DIME stands for Development of Ideas in Mathematical Education. Naturally, the program was invented by an Australian, pioneered in Scotland, and printed in Canada—Americans today are too strung out over basic skills to pioneer something this fun and effective. The DIME Build-Up program is good for grades K–6. Further DIME sketching programs are available.

NEW!
Drawing Kit for Geometry

Grades 3–6. $12 plus shipping.
Activities for Learning, 21161 York Rd., Hutchinson, MN 55350. (800) 593-7030. Fax: (320) 587-0123. Email: joancott@hutchtel.net.

NEW!
Janice VanCleave's Geometry for Every Kid

Grades 3–6. $11.95.
John Wiley & Sons, 1 Wiley Drive, Somerset, NJ 08875. (800) 225-5945. (732) 469-4400. Fax: (800) 597-3299. Web: www.wiley.com.

Exciting ideas, projects, and things to do!

ties use simple materials—hammer and nail, straws, toothpicks— to demonstrate or model geometric concepts. Trust me; these activities are *very* fun!

Here's what it covers. Identifying lines, line segments, and rays. Measuring angles of straight-sided figures. Identifying intersecting, parallel, and perpendicular lines. Identifying triangles. Identifying quadrilaterals. Determining different ways polygons can fit together. Identifying congruent polygons. Making pentominoes. Learning about curved geometric figures. Identifying and drawing the parts of a circle. Drawing and measuring central angles. Tracing plane geometric figures. Determining lines of symmetry. Using plane geometry to make artistic designs. Extending and relating geometric patterns. Calculating the area of a rectangle. Calculating the area of a rhomboid or rhombus. Calculating the area of a circle. Using graph paper to calculate the area of plane figures. Identifying solids. Determining the number of faces, edges, and vertices of a polyhedron. Calculating the surface area of rectangular boxes. Changing one geometric figure into another by moving one side at a time. Using coordinates to graph figures. Using perspective to draw three-dimensional figures. If you don't remember what some of these words mean, don't worry. They're defined in the text and in the glossary. An index is also included. *Mary Pride*

Sir Cumference and the First Round Table, a 32-page illustrated softcover, illuminates mathematical ideas by twisting them into a classic tale. It tells the tale of how Sir Cumference and his wife, Lady Di of Ameter, and their son Radius help solve the problem of the too long rectangular table at which the knights sit. Ever frugal, the family come up with different ways to cut the existing table into a shape that might make the meetings work better. The illustrations show how to cut one shape and form it into another—a neat trick when trying to explain how to find the area of different shapes. Each table has its own unique problems (triangular tables have corners that are as sharp as sword points, regular-shaped polygons didn't always have an edge for each knight). Eventually—and I don't think I'm giving too much away here—the knights settle for a *round* table. A book that is definitely *not* for mathematical squares. *Teresa Schultz-Jones*

Are you having problems describing an icosahedron or an octahedron to your children? If you're like me, not only can you not describe them, you can't even visualize them. The **Vector Flexor** Fold-A-Form geometry toy helped solve that dilemma for me.

Vector Flexor is made up of 24 primary-colored sticks which are joined together with flexible rubber tubing. Fortunately, no assembly is required. When you take your Vector Flexor out of the package, it immediately opens up into a vector equilibrium. As you follow the instructions, your Vector Flexor will change from a vector equilibrium to a icosahedron, then to a octahedron, then to a large triangle, then to a tetrahedron, then to a small triangle.

Following the skimpy, one-page directions is the hard part, at least for those lacking in the area of manual dexterity. Here are the directions for going from the octahedron to the large triangle:

> *Now hold the top triangle like a steering wheel, release it slightly and then turn it 180 degrees either way until you have a LARGE FLAT TRIANGLE. Be sure to keep the large triangle always directly over the bottom.*

You may initially have a hard time learning how to "steer" an octahedron, but with a little bit of perseverance, you'll soon get the hang of it.

NEW!
Sir Cumference and the First Round Table

Grades 1–5. $6.95 plus shipping. *Charlesbridge Publishing, 85 Main Street, Watertown, MA 02472. (617) 926-0329. Fax: (617) 926-5720. Email: books@charlesbridge.com. Web: www.charlesbridge.com.*

NEW!
Vector Flexor

Grades 1–6. $8 postpaid. *Tobi Toys, PO Box 10, Gepp, AR 72538. (870) 458-2562. Email: tobi@centuryinter.net.*

Once you do, you'll have a great tool for teaching those hard-to-comprehend geometrical shapes. (If you are really captivated by these geometric shapes and want to learn more, the owner of Tobi Toys recommends the book *Synergetics* by R. Buckminster Fuller.)

A one-page example of 16 different forms such as pentagons, stars, and double tetras is included. The directions for making those 16 forms are not included. However, most children will figure out how to make not only those shapes, but many others as well.

In spite of the skimpy directions, you will have a lot of fun figuring out exactly what you can do with the Vector Flexor. You may find yourself manipulating this toy into forms that go far beyond commonly known geometrical shapes. And best of all, there are no small parts to lose! *Rebecca Livermore*

So what, you ask, is **Visual Thinking**? Good question. In this case, it's the title of two boxes full of colorful task cards (100 per box) designed to teach visual thinking skills. And now, since I have not yet told you what visual thinking really *is*, and I don't want to leave you gnashing your teeth in frustration, here's a definition of visual thinking straight from the teacher's guide included with Set A:

> *Visual thinking is an integral part of our society. On any given day we might need to be able to interpret a graph, map, photograph, sculpture, graphic symbol, and/or body language. In order to understand a book or something told to us orally, we must be able to visualize characters, settings, and physical objects from the words that are given. And, in order to efficiently solve a problem, we need to be able to visualize possible approaches to solving it or to draw a picture of the elements of the problem.*

So Dale Seymour's Visual Thinking series is designed to help fourthgraders and up acquire spatial perception skills. This is important because studies have shown that many students lack these skills. Success in geometry class, engineering, and even in art is based on the ability to interpret, remember, and mentally manipulate visual symbols.

So much for theory. What you get in each box is 100 task cards and a very short teacher's commentary with an answer key for the cards. The box itself, I might add, is very sturdy and attractive, looking as if it were designed by the people who do those upscale cheese popcorn bags. Each task card has a single assignment laid out on it, which should take between three and 15 minutes to complete. These are fun assignments, ranging in Set A from a set of five strings of colored circles with the instruction to "find the two designs that are exactly the same" to Card 100 which shows three different views of the same solid and asks how many triangular faces, edges, and vertices (corners) the solid has. (This is not as easy to figure out as you think, since you are looking at two-dimensional pictures of only part of a three-dimensional object!) In between you'll find problems asking you to draw spatial forms, count bricks in a stack (including the ones you *can't* see), find the missing puzzle piece, and all sorts of other ingenious ways to limber up your spatial sense. Problems become more difficult as you move through the cards. Set B is harder than Set A.

These sets are just excellent. The exercises really can improve your spatial skills, and they are lots of fun besides! The task card format means you can use the program just a little bit at a time, or do a whole lot at once—it's up to you. The durable cards should last for years; you can use them with every child in your family, and the grownups, too. Girls should especially benefit, as in general girls have weaker spatial skills than boys. Recommended. *Mary Pride*

Visual Thinking, Sets A and B
Grades 4–12. $32.95 per set. Both sets, $54. Shipping extra.
Dale Seymour Publications, PO Box 5026, White Plains, NY 10602. (800) 872-1100. Fax: (800) 551-7637. Web: www.cuisenaire-dsp.com.

Homeschool Geometry of the Future

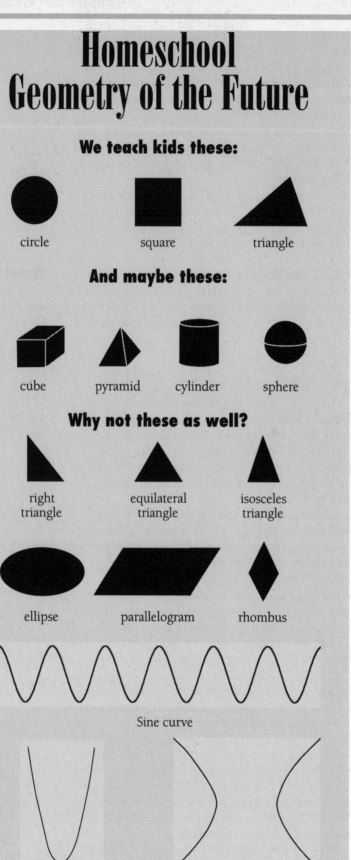

We teach kids these:

circle   square   triangle

And maybe these:

cube   pyramid   cylinder   sphere

Why not these as well?

right triangle   equilateral triangle   isosceles triangle

ellipse   parallelogram   rhombus

Sine curve

parabola   hyperbola

CHAPTER 29

Math Drill Materials

Math computation is the only area in which public schooled children beat homeschooled children on standardized tests.

The reason? At home, we have all the time in the world to teach each subject. There are no bells ringing to summon Tawana and Jose to their next class. So we tend to let the kids take all the time they want with their assignments.

That's fine when it comes to pursuing a science unit study, but not so great when it comes to speedy math computations. It's all very well that the kids *understand* their math, but in the real world, and even the Twilight Zone of standardized tests, it helps a lot if you can work through a math problem quickly.

Therefore, we have assembled the following drill resources. My hope is that you all will use them, and the next time we put out a new *Big Book* edition, homeschooled kids will be tops in *everything!*

Timed Drill Sheets

Providence Project's **CalcuLadder Series** is a set of calculation drill sheets, starting with numeral recognition in level one and winding up with fractions, percents, and all that other lovely pre-algebra stuff in level six. Each level consists of 12 copies of 16 different worksheets. Your child works a sheet once a day until 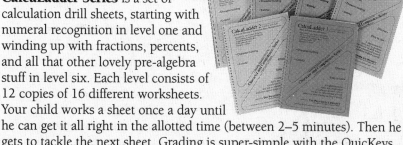 he can get it all right in the allotted time (between 2–5 minutes). Then he gets to tackle the next sheet. Grading is super-simple with the QuicKeys grading key (just turn around the sheet, lining up the rows, and instantly see if your answer is correct). An Instructor's Guide is included for each set. Colored paper, cute visuals in the margins, and a Bible verse on the bottom of each page are freebie extras. The whole program only takes about five minutes a day, and let me tell you, it really does increase calculation ability and speed! Plus, each level now comes neatly spiral-bound, so you won't be chasing worksheets all over the house.

I recommend this supplemental program for all home schoolers whose children are anything short of supersonic in their math computation speed and understanding. *Mary Pride*

- **CalcuLadder 1:** Basic addition and subtraction for grades 1 or 2 or remedial. 2- and 3-minute drills.
- **CalcuLadder 2:** Advanced addition and subtraction and basic multiplication. Grades 2 or 3 or remedial, 3- and 4-minute drills.
- **CalcuLadder 3:** Intermediate and advanced multiplication and basic division. Grades 3 or 4 or remedial, 4- and 5-minute drills.
- **CalcuLadder 4:** Advanced multiplication review, intermediate and advanced division, place values, product estimation, basic fractions, and decimals. Grades 4 or 5 or remedial. 5-minute drills.
- **CalcuLadder 5:** Advanced division review, intermediate and advanced fractions. Grades 5–7 or remedial. 5-minute drills.
- **CalcuLadder 6:** Fractions review, percents, English & metric units, pre-geometry, more. Grades 6–8 or remedial. 5-minute drills.

Math drills! Does this thought make you smile with delight or cringe with dread? Whether they are a necessary evil or a delightful pastime in your life, this math series can supply you with a complete drill system.

Addition Facts in Five Minutes a Day is now perfect-bound. **Subtraction Facts in Five Minutes a Day**, and **Division Facts in Five Minutes a Day** both are spiral-bound. Each includes reproducible masters for the drill sheets. They are printed in black and white, with no frills. Each book contains a recordkeeping section, a reproducible flashcard section, and a games and activities section.

You are instructed to administer daily timed tests, using a photocopy of the current drill page. Although they were intended for classroom use, they can be easily altered to meet the needs of a homeschool setting. Your child repeats each sheet (that's why they need to be photocopied!) until he reaches a completion time of three minutes with 100 percent accuracy.

The drills are designed to be competitive in nature. Your child can either compete against himself or against siblings (or you can skip the competitiveness altogether).

Each book is designed to take a whole school year to complete. The author stresses the importance of over-learning math facts.

You will need access to a copy machine to use this series. Some directions need to be altered for home use. *Maryann Turner*

NEW!
Five Minutes a Day! series

Grades 1–3. Addition Facts, Subtraction Facts, Division Facts, $11.95 each. Multiplication Facts, $13.95. Shipping extra.
Instructional Resources Company, P.O. Box 111704, Anchorage, AK 99511. Orders: (800) 356-9315. Inquiries: (907) 345-6689. Fax: (907) 345-6689. Email: santhony@alaska..net. Web: www.alaska..net/~santhony.

NEW!
Math-n-Works series

Grades 2–5. $24.95 each postpaid.
Keys For Learning, PO Box 1898, Forks, WA 98331. (800) 850-4835. Fax: (360) 374-3316. Email: kfl@olypen.com.

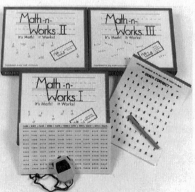

The idea of **Math-n-Works** is simple: daily speed tests will help you remember the basic arithmetic facts. Each day you take a timed 100-question arithmetic quiz and record your scores and how long it took. As you take the tests, your speed should improve until you can recall the facts instantaneously. The recommended goal is the ability to complete 100 arithmetic facts in under three minutes.

Math-n-Works improves upon old-fashioned drills by providing a stopwatch and a unique quick correct sheet. To correct problems, you place your worksheet under a sheet of clear plastic which contains the answers, allowing you to quickly see which problems were done wrong. This can be a bit awkward, since you have to lift the clear plastic up each time you are marking an answer wrong. (Why couldn't the *worksheets* be clear plastic and the *answer sheet* be paper?)

Each set of Math-n-Works comes with

- Quick correct sheets
- Table with 45 double-sided test pages
- Stopwatch
- Highlighter (to correct the problems)
- Fact sheet with all of the arithmetic operations included in the tests
- Progress booklet
- Directions

The first two packages, *Math-n-Works I* and *Math-n-Works II*, are designed to put the 400 basic arithmetic facts into long term memory. On these sheets, the problems are presented vertically. *Math-n-Works III* presents the problems horizontally and is designed only for review, since it does not provide all of the math facts on each page.

I was surprised that my kids enjoyed the speed tests, since they usually don't like this sort of thing. The stopwatch, although somewhat gimmicky, inspired them to improve their speed. *Teresa Schultz-Jones*

Math Songs

Addition Songs. Why count sheep at night, when your child could drift to slumberland memorizing his addition facts? This tape includes a 25 x 36" sing-along poster which lists the numerals 1–20 and the addition tables 1 + 1 to 9 + 9. The first song counts from 1–20 followed by the tables sung as, "1 + 1 is 2, . . . 1 + 9 is 10" Each table is repeated with no answer. Your child only has to add one to the previous answer in each table to come up with the next answer in the series, limiting this product to an introduction of the addition tables. No tips are given for handling the trickier tables. No mixed review is given. The music was light and enjoyable to listen to, a pleasant diversion in the car.

Subtraction Songs. Same format as the addition tape. Covers all the subtraction facts from 1-1 to 20-12. Each table is sung in a different catchy tune. Tape packet includes a poster of all the tables.

Fraction Drills Workbook. Used with *Multiplication Songs* from Audio Memory. Reproducible. Also available is a **Division Drills workbook**.

After memorizing the multiplication facts using the tape, your children will know that 3 x 12 is 36. With this workbook, they will see that $\frac{36}{3}$ reduces to 12. Students work their way from $\frac{3}{3}$ is $\frac{1}{1}$ to $\frac{36}{3}$ which is $\frac{12}{1}$. The book contains straightforward problems with no visual appeal. While fraction reduction is often a confusing part of a fractions, this is not a whole fraction course. *Katherine von Duyke*

International Learning Systems' "Songs that Teach" lineup also now includes two **Musical Math Facts Kits**. These teach all the addition, subtraction, multiplication, and division facts with recorded songs. The laminated books have sing-along charts and speed tests following a careful sequence.

The **Level 1** Kit teaches the addition and subtraction facts. It comes with a 30-minute cassette of songs that correlate with the charts in the wipe-off

Here are the topics covered in each set:

- *Math-n-Works I*—Addition and subtraction.
- *Math-n-Works II*—Multiplication and division.
- *Math-n-Works III*—Mixed addition/subtraction and mixed multiplication/division.

Since only two answer keys are provided with each set, there is a limit on how many variations of worksheets there can be. As a result, there are only three different addition worksheets, three subtraction worksheets, and so on. I have mixed feelings about this, since it's possible that some children will memorize the order of the answers without associating them with the problems.

NEW!
Audio Memory Math Songs & Workbooks

Grades pre-K–2. Addition and Subtraction songs, $9.95 each. Fraction and Division workbooks, $5 each. Shipping extra.
Audio Memory, 501 Cliff Dr., Newport Beach, CA 92663. (800) 365-7464. Fax: (949) 631-1150. Email: emily@audiomemory.com. Web: www.audiomemory.com.

NEW!
Musical Math Facts Kits

Grades 1–6. Level 1 (ages 5 and up) and Level 2 (ages 8 and up), $36 each.
International Learning Systems, 1000 - 112th Circle N., Suite 100, St.

Petersburg, FL 33716. (800) 321-8322. Fax: (813) 576-8832. Web: www.singspell.com.

NEW!
One Hundred Sheep

Grades K–6. $10.
Common Sense Press, P.O. Box 1365, Melrose FL 32666. Call (352) 475-5757 for a retail store near you; they do not sell retail themselves. Email: service@cspress.com. Web: www.cspress.com.

NEW!
Rap with the Facts: Multiplication

Grades 1–6. Cassette, Workbook, $9.98 together. Add $3.50 shipping. *Twin Sisters Productions, 1340 Home Ave., Suite D, Akron, OH 44310. Orders: (800) 248-TWIN. Inquiries: (330) 633-8900. Fax: (330) 633-8988. Web: www.twinsisters.com.*

NEW!
Rock 'N Learn Math

Grades 2–6. Audiocassette/activity book combos, $9.95 each. Multiplication Rap, Multiplication Rock available in CD/activity book combos, $12.95 each. Shipping extra. *Rock 'N Learn, Inc., P.O. Box 3595, Conroe, TX 77305. Orders: (800) 348-*

book. Manipulatives (popsicle sticks and counting chips) are also included for hands-on proof of the facts students are memorizing through song. Oral and written timed speed tests are also built in to the program. **Level 2** teaches all the multiplication facts through 12 x 12 and all the related division facts. It also includes a 30-minute song cassette.

A little felt chalkboard eraser is included in each of the math facts kits. *Mary Pride*

Roger Nichols invites us to increase the math capability of our children by learning the process of skip counting with his **One Hundred Sheep** audio tape and song book. The process of skip counting, by 2, 3, 5, 10, etc., is used in every math process, and so the ease of using the method is well worth the effort of learning it. Mr. Nichols' painless approach uses stories from the Gospels as a basis for his cassette tape. The variety of instruments used, combined with smooth harmonies, make each song come across as much more than a math lesson. Scriptural background for each song can be researched by the parent, but there are no suggested guidelines for usage. The 10-page booklet neglects ideas for practice, but does provide the complete words for each song.

Perfect for a ride in the car, or a quiet afternoon, *One Hundred Sheep* can be an asset to any beginning math curriculum with a little forethought and planning. *Lisa Mitchell*

"We're going to learn our multiplication facts, because school and learning is where it's at . . ." This is how the **Rap with the Facts** multiplication cassette tape introduces itself. Facts begin with the 2x table and progresses through the 12x table, each table being multiplied through twelve with a short musical interlude between tables. The second side drills the same facts, saying the problem and leaving space for an answer. Because the facts are presented in order, the children are really skip counting through each table. It's too bad it doesn't include another rap of mixed review.

The rap music is light, with background accompaniments that remind me of arcade themes. The 48-page reproducible workbook available with the tape includes timed drill sheets, mixed drill practice and word problems. The word problems are easy to figure out and present mixed problems in a verbal format. If your curriculum already includes timed drill sheets or fact pages, you can skip this workbook and just get the tape. *Katherine von Duyke*

Facts to music! Not exactly a new concept, but here is a series of audiocassette tapes that combine learning math facts with music from different musical styles. You can choose the style of **Rock 'N Learn Audiocassette Tapes** that best suits your family.

Available tape sets are:

Multiplication Rap, Multiplication Rock, Multiplication Country, Addition & Subtraction Rock, Addition Rap, Subtraction Rap, Division Rap, Division Rock.

Educators and musicians worked together to create these tapes. They are catchy and make memorizing the facts easier. There are no objectionable lyrics, and the tapes are educational. A reproducible activity book is included with each tape. The activity book has game, puzzle and worksheet pages. Each tape helps develop memorization of facts through 12. The facts on the worksheets are written in a vertical format to encourage your child to memorize them in the format that they see most often.

If you like one of these music styles, this is a cute, easy way for your child to memorize their math facts. *Maryann Turner*

Sara Jordan Presents Math is a ear-enticing, classy series of audio CDs: *Addition Unplugged*, *Subtraction Unplugged*, *Multiplication Unplugged*, and *Division Unplugged*. She uses memorable lyrics, fun music, and student involvement to drill math facts. Not only are the basic facts included, but practical suggestions to help memorize the facts are incorporated into the songs.

Unlike some other audio drill materials we've used in the past, this one holds your child's attention (at least for a few minutes). The lyrics book contains over a dozen worksheet pages which can be reproduced for additional students. *Maryann Turner*

When I was in grade school, I refused to memorize the multiplication tables and my math grades suffered because of it. If only I had had Skip Count Kid's tapes, I may have found multiplication easy.

The Skip Count Kid tape contains 10 songs, one each about counting by 2s, 3s, etc., up to 10s; and then a song about how 10 + 1 = 11, 10 + 2 = 12, etc., titled "You Must Have 10 to Make a Teen." The simple lyrics are arranged so that the counting sequence is repeated throughout the song.

The Skip Count Kid's Bible Heroes contains nine songs using skip counting (2s, 3s, etc., up to 10s), each song telling a Bible story as well. Most of the songs count up to 9 times the number by which they are counting.

The tapes could be listened to by a child independently, but the author intends that parents or teachers introduce them one by one. A teachers' manual booklet comes with each tape. The book contains the lyrics of each song, explanation of hand and body motions meant to go along with each song, other teaching tips, and some simple illustrations. *Melissa Worcester*

Math Drill Games

Practice your fractions, decimals, and negative numbers while infiltrating an enemy beehive and capturing its queen!

Hive Alive is like a small-scale math-based *Stratego*. Like *Stratego*, you have two players and markers you try to place in strategic positions on the gameboard. The markers have numbers on the back, except for the Killer Bee and Queen Bee markers. As you move about the board, occasionally you can challenge (attempt to "sting") a neighboring marker. If the number on the back of your marker is higher, you win.

At the primary level, you play with whole numbers only. At the "Fraction Faction" level, markers have fractions on the back. The "Droves of Decimals" markers have decimals on the back. The "Anything Goes" level mixes it up, with everything but whole numbers, plus some negative numbers.

Where does the math come in? Well, you have to translate fractions and decimals and figure out which represents a larger number. Decent practice for an area of math that often doesn't get the practice it needs. *Mary Pride*

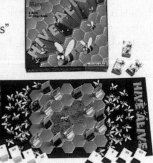

NEW!
Delightful Dice Math Games

Grades 3–6. $5 plus $1.25 shipping. *Mark Dickey, 181 Cleveland Drive, Croton-on Hudson, NY 10520.*

Did you know that three dice can be used to teach:

- computation
- place value
- factors
- least common multiples
- fractions and improper fractions
- prime factoring, and more?

Delightful Dice Math Games were developed by homeschooler Mark Dickey. They come in a zip-lock bag containing the game rules booklet, a helpful hints booklet, and three differently colored dice.

The rules booklet explains how to play each of the 12 games and references which section of the Helpful Hints booklet explains the math behind that game. Players' turns generally consist of rolling the dice to set up and solve a math problem, and games are open-ended, letting you play however many rounds you want.

Games vary in complexity. In "The Bigger, the Better," players learn how to read big numbers as they roll two die. You write the number from the first die, and use the second die to determine how many zeroes to write after it. A roll of 5 and 4 produces 50,000 or "fifty thousand." The winner of the round is the person who rolled the highest number. A more complicated game teaches about mixed-number fractions by having you rewrite the improper fractions that some rolls produce (the value of each dice corresponds to a whole number, numerator, or denominator).

My only complaint about the Delightful Dice Games is that the scoring sometimes seems unnecessarily complicated, but there is no reason you can't change how you score the game. After playing Delightful Dice Games, you may find yourself throwing dice in other games and calculating prime numbers and fractions! *Teresa Schultz-Jones*

Educational Insights Math Games

Readiness Math Games, Primary Math Games and Intermediate Math Games (3 games in each), $29.95 each set. Plus 'n Minus Game, $19.95. Fraction Match-Up, Thinkfast!, Gotcha!, and Capture the Flags, $6.95 each. Presto Change-O, $24.95. Shipping extra. *Educational Insights, Inc., 16941 Keegan Ave., Carson, CA 90746. (800) 995-4436. (310) 884-2000. Fax: (800) 995-0506. Web: www.edin.com.*

Readiness Math Games consists of three games: *Which One, How Many,* and *Adding it Up.* **Primary Math Games** is a set of three games— *Sum Buddies* for basic addition, *Minus Maze* for subtraction, and *Time Out* for time telling—all colorful and actually fun to play. **Intermediate Math Games** consists of *Prehistoric Times* (multiplication), *Dinosaur Division* (division), and *Ballpark Figures* (estimating skills).

Plus 'n Minus Games is math drill made painless as students must add and subtract to find their way around the game board. The double-sided board (one for addition, one for subtraction) comes with a reproducible activity workbook.

Thinkfast!, **Gotcha!**, and **Capture the Flags** are high-speed math competition using all four basic arithmetic processes: addition, subtraction, multiplication, and division. *Thinkfast!* is for two players only, and can be played using addition only, or subtraction only, etc. In *Capture the Flags!*, players roll dice and try to capture the cards laid down by finding one that equals any combination of the dice. If the numbers 2 and 3 are rolled, for instance, you can take a 5 (2 + 3), a 1 (3 - 2), or a 6 (2 x 3). But you have to be the first! *Gotcha!* players win by capturing the opponent's cards. If my 4 and 2 equal your 5 and 1, I can take them—if you don't figure it out first! In **Fraction Match-Up** you win by matching fractions.

Presto Change-O helps kids learn to make change as they roam about the game board collecting an allowance, doing chores for cash, and blowing their stash on treats. *Mary Pride*

Instead of dull, dreary flash cards, why don't you try **Match-A-Fact** for your math drill? Each set of cards comes with nine games: *Concentration, Winner Takes All (War), Lucky Seven (Old Maid), Draw One (Go Fish), Solitaire* (two versions), *Match-A-Fact, Beat the Clock,* and *Flash Card Frustration.* You get a problem deck (cards with math problems like 2+5 on them), an answer deck (whole number cards—1, 2, 3 . . .), a self-checking answer key, instruction booklet, and progress chart. *Match-A-Fact* is no kitchen-produced job, either. The cards are real playing card quality, and the packaging would look quite at home in any school supply store.

How does it work? Some games use both decks, some just one. For *Winner Takes All,* children deal the cards in the "problem" deck. The child whose answer is a higher number takes both cards. You remember the game from your youth. Thus 8 - 1 beats 5 - 4, for example. Kids can resort to the answer key if they forget the answer. You can see how much drill they get in math facts from just this one game! *Concentration* involves spreading all the cards in both decks face down, and turning over two at a time. If you match a problem with its answer, you may keep the cards. This is a great memory and math drill. Don't forget, each box has seven more games, and you can invent games of your own.

Match-A-Fact has gone over big wherever it has been used. Children request it for birthday presents, and parents who see it used at school buy their own copies for home. It really is fun to use, and not much more expensive than a batch of commercial flash cards. *Mary Pride*

Cathy Duffy, author of the *Christian Home Educators Curriculum Manuals,* is the inventor of the **Math Mouse Games**. Her only distinctively Christian game is the *Gardening* game, where Scripture references to sowing, weeding, watering, and reaping are included on the game board. The other games are math drill with a lot of soul. In *Grocery Store,* for example, you visit the four food groups and try to spend a total of $40 on your trip. But be careful: you can't spend more than $10 in each category! *Grocery Store* is played with a game board, pawns, dice, and Math Mouse Money. The set as a whole contains six game boards, printed back to back on folding cardboard, a fraction/decimal card deck, four special dice, a number line, pawns, spinner, play money, round markers to cover up spaces in some games, and an instruction book. Games are *Gardening, Grocery Store, Blast Off, Space Race, Roll a Problem, Multiplication Board, Add Off, Fractions and Decimal War,* and *Gobbling Fractions.* All basic math concepts are practiced. The learner also gets an introduction to economics in the grocery store and the garden.

These games are really cute, kid-appealing, and are now professionally printed in full-color. You get a lot for your money. *Mary Pride*

Match-A-Fact card games

Grades K–6. Addition, Subtraction, Multiplication, and Division $9.95 each, Set of all four, $36. Shipping extra.
Margwen Products, 382 34th St. SE, Cedar Rapids, IA 52403. (319) 365-6398. Fax: (319) 365-6398. E-mail: Matchfact@aol.com.

Math Mouse Games

Grades K–6. $21.95 (9 basic games plus variations) plus shipping.
Grove Publishing, 16172 Huxley Circle, Westminster, CA 92683. (714) 841-1220. Fax: (714) 841-5584. Web: www.grovepublishing.com.

Math Safari is a large electronic math drill machine. It has 10 different problem books available, each with 40 lessons. Each page has a lesson in the middle of the page and several questions around the edges. The Math Safari machine works similarly to its GeoSafari namesake. You turn it on, type in the lesson code, and tell it the number of players and the time each has to answer each question. After you tell it to start, it blinks a light next to the question and you type in the answer on the numerical keypad.

You can play Math Safari with either one or two players. If you play competitively, you take turns and the goal is to answer more questions correctly than the other player does. If you play alone, the goal is to answer all the questions correctly. If a player answers all the questions on the page correctly then the Math Safari will play a quick tune and flash all the lights on the board in sequence for a very satisfying streaming effect. If a player does not answer all questions correctly, Math Safari will tell him how many he answered right.

MathSafari Lesson units include:

- Ready, Set, Count! (Grades PreK–1)
- Addition Fun! (Grades K–2)
- Subtraction Fun! (Grades 1–2)
- Addition-Subtraction Fun! (Grades 2–4)
- Multiplication Fun! (Grades 2–5)
- Division Fun! (Grades 3–5)
- Fraction Fun! (Grades 3–6)
- Fractions, Decimals, and Percents Fun! (Grades 4–7)
- Ready for Algebra (Grades 5 and up)
- Gearing Up for Geometry (Grades 5 and up)
- More Addition Fun! (Grades 2–4)
- More Subtraction Fun! (Grades 2–4)
- More Multiplication Fun! (Grades 3–5)
- More Division Fun! (Grades 3–5)
- More Multiplication and Division Fun! (Grades 3–5)
- More Mathematics Fun! (Grades 5–7)

Computer software can do all the above, of course. But if you don't have a computer, or prefer to use a portable drill device that doesn't need a long time to "boot," Math Safari is just as fun as most computer programs, and easier to use competitively. *Joseph Pride*

Here is an entertaining way to keep your children's math skills sharp over the summer break. **Math Smart Master Edition** is a collection of four card decks—one for each of the four basic math operations: addition, subtraction, multiplication, and division.

The right side of each card has a mathematical equation and the left side has an answer to an equation. The game is played in a manner similar to dominoes, with players matching the equation to the corresponding answer.

To maximize the retention potential of the drill, the cards used could be the tailored to the need of the individual child. For instance, you might choose to drill only the cards that have an addition sum of ten, or perhaps only the nine times table. The different decks can be combined to increase the difficulty and interest. Reviewing math operations in this way could be a pleasant diversion from more traditional drill methods. *Barbara Petronelli*

Math Spin comes with eight ten-sided, colorful magnetic wheels that you can turn around and lock together with very little effort. Six of the wheels display the digits in order from 0 to 9. One wheel has the math operations on it, while the other has the signs for equals, greater than, and less than. To teach place value you add a number wheel at a time to create larger numbers up to 9,999. For the math facts, you can create math sentences such as 8 + 4 = 12 or even 85 + 14 = 99. You can also construct inequalities such as 10 + 4 > 11.

Instructions that come with the product explain how to use it in your home teaching; the instructions include four simple games that introduce math concepts sequentially.

While this doesn't have as high a "wow" factor as an electronic product like Twist & Shout (see review below), it's a lot quieter—makes no noise at all, in fact!—and is less expensive and more versatile. Once the child learns enough math to use it properly, it makes a great travel toy, too. Just don't store it on top of your disk drive or with your videotape collection. *Mary Pride*

To get a feel for **Mental Math Card Games**, picture your whole family enthusiastically calling out answers to multi-step mental math problems as quickly as possible, the younger ones laughing when Mom or Dad hesitate, and everyone encouraging everyone else to do his best. Due to the unique design, players can't tell whose turn it is until they've figured out the answer, and they stay alert the whole time, and solve *every* problem.

Try these when most of your kids know how to multiply and divide (the older ones can help the younger ones after that). Series I has two levels through division. Series II includes squares, roots, and a few cubes and primes. *Kim O'Hara*

Kids can give adults a hard time (which they love!) with this game. I know this is true, because my daughter Sarah beat the creator of **Muggins** at his own game when they played it at the Glorieta Homeschool Conference in August 1997!

Muggins is an arithmetic drill and thinking skill game played with marbles on a beautiful wooden board. The board has a groove around it (for marble storage while playing), and 36 numbered holes.

The object of *Muggins* is to get your marbles in as many rows as possible, while blocking your opponent's attempts to do the same. You move by rolling three dice and (1) adding, subtracting, multiplying, or dividing the numbers on the first two, and then to that total doing the same with the third die. E.g., if your numbers are 2, 6, and 3, some possible moves are:

- Divide the 6 by the 2, add the 3. (Answer: 6)
- Multiply the 2 by the 3, multiply by six. (Answer: 36)
- Add the 2 and the 6, subtract the 3. (Answer: 5)

You move your marble into that slot on the board.

There are a few other rules, such as the automatic "bump," where anyone rolling triples gets to remove one of his opponent's marbles, but you get the general idea.

New variations now included in *Muggins*:

- *Muggins, Jr.* (for kids ages 8–10): add and subtract only, using the three included 12-face polyhedrons.
- *Super Muggins* (advanced skill level): add, subtract, multiply, and divide using the polyhedron.

NEW!
Math Spin

Grades preK–8. $6 plus shipping. *Geospace International, 1546 NW Woodbine Way, Seattle, WA 98177. Orders: (800) 800-5090. Inquiries/fax: (206) 365-5241. Email: debink@gte.net. Web: www.spingames.com.*

NEW!
Mental Math Card Games

Grades 4–8. $8 plus shipping for each series of 2 decks. *Midmath, Ellen Hechler, PO Box 2892, Farmington Hills, MI 48333. Fax: (248) 737-6917.*

Muggins

Grades 3–adult. $26.95 (reversible game board, $38.95) plus shipping. *Old Fashioned Products, 4860 Burnt Mtn. Rd., Ellijay, GA 30540. (800) 962-8849. Inquiries: (706) 635-7612. Fax: (706) 635-7611. Email: muggins@ellijay.com.*

- *Dishes* (motivational version): dice is thrown only once. Players alternate making totals. First player unable to make a new total has to do the dishes!
- *Bluffing* (optional): encourages players to check each other's math for continual involvement.

Unlike all other math board games I have seen, *Muggins* is fast-paced, uses all the arithmetic operations, and involves a lot of mental math and strategy. Plus it's elegant, in a rustic, unstained kind of way. High-class math drill for families with brains who aren't afraid to use them. *Mary Pride*

"Hit it! What plus 8 is 12?" The voice is a cheery male. The product is **Twist & Shout Addition**. The part you are supposed to "hit" is the end of the tube. This is like hitting "enter" on a computer—it lets the gizmo know you're ready for action. It also makes a sound like a small explosion. You rotate the yellow band to select one of three games.

The exclamation mark selects the "Learn" game. Here, you build an equation by rotating the two blue number bands. Twist & Shout supplies the answer, both verbally with music and beat, and visually on its LCD screen. If you pick "3 + 4," for instance, Twist & Shout informs you, "Three plus four is seven . . . number heaven!" If you select the lightning "wild-card" symbol for one of the numbers, it will run through the entire family of addition facts for that number family in sequence.

The question mark selects the "Quiz" game. Here, you are supposed to hit the end of the tube when Twist & Shout tells you the right answer for the problem selected. Again, if you select the lightning symbol, you get to quiz yourself on an entire addition facts family.

The lightning symbol selects the subtraction game. Now we're back to "What plus 8 is 12?" You are supposed to rotate the number band to arrive at the correct answer, and then hit the end of the tube to select it.

Twist & Shout Multiplication works the exact same way, and can be used to practice up to the 12s tables. As with the other one, batteries are included, as is a handy carry strap. A neat way to practice math that's really different from computer programs or flashcards. *Mary Pride*

NEW!
Twist & Shout Math Toys

Ages 3–9 (Addition), grades 2–5 (Multiplication). Each Twist & Shout, $19.99. Shipping extra. *LeapFrog, 1250 45th St., Emeryville, CA 94608. (800) 701-LEAP (5327) or (510) 595-2470. Fax: (510) 595-2478. Email: custserv@leapfrogtoys.com.*

Do you need a fun, multi-sensory approach to teach math facts? The **U Can Do Exercise and Memorize** series combines learning math facts and a basic skills exercise program. It incorporates all learning styles, allowing your child to learn using their preferred learning style while also making use of the other styles. Your child sees the facts, hears the facts, sings along with the facts, exercises to the facts, and then writes the facts in their workbook. A video, a student book and a teacher's guide is included with each program. The videos are low key and non-glitzy. The children are cute and wholesome.

The four videos in the series cover the four basic arithmetic operations:

- *Addition Adventure*
- *Subtraction Safari*
- *Multiplication March*
- *Division Detectives*

NEW!
U Can Do Exercise and Memorize Math Series

Grades preK–6. Video programs, $19.95 each. Shipping extra. *U Can Do, 17900 Dolores Lane, Sonora, CA 95370. (800) 286-8585. Fax: (209) 533-8585. Email: Laura@candokids.com. Web: www.candokids.com.*

In each video, a group of children, dressed in various costumes, do simple exercises while repeating basic math facts. After reviewing the video, your child then completes the answers in the small 45-page workbook. The workbook sections are short and easy to complete. The series focuses on basic math facts and includes a teacher's guide with additional suggestions for teaching the facts. *Maryann Turner*

PART 6

Know-How

Eight-year-old homeschooled third-grader James Hicks has had a flair for electronics for some time. After watching a video on Thomas Edison, he decided to create a model telegraph. This telegraph's lights and loud buzzers made it easy to tell whether the operator was typing a dot or a dash. After James completed his telegraph, he signed up for a Harvest Home Educators science fair in Atlanta, GA.

As you can see by the picture, James presented his telegraph quite well. Due to the amount of noise it produced, the telegraph was the most popular entry with younger children. James won first place and took home a fantastic microscope.

Eight-year-old Molly St. John from Fraser, Michigan was presented with the Indiana Junior Naturalist Patch and Certificate at Shakamak State Park in Jasonville, Indiana. To earn the patch, Molly was required to perform three hours of park service, attend five naturalist activities, do a nature project to be presented to the naturalist, and do a nature identification hike to observe ten species of forest life.

For her service projects, Molly cleaned the nature center, performed a presentation on a slug that taught people about its habits and interesting qualities, and prepared for other naturalist activities. After the presentation, Molly's sister Sarah (17) and her two cousins went on a night walk through the forest with the naturalist. As Molly said, "If science is done right, it is fun!"

Molly enjoys earning patches. Last year she earned the Smokey patch, and next year she plans to earn her Junior Ecologist patch.

CHAPTER 30

Creation Science vs. Evolution

"What is the meaning of life?"
That's the question that theories of origins attempt to answer.

According to Darwin, the purpose of life is "survival of the fittest." Bare, naked survival. The universe is run by random chance.

Ever since Darwin, philosophers have struggled to find a reason for beauty, compassion, honor, love, self-sacrifice, and everything else that makes life meaningful. As the history of our century shows, they have failed. "Nature red in tooth and claw" fit just great into Stalin's Russia or Pol Pot's Cambodia or Hitler's Germany, but transcendent values such as kindness to outsiders and the weak didn't.

Of course, other answers besides Darwin's exist. Eastern religions teach that the purpose of life is to avoid pain, and eventually to avoid life. You don't want to become too attached to anyone or anything, because everything is ultimately an illusion, and (here's the part that Zen masters don't tell you) it *hurts* to lose your illusions. Be passionless. Uninvolved. Get off the wheel of karma and achieve nirvana. In this worldview, the world, which is just an illusion anyway, constantly recreates itself, going through cycles of death, destruction, and rebirth. There is no clear line between animal and man; in fact, kindness to rats and cows may be more important than feeding your own children.

The Western religious tradition teaches just the opposite. Here, the purpose of life is to "glorify God and enjoy Him forever." To do so, you have to find your mission in life and fulfill it. You don't want to escape life; you want to make the most of it, in service to God and others. In this view, the entire human race is important, having been created by God for a purpose. Everything had a definite beginning during Creation Week, and since then our history is the story of battles fought and won or lost for the sake of the kingdom of Heaven—not literal battles, but choices individuals and societies make to embrace righteousness or flee from it. The family is not just a temporarily useful evolutionary device, but God's perfect design for how men and women should live together and children should be raised. Animals are not people, and people are not animals.

As you can see, **quite a lot comes bundled with each theory of origins.** By picking a particular point of view, you are implicitly teaching all the religious and moral baggage that comes along with it. This is one reason why millions of families have left the public education system—it has adopted Evolution as a state religion. Or, if you prefer, a state *anti*-religion—because fans of evolution are terribly anxious that creation *not* be taught.

One reason for this might be that **evolution just doesn't stand up well to questioning.** Whether you look at the evidence of genetics (acquired characteristics are *not* inherited, so Darwin's whole proposed mechanism for evolution falls to the ground), or information theory (evolution has been shown again and again to be statistically impossible), geology (why is the "geological column" not to be found anywhere on the face of the earth, how come layers that are supposed to be *earlier* are often *on top* of layers that are supposed to be later, and how come fossil trees have been found sticking up *through* rock layers that supposedly took millions of years to lay down?), ecology (how did any of the dozens of symbiotic relationships develop, in which each species needs the other for survival?), or simple common sense (what *is* the evolutionary stage between scales and feathers, and what good would it do any creature to be covered with "sceathers"?), evolutionary theory is surrounded with clouds of questions that don't have answers. That's why evolutionists, and evolutionary texts, invariably attack the scientific credentials of creationists rather than discussing the actual scientific issues involved. It's so much easier to state (incorrectly) that "No reputable scientists believe in creation" or "All scientists today believe in evolution" than to *prove* evolution or *disprove* creationism.

If creationism was *really* a hare-brained belief held only by crackpots, evolutionists would *enjoy* demolishing it. Instead, they do everything they can to prevent you ever hearing the creationist side of the argument. All the more reason to give your child "both sides now"!

For the evolutionary point of view, any library trip will do. For the other side, check out the resources below.

Creation for Kids

More than just a Creation vs. Evolution Ministry...

Write these people. Ask for their catalog. Ask to be put on their newsletter mailing list. As the current **Answers In Genesis** catalog says, they are "more than just a Creation v. Evolution ministry." These are the people who bring you the excellent *Creation* magazine, and its companion, *Creation Ex Nihilo Technical Journal.* The staff travels widely, giving seminars in churches and other venues, and debating evolutionists. Tapes and videos of these seminars and debates are available through them, as are creationist children's materials, Christian biographies, a nice selection of worldview and science materials for homeschoolers, creationist books for family study, tracts, technical materials, and books on the relevance of Creation. They have tons of books and videos on theology, history, biology, geology, archaeology, and astronomy. The catalog even carries neckties, t-shirts, sweatshirts, and Christmas cards, all with a Christian or creationist message!

All right, I'll admit it; the neckties don't send me. However, AIG, as they are fondly known, have more going for them than fashion neckwear. These are the people trying to build a creation-science museum in Kentucky. As I write this, it look like the zoning approval is finally going to come through, after a long battle with anti-creation zealots from inside and outside the local community. AIG has a million bucks' worth of exhibits ready to go (many picked up for pennies on the dollar from other science museums), so this should be something to see when it's finally ready.

What's all the theology and such doing in their catalog? It's there because AIG considers their mandate to be "Defending the Bible from the very first verse!" This gives them a well-balanced outlook, as much of their work involves convincing people that the Bible is relevant today. This worldview emphasis means that their catalog is a great resource for world-view materials.

You might be interested in this: Answers In Genesis offers an instant library of their best, most current books, videos, CDs, and cassettes, called their "Max Pack." Individually, these titles retail for $1,635.40, but as a set you can get them for $899. This is not a motley assortment of leftovers; I've read most of them, and can testify that this is a good, wide selection for all ages that covers all the major areas of creationist and worldview controversy. A super support-group purchase, and not unreasonable for the well-stocked home library of the well-heeled homeschool family. *Mary Pride*

These folks have done us all a great service. They have written a fine creation science curriculum and included an entire lesson plan for every week of the school year.

The **Considering God's Creation** set includes a gigantic three-ring binder divided into a teacher's manual and a student section, and a cassette tape with 23 original songs about God's creation.

The teacher's manual contains suggestions, ideas, songs, Bible verses, "evolution stumpers," vocabulary lists, activities, and review questions. Lectures are pre-written for you, and they are good. This teacher's manual takes up the first 100 pages of the 270-page binder.

The student section is teeming with worksheets. Armed with scissors, glue, and a box of crayons, your student will classify animals, compare animal tracks, order the solar system, identify cloud types, learn plant characteristics, and draw conclusions about God's world.

Too often workbook illustrations are mere line drawings. Here, the authors have set up real challenges for the students. Each page is busy with concepts and expert drawings. An amphibian page, for instance, will actually become a field guide, helping the student identify the animals by comparing key characteristics. The next page features a make-your-own booklet on the frog's life cycle.

The order of this product is wonderfully logical. We begin with creation, and end with human anatomy and genetics. My favorite feature in this last section is called "Scientist Detective." Here you will choose a scientist and research his life. The worksheet includes a timeline, space for you to add nationality, religion, field of contribution, and other distinguishing information. I believe that many times science forgets the persons who put so much effort into their work. It's great to see a place for this. *MacBeth Derham*

Colorful, earnest, and readable, **Creation** magazine is a great introduction to creationism. The kids will pick this one up and read it—no question. Covers topics such as "Was Archaeopteryx an 'intermediary form' between birds and reptiles?" "Fossil hat found in Australian mine" "How fast can trees be petrified?" Many photos illustrate the articles, and the authors are careful to avoid and identify any questionable sources. A special "kiddie" section is included, so the younger set will have something they can read on their own. Good family reading. *Mary Pride*

Eagle's Wings
Considering God's Creation
A creative biblical approach to natural science

Mortimer and Smith

CREATION
TOP SCIENTIST: 'No' to evolution
ABORIGINAL MYSTERY CREATURES
CLONING...
Unique black/white family defies racism

Dinosaurs by Design Dry Bones . . . and Other Fossils

Grades 2-4. Dinosaurs by Design, $12. Dry Bones . . . and Other Fossils, $10. Shipping extra. *Institute for Creation Research, 10946 Woodside Ave. N., Santee, CA 92071. (800) 628-7640. (619) 448-0900. Fax: (619) 448-3469. Web: www.icr.org.*

NEW!
Evolution vs. Science and the Bible

Grades 2–adult. $7.95. Teacher Guide, $5.95. Shipping extra. *Bob West Graphics, RR4, Box 175-C, Brevard, NC 28712-9417. Phone/fax: (828) 885-2516. Email: theophilus@cit-com.net. Web: www.theophilus.org.*

NEW!
Dr. Kent Hovind Creation Seminar

All ages. Complete 11-hour seminar (7 videos plus free seminar note-book), $99. Individual videos, $17.95 each. Seminar notebook, $7. Other items also available. Shipping extra. *Kent Hovind, 29 Cummings Rd., Pensacola, FL 32503. (850) 479-DINO. Fax: (850) 479-8562. Web: www.drdino.com.*

Seminar tapes are each two hours long and include:
- Part 1—The Age of the Earth
- Part 2—Dinosaurs and the Bible
- Part 3—Leviathan, Fire-Breathing Dragon (includes interviews with people who claim to have seen living dinosaurs, plus actual photos and video footage of several encounters)
- Part 4—What is In the Textbooks

Major source of creation-science materials, all produced by scientists and writers associated with ICR. Large catalog, attractive and professional materials. ICR now has a strong line of creation science books for little kids. Some popular titles for younger children: **Dinosaurs by Design** (dinosaurs from a creationist viewpoint . . . including some mighty interesting speculations about what exactly were Leviathan and Behemoth), **Dry Bones . . . and Other Fossils** (find out all about fossils as you hunt 'em with the Parker family), and the two-model series designed for public schools that includes creation/evolution discussions on a kid's level **(Dinosaur ABC's and Fossils: Hard Facts from the Earth)**. *Mary Pride*

Evolution vs. Science and the Bible (87-page paperback book, newly revised), originally published in 1974, is now back by popular demand. The format is simple: present evolution, present the biblical view, show errors in evolutionary theory, finish with a quiz. The author, Bob West, uses well-written text, cartoons, and the Bible to get the message across.

In a debate format, the author first discusses the evolution theory. I believe that the best way to argue against something is to know all of the arguments for it, and refute them. In most instances, the author succeeds.

The quizzes follow each chapter, and the answers are right from the text. Did life begin without God? Check out chapter four for the exciting answer to that question. Want to know the "proof" of evolution? You'll find it in chapter nine. The cartoon character Theophilus will keep you giggling as he watches his evolutionist friend get tangled in his own logic. *MacBeth Derham*

I've seen a lot of creation-science resources, including videos, and these are definitely the best. **Dr. Kent Hovind's Creation Seminar** recently won third place in the Educational Video category of our Reader Awards, just behind 90-pound gorillas such as Moody's science videos and the History Channel.

These are not boring talking-head videos. Seminar presenter Dr. Kent Hovind does everything but bounce off the walls as he cracks jokes, shows slides and video clips, and generally demolishes the arguments for evolution while presenting the best current scientific creationist research, all in front of live audiences who are literally sitting on the edges of their seats. The acid test—*my* kids (ages 3 to 17 when this review was written) were on the edge of *their* seats, too (when they weren't rolling on the floor laughing)!

You know me—I can find something to quibble about. In this case, I don't think the "dumb and talkative women" jokes that occasionally crop up are really helpful in an evangelistic ministry. Way to go to convince feminists the Bible doesn't oppress women, right? (Of course, even *those* jokes were funny—I hated myself for laughing at them!)

Unlike just about every other writer and speaker, Dr. Hovind does *not* copyright his material. So you can duplicate these tapes for friends who need to hear the creation and salvation messages. All the same, over 350,000 video tapes have been ordered from his ministry since it started six years ago. Impressive. *Mary Pride*

The **Master Books Catalog** is a motherlode for creation science materials. Hundreds of products in all. Convenient discount packages for different ages and interests, from children to high school and up. *Mary Pride*

As homeschooling parents, we are often in search of the ultimate "guide" to help us through a difficult subject. In science, finding a guide based on biblical truth is a challenge. Too often, creation science resources are added as a perfunctory addition to an otherwise evolution-oriented text. The **Media Angels** team, Felice Gerwitz and Jill Whitlock, have put together a series of resource books for science that make creation a priority, not a curiosity. These guides are valuable, and a good value. The series includes:

- *The Science Fair Project Handbook* (reviewed in chapter 36)
- *Teaching Science and Having Fun* (reviewed in chapter 31)
- *Creation Anatomy: A Study Guide to the Miracles of the Body* (reviewed in chapter 32)
- *Creation Geology: A Study Guide to Fossils, Formations and Floods* (reviewed in chapter 34)
- *Creation Astronomy: A Study Guide to the Constellations* (also reviewed in chapter 34)

Most relevant to this chapter, Felice Gerwitz has teamed up with creation scientist Jill Whitlock for *Creation Science: A Study Guide to Creation.* It is similar in format to the *Geology* guide, with an outline for each grade group (K–3, 4–8, 9–12) on the study of creation and a reference outline with a marvelously in-depth discourse on the subject. Each grade group has suggestions for art, language, math and science, as well as strong vocabulary and spelling lists.

What a team! Whitlock's knowledge of creation is vast. Combine that with Gerwitz's winning format, and you get a truly Christian science guide book. How many science experiment books will have suggestions like, "Demonstrate the vapor canopy?" My favorite suggestion for fourth through eighth graders is a mock interview with Darwin! While they list a few questions, you can always add your own. Your eleventh grader might try writing an expose on evolutionary hoaxes. These ideas are just a few of many in this guide. Of course, bibliographies and other reference materials round out the information packed in this 122-page perfect-bound oversized book. And the reference outline is fully biblical and a pleasure to read! *Creation Science: A Study Guide to Creation* is a valuable resource for students and adults. *Macbeth Derham*

The Evolution Revolution is a song-and-story lighthearted introduction to some of the issues in the creation/evolution controversy. It tells how Patch the Pirate and his crew (Pixie, Peanut, Princess, etc.) come to I.Q. University, to check up on Derwin, a twelve-year-old who graduated from high school at age ten. It seems that he has gotten mixed up with a group called A.P.E. (Association for the Preservation of Evolution). Once there, they discover that professor Lambourghini, the founder and director of A.P.E. Men, is missing. Patch, crew, and Derwin go to the professor's place,

- Part 5—Evolution, the Foundation for Communism, Naziism &Socialism, & the New World Order
- Part 6—The Hovind Theory
- Part 7—Questions and Answers

The Master Books Catalog

All ages. Free catalog.
Master Books, PO Box 727, Green Forest, AR 72638. (800) 999-3777. Fax: (870) 438-5120. Email: mbnlp@cswnet.com.

NEW!
Media Angels Creation Science Series

Grades K–12. Creation Science, $16.95. Creation Astronomy, $18.95. Creation Anatomy, $18.95. Creation Geology, $18.95. Geology and Creation Science Activity Pack, $12.95. Teaching Science and Having Fun, $12.95. Science Fair Project Handbook, $5. Add 15% shipping.
Media Angels, 16520 S. Tamiami Trail, #18-193, Fort Myers, FL 33908. (941) 433-2097. Fax: (941) 489-1060. Email: MediAngels@aol.com. Web: www.mediaangels.com.

This photo shows the previous edition of the Media Angels series. The new edition is perfect-bound with color covers.

NEW!
Patch the Pirate Evolution Revolution

Ages 4–12. Cassette, $10.98. CD, $14.98. Choral Book, $5.95.
Majesty Music, PO Box 6524, Greenville, SC 29606. (800) 334-1071. Fax: (800) 249-2117. Email: info@majestymusic.com.

and are talking with his butler when he (and his car) suddenly appear in the garage. Then the fun really begins! Besides the basic story, it also features 12 songs, such as "Dry Bones" and "Our God is Able." The cassette and CD contain the entire creationist episode, beautifully rendered by Patch (Ron Hamilton) and company (his wife, children, church choir, and various others). The choral book contains the text of the story and the songs. These are all high-quality, and well worth the cost.

For a review of the many other titles in this series, see the Character Education chapter. *Ted Pride*

I wouldn't want you to think that the folks at ICR never sent me *any-thing*. They did send me two of their **Relevance of Creation** video seminar tapes.

What Really Happened to the Dinosaurs?, led by Ken Ham, is his presentation in front of a large group of elementary-age children. Mr. Ham is an excellent speaker and teacher. Armed only with a craggy face and an Australian accent, he not only keeps the kids in line, but changes their minds about creation science before your very eyes! See the amazing Fossilized Hat (a miner's hat that fell into an Australian mine 70 years ago). Learn the one question an evolutionist hopes you'll never ask—"How do you know? Were you there?" Now everyone in our family can say Mr. Ham's definition of fossils:

> *Billions of dead things*
> *Buried in rock lyers*
> *Lide down by wooter*
> *Owl ovah thee urth*

Just like an Australian! *Mary Pride*

Relevance of Creation video series

Grade 1–adult. $14.95 each video or $73 for all 6. Shipping extra.
Institute for Creation Research, 10946 Woodside Ave. N., Santee, CA 92071. (800) 628-7640. (619) 448-0900. Fax: (619) 448-3469. Web: www.icr.org.

Other videos in this series are addressed more to teens and adults. These include:

- *Creation Evangelism* (Ken Ham)
- *The Dinosaur Mystery Solved* (John D. Morris)
- *Genesis and the Decay of the Nation—The Relevance of Creation* (Ken Ham)
- *Genesis 1–11: An Overview—The Most-Asked Questions on Genesis Answered* (Ken Ham)
- *Creation and the Last Days* (Ken Ham)
- *What Really Happened to the Dinosaurs?* (Ken Ham)

A good buy for your church or home school support group, but not as good as Dr. Kent Hovind's series.

CHAPTER 31

Elementary Science Curriculum

"Oooh! Look, Mommy! There in the puddle! I see a . . . thing!"
"What's the 'thing' doing, Jimmy?"
"It's kind of swimming around."
"What does it look like?"
"It's small and green."
"What happens if you try to touch it?"
"It JUMPS!"
There you have it. Science in the raw. What does it include?

- Wonder ("Oooh!")
- Observation ("Look!")
- Description ("It's small and green!")
- Experimentation "(What happens if you try to touch it?")
- Logic and deduction ("I bet it's a frog")
- Terminology ("It's a *Froggus Puddlelovingus*")

What's In a Name? Beating the System

Terminology, or giving things their proper names, comes last in this list, but it should probably be closer to the top. Adam's first job was naming the animals, after all. Giving things names is the real "oldest profession."

Science as taught in the schools used to include a *lot* of "naming." Kids went on nature walks and field trips (literally, into the fields) and came back with samples of all kinds of plants and minerals and sightings of all kinds of birds and animals. Then the teacher told them what they'd found. Since kids love, nay, demand to know the names of everything they see, starting off by learning the names of the different kinds of birds, clouds, trees, insects, plants, animals, and rocks made science fun and instantly useful.

Today, however, schoolkids spend more and more time studying *systems* instead of *names*. They are taught about "the food chain," "the water cycle," "the reproductive cycle," and so on. They learn the names of the parts of a flower (because that is important in order to understand plant reproduction), but are not taught the names of the flowers themselves.

A More-or-Less A to Z List of Science Topics for Elementary Grades

Anatomy (skeleton and organs)
Botany (plants and gardening)
Chemistry (simple facts about mixtures, solutions, acids, and bases)
Deep Space (solar system, constellations)
Electricity and Ecology
Food webs and **Flight**
Geology (rock identification, for starters)
Health (hygiene, nutrition, exercise)
Insects
Journaling observations & experiments
Kitchen Science
Light
Microscope work and **Magnetism**
Nature Study
Oceanography (only if you live near one)
Pets
Reproduction (keep it simple)
Sound
Technology (simple machines, computers)
Very Important People in science history
Weather
X-rays and other forms of energy
Zoology (animal identification and behavior)

Lost in the Machine

I think this is because the leaders of our society are increasingly infatuated with the idea of controlling large systems. Ever since the Industrial Revolution, it has become more and more fashionable to think of everything as a machine, just one large system made up of little parts. This way of looking at the world, or *paradigm*, has been made to fit society, businesses, and even the human body. Devotees of the machine outlook see individuals of all kinds (even individual plants and fish) as unimportant, except for how they fit into a system.

Little kids' minds don't work this way. The early years are when it's easy to memorize lots of names, and when kids feel a strong need to know everything's name. Insofar as it is needed at all, the study of processes and systems fits better into an older student's education, once he has become comfortable with abstract thinking.

So let little kids make friends with the animals, plants, and minerals that make up the physical world. Let them learn the names of the "creatures great and small" (and maybe read them some James Herriot books, too!) Encourage their sense of wonder right along with their skills of observation and description. Teach them the scientific method and basic logic. Show them how to construct simple experiments. Take them out into the fields and see what they can see. That's the way young children learn science best!

Curriculum

This general science book is stuffed with information. Each topic is clearly discussed. **101 Things Every Kid Should Know About Science** covers Chemistry, Physics, Geology, Oceanography, Meteorology, Astronomy (the Big Bang viewpoint), Biology (evolutionary), Botany, Zoology, The Human Body, and Technology. The diagrams are clear and easily understood by young children.

Topic 7 is one of my favorites in the book. This section is entitled "All matter has mass and density." There is an ample explanation followed by a discussion of how Archimedes did an experiment on density, followed by a hands-on activity for the child to work with density.

Tucked here and there are "Fun Facts" and "A Brief Bio." These tidbits are food for the curious and are written on an interesting level.

I enjoy this type of book because the lessons are concise but clear. On some of our favorite points we used the encyclopedia to provide additional information. *Michele Fitzgerald*

A Beka's economically-priced **science textbooks** cover the gamut from K–12. As with all other science series I have seen, I'd skip the first few grades. You start getting some serious information in third grade. A Beka follows the encyclopedic format—lots and lots of facts and terminology. These are great books for browsing, but hard work to study through.

A Beka has been justly criticized in the past for the pedestrian artwork in its books, but the new editions of *Investigating God's World*, *Observing God's World*, and *Understanding God's World* look like they are following the winning visual format of the Usborne series. The catalog says that the book shows students "how to make an insect zoo, how to recognize the plants they see every day, how to attract birds to their own back yards, how to use field guides, how to interpret cloud formations, and how to identify rocks."

Seed germination, the causes of weather, God's design of the heavens, ecology of the ocean depths, and "many other aspects of God's creative genius" are also covered.

These new books are only 27-week courses, intended to be followed by the A Beka nine-week health courses for those grades. The books for grades 1–3 and grade 6 are regular 36-week science courses. *Mary Pride*

Bob Jones University Press has a **textbook science series** for Christian schools that has met with a great deal of approval in home schooling circles. The first few grades, as usual with science series, are rather lightweight, but starting in grade 3 you get an excellent, lean, presentation of science. Topics range widely in any given volume, just as they do in the public school science curriculum (and just about everyone else's, too).

Grade 3 topics include classification of animals, the solar system, skin, photosynthesis, birds, mass, and weight. **Grade 4** "presents God as the Author of order." Beginning with a study of the moon, in which the theories of creation and evolution are compared according to the evidence, it continues to the topics of insects, light, electricity, area and volume, simple machines, digestion, animal defenses, trees, erosion, and simple insect classifications. The **grade 5** book presents the limits of science (compared to the infinite knowledge of God). Topics are fossils, airplanes, thermal energy, atomic theory, weather, plant and animal reproduction, oceans, forces causing wind, and animal tracks. The new **grade 6** book explores earthquakes, volcanoes, the stars, nuclear energy, chemistry, circulation, space exploration, laws of motion, respiration, animal behavior, and the balance of nature (basic ecology).

BJUP attempts to combine factual learning with process skills and experimentation. Each chapter in each book has experiments or activities based on its topic; students are taught to observe and record their experiments. The teacher's manuals add considerably to the cost of this program, but for a full-scale science program you will find them worth it. Note: special home-school science teacher's editions for grades 1–6 are now available; These cost considerably less, and are designed especially for home use.

BJUP also carries most of the lab apparatus you are ever likely to need and chemicals in homeschool-sized portions. *Mary Pride*

Quite a bit of nature lore is included in this unpretentious spiral-bound book. **Science in Rhyme** is 100 wide-format pages of poems, and questions to answer based on the poems. Many of the poems come with pictures to color, e.g., birds, fish, leaves, flowers. You'll learn tree identification, bird identification, weather facts, seasons, time, major heavenly bodies, and more. The poem format is more appealing to small children than reams of textual facts, and the question and answer exercises ensure the new facts are retained. Very simple, old-timey format—don't expect glitz and glitter. Recommended. *Mary Pride*

The author of this 126-page softcover, Robert Philbin, is a little bit like a matchmaker. He wants you and your children to fall in love with science. He states in his introduction to **Doing Science: A Guide for the Perplexed**: "I have taught science at many levels and know that most students—and parents—think that science is facts. They come to me with very little enthusiasm for a lively subject because they have never really experienced, never really done, science . . . those who continue at the college level in science need a solid grounding in the process of science first; the facts will follow."

A Beka Book, Box 19100, Pensacola, FL 32523-9100. (800) 874-2352. (850) 478-8933. Fax: (800) 874-3590. Web: www.abeka.com.

BJUP Science for Christian Schools

Grades 1–6. Student worktexts, $13.50 each (softbound) or $22 each (hardbound). Teacher's editions, $22 each. Homeschool kits available. Shipping extra.
Bob Jones University Press Customer Services, Greenville, SC 29614. Orders: (800) 845-5731. Fax: (800) 525-8398. Web: www.bjup.com.

NEW
Carden Science in Rhyme

Grades 1–3. $10.20 plus shipping.
Carden Educational Foundation, PO Box 659, Brookfield, CT 06804-0659. (860) 350-9885 Fax: (860) 354-9812. Email: carden@cardenschool.org. Web: cardenschool.org.

NEW!
Doing Science: A Guide For the Perplexed

Parents. $12.95 plus shipping.
Inside Out Educational Services, PO Box 718, Trinidad, CO 81082. (719) 846-0300. Email: philbin@activematrix.net.

This book shows you how to help your child think scientifically. Robert spends the first part of the book introducing you to scientific method and technique, and encourages you to let your child's interests frame experiments and experiences. He uses the same two examples (weather and the workings of a ceiling fan) to show how asking the question "what if?" in a scientific context can lead to a whole lot of learning. The rest of the book offers a look at the scientific disciplines of astronomy, geology, physics, chemistry, biology, and mathematical experiments through the same lens. A very nice resource section rounds out the book. Specific textbook recommendations, Internet sites, and a listing of hands-on serious science journals are worth the cost of the book alone.

Mr. Philbin's homeschool philosophy runs toward the Moores/unschooling/delight-directed learning camp, which means that it takes a parent willing to cut loose from a textbook to do well with his approach. He says that he almost titled this book *Suzuki Science* after the very successful method of teaching children the violin or piano by having the parent learn right alongside the child. If you are willing to plunge in and investigate the world of science together with your child, then this is the match for you. *Michelle Van Loon*

Good Science for Home Schools

Grades preK–6. Volumes 1 (preK–3) and 2 (grades 4–6), $49.95 each. Workbooks, $10 each. Shipping extra. *Institute for Creation Research, 10946 Woodside Ave. N., Santee, CA 92071. (800) 628-7640. (619) 448-0900. Fax: (619) 448-3469. Web: www.icr.org.*

A materials kit is included with each volume. Volume 1 comes with BTB (a chemical you stick in water and bubble gases through to watch the color change), copper chloride, a hand magnifier, a battery holder, a few wires and alligator clips, and some teeny bulbs and teeny bulb holders. The materials kit for Volume 2 is much the same, except that this one has a mini ¼" lamp with two wires connected and a thin strip of metal instead of the poisonous copper chloride for Volume 1. You get to round up the rest of the materials: the aquarium, terrarium, mealworms, crickets, daphnia, guppies, chlamydomonas, hydra, euglena, brine shrimp eggs, duckweed, snails, amoebae, paramecia, chameleon, aphids, frogs, grass seed, clover seed, bean seed, cockroaches, and sowbugs (for the Life Sciences units), and styrofoam cups, magnets of various types, compasses, rivets, batteries, circuit tester, switches, bleach, batteries, vinegar, vials, bags, straws, and so on for everything else.

Good Science for Home Schools is a "process skills" program. Like *Science: The Search* it teaches clinical vocabulary and concentrates on the discovery process more than individual facts.

The Institute for Creation Research originally developed the Good Science program for Christian schools. Their Good Science Seminars began to attract homeschoolers, hence this targeted curriculum. Although the ICR staff still feels you will be best introduced to the program by attending a seminar in your area, they have provided a set of audiocassettes (in nice binder) recorded at a seminar to accompany each volume of this program. The cassettes provide how-tos and program philosophy for each of the topics studied.

The program's author, Dr. Richard Bliss, has worked 25 years in the public school system, and it shows throughout this course, from the terminology of "learning objectives" and "cognitive domain" in the introduction to the author's stated dependence on secular learning theories. His Christian convictions show in the occasional devotional thoughts incorporated into the activities and the attempt to "study science under the attributes of God." This means that, for each lesson, the pupil is supposed to think of an attribute of God that relates to the topic studied. When observing and classifying different kinds of buttons, for example, the pupil might think about God's *creativity* in making a world with such a variety of materials, or how He created man in His own image to be creative in designing buttons!

Surprisingly, there is not much mention of creation v. evolution after the introduction (which is written to the parents). The program also uses the dispassionate vocabulary of food webs, organisms, objects, ecosystems, etc., rather than Biblical vocabulary.

You'll find almost 80 lessons in Volume 1 and about 50 in Volume 2.

Volume 1, for the K–3 crowd, starts off with the typical smell-taste-touch-observe-sort-classify exercises found in preschool programs. Kids also do some simple chemical, electrical, and machines experiments (no magnetism), grow and kill plants, and grow and kill small vermin. Great stress is placed on learning the terminology of "objects," "systems," "interaction," and the like.

Volume 2, for kids in grades 4–6, starts out with "relativity," which in this course has nothing to do with Dr. Einstein. Kids will be determining relative motion and position and graphing these in various ways. Next on the list is habitat and environment. "Environment" is defined in the text as "the total of all the living and non-living beings affecting an organism." Oddly, although the book keeps urging students to "state an attribute of God" in connection with each exercise, God Himself is not ever mentioned as an environmental factor. The unconscious assumption taught is that the spiritual and natural world are closed systems, not affecting each other. I'm sure this is not what the curriculum designer had in mind—just as he did not intend to convey that God's Word has no rules regarding how people should handle plants and animals—but Good Science teaches absolutely nothing about these subjects.

Moving along in Volume 2, we come to a series of simple physics experiments. Although many of these resemble experiments I remember from high school, the kids aren't taught any of the underlying principles and formulae. In the next Life Science level, kids grow and stunt plants and grow critters and watch them eat each other. The Physical Science level following has some work on electricity and magnetism. Finally, the pinnacle of the program comes in the last Life Science level, where kids get to study ecosystems (e.g., a stocked aquarium and terrarium). *Mary Pride*

Creating a hands-on science program for grades K–6 is a pretty large order, since the abilities of children during these years varies so much. Liz Brough has built a lot of flexibility into her **Hands on Science** program, for this very reason. Beginning with a list of materials that you will need to have on hand to complete the experiments (most of which are normal household items) she walks you through the basics of using her curriculum, addressing what each age group can be expected to do and to understand. Each succeeding chapter encourages you and your child to explore a force of nature by performing a simple experiment. Thermodynamics (the study of heat), density of liquids, climate and air pressure, erosion and barometric pressure are just a few of the topics covered. Volume 1 includes one year's worth of material. Volume 2 will cover chemistry, biology, and nature science. Further volumes are planned.

The tone of the curriculum is quiet, relaxed, and self-paced. The book even reassures parents and students that failed experiments can be a "good" thing—leading to an opportunity for further exploration and a better understanding of the principle being studied!

The only thing I would add would be a plastic cover on the book for protection (quite a few experiments use liquids!) and some more pictures and diagrams for added clarity on some experiments.

Well written, heavily emphasizing the scientific method of discovery, using common household items, and built to stand alone, this is a good choice for early science education. *Teresa May*

If you are looking for an outstanding elementary science text, Rod and Staff has it. **God's Protected World**, their third grade science text, is a simple yet challenging introduction to chemistry, biology, and physics.

Clear, accurate drawings help tell the story of science. The text unfolds God's creation with joy, grabbing your attention and compelling you to read more. This is quite an accomplishment for an elementary text in any subject!

Each unit begins with Noah interacting with God and the resources that God has given us on Earth. Unit 1 is about water. Noah encountered water (lots of water!). He learned about water from God. Similarly, units on animals, raw materials, etc., also begin by examining Noah's life. This is an inspiring way to begin the study of science!

Each unit is divided into lessons. The lessons are clearly written and include vocabulary lists, a section to be read with the parent or teacher, a section for your child to read alone, and questions about the lesson.

NEW!
Hands on Science Volume 1: Particles in Motion

Grades K–6. $24.95. Shipping extra.
Castle Heights Press, Inc., 2578 Alexander Farms Dr., Marietta, GA 30064. (800) 763-7148.
Fax/Phone: (770) 218-7998.
Email: julicher@aol.com.
Web: www.flash.net/~wx3o/chp.

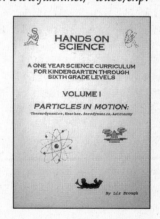

NEW!
Rod & Staff God's Protected World

Grade 3. Student edition, $9.45. Teacher's edition, $10.10. Exam booklet, $1.10.
Rod and Staff Publishers, Box 3, Hwy 172, Crockett, KY 41413-0003. (606) 522-4348. Fax: (800) 643-1244.

An exam book has tests for the end of each unit. The tests are fair assessments of the information your child is learning. The types of questions are short answer, yes or no, multiple choice, and long answer.

A teacher's edition of this text has suggestions for introducing the lesson, extra information, a quiz for each lesson, the answers to lesson questions, and answers to the exams. It includes a reduced copy of the student text on corresponding

Science: The Search

Grades 1–8. $25 each book. Add 10% shipping.
Cornerstone Curriculum Project, 2006 Flat Creek, Richardson, TX 75080. (972) 235-5149. Fax: (972) 235-0236. Web: www.cornerstonecurriculum.com.

The program stresses clinical terminology. Example:

Give your child a pair of shoes that need polishing, shoe polish, brush, and cloth.

"WHAT CAN YOU DO TO MAKE THESE OBJECTS INTERACT?"
[Your speaking part is always capitalized and enclosed in quotes.]

After they polish the shoes . . .

"WHAT EVIDENCE IS THERE THAT THESE OBJECTS HAVE INTERACTED?"

Lessons are supposed to be completed at the rate of one a week, but you should know that some of these lessons take a month or even a year to finish. You'll be watching little bugs grow, die, and eat each other for a long time.

Extra activities at the end of each lesson are simple experiments. In Unit 2, "God Gave Us the Materials We Need," one experiment asks your child to test the hardness of wood by hammering nails into wood scraps. Unit 6, "God Cares for the Animals," suggests bird-watching. Most of these extra activities can be done with materials you have at home and may require some guidance from you.

As I read this book for review, I learned how oil is refined. I was impressed by the clarity of text and illustrations, and by the strength of the vocabulary. Too many elementary texts simplify the language for children. Not so with *God's Protected World*! This third grade text has a vocabulary usually reserved for fourth and fifth grade public school texts. Words such as evaporate, condense, distill, and refine make this text a satisfying challenge.

This is an outstanding text. I recommend *God's Protected World* without reservation. *MacBeth Derham*

Science: The Search has four books. I saw Books 1 and 2. This is a process skills and terminology program, not a facts program. Kids learn by observation and experimentation, not by lecture and memorization.

Each volume is packaged quite nicely in a handsome spiral binder, and includes a Materials Kit. The Materials Kit for Book 2 includes two bar magnets, container of BTB, and a gear set including a base, cover, handle, and pointer plus two each of small, medium, and large plastic gears.

Each activity begins with a list of materials needed, a lesson topic, and a step-by-step lesson plan that tells you exactly what to do and say. The brochure claims that most of the materials and supplies can be found in the home, grocery store, or pet supply store. The list of supplies needed for the volume takes five index columns, and includes such items as color chips from a paint store, different colors and grits of sandpaper, a circuit tester (flashlight battery, bulb, and wire), fabric pieces, and red yarn. As you can see, you will have to visit quite a few places to pick up the materials.

The first 19 lessons are all typical sorting, classifying, and observing activities found in the better preschool programs. Life Sciences activities are most of the environmental type, involving life cycles, food webs and chains, groups of organisms, and habitat. A few kitchen science activities are thrown in, plus a goodish chunk of engineering (gears, electricity, magnetism) in the last half of the book.

The life cycle and populations activities are not for those with squirmy stomachs. You'll be growing mealworms in the privacy of your home and graphing how many aphids your crickets ate and how many live crickets your chameleon ate. Beverly Cleary's fictional Ramona threw up observing the classic mealworm experiment, and I'm with her.

The gears lessons are the best. You make a "black box" system by putting gears together and closing the plastic case provided. The children have to duplicate the gear setup without seeing it. Clever!

Although its author considers it a Christian program, *Science: The Search* is not very spiritual in its observations of nature, weather, aquarium animals, and so on. You won't find any "Praise the Lord!" excitement here. It's a dispassionate, clinical approach—students are not encouraged to relate to or enjoy the animals and plants observed, and reverence for life and death is not taught. Instead, the spiritual emphasis consists of four separate Spiritual Application activities: studying the names of God, writing down the attributes of natural/spiritual/carnal men, studying a dispensational seven-interactions-of-God-in-history, and a look at the church as "God's supernatural system." *Mary Pride*

The **Solomon Resource Guides** are colorfully-indexed volumes that put science units at your fingertips. Volume I covers weather, the solar system, plants, animals, and energy. Volume II covers natural resources, habitats, the human body, matter, and ecology. Based on a "whole language" and "unit study" approach to learning, the guides list concepts, resources, experiments, more resources, tests and answers. Authors Amy Bain, Janet Richer, and Janet Weckman strive to include many different angles on learning, from traditional to multicultural. With a resource list as long as theirs, you can pick and choose, avoiding the resources which don't fit your criteria (each resource includes a brief description . . . enough to get the flavor). The authors have included a list of creation science resources on a separate sheet of paper.

The Guides can be used for all levels. Consider the unit on plants. Your young children may be ready for the "Primary Concepts," which includes identifying parts of a seed (my three-year-old always asks me, "What's inside peas?"). Intermediate concepts in this unit include classification. The upper concepts include the anatomy and physiology of plant groups. I appreciate that the authors didn't separate the concepts by grade level, since some very young children are adept at classification, while some older children find it complex. Ideas for creative writing and art are also included for each level. With this format, you can mix and match a bit.

This is not a textbook. It does not tell you how to teach. It provides you with a flexible way to look at different topics in science. While it does provide you with sample tests, you can use them or ignore them as you see fit. The authors also provide extensive teacher resource lists, and while the children's lists are for grades K–8, a high-school student could easily adapt the teacher's list for himself. *MacBeth Derham*

Still nervous about teaching science? Felice Gerwitz has a book just for the reluctant science teacher. **Teaching Science and Having Fun** is a crash course in teaching science and the scientific method. Here, you won't find experiments, but you will find a simple and straightforward guide to *running* science experiments. Topics covered include the scientific method, picking materials for a small lab, microscopes and telescopes, flexibility and scheduling, copy pages, and "What to do when I don't know what to do!" Toward the end you will find a science experiment planning guide and last-minute advice.

The format here is question and answer, rather like an advice column. The advice is solidly relevant to the home school. Gerwitz leaves out the jargon that makes so many science teacher guides inaccessible to busy parents. Her relaxed manner will assure you that you can teach science *and* have fun. *MacBeth Derham*

This revised edition of the pop-up **TOPS** task-card science modules comes in a bound workbook complete with an introduction to the TOPS philosophy, teaching notes for every task card, a set of review/test questions with answer key, and two-up sheets of reproducible task cards in the back. This new format is a dream for the home teacher. Every single concept and activity is explained in full in the teacher notes, which consist of a copy of the task card at the top of the page and all answers, materials needed, and teaching tips at the bottom of the page.

OK. So we like the new format. Now what is TOPS? First, it's an attempt to combine both the "process" approach and the "traditional knowledge" approach to science. Kids learn facts *and* do open-ended experiments. Just about the entire field of science is covered, as a series of separate topics. Second, TOPS is science with simple things. No need for expensive kits of chemicals, miles of glass tubing, Bunsen burners, and so on.

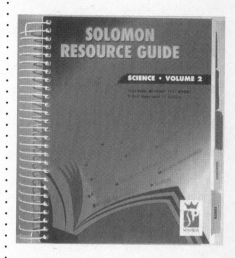

Timberdoodle presently offers the TOPS modules for electricity, solutions (stuff dissolved in liquid), electricity, magnetism, animal survival, *Rocks and Minerals*, *Analysis*, and *Earth, Moon, & Sun*. No evolutionary preaching in any of these modules. All mostly use simple materials found around the house. For example, the *Electricity* TOPS module has your child building bulb holders, battery holders, and switches out of paper clips, rubber bands, clothespins, aluminum foil, and pennies. Any additional materials are clearly listed at the beginning of each book.

What this all means is that for around $15 you can have 4–5 weeks of real science experiments with easy-to-gather materials like paper clips, string, test tubes, and candles. *Mary Pride*

Usborne Starting Point Science series

Ages 3–8. $4.95 each plus shipping. *EDC Publishing, Division of Educational Development Corporation, 10302 East 55th Place, Tulsa, OK 74146. (800) 475-4522. Fax: (800) 747-4509. Web: www.edcpub.com.*

The Usborne **Starting Point Science** series for young children features simple text and lively explanatory cartoon illustrations. The question in each title is answered step-by-step. Each book also includes simple experiments.

Unlike some Usborne books, whose pages are so loaded with sidebars and graphics that your eye just has to jump from thrill to thrill, you can actually read the Starting Point Science books to your children from start to finish. Older children can read them by themselves. Lots to look at and discuss on every page. Evolutionary content in *What's Under the Ground*, *Why is Night Dark?*, and *What's Out in Space*. Other nature study titles in this series: *What's the Earth Made Of?*, *How Do Bees Make Honey?*, *What Makes You See?*, *What's Under the Sea?*, *Why Are People Different?*, *Why Do Tigers have Stripes?*, *Why Do People Eat?*, *Where Did Dinosaurs Go?*, *Where do Babies Come From?*, *How Do Animals Talk?*, and *How does a Bird Fly? Mary Pride*

NEW!
ElementO

Grades 3–adult. $31.95 plus $3.95 shipping. *Lewis Educational Games, PO Box 727, Goddard, KS 67052. Orders: (800) 557-8777. Inquiries: (316) 794-3463. Fax: (316) 794-8239. Email: lewisbolay@aol.com. Web: members.aol.com/dickwlewis.*

Head Start

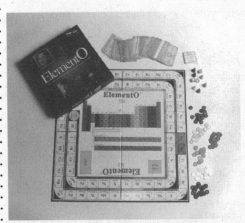

The **ElementO** board game teaches you about elements and the periodic table . . . and makes it such fun that your eight-year-old will beg to play.

This elegant game plays a little like Monopoly—you're trying to "buy" the elements you land on, so you can charge other people the number of protons in that element if they land on it. If you have the whole family of that element, whoever lands on one of them has to pay you the total number of protons in the whole family. You'll learn the element symbols and names without thinking about it. What a great way to give kids a head start on chemistry! *Mary Pride*

Janice VanCleave's Chemistry for Every Kid:101 Easy Experiments That Really Work features experiments simple enough for a kid who doesn't know scientific terminology. Many have dramatic results—clear liquids transform into a green blob, pennies grow a green coat, celery changes color, magic writing appears.

The "common household supplies" you'll need for this book include a few you may need to step out to the pharmacy for (e.g., tincture of iodine and hydrogen peroxide). Be sure to read ahead each week and figure out what supplies are needed in advance.

Each experiment is laid out as a two-page spread. On the left page is a brief statement of purpose, materials list, "cookbook" set of procedures to follow, statement of the expected result, and explanation of the science principle being demonstrated. Occasionally text from the left page continues on to the right page. Also on the right page are one or more line-art illustrations of the experiment setup and its stages.

Topics demonstrated include properties of matter, forces (mostly involving the bonds between water molecules), gases, physical changes, phase changes, solutions, heat, and acids and bases.

Despite the title, you couldn't use this as a "chemistry" (e.g., high school) lab book and get away with it. However, *Chemistry for Every Kid* is a fine, demystifying introduction to the subject for preteens. *Mary Pride*

Janice VanCleave's Physics for Every Kid: 101 Easy Experiments That Really Work is a systematically organized set of 101 experiments and demonstrations. Experiments include the classic conductance experiment in which you make a simple test apparatus with a lightbulb and battery to determine if each material you test conducts electricity or not. Demonstrations include the equally classic twirling color wheel that shows how white light is actually made up of all colors. The difference is that in an experiment, you are actually *testing* and *observing* the object or force itself. In a demonstration, you are *modeling* the object or force.

Each experiment or demonstration is laid out as a two-page spread. On the left page is a brief statement of purpose, materials list (only readily available materials are used), "cookbook" set of procedures to follow, statement of the expected result, and explanation of the science principle being demonstrated. Occasionally text from the left page continues on to the right page. Also on the right page are one or more line-art illustrations of the experiment setup and its stages.

Physics for Every Kid is divided into these sections: Electricity, Magnets (including one experiment using iron filings, and unbelievably featuring an illustration of a girl actually *touching* the filings, that I suggest you skip for safety reasons: read my note in the review of *Earth Science for Every Kid* on page 400), Buoyancy, Gravity, Balance, Flight, Simple Machines, Inertia, Motion, Light, Heat, and Sound. As you can see, all the major physics topics are covered, on a level simple enough for preteens. What a wonderful head start! *Mary Pride*

Unique among science curricula for homeschoolers, **Lyrical Life Science** teaches through the ear. Students listen to the songs (sung by popular "Songs of the Confederate and Union Armies" artist Bobby Horton) until they know them by heart. They read the text, which has complete lyrics and music for the songs, plus lots of other background information. Then they fill in the blanks and do the exercises in the workbooks. That's it!

Other educational song tapes are fun, but may spend an entire song teaching one or two words. Textbooks present lots of words and concepts, but tend to be a snore. Lyrical Learning's songs are fun *and* thorough. They pack in tons of terminology, in easy-to-remember fashion.

NEW!
Janice VanCleave's Chemistry for Every Kid
Grades 3–6. $12.95.
John Wiley & Sons, 1 Wiley Drive, Somerset, NJ 08875. (800) 225-5945. (732) 469-4400. Fax: (800) 597-3299. Web: www.wiley.com.

NEW!
Janice VanCleave's Physics for Every Kid
Grades 3–6. $12.95.
John Wiley & Sons, 1 Wiley Drive, Somerset, NJ 08875. (800) 225-5945. (732) 469-4400. Fax: (800) 597-3299. Web: www.wiley.com.

NEW!
Lyrical Life Science, Volumes 1–3
Grades 4–9. Each text/cassette set, $19.95. Each text/cassette/workbook set, $25.50. Add $3 shipping for first set, $1 for each additional.
Lyrical Learning, 8008 Cardwell Hill, Corvalis, OR 97330.
Phone/fax: (541) 754-3579.
Email: lyricallearning@proaxis.com.

Volume 1 of Lyrical Life Science is divided into eleven chapters (The Scientific Method, All Living Things, Invertebrates, Cold-blooded Vertebrates, Birds, Plants, Algae, Fungi and Nonvascular Plants, Vascular Plants, Protozoa, Genetics, Viruses and Bacteria).

The 15 chapters of **Volume 2—Mammals, Ecology, and Biomes** cover Mammals, Monotremes & Marsupials, Carnivores & Pinnapeds, Ungulates, Primates, Rodents, Rodent-Like Mammals, Bats, Insectivores, Toothless Mammals, Whales, Sirenians, Single-Family Orders, Ecology, Biomes.

Volume 3—The Human Body covers this topic in 13 songs. Hot off the presses (I am holding one of the very first advance copies in my hand), it includes a song about each major body system: Introduction to the Human Body, Skeletal System, Muscular System, Nervous System, Sensory System, Reproductive System (tastefully done), Digestive System, Excretory System (again, tastefully handled, nothing gross), Circulatory System, Immune & Lymph Systems, Respiratory System, Endocrine System, and an interesting song entitled "Ologies" that teaches what the name of each science is that involves anatomy (histology, cardiology, neurology, etc.).

NEW!
Beautiful Feet Books History of Science Course

Grades 3–7. Science Pack including *The Way Things Work*, $134.95. Science Pack without the book, $103.95. Study Guide alone, $10.95. *The Way Thing Work* CD-ROM, $39.95. Books also available individually. Shipping extra.
Beautiful Feet Books, 139 Main St., Sandwich Village, MA 02563. Orders: (800) 889-1978. Inquiries: (508) 833-8626. M–F 9–5 EST. Fax: (508) 833-2770. Web: www.bfbooks.com.

Each chapter of each volume begins with a song. The tune is borrowed from a song that nearly everyone will already know (examples: "Dixie," "If You're Happy and You Know It . . . "), but the new words really pack an educational wallop. Here's an example, "Viruses cause many different in-fect-ious diseases! Influenza, common colds with fevers, coughs, and sneezes—AAAHHHCHOOO!" (Sing this to the tune of "Yankee Doodle" and see if you can do it without a giggle or two! We couldn't!)

Following this lyrical introduction to the material, the main text continues with several pages of textbook-type information which expands upon and reinforces what the student has learned in the song, and ends with a bibliography of resources for further study and an index. The accompanying workbook tests your student's memorization of the knowledge presented in the chapter. Comprehension of the presented material is evaluated with a set of short essay questions. Your student is then given the chance to apply what he or she has learned in the "Digging Deeper" section. The activities in the Digging Deeper area range from discovering what the difference is between a "theory" and a "law" to reasoning out why you would not likely "find a snake crawling on the snow in Alaska in the winter." Answers to questions are found in the back of each workbook.

Memorization of complicated terms and classifications is a very important part of serious science study, but is often considered the most difficult and boring of tasks by students and teachers alike. Hats off to Lyrical Learning for adding some fun to the process—and making it so much easier! *Teresa May and Mary Pride*

History of Science

Beautiful Feet Books History of Science course, "a Literature Based Introduction to Scientific Principles and Their Discoverers," uses biographies of famous scientists, as well as hands-on experiments that demonstrate the truth of their discoveries. Scientists studied include Archimedes, Galileo, Benjamin Franklin, Pasteur, Marie Curie, Thomas Edison, and Einstein. Students read biographies about each of these famous scientists. Additional scientists are found in *The Picture History of Great Inventors* (also included) and David Macaulay's *The Way Things Work,* an excellent book that shows the history of engineering and "how things work." *The Way Things Work* is optional, but I highly recommend you get it (see its review for more details). For experiments, *Science Around the House* and *Explorabook* (also reviewed in *Big Book*) are included.

I am happy to report that all the biographies are well-chosen. I only regret that there's no way at present to purchase all the additional titles that the study guide suggests for supplemental reading!

The experiment books are equally well chosen. *Science Around the House* is a logical sequence of experiments designed to teach children about the

physical properties of matter—mass, volume, density, viscosity, and much more. Instead of going for the typical flashy activities, which may be fun but don't teach kids a whole lot, the author is giving your kids a solid foundation. I appreciated that! The *Explorabook* doesn't cover many topics—magnetism, bacteria, air flow, and optical illusions—but here is the big science fun you're also looking for.

The 67-lesson course is not all just reading and experimenting. You'll be writing Bible verses, scientific terms, experiment results, and reports on science history in a science notebook (not included). You'll also be sketching maps, simple machines, and more in that notebook. For younger children (grades K–2), you can just read the books, saving the experiments and activities until they're a bit older.

Probably the best way to use this course is for two lessons per week, during a regular 36-week school year. That way you can spend a couple hours on each lesson, which may be needed for doing all the experiments and notebook work. Your kids will learn a lot more science than with a typical elementary-school science course, and I bet you'll enjoy it more, too! *Mary Pride*

Duplicate famous milestones in the history of science—all from the comfort of your own kitchen! The **Famous Experiments** series of scientific exploration books answers young scientists' questions, and enables them to see not only *what* makes things work, but *why*.

This series is not just a set of cookbook type experiments, but rather a set of launching points for other scientific discussions. Each lesson begins with a question and follows with a related activity. You will need to help your child with some of the experiments.

Divided into four categories, **Who? Famous Experiments for the Young Scientist** begins each chapter by asking a question about a basic principle of science. "Who invented the hang glider?" is one example. Turning to that chapter, you will find a materials list (common household items), step-by-step instructions for completing the activity, and an accounting of the results to be expected from the experiment. To answer the "who?" question, a scientist or inventor is profiled—basic biographical information plus a more detailed list of his or her scientific accomplishments (including the one under study). After this you will find a list of topics for further study, and some interesting trivia tidbits.

Where? Experiments for the Young Scientist follows the same basic pattern. However, it is divided into five categories and, as can be expected from the title, answers questions from a different perspective. The chapter headings, "Where was the first airline started?" "Where can you see electricity producing light/heat?" and "Where did Celsius/Fahrenheit come from?," give you an idea of the range of activities included.

Be aware that several of the books talk about evolution as a proven fact and pagan gods as if they actually exist. Oddly, the study guide, meant for Christians, never points out the places in the books where these things happen, or give suggestions as to how you might deal with them. In the case of the pagan gods, the author of the Archimedes book is obviously using literary license to place the reader in the mindset of Archimedes' time. A note to that effect in the study guide would have been appreciated.

NEW!
Famous Experiments for the Young Scientist series
Grades 3–8. Each book, $10.95. Shipping extra.
TAB Books, A division of McGraw-Hill, Order Services, PO Box 545, Blacklick, OH 43004-0545. (800) 338-3987. Fax: (614) 755-5645.
Web: www.mhhe.com.

What? Experiments for the Young Scientist is an easy to use 142-page paperback with 34 carefully chosen experiments. The author, Robert W. Wood, has reunited science experiments with history. Evangelista Torricelli, Edison, Tesla, and even Daniel Boone are among those mentioned in this book. Each unit is a specific topic in science: The Young Engineer, The Young Astronomer, the Young Chemist, etc., all including experiments easily done at home. Icons at the beginning of each experiment indicate potential hazards, and adult supervision is recommended for many procedures. Your young physicist will bend light. Your young chemist will change the density of water. Your young meteorologist will make clouds. And when you have finished, follow up activities in science and history will keep you busy for a while.

When should you use **When? Experiments for the Young Scientist**? When you want to know the history, as well as the science, behind such everyday objects as the battery, the thermometer, and paper. When you want to know when you can see the planet Venus. When you want to find out about taste buds. *When?* leads you to the answers in such a short time, your kids won't ask, "When will the experiment be over?," but rather, "When can we do the next chapter?"

Consider the question, "When was the first battery made?" This chapter will send you to the kitchen for a lemon to make a small acid electric cell. The directions are very clear, and, like most activities in the book, this takes less than half an hour. While this kind of experiment can be found in most elementary science books, the real difference in *When?* is the follow-up. Each chapter ends with facts about the people or events behind the original invention. This chapter ends with brief anecdotes about the moment of discovery, featuring Luigi Galvanic and Alessandro Volta. Other intriguing chapters are, "When Does Light Bend?," "When does Paper Contain Starch?," and "When Was the First Zipper Used?" In all, you get 38 experiments that can be performed easily in a kitchen. The word "When" is written boldly over an illustration of a dinosaur on the front cover. Despite this dubious beginning, only one of the 38 experiments in this science book is objectionable from a creation science point of view.

According to the literature included with the review books, there is one more book in this series, entitled *Why?*

Please note that this is not meant to be a complete science course, but we recommend this series as a hands-on supplement to an upper elementary and junior high level science curriculum. *Teresa May and MacBeth Durham*

NEW!
Nerd Kards

Grades 4–adult. $14.95 plus shipping.
Activity Based Supplies, PO Box 408, Pittsburg, KS 66762. (800) 469-8070. (316) 232-3359. Fax: (800) 237-3504. Web: www.absupplies.com.

Nerd Kards are a fun way to learn about the history of science. This deck of 102 cards comes in a handy plastic box. Each card has a photo or portrait of a scientist on the front, and facts about his life and work on the back. (Yes, "his." Madame Curie is the only woman included; she shares a card with her husband.) The selection consists of major figures in science history (Aristotle, Galileo, and so on), plus Nobel Prize winners. You've probably never heard of most of the latter, so this is your chance to learn something! The deck comes with instructions for three games, or you can just browse the cards to get a sense of who these famous science guys are. *Mary Pride*

CHAPTER 32

People

Health education in the schools focuses on fitness, nutrition, and simple anatomy lessons, with sex education, AIDS education, and safety lessons thrown in.

At home, you don't need to worry about sex ed and AIDS ed much in the early grades. Simple training in modesty, the use of disposable toilet seat protectors when traveling, and good handwashing skills are all the instruction the average homeschooled child needs. "Where babies come from" is a topic that arises spontaneously and can be handled without any need for embarrassment. Most little kids are quite happy to know that a baby grows inside of Mommy without needing detailed explanations of Daddy's contribution and how exactly it got there. Nor do they need explicit details of venereal diseases and how to catch them, or X-rated lessons in sexual how-tos, as are becoming distressingly common in public and private schools.

The time schools spend on these topics would be much better spent, with far better results for kids' health, if they taught kids *real* first aid (including CPR and the Heimlich Maneuver), *real* nutritional facts (including the uses of herbs and vitamins), and how to prevent disease through fitness and avoidance of unclean lifestyles and bad companions. Yeah, smoking is bad, but I can think of a few things that are worse.

IN THIS CHAPTER
Resources for health education, human anatomy education, and safety education. For first aid resources, see page 546.

Health

A Beka's bright, cheery, colorful **Health, Safety, and Manners series** for grades 1–3 follows the typical A Beka "programmed" format, where the text talks to the child in the first person (e.g., "I will take care of my body"). I was impressed by the thoroughness of this series, and enjoy the emphasis on manners. *Mary Pride*

A Beka's Health, Safety, and Manners
Grades 1–3. Grades 1 & 2, $9.10 each. Grade 3, $9.20. Add shipping.
A Beka Book, Box 19100, Pensacola, FL 32523-9100. (800) 874-2352. (850) 478-8933. Fax: (800) 874-3590. Web: www.abeka.com.

NEW!
The Brain Train

Grades 3–6. $4.95 plus shipping.
*Safe Goods, P.O. Box 36, East Canaan,
CT 06024. (860) 824-5301 or (800)
903-3837. Fax: (860) 824-0309.
Email: safe@snet.net.
Web: www.animaltails.com.*

NEW!
Five Kids & A Monkey

Grades 2–5. Books, $7.95 each.
Corresponding unit studies, $5
each. Shipping extra.
*The Creative Attic, Inc., PO Box 187,
Canterbury, NH 03224-0187. Orders:
(888) 566-6539. Inquiries: (603) 783-
9103. Fax: (603) 783-0118.
Email: the5Kids@aol.com.*

Life Before Birth

Grades 3–8. $12.95, Video $19.95.
Shipping extra.
*Master Books, PO Box 727, Green
Forest, AR 72638. (800) 999-3777.
Fax: (870) 438-5120.
Email: mbnlp@cswnet.com.*

NEW!
Movin' and Groovin'

Grades 4–6. $12.95 plus shipping.
*The Learning Works, Inc., P.O. Box
6187, Santa Barbara, CA 93160.
Orders: (800) 235-5767. Inquiries:
(805) 964-4220. Fax: (805) 964-1466.
Email: LESatTLW@aol.com.
Web: www.thelearningworks.com.*

The Brain Train is a book geared for children that explains how the brain works and what your children can do to keep their brains healthy and working optimally. It is a 26-page paperback book with cute line drawings that capture your child's attention. It explains how important proper nutrition, water and exercise are in keeping your brain healthy. There is also a progress chart that your child can fill out to see how he scores in the "keeping the brain healthy" department. Include in the back is a "Notes to Parents and Teachers" section that addresses the topics covered in the book. There is also a resource directory that reads a little bit like an advertisement. The bibliography section lists other books that are recommended to further educate you about the various topics. *Maryann Turner*

Each of the three 32-page non-consumable **Five Kids & a Monkey** books cover a specific health-related topic:

- *Five Kids and A Monkey Investigate a Virus* covers germs and the immune system
- *Five Kids & A Monkey Solve The Great Cupcake Caper* covers healthful eating and exercise
- *Five Kids & A Monkey Banish the Stinkies* covers keeping clean and healthy

Questions are sprinkled throughout the book; the answers are located in the back. Each book also contains a page of "Dynamic Definitions" of words used in the book. For instance, in *Investigate a Virus*, the word *virus* is defined as "The smallest type of germ. Viruses can only be seen by a very powerful microscope."

Each book concludes with experiments and/or activities. In addition, each book contains lessons in character qualities such as loyalty, honesty and responsibility. The unit study books contain activity ideas plus five reproducible handouts.

Although the Five Kids & A Monkey series isn't comprehensive enough to make up the core of your science curriculum, it may provide a nice change of pace in your homeschool. *Rebecca Livermore*

You will adore this cute, colorful hardcover book from Master Books. **Life Before Birth: A Christian Family Book** is written as a series of dialogs between Dr. Gary Parker and his children. Crammed with colorful cartoon illustrations, it not only gives the facts of life, but a Christian pro-life and creationist outlook as well. Topics like abortion and birth defects are presented to your children in a way that will make them want to stand for life and love. All is done in good taste: nothing gruesome. You can get it three ways: the book alone, the book and a read-along cassette in a plastic pouch, the book and cassette and a six-minute VHS video that capsulizes the book's message. Nicest looking book on the subject I have ever seen. Highly recommended. *Mary Pride*

After reading through **Movin' and Groovin'**, I believe this book could be used as a text for teaching health. Though the bulk of the book is exercise ideas, the remainder of the book is chock-full of information on physical fitness and nutrition, including:

- 20 pages of information about fitness, exercising and muscles, including simple diagrams with various muscles labeled
- 70 pages of slightly off-beat exercises to be done in various rooms in the house: bedroom, kitchen, family room, and out-

side. Examples include shooting laundry into the basket and using canned beans as weights
- 10 pages of nutritional information including a food pyramid diagram, discussion on size of servings, and instructions on how to read food labels
- 30 pages of nutritional recipes for breakfast, lunch, dinner and snacks

There are black-and-white illustrations on practically every page, and the text is simple enough to be read by a fourth grader. One minor warning: there is no section discussing food preparation and kitchen safety tips, like many cookbooks meant for young children contain. Parental supervision will be required in using the recipes. There are, however, safety tips for the exercise portion of the book. *Melissa Worcester*

Perhaps the best introduction to public-school nutrition ideas is Educational Insights' **Nutrition Box**. "A complete self-contained kit on nutrition," this low-priced kit consists of 50 cards, each with background info and suggested follow-up activities, neatly stored in a handsome box. Topics include vitamins, minerals, and proteins (a more sensible approach than solely concentrating on the Four Food Groups), nutrition around the world, and proper food preparation. The Nutrition Box is suggested for grades four and up, but at home could be used to some extent even with preschoolers. *Mary Pride*

Human Anatomy

The **Some Body** game from Aristoplay is the simplest, most fun, hands-on body parts instruction I have yet seen. You can play it right out of the box, after a little time spent parting the peelable vinyl body parts from their storage sheets. Basically, the idea is to place body parts in the correct places and the correct order (from back to front) on the game board, an outline drawing of a child's body. You get four *Some Body* game

boards with outlines showing where body parts go, four Body Part sheets of labeled vinyl body part peel 'n stick cutouts, one reference chart showing you where's what in the human body (inside the box top), 50 Body Part cards with questions and experiments, four wild cards, and the indispensable instruction sheet. New edition will include 50 Muscles & Bones cards.

Savvy home schoolers will immediately think of all kinds of ways to teach anatomy using the peel 'n stick body parts and the game board. Or you can just play the games suggested. Draw cards to find which body part you can place on your Body Board. More difficult version: answer questions about body part functions before you get to place an item on the body board. Cards-only version: match questions and answers about body part functions. *Mary Pride*

The Nutrition Box
Grades 4–8. $9.95 plus shipping. *Educational Insights, Inc., 16941 Keegan Ave., Carson, CA 90746. (800) 995-4436. (310) 884-2000. Fax: (800) 995-0506. Web: www.edin.com.*

Aristoplay Some Body game
Grades 1–6. (they say), but fun for all ages. $25 plus shipping. *Aristoplay, Ltd., 450 South Wagner, Ann Arbor, MI 48103. (800) 634-7738. (734) 995-4353. Fax: (734) 995-4611. Web: www.aristoplay.com.*

NEW!
Bones Skeleton & Book

Grades 2–8. $15.95 plus $3 shipping.
Home Life, Inc., PO Box 1190, Fenton, MO 63026. (800) 346-6322.
Email: orders@home-school.com.
Web: www.home-school.com.

Cuisenaire Your Amazing Senses Discovery Book

Grades K–6. $9.95 plus shipping.
Cuisenaire Company of America, 10 Bank Street, PO Box 5026, White Plains, NY 10602. (800) 237-0338. Fax: (800) 551-7637.
Web: www.cuisenaire.com.

Educational Insights 3-D Human Body Charts

Grades 4–8. $39.95 plus shipping.
Educational Insights, Inc., 16941 Keegan Ave., Carson, CA 90746. (800) 995-4436. (310) 884-2000. Fax: (800) 995-0506. Web: www.edin.com.

NEW!
Educational Insights Anatomy Apron

Age 3–8. $22.95 plus shipping.
Educational Insights, Inc., 16941 Keegan Ave., Carson, CA 90746. (800) 995-4436. (310) 884-2000. Fax: (800) 995-0506. Web: www.edin.com.

NEW!
Janice VanCleave's Human Body for Every Kid

Grades 3–6. $12.95.
John Wiley & Sons, 1 Wiley Drive, Somerset, NJ 08875. (800) 225-5945. (732) 469-4400. Fax: (800) 597-3299.
Web: www.wiley.com.

The **Bones Skeleton & Book** is a real kid-pleaser. Put together your own 12" tall, 25-piece skeleton with actual moving joints. Read the included 64-page book—it's a detailed, fun course in human anatomy, from bones to muscles to body systems (circulatory, respiratory, and digestive) and much more. What a great way to give your kid's a complete human anatomy unit, while they think they're just having fun! *Mary Pride*

Planning a unit on the senses: sight, hearing, touch, smell, taste? **Your Amazing Senses Discovery Book** is the name of a really neat book that will teach your children what they need to know (and more!) while entertaining the whole family. This extraordinary full-color book has things that pop up, things to pull, trick eyeglasses to look through, optical illusions, scratch 'n sniff, a reflex-testing experiment—over 30 activities in all, and all built into the book! Nothing for you to do but leave it out where Junior can find it. *Mary Pride*

You've seen 3-D maps; the mountain peaks literally stand out. This set of eight **3-D Human Body Charts** works the same way. You can *see* the body parts in full color, and *feel* them, too, getting an idea of their volume and shape as well as of their outlines. Each chart has exploded views of important features. The Circulatory Systems chart, for example, shows the inside and outside of the heart, as well as a full-body view of the circulatory system. All parts are clearly labeled.

The set includes charts of the circulatory, digestive, muscular, nervous, respiratory, and skeletal systems, plus one each for eye-ear-skin and smell-and-taste. If you purchase it, you'll have hands-on access to more anatomical information than Leonardo da Vinci possessed in his pre-grave-robbing days. *Mary Pride*

So you want to teach a houseful of kids where their internal organs are. How are you going to do that? Buy an **Anatomy Apron** and show them how to velcro their "guts" onto it! What could be more fun?

The Anatomy Apron itself is a plastic apron in a fairly small size. It comes with adhesive velcro pieces and a sheet full of "internal organs"—colorfully drawn on nice cloth—that will attach to velcro. The theory is, you stick the velcro onto the apron and then you describe what your child's internal organs do, while illustrating exactly where they go by attaching big, red, spongy "organs" to the velcro. It gets the idea across much better to small kids then pointing to their stomach and saying, "This is where your large intestine is." Then you take the organs off and have Johnny put them on again. He'll love it! *Joseph Pride*

Janice VanCleave's Human Body for Every Kid takes the "molecules to man" approach. Starting with the basics of cell theory, it proceeds to the brain and autonomic functions, your sense of balance, how your body monitors its temperature, reflexes, skin and the sense of touch, hair and nails, eyes, voicebox, sense of smell, sense of taste, ear and the sense of hearing, respiration, blood and circulation, heart, digestive system, skeleton, muscles, reproduction, and genetics.

Each chapter starts with a "What You Need to Know" introduction to the chapter subject, "Let's Think It Through" questions and puzzles to solve using the information from the introduction, answers to the above, application exercises, a step-by-step activity (typically, a demonstration or modeling of facts taught in the chapter), line-art charts and illustrations, and solutions to the exercises.

Genuine scientific terminology is used throughout. Each new word is defined when first introduced, and also included in the glossary at the end. An index is also included. *Mary Pride*

Media Angels Creation Anatomy: A Study Guide to the Miracles of the Body is a unit study with over 300 activities divided into grade levels K–3, 4–8, and 9–12. Its 170 oversized perfect-bound pages contain:

- a 42-page Teaching Outline (more on this later)
- separate Teaching Outlines for each grade level (K–3, 4–8, and 9–12), each with a reading list, a list of selected books of experiments and activities, vocabulary/spelling/grammar ideas, language arts ideas, math reinforcement ideas, science activities and experiments, geography/history ideas, and art/music ideas
- resource lists galore: books, videos, software, science and government addresses
- short materials list of items you'll find useful doing this unit
- field trip guide
- forms for noting your star discoveries and science experiments
- glossary
- bibliography

Topics covered in detail in the Teaching Outline are, first, the "Body Analogy"—how the parts of the body are used symbolically in Scripture. Then, blood/heart/respiration, injuries and healing, skeletal system and muscles, digestive system, nervous system and brain, reproductive system (where did it come from? how does it work on a cellular level?), DNA and the origins of life, senses, language, races (from the point of view that we are all descended from Noah), and human history.

This glossy book will save you hours of work preparing your own anatomy unit study. So, if you are a fan of unit studies, and agree with the authors' outlook, or would like to learn more about it, why not get it? *Mary Pride*

Systems of the Human Body is a nice thorough overview of the human body, with 12 of Milliken's famous full-size, full-color transparencies. Covered are the following body systems: skeletal, muscular, nervous, brain, eye and ear, circulatory, respiratory, digestive, excretory, endocrine, reproductive, and skin.

The transparency of the reproductive system is tastefully done, focusing on the inner organs. Milliken's pictures present only the body systems under discussion, using gender-neutral body outlines to avoid focusing kids' attention where it doesn't belong.

The built-in teacher's guide gives background information and answers for each worksheet, plus optional enrichment activities. Twenty worksheets cover all the topics, plus provide tests and reviews.

For low-cost anatomy studies you might also want to consider Milliken's

NEW!
Media Angels Creation Anatomy
Grades K–12. $18.95 plus shipping. *Media Angels, 16520 S. Tamiami Trail, #18-193, Fort Myers, FL 33908. (941) 433-2097. Fax: (941) 489-1060. Email: MediAngels@aol.com. Web: www.mediaangels.com.*

Milliken Systems of the Human Body
Grades 4–9. $14.95 plus shipping. *Milliken Publishing Company, 1100 Research Blvd., St. Louis, MO 63132. Orders: (800) 325-4136. Inquiries: (314) 991-4220. Fax: (800) 538-1319. Web: www.millikenpub.com.*

full-color Diagrammatic Study Prints. *Systems of the Human Body* and *Organs of the Human Body* are each a set of eight poster-size prints with anatomical items clearly labeled. Each comes with four review sheets and a teacher's guide. *Mary Pride*

My Body

Grades preK–6 (adult help needed). $7.95 plus shipping.
Teacher Created Materials, 6421 Industry Way, Westminster, CA 92683. (800) 662-4321. (714) 891-7895. Fax: (800) 525-1254. Email: custserv@teachercreated.com. Web: www.teachercreated.com.

My Body is an anatomy book with a difference! Along with handwritten explanations of body parts, you get patterns for making your own life-sized illustrated person. You start by tracing your child's body on tagboard or other sturdy paper. Then photocopy the pattern pages and color as directed. Place as directed on the paper body. Some organs will "lift up" to expose others beneath when finished. A neat project for hands-on (lungs-on, heart-on . . .) learning! *Mary Pride*

NEW!
Newton's Body Shop

Grades 3–8. $19.99 plus shipping.
The Wild Goose Company, PO Box 35171, Greensboro, NC 27425. (801) 363-0696. Fax: (801) 535-2669. Email: wgoose9150@wildgoosescience.com. Web: www.wildgoosescience.com.

Biology in a box for the younger set! **Newton's Body Shop** is a fun way to learn about anatomy from the inside out. Your child gets to build working models of the inside systems of their bodies. The activities and experiments are sure to keep the attention of your child. He can build a model of muscles and bones using paper tubes, acetic acid, one craft stick, elastic cord, ping-pong ball, pipe cleaner, white vinegar, red crayon, and an egg shell or chicken bone. The questions following each activity are designed to magnify the learning experience.

The eyes, ears, respiratory system, circulatory system, and digestive system are all covered. The hard-to-find items are all included in the kit, including a sheep's eye.

Newton's Body Shop is based on the PBS television show, *Newton's Apple*. The show was created to help "scienceophobic" people discover how much fun science can be. This science kit does just that! *Maryann Turner*

NEW!
Science Questions and Answers—The Human Body

Grades 1–3. $5.95 plus shipping.
NTC Publishing. 4255 West Touhy Ave, Lincolnwood, IL 60646. (800) 323-4900 x 147. Fax: (800) 998-3103. Email: ntcpub@tribune.com. Web: www.ntc-school.com.

I am always searching for interesting texts to meet our health requirements and I have not been impressed with regular health textbooks. Luckily, **Science Questions and Answers—The Human Body** is not your regular run-of-the-mill human body book. One of an extensive series of "Gifted and Talented" question and answer books by Lowell House (now carried by NTC Publishing), this 63-page book is packed with information for the curious child. It's ideal for a science or health class, or as a great supplement for a unit study on the human body that's free of the new age attitudes found in many contemporary health texts.

Fifty topics are covered in the text—ideal for a weekly health class. A concept is usually covered in one page and is followed with fun questions that will trigger great discussions. The answers for these questions are located in the back of the book.

Science Questions and Answers starts off with "What are cells?" There is an approximately 100-word explanation followed by six unusual questions. The question "Why does our body need different kinds of cells?" provided our family with some great discussion and sparked some further research. These questions are fun and interesting and you can involve children older than the recommended eight years in the readings and discussion. The older ones in our house pull out the encyclopedia and expand the lessons with further independent study.

Our children have kept a Health Notebook with drawings of all of the book's diagrams. These high-quality diagrams are clear, not overloaded with gigantic technical terms, and are easily understood by children as young as five and six. The order of the presentation held their interest. In many of the sections there are "One Step Further" activities which are pleasurable learning experiences.

We are using this as our Health text this year, so we read from this book before lunch on Friday and discuss the questions during lunch. This book is downright fun and has provided many insightful discussions at our Friday lunches. *Michele Fitzgerald*

Usborne **How Your Body Works** is not just another pretty skeleton. Take a trip through the Body Machine with this incredibly visual kids' introduction to the human body and how it works. See the white blood cell "police" chase down germs. Learn how the bones and muscles and reproductive organs function. Terrific cartoon-style illustrations make the concepts vivid. One of our kids' favorite science books. *Mary Pride*

Using terms a child who has never studied science before can understand, **Understanding Your Brain** explains all about our brains—how they work, what makes them work, why some people can learn faster than others, etc. Even I, who hate science, ended up reading it all the way through and doing the I.Q. puzzles, etc. (I got them all correct! Hah!) This book really grabs your attention and keeps it, besides being factual. Full-color, cute illustrations. Also in the "Science for Beginners" series, *Understanding Your Muscles & Bones. Sarah Pride*

Usborne How Your Body Works
Grades 2–8. $8.95 plus shipping.
EDC Publishing, Division of Educational Development Corporation, 10302 East 55th Place, Tulsa, OK 74146. (800) 475-4522.
Fax: (800) 747-4509.
Web: www.edcpub.com.

NEW!
Usborne Understanding Your Brain
Grades 3–8. $6.95 plus shipping.
EDC Publishing, Division of Educational Development Corporation, 10302 East 55th Place, Tulsa, OK 74146. (800) 475-4522.
Fax: (800) 747-4509.
Web: www.edcpub.com.

Safety

Bicycle safety is important for most of our children. Whether you live out in the country, in the suburbs, or in a busy city, most likely your child rides a bicycle. The **Bicycle Safety series** videos were designed to encourage safe riding practices regardless of where your child rides.

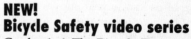

The *Bicycle Zone* video is particularly geared toward the younger crowd. It stresses the rules of the road and safety in simple terms, although it does depict the adults (parents in this case) as being somewhat ignorant of bicycle safety. It does get the point across, in spite of making the parents look less than intelligent.

Pedal Smarts and *Getting There By Bike* are for the older bicyclist. All three videos in the series are informative and contain information that is "a must" for children to know in order to be safe while cycling. I found *Getting There By Bike* motivating as well. After viewing it, I was all geared up to work on my rusty bicycling abilities! *Maryann Turner*

NEW!
Bicycle Safety video series
Grades 1–6, The Bicycle Zone. Grades 7–12, Pedal Smarts. College and adult, Getting There by Bike. First video, $22 postpaid; additional videos, $15 each.
Taps Trailer, 22-D Hollywood Ave., Hohokus, NJ 07423. (800) 343-5540.
Fax: (201) 652-1973.
Email: tmcngy@aol.com.

NEW!
Freddie Firefighter's Fire Safety and Burn Prevention Activity Packet

Pre K–K, 1–2, and 3–4. $2.50 per packet. Discounts for large quantities. Shipping extra.
Genecom Group, Inc., PO Box 47302, Plymouth, MN 55447.
Phone/fax: (612) 536-3513.

Jellybean

Parents. $24.95.
M R K Publishing, 448 Seavey, Petaluma, CA 94952. (707) 763-0056. Fax: (707) 763-1539. Can only order through local bookstore.

A partial list of fatalities from dog bites in one year shows that half the victims on the list were babies ages 18 months or less, right down to 5 and 6 days old. All but four of the 22 fatalities were inflicted by huskies, German shepherds, wolf hybrids, chows, malamutes, pit bulls, or dogs with one parent from those breeds. If you own one of these dogs, it is especially important for you to read this book. Also note that, for every dog-bite fatality, there are hundreds or even thousands of non-fatal dog bites, many of which are disfiguring and painful. Dog-bite *deaths* occur mostly to toddlers-and-under and senior citizens. Dog-bite *injuries* can happen to anyone.

Thanks to Rob and Cyndy Shearer's tape on Twaddle-Free History, we've learned to get beyond social studies lessons on "the fireman is your friend."

Now here come **Freddie Firefighter** and company to remind us that playing with matches is dangerous. These 12 worksheets cover the basics of fire safety including stop-drop-roll, calling the fire department, crawling to escape a smoke-filled room, what a smoke alarm sounds like, kitchen safety, and (of course!) the fireman is your friend. The only difference between the levels is the difficulty of the blanks to be filled in. Preschoolers get coloring sheets, older kids get word searches. This material might be appealing and helpful to younger children, especially if combined with a field trip to the fire station.

What you don't get is information on putting out fires, how to recognize the famous "fire triangle," how to operate a fire extinguisher, or any material on campfire safety.

While parents are assumed to be teaching this to their children, the tone throughout is condescending. "Contact your local fire department for more information," is stated repeatedly, even to the point of getting their help to "treat any continued unsafe fire-related behaviors you may observe." Now the firemen aren't just our friends, they're our children's disciplinarians as well? *Renee Mathis*

Every year, hundreds of children are bitten seriously by dogs—sometimes even their very own pets. Yet "dog safety" and "proper dog handling" are not subjects commonly taught in safety courses. Dog psychologist C. W. Meisterfeld, a man with lots of experience reclaiming dogs that have been turned vicious through the foolish mis-training provided by their owners, has written a book on this subject. This is it: **Jelly Bean versus Dr. Jekyll & Mr. Hyde: Written for the Safety of Our Children and the Welfare of Our Dogs**. The strange title refers to an actual case (described in the book) of a dog with excellent breeding and loving owners who turned into a menace,

but was reclaimed by Dr. Meisterfeld. The book itself, besides the story of Jelly Bean, explains how dog personality and dog behavior work, why dogs "go around the bend" and start attacking their own owners, and Dr. Meisterfeld's own "totally positive" system of dog training, as contrasted with the jerk 'em-around school of thought. The book includes numerous other case histories (with photos) along with Jelly Bean's. One photo shows a child whose dog bit him in the face, and it'll cure you instantly of the idea that dog safety is some trivial little thing we can easily ignore.

One warning: in some short sections of the book a California child psychiatrist makes some analogies between dog psychology and the training of human children. This sounds very plausible, and some of his ideas are good, but human beings are not mere animals acting on instinct. The point of child training, for Christians, is not just to get the child to behave, but to teach him how to relate to God, who does not rely totally on positive incentives alone in His relationship with His wayward children. Otherwise, recommended. *Mary Pride*

Safety is a big issue in our modern, fast-paced society. Our children have more safety-related topics to be concerned about than ever before in history. Not only do they have to learn the basic safety rules from days gone by, like:

- Don't chase the ball into the street!
- Look both ways before crossing the street!
- If your clothes catch fire, stop, drop and roll!

But there are all the additional warnings that our modern era has brought into our children's lives.

- Don't talk to strangers!
- Instructions about dealing with obscene phone calls.
- How to handle improper touching.
- What to do if you find a bag of pills in the park.
- And a multitude of others.

If all our modern hazards cause you to worry about whether you've covered all the bases with your children, **The Safety Book For Active Kids** is a useful reminder of most of the various hazards we face in life. It includes helpful information about how to handle each situation. The format introduces the child to the particular problem or peril on one page, and offers ideas and solutions on the following page. The art work is simple black-and-white illustrations, and the book is uncluttered and parent/child friendly. It includes a wide variety of situations to help your child develop important problem-solving skills. There are two pages that discuss trick-or-treating safety. If you find that offensive, the pages can be easily removed (they are front and back of the same page). There are fun activities and checklists for parents at the end of the book. The book is a very useful tool to help you approach the many dangerous everyday safety issues that we all face. *Maryann Turner*

Safety Zone is a fun, simple game that helps your child feel more prepared for safety hazards should they occur. It helps him become aware of, and learn skills needed to avoid, many of the dangers he might face. It builds self-confidence in your child and his decision-making abilities.

The game comes in a cylinder. The game board is unrolled and white board bars are slid onto the curled sides of the game board—that, in itself, was fun for my 7-year-old. (The Bossy girl and Bully boy depicted on the game board are somewhat obnoxious-looking, but not too offensive.) Your child advances around the board by rolling dice. If he lands on a yellow, blue, or red box, he draws a card of the same color. Your child draws the card, but it must be read by you or another player. Depending on the question, the correct answers are marked with a *, or the reader may find examples of several acceptable answers. If your child answers correctly, he may advance 2 spaces and read the new box. If the answer is incorrect, he may not advance and you should discuss the correct answer with him. A correct answer to the Daily Double moves the player 4 spaces. The "Bossy & Bully" cards can elicit answers from your child that may differ with the card's answers; the parent is the final judge. All players to reach the Safety Zone are winners . . . so there are no losers! *Maryann Turner*

Personal Safety, from **TREND's** popular **Fun-To-Know series**, teaches kids how to handle possibly life-threatening situations. Each card gives an illustrated safety rule on the front. "Be safe in stormy weather," for example, shows a child sitting safely indoors reading a book while lightning flashes outside. The back of the card contains more information about safe-

NEW!
The Safety Book For Active Kids
Grades preK–3. $12.95.
The Learning Works. PO Box 6187, Santa Barbara, CA 93160. Orders: (800) 235-5767. Inquiries: (805) 964-4220. Fax: (805) 964-1466.
Email: LESatTLW@aol.com.
Web: www.thelearningworks.com.

NEW!
Safety Zone
Ages 6 and up. 2-4 players. $19.95.
Life Lessons, 4804 Belvedere St., Austin, TX 78731. (512) 451-1394.

TREND Fun-To-Know Safety Flash Cards
Grades preK–6. Personal Safety (#T-1652) and Signs and Symbols (#T-1655) Fun-To-Know Flash

Cards, $4.59. Shipping extra.
*TREND Enterprises, Inc., PO Box
64073, St. Paul, MN 55164. (800) 328-
5540. Fax: (800) 845-4832.*

ty in that situation, plus a "What If?" exercise that presents a safety dilemma plus three possible solutions. The best choice is given and explained.

Swimming safety, fire safety, street safety, car safety, and personal safety are among the topics covered.

I especially appreciate the way these cards give kids the *reasons* behind the rules. The "What If?" scenarios only take a few seconds to introduce and read, and can be quite involving.

Another entry in TREND's Fun-To-Know series, *Signs and Symbols* is a set of 26 flash cards. Each has a symbol on the front, e.g., a STOP sign or the international handicapped symbol of a person in a wheel-chair. On the back are questions designed to teach the social rules and laws pertaining to the sign. For example, on the back of the Phone card, question 4 asks,

> *What is your home phone number? The Police? The Fire Department? A Poison Control Center? Hospital Emergency? Why is it important to know these numbers and post them near telephones whenever possible?*

Ages 4 and up will enjoy learning to spot these signs, while older children will benefit from learning to apply these simple survival skills. *Mary Pride*

NEW!
Yellow Dyno Safety Series

Grades preK–4 (Yellow Dyno's
Can't Fool Me). Grades 3–6 (Tricky
People). $29.95 each. $79.95 for a
complete kit including Yellow
Dyno's Can't Fool Me, 200-page
manual, coloring books, and more.
Shipping extra.
*Nest Entertainment, 6100 Colwell
Blvd., Irving, TX 75039.
Phone: (888) 954-5437.
Fax: (800) 221-8729.
Web: www.nest-ent.com.*

Mix Elvis and Little Richard together and *voila!*—you've just met **Yello Dyno**, the superhero type leader of an all-kid band. What makes him special? His desire to educate and inform his band members and ultimately you through his music about "tricky people," which is really just a kinder name for a child abuser and/or molester.

This stage for *Tricky People: Safety Rules from Yellow Dyno* is set when we meet Reginald Charming, a man who sponsors and promotes children's bands and other activities. He preys upon young girls through various predator tactics including flattery, baiting, and bribery. The video confronts this sensitive issue head-on and addresses coping with uncomfortable pressuring and post-abuse situations. Because of this, parental involvement in the viewing is advised.

Though the message is extremely noble, parents need to fill in some gaping questions left behind as some scenarios are left vaguely unconcluded. My 8-year-old reviewer was full of questions throughout, as many scene outcomes were based on assumptions. In addition, a large, gruff, singing dinosaur aimed at this age group seemed "babyish" to my reviewer, who at eight, is beyond costumed pals. You may be disappointed to see normalcy portrayed as loosely supervised children, who at 8 to 12 are allowed freedoms that driving teenagers should just be earning. For example, the children come and go to the mall without telling any adults where they are going (no adults are around to tell). They seem to have dropped off the kids for the day in no one's care. Despite that, the music is catchy and upbeat, and the overall intent to educate good, though corny at times.

The *Yellow Dyno's Can't Fool Me* video covers the same points and situations as *Tricky People*, but in a much more fragmented way. Story examples were left unconcluded, undefined, and vague, perhaps because it is aimed at a younger audience. Nevertheless, some scenarios were left dangerously unaddressed as to their outcome. For example, a man lures a child to his car to get a kitten, but doesn't show the child's method of escape or how to handle the situation appropriately. The story simply goes on to another issue. If you chose to purchase this, it should in my opinion only be watched following the viewing of *Tricky People*, to avoid confusion. The two are sold as a unit or separately. The same catchy songs and excerpts from *Tricky People* are repeated in this video, which makes this video basically a scaled-down repeat aimed at the younger audience. *Shari Fooshe*

CHAPTER 33

Plants & Animals

Nature study is science on a human scale. Mostly, it's about what you can see with your eyes, unaided by anything except your glasses. Plants. Animals. Rocks. The stars in the sky.

Ecology is about what you *can't* see—how entire populations of plants and animals interact with each other, with their surroundings, and with us.

Young kids aren't capable of actually *doing* ecology, because they don't have the time or expertise to take down the hundreds of necessary field measurements, or the statistical expertise to model the results on computers. Young kids have to take ecology on faith. Which may not be such a good idea.

Today's ecological models tend to assume that most species and the environment are *fragile,* that humankind's presence is invariably *harmful,* and that slight variations in measurements are *meaningful,* to list only three assumptions. Thus, children are led to believe that if all the rabbits in an area die, all the foxes will die too, as in one especially popular "populations" example. They are not led to even consider the possibility that the foxes could switch to eating mice, or garbage, or cats, or that the foxes could migrate, or even that some concerned citizens could "adopt" foxes and provide food for them until the crisis abates. Black and white. Dead rabbits, dead foxes.

The older, nature-study approach would have been to get out there in the wild and try to spot a fox. Or at least some fox droppings and other evidence of where the fox had been. The even older pioneers-and-Indians school of education would have taught the kids how to walk quietly through the woods, how to construct blinds, and how to hunt what they needed for food (which does *not* include foxes but *does* include rabbits!).

Getting out in the woods teaches kids that the real world is a lot more complex and beautiful than the computer-generated models in their textbooks. In the field, kids can see the good and bad of what human beings do, too. Walking through a burned-out area thoroughly impresses Smokey Bear's warnings on you, while visiting a coppice shows how people can "garden" trees in a self-sustaining way that creates beauty while it provides needed wood. Similarly, farm visits are way more educational than graphs of annual beef production or political tirades about farming methods.

While nowhere near as valuable educationally, watching videos about natural phenomena can also teach kids a lot. Look how much gunk Mt. St. Helens blew into the air. See how many square miles of trees this one volcanic explosion flattened. That might provide some perspective the next

IN THIS CHAPTER

Resources for nature study, gardening, and ecology.

Two scientists, looking at the very same ecological system, can come up with totally different opinions. That's because a complex model changes drastically when you

(1) **Change any of the presuppositions** governing the model.

(2) **Decide which data is critical** to the model and which should be left out as irrelevant.

(3) **Know your funding will evaporate** if you get politically incorrect results.

time someone starts complaining about how all pollution everywhere is caused by human beings.

Christian Liberty Nature Readers series

Grades 1–5. Book 1, $6. Book 2, $3. Book 3, $3.50. Book 4, $4. Book 5, $5. Shipping extra.
Christian Liberty Press, 502 West Euclid Ave., Arlington Heights, IL 60004. (847) 259-4444. Fax: (847) 259-2941. Email: enquire@homeschools.org. Web: www.homeschools.org. They take credit card orders, but not over the phone. Any other contact method will work.

NEW!
Crinkleroot Series

Grades 3–6. Each book, $12.95–$14.95. Shipping extra.
Greenleaf Press, 3761 Hwy 109 N., Unit D, Lebanon, TN 37087. Inquiries: (615) 449-1617. Orders: (800) 311-1508. Fax: (615) 449-4018. E-mail: Greenleafp@aol.com. Web: www.greenleafpress.com

NEW!
The Equinox Guide Series— Nature Study Books

Grades 2–8. Each book, $7.95–$9.95. Shipping extra.
Greenleaf Press, 3761 Hwy 109 N., Unit D, Lebanon, TN 37087. Inquiries: (615) 449-1617. Orders: (800) 311-1508. Fax: (615) 449-4018. E-mail: Greenleafp@aol.com. Web: www.greenleafpress.com

Nature Lore

In Victorian times, adults wrote hundreds of books designed to spark children's interest in God's creation. Continuing in this tradition, the **Christian Liberty Nature Reader series** "takes your children into the fascinating world of tiny creatures such as spiders, bees, hermit crabs, wasps, and turtles." Ol-timey writing, facsimile illustrations, smallish print. Good if you have time to read aloud, probably not enticing enough for most kids to want to read on their own. One book each for grades 1–5. *Mary Pride*

Crinkleroot is Tarzan for the '90s. Instead of being raised by apes, he was "born in a tree and raised by bees." Like Tarzan, he may live in the deep woods, but Crinkleroot's favorite food is that munchie of couch potatoes everywhere—popcorn. The Big C can "whistle in a hundred languages and speak caterpillar, salamander, and turtle." Considering that whistles sound the same in most languages, and that caterpillars are not known as big talkers, we start to suspect that author Jim Arnosky is having some fun with us. Which he is.

The Crinkleroot series, which includes Crinkleroot's guides to *Animal Tracking, Walking in Wild Places, Knowing the Birds,* and *Knowing the Trees,* reads like a typical children's book. Whimsical cartoon illustrations accompany Crinkleroot's narrated wildlife tours. Typical sample: "Look! A song sparrow nestled on her eggs. Let's tiptoe back and away so we won't disturb her." When Crinkleroot finds a tick on his pants, he not only tells you how and why to remove ticks, but you get a full page of "tick facts." When Crinkleroot takes you on a tree tour, he tells you how to identify trees, the parts of a tree, and how a forest looks and smells. Unusual for a nature book today, there is no eco-whining or commands to write your Congressperson. Crinkleroot just plain enjoys nature, and you just can't help picking up some of that enjoyment while reading these gentle, friendly books. Recommended. *Mary Pride*

The photography in these books is terrific! Have you ever seen a close-up of whale lice? Have you ever wondered how many bluebirds fit into a nest cavity? Do insects pique your curiosity? These 60+ page paperbacks (*Bluebird Rescue* is 48 pages) are stuffed full of top-quality photos. The authors often speak in the first person, letting you know just how it feels to look for insects in a rain forest, or how to find the increasingly rare bluebird. The photos and the personal touch make this series special.

Bluebird Rescue examines the plight of the bluebird. Since the introduction of the starling and English sparrow, the lovely bluebird has had fierce competition for nesting places. The author lets you know how to help (and attract) bluebirds with nest-box plans. You will also find out what berries the bluebird will eat. Photos include eggs, nests, hatchlings, nestlings, fledglings, and adult birds.

The Architecture of Animals examines animal homes, from insect nests to mammal burrows. Amazing photos of paper wasp nests, spider orbs, swallow dwellings, and beaver lodges.

Similarly, the winning photos in **Exploring the World of Insects** makes the book. That is not to say that all of the photos are beautiful. Some, like parasitoid wasps on a hornworm, are repulsive (though I have come to appreciate their tomato-saving qualities!).

Meeting the Whales and **Riding with the Dolphins** include complete surveys of different species. Despite the great photography, these books suffer from evolution-as-fact, man as the enemy, save-the-whales rhetoric.

Each of these books is rather like an encyclopedia entry, but again, the photography makes each worthwhile. The friendly first-person narration reads very smoothly. *MacBeth Derham*

Everything You Never Learned About Birds has as many facts as an Eyewitness Book or Usborne Book, but is better arranged and more friendly. Author Rebecca Rupp's colorful book is packed with illustrations and photos, nature lore and "bird words," bird legends and hands-on projects, all in easy-to-digest mini-sections. For example, the two pages on birds' feet tell you everything from basic bird leg construction (illustrated with a drawing of a bird leg *v.* a human leg), to the Latin words for various bird foot types, to bird footprints, to how the jacana walks on lily pads, to a legend about the curative value of owls' feet. Don't miss this one when you do your unit study on birds. *Mary Pride*

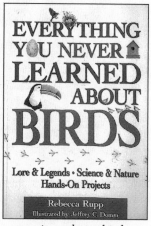

Buzz, Chirp & Hum: A Study of Insects is another of the **Helen Nelson** 12-week science unit studies. This has serious instruction in how to classify insects properly, but Nelson's art background also comes through in many fun art projects for young children. The comb-bound unit volume includes a choice of one ongoing project and numerous one-shot activities in the areas of reading, science, art, and language arts. The best large project is an insect collection and field guide to be assembled according to the 15 orders and bound at the end of the unit. One meaningful option in the final unit is a comparison of grasshopper devastation in *On the Banks of Plum Creek* and in Exodus 10. The finished large projects can be laminated, bound, or otherwise preserved as lasting records of the students' work. An extensive bibliography is included. *Cindy Marsch*

NEW!
Janice VanCleave's Biology for Every Kid

Grades 3–6. $11.95.
John Wiley & Sons, 1 Wiley Drive, Somerset, NJ 08875. (800) 225-5945. (732) 469-4400. Fax: (800) 597-3299. Web: www.wiley.com.

NEW!
Moody Science Videos

All ages. Moody Science Classics, $9.95 each. Moody Science Adventures, $14.95 each. Forces of God's Creation, $49.95 set, $19.95 each. The Edge of Creation, $29.95 set, $19.95 each. Wonders of Creation, $44.95 set, $14.95 each. Shipping extra.
Moody Video, 820 N. La Salle Blvd., Chicago, IL 60610-3284. Orders: (800) 842-1223. Fax: (800) 647-6910. Web: www.moody.edu.

Janice VanCleave's Biology for Every Kid: 101 Easy Experiments That Really Work has more genuine hands-on experiments than the other books in this series. Thanks to the fact that biological life is all around us (plants, molds, insects, our own bodies), it's easy to find actual material to experiment on, rather than having continually to resort to modeling how systems work, as in the other books.

Each demonstration or experiment is laid out as a two-page spread. On the left page is a brief statement of purpose, materials list, "cookbook" set of procedures to follow, statement of the expected result, and explanation of the science principle being demonstrated. Occasionally text from the left page continues on to the right page. Also on the right page are one or more line-art illustrations of the experiment setup and its stages.

Among the topics covered in this book are a wide variety of plant parts and properties, molds, fungi, small organisms, insects, fish, earthworms, birds, and human anatomy. It's all very organized and thorough. Probably every plant experiment in your science text is there, plus dozens more. As with every book in this series, all experiments use common household items and are easy to set up.

There are enough human body experiments in *Biology for Every Kid*—45 in all—that you might be tempted to skip *Human Body for Every Kid* (reviewed in chapter 32) and just make do with this book. That's fine, if you have a science text that covers anatomy well and all you want is the experiments. Remember, the *Human Body* book is a teaching text as well as an experiment book. *Mary Pride*

We have a lot of videos to talk about here, but it's worth taking the time, because your fellow homeschoolers have voted these science video series #1!

Let's start with **the Moody Science Classics** (28 minutes each). Produced over 40 years ago, they include *Faces of Faith, Dust or Destiny, Hidden Treasure, Where the Waters Run, Red River of Life, City of the Bees, Prior Claim, Signposts Aloft, God of Creation*, and *Empty Cities*. These excellent videos explore all of the sciences, demonstrating the wonders of God's world through observation via telescope, microscope, time-lapse photography, etc.; through experiments; or through models, diagrams, and animations. God is explicitly praised as the designer and creator of everything shown. Every video ends with a gospel message.

The Moody Science Adventures series includes four 30-minute videos, each divided into three 10-minute episodes. The videos in this series are *Treasure Hunt, The Power in Plants, The Clown-Faced Carpenter*, and *The Wonder of You*. They include some footage you will recognize if you have seen the Classics series.

Recently, Moody has produced three stunning video boxed sets: **The Wonders of Creation** (*Human Life, Animal Kingdom*, and *Planet Earth*), **The Awesome Forces of God's Creation** (*Whirling Winds, Roaring Waters*, and *Thundering Earth*), and **Journeys to the Edge of Creation** (*Our Solar System* and *The Milky Way & Beyond*). These are as good science as the previous ones and more up-to-date, while noticeably less evangelistic.

The Discovering God's Creation series with Professor Schnaegel is the only clinker. This attempt to woo young viewers with MTV-like camera angles and goofy antics also teaches a politically correct version of ecology ("exercising dominion" now becomes "hands off the habitat"). It even opens with a sequence that could be taken as dissing Moody's other beautiful science videos. With this exception, Moody's videos are highly recommended. *Mary Pride*

Did you know that there are about a billion, billion insects in the world? That there are a million insects for every person on earth? Are you aware that the insects of the world weigh twelve times what the people weigh? Did you know that a single cabbage aphid can have 906 million *tons* of descendents in one year? **The Naturalist's Handbook** is brimming with such facts.

The Naturalist's Handbook was compiled to stimulate and direct young nature explorers in their study of life science. The author encourages would-be naturalists to consider themselves detectives and to fine-tune their skills of observing, questioning, measuring, comparing, and interpreting their findings.

The handbook is divided into units on plants, bugs, mammals, birds, and water. Each unit is further subdivided into an introduction to the life form being studied, a checklist for identification purposes, interesting sidebar definitions, and at least one follow-up activity. The activities include simple inside tips well known to experienced naturalists, such as the optimal weather conditions for a butterfly hunt, how to move during your hunt, and where to hunt.

Each child's copy of *The Naturalist's Handbook* will be unique, as a journaling section is included after each unit. The author urges children to make detailed field journals and suggests ideas for what kinds of things to record. Unfortunately, after the high-quality instruction in journaling, very little space is allowed for such journaling on the workpages. This could be made up for by using a separate notebook for recording, which would also make the handbook non-consumable (so you wouldn't have to buy extra copies!).

Sturdy and well bound in an enclosed spiral-style construction, which makes it easy to handle, *The Naturalist's Handbook* could be used as a complete year of elementary life science study. *Barbara Petronelli*

Aimed at readers from preschool to early teens, this monthly Christian magazine includes read-aloud stories, science articles, a readers' forum, child-submitted pictures and poems, "You Can Draw" pages that guide children to produce their own nature drawing, and activities, projects, and puzzles. With a creationist emphasis, and a smorgasbord of nature books and products offered for sale through the magazine, **Nature Friend** sounds like everything a Christian family could wish for in a nature magazine.

Nature Friend's **Nature's Workshop Catalog** features tested nature-study products and books, plus some science equipment and art supplies. Books are either evolution-free or have "guideline sheets" included. Bird feeders, binoculars, ant farms, telescopes, microscopes, lab equipment, art supplies, puzzles, nature study guides, nature coloring books, and lots more are all offered. *Mary Pride*

A Pinky Is a Baby Mouse is not only a cute, illustrated, rhyming nature book for young children. It's a vocabulary book for all of us who don't know or can't remember what you call a baby bear, buffalo, dolphin, eel, firefly, and more—100 creatures in all. Let's see how you do. Quick—what's a baby gorilla called? A baby dove? A baby partridge? A baby firefly? If you don't know the answers, this book is your answer. *Mary Pride*

NEW!
The Naturalist's Handbook
Grades 3–6. $14.95 plus shipping.
Gibbs Smith Publisher, P.O. Box 667, Layton, UT 84041. (800) 748-5439. Fax: (800) 213-3023. Web: www.gibbs-smith.com.

Nature Friend magazine
Grades preK–9. 12 issues per year. $22 (Canada $25, other countries $30). Catalog, $3, refundable with first order.
Nature Friend Magazine, 2727 Press Run Road, Sugar Creek, OH 44681. (800) 927-4196. Fax: (330) 852-3285.

NEW!
A Pinky Is a Baby Mouse
Grades preK–3. $5.99 paperback, $14.45 hardcover.
Time Warner Trade Publishing, C/O Order Entry, 3 Center Plaza, Boston, MA 02108. (800) 759-0190. Fax: (800) 286-9471. Email: cust.service@littlebrown.com. Web: www.littlebrown.com.

Usborne Nature Books

Grades 1–8. Mysteries and Marvels of Nature series (Bird Life, Insect Life, Reptile World, Animal World, Ocean Life, Plant Life), $6.95 each (paperbound) or $14.95 (library bound). First Nature series (Creepy Crawlies, Butterflies and Moths, Fishes, Birds, Flowers, Trees, Wild Animals), $4.50 each (paperbound), $12.95 each (library bound), or combined into The First Book of Nature, $16.95. Shipping extra.

EDC Publishing, Division of Educational Development Corporation, 10302 East 55th Place, Tulsa, OK 74146. (800) 475-4522. Fax: (800) 747-4509. Web: www.edcpub.com.

NEW!
Garden Crafts For Kids

Grades 3–12. $14.95 plus $5 shipping.
Sterling Publishing Co., Inc., 40 Saw Mill Pond Rd., Edison, NJ 08837. (800)367-9692. Fax: (212) 213-2495. Web: www.sterlingpublishing.com.

KidsGardening

Grades 3–12. $13.95 plus $3 shipping.
Home Life, Inc., PO Box 1190, Fenton, MO 63026. Orders: (800) 346-6322. Inquiries: (636) 343-7750. Fax: (636) 343-7203. Email: orders@home-school.com. Web: www.home-school.com.

In the natural-science area, Usborne offers several series for different age levels. (My personal experience indicates that 42-year-olds should be included in these age levels!) The **Mysteries and Marvels series** is a show stopper. As the catalog says, it's a "dramatic and detailed look at the amazing, the unexplained, and the mysterious in nature." *Mysteries and Marvels of Ocean Life*, for example, has chapters on ocean giants, the miniature sea world, twilight and deep sea fish, lights and electricity, colorful characters, living together (symbiotes), mimics, marine hitchhikers, sea changes, the hunters' weapon, defense and escape, beware—poison!, unusual events, and record breakers. Throughout the book, true-or-false questions appear. These are finally answered in the back, just before the index. In theory, "these books will delight 8–11 year olds"; in practice, our two-year-old loves them as much as the rest of us do!

Moving along, the **First Nature series** has larger text and less detail, this being aimed at the six-and-up crowd. Get this series (either individually or in the durable combined volume) and you won't have to worry about what to do for science hour! Again, the illustrations are almost unbearably good and the text is filled with colorful details. Bet you can't buy just one!
Mary Pride

Gardening

WARNING: This book may be dangerous to the state of your backyard! After reading **Garden Crafts For Kids** our oldest daughter was brimming with new gardening ideas, from planting a pole bean teepee to growing loofah sponges. If we'd let her she would even grow a patchwork flower "bed" set in a real metal bed frame! (It's gorgeous in the photo, but not in my yard, thanks!)

Seriously, this is an outstanding gardening book, terrific for an entire horticulture unit or as inspiration for just a few green-thumb projects. If you've never planted a garden before you can find sound, thorough advice about soil preparation, planning your garden, and choosing easy vegetables to grow. More experienced gardeners may appreciate the sections on building a cold frame, diagnosing plants' nutritional needs, and much more. Crafts abound: some are products to use while you garden (painted tools, apron, seed caddy, and more) and some are ideas for using your harvest. Among other projects, you'll find clear instructions for making a topiary, herbal body powder, and pressed flower cards. And what better way to enjoy the fruit of your hands than by eating it? You'll find recipes for gourmet flower cupcakes, forest honey made from pine needles, and zucchini tea cake. You'll even find serious science experiments, such as testing soil pH with violets or using an onion to make electricity.

Gloriously illustrated with stunning photos, this 144-page paperback is the best gardening book I've seen for kids. From bizarre but fun (a bathtub garden or a firefly flashlight) to practical (homemade bug spray) to aesthetic (dried floral wreath) *Garden Crafts for Kids* offers something for just about everyone.
Anne Wegener

How can anyone not like a book with a title like **KidsGardening: A Kids' Guide to Messing Around in the Dirt?** Gardening is ecology in the useful sense, and this is *the* gardening book to get your urchins. For one thing, it comes with five packets of kid-friendly seeds: good strong growers that also are annual favorites. Irresistible illustrations on the seed packets make even a blister-conscious adult anxious to plunge that old hoe into the dirt! The seed packets are bound right onto the outside of the book, so they stay where you want them until it's time to plant.

This book has wire spirals, so it will stay conveniently open, and sturdy, jelly-proof pages. The usual colorful, goofy, illustrations lead you right into the mostly

hand-lettered text. This is brilliantly organized, starting with info on what plants need to grow and how to prepare your soil, moving on to the wonders of composting and transplanting, and how to battle the bugs organically. Separate sections are devoted to veggies, flowers and herbs, and indoor gardening. You even get recipes for yummies like garlic bread and guacamole (made with your homegrown garlic and avocados, of course!). *KidsGardening* closes triumphantly with directions for worm farming in a box and how to make a scarecrow.

I just have to give you a taste of the book's memorable style. How about this one: "Mulch is like a blanket that covers your garden and keeps weeds from growing and keeps your garden soil moist and soft." Next to this sentence is a picture of a flower snuggled in bed under a blanket of leaves. You can bet any kid reading this will remember what mulch is and what it's good for! Or how about this definition of weeds: "Weeds are any plants that grow where you don't want them." I've seen people write for pages about which plants are weeds and which aren't without saying it this well! *Mary Pride*

The **Starting Gardening Kit Kit** comes with the Usborne First Skills book *Starting Gardening*, a kid-sized plastic trowel, a few plastic garden markers, and packets of easy-to-grow seeds. The kit I saw came with labeled packets of California poppies (for flowers) and chives (for herbs), along with unlabeled ziploc packets of whole red lentils and chick peas (for sprouting). The only instructions are what you'll find in the book or on the seed packets. Additional supplies, such as seed starters, flowerpots, garden tools, and so on are needed (of course!). The main point of including the "extras" is to get kids excited in a way a book alone can't manage. Once excited, they'll want to at least plant the plantable seeds and sprout the sproutables. From there, the book suggests many other kid-friendly gardening projects, including ferns, a wildlife garden, an alpine garden, and drying and pressing flowers, along with the gardening basics shown step-by-step in its 32 colorfully illustrated pages. *Mary Pride*

Ecosystems & Ecology

Nate and Nell Kidd's mom is an ecologist. They travel with her to exotic locations, where they catch everyday eco-crooks such as cactus thieves. If this sounds like the Hardy Boys and Nancy Drew meet Rachel Carson, you're right. So far the series includes: *The Condor Hoax, Robbers of the Giant Cactus, Monarchs at Risk, Troubles in the Rain Forest,* and *Threat to the Sea Otters.*

The Ecology Kidds are part of High Noon's high interest, low vocabulary series of books for slow or reluctant readers. The interest level of these books appeals to children ages 8–16, but the readability is at a second grade level. Surprisingly enjoyable, with a focus on species conservation rather than abstract (and scientifically controversial) issues such as ozone depletion. *Mary Pride*

Facts not Fear should be mandatory reading in ecology classes . . . if I believed in mandatory education in the first place! Unlike the unscientific doom-mongering found everywhere from school texts to TV shows, here are the scientific facts that debunk all the common ecology apocalypses. Written in consultation with a distinguished academic and scientific advisory professional, this book presents both the "fears" (what school kids are taught) and the "facts" (what the research really says.

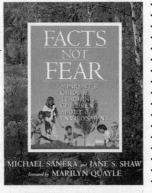

Part 1 explains the problem—how "phony science" and eco-activism have become entrenched in schools. The book then devotes a chapter each to these questions:

- Will Billions Starve?
- Natural Resources on the way out?
- Are Our Forest's Dying?
- The Rain Forest—One Hundred Acres a Minute?
- American Wildlife—On the Edge?
- Where Have All the Species Gone?

- The Air We Breathe
- A Hotter Planet
- Sorting Out Ozone
- Acid Rain
- Not a Drop to Drink!
- Don't Eat the Apple!
- A Garbage Crisis
- The Recycling Myth

Easy-to-read format, plus booklists for further study, make this an indispensable homeschool tool. *Mary Pride*

Janice VanCleave's Ecology for Every Kid is the ecology course you should be using. It covers all the scientific terminology and concepts you can expect to find in a textbook, plus fun thought experiments and demonstrations to make them memorable. Its treatment of topics such as acid rain and the ozone layer, while taking the view that these are indeed problems, is not hysterical or gloom-inducing. Kids are not guilted into become little political radicals; in fact, Mrs. VanCleave expressly says, "Many of the solutions are adult decisions." The emphasis is on teaching the science facts and terms, and mildly encouraging personal conservation (e.g., not wasting water).

The book is designed in an open "chapter" format. Each chapter of the starts with a "What You Need to Know" introduction to the chapter subject (including definitions of the important terminology), "Let's Think It Through" questions and puzzles to solve using the information from the introduction, answers to the above, application exercises, a step-by-step activity (typically, a demonstration or modeling of facts taught in the chapter), line-art charts and illustrations, and solutions to the exercises. Genuine scientific terminology is used throughout. New words are introduced in boldface and defined on the spot. A glossary and index are included.

Chapters cover basic ecological definitions (what is an environment, how species affect each other), social groupings, mutualism/parasitism/commensalism, food chains and webs, weeds, oxygen cycle, water cycle, adaptation, ecosystems and biomes, tundra and polar lands, woodlands, grasslands, deserts, mountains, ocean ecosystems, water pollution, global warming (she is careful to point out "many," not "most" or "all," scientists support this prediction), the good and bad side of plastic, acid rain, ozone layer, garbage and recycling, renewable energy sources, endangered animals, and my personal favorite, "How Farmers and Ranchers Produce Food While Protecting the Earth's Limited Natural Resources."

I suggest that, you, the parent, read *Facts Not Fear* (reviewed above) before teaching this course, so you can present both sides of the controversies surrounding global warming, acid rain, and the ozone layer. Regardless of your own views on the matter, it's important to know these *are* controversies, not matters of settled scientific fact. If a few sentences pointing this out were put in the next edition of *Ecology for Every Kid,* this book would be just about perfect. *Mary Pride*

NEW!
Janice VanCleave's Ecology for Every Kid

Grades 3–6. Each book, $10.95.
John Wiley & Sons, 1 Wiley Drive, Somerset, NJ 08875. (800) 225-5945. (732) 469-4400. Fax: (800) 597-3299. Web: www.wiley.com.

CHAPTER 34

Earth & Space Science

In elementary school, Earth Science is not taught as a separate subject. Like the other sciences, bits and pieces of it are tucked into each year of the science curriculum. In junior high, children get a year of Earth Science (which, oddly, includes Space Science). Then, in high school, no Earth Science or Astronomy at all, unless they're available as electives.

There's something to be said for skipping Earth & Space Science entirely until eighth grade. A serious course on the subjects will yield better results if the student hasn't been confused by years of cutesy terminology and oversimplified facts.

Or you could teach your kids serious Earth & Space Science *right now*, using the resources in this chapter.

Earth Science

"Science sings the glory of God!" exults the brochure for these four unit studies designed for Christian homeschoolers, and indeed **Helen Nelson** has a reverent, academic, and child-appealing approach to these broad areas of study.

At times the sophisticated vocabulary and concepts seem disjointed from the simpler reading, science, art, and language projects, but a discerning parent can harmonize them without much difficulty. The twelve-week units will need day-to-day breakdown for each family based on the flexibility allowed by extensive bibliographies and project lists, and each comb-bound unit volume includes a choice of one ongoing project and numerous one-sitting activities. The finished large projects can be laminated, bound, or otherwise preserved as lasting records of the students' work.

Buzz, Chirp & Hum: A Study of Insects is reviewed in the Plants & Animals chapter.

The Deep Blue Sea: A Study of Oceans includes outlines, vocabulary lists, reading lists, and projects (as do all of the volumes in this series) on many aspects of oceanography, including currents, weather, and physical features, with plants and animals covered in the second half of the unit. Rich literature selections enhance this volume—I long to do the critical study of Winslow Homer's ocean paintings.

The Sun and Beyond: A Study of the Solar System is reviewed in the Space section of this chapter.

Earth Science Covers:

- Geology
- Meteorology (weather and atmosphere)
- Oceanography

Space Science Covers:

- Constellations
- History of the Space Program
- Solar System

NEW!
Helen Nelson science series
Grades 1–8. $14.95 each.
Shipping extra.
HN Studies, PO Box 251, Wheaton, IL 60189. (630) 653-8750. Fax: (630) 510-0330. Email: Lhs73@aol.com.

Terra Firma: A Study of Geology has perhaps the best science projects and models of the series, including crystal-growing, a model glacier, and edible "rocks." Several Bible projects include Joshua's stones of remembrance, heavenly jewels, and the wise and foolish men's house foundations, but the science/Scripture linkage here seems more coincidental than educational. *Cindy Marsch*

Janice VanCleave's Earth Science for Every Kid is "101 Easy Experiments That Really Work." In most cases, these are *demonstrations* that really work, not experiments *per se*. You will be mostly modeling principles of earth science, not observing them directly using the earth itself.

Each demonstration or experiment is laid out as a two-page spread. On the left page is a brief statement of purpose, materials list, "cookbook" set of procedures to follow, statement of the expected result, and explanation of the science principle being demonstrated. Occasionally text from the left page continues on to the right page. Also on the right page are one or more line-art illustrations of the experiment setup and its stages.

Topics covered in this book are Earth in Space, Rocks and Minerals, Crustal Movement, Erosion, Atmosphere, Weather, and Oceans.

A few of the Erosion demonstrations follow the evolutionary view of geology (slow, gradual change formed major geological features) rather than the catastrophist and creation science views (mountains and other geological features were formed swiftly in times of catastrophe). Most of the book, however, covers currently observable phenomena.

Some of these demonstrations are *very* simple—using a peanut butter and jelly sandwich to demonstrate sedimentary layers, for example. Others, such as constructing a small dynamo with wire, iron nail, battery, cardboard box, and iron filings, require a little more work.

Overall, *Earth Science for Every Kid,* with its many fun and easy demonstrations and experiments, and its wide coverage of earth science topics and terminology, would make a wonderful companion to any earth science course—or an elementary earth science course by itself. *Mary Pride*

Does your kid want to be a marine biologist? Are you one of those Janice VanCleave fans who just can't resist her books? Then you might be interested in **Janice VanCleave's Oceans for Every Kid**, a fun introduction to oceanography.

While the book includes numerous experiments and demonstrations, this falls in the family of books that teach the subject matter. Each chapter starts with a "What You Need to Know" introduction to the chapter subject, "Let's Think It Through" questions and puzzles to solve using the information from the introduction, answers to the above, application exercises, a step-by-step activity (typically, a demonstration or modeling of facts taught in the chapter), line-art charts and illustrations, and solutions to the exercises. New scientific terminology is boldfaced and instantly defined, plus there's a glossary of all such terms, and an index.

So, what are you studying? The distribution of land and water around the earth. The four basic oceans. Techniques and technology of early ocean studies. Past and present oceanography tools. Features of the ocean floor. How scientists determine the depth of the ocean floor. Current. Waves. How waves change shorelines. Tides. Differences in ocean temperature. Water pressure. Why the ocean is salty. Problems and solutions of ocean pollution. How the oceans affect our weather. Icebergs. Ocean life and how it is "layered" according to depth. Ocean food web. How marine life moves. Whales. How some ocean creatures see. The sensory system of fish. Plus an annotated bibliography of more books on the subject.

NEW!
Janice VanCleave's Earth Science for Every Kid

Grades 3–6. $12.95.
John Wiley & Sons, 1 Wiley Drive, Somerset, NJ 08875. (800) 225-5945. (732) 469-4400. Fax: (800) 597-3299. Web: www.wiley.com.

IMPORTANT NOTE: loose iron filings are a health hazard. If you get them on your fingers and rub your eyes, they can embed in your eye. Once there, they can remain unnoticed until you have to have an MRI (magnetic resonance imaging) scan done someday. The scan will agitate them and perhaps blind you. Sadly, there was no safety note in the book on this topic, which is why I'm mentioning it here.

NEW!
Janice VanCleave's Oceans for Every Kid

Grades 3–6. $12.95.
John Wiley & Sons, 1 Wiley Drive, Somerset, NJ 08875. (800) 225-5945. (732) 469-4400. Fax: (800) 597-3299. Web: www.wiley.com.

Like most Janice VanCleave books, *Oceans for Every Kid* is so well organized that you learn something even while skimming it. I'm not all that interested in oceanography, but I found myself thinking, "Hmm. This looks interesting. I'd like to do that activity. Here's a new word I didn't know!" Reading this book is like a day at the beach! *Mary Pride*

Media Angels Creation Geology: A Study Guide to Fossils, Formations and the Flood is an excellent unit-study resource. Outlines, reading lists, vocabulary and spelling lists, math ideas, history, geography and field trips,and more are included in this 194-page oversized perfect-bound manual. Divided into easy-to-reference grade levels, each topic covered has creative and compelling ideas for in-depth study.

Suppose your sixth grader is studying geology, and you want to help make it real. Turn to the section called Geography and History Ideas. Here you will find field trip suggestions, map reading and plotting ideas, and some time-line assignments. Your high-schooler might take the task further, and write a biographical sketch of an early geologist, or do an in-depth study of plate tectonics. Math ideas for the young include grouping and measuring, while the older students will be graphing and plotting.

Over 300 activities are included. Many integrate geology with other curriculum areas, such as spelling, vocabulary, math, art, and music.

The assignment ideas are clear and easy to understand, and the extensive background information and bibliographies will help get you started. Still, there is some room left here for the older student to seek out reference materials on his own.

Units are included for grades K–3, 4–8, and 9–12. The high-school vocabulary is challenging (I even had to look up a word or two!). There are also reproducible science experiment sheets to help your student get the hang of writing scientifically. An optional Activity Pack includes ready-made crossword puzzles, games, activities, and experiments correlated with this book and the Media Angels Creation Science book. *Macbeth Derham*

A child's curiosity knows no bounds, especially when the subject is the complex and changing weather that forms the backdrop to our busy lives. **Weather Whys** is a colorful and cleverly illustrated book written to give children the answers they need to understand a bit more about the way our atmosphere works.

Covering weather variables like air pressure, sun, ultraviolet light, temperature, wind, fog, and seasons, each *Weather Whys* chapter begins with a question. For example, "Why do we need to know about the weather?" relates the variables of weather to the ways that we dress, the activities we plan for each day, the dangers we may face, and the fact that certain kinds of weather are vital to life. Thermometers, barometers, anemometers, and other tools of the meteorological trade are examined, as well as the way meteorologists use these tools to forecast the weather.

Some time is also spent on safety—preventing heat stroke, lightening strikes, and eye damage from improperly viewing a solar eclipse. "Stuff You Can Do" and "Fast Facts" are scattered through the pages to provide fuel for interesting weather discussions. "A Wonderful Wheel of Weather Words" is included as an interactive tool to help children memorize weather vocabulary. Turn the wheel to the new word, and the definition and an illustration appear in the next window! (Both sides of the wheel are printed for a total of 16 vocabulary words and definitions.)

Weather Whys would make a good basic introduction to weather for children in grades K–3. *Teresa May*

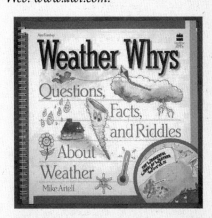

Space Science

Both **Exploring the Night Sky** and **Exploring the Sky by Day** are award-winning books. The former is an astronomy overview, complete with "big bang" references, while the latter is a meteorology guide. Like the other books in this series, both have great photography. The astronomy book also includes some drawings of landscapes on other planets, and some fanciful "extra-terrestrial" art work, as well as star charts, real photos and enhanced photos of the solar system. The weather book includes some very fine photos of atmospheric conditions: Tornadoes, water spouts, hurricanes, etc. *MacBeth Derham*

The Sun and Beyond: A Study of the Solar System, a unit study by **Helen Nelson**, begins with a lovely reminder that "the heavens declare the glory of God . . . night after night they display knowledge." Nelson also tackles the need to learn secular humanist thought while defending God's supremacy, preparing the teacher for the mostly-secular resources available in this study. Aside from the expected weeks devoted to pairs of planets and our moon, one chapter introduces great astronomers of history, and others cover comets and space exploration.

With the right source books, the astronomer study could be very faith-building, but with the wrong source books, it could be no better than what the local government school offers. *Cindy Marsch*

Janice VanCleave's Constellations for Every Kid does more than teach what constellation is where. You get a complete introduction to stellar cartography and many astronomical techniques. As with her other books, the evolutionary timeframe is used throughout and assumed to be correct.

Each chapter of *Constellations* starts with a "What You Need to Know" introduction to the chapter subject, "Let's Think It Through" questions and puzzles to solve using the information from the introduction, answers to the above, application exercises, a step-by-step activity (typically, a demonstration or modeling of facts taught in the chapter), line-art charts and illustrations, and solutions to the exercises. Three appendices are included: a star map of each seasons, a list of constellations with pronunciations, and a list of major stars with pronunciations and the constellations to which they belong.

I personally found the *Constellations* book to be overkill and somewhat confusing, due to the way the astronomical information was mixed in. H.A. Rey's book on the stars (available at your library) or Rod and Staff's will both get you up to speed much more quickly.

If you're using a Christian curriculum, **Janice VanCleave's Astronomy for Every Kid** might be a better bet. You get "101 Easy Experiments That Really Work," designed to illustrate the principles of astronomy you are already studying in your course. Each experiment or demonstration is laid out as a two-page spread. On the left page is a brief statement of purpose, materials list, "cookbook" set of procedures to follow, statement of the expected result, and explanation of the science principle being demonstrated. Occasionally text from the left page continues on to the right page. Also on the right page are one or more line-art illustrations of the experiment setup and its stages.

The *Astronomy* book is divided into seven sections: Planets (topics such as surface temperature and how light bends in the atmosphere), Space Movement (topics such as the effect of distance on the speed of planets and why planets don't fall into the sun), Sun (topics such as eclipses and the solar spectrum), Moon (topics such as how long it takes light from the moon to reach the earth), Stars (topics such as why some of them seem to move in a circle and how to figure out which star is closest), Space Instruments (topics such as how light travels through a telescope, how different types of telescopes work, and how mass can be measured in space), and Space and Space Travel (topics such as escape velocity and weightlessness). You'll pick up a lot of facts without having to sift through the differences between modern hypotheses and demonstrated scientific fact. *Mary Pride*

Its nose cone lights up! Its cargo bay doors open and close! It has a built-in display stand and card storage compartment in the back! It comes "batteries included" with 25 talking Space Cards (a set of 35 additional cards is available separately). It's the **LeapFrog Space Shuttle**, and it's designed to teach hundreds of facts (some factual, some evolutionary) about the solar system, stars, space exploration, astronomers, and more.

How it works: Place one of the Space Cards in place. Hidden sensors read punch holes in the bottom of the card, letting the gizmo know what the questions and answers are. The Space Shuttle will then verbally ask and answer questions, in a young male voice. You can choose one of three games: Fact-Finding Mission (the voice tells you facts about the object pictured in full-color photo on the card), Mission Control Space Quiz (you are asked questions about those facts), and Ultimate Space Challenge (random questions about any of the cards). Questions are true/false. You are told how many right you got out of every 5, 10 or 20 questions.

This is a lot of packaging for a relatively small amount of data. You can buy an Usborne, DK, or Millbrook book that will teach you lots more about space for a lot less. However, they won't have anywhere near the "fun factor" of this product, making it a great gift for a space-minded kid. *Mary Pride*

Media Angels Creation Astronomy: A Study Guide to the Constellations is a unit study you won't soon forget! In these 170 perfect-bound pages, you'll find

- a 25-page Teaching Outline with detailed background information about the histories and areas of conflict between creation astronomy and "Big Bang" astronomy
- separate Teaching Outlines for each grade level (K–3, 4–8, and 9–12), each with a reading list, a list of selected books of experiments and activities, a vocabulary/spelling list, language arts ideas, math reinforcement ideas, science activities and experiments, geography/history ideas, and art/music ideas
- resource lists galore: books, videos, software, Internet, space and science resources, astronomy science and government addresses
- short materials list of items you'll find useful doing this unit (wish it was in the *front* of the book!)
- field trip guide
- Gospel Message in the Stars constellation chart
- forms for noting your star discoveries and science experiments
- bibliography

Now, if you were a good boy or girl, and didn't skip over the list above, you're asking, "Whoa! 'Gospel Message in the Stars'? What's up with that?"

Here's what the authors have to say:

A study of the original 48 constellations is used in this study of Creation Astronomy. Later or modern constellation names are not included. Most Christians avoid studying the stars because of the association with the wickedness of astrology, but God created those stars and He designed them to speak and show knowledge of Him; we need to get excited about the things that His Creation can teach us.

Just look at the constellations! There, right in front of us is the Virgin, the Mother and Child, the Serpent, the King, a Crown, the serpent going after the crown, the Great Physician grasping the serpent, the serpent striking a man's heel, the dying sacrifice, and the living fish, which is the symbol of the Church. There is an altar, an arrow, a Cross, a stream of water symbolizing the Holy Spirit being poured out into the fish's mouth, and of course, the Lion returning. Jesus was called "The Lion of Judah."

NEW!
Millbrook Children's Space Atlas

Grades 5–12. $14.95.
The Millbrook Press, PO Box 335, 2 Old New Milford Rd., Brookfield, CT 06804. Orders: (800) 462-4703. extension 3034. Inquiries: (203) 740-2220. Fax: (203) 740-2223.

NEW!
Millbrook Future Files series

Grades 4–12. Each book, $22.50 hardcover.
The Millbrook Press, 2 Old New Milford Rd., Brookfield, CT 06804. Orders: (800) 462-4703. Inquiries: (203) 740-2220. Fax: (203) 740-2223.

Moonwalk videos

Grades K–12. $15 each (VHS only) plus $3.50 shipping.
Charlie Duke Enterprises, PO Box 310345, New Braunfels, TX 78131-0345. Email: cdmoon16@sat.net.

That's what makes this unit study so fascinating. You'll be learning the original Greek and Hebrew names of the stars, and the "original 48 constellations."

The descriptions of the constellations and stars used in this unit study come from an 1882 book titled *The Gospel in the Stars,* by Joseph A. Seiss. The background information, resources, and over 250 activities come from the authors. Together, they provide an excellent introduction to the scientific terminology, history, and concepts taught in a regular school, plus enough information to question the billions-and-billions-of-years party line. You'll look at the night sky a whole different way after using this unit. *Mary Pride*

The Children's Space Atlas, like other Millbrook Children's Atlases, is organized geographically. In this, the sections are Introduction, Solar System, Night Sky, Stars and Galaxies, and Exploring Space. Each section is made up of oversized double-page spreads, loaded with photos, diagrams, illustrations, charts, and text. You could easily use this atlas as the basis for a unit on astronomy; unlike other "reference" books, its 96 pages are designed to be *read*, not just referred to. *Mary Pride*

Today's science writing often ventures into speculations about future inventions and discoveries. **Millbrook's Future Files series**, which at present is just two books (*Cosmic Journeys: A Beginner's Guide to Space and Time Travel* and *Superhumans: A Beginner's Guide to Bionics*) introduces you to these brave new worlds. If you're unfamiliar with starwisps, event horizons, lightsails, cryogenics, cyborgs, fuzzy logic, virtual pop stars, and so forth, this book is an eye-opener. Illustrated with scenes from movies about most topics mentioned, along with gorgeous 3-D rendered illustrations of technology as it might exist someday, these books are just the sort of slick eye candy to appeal to the average techie kid. Employing a visual device that lets you see how likely—or unlikely—it is that we will ever see nanites or use a black hole for time travel, this series helps you understand modern science fiction—and unscramble it from modern science facts. *Mary Pride*

Now the Apollo flight is on video, starring Charlie Duke, one of the crew members on that historic space mission. So what, you say? Well, what we have here is an educational space video. Charlie shows how an astronaut gets into his space suit, how he eats (with footage from the flight of astronauts chasing grapes around the capsule), and even explains what every kid wants to know, how they went to the bathroom when there were no bathrooms on the moon. He also shares a lot of behind-the-scenes details of things that went wrong and that *almost* went wrong. Plus you get some fantastic views of the flight itself and the moonwalk.

Since going to the moon, Charlie has become a Christian. That's why Charlie Duke Enterprises has *two* videos available. **Walk on the Moon, Walk with the Son** includes his Christian testimony. **Charlie Duke, Moonwalker** lacks the testimony but in consequence spends more time covering an astronaut's work. We enjoyed them both.

The whole story is also available in book form. Entitled (what else?) *Moonwalker,* it is available from Charlie Duke for $15. *Mary Pride*

CHAPTER 35

Engineering

I f you'd like to teach the world to sing, call a musician. If you'd like to build a road, or design a computer, or invent a new kind of packaging, or put up a building that won't fall down, call an engineer.

Engineering is where the rubber *really* meets the road. The reason tires last for 40,000 miles and up these days, as opposed to the couple of hundred miles (at most) that the first tires were good for, is because generations of engineers have been busy redesigning tires . . . *and* the roads they roll on.

This takes a special kind of mind. A can-do mind. A "how does it work?" mind. A mind that likes to solve problems. A mind that is *not* comfortable with the idea that everything is changing all the time. (Engineers know about things like gravity and friction that are always with us.) A mind that is obsessed with making things that work better and better.

If you are beginning to sense that engineers aren't the touchy-feely type, give yourself two points. If you are beginning to fear that your child may grow up to become one, give yourself four points. If you feel like saying, "Proof: trivial" and skipping to the next section, you *are* an engineer.

Some Things You Need to Know About Engineers

Engineers like to think they are smarter than the rest of us.

That's because they are. (Or maybe I just think so because both of my degrees are from an engineering school!)

Engineers are often considered socially inept.

That is because, as *Dilbert* cartoonist Scott Adams has pointed out, engineers have different social goals than the rest of us. Much of what passes for conversation seems to engineers like a total waste of time, not directed to solving any problem anywhere. Engineers feel that, if you can't be solving problems, you should be impressing people with how much more likely to solve problems you are than they are. Non-engineers feel like *this* is a total waste of time. So conversation lags.

Sad but true: most people would rather have you pat their shoulder than solve their problems. This is why few engineers are successful politicians. And why I wish more politicians were engineers!

If you have a future engineer at your house, be glad! Your way is paved before you. The kid *wants* to study. Even college won't be a big problem, because engineering courses are about as far from politically correct as you can get. There's no chance the Supreme Court will repeal Newton's Laws of

How to Spot a Future Engineer

Here are some ways to spot a future engineer:

- **Lego obsession.** Actually builds things with them. Never the things pictured in the gaily illustrated instructions.
- **Takes things apart a lot.** How this differs from simple vandalism: the future engineer attempts to put the things back together again.
- **Fascinated with tools.** Especially those he is not supposed to touch.
- **Prefers to play alone.** Exception: cut-throat strategy games.
- **Needs to be peeled away from the computer** for little things, like eating and sleeping.

Motion anytime soon. And you have years and years to teach him or her the social skills, if desired. In the meantime, you can give the little nipper a head start with the nifty hands-on goodies below.

Electricity

The neatest introduction to the study of electrical wiring and currents that I've seen, Ampersand's **AC/DC Electric Circuit Game** is played with a deck of special cards. Cards depict energy sources, wires, switches, energy users, and fuses. The object of the game is to construct workable circuits. Players may get "shocked" or "shorted," so watch out! You can't help but learn the rudiments of electricity playing *AC/DC*. I wish someone had given me this game before I went to engineering school (but then, it probably hadn't been invented way back then!). *Mary Pride*

For those unfamiliar with the concept, unit studies involve a single topic that is analyzed and studied from various angles and viewpoints, often incorporating other academic subjects into the area being studied. For example, a unit study on medieval art may deal with its influence on the writing of that period. Most unit studies require loads of time and research. **Amanda Bennett** has come to your rescue and saved you precious time with her unit studies.

One of her most recent unit studies is **Electricity**. This wonderful non-consumable paperback is just over 100 pages. It may be short, but the ideas and information presented are tremendous! Mrs. Bennett incorporates several items into her books: an outline of the topic, spelling and vocabulary lists, reading lists, reference lists, suggested software, games, and videos lists, an activities and field trip list, and for those with Internet access, an Internet resources list. The outline itself is fairly simple, but is detailed enough to be a stand-alone lesson. The section on scientists and inventors has more information in the outline than some science textbooks ever mention on some of these wonderful people.

There is so much information and so many ideas are presented in *Electricity* that you could spend months studying and still have more to cover. Anyone wanting to learn about electricity can do so with this guide. If you have no background knowledge, you have an excellent framework to aid your journey and if you are experienced in unit studies, you are presented with more ways for expanding your knowledge of the subject. This book rates a definite thumbs-up! *Barbara Buchanan*

Inside Out

If you like David Macaulay's books (*Pyramid*, *Castle*, etc.), you'll love Peter Bedrick Books' **What's Inside series**. Bright, colorful cross-sections make the construction or anatomy of each book's subject perfectly clear. The *What's Inside Buildings?* book, for example, presents basic building types (e.g., skyscrapers, tunnels), famous historical buildings such as the pyramids and the

AC/DC game

Grades 3–12. $9.95 plus shipping. *Ampersand Press, 750 Lake Street, Port Townsend, WA 98368. (800) 624-4263. (360) 379-5187. Fax: (360) 379-0324. Email: erh@olympus.net. Web: www.ampersandpress.com.*

NEW!
Electricity (An Amanda Bennett Unit Study)

Grades 4–8. $13.99 plus shipping. *Holly Hall Publications, Inc., 255 S. Bridge St., Elkton, MD 21921. Orders: (800) 211-0719. Inquiries: (410) 392-5554. Fax: (410) 392-0354.*

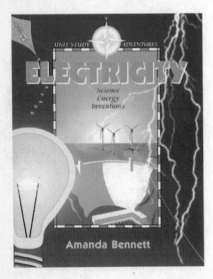

NEW!
Bedrick What's Inside series

Grades 3–8. $17.95 (hardcover) each plus shipping. *Peter Bedrick Books, c/o NTC Contemporary Publishing, 4255 W. Touhy, Lincolnwood, IL 60646. (800) 323-4900. Fax: (800) 998-3103. Email: ntcpub@tribune.com. Web: www.contemporarybooks.com.*

Colossus of Rhodes, building basics (arches, columns, vaults, etc.), but takes you through all the parts of building construction, from footings and foundations to utilities such as electricity and heating, illustrated with famous examples. Well-written accompanying text adds interesting facts and shows you what to look for in the spectacular full-color illustrations.

The series so far includes

- *What's Inside Airplanes?*
- *What's Inside Buildings?*
- *What's Inside Everyday Things?*
- *What's Inside Plants?* (a particularly excellent book that presents plant and cellular biology better than any textbook I've seen)
- *What's Inside the Human Body?* (just out)

The entire series is highly recommended. *Mary Pride*

A book to make Dilbert scream with joy. David Macaulay, that British-born fellow who insists on giving us the "inside view" of such items as pyramids and cathedrals, gives us a *deep* look at engineering in **The New Way Things Work**. Assisted by a crew of wooly mammoths (don't ask) he moves quickly from motions and forces to inclined planes and wedges (how to use them for catching a mammoth, for making locks and keys, or in a can opener, plow, or zipper) . . . and that's just the first 22 pages of this massive (dare I say "mammoth"?) 384-page book.

Not to keep you in suspense any longer, this popular book's main parts cover the mechanics of movement, harnessing the elements (from water power to nukes—"flower power" wasn't mentioned), working with waves (light, sound, electromagnetic, x-ray, etc.), electricity and automation, and machines. You'll encounter more "everyday objects" and "high-tech objects" than you can shake a tusk at, each explained and illuminated with wild and wooly text and Macaulay's trademark large cross-hatched drawings, some colored, some not.

Any kid who studies and understands this book has already received half of an engineering-school education. *Mary Pride*

For younger children who wonder how things work, **Millbrook Cutaway Books** have the answers. With smaller pages, easier-to-read "Roman" text, as opposed to the "italic" text in the Fantastic Cutaways series reviewed below, and simpler illustrations, this series includes great "peel-back" layered artwork that exposes the inner workings of high-

interest vehicles. Books in this series: *Racing Cars, Space Vehicles, Trucks,* and *Firefighters.* Fun! *Mary Pride*

Millbrook Fantastic Cutaway Books

Grades 2–8. Each book, $9.95.
The Millbrook Press, PO Box 335, 2 Old New Milford Rd., Brookfield, CT 06804. Orders: (800) 462-4703. extension 3034. Inquiries: (203) 740-2220. Fax: (203) 740-2223.

Another **Millbrook** series originally published by Aladdin Press in England, the **Fantastic Cutaway Books** have the terrific art and photographs and gripping text I've come to expect from the folks at Aladdin. Don't be misled by the series title; though each book does include "cutaway" full-color illustrations of the kinds of machines kids love to read about, you'll also find many photographs of the real machines and illustrations of the machines in action. The lush art (is it digital or airbrushed? hard to tell) makes the machines look like works of art themselves. With this series, both boys and girls will learn a lot of basic engineering principles without even trying. So far, the series includes *Flight, Spacecraft, Giant Machines, Speed, Giant Buildings,* and *Rescue.* Bonus: each book comes with a detachable fold-out poster showing many of the machines (or buildings) in the book, plus text. *Mary Pride*

Usborne Cutaways series

Grades 5–12. $7.95 each plus shipping.
EDC Publishing, Division of Educational Development Corporation, 10302 East 55th Place, Tulsa, OK 74146. (800) 475-4522. Fax: (800) 747-4509. Web: www.edcpub.com.

The **Cutaways** series are amazingly detailed books, full of factual information. In the center of each double-page spread, there is a lushly airbrushed picture, showing all the important parts of whatever vehicle is being discussed. Around the picture, there are detailed facts and descriptions of each part. Give these to the aspiring engineer in your family.

Books in this series so far are: *Cutaway Planes, Cutaway Cars, Cutaway Boats. Sarah Pride*

Usborne Technology series

Grades 2–12. Young Machines series: Diggers and Cranes, Tractors, Racing Cars, Planes & Helicopters, and Trucks, $6.95 each. Beginner's Knowledge series: Railways & Trains, Castles, Pyramids, & Palaces, and Ships, Sailors, & the Sea, $8.95 each (paperback). How Machines Work, $8.95. Explainers series: How Things are Built, and How Things are Made, $4.50 each. Introduction series: Robotics and Lasers, $7.95 each (paperback) or $15.95 (library-bound). Shipping extra.
EDC Publishing, Division of Educational Development Corporation, 10302 East 55th Place, Tulsa, OK 74146. (800) 475-4522. Fax: (800) 747-4509. Web: www.edcpub.com.

Let's start with the little kids. The **Young Machines series** looks extremely promising. Each book explains how a class of large vehicles works (with large, bright pictures), what jobs they do, and even a history of some of the machines. Parts are named, and you get to see many different types of that machine. A visual index in the back of each book has smaller pictures and facts about each individual machine.

On to the **Beginner's Knowledge series**. This, too, is brand-new. Find out how trains, tracks, and railways were invented and improved through time. See how castles, pyramids, and palaces were built. And what about those sailing boats, from Egyptian reed boats and clipper ships to ocean liners? A visual time line in the back of each book shows how each artifact developed over time. (A neat feature in the *Castles* book: an illustration showing many famous buildings in the same picture, so you can see their relative sizes.)

How Things Work explains . . . how things work. Basic physics for the preteen set from the **Simple Science series**.

From the **Explainers series**, *How Things are Built* and *How Things are Made* take a different tack. *How Things Work* is more scientific; the Explainers books get into the nitty-gritty of engineering, construction, and assembly lines. Lots of terrific illustrations make it all clear.

In theory, the **Introduction series** is for teens and adults. In real life, I've found our six-year-old browsing these books. (She started reading when she was four.) Any seven- or eight-year-old who is a good reader should find these how-things-work books fascinating. They go into greater detail than the Explainers series, and cover more futuristic technology. *Mary Pride*

I don't know about you but I enjoy good artwork when I'm learning about something new. In the **Wonders of the World** books, good art is mixed with a few photographs and together they make the story of the wonder come alive. Each of the books about an interesting man-made structure has an easy-to-read story format about the designers and builders. *The Roman Colosseum* and *The Great Wall* have a map and a time-line in back. The other two books, *The Brooklyn Bridge* and *The Panama Canal* have a fact sheet. Each book describes the purpose of the Wonder: why it was built, by whom, what it was used for, why it was so wondrous. *The Roman Colosseum*, while mentioning the gladiators and the lions, does not mention the persecuted Christians. Even so, these books would make a welcome addition to your curriculum. *Barb Meade*

Construction Systems

These **Baufix** sets are really neat. It's a construction kit for kids ages three through 10, with large, chunky pieces cleverly designed to introduce young kids to simple mechanical and technical skills.

The **Two-Student Baufix set** includes an assortment of 34 wooden bolts of different lengths, all color-coded; six wooden block nuts; a collection of three-hole, four-hole, five-hole, and seven-hole connecting bars; four wheels with tires you can stretch over them; several sizes of base plates; nine wooden diamond nuts; spacers and washers galore; and a wooden wrench. The included wordless manual has visual instructions for nine projects, but of course your children can make hundreds of models with these open-ended materials.

The **Baufix Cog Wheels and Propulsion Parts set** comes with two large (3.75") gears and six small (1.25") gears, along with two hooks, cranks, lots of spacers, and a goodish number of shafts and locknuts. Unhappily, you can't make any of the projects in the included wordless manual, because they all require a wooden baseplate or three-hole threaded blocks, neither of which are included in either Baufix set from Cuisenaire Company.

Even little kids can handle the Baufix materials, screwing bolts into block nuts and sliding spacers on bolts. My son built the first project—a rather complicated vehicle—on his fourth birthday!

Baufix is a great toy that beats Duplos, Erector sets, and Lincoln Logs. Now what we need for full educational value are (1) pulleys and (2) a separate project manual or set of task cards along the lines of the LEGO Dacta Technic materials. Even without these goodies, Baufix is a lot of creative fun. With them, it would be a deserving candidate for Educational Product of the Year. *Mary Pride*

Capsela kits are a system of motors and gears housed in see-through capsules with an assortment of moving accessories. You can easily snap together the components to create all sorts of vehicles, devices, and machines: a racing car whose speed you can gear up or down, a vacuum that cleans, a fireboat that sprays water, even a computerized remote control robot with a 96-command memory, and many more that really work. The possibilities are limitless as all sets are totally interchangeable.

NEW!
Wonders of the World Books

Grades 1–8. The Great Wall, $18.95. The Brooklyn Bridge, The Roman Colosseum, The Panama Canal, $19.95 each. Shipping extra. *Mikaya Press, Inc., 12 Bedford Street, New York, NY 10014. (212) 647-1831. Fax: (212) 727-0236. Email: waldman@mikaya.com. Web: www.mikaya.com.*

Baufix sets

Grades preK–4: two-student Baufix set, $30.95; six-student Baufix set, $89.50. Grades 1–4: Baufix Cog Wheels and Propulsion Parts set, $17.95. Wood Base Plates, discontinued. Shipping extra. *Cuisenaire Company of America, PO Box 5026, White Plains, NY 10602-5026. (800) 237-3142. or (914) 328-5487. Fax: (800) 551-7637. Email: info@awl.com. Web: www.cuisenaire.com.*

Capsela Kits

Grades 1–adult. Introductory 175, $15.99. Starter 200 (makes 10 projects and models), $21.99. Explorer 250 (20 projects and models), $28.99. Intermediate 400 (22 projects and models), $34.99. Inventor 450

(30 projects and models), $49.99. Advanced 500 (39 projects and models), $46.99. Deluxe 700 (56 projects and models), $69.99. Expert 1000 (100 projects and models), $84.99. Capsela Scientific course: set of Capsela Scientific components, $120; Capsela Scientific manual, $30; 3-lesson sampler workshop, $30; hand generator kit with lamp, $20; storage bag, $12. *Playtech. (212) 242-3020. Fax: (212) 242-3087. They do not sell mail order.*

Dr. Drew's Blocks

All ages (really!). 72 blocks with canvas bag, $47.95. 108 blocks with wood tray, $77.95. 288 blocks with cardboard box, $129.95. 180 blocks with wood tray, $97.95. Shipping extra. *Dr. Drew's Toys, Inc., PO Box 510501, Melbourne Beach, FL 32951. (407) 984-1018. Fax: (407) 984-9090. Email: dr-drew@iu.net.*

Each set also includes the *See How It Works* 32-page science booklet that explains how and why things work. This is an abridged version of the Capsela Scientific curriculum guide.

For classroom teachers, there's Capsela Scientific, a hands-on science curriculum with a 25-lesson manual written by Dr. Clifford Swartz. The kit includes teacher overviews, notes, and student hand-out masters, along with the Capsela parts to build over 110 high-interest working models. For example, students build a propeller boat to demonstrate buoyancy; a car demonstrates friction, traction, motion, and movement; a blinkmobile demonstrates blinking light behavior; and so on. Lessons also cover the concepts of electricity, Newton's Third Law, work, force, energy, and more.

Capsela is just buckets of fun for kids of all ages—even those with moustaches and beards! *Mary Pride*

Dr. Drew's Blocks are made out of hardwood, not your typical soft pine. This means they clack together in a satisfying fashion and they don't immediately develop a leprosy of dings and dents like common blocks. Dr. Drew's blocks are also slim and rectangular (3 x 2 x ½"), so babies can grasp them easily and adults can build terrific constructions (see the accompanying photo). The blocks come in a natural, splinter-free finish that go with any decor except Recent Plastic. They are truly a "discovery" toy, limited only by your imagination and the size of the set you purchase. The whole kit and caboodle comes with a durable and attractive canvas bag, so you have someplace to put them (most other sets come with a cardboard box that immediately generates into a ragged eyesore). Now you know why Dr. Drew's Blocks received a "Toy of the Year" award from the Parents Choice Foundation.

Oh yes: the inventor, Walter F. Drew, is a for-real Ph.D. and early childhood educator. He would say that the simplicity and uniformity of his blocks make it easy for children to discover number relationships and basic geometric patterns and to develop their creativity through construction and free play. He would also point out that all ages can play with the blocks together. I will just say that these blocks are *fun!*

We've owned a variety of these sets, from the biggest to the smallest, in cardboard boxes, bags, and wooden trays. My advice is to go for their bestseller, the set of 108 in the wood tray. The wood tray makes it much easier and neater to pack away, as well as teaching all sorts of basic sorting and arranging skills, and you get enough in the set to build some really great constructions. A family heirloom you can pass on to your grandkids! *Mary Pride*

NEW!
FischerTechnic Pneumatic Kit

Grades 5–12. $105 plus shipping. *Timberdoodle Company, 1510 E. Spencer Lake Rd., Shelton, WA 98584. (360) 426-0672. Fax: (800) 478-0672. Email: mailbag@timberdoodle.com. Web: www.timberdoodle.com.*

If your kids are into building complex working machines, then the **FischerTechnic Pneumatic kit** is for you! It uses the basic FischerTechnic building materials, blocks with slots and/or pegs on them that attach together fairly easily. However, unlike most FischerTechnic kits, the pneumatic set also has pneumatic pistons, air-flow switches, an air compressor, and a large length of pneumatic tubing. The kit has instructions for building six different machines ranging from bull-dozers to cranes. And due to the FischerTechnic building materials, any machines you make are not going to fall apart. The set includes over 500 pieces, and the pneumatics have no leaks, which is quite amazing in a plastic construction kit. You place a machine in a certain position and close the pneumatic air switch and when you come back tomorrow it will still be exactly the way you left it. *Joseph Pride*

Seymour Papert, inventor of the LOGO computer language, says his interest in math started with a fascination for gears. Here is a great product for budding mathematicians and mechanical engineers, or any child or adult who'd like to improve their spatial skills while having fun. **Gears! Gears! Gears!** sets are collections of brightly colored, chunky plastic gears made to mesh with one another and turn on axles attached to interlocking bases. The bases are sized so that gears on one base will mesh with gears on the next one. Pile the gears up and drive them from the gears on the base. If you join two towers together, you can make bridges of gears. Add pulleys to increase the complexity of your creations. Attach springs and propellers for more fun action.

The basic **Activity Set** contains 95 pieces, including small gears with several bases capable of holding four gears apiece. The Activity Set also includes pieces needed to make towers and bridges. You can add to this with more of the same with a **Gears Too! Add-On Set** containing 64 more pieces, or start with a **Super Set** of 150 pieces.

The new accessory sets add more options—and more fun! The **Whirligigs** set contains three different sizes of gears with colorful decals on them and bases that fit them, plus a pinwheel, a propeller, and a spring. The spring can be used to attach two gears either in a straight line, or at an angle so that one gear will drive the other. The **Pulleys Plus** set contains three different sizes gears and bases with pulleys that attach to the gears. This set gives kids the chance to see how pulleys work and to contrast that with the operation of gears. It also comes with a worm gear, which can easily be made to work as a shaft joining two gears, and may with a little ingenuity be made to work as a worm gear and drive one of the normal gears. The **Round-About** set contains a large spin wheel with L connectors and gears that attach to the large wheel. Finally, the **Gizmos** accessory set has decorative gears of three different sizes, plus one rack-and-pinion gear, two springs, one crank, one airplane-style propeller, and lots of bases and joining pieces.

If you'd like to start with someone else's illustrated step-by-step instructions, get the *Building Activity Book*. You'll need an Activity Set or Super Set in order to follow its instructions, since all the wordless instructions in this spiral-bound book require four-gear bases. Although it's only 13 pages long, this book shows you how to build just about every basic type of gear configuration: snakes, towers, bridges, flags, carnival, stacks, factory, and more.

If you can afford it, the Super Set is the best deal. Among other things, it comes in a handy and sturdy plastic storage bucket. Of the accessory sets, the one I'd go for first for educational value is the Pulleys Plus set. A truly wonderful gift. *Bill Pride*

LEGO DACTA

Grades 2–12. TECHNIC 1, $67.
Teacher's guide, $13.25 each.
Shipping extra.
*LEGO Dacta, PO Box 1707,
Pittsburgh, KS 66762. (800) 362-4308.
Fax: (888) 534-6784.
Email: legohelp@pitsco-legodacta.com.
Web: www.pitsco-legodacta.com.*

I love 'em, I love 'em, I love 'em, I love 'em. After years of wishing for a systematic hands-on engineering curriculum, my wish has been granted. The **TECHNIC** kits from **LEGO Dacta** are everything I wished for, and more!

First of all, the kits are beautiful. Pieces are constructed of colorful, sturdy plastic and beautifully engineered. Second, the brilliant designers of this program (God bless 'em!) have put the pieces together in a compartmentalized molded-plastic storage case. This means *no* little TECHNIC pieces crunching underfoot or getting eaten by the vacuum cleaner. In fact, the first exercise in each kit is taking the pieces out of the little plastic bags and learning to put them away neatly in their proper places! Third, the 20 step-by-step Activity Cards included in each kit are *wonderful*. Full-color illustrations show real-life examples of the principles you are learning right along with drawings of the models you are constructing. The accompanying teacher's guide to each kit explains the assignments, gives in-depth instruction in the engineering principles, and provides numerous follow-up activities. *You need the teacher's guide for each kit,* since there are no words on the cards, just illustrations of the project steps.

Here's how it works. You open the kit. You take out an activity card. You do the activities on the card. After you've finished one card, move on to the next. Can it get any simpler than this? Not only that, individual activities can be completed within 20 minutes!

TECHNIC 1, the "Simple Machines" set for children ages 7 and up, starts with simple frames and how to make frames rigid. Further activities teach principles of levers, moving objects by sliding and rolling, gears, rotation, transference of energy from one form to another, ways of lifting, steering, and wind and water power. No complicated terminology—you *do* things and then discuss them in everyday language. Each model can be built within 20 minutes using some of the 179 pieces!

Until fischertechnik decides to produce simple, sequential activities *in English* and inexpensive compartmentalized boxes for its kit pieces, these new LEGO DACTA kits will remain, in my opinion, the best engineering education buy. *Mary Pride*

OWI's line of **MOVIT** kits is a series of computerized, logic-controlled battery robot kits designed to teach the basic principles of robotic sensing and locomotion. Each comes with pre-assembled PC boards, hardware, and mechanical drive systems. Parts come in little numbered plastic bags. Instructions refer to the numbers on the bag, so you can always tell what part they are talking about. You only need basic hand tools to put these little critters together, and most little human critters over the age of ten are supposed to be able to handle the job.

Each robot uses a different type of movement or has a different sensor. "Soccer Robot," for example, has six insect-like legs, two-speed movement, and a control box. He can run or walk forward or backwards, or even turn in circles. You can program him, or use the wired control to make him play slow-mo soccer, etc. "Hyper Peppy," a kit we put together as a family project, is lots of fun to run around the room. When its sound sensor comes into contact with a wall or other obstacle or hears a loud noise, such as a hand clap, it automatically reverses direction for a preset time and then zooms off on a new course to the left of its first one. "Line Tracker" follows a black line drawn on white paper, using a photo-interrupter "eye." "Robotic Arm" can be programmed to perform simple tasks, using the attached three-button input device. These are just a few of the available kits, with more coming out all the time. *Mary Pride*

You've seen construction kits with interchangeable, interlocking pieces before—but not like this. The award-winning **Robotix Construction System** allows kids to build, power, and control intergalactic space vehicles and motorized robotic creatures. These kits are a great way for kids to learn principles of robotic engineering . . . as well as eye-popping gifts for kids of any age (such as you, the homeschool parent).

Least expensive are the **non-motorized sets**. The Stealth Explorers and Terrestrial Construction Unit each come with instructions for building three different machines. To add a motor and controller, purchase the Action Pack.

Next are the **single-motor sets**.

The impressive Vox Centurion

Each comes with either an Action Pack or a Wireless Turbo Chassis and Controller. Sets include the Galactisaurs and Remote Speeders. Remote Speeders 2.0 comes with double the parts and two Wireless Chassis and Controllers. With this you can build three different speeders in two color combinations—and race them!

With **three motors**, Galactisaurus Rex, when connected to the included Wireless Action Controller, has genuine foot-stomping ability, plus you can use his over 250 pieces to build Robo-Dragon (he flaps his wings!) and other robots of your own design.

At the **four motor** level are our friend "2K-9" the Robo-Dog—over 150 pieces

Galactisaurus Rex

The Stealth Explorer

The Terrestrial Construction Unit

2K-9, the Robo Dog. This unit resembles the previous version, but it now sports colored pieces

Remote Speeder

come with this puppy—and the towering Vox Centurion (pictured on the previous page). Over three and a half feet tall, with over 425 parts, the Vox Centurion is the "top of the line" in more ways than one.

All these models listed above are the new Fall 1999 lineup. We reviewed the previous year's models, as the newer ones were not available at press time.

Putting together the Robot Commander (an earlier model that has now been replaced by the Vox Centurion), we found that it came with a five-switch control console. You attach a line from a motor into the plug next to a switch, then rock the switch "on" or "off" to control that motor. This is pretty simple for even a young kid to understand. By installing the motors in various places, you can make the robot turn his head, grip with his hand, move his arm, open and close his mouth, move his face shield up and down, light up his eyes, and so forth. By installing several motors in one arm, you could make the robot raise his arm, bend his elbow, grasp an object . . . or do all of these at once!

Very cool are the materials that came in the Robot Commander kit. The sheet of colored decals. The Space Scout action figure. The scissor claw. The light unit. The wordless, illustrated step-by-step instructions for building the robot one section at a time, with introductory comments in about a zillion different languages. (Fishertechnik fans are familiar with this sort of instruction guide.) Not quite so cool is the lack of a permanent storage solution for the kit parts. Though the kit itself comes in a nifty cardboard suitcase, the parts are packaged in two layers of corrugated cardboard compartments. It's doubtful you'll ever get them back in their original spots, even if you have the foresight to write down exactly what came from where as you take it out of the suitcase the first time. I suggest ziploc bags for the smaller pieces as a partial solution.

Any of the Robotix kits makes a wonderful present for a hands-on type kid. The larger kits are also fun to work on as a family, like we did. *Mary Pride*

CHAPTER 36

Science Experiments & Activities

Science experiments come in three flavors:

- **Step-by-Step Recipes.** A pinch of this and a dash of that. Apply some heat or add an ice cube. Stir, shake, or add electricity. You follow the instructions to create a predetermined result.
- **Bug Eyes.** You look and make observations, but do little or nothing to affect what you're looking at. Microscope and telescope work come under this heading.
- **Twilight Zone.** You look into . . . the future. You predict what will happen next, based on the change you are about to make to your mixture, circuit, aquarium, or whatever.

Each of these has its value. Following a recipe is the quickest and probably safest way to get used to new equipment. Bugging your eyes out at a series of slides is the only way to step into the world of microscopy. Setting up a system and then throwing something into the works is more valuable educationally if you have already thought about what is likely to happen as a result of what you did.

Builders, Not Destroyers

The only type of scientific experiment I would like to discourage is the **Destruction Experiment**. In its various forms, this involves wrecking or killing something just to see what will happen. For example, the Dying Plant Experiment. To do it, you take two or more healthy plants. You treat one nicely, giving it plant food, water, and sunlight. You torture the other one by depriving it of light, water, and/or food. Then you compare them. Oh, surprise! The mistreated plant is withered and dying.

Similar to this, in my mind, is killing frogs and fetal pigs for the sole purpose of dissecting them later. It's one thing to dissect a byproduct of the food processing industry, such as a (oh, yukky) cow's eyeball. That cow

> The difference between "Activities" and "Experiments" is that activities *demonstrate or model* science facts, while experiments *test* science facts directly. Experiments are what scientists do; activities are a teaching device to help you remember your science lessons. Both have their place in the homeschool.

was *gone,* whether you salvaged the eyeball or not. But killing frogs and pigs and plants just so we can see how they look when they are dead seems to me to teach unintentional lessons in callousness.

In contrast, asking kids to raise the biggest, healthiest plants (or frogs, or pigs) possible provides them with just as much scope for experimentation, but also feeds their natural, kindly impulses. As my husband Bill is fond of saying, "Let's learn to be builders, not destroyers."

Getting Started & How Tos

My First Science Notebook and **My Science Notebook 2** are both elementary-level science aids. The notebooks can be used to start young scientists using science skills, e.g., observation, measurement, record keeping, etc. Drawing and measuring lead to graphing and mapping. Experiments and notes are kept together in the notebooks. *MacBeth Derham*

Project-Oriented Science is designed to help you plan science projects appropriate for your children. It has two parts: a planning section and a science skills section. The first section leads a teacher through the steps of creating a plan for a science course centered around a few good experiments. It helps you use any text book more efficiently by understanding how to fit the experiments into the book's plan. The author, Kathleen Julicher, sets it up simply using a seven-step system. She shows how to integrate skills, principals, topics, and projects into the plan. She includes planning sheets for the year, month, or whatever time period you need.

The second section consists of reproducible skillsheets to be used in building a science notebook. *MacBeth Derham*

Now, this is a really charming set of science education books! The **Science Spiders series** combines experiments and thinking skills, via charming plots about a family of science-minded spiders. Mom is a scientist. Kids Namila, Fets, and Pro learn science facts and experimental procedures by trying to solve science questions arising out of their home and school life. Each 32-page book is fully illustrated in color, and an equally fun read for kids and adults. Activities and experiments based on the story line are included at the back of each book. Best of all, in the story itself, experiments don't always go as planned, and the family interactions are genuine (e.g., kids having sword fights with the spaghetti sticks they are supposed to be using for the experiment). Learning how to deal with mistakes and unexpected results is a skill *never* taught in science class, yet needed every day in the world of real science.

In *Broken Bones,* the family learns about x-rays, exothermic reactions, and forces, while trying to figure out why Namila keeps breaking her arm when she falls down. In *First Science Fair,* second-grader Pro makes cupcakes with different missing ingredients for his first science fair contest. A fine introduction to science fairs *and* the scientific method! In *Surprise*

NEW!
My First Science Notebook
My Science Notebook 2
Grades 1–6. $9.95 each plus shipping.
Castle Heights Press, Inc., 2578 Alexander Farms Dr., Marietta, GA 30064. (800) 763-7148.
Web: www.flash.net/~wx3o/chp.

NEW!
Project-Oriented Science: A Teacher's Guide
Parents. $14.95 plus shipping.
Castle Heights Press, Inc., 2578 Alexander Farms Dr., Marietta, GA 30064. (800) 763-7148.
Fax/Phone: (770) 218-7998.
Email: julicher@aol.com.
Web: www.flash.net/~wx3o/chp.

NEW!
The Science Spiders series
Grades 1–6. $5.95 each; buy 5, get 1 free. Shipping extra.
Ranch Works, PO Box 23565, Columbia, SC 29224-3565. (803) 736-9797. Fax: (803) 736-5362.
Email: ranchworks@sciencespiders.com.
Web: www.sciencespiders.com.

Explosions, Mom is invited to demonstrate science principles for Namila's class. Her experiments on how chemicals react have some unexpected results. In *Secret Tricks,* Mom surprises Namila's class with demonstrations of how air pressure works. In *What Can I Do?,* bored preschooler Fets learns how to test foods for acid and base (it's hours of fun!). Finally, in *The Experience,* Fets learns some color science by doing "experiences" (her word for *experiments*). A good book for teaching us adults how to handle a mess-making little scientist!

I did wonder why Dad is never present, but then I remembered, this is a *spider* family . . .

I recommend this entire series, and believe you will like it, too. *Mary Pride*

Science Fairs

All About Science Fairs is the best workbook I have seen for actually getting home-taught kids rolling with a science fair project. The book was written for school classes, not homeschools, and is full of busywork. So what makes it so good?

- The bound-in comic book, in which a goofy alien explains to the earth kids what science fairs are all about and how to design a project. Simple, memorable explanations.
- The Science Project Checklist. Follow the steps for success!
- The list of 120 science project ideas—divided into three ability levels.
- The teacher's guide in the front, which goes through the whole project development process step by step. The guide also neatly explains how to use graphs, data charts, and so on effectively in your science project.

The worksheets, designed to provide practice in scientific procedures, are not the high point of this book. No need to actually fill them out—just read 'em and you'll get the idea. *Mary Pride*

"Where can you find lots of interesting ideas? How do you begin a project? How can you create an eye-catching display? What can you do to impress the judges?" These are among the practical questions answered in **Janice VanCleave's Guide to the Best Science Fair Projects**, an oversized 160-page hardcover.

The first nine chapters explain the scientific method, how to select a topic, categories in which you can enter your project (a brief descriptive list of the sciences and their sub-disciplines), how to do primary and secondary research, going step by step through a sample project, how to create a project report, do's and don'ts for your project display, how to present yourself and your project, and how you will be judged.

The remainder of the book is 50 science fair project ideas in the areas of astronomy (two projects), biology (16 projects), earth science (16 projects), engineering (two projects), physical science (12 projects), and mathematics (two projects). Each project takes up a two-page spread in the book, and follows the same format as those in Janice VanCleave's Spectacular Science Projects series.

There is also an appendix of science project and experiment books, divided by category, which oddly doesn't include any Jane Hoffman (the Backyard Scientist) books; an appendix of reference books; an appendix of scientific suppliers; a glossary; and an index. Recommended. *Mary Pride*

NEW!
KidSource: Science Fair Handbook

Grades 3–6. $9.95 plus shipping. *NTC Publishing. 4255 West Touhy Ave, Lincolnwood, IL 60646. (800) 323-4900 x 147. Fax: (800) 998-3103. Email: ntcpub@tribune.com. Web: www.ntc-school.com.*

NEW!
Media Angels Science Fair Project Handbook

Grades K–12. $5 plus shipping. *Media Angels, 16520 S. Tamiami Trail, #18-193, Fort Myers, FL 33908. (941) 433-2097. Fax: (941) 489-1060. Email: MediAngels@aol.com. Web: www.mediaangels.com.*

Everyday Science Sourcebook: Ideas for Teachers in Elementary and Middle School

Grades 1–8. $19.95 plus shipping. *Dale Seymour Publications, PO Box 5026, White Plains, NY 10602. (800) 872-1100. Fax: (800) 551-7637. Web: www.cuisenaire-dsp.com.*

Does the thought of your support group's annual science fair send cold shivers up your spine? Relax! The **KidSource Science Fair Handbook** will walk you through all the steps needed to produce a top-notch exhibit.

This is one thorough book, yet its 112 pages illustrated with cartoon-like drawings should not prove intimidating to most students (or moms!). From an explanation of what a science fair is and how to design an original project to recording your data and building your display, you'll find instructions and examples.

You will also learn about the scientific method and how to perform library research. Lists of organizations complete with addresses and web sites will help you find information and supplies. Sample projects show what is possible and realistic. (Not surprisingly, evolution makes a brief appearance in "Roadside Geology," the earth science project.)

Throughout this softcover book you'll find helpful tips, even some for when you've procrastinated too long and are running out of time. Stories of research performed by both professional scientists and award winning student scientists will serve to inspire you. (One girl created an automobile engineering project by building little cars from pasta!)

A science fair is a great way to learn a lot of science and research skills, and this book can help to make it a less stressful, more productive event. *Anne Wegener*

The **Media Angels Science Fair Project Handbook** is a simple booklet with practical steps to follow for most science fairs. Included are sections on scheduling time, finding a topic, displays, scientific method, what judges are looking for, and resources. The author also includes a list of science contests and federal agencies with which you may need to check (for information about experimenting on animals, for instance). Illustrations include a sample data sheet and a display table format. If your child is thinking about a science fair, this booklet will give him or her a real head start. *Macbeth Derham*

Activities

We're all hearing a lot about "process skills" these days. In science, this means the ability to tackle and solve a scientific problem, as opposed to encyclopedic knowledge of scientific facts. **Everyday Science Sourcebook** is a great tool to help you develop science process skills in your children.

First, what the book is not. It is not a science program. It is not a "how to teach science" book. What you get are lots and lots of hands-on activities, organized in ways that make this book really easy to use.

Activities are in developmental order, first of all. That means that activities for teeny kids come before activities for teens. The theory subscribed to by this book is that kids start learning science by *observing* (ages 1 and 2), *communicating* (ages 2–4), *comparing* (ages 4–6), *organizing* (ages 6–8), *relating* (ages 8–12), *inferring* (ages 12–15), and *applying* (ages 15–adult). Activities are therefore provided in that order.

Activities are also arranged numerically by categories: inorganic matter, organic matter, energy, inference models, and technology. These are further subdivided into topics. For example, the category "inorganic matter" breaks down into solids, liquids, gases, geology, oceanography, and meteorology. Each activity has a letter code that tells you exactly which skills and age level it is designed for.

So, need a science activity to correlate with your unit study or textbook? Look no farther . . . it's all here. *Mary Pride*

Have a blast exploring science with your youngest students with **The Giant Encyclopedia of Science Activities for Children 3 to 6**! Superbly organized, finding an activity to meet your needs in this oversized paperback is simple. From "Air" to "Magnets," "Nursery Rhymes" to "Winter," the table of contents lists more than 600 activities under nearly 50 alphabetic categories.

Perhaps you want to teach your preschoolers about birds. Would you like to build nests from strings, grasses, and yarn? Maybe you'd like to try building real nests with mud and straw. Then again, you might put out dryer lint and yarn for live birds to use in their nests. You can also examine feathers, make a Christmas tree for birds, create paper-bag ducklings, and more. Most projects require easily-found materials, and fairly short planning and setup times. After each of the 10 bird activities you'll find many extension ideas for more science, math, art, field trips, games and original songs and poems. I especially like the lists of related literature which accompany many of the projects.

Though written by (classroom) teachers for teachers, nearly all of the activities in the *Giant Encyclopedia of Science Activities* work well at home with minimal, if any, changes. (Granted, at home you probably will not choose to make paper pizzas to teach nutrition.)

With this 575-page resource on your shelf you won't have to leave your little ones out when you study science. You can teach science topics to your preschoolers alone as well as find creative activities related to the studies of their big brothers and sisters. Recommended. *Anne Wegener*

Don't be misled by the title. **Science Is Fun** is not just another superficial science activity book. Inside this oversized, 198-page book you'll find both well-organized science facts covering just about everything you expect to study in elementary school and hundreds of fun activities.

All the book is on this simple, enthusiastic, direct level. No gross "Squirmy Science" activities—lots of respect for God's creation. None of the activities takes a lot of time or gets very complicated for either mom or child. Great backyard and kitchen science for this age group.

The book is designed to foster a sense of wonder, yet although it's not written from a biblical point of view it manages not to slip into the fuzzy New Age thinking so often associated with nature exploration books these days.

Science Is Fun is fun to read. Liberally illustrated with many small line-art drawings, it also employs special symbols to alert you to upcoming science facts, experiments, ideas to try out, and so on. Contents are organized logically into teaching tips ("How to Use This Book"), tips on exploring/collecting/saving natural items (and which items not to collect), tree science, bug science, wild animal facts and identification (and food chains), window-sill gardening (very detailed and helpful instructions), "The Wonders of Our World" (facts and experiments designed to illuminate astronomy, weather, the three states of matter, and other physical-science basics), recycling, and fitness and nutrition. The last two chapters present a mainstream view of these topics.

Each chapter is followed with a well-chosen list of library books you can check out to follow up on the science you have just studied. The book closes with an assortment of fun and easy recipes meant to add some fun to your science explorations, from Dirt Cake (serve it in a flowerpot!) to play-dough (not for eating!). There's even an index to instantly direct you to any individual science topic covered in the book.

Author Carol Oppenheim has spent years teaching science to young children. Her experience shines through on every page. She knows what

NEW!
The Giant Encyclopedia of Science Activities for Children 3 to 6
Ages 3–6. $29.95 plus shipping.
Gryphon House, Inc., P.O. Box 207, Beltville, MD, 20704-0207. (800) 638-0928. Fax: (301) 595-0051.
Web: www.ghbooks.com.

NEW!
Science Is Fun
Ages 3–10. $25.95 plus shipping.
ISBN: 08-2737-3368
ITP, PO Box 6904, Florence, KY 41022. (800) 347-7707. (606) 525-2230. Fax: (606) 647-5023.
Web: www.thomson.com.

Typical Activity:

Earthworms!

Hold a cool, moist, wiggling earthworm in your hand (smiley face picture). Be gentle—it can't hurt you. If you show the children that it is fun, they will try it, too!

Picture of earthworm, identifying clitellum (band in the middle of the worm) and castings (earthworm droppings)

Earthworms are interesting and helpful:

- They work like plows mixing and loosening the soil.
- They don't have eyes or ears but they can tell light from dark and feel every vibration.
- They have no bones or lungs. Oxygen passes through their skin.
- They have 5 pairs of hearts.
- Their castings (elimination) enrich the soil.

Dig Up A Few Earthworms and put them in a box with a thin layer of soil. Watch how they move—examine them with a magnifying glass—look for the clitellum—let them go so they won't dry out! Earthworms must be moist or they will die!

kinds of activities children enjoy doing, how to prepare the activities with a minimum of fuss, what safety rules you should follow, and a lot more you don't find in typical science activities books. Recommended. *Mary Pride*

Experiments

UPDATED!
Backyard Scientist Books

Grades preK–6: Exploring Earthworms, Original Backyard Scientist, Series One, Series Three, Series Four. Grades 4–9, Series Two. Each book, $8.95. Shipping extra. *Backyard Scientist, PO Box 16966, Irvine, CA 92623. (949) 551-2392. Fax: (949) 552-5351. Email: Backyrdsci@aol.com.*

The way the series currently breaks down is this:
* *The Original Backyard Scientist* and *Backyard Scientist, Series One*— introductions to science via simple experiments
* *Series Two*—for older children, this one focuses on experiments in chemistry and physics
* *Series Three*—life science experiments
* *Series Four*—chemistry and physics investigations for all ages. 24 experiments, from "Cleaning a Penny with Electricity" to "Density of Gasses." Super-duper dry ice experiments, too!
* *Exploring Earthworms*—the first Backyard Scientist book to work with living animals. (Please, Jane, don't ever do one on maggots and fruit flies! Remember Ramona!)

Backyard Scientist series author Jane Hoffman, the human whirlwind, can be seen at many homeschool conferences, as well as on TV and radio shows nationwide. Her books have been homeschool favorites for years.

For you who have not yet encountered Jane or her series (it does get isolated out there on the space station, doesn't it?), the Backyard Scientist formula is simple: Take everyday questions, mix with everyday items (found around the house or easily purchased), add a dash of concept, and *voila!* What you get is a handy small book of science experiments with lots of enthusiasm and personable drawings, actual educational value, and no busy-work or twaddle. You and your child have learned something, and it was *fun!*

Jane has also come out with some great kits. Check them out in the Science Kits & Equipment chapter! *Mary Pride*

NEW!
Barron's Science Wizardry for Kids

Grades 5–8. Book, $13.95. Package, $21.95.
Barron's Educational Series, Inc., 250 Wireless Blvd., Hauppauge, NY 11788. (800) 645-3476. Fax: (516) 434-3217. Web: www.barronseduc.com.

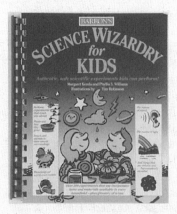

Your basic kitchen chemistry, backyard biology, and fun physics. **Barron's Science Wizardry for Kids** includes over 200 kid-proof science experiments and activities with common household objects. Spiral-bound, it's printed in two colors (orange and blue), illustrated with whimsical cartoons, and accompanied by a portable indoor/outdoor microscope with belt holster.

I like this better than its sister volume (*Barron's Math Wizardry for Kids*, also by the same authors). The experiments and activities are mostly classics, from Make Your Own Volcano to counting tree rings to making a kaleidoscope. The inevitable environmentally-correct section is mercifully small (16 pages out of 316). The spiral-bound format is great for an experiments and activities book. The hints, tips, and instructions really teach you something. All this plus a science glossary and an index, too! *Mary Pride*

Exploring God's Creation is the second-grade science experiment book in a series. Based on the concept of earth stewardship, students learn about God's creation through a series of activities in earth and life sciences.

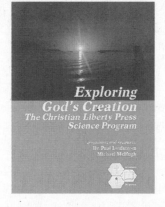

Each unit opens with a message to the parent/teacher from Dr. Paul Lindstrom, superintendent of the Christian Liberty Academy. Part inspiration and part practical suggestion, Dr. Lindstrom's message will help prepare you to teach the upcoming unit. He even includes Bible verses and field trip ideas!

The units are divided into chapters with one experiment in each. Photos help illustrate the procedure, and there are warnings on potentially hazardous sections. You should do these experiments with your children.

The chapters are followed by unit reviews and a "checkout" quiz. The quizzes are fair assessments of the material. The vocabulary is not too difficult. This is a good basic book of science labs, and the price is right. *MacBeth Derham*

Hands-on, minds-on. The **Science Explorer** books wonderfully flesh out this guiding principle of San Francisco's world famous Exploratorium museum, publisher of this series. These are science activity books with a difference: they are designed for families to use together. While kids alone can carry out many of the experiments, many require parent/child interaction. Parents serve as fellow explorers, and help foster their children's curiosity and creative inventiveness.

Two titles are currently available:

- *The Science Explorer: Family Science Experiments from the World's Favorite Hands-on Museum*
- *The Science Explorer Out and About: Fantastic Science Experiments Your Family Can Do Anywhere*

Both books offer around 50 easy-to-perform, largely original experiments arranged thematically on topics such as bubbles, optical illusions, things that fly, sound, mirrors, architecture, and shadows. Field-tested by hundreds of families, these experiments are educationally sound and loads of fun.

Want to investigate mixtures? *The Science Explorer* encourages you to puff marshmallows in your microwave, make a milk/dishwashing soap kaleidoscope, create "Exploragoo" (like very slippery Silly Putty), and make and play with "Outrageous Ooze," a strange colloidal suspension of cornstarch in water. A "What's Going On?" section simply explains scientific concepts and gives ideas for related activities. If you want to impress your friends, after making the "Outrageous Ooze" read the explanation and you can talk knowledgeably about colloids, non-Newtonian fluids, and thixotropic substances!

The Science Explorer Out and About offers more of the same, but this book also includes non-traditional field trips which encourage you to further explore the world right around you.

You might use these super books to find experiments to add to a textbook-based science program or science unit studies. But some of these activities, like Bubble Bombs, Mirrored Sunglasses, or Exploragoo are so much fun you may choose to include them at your next birthday party! *Anne Wegener*

NEW!
Exploratorium To Go

Grades 2–6. Hands on Science, Exploring Electricity and Exploring Food, $5 each. Finding Your Way, $5.95.
Exploratorium Mail Order, 3601 Lyon Street, San Francisco, CA 94123. (415) 563-7337 ext 393.
Fax: (415) 561-0370.
Web: www.exploratorium.edu/store

NEW!
Genesis For Kids

Grades 3–8. $12.99 plus shipping.
Tommy Nelson Publishers, PO Box 141000, Nashville, TN 37214. (800) 933-9673 ext. 2039. Fax: (615) 902-2450. Web: www.nelsonword.com.

NEW!
Gobble Up Science

Grades K–6. $10.95 plus shipping.
The Learning Works, P.O. Box 6187, Santa Barbara, CA 93160. (800) 235-5767. Fax: (805) 964-1466.
Email: LESatTLW@aol.com.
Web: www.thelearningworks.com.

The **Exploratorium**, that famous science museum in San Francisco, can now come a little closer to your home through their catalogue and publications. They sell games, gadgets, and books that can change your home into a science museum.

Hands on Science, Exploring Electricity, and *Exploring Food* are all based on museum exhibits, redesigned to work in your home. Each contain experiments, such as how to make batteries from fruit, but also include the history of the subject. There is even a timeline of electricity included, starting with Ben Franklin's famous kite-flying experiment. You can make a fog chamber or a pickle battery.

Yet another publication is *Finding Your Way.* This covers basic orienteering, map making, topography, and surveying. You will learn how to tell time using the sun, how to get your bearings using a compass, how to make a three-dimensional map, and much more. There is an extensive bibliography, so follow-up reading is easy.

These books can be used on several different levels, with parents helping the younger children, and older children using them to supplement study of physics or chemistry. Oh, and get a copy of the catalog. It's full of things you might like to explore! *MacBeth Derham*

What do you get when you cross Sunday School-flavored curriculum, creationism, and lots of whiz-bang hands-on science experiments? **Genesis For Kids**, subtitled "Science experiments that show God's power in Creation!" This 160-page oversized paperback from Tommy Nelson Publishers, the children's imprint from the Christian publishing giant Thomas Nelson, walks you through the creation week, accompanied by "tour guides" Dr. Lenslo and Dr. Paige, two cartoon characters that introduce each topic with lots of exclamation-point loaded dialogue ("Science is sooooo awesome!" declared Dr. Lenslo.)

Each of the seven sections corresponds to a day of creation. Other than a "toolbox" interlude in each section in which Drs. Lenslo and Paige discuss basics of science such as classification and drawing conclusions, the book is packed with lots of nifty hands-on experiments. All use readily available materials, and each one highlights God's creative nature. For example, there are 18 different experiments in the "Day 5: God made the birds and the fish" section. Typical is an observation exercise: you are to soak chicken bones in vinegar for 3 or 4 days. The vinegar leaches the calcium out of the bones, making them rubbery. The point of the experiment is that bird bones work especially well in this experiment because they are already lighter weight, being planned by God for flight.

An appreciation for God's design is obvious in each segment of this book. The text has lots of light humor, and assumes that the children reading it will be performing the experiments with the help of adults (rather than the other way around). The downside is that the material often reads as if its authors are a bit too anxious to make friends with their readers. However, the concepts and experiments are accessible and fun, and make a simple introduction to hands-on science for your elementary age student. *Michelle Van Loon*

In **Gobble Up Science**, a consumable—but inedible—136-page softcover book full of science experiments you can whip up in your own kitchen, you'll learn about taste, nutrition, water, mixtures, reactions, color, digestion, crystals and more. Each experiment lists:

- Its objective(s) in the form of questions that you'll be able to answer when you're done

- What you'll need
- List of steps
- Questions or tables to fill in as you go
- A relevant science fact
- A happy/sad face indicating whether the results are edible

You'll find everything you need at home for the 94 experiments in this book. The most exotic items are wine glasses for prisms and red cabbage for an acid/base indicator. Who would have thought that you could learn about the differences between solutions, suspensions and colloids while you make soup, jello, and meringues? And you won't need fancy lab equipment for paper chromatography—you just need some glasses of water, paper towels, and markers.

Gobble Up Science could be used as a course by itself if you did two or three activities each week for young children. For older kids, simply add some supplemental reading.

The Gobble Up series (which also includes *Gobble Up Math*—see review in chapter 25—have all the elements of good project books. They teach the concepts (not just the tricks), are quick and easy to set up, are fun to do, and don't require anything unusual. *Bon appetit! Teresa Schultz-Jones*

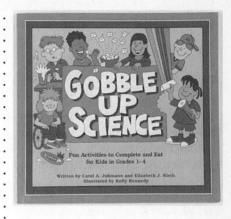

These full-color, hardbound science books include approximately one experiment or activity for every two pages. For example, the **Science Book of Light** has experiments for making a periscope, kaleidoscope, seeing how water distorts vision and at least eight more besides.

All the experiments are fascinating. You get step-by-step instructions with accompanying high-quality color photographs for each step. After each activity is a brief explanation of why it works. What's missing is a description of the scientific principles involved. For that, whatever science textbook or library books you use will usually provide the answers.

This series includes *Light, Color, Gravity, Energy, Sound, Weather, Air, Electricity, Hot and Cold, Machines, Magnets, Motion, Senses, Things That Grow, Numbers,* and *Water.* If you get them all, you'll be covering most elementary-school science topics, with the exception of animals. Recommended. *Sarah Pride*

NEW!
Gulliver Science Book of . . . series

Grades 2–5. $9.95 each plus shipping.
Harcourt Brace, 6277 Sea Harbor Dr., Orlando, FL 32887. (800) 543-1918. Fax: (800) 235-0256. Web: www.harcourtbrace.com.

If there is one thing my family loves, it is a great science book and the **Home & School Activity Book** fits the bill!

There are many children's science experiment books on the market. So what makes this book so different? First, instead of just telling kids the facts, it introduces each topic with a good question, provides a multiple-choice selection of answers, then gives a concise, but not watered-down answer. The highlight of each topic is the experiment that explains or demonstrates it without requiring $10,000 worth of equipment. Nothing is more frustrating than interrupting the learning process to search for a specific experiment to reinforce an idea. I never seem to have all the items required. The *Home & School Activity Book* only requires pennies, a globe, a milk carton, a flashlight, a glass, and a few other simple things.

While the equipment and supplies sound simple, the underlying great ideas are definitely not! The book is divided into four main parts. The first three—Astronomy, Physics, and Chemistry—are straightforward explanations of fundamental scientific concepts. The fourth part, Interesting Information, contains great informational sections on optical illusions and great inventions and discoveries. My nine-year-old son loves the diagrams. The diagrams are very clear, not glitzy, and a child can easily concentrate on them.

NEW!
Home & School Science Activity Book

Grades 1–4. $8.50 plus shipping.
Pigeon Press, PO Box 2788, Clarksville, IN 47131. (812) 283-4921. Fax: (812) 282-0127. Email: pigeonpres@aol.com. Web: home.earthlink.net/~kgrizwald.

At the very end of this book is a coupon to join The Home & School Science Club for $5.95. The club will provide a newsletter filled with science experiments, information and science facts. The club member will also receive a free science gift for joining. I do not usually join clubs but we are have mailed off our card because we really enjoyed this book. *Michele Fitzgerald*

NEW!
Janice VanCleave's Spectacular Science Project series

Grades 3–7. Each book, $10.95.
John Wiley & Sons, 1 Wiley Drive, Somerset, NJ 08875. (800) 225-5945. (732) 469-4400. Fax: (800) 597-3299. Web: www.wiley.com.

The **Janice VanCleave's Spectacular Science Project series** currently includes these titles: *Animals, Earthquakes, Electricity, Gravity, Insects & Spiders, Machines, Magnets, Microscopes & Magnifying Lenses, Molecules, Plants, Rocks & Minerals, Volcanoes,* and *Weather.* Each book is paperbound, 96 pages, and practically square in size. Each book includes 20 simple and fun experiments designed to answer questions kids often ask about the book's topic, plus suggestions for customizing your own science fair projects.

If you'd enjoy making models of rocks and minerals with gumdrops, toothpicks, and plastic bags; if you'd like to make your own barometer from a soda bottle, straws, modeling clay, and colored water; if you'd like to grow penicillium mold (not by accident, as usual); if you'd like to find out how a box of marbles can teach you how lava forms into rocks; then you're a likely candidate for one or more of these books.

Each chapter includes the following sections: Problem (the question you'll be answering, a materials list, and step-by-step experiment instructions, plus one or more line-art illustrations), Results (what should have happened?), Why? (what does it all mean), Let's Explore! (in which you are encouraged to vary the experiment design and inputs to see what happens), Show Time! (more info to help you design your own experiment), and Check It Out! (leads for further research).

One great thing about this series: it teaches genuine science terminology. New words are introduced in boldface, explained right in the text, and also found in the glossary at the back of each book. So now your eight-year-old can know what *geotropism* and *calderas* are. What a great head start on high school science! *Mary Pride*

NEW!
Science in Seconds at the Beach

Grades 3–6. $12.95 plus shipping.
John Wiley & Sons, 1 Wiley Drive, Somerset, NJ 08875. (800) 225-5945. (732) 469-4400. Fax: (800) 597-3299. Web: www.wiley.com.

Tired of the run-of-the-mill science texts? Sick of mixing vinegar and baking soda or playing with magnets? If you answered yes, I have the book for you.

Science in Seconds at the Beach falls in the "Unusual" category. With this book you can turn a trip to the beach into a science class, plus a lot of family fun. Our family did just that on a trip to the coast of New Jersey. We studied sand, seaweed, seabirds, water motion, seashells, and bi-valves.

Science in Seconds provides 100 exciting experiments that can be done in 10 minutes or less. But you don't have to pack up the family and travel for hours to get to the ocean. Many experiments can be done with items and books that you have around the house. There are a few that do require a real beach.

The instructions and diagrams are superb. Each page contains an experiment broken down into three easy to understand parts: Materials, Procedure, and Explanation. I have found that older children enjoy doing additional research on the different topics. There is a list of Marine and Wildlife Organizations in the back of the book, which the older children found exciting. They wrote to all of them, which provided great letter-writing practice. Their goal is to make a collage with the information they collect.

To make this book complete there is a comprehensive, five-page glossary. These words were easily incorporated into our vocabulary and spelling lists.

By adding the resources of our encyclopedia, we found sufficient material to use this book for our science lessons for about six weeks. With a little imagination, you could develop this into a dynamite unit study. *Michele Fitzgerald*

Written by Jean Potter, former kindergarten teacher, state education director, and Acting Assistant Secretary for Elementary and Secondary Education for the United States, **Science in Seconds with Toys** uses a fresh approach to teach physical science concepts to preteens and their moms. Using time-tested toys, such as Slinkies, Hula-Hoops, Silly Putty, marbles, squirt guns, Jack-in-the-boxes, sliding boards, and see-saws, science concepts are brought to  life. Make your own Silly Putty and learn about non-Newtonian fluids. Conjure up some "play plubber" and discover a plastic-like polymer. Dig out the marbles and Matchbox cars to experiment with friction, force, and kinetic energy. Find out how your Etch-a-Sketch and ViewMaster work. Construct a kaleidoscope. Grab the wax paper and head for the nearest sliding board for a first-hand, bottoms-on, state-of-the-art experience in friction reduction. (Oh, and while you're at the playground, don't forget to consider the amazement and amusement of the lever and fulcrum . . . I mean the teeter-totter.) You get the idea.

On each page, along with labels of the concept covered, are a list of needed materials, clear step-by-step procedure, and a follow-up explanation of the laws behind the experiment. The explanations are brief and could be extended with further reading if there is the interest or the need.

Who said science is dry or boring? I can't wait to get out the blow dryer and ping-pong balls to find out for myself about Bernoulli's Law! *Barbara Petronelli*

Are you looking for a way to teach your children the basics about *Plants, Simple Machines, Solids, Liquids and Gases,* or *Living Things?* If so, the **Starting With Science** series is just the thing for you. These four books are superb for demonstrating basic concepts using household items.

Each book includes 15 topical lessons in its 32 pages. Each lesson topic is introduced in a few short sentences. Then, on to the "demonstration" (e.g., the simple experiment that demonstrates that science topic). You are given a list of items needed and instructions on what to do. After the demonstration is complete, you are also given details on what results the experiment should have, and why. This is helpful in case you cannot do the demonstration and just want to discuss the topic. Further definitions are also given as needed.

The photographs are outstanding. Each lesson includes a clear, colorful photo of the lesson. Sometimes it will show how to do the demonstration, other times, it shows the results.

So, if you want to teach your child about inclined planes (and eggs) or a plant's need for water (and food coloring) or solids and liquids (and cornstarch) or photosynthesis (and tattoos), then these books will be a great addition to your main science texts. If you want to know how each of the items in parentheses relates to the item before it, buy the books and find out! *Barbara Buchanan*

NEW!
Williamson Super Science Concoctions

Grades 1–6. $12.95 plus shipping. *Williamson Publishing Company, Church Hill Road, Charlotte, VT 05445. (800) 234-8791. Fax: (802) 425-2199. Web: www.williamsonbooks.com.*

Usborne Science Activities Series

Grades 1–5. Individual books, $4.95 each paperbound, $12.95 each library-bound. Collections: each hardcover volume, $12.95. Shipping extra. *EDC Publishing, Division of Educational Development Corporation, 10302 East 55th Place, Tulsa, OK 74146. (800) 475-4522. Fax: (800) 747-4509. Web: www.edcpub.com.*

Titles in this series: *Science with Weather, Science with Your Body, Science with Batteries, Science with Magnets, Science in the Kitchen, Science with Air, Science with Light & Mirrors, Science with Water,* and *Science with Plants.* The following collections are also available:

- *Usborne Book of Science Activities, Volume 1.* Includes *Light, Water,* and *Magnets.*
- *Usborne Book of Science Activities, Volume 2.* Includes *Plants, Kitchen,* and *Air.*
- *Usborne Book of Science Activities, Volume 3.* Includes *Weather, Body,* and *Batteries.*

If you are tired or leery of the textbook approach to learning science concepts and looking for a solid introduction to the science of chemistry, get this book. **Super Science Concoctions** uses 50 homemade mixtures to investigate basic science principles. Your kitchen is the lab and directions are given for science safety, steps, and supplies. The supplies listed are usually already in your home or readily available from your local grocery store or pharmacy.

Some of the projects involve experiments with molecules in motion, solvents or solutes, chromatography, and crystal growing. Phase changes are explored as kids melt paraffin and chocolate. Chemical changes are observed as they create a volcano with sand, baking soda, and vinegar or give an egg an acid bath. Children will learn living definitions of terms like volume, shape, viscosity, miscible and immiscible, as they experiment with liquids. Learning scientific vocabulary in this way prevents the strain of learning it as more difficult upper-level science courses are studied.

Create weird substances, such as "Gooblek" and "Blobber." These strange substances don't behave like solids, liquids, or gases and are just plain fun to play with: gelatin worms, blubberscotch, and terrific taffoid are just a few. Polymer chains are even made with a concoction of glue and Borax. The result is a type of plastic.

This hands-on method is an ideal way to introduce your six-to-twelve-year-old youngsters to science that's much more fun out of a text than in it. *Barbara Petronelli*

I've just seen the first book in the new **Usborne Science Activities series** for young children. It's *Science with Water,* and it's excellent! Its 24 pages are a series of simple step-by-step illustrated experiments, capped by notes for parents and teachers explaining the scientific topics covered and a complete index. Topics include surface tension, volume, boat design, evaporation and condensation, solutions, water power, air and water tricks, absorption, and ice. These technical terms aren't used in the book: instead it talks about water's "skin," floating, fun with boats, and other non-threatening terms. The experiments are all doable, requiring no fancy equipment nor much preparation time. This kid-pleasing series is great for injecting a dose of science into even the heaviest home schedule.

If you are interested in this series, I recommend you buy the collections rather than individual books. For less than the cost of three individual paperbound books, you get them bound together as a much more durable hardcover. *Mary Pride*

CHAPTER 37

Science Kits & Equipment

Years ago, when I told a new acquaintance that we were homeschooling our children, one of the first things they asked was, "What about computers? Won't they be missing out? After all, the schools have all those computer labs filled with wonderful new machines like PCjr's and Apple IIs!"

As you can imagine, people don't ask me any more if we're worried about our children missing out on computer experience. The typical homeschool now has *better* computers than the local school's computer lab—which is well stocked with an abundance of outdated machines!

As usual, though, the skeptics always come up with something new. As our children reach college age, I'm hearing, "What about lab science? Sure, you can teach science from workbooks, but how can you possibly set up a lab in your home?"

Why Lab Science Matters

If you've never been asked this, you might think, "What does it matter? After all, videos featuring lab demonstrations are available from A Beka, Alpha Omega, Bob Jones University Press, and School of Tomorrow. If we *see* how it's done, do we really need to bother doing it ourselves?"

It depends on your child's goals. Obviously, if he hopes for a career in science or engineering, high-school lab science is a must. What you—and he—may not realize, though, is that selective colleges and universities typically require *all* applicants to have completed several years of lab science—even if they plan to go into basketball coaching or fine arts!

Lab science has benefits beyond impressing admissions officials. It teaches precision, thoroughness, record-keeping, honesty (it's a huge scientific sin to erase or change any data in a science notebook), self-confidence, and of course, a deeper knowledge of science.

Lab Science for Young Kids

That's why, even in the early grades, most homeschool families opt for some flavor of "kitchen" or "backyard" science using common household materials, rather than relying solely on books and textbooks. However, the more scientifically dedicated parent has some options beyond this.

DEFINITIONS

- "Kitchen Science" is experiments with common household substances.

- "Backyard science" among homeschoolers commonly refers to the kitchen-science-style experiments of Jane Hoffman, the Backyard Scientist.

- "Lab science" uses real lab chemicals and equipment *not* commonly found in your home.

- "Science kits" come with all the lab science supplies needed to perform the experiments. You may need to provide common household substances.

Homeschool Lab Supplies

The most natural source of homeschool lab science is your curriculum provider—assuming they offer lab science. If you use **A Beka**, **Alpha Omega**, **Bob Jones**, or **Christian Light**, you are in luck; your science curriculum already includes lab work. All you have to do is purchase the equipment and supplies. This, however, is not as easy as it sounds. Even if you want to buy every item needed for a grade level, only Christian Light offers a "package" deal. (You need their Core Unit *plus* the unit for the desired grade, by the way.) And if you hope to save a few dollars by only doing the most important labs from your curriculum, you have to spend hours flipping through the lab book to figure out which materials on the price list you can skip.

This is where **Home Training Tools** comes in. They have researched what materials are best for homeschool use with the science curriculum of six different publishers. They have special order forms for each grade level of A Beka, Alpha Omega, Bob Jones University Press, and Christian Light Education. They also have order forms for levels 1–3 of Apologia Educational Ministries and levels 1–3 of the Castle Heights Press "Exploring Creation" series.

I asked Frank Schaner, owner of Home Training Tools, how those special forms work. He told me:

NEW!
Home Training Tools
2827 Buffalo Horn Dr, Laurel, MT 59044-8325. (800) 860-6272. Web: www.HomeTrainingTools.com.

A Beka Book
Box 19100
Pensacola, FL 32523-9100.
(800) 874-2352.
Web: www.abeka.com.

Alpha Omega
300 N McKemy Ave, Chandler, AZ 85226-2618. (800) 622-3070.
Web: www..home-schooling.com.

Bob Jones Order Forum
Customer Services, Greenville, SC 29614. Orders: (800) 845-5731. Fax: (800) 525-8398. Web: www.bjup.com.

Christian Light Publications Lab Materials
PO Box 1212, Harrisonburg, VA 22801-1212. (540) 434-1003. Fax: (540) 433-8896.
Email: orders@clp.org.

School of Tomorrow
PO Box 299000, Lewisville, TX 75029-9904. Orders: (800) 925-7777.
Inquiries: (972) 315-1776.
Fax: (972) 315-2862.
Email: info@schooloftomorrow.com.
Web: www.schooloftomorrow.com.

The major Christian homeschool suppliers all carry lab materials or lab science videos, or both. But it's not always easy to figure out just what equipment and supplies you need.

The forms list everything you need to do the lab portion of an individual course. You can buy items individually, or in some cases you can buy a kit with all the materials for an entire course.

When we are researching a form, we buy the curriculum and go through it asking, "I'm teaching this to my children at home. How would I do this?" This is necessary because sometimes a curriculum is written from a school perspective rather than for homeschoolers. We simplify the material needs and suggest low-cost methods for a particular lab.

The customer decides how much he wants to spend,. For example, he might say, "I want Bob Jones University Chemistry lab, and I only want to spend $100." We send the BJU Chemistry order form out to him for free. He decides which labs he will do and which he will skip so that he only needs to pay $100.

Even if you're not using one of these curricula, Home Training Tools has what you need for lab science at home. They carry a broad range of science equipment and science learning tools: telescopes, microscopes, sphygmomanometers, stethoscopes, barometers, hygrometers, rock collections, chemistry sets . . . just about everything. *Mary Pride*

School Science Suppliers

I don't need to spend much time with these. Schools buy their science supplies from catalogs like these. Bright, colorful, many kit items, some more affordable than others. We've listed contact information for four of the most popular: **Carolina Biological Supply** (their new catalog has Janice VanCleave on the cover!), **Cuisenaire** (also home of the famous Cuisenaire rods), **Delta Education** (very high quality science and math equipment), and **NASCO** (they like homeschoolers enough to occasionally advertise their catalog in homeschool publications). I suggest you pick one person in your support group to request these catalogs, and then pore over them together. Many of their items make more sense as shared group purchases.

Science Catalogs

"Hands on science and technology products" are the stock in trade of **Activity Based Supplies**. Founded by a group with years of experience in school sales, this catalog does *not* include products you can get in stores like Toys "R" Us. They have an entire catalog of LEGO materials, from LEGO PRIMO and DUPLO to the more advanced LEGO TECHNIC. Their second catalog includes model dragsters and race kits (used widely in school "technology education" programs to study physics principles), model planes and rockets (and an entire "rocketry curriculum," plus a book on science fair projects with rockets), engineering kits and books of all kinds (including K'Nex), plus ingredients to make all sorts of your own creations (e.g., pulleys, fiber optic cables, gearbox kits, motors, etc., etc.). You'll find some classroom bulk kits, but just about everything also comes in individual student packs, for home use. *Mary Pride.*

Carolina Biological
2700 York Rd, Burlington, NC 27215. (800) 334-5551. Web: carolina.com.

Cuisenaire
PO Box 5026, White Plains, NY 10602-5026. (800) 237-0338. Web: www..cuisenaire.com.

Delta Ed
PO Box 3000, Nashua, NH 03061-3000. (800) 442-5444. Web: www.delta-ed.com.

NASCO
901 Janesville Ave, Fort Atkinson, WI 53538. (800) 558-9595. Web: www.nascofa.com.

NEW!
Activity Based Supplies catalog
Ages 6 months–18. Free catalog. Activity Based Supplies, PO Box 408, Pittsburg, KS 66762. (800) 469-8070. Fax: (800) 237-3504. Web: www.absupplies.com.

Edmund Scientific Company

Edmund Scientific Company, Consumer Science Division, 101 East Gloucester Pike, Barrington, NJ 08007. Orders: (800) 728-6999. Inquiries: (609) 547-8880. Web: www.edsci.com.

NEW!
Tobin's Lab

Tobin's Lab, PO Box 6503, Glendale, AZ 85312-6503. (800) 522-4776. Web: www.tobinlab.com.

NEW!
Science Labs-in-a-Box

Ages 5 and up. $92.50/month/topic plus $100 deposit. Biology and Chemistry, $102.50/month/topic plus $100 deposit.
Science Labs-in-a-Box, Inc., 13440 Floyd Rd. #7, Dallas, TX 75243. (800) 687-5227 or (972) 644-4452. Fax: (972) 669-1518. Web: www.sciencelabs.com.

Science Labs in a Box Topics kit

The **Edmund Scientific's Catalog** has all the basic science equipment you need. Microscopes, telescopes, stethoscopes, orotoscopes, binoculars, and the ever-popular sextant. This catalog's main claim to fame is their zany science gifts, from quarters that "blast off" when you tip the waiter, to your personal robot. Plus a pile of science kits with kid-appeal. This is not a catalog designed for homeschoolers per se, but for adults who like science and parents who want to add a dollop of hands-on science to their child's world. *Mary Pride*

The **Tobin's Lab catalog**, on the other hand is designed for homeschoolers. This could be your one-stop shopping source for homeschool science equipment and supplies, especially for the early grades. Produced by the Duby family (Mike, Tammy, Tobin, and Megan), this 88-page catalog has everything from binoculars and microscopes to space games, crystal kits, and dissection specimens. Laid out in the order of the Days of Creation (first day is chemistry, physics, light, color, and solar power, for example), this has everything scientific except the science curriculum itself (though they do offer World Book products and a hefty sampling of Usborne books). Need a Moo Magnet? Some silkworms? A see-through bat model? A triple-beam balance? An Instant Fish kit (just add water)? If you've ever wished for a rock pick for your speleological expeditions, or a dissecting kit for that ginchy KONOS cow eyeball unit study, this is the place to get it. *Mary Pride*

Lab Kit Rentals

A knock at the door. You step outside to be greeted by the friendly UPS guy delivering a *large* box. What's inside? A month's supply of scientific experiments, instructional videos, and lab equipment, all delivered directly to your home. The **Science Labs In-A-Box** program, offering a convenient "pizza-delivery" approach to science instruction, is one of the most innovative options for homeschoolers introduced in recent years. And it is a terrific option for those of you who are serious about science.

As the name implies, every month a box arrives at your house, including all the lab apparatus and ingredients needed for school-quality science—eight monthly boxes containing a total of more than 30 labs. Each box has enough materials for two children to do the experiments. When you finish the experiments in one box, you simply arrange to have that box returned and order the next box in the series. In effect, you're renting up to $2,000 worth of equipment and getting all of the materials prepackaged for you, ready to use.

We've received many of these boxes, and can tell you the equipment and materials are all first-class. All necessary materials are included. And I mean *all*—even down to the roll of tape necessary to repackage the box! For example, the chemistry boxes include a Periodic Table chart, goggles and lab smock, lab instruction videos (hosted by Science Project's own Mr. B. in a classroom setting), textbook and teacher's guide, filter paper, various containers (beaker, flask, graduated cylinder, etc.), a broad assortment of chemicals and substances, and much more. All the equipment you need for in-depth hands-on chemistry. Each lab exercise also includes a Biblical perspective, highlighting a principle from the lab and applying it to the Christian life.

Available lab courses include:

Science Labs in a Box General Science I kit

- *Topics* (ages 5–8) includes earth science, weather, physical changes, chemical changes, light, sound, health, magnetism, electricity, and more.
- *Topics II* (ages 5–8) lets you study rainbows, kinetic energy, the water cycle, simple machines, emulsions, airplanes, and more. Available fall 1999.
- *General Science II* (ages 9–11) includes paleontology, life science, physical science, chemistry, biology, and more.
- *General Science III* (ages 9–11) includes earthquakes and volcanoes (make and record your own mini volcano!), astronomy (build and launch your own rocket!), respiratory system, and more.
- *Earth Science* (ages 12–14) includes meteorology, geology, oceanography, astronomy, and more.
- *Life Science* (ages 12–14) includes classification, cells and Biblical creation, life processes of organisms, genetics, and more.
- *Physical Science* (ages 14 and up) includes scientific method, metric system, introductory chemistry, introductory physics, and more.
- *Biology* (ages 14 and up) includes cells, classification, microbiology, genetics, dissection, botany, body systems, and more.
- *Chemistry* (ages 15 and up) includes mixtures and alloys, solvents, water testing, petrochemicals, foods, radioactivity, atmospheric chemistry, consumer chemistry, and more.

Science Labs in a Box General Science II kit

If, after you've completed the experiments, you would like to purchase one of the items to keep (e.g. a microscope), just read the price off of the enclosed checklist, and include payment along with the rest of the items being returned in the box. Co-op prices are available—share with a friend if you'd like to save more money and double your fun! *Mary Pride*

Kits

The **Alien Slime Lab** (a disguised biochemistry kit) contains seven chemicals, including the "alien blood," a test tube stand with micro-reaction chambers, a measuring cup, an electrical conductivity meter, four test tubes, a funnel, protective goggles, five eyedroppers, plastic gloves, tweezers, a stirring stick, a magnifying glass, a magnet, an "alien skin" specimen, a pH chart, pH paper, ammonia test strips, color vision DNA test paper, chromatography paper and cobalt chloride paper. Using all this equipment, you have to analyze the "alien skin" and "alien blood" to find out if there are any signs of life.

The experiment booklet included holds 10 experiments for this task, from checking fluids for conductivity to making "new aliens" with the DNA. This is a really fascinating kit, and the skills learned from it will last you for years. It's great for adults as well as kids, and kept us busy and interested for quite a while. *Sarah Pride*

NEW!
Alien Slime Lab
Grades 5 and up. $14.95 plus shipping.
Educational Insights, Inc., 16941 Keegan Ave., Carson, CA 90746. (800) 995-4436. (310) 884-2000. Fax: (800) 995-0506. Web: www.edin.com.

Alpha Omega Elementary Science Kit

Grades 2–8. $209.95. Prepared Slides, $11.95. Microscopes also available. Shipping extra.
Alpha Omega Publications, 300 N. McKemy, Chandler, AZ 85226. Orders and inquiries: (800) 622-3070. Fax: (480) 785-8034. Web: www.home-schooling.com.

NEW!
Backyard Scientist Kits

Grades K–8. $12.95 each. Postpaid.
Backyard Scientist, PO Box 16966, Irvine, CA 92623. (949) 551-2392. Fax: (949) 552-5351. Email: Backyrdsci@aol.com.

UPDATED!
Butterfly Garden and Butterfly Garden School Kit

Ages 2–14. Basic Garden (3-5 caterpillars), $21.95. School Kit (33 caterpillars), $45.95. Shipping extra.
Insect Lore, PO Box 1535, Shafter, CA 93263. (800) LIVE-BUG. Inquiries: (661) 746-6047. Fax: (661) 746-0334. Web: www.insectlore.com.

There is a small brochure in the kit with some basic information about the butterflies, but you will need to supply age-appropriate books to help your family to get the most from the kit. The smaller kit would be great for any family that wants an interesting experience to spice up their science studies (my kids were enthralled, and even my husband spent quite a bit of time watching!) The larger kit might be a better way to go if you know several families who are also interested in participating.

The Insect Lore catalog also includes lots of kits and books from suppliers reviewed in this volume of *Big Book*. The Educational Insights *Adventures in Science* kits and *Discovery* collections. Usborne nature and science books. Games from Ampersand Press. Plus videos, puzzles, puppets, and coloring books, all with a nature theme.

Here's a conveniently packaged kit of basic lab equipment designed for use with Alpha Omega courses.

The **Elementary Science Kit** includes all the basic equipment and supplies you need to set up a home, school, or support group science lab: beakers of various sizes, wire, clamps, a graduated cylinder, pipette droppers, filter paper, Erlenmeyer flask, funnel, stirring rods, test tubes of various sizes, test tube rack, thermometers, tubing, and bunches more. You can add specialty items (which Alpha Omega kindly lists by the LIFEPAC in which they are needed) in order to do all the experiments in Alpha Omega's grades 2–8 courses. *Mary Pride*

Backyard Science Kits—*Magical Slime! Magical Super Crystals! Magic Rocks!* What kid could resist science kits with names like these? Especially when each comes with all the ingredients for parent-supervised scientific fun, and a 24-page experiment booklet with complete step-by-step instructions and room for writing your scientific observations, all in a handy reusable zip-loc bag? (You'll still need to supply some common household items, such as aluminum foil, sugar, and water. No biggie.) *Mary Pride*

This turned out to be a delightful project that fascinated our whole family. Insect Lore has put together a butterfly-growing kit that takes almost all of the anxiety out of growing Painted Lady caterpillars from tiny newly hatched larvae into beautiful live butterflies!

Each **Butterfly Garden** kit comes with caterpillars, a plastic container (or in the case of the larger "School Kit," several containers) to house the larvae in, "larvae culture" for the caterpillars to eat, and a butterfly "house" with clear windows for observation, complete with a fake flower for feeding your bugs sugar-water.

Everything you need is in the kit, except the caterpillars, which are either ordered at the same time and delivered with the kits, or which can be ordered with a coupon to be delivered at a later date. Once you have unpacked your kit and proceeded with the minimal preparation required, your caterpillars will be fully self-contained, living entirely on the "culture" included until after they have become chrysalides and are ready to be transferred to the butterfly house to hatch.

Although I was a little concerned about the mountains of caterpillar "frass" that piled up in the jars during the process, every single one of our caterpillars from both kits hatched out into beautiful butterflies.

The Insect Lore Customer Service folks were great to deal with and very helpful when our first school kit caterpillar order form went astray in the mail, replacing our order quickly and with little fuss.

All in all, highly recommended. *Teresa May and Mary Pride*

It's not cheap, but if you want science equipment to perform all your science experiments, **Christian Light Publications** has it. Their **lab materials** are available in complete sets or as individual components. Sets are correlated with their science worktexts (a Mennonite-approved updating of the original Alpha Omega Publications texts). *Mary Pride*

Crash and Burn Chemistry is a wonderful introduction to chemistry. The experiments are short and easy to do, and most of the items needed are included in the kit. Items not included are easily found around the house. Numerous chemicals are used to acquaint your child with different areas of chemistry. Your child learns about physical and chemical changes.

The title of the kit explains how the experiments work. A "crash" in chemistry is the product of a chemical reaction. When two chemicals are mixed in a solution and solid precipitate is formed, the solution is said to have crashed. A "burn" is something that is experiencing rapid oxidation. According to the booklet that came with the kit, a smoke screen, fire, or explosion is a burn. The experiments in the kit give you many examples of physical versus chemical changes. Best of all, most children adore messing around with chemicals so it's easy to get them interested. Make sure that the kit is used with parental supervision, because some of the chemicals could be harmful. Always follow the directions! *Maryann Turner*

The **Adventures in Science Kits** are the perfect drop-of-a-hat set of science experiments. The projects in this series are great for young children just starting science. Each kit includes a lesson manual and all materials needed for the experiments. The manual first teaches a science concept, such as how mirrors reflect light, and then gives you instructions for an experiment, such as building a periscope. Each kit has 21 such lessons, presented systematically in a logical sequence and includes a few ingredients not normally found around your house.

Inside each booklet are some introductory thought questions, a list of materials needed, and step-by-step instructions for one or more discovery experiments. Often you will be observing strange things, like paper inside an underwater glass remaining dry or a balloon full of air weighing more than an uninflated balloon. The scientific processes causing these phenomena are explained on the last page of each booklet.

The Adventures in Science format is super handy for quickie experiments. Just grab the first little booklet you haven't yet completed, round up

Christian Light Publications Lab Materials

Christian Light Education, PO Box 1212, Harrisonburg, VA 22801-1212. (540) 434-1003. Fax: (540) 433-8896. Email: orders@clp.org.

NEW!
Crash and Burn Chemistry

Grades 3–8. $29.99 plus shipping. *The Wild Goose Company, PO Box 35171, Greensboro, NC 27425. (801) 363-0696. Fax: (801) 535-2669. Email: wgoose9150@wildgoosescience.com. Web: www.wildgoosescience.com.*

Educational Insights Adventures in Science kits

Grades 3–8. $9.95 each plus shipping. *Educational Insights, Inc., 16941 Keegan Ave., Carson, CA 90746. (800) 995-4436. (310) 884-2000. Fax: (800) 995-0506. Web: www.edin.com.*

The Adventures in Science series includes:

- *Color & Light*—Build a periscope, shadow clock, kaleidoscope, spectroscope, water magnifier, model of the human eye. Explore color illusions and the effect of light on plants. Play with mirrors.
- *Sky Science*—Build a barometer, anemometer, weather vane, salad dressing bottle thermometer, rain gauge, hygrometer, and weather map, and put them together to make a complete weather station. Make a sundial, lunar eclipse model, model solar system, moon craters, refracting telescope, bearing dial, constellarium, model galaxy, balloon space ship. Perform magic tricks, like turning a glass full of water upside down without spilling it. Learn about air, weather, the solar system, spaceships. A terrific kit!
- *Electricity*—comes with light bulbs, insulated wire, light sockets, and battery clips. Build an electronic quiz game, parallel and series circuits, galvanometer, telegraph, and rheostat. Learn principles of electrical safety, battery handling. Split water molecules with electricity.
- *Backyard Science*—magnifying bug viewer, copper wire, beads, metal washer. Build bird feeder, butterfly model, tetrahedral

kite, astrolabe. Print with leaves. Collect and observe bugs. Learn to recognize the constellations.

- *Magnetism*—includes horseshoe magnet, disk and bar magnets, nails, insulated wire, iron filings. Build electromagnets, other magnets, floating polygons. Go on a magnetism treasure hunt.
- *How Things Work*—non-toxic stamp pad, magnifying glass, medicine cups, cup hook. Build a balloon-powered "rocket boat," pin piano, and more. Learn about inertia, friction, simple machines, levers and pulleys, sound and sonar.
- Other kits in the series are *Dinosaurs & Fossils*, *Spy Science*, *Eco-Detective*, *Science Magic Tricks*, and *Human Body*.

Educational Insights Discovery Collections

Grades 3–8. Seashells, Fossils, Gems, and Rocks, $17.95 each. Exploring Nature, $34.95. Nature Lab, $49.95. Shipping extra.
Educational Insights, Inc., 16941 Keegan Ave., Carson, CA 90746. (800) 995-4436. (310) 884-2000. Fax: (800) 995-0506. Web: www.edin.com.

NEW! Professor Pete's Portable Science Kits

Grades 3–8. $18.95 each plus shipping.
Delta Education, 80 Northwest Blvd, Nashua, NH 03063. (800) 442-5444. Fax: (800) 282-9560. Email: Matthew@delta-ed.mv.com. Web: www.delta-ed.com.

the materials, and do the experiments! Or, if you prefer, browse through the booklets until you find one that meets your fancy.

The scientific equipment included in each kit is not terribly deluxe. The Sky Science kit includes a teeny-tiny compass, a test tube, a packet of balloons, and a thermometer. The Light kit includes a small prism, several sheets of colored cellophane (the "colored and polarized filters"), a piece of silver plastic (that's the "reflective surface"), and a small piece of clear plastic with zillions of teeny, invisible lines (the "diffraction grating"). Hey, at the price of these kits, we can't expect them to throw in a stereo microscope!

Between these 11 kits, you get more hands-on science and *memorable* exposure to more science topics than most schoolkids get in grades K–12. No miserable workbook pages or opaque directions—just lots and lots of *fun! Mary Pride*

Nothing is more frustrating than a natural science unit about the ocean when you live in Missouri. Your science text suggests, "Go to the beach and find a starfish, a sand dollar, and a barnacle." "Right," you think. "I'll just slide down to the ol' Mississippi and pick up some floating pop bottles instead." Now, thanks to Educational Insights, you can bring the great outdoors home without going outdoors.

The **Discovery Collections** are boxed sets of labeled specimens plus storage/collection bag, an identification/activity guide, an ID chart, and a magnifying glass with measuring rule.

Seashells has 21 authentic seashell specimens. Learn about the different shells and the creatures that live in them.

Fossils provides 10 authentic specimens (like trilobites, dinosaur bone, a shark's tooth, and petrified wood) from the supposed Paleozoic, Mesozoic, and Cenozoic eras in a sectioned plastic tray.

Rocks lets you practice geological identification with 16 neatly packaged and numbered specimens (including the ever-popular quartz, pyrite—"fool's gold," and obsidian).

Gems has 12 specimens of gems and semi-precious stones (sorry, no diamonds!), and includes information about mining and crystal growing.

If you *love* to get your hands on specimens, EI's **Nature Lab** has both activities (over 50 of 'em) and lots of fun specimens. Grow living Sea Monkeys from eggs. Grow plants from seeds. Mess around with fossils. Identify rocks. Fiddle with seashells. Lots more included, plus a lovely full-color 32-page activity book. *Mary Pride*

Professor Pete's Portable Science Kits is a dream come true! Everything you need for a science experiment, all stored in a convenient, sturdy, reusable plastic container.

In our house getting supplies together for a science experiment can be time-consuming. I know that wire is somewhere, but *where*? I will probably find that wire a month after we wanted to do the experiment, when we are in a different science area all together. I try to keep all the stuff in plastic containers but for some unexplainable reason, the item I need is never there.

Professor Pete's Portable Science is a relief. Everything that is needed, except tape, sandpaper, a meterstick, and scissors, is included. Not only is everything included, but the experiments are very interesting.

The booklet that comes with each kit contains eight very detailed experiments. My youngest son worked on these by himself and he enjoyed the clear instructions and diagrams. He was able to follow all the experiments on his own. Each booklet contains "Did You Know," "Bright Idea," and "Points to Ponder" sections which create further interest and research. My son worked for hours with these and continues to re-do experiments.

So far this series includes kits for the following: Flight Follies (#750-9028), Cruising the Circuit(#750-9006), and Current Attraction(#750-9017).

The supplies are excellent quality and will last through many children. These kits met both mom and child requirements and are easy to store. The kits might seem a bit pricey but you may find that the savings in time, gasoline, and shipping definitely made up for it. *Michele Fitzgerald*

Each of the **Science in a Nutshell** kits comes attractively packaged in a durable, lock-tight plastic tote. That alone is enough to endear this series to homeschool moms who are tired of "creative" messes. But there's more! Specially designed for either small-group (e.g., your family) or individual (one child) use, each of these self-contained kits comes with sturdy, reusable items, plus enough consumable materials to use it over and over again. Also included: an easy-to-use guide to 8–12 activities *and* a a preformatted fill-it-in student activity journal for recording experiment observations. The habit of scientific note-taking is absolutely essential to any real scientist, but most science kits today do nothing to encourage it. Kudos to Delta Education for going the extra mile here!

We reviewed the *Electrical Connections* kit. It came with two yellow plastic battery holders, two "D" batteries, one rectangular piece of pine, lots of insulated copper wire, some bare copper wire for testing conductance, a bag of contact clips and other metal pieces, lightbulbs, three multi-clip lightbulb holders, a couple pieces of white tagboard, and a box of thumbtacks. Armed with these mostly reusable components, you can embark on nine activities that introduce youngsters to basic electric circuits, including building two battery-powered games. Very tidy and organized.

Kit titles include *A Peek Inside You, Body Basics, Bubble Science, Charge It Static Electricity, Clever Levers, Crystal Creations, Detective Lab, Electrical Connections, Electromagnetism, Energy & Motion, Flight! Gliders to Jets, Fossil Formations, Gears at Work, Human Machine, Magnet Magic, One and Only You, Our Changing Earth, Pulley Power, Rock Origins, Seed Mysteries, Smell/Taste/Touch, Soil Studies, Sound Vibrations, Vision & Hearing, Water Cycle, Weather Wise, Wheels at Work,* and *Work: Plane & Simple.*

Compared to the price and quality of other for-sale or for-rent kits, these are an excellent buy—even better as a support-group purchase. The containers stack, so they won't take up much space in a support-group library, and 10 or 20 families could easily club together to buy the entire set. *Mary Pride*

Ever start to demonstrate a particular science lesson, only to find you don't have all the necessary items? Well, Steve Colgan of **The Science Connection**, has rectified that problem. He has put together six **science kits**: *Chemical Reactions, Crime Lab Chemistry, Convection, Earth, Moon and Stars, Fingerprinting,* and *Hot Water and Warm Homes from Sunlight*

Each kit contains a teacher's guide, student copies of pages from the guide, and the needed materials for the activities, all boxed together in a clear Rubbermaid tub.

These are basic science kits—great for introducing your students to basic principles. The kits are enjoyable for all ages. Even my four-year-old enjoyed a couple of them.

Let's take a look at how these kits work. In *Crime Lab Chemistry,* for example, you test several black felt tip pens (included) to determine which was used to write a note. After labeling each pen and a clear cup, you draw a horizontal line on paper towel strips with each pen. The strips are then

NEW!
Science In a Nutshell series
Grades 3–8. Each kit, $32.98. Shipping extra.
Delta Education, 80 Northwest Blvd, Nashua, NH 03063. (800) 442-5444. Fax: (800) 282-9560. Email: Mathew@delta-ed.mv.com. Web: www.delta-ed.com.

NEW!
The Science Connection Kits
Grades 2–10, depending on kit. Each kit, $29.95. Shipping extra.
The Science Connection, 17904 82nd St. E, Sumner, WA 98390. (253) 863-9118. Email: steve.colgan@gte.com.

The only drawback to these kits is the price. For about half the retail price, you can put the kits together yourself. The teacher guides are GEMS Guides; these are available from *Lawrence Hall of Science, University of California, Berkeley, CA 94720-5200, (510) 642-7771, Fax (510) 640-0309.* The price of the guides range from $9 to $14, and most of the materials you'll need are things you might already have around your house; a few supplies might need to be purchased.

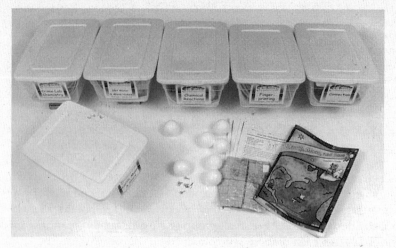

taped to pencils and lowered into water in the bottom of each cup. The colors used in making the ink will then separate out. Each of the pens included produced a distinct pattern on the paper towel strip. Thus, the principles of chromatography are taught. Follow-up activities include discussions on when this would be practical outside the classroom.

If you prefer prefab kits, these are a good choice. *Barbara Buchanan*

NEW!
Worm Acres
$34.95. Additional worms (250), $13.95.
Insect Lore, PO Box 1535, Shafter, CA 93263. (800) LIVE-BUG. (661) 746-6047. Fax: (661) 746-0334. Email: insect@lightspeed.net. Web: www.insectlore.com.

Nobody likes me, everybody hates me, guess I'll go eat worms . . .

Usually I get home-ec products in the mail to review. Imagine my surprise at finding *this* on my doorstep! For the squeamish among you, **Worm Acres** is about as ick-free as you can get in a science kit, considering you're dealing with your basic garbage here. Worm Acres includes a heavy-duty, dark green plastic bin, a supply of dirt, some cute stickers to jazz up your Worm Farm, a coloring book, some garden seeds, suggestions for experiments, and a plastic spray bottle to mist the little creepy crawlies. (What could be worse than live worms? Dried ones!).

The concept is similar to the ant farm or butterfly garden. You mail the enclosed coupon and the live animals are shipped directly to you. My first shipment contained less than the promised 250 earthworms (I didn't count each one; but the lack was obvious) and Insect Lore was very nice about sending me a replacement batch.

While the main advantage here is the ease of use—after all *you* aren't the one digging up the worms—there are several things to keep in mind before shelling out a lot of money for this kit. Butterfly gardens let you watch metamorphosis in action. Ant farms let you see the little tunnel builders up close and personal. Worm Acres lets you see . . . not much. Yes you can poke around and dig them up. Yes you can see the organic material being turned into compost (looks like rotting garbage) but that's about it. There's nothing here that you couldn't gather on your own, and for a lot less money too. When it comes to getting children interested in science, I'd go for something that offers a lot more whiz-bang for the bucks. *Renee Mathis*

PART 7

Social Studies

Homeschooler David Hammond (9) recently was awarded Scouts Canada's Fortitude Award. It is given "for eagerly and enthusiastically participating in Scouting activities despite adversity." David is a multiple amputee.

He also showed his skill at the pinewood derby competition, earning first place in his pack's Kub Kar competition.

Homeschoolers know how to make the details fun! Take the brother-sister duo of Eric and Deborah Francisco. At 10 and 8, respectively, they drew pictures of what they studied in history on pieces of cloth. When they had enough pieces for a quilt, they learned how to sew and gradually put the pieces together. In recognition of their accomplishments, the completed quilts were displayed at the county library for several months. What they learned about history was reinforced with a proud sense of accomplishment.

CHAPTER 38

How the World Works

Many kids today are out of touch when it comes to work and money. I mean *really* out of touch. In outer space somewhere, slowly circling the planet Saturn.

A while ago Focus on the Family's *Clubhouse* magazine asked kids to write in with their answers to the question, "Should kids have to do chores?" Here are some of their answers:

> *"I don't think kids should have to do chores because they might get dirty."* Jennifer, age 11, from Oregon.
>
> *"I think kids shouldn't have to do chores, because you don't want to wear out a kid."* Matthew, age 8, from Montana.
>
> *"I think the only reason God made parents is to clean my room, and I should get my allowance for nothing."* Sam, age 9½, from Alaska.

This neatly parallels what author Jean Ross Peterson observed when interviewing children for her book on money management. In her own words,

> *My eyes were opened when I interviewed children whose ages ranged from six to fourteen:*
>
> *Susan, age thirteen, "I'm going to be a model and a fashion designer."*
>
> *Dave, also thirteen: "I'll be a world class swimmer and a Supreme Court judge."*
>
> *Eric, age twelve: "I'm going to own hotels and travel on my boat."*
>
> *Beth, age seven: "Someday I'll be like a famous person on TV, or a model."*
>
> *Steve, age eleven: "I want to be a private eye."*
>
> *Rick, age nine: "I'm going to have my own business, be on a SWAT team, and live on a horse ranch."*

Give Me Liberty!

- People act in what they perceive to be their own best interests.
- Politicians are people. Most of them, anyway!
- Therefore, government will tend to be used for the perceived interests of politicians, government workers, and the people with big money who put politicians into office.
- Every time you say, "The government should do something about that," you're asking for more of your rights and money to be given to other people.
- Every time you say, "I and my friends/family/church/support group should do something about that," you're preserving your liberty.
- Homeschooling is one small step back to liberty.

The American Dream

People wonder what the "American Dream" is. Many today think the American Dream is the chance to make more money or even get rich. That's not right. The American Dream has always been the chance to run your own life, under God, without interference from kings or tyrants.

This is a random sample from over one hundred children who told me what they intended to do when they grew up. It's interesting to note that when I asked each child if he or she knew how to become whatever occupation was selected, the unanimous answer was, "Go to college."

We'll have more to say about the College Thing in Volume 3. Right now all I can say is, "Good luck, kids," because as Mrs. Peterson notes, no less an authority than the *Wall Street Journal* has discovered that today's typical kid expects "to make a lot more money than my folks do, but I won't have to work as hard to get it."

Bringing up kids with financial and career expectations like this is a major mistake. The real world doesn't work like this. Never has. Never will. The kids will find this out, too, when their VISA bill rises up and eats their new car or their spouse divorces them because they financially ruined the family.

So, How DOES the World Work?

Where does money come from? Where does it go? And why does it disappear so soon? How does the stock market work? The government? Business? Farming? What's happening in the world out there? Are we happy about it? Should we change it?

We have squirreled together a few resources for you, and we'll bring them up later in this chapter. But here first, for your viewing pleasure, is a capsule description of How the World Works.

How Money Works

It doesn't grow on trees. And you don't own a government printing press. So you have to *work*. What you earn, minus what you are forced to pay to the government in taxes, minus what you choose to give away as tithe or donations, is your income. Out of that you have to pay for rent, utilities, gasoline, and other items kids often think are taken care of by magic. With what's left over you can go shopping for clothes, food, entertainment, health products, and subscriptions to *Practical Homeschooling*. (Please!) If you pay your credit card bill each month, you never have to pay interest. If you don't have a credit card at all, you won't be tempted, but you won't be able to do much shopping by telephone, either.

WHAT TO TEACH THE KIDDIES: Work, by definition, is not always fun. It just has to be done. Work is like eating: veggies come first, *then* dessert. Spending is the same: first the veggies (taxes, rent) *then* the dessert (CDs and new sneakers). Daddy makes more than you because he knows more and has more experience. If you want a better job than Daddy, study harder than he did. Flipping burgers is not a permanent career path. If you don't have it, don't spend it. A penny saved is a pain in the neck. Collect enough and they tear a hole in your pocket. A dollar saved is a dollar earned—actually, more like *two* dollars, because you have to *earn* two dollars to have the same amount, after taxes, as you get when you *save* one dollar. Don't be a tightwad. Don't be a spendthrift. The best things in life are free (at least, they don't cost any money). Most old proverbs are true.

How the Economy Works

Economics for kids in one lesson: in theory, "the economy" is the sum of individual people's transactions. Smith wants Sullivan's product. He pays

Sullivan some money for it. Now Smith has the product and Sullivan has the money. That's "free market" economics. In "socialist" economics, the government owns all the products and the people buy them from the government with the wages the government pays them. In "mixed" economies, some people and products belong (in a manner of speaking) to the government, and others to the "private sector." The "private sector," however, is constantly being told by the government how to conduct business. When the government completely regulates all aspects of the private sector, while still allowing private ownership of the means of production, the technical term for this is "fascism."

WHAT TO TEACH THE KIDDIES: Got all that? Great! Now if you can explain it to your kids, they'll know more about economics than some folks who write economics columns for major magazines, not to mention most members of Congress!

How the Stock Market Works

THEORY: People believe in a company and purchase its stock, thus providing the company with needed cash (at least during the IPO, or Initial Product Offering).

PRACTICE: People treat the stock market like a lottery, "betting" in the short term on what they hope will be winners and even taking "bets" on whether stock prices will rise or fall. (If you take a "put" option on a stock, you make money if it *loses* value.) What's more, nowadays people don't even have to put up the full amount of the stock they purchase, thanks to trading "on margin."

LIKELY RESULT: we are all doomed. Or at least our money is. (If it worries you to share this thought with the kiddies, remember that Politically Correct types write entire books telling kids the *planet* is doomed!)

WHAT TO TEACH THE KIDDIES: Gambling is wrong. Investing is OK. You can tell the difference by how long you plan to stay with a company's stock. If you invest, you should pick companies that (1) know how to make a profit and (2) are making the world a better place. Try to avoid investing in Strip Mines 'R Us.

How the Banking System Works

You are a banker. You have *x* dollars in your coffers. Thanks to fractional-reserve banking laws, you can make, say, 5*x* dollars worth of loans. Then the loans themselves become collateral, so you can loan even more.

WHAT TO TEACH THE KIDDIES: "If you don't understand how banks make money out of nothing, and how some manage to fail when they have this amazing power, don't worry, kiddies—I don't either."

How the Court System "Works"

CASE 1: You are a vicious criminal. You are clearly guilty. So you "plea bargain." That means you are assigned a fraction of the sentence you richly deserve. Then, in jail, you are released even earlier thanks to "overcrowding" or parole. You then commit more crimes.

CASE 2: You peacefully protest a government policy, but make the mistake of picking a politically incorrect cause. You go to jail. You stay there. You don't get a reduced sentence. You get a sentence longer than some murderers get.

This isn't the whole story. Has anyone else noticed that we are no longer a republic, or even a democracy, but a "judge-ocracy"? In more cases than I

Think You're Free?

Then imagine life with
- no income tax
- no business licenses
- no social workers
- bank privacy
- no search or seizure without a duly authorized warrant
- no phone taps
- no federal databases
- no centrally controlled media (every town having two or more independently owned newspapers)
- no political correctness
- hardly any lawyers
- never having to ask permission to do just about anything

America used to be like this!

could fit in this book, *one* man or woman, or at most five men and women, have overturned laws that entire legislatures labored to create, or that have been on the books since the republic was founded, or that millions of citizens have passed by referendum. Every time a law is passed that looks like it may give small businesses, taxpayers, or families some relief, some judge somewhere stops it flat in its tracks. (With the one very positive exception of the laws regarding homeschooling. The only explanation for this is that God is on our side!) And how about the laws that judges *create* out of thin air, or the taxes they illegally impose to enforce their view of the perfect society?

WHAT TO TEACH THE KIDDIES: Little kids don't need a lot of grief and stress. But maybe, while we're telling them how the world *ought* to work, we should occasionally admit that it doesn't work very much like it ought to. When they grow up, maybe they can do something about it.

Business & Economics

Aristoplay "Made for Trade" game

Grades 3–adult. $25 plus shipping. *Aristoplay, Ltd., 450 South Wagner, Ann Arbor, MI 48103. (800) 634-7738. (734) 995-4353. Fax: (734) 995-4611. Web: www.aristoplay.com.*

Historical board game that teaches economics lessons. In **Made for Trade**, you play the part of a character such as Makepeace Middleton, a continental soldier, or Eliza Oglethorpe, tavern maid. After escaping indentured service, you try to earn shillings and barter for goods in the town shops while avoiding taxes. Find out what a free-market economy was like, and how taxation without representation messes things up. Work your way up from indentured service to colonial prosperity. Historical events crop up now and then, to which you must respond. Congress, for example, might authorize the establishment of a navy and you, as shipowner Christian Fairhill, collect four shillings in increased profits. Some fun touches: if you visit the tavern you lose a turn for self-indulgence, and you have to pay a church tithe every time you pass the meeting house.

Like other Aristoplay games, *Made for Trade* is a work of art as well as educational. You get a lot for your money: the colorful game board (laid out like a colonial town for atmosphere), eight character cards with stands, eight inventory lists, 48 object cards (things you can buy or barter), 30 Event I cards, 30 Event II cards, 60 plastic shillings, and one pair of dice. In addition, *Made for Trade* includes a special information sheet compiled by the staff of the Winterthur Museum. This sheet describes all 48 objects and adds extra historical interest to the game. Two to four characters can play at any of the four play levels. *Mary Pride*

Biblical Economics in Comics

Grades 3–adult. $9 plus shipping. *Vic Lockman, 233 Rogue River Highway #360, Grants Pass, OR 97527. Fax: (541) 479-3814.*

Our kids have just about worn the covers off five copies of Vic Lockman's **Biblical Economics in Comics**. This is undoubtedly partly a tribute to Mr. Lockman's cartooning skill—after all, the man has put in more than 30 years in the comic book industry, authoring over 7,000 comic book stories and publishing more than 100 cartoon booklets. The rest of our youngsters' fascination with this 100-plus page small paperback stems from the intriguing storyline. In Mr. Lockman's hands, economics is transformed from the "dismal science" into a series of cartoon vignettes featuring mice, rats (Bureau-Rats!), and cats.

Episode One, "The Market," starts with Adam Mouse shipwrecked on an island. There he is joined by a lady mouse, and bingo! the division of labor. They next have a family, which works as a mini-marketplace (more division of labor). When Junior gathers so much fish it begins to spoil, Pop diverts Junior's efforts to wood chopping . . . "and so, production is diverted to fill a greater demand!" The principles of exchange, competition, supply and demand, medium of exchange, capital and savings, loans and interest, profit and productivity, taxes, and even international trade are all explained so clearly a six-year-old can understand them. (I know. I asked my six-year-old.)

Next, Mr. Lockman starts explaining some of our economic woes. Enter the Bureau-Rats, who, taking their lead from Karl Marx, inflict a graduated income tax on Mouseland. (I say this as someone who most of her life has honestly qualified for one of the bottom tax levels!) This is swiftly followed by a central bank, fiat money, inflation through expansion of printed money, checkbook money (the money printer got tired), tariffs, immigration quotas, public works, government aid to farms and industry, minimum wage laws, price fixing, rent control, public housing, welfare, monopolies, and that eternal favorite of Keynesian economists for stirring up sluggish economies, war. The rest of the book is devoted (still in cartoon form, but without story plots) to an exposition of the proper roles of government, law, money, and taxes, all from a specifically biblical viewpoint.

The revised edition of *Biblical Economics in Comics* includes a new 12-page cartoon section on usury: what it is, what the Bible says about it, and how to live without it. Excellent teaching on this complex subject, simple enough for a child to follow. *Mary Pride*

What's a "fwat"? It's the product of Ump's business. Ump is a caveman who excelled with the fwat in the game of fwap, and **Ump's Fwat** is the story of how he made his fortune manufacturing fwats for other cavemen. This fanciful tale is used to illustrate many of the concepts and terms used in economics, business, and investing. Scarcity, resources, savings, marketable product, investor, employer, etc. are many of the terms you'll find used in the story.

If I were to criticize anything about this thoroughly winsome booklet, it would be the constant emphasis on how Ump's fwat business is so great at creating jobs. I believe that the ideal is for every man to sit under his own vine and fig tree, i.e., to have his own business and not have to work for someone else's. Since *Ump's Fwat* is written from the entrepreneur's perspective, this is not a major problem.

Also available: an instructor's guide, an eight-minute animated video retelling Ump's success story, and **The Economic Baseball Game**. The latter is a supply-and-demand simulation in which players buy and sell baseballs, and is designed for ages 10 to adult.

I have not seen the instructor's guide, the video, or the *Economic Baseball Game*. Myself, I can get a lot out of the *Ump's Fwat* book, but if you are not already knowledgeable about free-market economics the instructor's guide and game might be helpful. The video is too pricey for single-family viewing. *Mary Pride*

My sixth-grade teacher explained inflation and depression to us, using many historical examples. "Why doesn't our government know this stuff?" I wondered all through my teens. Perhaps because the members of our government took college economics classes similar to the one I later did, taught by people with Marxist leanings.

Richard J. Maybury (Uncle Eric) believes, as did my sixth grade teacher, "You can understand almost anything if it is explained well." And explain it well he does, in the form of letters written from "Uncle Eric" to his nephew.

Whatever Happened to Penny Candy? covers the origin and history of money, the origin and history of the dollar, the business cycle, inflation, recession, depression, foreign currencies, why governments try to tinker

with the market and always fail, and more, with very practical advice on how to tell what's really going on as opposed to how the media might be "spinning" it. Includes glossary of terms, resource list for further reading, and a bunch of great quotes that distill economic wisdom into its purest form.

If your children (or you) want to understand what is going on with our economy, this book is a must. Recently updated with current information for the 1990's, it is a treasure trove of interesting information and resources for further study. While it paints a realistic view of our future, it is neither frightening nor alarmist. If only I could afford enough copies to send to everyone in Washington D.C. . . . *Rebecca Prewett*

Law & Politics

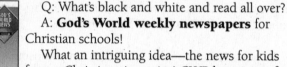

Going to the Bottom of the Earth
➤ Three men are skiing to the South Pole and back. It will take them about three months.

Q: What's black and white and read all over?
A: **God's World weekly newspapers** for Christian schools!

What an intriguing idea—the news for kids from a Christian viewpoint! GWP has papers for all different reading levels from kindergarten to adult. The papers for children are carefully matched to their interests and abilities. Following a newspaper format, you get feature stories, reports on hot news items, editorials, cartoons, and letters to the editor. Papers for the kindergarten through junior high set also include activities for kids and seven full-color posters. A teacher's guide is included with each edition. No fuzzy-wuzzy copouts here either; the editors of the children's editions know what the Bible says and aren't ashamed of it. The adult magazine tries to be more intellectual, and thus sometimes sounds a more uncertain trumpet (especially in the Arts section). *Mary Pride*

God's World Newspapers

Grades K and up. PreK–1 edition, $17.95. Edition 2–3 (grades 2-3), $17.95. Upper edition (grades 4-6), $19.95. Senior edition (junior high), $19.95. World (senior high and adult), $49.95 for 50 issues. World student rate (26 issues), $25.95. Each paper 26 issues, September to May, except World (40 issues). Substantial discounts for more than one paper going to the same address.
God's World Publications, PO Box 2330, Asheville, NC 28802. Orders: (800) 951-5437. Inquiries: (828) 232-5459. Fax: (800) 537-0447. Email: service@gwnews.com. Web: www.gwnews.com.

NEW!
Whatever Happened to Justice?

Grades 5–adult. $14.95 plus shipping.
Bluestocking Press, PO Box 2030, Shingle Springs, CA 95682-2030. Orders: (800) 959-8586. Inquiries: (530) 621-1123. Fax: (530) 642-9222. Email: uncleric@jps.net.

A thief robs you of your money, is caught, and ends up in jail. You are still minus your money—and you have to pay taxes to convict and incarcerate the criminal. In some parts of the country, property owners cannot clear brush off their own land lest they disturb the habitat of an endangered rat. Our country mandates compulsory education for children. Laws determine the prices of various goods. Is this justice?

Whatever Happened to Justice asks, "What is justice, anyway?" What is the difference between common law, natural law, and political law? What two laws should form the basis for every society—two laws upon which people everywhere, of every religion, can agree?

Written in the same format as *Whatever Happened to Penny Candy?* (a series of letters from "Uncle Eric" to his nephew Chris), this book explains the basis for true justice, what principles motivated the founders of our country, and what has gone wrong since then.

This excellent book belongs on every family's bookshelf and is must reading for everyone ages ten and over. It will provide the ammunition you need to counter the argument, "You're just trying to legislate your morality." *Rebecca Prewett*

Money Management for Kids

First you make it. Then you spend it. Ain't that life?

Moneywise Kids first sets kids the task of earning $100. At each turn, you roll the dice and pick up the designated amount of money. You also exchange smaller bills for bigger bills. As soon as you've hit $100, you've won the first game out of two.

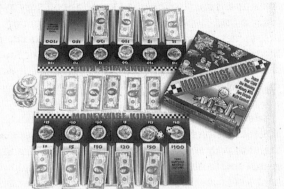

The second game starts the same way. You roll the dice and get the designated amount from the bank. Then you pick up a Moneywise marker which tells you what you'll need to buy this turn: medical care, transportation, clothes, food, taxes, or shelter. If you can afford it and need it, you purchase the marker. The object of this game is to end up with one of each marker.

This simple little game, which includes play money bills but no coins, is easy to play. It's a good way to practice addition and subtraction and to learn from the start that the essentials of life don't grow on trees. To make it perfect, add your own "Gifts and Charities" marker. *Mary Pride*

Is money management a problem for your kids? Would you like them to learn to earn the cash they need to finance their interests? Here's your chance to enroll them in **Cash University**, the money management system for kids!

The makers of Cash U encourage parents to participate with their children to help them learn lifetime skills including setting goals, earning rewards, using a checkbook, achieving goals and being responsible.

The tools needed to help reach these goals come attractively packaged in an 8 x 11" box. See sidebar for list.

After reading the instructor's manual and listening to the cassette which explains Cash University's philosophy, Mom or Dad sits down with Junior and explains how he will choose a coveted item to work toward—something he could earn in about a month's time.

A photo or hand-drawn picture is attached to the provided clip on the Goal Reminder Sheet. The dollars needed and the dollars saved are recorded on the wipe-off board.

How will Junior earn the money for his goal? The "allowance calculator"—another wipe-off board—charts days of the week and chores to be completed. For each chore done to the supervisor's satisfaction, Junior earns an agreed-upon sum. But wait: just as in real life, Junior can be penalized for socially unacceptable behavior. That's right! Fines for not listening, interrupting, leaving a mess, unfinished schoolwork, etc. will be recorded. It's up to the Job Police to do the enforcing.

After the first week's allowance is calculated, Junior's total is recorded as the beginning balance in his very own checkbook. When he needs some incidental spending money or when he reaches the amount needed to purchase his goal item, Junior writes *you* a check, which you cash for him from his accrued savings. Junior then learns to record his debit, just like in real life.

Junior is also taught to plan for the distant future—college! Yes, he begins to contribute through performing special jobs that enable him to earn

A new mini-kit is now available. This contains the goal reminder sheet, allowance calculator sheet, checkbook, and erasable marker—basically all the disposable and personal items in the kit. Useful for additional children in the Cash U program.

NEW!
Money Skills: 101 Activities to Teach Your Child About Money

Ages 3 and up. $9.95 plus shipping. *Career Press, PO Box 687, Franklin Lakes, NJ 07417-0687. (800) 227-3371. Fax: (201) 848-1727. Web: www.careerpress.com.*

funds to be tucked away for the rapidly rising cost of higher learning. On the College Savings Board, there is a place to record the name of a college that Junior might like to attend.

Coupons are also included for non-monetary awards: a trip to the library, a read-aloud, or a special date with Mom or Dad. Upon reaching his first monetary goal, Junior earns his first Associate Degree in Money Management. Fill out the application and return to Cash University, with a small fee, and Junior will receive his personal diploma. Advanced degrees may be awarded upon completion of subsequent goals. *Barbara Petronelli*

Money Skills by Bonnie Drew is a homeschooler's dream! The learning activities are broken down into three age groups, making this something useful to your entire family. Kids ages 3–5, 6–8, and 9–12 each have projects geared specifically for them. There are enough additional resources listed to help you create an in-depth unit study on money, or you could simply choose to focus on one or two family projects. Learning skills and objectives are clearly explained, giving you an idea of just what each activity is supposed to teach. No more mindless dog-and-pony shows!

While not specifically Christian, this book unashamedly promotes thrift, delayed gratification, entrepreneurship, and unselfishness. Talk about family values!

The emphasis for each age group is slightly different. Younger children are mainly exposed to Money Facts: How much is a nickel? What is money used for? Middlers are taught in terms of Money Skills: How to make change, how to estimate costs, how to save for long term purchases. Older kids are learning Money Smarts: comparison shopping, checking accounts, and compound interest.

While this isn't a workbook, there are a few reproducibles included to help you get started (sample checks, budget chart, coin flash cards, and even a credit application).

Bravo to Bonnie Drew for only including activities that are based on real life, that are inexpensive, yet have solid educational value. *Moneyskills* is worth its weight in gold. *Renee Mathis*

CHAPTER 39

Map Skills

How do you start a little kid studying geography? By teaching him or her

- how to read a map
- the names of geographic features
- what is where: states & capitals, countries, famous landmarks.

How to Read a Map

"This direction is *north*. The opposite direction is *south*. *East* is to the right when *north* is up. *West* is to the left. Good!

"Now, you have to learn that on a map various symbols 'stand for' different things. Here is a small drawing of a house with 'Wilson' written on it. That *stands for* the Wilson's house. This is the road. Here is the park."

Usually, the first maps a child is asked to read in school are neighborhood maps with just a few roads running north-south and east-west, and little drawings of houses, schools, and so forth. Sometimes the child is asked to draw a map of his own neighborhood, or even his own room. He may be given navigation exercises, such as "You are here. Go one block east and two blocks south. Where do you end up?"

In real life, of course, this is not the kind of map grownups use. We use *road* maps. So as soon as a child is able to read the small print on a local road map, why not let her start trying to plot the route from your house to, say, the science museum? Or, if you take a long trip, the kids can help you figure out the best interstates to take and calculate how many miles between various road stops.

Other types of map abound: political maps, topographic maps (these show the relative height of land features, physical maps (these show features such as mountains, rivers, and forests), and more. Learn to read and use all these with the resources below!

> Once your child has learned to read a map, *you* can ask *him*, "Are we almost there?"

Educational Insights 3-D Landform Maps

Grades 3–8. $19.95 plus shipping. *Educational Insights, Inc., 16941 Keegan Ave., Carson, CA 90746. (800) 995-4436. (310) 884-2000. Fax: (800) 995-0506. Web: www.edin.com.*

Golden Educational Center Outline Maps

Grades 2–adult. Forty-six 11 x 17" maps (2 each of 23), $13.95. Set of 50 of the same map, $6.90. Shipping extra. *Golden Educational Center, 857 Lake Blvd., Redding, CA 96003. (800) 800-1791. Fax: (530) 244-5939. Email: rlw@iname.com. Web: www.goldened.com.*

NEW!
Janice VanCleave's Geography for Every Kid

Grades 3–6. $12.95. *John Wiley & Sons, 1 Wiley Drive, Somerset, NJ 08875. (800) 225-5945. (732) 469-4400. Fax: (800) 597-3299. Web: www.wiley.com.*

NEW!
Map Mysteries
World Geography Mysteries

Grades 4–6. $10.95 each. Shipping extra. *The Learning Works, Inc., P.O. Box 6187, Santa Barbara, CA 93160.*

This really is hands-on learning! **3-D Landform Maps** is a set of (1) three full-color raised-relief maps of an imaginary land, showing the 44 most popular geographic features, (2) a teacher's guide bound together with (3) six reproducible worksheets. Your students literally get their hands on the map and *feel* the shape of a mountain range, peninsula, or delta. You start to feel eerily like a giant looming over the earth after you've used this ingenious educational tool for a while. A fun way to learn about geographic features, with no sermonizing about how the features may have gotten there. *Mary Pride*

From the publishers of the *Creating Line Designs* and *Designs in Math* series, yet another tool for integrating your artistic side with your intellectual one. We're talking about a package of black-and-white **Outline Maps** for your students to label and/or color in themselves. The size is a comfortable 11 x 17"—easy for children to work with. Price is right, too.

Set includes World (outline and political boundaries), United States (outline, waterways, state boundaries), Africa, Asia, Australia, Europe, North America, and South America (separate maps for outline, waterways, and political boundaries of each). By looking up and labeling states, countries, rivers, and so on, your student will really learn where these things are. The open-ended format of white spaces to fill in also means you or he can add notes of interest—historical, cultural, or whatever. I haven't found a package like this anywhere else. *Mary Pride*

Janice VanCleave's Geography for Every Kid is subtitled "Easy Activities That Make Learning Geography Fun." But this book is much more than "activities." It's really a mini geography textbook, complete with hands-on activities to make geography concepts memorable.

Each chapter starts with a "What You Need to Know" introduction to the chapter subject. This is where new information and terminology is introduced. "Let's Think It Through" questions and puzzles to solve using the information from the introduction, answers to the above, application exercises, a step-by-step activity (typically, a demonstration or modeling of facts taught in the chapter), line-art charts and illustrations, and solutions to the exercises round out each chapter.

While this is not a "learn where everything in the world is located" book, it does a good job of covering geography terms and concepts—especially map skills. Chapter topics are models of the solar system (Ptolemy v. Copernicus), how to use ancient mapmaking symbols and techniques, how early explorers navigated by maps and stars, latitude and longitude, globes v. flat maps, using a map scale to determine distance, how to read and use a grid map, how to use a map legend, geographic north v. magnetic north, using a compass rose, how to determine the depth of the ocean floor, how to read a topographic map, tracking the path of a hurricane, how the sun affects the seasons, time zones, atmospheric circulation, water and climate, climate regions, identifying and locating the seven continents and four oceans, and world population and location. *Mary Pride*

Would your children like to to discover new places and people? Then these books from Learning Works are for you!

In **Map Mysteries**, one chapter is "Geography by the Numbers." The activities describe the towns or areas and their main features. You must locate them on the map by using longitude and latitude readings. Each chapter includes something for science, history, literature or math. You discover tidbits about monuments, space, movies, mainly in the United States.

World Geography Mysteries is more of the same exciting activities involving the Western and Eastern hemispheres, Australia, South America, and all points in between. Also included are a few chapters on different cultures of the world.

The instruction are easy to follow and self-explanatory. Your children will learn their way around an encyclopedia and library using these books. They would make excellent supplements to any curriculum or learning style. *Barb Meade*

Your mission: to use the maps found in the **Mapped Out! The Search for Snookums** book along with your logical thinking skills to navigate the city of Spittsburgh and find Snookums, a petnapped iguana.

That's right, this interactive book attempts to teach map reading while having your child follow clues to solve this far-fetched mystery. In order to chase down this endangered reptile you will have to read a subway map, a train timetable, a mall directory, and more, while continually referring back to the enclosed city map of Spittsburgh. Watch out for red herrings! If you make a navigational mistake you will end up on the wrong page and will have to backtrack. Along the way you will find notes in actual envelopes, lift 'n' look flaps, and other fun manipulatives.

Several things about this book seem designed to appeal to TV-watching kids, from the intensely colored animated illustrations to the humor which occasionally is slightly off-color. (One of the lift 'n' look flaps is of a toilet!) Also, the detective for whom you are supposedly working, Bianca Beare, is known as Ms. Beare, rather than Mrs. or Miss Beare.

Is this a useful tool for teaching map skills? For children already versed in using maps, this book can be a fun way to challenge their expertise. For those who have not had much exposure to maps, *Mapped Out!* does give adequate explanations and plenty of incentive to try their new abilities.

So, if the theme and humor appeal to you, you might want your child to spend a few hours with this witty book as a lightweight but enjoyable means to reinforce or teach city map skills. *Anne Wegener*

Are you looking for a map series that will complement your other studies in geography? If so, **Maps My Way—U.S.A.** may be for you.

Maps My Way—U.S.A., developed by Elizabeth Nicholson, a homeschool mom and former elementary school teacher, includes maps of all 50 states and a full U.S.A. map in two versions: blank student maps and teaching maps. The teaching maps contain helpful information such as state and river names. Small states, and states that are logically related, like Virginia and West Virginia, are shown together.

This 46-page reproducible map series is printed on slick, good-quality paper and is three-hole punched, which makes photocopying a breeze.

There aren't any lessons *per se*, but suggested lesson topics are included. For instance, you might use the state maps to find cities at given coordinates, identify mountain ranges and rivers, find the distance between given cities, etc. Other suggestions include tracing your family history, creating weather maps from newspaper data and tracing routes of explores, traders, and so on.

If you like a lot of structure, and clear plans for each individual lesson, you may find this resource to be overwhelming. But if you want a curriculum which offers flexibility and endless possibilities, check this one out—especially at its new, lower price! *Rebecca Livermore*

Orders: (800) 235-5767.
Inquiries: (805) 964-4220.
Fax: (805) 964-1466.
Email: LESatTLW@aol.com.
Web: www.thelearningworks.com.

NEW!
Mapped Out! The Search For Snookums
Grades 3–6. $19.95 plus shipping.
Gibbs Smith Publisher, P.O. Box 667, Layton, UT 84041. (800) 748-5439.
Fax: (800) 213-3023.
Web: www.gibbs-smith.com.

NEW!
Maps My Way—U.S.A.
All ages. $14 plus shipping.
AlmaNichePublishing, LLC, 310 Williams St., Hattiesburg, MS 39401. (800) 299-6974.
Inquiries/fax: (601) 584-8932.

NEW!
Mapworks

Grades 4–8. $10.95 plus shipping.
*The Learning Works. PO Box 6187,
Santa Barbara, CA 93160. Orders:
(800) 235-5767. Inquiries: (805) 964-
4220. Fax: (805) 964-1466.
Email: LESatTLW@aol.com.
Web: www.thelearningworks.com.*

NEW!
Mighty Maps!

Grades 3–6. $9.95 plus shipping.
*Teaching and Learning Company,
1204 Buchanan St., PO Box 10,
Carthage, IL 62321. Orders: (800)
852-1234. Inquiries: (217) 357-2591.
Fax: (217) 357-6789.
Email: tandlcom@adams.net.
Web: www.ierc.com.*

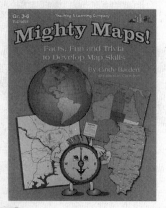

NEW!
Scholastic Map Crosswords

Grades 4–8. $9.95 plus shipping.
*Scholastic Professional Books, 2931
East McCarty St., Jefferson City, MO
65102. (800) 724-6527. Fax: (800)
223-4011. Web: www.scholastic.com.*

When you already know how to read maps, but you're just beginning to glimpse how much more there is to geography, you're ready for a book like **Mapworks**. Thirty-nine pages of scavenger-hunt-style activities will send you, not house-to-house, but from atlas to globe to encyclopedia to almanac. When you're done, you'll have "explored" the United States, Canada, and the world. You'll have found over 500 bodies of water, continents, deserts, mountains, islands, countries, states, and cities, and learned to use compass directions, latitude and longitude, map indexes, and map scales. Illustrations on each black-and-white page are attractive, appealing, and appropriate. Reproduction limited to a single classroom. *Kim O'Hara*

Would you like to be able to teach map skills with your eyes closed? With **Mighty Maps!** you can almost do that! This resource is laid out in a user-friendly format that requires almost no preparation. The material is presented in such a way that even parents and students with no previous map skills can understand.

This 92-page reproducible book contains 75 one-page lessons which cover 17 different categories, such as using an atlas, using map grids, time zones, map keys, and longitude and latitude. Two of the lessons contain simple skill-building activities, such as building a compass. These activities require basic supplies, such as string, magnets, needles, etc.

Mighty Maps! also contains a list of 18 challenge questions such as, "Wind direction can be important to people like pilots and firefighters. Why? What about people in other occupations or hobbies? Why would wind direction be important to them?" The questions are separate from the lessons and are optional.

Reproducible maps of the United States, Canada, Mexico, and the seven continents are included, along with several suggestions for using them.

Mighty Maps! is a great resource if you want to simply introduce your children to various map skills; they most likely won't master the concepts because the lessons are very brief with little or no repetition. If you crave hands-on lessons, you will be left wanting with this resource; but if you enjoy workbooks, and easy preparation, it's perfect! *Rebecca Livermore*

Crossword enthusiasts, take note! **Map Crosswords** is a unique way to teach geography skills through crossword puzzles!

This 64-page book by Spencer Finch has 25 two-page lessons, arranged in ascending order of difficulty. Each lesson contains a map with directions for using the map. For instance, the map used to teach scale says, "Scale is the relationship between distances shown on a map and the real distances on the earth. Maps with large scale, such as Map B, show more detail than maps with smaller scale, such as Map A. The scale of a map is shown by a straight line divided that tells how many miles or kilometers equals one inch. Using this scale, you can measure a distance on a map and then figure out the real distance in miles or kilometers on earth. You will need a ruler to answer some of the questions in this puzzle." The opposite page contains a crossword puzzle directly related to the preceding map. You practice newly learned map skills as you work the puzzles.

The book contains a variety of maps—everything from highway maps to subway maps to population cartograms. An answer key is included in the back of the book. *Rebecca Livermore*

CHAPTER 40

U. S. Geography

United States geography, as taught in schools, is mostly

- knowing which state goes where on a map
- knowing the capital of each state
- a mish-mash of poorly related information about imports and exports, tourist attractions, state nicknames, and so forth
- a more detailed study of your state's geography

We can help you with what you need to know about what state goes where and what its capital is. I see no real point in studying the "mishmash." Who cares how many tons of wheat are produced annually in Nebraska? This sort of information changes yearly, can be found in reference books if you ever need it, and makes no difference whatsoever to your daily life, unless you are a Nebraska wheat farmer.

On the other hand, knowing about the major physical features of the USA—its main rivers, mountain ranges, the Great Lakes and the midwestern plains—is useful. So is knowing the time zones, and the Post Office abbreviation for each state's name. You'll want to know in later years that, when planning a skiing trip, there's more snow in Colorado than in Missouri. When calling a friend or relative elsewhere in the country, it helps to know if you're an hour ahead of them or two hours behind. When writing letters, you need to know the state abbreviations.

Knowing what a city or area is famous for also increases your cultural literacy. Boston, Massachusetts, is famous for the number of colleges dotted around its metropolitan area, and also for the "Route 128" strip of high-tech companies just outside the city. The U.S. Naval Academy is in Annapolis, Maryland. Florida has lots of people from Cuba, while California has lots of people from Mexico. "Silicon Valley" is in California. Microsoft is in Redmond, Washington. This is the sort of information adults pick up by reading newspapers and magazines or by watching documentaries and the TV news. Why not make a habit of taking out the atlas and looking up areas when you read about them or they touch your lives in some way?

NEW!
Beautiful Feet Books "Geography Through Literature"

Grades 3–7. Geography Pack, $59.95. Geography Pack with hardbacks, $99.95. Study Guide, $8.95. Set of 4 maps, $16.95 for first set, $12.95 for additionals. Shipping extra.

Beautiful Feet Books, 139 Main St., Sandwich Village, MA 02563. Orders: (800) 889-1978. Inquiries: (508) 833-8626. M–F 9–5 EST. Fax: (508) 833-2770. Web: www.bfbooks.com.

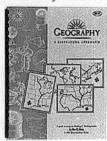

NEW!
Hewitt Across America

Grade 2. Complete program, $129.95. Teacher's Manual, student workbook, and reader *only*, $99.95. Additional student workbooks, $30 each. Reader, $13.95. 3rd and 4th grade supplement, $29.95.
Hewitt Homeschooling Resources, PO Box 9, Washougal, WA 98671. Free catalog: (800) 348-1750. Orders/Inquiries: (360) 835-8708. Fax: (360) 835-8697.

I would want to flesh out the history with a basic overview that would help tie everything together in the student's mind.

I would also add more depth and systematic study of Scripture to the Bible/Character studies. I thought this was the weakest part of the curriculum.

I enjoyed the way many of the math word problems tied into the state being studied. However, this assumes that your child will be "on target"; if he isn't, the word problems might not be quite as fun or meaningful.

Curriculum

Beautiful Feet Books Geography Through Literature course is based on four award-winning classics by Holling Clancy Holling. To give you the flavor of these old-timey books, written decades ago, here's the story of *Paddle-to-the-Sea*. A lonely Native American boy carves a little wooden canoe with a wooden boy like him in it. He puts the canoe into a little brook at the headwaters of the Great Lakes and lets it go, hoping it will make it all the way down the St. Lawrence river to the Atlantic Ocean. The story follows the adventures of the little wooden canoe. No, the canoe does *not* talk and the wooden boy does *not* come to life! Instead, various kind people read the message on the bottom of the canoe and help it back into the river. Eventually, the canoe does make it to the sea, and then . . . but you'll have to read the book for yourself to find out. For our purposes, you just need to know that the canoe's trip introduces the reader to the geography of the river: the communities around it, the wildlife, the plants, and much more.

Three other books are included with this course: *Minn of the Mississippi, Seabird,* and *Tree in the Trail.* Between all four, you encounter three regions of the USA, plus some world geography as well

The study guide provides daily lesson plans, with assignments for the parent to read aloud to the student . Four 18 x 24" maps are also included in the Geography Pack, for the student to label and color. Or you can purchase, maps, study guides, and books separately.

This is way too much fun. You probably won't believe you're *really* doing geography. So now where is the world geography course, already? *Mary Pride*

Across America is aptly named—a "trip" across our country, from Maine to Hawaii and the U.S. Territories, in the form of a unit study integrating Bible/Character, Social Studies with a geography emphasis, Science, Health, Language Arts (including reading, spelling, and ball-and-stick penmanship), Study/Thinking Skills, Math, P.E., Music, and Art. The package includes:

- **Teacher's Manual.** Over 400 pages of learning objectives, instructions and lessons. Also includes an appendix containing maps, project patterns, Xerox masters, and other resources.
- **Student Workbook.** 250+ pages containing all of the worksheets your student will use for the year.
- **Across America Reader.** 51 stories, one based on each state plus one for the Territories.
- **States and Capitals Kit.** Includes a cassette tape, large map and state flag stickers.
- **Rummy Roots** word game.
- **Critical Thinking for the Primary Grades.**

You will need to provide basic school supplies, a picture dictionary, old magazines and newspapers to cut up, index cards, and 20 small manipulatives for Math (Lego bricks are fine; so are beans). A local library is a big plus.

The course is divided into 38 easily taught units, one per week. It's assumed that you will spend additional time studying your own state. In Unit 36, for example, you study California. The character trait is, "Realizing that big goals may be achieved a little at a time." Several Scriptures are given to study and memorize. Your child will learn some basic history of California, complete a state map, look at pictures of California which you provide, make and eat a "California" salad, learn some Spanish terms, studies beetles and frogs, read a story about a boy spading his garden during the California gold rush, learn spelling words, study apostrophes, learn about simple fractions (halves, thirds,

fourths), jump rope, learn some basic gymnastics, sing songs about California, learn the Mexican Hat Dance, and press flowers to make a bookmark.

My second-grader liked the history/geography activities we did, especially the map work. Two of our children eagerly began geography notebooks; the history/geography portion is easily adaptable to a range of ages. My daughter liked the reader. I wish that the stories did a better job of depicting the history or the "flavor" of the state being studied. Instead they were based more on the character trait for that week with sometimes only the vaguest connection to the particular state.

Unlike some unit study curriculums that require a great deal of teacher preparation or are intimidating for novice homeschoolers, this one has done most of the work for you and is simple to use. *Rebecca Prewett*

Memorizing States & Capitals

The **Audio Memory States & Capitals** tape set includes a 25 x 36" United States poster for older children to color, with 172 items to label. The poster includes the words to the eight catchy songs and a self-quizzing format.

The unique aspect of this mini-course is that the states and capitals are not taught in alphabetical order, but rather by location—which makes sense, considering we are trying to learn *where* things are! In the States Songs, the states are sung in order, according to the part of the U.S. border they form; and each state is connected geographically to the next one in the song. On the flip side, the capitals songs sing through the states naming their capitals in the same order as the States song. The capitals songs are sung in echo fashion and repeated for self-testing.

I found myself better able to place the states after learning these songs with my children. *Kathy von Duyke*

How can a set of 56 8½ x 11" illustrated flash cards help your youngsters memorize the capital of every U.S. state, and each state's general location? What if I told you that one flash card has a picture of a big ARK on top of a LITTLE ROCK and another shows the BOYS watching while IDA HOES potatoes? Yes, **Arthur Bornstein** has struck again. The outrageous associations and goofy scenes in his States and Capitals Kit make it easy to remember which capital goes with which state. More: the back of each card shows the state's outline and relative size, its abbreviation, nickname, flower, tree, bird, and date of entrance into the Union, plus teaching tips. Accompanying booklet and cassette tape explain whatever else you need to know about using this kit. Then, when your students have finished giggling their way through all fifty states, cards 51–56 feature a map of states and their capitals, and memory associations for the 13 original states, Western states, Midwestern states, Southern states, and Northeastern states. Exaggerated cartoon-style, busty females in low-cut dresses, quite a few Catholic and Christian allusions (Mass for Massachusetts, Ark for Arkansas, St. Paul's Cathedral for St. Paul). Very easy to use. Mary Pride

TREND has packed an awful lot of information on the **States and Capitals Fun-to-Know Flash Cards**, while keeping all that information accessible. On the front of each card: state outline, location on a U.S. map, capital location, year of statehood. On the back: the state's capital, nickname, date and number of statehood, flower, bird, industries, attractions, fun facts about the state, and a couple of quiz questions, plus a mini re-

NEW!
Audio Memory States and Capitals Songs
Grades K–6. $9.95 plus shipping.
Audio Memory, 501 Cliff Dr., Newport Beach, CA 92663. (800) 365-7464. Fax: (949) 631-1150. Email: emily@audiomemory.com.

Bornstein States and Capitals Kit
Grades 2–adult. $39.95 plus shipping.
Arthur Bornstein's Memory Training Programs, 11693 San Vicente Blvd., Los Angeles, CA 90049. (800) 468-2058. In LA: (310) 478-2056. Fax: (310) 207-2433. Email: abornstein@aol.com. Web: www.bornsteinmemory.com.

TREND Fun-To-Know States and Capitals Flash Cards
Grades 3–8. $5.79 plus shipping.
TREND Enterprises, Inc., PO Box 64073, St. Paul, MN 55164. (800) 328-5540. Fax: (800) 845-4832.

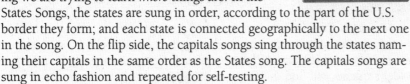

gional map with the state highlighted. Fifty cards in all (if New York State ever gets smart and secedes from New York City, that'll be 51). *Mary Pride*

"Memorize . . . all [the state capitals] *forever* in 20 minutes without trying!" Sounds too good to be true? It is. It took me 30 minutes. But then, I stopped to read some of the fun facts about each state along the way.

Just like *Yo, Millard Fillmore!* (which teaches you the Presidents in order), **Yo, Sacramento!** employs the memory device of outrageous cartoons to help you remember each state and its capital. For Missouri, whose capital is Jefferson City, the "chef's son is sitting in misery" because his dad punished him for making a mess. "Chef's son sitting" sounds a bit like "Jefferson City," and "misery" stands for "Missouri." Lame, you think? Yes, but highly visual (thanks to the cartoon) and memorable.

You can just look at the cartoons and captions and inside 30 minutes learn the states and capital. (Expect little kids, who don't even know the state names, to take somewhat longer.) Or you can also read the introductions to each region, study the outline maps, and read the facts about each state (on the left-hand pages, opposite the cartoons on the right-hand pages). That will take a little longer, but enable you to play the 75-question Jeopardy-style quiz in the back of the book (answers are provided). Maybe you'll even feel brave enough to play Name That State on the U.S. map page. It's not a complete U.S. geography education, but it's a start. *Mary Pride*

NEW!
Yo, Sacramento!

Grades 4–adult. $6.95.
The Millbrook Press, PO Box 335, 2 Old New Milford Rd., Brookfield, CT 06804. Orders: (800) 462-4703. extension 3034. Inquiries: (203) 740-2220. Fax: (203) 740-2223.

NEW!
Audio Memory 50 States Crosswords

Grades 3–12. $9.95 plus shipping.
Audio Memory, 501 Cliff Dr., Newport Beach, CA 92663. (800) 365-7464. (949) 631-0501. Fax: (949) 631-1150. Email: kathy@audiomemory.com. Web: www.audiomemory.com

Lauri Fit-A-State Puzzle

Grades 3–12. $19.95 plus shipping.
LAURI, PO Box F, Phillips-Avon, ME 04966. Orders: (800) 451-0520. Inquiries: (207) 639-2000. Fax: (800) 682-3555.

Activities

50 States Crosswords is a stimulating supplement to the study of U.S. history and geography, no matter what grade level your child is in. Upper-elementary students can easily rise to the challenge of these puzzles, and older students will find their memories refreshed.

This crossword-puzzle workbook comes spiral-bound for ease of use and covers each of the 50 states, plus Washington D.C. Historical and geographical facts are included, as well as information about famous people and places in American history. Each puzzle is in a large black and white print suitable for reproduction. There are many questions for each puzzle, with an accompanying word list. A handy answer key is found at the back of the book.

Don't be misled to think this workbook is simply a book of crossword trivia. The questions used by the publishers have been critically selected to include key information all students should know about the United States. Parents may find the workbook so much fun that this lesson enrichment becomes a family affair. Audio Memory Publishing is to be commended for such a creative addition to the study of our country. *Lisa Mitchell*

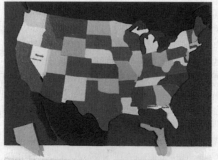

I went out and paid money for Lauri's crepe rubber Fit-A-State Puzzle. If you knew how stuffed my storage cabinet already is with things geographical, you'd realize how great I think these Lauri maps are! First, they are beautiful. States are different colors of crepe rubber. Second, they have texture and heft. The pieces are ⁵⁄₁₆-inch thick and feel great. Third, they are puzzles. You have to learn something about geography just by putting the puzzles back together! Novices quickly learn to look for clues: the funny-shaped, tiny states come from New England,

and the big blocks from out West. Unlike most U.S. state puzzles, this set includes pieces for all 50 states! State names are shown on the underlay, so you can see what you are looking for. And if you lose Rhode Island, Lauri will replace it for 50¢. *Mary Pride*

McClanahan publishes beautiful full-color sticker books. The **State Sticker Book** is no exception. It has three stickers for each state: a banner with the state's name, the state flag, and a picture of the state flower. You stick these in marked spots on each state. Every state has a page, with a few interesting or weird facts about that state and nice cartoony illustrations of those facts.

There's a little prehistoric mumbo-jumbo, but nothing a little magic marker couldn't fix. All in all, this is an excellent book, and one sticker-loving kids will enjoy. *Joseph Pride*

Games

Games are a great teaching tool, as long as they are fun and packed with useful information. **Discover America** is such a game!

Two to four players or teams travel around the board with Washington, DC, as their final destination. When the last person arrives in Washington, DC, each player adds up his money. The player with the most money wins.

To progress around the board, players choose to either spin the "state selector" and name a state capital, or roll the dice and follow an instruction card. For example, if a three is rolled, the card tells you, "Move 3 spaces, collect $30, and pass the dice." If a seven is rolled, the card instructs you, "Take a quiz card; if correct, move 1, earn $10 and play again." Quiz cards contain questions ranging from the founding of our country to the space age. And to add excitement, players occasionally draw lucky cards or sorry cards.

If your family is out for a drive discovering America yourself, you may also be interested in the travel version—a team game which has players look for license plates and road signs while gathering other information about the 50 states.

If you tend to play games insatiably, you might want to consider purchasing the sturdy deluxe edition. My family voted this game a "keeper." *Rebecca Livermore*

United States Geography Journey is a workbook and game rolled into one. First, the workbook. It's divided into six sections. The first section, "General Geographic Facts," teaches kids how to read maps of all kinds. Each of the next four sections focuses on one particular region—southern, northeastern, central, and western—of the U.S.A. Activities include matching states to their outlines, matching states to their geographic features and locations, and a detective story that the reader can follow on his map. The sixth section, "Just for Fun," has quiz questions covering all states and regions.

Included with the workbook are six 8½ x 11" Colorprint U.S. maps, a large U.S. outline map, and 128 U.S. Geography Grab Bag game cards

NEW!
McClanahan State Sticker Book
Grades 2–5. $6.95 plus shipping. *McClanahan Book Company, Inc., 23 West 26th Street, New York, NY 10010. Orders: (800) 395-8594. Inquiries: (212) 725-1515. Fax: (800) 372-9170. Email: info@mcclanahanbooks.com. Web: www.mcclanahanbooks.com.*

NEW!
Discover America
Ages 9–adult. 2–4 players. Retail edition, $35 postpaid. Deluxe edition, $45 postpaid. Travel edition, $12 postpaid. *Second Avenue Creations, 108 S. Fourth Ave., PO Box 472, St. Nazianz, WI 54232. (800) 713-1105. Fax: (920) 773-2927. Email: second@discoveramer.com. Web: www.discoveramer.com.*

United States Geography Journey
Grades 4–8. Workbook only (no maps), $6.95 plus shipping. *The Learning Works. PO Box 6187, Santa Barbara, CA 93160. Orders: (800) 235-5767. Inquiries: (805) 964-4220. Fax: (805) 964-1466. Email: LESatTLW@aol.com. Web: www.thelearningworks.com.*

(printed in sheets of eight questions per sheet). Using the maps, a whole group of students and their teacher can solve the quiz problems at once.

U.S. Geography Grab Bag is a look-it-up game. Categories for the question cards include Using a Map Scale of Miles, Which is Farther?, Rivers-Lakes-and-Seas, Latitude and Longitude, North-South-East-or-West, Borders and Boundaries, Comparing Size, and The Name's the Same. Each category includes 16 cards, color-coded to the category. These are not "knowledge" questions, but look-it-up questions, such as "The distance between Columbia and Sumter, South Carolina, is about 50 miles—true or false?"

When you get a card, use your U.S. map to determine whether the information on the card is true or false. If true, place your card in the True box on the game sheet (or in a box labeled "True" on any old plain sheet of paper). If false, place it in the False box. Game variations include moving markers across individual U.S. maps, or claiming states with different-colored markers for each student on a large U.S. map. Answer key is in the back of the workbook.

U.S. Geography Journey has more map work than any other single program I have seen. Good for larger families (who can use more of the maps!) and as a unit to train kids in map work. *Mary Pride*

CHAPTER 41

World Geography

QUESTION: Who cares about tundra and plains and mountains, anyway? ANSWER: These geographical features are extremely important in understanding the *people* who live on or near them, and in understanding the history of those people. Settling on a narrow strip of fertile land between the craggy fjords and the ice-capped mountains produces a different way of life than putting up a hut on an island where the coconuts literally fall into your lap. Life on the plain between warring empires is almost guaranteed to be exciting, while having an ocean between you and your nearest potential enemy makes it easy to give peace a chance.

It's boring to watch a hockey game if you don't know anything about the teams or players. It's just as boring to look at places on a map and not know what happened there. That's why **the best way to study geography is in terms of history and culture.** Once you know how important the Nile River was (and is) to the Egyptians, it's simple to remember that the Nile is in Egypt.

When studying **shapes** (the outlines of nations, states, and continents and the course of rivers, etc.), the best way to get these into the brain is to copy the shapes. I am not a particularly kinesthetic learner, but I will forever remember that Italy looks like a boot because I had to copy its coastline as an exercise in sixth grade.

Drill has its place, in my opinion, and as far as geography is concerned that place is supplying simple facts and shapes again and again until we are comfortable with them. It then is easier to fill that data with content. When the Sudan comes up in dinner conversation, you'll at least have a vague idea that it's on the other side of the world. You won't think it's one of the fifty states or a province of Mexico!

We are now blessed with a superabundance of colorful and fun geography products. There are books to introduce geographic concepts, hands-on projects, drill products, and maps and atlases and globes. All of these (1) help you get from point A to point B in your personal travels or (2) provide the "where" of "Who did what where?" If these points are kept firmly in mind, geography study can be a thrilling journey of discovery!

Curriculum

Alpha Omega History & Geography LIFEPACs

Grades 1–12. 10 LIFEPACs per grade. LIFEPACs: Grades 1–10, $3.50 each LIFEPAC. Set of 10 for $34. Grades 11–12, $2.95 each. Set of 10 for $28.50. Teacher's guides and answer keys extra. Shipping extra. *Alpha Omega Publications, 300 N. McKemy, Chandler, AZ 85226. Orders and inquiries: (800) 622-3070. Fax: (480) 785-8034. Web: www.home-schooling.com.*

Alpha Omega's History & Geography LIFEPACs cover history, geography, economics, citizenship, and a whole lot more. Here's the scoop on these worktext-based courses:

Grades 1 and 2: almost no geography is covered. **Grade 3** is a whole year spent on American cultural anthropology. In other words, it's a simplified field trip around the country. Units are: *A Fishing Community, A Farming Community* (Kansas), *A Fruit-Growing Community* (Washington), *Oregon: Land of Forests, A Golden Land* (California), *Cattle Raising in Texas, Coal Mining and Pennsylvania, Manufacturing Community* (Michigan), and *Florida: Gateway to Space.*

Grade 4 examines the geography and cultures of geographic areas around the world. It begins with a touch of world geography, then looks at two island countries (Japan and Hawaii), two mountain countries (Peru and Switzerland), the polar regions, tropical jungles (Amazon and Congo), grassland regions (Kenya, Argentina, U.S.A.), desert lands, and seaport cities (San Francisco, Hong Kong, and Sydney). The last LIFEPAC, *The United States: Your State,* teaches basic U.S. history, geography, and government, plus activities for doing your own state report. Each unit on a country or area includes information on its history, geography, culture, and industries, from a Christian perspective. For example, the unit on Hawaii tells how the missionaries came to Hawaii and what effect they had (Hawaii was once a Christian country!).

Grade 5 mostly focuses on U.S. history. LIFEPACs 7–9 of this course cover geographic regions of the U.S., "Our Southern Neighbors" (Mexico, Central America, and Caribbean), and Canada.

Grade 6 tackles world history. For more details, see the review in chapter 43.

All Alpha Omega levels are very easy to use, as long as you keep up with your grading of workbook exercises and writing assignments. The tests are right in the workbooks, as are pre-tests and teacher checkpoints. Alternative tests for all subjects and LIFEPACs can be found in all Alpha Omega teacher's editions. *Mary Pride*

Audio Memory Sing Around the World Kit

All ages. Sing Around the World Geography Kit, $19.95. Sing Around the World book, $6.95. Coloring map of world (U.S.A.), $3 each. History and Bible Songs, $12.95 each. Shipping extra. *Audio Memory, 501 Cliff Dr., Newport Beach, CA 92663. (800) 365-7464. (949) 631-0501. Fax: (949) 631-1150. Email: kathy@audiomemory.com. Web: www.audiomemory.com.*

Learn what's where by singing along with tapes! Audio Memory Publishing's updated **Sing Around the World kit** has one long-playing cassette with 23 songs, a 72-page songbook with all the lyrics plus regional maps to color, and several pages with pictures of landmarks to color. To make things more lively, the book also features many pictures of the people, pastimes, landmarks, and cultural detritus of each area.

Song topics include Southeast Asia, the Middle East, Australia, New Zealand, Canada, Central America, South Asia, Mexico, Asia, Greenland, Oceania, South America, Africa, West Indies, United States, Continents and Oceans, the Solar System, Eastern Europe, Southern Europe, Scandinavia, Western Europe, the British Isles, and the former USSR.

How helpful will these cassettes be? It's all up to you. If you and your kids are the type who like to have music playing, sooner or later you will pick up the lyrics to all of these songs almost unconsciously. They won't *mean* anything, though, until you get out the songbook and start locating the countries you are singing about. They are numbered in the same order as they are sung on the 23 book maps. This has 171 numbers listed on the side, corresponding to numerals on the map. *Mary Pride*

Can your child answer these questions:

> 1. What two oceans do not touch Australia?
> 2. The Prime Meridian passes through which three continents?
> 3. Two countries in South America are totally landlocked. Bolivia is one; what is the name of the other country?

Dollars to doughnuts he can't. The amount most kids today know about geography is pitiful. You know that. I know that. So what are we going to do about it?

How about a geography program that takes 5–10 minutes a day, and teaches kids not just the simple stuff like, "Find Florida on this labeled U.S. map," but how to answer toughies like the questions above? **Daily Geography** is a set of teacher's manuals with geography questions and answers for every week of the school year, plus a scope and sequence, glossary of geography terms, and simple teaching suggestions. The teacher's manuals for grades 2 and 3 have six geography questions a week. The manuals for grades 4–11 have eight questions a week. If you use the entire program, your child will have worked through nearly 2,500 sequenced geography questions.

Here's how it works. You write two geography questions on the chalkboard. (Every home teacher needs a chalkboard, anyway.) Your child then copies the questions into his geography notebook and looks up the answers using maps, globes, and atlases. He then reports his answer orally and/or shows you the answer on the map. Correct answers are recorded in the geography notebook. You can either do one or two geography questions every day, or have a single, longer geography session once a week.

The questions for each week fit on a single page of the manual, and are divided according to concept. These are *not* multiple choice—the student has to figure out the answers himself. Concepts taught run the gamut from states and capitals to map reading, relative positions of geographic features (e.g, "Which of the Great Lakes is farthest east?" and "If you were in the Gulf of Bothnia, between what two countries would you be located?"), and "thinking questions" like, "Look at a map of Asia. Why would you find little farming in Northern Asia?" (answer: It's very far north and very cold). The Grade 2 work starts off slowly with questions like, "Is the United States a city, a state, or a country?" and by grade 10 you are finding your way about the Gulf of Bothnia.

The Daily Geography program builds on itself. Your average eighth-grader would have trouble jumping right in with the eighth-grade book, in my opinion. The solution is to order all the levels up to and including your student's grade level, and to do extra questions in each geography session until he is caught up. All the school-age children in a family can learn their geography at once, although you may need to write separate questions for each grade level. *Mary Pride*

Essential Learning Products Company publishes a concise group of workbooks for studying geography. The **It's Our World Geography Series** comes in levels A–F, accommodating the six elementary grades. However, middle grade students could also profit from the reinforcement of books E and F without becoming bored. These consumable practice books are 96 pages long, bound with sturdy paper, and are printed in basic colors of black, white, and blue.

Daily Geography program
Grades 2–11. $19.98 plus shipping. *Great Source Education Group, 181 Ballardvale Street, Wilmington, MA 01887. (800) 289-4490. Fax: (800) 289-3994. Web: www.greatsource.com.*

**NEW!
ELP's Geography Series**
Grades 1–6. $3.99 per book. *ELP (Essential Learning Products), P.O. Box 2590, Columbus, OH 43216-2590. (800) 357-3570. (614) 486-0633. Fax: (614) 487-2272. Email: buckeye427@email.msn.com.*

This series follows the traditional public school model of "widening circles." The student starts with himself, his family, and neighborhood, and progresses gradually outwards until he is studying world geography. Books A–C present the special places in a child's life: home, neighborhood, and earth. Methods of going to school are addressed in book B and could be used as map and transportation lesson for homeschoolers. Middle books D and E introduce the use of a globe, as well as map reading and our environment. All the crucial skills which apply to geographic terms are sufficiently covered, and several of the workbooks include activity ideas which supply added enrichment to this topic. The last book in the series, book F, instructs students on subjects such as biomes, international and political boundaries, and transportation networks.

Few sources cover such a wide range of skills in this efficient manner, and parents will be additionally pleased that these lessons require little or no preparation time. *Lisa Mitchell*

Geographic Literacy Through Children's Literature is a 200-page softcover teacher's manual that bases its lessons on the five themes of the National Geographic Standards. They are discussed in their own chapters as follows:

- Location—Position on the Earth's Surface
- Place—Physical and Human Characteristics
- Human-Environmental Relations—Humans and Environments
- Movement—Humans Interacting on the Earth
- Regions—How They Form and Change

The author leads you through these themes using hands-on student-centered activities, such as making a cootie-catcher game for use in learning landforms, and many other creative ways to make the concept stick in the student's mind. These ideas are designed to be interlaced in other subjects. The best feature of this program is the use of children's picture and reference books—160 of them, to be exact! In the back of the manual, the books are listed by author with a description by grade level.

All of this information is presented to you in a chatty conversational format, as if you are sitting down to tea with your next door neighbor. By the time you finish reading the book, you will feel comfortable with your new neighbor and will be at ease teaching geography.

I would recommend this book to geography novices teaching the subject for the first time. The only drawback I found was that the teaching idea sections seemed to cover grades K–6 well, but for grade 7 and up they were overly brief. *Toni Clark*

NEW!
Geographic Literacy Through Children's Literature

Grades K–12. $22 plus shipping.
Teacher Ideas Press/Libraries Unlimited, P.O. Box 6633, Englewood, CO 80155-6633. (800) 237-6124. Fax: (303) 220-8843. Email: lu-books@lu.com. Web: www.tip.com.

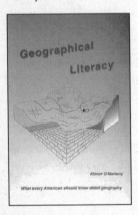

NEW!
Hands-On Geography

Grades 1–6. $15.
Geography Matters, Inc., PO Box 92, Nancy, KY 42544. Fax/phone: (800) 426-4650. (812) 473-4129. Email: geomatters@earthlink.net. Web: www.geomatters.com.

Hands-On Geography is the creation of two homeschoolers who couldn't find a Christian geography curriculum to suit all their needs. While it may not be a complete geography course for your sixth-grade child, the activities in this book are fully sufficient for younger children, and just challenging enough to enhance the curriculum for older children.

Eleven chapters take the student around the geographical world, from home back to biblical geography, and to points all over the globe. Activities are divided by grade level, so you can use the handbook all through early education. However, with a little tailoring, all activities can be altered to an enjoyable level for students beyond the middle grades. There are chapters on games, notebook ideas, luncheons, current events, creative thinking, map studies, and more. The chapters on Joseph's

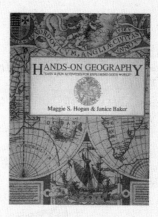

Biblical Journey and Missionary Geography provide a stimulating look at Christian life in geography, a rarely addressed theme that is well developed by the authors.

This book has been wisely published on sturdy, endurable paper. Printed in bold, black ink, pages are suitable for reproduction—and the authors grant this permission for student's activity sheets.

Each activity estimates preparation time at the top of the page, as well as items needed. There is also a somewhat limited list of resources in the back of the book.

Support groups should take note that some of the activities in *Hands-on Geography* are targeted for use by several families or homeschool groups. They require minimal cost and could be the focal point of any gathering. *Lisa Mitchell*

Visit 26 exciting landmarks from around the world with **Famous Places Fun-to-Know Flash Cards**. Each landmark is illustrated in color on the front, while on the back it's located on a mini-world map and its history is described. A "Think About It!" section provides fun facts about the landmark and asks "thinking" questions about it, e.g., why did the Eiffel Tower take less time to construct than St. Peter's Basilica or the Great Pyramid when it's twice as tall as each of them? The illustrations aren't all that detailed, but then, look at the price!

Take one part teaching manual, one part almanac, one part unit study guide, one part timeline figure blackline masters, mix in more information and ideas than any one family could consume in a homeschooling lifetime, and you'd have **The Ultimate Geography and Timeline Guide**. "Ultimate" truly is the operative word here. This 353-page guide will help you incorporate quality geography study into your curriculum, no matter what your teaching style is.

The book begins with an overview on teaching geography. The authors, both homeschooling moms themselves, use a helpful, encouraging tone that make it sound as if a coach was standing inside the pages of the book. "Help your student develop sound, life-long learning habits by modeling the best 'look-it-up attitude' . . . It really does not take that long to look up a word in the dictionary or a place in the atlas. Go ahead! Grab a dictionary and prove it to yourself." There are very detailed and complete units on incorporating geographic thinking into your studies in fun and creative ways, from collecting coins to creating a compass-based treasure hunt. You'll learn how to teach geography across the curriculum with unit-study plans (the geography-focused literature study using the classic book Hans Brinker is excellent!) and a section on researching using the Internet. They also delve into how to teach "pure" geography (with great reproducible questionnaire activity sheets). You get tons of map masters along with more creative activity sheets that are keyed to hands-on, experiential learning, and a thick section on timelines filled with both teaching tips and masters of attractive timeline figures (printed on little squares so they're easy to cut out after you've copied them).

Whether you are a unit study buff, do literature-based curriculum, or work through a stack of textbooks each year with your children, you will find this guide works for you. Textbook users can use this for inspiration to spice up their study. Others can find ample material here to plan a wonderful and inventive study of their own using the reproducible scope and sequence grids. Simple, accessible presentation, attractive graphics, information galore, and a bazillion do-able ideas from which to choose make this book a winner. Recommended. *Michelle Van Loon*

TREND Fun-To-Know Famous Places Flash Cards

Grades 3–8. $4.59 plus shipping. *TREND Enterprises, Inc., PO Box 64073, St. Paul, MN 55164-0073. (800) 328-5540 or (612) 631-2850. Fax: (800) 845-4832. Email: SPetersen@trendent.com.*

NEW!
The Ultimate Geography and Timeline Guide

Grades K–12. $34.95 plus shipping. *Geography Matters, Inc., PO Box 92, Nancy, KY 42544. Fax/phone: (800) 426-4650. (812) 473-4129. Email: geomatters@earthlink.net. Web: www.geomatters.com.*

NEW!
Gospel for Asia Window To Our World

All ages. $20 suggested donation for 2-year subscription.
Gospel for Asia, 1932 Walnut Plaza, Carrollton, TX 75006. (800) WIN-ASIA. Fax: (972) 416-6131. Email: info@gsa.org. Web: www.gsa.org.

NEW!
Link International/ Voice of the Martyrs

Parents: Voice of the Martyrs. Grades K–8: LINK. Both newsletters are free, but donations are appreciated.
The Voice of the Martyrs, PO Box 443, Bartlesville, OK 74005. Credit card orders: (800) 747-0085. Inquiries: (918) 337-8015. Fax: (918) 338-0189. Email: linkinternational@vom-usa.org. Web: www.linkingup.com.

NEW!
The Personal Prayer Diary & Daily Planner

Ages 12–adult. $16.99.
Youth With A Mission, Box 55787, Seattle, WA 98155. Orders: (800)922-2143. Inquiries: (425)771-1153. Fax: (425) 775-2383.

Make It Real

A heart for missions doesn't just happen. It can take root in your life as you serve those in your home and neighborhood. But cultivating a missionary heart should also happen by sharing information and testimonies of those on the front lines in far-away places. **Gospel for Asia**, an organization that raises support in the west for native missionaries in Asia, has developed a nifty "across the curriculum" supplement that you can use to help your child connect with what God is doing on the other side of the globe.

Window To Our World is a 16-page magazine that shows and tells about life inside the 10/40 window, missiologist shorthand for the unreached people groups found on a map between 10 and 40 degrees north latitudes. The first issue includes a testimony of a 100-year-old woman from India who responded to a simple gospel message, a social studies activity page (which includes ideas like pretending that you live in the Third World and living for a few hours without electricity, running water or other conveniences), a science object lesson, vocabulary, craft and food ideas, a brief overview of the history of missions, and more. This is meaty material, attractively presented. The many ideas and discussion topics can be easily integrated into whatever curriculum you are using. Open this *Window* and get a bird's eye view of front-line missions today. Highly recommended! *Michelle Van Loon*

The Voice of the Martyrs (VOM) is "a Christian missionary organization dedicated to serving today's persecuted church" around the world.

The **LINK International** homeschool edition is their free quarterly full-color publication designed to introduce homeschool families to the geography, culture, history, and spiritual needs of other countries. Each issue features a different country. What's more, readers are given opportunities to donate to specific projects to help Christians in that country. For example, the Spring 1998 issue about Bangladesh explained how Christians there are often not allowed to drink from the public wells (on the grounds they will "poison" the water). For $80 to $200 per well, VOM can help local Christians dig their own well. Another need is for tools to earn a living. Former Muslims who convert to Christianity in Bangladesh lose their inheritance. VOM has a project supplying sewing machines to new Christians, so they can make a living by sewing. Relatively little of each newsletter is devoted to these donation opportunities. Most is solid educational content about the country of the issue.

The "parent publication" of LINK is a monthly 16-page newsletter called **Voice of the Martyrs**. This has similar content, but at a more extensive and adult level. Our 13-year-old daughter, Magda, has been a subscriber to this one for several years, and likes it very much. *Mary Pride*

For years I have been searching for tools to provide our family with a Christian world view. I may have just found one! Youth With A Mission's **Personal Prayer Diary and Daily Planner** is an integrated prayer journal, planning calendar, and mini social studies curriculum, all bound into an attractive 192-page spiral-bound diary with silver-stamped simulated leather cover (your choice of navy blue, burgundy, or dusty rose).

The introductory section gives elementary instruction on Christian devotion: worship, quiet time, intercessory prayer and prayer for the nations, meditation, memorization, and restoring relationships, among others.

Before each month, another section points out unreached peoples groups that have not yet heard the gospel message or world class cities like Boston and New York that definitely need prayer.

Cultural information about each group and city is supplied, as well as specific prayer requests.

The heart of the diary, the week-at-a-glance planning calendar, provides a place to write notes and "things to do," a nation per day to pray for, a particular Unreached People Group of the day, and a Bible passage to read. These passages are planned to take you through the Old Testament once and Psalms, Proverbs, and the New Testament twice in a year.

And there's more: maps, a country-by-country brief description of each nation's spiritual and material outlook, a prayer journal where you can write down your prayers and their answers, a yearly planner for this year and the next, a listing of weekly prayer responsibilities designed to help you pray systematically for the opinion-molders in every society, etc.

You really can use the *Personal Prayer Diary and Daily Planner* as a daily planner, since its basic week-at-a-glance design resembles the planners used by businessmen. Like the fancier business diaries, it includes a year-at-a-glance planning section for this year and the next as well as an area for notes, addresses, telephone numbers. If you use it conscientiously, you also have a Bible study plan, a nation to pray for, an unreached group to pray for, and a social organization (the church, the family, media, government, education, business, or the arts) to pray for each day. This is not at all an overwhelming task, given the excellent design of this prayer and personal-organization aid.

My one real suggestion for improvement concerns the daily prayers for nations. These are presented in strict alphabetical order, unlike the Unreached Peoples material, which is grouped by region. This diary would be worth far more educationally (meaning that it would be easier for users to remember something about the nations we were praying for) if the nations also were grouped by region, with perhaps a little historical and cultural introduction to each region.

A review of this diary in the now-defunct *Family Resources* magazine suggested that you supplement the diary's maps with globe work and encyclopedia research. I heartily concur. Take the time to look up the country of the day on the globe and read about it in the encyclopedia, taking care to translate the inevitable humanistically-slanted and socialist viewpoint from which most modern encyclopedias are written. Also take the time, if possible, to share stories you have heard from that country's history. Your children won't remember all this the first time around, but if you continue to buy and use this prayer diary for several years, they will gain a Christian outlook on the world that is priceless. *Mary Pride*

Part of a real education includes learning what life is *really* like in other countries. Wealthy parents, understanding this, used to send their sons on the Grand Tour, a worldwide tour lasting up to two years after they graduated from the university. Few of us can afford the Grand Tour, but now there's an affordable alternative!

I am really excited about Quantum Communications' fabulous **Traveloguer Collection** of travel videos. Now, I know what you're thinking. "*Travel videos?!?* What's so great about those?" Too many travel videos are the updated equivalent of Uncle Harry's slide show of Europe, long on tourist attractions and short on descriptions of the real countries and their people.

Not so with the Traveloguer Collection! These 60-minute videos are adapted from films produced by real "traveloguers." Traveloguers are independent film producers who spend years studying what makes a country unique, as well as spotting the best film shots. They then present their films to live audiences of thousands throughout North America. The best

Traveloguer Collection
All ages. $24.95 each. Quantity prices: 3 or more tapes, $19.95 each. Shipping extra.
Mentor Productions, PO Box 1148, San Clemente, CA 92674-1148. (800) 521-5104. *Inquiries/fax:* (949) 498-3954.

The videos come in impressive, durable gold-stamped cases that will look lovely on your shelf. Tapes available: *Song of Ireland, The Romance of Vienna, Austrian Odyssey, ¡Si Spain!, A Russian Journey, Treasures of Italy, Bonny Scotland, Byways of Britain, Bonjour France, The Spirit of Sweden, Discovering Denmark, The Glory of England, Romantic Germany, This is Switzerland, The Wonders of Norway, Americans in Paris, Eternal Greece, The Charm of Holland,* and *Portugal and the Azores.* The Germany video has been recently revised, by the way, and is even better than the original. Great footage of those kids taking down the Berlin Wall!

of these films of European countries have been brought together into the Traveloguer Collection.

Not only is this some of the most spectacular film footage I have ever seen, narrated by people who obviously know what they're talking about, but these videos have tremendous educational value (again setting them apart from other travel videos series).

The videos teach you *geography,* as every visit to a new part of the country is introduced by highlighting the parts you are about to visit on a video map, and the videos each make a point of showing you each country's distinctive terrain. The *culture* and *history* are introduced, through visits to dozens of important cultural events and historic sites. The traveloguers also make a point of introducing us to interesting craftsmen and businesses in each country, and showing us in detail how several local crafts are made (e.g. Swedish wooden horses, Irish porcelain baskets).

You find out about the day-to-day life of both urban and rural inhabitants, and what they do for sport and entertainment. The traveloguer narrator gives you a verbal picture of the social and political structure of the country while showing you examples of government buildings and state institutions.

You are also treated to a trip down the major waterway of each country, and taken to the home of a typical inhabitant.

Lest all this sound dull and dry, let me hasten to assure you that these are tremendously entertaining videos, put together with a lot of intelligence and wit. I won't soon forget the spectacle of the kilt-clad Scotsman doing his best to hurl a 300-pound telephone pole end over end! (That's a national sporting event, believe it or not!) You get a real "feel" for countries that previously were just names on a map.

I can heartily recommend 16 out of the 19 Traveloguer videos. The remaining three require more serious consideration, for the following reasons. *Eternal Greece* starts with a squirrelly sequence featuring a girl posing as Gaia, the earth goddess, and presents paganism throughout in rather too glowing terms to make Christians comfortable. (This is not at all true of the other videos in the series, by the way—they mention each country's Christian heritage in very positive terms.) The *Americans in Paris* video also has a brief nightclub sequence (the only one in all 17 videos), and if you know anything about Paris nightclubs, this is not something you want the children watching. *¡Si Spain!* also has a brief shot of a portrait of the nude wife of a Spanish nobleman. Said portrait created a scandal at the time it was painted, and it doesn't really belong on a family video. I'm telling you about this only so you are forewarned.

I don't want you getting the impression that the rest of the videos suffer from these problems. Even in the case of the Paris and Spain videos, these are only lapses in what are otherwise fine videos. In general, the traveloguers have done a commendable example of showing us what is worth showing and depicting a society honestly, without dragging us through its seamy side or pushing any propaganda. These are videos you can watch again and again, learning more and enjoying them more each time. *Mary Pride*

Games

You can really learn some rote geography—what is where and what goes on there—with **Where in the World?,** a colorful set of four games in one. Starting with the simple *Crazy Countries* card game, played like Crazy Eights, you progress to the *Statesman, Diplomat,* and *Ambassador* board games.

First, *Crazy Countries.* As in Crazy Eights, you try to follow suit (region, in this case) or put down a card with the same number. In level 2, you follow suit by putting down a country with the same religion, literacy rate, population level, or whatever. It's doubtful that kids will really bother to stop and memorize much about countries at this level, but they are getting familiar with the idea of different countries, each with its own characteristics.

In level 3, the *Statesman* game, you learn the location and relative sizes of countries. Select the color-coded cards for a particular region and pass them out. Then pull out the Region Board for that region. Each country on the board is colored differently than its neighbors and numbered according to size—largest with the lowest number, smallest with the highest number. Now, draw a card and read the name to the player on your left. He must locate the country by either locating its size number on the Region Board or spinning the Spinner and giving the right answer for the category selected. Each correct answer wins you a country. Add up the country numbers at the end. Highest score wins. Since the smaller the country the higher its number, you have much incentive to learn the location of the hard-to-remember little countries.

Diplomat is played the same way, except that you have to provide the answer to a preselected category. The *Ambassador* game takes this to a new level of challenge by making you guess the name of the country from clues, instead of answering questions about a known country. At the Junior level, clues are taken from categories on the cards themselves. At the Senior level, players are supposed to invent their own clues. A clue for U.S.A., for instance, might be "Blue jeans and cowboys."

You get a lot for your money: six durable, colorful Region Boards; 194 playing-card quality Country Cards, each listing capital, population, monetary unit, literacy rate, major languages, major religions, major export, major import, and major seacoasts; seven Wild Cards; a Category Spinner; 120 playing pieces in six different colors (for placing on countries you identified); game instructions; neat, durable box. *Mary Pride*

Race around the world, as represented on the **National Geographic Mystery Voyage** game, collecting the clues you need to reach one of 60 mystery destinations, each with its own photograph card. Each clue card and mystery card has three clues on the back. The difference is that everyone in the current area of the board gets to see the clue card, while only the player who lands on it gets to see the mystery card, unless of course some quirk of gameplay forces him to reveal it to an opponent. Each destination has four mystery clues and four regular clues, for a total of 480 clues on 160 cards. Some sample clues:

- Contains most of Earth's second-longest river.
- Contains snakes big enough to swallow a deer.
- Home to a wooly spider monkey.

Aristoplay "Where in the World?" game
Grades 3–12. $32 plus shipping. *Aristoplay, Ltd., PO Box 7529, Ann Arbor, MI 48107. (800) 634-7738. (734) 995-4353. Fax: (734) 995-4611. Web: www.aristoplay.com.*

The categories provided are useful, but somewhat sterile. It would be great if Aristoplay could give us bigger cards with categories like culture, racial composition, art, musical instruments and music styles, governmental form (totalitarian, democracy, republic, canton republic . . .), major lifestyles (urban, rural, jungle). I'd gladly trade Literacy Rate and Imports and Exports for some of these.

NEW!
National Geographic games
Grades 3 to adult. Mystery Voyage, $22. Pictures of the World, $5. Shipping extra. *University Games, 1633 Adrian Rd., Burlingame, CA 94010. Call (800) 347-4818 to find a store near you. Fax: (650) 692-2770. Web: www.areyougame.com. You can't order direct from any of the above, but you can find a retailer near you which sells the game.*

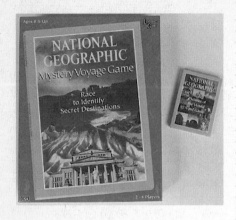

You guessed Brazil, right? If not, sentence yourself to watch the movie *Anaconda* at once!

If all this traveling around the gameboard seems to you like an annoyance designed to prevent you from rapidly answering a lot of questions, take a look at the **National Geographic Pictures of the World** card game. Lacking the two "Magic Slate"-style writing pads, complete with wooden pencils, this easy-traveling game is a deck of 30 picture cards and 25 question cards. Your goal is to be the first to collect 5 question cards. There are 25 questions that work with each card—the usual wacky geography facts, such as "What language is spoken most often in the country where this picture was taken?" and less typical questions, such as "Was this picture taken within 5,000 miles of Tokyo?" Your real goal is to not end up with the photo of a red phone booth, which coincidentally has Big Ben hiding behind it. At first I thought the question for that picture would be, "Has Superman ever changed here?" Further fascinating fact: Protestant and Catholic religions are further defined as "(Christian)," whereas Russian and Greek Orthodox are not. But seriously, you can learn a lot of useful facts in a friendly way for just a few bucks playing this game. *Mary Pride*

Take-Off!

Grade 1 to adult (they say); Grade 3 to adult (I say). $29.95 plus shipping. *Resource Games, P.O. Box 151, Redmond, WA 98053. (800) 275-8818 or (425) 883-3143. Fax: (425) 883-3136. Email: smartfun1@aol.com. Web: www.resourcegames.com.*

Take-Off! from Resource Games, Inc. is more absorbing and educational than many other geography games I've seen. For one thing, it's a real game, not just flash cards with a game board. Here's how it works:

1. Uncork the navy blue tube and pull out the contents. These turn out to be a full-color, laminated 56 x 24" map, two decks of capital city/flag cards, two weird-looking eight-sided dice, and a rules sheet with a pronunciation guide for all those "furrin" places.
2. Unroll the 56 x 24" map. Notice it is about as long as your ten-year-old. You're going to have to clear either the table or the floor to play this game!
3. Scrap the crummy little plastic bag you ripped apart to get the playing pieces. Replace it with a ziplock bag.
4. Pick a color . . . any color. You have six fleets of jets to choose from: red, orange, blue, green brown, and yellow. (Incidentally, when will games manufacturers realize that red and orange look very much alike in dim indoor lighting?)
5. Pick a number from one to four. That's how many jets you will be using per player. (Yeah, the game directions say you have to use at least two jets, but no lightning bolts will zap you if you use only one jet when playing with your four-year-old.)
6. Roll the dice. If a color comes up, move one of your jets from its present location along a line of that color to the next location. (Some people let you go backwards, if that's the only way you can follow a line of that color. Some prefer to just skip a turn.) If a jet symbol comes up, move along any color route to another city. If a *TakeOff!* facet comes up, pick a *TakeOff!* card.
7. What's this? The *TakeOff!* card has a city name on it and a flag. But you haven't the faintest idea where "Ouagadougou" is. Here's where the intellectual stimulation comes in. Around the edges of the map are flags of the countries. Flags of North America are together, as are flags of Central America, South America, Africa, etc. It is merely child's play to match the flag on the card to the right flag on the map. Literally child's play, since this is exactly the sort of matching activity they do in preschool. The country's name is under the flag. So now you know Ouagadougou is in—where else?— Burkina Faso. And, since the flag was with the other Africa flags, Burkina Faso is in Africa. A bit of staring at the countries and capitals on the Africa portion of the map, and *voila!* You can now move your jet to Burkina Faso.

8. But there's already a jet in Ouagadougou. Too bad for him. He has to go back to start.

9. All jets start in Honolulu. You win by getting your jets around the world and back to Honolulu.

10. To make your life slightly less complicated, the board is divided into East and West. A line smack down the middle of Africa separates the two. The 169 capitals cards are also divided into two color-coded decks, so you only have 85 (at most) possible flags to check out before you find Burkina Faso.

11. You will notice there is no well-meant teacherly rubbish about "Tell me how many people live in Burkina Faso and what its chief exports are before you can fly to the next city." Play is fast-paced, and the educational value comes directly through playing the game. The game gives its players a need to know where all these places are and satisfies the need, all at once.

We've been told, "Students who played this game only 14 times improved their test scores on the average of 340 percent!" *Mary Pride*

Globes & Tools

The **GeoSafari** electronic learning game was the hit of the Toy Show when it first came out, winning dozens of awards. Since then new versions with fancier features keep coming out, as well as more lesson units.

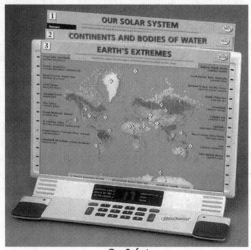

GeoSafari

Here's how it works. You choose a lesson card, place it on the front of the GeoSafari, and type in its code. Then you select how many players (1 or 2), and the amount of time each player has to answer a question (from 1 to 99 seconds, with 20 seconds as the default).

When it's your turn, you hit the appropriate button and are given a question. This takes the form of lights flashing around the edges of the lesson card. When the light stops beside one of the questions, you then find the right answer, which always has a number associated with it. For example, you may have a U.S. map with numbers on some of the states. The names of the states are on the sides of the card, and the light stops next to "Montana." You then have to find the state of Montana, which has a "16" on it, and type in "16," followed by the Enter key, before your time runs out. If you get it right, the game warbles an electronic tune and you get a point added to your score. If not, you hear a beep. For a hint, you can press the "Help" button. You can also choose to have the game quiz you on questions you missed until you get them right—the very handy Review mode.

The first new GeoSafari feature is the pair of "Go Pad" buttons you can hit to stop the timer when you have the answer, just like on a TV quiz show. This means you can either play in "alternate" mode, with each of you answering a question in turn, or in the new "quiz show" mode, with whoever has the answer first getting to give it. You have to hit the Go Pad by the first response time, and then give the answer before the second timer goes off.

GeoSafari lesson units each contain 20 double-sided colorful cards and come in a convenient see-through plastic pouch with a velcro closure. The first GeoSafari lesson units were on geography. However, the makers quickly realized that this device was adaptable to drilling all sorts of facts for all sorts of subjects, including: *More U.S. Geography, More World Geography, Animals of the World, U.S. History, Puzzles and Thinking Games, Science, Wonders of the Smithsonian, World History, Learn Basic Spanish, Learn Basic French, Earth's Ecosystems, Sports, Exploring Stamps, Learn Basic English, World of Art, 3D Reefs and Oceans* (16 lessons), and *3D Wildlife Wonders* (16 lessons).

GeoSafari Jr. lesson units include: *Reading Games*, *The Busy World of Richard Scarry*, *Phonics*, *More Learning Fun*, *Sight Words*, *Getting Ready for School*, *Science Fun*, and *Eye Clue* (perception training: searching for objects in a picture).

NEW!
GeoSafari Talking Globe

Grades 3–adult. $99.95 plus shipping. $9.95 adaptor recommended.
Educational Insights, Inc., 16941 Keegan Ave., Carson, CA 90746. (800) 995-4436. (310) 884-2000. Fax: (800) 995-0506. Web: www.edin.com.

NEW!
Odyssey Atlasphere

Ages 4–adult. Basic Atlasphere, $299. GeoMania, $39.95. Metropolis, $69.95. Shipping extra.
Home Life, Inc., PO Box 1190, Fenton, MO 63026. Orders: (800) 346-6322. Inquiries: (636) 343-7750. Fax: (636) 343-7203. Email: orders@home-school.com. Web: www.home-school.com.

The second new feature is "Bonus Points." This allows you to give a weaker player extra points for each correct answer, making it even easier for two players of unequal ability to have a good game.

More sets keep appearing, both from Educational Insights and from other companies who create "specialty" sets for their own customers.

The **GeoSafari Jr** is really just the same electronic device with brighter colors to appeal to little kids and a different set of introductory preschool and early-elementary lesson cards.

Lesson units are interchangeable between GeoSafari and GeoSafari Jr units. Some lesson sets are also available in Spanish. You can also make your own lesson units from the Make-Your-Own lesson cards.

These are *very* sturdy devices, designed to withstand a lot of hauling into and out of closets. We've never known one to fail. Plus they come with a one-year limited warranty.

Be sure to buy the adapter, or you'll end up spending a fortune on batteries. The carry case is also worth it, making it easy to store and transport a GeoSafari and its lesson units.

Even families that try to resist electronic devices love GeoSafari. It's a great way to get the kids practicing their school facts. Even Mom and Dad will enjoy going a round or two! *Mary Pride*

The **GeoSafari Talking Globe** allows up to four players to play against each other at three different skill levels. The idea is that you will learn your way around the globe itself, as well as eventually memorizing lots of geography facts.

Here's how it works. The base on which the globe sits includes all the electronics. It asks you questions in its two programmed voices. You then look for the answers to questions on the colorful 12" geopolitical globe. ("Geopolitical" means it shows you geographical features, such as mountains and rivers, as well as political outlines of countries and states.) You enter answers by typing in a code on the base. All the questions are difficult, but not so difficult as to make you give up hope (at least in Beginner level) and kept me and my siblings engrossed for hours. With 10,000 pre-programmed questions, you won't be repeating the same batch of questions anytime soon.

This is a great tool for studying for Geography Bees, as are all of the GeoSafari line. Finally, I can compete at geography with my mom! (With me at Beginner and her at Expert, that is.) *Sarah Pride*

I can pretty much sum up the **Odyssey Atlasphere** in three words; it is awesome. Imagine . . . a talking globe that, when you press a stylus to, or even *near*, any point on the globe, tells you the country's name. In a normal human voice, not weird synthesized speech.

But more than that, upon request (by touching a category on the console, or just repeatedly pressing Play) it will tell you all the following:

- **Country**—place name, capital city/cities, type of government, political status, political divisions, date of independence/founding/admitted to a union
- **People**—population, population density, percent urban, population growth rate, population doubling time, life expectancy (males and females), birth rate, death rate, number of people per telephone, adult literacy rate, major religions, common languages
- **Land**—total area, maximum/minimum elevation, maximum depth of oceans and lakes, world circumference and diameter
- **Money**—type of currency, gross domestic product per capita, purchasing power parity, income distribution, energy con-

sumption per capita, energy production per capita, government budget, total imports/exports, import/export partners, average income (U.S. states and Canadian provinces only)

- **Climate**—annual precipitation
- **Sounds**—local music, national anthems (some countries)
- **Time**—set your home location and time/day, then touch any location on the globe to hear the time and day
- **Distance**—between two points, estimated travel time between two points walking/driving/flying, length of a line traced with the styles, total distance between a series of points, estimated travel time between a series of points
- **Compare**—any of the themes above for two places; e.g., population density of USA and Norway

More than that, you can find the location of a country by spelling out its name via touching letters printed on the globe.

More than *that,* you can drill yourself on all the countries of the world with your choice of three games for one to six players (all included in the basic GeoZone game cartridge that comes with your Atlasphere). Each player has an assigned name and can choose a proficiency level of one to four.

- **Eureka** asks you to locate as many countries as possible in four rounds of 45 seconds each
- **Globesurfer** asks you to locate several countries, then answer questions about them
- **Solo Trek** asks you to locate every country on earth in the minimum number of rounds

Even more than *that,* every game gives you verbal hints, such as "Look in Asia" or "Try 2,000 miles northwest."

With the additional "Metropolis" game cartridge, you can learn and test yourself on cities of the world as well.

Any child who can read and understand north/south/east/west can hardly help learning tons more geography than all the other kids on his block with the help of an Atlasphere. Plus, he'll beg you for the opportunity to learn all this! No other product, including software packages, can provide this level of hands-on interactive discovery.

Since the Atlasphere, amazing as it is, doesn't include photos or detailed text about individual countries, for a really super no-hassle world geography course, combine it with Rand McNally's *The World: Afghanistan to Zimbabwe* (see last review in this chapter).

This got my nod as the Best New Educational Product of 1998. *Mary Pride*

Replogle is to globes what Arm & Hammer is to baking soda. If you have a globe, it's likely a Replogle. What you may not know is that Replogle offers many more models of globes than the inexpensive world globe you picked up at the teacher's store. Some examples:

- The **Locator** provides a cool way to reinforce your geography lessons. Its included reference guide gives latitude and longitude for more than 25,000 cities and rivers. Turn the dials at its base to a particular setting, and an internal spotlight pinpoints that location! Solid wood base.
- The **Day/Night** comes with hour and month dials. Use these to visually demonstrate what parts of the globe are in darkness or light at any hour of any day of any year. Also useful for

So far, my family has spent approximately 12 hours playing with the Atlasphere, and we haven't even made it through all its features yet. What we *have* accomplished is to amazingly improve our geographical knowledge. Go ahead, ask my daughter Sarah where Burkina Faso is . . . or the Maldives. We have the Educational Package, which also includes an excellent activity guide and the Metropolis game cartridge, so you can also ask me about capital cities and state/province capitals. And I'll even know how to *pronounce* them correctly!

NEW!
Cool Replogle Globes
All ages. Locator, $129.95. Day/Night, $99.95. Starlight, $49.95. Constellation, $59.95. Moon, $42.95. Atlantis, $42.95. Discovery, $49.95. Shipping extra.
Replogle Globes, Inc., 2801 S. 25th Ave., Broadview, IL 60153-4589.
Orders: (800) ASK-4GLB.
Inquiries: (708) 343-0900.
Fax: (800) 4-GLOBES.
Email: replogleglobes@compuserve.com.

demonstrating seasons and lands of the "midnight sun." Bonus: when lit, political boundaries are visible. When not lit, you see land features instead.

- The **Starlight** is a classic style from the '40s and '50s, updated with today's cartography. This very cool globe has the oceans in black and extremely bright colors for the countries, all on a chrome metallic base. Gyroscope-style mounting.
- The **Constellation** is another illuminated globe. With the light off, you see stars, constellations, and nebulae. With the light on, "celestial images," e.g., zodiac illustrations and art depicting other such features, appear.
- The **Moon** is a NASA-approved globe of—what else?—the moon.
- The **Atlantis** has raised and indented relief, true-life colors in land areas, and richly detailed underseas physical features. Gyro-matic mounting with numbered full meridian lets you swing the globe up or down to bring any area into close view.
- The **Discovery** lights up to show land and sea features ("physical" map), while unlit it shows standard political boundaries. They say kids can also use it as a night light, but I'm wondering how long the bulb can last.

All the above globes are 12" in diameter, except the 10" Discovery. Replogle also has an extensive line of inflatable globes, plus library-stand globes, bank and pencil-sharpener globes, and lots more. Everything for the middle-market cartophile! *Mary Pride*

Reference

Rand McNally's The World, Afghanistan to Zimbabwe

Grades 4–adult. $39.95 plus shipping.
*Rand McNally & Company, 150 South Wacker Dr., Chicago, IL 60606. (800) 234-0679. (312) 332-2009
Fax: (312) 443-9540.
Web: www.randmcnallystore.com.*

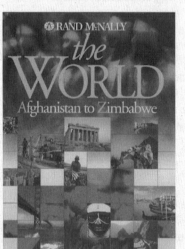

One of the very best ways to study geography and world cultures is to focus on a country-of-the-week or month. **Rand McNally's The World, Afghanistan to Zimbabwe** presents 236 countries in alphabetical order. Each country has a map locating it in relation to its neighbors . . . a fact box or two giving key facts and figures . . . a more detailed map of the country itself showing cities, mountains, lakes, and rivers . . . a concise country profile . . . and (usually) a photo or two showing interesting sights. Just enough information for a child to actually remember.

At the front of the atlas is a 24-page section entitled "World Superlatives and Information Tables." This colorful and highly illustrated section contains all the facts people want to know most about geography: What is the longest river in the world? How about the highest mountain? It's all there with lots of other fascinating facts.

This book, plus the Odyssey Atlasphere, will teach your child more world geography than even the brightest of today's high schoolers can dredge up when tested. *Mary Pride*

CHAPTER 42

U. S. History

Filmmaker George Lucas says he got part of the inspiration for his epic *Star Wars* trilogy from the conflict between the British Empire and the American rebellion. The parallel holds up: in *Star Wars,* the Imperial officers share the arrogance, brutality, and even accents common to British officers at the time of the War of Independence. (I'm not overstating how nasty the British military were; we *did* have good reasons for wanting to be rid of them!) As in *Star Wars,* the American "rebel alliance" sought freedom from the tyranny of the Empire, and the Empire's professional soldiers had contempt for the "rebel scum" (this is the true theme of the song, "Yankee Doodle Dandy").

In *Star Wars,* the "rebels" aren't *really* rebels; they are *conservatives* who want to return to the freedoms of the Old Republic. Emperor Palpatine is a usurper who had no right to overthrow the Old Republic and establish his despotic rule. In other words, this is another exact parallel between Lucas's fictional universe and our real one. Unlike the Marxist-Leninist revolutions that led to bloodbaths and decades of oppression, the American "Revolution" quickly led to the establishment of a stable form of government meant to preserve the traditional "rights of Englishmen" for which the colonists had petitioned in vain.

So today's American history textbooks are right when they cast the American story as a quest for liberty.

The question is, "What *kind* of liberty?"

According to today's school textbooks, it works like this:

- Most Americans used to be seriously oppressed by other Americans. Including by those oppressive patriarchal rats, the Founding Fathers.
- Only government bureaucracies and regulations could save them!
- We *needed* a progressive income tax, a welfare society, "speech codes" on college campuses, abortion rights, NAFTA, and a New World Order!
- Hallelujah! *We got what we needed!*
- But it wasn't enough. Tons of people are still seriously oppressed, and *more* bureaucracy and regulations are needed to crush their would-be oppressors.
- When the government controls every single bit of our lives, enforcing Political Correctness on everything from who is allowed to have children to when we have a "duty to die," then we will have achieved the American Dream.

> America, America
> God mend thine every flaw
> Restore thy soul in self-control
> Thy liberty in law.
> —*from "America the Beautiful"*

> The British Dream was Empire.
>
> The American Dream was Lawful Liberty—liberty restrained only by the laws of God.
> *See poem above.*

Just for the Record

Our forefathers founded a *republic*, not a *democracy*. "Democracy," meaning direct government by the people, which they considered "mobocracy," was anathema to them. A "republic" is a government where (1) the leaders' powers are restricted by law and (2) the people elect representatives rather than voting directly on all matters.

For what it's worth, we aren't living in a democracy, anyway. When's the last time you voted directly on the Federal budget?

Huh? Did I miss something here? This sounds more like *The Empire Strikes Back* than *A New Hope!* Emperor Palpatine would have loved these guys!

The sad truth is that, in today's textbooks, the story of American *liberty* has become the story of American *oppression*. True liberty now supposedly equals total state control of everything except your criminal urges. Those, you should feel free to indulge.

Of course, it's rarely stated this blatantly. What I've listed above is the *unconscious impression* kids get reading the current crop of public-school texts. Never is the individual considered able to solve his own problems. Nor are problems ever solved in face-to-face relationships. Charities, churches, families, and community organizations of all sorts are not mentioned as viable institutions that can improve society. Nor is it *ever* considered that we might get rid of new approaches that don't work and return to old laws or ways of doing things. In fact, the old ways are often censored out. How many schoolkids ever learn that Americans didn't have a personal income tax until 1916, for example? How many books include discussion questions that bring up how America survived for so long without an income tax, or ask what would happen if we tried to do this again?

Instead, today's social studies and history texts have only One Final Solution to every problem:

MORE GOVERNMENT

Here is its corollary:

> It's OK to have our laws overthrown by small groups of judges, and to have them create brand new laws that explicitly contradict the Constitution!

The entire American experiment was founded on the idea of *less* government. We didn't get rid of the Empire to build a bigger Empire. The "liberty" the colonists were seeking was the right to live their own lives *without* undue government interference.

People were presumed innocent until proven guilty. Laws were not founded on the presumption that all our fellow citizens are racist polluting wife-beating child abusers who need constant oversight and scrutiny lest they indulge their evil tendencies. Nor were appeals to "the courts" seen as a legitimate way to *make* laws. Separation of powers, remember?

The American Revolution's war cry was "No Taxation Without Representation!" The soldiers at Valley Forge left bloody footprints in the snow in their quest to live under laws created by their duly elected representatives, who themselves would be limited in the areas about which they could legislate. The joy of living under laws invented in ACLU lawsuits had not entered their minds. If anyone had ever told them that they were fighting to have pornography declared a "First Amendment Right" and to have American kids forced to attend schools where it would be *illegal* to teach them the Bible, the whole Continental Army would have packed up and gone home.

In short, American history *as it really was* is considerably different from the brand now taught in the schools. Which alone might be enough good reason to educate your children at home, using some of the resources below.

Curriculum

As is generally true with history textbooks, those in this strongly evangelical Protestant series for the first three grades are skippable. Things pick up in grade 4, with the new **History of Our United States** textbook, and go on swimmingly to cover Old World history and geography and New World history and geography. These volumes have a semi-encyclopedic format, with tantalizing bits of information tucked away under pictures and in sidebars. Teacher's editions are available for all books. They include the complete text of the student book, so if you get the teacher's edition, you may be able to live without the student book.

The new *History of Our United States* has an emphasis on sung and unsung American heroes, including inventors, evangelists, missionaries, and entrepreneurs (*much* more interesting than just memorizing dates!). It is a fresh, readable, beautifully illustrated and laid-out book, with good coverage of all the important historic events. Some of the historic interpretations are open to question (e.g., that the Aztecs were merely innocent victims of the greedy Spaniards, that Lincoln was justified in committing the Union to war, that Sherman was justified in destroying Georgia, and that John D. Rockefeller Sr. greatly benefited American civilization). Others are a little hard to understand, such as the consistently pro-public school tone taken by this textbook written for Christian schools and home schools! Otherwise, the book is, as expected, conservative and pro-free market. I'm probably going to use it myself, taking care to give "the other side of the story" where necessary (did you know Cortez preached to the Aztecs that they should give up human sacrifice, and that the other Indian tribes gladly cooperated with him to rid themselves of the hated Aztecs?). It's worth going to a little trouble of this nature, because *History of Our United States* really is about the easiest-to-use, most thorough, elementary-school history text I've seen. *Mary Pride*

Grade 3 of the **Alpha Omega History and Geography LIFEPAC** worktext curriculum tours the U.S. Grade 4, LIFEPAC #9, has good state history instruction. Grade 5 is mostly U.S. history. For details, see review in chapter 41. *Mary Pride*

Beautiful Feet Books is a Christian publisher offering a "literature approach to history" (and now, to science and geography as well).

Beautiful Feet study guides provide daily lesson plans, with assignments for the parent to read aloud (elementary grade levels), or for the student to read on his own (junior and senior high levels). Students build and color their own timelines, and create their own journals or notebooks, too. A typical notebook includes Bible verses and biblical principles, book reports, vocabulary word definitions, maps, poetry, comments on the character qualities of the people being studied . . . and the student's own illustrations. The goal is to produce a notebook that is a work of art the student will be proud to show to others.

A Beka History Grades 1–4

Grades 1–4. My America and My World, $8.75. Our America, $8.75. Our American Heritage, $10.95. The History of Our United States, $13.95. Shipping extra.
A Beka Book, Box 19100, Pensacola, FL 32523-9100. (800) 874-2352. Fax: (800) 874-3590. Web: www.abeka.com.

Alpha Omega History & Geography LIFEPACs

Grades 3–5. 10 LIFEPACs per grade. LIFEPACs: Grades 1–10, $3.50 each LIFEPAC. Set of 10 for $34. Grades 11–12, $2.95 each. Set of 10 for $28.50. Teacher's guides and answer keys extra. Shipping extra.
Alpha Omega Publications, 300 N. McKemy, Chandler, AZ 85226. Orders and inquiries: (800) 622-3070. Fax: (480) 785-8034. Web: www.home-schooling.com.

NEW!
Beautiful Feet Books "History Through Literature" Curriculum for elementary grades

K–12. Early American History/Primary, grade K–3: Study Guide, $12.95; Jumbo Pack, $189.95; Literature Pack, $99.95; Semester Pack I and II, $99.95 each. Early

American History/Intermediate, grades 5–6: Study Guide, $13.95; Jumbo Pack, $174.95; Comp Pack (for those who already have purchased the K–3 Jumbo), $94.95; Semester Pack I and II, $84 each. California History, grades 4–6: Jumbo Pack, $104.95; Literature Pack, $52.95; Study Guide, $12.95. History of Horse, grades 3–7: Equine Pack with hardbacks, $132.95; with paperbacks, $81.95; Study Guide, 10.95. Timelines available: Early American History, Medieval History, California History. Prices for each timeline: single student, $8.95; two student, $13.95; classroom version for 15 students, $49.95. *George Washington's World, World of Columbus and Sons, Augustus Caesar's World, World of Captain John Smith,* $13.95 each. Books also available individually. Shipping extra. *Beautiful Feet Books, 139 Main St., Sandwich Village, MA 02563. Orders: (800) 889-1978. Inquiries: (508) 833-8626. M–F 11–5 EST. Fax: (508) 833-2770. Web: www.bfbooks.com.*

As you can see, more than just history is being studied here. The student is learning and practicing English composition, literary analysis, map studies, character qualities, art, and Bible. As you can also see, this curriculum incorporates elements of both classical education (with its emphasis on history and fine literature) and the Principle Approach (including its basic principles and its emphasis on recording what is learned in a notebook).

Beautiful Feet study guides are now available for most of Western historical studies: Ancient History, Medieval History, Early American History, and Modern US and World History. Other courses are available, too.

Here are the time frames covered:

- **Ancient History** Ancient Egypt, Greece, and Rome—see review in Volume 3
- **Medieval History** Magna Carta in 1215 through Elizabethan England of the 1600s—see review in Volume 3
- **Early American History/Primary** Vikings through the Civil War
- **Early American History/Intermediate** Viking through the Civil War
- **Modern US and World History** Civil War through Vietnam—see review in Volume 3
- **History of Science** covers from ancient Greece to current times. See separate review in Chapter 31
- **History of the Horse** will especially appeal to preteen girls. Covering the period from 1700s through early 1900s, you'll read lots of famous "horse" books (e.g., *Black Stallion, Justin Morgan Had a Horse*), learn how to identify horse breeds, practice drawing pictures of horses, chart blood lines, and learn Bible memory verses about horses in this one-year course.
- **Geography Through Literature** covers most of the regions of the U.S. See separate review in Chapter 40.

Beautiful Feet Books lets you buy just what you want. You can purchase individual study guides and try your luck with finding all the books in the library. You can buy just the books you don't already own. Or you can buy complete "packs" for each course.

Jumbo Packs include *all* the reading books, supplementary material (including timelines, if available), a student composition notebook, and the appropriate study guide. Semester Packs divide the course into two semesters. If you order both semesters, you get exactly the same materials as if you had ordered a Jumbo Pack. For Early American History/Primary and California History, the Literature Pack includes most, but not all, of the books, and none of the supplemental materials. A "Comp Pack" is also available for Early American History/Intermediate. This is intended for those who have already purchased the Early American History/Primary Jumbo Pack; it includes just the additional books you need for the Intermediate level.

Beautiful Feet Books' educational philosophy, and passionate desire to give children a love of greatness, can be best seen by this extract from one of their recent catalogs:

It has been said, "There is no greater proof of a man's own littleness, than his disbelief in great men."... Sadly, our society doesn't present us with much that is uplifting or ennobling....

The mainstream publishing industry's attempt to destroy all the heroes of our past is only a symptom of the moral and spiritual vacuum in which we live. It it positive proof of their very "littleness."...

In order to teach a large number of students all the same information at the same time, the textbook was invented.... The history textbook spelled the death knell for inspiring any love or passion for history. Previously, history was learned by reading the "masters."...

As homeschooling families desiring to restore a classical approach to education, we would be wise to imitate, as much as possible, our wise predecessors. Starting with the youngest grades, we can be constantly exposing our children to the very best children's literature, elevating their thoughts, expanding their vocabularies, "forming their palate" for that which is truly noble and enduring.

The question then is often asked, "But how do I teach a comprehensive course in history using just children's books?" We think that Ralph Waldo Emerson answers that concern best: "There is properly no history, only biography." As Christians, understanding the sovereign hand of God over the affairs of men, the study of history becomes part of our heritage.... By simply arranging the stories of people in chronological order, we can study history in the most rewarding manner. That is what we have attempted to do with our guides.

I have read almost every book used in these courses, and can recommend Beautiful Feet Book's choice of literature as both well-suited for the indicated grade levels and plain all-around good reading. Their courses are well-designed, easy to use, and should appeal to children who are not allergic to writing. (Suggestion for reluctant writers: teach them to keyboard and let them input their "notebooks" on the computer.)

Not every book is "uplifting," as the catalog copy seems to suggest; you'll find a hefty dollop of books about suffering and injustices of many kinds. Thankfully, these are mostly for the older grades.

The study guides as a whole are markedly Christian, teaching biblical principles and Bible verses galore. Be aware, though, that although these courses are explicitly designed for Bible-believing Christians, several of the books talk about evolution as a proven fact and others talk about pagan gods as if they actually exist. In the case of books like *Leif the Lucky*, the references to pagan gods are clearly meant to place the reader in the mindset of the time. A note to that effect in the study guide would have been appreciated.

Thousands of families have bought and enjoyed these books and courses. They are attractive, relatively easy to use (kids still have to take notes and write reports), and the mostly secular books used in the courses are well-written and fun to read. Your kids will definitely learn—and remember—more history this way than they would with textbooks alone. I only wish they'd taught history this way when I went to school! *Mary Pride*

Beautiful Feet Books is also in the process of republishing the classic Genevieve Foster "World" books. Each oversized volume has chapters about people and events that were going on worldwide at the same time. *George Washington's World*, for example, lets you know about major personalities of George Washington's day, in the U.S., Europe, and elsewhere. It's a fascinating way to make the pieces of the history puzzle fit together. Each book is well written, with each chapter reading like a story, and packed with timelines, charts, maps, and illustrations. The religious outlook is eclectic: Asante myths and Native American shamans are treated with the same respect as Catholic missionaries and humanist thinkers. Currently available: *George Washington's World*, *Augustus Caesar's World*, *World of Columbus and Sons*, and *World of Captain John Smith*.

NEW!
BJUP Heritage Studies 1–5

Grades 1–5. Student text, $15.50. Teacher's edition, $37. Shipping extra.

Bob Jones University Press Customer Services, Greenville, SC 29614. Orders: (800) 845-5731. Fax: (800) 525-8398. Web: www.bjup.com.

NEW!
Brown Paper School USKids History

Grades 3–8. Prices for individual books vary from $10.95 to $12.95. Shipping extra.

Little, Brown, and Company, 3 Center Plaza, Boston, MA 02108. (800) 759-0190. (617) 227-0730. Fax: (800) 286-9471. Web: www.littlebrown.com.

Bob Jones University Press has always had a kitchen-table friendly reputation. The 1998 teacher's edition for **Heritage Studies 1** upholds this fine reputation. It lays each day's lesson out for you in a simple, easy-to-use format. The 212-page, spiral-bound book uses the student text as a starting point for lots and lots of activities.

Lesson 18, entitled "John Smith Leads the Way," is typical. The preview lays out the main ideas of the day's lesson, along with an objective, a listing of any additional materials needed, and teacher's notes with a short paragraph about the half-timbered structures that were prevalent at Jamestown. The lesson opens with a short story about John as a boy that you read to your children. Pictures of each page in the student book are copied in black and white on the corresponding pages of the teacher's guide. After the story is read aloud, you are directed to read the student text to your child. Discussion questions for each page of student text ("Did John Smith ever sail the sea?" "What help do you think the ladies offered for the new settlement at Jamestown?") help you evaluate your child's understanding of the material. A coloring and sequencing activity is used to wrap things up. There is also a section for each lesson called "Going Beyond." The John Smith chapter's activity has instructions for helping your child create a model wattle and daub house such as was found at Jamestown, along with other background material about Smith and Pocahantas.

There are additional maps and worksheets, a scope and sequence, and listings of Scripture that highlight the truths taught in the text. This is a complete package. If you simply try to use the student text, you will be missing about 75 percent of the material that BJUP intended when they created this curriculum. And it is high-quality material, from a very conservative evangelical perspective.

If this sounds good to you, be aware that revised editions of grades 2–5 of this series are also available. Where before the elementary texts followed a "near-to-far" framework, the first to fifth grades now teach (mostly) American history using a considerably more sensible chronological sequence. Grade 6 introduces world history; see separate review in the World History chapter. *Michelle Van Loon*

The **Brown Paper School USKids History** books use stories and games to teach their lessons. The stories are well written for the third to eighth grade range, and are rather interesting. The games and activities are fascinating, and have great directions.

The books are in double-page-spread format, and are full of black-and-white drawings of fairly good quality. The writing is superior, and grabs your attention quickly.

Books available in this series are:

- *Book of the American Indians* (some sample activities—play the "Stick in the Sand" game, make a number of musical instruments, make a basket, make a tipi, and make a pair of suede moccasins)
- *Book of the New American Nation* (build a model flatboat, a "Cabinet Game" to help you learn about how the President delegates to Cabinet members, make a "mill doll" like the factory children did, rope-spinning, and more)
- *Book of the American Revolution* (make a paper quilt, play the "Catch a Tea Smuggler" simulation game, putting on a "Boston Massacre" play, send secret messages, build a fort, and more)
- *Book of the American Colonies* (writing a family saga, make a compass, draw up a peace treaty, play the "Road to Freedom" game, make natural dyes, and more)

Things to look out for: The *American Indians* book has a lot of naked people running around in it, more than can be justified by appeals to "historic accuracy." Native Americans could justly be offended by the way the art goes out of its way to depict them as naked savages. Also, it asks the reader to engage in a number of pagan religious activities, such as constructing a "spirit figure" and a rainmaking device. Many of the stories in this book either are Indian myths or refer to Indian myths and religious teachings. These teachings are presented as fact, e.g., "A hunter knew he was powerless unless he honored the spirit connected to the deer." Not "a hunter *thought* he was powerless . . . ." All the other books in this series seem to be fine. *Sarah Pride*

America is beautiful in these patriotic history books. **Christian Liberty History Book B** is a 96-page two-color workbook designed for use at the first or second grade level. In huge print and easy language, it introduces American history from Pilgrim days through the Industrial Revolution, plus a smidgin about the three branches of government and a speck of geography (continents and oceans). The book is pro-industrial capitalism and favors traditional American freedoms.

A Child's Story of America, for third and fourth graders, reviews the history of America from Columbus to the 1990s. Each chapter ends with review questions. The book's tone makes it evident that it is adapted from an older work, with more recent history added later, but no information about the original edition is given. Like American history books of a bygone era, it tells kids right from wrong, according to the lights of that period. America is great and wonderful, and there are good guys and bad guys. George Washington is brave and gallant; the Indians are cruel fighters; Daniel Boone is an admirable woodsman. You find out some surprising facts of colonial life and some stories you may not have heard, such as the sad fate of the Acadians, French-Canadian settlers in what is now Nova Scotia, who were deported by the British on just a few hours' notice. You also find out about the explorers, different ways of life in each colony, pre-revolutionary life, Revolutionary War adventures and heroism, the founding of the republic, American inventiveness (and the fate of several inventors), and our subsequent wars, winding up with the Cold War.

Exploring American History, for fourth and fifth grades, takes a biographical approach. You follow the life of one famous man and what was happening during the time he lived. It covers each of the major characters and events of American history from Columbus to George Bush. The final chapters cover the major events and personalities of the 20th century. *Mary Pride*

"History • Adventure • Drama • Great Stories." The blurb on the box sayeth sooth: this is an extremely dramatic, readable set of history books. In fact, it's *more* than that. Divided into chapters (*not* two-page spreads), each page is packed with memorable graphics and juicy historical tidbits. Tying it all together is author Joy Hakim's sprightly, politically-correct prose. For yes, indeed, **A**  **History of US** might as well have been named *A Civil Rights History of the US*. It turns out to be replete with sympathy for leftist causes such as handgun bans, and to have as its unifying theme the struggles of minorities, women, Native Americans, immigrants, blue-collar workers, etc., to grab a slice of the American political pie. This also happens to be the unifying theme of every committee-written school history textbook minted since the 1970s, although they have nowhere near the energetic style and "fun factor" of *A History of US*.

Christian Liberty Press History Books

Grades 1–5. History Book B, A Child's Story of America, and Exploring American History, $5.50–$8.95 each. Shipping extra. *Christian Liberty Press, 502 West Euclid Ave., Arlington Heights, IL 60004. (847) 259-4444. Fax: (847) 259-2941. Email: enquire@homeschools.org. Web: www.homeschools.org. They take credit card orders, but not over the phone. Any other contact method will work.*

Christian Liberty Press also has a number of miscellaneous patriotic biographies (Robert E. Lee, George Washington, Stonewall Jackson, the Mayflower Pilgrims, *Stories of the Pilgrims, Boys and Girls of Colonial Days*). Just released: a biography of J. E. B. Stuart, and a new third-grade reader entitled *History Stories for Children*. All are quaint, inexpensive, and old-timey in flavor, strongly preaching the importance of hard work, selflessness, courage, and godliness.

NEW!
A History of US series

Grades 3–6. 10-volume boxed set, $153.45 (paperback) or $219.45 (hardcover). Individual volumes: paperback, $13.95; hardcover, $19.95. Shipping extra. *Oxford University Press, 2001 Evans Road, Cary, NC 27513. (800) 451-7556. (919) 677-0977. Fax: (919) 677-1303. Web: www.oup-usa.org.*

The *A History of Us* series includes

- *The First Americans*
- *Making Thirteen Colonies*
- *From Colonies to Country*
- *The New Nation*
- *Liberty for All?*
- *War, Terrible War*
- *Reconstruction and Reform*
- *An Age of Extremes*
- *War, Peace, and All That Jazz*
- *All the People*

If you have a serious "down" on President Reagan, you'll love the way he's dissed in the last chapter. If not, that chapter will give you lots of insight into the outlook of the rest of the book. *Mary Pride*

I really don't have time to write this, but I have just to squeeze it in at the last minute. **The History of the United States and Its People** is a reprint of a text used in school 110 years ago. A ground-breaker in its day, this 419-page hardcover divides U.S. history up until 1889 into 61 readable chapters, each with a single topic. Instead of a strict chronological approach, in which each individual thread is picked up and dropped as the text skips from theme to theme, author Edward Eggleston's method allows children to link causes and effects.

Amply illustrated with engravings and line-art illustration on just about every page, and with maps designed to focus on just the places being studied, this handy-sized book has enough eye candy to attract modern children.

Parents will appreciate the "Questions for Study" and "Study by Topics" built into the end of every chapter. These lend themselves particularly well to the Charlotte Mason "narration" style of study.

The main virtue of this book, besides its numerous learning aids, is its readable and straightforward text. Written in an era before political correctness, the author tells it like he knows it, with no special consideration given to any group, even his own. There is simply no agenda behind these pages; just a desire for historical truth. How refreshing!

Overall, I would say that, for the period it covers, this is the best history text for young people I have yet seen. *Mary Pride*

NEW!
The History of the United States and Its People

Grades 4–8. $24.95 plus shipping.
Lost Classics Book Company, PO Box 1756. Port Collins, CO 80522. 970-493-3793. Fax: 970-493-8781.
Web: www.lcbcbooks.com.

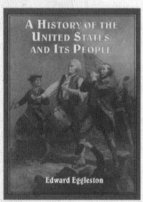

NEW!
Life in America Unit Study series

Grades 3–6. Each volume $54.95.
Shipping extra.
Heart of Wisdom Publishing, Bookmasters, Inc., PO Box 388, Ashland, OH 44805. Orders: (800) BOOKLOG. Inquiries: (419) 281-1802. Email: order@bookmaster.com.
Web: www.heartofwisdom.com.

Some of you may be turned off by unit studies. OK, how about if I tell you about a wonderful new series of cross-curricular history books instead?

Each hefty 360-page paperback volume is designed to cover one semester of American history, chronologically. **Life in a New World**, the volume I (Renee) reviewed, covers the years 1000–1763. Its six main sections are each subdivided into six lessons, working out to around two lessons per week.

Each lesson is structured using the "4 Mat system": *Excite* (introduce the lesson), *Examine* (present the lesson), *Expand* (practice the lesson), and *Excel* (respond to the lesson). This is great methodology for any subject, by the way.

The basic history text is written into the book, and it's interesting to boot! In addition to a few novels (adjust these up or down depending on age levels), you'll want to add the recommended supplements. Plan on buying Parson's *American History Explorer* on CD-ROM, Joy Hakim's *A History of US* (volumes 1 and 2), and *Writer's Express* from GreatSource publications.

The approach here is solidly biblical, but if your own history background is weak you may want to supplement with some other materials, especially those outlining America's Christian history, in order to combat the secular viewpoint in the recommended resources. (Frankly, I think the authors are much too sympathetic toward Roger Williams. Listen to Steve Wilkins' *America: The First 350 Years*, reviewed in volume 3, for the rest of the story.)

Lessons open with an overview of which subjects are emphasized, approximately how many days to spend, clearly defined objectives, and a list of optional resources.

The style is clean and crisp. Icons alert you to types of activities (36 in all, but you'll quickly get used to them). The numbering system for lessons, on the other hand, seemed overly complicated. I ignored it. What would be helpful is an index of activities, or at least a loose grouping by type. The authors affirm that the national history standards are met, yet it would be nice to be able to pick up this book and see at a glance which subjects are covered.

Life in a New World contains no reproducibles, tests, or other worksheets. Instead, students are encouraged to keep a detailed portfolio of all their work. Thankfully, almost all the lessons include at least one portfolio activity and plenty of questions and opportunities for discussion.

The use of multimedia combined with the unit-study format puts this one on the cutting edge. Impressive book!

The next volume in the series, **Life in the Colonies: 1764–1800**, also is an in-depth study of American history, science, literature, geography, culture, music, and so much more.

Although the book says it's for grades 3 to 6, it can be used from the youngest children in your class to the oldest. It has a myriad of activities and supplemental reading suggestions that it would (and should) take several years to cover it all.

At first glance, it looks rather awkward; but once the overview and introduction is read, it becomes clear that this curriculum uses many resources. Children are asked to write a portfolio, read many books, play different games, make their own maps and timelines. They get to explore life two hundred years ago in a manner that doesn't always seem like book-learning.

The basic book is a little steeply priced; but since it lasts many years, it's well worth the initial investment. *Renee Mathis and Barb Meade*

Those of you who attend home school conventions have heard of, or even seen, **Richard "Little Bear" Wheeler** doing his historical reenactments wearing period costumes and carrying period artifacts. So have those of you with camp ministries.

Mr. Wheeler has a particular burden for the revival of true history. Towards this end he has prepared a series of audiocassettes in which he reads and reenacts historical accounts from the 1300s to the 1800s. Each volume of this series has twenty 3–15 minute long historical accounts with biblical application, narrated by Mr. Wheeler, with music and sound effects. Each volume also has an accompanying reproducible workbook, with spaces for students to fill in answers to the questions, plus selected color illustrations and/or projects. Here they are:

- **Volume 1:** 1300s–1620. Wycliffe, Tyndale, Columbus to the Pilgrims.
- **Volume 2:** 1607–1775. Jamestown to Paul Revere's ride.
- **Volume 3:** 1775–1781. God's providence during the American Revolution.
- **Volume 4:** 1775–1781. Heroes of the American Revolution.

Is it complete? Considering that most of what passes for elementary grade science is fluff, all the science activities contained here will give you a good variety of experiences. But they are not organized for you, indeed, you may not even choose them at all. Same with the writing assignments. *Writer's Express* is an outstanding resource, but it is possible to complete entire *Life In a New World* lessons and do no writing at all. Balance is the key here! Be sure to require a variety of activities that will challenge your child.

Also available to accompany the book are CD-ROMs that enhance the learning that is presented in the guide book. Though the CDs aren't necessary to cover this curriculum in depth, they would be a delightful addition.

Little Bear series
Grades 3–12. Tape series: volumes 1–11, $16 each; volume 12 &13, $12. Workbooks, $4 each. Shipping extra. *Mantle Ministries, 228 Still Ridge, Bulverde, TX 78163. (830) 438-3777. Fax: (830) 438-3370. Email: mantle3377@aol.com. Web: www.mantlemin.com.*

- **Volume 5:** 1803–1806. Highlights of the Lewis and Clark Expedition.
- **Volume 6:** 1806–1861. Davy Crockett, Kit Carson, Oregon Trail, and Westward Movement.
- **Volume 7:** 1861–1865. The Civil War.
- **Volume 8:** 1865–1890. Cowboys, Indians, soldiers, and gunfighters of the Old West.
- **Volume 9:** 1620–1880s. Twenty stories from the book *American History and Home Life.*
- **Volume 10:** 1700s–1900s. Ten godly presidents and ten valiant women of God.
- **Volume 11:** The Holiday Series. Twenty of our national holidays from a Biblical perspective.
- **Volume 12:** Highlights of previous volumes.

Mantle Ministries has republished a number of historic books suitable for teens and adults, and is in the process of producing several videos featuring "Little Bear" in his period roles.

"Little Bear" also has a resource catalog, called "Little Bear's" Resource Guide, for those of you who'd like to have access to his sources of period clothing and personal effects, instruments, and weaponry. *Mary Pride*

Our Christian Heritage workbooks

Grades 1–6. New books, grade 1–2, $8.50 each. Grade 3–4, $9.50. Grade 5–6, $10.50. Teacher manuals, grade 1–2, $23.50. Grade 3–4, $25.50. Grade 5–6, $27.50. Old series, complete set of 5 books $28, Books A–E, $5.95. Add 10% shipping.
Our Christian Heritage, 6335 Oberon Rd., Arvada, CO 80004.
(303) 421-0444.

Workbooks based on the Principle Approach for grades 1 to 6 with a Scriptural approach to the studies of geography, history, and government. History is the biggest component of the three **Our Christian Heritage** workbooks. These workbooks are well liked by Reconstructionists. Christian Liberty Academy uses some of the volumes. Inexpensive.

There is now a new series of the books, containing about 50 percent more material. The manuals contain tests, answer keys, maps, charts, et cetera, making the course complete. The old series is still available, but the new series seems far more popular. *Mary Pride*

NEW!
Ballads of American History

Grade 2 and up. $24.95 plus $3 shipping.
Noble Publishing Associates, PO Box 2250, Gresham, OR 97030. Orders: (800) 225-5259. Inquiries: (503) 667-3942. Fax: (503) 665-6637.

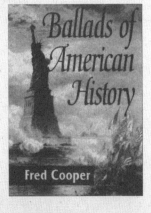

Songs of the Times

A lost colony. A providential Indian. Courageous settlers and pioneers. A race to build a transcontinental railroad. Who doesn't love a good story? And the stories of our American heritage are some of the best. Put those tales to music and you have **Ballads of American History**, a superb book and CD set.

Fred Cooper has written nine original ballads which tell the tales of pivotal periods of American history. Musical styles, which are written in keeping with the historical eras, range from bluegrass ("Transcontinental Railroad") to high church music ("Pilgrims") to a classical music gavotte ("The Constitution"). Gregg Harris performs the vocals with a deep, clear voice, well suited to the ballad style. The lyrics are easy to understand and the songs are quite singable. In true ballad fashion these songs are loooooong, so you will hear and sing oodles of facts, dates, names and events.

After familiarizing yourself with a song, say, "The American Revolution," you turn to the accompanying 159-page book. Here you will learn why the composer chose to use a fife-and-drum style for this piece, what other instruments are heard, and why it is in a major key. Then you will read a thorough summary of this war which gives a deeper understanding to the words of each verse. Review questions found at the end of the chapter can serve as discussion or essay starters. Musicians will appreciate the music in the songbook section, though it includes only the melody line and chords.

Both textbook and unit study teachers will find *Ballads of History* to be a great way to add some pizzazz to their American history courses. *Anne Wegener*

Bobby Horton is just plumb amazin'! Here's a man who can play *dozens* of instruments and who forms his own vocal group by singing different parts and combining them in the studio. Now he is helping so many homeschool families study the Civil War era in a whole new way—through its songs!

Much historical research went into reconstructing (pardon the pun!) the original lyrics and tunes, and reproducing them faithfully on period instruments. The result ranges from the comical "Mister, Here's Your Mule" and "Corporal Schnapps" (nothing to do with liquor—it recounts the trials of a German enlistee whose girlfriend returns to Germany with another man), to the boisterous "Richmond is a Hard Road to Travel," to the patriotic "We are Coming, Father Abraham" (it refers to Abraham Lincoln) and equally patriotic "Dixie," to the heartbreaking "Shiloh." You'll experience the Civil War era from the *inside*—through the hearts and minds of the soldiers, lovers, mothers, draftees, and just plain folks who lived through it.

Each cassette and CD includes about 18 priceless Civil War songs, plus a paragraph of background info about each song. Complete handwritten lyrics for each song are available separately.

Bobby Horton's output now includes:

- *Homespun Songs of the Union Army* —Volumes 1 & 2
- *Homespun Songs of the CSA (Confederate States of America)*— Volumes 1–5
- *Songs of the Union Army*—Volumes 1–3
- *Songs of the CSA*—Volumes 1–5
- A video, *Music & Memories of the Civil War*
- *Homespun Songs of Faith 1861–1865* is historic Christian hymns performed in the same style as the Civil War recordings
- *Homespun Songs of the Christmas Season* is more Christian hymns in the same style, this time with a Christmas theme
- *Homemade Songs of Vicksburg,* Bobby's latest, is an original instrumental soundtrack of the Vicksburg National Military Park Video Tour

CAUTION: To keep the songs historically accurate, volumes 1 and 2 of the CSA tapes each include one strong word pertaining to the everlasting destination of the unrighteous. Even so, the vocabulary is considerably milder than what you'd hear on any prime-time TV show these days. *Mary Pride*

The **Songs of America's Freedoms Kit** is now repackaged. It includes a 30-minute song cassette that teaches children about the Bill of Rights, five "sing along and point" coloring place mats, a constitution booklet, a set of colored markers, and a manual. The publisher has heard of three teachers who separately won "Teacher of the Year" awards for putting on the assembly program presented in this kit.

The **Songs of the U.S. Presidents Kit** includes six "sing along and point" coloring place mats, a song cassette, and the Safari *Presidents* game. Of these, the most significant component is the song cassette itself. This is being used even in daycare centers to teach preschoolers all the presidents in order! *Mary Pride*

NEW!
American Adventure series

Grades 3–8. Single books, $5.95 each. Book club members: first two-book shipment, $3.99 plus $1.98 shipping; subsequent two-book shipments, $7.98 plus $1.98 shipping. Ask about special pricing for the whole set. Shipping extra. *American Adventure Book Club, PO Box 722, Uhrichsville, OH 44683-0722. (740) 922-7280.*

Eight more titles will soon be added to this series in the summer of 1999. The first two, *Black Tuesday* and *The Great Depression*, round out the Minneapolis Period. The next six, *Starting Over, Changing Times, Rumblings of War, War Strikes, The Home Front, and Coming Home,* are the Seattle Period.

Story Books

Increasingly popular among homeschoolers, because it teaches the high and low points of American history and culture with no more effort than reading through a set of Nancy Drew or Hardy Boys stories, each book in the **American Adventure series** is a 144-page kid-sized paperback. The stories are based on historical fact and feature historical characters, for example William Bradford in the *Mayflower Adventure* book.

The series covers the multi-generational story of a fictional family, from their arrival on the Mayflower to the dramatic conclusion of World War II.

These books are written in a lively style and the historical facts are introduced in a natural way within the framework of the novel. The central characters in each book are the fictional child hero and heroine. Although the series doesn't gloss over evils such as slavery, it helps correct today's common view that our history is nothing but a sad tale of exploitation, cruelty, and abuse. In each time period, the story children encounter people of strong character whose lives embody Christian virtues.

The books in this series currently available are:

• *Mayflower Adventure*	• *Danger on the Railroad*
• *Plymouth Pioneers*	• *Time for Battle*
• *Dream Seekers*	• *Rebel Spy*
• *Fire by Night*	• *War's End*
• *Queen Anne's War*	• *Centennial Celebration*
• *Danger in the Harbor*	• *Great Mill Explosion*
• *Smallpox Strikes*	• *Lights for Minneapolis*
• *Maggie's Choice*	• *Streetcar Riots*
• *Boston Revolts!*	• *Chicago World's Fair*
• *Boston Massacre*	• *A Better Bicycle*
• *American Revolution*	• *New Citizen*
• *American Victory*	• *San Francisco Earthquake*
• *Adventure in the Wilderness*	• *Marching with Sousa*
• *Earthquake in Cincinnati*	• *Clash with the Newsboy*
• *Trouble on the Ohio River*	• *Prelude to War*
• *Escape from Slavery*	• *Great War*
• *Cincinnati Epidemic*	• *Flu Epidemic*
• *Riot in the Night*	• *Women Win the Vote*
• *Fight for Freedom*	• *Battling the Khan*
• *Enemy or Friend?*	• *Bootlegger Menace.*

These cover the Plymouth Period (1620–1634), the Boston Period (1635–1808), the Cincinnati Period (1808–1865), and the Minneapolis Period (1876–1935).

You can purchase these books three ways: as individual volumes, as a complete set, or through membership in the American Adventure Book Club. Book club members receive some additional benefits. A large, colorful poster accompanies your first installment. If you decide *not* to join, return *Plymouth Pioneers* within 15 days and you still get to keep *Mayflower Adventure* for free. Every month, you get stickers to place on the poster, to mark your historical reading progress, and a newsletter with related topics for further exploration and puzzles that can only be solved when you've read that month's books. When you finish reading every book in the series, you get a completion certificate declaring you "A Junior American Historian."

This set makes good wholesome and edifying reading for the whole family, especially when you see the alternatives available in the bookstore. *Mary and Sarah Pride*

Facsimile reprints of old-timey history stories. Original art, paperbound. A point of view increasingly hard to find at the public library. **Stories of the Pilgrims** tells the history of the Pilgrims from the beginning at Scrooby Inn to the death of the Indian chief Massassoit and the adventures of some Pilgrim children with unfriendly Indians. A good read-aloud book for younger children, or for preteens to read on their own. Lots of stories on these 240 pages! **Boys and Girls of Colonial Days** tells stories about children from the times of the Puritans onward to Betsy Ross, Benjamin Franklin, and George Washington. *Mary Pride*

In God We Trust: Stories of Faith in American History (224 pages, hardbound, with glossary and bibliography) tells of 50 important Christian Americans. Covering 800 years of history, from Leif Ericson in 1000 A.D. to Katherine Lee Bates, author of "God Bless America" in the early 1900s, it combines large-print, easy-reading text with color illustrations of each historical personage. Occasional "fun facts" and quotes appear in sidebars. These take the form of grey boxes, with a row of stars on the top, placed in the text itself, instead of in a separate margin.

Many famous people are highlighted throughout the book: Paul Revere, Sojourner Truth, Francis Scott Key. Others are less well known: John Peter Gabriel Muhlenberg, Charles Cotesworth Pinckney, Eusebio Fancisco Kino. Regardless, you will learn about what they all did, and how their Christian faith changed their lives . . . and our country. A great family read-aloud book. *Mary Pride*

From the prolific Carole S. Marsh, here are two titles of her *Our Black Heritage* series.

Out of the Mouths of Slaves is billed as "wisdom, trauma, humor—an authentic oral history experience for young readers." Along with a brief history of black civil rights and wrongs, you'll find lots of quotes from a wide spectrum of Southern blacks. Slavery, slave ships, rebellions, the Civil War, and the dreary lives of sharecroppers are chronicled, along with the black community's attempt to withstand the Ku Klux Klan. I was surprised to hear that, in at least one area, the authorities instructed blacks to form a militia and defend themselves—which they did with success.

All in all this is a balanced book, quoting both contented slaves and runaways, success stories and failures. If anything, it gives you an appetite for further reading and a deeper understanding of the financial and emotional frustration that finally boiled over in the Civil Rights Movement.

The Best Book of Black Biographies has an assortment of inspirational long and short biographies of famous and not-so-famous blacks. Slaves. Sopranos. Musicians. Pioneers (including the founder of the city of Chicago). Scientists. Pilots. Symphony conductors. Plus a smattering of the usual politicians, singers, and sports stars. Kudos to Mrs. Marsh for celebrating the diversity of talent in the black community: Michael Jackson gets less space in her book than William Henry Hastie (the first black governor of a U.S. territory, in case you didn't know)! *Mary Pride*

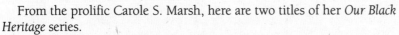

Source Documents

That for Which Our Fathers Fought and *That of Which Our Fathers Spoke* are two booklets loaded with essential American source documents. "Source documents" are the original words themselves: not censored, not

Trivium Pursuit, 139 Colorado Street, Suite 168, Muscatine, IA 52761. (309) 537-3641. Email: trivium@muscanet.com. Web: www.muscanet.com/~trivium.

paraphrased, not reinterpreted. These speeches, laws, covenants, and quotations give us a window into what our forefathers were really like, and what their deeds really meant.

That for Which Our Fathers Fought includes:

- Magna Carta (English translation from the Latin of the historic document in which King John ceded some civil rights to the barons)
- Mayflower Compact (in which the Pilgrims pledged their colony to God)
- Declaration of Rights of the Continental Congress
- Virginia Bill of Rights (predecessor to the Constitutional Bill of Rights)
- Declaration of Independence
- Constitution of the United States of America
- Bill of Rights and all other Amendments to the Constitution
- All four stanzas of the "Star Spangled Banner," our national song

That of Which Our Fathers Spoke includes:

- The Rights of the Colonists, adopted by the Boston Town Meeting of 1772
- Patrick Henry's "Give me liberty or give me death!" speech
- George Washington's First Inaugural Address
- George Washington's Thanksgiving Proclamation
- George Washington's Farewell Address
- 60 additional selected sayings by Washington, MAdison, Jefferson, Franklin, Monroe, Adams, etc. between 1750 and 1830.

The heart of the *real* American dream, inexpensively preserved for you. *Mary Pride*

Teaching Aids

American History in Verse is just what the name says: poems about every major incident and personage in American history by a hodgepodge of bards, many contemporaries of the persons or events. You get some queer gems here, as well as many poems rollicking, tender, tragic, and even ludicrous. Find out what the Man in the Street used to think about American history, back when he used to know enough to think something about it. *Mary Pride*

I can't think of a better way to spend 63 minutes than watching **Bobby Horton** sing and play the guitar, fiddle, and banjo and tell stories.

On his **Music & Memories of the Civil War video** you will hear over 18 songs—some that were popular in the North, some in the South, and many in both—that give you insight into the people who fought in the war and those who remained behind and kept the home fires burning. You learn that many of the tunes were sung on both sides, but with different lyrics, and that "Dixie" was written by a Northerner. You learn about the town in North Carolina where all men aged 17–45 died in one day. And you learn about the song sung by both North and South, written after the battle of Shiloh Hill.

Bobby Horton is a seasoned professional who contributed to the soundtrack of Ken Burns' series, *The Civil War.* His knowledge of the time period

American History in Verse

Grade 5–adult. $11.95 plus shipping.
Bob Jones University Press Customer Services, Greenville, SC 29614. Orders: (800) 845-5731. Fax: (800) 525-8398. Web: www.bjup.com.

NEW!
Bobby Horton's Music & Memories of the Civil War Video

Grade K–adult. $25 postpaid.
*Bobby Horton, 3430 Sagebrook Lane, Birmingham, AL 35243. (205) 967-6426. Fax: same number, dial *51.*

is amazing and will keep you glued to your seat. Throughout the video you see him in different outfits—sometimes the genteel Southern gentleman, sometimes a soldier, and sometimes a common man. The settings add to the appeal as you're taken from the porch of a small, wooden house where he plays with his friend, Bill Foster, to a steamboat on the Mississippi. He never loses your attention as you listen to the songs and the stories behind them. These tunes are boastful, optimistic, patriotic, and mournful and they remind you that individual people and lives are forever changed by war.

I cannot tell a lie. This is history at its best! *Marla Perry*

Education writer Ruth Beechick recommends that young children study history with a simplified time line. The idea is to start with big chunks of history—say Middle Ages and The Age of Exploration. Then, as your child matures, you divide these up into smaller chunks and add more information. That way he has a complete world history framework from the beginning.

Now Creation's Child has a set of two time lines based on this philosophy. The **Simplified U.S. Time Line** covers the highlights of U.S. history from the 1400s to 1989. Events such as Gutenberg's invention of modern printing and Columbus's first voyage are shown, sometimes accompanied with old-timey engravings. It's printed on heavy brown paper stock.

The **Activity Time Line** provides a guided way for your child to get personally involved in making his own time line. You get a ruled time line and sheets of events and people for him to cut out. A typical event will be enclosed in a ruled box and described with both words and a picture. Your child cuts out the box and pastes or staples it to the time line in an appropriate place. "Period" dates for the event boxes are provided so your child will know exactly where on the time line to place them.

Also from Creation's Child: **The United States Time Line 1400–1900** is organized in general horizontal bands. The top row pertains to England and Europe. The areas of religion, education, publications, presidents, government, economy, industry, arts, science, and health are presented from top to bottom on each panel. The time line is printed in black on heavy white paper, with many line art illustrations and engravings of people and events. You get six 17 x 22" panels, each covering 50 years, plus an extra panel for 1775–1800, which has been expanded to include more details of this interesting period in our history, plus the 1900s panel originally developed for the Junior version, which is half as tall as the other panels.

The **Junior Version U.S. Time Line** includes many of the same pictures and the most important information from the larger U.S. Time Line. Again, blank lined student panels are available separately, for adding extra information. One century per 8½ x 22" panel.

If you have young children around, the laminated version is a definitely better buy, as it takes little fingers no time to rip and dog-ear your carefully tacked-up time lines. *Mary Pride*

"Build your knowledge of history with fun, self-checking quiz wheels!" Here's how it works. Slip one of the compact 7" **Windows of Learning** question-and-answer disks into the circular case. A question will appear in the cutout window at the top. Look in the window on the other side for the answer. Then rotate the disk for the next question. Keep track of how you're doing with the handy scorekeeper. Practice by yourself or with a friend. Set contains scorekeeper, map case, and five two-sided disks with 10 questions on each side, for 100 questions in all. *Mary Pride*

Creation's Child Time Lines
Grade 4 and up. Simplified U.S. Time Line, $5.50. U.S. Activity Time Line, $6.95. Junior version U.S. Time Line, $7.95. Large U.S. Time Line, $8.95. Shipping extra. *Creation's Child, PO Box 3004 #44, Corvallis, OR 97339. Phone/fax: (541) 758-3413. Send SASE for free brochure.*

Educational Insights Windows of Learning, U.S. History
Grades 5–adult. $1.70 plus shipping. *Educational Insights, Inc., 16941 Keegan Ave., Carson, CA 90746. (800) 995-4436. (310) 884-2000. Fax: (800) 995-0506. Web: www.edin.com.*

NEW!
Pioneer Skills Video Series

Grades 3–adult. Videos, $20 each. Workbooks, $6 each. Kits, $17 each. All 8 tapes and 2 workbooks, $150. Postpaid.
Historic American Productions, Inc., PO Box 763, Addison, TX 75001. (800) 715-6337. (972) 416-4323. Fax: (972) 416-5328. Email: hap@cyberramp.net. Web: www.cyberramp.net/~hap

TREND Presidents of the United States Fun-To-Know Flash Cards

Grades 4–12. $5.59 plus shipping. *TREND Enterprises, PO Box 64073, St. Paul, MN 55164. (800) 328-5540. (651) 631-2850. Fax: (800) 845-4832. Email: customerservice@trendent.com.*

NEW!
Yo, Millard Fillmore!

Grade 4–adult. $6.95.
The Millbrook Press, PO Box 335, 2 Old New Milford Rd., Brookfield, CT 06804. Orders: (800) 462-4703. extension 3034. Inquiries: (203) 740-2220. Fax: (203) 740-2223.

Time was, when an American equipped with a handful of prairie grass and a couple of sticks of wood could twist himself a rope that would get his wagon the rest of the way over the Oregon Trail. Meanwhile, Mama could take wool from right off the sheep and turn it into finished clothing. Ever wonder how they did that?

Each of these 28-minute **Pioneer Skills** videos includes a fascinating historical introduction to the craft in question (going back as far as ancient times!), a real-life demonstration by a working craftsperson, and (most unique of all) a set of 10 questions posed at the end of the tape, with answers supplied later, that check whether you were really listening.

The series includes *The Saddlemaker, The Blacksmith, The Ropemaker, The Wagonmaker, The Spinner, The Weaver, The Potter,* and *The Basketmaker.*

While you won't master any of these crafts with this short an introduction, each is sufficient to fill you in on how the pioneers themselves did it. A great set for your support group library. *Mary Pride*

A colorful portrait of each president on the front, with his dates in office and the number of his presidency. Biographical details, noteworthy events of his presidency, and fun facts on the back. Forty-two **Presidents of the U.S. Flash Cards** in all. Inexpensive, worth it. Get an extra set to staple on your time line. *Mary Pride*

Yo, dear reader! You should definitely buy **Yo, Millard Fillmore!** I've just spent 30 minutes with this book and I can

- recite every President of the United States in order
- tell you what number President each one was
- tell you all kinds of fascinating facts about each President

Using the familiar memory tactic of matching each President to an outrageous cartoon (e.g., Madison to a "mad sun"), this book goes several steps further by

- making it into a crazy story ("the mad sun . . . opens his mouth and out flows a boiling river . . . In the river is some money row-ing a boat") that connects all the Presidents in order
- adding number clues along the way for every fifth President (the money rowing the boat is a five-dollar bill, because Monroe is the fifth President)
- giving you a full page of fascinating facts about each President opposite his cartoon-story page
- reviewing what you've learned after every tenth President
- providing a Jeopardy-style quiz of 112 questions (with answers) to test your knowledge of the fascinating facts
- even throwing in a bibliography for further reading about the Presidents!

So, quickly now: Who was the seventeenth President? Who was known as "Old Kinderhook"? Who was "the President without a party"? If you or your kids don't know the answers to these questions, grab this book. *Mary Pride*

CHAPTER 43

World History

It's a big world out there, and it's been there a while. One semester in high school isn't enough to learn about everything that's gone on in it since the beginning of time. That's why homeschoolers have rediscovered the value of teaching world history in the *early* grades.

Here's a world history sequence many have found helpful:

- **Old Testament history.** This is essential for understanding classic literature and much of the history of the Western world, as well as essential for understanding the teachings of the Christian and Jewish religions.

- **Mythology.** The Greek, Roman, and Norse myths are great stories, and provide important background for understanding classic literature, as well as for understanding ancient history.

- **The histories of ancient Greece and Rome, with a dash of Egyptian history thrown in.** Why Greece and Rome? Because the history of the West has two parallel strands, often referred to as "Athens and Jerusalem." From "Jerusalem," namely the Bible, we get our code of ethics and the stories that give these rules and relationships flesh. From "Athens" we get the Greeks' experiments in democracy and philosophy, and the beginnings of scientific inquiry. The Romans conquered the Greeks and carried classical civilization forward. Why Egypt? The Egyptians predated the Greeks, and as well as filling supporting roles in the Old Testament. They also left their mark on ancient classical civilization.

- From there, you can segue into **the fall of Rome** and **the rise of the barbarians** during the Dark Ages. Here we pick up on the Norsemen, those white guys in the funny hats with horns sticking out of them.

- **From the Norsemen,** the stream of Western civilization moved on **to the "Normans,"** Norsemen who settled in what is now France. The Normans under William the Conqueror (formerly known as "William the Illegitimate," so he had strong incentive to do something that would change his title) successfully invaded England in 1066.

- At this point, world history courses of the past usually continued with a scrutiny of **British history**. Since the British had quite an effect on everyone else, and the Reformation (which was strong in Switzerland, Bohemia, and Germany) had quite an effect on Britain, this involved the student in quite a bit of European history, too. Why British history?

Yes, little kids can learn world history! If today's kids can name all the characters and repeat the plot of their favorite TV show or video, which we all learn they can, then our own children can as easily learn the characters and plots of the dozens of fascinating stories that make up world history.

Because American culture and law took its largest drink from the British culture and common law.

- Following the footsteps of the British leads naturally to **American history**, since the War of Independence (otherwise known as the American Revolution) was a story of American colonist versus the British Empire.

This gives kids the "big picture," from Creation through the present day. They can see history as the development of their own civilization.

Multicultural Musings

"Multiculturalism" is a word that has been much abused of late. Insofar as it reminds us that our *shared* civilization is made up of strands from many cultures, it's helpful. When it's used to fragment us into a Balkanized bunch of *separate* little "cultures," it's dangerous.

One sure way to tell the multicultural baddies from the goodies is the way they treat history. According to the baddies, all of history is the struggle of oppressed peoples against straight white Christian males. Thus, history is turned on its head. Every advance in civilization is seen as yet another atrocity for which apologies and reparations are required.

But, in *real* history . . .

If your ancestors were European, they might have looked like this.

- **Every nation kept slaves,** including blacks, Asians, Muslims, and even Native Americans.
- **White people were slaves too.** The word "slave" comes from "Slav." That's because white Slavic people for centuries were the slaves of choice for the more dominant Asian peoples in their part of the world.
- **Those white people who weren't slaves** may have been called "serfs" or "peasants." This sounded better, but amounted to the same thing. You had to work for the lord, you couldn't leave for another job, you had practically no rights, and you might even have had a slave collar to wear to remind everyone of your status.
- **The serfs, peasants, and slaves outnumbered the aristocracy** by vast numbers. Thus, most white people today are descended from slaves.
- While we're at it, **most white people today are descended from strange tribal folk** who practiced odd religious rituals, liked to fight a lot, and had very little hygiene. The Vikings and the Zulus, before they were reached by Western civilization, had more in common with each other than they do with you or me. We all started in the same place.
- **The Christian nations abolished slavery** *without* any noticeable pressure from minorities to do so, since in those days minorities had no political or military power to speak of.
- **Very few white people are descended from anyone important.** So are very few black people, or Asian people, or Amerindians. So what? We *all* inherit what our "forefathers" created, even if they were never related to us.

George Washington never had any children, yet he is considered the "Father of his country." That makes sense, because *all* Americans, even brand-new immigrants from the other side of the world, inherit the results of George Washington's life. The alternative is to preach racial hatred, as each group insists it will *only* accept what *its own* forebears invented. That's why there's such a big fuss over "Afrocentric" education; some educators foolishly believe it will wreck black kids' self-esteem if they learn most of our civilization was created by white people (which it was—big surprise, since after all the whites in Europe and America vastly outnumbered the blacks and had almost all the power and money).

They're missing the point here. How could anyone expect Africa to have been the biggest influence on Europe? If everything wonderful was supposedly *invented* in Africa, how come it only *developed* in Europe? (What actually happened, in case anyone's interested, is that the tribal Europeans got the Christian gospel before the tribal Africans, and it changed them into productive, inventive, responsible, scientifically-oriented peoples. Just like it will do for any nation or tribe that surrenders to Jesus.)

Without any historical evidence, the Afrocentrists are teaching a doctrine that evil white people *stole* all the achievements of Africans and *lied* about it for centuries. What a great way to teach racial harmony. But probably racial harmony is not the objective here, since such "history" is usually couched in Marxist-Leninist terms of "struggles" against "oppressors." The interesting thing is that when Marxist-Leninist doctrine starts being taken seriously, the society in which it happens gets treated to a bloodbath followed by decades of poverty and *real* oppression.

I'm saying that the people who try to divide us this way have *their own* agenda and could care less about increasing anyone's rights. Where you see hate preached against *any* race, it's not God who is behind it, you can be sure.

> If your own ancestors come from Latin America, Asia, or Africa, you may naturally want to pay additional attention to the history of those regions. That's fine ... homeschool is *your* school and *you* determine the curriculum!

Important Thoughts

We need to study history as it really happened, not as we would have liked it to have happened. Or very soon we will end up knowing nothing real about history at all.

We also need to stop thinking so much in terms of races and peoples and more in terms of civilizations. Many races and peoples can make up a civilization. We don't all need our own private civilizations—instead, we should be contributing to the one we all share.

Finally, we need to remember the past *is* the past. So my ancestors or your ancestors were mistreated and didn't get to become important and famous. That says nothing about what you or I will do with our lives. If anything, it makes it easier to leave your mark. Being the first in your family to graduate high school (like my father, who went on to get a Ph.D.) is more of an achievement than just graduating high school as all your umpteen relatives have always done. There's still room out there for the first black President, the first Asian attorney general, and the first white woman in a *long* time to win an Olympics race. Go for it!

Sources for History Stories

Since the word "history" includes the word "story," world history is best taught with plenty of stories of important individuals and events along the way. These stories then serve as "reference pegs" on which to hang the broader spans of decades and centuries.

Movies. One easy way to do this is to rent videos about historical personages and events. Hollywood used to churn out lot of these historical spectaculars, and even if they weren't always totally accurate historically, generally the costumes and sets were fairly authentic. Some that come to mind are:

- *Alexander the Great*
- *The Egyptian*
- *Cleopatra*
- *Julius Caesar*
- *Spartacus*
- *The Vikings*
- *Henry V*

Sadly, much of history is bloody, and rulers often behaved with less than perfect personal morality, so these movies may not be suitable for young children.

Documentaries. Over the years, hundreds of history documentaries have been produced. You generally can't find them at Blockbuster Video, though. If someone could pull together a catalog of quality history documentaries and literature-based movies, this would be much appreciated.

Biographies. Oh, yes. Your local library has lots of these. I read *every* biography in the Children's Library when I was young and loved it!

Historical fiction. Good historical fiction serves much the same purpose in giving kids a taste of life in different time periods.

Below are some additional resources that may help with your world history program.

World History Curriculum

A Beka has a wealth of **world history books and teaching aids** written for differing age levels. I'm starting with the fifth- and sixth-grade books, because I believe most middle- and high-schoolers have *not* mastered the history and geography run by them in elementary school and because A Beka's history books for earlier grades aren't really as good as these. Personally, I'd rather read the kids the fifth- and sixth-grade books, and amplify with library books, than settle for the oversimplified material in A Beka's early-grades books.

Old World History and Geography and **New World History and Geography** study the world's history by geographical regions. These books present history and geography in context, introducing the forms of government, important people, national heroes, and culture of each area as they change over time. Both texts are packed with beautiful full-color photographs and illustrations and loaded with maps and other visual aids. Strong Christian and anti-Communist emphasis: lots on missionaries. Rather encyclopedic reading; A Beka believes in giving you a *lot* of information.

In the Beginning and **The Modern Age** are the seventh- and eighth-grade world history books, respectively. *In the Beginning* attempts to tell history as "His Story," taking a providential view, from the Garden of Eden through the Renaissance. *The Modern Age* picks up the threads and follows them from the Reformation to modern U.S. history. Both books are designed for ease of studying. Key events are emphasized in the text, and paragraph headings and summary statements are accented by color or boldface. Lots of support materials available for these books. *Mary Pride*

Grade 4 of this worktext series includes some history of various countries.

Grade 6 tackles world history. First there's a very good unit on world geography, then we move from the *Cradle of Civilization* (excellent background for your Bible studies) to *The Civilizations of Greece and Rome, Life in the Middle Ages,* and one unit each on Western Europe (from the Renaissance on) and Eastern Europe (from Byzantium to the Space Age). This sequence is interrupted by two mostly geographic units on South American countries and one on Africa (tucked in right before we move to Europe). Each history unit includes information about the geography of the time and place being studied, along with information on daily life in that time period, plus its social institutions, and economics. The units on geographic regions (South America and Africa) include history, geography, types of people who live in each country, industries, major cities, and holidays.

Each grade level is 10 worktexts. For more information on this series, see the review in chapter 41. *Mary Pride*

A Beka History and Geography

Grades 5–8. Old World History and Geography: student book, $13.95; teacher's edition, $21.70; maps, tests, review sheets also available. New World History and Geography: student book, $14.90; teacher's edition, $22.60; maps, tests, review sheets also available. History of the World, $18.20. The American: Land I Love, $18.20. Teacher's editions, $24.95 each. Shipping extra.
A Beka Book, Box 19100, Pensacola, FL 32523-9100. (800) 874-2352. (850) 478-8933. Fax: (800) 874-3590. Web: www.abeka.com.

Alpha Omega History & Geography LIFEPACs

Grades 4 and 6. $3.50 each. Set of 10, $34. Teacher's guides and answer keys extra. Shipping extra.
Alpha Omega Publications, 300 N. McKemy, Chandler, AZ 85226. Orders and inquiries: (800) 622-3070. Fax: (480) 785-8034. Web: www.home-schooling.com.

Heritage Studies 6, the most recently published revised Bob Jones history text, is a complete departure from the first edition. Previously the sixth grade material covered the eastern hemisphere (the limits of "far"), but the new version is the first half of a survey of ancient and medieval world history. The publishers split the material found in the current seventh grade **World Studies** book into this new book and a future seventh grade text, expected to be published by fall of 1999.

This is an attractive text! Appealing graphics—colorful drawings, photographs and maps—grace nearly every one of the 315 pages in this softcover book. Using a cultural, not a biographical, approach, *History 6* gives a taste of past civilizations from around the world from Mesopotamia to Medieval Europe. Sprinkled throughout the twelve chapters you will find interesting side articles on such things as "In the Bible," "Discovering How," "Things People Did," and "Echoes from the Past."

The text addresses the student almost conversationally, periodically throwing in a few questions for the reader to ponder. For review and reinforcement you can turn to the Student Notebook, a 3-hole-punched consumable set of 86 creative worksheets.

History 6 can be of use to even those of you who normally are not textbook fans. A fantastic co-op in my area uses the current *World Studies* for their unit study framework. And it would also serve as a great read-aloud text for your younger children. I, for one, am looking forward to reading the chapters on Mesopotamia, Egypt and Israel with my little ones as my older ones study these same topics. *Anne Wegener*

World history from creation through the present for first and second graders? Really?

Yes, really. Though the subject matter seems like a lot to bite off, Christian Liberty's **History for Little Pilgrims** text reads like a fascinating story. Your little one will meet all sorts of characters from Boniface (an early missionary who behaved a bit like Elijah when he chopped down a huge oak tree that the people were using to worship Thor, in order to prove that the God of the Bible was the only true God) to Douglas MacArthur. Accompanying detailed lesson plans flesh out the text and are quite easy to follow. This well-written and colorful 122-page text tells a big story plainly.

However, the teacher's manual takes the simple text and adds perhaps too much for many first- and second-graders. Schoolish instructions like "Read the section entitled 'Thomas Jefferson' to your student and explain the term 'Louisiana Territory'" (plus three pages of background about Jefferson) may give beginning homeschoolers the idea that they need to attempt to cover all this material. Those of you who are interested in introducing formal history to your little ones may be better served by simply reading and enjoying this story of God at work in the affairs of men, and leaving aside the "school" part of this history study. *Michelle Van Loon*

The **Greenleaf Press Famous Men series** broke new ground among homeschoolers when it first appeared in 1989. Founded by homeschool parents Rob and Cyndy Shearer, Greenleaf's philosophy is, "To spread world history over the elementary school years and proceed at a leisurely pace that would allow the child to live with the material for a period of months." Popular among the elementary-school set, these history packages also make a fine, slower-paced introduction to world history for students in the middle grades.

The Greenleaf approach gets kids familiar with the basic setting and people from each historical time period *before* they enter high school. Perhaps the best example of how this works is the Ancient Egypt Study Package. The **Greenleaf Guide to Ancient Egypt** stands alone, not having

NEW!
BJUP Heritage Studies 6

Grade 6. Student text, $18.50. teacher's edition, $37. Student Notebook Packet, $6.50. Test Pack, $8. Answer Key, $4.50. Shipping extra. *Bob Jones University Press Customer Services, Greenville, SC 29614. Orders: (800) 845-5731. Fax: (800) 525-8398. Web: www.bjup.com.*

NEW!
Christian Liberty History for Little Pilgrims

Grades 1–2. Softcover text, $9.50. Teacher's manual, $5. Shipping extra. *Christian Liberty Press, 502 West Euclid Ave., Arlington Heights, IL 60004. (847) 259-4444. Fax: (847) 259-2941. Email: enquire@homeschools.org. Web: www.homeschools.org. They take credit card orders, but not over the phone. Any other contact method will work.*

UPDATED!
Greenleaf Press Famous Men series

Grade 4 and up. Famous Men of Greece, Famous Men of Rome, Famous Men of the Middle Ages, Famous Men of the Renaissance & Reformation, $15.95 each, Greenleaf Guides, $7.95 each except Middle Ages, $9.95, and Old Testament

History, $10.95. Study Packages: Old Testament #1, $32.25; Old Testament #2, $50.25; Ancient Egypt, $38.95; Egypt for Older Students, $54.75; Ancient Greece, $52.70; Ancient Rome, $42.95; Middle Ages, $57.95. Ancient Rome Study Package, $42.95. Many supplemental materials available for each time period. Shipping extra. *Greenleaf Press, 1570 Old Laguardo Rd., Lebanon, TN 37087. Inquiries: (615) 449-1617. Orders: (800) 311-1508. Fax: (615) 449-4018. Email: Greenleaf@aol.com. Web: www.greenleafpress.com*

a Famous Men book to accompany it. To make up for this, the people at Greenleaf have put together several Usborne books (*Time-Traveler Book of Pharaohs and Pyramids* and *Deserts* from the First Travelers series), a book on King Tut's mummy, David Macaulay's great book *Pyramid* that shows the construction of the pyramids, and a history book entitled *Pharaohs of Ancient Egypt*, written at a fourth-grade reading level.

Using these as the basic texts, the Greenleaf Guide pulls it all together with reading assignments, salt dough maps, modeling activities, and discussion questions. It's an absolutely enthralling introduction to this time period, designed so the whole family can study the same lessons at once.

Famous Men of Greece, **Famous Men of Rome**, and **Famous Men of the Middle Ages** are updated reprints of three works originally published in 1904. The Greece and Rome books present Greek and Roman mythology along with short biographies of famous men from each area, while the Middle Ages book is pure history, from the Germanic chiefs who overpowered the Romans to notables such as Charlemagne, St. Francis, Marco Polo, and Joan of Arc (an honorary Famous Man). All are written at a fifth-grade reading level.

Famous Men of the Renaissance & Reformation is a Rob Shearer original. The first Famous Men book to include illustrations, it boasts over 75 images of famous men, women, and artworks from this period. It covers western European history from 1300–1550, with separate chapters on over 30 Renaissance and Reformation notables. Same easy-reading style as the other Famous Men books.

Those who know enough about Greek and Roman history to notice may observe that statism was exalted in previous editions of *Famous Men of Greece* and *Famous Men of Rome*. Lycurgus, for example, who persuaded the Spartan citizens to divvy up their property and slaves, kill their feeble and deformed babies, and live on the simplest food served in a communal dining hall, was called "one of the wisest and best men that ever lived in Greece." The new edition does not personally commend Lycurgus, though it still describes him rather favorably.

That's why Greenleaf wrote study guides: to highlight some of these problems in past culture and encourage readers to judge ancient customs by biblical attitudes. These Greenleaf Guides are really well-organized and thorough. Each chapter of the corresponding Famous Men books is covered separately, with vocabulary word lists and discussion questions. Background information is provided where necessary.

The **Greenleaf Guide for Greece** includes supplementary reading assignments from Homer's *Iliad* and *Odyssey* and selections from Plato. The guide for Rome assigns supplementary readings from Foxe's *Book of Martyrs*, Virgil's *Æneid*, Macaulay's *City*, and more. Geography is covered (via salt dough maps), and story characters are analyzed in terms of biblical standards of righteousness. The **Middle Ages guide** directs you to reading Macaulay's *Castle* and *Cathedral*, and uses Facts on File's *Cultural Atlas of the Middle Ages* for detailed reference readings. The **Old Testament guide** relies on the *Children's Atlas of the Bible*, *How the Bible Came to Use*, and *Chronological and Background Charts of the Old Testament*.

Greenleaf Press may not have written any test sets, but they have tried to make your life easier in other ways. Case in point: they created **Study Packages** for each time period. These include the Famous Men and Greenleaf Guide for that period, plus the major supplemental books. (Note: the only difference between Old Testament packages #1 and #2 is that #2 includes *Chronological and Background Charts*, while #1 does not.)

In addition, Greenleaf Press's catalog lists hundreds of resources organized by time periods, so your children can cut out historically-accurate models, see how cities and towns were built, and read the history of each time period both as straight history and historical fiction. Plus tons of the very best resources for art, music, and nature study. I once spent an entire speaking fee on Greenleaf's goodies, and highly recommend their products and service. *Mary Pride*

If you enjoy unit studies, and if you're interested in the medieval/renaissance period, you'll love **Rebirth and Reformation: A Unit Studies Guide to the Medieval/Renaissance Period** by Vivian M. Doublestein.

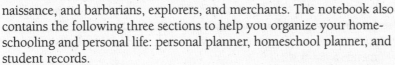

The first thing that caught my attention with this curriculum is how pleasing to the eye it is. The book is printed on top-quality paper and has beautiful artwork sprinkled throughout. The large, 3-ring binder contains well over 100 pages of instructional material which covers the church, medieval life, the renaissance, and barbarians, explorers, and merchants. The notebook also contains the following three sections to help you organize your homeschooling and personal life: personal planner, homeschool planner, and student records.

The primary drawback to the curriculum is the large amount of preparation time. Be prepared to spend a lot of time at your local library, digging up the necessary information to complete the assignments.

If you like curriculum that holds your hand and provides step by step instructions, you may be overwhelmed by this unit study. But if you like biblically based unit studies that point you in the right direction and stir up the artist in you, you'll love Rebirth and Reformation! *Rebecca Livermore*

Activities & Games

Aristoplay has designed a game package to delight your budding historian with the peculiarities and particulars of Ancient Egyptian culture. Eight competitive and cooperative games of varying degrees of difficulty and fun will familiarize your Egyptologist with life as it was over 4,000 years ago. You'll learn about Egyptians gods, King Tut, the pyramids, scarabs, and

For years, I have been wishing that these guides included quizzes with answer keys. How else is a simpleminded parent such as myself supposed to know whether my kids are doing the activities right and learning all the facts? Recently, Covenant Home Curriculum has solved this problem by releasing their own Test Sets for several of the Greenleaf Guides. Greenleaf plans on carrying these tests in the next edition of their catalog.

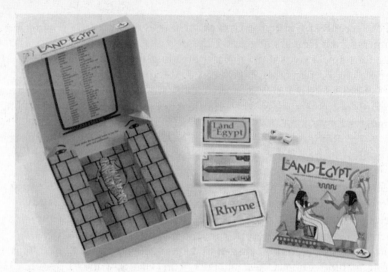

more. **In The Land of Egypt** will also encourage observation, problem-solving and thinking skills. Your student will learn as he deciphers rhyme puzzles, reads or listens to a story and later narrates it back to you, or plays Concentration-like matching games with Egyptian symbols.

This is a great way to enhance a study of the time period and to complement a more traditional course of study, such as the *Greenleaf Guide to Ancient Egypt* or the second grade history curriculum from Veritas Press. The games are recommended for ages eight and up, but a younger child could participate, with the guidance of a parent or older sibling. *Barbara Petronelli*

NEW!
Classical Kids: An Activity Guide

Grades 1–6. $14.95 plus shipping. *Chicago Review Press, 814 North Franklin St., Chicago, IL 60610. Orders: (800) 888-4741. Inquiries: (312) 337-0747. Fax: (312) 337-5985. Web: www.ipgbook.com.*

Friends, Romans, and homeschoolers, lend me your ears! I come not to discourage you, but to encourage you to take a close look at this book for your unit studies on Ancient Greece and Rome. Even Brutus and Cassius would be impressed by **Classical Kids: An Activity Guide to Life in Ancient Greece and Rome**.

Dress in the manner of the Greeks and Romans and make your own *chiton* and *peplos*! Find out the origins of birthstones! Prepare a feast of baked fish in grape leaves or crustulum! Discover the secrets behind magic squares, the moving coin, and the abacus! Build your own volcano and aqueducts!

With 182 pages of instructions and illustrations, this is a veritable treasure trove of activities to enhance any unit study or textbook in the study of the Ancients. Included are several maps and a brief timeline. This book is well worth the price for hours, nay, years of fun and learning. Recommended. *Barb Meade*

NEW!
The Millennium Paper Doll Book

Grades 1–5. $9.95 plus shipping. *The Learning Works. PO Box 6187, Santa Barbara, CA 93160. Orders: (800) 235-5767. Inquiries: (805) 964-4220. Fax: (805) 964-1466. Email: LESatTLW@aol.com. Web: www.thelearningworks.com.*

Dress up your child like a medieval knight or damsel. How about in Japanese kimonos? Or as a pilgrim or pioneer? With the paper doll cut-outs in **The Millennium Paper Doll Book**, you can find a picture of your child and glue it to the doll so your virtual "child" can dress up in period costumes. There are costumes for both boys and girls from 1,000 years of history. Your children can color and design the outfits however they see fit. Each outfit has its own description and ideas on decorating.

With the exception of the 70's miniskirt and the 80's off-the-shoulder T-shirt, the outfits are fun and the dolls could be a different type of addition to any unit study. *Barb Meade*

Suppose you've been given the job of planning the grand finale for your homeschool group's study of ancient Greece. Perhaps an Olympic day or a Greek feast might be fun, but where can you turn for ideas? Filled with activities which are not just exciting but are actually doable, **Spend the Day in Ancient Greece** by Linda Honan may be just what you need.

Honan sets the 30 activities in this book into a fictional story of a "typical Athenian family." As you accompany the two children through the events of a single day (the birthday of Athena), you will find instructions for preparing foods and for making clothing, jewelry and items from a water clock to a model Greek boat. Background information in each of the 11 short chapters will give more meaning to your projects.

In one chapter you will learn about the Hoplites, the best foot soldiers in the Athenian army and about the relative importance of military service to the Athenians (fairly important) and the Spartans (extremely important). Brief sidebars will tell you about Alexander the Great and the first marathon. Arming your little soldiers will be a breeze with the clear, well-illustrated instructions for making an impressive Corinthian helmet from a paper paint bucket, as well as greaves and a shield.

Though there are some super projects here, there are some questionable activities and descriptions because the story is based on following the family as they celebrate the birthday of a goddess. For this reason this book serves best as a parent idea resource.

Now about that Olympic Day. How about having the kids make Hoplite helmets and greaves for a foot race, model chariots, a discus and javelin for two events of a pentathlon and winners' crowns and clay amphoras for prizes. As for a Greek feast . . . now it's possible! *Anne Wegener*

Fact Books

Ever wish you could go back and live during another era? This set of books gives you an opportunity to see what the "everyday" man lived like in days gone by. You can get inside their lives and see what their civilizations were like. Each double-page spread contains one event and beautiful color paintings that tell you the story of how they lived their lives. There is some nudity in the *Greek Potter* book.

This series includes:

- *A Cathedral Builder*
- *An Egyptian Craftsman*
- *A Florentine Merchant*
- *A Greek Potter*
- *An Ice Age Hunter*
- *A Roman Soldier*
- *A Viking Settler*

These historical accounts make a wonderful addition to anyone's home-school library. They will be read and enjoyed by everyone interested in learning about earlier civilizations. *Maryann Turner*

The **First Facts series** includes books on five ancient cultures: *Ancient Egyptians, Ancient Greeks, Ancient Romans, Middle Ages,* and *Vikings*—and one book on the *American Frontier,* half of which is about Native Americans.

After the introduction, each two-page spread starts with a "fact"—e.g., "Vikings were fine sailors"—and then

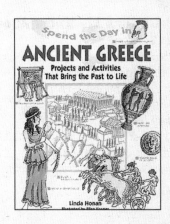

expands on it with a paragraph or so of text, detailed full-color illustrations, and sidebars loaded with factoids. The "fact" approach makes this more memorable than other books organized by subject. "Rich Romans ate flamingoes and peacocks" helps engage the interest and memory more than a spread about "Food the Romans ate," for example. In all, decent introductions, with a reading level suitable for upper elementary, each ending with a glossary and an index. *Mary Pride*

Each book in the **How We Know About series** begins with a few pages on the archaeological and written evidence for what we know about the civilization. The rest of the oversized, fully illustrated book then takes the usual two-page-spread, "fact" book approach, with loads of captioned illustrations and a fair amount of text about a number of lifestyle topics: their tools, homes, work, and so forth. Each of the spreads displays some artifacts, with text about how the artifacts were found and what that tells us about the civilization. Books in this series: *Egyptians, Greeks, Romans,* and *Vikings.* You may prefer to start with books such as these, instead of a regular fact book, so your kids can see for themselves that historical "facts" need to be based on hard evidence. *Mary Pride*

NEW!
Bedrick How We Know About series

Grades 4–8. Each hardcover book, $17.95. Shipping extra.
Peter Bedrick Books, c/o NTC Contemporary Publishing, 4255 W. Touhy, Lincolnwood, IL 60646.
(800) 323-4900. Fax: (800) 998-3103.
Email: ntcpub@tribune.com.
Web: www.contemporarybooks.com.

NEW!
Candlewick History News series

Grades 5–8. Each hardbound book, $15.99 or $16.99. Shipping extra.
Penguin-Putnam Inc., 405 Murrey Hill Parkway, E. Rutherford, NJ 07073. (800)331-4624.
Fax: (201)933-2903.
Web: www.penguinputnam.com.

The **Candlewick History News series** is a hoot! Perfect to add some "zing" to your history studies, each oversized hardbound book is loaded with illustrated "newspaper" stories about the civilization or era in question. For example, *The Greek News* includes pieces on how the Greeks started new colonies, the history of Athens, the war with Persia, and other traditional historic events and eras of importance. But instead of dry textbook commentary, you get headlines such as "Greece in Peril" and "Xerxes Crushed" and sidebars such as "Our Brave Boys," which starts, "No matter how long our history, our warriors' brave stand at Thermopylae will never be forgotten . . ." Lifestyle pieces explore issues such as the treatment of women in ancient Greece (interviews with a married woman from Rhodes and a 14-year-old bride-to-be from Thebes), theatre news, school life, the Olympics, and much more. Learn about the pieces that make up Greek armor . . . view a sea battle . . . see a trireme (Greek ship) . . . check out Greek fashion . . . The factoids and fake ads are also a learning experience. Fancy life as a shipyard worker? Want to brush up your orating skills? Curious about the fate of runaway slaves or cowards in Sparta? It's all in *The Greek News*!

The facts are all accurate, and not mangled for the sake of inside jokes. Unlike textbooks, the facts are presented memorably, in a way students are familiar with.

Be aware that, in each case, the newspaper articles are written from the point of view of the civilization studied. So, for example, the *Aztec News* has a piece on why human sacrifice is important and the foreigners are wrong to try to end it, and the *Greek News* has an article about why slaves are a good investment. You are expected to read "past" the clearly false or outdated ideas in such pieces, to understand the people of the times without being influenced by them.

The series includes a book for just about every major ancient civilization you'll study: *Stone Age News, Egyptian News, Viking News, Greek News, Roman News, Aztec News,* and *Explorers.* There is also a book on *Medicine*— great for your history of science unit study! *Mary Pride*

While reviewing the **Gulliver Living History** books it was all I could do to keep my children, from tots to teen, from running off with them. With large rich photographs which engage even little ones and a text written at an upper elementary level, the *Living History* series appeals to a wide range of ages.

What sets these books apart from other history books are the striking color photos of models reenacting past cultures and events. Using computer technology, these pictures place the actors and artifacts into locations from Iceland (Vikings) to the Caribbean islands (Columbus). While some of the pictures are obviously staged, especially those in *Ancient Egypt*, others are so realistic you may almost forget that they are of actors.

The clear text, though sometimes overshadowed by the dramatic photos, adds depth and detail. Topics, arranged thematically on two-page spreads, will help you "see" into the lives of peoples of the past. What would it have been like to spend the winter in a Viking settlement, to paint a Renaissance fresco, or to attend a feast in ancient Rome?

Though these are not Christian books, Christianity is neither ignored nor treated disrespectfully. Be aware there is some nude art typical of the times in the *Greek* and *Renaissance* volumes.

The addition of accurate maps and a timeline on the endpages increases the value of these 64-page hardcovers as reference tools. A "How Do We Know" section describes archeological and historical evidence for what is known about each culture. The quality and sophistication are highest in the most recently published titles (*Italian Renaissance, First World War,* and *Industrial Revolution*).

Titles available in this series include *Ancient Greece, Classical Rome, First World War, Fourteenth-Century Towns, Industrial Revolution, Italian Renaissance, Knights in Armor, Pyramids of Ancient Egypt, The Vikings,* and *The Voyages of Christopher Columbus.*

Finding resources that work for the multi-age situation so many of us have in our homes is rare. With these books you can gather your whole family, snuggle down with your youngest nearby to see the pictures and enjoy history together! *Anne Wegene*

Millbrook's Mystery History series spares no effort to get kids involved in history. Each double-page spread includes *all* the following features:

- Three questions about the historical event or place pictured, with answers on the bottom of the page
- Hidden pictures to spot within the main picture (e.g., a yo-yo, stamped envelope, road sign, ticket, and roller skates) and determine which don't belong within the scene
- Clues to find a mystery personage (e.g., a person plotting against the Roman Emperor Diocletian) from among a number of suspects at the end of the book
- "Hidden history" questions, with answers at the back of the book
- A puzzle or activity related to the scene

In addition, each page includes informative text about the scene pictured, some pages have true/false questions (answers, again, are at the back of the book), and the final spread is a game to play.

Some of the information will look familiar to readers of Millbrook's Fact or Fiction series, which emphasizes many of the same facts, but the full-color drawings are completely different. Be aware that one scene in the

NEW!
Gulliver Living History Series
Grades 4–12. (to read themselves), grade preK–4 (read aloud by parent or older child). Hardcover, $16.95. Some titles available in paperback, $9. Shipping extra.
Gulliver Books/Harcourt Brace, 6277 Sea Harbor Dr., Orlando, FL, 32887. (800) 543-1918. Fax: (800) 235-0256.

NEW!
Millbrook Mystery History series
Grade 4 and up. Each book, $9.95, except Pirate Galleon, $10.95.
The Millbrook Press, PO Box 335, 2 Old New Milford Rd., Brookfield, CT 06804. Orders: (800) 462-4703. extension 3034. Inquiries: (203) 740-2220. Fax: (203) 740-2223.

Pirate Galleon book shows blood on the deck and on the clothes of two brawling pirates. The cover of the *Roman Colosseum* book has a scene of lions attacking some gladiators, one of whose legs is bleeding from shallow scratches. The scene of entire Christian families, including young children, about to be attacked by wild animals in the Colosseum might also scare some younger readers. None of the other books have any blood, even in war scenes showing fallen warriors with arrows sticking out of them. Male rear nudity is visible at a distance in the Roman bath scene, and some male and female rear nudity in the *Trojan Horse* book (a picture of Spartans exercising).

Books in this series include *Medieval Castle*, *Pharaoh's Tomb*, *Pirate Galleon*, *Roman Colosseum*, *Trojan Horse*, and *Viking Longboat*. *Mary Pride*

NEW!
Oxford's Smelly Old History

Grades 2–8. Each book, $7.95.
Oxford University Press, 2001 Evans Road, Cary, NC 27513. (800) 451-7556. Fax: (919) 677-1303.
Web: www.oup-usa.org.

Want to scratch and sniff your way through history? Be warned; it's no bed of roses! That's the idea behind the **Smelly Old History** series from Oxford University Press.

It's safe to say you'll be getting a whiff of history that's usually not covered in textbooks. Oh, yes, these 32-page paperbacks have the usual glossary and index. But you'll find a real difference in their two-page spreads. Like an Usborne book, these include lively four-color cartoon illustrations and bouncy text. Like an Eyewitness book, they also include photographs of historical artifacts. Unlike either, they have scratch-and-sniff panels to bring the historical smells you'll be reading about to life. Often, vile and reeking life. For, as the names of the books imply, the past was often odiferous.

Just look at these titles: *Mouldy Mummies*, *Greek Grime*, *Roman Aromas*, *Vile Vikings*, *Medieval Muck*, *Tudor Odours*, *Victorian Vapours*, *Reeking Royals*, and *Wartime Whiffs*. The slight naughtiness continues in the books themselves. In the *Mummies* book, for example, you see a photograph of an actual naked mummy, as well as the cartoon backside of a lady bather. A guest is shown throwing up at a banquet, and the little artistic squiggles that include "bad smell" are rising off the pictures on at least half of the pages. Spread titles include Smells Divine, Deadly Deodorant, Spicy Stuffings, Foul Pharaohs, Meaty Mummies, Fragrant Feasts, Lotions and Potions, Egyptian Effluence, and more. The scratch-and-sniff smells are overripe mummy, frankincense, a Pharaoh's cheesy feet, cat's grease and gazelle dung, and roses on Cleopatra's barge. Packed with memorable historical tidbits, these are books the kids will go for, assuming you, the parent, don't turn up your nose at the whole series concept. *Mary Pride*

Usborne History books

Grades 2–8. First History series, $4.50 each. Starting Point History series, $14.95 each. Time Traveler Series, $6.95 each. Combined volume, Time Traveler Books, $22.95. Children's Picture World History series, $6.95 each (paperback) or $14.95 each (library-bound). Combined volume, The Usborne Book of World History, $24.95. Living Long Ago books, $4.50 each (paperback) or $12.95 each (library-bound). Shipping extra.
EDC Publishing, Division of Educational Development Corporation, 10302 East 55th Place, Tulsa, OK 74146. (800) 475-4522.
Fax: (800) 747-4509.
Web: www.edcpub.com.

The most fascinating, child-appealing "history books" I have ever seen. The books in the **First History series** each follow one boy's daily life and family through town and country. Emphasis is on everyday life, but because of the superb full-color illustrations you can't help noticing the architecture, furniture, clothing, and artifacts of each time period. The series includes *Prehistoric Times* (the "caveman" viewpoint is followed), *Roman Times*, and *Castle Times*.

The colorful **Starting Point History series** teaches ancient history almost painlessly. Using a question/answer format, your children will find many of the answers to questions they may have asked before, and also some interesting facts. Books in this series are: *Who Were the First People?*, *Who Were the Romans?*, *Who Were the Vikings?*, *What Were Castles For?*, *Who Were the First North Americans?*, and *Who Built the Pyramids?*

For slightly older children, the **Time Traveler series** takes a child back in time to see how life really was for the high and lowly in ancient Egypt (the *Pharaohs and Pyramids* book), Rome (*Rome and Romans*), Norseland (*Viking Raiders*), and medieval Europe (*Knights and Castles*).

The **Children's Picture World History series** does the same for *First Civilizations* (strong evolutionary outlook); *Empires and Barbarians*; *Warriors and Seafarers*; *Crusaders, Aztecs, and Samurai*; *Exploration and Discovery*; and *The Age of Revolutions*. All are full-color throughout, 8½ x 11", in quality cartoon style on glossy paper, with plenty of descriptive text. See how Baron Godfrey's castle defenses were designed, or how the Egyptians turned papyrus into paper! Watch the Vikings build their ship, or the Romans prepare a feast! Kids can't put them down (and neither could I). Slight Magic Marker-ing needed in a few places (Cretan ladies dressed like Playboy models).

The Living Long Ago books from the **Explainers series** includes *Food and Eating*, *Homes and Houses*, *Clothes and Fashion*, and *Travel and Transport*. Each book chronologically follows its theme through the following se- quence: primitive times (mostly speculation), ancient Egypt, Rome, Vikings, medieval period, European, early American, and modern times. You find out how things were made and used (again, with great illustra- tions). Activities in each book include such things as making your own me- dieval fish pasties, model coracle, or model teepee. Nice open page layout. *Mary and Sarah Pride*

Teaching Aids

The timeline dilemma is a familiar one to homeschoolers, namely, "Where do you put it?" Most of us barely have enough wall space for our family photos, much less something spanning eras and eons.

Bonnie Dettmer has come to our res- cue. How about a "timeline on a shelf"? Her **Book of the Centuries** is a large 7- ring binder filled with blank pages just waiting for your personal touch.

Several nifty features make this much more appealing than just notebook-pages-in-a-binder. (Which you could do and accomplish the same thing, but it wouldn't be nearly as much fun!) All the pages are heavyweight and have the dates marked along the top edge. Spanning recorded history from Creation to the present, the incre- ments vary from 100 to 25 years per page. Also included are shorter pages, lined and labeled for "notes." These are meant to be interspersed among the pages and allow you to include even more information, while still keeping the years in view.

The possibilities for this kind of book are endless. You may want to in- clude maps, photos, reproductions of famous artworks, biographies, family trees, drawings of clothing and costumes, inventions, discoveries, explo- rations, summaries of historical fiction read, or whatever else your imagina- tion can conceive. With "scrapbooking" such a popular hobby these days, just think of what you could do with some fancy stickers, stamps, and col- orful mats for your illustrations.

Being able to refer to this for years to come makes this a wonderful in- vestment. *Renee Mathis*

Creation's Child Simplified World Time Line, contained on seven pieces of 8½ x 11" cardstock, covers the period from 4600 BC to 2000 AD, including key events, people, and black line illustrations. Bible characters are shown as well.

NEW!
Book of the Centuries
Grades 3–12. $29.95 plus shipping. *Small Ventures, 11023 Watterson Dr., Dallas, TX 75228. Phone/Fax: (972) 681-1728.*

Creation's Child Simplified World Time Line
Grades 1–12. Simplified World Time Line: regular, $6.50; laminated, $10.95. Shipping extra.

Creation's Child, PO Box 3004 #44, Corvallis, OR 97339. (541) 758-3413. Send SASE for free brochure.

NEW!
Veritas History Flashcards and Tapes

Grades 2–6. Each card set, $19.95. Each audiocassette, $6.95. Each card/audiocassette set, $24.95. Classroom kits include 16 of one flashcard set, one audiocassette: $274.95 each. Shipping extra. *Veritas Press, 1250 Belle Meade Dr., Lancaster, PA 17601. (800) 922-5082. Inquiries: (717) 397-5082. Fax: (717) 397-6544. Email: Veritasprs@aol.com. Web: members.aol.com/Veritasprs.*

Also included are instructions, extra pages of important dates, short lists of key people, and a reproducible lined page so students can add information to the chart from their own independent studies. *Mary Pride*

Veritas Academy is a classical and Christian grade school. Like other such schools, it has pioneered some of its own curriculum. Unlike most such curriculum, the resulting history flashcard and tape series has no whiff of the mimeo machine about it. These high-quality materials look like they belong on store shelves—and I hope the stores are smart enough to figure this out!

Each **Veritas History Flashcard Set** includes 32 oversized, colorful, glossy cards, designed to cover a year of history study, with one event studied per week. After five years of using this program, a child will be familiar with 160 of the most important events in human history.

Each card is topped with a color-coded bar which indicates which series it belongs to. If the event in question is found in Scripture, a purple bar is beneath the top color bar.

One side of each card has a full-color illustration, with the work's author and title when known, and the major event or time period named in large type, along with the Scripture reference, if applicable. The other side of each card has its name and number, along with more detailed information about the event or person named, including its date.

Cards can have up to three numbers: one for the card's place in the particular series, one for its place in the Bible series, and one for its chronological number in the combined Bible/history series.

A short list of resources for further study, with page numbers so you can look up the precise information, is also on the back of each card. Resources mentioned include the Greenleaf Guides; *Streams of Civilization*; Eerdman's *Children's Story Bible*; Dorling-Kindersley *Children's Illustrated Bible*; Kingfisher *Illustrated History of the World*; the *Iliad* and *Odyssey*; various Usborne, Bedrick, and Eyewitness books; and other resources likely to be found on a well-stocked homeschool or library book shelf. An enclosed resource sheet tells who is the publisher of each resource and gives their 800 number, if it's not a title sold exclusively through bookstores.

A music audiocassette tape is available for each series. The **Veritas History Tape** puts the events on the cards in a song sequence, to help children remember them in order. You can use the flashcards, and associated resources, as a history curriculum, and the songs for additional (and painless) reinforcement.

Teacher's manuals are available for all five sets of flashcards. I saw the manual for *Old Testament/Ancient Egypt*. Marlin and Laurie Detweiler, authors of the flashcards, inform me that this manual was inspired by the work of Rob and Cyndy Shearer of Greenleaf Press. It's a small world, isn't it? The large, spiral-bound manual includes teaching instructions plus a worksheet, one or more projects, and a test for each flashcard. In addition, a literature unit based on *The Pharaohs of Ancient Egypt* by Elizabeth Payne, recipes for giving an Egyptian feast, and some other matter is included at the end of the manual.

The author suggests you laminate the cards, punch them, and put them in sequence on a large ring. This is a good way to keep them organized and in chronological sequence, and not too much work for such a helpful, easy-to-use history study tool. *Mary Pride*

Available on both flashcards and tapes are:
- Old Testament/Ancient Egypt
- New Testament/Greece/Rome
- Middle Ages/Renaissance/Reformation
- Age of Exploration and Discovery (up to 1815 A.D.)
- Modern World History (1815 to present)

Coming soon will be three sets of Old Testament flashcards and two sets of New Testament.

PART 8

Arts & Sports

Aaron Yamagata, an 8-year-old from Encino, CA, won the UNICEF "Kids Helping Kids" card contest, in the face of a good deal of competition. A homeschooler, Aaron has wanted to be a famous artist for some time now, and has already astounded many of his elders with the success he's had so far. He's an accomplished artist already, and fame seems to be on the way.

Koleesa, Kevin, and Kurtis Amundson (from left to right in the picture) are not to be trifled with . . . At a tournament in Abilene, KS, Koleesa, a brown belt, took third place in defensive sparring, Kevin, 2nd Degree-Decided black belt, took second place in defensive sparring and presentation of form, and Kurtis, the same rank as Kevin, took first place in presentation of form and third in defensive sparring. Koleesa is 7 years old, and the two brothers are 9. All three are privately trained in karate at Taekwondo USA/Karate for Kids in Burnsville, MN. They've all been at it since they were about five years old. How many ranks are left?

CHAPTER 44

Drawing & Cartooning

Is art just a pastime for special people with enormous talent?
Not in my book!
You might squawk, "Hey, not me! No way! I can't even draw a straight line!"

Well, first of all, **drawing is not drafting**. You can always use a ruler or a computer to draw a straight line. *Drawing* is about making curved lines and wiggly lines and crosshatching and such until the final result looks like something. *Drafting* is about defining the outlines of manmade structures—and I don't know any mechanical designers who try to produce straight lines freehand, either!

Second, and far more important, is the fact that, rare cases aside, **most people need to be *taught* to draw**—and almost none of us have received this training. The reason? Somehow the idea has taken hold in art instruction circles that the way for people to learn art is for each of us to make "five thousand mistakes" on our own. Then, after we've made all these mistakes, the talented will emerge and the rest of us will sink back into the dregs. This is the way the schools teach reading, and it of course produces the same sorry results.

Contrast this with the ancient and honorable **apprenticeship system**. There the would-be artist worked under the direction of a master in his craft. At first, the apprentice spent most of his time doing mechanical tasks: rehairing brushes, mixing paints, and so on. During this phase he was learning to handle the physical tools of his art. Then the master would let him try some small exercises, and if the apprentice was successful he would perhaps get to contribute a minor part to one of the master's own projects. In time, he would learn most of the master's techniques (canny masters kept some back!) and would be ready to try something new on his own.

At each step the apprentice was taught the skills he needed. He saw all the stages artwork goes through; he saw the finished result; he heard the master criticize his efforts and make suggestions for improvement. He did *not* blunder about making five thousand mistakes, as the master wanted a productive apprentice, not a nitwit.

As someone who has never been accused of possessing great artistic talent, I am here to tell you that today you can start learning to produce really nice drawings, even if you never have before.

Over the last few years a number of really fun and easy-to-follow drawing programs have been developed. These all follow the time-tested method

Every person reading this book can learn to draw.

It is being overly generous to say that 5 percent of our college graduates know how to draw. There is no successful drawing program in our public schools and educators know it . . .

If you will evaluate our public-school art program, do not ask the art supervisor. The reply would probably sound much like the weavers' description of their goods in the tale, The Emperor's New Clothes. Instead, ask yourselves and your neighbors because you are the products of the public-school art program and NO EDUCATIONAL PROGRAM IS BETTER THAN THE PRODUCT IT TURNS OUT . . .

Many art supervisors and teachers maintain that there is no "right" and "wrong" in drawing . . . In a drawing program where there is no right and wrong and no rules, the children have nothing tangible to grasp and nothing to take home. They do not learn the right way; they do not learn the wrong way; they do not learn . . .

One of the main objectives of today's public-school art program is "Free Expression (creative self expression)." We know that people who do not know how to draw cannot express themselves freely . . .

—Bruce McIntyre
Author, Audio Visual
Drawing Program

of introducing skills one at a time, rather than mindlessly urging the student to be "creative." Below you will also find a number of excellent resources that introduce you to other media and techniques besides drawing.

Art Curriculum

Simple, really sweet, step-by-step art courses for grades 1-8 that teach drawing, coloring, lettering, painting, and paper cutting. The art has a Mennonite flavor: simple dress, gentle little girls with braids, Christian messages.

Art with a Purpose comes in eight levels. **Artpacs 1** and **2**, for grades 1 and 2, cover simple drawing, including drawing with grids, tracing, craft projects, and simple one-point perspective. **Artpac 3** covers drawing animals using simple shapes, proportions of a face, and how to make a face happy or sad. **Artpac 4** includes 3-D shading, illustrating a little story book, and elementary perspective drawing. **Artpac 5** includes advanced shading techniques; lettering, layout and design; and how to mix, paint, and blend watercolors. **Artpac 6** covers shading with colored pencils, perspective, drawing faces, and more freehand drawing. **Artpac 7** includes advanced grid drawing including accurate reduction and enlargement, attractive calligraphy, and advanced painting in full color. **Artpac 8** deals exclusively with illustration techniques with pen and ink.

Each Art Pac includes instruction sheets for the teacher which present the lessons' goals and provides teaching guidelines.

Art with a Purpose was designed specifically to lighten the teacher's workload and to provide truly Christian art instruction. It succeeds at both. For these reasons, it has become the core art course of choice among Christian home schoolers. *Mary Pride*

Bruce McIntyre was a veteran public school art instructor who also put in a decade as a Walt Disney artist in the era when Disney's art was really something. His first book, aptly named **Drawing Textbook**, explains in crystalline detail why public school (and most private school) art programs fail to produce students who can draw. His analysis of what went wrong is combined with a stirring call to achieve drawing literacy in our day, and takes up the first 13 pages of the book. Find out why the ability to communicate visually makes such a difference, and the one approach to art instruction that provides it. Then you and your children can tackle the 222 graduated exercises that make up the rest of the book! These start with simple stuff—a birthday cake, a TV set—and progress along merrily introducing the Seven Laws of Perspective (surface, size, surface lines, overlapping, shading, density, and foreshortening) and other goodies until by lesson 58 you're drawing realistic skyscrapers, by lesson 94 you're getting down on paper a twisted candle that would make the Hildebrandt brothers proud, and by the last lesson you can draw *anything!*

Once you've finished *Drawing Textbook*, **Drawing in Three Dimensions** gives you 12 "clubs" (actually, 12 timed drawing exercises of increasing difficulty) and a more in-depth explanation of each drawing principle—plus tips on how to make your drawings more attractive by adding tapering, texture, repetition, S curves, variety, color, value, and distribution. This is an updated and improved version of Bruce's original *Big Easel II* book. **Art Elements** takes up the theme of how to make your drawings more attractive, with more input on the "25 elements of art," including those mentioned above. From here on in, it's merely a matter of adding to your visual vocabulary with his supplementary books, such as *Cute Animals, Things for Sports, Scenery,* and *Flowers and Trees*. Each of these

Art with a Purpose

Grades 1–8. Art Pac for each level $5. Shipping extra.
Share-A-Care Publications, 240 Mohns Hill Road, Reinholds, PA 17569. (717) 484-2367. Email: myronweaver@juno.com.

Audio-Visual Drawing Program

Grades 3–12. Drawing Textbook, $8. Drawing in Three Dimensions, Art Elements, Cute Animals, Scenery, Flowers and Trees, $6 each. California Easel Drawing Lessons (originally broadcast on TV), $576 for entire set. Individual tapes (7 lessons each), $96 each. Shipping extra.
Audio-Visual Drawing Program, PO Box 186, Ridgecrest, CA 93556. (760) 375-2892. Email: info@avdp.com or orders@avdp.com. Web: www.avdp.com.

shows how to apply the seven elements of drawing to a particular class of objects.

Freehand Sketching is the book for teens and adults. It covers the same basic seven principles of drawing, plus info on positioning and aligning.

The only problem with this series is the poor reproduction (photocopy or mimeo quality), which makes some drawing details hard to follow.

Based on the *Drawing Textbook*, Bruce McIntyre's **Self-Study Drawing Course** is a set of 37 lesson booklets, each containing six drawing lessons. Or, for those who prefer video, the same program is available as the *California Easel TV Series*—again a set of 37 lessons, six exercises each. Bonus Lessons, to accompany the video series, focus on drawing particular objects, such as holiday pictures, flowers, fire, people, and space. *Mary Pride*

The Beginning of Creativity is a splendid approach to helping your children learn to draw! The seven days of creation are the theme for a series of easy exercises. The author shows you how to build a drawing step by step, instead of asking you to copy a finished drawing (which is often so difficult that it's discouraging). The lessons are built in such a way that no matter what your artistic level, you will be much better at drawing after completing this course.

All of the basics of drawing are covered: line, shape, shading, perspective, design and pattern, and how to critique your work. Best of all, it shows that creativity is biblical. An excellent value. *John Nixdorf*

When it comes to cartooning, Vic Lockman is the Old Master. His **Big Book of Cartooning in Christian Perspective series** introduces cartooning techniques step by step. Each book is spiral-bound, with plenty of blank workspace opposite the lavishly illustrated instructions, so you can practice your new skills and compare them to Vic's work at the same time. Bible verses are scattered throughout these books, hence the "Christian perspective."

Big Book I teaches how to combine shapes to make any person or objects, faces, hands and feet, wrinkles and folds, emotion and "breath of life" action, perspective, animals, scenery, weather, inking, lettering, and lots more in its 99 full-size pages.

Big Book II quickly recaps the basic lessons, and explains how to draw all sorts of cartoon animals. The two pages devoted to horses, for example, show how to draw a correctly proportioned horse, a "cartoony" horse, a number of horse gaits, horse hooves, and horse ears. This book does not include blank workspace, which is why it is shorter (46 full-sized pages).

The Big Book of Cartooning Machines isn't really that big (46 half-sized pages). It covers all sorts of popular cartoon machines in detail, from Grandpa's car to space ships. Limited space in this one to draw your own art.

Drawing for Girls (68 full-sized pages) covers similar topics to Book I, and some of the animals in Book II, but also features "girlish" topics such as how to draw paper dolls and brides. Vic came up with this book to entice girls, who are not always as interested in cartooning as boys.

Each book of **Cartooning for Young Children** is a smaller, handy size, with instructions broken down into even smaller steps and with plenty of workspace. Workspace drawings have dashed outlines to help younger children get started. For these books, it's more a case of "copy this drawing" than learning basic rules.

Miracle Art shows you how to do "trick" art—turning a letter into a person, an anchor into a sailor, a star into a sheriff . . . The book also includes some "Gospel Quickies," short Bible talks you can illustrate with one drawing that turns into another related to the talk. Compulsive doodlers will love this book.

Questionable features: Unscary Frankenstein monsters and other popular cartoon symbols appear in these books, as do intelligent animals, talking trees, and so forth. These all form part of the standard "cartoon vocabulary" and are not meant to be taken literally. *Mary Pride*

Big Yellow Drawing Book

Grades 2–adult. $10 plus shipping.
Hugh O'Neill and Associates, Box 1297, Nevada City, CA 95959. (530) 265-4196. Email: honeill@gvnet.com. Web: www.oddbodkins.com.

And while we're concentrating on drawing as the foundation of all art, don't miss **The Big Yellow Drawing Book**, a product of the O'Neill clan. Dan O'Neill is a cartoonist of repute in flower child circles. His "Odd Bodkins" comic strip gained quite a following in the sixties and seventies. His father Hugh (a genuine Ed.D.) helped by insisting that his wife Marian, an accomplished artist, and son Dan, the cartoonist, adhere to the known principles of learning. The end result of their labors is an extremely charming, simple introduction to drawing (in general) and cartooning (in particular) that has been proved 99 percent successful in teaching people of all ages to draw.

You begin by drawing cartoon faces—big round circles with eyes and mouths. Learn to convey emotion via eyebrows and eyelids. Learn to draw shapes, to place objects in the foreground and background, and to use simple perspective. Ample workspace on every page, plus step-by-step instructions about what to put into that workspace. Mischievous but wholesome cartoon examples are just slapdash enough to avoid intimidating a beginner.

Doesn't go as far as Vic Lockman's cartooning series (reviewed above); recommended as your child's first cartooning experience. We got one for each member of our family. *The Big Yellow Drawing Book* makes a great stocking-stuffer (as long as you wear tights—the book is 8½ x 11"). *Mary Pride*

NEW!
Calvert Discovering Art

Grades 4–8. First student, $200.
"Group" enrollment for additional student, $60.
Calvert School, 105 Tuscany Rd., Baltimore MD 21210-3098. (410) 243-6030. Fax: (410) 366-0674, E-mail: inquiry@calvertschool.org. Web: www.calvertschool.org.

Calvert's video course, **Discovering Art**, shows the same attention to detail that characterizes their other offerings. The six videocassettes include 32 art lessons intended to span a school year. The story line features both child actors and professional artists—including a computer animator, a paper artist, a sculptor, and an artist who assists "Peanuts" creator Charles Schulz on special projects. Lessons are TV-quality and cover both art appreciation (works from all eras are shown) and artistic techniques.

In a typical lesson, the video children encounter an artist, ask questions, and are shown how to handle some artistic problem—line, shading, perspective, etc. Your own children are then given a project that employs the new techniques: for example, using contour lines to draw the outline of a plant. By the end of the course, you will have seen hundreds of paintings, prints, drawings, sculptures, and photographs and created dozens of art projects. You will have studied dozens of art forms: drawing, painting, sculpture (with a variety of media), computer art, photography, fabric art, and so on. You will have a solid background in the basics of color (hue, value, and chroma), lighting, shape and lines, perspective, positive and negative space, and other foundations of art theory.

You get more than videos, of course. The course includes a 178-page, spiral-bound guidebook, project instructions for one student, six fine art postcards, and an art kit, as well as the videos. The teacher's guidebook has complete step-by-step lessons, as well as voluminous suggestions for further reading and art study. The art kit comes with tools and materials of the highest quality: an abundance of different kinds of art and construction paper, a rubber brayer and block ink, colored chalk, washable markers, colored pencils, washable tempera paint, drawing pencils, a black marker, foam board and a foam block for carving, oil pastels, watercolors, crayons, white glue, yarn, masking tape, a pencil sharpener, a kneaded eraser, safety scissors, a ruler, and a camel's hair brush, all in a convenient cardboard suitcase with a carry strap. One art kit is included in the basic program, and another complete art kit and project instruction booklet comes for each additional enrolled pupil. If you bought the art supplies separately, it would likely cost you more than the price of enrolling an additional pupil.

Our kids, as is normal, squirmed during some of the contrived video scenarios, but loved the projects. I appreciate the effort the Calvert staff put into pulling together so many art examples to illustrate each point, and their suggestions for additional reading, study, and field trips are excellent. *Mary Pride*

Questionable features: (1) One of the earliest projects, in lesson 3, asks your child to imagine he is an alien from another planet trying to describe an Earth object. (2) Lesson 11, on African art, shows masks used in pagan rituals and endorses their artistic qualities while carefully saying nothing negative about paganism itself. (3) The professional artist in lesson 17 likes to use skeleton shapes and Buddhas in her work, thanks to her religious outlook. (4) In lessons 28 and 29, the video children are creating Earth Day posters (Earth Day has rapidly become the politically correct substitute for Easter), and your children are supposed to invent a planet in another solar system (no problem, as long as they are aware nobody has ever proved that planets exist anywhere except in our solar system!). (5) Occasional works with pagan themes are dotted throughout the course, e.g., *Isis Nursing the Child Horus* in lesson 1. Forewarned is forearmed, and you can easily work around any of these features that bother you by reading ahead in the guidebook.

NEW!
Choose Art

Grades 2–4. $13.95 for the student book, $13.95 for the teacher's manual. Reproducible Blackline Masters, $109.

Choose Art Publishing, PO Box 26005, Saskatoon, Saskatchewan, Canada S7K 8C1. (306) 931-4183. Fax: (306) 931-4150. Email: art@chooseart.com. Web: www.chooseart.com.

This Christian-based art curriculum adeptly organizes things to let you successfully:

- create art projects
- provide a program for one or many
- instruct children of different levels and abilities
- build upon previous lessons, and have fun (all at the same time)!

The project directions are well written and explicit enough to guide even the most reluctant teacher—as we found out the week we planned to test a lesson out on a group of children. I came down with the flu and one of the other mothers was able to step in and present what became one of the favorite meetings. The directions for setting up the work areas are especially well-thought out.

The tips and suggestions for setting up work areas reflect that this art curriculum is a well-tested program. It is being used in many Christian schools in Canada and has been selected for the School of Tomorrow's art curriculum. And Choose Art has just released a similar program for grades five through seven.

NEW!
Doodle Series

Grades K–4. Build a Doodle Series, $3.95 each. Grades 1–6. Super Doodle Series, $4.95 each. Shipping extra.
The Learning Works. PO Box 6187, Santa Barbara, CA 93160. Orders: (800) 235-5767. Inquiries: (805) 964-4220. Fax: (805) 964-1466. Email: LESatTLW@aol.com. Web: www.thelearningworks.com.

NEW!
Doodles and Oodles of Art

Grades pre K–3. $13.95 plus shipping.
Teaching and Learning Company, 1204 Buchanan St., PO Box 10, Carthage, IL 62321. Orders: (800) 852-1234. Inquiries: (217) 357-2591. Fax: (217) 357-6789. Email: tandlcom@adams.net. Web: www.ierc.com.

The **Choose Art** program is deceptively simple, since the hard work of sequencing and designing the curriculum has already been done for you. Each of the three programs for this age group (*Flowers and Bulrushes*, *Peaceful Pastels*, and *Butterfly Wings*) contains 32 one-hour lesson plans. The programs can be used in any order, and offer three years of art lessons.

Each program contains seven units (four lessons each) designed around a different scriptural verse and an additional unit of holiday-themed lessons.

You get a 200-page spiral-bound 9 x 11" teacher's manual, a student binder with 140+ pages, scriptural theme mini-posters, and certificates of completion.

The teacher's manual clearly explains the objectives of each lesson, materials and preparation, how to present the lesson (and what to expect), answer sheets and copies of the student workpages. A typical lesson starts by discussing the scriptural theme (sometimes with a story), discussing the art concepts or techniques related to the lesson, followed by an art project. There may be worksheet pages with vocabulary or drawing exercises included as well. Two levels of exercises are provided which allow you to tailor the program to fit your child's needs (or to teach to more than one age group). As you work through the lessons, the children fill their student binders with their completed worksheets and lessons.

Line, shape, color, texture, pattern, form, and space concepts are introduced gradually by teaching how different techniques produce different results. The projects allow you to explore each new technique and to be creative, but are structured to ensure success. This is especially important when teaching art, because if you are successful at using a new technique, you'll be more likely to use it again on your own. As you progress through the Choose Art program, you're given opportunities to practice the techniques from previous lessons. *Teresa Schultz-Jones*

What a fun way to build perceptual skills! Shape recognition, sequencing, following directions, patterns are all covered in **Build a Doodle** (but don't tell your kids that!). Not touted as a drawing book *per se*, your kids nevertheless will be thrilled at their creations, ranging from jet fighter planes to the widest variety of animals you've ever seen.

Pages are simple and similar to Ed Emberley's drawing books, where each square contains a portion of a drawing. Start with a basic shape, add a line or two here and there and *voila!* All you have to supply is a pencil and paper.

Slightly more complex, each **Super Doodles** include a fun fact about each drawing and a suggestion for expanding the drawing. "Draw a long row of red-eared sliders (type of turtle) sunning themselves on a log in a pond. Add cattails, dragonflies, and a swimming snake to the scene." The 11-book series includes the following titles: *Dinosaurs*, *Endangered Animals*, *Insects*, *Mammals*, *Marine Life*, *Pets*, *Rain Forests*, *Reptiles*, *Sports*, *Vehicles*, and *Zoo Animals*. Great for illustrating stories or having fun on rainy afternoons. *Renee Mathis*

In **Doodles and Oodles of Art**, you are warned up front, "Some of the best art never makes it to paper. It is on the children's hands and faces and in their minds as they explore and think about the process."

This 136-page softcover book is full of ways to help your child explore art that you have probably never even considered. You will find an entire chapter devoted to art techniques using joint compound—yes, that's the stuff used on walls! You will learn how to make butterfly collages out of sealable sandwich bags and fish from aluminum foil, tissue paper, liquid starch, toothpicks, a Styrofoam ball, and wiggly eyes. In fact, by the time you get through the book, everything you look at may be a candidate for your next art project!

Each project has a list of required materials (fascinating reading!), clear directions on the process to follow and an illustration of what the finished project looks like. All of these very original projects appear quite doable, quite possibly messy, and genuinely fun. The only problem I found in the book was its constant references to a supply list that wasn't included (though it is available upon request). *Teresa Schultz-Jones*

The **Draw Today** program uses features found in the best drawing courses—teaching students to draw contours, to shade, to visualize positive and negative space, to draw objects "upside down" in order to see them more clearly—but adds an unusual twist or two.

First, you use no media except pencils, charcoals, and erasers. Your stick eraser acts as a pencil and is a major art tool in this program. By using charcoal instead of ink, you can add to a drawing *or* take away from it, enabling you to correct your work instead of having to totally redo it.

Second, the publisher guarantees you will learn to draw in less than a day and will be able to create realistic portraits in only a few days, or your money back. They have hundreds of testimonials from people who learned to draw with this program to prove it! Many of those writing the testimonials had never been able to draw well before.

The **Parent/Student Set with Video**, their most popular kit, comes with a 56-page instruction book. Besides the how-to instructions, you get 30 images to use for drawing practice. Some are portraits; others, animals, landscapes, and flowers. The kit also contains a 75-minute video divided into lessons, a parent curriculum guide, and many other ingredients, including charcoal pencils, three kinds of erasers, drafting tape, ruler, transparent grid, squint sheets, special paper, and other special materials, as you can see in the picture below. Plus, there's a toll-free help line if you need it!

For families with several children, each **Additional Student Set** includes everything in the Parent/Student set except the video and curriculum guide.

Draw and Paint Today takes the concept one step farther. This is basically the same course as Draw Today, with some extra lessons and supplies, including acrylic paints and brushes.

The *Draw and Paint Today* book starts off the same as the *Draw Today* book, but a Part II, "Painting," has been added. Again, we are treated to a completely new method, unlike anything you're likely to find in a local art class. Or should I say, "a completely *old* method," because you will be learning to "glaze" your painting, and glazing is a technique that is over 500 years old. Here's how it works. You start with an underpainting, which by an amazing coincidence turns out to be the kind of charcoal drawing you have just learned to do. You fix or seal it, then "glaze" it step-by-step, overpainting with a mixture of acrylic paint and medium. Color photos show you just how to do it. The final result is amazingly professional.

Two optional accessories can help you extend your new skills. The **Adjustable Image Framer** helps to isolate your subject, figure out the focal point, and determine an appropriate composition shape (horizontal or vertical, large or small). This well-made product comes with a locking device and complete instructions.

The **DaVinci Perspective Grids**, named after the ubiquitous Leonardo, help you achieve the proper proportions and perspective when drawing real-life objects.

NEW!
Draw Today Homeschool Program

Grade 5–adult. Parent/Student Set with Video, $49.95. Additional student set with supplies, $29.95; without supplies, $17.95. Draw and Paint Today Set with Video, $79.95. Image Framer, $9.95. DaVinci Perspective Grid, $19.95. Supplies all available separately. Shipping extra.
Artskills, 217 Ferry Street, Easton, PA 18042. (800) 552-3729 or (610) 253-6663. Fax: (610) 253-0715. Web: www.artskills.com.

Contents of the Draw Today Kit

For the drawing and painting skills they promise to teach you, Draw Today (and Draw and Paint Today) *are* easier than other methods, they *do* yield amazing results, and they *are* guaranteed. Highly recommended. *Mary Pride*

NEW!
Draw•Write•Now Books 1, 2, & 3

Grades 1–4. $10.95 per book. Shipping extra.
Barker Creek Publishing, Inc., PO Box 2610, Poulsbo, WA 98370. Orders: (800) 692-5833. Inquiries: (360) 692-5833. Fax: (360) 613-2542. Email: publisher@barkercreek.com. Web: www.barkercreek.com.

My one complaint about the product was that the softcover binding did not allow for the book to lie flat easily when open to a lesson. A spiral binding would eliminate this but would probably also increase the price. Offering all of the books together in a three-ring format would also be nice.

NEW!
How Great Thou Art

Ages 3–5: Baby Lambs Book of Art, $14.95. Grades preK–4: Little Annie's Art Book, $14.95. Grades K–3: I Can Do All Things, $42.95. Grades 3–8: Lamb's Book of Art I or II, $14.95 each. Grade 3–adult: Feed My Sheep, $42.95; God & the History of Art, $73.95. Videos plus text combos: I Can Do All Things, $129; Lamb's I, $69; Feed My Sheep, $179.95. Lamb's I & II Teacher's Manual, $7.95. Extra paint cards, other supplies, text plus teachers manuals combos also available. Shipping extra.

When she taught school, Marie Hablitzel started every day of the school year with a drawing and handwriting lesson. She sent some of the lessons to her grandchildren. Marie's daughter, Kim Stitzer, encouraged her to publish them, and co-authored **Draw•Write•Now**. Books One, Two, and Three are available now, with five more to come.

Hablitzel uses the same methods used by Mona Brookes in *Drawing with Children*. By breaking complex objects down into simple shapes, children are able to draw almost anything and practice their fine motor skills at the same time. Each lesson combines drawing and handwriting practice in a way that is both creative and straightforward. Unless you plan to adapt or change it in some way, no preparation time is required; adapting it would not require much time, either. Most children could complete the lessons on their own with no adult help.

Each colorful, reasonably-priced book contains 21 lessons in three units (four to eleven lessons per unit). Each unit (complete on a two-page spread) contains an example of the finished drawing, a step-by-step, shape-by-shape breakdown of how to draw the main subject, four printed-out sentences pertaining to the subject (for handwriting practice) and a question leading to further learning on the subject. The best part about each lesson is the drawing, which is presented in a simple, easy-to-follow way that even four-year-olds can draw.

Each book also contains general tips on how to use and adapt the program, two pages per unit of suggested additions to the drawing (backgrounds, settings, composition, details, etc.), and one page per unit of the answers to the questions posed in each lesson. This latter page serves as a good jumping-off point for unit study, including books to read and projects to do. These pages also make the books more interesting for older children.

Book One contains the following units: On the Farm, Kids & Critters, Storybook Characters. Book Two contains: Christopher Columbus, Autumn Harvest, The Weather. Book Three units: Native Americans, North American Geography, and The Pilgrims. Books Four through Eight will contain units including Polar Regions, Abraham Lincoln, George Washington, and Animals of the World. *Melissa Worcester*

Winner of two out of three *Practical Homeschooling* 1998 Reader Awards in the Art category, the **How Great Thou Art** family of art courses by instructor Barry Stebbing has certainly made an impact on the homeschool community. Growing rapidly from one course (the original "How Great Thou Art") to 10 courses for all age levels, and with video lessons and supplies packages now available for many of these courses, it's easy to be confused by the wide range of options available from this publisher.

Here's what I found by examining the How Great Thou Art catalog:

- You can't just go by age level when purchasing these courses, because typically each age level will have two or more courses available.
- Special combo prices are often available when you purchases videos or a teacher's manual at the same time as the course text. So it really helps to know if you'll want any of these additional items *before* you buy.

How Great Thou Art Publications, Box 48, McFarlan, NC 28102. Orders: (800) 982-3729. Inquiries: (704) 851-3117. Fax: (704) 851-3111. Email: howgreat@vnet.net. Web: www.howgreatthouart.com.

In a minute, I'll describe How Great Thou Art's educational philosophy and methods. But first, let's get the individual courses straight.

Baby Lambs Book of Art is the preschool book. It provides very, very simple instructions to drawing (in the cartoony style used in all the courses for younger children) and color (primary and secondary colors on the color wheel, warm and cool colors). It also includes a few pages each of practice in manuscript printing, numbers, simple arithmetic, and puzzles (one maze, one hidden picture, and two "what's wrong or missing" pages). There's also an alphabet coloring book section, with fairly detailed drawings and a Bible verse for each letter, and a cut-and-paste crafts section. Bible verses and retold Bible stories are found throughout the book. You will need additional resources from other publishers to seriously teach printing, numbers, and arithmetic, but it doesn't hurt anything to have these extra practice-and-coloring pages included. No video is currently available to go with this book.

I Can Do All Things is really for ages 5–8, although the catalog currently lists it as for ages up to 11. This three-year course covers similar material to those for older age levels, but the beginning lessons start off easier. Intended for use as a three-year course, its 180-plus lessons cover cartoon-style drawing for beginners, and beginning color theory and techniques with colored markers, colored pencils, and acrylic paints. Your supplies cost is kept low, because students learn to mix their own paints from the three primary colors plus white. Video lessons and art supplies for this course are available from How Great Thou Art.

When you arrive at age 8, you have to make a choice: **Lamb's Book of Art I and II**, **Feed My Sheep**, or **God & the History of Art**. They all cover the same topics—color theory, cartoon-style (as opposed to photorealistic) drawing, anatomy, perspective, nature studies, portraits, lettering, and so on. Here's the difference:

- *Lamb's Book of Art I* is the budget one-year course suitable for the family that wants to try a taste of the "Barry Stebbing method." In addition, a supplementary volume, *Lamb's Book of Art II*, is available for those families who bought the first volume and want additional, inexpensive activities. A single teacher's manual that covers both volumes is available; videos are only available for *Lamb's Book I*.
- *Feed My Sheep* is the mid-priced three-year course that provides more in-depth instruction for the family that is serious about art as a regular, ongoing part of the curriculum. Video

The cartoon style taught in the books for younger children is not superhero or "comic-book" style art. It's basically classic "kid art"—simplified. geometric (lots of circles, ovals, and egg shapes) representations of the subjects. For example, a flower might be drawn as a circle surrounded by oval petals, on a wavy stem with two stylized oval leaves. Fun characters such as "Wally the Worm" are used to introduce basic drawing techniques. Young children are also taught to color in backgrounds by drawing colored lines, rather than coloring every inch. This looks strange at first, but results in many more completed pictures.

All the courses except Baby Lambs and Lamb's Book come with "paint cards." These are sturdy preprinted pieces of oversized cardstock with paintable surfaces. Marker and paint work is done on those cards, instead of on the thinner book pages, so it will turn out nicely. You can purchase extra sets of the paint cards for additional students.

Now, the big question: is it worth buying the videos, if you purchase a course that has videos available? Yes! On the videos, the affable and energetic Barry Stebbing shows you step by step how to do each assignment, often adding visuals of completed student art. This makes it *so* much easier to see what you're aiming for! Your comfort factor—and motivation—will go way up if you get the videos . . . and while you're at it, make it easy on yourself and get the art supplies from them, too.

I Want to Paint a Zebra, But I Don't Know How

Ages 3–8. $14.95 plus shipping. *Small Business Press, Inc., PO Box 871284, Dallas, TX 75287-7284. (214) 392-0950. Fax: (214) 233-6195.*

lessons and supplies are available for both courses. Videos and art supplies are available, but no teacher's manual.

- Think of *God & the History of Art* as the deluxe course. Like the others, it includes "Barry Stebbing method" lessons in beginning drawing and painting, but this time they are designed to complement the many art period and artists you will also be studying. This book also includes many examples of student artwork based on Bible stories, and is intended for use as a four-year curriculum. Neither a video nor a teacher's manual are available initially, but the student art examples included in the text, and the 34 postcards of famous art, should provide enough visual information for you to easily handle the lessons.

When it comes to Christian content, these courses aren't heavy on theology. You'll find some examples of praise to God for His role as Creator and as the reason for our creativity, and some Bible verses and Bible stories, especially in the products for younger children.

Techniques such as color creation, stippling, cross-hatching, overlapping, and lights and shadows are taught in all the books for ages 5 and up. More advanced techniques—e.g., 2- and 3-D perspective, anatomy proportions, and composition—are taught starting at age 8.

Are any—or all—of these the art courses you are looking for? It depends on what you want to spend and what you're looking for. If you want a course that uses modern methods (rather than an "Old Masters") approach . . . if you're looking for a one-book course (rather than one with lots of workbooks) . . . if a Christian tone appeals to you . . . and if you want something that's easy to use, with little time required to set up for a lesson . . . give the How Great Thou Art family a chance! *Mary Pride*

First things first: **I Want to Paint a Zebra, But I Don't Know How** will not show you or your child how to paint a zebra. However, in author Elaine Heuer's own words, "It will help set up an environment that will leave the children free to create their own unique zebra, however they may see it."

Whenever I see that a Montessori teacher has written a book, I am pretty sure that it will be well-organized, proceed in a sensible step-by-step fashion, and cover the ground thoroughly. No surprises here: this is exactly what *I Want to Paint a Zebra* does. This basic-skills book shows young children how to cut, glue, make collages and prints, work with clay, and paint with tempera and watercolors. (Digression: Why do early-elementary and preschool teachers always stress *watercolors*, the hardest-to-use painting medium, when *temperas* are ideal for little kids?)

When I said this book went step by step, I meant *step* by *step*. The first exercise in cutting with scissors includes teaching the child how to properly move his hand muscles in order to make a successful cut, as well as how to hold the scissors and paper. The parent or teacher is urged to use tagboard at first, as it is "the best weight paper for this activity—not too light or too heavy." The author obviously knows her stuff, including everything that can go wrong with each activity and how to guard against it.

I Want to Paint a Zebra has a nice, open format with many "how-to" illustrations. Don't let the book's apparent simplicity fool you, though. You are getting a method that has been tested for years in preschool, elementary, and Montessori classrooms. If you've never tried teaching basic art skills to a child before, you'll save yourself a lot of grief with this book. If you *have* tried teaching basic art skills before, you are perhaps even more likely to appreciate the 30 art activity "recipes" that make the whole thing so easy and so much more fun. *Mary Pride*

CHAPTER 45

Art History & Appreciation

Children today and their parents, namely us, need more than ever to be exposed to the art of the past. If you're looking for beauty, truth, nobility, purity, or anything uplifting or basically honest, your chances of finding it are a lot better in the seventeenth century (or the seventh, or the seventh B.C.) than in the twentieth. Whatever their faults, artists of the past at least tried to deal with sublime themes. Throwing cultural temper tantrums was not "in" in the days of Fra Angelica, Michelangelo, Rembrandt, or even Winslow Homer. Technical expertise, an eye for beauty, and an ability to separate the significant from the trivial, was.

Art history, presented well, can speak to you in a way that those weird modern sculptures in front of the downtown bank never will. Learning from the past is the first step to producing something worthwhile in the present. And, unlike grim pilgrimages to the latest mind-numbing happening at the Museum of Trendy Art, it is *fun!*

So let's take a tour of the art of the past. Meet great artists whose work will impress you and who we know you will enjoy.

Art for the Smart

I am really impressed by the three-year **Adventures in Art** art history and appreciation program. Each year's offering includes 17 museum-quality full-color reproductions (up to 11 x 17" in size) of major artworks spanning the time frame from Byzantine art through the modernists, a parent study guide, an art comparison sheet, and instructions on how to set up an art time line. You also get a 75-page study guide, with a sheet containing historical commentary for each painting and background information about each artist.

The program itself follows the five steps of observing single paintings, comparing paintings by the same artist, comparing paintings of different artists, developing an art history time line, and finally classifying paintings by schools of art.

Year 1 includes *Madonna and Child on a Curved Throne* (Byzantine), Cimbue's *The Crucifixion*, two paintings by Duccio, three by Da Vinci, three by Rembrandt, three by Monet, three by Cezanne, and one by Picasso. One of the Rembrandt prints is his *Raising of the Cross,* suitable for display in

Adventures in Art
Grades 2–12. Galleries I–III, $60 each. Portfolio, $30. Shipping extra. *Cornerstone Curriculum Project, 2006 Flat Creek, Richardson, TX 75080. (972) 235-5149. Fax: (972) 235-0236. Web: www.cornerstonecurriculum.com.*

If you get this series you definitely should purchase the portfolio, unless you plan on framing the prints or otherwise providing a way to preserve them. It would be a shame to have these fine prints ripped up or wrinkled, as is all too likely to happen when such large prints are being handled by little hands.

Aristoplay Artdeck

Grades 5–adult. $15 plus shipping. *Aristoplay, Ltd., PO Box 7529, Ann Arbor, MI 48107. (800) 634-7738. Fax: (734) 995-4611. Web: www.aristoplay.com.*

NEW!
ARTEXT Prints

Grades 1–9. Artext Juniors: 30¢ each; set of 10 Modern Art Subjects, $2.75; set of 30 Primary, Intermediate, or Upper Level Subjects, $7/set; complete set of 100 prints, $22.50. Artext Prints: $2 each; set of 10 Modern Art Subjects, $16; set of 30 Primary, Intermediate, or Upper Level Subjects, $45/set; complete set of 100 prints, $130. Accompanying text, $15. Minimum order size, $15. Add $4 shipping. *Art Extension Press, PO Box 389, Westport, CT 06881. (203) 256-9920. Fax: (203) 259-8160. Web: www.home-school.com/Mall/Artext. Server is case sensitive.*

your home and exclusively available through Cornerstone Curriculum Project. By the time you have finished all four years you will have also sampled Giotto, Van Eyck, Massaccio, da Vinci, Michelangelo, Dürer, Renoir, Degas, Van Gogh, Gauguin, Seurat, Kandinsky, Pollock, and Dali.

Cornerstone Curriculum Project is serious that children should discover about art on their own, to the point of discouraging parents from telling children about the various schools of art. I understand their point, but all the same I do wish the program included more specific questions directed to the individual works and artists. The publishers should also consider making available books on each artist, for those who want to pursue a particular artist further. Art observation, after all, is supposed to generate interest in the artist. Museums understand this; when we went to the George Caleb Bingham exhibition at the St. Louis Art Museum, we were able to buy a book about Bingham with excellent reproductions of his paintings, as well as prints, postcards, and even buttons! Being able to satisfy your curiosity like this provides a wonderful feeling of closure. Even *without* these goodies, Adventures in Art is a wonderful program. With them, it would be phenomenal! *Mary Pride*

Artdeck, subtitled "The Game of Modern Masters," is a beautiful card game composed of a mini-collection of 52 major works of modern art by 13 of the most famous artists. The game involves collecting "suits" of cards in a fashion similar to *Rummy*. All the aces, for example, are paintings by Joan Miro. The Artist Card for each suit gives pertinent facts about the artist, including a brief overview of his style and the titles of the works on the other cards. The cards are top quality. Shiny and colorful. No wonder art museums carry this game. Now, the $10,000 question: *Why only modern masters?* The same game format would work with medieval art, or Renaissance art, or traditional English art . . . This could be done by either enclosing a flyer offering additional card sets, or by producing "new" games with different cards but otherwise the same format. Would you be interested in this? Well, it seems Aristoplay has anticipated my question, as they now offers card games of Mexican artists and African artifacts.

Let me mention in passing that exposure to real art, even on this small scale, has sparked an interest in looking up the artists in our encyclopedia. One little thing leads to another. *Mary Pride*

Artext Prints are quality four-color reproductions of masterpieces from around the world. These handy study prints, popular with homeschoolers, average in size from 7 x 9 to 8 x 10 inches, making them suitable for hand-held study, three-hole-punching and binding, or framing on the wall. The complete set of 100 prints includes 35 modern paintings, 40 old masters, and 25 depicting historical events, period costumes, social studies topics, and other academic subjects.

Artext Juniors are the smaller, more affordable size. Averaging 3 x 4 inches, they can be used for card games (putting together sets of paintings from the same "school" of painting, for example) or just as carry-around study prints.

I don't have space to list *all* the artists included in this series, but here are a few in no particular order: Van Gogh, Corot, Rapahel, Goya, Miro, Matisse, Picasso, Renoir, Fra Angelico, Brueghel, Valasquez, Gainsborough, Klee, Verrmeer, Cezanne, Gauguin, Constable, da Vinci, and Whistler. Most artists only have one painting included (in fact, Raphael was the only one I noticed having more than one print), so the series can include as many artists as possible.

The accompanying text, **Learning More About Pictures** by Royal Bailey Farnum, has been recently revised to include the work of 10 outstanding modern painters. Small illustrations identify the 100 pictures, selected and graded for season and age level application. Art appreciation notes are included for each picture. The handy-sized 100-page volume also includes biographies of each artist, tables showing how to integrate the prints into your entire curriculum, a glossary of art terms, and a bibliography. *Mary Pride*

Thanks to **Art Through Children's Literature**, your child can learn to draw 57 different styles of art by studying the art in a like number of Caldecott Award-winning books, including *Make Way for Ducklings* and *Madeline's Rescue*. There are three lessons for each book's art style, making a total of 171 lessons. Black-and-white drawings illustrate each lesson, showing an example of what looks like a typical child's drawing of the concept.

This book goes from contour to perspective drawings, and anywhere around and in between. It also suggests many different styles of art that I had never even thought of before, like making an outline of a person and filling it with lines, or using an eraser to draw lines on a grey background. Each lesson has a complete list of supplies needed, most of which don't go beyond tempera paints, watercolor paints, pencils, crayons, paper, chalk, markers and/or paintbrushes and sponges. The only thing I didn't like about this book was that most of the projects wanted you to reference the style of art in the children's book from which it came.

The good news: all libraries everywhere stock the Caldecott Award winners. The bad news: if you don't watch out, this book may end up causing you some extra library trips. *Sarah Pride*

A terrific innovation in teaching art appreciation, **Child-Size Masterpieces** (formerly known as **Mommy, It's a Renoir!**) begins with a manual outlining a course of study based on Montessori principles and using art postcards. First, very young children practice matching identical postcards. They then try pairing two different paintings by the same artist and grouping four paintings by the same artist, eventually progressing to recognizing any studied artist's style in any context. Control cards teach the names of well-known artists and their famous paintings. The manual does not include any of these cards, but does contain renditions of 71 works of art.

A series of seven art postcard books is used with the manual. You cut out the cards on the dotted lines and file them in pocket-folders. An extra, smaller card is included for each step for the cover of each folder. Volumes now available include:

- *CSM—Easy* (ages three to six)
- *CSM—Intermediate* (ages three to six)
- *CSM—Advanced* (ages three to six)
- *CSM—Black Artists* (ages three to eight)
- *CSM—Names of Artists* (ages six and up)
- *CSM—Famous Paintings* (ages six and up)
- *CSM—Transportation in America* (ages eight and up).

The first three volumes cover the first three steps (matching identical paintings, pairing companion paintings, and grouping four paintings by one artist) in increasing levels of difficulty. One volume each teaches the names of artists and the names of famous paintings.

You'll find a wide variety of artists in this series, from Renaissance to modern. The reproduction is excellent. *Mary Pride*

Gallery: The Art Appreciation Game is an art card game played rather like Go Fish. The game comes with 40 full-color, 3½ x 5⅜" cards displaying four artworks from each of 10 famous artists—Corot, Copley, Cezanne, Cassatt, Cole, Degas, Renoir, Monet, Chardin, and Rembrandt. Each card has a small picture on it, along with a capsule description of the artist and a list of the paintings of that artist included in the game. Each 2 x 2¼" picture is a reproduction of originals found at the National Gallery of Art in Washington, D.C. Simple rules allow players to concentrate on the art, the artists, their country, their style, and the age in which each painted. Rules for young children are also now included in every game.

Each artist included in *Gallery* was chosen "for their classic style and value." The publishers of *Gallery* believe each artist they have included "was first in his area of influence for some reason." Chardin was first in presenting the common man and his interests. Corot was a pioneer in presenting landscapes realistically rather than romantically. Rembrandt was the greatest Dutch painter. Cole was America's first serious full-time landscape artist. Copley was the first American portrait painter to put backgrounds and other people into his scenes. Mary Cassatt was the First Lady of American Impressionism. And Degas, Renoir, Cezanne, and Monet, Impressionists all, were all pioneers in their way. *Mary Pride*

Gallery

Grade 6–adult. Gallery, $14.50 postpaid. Background Notes, $12.50 postpaid.
B & I Gallery Specialists, 609 Lincoln Terrace, Moorestown, NJ 08057. (609) 235-4943. Fax: (609) 231-1546. Email: benirm9@mindspring.com.

Now you can also get **Background Notes** to accompany *Gallery*. The spiral-bound set includes eight artists: Rembrandt, Chardin, Corot, Copley, Cole, Cassatt, Degas, and Monet. These include historical information about each artist, analyses of the paintings included in *Gallery*, and suggested activities and bibliographic references, as well as any spiritual searches or faith confessions made by the artist. Some of the paintings' details highlighted in the *Background Notes* are impossible to see on the cards, due to their small size. However, if the descriptions spark your interest, you can always buy a large-sized print of the painting—and *Gallery* would have served its purpose!

KONOS Artists and Composers Timeline

Grades K–8. $20 plus shipping.
KONOS, Inc., PO Box 250, Anna, TX 75409. (972) 924-2712. Fax: (972) 924-2733. Email: konos@konos.com. Web: www.konos.com.

Timelines are one of the best ways to learn history. Your child can get a real feel for art and music history, with the **KONOS Artists and Composers Timelines.** You get five laminated blue sheets of figures to cut out and attach to a time line. Each painter holds a major work; each composer holds a major composition. Artists and musicians included range from Renaissance to modern, with most concentrated in between. A fun, hands-on way to study art history, and a natural taking-off point for study of individual musicians and schools of music. *Mary Pride*

Usborne Story of Painting

Grades 4–12. $6.95 plus shipping.
EDC Publishing, Division of Educational Development Corporation, 10302 East 55th Place, Tulsa, OK 74146. (800) 475-4522. Fax: (800) 747-4509. Web: www.edcpub.com.

Colorful, copiously illustrated introduction to art through the ages. **Usborne Story of Painting** includes information on how artists lived and materials they used, as well as introducing several important artists. Starts with cave painting, ends with modern art. Suggested for ages ten and up, but children of any age will enjoy looking at the pictures and listening to the text. *Mary Pride*

CHAPTER 46

Making Music

If you're like me, you see music lessons as a way to learn to play an instrument, not to learn *about* playing an instrument. I myself quit taking piano lessons when my teacher refused to let me attempt Tchaikovsky's *Nutcracker Suite*, condemning me instead to more weary months of Bartok piano exercises. I liked Tchaikovsky; I was familiar with the music—unlike Bartok's, which always sounded to my youthful ears like a mistake. So why didn't my teacher let me try it?

That question propels us into a hot debate among music teachers. Do people learn music best by proceeding step by cautious step and not being allowed to try advanced pieces until they have been taught how to play them? Another issue: Is it a good idea to concentrate on learning pieces you have never heard? One more question: Is it best to learn theory *before, during,* or *after* having mastered elementary playing techniques?

The Suzuki Method

It is a good idea to become familiar with how a particular piece sounds before trying to play it yourself. Listening to music builds up your "data" on which your musical knowledge will be based. It would also be a good idea to mess about on the instrument before settling down to serious learning. Playing provides tactile data—you discover what movement makes what sound. Sight reading, a highly refined skill, would follow playing by ear in this view. You'd want to get a "feel" for the instrument and for music in general before attempting to delve into the complexities of music notation and theory.

Part (not all) of the musical approach outlined above is the famous Suzuki method. **Shinichi Suzuki,** a Japanese man, developed a method of music instruction that begins by exposing the student to lots of good music—in fact, the very pieces he will learn to play. Once he has become thoroughly familiar with these pieces, he is allowed to begin lessons. Music theory is only introduced after the student has already been playing for some time.

Mr. Suzuki had some other ideas as well. Children's parents are present for all lessons, and are encouraged to learn along with the children. Students also spend some time in group lessons and recitals, where they get to hear musicians of various ages and skill levels play. This gives them a

Steps on the Road to Making Music

- Listen to the music you want to play.
- Learn to sing *a capella*.
- Pick the right instrument. Size does matter!
- Mess around with your instrument.
- Learn to play "by ear."
- Learn how to read and interpret written music (this is called "music theory").
- Practice, practice, practice. But only songs you *like*. Mix in some fun, simple pieces along with the new, tough ones.
- Formal recitals are for parents, teachers, and prodigies. Shy kids should be excused.
- Family music evenings and neighborhood hootenannies are great! Turn off the TV and make music like your ancestors did.

Picking an Instrument

When should your child start learning to play an instrument? And *Which* instrument should he learn to play? Let me share with you what a reader (Colleen Story) shared with me.

The Right Instrument for Your Child, by Atarah Ben-Tovim and Douglas Boyd (Quill imprint of William Morrow, Inc., 1985), a $12.95 paperback, is a must for anyone considering starting a child on a musical instrument. The authors did 10 years of research and concluded choosing the wrong instrument was the most common factor in musical failure—not lack of "musicality" or music potential. The second most common factor was starting at the wrong time— too early. They felt their research indicated that, for 95 percent of children, the best time to begin an instrument is between eight to eleven years old. The book is designed to help you determine, through questionnaires and profiles of musicians who like specific instruments, which instrument(s) are best suited to your child's temperament, physical characteristics, and readiness. The one instrument suggested for six to eight year olds is the recorder . . .

Thanks, Colleen. I suspected as much. In spite of all the frantic rush to get nurslings involved with a musical instrument, *spiritual* readiness (the ability to persevere and the desire to create a work of art) still seems a logical prerequisite to serious musical instruction.

Play around with music all you like; expose your children to great music and let them fool with instruments, by all means. But if you want to nurture a lifelong love of music, you might be better off telling your youngsters to wait until they've shown they're mature enough to make good use of official music lessons.

taste of what they can look forward to accomplishing, as well as getting them used to playing before a friendly audience. All is ideally done in a spirit of helping and comradeship. Using this method, very young children have demonstrated amazing musicianship.

True, Suzuki follows the "mastery learning" approach of forbidding children to tackle anything new until the old is thoroughly learned. And controversy swirls about the questions of how much and if and when parents should make children practice, an issue over which Suzuki teachers have split. But access to an instrument of the right size; a wide mental library of good music; the support of other musicians and the encouragement of one's family; putting off academic studies until the student can see the need for them—these old-fashioned ideas, so well proven in the lives of musicians like Mozart and Bach, are again gaining ground.

Kodaly and the Art of Singing

Another big name in music instruction is **Zoltan Kodaly,** a Hungarian man. Kodaly was vitally interested in singing as the best introduction to music of all kinds. As Laszlo Eosze relates in *Zoltan Kodaly: His Life and Work* (Crescendo Publishing Company, 1962),

"That the teaching of music is best begun with singing," he writes, "that it is through singing, and before ever touching an instrument, that the child should learn to read music, are recognized as truths by a good many people . . . Mechanical training in instrumental playing, without corresponding theoretical education; music-making with the fingers instead of the soul; the omission of any thorough musical grounding; and neglect of solfeggio—these are the direct causes of the present decadence of singing and of the increasing number of second-rate professional musicians . . ."

Kodaly's great desire was to revive *solfeggio*, the art of being able to recognize notes and intervals by ear in any key and sing them. We are familiar with this as Do-Re-Mi-Fa-Sol-La-Ti-Do style singing. In this way, the student would be able to pick up a score of music, once trained in sight reading, and hear it in his head. He would also be able to translate music into staff notation, and duplicate it by ear in his instrument.

Kodaly was also a champion of Early Childhood Music Education. He deplored the use of the piano in teaching songs and choral music as a (possibly untuned) crutch that prevented children from appreciating pure, virginal melody. Kodaly was active in encouraging music societies and choral singing, writing a number of volumes of choral exercises for young people. He also worked on popularizing the pentatonic scale, in an attempt to revive a national Hungarian musical consciousness.

The Family that Plays Together

Suzuki has been popularized for the family music market much more than Kodaly. This can perhaps be attributed to Suzuki's firm insistence that parents spend time with their children during music lessons and practice. In today's society, this is one of the few excuses for family togetherness left for upscale parents! *Any* educational method which brings parents and children together unleashes dynamic possibilities far beyond the lessons' content.

Take Suzuki's stress on exposing the student to lots of good music and a supportive atmosphere. Mix in Kodaly's singing and solfeggio training. Add the common-sense idea that music is for *playing* and *enjoying*, not for showing off. What do you get? The family that plays together . . .

Who ever said learning to play music was just for kids, anyway? If you want to be a concert star, perhaps it helps to start practicing two hours a day at the age of four. But if you want to *play*, the time to start is now!

How to Teach Music

"Music making is not optional for God's children," says this musician, educator, music therapist, and author. Not to worry, non-musicians! Dr. Mary Ann Froelich has written a wonderful guide for meeting the obligation to bring up our children in musical nurture and admonition. She emphasizes the importance of music as ministry: parents as music ministers to their children, and children becoming music ministers to their community.

Music Education in the Christian Home is liberally sprinkled with Scriptural references to the power, health, and joy which comes from music, and discussion of music as an essential part of worship. She compares and contrasts the major music education methods and shows how to choose the best one for your child. You learn how to develop a total musical program of listening and music history, as well as performance.

More than half of the 240-page book is made up of appendices and resources to help parents and teachers restore music and joy to children's lives. Included are Basic Music Theory for Parents, Songs for Music Therapy and Pastoral Care, Improvisation Guide, Music History, and Biblical References to Music and Dance.

I hope many mothers of infants will find this book in time to make the most of the wonder years, but even if the children are past that age, it is not too late to profit from this book. Adults also receive a musical education as they teach their children, and gain confidence in their musical selves. *Anne Brodbeck*

Musical choices can be bewildering without sound advice. **Sound Choices**, a 374-page quality paperback book is packed with solid answers to every question a parent could possibly imagine about how to teach music at home, and even more information and advice we never knew we needed. The layout and icons make it easy to spot tips for different ages, stages and needs. (Special attention is given to overcoming or accommodating handicaps.) Each chapter includes a whole catalog of varied resources. Abundant  photographic illustrations and quotations from prominent professional musicians help inspire children's musical growth. I recommend *Sound Choices* to any homeschooling parent, musically-inclined or not. *Anne Brodbeck*

The Phonics of Music

And here's where to start. Learning to read music is like learning to read English. Not altogether easy. The way you are taught to read music makes a real difference in how (or if) you learn.

I find that the resources available for learning to read music break down into these categories:

- **Activity-oriented materials for young children.** Teaching kids to read music this way can be rather exhausting for the parents, but is a blast for the kids.

- **Sobersides adult programs.** These lay it out like so: "This is a treble clef. (See illustration.)"

Just as with phonics instruction, a skilled teacher doesn't really need a course, manipulatives, or activities. However, since lots of us parents don't really understand how to read music ourselves, you may find that it's worth investing in the goodies.

If you're determined to skip the process of learning to read music, your choices narrow down to playing everything entirely by ear or getting songbooks written in note-and-chord notation. Davidsons Music has lots of these kinds of materials. If, however, you want to sing along with everyone else on Sunday morning or play tunes out of a regular songbook, here's how.

Basic Music Curriculum

NEW!
Burst Into Music
Ages 3–8. $12.95.
J&S Publishing, 1832 Adams Street, Prescott, AZ 86305-1310. (520) 445-0487. Email: mojadoaz@northlink.com.

Less experienced music teachers will really appreciate this handy manual, especially good for teaching music theory to young children. An attractive 112-page large-format paperback book, **Burst Into Music** has more than 50 simple reproducible drawings for flash cards, coloring pages, and games. There are introductions to musical instruments with directions for making some simple ones and six easy songs with music. A wealth of ideas for having fun with music and children. *Anne Brodbeck*

Davidson How to Read Music
Grade 5–adult. $7.95 plus shipping.
Davidson Music, 6727 Metcalf, Shawnee Mission, KS 66204. (913) 262-6533. Fax: (913) 722-2980. Web: www.davidsonsmusic.com.

Davidson Music has been around for years and years. It is a publisher of simply-produced how-to-play music books, all written by music teacher Madonna Woods, and originally aimed at nice middle-aged or older Christian people who have "always wanted to learn to play the piano or organ someday," or who want to upgrade their music-playing skills.

How to Read Music is Davidson's book that "reduces music reading to its simplest form." From the catalog description:

You learn to read treble clef and professional secrets on how to remember your notes. You're shown a short cut to learning bass clef notes. Rhythm is explained in an easy to understand way. You learn time values of notes and how to tell how many beats the different notes get. Time signatures are explained and you are shown how to count.

The various key signatures also are explained, showing you how to tell what sharps and flats to use . . . Everything clearly illustrated.

I got a copy of this oversized booklet and can tell you that the catalog description is right-on. Madonna Woods is a truly excellent teacher. Everything is presented step by step with lots of explanation and encouragement. You feel like you are taking personal music lessons with an unhurried, traditional teacher. She not only explains how to read music, starting with the clefs and the notes, but tells you how to maximize your learning—what new concepts you should study and restudy, for example. I surely wish *my* music theory teacher had urged me to take the time to be perfect at locating the individual notes, like Madonna Woods does, before pressing on to more complicated things. Recommended. *Mary Pride*

The **Early Childhood Homeschool Kit** is designed to be a beginning step which will encourage your child to love playing and listening to music. You are provided with the *Songs I Can Play* student and teacher books, an eight-bar number xylophone, piano guides, and a numeral strip. There is no need for reading skills or knowing musical notation. You simply have your child match the numbers on the large stand-up book to the corresponding numbers on the xylophone or piano. Familiar songs like "Three Blind Mice," "Jingle Bells," and "Row Your Boat" are included for easy learning. Cute pictures adorn the pages of each of the songs and large numbers and words are used for easy readability (that is for those who are reading). Use octave matching games to teach the concepts of high, middle, low, up, and down. You also learn left to right reading, number concepts, eye-hand coordination, sequencing, and matching.

This system was developed for teaching to individual 5-year-olds and small groups of five or six with parents. The teacher's book is full of instructions on what you should say to your student and when. They are very detailed and tend to be overwhelming. "Say to the children . . ." is used quite frequently and each step is painstakingly laid out for you, from taking out instruments to setting up the music. Larger families will find there is little time for its "sit down and pay attention" approach.

Though the material is a bit heavy-handed and school-ish, it can be adapted for home use. Best use: group situations. *Marla Perry*

Let's Learn Music takes up the challenge of making workbooks and drills absorbing and fun. It succeeds—to a degree. The three booklets are geared to early readers, using simple words in a large typeface and plump musical notation, easy for young eyes to read.

Don't mistake these for self-teaching texts. The workbooks are best used to supplement your teaching rather than supplant it. Some exercises are "cute," others merely drill. Your child may search for two whole notes on "Mr. Rabbit" on one page and a few pages later tackle a matching exercise. You'll need plenty of colored markers or crayons if you plan to have your child follow the instructions in the books.

Unlike most music programs which begin with rhythm and then go to notation and music theory, this series first introduces your child to various notes (whole, half, quarter, etc.), rests, the staff, and then the scale. Rhythm is finally introduced with the first "real" song.

Teacher's notes, while useful, appear in the same typeface as the child's text and in some cases aren't clearly addressed to the teacher.

The level of music theory presented as you progress through these workbooks seems to accelerate much faster than the implied reading level. For example, whole and half steps and scales (Chromatic, Minor and Harmonic Minor) are introduced in book three.

Let's Learn Music can be a valuable supplement to a well-organized music curriculum but falls just short of its goal of making workbooks and drills fun and absorbing. It comes close with "Find 2 whole notes on Mr. Rabbit," or "Follow the dots up the scale. . . . Color the bird," and then follows the old vaudeville maxim, "leave 'em wanting more." *Tony Silva*

In this intermediate music series, you meet Mrs. Treble Clef who had so many children (notes) she didn't know what to do. No problem, she had Mr. Bass Clef build her a staff. This clever story is the hook on which a fairly thorough presentation of basic music theory hangs.

Mrs. Treble Clef prepares her little notes for a trip to the Orchestra Hall where they meet the four families of instruments. As an educational story time, this approach would be hard to beat. After a few brief stories about

Keyboard Capers

Grade preK–6. Book, $18.95.
Laminated Manipulatives, $37.95.
Manipulatives & book, $51.95.
Shipping extra.
*Elijah Company, 1053 Eldridte Loop,
Crossville, TN 38555. Orders: (888)
2ELIJAH. Inquiries: (931) 456-6284.
Fax: (931) 456-6384.
Web: www.elijahco.com.*

NEW!
Little Composer

Grades preK–4. $34.99 plus
shipping.
*Leapfrog, 1250 45th Street, Suite 150,
Emeryville, CA 94609. (800) 701-5327.
Fax: (510) 595-2478.
Email: custserv@leapfrogtoys.com.
Web: www.leapfrogtoys.com.*

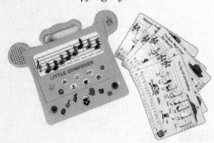

great composers, it's back to work . . . and drill . . . and work . . . The rest of Book 2 takes your child a little deeper into music theory and notation, singing and writing simple songs.

Book 3 begins with a section on the origin and development of music which grown-ups will find fascinating. Back to more theory with chords and most scales. Then more instruments. Then more theory—including a primer on musical forms, elements of music and ample review questions on all the material covered.

As with Hayes Let's Learn Music Series, **Hayes Music Series** is great as a supplement to your regular music curriculum. The stories in Book 2, while not exactly classical literature can be a refreshing—and educational—change of pace at story time. *Tony Silva*

Keyboard Capers, a terrific music-reading program for kids, consists of 100 easy activities for parents and teachers of children age 4 and up. It covers everything: learning the letters A–G forward and backward, staff and clefs, locating keys on the keyboard, rhythm, intervals, notes, music words and signs (e.g., pianissimo), ear training, and major scales.

I *like* this book! Author Rebecca Doyle Stout has managed to come up with 100 easy activities "for parents and teachers of Suzuki piano students age 4 and up" that actually teach kids (whether Suzuki-ized or not) to read music *without any struggle!* Sample activity: practice rhythm using the pink (half-note), purple (whole note), and blue (dotted half-note) cards.

This is the easiest, most fun music-reading course I've seen.

The program relies heavily on manipulatives, for which patterns are included. If you decide to manufacture the manipulatives yourself, no supplies more complicated than Magic Markers, index cards, posterboard, scissors, and tape are needed. Or you can buy a beautiful set of colorful, laminated (or unlaminated) manipulatives for *Keyboard Capers*. It takes quite a while to make the manipulatives from scratch, so I'd suggest buying the prefabbed set if you're strapped for time. *Mary Pride*

Perhaps this was designed for the younger crowd, but at my house everyone got involved. **Little Composer** is a toy designed to introduce your child to fundamental music concepts. It helps establish the relationship between notes and sounds. This little plastic, hand-held box has many features including:

- Instrument Buttons: Your child can press different buttons to hear various instruments and "voices" sing the notes (voices include dog, cat, woman playing the flute, or LeapFrog)
- Moveable Notes: Your child can move the note button up or down to hear and see that notes have sounds and names.
- Song Buttons: Here your child can learn various songs, such as: *Twinkle Twinkle Little Star, Mary Had a Little Lamb, Row Row Row Your Boat, Itsy-Bitsy Spider, I'm a Little Teapot, Baa Baa Black Sheep, London Bridge is Falling Down, Wheels on the Bus,* and *BINGO.*
- Song Cards: Cards with cut-out slots that fit over the notes on the Little Composer. Your child then slides the notes up into the position of the slots on the cards to match the note position. Once in the proper position Little Composer will play the song on the card when the play button is pressed.

One other neat feature: your child can create his own songs by placing the note buttons as he likes. Then he can press PLAY to hear his composition! This toy is sure to entertain for hours! There is a lot of music education packed into this little box. *Maryann Turner*

Wonderful Marcy Marxer teamed up with delightful Cathy Fink for another video you'll love, **Making and Playing Homemade Instruments**. Watch the dynamic duo and three children make and play fanciful instruments such as the Yardstick Mouthbow, Oatmeal Box Banjo, Bottle Cap Castanets, and Washtub Bass, among others. Needs a few simple tools and household supplies. 60 minutes. (HOMESCHOOL INSIDE TIP: You can also see Cathy and Marcy on the Calvert School "Melody Lane" music-appreciation video series!) *Mary Pride*

Try to imagine cramming eight years of in-depth music theory and music appreciation onto the last few inches of your bookshelf. Try to imagine what eight years of in-depth music instruction would do to your budget . . .and then be prepared for a pleasant surprise.

Music, It's Great doesn't take much space on the shelf. The teacher's manual and piano accompaniment book come in two small binders. Virtually all of the remaining resources could fit comfortably into another somewhat larger binder. If you use the program from Grade one through eight, the cost is less than $10 a year. This small and relatively inexpensive package amounts to a comprehensive—you might even say "exhaustive"—course with an emphasis on fundamental theory, great themes, and lots of singing.

This curriculum is very structured, leaving little to chance or imagination, yet its approach doesn't limit the fun of learning and making music. It also doesn't relieve teacher and student of the joy of hard work. While Grace Bartel, the program's designer, worked hard to adapt the original course to homeschool use, the marks of a product created by a professional educator for classroom use remain.

Here is what you get with the basic course:

- 130-page teacher's manual with detailed daily lesson plans
- 62 worksheets for each grade
- Packet and cassette tape for teaching themes from the works of the great masters
- Complete recorder course
- Songbook with 147 well-loved songs with easy piano accompaniment
- Rhythm instrument instruction and accompaniment for most of the songs
- Permission to copy all the materials for use of the purchasing family

If you opt for the complete course, you also get:

- First and second voice parts for almost all the songs
- A 220-page manual instead of the 130-page one
- Orff instrument instruction and accompaniment (xylophone, bells, etc.)
- Guitar accompaniment
- Listening cassette tape
- Listening skills packet

You'll find 12 pages of numbered notes at the beginning of the teacher's manual. Don't spill coffee on these: they're your secret decoder ring, and without them none of the course makes any sense. Each daily lesson plan (there are 160 of them) gives you all the basic information needed to teach a single concept to one or more grade levels. Some days skip whole grade

UPDATED!
Making and Playing Homemade Instruments
Grades 3–8. $19.95 plus shipping. *Homespun Tapes, PO Box 340, Woodstock, NY 12498. (800) 338-2737 or (914) 246-2550. Fax: (914) 246-5282. Email: hmspn@aol.com. Web: www.homespuntapes.com.*

NEW!
Music, It's Great
Grades 1–8. Basic course homeschool version, $70. Complete course (with voice, guitar chord, and xylophone accompaniments), $105. Lives of the Composers supplement, $12. Shipping extra. *Grace Bartel, 4718 Regent St., Apt. 94-A, Madison, WI 53705. (608) 238-7069. Email: musicits@juno.com.*

Rather than print up a flashy stack of flash cards, the kids create their own, printing a symbol or concept on one side and its meaning on the other. If you follow Grace's instructions for making the cards, you'll end up with something akin to Bible memory cards. These are held together with rubber bands in categories such as "Know" and "Don't Know." As with everything else in the course, instructions for making the cards and the "Memorization System with 12 Boxes" are provided. Here, you're advised to "get a whiskey or wine box with dividers for 12 bottles in it." If you're not into rooting through dumpsters behind liquor stores, check a local bookstore for used cardboard displays instead. The displays for those popular "Teeny Weeny Books" are ready-made and won't ruin your reputation as a teetotaler.

levels and others skip lessons altogether, focusing instead on reviews of songs learned, great themes, or flash card drills.

Preparing for lessons requires use of both the lesson plans and the notes—the latter to interpret the former. At first blush, this seems like a paradise for folks who like to build nuclear devices from spare parts, but it gets easier with practice, and it's a key to the curriculum's compactness.

All the worksheets in the course are hand-drawn (for that "warm, fuzzy" look) and reproducible. Those from the higher grade levels are a bit confusing because more information is drawn into the same space. There's something nice about hand-drawn worksheets, and Grace's printing, neat and inviting, betrays the fact that she's a seasoned classroom veteran.

Like the worksheets, the *Great Themes* and *Listening and Dictation* tapes are decidedly homegrown. You get real kids singing the way real kids normally sing at the grade level represented on the tape. The *Great Themes* tape presents music of great composers with catchy lyrics designed to make them memorable to kids. You haven't lived until you've heard the joyous strains of "Hallelujah . . .Hallelujah . . . It's a chorus . . .Handel wrote it!"

Overall, the music is fairly easy, with the teacher's accompaniments at a moderate level. The course doesn't require that the teacher be an accomplished musician, but an ability to read and play simple music is almost a necessity, especially when the time comes to expose kids to actual instruments. The accompaniments are designed to include second-voice singing if you wish to include it in your program—and if you have enough voices.

The **Lives of the Composers** supplement consists of 32 little booklets, one for each of the composers covered in the course. Each booklet consists of one piece of paper which can be folded down the middle to make 4-pages. Each booklet contains a short biography of one composer with a few quiz questions at the end. An answer key and a short history of music. are also provided in the packet.

If you're looking for a comprehensive and structured music instruction program, this could well be your pick. *Tony Silva*

Praise Hymn Music series

Grades K–7. God Made Music student book, $4.98 each grade. Teacher's manual, $10.98 each grade. Sing-A-Long: Cassette, $7.98 each grade; CD, $12.98 each grade. Shipping extra.
Praise Hymn, Inc., PO Box 1325, Taylors, SC 29687. (800) 729-2821. Fax: (864) 322-8284. Email: prazhyminc@aol.com. Web: www.praisehymninc.com.

Christian music-reading instruction. Praise Hymn's bag of tricks includes **The God Made Music series** (K–7), with accompanying Teacher's Manuals for K–6 (the grade 7 book can be studied alone or with an instructor). For K–2, the instructor may have only a limited musical background; for grades 3–7, the instructor needs to understand basic music concepts. This is a much more complete musical program than *Your Musical Friends* (see next page), covering music theory, band and orchestra instruments, music reading, singing, classical music introduction (with the recommended selections available on correlated records and cassettes), music styles, Old and New Testament music, and lots more. Of course, this also requires a deeper commitment on the part of both parent and child.

Plus correlated filmstrips, classical records and cassettes, felt board and music symbols, and an Instruments Picture Poster. *Mary Pride*

Rhythm Band is the place for music-reading games! Let's see how well I can distill down for you the two of greatest interest to homeschoolers.

Fun with Music Symbols is an entirely different type of game invented by the wife of Rhythm Band's founder, Mrs. Laura Bergin. Hang up the white foamy fabric sheet on the wall. On it is printed a target; on the target are printed 16 note values, rests, and other musical symbols. Heave a velcro ball at the target. Call out the name of the musical symbol it hits and get five points. Any number can play. Lots of fun, inexpensive.

Music Bingo is a traditional bingo-type game. Music Bingo can be used for prosaically drilling names, descriptions, and uses or music symbols. For two to 36 players. *Mary Pride*

The **Your Musical Friends** workbook series is a music reading program for little kids. Each musical symbol is carried by a cartoon animal. Quacker Treble Clef, for example, has a body made of the treble clef, a tail like a bass clef, and quarter notes for feet! There's Crescendo Whale, Forte Lion, Sixteenth Note Bird, Ritard Turtle . . . 29 animals in all.

The kindergarten book introduces the characters in the form of a coloring book. The first grade book, *Fun with Your Musical Friends,* gets into the two staffs and notes and rests. The second grade book, *Enjoying Music with Your Musical Friends,* looks at line and space note values and the loud and soft signs. The third grade book, *Learning More with Your Musical Friends,* includes sharps, flats, tempo, repeats, and accents. Finally, the fourth grade book, *Reading Music with Your Musical Friends,* covers the last details of dotted notes and so on, and launches into actual sight reading.

Each book begins with a review of the previous book. The exercises and stories are fun and colorful and *very* Christian. An example: a fill-in-the-blanks-with-the-note-name exercise in the fourth grade book about how Isaac Watts' mother had to spank him for continuing to drive her crazy by always speaking in rhyme gives Isaac's reply: "Mother, do some pity take. I will no more verses make!"

The instructor needs no musical background.

Because the publisher strives to keep costs low and therefore uses medium-grade paper, the art is muddy, but that is my only quibble.

New: cassette tapes to accompany each workbook. The Musical Friends animal characters lead your child through each workbook. Each character has his own voice and personality, as well as a Scripture verse representative of his or her musical function. A song tape called *Your Musical Friends Songs, Plus More!* (with corresponding songbook) is also available.

If your children want to know what all those funny little squiggles in the hymnbook mean, this is the easiest-to-use series around. *Mary Pride*

Band Instruments

MVP may be the answer to your musical prayers! The list of videos this company manufactures is unbelievable. If your child is interested in anything from the piano to the tuba to the conga drum, then you can find it here. There are even courses on how to read music.

The Maestro series includes beginning lessons on all common band instruments. Each 52-minute video contains between six and ten lessons. The instructor, introduced on the cover of the video, includes his or her specific credits and musical degrees. MVP uses actual students in each lesson to illustrate specific techniques as well as basic notes. Reading music is covered in a concise, straightforward approach, but some reinforcement should be considered. Students learn simple songs as well as the assembly of the instrument, hand positions, breathing (on wind instrument videos),

Rhythm Band Games

Grade preK–6. Fun with Music Symbols, $8.50. Music Bingo, $14.50. Shipping extra.
Rhythm Band Instruments, PO Box 126, Fort Worth, TX 76101-0126. Orders: (800) 424-4724. Inquiries: (817) 335-2561. Fax: (800) 784-9401. Web: www.rhythmband.com.

Your Musical Friends

Grades K–4. Workbooks, $9.95 each. Teacher's guides: 1–4, $2.95; level 5, $3.95. Special offer (includes all above), $59.95 (includes US shipping; Canada and overseas add shipping). Corresponding teaching cassettes: Levels1 & 5 (two cassettes per) $10.95 each. Levels 2–4 (single-cassette), $9.95 each. Special offer including cassette tapes, $104.95 (includes US shipping; Canada and overseas add shipping). Songbook, $4.95. Corresponding tape, $7.95. Shipping extra for orders other than special offers.
Parsonage Enterprises, Christian Education Music Publishers, PO Box 388, Brook, IN 47922. (800) 573-6127. (219) 275-6397. Phone/Fax: (219) 275-6553. Email: parsonage1@yahoo.com.

The Maestro series

Grade 1–12. $19.95 each plus shipping.
Music Video Productions, Inc., 9030 Eton Ave., Canoga Park, CA 91304. (888) 325-0049. Fax: (818) 709-7846.

care of the instrument, and posture for proper playing. While they may not be sufficient for the advanced student, this multimedia format can certainly get your child on the road to learning a band instrument.

Each video comes with a booklet to assist in getting the most out of each lesson. Suggestions on how to buy a used instrument are especially useful, as well as the proper handling of the instrument. Parents with little or no musical background will find this an advantage as they teach their child. Parents should order a catalog of the full range of products from MVP. Prices vary on the videos, but the Maestro Series is a homeschool bargain. *Lisa Mitchell*

Keyboard Instruments

Almost every piano teacher I have met uses **Alfred's Basic Piano Library** as one of their basic curriculum options. Published by a third-generation family-owned company founded in 1922, this flexible and easily interchangeable piano-teaching system has stood the test of time.

The Basic Piano library is a collection of lesson books and recital books in up to 7 levels (1A, 1B, 2, 3, 4, 5, and 6), with teacher's guides. For the average student, covering the material should take about three years. The list of titles and prices in the margin is only a small sampling of the materials available, all correlated page-by-page to the basic lesson books. Also available are Theory Books, Technic Books (for technical drills), Activity & Ear Training Books, Solo Books, Sacred Solo Books, Repertoire Books (with selections from the Baroque, Classical, Romantic, and Modern periods), Christmas Joy! books, and Flash Cards.

Alfred uses overlapping concepts, like an incremental approach, to prevent learning gaps. Units are not used, to encourage progress at the student's own pace. "When the student . . . understands the concepts . . . **TURN THE PAGE!"**

Ear, eye and hand training all go together throughout. The music is carefully chosen to appeal to each age group, including adults. When students successfully complete the six levels of the basic piano course, they are prepared to play basic classical piano repertoire.

The Basic Piano Library starts off easy. Little children are not confronted with the fraction concept of notes in the Prep course, but learn quarter notes first, and progress from there to half and whole notes. Eighth notes are introduced in book 1-B, the second half of the course after the Prep course. (This is the beginning level for six- or seven-year-olds. The **Young Beginner Prep Course** is for pre-readers.) The 48-page children's books are colorful and inviting, with activities such as coloring and games for young beginners, providing about a half year's worth of lessons in each book. All of the music in level A of the Prep set is taught by repeated notes or by single steps (adjacent notes) up or down. The Prep B level book introduces skips. The 64-page books for older children use illustrations, exercises and puzzles to engage and teach music skills and theory.

For eight- and nine-year-olds, Lesson Book 1 of the **Later Beginner Prep Course** Lesson Book 1 covers the same fundamentals as Levels 1A and 1B of the Basic Piano Library, but in fewer pages—72 rather than 112. All the supplementary volumes are available: Theory Books, Recital Books, Fun Books, Technic Books, Ear Training Books and much more, each correlated page-by-page with the Lesson Books.

For those who prefer the savings and convenience of not having to carry multiple books around, Alfred has a **Basic All-in-One Piano Course**. It includes all the pages from Lesson Books 1A, 1B, and 2 of the Basic Piano Library, plus a selection of pages from the Theory, Recital, and Fun Books,

NEW!
Alfred's Basic Piano Library

Ages 3–adult. Teachers' editions are free. Young Beginner Prep Course, 2 lesson & 2 activity & ear training books, A-C $5.95 each; D, $5.50; E, $4.95; F, $4.95. Beginner Alfred's Basic: 1A, $6.95; 1B, $6.50; 2, $8.50; all others $6.50. Beginner All-in-One Course: books 1 and 2, $6.50; books 3-5, $5.95 each. Later Beginner Alfred's Basic: book 1, $8.50; book 2, $6.95. Later Beginner Chord Approach: level 1, $7.95; level 2, $7.50; theory book 1, $6.95; theory book 2, $6.50. Adult All-In-One Course, 3 books, $14.95 each. Shipping extra.

Alfred Publishing Co., P.O. Box 10003, Van Nuys, CA 91410-0003. Orders: (800) 292-6122. Inquiries: (818) 892-2452. Fax: (800) 632-1928. Web: www.alfredpub.com. Call or fax to find a store near you; Alfred Publishing does not do direct sales.

all combined into a five-book sequence. An **All-in-One Sacred Course** for young beginning students, with the same musical approach but featuring lyrics and illustrations that teach Christian principles, is also available.

The 96-page **Later Beginner Adult Piano course** books are not as charmingly illustrated, but have appropriate illustrations to make lessons clearly understandable. The adult books with accompanying audio CD's are fine for self teaching. They move faster than the children's books, and in two levels reach basic musical competence to a level of playing confidently for fun. Even adults are sure to be thrilled at how quickly they can play recognizable and full sounding music. An **Adult All-in-One Course** is also available, as are are **Basic Jazz/Rock Course**, **Basic Electronic Keyboard Courses**, **Basic Adult Piano Course for Windows**, **Basic Piano Library Theory Games Software** for levels 1A–5, and MIDI accompaniment disks for at least several books of all the courses Alfred offers.

Usually a teacher will expect to work through two books in a year's time, but of course, that depends on the student's progress and the number of correlating activities and materials chosen.

Although the children's books have teacher's guides available, which tell you page by page exactly what to do, a non-musician parent might prefer to have an experienced music teacher demonstrate, guide, and evaluate progress. By using the available CD's or cassettes, so you can tell what sound you are aiming for, a determined parent can teach these courses without the expense of an outside instructor. For this purpose, the All-in-One courses make the most sense. *Anne Brodbeck*

Just think of it . . . a piano instructional that boosts your child's self-esteem and makes him popular at parties, church gatherings, and major summit conferences! OK, so we exaggerated. This video program doesn't mention summit conferences. Once you get past the initial "great expectations" hype, you'll

discover an efficient and somewhat enjoyable method for learning piano.

The first in a series, **The Adventure Begins** introduces all of the keys on the piano and has the student actually playing a song before getting into any theory. Although "incremental" in its presentation, far too much material is covered in the last lessons. These would have better served beginning students if they had been broken down into smaller bites. It's not likely that anyone can learn rhythm, timing, and the entire Grand Staff in one sitting—even though the video format allows you to easily repeat a lesson.

Each lesson begins with a brief review of previous material and ends with instructions to stop the tape and perform an exercise.

As you might expect, this video is short on feedback. If you are clueless about whether your child is performing the exercises properly, you may need to ask a professional instructor.

The Adventure Begins is professionally produced with simple but effective graphics and a friendly narrator. Overhead shots of the keyboard—reminiscent of your favorite cooking show—give a full view of the action, but at such a distance it can be difficult to follow.

This program does a fair job of introducing the student to the piano. The video medium makes repeating lessons almost a snap and is an economical alternative to hiring a teacher. If you need the help of a professional piano teacher, *The Adventure Begins* can be a good supplement or review. *Tony Silva*

NEW!
Kopy-Keys Series: "The Adventure Begins"

Grades 1–5. $19.95 plus shipping. *Thelma Hrncir, Big Note Studio, 3102 Vicksburg, Corpus Christi, TX 78410-2436. (512) 241-3114.*

NEW!
Madonna Woods Piano Course for Christians

Grade 3–adult. Books, $7.95 each. Cassettes, $10.95 each. Book and cassette sets, $17–$27. Shipping extra. *Davidsons Music, 6727 Metcalf, Shawnee Mission, KS 66204. (913) 262-6533. Fax: (913) 722-2980. Web: www.davidsonsmusic.com.*

If there's such a thing as a comfortable balance between thorough thoroughness and simplicity, you'll find it in this offering from Davidson's Music. The **Madonna Woods Piano Course for Christians** opens in the customary "This is a piano" fashion and progresses through six levels of hands-on music theory. What makes this a "piano course for Christians" is the choice of music. You'll enjoy many familiar hymns, interludes, and Christian themes throughout. All the lessons end with an encouraging note and a "God bless you!"

Each workbook is packaged with one or more audio cassettes, and a very friendly—and easily decipherable—insert for the teacher or parent. Together, these resources provide everything necessary to build a solid foundation for the beginning piano student.

Exercises for each piece of theory presented help reinforce your understanding and skill. Quite a bit of instruction is built into the workbooks, but the tapes are indispensable for their examples and encouragement. The narrative and piano accompaniment on the tapes is much like having an expert piano teacher on hand for each lesson. You only have to watch and listen to your student and tell him how he's doing. If you're not proficient on the piano, you may want to find someone who is to provide that all-important feedback. Because of the way this course is designed however, it's not necessary to have a professional looking over your child's shoulder every minute. A periodic "checkup" will do just fine.

Any printed work is subject to typos, and the Madonna Woods course is far from an exception. Typos in and of themselves are harmless for the most part, but when they occur in the musical notation, it can become confusing. A case in point is the explanation of "staccato." The practice piece following an introduction of staccato has no notes marked for staccato play, even though the lyrics in the piece reinforce the concept.

You'll get everything you need for a thorough and enjoyable piano instructional experience in this course. Everything, that is, except the piano. It's complete, easy to follow, and a great place to start. For further instruction, Davidsons can also accommodate you, with literally dozens of graduated keyboard courses for piano and organ. *Tony Silva*

NEW!
The Progressive Pianist Series

Beginning Pianists. The Progressive Pianist kits (includes student book, two tapes and an answer key): Part One, $49.50; Part Two, $65; Part Three, $65. Student books alone: Part One, $21.95; Parts Two and Three, $30.95 each. Shipping extra. *Rainbow Re-Source Center, Route 1 Box 159A, 50 N 500 East Road, Toulon, IL 61483. Orders: (888) 841-3456. Inquiries: 309-695-3200. Fax: (309) 695-3042. Email: rainbowres@aol.com.*

For the non-musical parent and student, **The Progressive Pianist** is a very easy way to learn beginning piano or keyboard skills. The starter kit gives you everything you need to get started: the main student book, a performance pieces tape, an exercises tape, and an answer key to questions in the book.

You begin by learning about staffs and notes and the grand staff, bass, and treble clefs. Music theory is emphasized as a solid foundation for further study. The book has theory exercises throughout that reinforce the concepts taught. Finger exercises are also included to strengthen muscles. Very early in the program you are rewarded by being able to play easy songs!

The book is spiral-bound with some black and white pictures. It is designed to be consumable, so you will want one for each student.

Two cassette tapes are included. The first is a recording of all the pieces and the other has the exercises so you can hear what they should sound like. These make it easy to put notes and performance in context.

The *Hymns Book* and the *Christmas Favorites* give students a chance to practice their new skills. The Christmas songs are a combination of eight sacred and popular songs. Seven hymns make up the other book. Each book comes with a cassette tape which allows the student to hear the piece played correctly. The song is played twice, once with a metronome—to keep an even tempo, and once without; with fully orchestrated accompaniment—so that you can play along for enjoyment.

The Progressive Pianist is designed to be self-explanatory and is perfect for the homeschool family. And why shouldn't it be? Its author is an accomplished musician and homeschool parent. Enjoy. *Marla Perry*

Amazing! This one word describes the **Stewart Piano Course** by Elsie Stewart. Even the most skeptical must step away from this course in awe of Mrs. Stewart's efforts to provide an effective alternative to customary piano lessons! Each book of the Stewart Piano Course should be followed to take full advantage of the learning process, starting with The Beginners Book. It contains 25 ready-to-use lesson plans. Books are purchased separately, but each book is crucial to the continuity of this unusual approach.

Students learn the keyboard, how to get their fingers working, and then move on to the 12 major scales, transposing and chords. Hand-eye coordination transitions through a normal process without uncertainty or fear. As the author suggests: "If your child can recognize ABCDEFG and 1234567," then they can learn to play the piano with the Stewart Piano course.

These are complete teacher instruction books, with each step and procedure laid out in easy to understand language. Ideas are provided to make the learning process go smoother, but these lessons are each so well planned and motivating that parents can rest assured if they take on the responsibility to teach their own child. The effective use of Stewart Piano Course can enrich the musical talent of any age student, but may be most effective with those of early elementary age who are just discovering piano. Parents, take a close look at this option as you begin to consider the piano needs in your home! *Lisa Mitchell*

The **First Book of the Piano** and **The First Book of the Keyboard** are each 64 oversized, colorful pages. Friendly little colored Blob People give you a pile of information about music in general and how to play these instruments in particular.

Follow up with the colorful **Usborne Easy Instrumental Tunes** books. These include tunes in standard musical notation, plus lyrics and playing tips. Unlike typical beginners' series such as Bastien Piano, these don't keep adding a new, difficult technique at every lesson or two. With just minimal instruction, children can actually learn to play these tunes, and get a feeling of success at the beginner's level.

At present, the series includes these titles for keyboard instruments: *Easy Piano Tunes*, *More Easy Piano Tunes*, and *Easy Keyboard Tunes* Recommended. *Mary Pride*

String Instruments

How do you say charming, entertaining, educational, and fun? . . . **Fiddle For Kids 1 & 2**! This has got to be the easiest and quickest way to fiddle playing yet.

Luke Bulla and his younger sister Jenny Anne, both accomplished and talented young fiddle players, teach you step by step in 110 minutes of video. They are assisted by their seven-year-old brother Jed, who plays along with you.

You begin with the basics by learning the parts of the fiddle and bow, how to stand, how to hold them, and where to put your fingers. Next, you learn the names of the strings and how to tune by ear. By the end of the first tape you will have learned an easy exercise called, "Down Kitty Up Kitty" and your first song, *Boil the Cabbage Down*.

Part Two of this series continues by teaching you three more songs: *Old Joe Clark*, *The Tennessee Waltz*, and *Devil's Dream*. You don't play these songs all at once, but take them apart and learn them bit by bit. The only problem is that there's never a point where you learn how to read notes. Although the sheet music for these songs is provided and the letter names and finger numbers are given under each note, you aren't able to read the music without these extra notations. If you've already learned to read music on the piano or any other instrument, then this won't be a distraction.

This is charming stuff and the Bulla siblings, assisted by their father Brad, are a delightful family who make fiddle playing not only easy, but fun!

Also available for beginning string artists, **Ukulele For Kids 1 & 2**. These two videotapes (with 20 music lessons total) taught by Marcy Marxer and Ginger the Dog make a very good introduction to instrumental music for people too small to handle a guitar. The ukulele is a very non-threatening and fun small instrument. The videos, almost an hour each, feature conversations between a very talented puppet dog and Marcy.

Marcy, a professional musician, explains musical theory, parts of the ukulele (which many other stringed instruments share), and chording and strumming patterns. (Ukulele skills transfer nicely to guitar.) Old, familiar folk-nursery tunes gently lead a progression from bewildered beginner to almost accomplished junior entertainer.

There are very few flashy technical events in the videos (few fades, no camera angle changes, no exciting scenery changes, no races, no violence) but the pleasant banter between Marcy and the dog helps maintain the interest of children who want to learn music. *Marla Perry and Anne Brodbeck*

UPDATED!
Homespun Kids' Guitar 1 and Kids' Guitar 2

Grade 3–8. $24.95 each or $39.95 for both. Songbook, $14.95. Shipping extra.

Homespun Tapes, PO Box 325, Woodstock, NY 12498. (800) 338-2737 or (914) 246-2550. Fax: (914) 246-5282. Email: hmspn@aol.com.

Marcy Marxer, a well-known performer of children's music, teaches this hour-and-a-half video course of guitar basics for kids. **Kids' Guitar 1** follows the traditional method of starting with tuning and easy chords, and proceeds to simple children's songs. Marcy is cheerful and easy to follow. She also is well aware of the usual pitfalls of early guitar learning, and helps you avoid them. Good competent guitar lessons—nothing glitzy or unexpected. Course comes with booklet of song chords and lyrics.

Kids' Guitar 1 video has now been joined by **Kids' Guitar 2**. The new video starts with a quick review of tuning up and of the basic chords taught on tape 1. Then Marcy takes you through a series of songs, using each to introduce a new chord or fingerpicking style. Very patient, friendly teaching method uses chord diagrams, closeups of Marcy's fretboard and strumming positions, plus lots of good-natured monologue. Excellent chord-switching exercises help you build up speed. Songs include children's classics such as *Shortenin' Bread*, *O Susannah*, *When the Saints Go Marching In*, and so on. Comes with spiral-bound songbook and pick. Recommended. Video 1 is 90 minutes. Video 2, 75 minutes.

The first 11 pages of **Cathy Fink & Marcy Marxer's Kids' Guitar Songbook** cover guitar and ukulele chords, strumming and fingerpicking, walking bass lines, and transposing. Then you get lyrics and chords for 12 children's songs. The enclosed *free* CD allows you to hear a "slow" and "fast" version of each song, with audio introductions (usually) for each. Turn the stereo knob all the way to the right to hear mostly guitar, or to the left to hear mostly ukulele. What a well-designed and helpful package!

Why is there a track for ukulele, and ukulele chords, in this songbook/CD combo? Because Marcy Marxer is also the artist/author of Homespun Tapes' Ukulele for Kids 1 and 2. See review above. *Mary Pride*

Do you have a five- to ten-year-old in your family who is interested in the guitar, but you have ruled it out because of the cumbersome size and fingering of the instrument? Homespun to the rescue, again! This family-friendly company is offering a new approach to learning guitar for kids. It is called **SmartStart Guitar** and is taught by the animated Jessica Baron Turner.

Turner recommends the use of a child-sized guitar called the "Baby Taylor" (also available from Homespun). She begins with naming the parts of the guitar, the proper hold and playing posture. SmartStart tuning is open-tuned (D-G-D-G-B-D), as opposed to the standard tuning of E-A-D-G-B-E. This tuning produces a pleasant sound and allows for easy formation of chords. Turner places emphasis on maintaining a steady beat.

Use of the flatpick, the capo (device attached to the neck of the instrument to alter the key), and strumming techniques are covered. "Easy D," "Easy C," "E minor," and "Intermediate D" chords are taught, and after each chord an easy tune is introduced using that chord.

Tunes included are: *Twinkle Twinkle Little Star*, *Are You Sleeping?*, *This Old Man*, *Buffalo Gals*, *Kumbaya*, and *Joshua Fought the Battle of Jericho*.

This seems an ideal method for teaching young children, eliminating many common roadblocks, and would be easily followed by a more traditional course, such as the Homespun Marcy Marxer's Kids' Guitar course.

At the end of the lesson, the effervescent Turner congratulates kids with warm fuzzy feelings, encouraging them to reward themselves with a pat on the back and a big hug! Highly recommended. *Barbara Petronelli*

Shar sells the **Children's Music Series** by Evelyn Bedient Avsharian. This contains workbooks and games for teaching music reading by several innovative methods, plus fun and easy songs. Example: the Mississippi Hot Dog Lonely Hamburger Band is said to include "exciting pieces on A alone, E alone, and both strings. Duets and rounds in two basic Twinkle rhythms." Clever of them to make playing one string exciting.

Shar's listing of sheet music for string players and records and cassettes of string music is as complete as you can reasonably expect. Plus a large selection of hard-to-find video-cassettes of great string players and teachers, writers, artists, opera, and ballet. You will probably want to send for this no-frills catalog. *Mary Pride*

Vocal

The singing Lester family, who have been making music for homeschoolers since 1980, have put together a series of audiocassettes that teach your family to sing in harmony. Newest of these is **Favorite Traditional Hymns.** While the **Homestyle Harmony** and **Traditional Christmas Carols** presented full four-part harmony, most of the songs on *Favorite Traditional Hymns* are in two-part harmony, making it the perfect "starter" tape. For each song, first you hear it sung in harmony, then each part is sung separately, then it's sung in harmony again. You get a lot of songs, too. Here's what's on just this one tape: *Jesus Loves Me*, *Jesus Loves the Little Children*, *Anywhere with Jesus*, *God Will Take Care of You*, *Sweet Hour of Prayer*, *Allelujah*, *Jesus Thou Joy of Loving Hearts*, *He is Lord*, *For the Beauty of the Earth*, *Onward Christian Soldiers*, *Amazing Grace*, *What a Friend We Have in Jesus*, and the *Doxology*. Similarly, their **22 Traditional Rounds** tape includes tons of rounds, their *Homestyle Harmony* tapes includes many traditional "learn to sing in parts and harmony" songs, and the songs on their *Favorite Traditional Hymns* tape are just those you'll want to sing with your family or when you go a-caroling.

NEW!
Homespun SmartStart Guitar
Grade K–6. Instructional level 1 (no prior experience necessary). 50-minute video, $19.95 plus shipping.
Homespun Tapes, PO Box 340, Woodstock, NY 12498. (800) 338-2737 or (914) 246-2550. Fax: (914) 246-5282. Email: hmspn@aol.com. Web: www.homespuntapes.com.

Shar Products Catalog
All ages. Free catalog.
Shar Products, PO Box 1411, Ann Arbor, MI 48106. (800) 248-7427. Fax: (800) 99-STRAD. Email: sharnet@sharmusic.com. Web: www.sharmusic.com.

UPDATED!
Lester Family Music
All ages. $9.95 each. 3 for $25. Shipping extra.
The Lester Family, PO Box 203, Joshua Tree, CA 92252. Orders: (800) 793-5309. Inquiries: (760) 366-9684. Fax: (760) 366-3254. Email: newmoon@cci-29palms.com. Web: www.planesong.com/newmoon.

The Lester family sing with sincerity. There's nothing fake or overproduced about these lovely *a capella* tapes. And just think how much better your family singing will sound! *Mary Pride*

Wind Instruments

Have you ever dreamed of picking up an instrument and playing it? Almost immediately? No suffering through long lessons? Well, now you can.

The Homeschool Recorder Kit 1 comes with a *Let's Sing & Play, Book 1* student book, one German superior recorder in zip case, *My Write and Read Music Workbook*, a tutoring/accompaniment tape (or CD for $5 extra) for Book 1, and one *Recorder Teaching: A Homeschool Approach* manual. Everything you need to teach the recorder is included. And more.

You learn the basics first: how to hold the instrument, how to begin the tone and how to play the letters "B-A-G." This is taught in both student and teacher's book, as well as the cassette tape or CD. Each step goes slowly, with time for practice. Plenty of diagrams are included to show finger placement. MusicWorks uses the "point, say, and play" method. First you point to the letters on the page and say or sing their names. Then you say the names again while fingering each note on your recorder. Finally, you play the song. Students will be playing songs right from the beginning.

The cassette tape reinforces the auditory nature of the lesson. You hear how you are supposed to blow and how the songs actually sound. Don't expect that your efforts will sound exactly the same, since the songs have extra orchestration to give them a fuller sound.

The student book is the stand-up kind which allows it to be placed on a table at eye level. Each page shows the actual letters that you are to play, with the measures being set off by horizontal lines. The pieces include beginner songs, children's songs like *Mary Had a Little Lamb*, and excerpts from famous classical pieces such as the march from the *Nutcracker Suite*.

The music workbook begins the transition from letter notation to staff notation. Level one shows how the letters themselves sit on the lines of a staff and level two teaches the notes themselves. Don't let the musical terminology scare you. Even non-musical parents can learn this alongside their children.

The manual is school-ish in nature and you will probably find that many of the instructions are overly detailed and choreographed, such as explaining how to make your student book stand up (complete with picture) and what to say when talking to your child. I wasn't impressed with its tone, although there is some worthy information worth digging for.

The Homeschool Recorder Kit 2 includes one *Let's Sing & Play: Book 2* student book, Rhythm and Pitch Notation Charts—a 14 x 11" flipchart book, and the Book 2 *Recorder Concert Play Along* cassette.

You will need to complete MusicWorks' Level 1 program for the recorder before you tackle this, as it takes off where Level 1 ends.

A wide range of songs and styles are represented in the play book: pop, classical, folk, rock, patriotic and marches. Professional musicians on synthesizers provide the accompaniment for each song which can be used for concert or recital settings. A few songs have a definite rock beat.

The extra large, spiral-bound, stand-up flip charts teach musical notation and reinforce rhythm and pitch fundamentals. You will learn to quickly identify standard notation of quarter notes, half notes, eighth notes, dotted notes, and rests. Major scales, sharps and flats, and the treble and bass clefs are also taught. If you have a background in music, you'll be able to forego the flip charts, in which case you'll want to write or call for pricing information.

NEW!
Homeschool Recorder Kits

Grades 3–7. Kit 1, $56.20 postpaid. Extra recorders, $5.95 each. Kit 2, $41.20 postpaid. Mention homeschooler code HS-1 when ordering. *Peg Hoenack's MusicWorks, 8409 Old Seven Locks Road, Bethesda, MD 20817-2006. (800) 466-TOOT (8668). (301) 365-1818. Fax: (301) 469-9252. Email: phoenack@ix.netcom.com. Web: www.netcom.com/~phoenack.*

Carols & Holiday Songs provides typical Christmas songs easily played at this level—some sacred and some popular. MusicWorks also sells the *Hansel and Gretel* opera with piano accompaniment for an additional cost. Because of its nature, it would work best with larger groups.

A bit plodding and detailed, this does the job. If you can remember the music program in the public schools twenty-five years ago, then you'll have a good idea of what it's like. *Marla Perry*

I remember my first experience with a recorder vividly—the instructions were in German! Fortunately for homeschoolers looking for an economical and easy alternative to piano lessons (and pianos), the **Nine-Note Recorder Method** is written in English.

Homeschooler Penny Gardner disposes of the music theory in one page and you're off! She provides little additional instruction beyond the brief explanation of notation, rhythm and how to hold the recorder, but very little is needed for this instrument. The method is limited to nine notes (plus a tenth "bonus" note in the last selection.)

The music is easy to play and professionally typeset. Notes appear on wide staves and are plump as notes go, making them easier to distinguish by people new to reading music. By the end of the first book, you're doing simple duets.

A second book, **Easy Duets for Christmas** adds to your repertoire for Holiday performances.

The Nine-Note Recorder Method is proof that you don't have to master the entire Grand Staff and all of the nuances of music theory to make music—and have fun in the process. *Tony Silva*

The **First Book of the Recorder** is 64 over-sized, colorful pages. Friendly little colored Blob People give you a pile of information about music in general and how to play the recorder in particular.

For practice (and more instruction from the Little Blob People), try *The Usborne Book of Easy Recorder Tunes* and its sister volume, *More Easy Recorder Tunes*. Both are available combined into one bargain-priced volume, *200 Easy Recorder Tunes. Mary Pride*

NEW!
The Nine-Note Recorder Method
Easy Duets for Christmas

Grades 3–8. Both in one volume for $9.95. Add shipping.
Penny Gardner, P.O. Box 900983, Sandy UT, 84090. (801) 943-3146. Email: pennygar@aol.com. Web: members.aol.com/PG9Note/

Usborne Recorder Books

Grades 1–12. First Book of the Recorder, Easy Recorder Tunes, More Easy Recorder Tunes, $10.95 each. 200 Easy Recorder Tunes, $17.95. Shipping extra.
EDC Publishing, Division of Educational Development Corporation, 10302 East 55th Place, Tulsa, OK 74146. (800) 475-4522. Fax: (800) 747-4509. Web: www.edcpub.com.

CHAPTER 47

Music History & Appreciation

There *was* music before Madonna, Hootie and the Blowfish, and the artist formerly known as Prince and now known as "squiggle." Honest. Check it out!

Discovering Music of the Ages

Here is a truly remarkable music program. **The Basic Library of the World's Greatest Music** from World's Greatest Music is an 18-cassette collection of the greatest classic compositions, stored in a specially designed carrying case. At $144, this tape set is a great buy for the excellent music alone. Figure it out for yourself—that's only $8 per cassette!

But the cassettes are not all you can get! Basic Library of the World's Greatest Music is a complete classical music curriculum. Other components available are:

- Teacher's edition containing timetable charts, 31 chapters on the composers and their music, composer's pronunciation guide, a very helpful Music Glossary, 62 cooperative learning activities, suggestions for users, compendiums (comprehensive synopses of the lives of the great composers presented in an easily remembered format), answers to the questions in the chapters, word searches and crossword puzzles.
- Student Workbook of word searches and crossword puzzles
- Student Textbook containing Time table charts, the composers and their music, compendiums, music glossary.
- Video library
- Lecture Guide—This guide is designed to be used with the video series, but can be used by itself as a lecture tool.
- CD-ROM—the CD-ROM allows students to enjoy and learn about classical music on their computers. The CD contains key elements from the student textbook, more than 6 hours of classical music, and dozens of nature scenes.

Basic Library of the World's Greatest Music

Grades 5–adult. Teacher's edition, $33. Textbook, $25. Workbook, $4.50. Audio library, $144. Video library, $200. Lecture guide, $20. CD-ROM, $50. Shipping extra. *World's Greatest Music, PO Box 747, Lobeco, SC 29931. Orders: (800) 414-8003. Inquiries: (843) 846-1213. Fax: (843) 846-1324. Email: amw-lee@webtv.net. Web: www.amusicworld.com.*

Timetable charts in the teacher's edition include one each for the Baroque, Classic, Romantic, and Modern periods. They show the chief styles, chief vocal forms and instrumental forms, great composers of the period, and what was happening in literature, philosophy, architecture, the other arts, and general history of each period. This section is introduced with an ultra-simplified time-table showing all four periods at a glance—ideally suited for introducing anyone to music history.

Each chapter on a composer begins with an outline portrait and a brief outline of his life, followed by a more in-depth biography. Next comes a brief overview of the composer's works contained in the Basic Library. This is followed by listening activities and related activities, such as making up a story to go with the music, a short list of questions to ask the student about the composer's life and the musical selections, a word search, and a crossword puzzle.

NEW!
Calvert School's Melody Lane video program

Grades K–3. $150. Free shipping, domestic USA or regular surface mail to foreign addresses. *Calvert School, 105 Tuscany Rd., Baltimore, MD 21210. Orders: (888)487-4652. Inquiries: (410) 243-6030. Fax: (410) 366-0674. Email: inquiry@calvertschool.org. Web: www.calvertschool.org.*

World's Greatest Music is very easy to use. You can pick it up when you have time, work through a composer, and put it down until you again feel the energy to tackle musical studies. In the meantime, you simply play the cassettes you have studied or are about to study until they are second nature to the children.

The only other program that even comes close to this is Cornerstone Curriculum Project's Music and Moments with the Masters.

You might want to supplement Basic Library with Betty Carlson and Jane Stuart Smith's *A Gift of Music: Great Composers and Their Influence* (Crossway Books: $12.95 for the new edition) which gives more nitty-gritty details of the composers' lives and shows how their relationship to Christ, or rebellion from Christianity, affected their music. This book is included in the Cornerstone Curriculum Project program. *Mary Pride*

The 13-video library in the Basic Library of the World's Greatest Music includes: Handel's *Water Music*, Mozart's *Symphony No. 40 in G-Minor*, Schubert's *Unfinished Symphony*, Chopin's *Concerto No. 1 in C Minor*, Liszt's *Triangle*, Tchaikovski's *Symphony No. 6 in B Minor*, Haydn's *London*, Beethoven's *Eroica*, Mendelsshon's *Scotch*, Schumann's *Concerto in A Minor*, Brahms's *Symphony No. 1 in C Minor*, Dvorak's *From the New World*, and Summary Video. The classical music selection is played while the video shows pictures of classical art, nature scenes, or both.

Calvert School's "Melody Lane" video program is an excellent resource for teaching many children at once. Melody Lane, with its Misterogers/Sesame Street format, is designed for young children. Although older children find some of the segments a bit too precious, most of the lessons interest all age groups.

Basically, Melody Lane is a 32-lesson, six-video music-literacy video curriculum with lots of enrichment ideas in the accompanying manual. The first five lessons, introducing the instrument families, come from the Calvert First Grade supplement video program. After this, you learn about rhythm, beat, tempo, duration, and melody. An introduction to American and foreign folk music follows, then uses of music (movement, dramatic improvisation, and dance), two really fun segments on people who make instruments and how to make your own homemade instruments, four segments on famous composers (Bach and Handel, Mozart, Beethoven, and Aaron Copland), and four more segments on how to make and use various kinds of music (singing together, playing together, music as expression, music that tells a story, and music in religion).

I have not listed *all* the segments, but this will give you a fair idea.

Music styles covered emphasize the classical and folk side, but you'll find brief pop and jazz sequences as well.

All Calvert products are of excellent quality, and Melody Lane is no exception. The guidebook is first-class, with a week's worth (at least) of teaching tips and follow-up suggestions for each video segment. The video segments themselves are TV quality. These are not "talking-head" lectures, but visits to musicians' studios, demonstrations of musical techniques, play-along games, and much more.

Our family as a whole enjoyed the portions with professional musicians more than the segments featuring kids being taught by teachers. Marcy Marxer and Cathy Fink were *great* demonstrating folk instruments and American folk songs!

Your family won't learn how to read or play music from this series, unless you count those homemade instruments, but they *will* have a lot of fun and become musically literate. *Mary Pride*

Classical Kids' *Beethoven Lives Upstairs*, in my opinion the best title in this series, weaves the facts of the composer's life and excerpts from his works around the life of a fictional child. It is available both in video and audiocassette form.

Other music education titles available from Classical Kids:

- *Mr. Bach Comes to Call* (Bach and a magical orchestra and choir return from the grave to encourage a little girl to keep up her piano lessons)
- *Mozart's Magic Fantasy* (with the help of an overplayed conductor, a cutesy dragon, and a Dudley Do-Right variety prince, a young girl explores the world of Mozart's *Magic Flute*)
- *Vivaldi's Ring of Mystery* (a magical violin helps call a young orphan girl, Katrina, to the side of her long-lost grandfather)
- *Hallelujah Handel* (Katrina finds an otherwise mute orphan boy who sings like an angel, and through the magic of music he regains his speech)
- *Tchaikovsky Discovers America* (a girl and boy take the composer on a trip to Niagara Falls)
- New (and not seen yet by us): *Mozart's Magnificent Voyage*

Each audiocassette includes many excerpts from famous pieces by the composers. Oddly, the pieces are not played in reference to the composer writing them, or even introduced by name on the recording. They are mostly used as "mood music."

The teacher's guide includes plans for 45–minute lessons, including guided parent/child discussion. Additional activities and tidbits of social history, language arts, writing, geography, drama, dance, art, and thinking skills are also included. Most of the educational value of this series is in fact in each teacher's guide, in my opinion, since the storylines themselves blur fact and fiction.

Chronologically speaking, the first recordings in this series mentioned God when appropriate, while the later ones seem to go out of their way to leave Christianity out in favor of fantasy and magical elements. Also, in most cases, the music is used as a backdrop to the story, rather than individual pieces being identified and introduced. Frankly, I don't see what the big deal is about this series (with the exception of *Beethoven*). *Mary Pride*

Even parents with little musical experience can expect success as they and their children learn music together with games, singing, instruments, and music appreciation. Here is a complete music curriculum, scope, and sequence, for grades K–4.

God Made Music was originally intended for Christian schools, but will work well for homeschool. The music chosen for listening is of the standard classical repertoire, and the songs vary from old-fashioned nursery rhymes and folk songs to hymns and Christian holiday songs, carefully chosen to match the time of year. The authors add their own compositions to round out the program, designed to teach and reinforce specific skills.

Skills and concepts taught include intervals, rhythms, melodies, harmonies, basic keyboard, flutophone, and recorder. You will need a separate (inexpensive) student book for each student. *Anne Brodbeck*

NEW!
Classical Kids
Grade K–6. Cassettes, $10 each. CDs, $17 each. Teacher's guide, $10–$15 each. Shipping extra. *In the United States: Rounder Mail Order, 1 Camp Street, Cambridge, MA 02140. (800) 443-4727. Fax: (617) 868-8769. Web: www.rounder.com. The Children's Group Inc., 1400 Bayly Street, Suite 7, Pickering, Ontario Canada L1W 3R2. From the USA: (800) 385-6612. (905) 831-1995. Fax: (905) 831-1142. Web: www.childrensgroup.com.*

NEW!
God Made Music series
Grades K–4. Student books, $4.98. Teacher's edition, $10.98. Sing-along or classical listening cassette, $7.98. CDs $12.98 each. Shipping extra. *Praise Hymn, Inc., PO Box 1325, Taylors, SC 29687. (800) 729-2821. Fax: (864) 322-8284. Email: prazhyminc@aol.com. Web: www.praisehymninc.com.*

NEW!
The Joy of Music

All ages. $20 each video plus shipping. Free catalog.
The Joy of Music, PO Box 5564, Bloomington, IN 47407. (800) 933-4844 (ask for Donna).

NEW!
Lives of the Musicians

Grades 3–12. $20 plus shipping.
ISBN: 015-248-0102.
Harcourt Brace, 6277 Sea Harbor Dr., Orlando, FL 32887. (800) 543-1918. Fax: (800) 235-0256. Web: www.harcourtbrace.com.

NEW!
Making Music with John Langstaff

Ages 3–7 & 7–11. Making Music With Children (Programs 1 & 2), $24.95 each or $44.95 for both. Making Music in the Classroom (Programs 3 & 4), $29.95 each or $54.95 for both. Let's Sing! and Let's Keep Singing! (Programs 5 & 6), $19.95 each, $35.95 for both.

"The woman with flying feet" is how my kids describe Diane Bish. It's an apt description; she's the only person I know who can seemingly dance while seated behind an organ. Diane Bish is a concert and recording artist, composer, conductor, and international television personality. And each of her half-hour long television shows are now available on home video!

The following **Joy of Music** series are available (each video in the series can be purchased separately). **Music & the Bible** is a 12-video series which explores scriptures from the Old and New Testament which relate to praising God through instruments and song. A single instrument (harp, flute, strings & organ, bells, trumpets, etc.) is featured on each video, with one video featuring various instruments. **Musical Journeys** is a 20+ video series that will take you around the world. You will be able to "travel" with Diane Bish to cathedrals, cities, villages, and museums in such exotic places as Austria, England, Germany, Holland, and France. The **Great Composers** series features musical biographies of Bach, Handel, Mozart, and favorite hymn writers, both men and women. The **Christian Artist** series features nine different classical performers who discuss their faith with Diane Bish. **Great Cathedrals: Monuments of Faith** is a great way to learn the history of 30 of the world's great cathedrals and the faith of their builders.

Diane Bish does a masterful job of weaving together history, music, and Scripture. If you're looking for a way to get your kids excited about organ music while they "travel" around the world, and if you'd like their musical education to be punctuated by Scripture, these videos may be exactly what you're looking for! *Rebecca Livermore*

As you might suppose from the subtitle—"Good Times, Bad Times (And What the Neighbors Thought)"—this is a delightful collection of very brief biographies of the great composers, both classical and contemporary. While it has all the appearance of a coffee table book, **Lives of the Musicians** is a valuable tool for homeschool parents who know the virtue of rounding out the curriculum with good old fashioned story-telling.

The text is written in a friendly, almost conversational, style and each story is accompanied by a caricature watercolor worthy of its subject. Some of these, like the stories, don't flatter their subjects overmuch, but all are amusing.

While *Lives of the Musicians* doesn't suggest how you should use it, some possibilities leap from the page into your imagination. Try using the stories as "rewards" for identifying a piece of music by a given composer. You can let the composer's work continue playing while you treat your child to the companion story.

A word of caution is in order: Some of these folks were not as glorious as their music. Not all of the great composers were exemplary role models. *Tony Silva*

You have seen the news reports linking excellence in academics to early musical training. **The Langstaff Project** is the product of one of these researchers, Elizabeth Lloyd Mayer, Ph.D. and well-known music educators John and Nancy Langstaff. Four 60-minute videos, two 45-minute videos, four research-based how-to booklets, two curriculum guides by John and Nancy Langstaff, and a song booklet that comes with each tape all help teachers, librarians, or parents to develop a home music program.

Mr. Langstaff is a warm, grandfather figure who can inspire and reassure children and adults in their ability to join in and make music all together. He shows how to develop skills like singing on pitch, developing complex rhythm patterns, part singing, playing simple musical instruments, and moving to music. The music comes from many cultures, including folk songs, nursery rhymes, jingles, street vendor calls, traditional children's spirituals, and a song with Native American spiritual roots.

If you're longing for a break from TV-styled animation-learning, and like me you value warmth, quietness, sincerity, and quality teaching, you'll love this series. *Anne Brodbeck*

If you're looking for a real classical music curriculum with Christian content, that you can teach almost entirely by just turning on your cassette or CD player, here it is!

Cornerstone Curriculum Project's **Music & Moments with the Masters** series is a five-year music curriculum. Year 1 features J.S. Bach, Handel, Haydn, and Mozart. Year 2 has Beethoven, Schubert, Verdi, and Mendelssohn. Year 3 it's Schumann, Chopin, Verdi, and Grieg. Year 4 you get Wagner, Brahms, Tchaikovsky, and Dvorak. Year 5 is a four-part study called "Classical Composers and the Christian Worldview," an analysis of musical style in different periods based on the ideas of Dr. Francis Schaeffer. For each musician you get one professionally-narrated cassette tape that tells the story of the man's life interspersed with excerpts from pieces he composed during the period being narrated. You also get a second tape of the master's "Greatest Hits." Each year, then, has eight tapes in all. *The Gift of Music: Great Composers and Their Influence* (Crossway Books) also now accompanies this series.

Our resident Charlotte Mason expert recommends taking one composer at a time and playing their work extensively. That approach works great with this curriculum. For example, in Year 1, first you play Bach recordings for a month, then Handel for a month. Month 3 you play selections from the first two months, and the kids get to guess who is the mystery composer! In month 4, you play Handel, then in month 5 it's mystery composer month again, this time reviewing all the works studied to date. And so on.

The first four years of this curriculum use cassettes published by Allegro and Sony Records. The quality is superb, and they have great kid-appeal. Year 5 is currently being redesigned, since the recordings previously used have gone out of print. *Mary Pride*

Although **Music Homestyle** is billed as a progressive curriculum guide, it works more like a launch pad. The guide includes all the materials you need to start your own musical adventure. The five brief lesson plans cover patriotic music, reading music, famous composers, instruments, and storytelling music.

Author Robin Mazo explains in her introduction: "As with any curriculum, this is only a starting point. I encourage you to dig deeper and research more material . . ." Digging deeper is easy with this approach. Each topic is covered with just enough depth to gently nudge your curiosity. Take the National Anthem for example. It's generally known that few Americans can actually sing "The Star Spangled Banner." Even fewer are aware of its overtly religious lyrics, probably considered "unconstitutional" in a traditional public school setting. Each of the patriotic songs is introduced by a brief story, and all lyrics are included—even those that may frighten the political revisionists.

Reading music is covered in much the same way. Brief introductions provide you with enough information to launch your own studies of sound, music theory, and rhythm. All lessons have related worksheets, which are often starting points in themselves.

Additional books of words and music, $4.95 each; set of 4 Instructional booklets, $4.95. *Langstaff Video Project, 337 17th St., #207, Oakland, CA 94612. (510) 452-9334. Fax: (510) 452-9335. Email: sfbayrevels@earthlink.net.*

NEW!
Music & Moments with the Masters series
Grades K–12. Year 1, $55. Years 2–4, $45 each. Year 5, $TBA. Price listed is for cassettes; add $20 per year for CDs. Add 10% shipping. *Cornerstone Curriculum Project, 2006 Flat Creek, Richardson, TX 75080. (972) 235-5149 M–W 1–5. Fax: (972) 235-0236. Email: dquine@cornerstonecurriculum.com. Web: www.cornerstonecurriculum.com.*

NEW!
Music Homestyle Book 1
Grades 1–8. $15.95 plus shipping. *From the Robin's Nest, 10181 Tulane Dr., St. Louis, MO 63123. (314) 849-1587.*

The section on great composers gives a brief biographical sketch of each composer, with a suggested list of great themes at the bottom of each page. No audio is included; that would take away the fun of going to the library to check out a recording of *Suite in A minor* and a biography of Bach.

Instruments of the orchestra are presented along with suggested recordings which feature key instruments. The orchestra is divided into sections of related instruments, much as it would appear on stage. Again, you're launched into another adventure with a suggestion to visit an orchestra.

The guide concludes with a few stories about how music tells stories. *Peter and the Wolf, Grand Canyon Suite,* and *The William Tell Overture* are among the featured story-telling pieces. Books II and III are being developed and will offer different material using the same format.

Music Homestyle is an excellent way to bring the whole family into the experience of learning about music. It's approach is ideal for people who are more in need of seed-thoughts than the hand-holding offered by more traditional music programs. *Tony Silva*

NEW!
Tubby the Tuba and Friends
Grades 1–6. CD, $15.99. Cassette, $9.99.
Angel Records, 304 Park Avenue South, New York, NY, 10010. Available in book and music stores.

Do you desire to expose your children to the beauty and splendor of a symphonic orchestra but shudder at the thought of having to control their wiggles and giggles for two solid hours? Relax! Your journey into the world of the orchestra won't require expensive tickets or fancy patent-leather shoes. Interested? Good! Throw a blanket on the living room floor, put jammies on the kids, plug in the CD player, and prepare to meet "Tubby the Tuba."

Tubby the Tuba and Friends will help your child learn the sounds of the orchestra's instruments and discover which of them are likely to play fast, slow, high, or low. The recording is over an hour long. Tubby's story is woven into the following five songs: *Tubby the Tuba, The Story of Celeste, Adventures of a Zoo, Peepo the Piccolo,* and *Tubby the Tuba Meets a Jazz Band.* The music is performed by the Radio Orchestra of Bratislava under the direction of Stephen Gunzenhauser. The stories are written by Paul Tripp.

As an added bonus, the CD contains a booklet that opens up to a two-sided poster with the text of each piece on one side and cartoon characters of the instruments on the other side.

This recording is an updated version of an old favorite. It has been around for over forty years and has sold more than ten million records and books, introducing millions of young children to the wonders of the orchestra. Perhaps your child will also enjoy a journey into the world of musical instruments with Tubby the Tuba. *Rebecca Livermore*

NEW!
Tune In!
Three grade levels: K–2, 3–5, and 6–8. $44.95.
Parker Publishing Company, Order Processing Center, PO Box 11071, Des Moines, IA 50336. (800) 947-7700. Fax: (515) 284-2607. Web: www.phdirect.com.

Tune In! is the best music resource I have seen yet. Billed as a "Music Listening Discovery Kit," Tune In is a full music curriculum in one attractive vinyl case with three 60-minute tapes and a large-format paperbound book. There is a wide variety of music—folk, classical, instrumental, and vocal to illustrate musical principles.

The vocalist has a delightful voice, and the musicians are superb. The program engages children on an adventure of learning to develop musical awareness, ability, understanding and enjoyment. Plus, it isn't boring or annoying to adult listeners.

The author freely uses humor, games, and dance to interest the students.

The cassette tapes are crowded with an incredible amount of music, enough to last for almost a year of music theory on any of three levels, kindergarten through junior high. The author, Marie Meachen, is an accomplished musician and writes primarily for music teachers, so those parents who are inexperienced with music may have to seek outside help in using this curriculum.

Improvements: Rather than simply referring to "Tape One, Side One," many people would appreciate having the specific location on the tape. Musically inexperienced teachers could benefit from a few more specific explanations of some topics. *Anne Brodbeck*

Starting with music in the ancient world and proceeding to the different kinds of music around the world, this lively, colorful book covers music history from the Middle Ages to the present, including opera and a look at the orchestra. Musical techniques, instruments, and great composers are all introduced.

Like all the other Usborne books, the illustrations and quality of information in **Usborne Story of Music** are both fascinating and exceptional. You won't find a simpler, more fascinating introduction to music history anywhere. *Mary Pride*

If you're thinking "nursery rhymes," think again. Music history includes the history of children's music—and learning to sing classic children's songs is a great way to begin making music. Wee Sing authors Pam Beall and Susan Nipp have performed the formidable task of collecting the best classic children's music, arranging it into sensible order, and producing it with panache.

The **Wee Sing series** now includes the original *Wee Sing, Wee Sing Children's Songs and Fingerplays, Wee Sing and Play, Wee Sing Silly Songs, Wee Sing Around the Campfire* (this includes a section of campfire gospel songs), *Wee Sing Nursery Rhymes and Lullabies* (a story motif holds the songs together), *Wee Sing for Christmas, Wee Sing Bible Songs, Wee Sing America, Wee Sing Fun and Folk, Wee Sing Dinosaurs, Wee Sing Around the World, Wee Sing More Bible Songs,* and their latest production, *Wee Sing for Baby.*

Each cassette comes with an illustrated songbook containing all the songs on cassette, plus some extra. The presentation is so varied and excellent and the price so right that these are the best-selling children's cassettes today.

The *Wee Sing Together* video includes 21 songs from the series embedded in a fantasy plot about a little girl's birthday party. Other videos in this series are: *King Cole's Party, Grandpa's Magical Toys, Wee Sing in Sillyville, The Best Christmas Ever!, Wee Sing in the Big Rock Candy Mountains, Wee Sing in the Marvelous Musical mansion, The Wee Sing Train,* and *Wee Sing Under the Sea. Mary Pride*

Usborne Story of Music

Grades 4–12. $6.95 plus shipping. *EDC Publishing, Division of Educational Development Corporation, 10302 East 55th Place, Tulsa, OK 74146. (800) 475-4522. Fax: (800) 747-4509. Web: www.edcpub.com.*

UPDATED!
Wee Sing series

Ages 2–8. Wee Sing book/cassette sets, $9.95 each. Book/CD sets, $12.95 each. Book alone, $2.95 each. Wee Sing videos $14.95 each (VHS or Beta). *Putnam Publishing, 405 Murray Hill Pkwy., East Rutherford, NJ 07073. (800) 788-6262. Fax: (201) 896-8569. Web: www.penguinputnam.com.*

CHAPTER 48

Social Skills

"But what about socialization?"
We homeschoolers each have our list of favorite responses to this perennial question. But before we fall back too readily on our fund of quips and serious responses, let's take a minute to make sure we *are* doing a good job in this area.

Face it, kids aren't born with good manners or the ability to graciously stand up for their principles. Restaurant etiquette, shopping etiquette, church etiquette, and play etiquette have to be *learned*. Handling peer pressure is hard for adults; kids need to learn effective techniques in this area as well.

This may be the most life-changing chapter of this book, especially for those of us parents who had to pick up the social skills we possess out of thin air. We *can* do better than this for our own kids. Here's how.

Social Skills Training for Kids

"Feelings are wonderful . . . They aren't necessarily good or bad, they just are." So begins the **ABC Feelings** tape and your journey into the wonderful world of psychology.

Each page shows a letter of the alphabet with an accompanying feeling. *A* is for acceptance, *B* is for brave, *C* is for confused, and so on. A line drawing shows a young child experiencing that feeling. Here's a sample page: "L is for loving," it says. The picture shows a boy stroking his pet turtle. "I love my turtle just the way he is." The book guides you in the parent exchange. You say, "See that child petting his turtle, because he feels loving towards it. Once when I felt loving . . . " Now you share an incident in your life when you felt loving. Then you say, "Can you think of a time when you felt loving?" You wait for your child to answer. "Sounds like you felt warm and full of goodness, like everything was wonderful in your world. So now we know what that feeling is when we feel loving." You discuss other feelings that begin with *L*. After the discussion, your child can color the provided blank page. The book can be used alone or with the cassette tape. The tape has the author and two young children discussing their feelings and includes more advice on how to listen and discuss. Music accompanies each feeling.

Socialization = training kids not to rock the boat in a socialist state. (I know that's not the dictionary definition, but think about it!)

Social skills = the ability to interact graciously with others.

NEW!
ABC Feelings: A Coloring/Learning Book and ABC Feelings: A Fun Adventure into Music and Sound!
Ages 3–8. Book, $7.95. Cassette, $10.95. Both, $16.95. Shipping extra. *ABC Feelings, Inc., PO Box 2377, Coeur d'Alene, ID 83816-2377. Orders: (800) 745-3170. Inquiries: (208) 762-3177. Fax: (208) 772-0411. Email: feelings@iea.com. Web: www.home-school.com/Mall/ABCFeelings.html. Server is case sensitive.*

The author's goal is for children to develop a sense of empowerment, to avoid the role of victim, and to take responsibility for their feelings, to live a life of harmony and cooperation and to be in touch with their feelings. As a parent, you are to be a role model teaching responsibility, self-reliance *á la* Thoreau, and self-love.

If this sort of thing appeals to you, then you won't be disappointed. *Marla Perry*

"Mama! He took my toy!" "Well, he took it from me first!" "That's because he wasn't playing with it right!" I don't know about you, but I get tired of those interactions. **The Brother-Offended Checklist** is a tool that you can use to teach your children to implement Scriptural principles in response to those who have offended them and to confess and repent of sin. Furthermore, these materials will help you to act as a righteous judge and discipline in a godly way, rather than just to react. ("Can't you see that I'm busy? Here, if you're going to fight over that toy, just give it to me and go to your rooms!")

This spiral-bound book, written in beautiful calligraphy with line drawings, can be used by your entire family. Many Scriptures and Biblical examples are included. The 16 x 22" chart is a visual reminder for your children—showing the nine steps an offended child is to follow and including five steps to encourage the offender to repent. It has cartoon illustrations for each step and lists a number of Bible verses. *Rebecca Prewett*

"Self-Help for Kids," the trademark of Free Spirit Publishing, might seem unnecessary for homeschoolers—we go out of our way to protect and help our children ourselves. But if the little terror at co-op just won't let up, some tips in the **Bullies Are a Pain in the Brain** book may help.

No, bullies do not all have low self-esteem, but they do all want more power. And no, they won't necessarily go away if you ignore them, so then what can you do? This line-drawing-illustrated 120-page paperback blasts myths about bullies and offers coping strategies—run, find an adult, take self-defense classes. Note: includes slang you might not want in your home, "hip" tone. *Cindy Marsch*

Want to teach your kids basic rules of Christian behavior without a lot of fuss? Gregg Harris's **21 House Rules Preschooler's Training Kit** is for you! This wonderful kit provides a framework of totally reasonable rules for behavior that children themselves will agree with! Rules like, "We obey our Lord Jesus Christ . . . We do not hurt one another with unkind words or deeds . . . When someone is sorry, we forgive him . . . When we have work to do, we do it without complaining . . . When we take something out, we put it away." Following these simple rules will eliminate 80 percent of the parent-child strife around your house. Of course, *you will have to obey the rules too!* The kit comes with a reproducible training manual/coloring book that illustrates all 21 rules (some great drawings by Gregg's son Joshua), a laminated (jelly-proof) 21 House Rules Master Sheet to post on your fridge or bulletin board, 21 individual rule posters, and complete instructions. Over 3,000 satisfied families have used it. Very highly recommended.

Rules for Friends is just exactly what every family needs to keep "socialization" from becoming a social disease! Following the same format as the 21 *House Rules Preschool Training Kit, Rules for Friends* trains your chil-

NEW!
The Brother-Offended Checklist

All ages. $7.50 plus shipping.
Doorposts, 5905 SW Looking Glass Dr., Gaston, OR 97119. Phone/fax: (503) 357-4749. Email: Doorposts@juno.com. Web: www.lyonscom.com.

NEW!
Bullies Are a Pain in the Brain

Grades 3–7. $9.95 plus $3.25 s/h.
Free Spirit Publishing, 400 First Ave. N., Ste. 616, Minneapolis, MN 55401. (800) 735-7323. Fax: (612)337-5050. Email: help4kids@freespirit.com. Web: www.freespirit.com.

Gregg & Joshua Harris Child Training Kits

Ages 2–16. 21 House Rules Preschooler's Training Kit, Uncommon Courtesy for Kids, Rules for Friends $14.95 each. Shipping extra.
Noble Publishing Associates, PO Box 2250, Gresham, OR 97030. Orders: (800) 225-5259. Inquiries: (503) 667-3942. Fax: (503) 618-8866.

dren how to treat their friends and lets the children's friends know what is expected of them when they visit your home. This one is designed for somewhat older children.

Finally there's **Uncommon Courtesy for Kids**, co-authored by Gregg and Joshua. This "training manual for everyone" introduces the concept of courtesy to both kid and adult readers, then gives Six Manners of Speech, Four Words to the Wise, Five Rules for Public Transportation, Six Ways to Be Considerate to Adults, Six Table Manners, Phone Manners, How to Take a Phone Message, Seven Rules for Going to Church, Eight Rules for Traveling in the Car, Four Awkward Things That Happen to Everybody, and more! Each set of rules is illustrated with examples of people of all ages following (or not following!) the rules. Parents are also told how to train kids gently in these rules. Knowing what a wicked world this is, Gregg also includes instructions in when *not* to obey or follow adults. You'll get a lot more out of *Uncommon Courtesy* if you get the complete kit, which includes not only the basic coloring book manual but also a laminated poster summarizing all the rules and individual "rules" posters, plus instructions in how to use these materials to help your kids actually learn to be courteous. *Very* highly recommended! *Mary Pride*

No, this is not a game on etiquette while visiting the jungle; unless your everyday life with the children resembles a jungle! **Jungle Etiquette** is a wonderful board game that employs a jungle theme to teach proper etiquette to everyone playing. The aim of the game is to earn $10,000 or acquire the four royalty cards (throne, staff, crown, and robe) and make it to the top of the jungle temple first.

How do you earn the royalty cards or money? You roll the dice, move that number of spaces, and have another player read the etiquette question on the corresponding "animal" card. You earn gemstones (money) for each correct answer. The amount you earn corresponds to which animal the card was for. The royalty cards are earned when you land on the "Gorilla Wisdom" spaces. And, instead of a "go to jail" space, you have two Quicksand spaces, where you lose one turn, and a Hyena space. The hyena cards represent poor manners, thus you either lose a turn or a gemstone.

This is a fascinating way to teach proper etiquette to your children. Sometimes you take it for granted that they know all the basics and fail to teach some of the more specific things, such as the proper way to set a table for a formal dinner party. That question is included, along with the meanings of "a la carte" and "RSVP," the proper way to blow your nose in public, and much more.

It's never too early to teach proper etiquette. Our kids really enjoyed this game. And, as long as you have someone who can read the questions to them, even the littler guys can join in.

The only drawback is the length of time it takes to acquire the necessary gemstones and/or royalty cards. The game seems to drag on a little long for the younger kids and even the older ones get impatient for it to end soon. But don't you just love the company's phone number! *Barbara Buchanan*

Character training materials tend to start with character traits—from *inside* the student. Etiquette materials start with behavior—what the student *does*. Oddly, this often is more effective, especially when students are taught the reasons *why* they should follow the rules of etiquette.

Etiquette is really all about doing unto others as you would have done unto you. It's about being kind, considerate, thoughtful, respectful, helpful, generous, grateful, obedient to proper authority, protective of other's property and rights . . . Does this begin to sound like character training after all?

NEW!
Jungle Etiquette: the Game

Grade 2 and up. $29.95 plus shipping.

Youth Advantage, 22431-B160 Antonio Parkway, Suite 418, Rancho Santa Margarita, CA 92688. (888) IMPOLITE. Fax: (949) 589-2775.

NEW!
Oops, Your Manners Are Showing

Ages 4–7. Preschool teacher's book, $9.95. "Manners Can be Fun" audiocassette, $4.95.

Ages 8 and up. Student book, $11.95. Teacher book, $14.95. Shipping extra.

The Oops Group, Inc., PO Box 5868, Katy, TX 77491-5868. (888) 749-OOPS (6677) or (281) 347-1244. Fax: (281) 347-1277.

The "Oops" approach is available for two age groups:

- *Oops, Your Manners are Showing for Ages 4–7* is the name of the teacher's book for that age group, and *Manners Can Be Fun* is an audiocassette with that song on one side, and the soundtrack to it on the other.
- For ages 8 and up, both a teacher's book (with all sorts of suggested activities) and a student workbook (with some written activities, and all the step-by-step etiquette instructions) are available. Confusingly, they are also both entitled *Oops, Your Manners are Showing for Ages 8 and Up.* Clearly, you will have to specify age level and whether you want a student or teacher book for each book in this series that you order.

Each age level gets lessons on the same eight topics:

- Courtesy Begins at Home (what manners are and why we need to learn them)
- Introductions (how to introduce people to each other)
- Conversation (what's rude and what's not)
- Telephone Etiquette (how to answer the phone, take messages, call for information, and more)
- Guest Relations
- Manners Away from Home
- Table Manners
- Thank-You Notes

NEW!
Polite Moments
Grades 2–12. $2 plus shipping.
Plain Path Publishers, PO Box 830, Columbus, NC 28722. (828) 863-2736. Email: plain@juno.com.

Oops Group certainly thinks so! They have developed a set of etiquette training tools that many homeschoolers are now using. Originally used mostly in Christian classrooms, the "teacher" books include a wide variety of activities, including some (such as skits and team activities) that are unwieldy in the home setting. Italicized instructions provide suggestions for adapting the other activities to teaching one or a few students.

The "student" book (for ages 8 and up) has all the "rules" of etiquette, plus some fill-in-the-blank exercises, for which answers are given in the "teacher" book. The rules are *not* always repeated in the teacher book, so you will need both books. If you only have time to run through the material quickly, you can probably get away with just the student book.

The book for older children also extensively teachers table settings and table manners, course by course and item by item. If you ever wondered what to do with a finger bowl, this is your section. It ends with a "Manners to Grow On" section, with tips for a winning resume, how to behave at a job interview, on-the-job etiquette, and how to behave at weddings, hospital visits, and funerals.

You'll find a few Scripture verses scattered throughout, but mainly, the Oops! materials assume you know why you should be kind, thoughtful, and so forth. If you want to study these subjects in more detail, a good Bible-based character curriculum will complement the Oops! materials nicely.

Manners are important; safety is, too. The "telephone etiquette" section in the "ages 4–7" book teaches children to answer the phone with their own name and does not warn about giving out information to strangers. The book for ages 8 and up doesn't warn against answering with your own name, but does mention that you should not tell callers that you are alone at home. Keep this need for additional safety instruction in mind while using the Oops! curriculum. *Mary Pride*

The little **Polite Moments** booklet gives plenty of Biblical support, encouragement, and admonishment for everyday etiquette, such as "Train yourself to eat things that you don't like," "Always stand and meet the company," and even "Give your mother flowers."

Some might argue that etiquette is a cultural issue that the Bible does not address, and that "give your mother flowers" is found nowhere in Scripture. However, this booklet deals with a much deeper issue than societal norms of behavior—it deals with how the application of Biblical principles will result in actions that are polite and thoughtful. You won't learn about which fork to use at fancy dinners, but you will learn how to be a blessing to others as you treat them with courtesy.

This booklet was written for children, but many adults might benefit from it as well. (I was convicted at a few points.) I don't know about you, but this is a book we could use in our family. *Rebecca Prewett*

Sharon Scott, author of the books below, spent seven years with the Dallas Police Department as director of the First Offender Program. Working with "thousands of young people between the ages of 10 and 16 who had made such poor decisions that they had actually broken a law and been taken into custody (arrested)" she "began seeing that the number-one reason why kids were making bad decisions, including breaking laws, was because they did not know what to say to their friends when begged, bribed, dared, or challenged." It's easy to "Just Say No!" to some creepy guy hanging around the schoolyard, but not so easy to say no to your boyfriend, girlfriend, best friend, or the popular kids in school.

Sharon took this as a challenge to train teens in *positive* peer group techniques and peer pressure *reversal* techniques. So far she has trained over one million kids and adults in these techniques, and written several books, which have garnered endorsements from such sources as the Boy Scouts of America, the U.S. Department of Education, and the National Federation of Parents.

Mrs. Scott's **Positive Peer Groups** book gives instructions in how to set up a positive peer group program in your school. This book doesn't really apply to the home situation, but may be of interest to those of you with school connections. **When to Say Yes and Make More Friends** likewise is advice for kids on how to reach out and make good friends in school. The kids who most need this advice tend to be from broken or otherwise messed-up homes, as is evident by the case histories given.

The second edition of **Peer Pressure Reversal: An Adult Guide to Developing a Responsible Child**, a larger book, explains the Peer Pressure Reversal philosophy to parents and explains how to teach it to the kids, again by role-playing a number of situations. This takes 90-odd pages of the book. Section Four of the book has reinforcement suggestions ranging from the usual behavior modification techniques (positive reinforcement for encouragement and, for discipline, deprivation of privileges) to organized family activities and influencing the child's circle of friends.

Of interest to just about everyone is **How to Say No and Keep Your Friends** (now in its second edition) a book with the same message, but directed to teen and preteen readers. Mrs. Scott's philosophy is, "You can say no to trouble *and* be liked." The book's introduction provides statistics of how many teens get in trouble today and true examples of kids who messed up and then were introduced to her Peer Pressure Reversal system. The system includes these steps: Check Out the Scene (look and listen, ask yourself "Is this trouble?"), Make a Good Decision (think of the consequences on both sides and take action), and Act to Avoid Trouble (what to say and how to say it). This gets really specific. I'll list her 10 peer pressure reversal responses in the sidebar.

Each one of these responses is presented in detail, with cartoon illustrations, examples, and suggestions.

Learn other valuable techniques, such as the Thirty Second Rule (start trying to get out of the situation within thirty seconds or less) and the Two No Rule (never say no more than twice before leaving or changing the subject). This all takes practice, so the book provides numerous role-playing situations for kids to exercise their new skills.

Aside from the assumption that your child will be dating, the only area I really disagree with the author is her belief that *all* jealousy is wrong. Since God Himself is a jealous God, this can't be right. However, she's talking about overcontrolling girlfriends and boyfriends, who have made no marital commitment. With this in mind, her cautions are correct.

Sharon Scott's Peer Pressure Reversal Books

Ages 9 and up. Peer Pressure Reversal and Positive Peer Groups, $14.95 each. How to Say No and Keep Your Friends/How to Say Yes and Make Friends, $11.95 each. Package price for all four books (the "Teen Empowerment Collection"), $39.95. Shipping extra. *Human Resource Development Press, 22 Amherst Rd., Amherst, MA 01002. Orders: (800) 822-2801. Inquiries: (413) 253-3488. Fax: (413) 253-3490. Email: orders@hrdpress.com. Web: www.hrdpress.com.*

10 Peer Pressure Reversal Responses

1. Simply say no
2. Leave
3. Ignore the Peer(s)
4. Make an excuse
5. Change the subject
6. Make a joke
7. Act shocked
8. Use Flattery
9. Suggest a better idea
10. Return the challenge

Sample "Return the Challenge" Responses

When a friend says, "I thought you were my friend. If you were, you'd do this with me," you can use one of several comebacks:

"I am your friend; and that's why I'm not going to do this with you."

"If you were my friend, then you'd get off my back when I say no."

"With friends like you, who needs enemies? Stop trying to get me in trouble!"

"Best friends don't try to boss each other around. Please let me do my own thinking."

If your friend is being really unkind and pushy, a stinger zinger is: *"Who said you were my friend?" (You can soften it, if desired, by laughing.)*

Your child *will* face peer pressure sooner or later—even while living at home, if he has friends from outside the family. *How to Say No* provides the tools needed to resist peer pressure with style. Kids are unlikely to discover such tools on their own. Since the consequences of giving into peer pressure today range from date rape to car accidents to drug addiction to an arrest record, this is nothing to fool around with. I heartily recommend this book to every parent. *Mary Pride*

"Blessed are the peacemakers." The world, unfortunately, is filled with conflict. I was pleased to discover that **The Peacemaker: A Biblical Guide to Resolving Personal Conflict** by Ken Sande (which, while written for adults, formed the basis for this curriculum) was truly Biblical. It began with the concept that even our conflicts with one another can be used to the glory of God. While the book was written by an attorney, it did not only deal with legal conflicts. Instead, many types of relationships and conflicts were used as examples and illustrations. The book is divided into four sections: Glorify God, Get the Log Out of Your Eye, Go and Show Your Brother His Fault, and Go and Be Reconciled. A lengthy index in the back lists the numerous Scripture references used. This is the most exhaustive study of this topic I have ever read. However, it makes interesting, practical, and convicting reading.

Ken Sande's wife has taken this book, simplified it, and come up with a curriculum designed to teach children how to respond to conflict. **The Young Peacemaker** includes moving verse and visually appealing graphics, while the workbook teaches kids the following principles:

- Conflict is like a slippery slope.
- Conflict starts in the heart.
- Choices have consequences.
- Conflict is an opportunity.
- Wise-Way choices are better than my-way choices.
- The blame game makes conflict worse.
- The Five A's can resolve conflict.
- It is never too late to start doing what's right.
- Think before you speak.
- Respectful communication is more likely to be heard.
- A respectful appeal can prevent conflict.
- Forgiveness is a choice.

At first, I wasn't too impressed with these principles. However, I was impressed with the way in which they were developed. Your child will learn what causes conflicts, good reasons for some conflicts (e.g. standing up for righteousness), how to make good choices according to Scripture, how to avoid blaming others, how to seek forgiveness, what repentance really means, how to forgive others, ways to avoid conflict through communication, and how to make a respectful appeal. I have seen some of these issues dealt with superficially in other materials written for children. However, I have never seen such a thorough, Biblical approach that deals with heartfelt attitudes, rather than merely external behavior. This is taught in an interactive, discussion setting, with anecdotes children can appreciate and suggestions for further activities.

The accompanying workbook mostly consists of fill-in-the-blank type worksheets. I'm not much of a worksheet person, so I would probably do without it. I would suggest teaching the 11 lessons over a period of weeks, either as Bible/Character Studies or using it as the basis for a unit study. *Rebecca Prewett*

NEW!
The Young Peacemaker

Ages 9–12. Parent/Teachers Manual, $19.95. Cassette tape and study guide, $14.95. Shipping extra. *Institute for Christian Conciliation, 1537 Avenue D, Suite 352, Billings, MT 59102. (406) 256-1583. Fax: (406) 256-0001. Email: peace@mcn.net. Web: www.hispeace.org.*

CHAPTER 49

Domestic Arts

Cooking! Sewing! Cleaning! Can little kids really learn to do this? Sure!

By the time I was eight, my folks had taught me how to make bacon and eggs and brew their morning coffee. By the time my daughter Magda was nine, she was cooking dinner for the family. By the time my daughter Sarah was 10, she was sewing doll clothes for her little brothers' and sisters' stuffed toys and knew how to clean the bathrooms like a professional.

All of our children have, in their turn, learned how to do household chores from washing the dishes to washing the laundry. In our case it has been a necessity; there's no way I could write books, publish magazines, homeschool, *and* do all the chores for a family of 11 people. But it's also good for the kids. Learning these practical skills earns them self-confidence and helps them get ready for the day when they will have homes of their own.

Making Chores Pleasant
Here are some tips that make it easier to teach kids real-life skills:

1) Carefully explain each step of the job. Then let your youngster try it, with you helping on the tough spots.

2) Repeat step one again.

3) And again.

4) In short, don't expect a one-time lecture to do it all.

5) Count on inspecting their work forever. Everyone loves praise for a job well done, and everyone profits from immediate feedback and suggestions on how to improve a less-than-perfect job.

6) Also count on helping out every now and then, just to show that you're not dumping an unwanted job on the child. When you do the job, do it with great enthusiasm.

7) Have races every now and then. Who can fold the laundry fastest? Who is the fastest dishwasher? When it's impractical to have two or more people competing at once, time each person's work. You can try to beat your own best time, or someone else's. Racing adds energy to a task and also makes it clear how little time a task must take—an important lesson for dawdlers.

8) Important Tip: Insist on a cheerful attitude. I promise you, this will make a real difference!

Is There Life After Housework? video
Who Says It's A Woman's Job to Clean?

Ages 7 and up. Is There Life After Housework? video, $29.95. Who Says It's A Woman's Job to Clean?, $5.95. Shipping extra.
Home Life, Inc., PO Box 1190, Fenton, MO 63026. Orders: (800) 346-6322. Inquiries: (636) 343-7750. Fax: (636) 343-7203. Email: orders@home-school.com. Web: www.home-school.com.

NEW!
Healthy Snacks

Grades 2–8. $6.95.
Warren Publishing, PO Box 2250, Everett, WA 98203. Orders: (800) 773-7240. Inquiries: (206) 353-3100. Fax: (206) 355-7007.

The Kids' Multicultural Cookbook

All ages. $12.95 plus $3 shipping.
Williamson Publishing Company, Church Hill Road, Charlotte, VT 05445. (800) 234-8791. Fax: (802) 425-2199. Web: www.williamsonbooks.com.

KidsCooking

Ages 6 and up. $13.95 plus $3 shipping.
Home Life, Inc., PO Box 1190, Fenton, MO 63026. Orders: (800) 346-6322. Inquiries: (636) 343-7750. Fax: (636) 343-7203. Email: orders@home-school.com. Web: www.home-school.com.

Cleaning

See cleaning expert Don Aslett's techniques demonstrated in front of a live studio audience. Don is a natural comedian and showman—we were falling off our seats laughing the first time we saw the **Life After Housework video**! Kids *love* this video—we've watched it 20 times as a family!

Who Says It's A Woman's Job to Clean? is *the* book for teaching kids how to clean. A fun read with its cartoon-style illustrations, it also presents cleaning techniques in language simple enough for a kid. The streamlined techniques make cleaning much easier and more fun, too. Strange but true: this was my son Joseph's favorite book when he was seven years old! *Mary Pride*

Cooking

Healthy Snacks is a simple cookbook featuring recipes that contain no white sugar or refined flour. The title is a bit of a misnomer since there are several main dishes, soups, and breakfasts included. Nutrition information is given (fat, calories, protein, carbohydrates, and sodium). Although the recipes aren't written specifically to children, most of them are easy enough for children to prepare themselves. There's no reason for homeschool lunches to be boring or humdrum. Try a few of these treats and let others worry about "cafeteria food"! *Renee Mathis*

The Kids' Multicultural Cookbook contains interesting tidbits about kids all over the world, photos of them cooking or eating their native specialties, and recipes so easy that most can be made with little assistance. For creative cooks in your family, there are additional recipes that are a bit more complicated.
The author traveled the globe for one year in search of recipes that would be appealing to other children. A few here and there might be a tad too "exotic" for your tastes, but most of them contain ingredients that can be found in any large grocery store. Hint: Let your kids choose which treats they want to prepare. Their adventuresome choices just might surprise you!
Games, party ideas, traditions, customs, and manners all help to fill out the 160 pages. This one's a lot of fun. *Renee Mathis*

I love it! This is great! It's **KidsCooking: A Very Slightly Messy Manual.** It's bound with wire spirals, printed on wipe-clean heavy-duty cardstock, heavily illustrated with cute and corny full-color drawings, loaded with sensible instructions, and packaged with a "goodie"—a set of colored plastic measuring spoons.

All this nifty packaging wouldn't count unless the recipes were good. They are. Basics like four ways to cook eggs and three recipes for popcorn. Fudge brownies from scratch. Burritos. Spaghetti. Fruit salad. Chocolate chip cookies. Not-so-basics like homemade applesauce and carrot-raisin salad. Something for every meal course and time of day, from early morning breakfast to party desserts. Plus inedibles like play dough, face paint, finger paints, giant soap bubbles, and puppy crackers.

I could swear I've seen every recipe in this book (except the play dough and puppy crackers) at some potluck supper or other over the last 10 years, testifying to the all-American canniness of the recipe choosers. Sixty-eight parent-approved and taste-tested recipes in all, each explained so simply that the average preteen can make 'em. The best kids' cookbook; the bestseller. *Mary Pride*

For years I have been skeptical of unit studies that involve cookery. Usually Mom rushes around supervising the kitchen, and the children end up as go-fers instead of as cooks. But now Usborne has come out with a cookbook that actually makes it easy for children to experience the cuisine of many other countries. **The Usborne Round the World Cookbook** includes:

- Illustrated step-by-step instructions children can follow to create recipes from every major country and all continents. Each country has its own double-page spread.
- Background information on food production in each country.
- Small illustrations showing ethnic costumes for each country.
- Cooking and safety instructions.
- Complete index.

The recipes use readily-available supermarket ingredients, and represent the mainstream cuisine of each country (e.g., Hungarian goulash, Scottish scones). Our girls have made quite a few of them with total success. All the book needs to be perfect is a spiral binding—but for $8.95, who can complain?

Other Usborne cookbooks you might consider: *Hot Things, Party Things*, and *Sweet Things*. ($4.50 each). Small, handy format, with same double-page spread for each recipe. A team of tiny cooks demonstrates exactly how to perform each step. Good choice of recipes. Not as useful educationally as the *Round the World Cookbook*, but a decent introduction to cooking for its own sake. *Mary Pride*

This **Kid Kit** includes the book **Starting Cooking,** a mini-rolling pin, plastic measuring spoons, a wooden mixing spoon, a whisk and an apron. All of the utensils are fine, except the rolling pin, which bruises your fingers if you try to use it, due to it being so small.

The book is really great! It explains basic cooking terms and provides instructions on using the utensils at all points where they are needed. It teaches you how to make many different recipes of different kinds, including 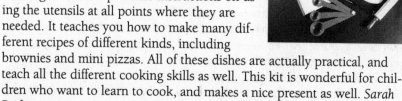 brownies and mini pizzas. All of these dishes are actually practical, and teach all the different cooking skills as well. This kit is wonderful for children who want to learn to cook, and makes a nice present as well. *Sarah Pride*

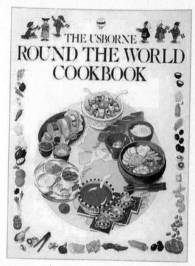

The Friendly Loom

Ages 7 and up. Twenty-four-inch Tapestry Loom, $179.95. 48-inch Tapestry Loom, $208.95. Lap looms: Size A with accessories, $39.95; size B with accessories, $49.95. Peg Loom with accessories, $18.95. Starter Kit, $33.95. Easy Weaver size A, $89.95; Size B, $134.95. Lap Loom Project Kits, $19.95 each. Mini Loom, $16.95. Yarn Ball Packs, $14.95. Shipping extra.
Harrisville Designs, Center Village, Box 806, Harrisville, NH 03450. (800) 338-9415. Fax: (603) 827-3335. Email: info@harrisville.com. Web: www.harrisville.com.

Fabric Arts

Our children have always been fascinated with weaving. One of son Ted's first independent purchases was a pot-holder weaving kit. But pot-holders rather limit the scope of one's imagination, and a real loom is exorbitantly expensive and space-wasting. Not to mention the way the kids would fight over it.

Our kids have all woven serious projects, all at once, on the same loom. How did this happen? The **Friendly Tapestry Loom** from Harrisville Designs. You get a pegged frame that you can adjust up and down, depending on how long you want your finished piece. This rests on a floor stand. You set up the loom quickly by running cotton warp back and forth over the pegs, then select whatever you want to weave through it and weave! Patterns and materials can be as wild or wooly as you wish: feathers, cloth or rag strips, grass bundles, plants, seaweed, twigs, vines, leather or fur strips, plastic bread bags, rolled or twisted paper bags, bead strings, bias tape, ribbons, ric rac, or even yarn! The accompanying booklet tells you how to set up and weave, and gives ideas for patterns. And because the Tapestry Loom is so wide, several children can work side by side on individual projects.

The Tapestry Loom comes in two sizes and new lap versions. The larger looms each have adjustable sides. You loosen or tighten a knob to adjust the height of your weaving space. Each fits flat along a wall when not in use. The lap looms come in a 12 x 16" size (size A) and the larger 14½ x 18½" size B. Each comes with an accessory package that includes one ounce of cotton warp yarn, wool weft yarn (four or six colors depending on size of loom), a plastic needle, wooden shed stick, and 6" wooden stick shuttle. This lap model is definitely preferable for home use. It's cheaper to buy one for each child than to get the floor model, and the lap model is much more portable, easier to store, and prevents sibling rivalry!

The **Peg Loom** uses the same technique as the lap looms, but is smaller and even less expensive.

The **Easy Weaver looms** come set up and ready to use. They work on a different principle from the Tapestry Looms and Lap Looms. These looms lie flat with the warp threads wrapped around two drums at either end. As you finish part of your project, you wind it onto the take up drum and let some more warp thread out of the supply side. The warp threads go through a device called a heddle which looks like a small picket fence—vertical bars with slots between them. Every other thread goes through a hole in one of the bars, and the rest go through the slots in between. You merely move the heddle up or down to spread the warp threads apart then send your shuttle through the gap. Easy Weavers come in two sizes: Size A weaves a cloth 6½" wide, and Size B weaves a cloth 15" wide.

Harrisville Design's **Lap Loom Project Kits** are designed to fit on the lap looms. Each kit includes complete instructions, plus enough 100 percent virgin wool yarn and any other materials necessary to complete the project. So far, nine kits are available. These include: Kit #31—Summer Flowers Mini Purse, Kit #30—Setting Sun Mini Purse, Kit #21—Winter Magic Purse or Pillow, Kit #20—Plumtree Purse or Pillow, Kit #40—Navajo Wallhanging or Pillow Design, Kit #42—Kente Design Pillow, Purse, or Wallhanging, Kit #44—Persian Tapestry or Pillow, and Kit #10—Wooly Sheep Wallhanging or Pillow. *Mary Pride*

If you want to teach your children to sew, look no further. These bright, spiral-bound books lie flat, burst with colorful illustrations, and have what you're looking for. Step-by-step instructions gently build skills in a completely non-threatening way.

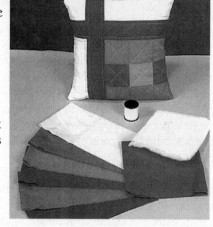

Sewing Machine Fun, the first book in this full-color series, starts by illustrating the parts of a sewing machine and telling you what each is for. You practice sewing first with a maze to stitch on paper. This teaches sewing in a straight line and pivoting your material. More such exercises follow, until following a pattern line becomes as familiar on the sewing machine as it was in handwriting class. Clear instructions show how to thread your machine; then you practice some "dot-to-dot" stitching. If you do it right, you have a picture! A bevy of simple sewing exercises follow, from a fabric greeting card to a "Possibility Pocket."

The other books build on these skills and add more skills and projects. How step-by-step are they? Well, a teenager could definitely teach himself the basics of machine sewing using these books. Younger children will need adult assistance (and a little supervision won't hurt even teens, who have been known to stick their fingers under the needle in the first excitement of sewing).

Book/kit sets, which include all fabric and supplies needed for the projects, are also available. A good deal, unless you enjoy extra trips to the fabric store. *Mary Pride*

My six-year-old son watched a TV show that demonstrated quilting and decided he wanted to make a quilt. Besides taking Home Ec. in eighth grade, I don't know much about sewing and I pictured a lopsided, crooked quilt. **Kids Can Paper Piece** gives instructions on a simple method that can make it possible for a beginner to have a chance to make a nice-looking quilt.

The basic premise is that you photocopy a blackline master and, following the step-by-step instructions in this book, sew the fabric directly to the paper, which is later removed.

The book is written for a child, but is meant to be used with adult assistance. The author gives hints on deciding whether your child is ready. There follow five pages of reproducible blackline masters to use as sewing practice—you actually place the paper in the machine instead of fabric.

The instructions for making the quilts are written in a clear and engaging style, explaining exactly how "paper piece" works and taking you through your first project step-by-step. They are followed by 23 different patterns plus four generic shapes to be used to complete various projects in the book. Many of the projects are simple geometric designs, but there are also some that make pictures such as a jack-o-lantern, Christmas tree and a house. Some patterns are simple and some seem pretty intricate. A good book that does a good job. *Melissa Worcester*

NEW!
The "I'll Teach Myself" series

Ages 7–17. Sewing Machine Fun: book only, $13.95; book/kit, $24.95. More Sewing Machine Fun: book only, $13.95; book/kit, $27.95. Step Into Patchwork: book only, $14.95; book/kit, $28.95. (Prices listed reflect special discount.) Shipping extra. *Farm Country General Store, 412 North Fork Rd., Metamora, IL 61548. Orders: (800) 551-FARM. Inquiries: (309) 367-2844. Fax: (309) 367-2844. Web: www.homeschoolfcgs.com.*

Harrisville Designs also sells the supplies you will need to get started weaving on the bigger models in the form of a Starter Kit. The kit contains four wooden maple shed sticks, four wooden maple stick shuttles, four brightly colored balls of thick 100 percent wool yarn (different colors), and one 440-yard cone of cotton warp. If you run out of yarn, they now sell packs of their 100 percent pure virgin wool, six one-ounce balls per pack.

NEW!
Kids Can Paper Piece

Grades 1–6. $14.95 plus shipping. *Hearts & Hands, 826 E. 49th Street, Indianapolis, IN 46205. (317) 923-7884. Fax: (317) 923-8874. Email: info@heartshands.com. Web: www.heartshands.com.*

First Aid

NEW!
CPR Prompt Home Learning System

All Ages. $60 plus shipping.
Timberdoodle Company, 1510 E. Spencer Lake Rd., Shelton, WA 98584. (360) 426-0672. Fax: (800) 478-0672. Email: mailbag@timberdoodle.com. Web: www.timberdoodle.com.

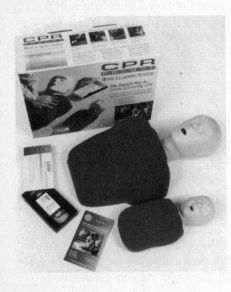

With homeschoolers' families being as large as they are, sooner or later someone is going to have an accident. When someone does almost drown or gets an electric shock and their breathing or heartbeat stops, knowing how to do CPR until the paramedics can get there may be the difference between saving or losing a family member. You could go to a YMCA or to a Red Cross CPR course, if you have these classes in your area and have the time to drive there and take the course, or you could get this kit from The Timberdoodle Company and learn CPR when you want to in the comfort of your home.

The **CPR Prompt Home Learning System** includes two figures with plastic heads and rubber clad bodies. The large figure can be set to simulate an adult (8 years and up) or a child (1 to 8 years old). You use the little figure to simulate doing CPR on an infant. You also get a 43-page Supplemental Learning Guide booklet, CPR Home Learning System video, and three each of Adult/Child and Infant replaceable lung bags. A number is given where you can order additional bags. Besides CPR, the booklet and video also cover rescue breathing (mouth to mouth), conscious choking (Heimlich Maneuver), and unconscious choking (abdominal thrusts).

The video is coded for age group and chapter with colored and numbered hearts in the upper corner of the video picture. Purple is for adults, green for child, and yellow for infant. The conclusion is coded with a blue heart. Each age group has three chapters, the first for CPR and rescue breathing, the second for choking unconscious, and the third for choking while conscious.

Instructions in the booklet are step by step and easy to follow. Each step is illustrated with a diagram. Troubleshooting tips are included for those occasions when things don't happen by the book.

This is a great little kit. I would recommend it for any family who does not have access to this instruction any other way, or who has many members all of whom want to learn these basic life-saving skills. *Bill Pride*

NEW!
Kids to the Rescue

Grades K–6. $7.95. With library binding, $17.95. Add $5 shipping.
Parenting Press, PO Box 75267, Seattle, WA 98125. (800) 992-6657. Fax: (206) 364-0702. Email: office@parentingpress.com. Web: www.parentingpress.com.

Ask your kids what they would do in the following situations: A strange dog bites them, their best friend steps on a rock and begins bleeding, or a younger sibling puts a pair of scissors in an electrical outlet. Did the answers surprise you? Sometimes it's easy to take for granted that our children have absorbed some basic, everyday, common-sense approaches to first aid. Of course this is one area of their education we don't want to intentionally neglect, but where to begin?

Kids to the Rescue is a short book of simple first-aid techniques that even young children can learn. Fourteen scenarios are presented, each with an accompanying pen-and-ink picture and a simple story. Emergencies covered are snake bites, nose bleeds, broken bones, dog bites, eye injuries, bleeding, insect stings, choking, poisoning, electric shocks, burns, unconsciousness, and clothing on fire. Following each situation are two or three illustrated steps a child can take on his own to be of assistance, all of which include going to a grownup for help. For example, in the case of a cut you would apply pressure, elevate, and seek help. The authors recommend that you read the book with your child, look at the pictures, discuss possible solutions, and role-play the first aid steps given on the pages. *Renee Mathis*

CHAPTER 50

Physical Education

For physical fitness, you need both a program that takes you through all the different stretching, strengthening, and coordination skills and a daily (or at least thrice-weekly) program of actual aerobic exercise—preferably exercise that increases your coordination while it tones your heart, lungs, and body. Your home program should not require gym facilities or expensive equipment. It should be tailored for use by individuals or small groups. It also should be interesting enough for your children to want to stick with it.

Community Fitness Options

You might want to work some team sports or YMCA courses into your physical education plan. But don't overdo it. It's easy to get the family's whole life revolving around one or two kids' sports schedules. If all you have is one or two kids, and both parents love to attend sporting events, that might not be so bad, but if you have more, it can be unfair to the less physically-talented kids. In either case, you don't want to forget the "home" in "homeschooling" because you're in the car so much!

Community sports options may not be available year-round. For example, my family pays to enjoy the swimming facilities of a condo development down the road. For less than $20 per person, we get to beat the Missouri summer heat and get some fun outdoor exercise. As long as summer lasts, that is! Come Labor Day, the only way the kids can go swimming is for us to drive them 20 minutes each way to the nearest YMCA. This year we weren't able to afford Y membership on top of the swim club membership, so walking and juggling had to substitute for swimming as the exercise of choice.

Fitness Programs for the Home

Physical education is more than just your favorite form of aerobics, of course. It involves understanding exercise—how and why to warm up, stretch out, and cool down—and how your body reacts—heart rate and body fat targets. It involves a number of skills, from ball handling to gymnastics, that aren't all included in any one sport. It also involves knowing the rules for popular sports. The resources below can help you with all this.

Besides Little League and the Y, here are some other community physical fitness options:

- Taking classes at a local martial arts academy
- Joining a health club (great for Mom and Dad, but probably not an option for young kids)
- Running in (and training for) local run-a-thons
- Walking in (and training for) local walk-a-thons
- Biking in (and training for) local bike-a-thons
- Playing tennis at the park
- Becoming part of the local street hockey scene
- Organizing a weekly pick-up baseball game
- Getting a local public or private school to let you on their sports teams
- Joining a skating club
- Joining a swim club
- Joining a country club (I wish!)

NEW!
All Fit

Ages 4–12. $19.95 each or $59.85 for set. Plus shipping.
Slim Goodbody Corp., PO Box 657, Camden, ME 04843. (888) 484-1100. (207) 230-0399. Fax: (207) 230-0795. Email: slimnyc@aol.com. Web: www.slimgoodbody.com.

Well, let's start with the content. Slim Goodbody, alias John Burstein, is wonderful as the host (and writer) of this series. **All Fit** is an excursion into exercise geared for kids. Slim is a body-suited fitness buff who explains the workings of the skeleton and muscles in a way kids understand and love. His enthusiasm and knowledge will have you pointing and flexing, stretching and rolling with the very first program.

Each program has a theme. Flexibility, Fitness, Balance, Coordination and Agility, are just a few of the topics Slim covers with his All Fit Team. A visit to the Body Lab helps Slim show you the anatomy. He explains these very clearly, using real muscle and bone names. His All Fit Team, made up of studio kids, help keep the pace up as they exercise and learn with Slim.

I thought at first that the segments were too short, but then I realized that many kids don't have the patience for exercise videos. With the anatomy lesson thrown in, and a "that's impossible" demonstration of something no one can do due to anatomical limits, exercise time is down to about five minutes. The length turns out to be just right.

The video set is accompanied by a teacher's guide. Vocabulary, pre- and post-viewing activities, concepts, objectives and activity sheets round out this program. *MacBeth Derham*

NEW!
Chicken Fat Kids—The Youth Fitness Video

Ages 2 and up. $14.95.
Kimbo Educational, PO Box 477, Long Branch, NJ 07740. (800) 631-2187 or (732) 229-4949. Fax: (732) 870-3340.

I guess I am too young to remember the "**Chicken Fat**" song which was popular in the 1960's, written by composer Meredith Wilson. The song in this video is based on that song, and it features children demonstrating the challenging workout developed for President Kennedy's famous youth fitness program. The video opens with a black-and-white clip of children from the 60's participating in the program. The idea is to "give the chicken fat back to the chicken" and your children will be singing "Go, you chicken fat, go!" after watching this video!

The rest of the video features 12 kids and an adult demonstrating various exercises (push-ups, toe touches, knee bends, marching in place, sit-ups, torso twists, pogo springs, jumping jacks, arm circles, bicycle ride, deep breathing, and running in place) with the chicken fat song in the background. The scene is a playground and a marina, with the kids exercising on a large dock. Though the video is 25 minutes long, the children are actually engaged in fast-paced exercising for only about 10–15 minutes of that time.

Safety tips are given before starting, such as drinking plenty of water, not overdoing it and wearing comfortable clothing. After the first round of exercises the kids take a break and hear an explanation of what exercises do for their body, and which parts are benefitted by which exercises. Then the round of exercises is repeated. At the very end you are invited to write in to join a club and "become a chicken fat kid." *Melissa Worcester*

NEW!
Converse All Star series

Grade 3–12. $12.95 each.
John Wiley & Sons, 605 Third Avenue, New York, NY 10158-0012. (800) 225-5945. Fax: (732) 302-2300.

Whether you're new to a sport or simply want to learn how to play better, the **Converse All Star series** of books may be the answer for you.

Each oversized paperback book is packed with history, rules, information on how to improve your technique and interviews with some of the stars of the sport. The first few pages of each book explain the background of the game, its rules, regulations and terminology. The main focus, however, is on techniques and strategy. The series makes good use of its many black-and-white photographs and line drawings to clearly illustrate all of the major points.

The technique and strategy chapters in each of the books vary according to the sport:

- *Converse All Star Baseball*. Batting, running the bases, and each of the positions (with infielders, middle infielders and outfielders grouped into three chapters).
- *Converse All Star Basketball*. Dribbling, passing, shooting, rebounding, offense, and defense.
- *Converse All Star Football*. The quarterback, running backs, receivers, offensive linemen, defense, the kicking game, and the game plan.
- *Converse All Star Soccer*. Training, dribbling, passing, receiving the ball, heading, shooting, goalkeeping, putting it all together, and restarts.

At the end of most chapters are games and exercises designed to strengthen your skills in that area. "Keep Focused" lists end each chapter with highlights to the important points.

Each book contains interviews with at least two heroes in the game, including players and coaches. (The soccer book contains an interview with a female player, but everything else—interviews and pictures—appear to be men.) Also scattered throughout the books are little snippets of fun facts and trivia. Key terms are introduced as they come up and are also contained in a glossary at the end of the book.

Even if you'd rather be playing than reading, these books have plenty of appeal for those times that you're on the sidelines. Each section is headlined to make what you need easy to find and the writing style is active:

"He brings the ball under control but the defense is all over him. He takes a quick dribble and sees an opening. His foot flies back, he kicks the ball, and it sails into the corner of the goal. Score!"

I especially like that teamwork skills resound throughout each of the books as a natural accompaniment to technical skills and positive thinking. Rather than stressing the importance of teamwork, each section talks about how that position or skill is performed in relation to the other players. *Teresa Schultz-Jones*

The books emphasize what players need to think about as they play. For instance, a football receiver must concentrate on: getting in the open to catch the ball, catching it and holding on to it. The books also emphasize what traits are important—in this case, a receiver needs to be "especially courageous," since you'll be catching many balls while you are off-balance and will need to be able to take the "hit." (They do not, however, go into the consequences of what could happen; this is positive thinking all the way!)

Creative Play Areas is a fantastic treasure trove of over 185 easy-to-make, inexpensive projects that families can make together to expand the children's imagination and ingenuity in a creative play environment. Everything from using scarves and hats as props for dramatic play to making your own floor "Road City Map." Find out the creative possibilities lurking in your card table, pillows, and stacks of old tires! Show your children how to make their own bows and arrows, obstacle courses, and instruments. Tons more, plus over 200 charming drawings, photos, and illustrations that show exactly how to do it. Great for kids from preschool to preteen (and even older, if they aren't too busy pretending to be cool).

The author pleads strongly for children to be allowed to be "their own engineers and custom designers," as in the days when kids made their own dolls and treehouses. As she says, "Children need an environment where they help build, where they can change and reconstruct and be responsible." Right on! *Mary Pride*

NEW!
Exercise Program for Young Children

Ages 4 weeks to 4 years. $11.95 plus $3 shipping.
Home Life, P.O. Box 1190, Fenton, MO 63026. Orders: (800) 346-6322. Inquiries: (636) 343-7750. Fax: (636) 343-7203. Email: orders@home-school.com. Web: www.home-school.com.

NEW!
Fitness at Home

Grades 1–12. Parent Kit, $4.75. Student Training Program, $2.95. Fitness Emblem, $2.25. Add 10% shipping.
Fitness at Home, 1084 Yale Farm Rd., Romulus, NY 14541. (315) 585-2248. Email: drk3@cornell.edu.

Fun Physical Fitness for the Home

Ages 0–10. $19.95 plus shipping.
Noble Publishing Associates, PO Box 2250, Gresham, OR 97030. Orders: (800) 225-5259. Inquiries: (503) 667-3942. Fax: (503) 618-8866.

This complete exercise program for children from 4 weeks old to 4 years old is divided by age group, with exercises for each group illustrated by photos of a mother and child doing them. Includes stretching, co-ordination, and strength exercises. Do these and your child will meet all the necessary physical—development timetables—especially important when a child spends most of his time at home and isn't involved in group fitness activities. Excellent, simple, safe. Modest dress throughout. *Mary Pride*

How many times have we sent the kids out to play, called it "physical education" for the day, and felt pretty good about it? When you think about it, we don't approach other subjects in such a haphazard manner, so why should this be any different?

Fitness at Home was designed by author David Kidd (BJU grad., coach, and homeschooling dad) to give children some basic, all-around fitness skills. The goal is not to push or pressure but to provide instruction in a systematic way. Students are expected to exercise five days per week, performing exercises from four different categories: flexibility, abdominal strength, endurance, and arm/shoulder strength. The student training program has a chart to keep track of days and progress, illustrations and descriptions of the different exercises, and a list of memory verses. The chart is reproducible, so the program can be used year after year. The Bible memory verses and discussion topics pertain to self-discipline and perseverance. The program is flexible in that you can substitute other sports activities for the daily requirements.

The parent's manual instructs you on the importance of fitness, how to find your child's target heart rate, and how to administer the pre- and post-tests. The test involves pull-ups (or flexed arm hang), sit-ups, sit and reach, and one-mile run.

The student training chart and a colorful award certificate are included with each Student Training Program. Only one parent's manual is needed per family, and one Student Training Program, but you'll need a new certificate for each participant. The emblem is an optional sew-on patch to identify the student as a participant in this program. There are three different award levels and everyone can earn one. The emphasis isn't worldly at all, rather it is in doing our best for the Lord to take care of the bodies He gave us. *Renee Mathis*

Sono Sato Harris' **Fun Physical Fitness for the Home** is an exercise and physical fitness guide that includes an array of indoor exercises to keep your child busy, active and fit during the long winter months. It is also great for the summer months! Not only does it include basic exercises, it also includes creative ideas to make physical fitness more fun.

Sono Harris draws upon her experience as a student, performer and teacher of ballet, modern dance, creative dance and gymnastics. Her love for dance and gymnastics is apparent throughout the book. The book is only 47 pages long, and includes black and white line drawn illustrations. There is a lot of material included in a small package. It begins with simple exercises like "The Russian Bear," where your child crawls on hands and feet, working up to straight knees and feet flat on the floor. Also included are stretching and tumbling exercises, as well as basic gymnastics. She gives tips on how to incorporate academics into your physical exercise and music programs through creative expression. A CD done by Craig Bidondo is included to provide motivational background music to the exercises.

The program is thorough and fun. It can be done by older children without a lot of supervision, once they learn the basic exercises. *Maryann Turner*

Gibby the Gibborang is a yellow monkey who tries to make exercising fun for children of all ages. This lively and humorous exercise video features Gibby and several of his friends demonstrating aerobic exercises against a jungle backdrop. The total playing time of the video is 45 minutes, with about 30 minutes of actual exercise including warm-up and cool-down. You are meant to exercise right along with the video, while watching Gibby and his friends demonstrate such aerobic moves as picking bananas, squashing mosquitoes (clapping), and monkeying around (monkey arm movements), all done with music in the background. These are not traditional exercises such as push-ups or sit-ups but rather aerobic exercises with a jungle twist.

Before the exercising (or, "Gibby-cizing") starts, Gibby explains some safety rules, encouraging supervision by parents and the advice of a physician before starting, proper clothing, plenty of water and pacing yourself so you don't over-do it. He also talks about ways to test your Exertion Level to make sure you are not working too hard: if you are breathing so hard you are having trouble talking, you should stop; and he demonstrates how to take your pulse and suggests that a parent or teacher should check with your doctor to find out what would be a good pulse rate. *Melissa Worcester*

Physical Education courses designed specifically for homeschoolers are hard to find. This one is top notch! I especially like the "Quick Start" section at the beginning of this spiral-bound 137 page book. This section gives you a jump start when beginning the program. For those of us that get bogged down in the how-tos, this added incentive makes the program very usable.

Home School Family Fitness was written by a homeschooling father of seven children, who just so happens to have a Ph.D. in physical education. He uses both areas of expertise to put together an excellent physical education manual for home educators. There are sections on strength, endurance, flexibility and aerobic fitness. The program is very family-friendly, using mostly equipment and ideas that are easily incorporated into your homeschool program. Physical fitness test, explanation of rules and more than enough activities to keep you busy for 40+ weeks are included. There are both indoor and outdoor activities, and technique checklists for baseball, soccer, volleyball, basketball, tennis, walking, running, and football.

If you need a comprehensive physical education manual that is easy to use, look no further. This one has it all! *Maryann Turner*

NEW!
Gibby the Gibborang Safari Exercise Video
Ages 2–12. $14.95.
Sports Specifics, Inc. 2383 Wine Ridge Drive, Birmingham, AL 35244. (888) GO GIBBY 464-4229. Inquiries: (205) 982-0763. Fax: (205) 403-8932.

NEW!
Home School Family Fitness
All ages. $18.75 plus shipping.
Home School Family Fitness Institute, 159 Oakwood Drive, New Brighton, MN 55112. (651) 636-7738. E-mail: whitn003@maroon.tc.umn.edu. Web: www.umn.edu/home/whitn003.

Home Life Juggling Products

Ages 4 and up. Juggling Step by Step two-hour video (VHS only) $29.95. Juggling scarves with instructions, $9.95. European beanballs (set of 3), $19.95. Soft & Safe clubs (set of 3), $35. Juggling Starter Kit (3 each of child-sized scarves and European beanballs plus video), $55. Juggling Deluxe Kit (same as starter kit plus set of 3 clubs), $109. Shipping extra.
Home Life, P.O. Box 1190, Fenton, MO 63026. Orders: (800) 346-6322. Inquiries: (636) 343-7750. Fax: (636) 343-7203. Email: orders@home-school.com. Web: www.home-school.com.

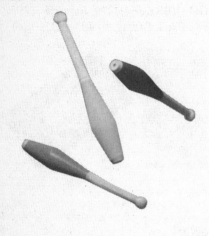

Here's why none of your friends can juggle—they started out with beanbags (or balls, or oranges). Here's what you should do; pitch the beanbags and try our **juggling scarves** and **Juggling Step-by-Step** video.

Scarves, the "training wheels of the juggling world," can repair your sagging confidence, and as an added benefit they won't knock over your vases. Once you have mastered scarves, *then* move on to beanbags, but *only after watching the video several times.* Juggling is just too hard to learn from a book for most of us; we need to *see* how it works. Even a juggling friend can't show you the moves in slow motion, but the video can (and does)! We sell smooth nylon juggling scarves, not the cheaper kind which disintegrates with use.

In the **Juggling Step-by-Step video** you meet Professor Confidence (a smooth fellow in top hat and tails who introduces the lessons and performs many of the moves), Won Israel (a colorful little clown), Amy (a beautiful Filipino girl), Andrew (an incredibly talented young juggler), John (a great club juggler), and Robert (a Huck Finn-type kid). Each of these has a particular specialty: balls, clubs, rings, scarves, devil sticks, diabolo, and team juggling are some of the topics covered.

Again, after the first lessons on basic moves, you are expected to pick up more advanced moves from simply watching the tape. The lessons and illustrative performances are set to music. As much fun to watch as a stage show!

The *Juggling Step-by-Step* video gives you a basic introduction to juggling scarves, beanbags, balls, rings, and clubs; and then goes on to more advanced routines with clubs and balls, unusual equipment like cigar boxes and hats, and even flaming torches! You'll also be introduced to team juggling, juggling with many objects, multiplex juggling, two-in-one-hand, and lots more. Each instruction sequence includes a routine by some really great jugglers. These videos are a quantum leap in juggling education.

One final word on juggling as the ultimate family sport: When's the last time you saw two guys throwing a football, baseball, soccer ball, or hockey puck back and forth on a street corner, with a hat beside them on the ground, and people throwing money into the hat? Now if they'd been passing *juggling clubs* instead . . . Get the picture? *Mary Pride*

NEW!
Millbrook "Fantastic Book of" series

Grades 3–6. Each book, $10.95.
The Millbrook Press, PO Box 335, 2 Old New Milford Rd., Brookfield, CT 06804. Orders: (800) 462-4703. extension 3034. Inquiries: (203) 740-2220. Fax: (203) 740-2223.

Interesting in snowboarding? Mountain biking? Gymnastics? Horses? In-line skating? Car racing? Find out more about the sport that grabs you with **Millbrook's "Fantastic Book of"** series. Each includes a eight-page fold-out section—more of a "play with me" novelty feature than an educational plus, since the spread is laid out as if it were separate pages, instead of using the extra width to show action from one side to the other. Lots of photos and illustrations demonstrate tips and techniques, and introduce each sport's purpose and history. Two-page spread format throughout, except for the fold-out. You couldn't learn a sport from one of these books, but you can easily see what will be involved if you do choose to get into it, as well as gaining more appreciation for the moves involved.

Finally! A physical education book designed not to intimidate most homeschooling families. What's more, this one is designed for multi-level teaching— what we all want and need! The six chapters in this spiral-bound book cover: foot manipulation/soccer, jump roping, volleyball, body coordination/exercises, hand manipulation/basketball, and racquet games. *Mary Pride*

Each chapter of **Physical Education for Homeschoolers** explains skills progression. Nice touch: instruction on building the basics with individual activities, all of which can be applied later in team situations. For example, soccer dribbling, trapping, and heading can be worked on alone or with a partner. All the lessons follow the same format: pick the level most suitable, work on the skills, and play some games. No need to worry if your children don't number enough to comprise their own team. Why not work on the activities at home, then gather with one or two other families and play together? How about a Saturday when the dads can join in?

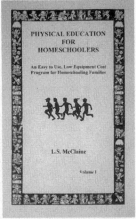

Needed: more detailed instruction for those of us lacking a little in the coordination department. Some of the jump rope routines had me tied up in knots. I was constantly wishing for a live-action video, or at the very least a photograph or two.

Preparation is minimal and the book contains lots of suggestions for turning common household items into PE equipment. *Renee Mathis*

Remember the **U Can Do Exercise and Memorize Series** of videos you read about in the Math Drill chapter? Well, here it is again!

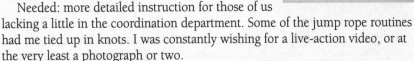

This is probably the only product that needs to be in two chapters of this book, because it covers two such different skill areas at once—learning math facts and a basic skills exercise program. Want to know more? Look at page 350! *Maryann Turner*

With the help of many photos and other illustrations, these four books teach you about picking your pony, how to get to know him, and how to take care of him once you have him. Specific topics taught in the **Usborne Riding School series** are:

- *First Pony*—choosing a pony, buying and trying out, where to keep him, choosing tack, becoming friends and checking his health, and more
- *Grooming and Stable Management*—grooming, feeding, clipping, hoofcare and shoeing, cleaning tack and health, among other things
- *Jumping*
- *Showing*

Inexpensive, attractive, and useful information if there's a horse in your future. *Sarah Pride*

NEW!
Usborne Soccer School series

Ages 8 and up. $5.95 each. Compilation volume (first four titles), $14.95. Complete Soccer School (all eight titles), $29.95. Shipping extra.
EDC Publishing, Division of Educational Development Corporation, PO Box 470663, Tulsa, OK 74147-0663. (800) 475-4522. Fax: (800) 747-4509. Web: www.edcpub.com.

NEW!
We Win!

All ages. $21.95 plus shipping. *Noble Publishing Associates, PO Box 2250, Gresham, OR 97030. Orders: (800) 225-5259. Inquiries: (503) 667-3942. Fax: (503) 665-6637.*

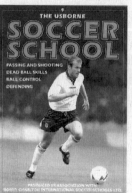

The **Usborne Soccer School series** will teach all the aspects of soccer, using Usborne's colorfully illustrated style. Each book is 32 pages of exercises, tips and tricks for improving your soccer game. Books available so far: *Ball Control, Passing and Shooting, Dead Ball Skills, Defending, Training and Fitness, Goalkeeping, Attacking,* and *Tactics*

A great series for aspiring and perspiring soccer players everywhere. *Sarah Pride*

We Win! is a complete noncompetitive physical education course for homeschoolers. It's Christian-based, but that doesn't mean poor tired Johnny on the floor over there has to say a Bible verse every time he does a push-up. This 170-page black-and-white book covers everything from noncompetitive sports to calisthenics and aerobics.

We Win! has a section on noncompetitive baseball, for example, which is just batting and trying to run around two bases with no scorekeeping. It's OK for the purpose of noncompetitive play, but your kids will be much more interested in the competitive version. Tag is a good noncompetitive game, also given some thought. The thing is, nobody knows who spent the most time as "it," so there's no way to win or lose, right?

In all, you get 36 chapters. The first three present the author's philosophy. The next two deal with planning your physical education program and some basic suggestions about equipment. Next come four chapters about general physical fitness, along with some suggested calisthenics, followed by four more "advice" chapters on skill development, work activities and units, and game organization. Then comes the meat of the book: units that teach the basic skills (but *not* the rules) of many popular sports, plus noncompetitive games to practice these skills. The sports covered include badminton, baseball, basketball, football, frisbee, gymnastic, handball, obstacle courses, paddleball/racquetball, ping pong, polo (as "pillow polo"), relay races, soccer, swimming, tennis, tetherball, track and field, and volleyball. You also get units on basic skill *types,* such as basic ball skills, locomotor skills, and hand/eye coordination.

The basic exercises in this book are described in detail, with plans on how to work up from fairly simple to difficult exercise programs. All exercises have nice cartoony illustrations showing how they work, too. If you want to get serious about your exercise program, this is the book for you—but you might want to add some of the "real" competitive games, as well. *Joseph Pride*

EXTRA INFO

Appendixes

The U.S. Constitution & What It Really Means

Do you ever get into arguments that go like this:
"XYZ is true!"
"No, it's not!"
"Is!"
"Is not!"

The only way to settle such an argument, we have found in our own family, is to consult an accepted authority. If, for example, we can't agree which land animal is the fastest, we check it out in the encyclopedia. If we are arguing over how to pronounce *progenitor,* we consult the dictionary. If son #1 thinks Ahab was a king of Israel, and son #2 thinks Ahab actually ruled in Judah, a concordance and the Bible will soon settle that question.

Political arguments can be just this dumb. Fur flies back and forth as the debaters fuss over which side has the most voters and which viewpoint ought to prevail. Rarely do they consult the authority—in this case, the United States Constitution—to see what the law of the land *already* says about the subject under discussion.

When it comes to politics, the law in America is supposed to be limited. Our lawgivers, for example, don't have the right to sell the citizens of Massachusetts into chattel slavery to the Japanese in order to balance the budget. Why? Because slavery is against the Constitution and because the Constitution (even *before* the anti-slavery amendment) never gave the government the right to enslave free citizens.

Our leaders—whether presidents, congressmen, or judges—have to swear to uphold the Constitution. They do *not* have the right to pass any law they wish, or to enforce unwritten laws.

Most political arguments these days tend to ignore the Constitution. The reason is that the vast majority of us have never read it, let alone studied it. It's not even that easy to find a copy—try to the next time you visit a bookstore or library. Failing such knowledge on the part of the citizens, our elected leaders and their unelected bureaucratic friends can, and do, regularly exceed their authority.

Think of this chapter as a free course on government as it *ought* to work.

To make it a unit study, read some biographies of the Founding Fathers, especially Thomas Jefferson, Benjamin Franklin, and the great George Washington. Get a copy of *Robert's Rules of Order* and hold your own family Constitutional Convention, making up an "ideal" constitution for the USA of the future. If possible, add a trip to your state capital or even Washington, D.C.

To make this more fun and educational, American Student Travel, 16225 Park Ten Place, Houston, TX 77084, (800) 688-1965, fax: (281) 647-7084, *www.astravel.com,* offers tours of Washington just for homeschoolers.

If all this sounds like too much work, just read the sidebars!

Schools go along with this by teaching kids about the "three branches of government," but not about the Constitution's limitations on government. So do educational publishers. Take *World Book Encyclopedia*, for example. Section 8 of Article I of the Constitution gives Congress the power "to coin money, regulate the value thereof, and of foreign coin, and fix the standard of weights and measures." The phrase, "to *coin* money" was deliberately introduced to prevent Congress from issuing paper money, as the Continental Congress had done (with disastrous results) during the Revolutionary War. President after president refused to countenance paper money or any central bank as utterly incompatible with this clear direction in the Constitution. Now see the World Book's comment on this section:

> *From this section, along with the section that allows the Congress to regulate commerce and to borrow money, Congress gets its right to charter national banks and to establish the Federal Reserve System.*

Tell it to Andy Jackson!

I could go through the Constitution, point by point, showing you how huge swaths of government policy and bureaucracy are illegal according to the highest law of the land. You could then say, "Ain't so! It don't say that!" We could argue back and forth. This gets us nowhere. So I decided instead, as a public service, to pay someone $100 to type the entire Constitution into my computer. Now you can read it *for yourself*. You can see what the Constitution *really* says. It's culture shock. Guaranteed!

Preamble to the Constitution

→ We the People of the United States, in Order to form a more perfect Union, establish Justice, insure domestic Tranquility, provide for the common defence, promote the general Welfare, and secure the Blessings of Liberty to ourselves and our Posterity, do ordain and establish this Constitution for the United States of America.

Article I [The Legislative Branch]

Section 1. All legislative Powers herein granted shall be vested in a Congress of the United States, which shall consist of a Senate and House of Representatives.

Section 2. The House of Representatives shall be composed of Members chosen every second Year by the People of the several States, and the Electors in each State shall have the Qualifications requisite for Electors of the most numerous Branch of the State Legislature.

No Person shall be a Representative who shall not have attained to the Age of twenty five Years, and been seven Years a Citizen of the United States, and who shall not, when elected, be an Inhabitant of that State in which he shall be chosen.

→ Representative and direct Taxes shall be apportioned among the several States which may be included within this Union, according to their respective Numbers, which shall be determined by adding to the whole Number of free Persons, including those bound to Service for a Term of Years, and excluding Indians not taxed, three fifths of all other Persons. The actual Enumeration shall be made within three Years after the first Meeting of the Congress of the United States, and within every subsequent Term of ten Years, in such Manner as they shall by Law direct.

Our forefathers made a BIG mistake in the Preamble, and we're still paying for it. They did not acknowledge Christ as the Lord of America. (On the bright side, they also did not acknowledge Mohammed, Buddha, Kali, or the Enlightenment's Goddess of Reason.) Thus, there is no absolute standard underlying the Constitution, unless (as some Supreme Court judges of the past have held) you simply assume that America is a Christian nation. For this very reason, descendants of the Scottish Covenanters for generations refused to take a loyalty oath to the Constitution, thus barring themselves from citizenship and from holding office. Sidelight: the U.S. flag is the first flag of a Western nation NOT to have a cross on it anywhere. This does not mean the Constitution isn't loaded with Christian principles (because it is), or that the Founding Fathers were some sort of deist conspiracy (because they weren't), but that at square one Christians unwittingly disenfranchised themselves from speaking politically in the Name of the Lord.

As you can see, federal taxes were to be raised by taxing states, not by taxing individuals. The states were to pay the federal government, thus allowing the states to exercise some control over how their money was spent. This is the opposite of today's "revenue-sharing," where the federal government exercises control over states by threatening to withhold its block grants from those that fail to comply with federal objectives, e.g., seat-belt laws.

The Number of Representatives shall not exceed one for every thirty Thousand, but each State shall have at least one Representative; and until such enumeration shall be made, the State of New Hampshire shall be entitled to chuse three, Massachusetts eight, Rhode-Island and Providence Plantations one, Connecticut five, New-York six, New Jersey four, Pennsylvania eight, Delaware one, Maryland six, Virginia ten, North Carolina five, South Carolina five, and Georgia three.

When vacancies happen in the Representation from any State, the Executive Authority thereof shall issue Writs of Election to fill such Vacancies.

The House of Representatives shall chuse their speaker and other Officers; and shall have the sole Power of Impeachment.

Section 3. The Senate of the United States shall be composed of two Senators from each State, chosen by the Legislature thereof, for six Years; and each Senator shall have one Vote.

Senators were originally appointed by state legislatures, giving the states some control in this area also. It also gave rural areas significant power, since state senates had a large proportion of rural representatives.

Immediately after they shall be assembled in Consequence of the first Election, they shall be divided as equally as may be into three Classes. The Seats of the Senators of the first Class shall be vacated at the Expiration of the second Year, of the second Class at the Expiration of the fourth Year, and of the third Class at the Expiration of the sixth Year, so that one third may be chosen every second Year; and if Vacancies happen by Resignation, or otherwise, during the Recess of the Legislature of any State, the Executive thereof may make temporary Appointments until the next Meeting of the Legislature, which shall then fill such Vacancies.

No Person shall be a Senator who shall not have attained to the Age of thirty Years, and been nine Years a citizen of the United States, and who shall not, when elected, be an Inhabitant of that State for which he shall be chosen.

The Vice President of the United States shall be President of the Senate, but shall have no Vote, unless they be equally divided.

The Senate shall chuse their other Officers, and also a President pro tempore, in the Absence of the Vice President, or when he shall exercise the Office of President of the United States.

The Senate shall have the sole Power to try all Impeachments. When sitting for that Purpose, they shall be on Oath or Affirmation. When the President of the United States is tried, the Chief Justice shall preside: And no Person shall be convicted without the Concurrence of two thirds of the Members present.

Judgment in Cases of Impeachment shall not extend further than to removal from Office, and disqualification to hold and enjoy any Office of honor, Trust or Profit under the United States: but the Party convicted shall nevertheless be liable and subject to Indictment, Trial, Judgment and Punishment, according to law.

Section 4. The Times, Places, and Manner of holding Elections for Senators and Representatives, shall be prescribed in each State by the Legislature thereof; but the Congress may at any time by Law make or alter such Regulations, except as to the Places of chusing Senators.

The Congress shall assemble at least once in every Year, and such Meeting shall be on the first Monday in December, unless they shall by Law appoint a different Day.

Section 5. Each House shall be the Judge of the Elections, Returns, and Qualifications of its own Members, and a Majority of each shall constitute a Quorum to do Business; but a smaller Number may adjourn from day to day, and may be authorized to compel the Attendance of absent Members, in such Manner, and under such Penalties as each House may provide.

Each House may determine the Rules of its Proceedings, punish its Members for disorderly Behaviour, and, with the Concurrence of two thirds, expel a Member.

Each House shall keep a journal of its Proceedings, and from time to time publish the same, excepting such Parts as may in their Judgment require Secrecy; and the Yeas and Nays of the Members of either House on any question shall, at the Desire of one fifth of those Present, be entered on the Journal.

Neither House, during the Session of Congress, shall, without the Consent of the other, adjourn for more than three days, nor to any other Place than that in which the two Houses shall be sitting.

Section 6. The Senators and Representatives shall receive a Compensation for their Services, to be ascertained by Law, and paid out of the Treasury of the United States. They shall in all Cases, except Treason, Felony and Breach of the Peace, be privileged from Arrest during their Attendance at the Session of their respective Houses, and in going to and returning from the same; and for any Speech or Debate in either House, they shall not be questioned in any other Place.

No Senator or Representative shall, during the Time for which he was elected, be appointed to any civil Office under the Authority of the United States, which shall have been created, or the Emoluments whereof shall have been increased during such time; and no Person holding any Office under the United States, shall be a Member of either House during his Continuance in Office.

Section 7. All Bills for raising Revenue shall originate in the House of Representatives; but the Senate may propose or concur with Amendments as on other Bills.

Every Bill which shall have passed the House of Representatives and the Senate, shall, before it become a Law, be presented to the President of the United States; If he approve he shall sign it, but if not he shall return it, with his Objections to that House in which it shall have originated, who shall enter the Objections at large on their Journal, and proceed to reconsider it. If after such Reconsideration two thirds of that House shall agree to pass the Bill, it shall be sent, together with the Objections, to the other House, by which it shall likewise be reconsidered, and if approved by two thirds of that House, it shall become a Law. But in all Cases the Votes of both Houses shall be determined by Yeas and Nays, and the Names of the Persons voting for and against the Bill shall be entered on the Journal of each House respectively. If any Bill shall not be returned by the President within ten Days (Sundays excepted) after it shall have been presented to him, the Same shall be a Law, in like Manner as if he had signed it, unless the Congress by their Adjournment prevent its Return, in which Case it shall not be a Law.

Every Order, Resolution, or Vote to which the Concurrence of the Senate and House of Representatives may be necessary (except on a question of Adjournment) shall be presented to the President of the United States; and before the Same shall take Effect, shall be approved by him, or being disapproved by him, shall be repassed by two thirds of the Senate and House of Representatives, according to the Rules and Limitations prescribed in the Case of a Bill.

Section 8. The Congress shall have Power To lay and collect Taxes, Duties, Imposts and Excises, to pay the Debts and provide for the common Defence and general Welfare of the United States; but all Duties, Imposts and Excises shall be uniform throughout the United States;

---

*All funding **must** be authorized by Congress. Do you see the words "Executive Orders" anywhere in this section?*

This is how a bill becomes a law. Do you see the words "Supreme Court" anywhere in this section? Or "judicial review"?

*Note that the **President**, not the Supreme Court, has the veto power, and the **Congress**, not the Supreme Court, has the sole right to create laws.*

*If it's a rule we have to obey under threat of penalties for noncompliance, it's a **law**. This means many so-called "court rulings" today are actually unconstitutional laws.*

Judges swear to uphold the Constitution. They ought to start by memorizing this section.

To borrow Money on the Credit of the United States;

To regulate Commerce with foreign Nations, and among the several ◄━━┊ states, and with the Indian Tribes;

To establish an uniform Rule of Naturalization, and uniform Laws on the subject of Bankruptcies throughout the United States;

To coin Money, regulate the Value thereof, and of foreign Coin, and fix ◄━┊ the Standard of Weights and Measures;

To provide for the Punishment of counterfeiting the securities and current Coin of the United States;

To establish Post Offices and post Roads;

To promote the Progress of Science and useful Arts, by securing for limited Times to Authors and Inventors the exclusive Right to their respective Writings and Discoveries;

To constitute Tribunals inferior to the supreme Court;

To define and punish Piracies and Felonies committed on the high Seas, and Offences against the law of Nations;

To declare War, grant Letters of Marque and Reprisal, and make Rules concerning Captures on Land and Water;

To raise and support Armies, but no Appropriation of Money to that ◄━┊ Use shall be for a longer Term than two Years;

To provide and maintain a navy;

To make Rules for the government and Regulation of the land and naval Forces;

To provide for calling forth the Militia to execute the Laws of the Union, suppress Insurrections and repel Invasions;

To provide for organizing, arming, and disciplining the Militia, and for governing such Part of them as may be employed in the Service of the United States, reserving to the States respectively, the Appointment of the Officers, and the Authority of training the Militia according to the discipline prescribed by Congress;

To exercise exclusive Legislation in all Cases whatsoever, over such District (not exceeding ten Miles square) as may, by Cession of particular States, and the Acceptance of Congress, become the Seat of the Government of the United States, and to exercise like Authority over all Places purchased by the Consent of the Legislature of the State in which the Same shall be for the Erection of Forts, magazines, Arsenals, dock-Yards, and other needful Buildings;—And

To make all Laws which shall be necessary and proper for carrying into Execution the foregoing Powers, and all other Powers vested by this Constitution in the Government of the United States, or in any Department or Officer thereof.

Section 9. The Migration or Importation of such Persons as any of the States now existing shall think proper to admit, shall not be prohibited by the Congress prior to the Year one thousand eight hundred and eight, but a Tax or duty may be imposed on such Importation, not exceeding ten dollars for each Person.

The Privilege of the Writ of Habeas Corpus shall not be suspended, unless when in Cases of Rebellion or Invasion the public Safety may require it.

No Bill of Attainder or ex post facto Law shall be passed.

No Capitation, or other direct, Tax shall be laid, unless in Proportion to the Census or Enumeration herein before directed to be taken.

No Tax or Duty shall be laid on Articles exported from any State.

No preference shall be given by any Regulation of Commerce or Revenue to the Ports of one State over those of another: nor shall Vessels bound to, or from, one State, be obliged to enter, clear, or pay Duties in another.

The "regulating commerce" clause referred to preventing economic warfare between states, not telling individual businessmen how to run their companies.

Congress was specifically forbidden by this line to issue paper money. They had to "coin" money, requiring a precious-metals standard. Coins aren't made out of paper. Nothing here gives Congress the right to give the Federal Reserve (a private bank) the right to create money out of thin air and charge the taxpayers for it.

The Founders were not fond of standing armies. For one thing, a standing army could be used domestically to suppress the government's critics or even to enforce totalitarianism. The idea that we "need" a huge army so we can send it overseas to fight on behalf of the United Nations is exactly the kind of "foreign entanglements" George Washington, our first Commander-in-Chief and our first President, warned against in his Farewell Address.

Very Important: *Look through Section 8. See if Congress has the power to transfer money from one group of people to another (welfare programs, entitlement programs, federal medical insurance, etc.); to regulate businesses in their way of doing business (e.g., mandatory parental leave, accommodations for the handicapped); to control education; to establish housing policies and erect public housing; to subsidize milk and tobacco production and to tell farmers what to grow on their own land; and so on. It just isn't there.*

No money shall be drawn from the Treasury, but in Consequence of Appropriations made by Law; and a regular Statement and Account of the Receipts and Expenditures of all public Money shall be published from time to time.

No Title of Nobility shall be granted by the United States: And no Person holding any Office of Profit or Trust under them, shall, without the Consent of the Congress, accept of any present, Emolument, Office, or Title, of any kind whatever, from any King, Prince, or foreign State.

In other words, states have no right to water down the marriage contract by no-fault divorce laws and other laws changing the status of the marriage covenant after a couple has already wed.

Section 10. No State shall enter into any Treaty, Alliance, or Confederation; grant Letters of Marque and Reprisal; coin Money; emit Bills of Credit; make any Thing but gold and silver Coin a Tender in Payment of Debts; pass any Bill of Attainder, ex post facto Law, *or Law impairing the Obligation of Contracts* [emphasis mine], or grant any Title of Nobility.

No State shall, without the Consent of the Congress, lay any Imposts or Duties on Imports or Exports, except what may be absolutely necessary for executing its inspection Laws: and the net Produce of all Duties and Imports, laid by any State on Imports or Exports, shall be for the Use of the Treasury of the United States; and all such Laws shall be subject to the Revision and control of the Congress.

No State shall, without the Consent of the Congress, lay any Duty of Tonnage, keep Troops, or Ships of War in time of Peace, enter into any Agreement or Compact with another State, or with a foreign Power, or engage in War, unless actually invaded, or in such imminent Danger as will not admit of delay.

Article II [The Executive Branch]

Section 1. The executive Power shall be vested in a President of the United States of America. He shall hold his Office during the Term of four Years, and, together with the Vice President, chosen for the same term, be elected, as follows.

Each State shall appoint, in such Manner as the Legislature thereof may direct, a Number of Electors, equal to the whole Number of Senators and Representatives to which the State may be entitled in the Congress: but no Senator or Representative, or Person holding an Office of Trust or Profit under the United States, shall be appointed an Elector.

The Electors shall meet in their respective States, and vote by Ballot for two Persons, of whom one at least shall not be an Inhabitant of the same State with themselves. And they shall make a List of all the Persons voted for, and of the Number of Votes for each; which List they shall sign and certify, and transmit sealed to the Seat of the Government of the United States, directed to the President of the Senate. The President of the Senate shall, in the Presence of the Senate and House of Representatives, open all the Certificates, and the Votes shall then be counted. The Person having the greatest Number of Votes shall be the President, if such Number be a Majority of the whole Number of Electors appointed; and if there be more than one who have such Majority, and have an equal Number of Votes, then the House of Representatives shall immediately chuse by Ballot one of them for President: and if no Person have a Majority, then from the five highest on the List the said House shall in like Manner chuse the President. But in chusing the President, the Votes shall be taken by States, the Representation from each State having one Vote; A quorum for this Purpose shall consist of a Member or Members from two thirds of the States, and a Majority of all the States shall be necessary to a Choice. In every Case, after the Choice of the President, the Person having the greatest Number of Votes of the Electors shall be the Vice President.

But if there should remain two or more who have equal Votes, the Senate shall chuse from them by Ballot the Vice President.

The Congress may determine the Time of chusing the Electors, and the Day on which they shall give their Votes; which Day shall be the same throughout the United States.

No Person except a natural born Citizen, or a Citizen of the United States, at the time of the Adoption of this Constitution, shall be eligible to the Office of President; neither shall any Person be eligible to that Office who shall not have attained to the Age of thirty five Years, and been fourteen Years a Resident within the United States.

In Case of the Removal of the President from Office, or of his Death, Resignation, or Inability to discharge the Powers and Duties of the said Office, the Same shall devolve on the Vice President, and the Congress may by Law provide for the Case of Removal, Death, Resignation or Inability, both of the President and Vice President, declaring what Officer shall then act as President, and such Officer shall act accordingly, until the Disability be removed, or a President shall be elected.

The President shall, at stated Times, receive for his Services, a Compensation, which shall neither be encreased nor diminished during the Period for which he shall have been elected, and he shall not receive within that Period any other Emolument from the United States, or any of them.

Before he enter on the Execution of his Office, he shall take the following Oath or Affirmation:—"I do solemnly swear (or affirm) that I will faithfully execute the Office of President of the United States, and will to the best of my Ability, preserve, protect and defend the Constitution of the United States."

Section 2. The President shall be Commander in Chief of the Army and Navy of the United States, and of the Militia of the several States, when called into the actual Service of the United States; he may require the Opinion, in writing, of the principal Officer in each of the executive Departments, upon any Subject relating to the Duties of their respective Offices, and he shall have Power to grant Reprieves and Pardons for Offences against the United States, except in Cases of Impeachment.

He shall have Power, by and with the Advice and Consent of the Senate, to make Treaties, provided two thirds of the Senators present concur; and he shall nominate, and by and with the Advice and Consent of the Senate, shall appoint Ambassadors, other public Ministers and Consuls, Judges of the supreme Court, and all other Officers of the United States, whose Appointments are not herein otherwise provided for, and which shall be established by Law: but the Congress may by Law vest the Appointment of such inferior Officers, as they think proper, in the President alone, in the Courts of Law, or in the Heads of Departments.

The President shall have Power to fill up all Vacancies that may happen during the Recess of the Senate, by granting Commissions which shall expire at the End of their next Session.

Section 3. He shall from time to time give to the Congress Information of the State of the Union, and recommend to their Consideration such Measures as he shall judge necessary and expedient; he may, on extraordinary Occasions, convene both Houses, or either of them, and in Case of Disagreement between them, with Respect to the Time of Adjournment, he may adjourn them to such Time as he shall think proper; he shall receive Ambassadors and other public Ministers; he shall take Care that the Laws be faithfully executed, and shall Commission all the Officers of the United States.

Section 4. The President, Vice President, and all civil Officers of the United States, shall be removed from Office on Impeachment for, and conviction of, Treason, Bribery, or other High Crimes and Misdemeanors.

Article III [The Judicial Branch]

Section 1. The judicial Power of the United States, shall be vested in one supreme Court, and in such inferior Courts as the Congress may from time to time ordain and establish. The Judges, both of the supreme and inferior Courts, shall hold their Offices during good Behaviour, and shall, at stated Times, receive for their Services, a Compensation, which shall not be diminished during their Continuance in Office.

Doesn't it sound like the Supreme Court is only supposed to mediate in quarrels between jurisdictions? Where is its power to annul duly-passed laws? Nowhere, that's where!

Section 2. The judicial Power shall extend to all Cases, in Law and Equity, arising under this Constitution, the Laws of the United States, and Treaties made, or which shall be made, under their Authority;—to all Cases affecting Ambassadors, other public Ministers and Consuls;—to all Cases of admiralty and maritime Jurisdiction;—to Controversies to which the United States shall be a Party;--to Controversies between two or more States; between a State and Citizens of another State;—between Citizens of different States;—between Citizens of the same State claiming Lands under Grants of different States, and between a State, or the Citizens thereof, and foreign States, Citizens or Subjects.

In all Cases affecting Ambassadors, other public Ministers and Consuls, and those in which a State shall be Party, the supreme Court shall have original Jurisdiction. In all the other Cases before mentioned, the supreme Court shall have appellate Jurisdiction, both as to Law and Fact, with such Exceptions, and under such Regulations as the Congress shall make.

The Trial of all Crimes, except in Cases of Impeachment, shall be by Jury; and such Trial shall be held in the State where the said Crimes shall have been committed; but when not committed within any State, the Trial shall be at such Place or Places as the Congress may by Law have directed.

Section 3. Treason against the United States, shall consist only in levying War against them, or in adhering to their Enemies, giving them Aid and Comfort. No Person shall be convicted of Treason unless on the Testimony of two Witnesses to the same overt Act, or on Confession in open Court.

The Congress shall have Power to declare the Punishment of Treason, but no Attainder of Treason shall work Corruption of Blood, or Forfeiture except during the Life of the person Attainted.

Article IV
[Laws Concerning the States]

Section 1. Full Faith and Credit shall be given in each State to the public Acts, Records, and judicial Proceedings of every other State. (*Nevada, in other words, should not have the right to cancel marriages made in Nebraska.*) And the Congress may by general Laws prescribe the Manner in which such Acts, Records and Proceedings shall be proved, and the Effect thereof.

Section 2. The Citizens of each State shall be entitled to all Privileges and Immunities of Citizens in the several States.

A Person charged in any State with Treason, Felony, or other Crime, who shall flee from Justice, and be found in another State, shall on Demand of the executive Authority of the State from which he fled, be delivered up, to be removed to the State having Jurisdiction of the Crime.

No Person held to Service or Labour in one State, under the Laws thereof, escaping into another, shall, in Consequence of any Law or Regulation therein, be discharged from such Service or Labour, but shall be delivered up on the Claim of the Party to whom such Service or Labour may be due.

Section 3. New States may be admitted by the Congress into this Union; but no new State shall be formed or erected within the Jurisdiction of any other State; nor any State be formed by the Junction of two or more States, or Parts of States, without the Consent of the Legislatures of the States concerned as well as of the Congress.

The Congress shall have Power to dispose of and make all needful Rules and Regulations respecting the Territory or other Property belonging to the United States; and nothing in this Constitution shall be so construed as to Prejudice any Claims of the United States, or of any particular State.

Section 4. The United States shall guarantee to every State in this Union a Republican Form of Government, and shall protect each of them against Invasion; and on Application of the Legislature, or of the Executive (when the Legislature cannot be convened) against domestic Violence.

Article V
[How to Amend the Constitution]

The Congress, whenever two thirds of both Houses shall deem it necessary, shall propose Amendments to this Constitution, or, on the Application of the Legislatures of two thirds of the several States, shall call a Convention for proposing Amendments, which, in either Case, shall be valid to all Intents and Purposes, as Part of this Constitution, when ratified by the Legislatures of three fourths of the several States, or by Conventions in three fourths thereof, as the one or the other Mode of Ratification may ◄━■━ be proposed by the Congress; Provided that no Amendment which may be made prior to the Year One Thousand eight hundred and eight shall in any Manner affect the first and fourth Clauses in the Ninth Section of the first Article; and that no State, without its Consent, shall be deprived of its equal Suffrage in the Senate.

Article VI [Transition to and
Upholding the Constitution]

All Debts contracted and Engagements entered into, before the Adoption of this Constitution, shall be as valid against the United States under this Constitution, as under the Confederation.

This Constitution, and the Laws of the United States which shall be made in Pursuance thereof; and all Treaties made, or which shall be ◄━━━━ made, under the Authority of the United States, shall be the supreme Law of the Land; and the Judges in every State shall be bound thereby, any Thing in the Constitution or Laws of any State to the Contrary notwithstanding.

The Senators and Representatives before mentioned, and the Members of the several State Legislatures, and all executive and judicial Officers, both of the

The Constitution can NOT be amended by majority vote of the Supreme Court, as at least one public-school booklet I saw claims! This, of course, hasn't stopped the Supreme Court, since the days of F.D.R., from doing just that. The judiciary now has open contempt for the people and the legislative process. Law students are even taught that it is a judge's DUTY to "make" laws—since it is so much harder to get policies beloved by the avant-garde enacted otherwise!

The Founders intended the "Treaties" spoken of to be treaties BETWEEN nations (e.g., a treaty with Britain regarding the rights of American and British shipping). Now that U.N. elites have private conferences at which leaders of many nations get together and sign "treaties" changing the political status of their citizen (example: the U.N. Treaty on the Rights of Children, which makes peer-group dependency and unrestricted access to TV commercials "rights" of children), this proviso has become the most abused line in the Constitution.

United States and of the several States, shall be bound by Oath of Affirmation, to support this Constitution; but no religious Test shall ever be required as a Qualification to any Office or public Trust under the United States.

Article VII
[Ratifying the Constitution]

The Ratification of the Conventions of nine States, shall be sufficient for the Establishment of this Constitution between the States so ratifying the Same.

AMENDMENTS TO THE CONSTITUTION

[The first 10 Amendments are called the Bill of Rights. They were ratified Dec. 15, 1791.]

Amendment 1
[Free Speech, Religion, Press, Assembly & Petition]

Congress shall make no law respecting an establishment of religion, or prohibiting the free exercise thereof; or abridging the freedom of speech, or of the press, or the right of the people peaceably to assemble, and to petition the Government for a redress of grievances.

The phrase "no law respecting an establishment of religion" meant, at the time it was written, that Congress should not establish a national religion. States were free to have state religions, as in fact several did for years after this amendment was passed. The amendment does NOT mean that Congress (and the states) must actively suppress all public religion, as the ACLU would have it. This is perhaps the most misunderstood amendment of the Constitution.

Amendment 2
[Gunowners' Rights]

A well regulated Militia being necessary to the security of a free State, the right of the people to keep and bear Arms, shall not be infringed.

A militia, by definition, is a citizen army. In America, historically the militia was organized town by town, not on the state or national level. The American Revolution started when some townsmen in Lexington and Concord refused to hand their guns over to the British.

Amendment 3
[No Quartering Soldiers on the People]

No Soldier shall, in time of peace be quartered in any house, without the consent of the Owner, nor in time of war, but in a manner to be prescribed by law.

Amendment 4
[Right of Privacy against Government Search & Seizure)

The right of the people to be secure in their persons, houses, papers, and effects, against unreasonable searches and seizures, shall not be violated, and no Warrants shall issue, but upon probable cause, supported by Oath or affirmation, and particularly describing the place to be searched, and the persons or things to be seized.

In other words, FBI, BATF and IRS guys are supposed to have a case against you and a list of what they want to take before they kick down your front door. They are also not supposed to randomly loot your property in hopes of finding something salable or incriminating. They are ESPECIALLY not supposed to be able to seize your goods first and THEN make YOU prove they made a mistake, as is currently the case under our unconstitutional and evil modern forfeiture laws. (Even USA Today has complained about these laws!)

Amendment 5
[Capital Crimes, Double Jeopardy, Self-Incrimination, Government "Takings"]

No person shall be held to answer for a capital, or otherwise infamous crime, unless on a presentment or indictment of a Grand Jury, except in cases arising in the land or naval forces, or in the Militia, when in actual service in time of War or public danger; nor shall any person be subject for the same offence to be twice put in jeopardy of life or limb; nor shall be compelled in any criminal case to be a witness against himself, nor be deprived of life, liberty, or property, without due process of law; nor shall private property be taken for public use, without just compensation. ◄--┈-

The "takings" clause here is our chief bulwark against the government seizing control of our land, in the name of "the public good." The Constitution does not recognize the doctrine of "the people's resources" or "the planet's resources" — it respects private ownership of property. Constitutionally speaking, if the government wants to force you to turn your land into a wildlife reserve or an unusable "wetland," they have to pay you for it.

Amendment 6
[Rules for Fair Trials]

In all criminal prosecutions, the accused shall enjoy the right to a speedy and public trial, by an impartial jury of the State and district wherein the crime shall have been committed, which district shall have been previously ascertained by law, and to be informed of the nature and cause of the accusation; to be confronted with the witnesses against him; to have compulsory process for obtaining witnesses in his favor, and to have the ◄-- Assistance of Counsel for his defence.

The JURY is supposed to try the case, not the judge. Also note that anonymous hotline tips and the like are not supposed to be evidence or cause for a criminal prosecution.

Amendment 7
(Right to Jury Trial)

In Suits at common law, where the value in controversy shall exceed twenty dollars, the right of trial by jury shall be preserved, and no fact tried by a jury, shall be otherwise re-examined in any Court of the United States, than according to the rules of the common law.

Amendment 8
[Bails, Fines, Penalties]

Excessive bail shall not be required, nor excessive fines imposed, ◄--┈- nor cruel and unusual punishments inflicted.

Capital punishment was not considered "cruel and unusual." Torture was.

Amendment 9
[Rights Not Mentioned are Still Rights]

The enumeration in the Constitution, of certain rights, shall not be ◄--┈- construed to deny or disparage others retained by the people.

Since the Constitution does not mention education, in-state business, charity, and hosts of other subjects, these areas are rights of the people to handle as we wish. We should not have to ask permission to make our own choices in these areas, since WE are the legal authorities over our own choices.

Amendment 10
[People and States Retain Rights Not Given to Federal Government]

The powers not delegated to the United States by the Constitution, nor prohibited by it to the States, are reserved to the States respectively, or ◄--┈- to the people.

For example, since education is never mentioned in the Constitution, according to this amendment the control of education is a right reserved to the States or the people. A "national education policy" and a Department of Education in the cabinet are clearly unconstitutional.

Amendment 11
[Federal Government Not to Decide Lawsuits Against States]

The Judicial power of the United States shall not be construed to extend to any suit in law or equity, commenced or prosecuted against one of the United States by Citizens of another State, or by Citizens or Subjects of any Foreign State. [Ratified Feb. 7, 1795]

Amendment 12
[Election Regulations]

The Electors shall meet in their respective States and vote by ballot for President and Vice President, one of whom, at least, shall not be an inhabitant of the same State with themselves; they shall name in their ballots the person voted for as President, and in distinct ballots the person voted for as Vice-President, and they shall make distinct lists of all persons voted for as President, and of all persons voted for as Vice-President, and of the number of votes for each, which lists they shall sign and certify, and transmit sealed to the seat of the government of the United States, directed to the President of the Senate;—The President of the Senate shall, in the presence of the Senate and House of Representatives, open all the certificates and the votes shall then be counted;—The person having the greatest number of votes for President, shall be the President, if such number be a majority of the whole number of Electors appointed; and if no person have such majority, then from the persons having the highest numbers not exceeding three on the list of those voted for as President, the House of Representatives shall choose immediately, by ballot, the President. But in choosing the President, the votes shall be taken by states, the representation from each state having one vote; a quorum for this purpose shall consist of a member or members from two-thirds of the states, and majority of all the states shall be necessary to a choice. And if the House of Representatives shall not choose a President whenever the right of choice shall devolve upon them, before the fourth day of March next following, then the Vice-President shall act as President, as in the case of the death or other constitutional disability of the President.—The person having the greatest number of votes as Vice-President, shall be the Vice-President, if such number be a majority of the whole number of Electors appointed, and if no person have a majority, then from the two highest numbers on the list, the Senate shall choose the Vice-President; a quorum for the purpose shall consist of two-thirds of the whole number of Senators, and a majority of the whole number shall be necessary to a choice. But no person constitutionally ineligible to the office of President shall be eligible to that of Vice-President of the United States. [Ratified July 27, 1804]

Amendment 13
[Slavery Abolished]

Section 1. Neither Slavery, nor involuntary servitude, except as a punishment for crime whereof the party shall have been duly convicted, shall exist within the United States, or any place subject to their jurisdiction.

Section 2. Congress shall have power to enforce this article by appropriate legislation. [Ratified Dec. 6, 1865]

Amendment 14
[Aftermath of Civil War]

Section 1. All persons born or naturalized in the United States, and subject to the jurisdiction thereof, are citizens of the United States and of the State wherein they reside. No State shall make or enforce any law which shall abridge the privileges or immunities of citizens of the United States; nor shall any State deprive any person of life, liberty, or property, without due process of law; nor deny to any person within its jurisdiction the equal protection of the laws.

"Mandatory voluntary community service," which the Ford Foundation and the other usual suspects are touting as the cure for teen gangs, dropouts, and crime, is an oxymoron. If it's mandatory (say, as a requirement for high-school graduation, as usually proposed and actually required some places), it's not "voluntary." That makes it involuntary servitude, e.g., slavery, whatever the courts might say and have said.

Section 2. Representatives shall be apportioned among the several States according to their respective numbers, counting the whole number of persons in each State, excluding Indians not taxed. But when the right to vote at any election for the choice of electors for President and Vice President of the United States, Representatives in Congress, the Executive and Judicial officers of a State, or the members of the Legislature thereof, is denied to any of the male inhabitants of such State, being twenty-one years of age, and citizens of the United States, or in any way abridged, except for participation in rebellion, or other crime, the basis of representation therein shall be reduced in the proportion which the number of such male citizens shall bear to the whole number of male citizens twenty-one years of age in such State.

Section 3. No person shall be a Senator or Representative in Congress, or elector of President and Vice President, or hold any office, civil or military, under the United States, or under any State, who, having been previously taken an oath, as a member of Congress, or as an officer of the United States, or as a member of any State legislature, or as an executive or judicial officer of any State, to support the Constitution of the United States, shall have engaged in insurrection or rebellion against the same, or given aid or comfort to the enemies thereof. But Congress may by a vote of two-thirds of each House, remove such disability.

Section 4. The validity of the public debt of the United States, authorized by law, including debts incurred for payment of pensions and bounties for services in suppressing insurrection or rebellion, shall not be questioned. But neither the United States nor any State shall assume or pay any debt or obligation incurred in aid of insurrection or rebellion against the United States, or any claim for the loss or emancipation of any slave; but all such debts, obligations and claims shall be held illegal and void.

Section 5. The Congress shall have power to enforce, by appropriate legislation, the provisions of this article. [Ratified July 9, 1868]

Amendment 15
[Voting Rights for Minorities]

Section 1. The right of citizens of the United States to vote shall not be denied or abridged by the United States or by any State on account of race, color, or previous condition of servitude.

Section 2. The Congress shall have power to enforce this article by appropriate legislation. [Ratified Feb. 3, 1870]

Amendment 16
[Income Taxes]

The Congress shall have power to lay and collect taxes on incomes, from whatever source derived, without apportionment among the several States, and without regard to any census or enumeration. [Ratified Feb. 3, 1913]

Amendment 17
[Senators Elected Directly]

The Senate of the United States shall be composed of two Senators from each State, elected by the people thereof for six years; and each Senator shall have one vote. The electors in each State shall have the qualifications requisite for electors of the most numerous branch of the State legislatures.

When vacancies happen in the representation of any State in the Senate, the executive authority of such State shall issue writs of election to fill such vacancies: *Provided,* That the legislature of any State may empower the exec-

There was NO federal income tax before this amendment was ratified. The government didn't need them then, and it doesn't need them now. Income taxes were established for socialist purposes, not out of economic necessity. Did you know that if ALL personal income taxes were abolished, it would mean scaling back to the government budget of just eight years ago? And did you know that the only reason income taxes weren't limited constitutionally to less than 10 percent (to honor God's supreme right to the greatest tithe) was that some legislators feared if 10 percent were explicitly mentioned, future lawmakers might exploit it by venturing to pass that high a tax percent?

This amendment destroyed the balance of power between rural areas and cities. Since then, city-based party machines have controlled Congress.

utive thereof to make temporary appointments until the people fill the vacancies by election as the legislature may direct.

➤ This amendment shall not be so construed as to affect the election or term of any Senator chosen before it becomes valid as part of the Constitution. [Ratified April 8, 1913]

Amendment 18
[Prohibition]

Section 1. After one year from the ratification of this article the manufacture, sale, or transportation of intoxicating liquors within, the importation thereof into, or exportation thereof from the United States and all territory subject to the jurisdiction thereof for beverage purposes is hereby prohibited.

Section 2. The Congress and the several States shall have concurrent power to enforce this article by appropriate legislation.

Section 3. This article shall be inoperative unless it shall have been ratified as an amendment to the Constitution by the legislatures of the several States, as provided in the Constitution, within seven years from the date of the submission hereof to the States by the Congress. [Ratified Jan. 16, 1919]

Amendment 19
[Voting Rights for Women]

The right of citizens of the United States to vote shall not be denied or abridged by the United States or by any State on account of sex.

Congress shall have power to enforce this article by appropriate legislation. [Ratified Aug. 26, 1920]

Amendment 20
[Lame Duck Amendment]

Section 1. The terms of the President and Vice President shall end at noon on the 20th day of January, and the terms of Senators and Representatives at noon on the 3rd day of January, of the years in which such terms would have ended if this article had not been ratified, and the terms of their successors shall then begin.

Section 2. The Congress shall assemble at least once in every year, and such meeting shall begin at noon on the 3rd day of January, unless they shall by law appoint a different day.

Section 3. If, at the time fixed for the beginning of the term of the President, the President elect shall have died, the Vice President elect shall become President. If a President shall not have been chosen before the time fixed for the beginning of his term, or if the President elect shall have failed to qualify, then the Vice President elect shall act as President until a President shall have qualified; and the Congress may by law provide for the case wherein neither a President elect nor a Vice President elect shall have qualified, declaring who shall then act as President, or the manner in which one who is to act shall be selected, and such person shall act accordingly until a President or Vice President shall have qualified.

Section 4. The Congress may by law provide for the case of the death of any of the persons from whom the House of Representatives may choose a President whenever the right of choice shall have devolved upon them, and for the case of the death of any of the persons from whom the Senate may choose a Vice President whenever the right of choice shall have devolved upon them.

Section 5. Sections 1 and 2 shall take effect on the 15th day of October following the ratification of this article.

Section 6. This article shall be inoperative unless it shall have been ratified as an amendment to the Constitution by the legislatures of three-fourths of the several States within seven years from the date of its submission. [Ratified Jan. 23, 1933]

Amendment 21
[Repeal of Prohibition] ◄-------

Section 1. The eighteenth article of amendment to the Constitution of the United States is hereby repealed.

Section 2. The transportation or importation into any State, Territory, or possession of the United States for delivery or use therein of intoxicating liquors, in violation of the laws thereof, is hereby prohibited.

Section 3. This article shall be inoperative unless it shall have been ratified as an amendment to the Constitution by conventions in the several States, as provided in the Constitution, within seven years from the date of the submission hereof to the States by the Congress. [Ratified Dec. 5, 1933]

Amendment 22
[Presidents Limited to Two Terms]

Section 1. No person shall be elected to the office of the President more than twice, and no person who has held the office of President, or acted as President, for more than two years of a term to which some other person was elected President shall be elected to the office of the President more than once. But this Article shall not apply to any person holding the office of President when this Article was proposed by the Congress, and shall not prevent any person who may be holding the office of President, or acing as President, during the term within which this Article becomes operative from holding the office of President or acting as President during the remainder of such term.

Section 2. This article shall be inoperative unless it shall have been ratified as an amendment to the Constitution by the legislatures of three-fourths of the several States within seven years from the date of its submission to the States by the Congress. [Ratified Feb. 27, 1951]

Amendment 23
[Washington, D.C. Gets Electoral Votes As If It Were a State]

Section 1. The District constituting the seat of Government of the United States shall appoint in such manner as the Congress may direct:

A number of electors of President and Vice President equal to the whole number of Senators and Representatives in Congress to which the District would be entitled if it were a State, but in no event more than the least populous State; they shall be in addition to those appointed by the States, but they shall be considered, for the purposes of the election of President and Vice President, to be electors appointed by a State; and they shall meet in the District and perform such duties as provided by the twelfth article of amendment.

Section 2. The Congress shall have power to enforce this article by appropriate legislation. [Ratified March 29, 1961]

Recently a Flag Protection Amendment to the Constitution was proposed. Again, the idea was to protect us from "Supreme" Court excesses. This time, the black-robed eminences wrongly "interpreted" the ACTIONS of flag burning and stomping on the flag as protected SPEECH, thus nullifying all kinds of state and federal laws against it. Concerned citizens flooded the airwaves with ignorant statements to the effect of, "You can't pass an amendment that contradicts the Constitution!" First, a Flag Amendment does NOT contradict our right to freedom of speech. Messing with the flag is not the same as speaking with your voicebox. Second, you CAN pass an amendment that contradicts the Constitution. (Not that I generally recommend this.) The Prohibition Repeal Amendment contradicted and in fact repealed the Prohibition Amendment. Being able to do this is the whole point of having an amendment process.

Amendment 24
[Non-Taxpayers Can Vote]

Section 1. The right of citizens of the United States to vote in any primary or other election for President or Vice President, for electors for President or Vice President, or for Senator or Representative in Congress, shall not be denied or abridged by the United States or any State by reason of failure to pay any poll tax or other tax.

Section 2. The Congress shall have power to enforce this article by appropriate legislation. [Ratified Jan. 23, 1964]

Amendment 25
[Presidential Replacement]

Section 1. In case of the removal of the President from office or of his death or resignation, the Vice President shall become President.

Section 2. Whenever there is a vacancy in the office of the Vice President, the President shall nominate a Vice President who shall take office upon confirmation by a majority vote of both Houses of Congress.

Section 3. Whenever the President transmits to the President pro tempore of the Senate and the Speaker of the House of Representatives his written declaration that he is unable to discharge the powers and duties of his office, and until he transmits to them a written declaration to the contrary, such powers and duties shall be discharged by the Vice President as Acting President.

Section 4. Whenever the Vice President and a majority of either the principal officers of the executive departments or of such other body as Congress may by law provide, transmit to the President pro tempore of the Senate and the Speaker of the House of Representatives their written declaration that the President is unable to discharge the powers and duties of his office, the Vice President shall immediately assume the powers and duties of the office as Acting President.

Thereafter, when the President transmits to the President pro tempore of the Senate and the Speaker of the House of Representatives his written declaration that no inability exists he shall resume the powers and duties of his office unless the Vice President and a majority of either the principal officers of the executive department or of such other body as Congress may by law provide, transmit within four days to the President pro tempore of the Senate and the Speaker of the House of Representatives their written declaration that the President is unable to discharge the powers and duties of his office. Thereupon Congress shall decide the issue, assembling within forty-eight hours for that purpose if not in session. If the Congress, within twenty-one days after receipt of the latter written declaration, or, if Congress is not in session, within twenty-one days after Congress is required to assemble, determines by two-thirds vote of both Houses that the President is unable to discharge the powers and duties of his office, the Vice President shall continue to discharge the same as Acting President; otherwise, the President shall resume the powers and duties of his office. [Ratified Feb. 10, 1967]

Amendment 26
[Voting Rights for 18-Year-Olds]

Section 1. The right of citizens of the United States, who are 18 years of age or older, to vote shall not be denied or abridged by the United States or by any State on account of age.

Section 2. The Congress shall have power to enforce this article by appropriate legislation. [Ratified June 30, 1971]

Suggested Course of Elementary Study

What should your child study when?

Until this point, most of us have been more-or-less following the typical course of study devised by the public-school curriculum designers. (For those of you who are interested, it is outlined in *Typical Course of Study,* a booklet published by World Book, Inc., and available from them for a nominal price.) Most published curriculum, whether Christian or secular, uses *Typical Course of Study* or some similar guide as a rule for what should be taught when.

Looking at *Typical Course of Study,* the first thing that strikes you is the **large number of skills** taught in each subject at each grade level.

The second thing that strikes you is the **totally arbitrary nature** of where many of these skills are placed.

The third thing that strikes you is **how often many of these skill and content areas are repeated** from grade to grade.

Let's look at some examples. "Presenting original plays" is listed as a grade 5 language arts skill. "Introduction to mythology" is listed as a grade 6 learning area. The two could easily be reversed, presented at lower grades, presented at later grades, or skipped altogether. Under Health and Safety, "sewage disposal" makes its one and only appearance in grade 5 (why grade 5?), while "dental health" or "dental hygiene" is presented and re-presented eight years in a row (does it take that long to learn to floss and brush your teeth?). Sentence grammar is first presented in grade 3 (simple punctuation), skipped altogether in grade 4, and then spread out over grades 5–8, only to pop up once again in grades 10 and 11. As one girl complained to me, "They keep teaching us this stuff again and again, and I *learned* it three years ago!" Science topics appear in an equally capricious fashion, with a dozen or more topics presented each year, some of which are repeated almost every year while others are not. The solar system, in various forms, is studied every year in grades K–5. Simple machines, on the other hand, pop up only in grades 1 and 3.

Another thing worth noting about the typical course of study is that *each skill and topic is given equal emphasis.* Learning to read and write are

The address to obtain *Typical Course of Study* is World Book Direct Marketing, PO Box 11370, Des Moines, IA 50350, (800) 504-4425, *www.worldbook.com.* There is a nominal charge for the booklet. Many other items of interest are available through their catalog, which you can request at the same time.

Many homeschool curriculum publishers also make their Scope and Sequence (an outline, by grade level and subject, of what is taught at that level) available free or at low cost. These are generally quite similar to what you'll find in *Typical Course of Study,* since these publishers also sell to Christian schools, which in turn base *their* course of study in large part on what the public schools are teaching. A big mistake, in my view.

just *part* of the language-arts program, which before children can even read already includes "simple pantomimes and dramatic play" and 15 other topics, including "development of class newspaper." "Dressing for weather and activity" and "neighborhood helpers" are not shown in any obvious way to be lower priority than "establishing sight vocabulary." This undoubtedly accounts for the huge number of cluttered projects teachers are always publishing in teachers' magazines, where first-grade kids spend a whole week making a cardboard box village in order to learn about "me and my neighborhood" rather than working on reading, writing, and arithmetic.

Our children need more than better educational resources. They need a better educational schedule. Here are what I see as the basic steps in that schedule:

1. **First give kids the tools of learning** (Bible, reading, writing, and arithmetic).
2. **Second, present them informally with lots of data** in all the subject areas.
3. **Third, tie it together** with organizing devices like time lines.
4. Once steps 1–3 have been accomplished, ***then* introduce formal study** of science, history, geography, art, and so on, while continuing to read voraciously and *discuss* what is read.

Step One: The Tools of Learning (Grades 1–3)

No matter how young or old your child is, here's where he needs to start once he's passed the "readiness" stage (can use crayons, scissors, hold a pencil properly, knows left from right, etc.).

1. **Bible**
    A. Memorize the names of the books of the Bible in order.
    B. Read through the entire Bible, with explanations of the difficult parts (many times).
    C. Memorize the Ten Commandments.
2. **Learn to read *well*.**
3. **Learn printing, handwriting, and keyboarding.**
4. **Learn to write *well*** (creative writing), including proper grammar and spelling. If your homeschool group has a Spelling Bee, your child can compete in the bee as early as first grade.
5. **Learn summarizing and narrating** (child is able to recount a story well).
6. **Learn basic arithmetic,** from numeral recognition up to decimals and fractions.

These are the *real* basics, to be studied together until mastered. Don't assume just because he's in fifth grade that he's on top of all these areas. Check him out with Step One skills first.

If your child can't read or write well, *don't worry* about teaching him Civil War history or cell biology. Get the reading and writing under control *first,* without distracting him with hours of studies in areas he can't handle due to his lack of language-arts skills.

Step Two: The Facts (Grades 1–3)

You don't have to let the science and social studies vanish during the time your children are mastering the basics. Here's some simple ways to provide social studies and science facts and experiences during the first three grades of school:

1. **History**
   A. Read historical biographies and fiction aloud. Good readers can read them to themselves. Try to focus on explorers, inventors, entrepreneurs, scientists, artists, musicians, preachers and evangelists, mothers, writers, and so on, not just on political figures. "Daily life" books that give a feel for the cultural setting of each time period are also good.
   B. Rent historical videos.
   C. Discuss the history of each holiday as it comes up.
2. **Geography**
   A. Look up locations on the map or globe as they come up in family conversation.
   B. Teach the kids to use a map and globe.
   C. U. S. and world puzzles.
   D. Geography games (optional, if you have the time) .
3. **Science**
   A. Read science books aloud, or have the child read them alone. Topics to cover: plants, animals, farming, rocks, weather, seasons, solar system and universe, measurement, human anatomy and senses, dinosaurs, magnetism, electricity, and simple machines.
   B. Nature walks and field trips (as time permits).
   C. Pet care (if desired).
   D. Simple experiments (if time permits).
   E. Basic personal hygiene (washing, brushing, flossing, putting dirty clothes in the hamper, etc.).

Here's what *not* to bother with:

- **Any K–3 formal social studies or science courses.** Without exception, these are all rinky-dink.
- **Units on transportation.** You could with equal justification study clothing, food preparation, architecture, or cosmetics (none of which I recommend bothering with). As your child studies history and drives in your car, he is bound to pick up transportation information without any special effort.
- **Units on "community helpers," "interdependence of people," "basic human needs and wants," and other code words for statism.** Community helpers units teach careerism (only paid jobs are represented, never volunteers or people who serve their families and neighborhoods) and subservience (self-employment and leadership positions are rarely presented). Units on interdependence and human needs invariably present gigantic institutional structures as *the* way to live.
- **All collective-guilt studies,** whether the guilt be racial, ecological, religious, economic, or whatever. These sometimes come disguised as "cultural appreciation" or "multicultural education" or "conservation" studies.
- **Complicated, cluttered projects** that "integrate skill areas" (e.g., handwriting assignments that include spelling words). It's safer to keep those skill areas separate until you're sure your child has actually mastered the skills!

If you want to integrate Bible with social studies and science, you can use Christian books or take the time to discuss what your children are reading (a good idea anyway!). It's always interesting to look up what the Bible has to say on a subject, too. Just pick your topic (e.g., "ear" or "liberty") and look up the references found under that topic in your concordance. You can pursue such studies further by adding cross-references. Example: "hearing" and "listening" fit naturally with a study of what the Bible says about ears, just as "freedom," "slave," "slavery," and "subjection" go along with a study of liberty. This can be done on Sundays or during family devotions time, if your regular home-school time is too short. You can also draw on the Bible for reading, literature, history, handwriting, drama, narrating, science (developing a proper attitude toward creation and the Creator), and even grammar assignments—McGuffey did!

The first three grades are also a good time to introduce the rudiments of baking, sewing, housecleaning, child care, and other daily-life skills. Again, with the exception of personal cleanliness and picking up after oneself, these can be fit in as time allows.

Step Three: Putting It All Together with Formal Studies (Grades 4–6)

We're only in the fourth grade at this point, so there is no reason to panic just because your son or daughter isn't sure whether Columbus discovered America in 1492 or 1776. (Let's keep this in perspective: a hefty minority of high-school graduates aren't sure about the dates either!) Up to this point we've been working on stories, not dates. Does your child know Columbus discovered America? Good: that's the first step! Now's the time to start your history time line, if you haven't already, and to perhaps work through a beginning history textbook. Now is also the time to get a bit more systematic about science (if desired), although serious science studies can really wait until junior high or even high school without major educational consequences.

I am not suggesting "dumbing down" the curriculum. I am suggesting that it's dumb to suffocate kids with more information than they are able to remember. Keep in mind also that the public schools teach kids all the information from this age onwards at least *twice*. The assumption is that they will *not* learn or remember most of it the first time around. My position is that **we shouldn't teach them material we don't expect them to remember in the first place.** Thus, it makes more sense to present the excellent fourth- through sixth-grade history and geography texts to seventh- through ninth-graders, who will actually be able to retain all that information, than to the age group for which they were written.

Therefore, here's what I suggest for grades 4–6:

1. **Bible studies**
   A. Time line.
   B. Maps (Middle Eastern geography).
   C. Memorizing the theme and a key verse for each book of the Bible.
   D. Knowing how to quickly look up any given Bible verse.
   E. Hebrew and Greek alphabets.
   F. Use of the basic Bible tools (dictionary, concordance).
2. **Reading: a lot.** Include good classic literature. Some Nancy Drew and Hardy Boys won't hurt, but don't let that level of book be *all* they read. If a child reads a lot, you can almost get away with skipping everything else except math. (I am *not* suggesting that you do this!)
3. **Handwriting:** developing a beautiful hand. Keyboarding should be taught now, if your computer crazy kid hasn't already taught himself.
4. **Creative writing:** all literary types (letters, journals, poems, stories, essays, plays, memos, reports, newspaper articles). Pen pals or key pals are great, as is writing for one of the homemade homeschool-kids

newsletters. Or how about entering the *Practical Homeschooling* Story Contest? There's a new one in every issue!

5. **Oral presentation skills.**
6. **Grammar: formal study.** It should only take a year or so to cover *all* of it at this age level.
7. **Spelling:** formal study if necessary (some children are naturally almost-perfect spellers). Use a rules-based program and child's own misspelled words, not canned "word lists." If your homeschool group has a spelling bee, now is the time to get more serious about prepping for the bee.
8. **Arithmetic:** continue. If finished, proceed on to pre-algebra, etc. If your homeschool support group has a Math Olympics team, now is the time to join it, since only children in grades 4–12 are allowed to compete.
9. **Geometry.**
10. **History.**
    A. Time line of U.S. history.
    B. Time line of world history.
    C. First history textbook (if desired: semi-formal study; read it as a book and *discuss* it).
    D. More mature history-oriented books from the library or EDC Publishing, etc.
    E. Bibliographies. There are literally hundreds written for children of this age level.
11. **Geography:** continue as above. Add geography quizzes and drills, if desired. Consider entering the Geography Bee.
12. **Science.**
    A. Engineering with construction kits (e.g., LEGO Dacta, fishertechnik).
    B. Simple experiments every now and then (child has more responsibility for setting up experiments on his own, calls you over to see the results).
    C. First science textbook (if desired; semi-formal study; do exercises, but don't worry about keeping up a standard classroom pace).
    D. History of science (through biographies or as a separate study). Can also be done later.
    E. If your child really loves science, and your homeschool group has a science fair, he might enjoy creating a project for the fair.
13. **Health and safety:** totally informal, as family situations arise (e.g., washing wound and putting on bandage, using Desitin on diaper rash, pointing pot handle to the back of the stove, etc.).
14. **Physical education:** pick a lifetime sport and get good at it.
15. **Home economics:** assign chores, let kids bake using simple recipe books. Weaving, knitting, and woodworking kits are also popular with this age group.

Of the above list, only Bible, grammar, and math actually need formal preparation time. Handwriting, creative writing, oral presentation, spelling, and engineering and science experiments require adult feedback, but not necessarily a lot of up-front teaching. If your child reads well and you get him good resources, he is able at this age to follow the instructions by himself.

For Those Who Want More

I personally feel that the elementary grades are also a fine time to introduce art, music, and foreign languages. Other subjects worth introducing in grades 4–6 are business, economics, and citizenship. Consider adding those subjects if any of the following apply:

- Your family considers such studies part of family play time, so they don't take any extra time from your day.
- Your family has a history of being musical (or artistic, or good at languages, or owning your own business) and you feel one of these subjects is likely to become your child's vocation.
- You are using resources that don't require you to prepare for the lessons.
- You are willing to take several weeks at a time off from your normal studies to really get into these new areas and get comfortable with them, or you have the basic studies under control and can afford the extra time for regular instruction in these areas.

Remember, the more time you spend on the basics, the more time you'll have later on to spend on everything else!

These are also the grades when you might want your child to take the Talent Search tests that may qualify him or her for one of the "talented youth" programs offered by various institutions. Upon qualifying, the child is eligible to take special correspondence or computer courses designed for young children who are capable of more advanced study. Volume 1 of the Big Book has the story on these talent-search programs, if you're interested.

Finally, if your child is *really* ready for more, get a copy of Volume 3 of *The Big Book of Home Learning*. You'll find everything you need for home study from seventh grade up to the college level in that volume. Happy homeschooling, and see you in Volume 3!

FIND IT FAST

Index

Find It Fast

Index

You've got the book.
Now get the magazine.

_____

_____

_____